JOHN GASSNER

MASTERS

OF THE

DRAMA

THIRD REVISED AND ENLARGED EDITION

DOVER PUBLICATIONS, INC.

C.B.S. Replacement
4.63
5-2-62 lyon
5-3-62 abu

TO MOLLIE AND CAROLINE

MASTERS OF THE DRAMA

JOHN GASSNER

MASTERS OF THE DRAMA

THIRD REVISED AND ENLARGED EDITION

DOVER PUBLICATIONS, INC.

C.B.S. Replacement
4.63
5-2-62 bpm
5-3-62 abw

TO MOLLIE AND CAROLINE

CONTENTS

APPENDIX

NOTES

BIBLIOGRAPHY

INDEX

ILLUSTRATIONS

SECTION I. STYLES OF THEATRE

xiv

THESE ILLUSTRATIONS ARE IN A GROUP
BETWEEN PAGES 604 AND 605

PREFACE TO THE THIRD, ENLARGED EDITION

THE MAIN feature of the present edition is Chapter XXXI, an extensive essay on playwrights who either won recognition or increased their international reputation after 1940. To this chapter I have added a midcentury summation of modern theatre and drama. The generosity of the publisher has also enabled me to append a Survey of Theatrical Styles to the revised photographic section on theatre from classic to modern times, and to add two sections of photographs, on Playwrights and an Album of Modern Stage Productions. It has been possible to augment the material on stage art in this book, which remains devoted essentially to playwrights, plays, dramatic theory, and criticism.

The table, Theatre and Man in the Western World, which suggests a relationship developed in the book between dramatic art and cultural history, has been brought up to date; and additional bibliographies and indices have been supplied.

For assistance in providing these additions and supplying new material at the end of a number of chapters, as well as making some necessary revisions, the author is indebted to his wife Mollie Gassner and to his friend, Dover Publications' president, Mr. Hayward Cirker. As the writing of the new section of the book was facilitated by the grant of a Guggenheim Fellowship and travel in Europe, I must also express my gratitude to the John Simon Guggenheim Memorial Foundation and its executive secretary Mr. Henry Allen Moe.

If *Masters of the Drama* has hitherto proved of sufficient interest to justify continued publication over a period of a dozen years, it may be hoped that the new enlarged edition will serve its readers and friends even better.

JOHN GASSNER

October 1951

PREFACE TO SECOND EDITION

FIVE YEARS of tribulation, during which civilization came close to perishing, have passed since this book was originally published by Random House. Now that the storm is passing and the lights go on again in the theatres of the world, it is a gratification for the author to see his book in print again. This, too, is a most appropriate occasion for reviewing the theatre's winding course through the millenia of man's aspirations and travail.

Fortunately, this reprint has also provided me with a long-sought opportunity to make a minimal revision: that is, to correct typographical slips and minor errors of fact, modify some ill-considered statements, add points of information at the end of various chapters, and supplement our chronicle with a résumé of the interim years of 1940-45. Space considerations and the paper shortage precluded my making a more amplified revision, but this is not altogether a misfortune, as a larger volume might have tried the reader's patience, if indeed it has not been already too severely tried.

In conclusion, I should like to pay a debt that has been long overdue to foster-parents of this possibly overambitious project. This book would have been considerably sparser but for my long association with the directors of the Theatre Guild as chairman of their Play Department; virtually all of the modern and contemporary drama came within its purview—many plays would have otherwise escaped my attention. Nor would the book ever have been undertaken at all but for Mark Van Doren, who introduced me to the not necessarily ignoble art of criticism by his teaching and example, which started precisely twenty-five years ago. Now that *Masters of the Drama* has survived, I may say without immodesty, the tests of critical and public reception, I have less hesitation in laying it in his lap. It is an ample lap on which the books of many of my contemporaries may be laid with more certainty that the effort has been worthy of his inspiration.

JOHN GASSNER

June 1945

PREFACE TO FIRST EDITION

THIS BOOK is an attempt to pay homage to one of the greatest mediums of human expression. It regards the drama as a comprehensive art that is inalienable from civilization.

The drama arose out of fundamental human needs in the dawn of civilization and has continued to express them for thousands of years. It represents humanity in moments of maximum tension, conflict, and crisis, and it tries to resolve them in broadly human terms. It brings the life of man visibly before mankind and levies tribute upon all the arts in order to achieve this purpose. Out of the word, the dance, music, and the plastic arts it builds one mighty synthesis of humanity's creative faculties. Its forms are manifold, embracing diverse conventions of theatre, and it pulsates in pantomime and recitation; in the relatively separate arts of the ballet, oratorio and opera; and in the newest products of mechanical progress, the films and broadcasting. Finally, the drama addresses itself not to isolated individuals but to mankind assembled in groups as if for a public function. It must be set down as the greatest collective enterprise that projects and interprets our common humanity.

If we retrace the course of the drama through the ages we cannot fail to acknowledge the validity of these claims. This is not less true today when the theatre has fallen upon evil days in many harassed countries, for the flaw has not been in the art but in humanity. And if the material conditions of production where the dramatist is still a comparatively free individual seriously handicap his creativeness, the fault rests likewise with the surrounding world. Nor is the pre-eminence of this art greatly reduced by obvious limitations in comparison with its present rival, the modern novel. What the play loses in extension it can generally retrieve with its economy and clarity, its formal beauty, and its immediacy.

Let us admit, of course, as we must, that this art has feet of clay and moves in the market place. The theatre is not a Sunday school, even if it was once a temple. Sometimes it bears closer resemblance to a circus. More often than purists can endure, it depends upon showmanship, strives for effect rather than meaning, and enjoys frivolity. It favors the most elementary forms of release along with the most redoubtable exaltations. It always oscillates between the sublime and the ridiculous, between the stars and the muck. The drama, in short, is as impure and frail as mankind itself. In the last analysis, however, this even proves to be an advantage, for the theatre has been so close to humanity precisely because it has feet of clay.

Needless to say, this is not an unmixed blessing. The stage can be guilty of much inexcusable banality and meretricious sensationalism. This is often, although not always, the case when mankind becomes too smug or suffers one of its periodic catastrophes. Because the theatre is so closely bound to man and to the world he makes (and that makes him), it may become under-nourished and may wilt in a general drought. Sometimes it even suffers more than a less susceptible human pursuit. But the theatre is never quite dead even when it produces few or no plays of consequence. The impulse for dramatization cannot be suppressed for long, and performers—from the humblest mime to the great Garrick—hold audiences in readiness for the drama that will be reborn under favorable conditions. There are many moments of decay and rebirth in this life-cycle. And here one may discern only the life-cycle of mankind as a whole.

This book is written for the general reader and student rather than for the specialist or the theorist. If historical tendencies and broad cultural trends enter into this story it is precisely because the theatre is so close to human history. Moreover, it is undeniable that the major dramatists were dominated by the drama of mankind and that their greatest work is devoted to its currents.

The merely clever practitioners of the art, who have no kernel of perception or vision, need not, of course, be scorned. They provide entertainment sufficient unto its day. In a painful world (and when was it not painful?), who are we to be ungrateful for a little pleasure from the stage! It is also true that plays are not important as plays in direct proportion to their significance or utility. First they have to be good plays; they must possess rich humanity and formal beauty. No record of the drama can be adequate if it considers ideas or reflected historical facts apart from the living quality of the play; that is, apart from its beauty of expression, its emotional power, and its nuances. One should not kill the protoplasm of the drama in order to study it.

Nevertheless, few products of mankind's dramatic talent can command much interest beyond their own day unless they arise from our understanding of individuals and of the world. The playwrights who have achieved permanence, or are likely to achieve it, have differed in this respect from the May-flies of the theatre. It is not some solemn academician or embattled propagandist but the theatre-wise critic John Mason Brown who warned his readers in *The Art of Playgoing* that "great plays are great for other reasons than that they are adapted to the stage. They soar above its physical limitation as the spirit of man transcends the body. It is to that spirit which they speak." This book strives, in the main, to describe the *concrete* manner in which the drama has spoken to the spirit.

The true drama is not, of course, "pure" literature. It was written to be read rather than produced only when dramatists had no alternative, or when for one reason or another writers failed to become *bona fide* playwrights; John Mason Brown has wisely declared that " 'the play's the thing'—in the library." This book therefore pays its respects to the living—or at least temporarily living—medium in which plays were created. Even when in a few instances some work not primarily written to be staged is considered in these pages, it receives attention largely because, despite its inherent inadequacies, it has revealed possibilities as acted theatre. The illustrations, assembled in a group, will also suggest the close relation that exists between script and stage.

Emphasis, however, has been placed largely on the literature of the theatre rather than on its associated arts. This should serve to repair the omissions and abbreviations that will be found in surveys of the theatre. These are excellent treatments of the theatre arts, but shortchange the very art that has made the stage a great organ of humanity. Even Stark Young, who can vie with anyone in sensitive devotion to the art of the stage, has not hesitated to maintain that "the dramatist is the most important figure in the eternal theater, the theater that outlasts one generation only. . . ."

Since a book must speak for itself, the author allows himself only one more comment. Some detailed consideration has been accorded to a number of plays which would strike most of us as at least partially dated. Some of these were used to round out this chronicle or to illustrate some general trend. However, most of them, when read with an alert sense of how they must have appeared in their own theatre, may surprise us with their persistent life. Time and again, moreover, supposedly outmoded works regain interest when actors and stage directors apply their intelligence to reviving them with appropriate reorientation or interpretation. The truth of this contention has been exemplified everywhere. There is an eternal recurrence in human experience to which it is wise to give heed, if we can.

In conclusion, the author wishes to express his gratitude to Messrs. Pascal Covici and Joseph Margolies for their initial interest in this book; to the editors of Random House who have co-operated most generously with him; and above all, to his patient wife and mainstay for invaluable assistance in the preparation of the manuscript.

Part I

PRIMITIVE PORTRAIT

LIKE everything else, the drama has a beginning. The *first* drama is, however, also the *last* drama. It is, in a sense, contemporary drama. It is still being practised by the primitive races that have survived into our own century; it still exists in the basic instincts and responses of modern man; and its cardinal elements still prevail, and will undoubtedly always prevail, in the theatre.

The "first playwright" is, necessarily, a composite portrait, in which different features become visible or merge at different stages. But in his totality he is already mankind grappling with the world, inner and outer, visible and invisible. It is no wonder then that his biography should tell us so much about ourselves.

I

THE FIRST DRAMATIST

1 AT THE FOUNTAIN

"THEY have twenty or forty yoke of oxen, every ox having a sweet nosegay of flowers tied on the tip of his horns, and these oxen draw home this Maypole (this stinking idol rather), which is covered all over with flowers and herbs, bound round about with strings from the top to the bottom, and sometimes painted with variable colors, with two or three hundred men, women and children following it with great devotion. And thus being reared up, with handkerchiefs and flags streaming on the top, they strew the ground about, bind green boughs about it, set up summer halls, bowers, and arbors hard by it. And then fall to banquet and feast, to leap and dance about it, as the heathen people did at the dedication of their idols, whereof this is a perfect pattern or rather the thing itself."[1]

So writes the Elizabethan Puritan Bishop Stubbes, who was so outraged by the fashion of ruffs in his day that he condemned starch as "that devil's liquour." Whatever we may think of his opinion of that innocent carbohydrate, however, the good Puritan was correct in ascribing pagan origins to Maypole dancing. He saw it for what it was—a spring rite. His successors even went further; they attributed paganism to the entire drama, charged it with sinister levity, and in 1642 padlocked all the public theatres in England.

The curious truth is that the modern historian can top any of their charges since there is not a single human impulse, moral or otherwise, that cannot be associated with the growth of the stage; the masters of the drama are, in short, the children of life. But this hardly discredits the theatre. It is, on the contrary, a sign of unassailable vitality that the drama should have come from the fountainhead of man's instinctive partiality for joy or emotional release and from his first efforts to master the visible and invisible world. The first playwright began indeed as a player and a magic-maker. But he gradually took the whole world of experience and thought for his field.

2 THE PLAYWRIGHT-PRIEST

Primitive man was an accomplished mimic and a creature of play. He was from the beginning an imitator who shared this attribute with

3

the higher animals but surpassed them in the flexibility of his body and voice, the developed consciousness of his will, and the ordering capacity of his mind. He also played like his animal brethren, discharging by this means his physical vitality. Wherever the theatre flourishes man is again unapologetically a superior animal or child imitating the creature world and enjoying the equally fundamental pleasure of playing with the aid of all his faculties from the most elementary physical movement to the furthest flights of fancy.

Still, instinct is inevitably harnessed to human aims and primitive man was too bedeviled by the struggle for existence to afford any wayward impulses. Instead he put them to work or they put themselves to work naturally. In copying movements or gestures, repeating sounds, and employing human, animal, and even vegetable disguises, primitive man was instinctively bringing himself in touch with his environment. And in playing he was not only discharging excess energy but preparing himself for purposeful action, a fact observed in both animals and children. He who plays at hunting or fighting prepares himself· for efficiency. England's battles were said to have been won on the cricket fields of Eton, and even the elaborate tournaments of the Middle Ages served the practical purpose of providing military training for the nobility.

Moreover, the struggle for existence forced a distinctly utilitarian or practical outlook on primitive man. Thus he made pottery at first solely for utility and only later did he begin to decorate it. In giving vent to his dramatic impulses he was likewise consciously practical. Like children and mentally diseased adults, he thought he could influence events by willing them. If he could only describe something he needed or if only he could think wishfully enough, he believed, he might get his heart's desire. In fact, we still make this assumption more frequently than we care to admit. And since man was not yet adept at uttering his thoughts, he resorted to action.

He wanted to eat regularly, to conquer his foes, and to be secure from attack, and curiously he soon learned that he could achieve his desires by dancing and acting out his desires. Although his theory is scientifically untenable, its effects were frequently valid since the results for which he strove magically might have been promoted by the inspiration and autosuggestion that the rite induced in the actors. By then, too, primitive man was beginning to think along lines that could only sharpen his awareness of nature and enhance his adjustment to it. Slowly piecing out the relationship between his food supply and the fruitful season of rainfall or maximum sunlight, he actually began to include some scientific thinking in his dramatic rite.

His means of expression might be as simple at first as the mimic tug-of-war of the Esquimaux: "In the autumn when the storms begin and the long and dismal Arctic winter is at hand, the central Esquimaux divide themselves into two parties called the Ptarmigans and the Ducks. The ptarmigans are the people born in winter, the ducks those born in summer. They stretch out a long rope of sealskin. The ducks take hold of one end, the ptarmigans of the other, then comes the tug-of-war." [2] If the children of summer win, there will be clement weather and the abundance with which this season is associated. The primitive Australian "paints the figure of the emu on the sand with vermilion drawn from his own blood, he puts on emu feathers and gazes about him vacantly in stupid fashion like an emu bird; he makes a structure of boughs like the chrysalis of a Witchetty grub—his favorite food, and drags his body through it in pantomime and shuffling to promote its birth." [3] Here it is the phenomenon of birth that is associated with the food supply.

Gradually the rites assumed greater complexity, dance rhythms, subtler symbolization, and more dynamic representation. Man danced out his desires until the pantomimic dance became the most finished early form of drama, and the first dramatist became a choreographer. At this point, moreover, we find an individual who transcends any single profession. We meet a priest, a scientist, a philosopher, and a social organizer —a multifarious specialist who holds in solution many functions that later became specialties. This dramatist is, in other words, a comprehensive personality rather than a stage carpenter. There is nothing humble about his profession, and an Aeschylus or an Ibsen merely continued the noble tradition when they encompassed a whole world.

The primitive playwright formulates and leads the pantomime since the form and execution of these performances require a guiding intellect. He also becomes, it is true, mechanically inventive, creating the theatre's first "props," as when he employs "bull roarers" and zigzag sticks to imitate the thunder and lightning that usher in the rainy season. He is, however, no mere mechanic but a priest who gives the act its content or meaning and teaches man the first uses of prayer. His rites, by which he allegedly harnesses providence, nature or God to the service of mankind, are simply a literal application of the early Christian slogan that to work is to pray—*laborare est orare*. It is, for example, significant that the word for dancing and working is the same in one Amerindian language, that when an elder of the Tarahumares tribe in Mexico reproves a young man for not joining the dance he actually says, "Why don't you get in there and work." [4] Moreover, this priest is a poet by virtue of the imaginativeness that enables him to animate nature or personify its forces as spirits; and he becomes simultaneously a scientist since he is a miracle worker, a witch doctor who exorcizes diseases (thus anticipating the healing or purging power of the drama by his literal medical practices), and a proponent of the idea that humanity can win mastery over nature.

He may not at first monopolize these attributes; but he certainly exercises them more conspicuously and consciously than other members of his community.

Finally, he is also a social philosopher, for it is he who organizes the performance as a communal activity and extends the psychological reality of the primitive commune. Nature under his leadership is not being mastered for the individual but for the tribe, and the primitive theatre that serves this purpose is a communion. Other rites directly related to primitive social organization are likewise developed under his tutelage—-the initiations of young men into the tribe and the various forms of ancestor worship which crystallize the concept of early society.

3 THE DRAMATIST AND THE GHOST

We must not, in fact, minimize the rite that centers in some ancestral figure or father image who was originally a patriarch, later a chieftain or king, and generally a priest as well. This hero is probably the first god, the character in whose image the spirits of nature and divine beings are created. Long before primitive man could conceive the abstract idea of a powerful supernatural agent, he had to cope with an all-powerful human being.

As potent as this figure was when alive, so potent could he be in death, for he might return as a ghost whose anger would have to be averted or appeased with tomb rites. He might indeed have good reasons for anger since he may have been killed by sons jealous of his autocratic control of the property and the women of the community. Perhaps, too, he was slain by the tribe which rebelled against him or which merely thought it expedient to transfer his strength-giving magical soul into the younger and more vigorous body of a new priest-king.[5] Even his natural death might fill his descendants with a feeling of guilt, for had they not often entertained unspoken and unacted wishes for his destruction, and are not thoughts winged agents of the will! Besides, the dead man's potency could be of a beneficent nature, for had he not led and watched over his people!

With this character, moreover, Death, the prime subject of tragedy, joins the theatre. One method of overcoming a difficulty is the standard one of undoing it in the mind! The trick is to be found in the lies and fantasies of children and adults, as well as in the process of magical "undoing" (Freud's concept of *Ungeschehenmachen*) noted in psychopathology. Primitive man denies death by bringing the deceased back in the form of spirits, and the rite of ancestral or spirit worship becomes a graphic representation of this resurrection. The tomb becomes the stage and the actors represent ghosts. Actual ghost scenes are, of course, abundant in the later theatre, and the spirit drama has one highly developed survival in the Japanese Noh plays. It is also known that many Greek tragedies, such as Sophocles' *Ajax* and *Oedipus at Colonus* and Euripides' *Hippolytus* and *Medea,* were related to rites commemorating a primitive hero or heroine. The drama still overcomes the prime dread when man, ennobled by his passionate struggle and his fortitude, survives in a spiritual sense. When Death entered the theatre at this early date tragedy was born.

If survival of the soul had terrors of its own because the ghost might be unfriendly, the danger could be lessened by rites of propitiation or by public exorcism of the hostile spirit such as the well-known custom of "spirit sweeping." Athens, for example, had the ancient festival of the Anthesteria at the end of February when the ghosts who were infesting the city at this time were placated and banished by means of revelry and dramatic dancing. Our Halloween is a survival of this widespread custom. Old European mummings like the traditional "St. George and the Dragon" play described by Thomas Hardy in *The Return of the Native* are similarly associated with ghosts who are frightened away by the mummers or swept out with a vigorously applied broom.

Man, moreover, discovered supplementary ways of negating mortality. Still the most effective means of overcoming the death rate is to increase the birth rate, and the latter was of the greatest importance to competing tribes. Performances which represented and induced procreation consequently assumed great importance, and it is not surprising that fertility rites for man, which had their counterpart in fertility rites for animals and vegetation, should arise early in history. Much revelry characterized phallic or sexual rites, as they tended to reproduce the euphoric elements of the sexual act. The pent-up libido was allowed complete release, sexual exhibitions were far more direct than even our burlesque shows, and badinage flowed freely. That the event proved a stimulus that had the required results nine months later is not remarkable, and if primitive man attributed them to magic it is too late to disillusion him. Out of these mummings, specifically, arose comedy, with its high spirits and with the laughter that silences many an anxiety or ache in the heart of the spectator. The proverbial "levity" of the stage is one of its oldest heritages; in sublimated form it is also a very precious one.

Life, we may add, was also asserted by the worship of potency in an animal (sometimes a plant, like the *soma* of the Hindus) in which the ancestral spirit and the tribe's unity were often incarnated. It became customary for the community to sacrifice a bull, horse, goat, or other creature and to incorporate its *mana* or magical power by partaking of its flesh and blood. Then, since it was serious business to kill the sacred animal, its death was symbolically "undone" in various ways. If, for example, the priest dressed up in its skin and danced, he could prove that the so-called totem was still alive and was in fact indestructible.

The addition of new adults to the tribe also called for rites of an initiatory character, and the ceremony showed the adolescent dying as a child and being reborn as a man. Sometimes the rites also warned the young man against transgressing tribal laws or overthrowing his .elders in the quest for property and women; the warning was given by means of a mimic execution or by the concrete act of circumcision.

In this bewildering complexity of ritual we see the content of the theatre broadening tremendously, and we also see its structure taking shape. Action and imitation, the first ingredients of the early play, began to follow a fairly fixed pattern once they assumed the form of a central struggle. Once the early playwright enacted the battle between the good season and the bad or between death and life, the dynamic principle of drama —*conflict*—entered the theatre.

4 THE PASSION PLAYS AND THE DEVELOPMENT OF "PLOT"

Only one more element is needed to complete the minimum requirements of the drama—namely, plot or story. Plot was already present in the earliest rites. Their simplest pantomime said in effect "I came upon a fierce animal, he growled and attacked me, I crouched, I cast my spear, released my arrow, killed him, and brought him home;" or "I met the enemy, we exchanged thrusts and blows, I pierced his heart, I cut off his head, I took his goods, and now I am secure and prosperous." Plot was then extended by the remembered deeds of the subjects of the tomb rites, and it acquired wonder and grandeur when the vegetation, as well as ancestral, spirits were endowed with remarkable characteristics and mythology was born. Myth, supplemented by saga material, became the matter of drama. The dramatized story now embraced individualized personalities who lived, worked, achieved greatness, suffered and died or somehow triumphed over death. Here, in short, is the same pattern that appears in later tragedy, and—with the omission of the final catastrophe—also in comedy.

The god or deified hero entered the theatre with aplomb, and his exalted character and importance could be honored only by all the resources that the early theatre can muster. The plays thus materialized were elaborate Passion Plays, like those of Oberammergau and other Central European towns, and it is natural that they should have arisen first in Egypt and Mesopotamia where civilization gained an early foothold. Best known is the *Abydos Passion Play* of Egypt.

The hero of the Egyptian dramas was Osiris, deified hero, corn-god, tree-spirit, patron of fertility, and lord of life and death. Born of the fruitful union of the earth and the sky, Osiris came down to earth, reclaimed his people from savagery, gave them laws, and with his sister-wife Isis taught them to cultivate the fruits of the soil. But he aroused the enmity of his brother Set or Death who prevailed upon him to enter a coffin, nailed it fast, and flung him into the Nile. Isis traveled far and wide in search of him, giving birth to a child Horus during her wanderings. With great difficulty she recovered his body only to lose it to his brother, who rent it into fourteen pieces and scattered them over the land. Ultimately Isis recovered the members of the murdered god, put them together, and fanned the cold clay with her wings. He came back to life as a result of these ministrations and became the ruler of the underworld.[6]

In the Passion Plays performed in honor of Osiris, the details of lamenting his death, finding the body, restoring it to life, and greeting the resurrected god with rejoicing were treated with great pomp. The play became part of an imposing and joy-giving festival lasting eighteen days and beginning, significantly enough, with a ceremony of plowing and sowing. To promote the magical purpose of the rite even further the Egyptians also made effigies of the god and buried corn with him, so that the sprouting of the seed which symbolized his resurrection might promote the growth of the crops. Other plays had related themes.

Syria's dramas revolved around the kindred figure of Tammuz or Adonis, god of the waters and of the crops that owed their abundance to the Mesopotamian rivers. His death was lamented ceremonially by the Syrian women, much to the dismay of the prophet Ezekiel who caught the daughters of Israel adopting the pagan custom. In the Passion of the Lord Tammuz, people mourned the fading and dying of the vegetation, and promoted its return. Each year the god died; each year he returned only to die again. Pots were filled with earth in which the seeds of vegetables and flowers were sown. Carefully watered and tended for eight days in the warm climate, the seed sprouted rapidly. But after the rootless plants withered, they were thrown into the waters with images of the dead Tammuz and mourned extravagantly.

Various myths told his story and personified this vegetation spirit. In Babylonia he was the handsome lover or young husband of Isthar, a mother goddess who represented the fertility of the earth. But since it was his sad lot to die every year and to pass into the bleak underworld, Isthar went down to the underworld in search of him, thus threatening all life with extinction. This serious problem came to the attention of the chief god Ea who finally prevailed upon the grim goddess of the underworld to allow Isthar to depart with Tammuz.

The Babylonian legends are supplemented by the Greek myth in which Tammuz, known as Adonis (originally merely his Semitic title—Lord, like the Hebrew word *Adonoi*) was beloved by Aphrodite. She hid him in a chest which she entrusted to Persephone, the queen of the underworld. Persephone, however, was so entranced with the youth that she refused to return him to Aphrodite. The goddess of love and life went down to the underworld to ransom him, but could not prevail upon the goddess of death to relinquish him until Zeus decreed that, like the vegetation, Adonis should divide his time between the upper and the nether world. The Greek myth, strongly reminiscent of the Babylonian rites in which the emphasis is on the death rather than the resurrection of Tammuz, has Adonis finally killed by a wild boar or by the war-god Ares or Mars in the shape of a boar. Ares' deed may have been the first crime of passion in the theatre, since as husband of Aphrodite he was jealous of the attention she lavished on the handsome boy!

In Alexandria, where the Greek version was favored, images of Aphrodite and Adonis were placed on two couches. Ripe fruits, growing plants, and cakes were set beside these patrons of fertility, and the lovers were married with pomp and cheer. But next day Adonis was dead and had to be mourned by the women with streaming hair and bared breasts. In token of their grief, the women of Phoenicia even sacrificed their virtue by yielding to strangers, and this in turn may have been a symbolic undoing of his death since it ensured their own fertility.[7] The ceremony ended with a song which foretold his return to the land of the living.

Tremendous advances in the theatre were ushered in by the Passions of Osiris and Tammuz. At most, the early dancers employed a variety of mimetic movements, covered themselves with skins, and wore masks representing animals known for their fecundating power. But the more elaborate ritual of the god added pageants and processions, images, and tableaux, like the one in honor of Aphrodite and Adonis. Stage "props" like the boat of Osiris which was attacked by his enemies became necessary, and some sort of scenery appears to have been suggested.

The leader of the primitive dramatic rite had to become a real stage director. The taxing function of organizing the Passion Play increasingly became a specialty, and it ultimately passed from the priesthood to the laity. In time the priest had to leave the theatre entirely, and at most he remained on its periphery like the priests of Dionysus who occupied thrones close to the stage but did not direct the actual proceedings or write the plays.* Since, moreover, the heroes of these Passion Plays were distinct individuals, the theatre was brought a step closer to individual acting, and the priest-actor was in time supplanted by the lay performer.

After the largely pantomimic Passion Plays only two more developments were needed to prepare the drama for its high estate in later times —completely human heroes, and dialogue. For this final stage we must

---

* It is significant, however, that the three masters of classic Greek tragedy, Aeschylus, Sophocles, and Euripides, were associated with the priesthood at one time or another. The transition of the playwright from priest to layman was gradual in Greece, as well as in the Orient and in medieval Europe.

not, however, look to Egypt or Syria where humanism could not reach
maturity owing to the dead-weight of despotism and hierarchy.

5 THESPIS AND THE DAWN IN GREECE

Destined to flower first and most completely as drama was the Passion
Play of Greece.

Like his fellow-man in Egypt or Syria the primitive Greek was steeped
in magic and ritual. The resurgence of spring he furthered and celebrated
in countless ways, enacting the uprising of the earth spirit Persephone
who in the familiar myth is carried off into the underworld by that formidable lover Pluto or Death. At Delphi the Greeks buried a puppet
"Charila," the grace-giving Spring Maiden, and then exhumed her to
represent, as well as to promote, the coming of the fertile season. Since,
moreover, winter is the great enemy, his representative, the great hunger
or "Ox-hunger," was cast out with great solemnity. A scapegoat in the
person of a slave was led forth, beaten with a rod cut from a magical
plant, and driven out of doors with the magical words: *"Out* with the Ox-
hunger, *in* with wealth and health!" [8]

A number of the cities resorted to animal sacrifice, slaying a sanctified
bull whose original may well have been the Minotaur of ancient Cretan
legend. In the Greek city of Magnesia in Asia Minor the finest bull was
set apart and made sacred at the beginning of seedtime. He was zealously guarded from contamination all through the autumn and winter
while he held the luck of the city conserved in his strong and beautiful
body. Then in April he was sacrificed solemnly and his flesh was eaten
by all the citizens in order that they might share his power or *mana*. Next
year a fresh bull was chosen and the cycle was repeated. This *Bouphonia*
or "ox-murder" was duplicated in Athens, with one significant addition
—the resurrection of the strength-giving quadruped. The Athenians
stuffed his hide and yoked it to a plow, as if he had not been killed at all.
To clear themselves of murder, moreover, "They fled, away after the
deed, not looking backwards; they publicly tried and condemned the
axe that struck the blow." [9] In their early history, the noble Greeks who
later gave us the philosophy of Plato and the sculpture of Phidias did
not differ greatly from the Indians on the plains or the Ainos of the island
of Sangalien who have a similar rite revolving around a sacred bear.

Another variously performed little drama was that of the new or "second" birth, a ceremony with which the young men of the Greeks were inducted into the tribe. Here again the ancestors of the Periclean sage and
artist did not differ greatly from the savages who have yielded their mysteries to modern anthropologists. Simulation of birth is a general feature
of this rite, as for example in British East Africa where the Kikuyu

mother stands over her crouching son and pretends to be having labor pains while he whimpers like a new-born infant.

But the Greeks developed under favorable conditions into a creative race which sublimated its superstition into highly personalized deities, beautiful stories, and vivid performances. Dionysus, created in the image of man, became the protagonist of the several functions of the primitive mind. He was recognized under several names as the Spring Spirit, the God of Rebirth ("The Divine Young Man" and "Bromius, He of the loud cry"), the Bull God or the Goat God, and the intoxicating power of procreation in all things. As god of the vine, the most common of his titles, he merely expressed one symbolic aspect of his energizing divinity. His rite, known as the dithyramb, was a "leaping dance" or dance of abandonment, accompanied by dramatic movements and supplied with appropriate hymns. The sacrifice of an animal, probably a goat, and much mummery by the dance-chorus dressed in goat-skins (thus resurrecting the Goat God symbolically) were also features of the rite. Moreover, the leaders of the dithyramb had an entire story to draw upon when they began improvising additions to the dance.

One myth made Dionysus the son of Zeus and Persephone, the spring or Corn Maiden; another called Semele, the Earth, his mother. In one version, Dionysus was born as the horned infant "Zagreus" and immediately mounted his father's throne. But he was overthrown by the Titans, whom he evaded for some time by assuming various shapes until his body was cut into little pieces (as in certain totemic bull-killing rites). Here again we find the essence of tragedy—conflict and death; Dionysus is simply another of those many gods who die. But in another account, prevalent in Crete where Dionysus was the son of an earthly king he is already on the way to resurrection. The pieces were put together at the command of Zeus and buried.

A Passion Play in Crete represented his tragedy in great detail. "All that he had done or suffered in his last moments was enacted before the eyes of his worshipers, who tore a live bull to pieces with their teeth and roamed the woods with frantic shouts." [10] In still other versions, his mother made him young again after piecing him together, or he rose from the grave and ascended to heaven by his own efficacy.

In time, moreover, the leaders of the dithyramb could include other related details taken from the many tales of ancestral and local heroes which were being recited by poets or enacted in tomb rites. Since these heroes, too, had accomplished great deeds in behalf of their people, since they too had had their *agon* or struggle with an opponent and had died, the nascent playwrights found it possible to fit them into the general mold of Dionysian drama. A tendency to substitute human for ritualistic detail made its appearance, and the trend was strengthened by the gradual waning of primitive religion, particularly in Athens where it was largely reduced to a festive formality. When skepticism struck off the shackles of superstition it released the essential drama in the rite from its primitive clogs. Finally the words associated with the dithyrambic dances, which had at first been spontaneous and fragmentary, became increasingly elaborate, this development being·facilitated by the rapid rise of Greek poetry. Soon the verses, which at first had been sung in unison or were at most divided between the chorus as in antiphonal singing, began to assume the form of individual dialogue.

When Thespis, a director of choruses, his face smeared with white lead perhaps in simulation of the dead god, stood on a table and addressed the leader of the chorus, dialogue was born in Greece. With his inspired step Thespis also created the classic actor as distinct from the dancer. His table, which probably served as an altar for the animal sacrifice, was moreover the first inkling of a stage as distinguished from the primitive dancing circle.

In inaugurating the reign of dialogue Thespis was probably not alone, for the give-and-take of Dionysian revelry was bound to suggest its use. He may have been anticipated by other leaders of the dithyramb, and it is known that the poet Arion had already inserted some spoken lines into the rite somewhat earlier. But it was the work of Thespis that made the strongest impression upon the Greeks, and his name has come down the ages as an important, if shadowy, figure. He appears to have employed dialogue more fully than any of his predecessors or contemporaries, and to have developed a fairly extensive dramatic plot. The wise rationalist, law-giver and censor of morals, Solon, is reported to have even rebuked him for his fabulous stories. "Are you not ashamed to tell so many lies?" Solon asked him. From an ingenious director of the dithyramb Thespis became a playwright and, in 535 B.C., the first prize-winning one. He even acquired a "theatre building" when his plays came to be performed in a permanent circular dancing ground of stone with a stone temple in the background.

A contest of plays in 535 arose when Pisistratus, the "tyrant" whom the common people of Athens invested, with power, brought a rustic Dionysian festival into the city. The "theatre" was constructed to accommodate the dithyrambs and early plays which comprised the major features of this democratic celebration. Unlike the ancestral spirits worshiped by the nobles, Dionysus the vegetation spirit was the property of all the people, and it was sound political strategy to celebrate his glory to the fullest extent.

A politician, we see, shares honors with Thespis in launching the Greek theatre. Without Pisistratus drama might have long remained a crude affair. Moreover, without his efforts to counteract the social pretensions of the aristocracy by giving the people a race of heroes who transcended any single family, completely human characters would have entered the Greek theatre more slowly than they did. It was largely owing to him that the vogue of the Homeric epics was established in the city. After that event it was a simple matter for the Homeric galaxy of heroes—Agamemnon, Odysseus, Achilles, and others—to take their place along with Dionysus among the *dramatis personae* of the theatre. Dionysus was never neglected by the classic stage, which paid tribute to the god by making him its patron, honoring him with an elaborate procession, and assigning to him the chief role in a number of plays. But the national heroes, along with several local ones like Theseus and Hippolytus, provided the classic playwright with decidedly greater variety of story material. Becoming the chief subject of the drama, the Homeric and ancestral characters transformed the theatre of God into the temple of Man.

It was under the influence of these developments that Thespis worked, and it is no wonder that he found it necessary to extend the boundaries of the choral theatre. How else could he have accommodated himself to the new humanistic spirit which made itself felt in Athens? Exactly to what extent he reaped the harvest of the cultural interests of his time it is impossible to say since his plays are completely lost. But others soon took up his work, and among them fortunately was Aeschylus the soldier, thinker, and prophet who responded to even greater historical forces and made the drama an instrument for the highest aspirations of Western humanity.

PART II

THE CLASSIC MASTERS

THE DRAMA first attains maturity in the classic age of Greece and Rome. It makes the first transition from ritual to art, and it marks the first advance toward characterization and broadly human content. The theatre, moreover, finally becomes a synthesis of the arts such as it has been since the fifth century B.C. Poetry and dramatic action, supplemented by nearly all the arts from music to painting, produce a potent organ for the expression of human experience and thought. The first masters of the drama are in a sense masters of life.

II

AESCHYLUS—"THE FATHER OF TRAGEDY"

I A PLAYWRIGHT AT THE CROSSROADS

IN THE year 525 B.C., Cambyses invaded Egypt, and Aeschylus was born. On the surface, a minor event in the history of Asiatic imperialism and the birth of the generally acknowledged "father of tragedy" have no visible connection. But the logic of cultural processes moves circuitously. It was the destiny of the theatre's first master to be linked with political and cultural history at almost every point in his exciting and moderately long life. No playwright ever found himself so frequently at the crossroads.

Every genius reveals a pattern of behavior. It was the pattern of the first great playwright, as it has been of many of his later compeers, to be always standing between two worlds or principles. What he was later to transcribe into plays was his in part by virtue of being alive in one of the critical periods of human history.

A second, and closer, thrust by the Persian empire occurred in his childhood when Darius invaded the Balkans in 512 as far as the mouth of the Danube. Thereafter, as Aeschylus grew to manhood, relations between the Persians and the Greeks became increasingly strained. When the Ionian colonies revolted against the Asiatic empire that had subjugated them many years before, he was twenty-six and old enough to feel the impact of the event. Four years later the Greeks of Asia Minor suffered a crushing defeat which resulted in the invasion of European Greece; and it was not long before his native state Athens, variously involved in the revolt, became the object of attack.

Appropriately enough, the world's first great tragedian matured on a volcano.

Ten years after Aeschylus made his debut as a produced playwright, in 490, he was on the plain of Marathon with the valiant band of Athenians that repelled the hosts of the greatest empire of his time. At the age of thirty-five he was a national hero: the theatre of Dionysus in Athens possessed a picture representing the heroism of Aeschylus and his brother Cynaegirus on this historic occasion. But there was to be no rest for the warrior playwright, and he was not destined for a complacent middle age. Ten years later, the memory of Marathon must have been ashes in the heart of the poet as he watched the hasty evacuation of his city.

The Persians had broken through at Thermopylae in overwhelming numbers. The Athenian populace was forced to take to its ships to avoid capture, and the proud city was razed to the ground by the invader. Aeschylus and Europe stood at the parting of the ways. The triumph of Persian arms would have turned Greece into a colony of the Orient, and it must have been evident to a thinker like Aeschylus that the collapse of Hellenic civilization would entail the destruction of a new viewpoint which embraced democratic principles and individual conscience and thought. From this fate Europe was saved by the momentous naval battle of Salamis when the Athenians, grappling with the Persian ships in hand-to-hand encounters, crushed the invaders. The forty-five-year-old Aeschylus returned with his fellow-citizens to rebuild Athens and make it the cultural and political capital of Hellas.

That he would never forget his participation in the great struggle by the side of his tribesmen and two brothers, one of whom was decorated for valor at Salamis, was inevitable. What thoughtful and imaginative man would forget a succession of crises and climaxes that could vie with any drama ever written? Aeschylus was to remember eight years later when he celebrated the victory and pondered on the fate of empires in *The Persians*. The epic sweep of his plays, their exalted dialogue, their broad strokes of characterization, and their situations which are fixed upon the peaks of titanic passion, belong to a heroic age. His orchestration favors trumpets, and his thought—no matter how subtle—rings with martial challenge. As he stands at the crossroads of ethics, he has the bearing of a soldier holding his ground against a horde of opponents, neither giving nor asking quarter. Moreover, for all his brooding upon human evil there is in his work a sense of resolute optimism: The right principle always wins in his philosophical and ethical conflicts as it won on the field of Marathon and the waters of Salamis. Even in his profoundest probings, always expressed in terms of colossal struggle, he remains a fighting poet.

Others were also to remember him as a soldier; not only the Athenians who recorded their victory in many a monument, but the citizens of Sicilian Gela where he breathed his last in his sixty-ninth year. On his tomb they set this epitaph:

> *Here Aeschylus lies, from his Athenian home*
> *Remote, beneath Gela's wheat-producing loam.*
> *How brave in battle was Euphorion's son*
> *The long-haired Persian can tell that fled from Marathon.* [1]

If, as it is believed, he wrote these lines himself, we have a good example of his self-appraisal.

No sooner, however, have the Persians been defeated than Greece begins to move toward another crisis. His city-state becomes an empire, and the struggle for hegemony in the Greek peninsula begins to occupy the poet. His plays contain topical allusions like the glorification of an alliance with Argos and contempt for the Thebans, who were enemies of Athens, in his first extant drama, *The Suppliants*. Watching the decline of a great empire like Persia, he was, above all, led to ponder on the destiny of nations and dynasties. He could not but consider the subject further when, elated with its victories, Athens began to acquire more power than it could use discreetly. It is not surprising that the subjects of *hubris* or catastrophic pride, and of nemesis or adverse fate, constantly occupied the mind of this thinking playwright.

Moreover, the problem of his country's future, which no Greek writer living in small and insecure states could ignore, was related to the whole question of government. The national events of the Persian invasion had long been paralleled by a local struggle between the aristocracy and the masses composed of those Athenian citizens who were less well stocked with ancestors, privileges, and wealth. In this class conflict which remained an issue long after Salamis, Aeschylus, the son of an ancient family of Eleusis, the Vatican City of Attica, was on the side of the nobility. Although it is difficult to gauge the full extent of his opposition to the new order, we know that he spoke slightingly of young power and of upstart rulers in *Prometheus Bound,* and it was believed that his loss of a prize contest to his young rival Sophocles in 468 was in the nature of a political repercussion. A number of years later he even went out of his way to glorify that aristocratic institution the Areopagus, the Supreme Court of Athens. The Franklin D. Roosevelt of the time, Ephialtes, deprived it of most of its powers, which included the right to punish public officials, supervise the administration, and censor the private lives of citizens. Little more than the right to try cases of homicide was left to that venerable body which consisted only of members of the richest families in the state. Aeschylus, who could only be perturbed by this loss of prerogatives, used the tragedy of his matricidal hero Orestes to buttress the tottering institution. Since Orestes in *The Eumenides* is tried and acquitted by the Areopagus, the honor of bringing light and peace into the ghost- and vengeance-ridden world is assigned to an institution which Aeschylus was inclined to support.

Even if the play tacitly accepts the reforms of Ephialtes by assigning a homicide case to the very first session of the Areopagus, this glorification of the court must have been offensive to democratic partisans. An ambiguous report of Aeschylus' life has him tried on a charge of impiety. Some allusion to the Eleusinian mysteries, which it was a crime to reveal, is given as the cause. But since impiety, like heresy, is an extremely elastic term, it is highly probable that his persecution was politically inspired.

The record also has him retiring on two occasions to the court of Hieron, the ruler of Syracuse. In Sicily, Aeschylus had no democratic faction to trouble him, and in this second home, which loaded him with honors, he died peacefully in 456.

So unconventional a thinker as Aeschylus cannot, however, be set down as a run-of-the-mine conservative. He had ringing praises for the early democracy of Athens in *The Persians,* and he reserved the most glowing praise for his city. He championed plain living and high thinking, and resented in the later course of Athenian democracy the prevailing tendencies of commercialism and demagoguery. The heroic age was being displaced by the rule of the trader, and the poet who sought nobility in all things may well have looked with longing on the old days of Marathon and Salamis. Even war had lost its idealistic façade, and battles were no longer fought for liberty but for commerce. When Aeschylus inveighed in his last trilogy against "War, who trades men for gold," he could not have been thinking of the battles in which he bore arms against the Persian invader. Politics no doubt exercised him more intensely than we shall ever know.

Nevertheless, it is his approach to religion and ethics that most affected the quality and significance of his tragedies. And again we find him standing between two worlds, for Aeschylus is both an Oriental mystic or Hebrew prophet and a Hellenic philosopher.

The most colorful part of his early training was his immersion in the mystic rites and speculations of Eleusis, the city of his birth where he was inducted early into the esoteric worship of the Mother and Earth goddess Demeter. Aristophanes makes Aeschylus apostrophize her:

> *"Oh, thou that nourished my young soul, Demeter,*
> *Make me worthy of thy mysteries."*

This cult appears to have been a survival of primitive worship, and the ecstasies associated with it were closer to the religious attitude of the East than they were to the rationalism of the Periclean age.

The Greeks considered Aeschylus a god-intoxicated man who achieved his effects by inspiration; according to Sophocles, he did "what he ought to do, but did it without knowing." The statement smacks of condescension, for the younger rival belonged to an age that regarded Aeschylus as a splendid barbarian. Athenaeus, a Hellenic Walter Winchell, retails information to the effect that he composed his plays while in his cups. Since the Greeks were boyishly fond of ridicule at the expense of offending artists and politicians, this story may have been, of course, a libel. Thus one particularly gleeful legend has it that Aeschylus met his death when an eagle mistook his bald pate for a rock and dropped a tortoise on it. . . . The bit of gossip passed on to us by Athenaeus may, however, have been an honest attempt to explain the rhapsodist in Aeschylus. According to another account apparently sanctioned by himself, he had once had a divine visitation. Once in his youth when he was set to watch the grapes ripening in the countryside, Dionysus appeared to him in his sleep and ordered him to compose tragedies. Obediently, the young man started a tragedy early next morning, and "succeeded very easily." Perhaps the hero of this story, which has its Anglo-Saxon parallel in the life of Caedmon, suffered hallucinations. According to some of our stage producers, he was not the last playwright to be thus afflicted.

Still, for all his cosmic imaginings and piety, he was also capable of developing an ordered philosophy, thereby proving himself as much a child of Greek reason as of Oriental rhapsody. Although he bears a strong resemblance to the later prophets of Israel, his view of divinity is compounded of Hellenic rationalism; in his first great trilogy, the Promethean one, he approaches God with his reason intact, and with a certain fearlessness. Not only did Aeschylus dismiss the polytheism of his time in favor of monotheism, but he regarded Zeus as the guardian of justice who is far removed from the willful and immoral divinities whose antics fill the Homeric poems. Moreover, he considered God a developing personality or principle which grows in goodness with the passage of time. Aeschylus may not have gone so far as to imply that since man creates his gods in his own image an improvement in the human species must be accompanied by an improvement in its divinities. But he makes it abundantly clear that he discerns an evolutionary principle in nature. Fate or Necessity, which orders everything, ensures the development of divine law in the direction of greater altruism and justice.

Similarly, in the province of human behavior, this earnest playwright arbitrates between the primitive blood-feud and civilized order. Investigating the problem of human suffering in his last trilogy, he arrives at the conclusion that it is the evil in man and not the envy of the gods that destroys happiness. "From of old," he says in *Agamemnon,* "hath this hoary tale been spread abroad among men, that when prosperity hath grown to its full stature it brings forth offspring and dies not childless; yea, that from a good hap a man's posterity shall reap unendingly a harvest of woe. But I stand apart from others, nor is my mind like theirs." Reviewing the history of royal families, he is ready to concede that the children's teeth are set on edge because the fathers have eaten sour grapes. But the hereditary taint is only a predisposition, which would disappear if it were not so tragically reactivated by human volition and perpetuated by the barbaric law of retribution. Such heroes as the fratricidal Eteocles and Agamemnon belong to families which are saddled with a curse, but the evil perpetuated in them is entirely of their own doing. Right reason and good will are the pillars of the first moral system that finds expression in the theatre.

Aeschylus appears to have believed that he stood alone in his philosophy. And at the beginning of his career he probably did. But his thought grew naturally out of a period which witnessed the transformation of Greek society. Later on, his intellectual peers expressed very much the same vision, and one of them, Pericles, even strove to give it concrete realization in the Athenian state. It was in the profoundly religious cast of his thinking that he differed from his younger contemporaries, as if he were bridging in his person the gulf between early religion and latter-day philosophy. In our own day he would perhaps strike us as a platitudinous moralist were it not that his plays are so instinct with life and transfigured by such glorious poetry.

2 AESCHYLUS AND THE GREEK THEATRE

For one who saw life so distinctly as a clash of principles, the nascent drama was of course a natural medium. At first, however, Aeschylus must have been torn between two allegiances. The poet in him could only be profoundly affected by the Homeric epics that had been collected, revised and arranged in Athens not so many years before his birth. Aeschylus rightly maintained that his tragedies were only slices from Homer's banquet, and most of them were based on stories contained in the cycle of epics among which those attributed to Homer were pre-eminent. Most of the tragedies possess Homeric qualities in the sweep of their narrative passages and in the heroic stature of their characters. Awed, however, by the virtually sacrosanct greatness of Homer, a young man would hesitate to invite comparison with him by composing epics. Moreover, an aspiring writer would naturally turn to the new form which was cracking its shell. Aeschylus, in particular, must have thrilled to the color and solemnity of the performances which had been growing in amplitude ever since dramatic contests had become a regular feature, ten years before his birth.

It remained for Aeschylus to broaden the form which won his interest. Even with the advances introduced since Thespis received the dramatic prize in 535, the plays were still little better than animated oratorios, strongly influenced by melic poetry which required instrumental accompaniment and by choral poetry which was supplemented by expressive dance movements. A chorus danced and engaged in dialogue with an actor who impersonated one or more characters by means of masks.

Tragedy, it is true, had acquired more scope in the hands of the playwrights Choerilus, Pratinas and Phrynichus who succeeded Thespis.

Phrynichus, in particular, made signal contributions to the early drama by introducing female characters and developing descriptive and lyrical passages greatly admired by the Greeks.[2] One of his historical plays, *The Phoenissae* which celebrated the Athenian victory at Salamis, remained popular throughout the fifth century. (It may have owed its excellence to the influence of Aeschylus, who had achieved importance by the time the play was introduced.) In general, however, not much action and characterization could be encompassed by the early plays, and only elementary conflicts could be enacted in them. The physical theatre was similarly rudimentary, and the stage as we now know it practically nonexistent. Nearly all the action took place in the circular dancing place called the "orchestra," that vestige of the old days when the drama had been little more than a circular dance around some sacred object. At best, there would be a hut, known as the *skene,* back of the "orchestra" in which the actors could put on and change their clothes and masks.

Again at the parting of the ways, Aeschylus had to choose between near ritual and theatre, between chorus and drama. As a professional dancing master or director of choruses, he would be partial to the sung and danced portions, especially as these afforded an outlet for his tremendous lyric talent. His choruses are the longest in Greek drama, and are remarkable for their metrical variety. Even in his most fully developed tragedy, the *Agamemnon,* there are only nine hundred lines of dialogue out of a total of about sixteen hundred seventy.[3] But he strove to make the chorus an active element in his theatre, as well as to reduce its length. The chorus of Elders in the *Agamemnon* quarrels with the queen's lover and is on the verge of hurling itself on him when stopped by the queen. The chorus of Furies in *The Eumenides* performs a dramatic function in actively pursuing the conscience-stricken son who murdered his mother.

Above all, however, Aeschylus proceeded to extend the acted portions of his plays, the parts which the Greeks called the "episodes" because they were not originally part of the drama and were only added to the performance. To develop the action was tantamount to making an interpolation, and this was no easy thing to do. In his attempt to overcome the inertia of the established form, Aeschylus took a great step when he added a second actor to tragedy. In time, he also acquired a third speaking actor, introduced by Sophocles, and so reached the ultimate range of individualization in Greek tragedy. If three actors seem pitifully inadequate to us, we must remember that they multiplied themselves by using masks, that they were augmented by mute characters like attendants and soldiers, and that mass effects could always be supplied by the chorus. In *The Eumenides* twelve mute judges try Orestes, and "supers" spread purple carpets under Agamemnon's feet when he appears in the first part of the trilogy accompanied by the other mutes who comprise his retinue.*

In broadening the theatre Aeschylus, moreover, was serving "show business" as much as the more ideal demands of drama, for the "father of tragedy" was one of the first of the long procession of playwrights who were also practical men of the theatre. If he was not an actor like his shadowy predecessors or like Shakespeare and Molière, he was an excellent stage director who knew the value of effective pauses and used them so frequently that Aristophanes took note of it in *The Frogs*. He also improved the tragic dance, developing a variety of postures and movements, since he trained his own choruses.

Aeschylus even favored sensationalism, in which he was only following the primitive love of masquerade. Many of his characters are weird impersonations of natural forces and fantastic mythological figures. Prominent among them are the horned Io, the curious Oceanus who rides a winged horse, the harpies who snatch food from Phineas in a lost play, and the titan Prometheus. The tragedies contain apparitions and ghosts, like the dead monarch Darius who is invoked in *The Persians* and the murdered Clytemnestra whose walking spirit harries her matricidal son Orestes in *The Eumenides*. Aeschylus could have given any of our stage directors close competition when he brought the Furies on the scene so realistically that he was reputed to have frightened children and caused miscarriages in the audience. To show "their symbolic torches, their snake-entwined tresses, their dreadful eyes, and nostrils snorting fiery breath" [7] was no mean assignment for the costume designer.

The costume designer was Aeschylus himself. Although Greek tradition probably erred in attributing the origin of the tragic costume to Aeschylus, he undoubtedly settled its important features. Resolved to make his actors as impressive as possible, a prime consideration in so vast a theatre as the Athenian one which seated as many as twenty thousand

---

* The development was undoubtedly a natural process, and the old dithyrambic goat or satyr chorus was inevitably divided and modified when dialogue was introduced. No great spirit creates quite alone or builds out of thin air. Gilbert Murray speculates interestingly in his *History of Ancient Greek Literature* (Appleton, 1916): "The Greek word for actor, 'hypocrites,' means 'answerer.' The poet was really the actor; but if he wanted to develop his solitary declamation into dialogue, he needed some one to answer him. The chorus was normally divided into two parts, as the system of strophe and antistrophe testifies. The poet perhaps took for answerers the leaders of the two parts. . . . The old round choir consisted of fifty dancers and a poet: the full tragic company of forty-eight dancers, two 'answerers' and a poet." This gives us *three* actors, as well as twelve members of the chorus once the performance began to consist of four plays—three tragedies [a trilogy] and a satyr-play. Professor Murray describes the tetralogy as an elaboration of the original dithyramb in which the chorus impersonated satyrs—"the tragic choirs were allowed three changes of costume [in the tragedies] before they appeared as satyrs confessed [in the satyr play that concluded the set of dramas]."

spectators, he added stature to his actors by developing the padded shoe or buskin, the *cothurnus*. Although Thespis used linen masks and Phrynichus introduced the use of female masks, it was Aeschylus who first employed expressive painted ones in response to the requirements of his progressively complex tragedies.

From costumes and masks to rudimentary scenic design was of course only a step, and one that so versatile a genius could easily take. He decorated his stage—that is, the scene-building which became a permanent set—with properties required by individual plays. He apparently also began to employ machinery and scenic effects successfully. His practical innovations make him the theatre's first notable showman as well as playwright. Aeschylus was, in short, the first important playwright, stage director, scene designer, costumer, and dancing master: a veritable O'Neill, Reinhardt, Robert Edmond Jones, Valentina, and Diaghilev rolled in one. He is the answer to Gordon Craig's prayer twenty-four centuries before Craig called for supermen in the theatre.

3 THE ATHENIAN THEATRE FESTIVAL AND ITS CONVENTIONS

The tragedies of Aeschylus, as well as of his successors, cannot be adequately understood without some picture of the conventions of the stage and some knowledge of the occasion for which they were written.

Greek plays were only produced at celebrations of which we still have such examples as the Malvern, the Ann Arbor Theatre, the Little Theatre, New Theatre, and Shakespearean festivals. It all began about the middle of the sixth century when, as we saw, the democratic tyrant Pisistratus transferred the old rustic Dionysian festival of the fruits of the earth to Athens. In the City Dionysia held at the end of March, the people acquired a splendid folk festival at which they could cement their interests and display the glories of their state to the visiting business men who filled the city at this time. An older but secondary festival known as the Lenaea, held about the end of January, also began to include tragic, as well as comic, contests. Later, other festive occasions in the towns and villages of Attica, known as the Rural Dionysia, began to favor dramatic productions, the most impressive being held in the seaport Piraeus. Frequently these festivals, the Greek equivalent of the "road," revived plays that had been produced at the City Dionysia but could not be repeated in Athens—until an edict legalized the revival of plays by Aeschylus after his death.

The City Dionysia, considered so sacred that minor violations were punished as sacrilege, began elaborately with a procession which escorted the ancient image of Dionysus, literally the "god-father" of the theatre, along the road toward the town of Eleutherae and then back to Athens by torchlight. The image was then placed in or near the orchestra of the theatre with appropriate rites, special seats or "thrones" being reserved for the elaborately dressed priests of the god. After two days of dithyrambic events, consisting of choral contests by choruses of men and boys, a day was devoted to comedies, with five playwrights competing; then three days were reserved for tragedy. Six days were devoted to the great festival; five, after 431 B.C. — during the last three days with five performances daily—three tragedies and a phallic "satyr-play" in the morning, and one or two comedies in the afternoon. Three playwrights competed for the prize in tragedy, each with three tragedies and a satyr-comedy, the plays being more or less related, although only Aeschylus appears to have written strictly connected trilogies or tetralogies.

Preparations for the contest were made some time before the festival. The plays were carefully selected by the first playreader of the theatre, the official or *archon* who also chose the leading player or "protagonist." Wealthy citizens were designated by law to bear the expense of a chorus of twelve to fifteen men, this being one of several state duties assigned to them until their impoverishment during the Peloponnesian War compelled the state to assume the burden. Rehearsals were arranged, the chorus being placed under a *didascolos* or trainer; properties were purchased, and a pipe-player was selected. Then a few days before the performance the playwright, actors, and chorus presented themselves in a place adjoining the theatre to give a *proagon*. Here, in lieu of billboards, advertisements and printed programs, the group announced the titles of the plays, the author's name, and similar details. Immediately before the contest the order of the contestants was determined by lot, and at its close the victors, judged by a committee also selected by lot, were crowned with garlands of ivy.

What the audience saw at a performance can be only roughly described, since production is the most mortal part of the theatre. But no doubt the artists of the Greek theatre strove for theatrical effect as ardently as any Max Reinhardt. An Athenian audience saw performances which, if not exactly realistic, were colorful, diversified, and impressive. There is no foundation for the myth of austerity foisted upon the Athenian theatre some twenty centuries later.

The masks, so frequently employed in primitive ritual, were not only a hallowed convention scrupulously retained by the Greek theatre, but a powerful means of attracting attention, creating excitement, and expressing essential drama. All the actors wore elongated grotesque masks of linen, cork, and wood, which grew larger and more curious with time. Although fairly stereotyped, portraying general attributes like cruelty, craft, and suffering, these disguises possessed considerable variety. Special masks would be required by mythological and allegorical characters like the horned Io, the multiple-eyed Argo, the snaky-haired Furies, and allegorical figures like Death, Force, and Frenzy. That even realism was attempted is shown by the fact that at the conclusion of Sophocles' *Oedipus the King* the mask of the hero depicted a bloodstained countenance with mutilated eyes.

The familiar boots or *cothurni* with their thickened painted soles and the high headdress (the *onkos*) above the mask made the actors appear taller than life. A six-foot actor would be raised to seven and a half feet or over, so that he was prone to tumble ignominiously if he took an incautious step. Mantles of saffron, purple and gold, and extravagant costumes, particularly in comedy, lent him color; and padded clothing balanced the height effected by the *cothurnus* and *onkos*. Characters were differentiated by means of the mask, the thickness of the *cothurnus*, the quality of the garments, and such details as the crowns worn by kings, the turbans of Orientals, and the crutches that assisted old men across the stage.

Heavily encumbered, the tragedians' movements were necessarily slow and their gestures broad. It is not surprising, therefore, that violent physical action was generally avoided, deaths occurring offstage and being related by a character known as the Messenger. Nevertheless, it was unlikely that the playgoer was bored by such static devices, for there was always more than enough movement in the chorus, in the orgiastic satyr-plays which came at the close of the morning's tragedies, and in the comedies that followed in the afternoon.

Facial play was of course concealed by the mask, but this, too, was no great loss in so vast a theatre as the Athenian. Nuances of emotion were expressed for the most part verbally, although mimetic gestures and expressive masks would be of help. Fortunately, the acoustics of a Greek theatre were excellent, and the voice of the actor could be projected to the utmost tiers with the aid of the open-mouthed mask that served as a sounding board. Actors were in fact chosen for their voices. Good actors were so greatly in demand that they soon commanded enormous salaries, and in later times, when playwriting talent had become scarce, acting assumed greater importance than the drama itself. It even became customary to have contests between actors as well as plays. The abused "star system" began among the allegedly austere Athenians.

The stage effect was vastly enhanced by the presence of the chorus that marched in with aplomb in ranks and files from the wings, came and went as needed, and mixed with the actors from time to time. In lieu of a curtain, every new scene was ushered in and followed by a chorus, and any amount of time could be assumed to elapse during the singing of the *stasimon* or choral ode. Like the actors, the chorus was variously costumed and wore masks appropriate to the age, sex and character of the persons represented. Especially varied was the costuming of the chorus in comedy, and the design of the clothing might contain considerable exaggeration for purposes of humor.

The chorus sang or chanted odes with appropriate, highly stylized movements. A dignified dance form called *emmelia* (harmony) accompanied the more stately odes, while odes of ecstatic emotion or gladness were accompanied by a lively dance. Much of the dancing was decidedly mimetic. One favorite dancer employed by Aeschylus was famous for his ability to describe dramatic events by means of gestures.

Even when the chorus remained passive this body did not stand frozen in a tableau, as has been supposed. It continued to follow the story with descriptive movements conveying emotions of anxiety, terror, pity, hope, and exaltation. Nor did the chorus always sing; for it sometimes used recitative and even conversational speech in addressing the actors. And it did not always sing or speak in unison. During the murder of the king in the *Agamemnon,* for example, the old men debate helplessly what to do and each member of the chorus voices his opinion. The songs were rendered with distinctiveness of utterance, each note corresponding to a syllable, and were accompanied by a wood-wind instrument resembling our clarinet. Later on, solos were added for greater effect and virtuosos made quite a practice of it much to the distress of the purists, who were not wanting in Athens. The use of a chorus in Greek drama certainly had its disadvantages because it slowed up and interrupted the dramatic portions of the play. But it greatly enriched the spectacular qualities of the Greek stage and introduced a musical component into the theatre, which has led writers to compare classic drama with modern opera.

It is no secret that in the physical theatre of the fifth century much had to be imagined or reconstructed by the audience from the suggestive background, the permanent scenic façade developed from the original dressing hut, and the descriptive passages of the play. Nevertheless, there was no dearth of color in the productions, and mechanical contraptions afforded some partially realistic scenery. The sound of thunder was given by a *bronteion,* and lightning was provided. A platform known as the *eccyclema,* a form of wagon-stage, was rolled out through the doors of the scene building or pushed out (in which case it was called an *exostra*) to reveal interior scenes. Trapdoors, aptly called "Charon's Steps," enabled ghosts to rise from the nether world. A crane-like contraption, the *mechane,* transported the actor who impersonated a god to the roof of the scene building, swept him across the acting area, suspended him in mid-air, and lowered him sensationally into the ·orchestra. Since he came by way of the machine, he was "the god from the machine" or "deus ex machina." Sometimes, too, the gods were exhibited in heaven on a special platform, called a *theologeion*, and there were such spectacular effects on the roof as Medea's departure in a chariot drawn by winged dragons. Even the settings were not so inadequate as has been imagined, since they could represent anything from a hill or countryside to a building or a series of structures. Occasionally, as in Aeschylus' *Eumenides* and Sophocles' *Ajax*, sets were even changed within a single play with the aid of revolving painted prisms called *periakti* set flush with the scene building on either side of the stage.[4]

Athenian playgoers did not differ from the rest of the world. They came to be entertained, enjoyed the spectacles and striking performances, and were not above political axe-grinding in the distribution of applause and prizes. Some ancient playgoers snored no doubt as blissfully as their modern counterparts, awaking only for the applause or the razzberries, which took the form of kicking one's heels against the front of the benches. Audiences rose at dawn, ate heartily, and took provisions with them to the theatre. Sometimes the actors were greeted with an avalanche of fruit, figs, and olives. What other annoyances plagued the anxious playwright and his players may be easily imagined. Some seventeen thousand people packed into an auditorium from dawn to dusk cannot be expected to behave like schoolgirls at commencement exercises.

As always, too, a spectacular production camouflaged the intrinsic merit of the dramatic composition, and a mediocre playwright who had a generous patron for his chorus stood a better chance of winning the prize. *Oedipus the King,* which is considered the greatest tragedy of antiquity, apparently lost first prize because its *choregus* or "backer" was niggardly. The "angel" who has been the butt of so many jests of the theatre is a more venerable institution than many of us would care to admit.

Certainly, neither the judges, who were not specialists like our drama critics, nor the audiences, interested themselves in the academic considerations of the three unities of time, place, and action which exercised critics during and after the Renaissance. When Aristotle declared in his *Poetics* that "tragedy endeavors, so far as possible, to confine itself to a single revolution of the sun or but slightly exceed the limit," he was merely making an observation, and a fairly elastic one, instead of laying down a law. There were practical reasons for this time-limitation, since Greek tragedies were as short as our long one-acters. That the Athenian playwrights should try to confine themselves to a single situation or a series of events transpiring in as short a time as possible was natural. Nevertheless, they followed no hard and fast rule. As noted before, any amount of time could pass during the singing of a choral ode; Aeschylus, for example, violated the "unity of time" in his *Eumenides* without the slightest scruple.

If the playwrights preferred a single locale or "unity of place" it was because the physical conditions of their stage favored "one-set plays." But here again they were not saddled with an inviolable law, as two-set plays like *The Eumenides* and *Ajax* prove. Unity of action they may have observed, like so many writers, as a principle of good taste and order, although here, too, there were violations. (Aeschylus' *The Seven Against Thebes* is a case in point.) If, unlike Shakespeare and other Elizabethans, Aeschylus and his successors did not as a rule encumber themselves with sub-plots, one good reason was probably the chorus, which could convey past and subsidiary events by means of vivid narrative. If the Greek playwrights did not clutter up their tragedies with extraneous clowning, a reason was probably the convention which enabled every tragedian to wind up his series of tragedies with a riotous and bawdy after-piece, the so-called "satyr-play." For the audience at large all these questions were, however, purely academic, and fortunately there were few Aristotles among them. Otherwise attendance at the theatre festival might have been considerably less exhilarating than it appears to have been.

4 THE EARLY TRAGEDIES AND DRAMATIC ART OF AESCHYLUS

The actual productions of the Athenian theatre, are, of course, as irretrievably lost as the snows of yesteryear. But even the literary precipitate of theatre which we call the drama is not always secure. Of the work of all the Greek playwrights who won the annual prizes only the plays of Aeschylus, Sophocles, Euripides, and Aristophanes have survived, and even these writers are represented only by a fraction of their writings. Of the ninety-two plays of Aeschylus only seven have come down to us.

Hundreds of scattered fragments and comments provide an inkling of some of the subjects he treated. The lost *Lycurgean* trilogy dealt with the struggle between Dionysus and a scornful Thracian king, the middle play treating the death of Orpheus who is torn to pieces by bacchantes because he too slighted the god. This trilogy is patently close to the Dionysian origins of the drama. In the *Women of Etna* Aeschylus told a local story, the founding of a new city by the playwright's Sicilian patron. Troy was celebrated by the playwright in another lost trilogy, the first part (*The Myrmidons*) dealing with the death of Achilles' friend Patroclus, and the last part (*The Ransom*) with Priam's visit to Achilles who finally permits him to inter Hector's body. Here Aeschylus is taking another slice from Homer's ample banquet. Ajax, another Homeric hero, who was at the same time a native son, is the subject of *The Thracian Women*. The poet's penchant for cosmic speculation appeared in *Weighing of the Souls*. Not much more is known about his lost plays.

Fortunately, however, the surviving tragedies are so well distributed over the playwright's entire career that they throw sufficient light on the development of his style and thought. All his tragedies are built on a large scale, and nothing short of trilogies could satisfy his Olympian genius. The characters are drawn in the large, without a multiplicity of subtle qualifications. The dramatic devices are direct and not conspicuously ingenious. Gilbert Murray rightly likens his early work to "one of those archaic statues which stand with limbs stiff and countenance smiling and stony." Of the dialogue another Greek scholar writes, "He wields the pen as one more familiar with the spear; the warrior of Marathon does fierce battle with particles and phrases." [5] It will be well to remember that the playwright's first audiences were decidedly unsophisticated and demanded no such subtlety and complexity as the next generation required of his successors. "You took over an audience who were mere fools," Euripides says to Aeschylus in Aristophanes' literary satire *The Frogs*.

Nevertheless, Aeschylus is a master of the picturesque. His characters are colorful creatures, many of them supernatural, Oriental or barbaric, and his speech is luxuriously metaphorical. Anarchy in the state is "the mixing of mud with water"; the sea "laughs in ripples without number"; winter comes "with snowy wings"; and the flame of the beacon announcing the fall of Troy "vaults over the back of the sea with joy." It "hands its message to the heights." Its "mighty beard of fire" streams across the gulf, and "swoops down" upon the palace of Agamemnon.[6]

At first, his success was anything but phenomenal. Aeschylus did not win a prize until he was forty-one. His progress in playwriting must have been exceedingly gradual, since the early plays reveal a preponderance of choral material and only the last works are well supplied with dramatic action. His approach to characterization became more careful and precise with time, and his matter became increasingly profound. But he remained throughout his work a rhapsodist who expressed himself in Oriental imagery bearing a close resemblance to Hebrew prophetic literature. Always, moreover, he was the exponent of conflicting principles.

His first extant work, *The Suppliants*, probably the first play of a trilogy, shows him still struggling with choral drama. The fifty daughters of the Hellenic patriarch Danaus seek refuge in Argos from the attentions of the fifty sons of Aegyptus. Descendants of the mythical Argive princess Io, they entreat the Argive king for succor. He heeds the laws of hospitality, and at the risk of a possible war saves the maidens who are being dragged away by heralds. The play ends with a tribute to hospitality, and a warning by the old father against unholy love. Not much dramatic action here, although the fact that the chorus is composed of the actors of the drama—namely, the Danaid girls—prevents the play from being wholly static. Moreover, this meager story serves chiefly as a springboard for the lost sections of the trilogy, in which Danaus delivers his daughters to their pursuers in order to prevent a war between Argos and Egypt but instructs them to murder their bridegrooms. One daughter, however, disobeys him because she has fallen in love with her husband, and this rebellion against patriarchal authority is defended by the goddess of love, Aphrodite. Hypermnestra has only followed the universal principle of love, which is superior to man-made prohibitions.

> *Pure Heaven is moved with yearning for the Earth,*
> *And Earth grows passionate for her Lord's embrace*

declares the goddess in the fragment of the play that has come down to us. The taboo against cousin-marriage is thus nullified.

Greater interest attaches to the second extant drama, *The Persians*, produced in 472, eight years after the battle of Salamis. Also part of a trilogy about which we know very little, the play recounts the defeat of the Persians under Xerxes and revolves around the reception of the news at the imperial court. The chorus describes the splendor of the army, but expresses anxiety for its welfare. Suddenly a Messenger arrives with the report of the catastrophe. Anxiety and pride struggle within the queen-mother Atossa as he recites the details of the rout. After a long silence, she speaks: "I have been silent too long. Who has *not* fallen?" The Messenger understands her, and replies that her son Xerxes, the King, is safe. This powerfully managed scene is followed by one of fantastic incantation when the ghost of Darius, the father of the defeated King, is raised from the dead to foretell the future. Darius prophesies more disaster and warns his people against the dreadful sin of *Hubris* or pride that is invariably punished by the gods. After this episode, which may well be described as the first ghost-scene of extant drama, Xerxes himself arrives. The degenerate son of a worthy father is broken in spirit, and the play ends with a long Oriental lament for the destroyed army. *The Persians*, too, is largely static drama, but its wealth of feeling and its mass effects create an intense play, while in the Queen we have the first extant example of dramatic characterization.

Among the many misconceptions regarding classic drama, there is one that this play does much to discredit—namely, the belief that Greek tragedy remained austerely aloof from contemporary events. *The Persians* deals with a practically contemporary event, and was obviously primed to arouse patriotic fervor. The defeat of the Persian host was a noble subject for epic drama, and it lent itself to some thinking on related subjects, such as the contrast between Greece and Asia, and between democracy and despotism. The patriotic dramatist exults in the independence of the Greek people who "call no man their master" and do not have to be driven to battle like unwilling slaves, while the moralist in Aeschylus regards the catastrophe as a punishment for overweening pride and desire for conquest.

Aeschylus was only one of the several classic dramatists who were not afraid of topical material, even if, like Euripides in *The Trojan Women* and elsewhere, they generally used legend and mythology as a thin disguise. And even in democratic Athens the course of the social drama did not always run smoothly. Aeschylus' contemporary Phrynichus was fined a thousand drachmas because a play he had written reminded the Athenians of the loss of one of their colonies owing to weakness or negligence on the part of the mother city.

5 A DIVINE COMEDY: THE PROMETHEAN TRILOGY

When, seven years or so after *The Persians*, Aeschylus turned to another epic tragedy he grappled with a subject which neither his contemporaries nor his immediate successors could treat with equal grandeur or profundity. The theme of the *Prometheus Bound* and its lost companion pieces was God himself.

Again we have what is probably a first play of a trilogy, and a tragedy in which there is little action. Nevertheless the *Prometheus Bound* is an unforgettable work, pregnant with beauty and thought and transfigured by that most inspiriting of characters, Prometheus, a rebel against God and a friend of man. It is true that Aeschylus regarded the titan as somewhat in the wrong and that the final part of the trilogy ended with the reconciliation of Prometheus and Zeus. Still, what Blake said of Milton —namely, that his greatest poetry was reserved for Lucifer "because he was a true poet, and of the devil's party without knowing it," appears to have been true of Aeschylus. Prometheus, the first humanitarian and rebel to be presented in the theatre, is the dramatist's noblest character. His tragedy is the prototype of a long line of dramas of liberalism.

When the tragedy opens, the titan is being fastened to a peak in the Caucasian mountains by "Force," "Violence," and the blacksmith god Hephaestus who performs his task unwillingly. Left alone at last, Prometheus addresses nature and above all his mother Themis or Earth in what is the first extant tirade of the theatre and is still one of the best. Being endowed with "forethought," he knew what he would have to endure if he brought fire to man and made his survival possible. Nothing did he fail to foresee, yet he defied the arrogant god Zeus out of pity for mankind. He will endure his fate, however, secure in the knowledge that Necessity or Destiny will ultimately end his struggle with the god and relieve his age-long torment. The sea-nymphs arrive as a chorus to assuage his suffering, and to them he explains his reasons for stealing the fire from heaven. No sooner had Zeus assumed power, he declares, than this upstart deity proposed to destroy helpless mankind and repopulate the earth with another race. As the principle of Pity and Progress, Prometheus, however, had contrary plans. First he freed men of the fear of death by causing blind hopes to dwell in their hearts, and then he gave them the gift of fire, which further delivered them of fear and enabled them to create tools. The elderly and comically presented Oceanus or Ocean arrives and discharges a pack of cowardly precepts urging submission to the new ruler of the world, but Prometheus spurns his advice and this early Polonius takes himself off in a huff. Left alone with the sea-nymphs, the titan further expounds his method of saving mankind by means of the arts and sciences in another passage that reads like a chapter by a modern anthropologist: Through Prometheus men won their minds, receiving from him the mother of all arts, Memory, and the indispensable science of healing.

Suddenly another victim of the Olympian gods appears—Io, the poor mythical maiden who is being driven from country to country by a gadfly sent by the young god's jealous wife Hera. To Io, who wants to kill herself, Prometheus confides the consoling news that Zeus is not everlasting. If the god marries a certain woman whose name Prometheus will not reveal, the child of their union will drive him from his throne. Only he can save Zeus, and he will not speak! Hermes, the cocky messenger of the god, appears with orders to discover Prometheus' secret, and when entreaties prove unavailing Zeus applies force. Amid the lightning and thunder which are hurled at him from heaven in a shattering climax the fire-bringing rebel remains fearless and silent.

The trilogy as a whole is not, however, a tragedy of rebellion but a Divine Comedy.[7] A lost third play, or the last two plays, described how Heracles, the son of Zeus by a mortal woman, pitied Prometheus, destroyed the vulture that fed on the titan's liver, and with the consent of Zeus delivered him from his bonds. The liberated rebel then imparted his secret to the god and became reconciled to him. By this time, too, Zeus was worth saving, for he had become friendly to mankind, even begetting leaders of the people or demigods like Heracles by cohabiting with mortal women. He had, in a sense, assimilated the pity and humanitarianism of Prometheus! The subject of the trilogy appears, then, to be the evolution of God in fulfillment of the law of necessity. From a young and willful tyrant Zeus becomes a mature and merciful ruler as unlike the Zeus of the *Iliad* as Isaiah's Jehovah.

6 HUMAN TRAGEDY—OEDIPUS AND AGAMEMNON

After establishing a moral providence in the universe it remained for Aeschylus only to make its will prevail among men. Inevitably Aeschylus turned from the drama of God to the drama of man in his last two surviving trilogies. In the first of them, an Oedipus tragedy with which Aeschylus won the tragic prize in 467, the subject is the domestic *Até* or family curse associated with the early history of the Theban state. The curse begins with Laius, a licentious homosexual who abducts a lad and is cursed by the latter's father Pelops. It works itself out horribly in the story of Oedipus who kills his father Laius unwittingly, marries his mother, and begets children by her. It continues in the children of this incestuous union when the two sons of Oedipus slay each other in a stubborn struggle for power.

Brooding upon the blood-streaked early history of man, Aeschylus dispensed with ready-made explanations. In reviewing the long record of parricide, incest, fratricide, and political conflict, Aeschylus went beyond the conventional Greek theory of the family curse. But he makes it abundantly clear in *The Seven Against Thebes* that heredity is little more than a predisposition. The crimes committed by the descendants of the corrupt Laius are the result of ambition, rivalry, and the insufficient sway of moral law during the legendary age.

Again only a single play was spared by that first and most drastic of book-burners, Time, but fortunately *The Seven Against Thebes* represents a climactic part of the trilogy. This tragedy opens with Eteocles rallying the Thebans to the defense of the city against Argive invaders led by his brother, to whom he had refused to cede the throne on alternate years as stipulated in their compact. A Messenger brings the news that seven renowned champions of the Argive army have planted themselves before the seven gates of the city. Learning that his brother Polynices will be at one of the gates, Eteocles hurries off to do battle with him, leaving the chorus to ponder on the curse which leads this family to destruction. Aeschylus makes the chorus of women plead with Eteocles not to fight at the seventh gate and become guilty of a brother's blood. But Eteocles merely blames Fate for his overpowering ambition and hatred. At six of the seven gates the Thebans conquer, but at the seventh gate the two brothers are slain by each other.

The penultimate scene is a moving lament by their sisters, Antigone and Ismene, and by the chorus of Theban women. They mourn the end of a dynasty and deprecate the vanity of the struggle for power:

> *They strove for land, and did demand*
> *An equal share.*
> *In the ground deep, deep, where now they sleep,*
> *There's land to spare.*[8]

But, as Antigone remarks, "Strife is the last of gods to end her tale," and a new conflict is indicated at the close of the tragedy. Although the Theban senate has forbidden burial rights for Polynices because he led an invasion against his country, Antigone is resolved to defy the decree. To man-made laws and to the primitive principle of retribution she opposes natural "piety" which, according to her, is timeless while in a state "what's right today is wrong tomorrow." The play ends with forebodings of fresh sufferings for the descendants of Oedipus.

There is a valid objection to ending the drama on a new and unresolved conflict, and too much of the action is relegated to narration. Nevertheless, Aeschylus was achieving new intensities in *The Seven Against Thebes* when he turned to human and individual tragedy. He reached them nine years later in his last and greatest trilogy.

The *Oresteia*, performed in 458 within two years of its author's death, is again the tragedy of a royal house. It deals once more with a hereditary curse, which began in the dim legendary world when Tantalus, admitted to the table of the gods, grew so vain that he revealed their secrets to mankind and was consequently cast into the pit of Tartarus. A son, Pelops, slew his charioteer and became the prey of the slain man's Fury or avenging ghost. Pelops' two sons Thyestes and Atreus murdered their step-brother. Fleeing to Mycenae, they attained power and affluence. But they became deadly enemies there when Thyestes seduced Atreus' wife. Pretending to become reconciled with Thyestes, Atreus slew his brother's sons and fed them to their father—a deed so abominable that the sun hid its face in disgust. Thereafter there could only be hereditary enmity between the two branches of the family.

When the first part of the trilogy, the *Agamemnon*, opens, Thyestes' son Aegisthus has been betraying Atreus' son Agamemnon with the latter's wife Clytemnestra. A watchman, posted on the roof of the palace, discovers from distant beacons that Troy has at last fallen. He is oppressed with premonitions of disaster, as are the old men of the chorus who were left behind when the Greeks, led by Agamemnon, departed for the siege. Among other things, they recall a dreadful deed—the sacrifice of Agamemnon's daughter Iphigenia by her father. He lured her to his camp and sacrificed her on the altar of Artemis merely to satisfy his ambitions, for without her death the army under his command could not have sailed to Troy. Agamemnon will soon return, and after the singing of another ode and the passing of an indefinite amount of time he appears, followed by captives and spoils of war. With him, too, is Cassandra, the Trojan vestal whom he has arrogantly taken for his concubine.

Clytemnestra receives him with forced cordiality as a conquering hero. Subtly and ironically she flatters his pride, making him walk to the palace on costly robes. Although hesitant at first, he accepts the honor. Casually, moreover, and quite unconsciously, he insults Clytemnestra by ordering her to take care of his concubine. She says nothing that would betray any resentment, but leads him to his bath, entangles him in a mesh, and murders him. Cassandra, who has sensed her doom and entered the palace knowing that there was no escape for her, is killed with him. Then Aegisthus appears, gloating over the dead, and arousing the fury of the old men who are about to hurl themselves on so vainglorious a weakling. They are cowed only by the demoniacal murderess, who is frankly exultant and maintains that she was only the ready instrument of the family curse and of the law of retribution; she had a right to kill the man who sacrificed her daughter.

> *From his seed she sprang, the flower I bore*
> *and wept for, Iphigenia slain.*
> *Oh, a worthy deed and a worthy doom.*
> *Will he boast in hell of the death he dealt,*
> *now the score is paid*
> *and the sword he slew with has slain him.*[9]

But, now, she wants an end to evil: "Enough, what is done is done." Her lover and she rule the city at last, and she promises that they will order things well.

So ends this incandescent tragedy in which Aeschylus creates living, three-dimensional drama out of the conventional subject of hereditary evil. The tragedy has been precipitated by the will of the protagonists. They may speak of the domestic *Até*, but the guilt of arrogance, brutality and illicit passion is entirely their own. Moreover, theirs is no conventional, no single-minded and unmitigated villainy even if Clytemnestra lays her plans carefully, never sways from them, and remains unrepentant to the end. Aegisthus may have originally intended to avenge his father by seducing his cousin's wife, but he appears to be genuinely in love with her. Clytemnestra, too, is guilty, but Agamemnon has given her ample provocation for revenge by his wanton sacrifice of her child. To this intensity of passion must be added the glorious choruses and Cassandra's rhapsodic tirades. The play is full of pity for mankind and is transfigured by a glowing certainty that suffering has a purpose. The visionary in Aeschylus foreshadows the triumph of right reason and good will in the sanguinary world: "Drop by drop, sorrow falls and opens our hearts to wisdom and the grace of God."

Some small portion of this wisdom comes to Clytemnestra in later years. But the consequences of her deed must darken her last days, and the second part of the trilogy *The Libation Pourers* or *The Choephori* is a revenge play. Sent away in childhood, Agamemnon's son Orestes returns many years later bent upon vengeance. He finds himself in a curious dilemma: in obedience to the primitive law of the blood-feud as expressed by the oracle of Apollo he must kill his father's murderers, but this can only make him guilty of matricide. He is aided somewhat by his sister Electra, Agamemnon's surviving daughter who has been persecuted by the murderers because she has remained unreconciled to them. After some intrigue and suspense, Orestes traps and kills Aegisthus and confronts his mother. She is alternately the unafraid queen who calls for "a man-killing axe" with which to defend herself and the mother who bares her breast to her son warning him against polluting himself with a dreadful crime the consequences of which will embitter his whole life. But the voice of the old law of vendetta, represented by his friend Pylades and by the primitive god Apollo, is too implacable to be resisted, and Orestes stabs her. No sooner, however, has Orestes justified his deed and claimed the protection of the god who ordered it than the Furies appear. Unseen by anyone but Orestes, these avenging spirits roused by his mother-murder drive him mad with terror and remorse. They pursue him angrily as he hastens away to seek shelter in Apollo's sanctuary.

A horrible crime, accentuated by a soul-shattering inner conflict and by a gripping climax, makes *The Libation Pourers* a worthy, if uneven, successor to the *Agamemnon*. In *The Libation Pourers* Aeschylus has reduced the law of the blood-feud to an absurdity, since followed logically it leads to an act even more intolerable than the original murder.

In the final part of the trilogy *The Eumenides*, the blood-feud is finally canceled. The chorus in the *Agamemnon* had already tellingly expressed the self-perpetuating nature of the law of retribution which now applies to the matricide:

> *Reproach in turn*
> *meets reproach. I know not*
> *who here can hold the balance.*
> *The spoiler is spoiled.*
> *Kill—your life is forfeit.*[10]

It is to this law that Orestes is delivered over, although in his case retribution is not easily distinguishable from subjective conscience. The Furies, who pursue him everywhere, beleaguer him even in Apollo's temple.

After many years, however, Orestes has finally expiated his deed by suffering. He escapes to Athens, and now that time has drawn the sting from his conscience he is ready to meet the Furies in open trial before the Areopagus, the High Court of Athens which has been specially established by the goddess Pallas Athene for this purpose. Although the vote is a tie, it is broken in his favor when Pallas Athene casts her ballot for his acquittal. It is, significantly, the goddess of reason who puts an end to the blind and self-perpetuating law of retribution. In this uphill struggle for a new vision and a new ethics it is Greek *sophia* or wisdom that has the last word.

Two years after the promulgation of this credo Aeschylus was dead. By then, however, he had notable successors. Sophocles and Euripides were polishing and extending his art, expressing new viewpoints, and employing somewhat modified techniques. His pioneering work was over. He had transformed ritual into drama, he had brought human character into the theatre, and he had brought spiritual vision into the drama. He had begun the stately march of tragedy. Now the procession could continue without him.*

I. Summary Note on the Greek Theatre: In the 5th century, the Theatre of Dionysus consisted of a semi-circular or horseshoe-shaped auditorium (*theatron*), a circular dancing area (*orchestra*) for the chorus, and behind it a permanent setting—the scene-building (*skene*), pierced by three doors. This background could be altered by various devices—perhaps by movable wooden panels, and later also by revolving prisms (*periakti*) with different scenes painted on the three sides. Immediately in front of this structure stood a low platform (*proskenion* or *logeion*) on which much of the acting took place, although the actors could step down into the *orchestra* or appear on the roof of the building. The *skene* also had wings (*paraskenia*) flanking the *proskenion*, so that the acting platform was framed on three sides by the facade of the scene-building. The *paraskenia* or wings could represent two additional buildings, and the actor moving from one wing to the other could probably create the illusion of traveling from one locality to another.

II. Summary Note on the Structure of Greek Tragedy: Tragedy had the following formal divisions: 1. *Prologue*, an introductory monologue or dialogue. 2. *Parodos*, the entrance and first recitation of the chorus. 3. The *episode*, a dramatic scene performed by the actors similar to our scenes or acts (the lines were written in iambic trimeter, for which the closest equivalent in English is blank verse). 4. *Stasimon*, a choral ode in intricate metres (without rhyme), followed by another *episode* or scene. There would be 4 or 5 episodes separated by choral odes, and the tragedy closed as a rule with a choral finale called the *exodos*. Occasionally the *stasimon* would be replaced by a song (a *commus*) sung by an actor alone or with the chorus.

* His two sons also wrote tragedies, now lost, as did his nephew Philocles, to whom Sophocles lost the first prize, although Sophocles competed with *Oedipus the King* for that particular play contest.

III

SOPHOCLES, THE SERENE

I THE HAPPY PLAYWRIGHT

"BLESSED was Sophocles, happy in his long life, his fortunes, his talent; happy to have written so many beautiful tragedies and made a fair end of a life which knew no misfortune." This portrait by a comic poet, Phrynichus, bears little resemblance to the Marathon warrior, voluntary exile and impassioned prophet who handed on his torch to Sophocles. "Sophocles is gentle here (in the Underworld) as he was in life," wrote Aristophanes who in all other instances would sooner stop writing than lose a jest. This picture too bears little resemblance to Aeschylus, whose pugnacity is celebrated in the same comedy that pays tribute to his successor's sweetness of temper.

Sophocles, born in 495, thirty years after his predecessor, in "white Colonus" about a mile northwest of Athens, enjoyed the comforts of a rich merchant's son and the advantages of a beautiful body, as well as the fruits of one of the most civilized epochs in world history. Sheltered in a village renowned for its loveliness and carefully trained in music by the celebrated musician Lampros, he grew in beauty of body and soul. So remarkable was he for physical grace at sixteen that he was chosen to lead the choir of boys who celebrated the victory of Salamis. After twelve years more spent in study and training, Sophocles was ready to compete with the established playwrights, and it was none other than Aeschylus who lost the prize to him. According to one story, feeling ran so high that instead of choosing the judges by lot, as was customary, the Archon in charge of the competition entrusted the decision to the Athenian board of generals.

Sophocles' success, however, proved to be more than a happy accident or a political maneuver. A hundred or more plays followed it, eighteen of them winning first prizes, the rest never failing to take second prize. That he was a natural genius is, moreover, attested by the fact that the composition of his plays did not absorb all his energy and interest. Like most of the writers of his time, he did not confine himself to literature, and foraged far afield. An accomplished actor, he performed in his own plays, winning fame for his acrobatic skill in the *Nausicaa,* in which he kept his public spell-bound with a ball-juggling act long remembered by his contemporaries. Only the comparative weakness of his voice, which probably made him choose a feminine role in the *Nausicaa,* led him to renounce the acting profession. He was also an ordained priest bound to the service of the two local heroes Alcon and Asclepius, the god of medicine. And although he appears to have been free from pronounced political convictions, he was twice elected to the Board of Generals who administered the civil and military affairs of Athens. One does not readily associate artists with high finance, but he was even a director of the Treasury Department which controlled the funds of the association of states dominated by Athenian imperialism known as the Delian Confederacy.

Sophocles was, in brief, the darling of the Athenian populace, one of the long line of writers who disprove the theory that genius must always be unrecognized in its own day. A social lion, he consorted with the Athenian galaxy which consisted of his fellow-playwrights Aeschylus, Euripides, and Aristophanes, of the great historians Herodotus and Thucydides, of the most brilliant of Greek statesmen Pericles, and of the greatest of all sculptors Phidias. His social charm was such that his epigrams were public property and he became the Joseph Addison of a long-remembered literary club. His life, which lasted fully ninety years, revealed no failing of his powers. It was clouded only by a law suit brought by one of his several sons Iophon, himself a playwright of some distinction. Iophon, who was jealous of his father's affection for an illegitimate son, wanted to have the aged man declared incompetent, but according to one report the charge was disproved when the poet recited portions of his last tragedy the *Oedipus at Colonus*. And just as his youth spared him the most harrowing details of the Persian invasion, so his death in 405 saved him from witnessing the final defeat and humiliation of his beloved city, which fell a few months later. No wonder Sophocles was declared fortunate even in his death! His memory was cherished by his harassed countrymen, who gave him the honorary name of *Dexion,* the Entertainer or Host, and brought yearly sacrifices to his tomb.

A remarkable personality was his, and Matthew Arnold was perhaps not greatly overpraising it when he coined his overworked phrase that Sophocles "saw life steadily, and saw it whole." He had enough experience to see it "whole," and the proper temperament for seeing it "steadily." Moreover, his endowments were invaluable to a dramatist. The man of the world mingled with people and learned to understand and delineate character; the conversationalist naturally mastered dialogue; the actor and the public figure could gauge the effect of his work on audiences. Better than any of his contemporaries who left their work to posterity, he knew how to construct finished plays.

This traditional account of a great artist is, nevertheless, distinctly superficial when left unqualified. If he had possessed no other attributes he might have been at most a superior Molnar or Rostand, and his posthumous honorary title of "The Entertainer" would have fitted him only too literally. Sophocles, as all the world knows, was a great deal more. He was a poet, with a purity of expression unparalleled in the theatre until Racine began to compose plays for the French court more than twenty centuries later. And like every major poet he knew the abysses as well as the heights. What mind-made demons he privately confronted can only be surmised from his tragedies, but these supply sufficient evidence to dissipate any pollyannic view of the man. At the close of a career which others would have considered a perfect vindication of human life, he could write, "Not to be born is, past all prizing, best; but when a man hath seen the light, this is next best by far, that with all speed he should go thither, whence he hath come."[1] Moreover, no one who spent a quarter of a century in a city ravaged by war and plague could possibly have been immune to anxiety and suffering.

At the heart of his thought was that "tragic sense of life" which the late Spanish philosopher Unamuno considered indispensable to maturity. Even Sophocles' lightest plays are anything but pollyannic in outlook and detail. True, he could create that dazzling girl Antigone, fresh as a morning glory in her courage and loyalty, he could write an idyl like the *Philoctetes* glorifying the impulsive nobility of youth, and he could compose in the *Oedipus at Colonus* the most beautiful picture of reconciled and serene old age in all dramatic literature. But the same writer appears to have been almost obsessed with an interest in horror and in mental and physical deformity. He favored the unpleasant themes of insanity, suicide, and torture in *Ajax, The Trachiniae,* and *Antigone.* A noisome physical disease is a main feature of *Philoctetes,* and his most famous character Oedipus appears in full sight of the audience with blood-streaked eyes. If there is truth in the report that he claimed to make persons as they should be, whereas Euripides made them as they were, he may have referred to an early period which is not represented by any surviving plays. In his seven extant tragedies he gives ample evidence of being able and willing to portray people as they are. He can be a realist and, now and then, even a naturalist along with the best of the fraternity.

The key to his work was provided by Matthew Arnold in the phrase to the effect that Sophocles possessed an "even-balanced soul." He comprehended both the joy and grief of living, its beauty and its ugliness, its moments of peace and its basic uncertainty so concisely expressed by his line, "Human life, even in its utmost splendor and struggle, hangs on the edge of an abyss." His serenity was born of knowledge, not ignorance.

There are two kinds of suffering in his tragedies—that which comes from an excess of passion, and that which flows from accident. Man-made evil is formed in the fixed mold of human character, and accident stems from the nature of the universe. Although Sophocles officially accepted the Greek gods, they did not affect his philosophy—formal acceptance is sometimes the best way of dismissing a moot point. Hardy's quatrain,

> *Crass Casualty obstructs the sun and rain,*
> *And dicing Time for gladness casts a moan . . .*
> *These purblind Doomsters had as readily strown*
> *Bliss about my pilgrimage as pain*

comes closest to expressing the Sophoclean viewpoint.

Still, Sophocles is not a paralyzing fatalist, even if it is chiefly from him that later scholars derived their exaggerated and much too literal opinion that Greek tragedy is the drama of Fate. Instead, he entertained a noble dream of humanity living by reason which he must have seen realized for a time in his own city, but which the philosopher Plato, who wrote after the defeat of Athens, was quick to return to the realm of speculation in his *Republic*. If man frequently fails to obtain control over his private demons, he can at least endeavor to check them, as Creon does rather belatedly in *Antigone;* or he can die nobly like the blundering hero of *Ajax*. And if the world order is beyond man's control, as it is in *Oedipus the King,* the victim must at least recognize his relative freedom from responsibility for what happened. Unlike Oedipus, who blinded himself upon discovering that he had married his mother, he must confront the horror of accident without losing his reason or dignity and without aggravating his condition with self-imposed suffering.

Man in the Sophoclean world must endeavor to introduce order into his own spirit. If the universe is devoid of justice, we must conclude that he can create that commodity himself—in his own person and in the world that is of his own making. Here again we are reminded of the thought of that other qualified fatalist, Thomas Hardy, who broached the idea that man's consciousness might somehow impregnate the "universal Will" with intellect and righteousness, "fashioning all things fair" if only

> *We would establish those of kindlier build,*
> *In fair Compassions skilled,*
> *Men of deep art in life-development . . .*
> *Men surfeited of laying heavy hands—*[2]

Regarding the "universal Will," however, Sophocles does not seem to have been too hopeful! His abiding faith could only be reserved for the world of art where alone mankind can "fashion all things fair." In fact, what he asks of his characters is only art in daily behavior—that is, order, taste, and balance. But he is realist enough to know that they cannot ordinarily grant his heart's desire as long as their demons prevail. It is chiefly in the artistry of his tragedies that Sophocles provides the order, taste, and balance so rarely discoverable in the actual world.

2 SOPHOCLES' ART OF THE DRAMA

Like every artist worth his salt, Sophocles did not of course achieve his stature at once; he experimented, tried different styles, and struggled painstakingly for perfection. How deliberate was his progress is shown by the conscious artistry of his composition and by his awareness of well-defined stages in his development. At first, he declared, he imitated the grandeur of Aeschylus; then he went to the opposite extreme of adopting an excessively spare and abrupt manner; and finally he struck a mean between the two styles, attaining that passionate yet restrained method which characterizes all his later plays—the only ones that have survived.

His progress was not, however, confined to style. The secret of Sophocles' triumph as a dramatist is that he learned to understand the nature of his medium more clearly than any other Greek dramatist. He could not, it is true, violate the unwritten injunction against enacting deaths on the stage; nor was he able to banish the particular convention which gave prominence to the chorus any more than could his successor Euripides. But Sophocles did the next best thing by reducing the chorus to a minimum and relegating it to the background. His chorus became primarily a group of spectators who follow the dramatic action closely, react to it emotionally, and comment on it without in the main losing themselves in irrelevant generalizations. These liberties he could take, and he also felt free to extend the boundaries of the dramatic complications of the play. In *Oedipus the King* he can stand comparison with Ibsen and O'Neill in the art of dramatic suspense and discovery.

A first step taken by him was the addition of a third speaking actor to Attic drama. A second step was the abolition of the trilogic form. Aeschylus used three tragedies to tell a story and therefore tended to embellish them with irrelevant lyricism and to mark time, especially in the middle sections. Sophocles used only one play for each plot and was consequently constrained to pack all his action into it. In all respects the shorter form offered the greater dramatic possibilities. Moreover, the titanic element was not to his taste; as Spengler has noted of all Periclean artists, Sophocles disliked anything that exceeded the human compass. His work bears a strong resemblance to the architecture and sculpture of his time which favored small temples and statues of gods who are not much larger than well-built human beings. Sophocles is precise rather than rhapsodic; and in the interest of definiteness he is even said to have turned to production problems, his contribution being the localizing invention of scene-painting by means of the *periaktoi* or painted prisms.

In the details of his dramaturgy Sophocles is likewise a fastidious craftsman who calculated his effects. He employs tragic irony or pathetic contrast with great skill, and how effective the device can be is shown in the powerful *Oedipus the King* where the hero, who is ignorant of his unnatural situation, tracks down every particle of evidence that ultimately brings him face to face with his own pollution. As a master of the nascent and difficult art of characterization, Sophocles knows how to create vivid contrasts which illuminate character and complicate the action. His recognition scenes—when, for example, Electra discovers her brother or Queen Jocasta learns that her husband Oedipus is her own son—are admirably managed. Expert too is the change of tempo and timbre in the extant tragedies; for example, the catastrophic struggle between Antigone and Creon, who denies her brother his burial rites, is preceded by a comic episode. It is noteworthy that Sophocles is the first writer known to have used some comic details in his tragedies, a procedure that could only be motivated by a desire for contrast and variety. Finally, Sophocles is a past master of the device of tragic suspense, of which *Oedipus the King* is a supreme example.

Sophocles, in brief, can teach the modern playwright more than one practical lesson. He also offers excellent instruction in the difficult matter of dialogue—this despite the inevitable interference of the chorus. His dialogue is remarkably crisp (sometimes even too crisp), his diction makes sparing use of adjectives and similes, and his exalted passages hew close to the line of conflict; they are never boring or grandiloquent. The perfection of his style leaves it almost self-effacing. Perhaps this is even his greatest fault for the modern reader, who may find his poetry a little too polished, a little too cold.

3 THE PLAYS OF SOPHOCLES

From various lexicons and allusions we learn the names of about a hundred lost plays attributed to Sophocles, and about a thousand fragments have been recovered by those busy gnomes, the scholars. Attic legends, the Trojan war, the return of the heroes, the adventures of Odysseus, the expedition of the Argonauts (Jason and the Golden Fleece), the wars of Thebes and Argos, the curse on the house of Agamemnon, and miscellaneous stories abound in his vast repertory. In one of the lost plays, *Thamyras*, Sophocles is said to have acted the part of a harp-player in a solo, an assignment that suited his musical talents. In another tragedy, he repeated the naturalistic conclusion of *Oedipus the King*, and the mask of his hero was distorted to show the effects of the blows the character had sustained. The survival of a host of titles and fragments also indicates that Sophocles wrote some very popular satyr-plays or comic after-pieces. Possibly his good taste toned down the orgiastic qualities of those hearty burlesques. That, on the other hand, he was sufficiently capable of robust jocularity is suggested by the fact that one of his lost satyr-plays was considered shockingly obscene by even so urbane a critic as Cicero.

From the recovered fragments, a number of which are surpassingly beautiful, it is also abundantly clear that his profundity and aliveness to the problems of his day were not confined to the mere handful of plays that have remained intact. Some of the fragments repeat the contention that excess of passion is folly and that violence even in a just cause is an error. Some of the quotations prove that Euripides was not the only liberal-minded poet among the later dramatists. Although Sophocles was not a crusader like his younger contemporary, his stand on social stratification and on the status of women in Athens must have been that of the inner Periclean circle to which he belonged. Three passages are particularly telling:

> *We, one race of mankind, by father, by mother,*
> *All came forth to the light of the selfsame day;*
> *No one man is born more great than another;*
> *But some are fed with a bitter bread. . . .*

> *And beside riches, to mankind all else*
> *Is second-rate; true there are some esteem*
> *A man in health; yea, to me, no man poor*
> *Appears to be in health, but always ailing. . . .*

> *I have regarded woman's fortunes thus,*
> *That we are nothing . . . Then when we come*
> *To full discretion and maturity,*
> *We are thrust out and marketed abroad,*
> *Far from our parents and ancestral gods,*
> *Some to strange husbands, some to barbarous,*
> *One to a rude, one to a wrangling home;*
> *And these, after the yoking of a night,*
> *We are bound to like, and deem it well with us.*

Only later in his old age, when Athenian demagoguery was reaping a harvest of military defeat and political chaos, does Sophocles show signs of conservative bias. During the short-lived revolution of the Four Hundred by the upper classes, the seat of the government was transferred to Sophocles' tranquil birthplace, where there would be no disgruntled masses to cope with. The *Oedipus at Colonus* gives, as it were, sanction to this anti-democratic move.

It is also evident from another fragment that Euripides was not the only dramatist to interpret the gods as natural forces. Sophocles describes Venus as an energy of life and destruction:

> *Death is her name, and Might imperishable,*
> *And maniac Frenzy, and unallayed Desire,*
> *And Lamentation loud. All is in her;*
> *Impulse, and Quietude, and Energy . . .*[3]

The extent of Sophocles' dramatic powers can, however, be gauged only in the complete tragedies available to us. Although characterization is always a prime feature, his extant work can be conveniently divided into three character plays—*The Trachiniae, Ajax,* and *Electra;* one social drama, *Antigone;* one idyl, *Philoctetes;* and two tragedies of fate, *Oedipus the King* and the *Oedipus at Colonus.*

4 CHARACTER PLAYS

One of the later plays, *The Trachiniae* or *The Women of Trachis,* is the feeblest of them all. Deianira, the wife of the national hero and demigod Heracles, being troubled by jealousy when he sends her a captive concubine, remembers a blood-anointed robe which the vengeful centaur Nessus had told her would recover her husband's affection. She sends it to her husband with a Messenger, and learns too late that it is poisoned. When her son returns with the news that his father is dying the distressed woman runs into the house and stabs herself. Then the tormented hero is brought in cursing her for a murderess. Her error being explained to him, he arranges his affairs, gives the young concubine to his son, and orders his body to be burnt.

The Trachiniae is weakened by disunity, since the interest is divided between Deianira and her husband, and the play uses more narrative than is customary in Sophocles' work. But the tragedy contains a powerful and touching study of a jealous woman. Deianira is affecting in her love for her husband and in her desire to recover his affections. There is no malice in her, she is kind to his concubine who reminds her of her own advancing years, and she dies nobly. Heracles, although not the most appealing of husbands, is an adequate portrait of a middle-aged man who turns to the enticements of youth, suffers for his infidelity, and is finally compelled to renounce his dream of emotional renewal. Realizing that youth calls to youth, he marries his son to the girl, "the flower of whose age is in its spring." *The Trachiniae,* which is devoid of cosmic and social questionings, owes much of its interest solely to insight into middle-aged characters.

More effective is the earlier tragedy *Ajax,* a penetrative analysis of a courageous but hypersensitive soldier who is destroyed by an excess of his finest qualities. His courage becomes overweening pride, his self-reliance leads to disdain of others, and his sensitiveness turns to morbidity when his self-esteem is wounded. When Achilles' armor is awarded to Odysseus instead of to himself, Ajax, who has a greater claim to the prize by reason of his valor, nurses his grievance until he resolves to murder the Greek leaders in their sleep. It cannot be said that some of them, particularly Agamemnon and Menelaus, were above goading a character like Ajax to desperation. But his criminal intentions, as well as his extreme self-confidence, arouse the anger of the stern goddess of reason Pallas Athene. Driving him mad, she leads him to vent his rage on an innocent flock of sheep whom he imagines to be the Greeks. When he recovers his senses he feels so humiliated that he falls on his sword.

The play is, in brief, a study of a tragic failing. Contrast is provided by Odysseus, who is described as a discreet, forgiving and comparatively humble man, and by a reasonable brother who succeeds in regaining for the dead hero the honor he has lost among the Greeks. Menelaus, the mean-spirited equivocator, and Agamemnon, the arrogant commander-in-chief, supply a different kind of contrast. By comparison with them Ajax is noble despite his failings, for not only is there no guile in him but he is capable of affection for his child, his parents, and his brother. Unlike Agamemnon he could never have sacrificed a child of his to enable the Greek fleet to sail for Troy. If Ajax seems callously indifferent to his loving slave wife, there is one excuse for him; he is too greatly absorbed in the wrongs and humiliations he has suffered.

Rounding out this character drama, Sophocles creates another of his well-realized women, the slave woman Tecmessa who attends her sullen soldier uncomplainingly, tries to lead him into the path of reason, and discovers his body after his death. Like Shakespeare, Molière and many another great playwright, Sophocles reveals a tender understanding and regard for womanhood. In a heroic saga like *Ajax* this feeling for the softer virtues is particularly valuable since it enriches the emotional content.

But Sophocles' greatest contribution to character drama is his *Electra,* in which he treats the theme of Aeschylus' *The Choephori* solely in terms of human personality. For Aeschylus the problem was an ethical one, the rightness of the blood feud. Sophocles dismisses the moral problem and accepts the mother-murder by placing it in distant antiquity; his intentionally archaic language in *Electra* sets the time element clearly. Having disposed of the ethical question, he addresses himself to the problem of character. What sort of woman was Electra who wanted to see her mother killed, and was ready to do the deed herself? The answer is to be found in her uncompromising spirit. Her sister Chrysothemis adjusted herself to the murder of her father and to her mother's marriage to Aegisthus. But Electra remained stiffly aloof and consequently became the object of mistreatment and abuse, which in turn only whetted her desire for revenge. An unbending and high-minded character, she is a living rebuke to her father's murderers, with whom she bandies words so courageously that she invites further perse-cution, especially on the part of the malicious upstart Aegisthus. When she is told that her brother Orestes is dead, she regards herself as his natural successor, and appeals to her time-serving sister to aid her in carrying out the revenge which according to primitive custom should have been his. When her mother is about to be slain inside the palace, Electra answers her desperate pleas with scorn and orders Orestes not to spare her. Nevertheless, her sinews are not wholly of steel, and her hardness can melt at times. After exchanging wounding words with her mother in the early part of the play she feels ashamed. When Orestes is reported to be dead she mourns him touchingly. When he reveals himself to her later, she almost forgets the object of his visit and jeopardizes their plans by holding him close to her. After her mother is killed, Electra is instinctively overcome with self-disgust.

Several of the other characters also possess vividly realized attributes. Clytemnestra is a dynamic woman who can be tyrannical and malevo-lent and yet is sincerely moved upon learning that the son appointed by primitive law to destroy her is dead. The *Paedagogus* or tutor who ac-companies Orestes is a single-minded representative of primitive law who is nevertheless capable of humor and understanding. To the brother and sister who are dallying before the house, he says drily: "If I had not been watching at the door from the first, your plans would have entered the house before your bodies." Only Orestes is a commonplace character who weakens the tragedy. Having been reared for his task from the beginning, he has no scruples and is not afflicted with remorse and madness like his more interesting counterpart in *The Choephori*. A primitive youth, he obeys primitive law; the merest shadow of doubt does appear, however, in his words to Electra after the murder: "In the house all is well, *if* Apollo's oracle spoke well." [4]

The characterization in this tragedy is, moreover, part of a carefully elaborated plot revolving around the manner in which Orestes gains access to Clytemnestra and Aegisthus. Sorrow and joy alternate through-out the play. Electra has reached the height of her grief for Orestes when he reveals himself to her. Aegisthus is called to see the body of Orestes who is reported to have died in exile, but his triumph is turned to horror; he uncovers the body and finds that it is his wife Clytemnestra who is dead. A notable example of ingenious dramaturgy is the manner in which the death of Aegisthus is reserved for the end. The more unpleasant detail, Clytemnestra's death, is forced into the background, and the sympathy of the audience is won for the children of Agamemnon when this contemptible bully is killed. Only the murder of Clytemnestra by her own son, callously presented without any reaction by Orestes, alienates the modern reader from the tragedy.

5 A GREEK IDYL

Nothing unacceptable to the taste of our day is to be found, however, in the character drama which the eighty-six-year-old Sophocles cast in the form of an idyl. *Philoctetes,* which exhibits the lighter side of his artistry, is a tragedy in the Greek sense only (because it is exalted drama); it employs no catastrophe at the end, and the spirit of the work is pastoral. Its background is a deserted rocky island full of wild scenery, and the hero, who had been left there by the Greeks when an adder bit him, lives in a cave. The idyllic spirit of the play is realized not merely in the vividly described natural surroundings but in the character of an unspoiled youth sent by the Greeks to lure Philoctetes to their camp because his bow is indispensable to their success against the Trojans. Neoptolemus, Achilles' young son, starts to do his duty, but treachery goes against his grain despite the wily Odysseus' instructions. Although he has gained possession of the bow and has tricked Philoctetes into boarding the ship that is taking him to Troy, Neoptolemus finally tells him the truth. Philoctetes, whose embitterment against the Greeks who had abandoned him amounts to an obsession, rages helplessly. For Odysseus, who has accompanied Neoptolemus, possession of the bow is sufficient, and he proposes to leave the ailing hero on the island. But generosity and pity for the man who is now having one of his spells and would die of hunger without his weapon lead Neoptolemus to restore the bow to Philoctetes. At this point the interest in character disappears and the idyllic element reasserts itself in the miraculous intervention of the demigod Heracles, who orders the wronged man to forget his wrongs and join the Greeks on the fields of Troy.

The play has darker elements in the physical agony of its hero, in his grievances against the Greeks, and in the representation of treachery and unscrupulousness in the darksome statesman Odysseus. Trenchant lines underscore Sophocles' comment on the way of the world: "War never slays a bad man," and "No gale blows adversely to plunderers." But the dominant atmosphere is one of sweetness and light, and the poet assures us, as it were, that the evil of the world is sometimes compensated by unsullied humanity. Neoptolemus is one of the most likable young men in the world of the theatre.

It is significant, however, that Sophocles reached his full stature only when, instead of contenting himself with mere character studies and with more or less fugitive observations on mankind, he followed the example of his exalted predecessor Aeschylus and turned to well-defined major themes. There are two of them in his extant work: man's respective relation to society and to the entanglements of fate.

6 SOCIAL DRAMA AND ANTIGONE

It is no secret that one of the great tragedies of the world's drama is *Antigone,* which was composed in 442 before any of the surviving character dramas. Sophocles applies himself here to a basic conflict, the rival claims of the state and the individual conscience. The philosopher Hegel formulated the conflict in *Antigone* as one between woman defending the family and man supporting the state. But this fairly literal interpretation does not exhaust the content of this tragedy, since two masculine characters in the play also defend Antigone's conduct. The fundamental question is how to mediate between these principles and avoid catastrophe to either the group or the individual. Moreover, the still more general opposition between love and hate casts its spell over the entire play.

The tragedy begins with a rush when Antigone enters the stage with a passionate speech expressing her intention to bury her brother despite the edict that forbids it. After a quarrel with her timid sister, she hurries away to pay him this last honor. Creon the king is informed by a humorous guard (in the first comic scene of any extant tragedy) that the dead man has been buried, and soon the sentinel, having caught Antigone, brings her before him. Instead of quailing before the new ruler of the city, she defies him. His law is not hers; "I was made for love, not hate," she exclaims. But Creon, "young in authority," will hear nothing in her defense. Even her sister's reminder that Antigone is betrothed to his son Haemon leaves him adamant, and Haemon himself pleads in vain for the great-hearted girl. Creon sentences her to be immured in a cave and left to die. Unrepentant, but bewailing her fate and recalling the tragic history of her family (she is the daughter of the unfortunate Oedipus), she is dragged away while the sent+entious chorus of Theban Senators intensifies her pathos by remaining deaf to her pleas and reproving her for her daring. They, too, are on the side of the implacable state.

But there is a sudden reversal of the situation when Tiresias, the blind priest and prophet, arrives to reprove Creon for desecrating the body of Antigone's brother and to warn him that he will be punished by the gods. Where is there valor in slaying the slain, he asks. And although Creon stubbornly accuses him of having been bribed and sends him away scornfully, he becomes strangely troubled by Tiresias' prophecy. It is bitter to submit, he declares, but submit he will, and he gives orders to release the girl. Anxiety seizes him as he fears he may be too late, and soon his forebodings are justified when a messenger brings him the report that Antigone hanged herself rather than await a slow death, and that Haemon, having found her dead, stabbed himself. The news spreads rapidly, and when Creon's wife hears that she has lost her only son she kills herself, too. Creon is heart-broken and can hardly find any consolation in the commonplaces uttered by his Senators.

Sophocles does not try to weigh the drama in favor of his heroine, for he recognizes the rights of the state and of public interest. Creon was, in a sense, justified in making a public example of a prince who brought an armed force against his own city. No matter how great the provocation, the latter should not have invaded his own country. But Antigone's claims are the stronger ones of piety and love. It is love, too, that asserts itself in the suicide of Haemon. As theatre convention discouraged the representation of romantic relations on the stage, the Romeo and Juliet of this play have no affecting scenes together, but the power of Haemon's love is fiercely attested by his death. Haemon's formal plea for Antigone in which he does not mention his love for her is, in fact, another of the many delicate touches for which Sophocles is famous.

Although Sophocles is not inclined to settle the dispute between the state and individual conscience, and contents himself merely with the observation that the consequences of the conflict are bound to be tragic, the momentum of his pity and of his characterization of Antigone throws the weight of sympathy, at least for modern readers, on the side of the noble girl. Like *Hamlet*, this dazzling tragedy holds in solution many problems that do not easily surrender their meaning to the casual reader. But by the same token *Antigone* is an excellent lesson to the modern social dramatist. He may see here how effective it is to express communal problems with measured objectivity through representative characters who speak for the whole human soul.

7 THE TRAGEDY OF FATE—OEDIPUS

The same wrestling with an important and difficult subject distinguishes the two great plays which raise the problem of fate. Accident is usually considered a cheap and easy device in the drama. But it is neither cheap nor easy in the *Oedipus the King*. The accident occurs before the opening of the play and ties circumstances into a knot that can only be resolved after a prolonged struggle. Fortunately, moreover, Sophocles was equal to his assignment. If he could not hope to solve the riddle of fate, he at least succeeded in writing one of the undisputed masterpieces of the world. And again it is his superb gift for characterization which endows the mere mechanics of dramaturgy with life, agony, and plausibility.

Oedipus killed his father and married his mother unknowingly, and nobody could prevent the consummation of the tragedy. Whatever explanations the Greeks might have proffered in an attempt to shift the responsibility of the crime to Oedipus, Sophocles discarded. As one who saw life "steadily" according to his pagan lights he refused to rule out the existence of accident in the tragedy. But Sophocles could not have woven a great tragedy around a passive victim. Oedipus is a superbly active personality, as if the Attic dramatist tried to tell us that fate works through the character of the victim. Destiny indeed finds a strong ally in this man of courage, nobility, and excellent intentions whose sole failing is his inflammable temper. Both his virtues and defects conspire with fate against him. Had he not been so impetuous and excitable he might never have quarreled with the arrogant old man who affronted him on the highway; he would never have struck him then, thus killing the stranger who later proved to be his father. Had not Oedipus been so high-hearted and quick-witted he might never have answered the riddle of the Sphinx, he would never have been made king of Thebes for ridding it of this monster, and he would never have married the widowed queen. When the play begins, the same admirable elements of his character conspire to open his eyes to his horrible deed. He is so resolute in ferreting out the person who is polluting the city with a secret crime that he discovers the guilt of parricide and incest in his own life. A less determined individual might never have pushed matters so far. Moreover, a less temperamental one would never have blinded his eyes in horror and so exacerbated his sufferings. Without being *morally* responsible, Oedipus is *psychologically* responsible for his sufferings. He is consequently a dynamic character and an active sufferer; he is in fact one of the great tragic figures of literature.

The psychological possibilities of the tragedy are of course not easily exhausted. Under the surface of Sophocles' story lie layers of primitive life that one can barely fathom. When Nietzsche wrote that the uncontrolled anarchic forces of passion and inner horror—the "Dionysian" element—lay behind the serene Apollonian mask of Sophoclean beauty, the German philosopher discovered a profound truth about Greek tragedy, and especially about *Oedipus the King*. The Oedipus story invites one into the depths of modern anthropology and psychoanalysis which have been intuitively plumbed by poets since time immemorial. We are reminded of the anarchic and incestuous impulses which have complicated the life of man and have expressed themselves in so many primitive taboos and civilized neuroses. Like all superlative works of art, this tragedy leads a double life—that which it expresses, and that which it reactivates.

One thing, however, is certain, and it suffices for the lover of the theatre: *Oedipus the King* provides overwhelming drama. The play is a marvel of suspense, pace, and mounting excitement. The experience provided by this play has no parallel in the theatre, except in *King Lear*.

The sequel to this tragedy, the serene and lovely *Oedipus at Colonus*, written many years later, is the Purgatorio and Paradiso to Sophocles' Inferno. The problem of inexplicable fate posed by *Oedipus the King* is not answered in the later work. But one solution is at least indicated: What man cannot *control* he can at least *accept;* misfortune may be borne with fortitude and be confronted without a sense of guilt. The exiled Oedipus has won the ultimate Sophoclean victory of freedom from perturbation. He can now regard his crime without heaping upon himself coals of fire mined from a morbid conscience. Like the patient in a Freudian analysis, who is said to have conquered his inner complications when he can regard them without the sense of guilt which calls for neurotic flight and self-torment, Oedipus is purged and healed. And with him we who followed him to the depths emerge released and strengthened.

He who was so abased that he was driven from his home by his sons is now lifted so high that Athens is sanctified by his presence. For anthropologists his magical efficaciousness harks back to the sanctification produced by the priest-king's death as described by Frazer in *The Golden Bough*. But the holiness of the dying Oedipus also has more universal connotations. One who has experienced the extremes of suffering has risen above common humanity. He has learned all there is to know about agony, and has been sanctified by this final knowledge. Beyond the utmost bounds of passion and pain there can be only enduring peace: Oedipus reaches at the conclusion of the tragedy the peace that truly passes understanding, and it is not difficult to make a sacrament of it. Reconciled with the world order, Oedipus washes himself, bids his daughters an affectionate farewell, answers the mystic voice that calls him, and goes unled to his grave, which is known to no man but the gentlemanly hero-king Theseus who succored him.

It remains to be added that this miracle play does not relinquish at any point its fidelity to human character. Before the mystic conclusion, Oedipus flares up again. One of the sons who allowed him to be cast out of Thebes tracks him down in order to win his blessing in the struggle for power which has begun between the brothers. But Oedipus, who remembers his son's unfilial conduct, sends him away angrily. Nor will the old man return to the city which mistreated him in his days of misery; instead he chooses to die in the commonwealth of Athens which befriended him. He is still the passionate Lear in the face of injustice. His serenity or sense of union with Nature comes only at the end.

It should also be remembered that the mystical conclusion was probably not entirely an end in itself for either Sophocles or his public. There are political connotations in the fact that the Thebans, who had cast out Oedipus and therefore forfeited the blessing he might have bestowed on them, were enemies of the Athenians in the war with Sparta. Although Thebes and Athens were friendly states at the beginning of the play, Oedipus had warned Theseus that this friendship might be broken. Chagrined by the enmity of Thebes and other formerly friendly cities, the Athenian public could take to heart the old king's prescient lines:

> *Faith dies, and unfaith blossoms like a flower.*
> *And who shall find in the open streets of men*
> *Or secret places of his own heart's love*
> *One wind blow true for ever?* [5]

According to the ancient tale upon which the play is based the sacred sufferer died in Thebes; Sophocles must have altered the legend deliberately when he had Oedipus buried in Attic soil.

Nevertheless, *Oedipus at Colonus*, like all great plays, transcends local interests. It remains Sophocles' valedictory to the inexplicable fatalities of life and an affirmation of the ultimate sanctity of suffering humanity. Both life and death lose their sting in this paean to the dignity of a broken soul.

Shortly after the production of *Oedipus at Colonus* in 405 Sophocles joined the shade of Aeschylus. Euripides, his younger contemporary and his intellectual peer, had died a few months earlier, and later in the same fateful year also died the glory that was Greece when Athens succumbed to the military power of Sparta. No master of the high art of tragedy flourished—or perhaps could have flourished—in Athens after Sophocles' death.

Nevertheless, it was given to Sophocles to see a worthy successor in his own lifetime and to watch him trace new paths for the drama And Sophocles may well have been bewildered and dismayed, as well as occasionally gratified, by what he saw. On the calendar Euripides was only some ten or fifteen years his junior, but in some respects he was twenty-three centuries in advance of every fifth-century Athenian playwright. In Euripides we meet ourselves, and in his plays we discover the modern drama more than two thousand years before its official birth.

IV

EURIPIDES, THE MODERN

I THE MAKING OF A LIBERAL

THE BEARDED MAN who lived with his books in a cave on the island of Salamis was a stranger among the men of his time. It was said of Euripides that he would sit all day long thinking, that he despised the commonplace, and that he was melancholy, reserved and unsociable. A portrait bust taken in his old age revealed a worn but beautiful face, thin hair, and tightly drawn lips. The very antithesis of the popular and socially successful Sophocles, his life was anything but a happy one. In fifty years of playwriting, during which he wrote ninety-two plays, he won only five prizes, the fifth being awarded after his death. A continual butt of the comic poets, especially of Aristophanes, he became the subject of the wildest calumnies and ridicule. Even his aristocratic mother was not spared when she was described as a green-grocer. His private life was invaded with charges to the effect that he was a betrayed husband and could not abide women. He was tried for impiety, and he left Athens under a cloud.

The Macedonian court of King Archelaus honored him and he found companions in exile there. But his life at the court was short, lasting only some eighteen months and being terminated by an accident. He was said to have been torn to pieces by the King's hounds, a rather strong possibility in savage Macedonia. His bones remained buried in foreign soil, for King Archelaus refused to surrender his body to Athens, which suddenly awoke to the fact that it had lost a great man but had to content itself with erecting a cenotaph. Euripides is, in short, the classic example of a misunderstood artist.

At the same time, we must not take the traditional portrait too literally. He was never entirely without admirers or without some form of social activity. Like every Athenian citizen he was a soldier up to the age of sixty, fighting intermittently on many fronts in the Peloponnesian War. Although Socrates does not appear to have been intimate with him, Athens' wisest man set him above all playwrights and never went to the theatre except when Euripides was having a play produced; he would even take the long road from Athens to the seaport of Piraeus to see a Euripidean tragedy. It is conceivable that Euripides could think of no greater tribute than approval from this quarter, since the two men thought alike even if they used different forms of expression. Just as Bacon was said to have composed Shakespeare's plays, there were stories current in Athens to the effect that Socrates wrote Euripides' plays or at least helped him with them. Nietzsche's statement that Euripides is to be considered "the poet of esthetic Socratism" [1] was anticipated by the Athenians themselves.

His wife's father Mnesilochus and his servant or secretary Cephisophon remained devoted to him to the end. Another friend was his protégé Timotheus, whose advanced program music was resented by conservative Athenians. Sophocles at least respected his fellow-playwright, even if he disapproved of his realism; he dressed his chorus in black when news of Euripides' death arrived. Even during his most difficult years, moreover, he had his supporters among the radicals and pacifists of Athens. When they assumed power temporarily, they selected him for the honor of writing an epitaph on the soldiers who had fallen at Syracuse. To set this poet down as an incorrigible eccentric and recluse would be a gross exaggeration. Euripides' story is merely that of a man who was out of tune with the majority. He was a free-thinker, a humanitarian, and a pacifist in a period that became increasingly war-mad and intolerant.

If Euripides was an embattled critic of his times he could, however, point out with justice that it was Athens, and not he, that had changed. His birth, traditionally given as the day of the battle of Salamis in 480 B.C. but probably occurring some four or five years earlier, coincided with the dawn of Athens' political supremacy. His youth was spent in an atmosphere of rising civilization which can only be compared to the Renaissance and the period of "Enlightenment" in eighteenth-century Europe. Rich, powerful, and cosmopolitan by virtue of its commerce and imperialism, the Athens of his youth attracted the most advanced thinkers and artists of the age, and provided the proper soil for the liberal philosophy which later fell upon such evil days.

The young Euripides was trained first as an athlete, but although he met with some success in athletics the future master of "mental fight" quickly tired of his profession. In later years he was to declare with characteristic violence, that "of all the million plagues of Hellas there is none worse than the race of athletes." Since he grew up amid the wonders of the new art, he was next attracted to painting; this at a time when he was also mastering music, which he was to practise with marked success when he provided elaborate and advanced scores for the lyrics in his plays. He who must have watched the superlative painter Polygnotus decorating the Acropolis and the sculptors at work in the temples or in the open air remained, in fact, something of an esthete throughout his life. He who saw the creators of beauty honored in his youth remained steadfast in his respect for art even when the Athenians began to regard it as an interloper and blamed Pericles for spending so much money on the beautification of the city.

It is also significant that, like Aeschylus, Euripides grew up amid the splendors of ceremonial worship. His native village Phyla was renowned for its many temples, and as a member of one of the first families of Athens he was among the select youths who participated in the services. Cup-bearer to the guild of dancers who performed at the altar of the Delian Apollo, and a torch-bearer to the Apollo of Cape Zoster who escorted the statue of the god from Delos to Athens annually, Euripides was in his youth closely associated with the religion he was to question later with such thankless perseverance. He was one of the many free-thinkers of Europe who were reared in a religious atmosphere, resembling in this respect Marlowe, who grew to manhood in the cathedral town of Canterbury, as well as Molière, Voltaire and Heine, all of whom received their training in Jesuit schools. A certain attachment to religion is perhaps always a prerequisite to active agnosticism.

Euripides remained susceptible to the esthetic values of religious worship to the end of his days. Some of the loveliest passages in his plays, in *Ion* and *The Bacchae,* recreate the beauty and wonder of divine worship. In celebrating Euripides the rationalist and the Socratic thinker we cannot ignore, as some writers have done, the poet in him. His fascination as a dramatist lies in this dualism between thought and fantasy, between emotion and reason. A more single-minded thinker would have written treatises instead of inspired literature.

Nevertheless, it was the philosophical "Enlightenment" in Athens that shaped his future course and marked him for life. The sophists, who questioned every doctrine and taught the deft art of reasoning, cast a spell on the impressionable and intelligent youth which never left him. Anaxagoras, the Ionian philosopher who came to Athens and spent some thirty years of his life there, was one of his masters. One of the first scientific thinkers of the world, Anaxagoras maintained that the sun was not a god driving across the sky in a golden chariot but a fiery mass of stone or earth whose immensity defied description. He taught the indestructibility of matter, the atomic nature of the world, and the existence of an ordering force in the universe. To Euripides he was not only a teacher but a friend. So was Protagoras who taught the science of language, developed a theory justifying democracy, and expounded the relativity of reality in the pregnant phrase "Man is the measure of all things." Of the gods Protagoras said that he had "no means of knowing whether they are or not." A number of other unconventional thinkers who expounded a variety of rationalistic and humanitarian doctrines or perfected the art of argumentation likewise imbued Euripides with a passionate love of rational truth. From them the first "modern" playwright developed the habit of casuistry in his dialogue and adopted a social outlook which maintained the equality of slaves and masters, women and men, and foreigners and natives. A man of his temperament and orientation was bound to have a pronounced attitude toward his country's policies, and it is not surprising that much of his work must be considered in relation to the political changes recorded by the Athenian historians.

At first Euripides could only swell with patriotic pride that so much enlightenment should scintillate in his native country. When Athens became engaged in the life-and-death struggle with anti-intellectual, provincial and militaristic Sparta he hurried to its defense not only as a soldier who bore arms for his city but as a propagandist who exalted its ideals. But the imperialism of Athens, following the momentum of all imperialist policy, became a ruthless instrument for the subjugation of her sister states, some of them as defenseless and comparatively neutral as Belgium had been in 1914. As the war with Sparta became prolonged and Athens suffered defeat after defeat, the people were in no mood for reason and tolerance. Militaristic demagogues whipped the masses into a *furor Teutonicus,* and the narrow-minded peasantry from the countryside, seeking shelter from invading armies within the city's walls, only swelled the ignorant majority that had no patience with the Enlightenment and even blamed it for catastrophes suffered at the front. The liberal statesman Pericles saw his influence wane, was compelled to let Anaxagoras and Phidias go into exile, and was even impeached. When he died shortly after from the plague—another disaster that exacerbated the intolerance of the Athenians—there was no one to stand between the people and their scapegoats. One by one Euripides saw his friends and masters driven from the city or silenced, and among them was Protagoras, who had read his iconoclastic treatise on the gods in Euripides' house. Soon the news came to the dismayed playwright that his friend was drowned at sea. The picture is unfortunately a familiar one to men of the twentieth century. Even book-burnings were not alien to Euripides' experience when Protagoras' treatise was consigned to the flames.

In the midst of these events Euripides continued to write plays which held in solution the teachings of the exiles, being saved from banishment himself partly because his heresies were expressed by his characters rather than by himself, and partly because the playwright cast his philosophy in a conventional mold. Employing gods who appeared in prologues and epilogues more frequently than in the work of his immediate predecessors, he was on the surface more formal than even Aeschylus had been. Cautiously, too, he left his argument in a state of suspension. The ordinary Athenian was placated with a conventional ending, the subtleties of the play could glide off his back like water, and his senses could be titillated by Euripides' sweet lyrics and colorful music which were popular with the masses. By these means Euripides could continue to function in Athens for a long time, even if he was regarded with suspicion and his plays were normally given second or third place by the watchful judges of the theatre festival.

That he was greatly restricted by this necessity to compromise with an inimical public is evident in the uneven and frequently cryptic artistry of his work. The prologues and epilogues, peopled with gods who often lack an apparent relation to his plays, are for the most part blemishes. His plays frequently have *two* endings—an unconventional one, dictated by the logic of the drama, for the skeptic; and a conventional one for the populace in violation of dramatic logic. The necessity of walking a slack-wire resulted in a certain oscillation of viewpoints; at one point Euripides is patently excoriating the gods of Greek mythology until they look like unadulterated scoundrels, if indeed they are allowed to exist at all, while somewhere else in the same drama they are very respectable divinities. In trying to seem noncommittal Euripides often used a tenuous dialectic by means of which various viewpoints are argued to no conclusion. His endeavor to sugar-coat his bitter pills led to the inclusion of solos that bear an uncertain relation to the dramatic action and serve only to titillate the senses or induce a torpid acquiescence to the drama as a whole. Unity of tone, action, and idea is poorly maintained in some of the tragedies. Occasionally, as in *Ion,* his dramaturgy is almost bewildering.

Euripides could, however, console himself with the thought that without such compromises he could not have spoken his mind at all. He might have believed (erroneously, one suspects) that he was subtly impregnating his fellowmen with ideas that would cushion the growing bigotry of the times. At least he might be able to counteract the rigid orthodoxy that had reasserted itself in Athens. He could raise his voice against the brutalities of militarism and imperialism by choosing legendary themes like the destruction of Troy. He could throw in a good word for the foreigner and urge some understanding for the latter in a play like *Medea*. And, no doubt, believing, like Ibsen, that society would be improved if women were emancipated and allowed to exert a humanizing influence, he could present the claims of womanhood by creating positive heroines. Even if his efforts were likely to be misunderstood, he may have felt that something could be gained by creating women who were complete persons instead of conventional figures. In making them real he naturally made them capable of evil as well as good, and it was perhaps inevitable that he should be set down in some quarters as a woman-hater. But he may have found solace in the expectation that in time the Athenians would learn to regard the other sex as composed of human beings, instead of designating married women as child-bearers one step removed from slavery.

2 THE BIRTH OF REALISTIC DRAMA

If Euripides sometimes bought his intellectual freedom at the expense of perfection, the purchase was a bargain in terms of dramatic progress. The nervous tension of Euripides' plays made him the most dramatic of Greek playwrights, as Aristotle realized. Most of his work contains a great deal of action, and his characterizations are complex and many-dimensional. While playing a game of blindman's buff with his audience, he managed to create the most forceful realism and social criticism of the classic stage.

Common people began to appear on his stage, and his upper-class Homeric heroes were frequently undistinguished or unpleasant characters. His Agamemnon and Menelaus are positively anti-heroic, as if Euripides wanted to show his audiences what conventional military heroes were really like. Other Homeric personages like Electra and Orestes are case histories dear to the psychiatric clinic of our own day. Euripides, moreover, is the first playwright to have dramatized conflicts within the individual without assigning the ultimate victory to the nobler urge. Superb examples of "split personalities" are provided in *Medea,* when the wronged wife struggles between her love for her children and a desire to punish their father Jason by slaying them, and in *Alcestis,* where Admetus oscillates between love of life and affection for the wife whose death alone will save him. Sometimes the psychological element even transcends the individual case, and becomes largely symbolic; the *Hippolytus* and *The Bacchae* pose the question of how far a man may go in denying the demands of some major life-force like sexuality or emotional release without being ultimately destroyed by it when it asserts its power. Euripides' work is unquestionably the prototype of the modern realistic and psychological drama.

His persistent social criticism also sounded a new note. Unlike Sophocles, Euripides did not maintain an impassive neutrality. Unlike Aeschylus, he did not confine himself to general ethical considerations. He devoted an entire play, *The Trojan Women,* to the evils of military aggression and imperialism. War that demands such sacrifices as the immolation of the maiden Iphigenia, who is slaughtered in order that the ships may sail to Troy, arouses his fiercest anger and contempt. Wherever his tragedies describe oppression Euripides speaks with a tongue of flame. Besides, Euripides sounds a grave warning to the oppressor. Let him not think that his victims will conveniently remain objects of innocent helplessness. Driven too hard, they may well become demons of fury and hatred, and like the Trojan queen in *Hecuba* they can in their despair destroy as well as be destroyed. The net result is a world almost equally darkened by the oppressor and the oppressed, a world which, in the words of Henry Adams, a sensitive man cannot regard without a shudder.

Rounding out his crusade, Euripides turns to the mundane and celestial leaders of mankind, and finds both of them largely contemptible. The former are schemers, cowards, and callous tyrants who are a far cry from their Homeric counterparts. They are capable of putting a just man like Palamedes to death, very much as the Athenians persecuted Anaxagoras and Protagoras. As for the gods, they are doubly dangerous, for not only do they reflect the primitive mentality of men but they serve as bad examples. The Delphic oracle is described by the embattled playwright as a fraud. Apollo who ordered Orestes to kill his mother is set down as entirely guilty in the *Electra*, and the same god is depicted as an unmitigated scoundrel, a rapist and a liar, in *Ion*.

In casting doubt on polytheism and demanding just gods, if there are to be any, he was of course only following in the footsteps of the exalted Aeschylus, whose plays he must have seen in his youth. But Aeschylus represented the Olympians or, more specifically, Zeus as developing into a great moral force. Euripides saw no such improvement because he found war-mad Athens returning to primitive worship and behaving as if its deities were absolutely devoid of conscience. One need only recall the cynical words of the imperialists who told the Melians, before demolishing their neutral city, "When you speak of the favor of the gods, we may as fairly hope for that as yourselves; neither our pretensions nor our conduct being in any way contrary to what men believe of the gods or practise among themselves." This is only a short step from Napoleon's opinion that God is on the side of the most efficient artillery. Euripides was clearly not an overbright sophomore or village atheist who denies religion because it is clever to do so.

By the time of his death in 406 he had advanced tragedy through his intense dramaturgy to a point reached only by the mature Shakespeare two thousand years later, and he had developed the problem play to a degree attained only by Ibsen and his successors after the lapse of some twenty-three centuries.

3 THE DEEPENING PERSONAL DRAMA

Euripides began pouring his new wine into the old bottle of conventional tragedy in his late twenties, one year after the death of Aeschylus, with a lost play *The Daughters of Pelias* which is significant on two counts. It shows the young playwright already concerned with the

Medea legend which he was to turn into one of his greatest tragedies, and it reveals him inclining strongly toward legends that required a very formal structure. Euripides, it was suggested, employed the conventional patterns of ritual, somewhat discarded by both Aeschylus and Sophocles, as a disguise for his iconoclasm. But it may well have been that he was also predisposed to such formalism by closeness, in his youth, to religious ceremonial. The epiphany or appearance of a god which he employed so often was a fairly fixed element in the ritual revolving around the Year Demon or vegetation spirit.

Another feature, the *sparagmos* or tearing of a god or totem animal to pieces, is strongly reflected in his *The Daughters of Pelias*. Here Medea wishing to avenge herself on King Pelias who has deprived her husband Jason of his patrimony, persuades his daughters that she can renew his youth if they kill him first. Euripides the psychologist is also in evidence in this first play, since it is the point of his drama that the barbaric Medea, whose code is so foreign to that of Greece, loses her husband's affection by the very passionateness with which she serves him. Euripides voices the sad truth that a woman may actually lose her lover through excessive devotion to him.

At the time of his first production, Euripides was not, however, burdened with personal and public griefs. Two of his next plays, *The Cyclops* and *Rhesus,* even reveal the young poet in a genial and romantic mood. *The Cyclops,* the only complete satyr-play in existence, is a charming rendition of Odysseus' encounter with the one-eyed cannibalistic Polyphemus whom he deceives and blinds in order to effect his escape. *The Cyclops,* which is full of grotesque humor, has the morning freshness of the *Odyssey. Rhesus,* if we are to accept the reliable opinions that attribute it to Euripides, is replete with adventure and romantic color. The play is a young man's dream of adventure in a strange country which bears points of resemblance to the cowboy-and-Indian films that used to delight young Americans. Only the magnificent touch when the soldiers stand embarrassed as a mother weeps over the dead body of her son foreshadows the later tragedies of this humanitarian who made the sufferings of mankind his special province. Even in 438, four years after his first victory with an unknown play, he was still writing romances like *Alcmaeon* and *Alcestis,* the latter being almost a fairy-tale unless one accepts the unnecessary and tenuous explanation that it is a rationalist tract.

Still, it is apparent that Euripides is already a skeptic and a satirist in *Alcestis.* He is not taking too seriously the old legend of the woman who died for her husband. The play extracts much humor from the demigod Heracles who becomes gloriously intoxicated and wrestles with Thanatos or Death for the body of Alcestis in order to restore her to her husband. Perhaps Alcestis did not even die but fell into a hypnotic faint, and perhaps Heracles' encounter with Death was merely a hallucination on the part of the temporarily irresponsible hero.

Already the playwright strikes a deeper note of skepticism and criticism. Admetus, the husband who is told by the gods that although he is slated for death he can escape his fate if somebody will die in his place, is not the conventionally heroic king of antiquity but a selfish bourgeois. He asks his parents to die for him, and when they refuse scornfully he is willing to accept his wife's sacrifice, even though he loves her and mourns her death sincerely. If many Athenians probably approved the conduct of Admetus, since a man (and a King to boot!) was considered a greater asset to the state than a mere woman, Euripides' viewpoint is transparent to the modern reader.

The two companion pieces of *Alcestis,* both lost, also reveal him grappling with characteristic themes. One of the plays, the *Telephus,* brought a beggar on the stage so realistically dressed in rags that it proved an affront to those who required ceremonial costuming in the theatre. The story, moreover, put the heroes of the Trojan expedition in an unfavorable light as ruthless, if unintentional, invaders of a neutral land. In the third tragedy, *The Cretan Women,* the author also made the tremendous innovation of dramatizing the love of a princess for a commoner. It was actually held against Euripides that he raised some doubt as to whether she had been wrong in seeking the *mésalliance* for which she was to be thrown into the sea. She is saved from a watery grave by a sailor (another common man, more humane than his masters!) who violates his orders and spares her life. Romance and realism appear simultaneously in *The Cretan Woman.*

Thereafter, Euripides began to take giant strides toward the modern drama. When we next meet a play of his seven years later, in 431, it is that incisive classic *Medea.* Jason, the hero of the Argonauts, having married the barbarian princess who saved his life at the expense of her father and brother, is growing tired of his wife. He has become a typical middle-aged husband who has wearied of romance, and now that love is no longer the whole of life in his estimation he has his eye on a politically convenient match with a Corinthian princess who will ensure his succession to the throne. But Jason has reckoned without his scorned wife. Goaded by the threat of exile and furious with jealousy, Medea murders the princess and the latter's father by means of a poisoned robe, and then kills her own children.

A remarkable study of the conflict of the sexes, a penetrative analysis of the relative interests of man and woman, and a powerful tragedy of frenzied jealousy, *Medea* is a landmark of realistic drama. If the murder of the children provides an unpalatable climax, it is nevertheless movingly mitigated by the inner struggle of the murderess. It is made comprehensible by her exotic temperament and the wrongs she is suffering, which include separation from her children who are to remain with Jason. Gilbert Murray rightly holds that portions of the dialogue could be labeled "Any wife to any husband" and "Any husband to any wife."

In addition to the striking reality of the personal drama and its sympathy for a murderess, the play is distinguished by its defense of women's rights.* Such feminism was a bold departure from the conventional attitude toward marriage between an Athenian and a foreigner. Marriage with a foreigner, even when contracted by an important leader like Pericles, was considered illegal in Athens. Yet here was Euripides treating a foreign wife of an allegedly inferior race with an impassioned sympathy that has been echoed down the ages by such modern writers as Grillparzer, Lenormand and Maxwell Anderson, all of whom returned to the Medea story. It is not surprising, therefore, that this great tragedy, so far in advance of its time, came out last in the theatre competition.

Three years later, we find Euripides again concerned with the theme of feminine passion. The *Hippolytus,* however, was composed in a tenderer and more poetic vein and even won first prize in 428, although an earlier version, *Hippolytus Veiled,* aroused no end of indignation because it represented the heroine Phaedra making advances to Hippolytus. In fact, even the rewritten drama, entitled *Hippolytus With the Garland,* was considered too sympathetic to a "shameless woman." Phaedra, the second wife of the Athenian king Theseus, falls desperately in love with his son Hippolytus, struggles in vain against her infatuation, and finally allows her nurse to reveal her passion to him. Outraged by such impropriety, Hippolytus scorns the proposal, whereupon the humiliated Phaedra accuses him of making improper advances to her. Unwilling to shame his father, the young man remains silent and allows him to invoke the god Poseidon against him. He is killed in a supernaturally induced accident. Then Phaedra, upon learning that he is dead, hangs herself.

Hippolytus is a tragedy of guilty passion the like of which, if we except a debased version by Seneca, did not appear in the European theatre until Shakespeare wrote *Antony and Cleopatra.* Phaedra, "shameless woman" that she was to the Athenians, is plainly a tragic woman who is under the spell of an overmastering emotion for a man of her own

* Medea declares: "Men say we women lead a sheltered life
　　　　　At home, while they face death amid the spears.
　　　　　The fools! I had rather stand in the battle line
　　　　　Thrice, than once bear a child."
This has rightly been compared to Nora's reply to her husband in *A Doll's House,* when he says that no man ever sacrifices his honor even for the one he loves. Nora replies, "Millions of women have done so!"

years. This is the work of "Aphrodite," who is considered by Euripides a cosmic force rather than a personal goddess.

This tragedy is, further, a unique psychiatric drama since Hippolytus is not simply any pious young man who respects his father's marriage. In our day he would be labeled a "case of arrested development" and his complex would afford a field-day for psychoanalysts. The servant of Artemis, whom the Greeks designated the goddess of chastity, as well as of the hunt, he is a frigid young man who is destroyed by the sexual force, "Aphrodite," which he has hitherto denied. In modern parlance, he is the victim of a repressed libido. The difference between *Hippolytus* and a modern psychiatric history—and a fortunate difference—is only the fact that the psychological conflict in Euripides' tragedy is presented poetically rather than clinically. The play is suggestive rather than matter-of-fact, and the atmosphere exudes the wonder and magic of ancient legend. Hippolytus is killed by a monster that rises from the sea and frightens his horses into overturning his chariot, and the victim's last moments are eased by the appearance of the goddess he had followed with such tragic single-mindedness.

4 EURIPIDES, THE HUMANITARIAN

Euripides could no doubt have continued creating powerful personal dramas *ad infinitum*. But life was becoming increasingly complicated for a humanitarian thinker. In 431, the year of *Medea*, Athens entered upon its long and disastrous war with Sparta. It was no time for a man like Euripides to concern himself with predominantly personal problems.

At first, as noted, he threw himself heartily into the cause which he also supported with shield and spear on the battlefield. Although he had reservations regarding the morality of warfare, he behaved like many a Wilsonian liberal in our own day. Viewing the war with militaristic Sparta as a struggle between darkness and light, without yet noting the militarism in his own back-yard, he thrilled with patriotic ardor. His Athens was a cultured democracy by comparison with Sparta, and it was only natural that the young liberal would give it due honor in so lovely a paean as he included in *Medea*. Athens in this ode is hailed not only as an old and happy land that has never been subdued by a conqueror but as a nation whose consuming desire is for "godlike behavior." Its children walk in the sunlight, and "Wisdom is the very bread they eat." Athens is said to be making the world safe for democracy. . . .

In the same spirit, two years after the beginning of the war, he wrote his *Heracleidae, Children of Heracles,* a somewhat mutilated and not particularly striking play in which Athens undertakes a war with Argos in defense of the wronged children of Heracles. The victorious city is here the champion of justice and humanity. A number of years later,

Euripides is again glorifying Athens—not Athenian imperialism, we must remember, but the humanitarian principle he saw embodied in Athens. In *The Suppliants,* the mothers of the Argive heroes slain before Thebes and lying unburied at its gates come to Athens to ask the city to intervene in their behalf. Theseus, the legendary Athenian king, urged by his mother who declares "Women in sorrow call thee, and men dead," promises to retrieve their dead and bury them. He sallies forth on his noble venture, burns the dead bodies, and brings their ashes to the grieving mothers. Only an occasional acrid comment on war and one touching cry that the Greeks would never have chosen war "if death had been present to their eyes" express a slowly growing disillusionment.

What Euripides so proudly calls a free city is also the theme of the beautiful *Heracles,* produced in the eighth year of the war. Heracles, driven mad by the jealous goddess Hera (although it is suggested in good rationalist fashion that Hera is merely a convenient symbol of his own psychic forces, since he is predisposed to madness), kills his children. Awakening to the horror of his deed, he is overcome with grief and wants to die when his old friend, again the Athenian Theseus, arrives to comfort him. Although Heracles is now, according to Greek custom, a pollution to anyone who touches him, the friend courageously puts his arms around him and takes him to Athens. Heracles, moved by his plea, "Benefactor of mankind and their great friend, . . . Greece will not permit thee to perish in thy blindness," goes with him to do what remains for him in a world which he has been clearing of monstrosities. This play of the year 429 has a number of rationalistic points, including Heracles' doubt of his allegedly divine origin, but is essentially a tribute to the Athenian spirit; it was the last of Euripides' works to sound the note of blissful patriotism.

By the year 425 B.C., indeed, Euripides had already written a stinging, if somewhat disjointed, indictment of war, *Hecuba.* In it he had described the cruelty of the Greek conquerors who enslave the Trojan Queen and sacrifice her daughter Polyxena at the tomb of Achilles. The evil of the world surges like a sea around the aged mother who soon learns that her youngest and sole remaining son, who had been sent away to safety, was killed by his greedy host Polymnestor. She seeks every means to avenge this last and most painful wrong, but finds the Greek leaders cowards at heart. Even Agamemnon, "the king of men," who is favorably disposed to her because he possesses her daughter Cassandra, is afraid to punish Polymnestor who is now the Greek's ally. Hecuba's outburst, freely rendered by Gilbert Murray, is memorable:

"Faugh! there is no man free in all this world.
Slaves of possessions, slaves of fortune, hurled

This way and that. Or else the multitude
Hath hold on him, or laws of stone and wood
Constrain, and will not let him use the soul
Within himself." [2]

Finally she takes vengeance into her own hands, thereby proving that the hate unloosed by the conquerors can also infect the conquered, a sound political doctrine that is still disregarded by the nations.

But it is the later events of the war and its increasing savagery that proved most distressing to Euripides. The *Ion,* a product of deep and complete disillusionment, is unquestionably the most blasphemous of his tragedies. Euripides' challenge to vested superstition is like Voltaire's, nearly twenty-two centuries later; *écrasez l'infâme* is his battle-cry. Apollo, a representative of the kind of gods the Athenians worshiped and a visible symbol of the people's growing moral degradation, is contemptible. He seduces a woman and then makes her husband believe that the child of the union is legitimate. The Athenians could not actually resent Euripides' charge that the Delphic oracle is an unvarnished fraud, since it supported Sparta during the war. But the whole spirit of the work is militantly anti-religious. Euripides, in fact, appears to have been so bitterly bent upon writing an exposé that his play, which is redeemed only by some lovely poetry, is sensational and melodramatic.

Even *Ion,* however, is moderate by comparison with the great tragedy which he wrote after the wanton destruction of Melos and the massacre of its men by an Athenian expedition in 416 B.C. The event was in fact only a climax to the desperate struggle between Athens and Sparta. Pericles, who had already warned his fellow-citizens that they had an empire to defend, had been succeeded by the demagogue Cleon who sounded a distressingly familiar keynote by warning his listeners not to be deceived by "the three most deadly enemies of empire—*pity* and *charm of words* and the *generosity of strength*." None of these "enemies" was evident in the seizure of Melos, and the event impressed itself upon Euripides with searing intensity. At the next festival, in 415, he gave the world its noblest pacifist play—*The Trojan Women*.

This lament in the wilderness of man's inhumanity to man opens with an overpowering sense of gloom. Troy has fallen, its men are all dead, and its shrines have been polluted by the conquerors who spared no one who sought refuge there. The gods are moody and angry, and they are all the more outraged since many of them had supported the Greeks in the war. Revolted at the butchery and impiety of the victors, the gods foretell evil days for them. Then the horrible day dawns, and instead of deities we see the broken women of Troy and hear them bewailing their fate as they await enslavement. They remember every wrong, every horror: "Around the altars they slaughtered us. Within, on their beds lay headless men." Soon the captives are allotted to individual conquerors. Even Cassandra, the Queen's daughter who is Apollo's priestess, is assigned to a master, the haughty Agamemnon; she is led away prophesying doom for the conqueror. As if to deepen their misery and the irony of fate, the only one among them to escape suffering is the self-assured adulteress Helen, who was the legendary cause of the war. But this is not the end of their travail by far. The virgin Polyxena, another of Hecuba's daughters, must be sacrificed at the tomb of Achilles, and Hector's infant son must be hurled from a tower to prevent his growing up into an avenger of his people. The Greek herald, a common man who is more humane than his masters, declares that he is ashamed of his orders; one who brings them should be a man who feels "no pity and no shame either." Finally, the city is set on fire, and the women, who have thrown themselves on the ground to invoke their dead since the gods above have remained deaf to prayer, are dragged away to the Grecian ships.

Never before had there been such an anguished cry for oppressed mankind; never again was it to be raised with such sustained utterance in the theatre. Although *Trojan Women* is a rather static, long-drawn out lament (even Euripides' greatest modern champion, Gilbert Murray, concedes that judged by common standards "it is scarcely even a good play"), this tragedy has a greatness all its own.

Nor was Euripides' quiver emptied by this onslaught on the powers of darkness. One companion piece, produced as part of the set of three tragedies which contained *Trojan Women,* was the lost *Palamedes* which had for its subject the destruction of a good man by a corrupt world. The idealist Palamedes incurs the enmity of the crafty politician Odysseus; he is falsely accused of treason and sentenced to death. A fragment of one of the choruses of the play sings a lament for him:

"Ye have slain, ye Greeks, ye have slain the nightingale:
The winged one of the Muses that sought no man's pain." [3]

Euripides is believed to have been referring to the exile and death of Protagoras, but his play, which also foreshadows the fate of Socrates, easily becomes a lament for all martyrs of reason and good will in a demon-ridden world. Another companion work, the lost *Alexander,* was in a less bitter vein, but made daring use of a slave (or an apparent slave) as the hero of a tragedy.

After the feverish creativeness of the year 415 there was a lull in Euripides' activity as a social dramatist. He turned the other way, seeking some escape from the realities with which he had been grappling. Like Shakespeare who wrote *Cymbeline* and *The Tempest* after *Hamlet* and

King Lear, Euripides began to write romances like the lost *Andromeda,*
a colorful love story of Perseus and the princess he saved from a sea-
monster. The year of the *Andromeda,* 412 B.C., marked the temporary
triumph of the Peace Party after the crushing defeat of the Syracusan
expedition. Prospects for peace were now brighter, and Euripides even
enjoyed a personal, if heavy-hearted, triumph when he was invited to
compose an epitaph on the Athenian dead. The year before he had also
written *Iphigenia in Tauris.* Although there is considerable religious
skepticism in this work, its effect is that of a happy reunion between
Iphigenia and her brother Orestes. Having shaken off half the furies
who have pursued him since the murder of his mother, he has been sent
to wild Scythia to complete his cure by fetching the statue of Artemis to
Athens. He is captured by the natives and brought to the temple to serve
as a human sacrifice but is saved by the priestess, who proves to be his
long lost sister. The same year as the *Andromeda* Euripides wrote another fanciful romance, *Helena,* in which the heroine is shown never to
have been at Troy. A deeper note is struck only when Euripides reflects
that the Greeks and Trojans fought a ten years' war over a phantom
Helen while the real one was residing in Egypt, an idea he took from an
old epic. The holocaust was caused by a delusion or phantom, and there
is sorrow for the city of Troy which was destroyed in vain: "To crimes
thou hast not committed thou owest thy ruin. . . . O Priam for how
frivolous a cause thou with thy Troy didst perish." [4] When a slave is reproved, "Wouldst thou a slave govern thy lord?", he answers like a true
Euripidean commoner, "Here reason is on my side." Nevertheless the
main effect is farcical, fantastic, and playful.

A year or two later, however, the note of pacifist protest is deepening
again. The war, for which Euripides saw a speedy end, did not stop;
instead it began to rage as violently as ever, and Athens was hurtling
down to defeat. In 409 or 410, his *Tyrian Women* or *The Phoenissae,*
the longest Greek play and apparently a unique attempt to write a trilogy in a single piece (a kind of modern three-act play), revives the sanguinary story of the siege of Thebes and the fratricidal conflict between
the sons of Oedipus. Only a certain degree of romantic self-sacrifice by
Creon's son lessens the impact.

Some three or four years earlier in *Electra* he had in fact returned to
the realistic study of mankind, but had confined himself to private drama.
The *Electra,* which treats the old story of how the children of Agamemnon avenge his murder by killing their mother and her new husband, is
decidedly a character play of the highest distinction and in some respects
a *tour de force.* Compared with the Electra plays by Aeschylus (*The
Choephori*) and Sophocles, it is distinctly modern. Euripides declares
flatly that Apollo who ordered the murder of their mother gave evil coun-

sel. The minor deities Castor and Pollux, who appear in the epilogue, can only shake their heads in dismay. Since Apollo is their superior, they cannot say much. "But though in light he dwell, not light was this," he showed Orestes, "but darkness." Answering the question of what kind of children were these who could kill their mother, Euripides makes Electra a sexually frustrated neurotic woman and Orestes a weak-willed lad who is swept on by her stronger will. To increase the pathos of the situation and one's repugnance to the murder, Euripides makes Clytemnestra a pathetic middle-aged person who wants peace at any price. She is even apologetic for the crime of passion she had committed in her youth. In short, the important characters of this play are all broken people. Finally, rounding out his unconventional clinic, Euripides adds a poor farmer, Electra's nominal husband, who is the only noble individual in this tragedy of diseased royalty. Both Orestes and his sister are overcome with remorse for their deed and are forced to separate sorrowfully after a cry of grief which rends the heavens.

Euripides returned to the same subject in *Orestes*, a psychological melodrama of uneven quality, in which Orestes is mad and Electra wellnigh deranged. The new democratic regime of Argos condemns them to death. Menelaus, their uncle who declines to help them because he hopes that Argos will fall into his hands once his brother's children are dead, is forced to save them after they murder his wife Helen and threaten to kill his daughter. This unpleasant portrait of Menelaus is another example of Euripides' deflation of the Homeric national heroes, though no doubt the Athenians were not displeased to see a Spartan ruler portrayed as a scoundrel. Euripides had, in fact, exposed him to ridicule in *Andromache*, an earlier play that was apparently sent to Argos for production following Alcibiades' success in persuading Argos and two other cities to form an alliance against Sparta. The psychological content of *Orestes* is, however, more enduring than its politics. Its hero's mental derangement and sundry descriptions of autosuggestion and hypnosis are worthy of a twentieth-century psychiatrist. Patriotism is at most a feeble spark in the play.

5 A PLAYWRIGHT IN EXILE

Certainly the aging Euripides did little to curry favor with his fellow-citizens. In fact, he became even more harassed by them than he had been while writing his bitterest social dramas. The war had become more disastrous and tempers were shorter than ever. He was pronounced blasphemous and casuistical. He was accused of concealing his wealth, and his oath on that occasion was questioned when a line from his own play, *Hippolytus,* was quoted in proof of the contention that he was capable of perjury. An undivulged private misfortune also befell him;

possibly his second wife betrayed him. According to the comic poet Philodemus, Euripides left Athens because almost the whole city "was rejoicing over him."

The septuagenarian poet now became a wanderer. First he went to Magnesia, in Asia Minor, where he had some connections and had been honored earlier by being assigned consular duties in Athens. But for some reason he did not remain there and went to Macedonia. Here at last he found respite from ridicule and rest for his bones. There was congenial self-exiled Athenian company at the court—Timotheus, the musician whom he had once saved from suicide, Agathon the esthete and playwright, Zeuxis the greatest painter of his time, and the historian Thucydides who had fallen out with the Athenians. Euripides joined a kind of University in Exile which may have reminded him somewhat of the glorious days of his youth when the high-priests of beauty were at work in Athens and men could speak their minds openly. One of his last acts was the characteristic one of saving a refractory Macedonian town from the King's wrath.

It was here that Euripides wrote his last two plays, each great in its fashion. Turning to the legendary sacrifice of Agamemnon's daughter Iphigenia, he wrote a stinging attack on superstition and cowardice in *Iphigenia in Aulis,* a play completed by another hand—possibly by his son's, who was also a playwright. Iphigenia is lured to the Greek camp on the pretext that she is to be married to the young hero Achilles. Agamemnon, weakling and egotist that he is, has enough conscience to rescind his invitation and to send a letter requesting his wife to keep their daughter home. But his brother Menelaus, the mean-spirited forerunner of all the cuckolds of the later European stage, who had not been above involving all Greece in a war so long as he recovered his flighty wife, captures the slave and destroys the message. Iphigenia, accompanied by her eager mother, arrives shy and expectant only to find that she is to be sacrificed on the altar of the goddess Artemis whom her father had offended. Achilles, whose youth endows him with some generosity and kindliness, is won over by Clytemnestra, and he promises to save the girl. But the mob spirit is as strong among the soldiers as it was among the Athenians Euripides had only recently left, and Achilles is stoned for his pains. Thereupon, Iphigenia, more courageous than the Homeric heroes, goes to her death voluntarily rather than risk the life of her defender. He promises, however, to stand by her side and to attempt to rescue her should she quail at the sight of the knife. The happy ending, which is not by Euripides, shows her saved by the goddess and transported to a far country.

The tragedy is all the more powerful for the searching quality of the characterization, which is full of light and shade. It is true that the evils

Euripides detested are told off with flaming anger: conventional heroism is shown to be so much poppycock. The gods are treated with bitter irony in the prayer, "To the dread power we make our vows, pleased when the blood of human victims flows." The irrational mob is assailed in Euripides' description of its conduct, and in the strong line, "The many are indeed a dreadful ill." [5] Nevertheless, the leading characters, with the exception of Menelaus, are not conventional villains. Agamemnon, who bears the chief responsibility for the sacrifice, shrinks from it and is dismayed when his wife and daughter arrive at the camp. But he is afraid to antagonize the Greek army, and is loath to dismiss the expedition which will bring him glory. Achilles may not be the intrepid hero of the *Iliad,* but he is at least capable of noble behavior—when prodded by Clytemnestra. Maidenly modesty and courage are beautifully realized in Iphigenia, and the deeply wronged and frantic Clytemnestra is not the callous murderess of Aeschylus and Sophocles.

As if to fix forever his dual tendencies, Euripides, moreover, left a second play of an altogether different stamp. Although *The Bacchae* shows a vengeful Dionysus confounding the guilty with the innocent and presents a psychological problem in the manner of *Hippolytus,* the work is shot through with fantasy and poetry. *The Bacchae* is equally great as a miracle play and as a symbolic psychological drama which repeats the immemorial conflict between reason and the irrational forces of ecstasy and religious release. Euripides may be indicting fanaticism and divine justice in this work, but he seems convinced that reason too has its limitations; that rationalism cannot wholly exhaust the truth about man or nature and cannot always overcome irrational promptings. Pentheus, the rationalist who despises the orgiastic worship of Dionysus, comes into conflict with this god who is here conceived as a natural force. Pentheus is destroyed by him very much as all those who deny nature are "shipwrecked in their ego," to lift a phrase from psychoanalysis. When Pentheus, a scion of the family that denied the divinity of Dionysus, tries to ban the exotic Dionysian religion he invites destruction. The god, who appears in the guise of a priest, performs miracles (which, it is suggested, may be nothing more than a hypnotically induced delusion), and finally turns the King's head. Bemused, Pentheus dresses up in feminine attire and spies on the bacchanals in the forest. Mistaking him for a lion's cub, the euphoric women attack him and rend him to pieces; and among his murderers is his own mother. This symbolic tragedy was Euripides' last testament, and a fitting one since it revealed him as both a realist and an imaginative poet, and as both a rationalist and a psychologist.

No sooner was he dead than the whole Hellenic world claimed him. He who had written "Unto the eagle all Heaven is free; to the noble heart the whole wide earth is home" became, in the words of F. L. Lucas, a veritable "poet of the Gentiles." Aeschylus was too rugged and Sophocles too aloof an Athenian to be as highly regarded as Euripides, whose cosmopolitanism and skepticism corresponded to the new spirit of the fourth century. When friends wrote his epitaph, "Euripides all Hellas for his monument hath won," they were not employing a pardonable exaggeration; they were stating a fact. His plays were, ironically enough, also of service to Athens in a manner which no local enemy of the supposedly unpatriotic poet could have anticipated. An Athenian ship escaping from pirates received shelter in Syracuse only because someone on board was able to recite his lines. And, according to one report, the conquerors of Athens, shortly after his death, decided to spare the city only when they heard a shepherd sing one of his lyrics. The very Oracle which he had assailed so trenchantly paid tribute to him by ranking him next to Socrates as the wisest of the Greeks.

6 CLASSIC TRAGEDY AFTER EURIPIDES

Imitators arose, and had to be warned by a poet of the Palatine Anthology that Euripides' "path is hard for a man to take." The host of minor playwrights of the fifth century, whose plays are now lost, left no particular mark in the theatre. Only Agathon, who used musical interludes and wrote one play for which he invented the plot and the characters instead of borrowing them from legend or history, may have advanced the drama somewhat. After Euripides' death, the fourth-century playwrights were merely successful day-laborers. Tragic contests or festivals continued for a long time, with an old play used as an introduction to the new ones, but the latter were comparatively weak, and the drama began to lose importance. Actors, scenic designers, and stage directors became more important than playwrights. Plays also began to be written at this time for the closet rather than the theatre.

The fourth century was also the age of criticism; it was the period of the sketchy *Poetics,* in which Aristotle described the principles of Greek dramaturgy as he found them in the works of his contemporaries and their predecessors. Aristotle wrote too late to affect the course of classic drama. His percipient definitions are, however, a landmark in the history of dramatic criticism even though their influence on the European theatre beginning with the Renaissance was in part unwholesome, largely because he was misunderstood and taken too literally. He set down the rather banal principle that stage drama is an imitation of an action, stressed the importance of a plot having a beginning, a middle, and an end; and favored unity of action (made interesting by several reversals of fortune and discoveries of the identity of characters) from which no part should be removable. According to the *Poetics,* moreover, the unraveling of the plot must arise out of the plot itself; *within the action* nothing must be irrational—a generally sound suggestion. Characters are to be revealed not only by what they do but by their moral bent (*ethos*) and by how they reason (*dianoia*).

Turning also to the general effect of tragedy, Aristotle developed the well-known theory of catharsis, according to which tragedy purifies the emotions through "pity and terror"—an enigmatic statement which has perhaps more than one flash of intuitive truth. We tend to interpret this idea as signifying a therapeutic process by means of which the spectator identifies himself with the sufferers on the stage and so rids himself of his own demons. The subject, which has been considered by Lessing, Goethe, and others, is, however, still susceptible of considerable discussion. A related idea fraught with suggestiveness is Aristotle's insistence on the importance of "recognition" (*anagnorisis*) or "change from ignorance to knowledge." [6]

In the third century B.C., the theatre enjoyed a period of success in Alexandria under the enlightened patronage of Ptolemy II, who made its library the repository of Greek culture until it burned down, to the irreparable loss of the world. At least five playwrights are known to have contributed to the twilight splendors of the period. But theirs appears to have been a borrowed glory. The first great cycle of world drama drew rapidly to a close after the Alexandrian period.

Rome, which adopted Greek culture after a fashion, did provide five respectable dramatists during the Republic, which came to an end in the second half of the first century B.C. But the lost plays of Livius Andronicus, Naevius, Ennius, and others were merely based on the work of Aeschylus, Sophocles and Euripides, with the latter especially singled out for this dubious distinction. At best the Roman fragments reveal some vigor and passion. Latin thunder takes the place of Greek harmony, and prose disguised as verse supplants poetry. Soon, moreover, the Roman plays became purely literary drama intended for private reading rather than for production, since the Roman masses, who were in a sense the original movie patrons, had no feeling for tragedy.

7 SENECA AND DECAY

Through the leading writer of closet drama, the stoic philosopher and Nero's tutor Seneca, Euripides, however, was destined to make himself felt in the world's second great period of dramatic production. Although Seneca was not the only Roman to imitate the master, it was his melodramas—*Medea, Phaedra, The Phoenissae, Thyestes, Troades, Hercules Mad* and other plays—that survived to influence the Renaissance. Euripides, who had launched such new forms as romantic drama and melo-drama upon the Attic stage, gave impetus to Senecan tragedy. From Seneca, in turn, the Renaissance dramatists adopted a good deal of their dramaturgy, including the five-act form, which this playwright developed from Euripides' custom of dividing his plays into five parts.

The want of sensibility and the formal character of the Latin language turned tragedy into the channels of recitation. Although Leon Herrmann[7] has argued with some plausibility that Seneca's plays might have been produced. the consensus is that they were merely declaimed by actors. Nearly all the action is relegated to description, the characters all shout in the same tone, and they are described with none of the subtlety required by the exigencies of production.

In behalf of Seneca it must be conceded that he reveals rhetorical in-genuity of a high order, and that a marked sense of dramatic effect—in speech, if not in action—appears in many forceful lines. Of this caliber are Jason's parting words to the departing murderess Medea: "Bear witness, grace of God is none in place of thy repair." The address of the chorus to Hercules' children who have been slain by his own hand in the *Hercules Mad* is another powerful example.

It is not wise to be overhasty, as has long been customary, in condemn-ing Seneca's plays as wholly undramatic. There is no single, unalterable convention of theatre, as this book shows, and recited drama is not necessarily undramatic. With characteristic acuteness, T. S. Eliot re-minds us in 1927 that the Roman philosopher's plays "might, in fact, be practical models for modern 'broadcasted dramas'." Since this statement was made we have had such distinguished examples of dramatic tech-nique in the field of radio as Archibald MacLeish's *Fall of the City* and *Air Raid,* which even the most captious critic could not call undramatic. A new development after 1918 and until 1937—first in Germany and then in America—was the mass chant, of which *Lynchtown* by Paul Peters and George Sklar and the poet Kreymborg's *America, America* are stirring examples. Another cousin of Senecan tragedy is the monodrama, as practised for instance by Cornelia Otis Skinner; and still another is Marc Blitzstein's exciting cantata, *The Cradle Will Rock,* which took Broadway by storm in the season of 1937-1938. T. S. Eliot's description of a Senecan performance, namely that the characters behave "like mem-bers of a minstrel troupe sitting in a semicircle, rising in turn each to his 'number,' " is a close description of the technique employed with dramatic success in *The Cradle Will Rock*. The debasement of Greek drama in Seneca's work is apparent not so much in the different and generally far less theatrical convention as in the too frequently fulsome rhetoric of the lines, the monotony of the verse, the want of sensibility in characteriza-tion, and the crudity of the melodramatic situations.

8 PLATO THE DRAMATIST

Although the pure flame of Greek tragedy died down rapidly, as we have seen, after Euripides, we cannot close this chapter without noting that it rose from its ashes in two novel forms: briefly in the Platonic dialogue, and in the comedy of manners which enriched the classic stage with the work of Menander and the Roman playwrights.

Euripides' desire to deflate the stock figures of antiquity had led him to create a form of tragi-comedy, and a few of his plays like *Helena* are close to comedy of character. In dissolving the rigid form of tragedy and filling his plays with anti-heroic characters, he paved the way for a form of comedy that has prevailed for more than two thousand years.

The other development, the philosophical dialogue, left practically no mark upon the theatre but cannot be dismissed because it gave the world's literature two or three semi-dramatic masterpieces. When Plato, who had written plays in his youth and had a bond with Euripides through his devotion to Socrates, turned to philosophy, he cast his disquisitions in the form of dialogues such as Euripides could have composed.

It requires no great imagination to define the three Socratic dialogues —the *Trial and Apology of Socrates,* the *Crito,* and the *Phaedo*—as a trilogy describing the martyrdom of a just man in an unjust world, a theme that had been treated earlier by Euripides in the lost *Palamedes.* As a matter of fact, these dialogues were scheduled for production by the experimental Gate Theatre in London in 1938, and were once considered by an American management. Socrates, killed by the Athenian state in 399, is the Euripidean hero of this philosophical (and for the stage necessarily discursive) tragedy. Accused of treason to the state, of misleading its young men and denying the existence of the gods, Socrates refuses to defend himself by a vulgar recourse to sentiment. He will not bring his wife and children to plead for him as is customary among the Athenians. Instead, he reaffirms his faith in Reason. The urge to propagate it is a sacred duty, which he calls his "daemon" or divinely inspired impulse. His is a new and more genuine kind of religion—"I believe as none of my accusers believes." Growing in dramatic stature, he also refuses to choose banishment and is therefore condemned to die. Offered an opportunity to escape, he prefers to attest his belief in free inquiry by draining the cup of hemlock prescribed by Athenian law. He continues to discourse on wisdom and immortality to his grieving friends as his limbs become numb and the poison reaches to his heart.

Thus Euripidean tragedy finds an apotheosis in philosophy. These dialogues, to which we may add by way of a prologue Plato's *Protagoras* or even some of the other dialogues (perhaps the beautiful *Symposium*), comprise in a sense a Passion Play of Reason. Socrates, the martyr of intellectual freedom who manages to be both congenial and inimitably noble, is a dramatic-character who has not lost his fascination for mankind even at this late date. His tragedy is profoundly poignant, though it can hardly be acted out in the theatre to any degree since so much of the matter is Socratic disputation. (This is true, even if snatches of dialogue and Socrates' trial speeches are superbly dramatic.) In any case, there is some significance in the fact that Athenian drama which started with a god dying for material human convenience should have found sublimation in the tragedy of a man who died for the freedom of the spirit.

FURTHER NOTES ON ARISTOTLE'S POETICS:

1. *Unities.* Nothing is said about "unity of place." Concerning the so-called *unity of time,* Aristotle merely stated that the later Greek dramatists tended to confine the action to "one revolution of the sun." He stressed only the organic nature, or unity, of action—that is, of the plot. The *Poetics* was not prepared by him for publication, came down to the later ages in fragmentary form, and the allegedly Aristotelian unities of time, place, and action were developed during the renaissance. They were foisted on the European theatre by the scholars of that time who were influenced by the practice of Seneca and the Roman writers of comedy, and by the critical dicta of Horace's *Art of Poetry.* They were sanctioned by the practice of the 17th century French dramatists Corneille and Racine.

2. *Hamartia.* Aristotle stressed that our sympathies in tragedy could be best engaged by a character who is not all evil (so that we can identify ourselves with him, instead of dismissing him as a monstrosity). The tragic hero would tend to be an acceptable human being if he were not under strain, but suffers from a defect or flaw in his character, the result of which is some action that leads to tragedy. This defect or flaw (I might add that, as in the case of Antigone, it might even be an excess of virtue) Aristotle calls *hamartia.*

3. *Spectacle.* Aristotle had the good sense to realize that the visual effect—or spectacle—was important, since a play for the stage is a story shown directly to an audience. And the Greek stage made abundant use of spectacle. Nevertheless Aristotle rightly considered "spectacle" subordinate to the intrinsic dramatic elements in a play. What Aristotle meant and what he was alleged to have meant is a vast subject. See Butcher's *Aristotle's Theory of Poetry and Fine Art,* with Introduction by John Gassner, Dover Publications, New York, 1951.

4. *"Pity and terror."* In genuine tragedy, we pity a credible character who suffers from an understandable mistake or act of violence. We experience fear because this or a similar evil might have befallen ourselves under similar circumstances. It is the question of how the arousal of pity and fear can relieve us that is subject to various explanations. Aristotle himself is not explicit on this point.

V

ARISTOPHANES, THE POET OF LAUGHTER

I THE PLACE OF COMEDY IN ATHENS

AT THE conclusion of Plato's *Symposium* we find Socrates arguing that comedy and tragedy are closely related, and that the same person could write both. Although the idea is apparently not broached elsewhere in Greek literature, it was pretty generally adhered to by the Athenians. The same playwrights who composed exalted tragedies were required to compose convivial after-pieces, and all the tragedians appear to have filled the prescription satisfactorily. As the art of the drama progressed, comedy was even introduced to some extent into tragedies, and finally, as we noted, a form of tragi-comedy made its appearance in the work of Euripides. The most conclusive evidence of this bilateral approach to life is, however, furnished by the Attic convention which added a contest of comedies to the Dionysian theatre festival.

The Athenians observed a theory of release which would have done credit to modern schools of psychiatry. They considered it sound practice to provide outlets to the normally restrained sexual instinct and to the reflex of rebellion against custom or vested power. Among the Athenians, moreover, a periodic release from convention was consonant with democratic institutions; one way to serve the goddess of Liberty was to offer her the burnt sacrifice of established reputations. The custom of comic mockery was indeed not remote from the political practice of ostracism by means of which men who waxed too powerful were banished from the state. To Americans, with their gloriously irreverent attitude toward aristocracy and authority, the principle underlying Attic comedy is certainly not foreign.

Just as we are greatly influenced by comic strips, cartoons, and dramatic travesties like *Of Thee I Sing* and *I'd Rather Be Right,* the Athenians were exceptionally susceptible to the suasions of the comic poets. The writers of comedy who threw the brickbats did not always care whose windows were broken. Nevertheless, theirs was a salutary art, and Aristophanes, who was technically on the side of aristocratic conservatism, was a democratic phenomenon.

The story of this art, however, is not primarily one of deliberate catharsis and democratic priming from the beginning. In developing comedy the Greeks displayed their characteristic genius of transform-

79

ing a primitive activity into a civilized function. Although Aristotle, writing in the fourth century, wrote that "comedy has had no history because it was not at first treated seriously," [1] the fifth-century Athenians were aware that they were putting an ancient ritual to new uses. The people of Athens, who like all sensible people could give themselves unreservedly to laughter, continued to regard comedy as a sacred function, giving it a place in the sacrosanct festival held annually in honor of Dionysus.

2 THE BIRTH OF COMEDY

In a somewhat earlier period there were no formal trappings to conceal the fact that comedy was originally fertility magic. While tragedy enacted the death of the god or ancestral hero, promoting fertility symbolically, comedy remained more literal. Finding a clear parallel between the procreation of nature and the procreation of man, primitive man sanctioned sexual display and even physical union, in the belief that nature would perform in the large what he enacted on a smaller scale. (In a distant sense, one might say that the sacred courtesans of the Mesopotamian temples were the first actresses of comedy.) It was not the death and resurrection of the god, as in tragedy, but his abundant energy or potency that was celebrated in primitive comedy once society began to canalize its imagination into anthropomorphic figures and substituted mythology for magic. It is not difficult to show that both euphoria and magic are still components of comedy; its rapt laughter is euphoric, and its destructiveness is of a magical nature—insofar as we attack an object with ridicule we employ the magical device of indirect, wishful annihilation.

From these rites of obscure times, Mediterranean civilization began to develop a number of somewhat differentiated performances which were destined to flower in those two more or less distinct forms, the satyr-play and Aristophanic comedy. Phallic mummeries representing nature both in its vegetational and sexual aspects acquired animal *dramatis personae* from totemism. The actors disguised as horses and goats or creatures half-man and half-goat known as "satyrs" disported themselves in honor of Dionysus, Pan and other gods of the field and the forest. The element of release inherent in the art and the grotesque animality of the characters inevitably produced comic effects. Combined with a hymn or dithyramb to the god (an innovation attributed to a certain Pratinas of Philus), and later acquiring a more or less developed story, this form of revelry became the after-piece known as the satyr-play.

That the satyr-plays remained so closely associated with tragedy is probably the result of a common origin, which is indicated by the very name for serious drama, since the Greek word *tragoedia* simply means "goat song." The latter may have soon used the goat merely as a sacrifice and later forgot the creature entirely, whereas the actors of the satyr-play actually incarnated the animal. Euripides' *Cyclops*, the only complete extant specimen of this type of play, shows how far it could go toward well-realized humorous action. But the association of the satyr-play with tragedy which began about 515 B.C. could only stunt its growth. The public that had patiently sat through three more or less harrowing tragedies tended to expect from the after-piece which closed the morning's performances nothing more than a relaxing bit of fluff. In time, therefore, this burlesque, which made so little progress toward dramatic sophistication, came to be discarded. After the fifth century it was customary to present only a single satyr-play at the beginning of the program, preceding the revival of an old tragedy. In this perfunctory manner, the Athenians continued to discharge a conventional obligation without being bothered with it during the remainder of the program.

A far nobler destiny, however, was reserved for the parallel development of "Comedy." For a long time it had been customary to celebrate Dionysus, who was the god of generation as well as of wine and vegetation, by means of masquerades and processions. Here in these so-called "comuses," from which the word "comedy" is derived, was the sexual rite in full bloom, with the actors (at first unspecialized citizens) disguised as birds, cocks, horses, and dolphins, carrying aloft a huge phallus on a pole and singing and dancing suggestively. Although the songs were incantations of fertility and therefore religious in character, the literal element in sexual magic provided much ribaldry. Moreover, the closely knit population of the towns and villages went a step further in applying their jests to individual citizens, a custom still not extinct wherever folk humor prevails.

Social satire became more firmly established when a crude form of farce or mime was imported from Sicily, where it attained some literary development in the work of the two poets Epicharmus and Sophron. Southern Italy continued this species of humor for several centuries and not only influenced Roman comedy but even outlasted it. Imported into Doric communities like Megara in the Greek peninsula, this type of farce was soon amalgamated with the native "comus," which had meanwhile pressed portions of the audience into its service and transformed them into a chorus. Perhaps harking back to the primitive conflicts enacted in imitation of the struggle between the good season and the bad, as well as responding to the rapid development of tragedy, the chorus became divided into two bodies which expressed their rivalry by means of antiphonal song.

The comic processions, now on their way toward full-grown drama, soon began to be held in an orchestra, and were finally brought to Athens, where they were officially recognized in 486. They became afternoon performances at the City Dionysia, and comprised the most prominent feature of the related festival at Lenaea where five comic poets competed for the prize. Sacred, not despite their connection with sexuality but because of it, the plays were supervised at the Lenaea by the same Archon Basileus or King-archon who supervised the sacrosanct Eleusinian mysteries.

Of the work of the early writers only fragments remain. We hear of a Cratinus, who won his first victory about five years before Aristophanes' birth and kept pace with the development of the art to such a degree that his *Wine Flask* defeated the younger man's *The Clouds;* and of a Crates, who developed satire and characterization. Lost, too, are the comedies of Aristophanes' contemporary, Eupolis, who often took the prize from him. Only the work of the greatest practitioner of the so-called "Old Comedy" remains—eleven plays out of a total output which exceeded forty.

3 THE COMIC ART OF ARISTOPHANES

The art which reached its zenith in Aristophanes holds in solution most of the elements we associate with comedy of any type. From the literal aspect of sexual ritual, it derived its comparative realism, its concern with the commonplace and the stupid. Hence its anti-heroic attitude, which made Aristotle declare that "Comedy tends to represent the agents as worse than the men of present day." From the associated element of release in sexual magic were born the addiction to unbridled fantasy and exaggeration of reality. Comedy has retained these features to various degrees throughout its venerable but irreverent course.

Nevertheless, Aristophanic comedy indulged a special spirit and followed a pattern uniquely its own. If Greek tragedy has been loosely compared to grand opera (with the proviso that in the former the dramatic elements far outweigh the musical ones), Aristophanic comedy can be described as a close cousin of light opera which finds its nearest modern parallel in the work of Gilbert and Sullivan. It also bears an affinity to burlesque and to topical musical revues like New York's *Pins and Needles* and to modern musical comedy, especially when the latter turns to political or social satire as in such American jollifications as *Of Thee I Sing* and *I'd Rather Be Right.*

The specific pattern of the Old Comedy, however, has no modern parallels. The comedy opened with an expository scene between the characters in which the setting and the story were disclosed to the audience. Then the chorus, fantastically garbed in costumes frequently suggestive of wasps, frogs, clouds, and birds, made its entrance with a song, the *parodos,* sometimes divided into two rival factions. Once on the stage, the twenty-four members of the comic chorus remained there throughout the action, participating in it variously and enjoying many liberties. A high point was the contest or *agon* in which two characters representing opposite views or interests contended until one of them downed his rival —generally with a torrent of Rabelaisian argument and vituperation. At this climax, while the actors withdrew from the stage, the chorus faced the audience and advancing toward it in military fashion delivered itself of a long and highly personal harangue. This speech, known as the *parabasis,* voiced the playwright's views, sometimes even chaffed prominent personages in the audience, and called a spade a steam-shovel. At the conclusion of the harangue, which could never have been permitted in an undemocratic community, the actors reappeared in a series of short scenes, and the play was brought to a conclusion with a representation of the consequences entailed by the *agon.* Complications might be added by means of two *parabases,* as in Aristophanes' *The Clouds* and *The Knights,* and variations in the general structure could be introduced by a freer treatment of the plot or by omitting the *parabasis* altogether, as in his *The Ecclesiazusae* and *Plutus.*

It was a gorgeous spectacle that the Athenians enjoyed as they watched the grotesquely dressed chorus, and the actors, sometimes made up to resemble some civic luminary who exposed himself as a fraud and a nincompoop. Fantasy, whimsy, and undisguised buffoonery characterized the story that unfolded itself. Badinage, ribaldry, and scolding such as would put any fishwife to rout spiced the dialogue and the songs. These proceedings would draw down the wrath of the censor in almost any part of the world today, and one can hardly blame Aristophanes' conscientious Victorian translator John Hookham Frere for referring dismally to the Greek text's "most profuse largesse of filth and trash." [2]

In intention, however, Aristophanes' plays were frequently as noble as the tragedies of Aeschylus, and it is not surprising that the comic poet should have referred so often to the heroic age of the Marathon soldier who brought tragedy to its high estate. If as Frere noted, Aristophanic comedy was "a great lie," it was intended to serve the truth—that is, as Aristophanes saw that elusive commodity. There was great keenness in the darts which Aristophanes hurled at error and pretence, and there was much stately indignation in his blasts against civic corruption. Above all, besides, he was a dramatic poet who could stand comparison with Aeschylus and Sophocles. His fantasy is alternately Rabelaisian and ethereal, and his lyrics are masterpieces of description and exaltation. To draw an accurate picture of Aristophanes' talent one would have to combine the topical humor of a Kaufman and a Hart, the apostolic zeal of a Theatre Union playwright, and the poetry of Shelley.

4 AN EMBATTLED CONSERVATIVE

Aristophanes was undoubtedly endowed with a disposition for slashing satire, and if we knew more about his life we might locate some of the sources of his gift in his personal history. (He apparently lost his hair early, but one cannot erect a theory of laughter on an impoverished scalp.) But he was just as assuredly the very antithesis of a cynic, for he believed strongly in the Athens of Aeschylus. He was no idle parodist of an idle day, for the Athens he travestied was fighting for its life, and his laughter is heavy with apprehension and grief. He was, in fact, a reformer and an ardent propagandist who did not always conceal his special pleading. That he could not abide an esthete is shown by his contempt for the tragic poet Agathon whom he accuses of effeminacy.[3] To the end of his days Aristophanes was an aristocratic conservative who regarded with disfavor all departures from the older and more fortunate Athens which he could have barely known since he was born about 445 B.C., fully three-quarters of a century after Aeschylus. To the democracy of his day he remained unalterably opposed, decrying hydra-headed government, large publicly paid juries, demagogic leadership, and the new sophistic philosophy which supplied the common man with the double edged refinements of casuistry.

Still, this picture of a grass-roots politician is an extremely one-sided one that does not do justice to either the artist or the political thinker in Aristophanes. Democracy at its best he never knew. By the time he was born it had lost much of its bloom, and by the time he was nineteen it had become maggot-ridden with corruption; the Athens he knew had become demoralized by the Peloponnesian War. Throughout the duration of the war, and especially after the death of Pericles, the Athenian populace was led by the nose by the unscrupulous politicians Cleon and Hyperbolus. It was in their interest to continue the hostilities which afforded them political power and to give the masses their head in little things in order to rule them in larger matters. Here were all the abuses of a democracy in decay, and behind them lurked, in fact, the same intolerance which is normally associated with extreme reaction. It was actually this false democracy that put a stop to free inquiry by exiling Anaxagoras and Protagoras, that frowned on the art of Phidias and ultimately killed Socrates.

Aristophanes no doubt had an aristocratic bias, and he was not concerned with an abstruse theory of democracy. But he was, whether he knew it or not, serving the cause of true democracy. It is to be remembered that the post-Marathon Athens he glorified in many an exalted lyric was not a tyranny or an oligarchy but a democracy. When he called upon his fellow-citizens to return to the old order, he was bringing them

back to a somewhat idealized democratic state before it had been corrupted by imperialism. Moreover, in flaying imperialism, with its attendant militarism and chauvinism, he was again only defending genuine
democracy. Aristophanes was a believer in patriotism rather than jingoism, which he satirized in three of his best plays; and although he never
speaks of *demos* without contempt, he championed democracy better than
he knew. More than he seems to have realized, this technically conservative satirist was on common ground with the radicals Euripides and
Socrates, whom he travestied.

It is only in secondary details—in his opposition to "new art" and
"new philosophy"—that he can be set down as an arch-cónservative. The
momentum of his thought carried him to irrational extremes in his constant attacks on Euripides and Socrates. However, his violence is largely
a form of dramatic generalization or extravagance. In order to attack a
particular abuse he would select a victim who was most likely to be familiar to the Athenians, even if the person in question was only loosely
associated with the satirized tendencies and only superficially tainted by
them. The method, like a good deal of "red-baiting" in any period, was
hardly fair, but it was decidedly effective. Moreover, an incisive satirist
like Aristophanes was apt to descry excesses latent in even an essentially
noble thinker.

5 POLITICAL SATIRE

His first two comedies, *The Banqueters* and *The Babylonians* brought
out under the name of leading actors in 427 and 426, were long ago lost
in the shuffle of time. We know, however that *The Banqueters,* which
is a satire on the new education, already sounded the note of Aristophanic
social criticism, and that *The Babylonians*—which is perhaps the world's
first political satire—attacked the internal and foreign policies in Athens.
He must have already matured considerably, since *The Banqueters* received honorable mention, being awarded second place. Two years later
he is already an accomplished satirist in *The Acharnians,* his first assault
on Athenian policies.

The Acharnians, written in the sixth year of the Peloponnesian War, is
the world's first anti-war comedy. Taking his cue from the sufferings of
the rural population of Attica which was exposed to continual invasion,
Aristophanes makes his hard-headed farmer Dicaeopolis conclude a private peace with the Spartans. Since no one listens to his plea for a cessation of hostilities, he despatches a messenger to Sparta on his own behalf
and receives an assortment of treaties. Dicaeopolis chooses one which is
especially to his liking, and the comedy concludes with a rustic celebration of the benefits of peace. Dicaeopolis is an excellent comic hero; his
unsentimental character is the illusionless Comic Spirit incarnate. Pep-

pered with allusions to the rapacity of the people's leaders (Cleon is accused of having accepted a bribe of five talents) and with a parody of Euripides' lost *Telephus,* the play is humorously topical.

When, for example, Dicaeopolis is denounced as a traitor by his fellow-citizens, who are charcoal-burners, he saves himself by threatening to destroy a charcoal hamper, very much as Telephus saved himself from the wrath of Agamemnon by threatening to kill the latter's infant son Orestes. Given an opportunity to plead for his life, he goes to Euripides to borrow his tragic stage effects. But when he inquires, "Is Euripides home?" he is answered by the casuistic playwright's servant in a characteristically Euripidean manner that "He is and he isn't; understand that, if you have the wit for it." Euripides lends him the pity-rousing rags of Telephus and adds other accessories of beggardom until his odd collection is almost exhausted. "Miserable man!" Euripides complains, "You are robbing me of an entire tragedy." Dicaeopolis then goes bravely to his trial. "I shall not please," he says, "but I shall say what is true." He knows what he is up against among the Athenian people: "I come to the general conclusion—we have no common sense."

Unexpectedly, however, he wins his case by means of telling pacifist arguments against Lamachus, a general of the day, and thereafter enjoys a busy and prosperous life. A Megarian war-sufferer who declares "We are crying with hunger at our firesides" sells him his starved daughters disguised as pigs, with farcical results that may be easily imagined. A Boeotian sells him eels in exchange for an informer, a commodity which was apparently as abundant in Athens as in any war-mad society. The Athenian general tries to enter Dicaeopolis' market but is not admitted. He is left to long for the pleasures of peace as the farmer enjoys a succulent feast and entertains himself with *two* courtesans.

But the chief object of Aristophanes' anger was Cleon, the militarist and demagogue who had succeeded the great leader Pericles. In *The Acharnians* the comic poet had threatened to "cut up Cleon the Tanner into shoe-leather." In his next play *The Knights,* which came a year later, he made good his promise. Although this time he did not venture to call the victims of his satire by their right names as he had in *The Acharnians,* everyone identified the Paphlagonian tanner as Cleon and his rival, the Sausage-Seller, as Cleon's successor Hyperbolus. There was a certain vindictiveness in this attack since Cleon, who tried repeatedly to have Aristophanes declared an alien, had charged the poet with slandering "the city in the presence of foreigners." But there was also considerable daring in this exposé of a politician who was then at the height of his power, as well as much patriotic fervor in Aristophanes' bitterness, since Cleon was the chief representative of the policies which the playwright considered ruinous to Athens. So great was Cleon's prestige at the time that no one dared to impersonate him and the actor who took his part had to dispense with the customary mask of the object of the satire. An unverifiable tradition has it that Aristophanes played the role himself, with his face smeared with wine-lees in mimicry of the demagogue's bloated and alcoholic visage.

The springboard of the satire and the reason for the play's title was Cleon's assault on the lower aristocracy of Athens, the Knights. Demos, or the Athenian people, is a credulous old gentleman who is wooed successively by the Paphlagonian and the Sausage-Seller. In an exchange of billingsgate it is the latter who wins, for he proves himself an even more incorrigible rogue than his predecessor and therefore has a better right to lead the Athenian populace. Nicias, the admiral of the Athenian fleet, and a vice-admiral Demosthenes are helpless against such egregious rascals. Nevertheless, Demos is liberated at long last when the fleet refuses to sail under the Sausage-Seller. Remarkably enough, *The Knights* received the first prize, even if its political results were nil.

The purely political character of the comedy and its relative want of invention do not commend it to modern readers, but the satire on politicians provides ample entertainment. When Cleon is confronted with his rival, he reflects: "It's certain he cannot be a greater thief, but perhaps he may be a luckier one." His opponent claims that he is well-prepared to lead the people since the school he attended was the kitchen, where he was taught with cuffs and blows. He sold sausages and lived licentiously, but above all, "I learnt to take a false oath without a smile, when I had stolen something." He is of the right breed, for does not Demos always respond warmly whenever an orator stands up in the Assembly and says "Demos, I love you ardently."

Two years later, in 422, in *The Wasps*, Aristophanes returned to his favorite theme—the deterioration of Athens. Here it was the judicial practice of the country and the passion for litigation that drew his fire. Considering the custom of large panels (often consisting of as many as five hundred paid dicasts or jurymen) a waste of time, a perversion of justice, and a ready instrument for demagogues like Cleon, Aristophanes invented the case history of an old man who becomes maniacally litigious and has to be confined in his house by his son Bdelycleon ("Enemy of Cleon"). This senile addict Philocleon ("Lover of Cleon") makes extravagant efforts to escape to the tribunal where cases are being tried. He is squeezing himself out through the chimney and pretending that he is only "smoke" when his son's retainers clap a cover on the top and weight it with a stone. He wriggles through a hole in the tiles and gets to the roof, pretending that he is only a "swallow," and has to be captured in a net. His fellow-jurymen, appropriately represented as wasps, arrive to rescue him. A compromise is finally effected whereby the father consents to remain at home if a mock trial is set up for him in his house. The house-dog, who happens to have stolen a Sicilian cheese, becomes the defendant, and is acquitted when the old man inadvertently casts his vote in his favor. Since he has never acquitted anyone before, Philocleon is sorely vexed. But he is consoled when, having renounced all jury duty, he turns in the manner of Molière's *Bourgeois Gentilhomme* to polite society, which he promptly upsets with his antics, throwing stones at people and abducting a flute-girl from a party.

That *The Wasps* is as diverting as it is colorful is self-evident. It attracted Racine, whose only comedy *Les Plaideurs* employs the incident of the mock trial of the dog. Farce, however, is not its sole claim to excellence. Some of the lyrics, which invoke Athens of old and exhort its citizens to return to the heroic age, are marvelously noble and spirited.

Having delivered himself of this general blast and call to action, Aristophanes returned next year with another of his anti-imperialistic comedies *Peace*, which again appealed to the people to come to an agreement with Sparta. He must have, in fact, reflected the temper of the people this time, since they signed the Peace of Nicias shortly after the play was produced. Here, as in the first of Aristophanes' pacifist plays, it is a farmer, the vine-grower Trygaeus, who strives to end hostilities. He mounts a huge beetle (another parody on Euripidean tragedy) and flies to Heaven in search of the goddess of Peace. Learning that the Greeks have imprisoned her in a dungeon and that the god of War is preparing to pound the warring communities in his mortar, Trygaeus liberates the goddess and ushers in a golden era of well-being. Here the satirist's nostalgia for peace reduces the burlesque elements of Aristophanic comedy, and *Peace* is most notable for its lyricism. The poet, recalling the once pacific beauty of the Attic countryside, dreams of the grapes and figs of Lemnos and of the simple possibility of at last

> —*Growing fat and hearty*
> *In the genial summer time.*[4]

The pacifist theme reappears ten years later in the famous *Lysistrata,* written in the twenty-first year of the war. A more light-hearted, risqué comedy can hardly be conceived, for there is rare sport in the conspiracy of the women who refuse all intercourse with their husbands until they stop behaving like fools and end the war. Their battle with the old men who have been left behind to safeguard the city, the vacillations of the women when their husbands arrive, the exasperations of the men, and the final victory of the women are delightfully farcical. Lysistrata, who leads the boycott of war, is Aristophanes' most completely realized character and strikes a note of high comedy rare in the fifth-century theatre. At the heart of all this banter was Aristophanes' brooding sorrow for the thousands who had recently lost their lives in the crushing defeat at Syracuse. But with fine and unwonted tact he does not stress the disaster. His plea for peace is fervent, but he behaves as if he realized that his fellow-citizens needed the balm of his laughter more than the vinegar of his scorn. He must have needed it too in those dark days.

It is, incidentally, worth noting that he who travestied the feminism of Euripides shares it when he makes the Chorus of Women say: "What matters that I was born a woman, if I can cure your misfortunes? I pay my share of tolls and taxes, by giving men to the state." To the men who reprove them, Lysistrata declares: "The War is a far heavier burden to us than to you. In the first place, we bear sons who go off to fight far away from Athens."

After *Lysistrata,* Aristophanes seems to have given up politics as a hopeless job. He did not devote an entire play to political questions until nineteen years later. By then Athens had lost her prestige, having been conquered by the Spartan alliance, and its liberties had waned to an extent that made it impossible to launch direct attacks on state policies. His play, *The Ecclesiazusae* (or *Women in Parliament*), presented at the City Dionysia in 392, is far less topical than his previous political satires. The play, which is largely fantastic, may have been intended as a travesty on Plato's *Republic,* published later but probably propounded by this time. The passion for ideal commonwealths receives in this comedy its most amusing and incisive treatment until the appearance of Aldous Huxley's *Brave New World* in the present century. Here it is the women who win ascendancy in the state by means of a ruse and establish a feminist utopia in which property and wives are held in common. The amusing consequences of this revolution comprise the bulk of the entertainment. And again as in *Lysistrata,* Aristophanes creates a well realized female character in a form of drama which ordinarily dispensed with rounded characterization; she is Praxagora, the leader of the women who tire of the dismal way in which men are running the world.

6 PHILOSOPHICAL AND LITERARY SATIRE

Political satire did not, however, exhaust the satirist's resources, and some of Aristophanes' sharpest sallies were reserved for the culture of his times. The first to feel the sting of his tongue was Socrates in *The Clouds,* which came early in Aristophanes' career in 423 B.C.

Strepsiades, driven to penury and despair by his son's extravagance, hears of the new art of argumentation as practised by the philosopher and enrolls in his *Phrontisterion* or Thinking Shop in order to be able to cope with the litigations entailed by his debts. But Socrates, swung aloft in a basket in order to be closer to the ether from which all his thought springs, and devoted to the deities Chaos, Clouds, and Speech, is too much for his pupil. Strepsiades therefore forces his son to take his place, and lives to regret his decision. The young man responds to the new learning so well that he is able to prove that he has a right to beat his father. The belabored parent is so enraged by this unfilial behavior that he sets fire to the alleged humbug's Thinking Shop. Since the comedy is supplied with a marvelous chorus of Clouds and is full of diverting situations, it has long been regarded as a masterpiece. It was not the least of Socrates' misfortunes that the work in which he is caricatured is so accomplished a travesty.

It was, however, Euripides, already ridiculed in numerous passages, who became the chief target of Aristophanes' fire. First, in 410, came his *Thesmophoriazusae* (*Women at the Festival of Demeter*), in which Euripides' alleged defamation of womanhood, a gross misunderstanding deliberately fostered by the comic poets, is resented by the women of Athens. Euripides prevails upon his father-in-law to plead his cause in feminine disguise and then enables him to escape the wrath of the assembly when his sex is discovered. Parodies of the styles of Euripides and of the younger dramatist and esthete Agathon enhance the variegated intrigue of what may be properly considered the theatre's first literary satire.

Five years later, in *The Frogs,* Aristophanes returned to his victim with added resourcefulness and verbal wonder. Since Sophocles and Euripides died within a few months of each other, Aristophanes made Dionysus greatly perturbed by the lack of a major dramatist on the stage. Resolved to bring Euripides back, Dionysus dresses up as Hercules, braves the three-headed dog that guards Hades, and prevails upon Pluto to let him retrieve the tragedian. But Euripides has two formidable rivals in the underworld and, although the urbane Sophocles gracefully retires from the conflict, the rugged Marathon-warrior Aeschylus has no intention of giving way to an upstart who has degraded his exalted art. After bandying lines from each other's plays in what appear to be the most remarkable parodies in literature, Aeschylus and Euripides finally decide to weigh each other's verses. Aeschylus has of course the weightier lines, and these tilt the beam so conclusively that Dionysus decides to return with the older poet, leaving Euripides permanently in the underworld.

The ingenuity of the plot, incidental extravagances, excellent serious lyrics, and scintillating parodies make *The Frogs* the greatest literary satire in any language. Two choruses are employed in the comedy: that of the frogs on the banks of the river Styx whose "Brekekekex, ko-ax, ko-ax" seems to be one of the first acquisitions of a college education, and that of the Initiates of the Eleusinian mysteries, who begin their great song with the beautiful lines,

Come arise, from sleep awaking, come the fiery torches shaking
O Iacchus, O Iacchus!
Morning star that shineth nightly,
Lo the mead is blazing brightly
Age forgets its years and sadness
Aged knees curvet for gladness.

The two remaining comedies of Aristophanes were of minor topical interest, though both have a significant place in the history of comedy. *The Birds* is pure fantasy free from direct topical allusions, which was probably why it lost the prize in 421 to Amipsias' *Revelers,* a satire on Alcibiades. In *The Birds* two gentlemen disgusted with the state of affairs in Athens depart for the land of the birds, "a city free from all care and strife." Restlessly conniving like the fellow-citizens they left behind them, they propose a scheme to the birds which will bring the gods to terms. By building the new city of *Nephelococcygia* or "Cloud-Cuckoo-dom," they intercept the stream of sacrifice to the Olympians and starve the gods into giving them a celestial bride. Much good-natured fooling, unfettered fantasy, and a parabasis which is one of the great poems of the Greek language make *The Birds* a delightful relief from topical cantankerousness.

Aristophanes' last play, *Plutus,* the revised and only extant version of which was produced in 388, satirizes the unequal distribution of wealth in a story of how the god of wealth, Plutus, was captured by an Athenian, healed of his besetting blindness, and enabled to discern between the deserving and the undeserving. Less brilliant and ingenious than the other comedies, *Plutus* is largely significant as a departure from Aristophanic topical satire which the collapse of Athenian democracy had made impossible. A new form of comedy known as Middle Comedy, which prevailed during the last three-quarters of the fourth century, was slowly displacing topical satire; it concentrated on love intrigue, dispensed with the free-spoken parabasis, avoided politics, and was comparatively tame in spirit. Aristophanes, however, was soon spared the necessity of subduing his spirit and guarding his tongue. He died in 385 B.C., three years after the production of *Plutus.*

VI

MENANDER, PLAUTUS, AND TERENCE

I MENANDER AND THE NEW COMEDY

It REMAINED for Menander and his contemporaries, more than half a century after the death of Aristophanes, to realize the possibilities of a form of comedy which is not primarily satire. By then Athens was under Macedonian rule. Playwrights were compelled to confine themselves to comedies of sentiment and private embroilments, and the taste of the day rewarded them with its favor. Many were the writers—sixty-four, to be exact—who responded to the new interest and created the form of domestic comedy or comedy of manners which has held the stage for twenty-two centuries with only minor modifications.

Unquestionably it made fewer demands upon genius than the Old Comedy, which needed men of the highest poetic endowment, imaginativeness, and political discernment. Every Aristophanic comedy displays fresh invention and offers original situations. The New Comedy, on the contrary, employed stereotyped plots, was decidedly less imaginative and ambitious than its predecessor, and possessed an essentially commonplace outlook. Fastening upon everyday characteristics and moving in ordinary grooves of behavior, it played gently on the surface of society.

Menander's plots are a wearisome repetition of young men who are in love with young girls, parents who are disturbed by the behavior of their children, intriguing servants who assist one side or the other, and long-lost relatives. With monotonous regularity, the comedies wind up their complications with a happy ending so facile that it would commend itself to any film addict. Although the plays and even the plots of his contemporaries are largely lost, there is no reason to assume that these sixty-three playwrights departed from the set formula. On the contrary, it is Menander who, according to ancient report, was the most gifted of them all and can be credited with the most inventive talent.

Undoubtedly, the new art of Philemon, Diphilus and Menander would have been scorned by Aristophanes and would have displeased fifth-century judges at the theatre festival. Comedy was infused with vivid observation of everyday details and supplied with a unified plot. Romantic love, long kept out of the comic theatre, was added to the inventory of dramatic situations and soon dominated the laughter of the stage as it has done up to our own day. Above all, comedy began to employ the perceptive art of characterization. Modern character-comedy and comedy-of-manners were born in the second half of the fourth century B.C.

Although Menander was not the most popular playwright of his time, winning only eight prizes and being frequently beaten by his rivals, he was ultimately accounted the best of them and held this eminence throughout classic times. The title of "father of modern comedy" is properly his, and a list of his lineal descendants, which would include Shakespeare and Molière, is long and honorable.

His fame, which we must largely accept by hearsay since most of his work has been lost, was due to his alleged mastery of characterization, his poetic style which was set on a par with Homer's, and his sympathetic tolerance for people—the one virtue to which Aristophanes was allergic. Each character had its stamp and was supplied with complex motives; slaves, as well as masters, were given distinct personalities; and within the limits of the romantic story, his people behaved with a plausibility which had not hitherto concerned the writers of comedy. It was these qualities that an ancient critic must have had in mind when he wrote his seemingly extravagant panegyric: "Oh Life, Oh Menander, which is the copy?"

Although the politically enfeebled Athens in which he was born in 343 or 342 was about a century removed from the Periclean age, it was still one of the great centers of civilization. The stimulus of a powerful social background or a vigorous commonwealth was not indeed granted to Menander, and its absence is reflected in the tameness of his genius which no amount of classic adulation can conceal from us. But the romantic afflatus of Alexander the Great and the trail he blazed through the eastern world exerted its fascination on Menander's youth. The liveliness of Menander's plots probably owes something to the adventure which took Hellas by storm and fired the imagination of all but the most disgruntled republicans.

The relaxed and hedonistic quality of the plays has an affinity to the philosophy of happiness taught by the great Epicurus, who was Menander's contemporary and fellow citizen. In Athens, too, was Aristotle, the philosopher of "the golden mean"—a cardinal principle in all genuine high comedy, in which sins of extravagance and excess are summarily punished with ridicule. Menander's greatest debt, however, was to his instructor, the philosopher Theophrastus whose *Characters* gave rise to the fashion of composing thumb-nail sketches of character types. Individuality, so nobly commemorated by Pericles in his famous funeral oration, was no longer passionately prized by the Athenians.

In this world flourished Menander, the child of a distinguished family and the nephew of Alexis, who had been writing comedies for a generation along with some thirty or more other playwrights of the so-called Middle Comedy. Menander grew into a cultured and sophisticated man with a squint and a passion for the fair sex. Society with its foibles and polite conversation claimed him, and Demetrius, the Macedonian ruler of Athens, was his friend. When the latter fell from power in 307 and a feeble democratic government was established, Menander found himself in disfavor, and one of his plays was refused a production. But by then his reputation was such that both Macedonia and Egypt offered him a haven at court, although he availed himself of neither invitation. Sixteen years later, in 291, he was accidentally drowned, being survived by his playwriting uncle and his rivals Philemon and Diphilus.

His posthumous fame grew by leaps and bounds, and his work, which came to be used as a model by teachers of rhetoric, was frequently revived. But to the hundred and five comedies he had written post-Roman times proved an unrelenting enemy. They were long available only in numerous fragments, until three comedies were partially recovered in 1905 when the explorer Lefebvre found an Egyptian papyrus codex that had been torn up to protect a variety of legal documents.

As in every epoch, the theatre of Menander had its well-defined conventions. The scene was in the street, and all action within the house was imparted to the audience in long soliloquies generally directed at the public. Various excuses were found for bringing characters out of doors. These devices did not, however, diminish the action but actually enlivened it, and there is room for lively complications in Menander's streets. The characters wore masks, as in the preceding century, but these had become exceedingly refined and expressive; perhaps they were not even so greatly removed from the grease-paint mask of modern times, and their use was not disadvantageous in the case of stock characters. The plays of Menander undoubtedly suffered less from the convention of the masks than did the highly individualized tragedies of Euripides. The proceedings were further enlivened with entertainments during the intermissions, for Menander's plays no longer employed a chorus to provide continuity of action but were divided into acts, probably five in number as in Roman drama.

Considerable growth is manifest from that early comedy of errors his *Samia* (*The Girl from Samos*), in which farce predominates, to his *Perikeiromene* (*The Shearing of Glycera*) and his *Epitrepontes* (*The Arbitration*), twenty or more years later. In *The Girl from Samos* a well-to-do genial householder Demeas has a mistress Chrysis whom he loves devotedly, although a formal marriage between them is impossible. His son, being in love with a cantankerous neighbor's daughter, pursues a clandestine affair with her, and the child of her union has to be carefully concealed. Thereupon Chrysis, the young man's stepmother in all but name, takes the infant into her house and pretends that it is hers. Complications arise when Demeas, who has just returned from a journey, misunderstands sundry remarks and concludes that his mistress has betrayed him with his son. Demeas drives Chrysis out of doors, and further misunderstandings ensue. But the Gordian knot is finally cut, Chrysis is taken back by Demeas, and his son is married to the neighbor's daughter. Menander's talent here combines a genial intrigue with much excellence of characterization; the two fathers and Chrysis are well-drawn and credible portraits in spite of the machine-made story. The dialogue is brisk and familiar for all its purity of diction, and well-turned colloquial phrases, reminiscent of a Kaufman "wisecrack," like "Cook, I'm damned if I know why you carry knives with you. Your chatter would reduce anything to mincemeat" contribute to the amenities of the comedy.

Although it exists only in a mutilated version, one finds in *The Shearing of Glycera* a less jerry-built plot which does not depend so greatly on comedy of errors. But misunderstandings abound and are in fact epitomized by an allegorical character called "Misapprehension." An elderly man who gave his two children away because he was too poor to care for them recovers both of them when a girl of uncertain status, who is being wooed by a soldier, turns out to be his long-lost daughter. Again it is characterization that provides the most lasting interest. Moschion, the girl's brother, is a particularly well-realized flighty youth who has been spoiled by his foster-mother, and the soldier Polemon who can fight faster than he can think is another vivid portrait.

The high water mark of Menander's extant work is, however, reached not in this facile comedy but in *The Arbitration,* which is quite modern in its implications. The sharp business man Simicrines marries his daughter Pamphila to the priggishly virtuous and frugal Charisius. As so often happens, however, theory and practice do not always recognize each other in this paragon of virtue. Four months before his marriage he became intoxicated at an all-night festival and assaulted an unidentified girl who could not identify him either. Five months after his marriage, during his absence, his wife Pamphila gives birth to a son. Since her husband could not seemingly be the father she makes every effort, with the aid of her nurse, to conceal the event, and the child is exposed in the countryside. Informed of these strange occurrences by an officious servant, the normally strait-laced husband renounces all staid behavior and goes away on an extended spree until his extravagance becomes a vexing problem to his father-in-law. Fortunately the young husband discovers that he is actually the father of the child;

the girl he has married proves to be the one he had assaulted! The un-
masking of a prig adds an incisive note to this the most completely
preserved of Menander's plays. It is easy to note its resemblance to
numerous exposures of puritanism and hypocrisy in modern comedy.

If the recovered plays of Menander will more than likely disappoint
a modern reader, the reason is not merely the makeshift quality of
his plots. If we can still derive enjoyment from the artifices of Sheridan,
we can readily accommodate ourselves to those of the fourth-century
Athenian. Nor is our disappointment a result of his fondness for doting
young men, angry fathers, ravished virgins, and intriguing slaves.
These types will be found in the inventory of the modern playwrights
whom so many readers and playgoers still favor. These characters are
further justified by their fidelity to Athenian life, for Menander took
his material from an age in which slavery prevailed and in which barriers to love-matches existed in the absolute authority of fathers. Moreover, his playful and indulgent attitude toward youth strikes a fairly
universal note; young men still go gallivanting, girls continue to be
responsive, and both still incline to find the whole world within the nut-
shell of a second-rate passion that looks like a first-rate one. It is the
fragmentariness of Menander's surviving work that leaves readers
somewhat skeptical of the evaluation put upon him by the ancient world.

Fortunately, however, the work of Menander was reincarnated in
the Latin comedies of Plautus and Terence. Generally uncreative without a foreign stimulus, Roman society turned to Athens for culture and
art, and the borrowings from Menander and his colleagues were not
only large but openly acknowledged, as if it were an honor to even
translate them into the Latin tongue.

2 PLAUTUS AND ROMAN COMEDY

A battered ex-actor with red hair, a paunch and very big feet, was
grinding somebody's corn and probably revolving in his mind the plays
of Menander when he decided to become a playwright. Plautus, born
in the town of Sarsina about 254 B.C., had led an adventurous life as
a Roman soldier, as an actor in crude native farces, and as an unsuccessful merchant who had rashly trusted his wares to the sea. Now at
the age of forty-five, he was reduced to the calling of an itinerant
miller who wheeled his hand-mill through the streets and ground corn
for householders. At first after his solemn decision to become a playwright he did not venture to renounce his humble occupation; his earliest plays, *Addictus* and *Saturio,* were written while he still plied his
hand-mill. Soon, however, his comedies began to suit the public taste,
for Plautus the adventurer and actor had a firsthand knowledge of his

TEXT CONTINUES ON PAGE 97 FOLLOWING THE PICTURE SECTION

The following section of photographs is intended to provide a rapid survey of main theatrical styles to which references occur throughout the book.

The Theatre at Epidaurus shows an open-air Greek theatre, with seats for the audience hewn out on the slope of a hill. The most prominent feature is the large dancing circle, or *orchestra*, for the chorus, which was so important an element in fifth century B.C. drama and theatre. At the side to the right, is one of the passageways, or *parodoi*, affording entrance and exit for the chorus and for processions. (Processions such as Agamemnon's return from Troy with his retinue of non-speaking supernumeraries in Aeschylus' *Agamemnon*, pp. 36–37.) At the back, are the ruins of the stone scene-building, the *skene*, which could represent a temple or a palace, and served as a permanent scenic background for the stage productions. Originally a simple wooden dressing-hut, the *skene* became a two-story stone building. During the 5th century B.C., the upper story, or *episkenion*, was used for the stage machinery, by means of which the gods were lowered to the stage level. The front of the lower story had a colonnade, or *proskenion*. Most of the acting during the 5th century B.C. probably transpired on a low platform in front of this structure, which had three doors and was flanked by projecting wings or *paraskenia*.

The theatre located in the Greek city of Epidauros belongs to the Hellenistic period (4th century B.C. and later), but the above-mentioned architectural features were also present toward the end of the 5th century B.C. in the theatre of Dionysos, where the great Greek plays were first staged.

During the Hellenistic period, stage productions became elaborate; more illusionism was sought, and more stage machinery for creating illusions was utilized. Now the *skene* was usually rectangular and divided into rooms. The front wall of the ground story had a series of pillars between which were set painted wooden panels, or *pinakes*. The actors usually performed on the second story level, so that the stage was about 9 feet high and from 8 to 10 feet deep, running the entire length of the building. At the back of this stage stood the colonnaded front wall of the second story, pierced by three doors, and served as the background. Between the columns of this upper

ILL. 1

colonnade, too, *pinakes* might be placed. The acting, then, was no longer close to the ground and there could be less intermingling between the actors and the chorus than in the fifth century. Since the chorus was no longer an important functional element in the later Greek drama, which was preponderantly comedy of manners and intrigue rather than classic tragedy and Aristophanic lyric-extravaganza, less intermingling was needed.

Later (after the 3rd century B.C.), under Roman influence, the Greek theatres underwent other modifications: the stage or acting-area was lower by a few feet but *deeper*, the frontage of the stage lost its colonnade but became a highly decorated scenic facade, and the *orchestra* was no longer a complete circle.

In the classic 5th century theatre, illusionism was not carried far. Tragedy would be stately and "ritualistic," and comedy would be broad and extravagant when written for an immense open-air theatre. Stage productions and individual performances had to be broad and, in the main, formalistic. Facial play by the actor would have been unnoticed; and none was needed, since the performers were masked. Stylized gestures and movements could be effective in this theatre, whereas our detailed and restrained realistic acting would have been lost on the audience. The actor needed, above all, a commanding physical presence and an effective voice. There could be no opportunity here for the external and inner realism required by modern stage directors such as Antoine or Stanislavsky after 1880. Stage direction, indeed, consisted mainly of training the chorus of a play in speech, dance, and pantomime.

Greek Comedy Scene provides an example of the extravagant appearance of the actors in the new type of non-choral comedy of manners called "New Comedy" developed in the fourth century B.C., first in Athens and then elsewhere in the Greek world: and then adapted and imitated by third and second century Roman playwrights, among whom Plautus and Terence became the most famous. (See pp. 92–104). Numerous costumes and masks were elaborated for comedy.

Reconstruction of the Frons Scenae at Aspendos gives us an impression of the later Roman theatre, which was notable for its impressive scenic facade. Here the separate elements of the older Greek theatre are fused, forming a single building, with a roof over the stage. Stage consists of an ornamental back wall of the stage — the *frons scenae* — and a platform for acting in front of it. At the side, may be seen one of the two entrances (also, of course, exits), called *vomitaria*. The *orchestra* of the Greek theatre was cut in half, becoming a semicircle. No longer used for a chorus, it provided space for extra seats, and it could be flooded for the presentation of nautical spectacles.

A View of Nō Stage provides an example of the stylized oriental theatre. This stage was and is used for the staging of the Japanese Noh (or Nō) plays, discussed on pages 130–35. Here the most prominent feature is the raised platform for the actor-dancer. The musicians who accompany his dramatic dance are seated in the background. At the side (left), will be seen a wooden bridge decorated with pine branches. It is across this bridge that the actors enter the stage. At the back of the platform, will be found the only scenery — and very formal scenery, at that. It consists of a wooden panel on which a pine tree has been painted. The plays written for this theatre are highly stylized dance-dramas, and the performance by masked actors is, of course, formal and extremely stylized. This kind of drama did not have its true Western counterpart until William Butler Yeats created his one-act "Noh" or "Nō" plays based on Irish legend, *Four Plays for Dancers* (1917–20), into which he poured his mature poetic powers. The Noh theatre is an example of oriental stylization, which prevailed more luxuriantly in the classic Hindu and Chinese theatres. (See pages 113–26.)

Medieval Stage: The Valenciennes Mystery Play is an illustration of the medieval multiple architectural stage, consisting of booths or "mansions" in front of which (an area called the *platea*) were enacted the different scenes or playlets that comprise a medieval Passion Play. (See pages 144–47). The stages were set up in the market place of the town, and the audience saw all the settings simultaneously throughout the performance, directing its gaze first at one booth, then at another, until the cycle of plays was completed. At the left, stands the "mansion" representing Heaven; at the right, Hell. The dragon's enormous jaws represent "Hell-mouth," through which "devils" emerged and "the damned" entered.

The Valenciennes setting is typical of medieval stage production on the European continent. In England, it was more customary to stage the Biblical plays on wagons known as "pageants." A succession of such "pageants," one pageant-wagon following another at a particular place where the public gathered, completed the production of an English passion play cycle. (See pages 145–46).

The Architectural Scenes for Comedy and Tragedy are Sebastiano Serlio's drawings in his book on architecture, *Architettura* (1551), for the kind of settings the Renaissance considered classically sanctioned. They represent a convention upon which numerous variations were made. The convention continued well on into the eighteenth century.

The settings developed during the Italian renaissance consisted of painted canvas flats (canvas stretched on lath frames) arranged in receding perspective, so that the space between these "side wings" was narrowest at the back, and there a painted flat or "backdrop" closed the gap. The "houses" nearest to the spectator were two-sided, the rest were simply "flats." In time, these were placed in grooves on the stage floor and could be slid in and out for rapid changes of scenery. By the eighteenth century, especially in Italy, numerous scene changes could be made by running off the painted canvas-and-lath flats at the sides, as well as by drawing them up to "the flies" beyond sight of the audience.

The Serlian setting for tragedy was designed to be more austere than that for comedy. In either case, the picture thus formed represented a street, where most of the action was expected to occur. Playwrights usually invented reasons for getting their characters to come out of their houses and meet on the street. This convention enabled playwrights to observe "unity of place," which, along with the "unities" of time and action, came into vogue when renaissance scholars and critics made Aristotle's *Poetics* (translated into Latin for Western Europe in 1498) the bible of playwriting and misconstrued and elaborated his statements. Here, then, we have the antithesis of the multiple-stage setting of the Middle Ages.

The Renaissance style is notable for the introduction of painted scenery in perspective and the advent of the so-called picture-frame stage, which came into existence when the setting was behind a formal *proscenium arch*. This arch served, too, as a masking frame later on, so that scenery could be changed without allowing the audience to see how this was done. Note that Serlio's stage has no proscenium arch, and there is no provision here for making changes of scenery. The first proscenium arch appeared at the Teatro Olimpico at Vicenza, Italy, completed in 1584. In consisted of an ornamented façade pierced by a large opening at the center and two smaller openings at each side; and into these archways were inserted permanent perspective settings representing streets leading to the stage. When later, in the Teatro Farnese at Parma (1619) and elsewhere, only one large archway was made, the architectural façade became a proscenium arch — that is, an architectural frame for the scenery, which occupied the entire visible stage but for the arch. It is to be noted, however, that most of the acting occurred on the platform space in front of the first side-wings. Although the Renaissance gave rise to the illusionist theatre — i.e., the pictorial setting — which led to the modern vogue of realistic scenery and acting, the staging of plays well on to the middle of the nineteenth century was by no means realistic or "representational." The actor declaimed, for the most part, in front of the scenery and often addressed himself to the audience. Playwrights, therefore, wrote long speeches regularly into their plays, employed the embellishments of rhetoric, and made free use of asides and soliloquies. In

England, indeed, a vestigial platform, known as the "apron," stood in front of the proscenium arch and accommodated most of the acting during the Restoration period and the 18th century.

Interior of the Globe Theatre, as reconstructed, gives an impression of the kind of stage for which Marlowe, Shakespeare, and other Elizabethans wrote. Unlike the Renaissance stage represented by the Serlio drawings, the Elizabethan "public," low-priced theatres, a development from the English inn-yards, retained the medieval features of a platform and multiple stage visible simultaneously — outer stage, inner stage, upper stage. The theatre building had no roof except a thatched one over the balconies and a portion of the stage. The main feature of the stage, which was architectural and did not accommodate painted settings, was the platform or outer stage that jutted out into the auditorium, so that the public, standing in the pit, surrounded the stage on three sides. The curtained alcove or "inner stage," flanked by doors, was used for *tableaux-vivants* and for some scenes supposedly occurring in a chamber, such as the Queen's "closet" scene in *Hamlet.* When the action mounted in excitement or extent, the actors probably moved forward and used the outer stage. The upper stage (the gallery above the stage) was also used somewhat; for some appropriate scenes, such as the balcony scene in *Romeo and Juliet.* The nature of this theatre and its effect on Elizabethan playwriting is described on pages 203–205.

An Exterior Setting by Giovanni Maria Galli-Bibbiena is an example of eighteenth century baroque design. Although the Elizabethan open-air theatre and the somewhat similar "bull-ring" type of theatre of the Spanish Golden Age served Shakespeare and Lope de Vega very well, the painted setting, comprising a "picture-frame" stage, became the established type of theatre throughout Europe, including England, whose first master of scenic design was Inigo Jones (1573–1652). The designers' settings became bolder in perspective, more elaborate, and, after 1700, truly monumental. The most famous designers of the Baroque period were members of the Bibbiena (or Bibienna) family. Scenic splendor, achieved mainly by means of skilfully painted flat wings, back-drops, and some built-up units such as pillars, began to overshadow playwriting, and theatrical production became increasingly operatic, so that the actor was dwarfed by the towering scenery. Ingenious scenic displays, including cloud effects and aerial chariots for gods, became the rage. This passion for stage spectacles coincided with the growing vogue of opera as theatrical entertainment.

Versailles Gardens 1673 Production of Molière's Imaginary Invalid and *Interior of Drury Lane* (1808) represent the prevailing "picture-frame" stage after the Renaissance. The picture of Molière's 17th century stage shows the actors performing in front of the pictorial setting. This setting within the frame is altogether formal, and is less conducive to the illusion of a real environment than the later Giovanni Maria Galli-Bibbiena setting shown on the preceding page. Note, for example, the chandeliers hung over the garden scene(!). Observe also the formal appearance of a Louis XIV garden at the sides, and the receding perspectives at the back.

The appearance of *Drury Lane Theatre* in 1808, before it burned down in 1809 and had to be rebuilt, is that of an opera house intended to accommodate specular productions. This picture also shows distinctly the forestage acting area or "apron," a reduction of the old platform of the Elizabethan period. The "apron" is flanked by the boxes and by the doors on the lowest level, so that the actors still play to the audience, instead of being separated from it by an invisible "fourth wall." Observe how the setting is framed by the rectangular arch, and gives the impression of a picture behind a frame. Note also how deep the stage is. When stages become increasingly shallow, later on in the nineteenth century, perspective settings of painted flats become ineffective.

The "apron" was cut down and was finally discarded entirely, after the middle of the 19th century. Once the actor played close to the scenery *within* the setting, as became customary, he was disproportionately tall and the painted scenery looked false. Stage illusion, painstakingly developed since the Renaissance, deteriorated. Therefore, the painted side-wing type of scenery was doomed after 1850.

Romantic Setting in Germany for an 1817 Production of Friedrich von Schiller's Romantic Drama "The Maid of Orleans": Here we see the new tendency to favor pictures of majestic and wild nature, and to depart from the conventional formalism in the neo-classic stage observable in the 17th century Molière and 18th century Bibbienna settings. The effect is pictorial rather than architectural. During the romantic movement, the settings for interiors were not radically altered, but exterior settings ceased to be formalistic. Nature, in short, was presented realistically, by means of built-up, painted, and transparent scenery broken up and arranged naturally. All this marked an advance toward illusionism and a veering away from formalism. This tendency began in the third quarter of the 18th century. It appeared in England in picturesque settings designed by the Alsatian artist Loutherbourg for David Garrick.

The scene from the Moscow Art Theatre production of *The Lower Depths* (1905) is an example of Naturalism — an extreme development of the stage realism that began to prevail after 1850. (See pages

402–403, 420, 514–16.) Painted flats are no longer used; the setting of this interior now consists of three walls and ceilings. We have here, then, an example of the "box-set." What the photograph does not show is that this setting also appears behind a proscenium arch, for the realistic theatre inherited the "picture frame" convention from the Renaissance. Here, moreover, the acting is entirely within the setting, and the solid set gives the illusion of a real and specific environment; the setting is no longer merely a conventionalized background. The actors conduct themselves as though they were concealed from the audience by a "fourth wall." They behave as though they were unobserved, living out their lives as they would in real life, instead of playing to the public.

The term "naturalism" is properly applicable to the extreme realism of the setting, the acting, and the costuming of this production of Maxim Gorki's picture of the "lower depths" occupied by derelicts. For a theatre dominated by this style of Naturalism, playwriting consists of colloquial dialogue and scrupulously maintained verisimilitude. There is no longer any justification for the drama's conventional asides and soliloquies in this style of production. Gone, too, are the set speeches and rhetoric intended for direct public address. Playwrighting, in short, becomes "natural." A play is no longer a dramatic poem intended for recitation and for displays of virtuosity by the performer, but a "slice-of-life."

Much of the world's greatest dramatic literature (Shakespearian drama, for example) does not fit into the above-described naturalistic style of setting. Nor do stylized modern plays written after 1890 by the poetic and fanciful writers who challenged the supremacy of realistic or naturalistic playwriting. A modern "symbolist" style of staging, therefore, began to gain adherents shortly after the establishment of dramatic realism, and this style was most pronounced in scenic design. Scene designers, indeed, became leaders of modern "art theatre."

Design by Gordon Craig for Sophocles' "Electra" (see pages 419–23) and the *Design by Robert Edmond Jones for "Macbeth"* represent this symbolist trend, characterized by a striving for atmospheric effect (facilitated by the introduction of electric lighting and the invention of the electric switchboard), suggestiveness, and simplification. In the *Macbeth* setting by Jones, the series of obliquely placed, seemingly toppling arches have a symbolic meaning; they are suggestive of the decline in Macbeth's fortunes. The arches, placed against a dark background, were used with different effect for different scenes by being variously placed and subjected to expressive electric illumination. Light is colored, dimmed, or brightened, and it is used directly or indirectly. It provides the magic that a poet such as Shakespeare supplied with the verbal beauty of his famous descriptive passages.

The influence of the simplification ushered in by symbolism may also be seen in the *Setting for Ampritryon 38 by Lee Simonson.* This setting was made for the Theatre Guild production of Jean Giraudoux' sophisticated version of classic comedy, in which Lynn Fontanne and Alfred Lunt played Alcmena and Zeus. Simonson represented a Greek interior with little more than a series of columns, draped for comic effect.

Design by Emil Pirchan for the Expressionist Leopold Jessner's production of "Richard III" (a violent German adaptation by Hanns Henny Jahn) shows simplification employed for dynamic expressionist staging. The steep flight of stairs symbolizes the power and royalty Richard III lusts after. Ascent and descent on these steps was precipitous, and the actors would often be expected to negotiate them rapidly and precariously. Expressionism in playwriting, especially in Germany immediately after the First World War, was stark, turbulent and even inchoate. The setting is a sort of stage stenography. It parallels the dialogue for the clipped, ejaculatory, sometimes hallucinatory lines of expressionist plays constituted stenographic dialogue.

Scene by Georg Grosz for an Erwin Piscator production represents another phase of modern stage production, also inaugurated in Germany during the nineteen-twenties. Here cartoons and sketches are projected on a screen, as if the action were intended to be seen against the background of a poster. The particular style of "epic theatre" employed by the German stage director Erwin Piscator at that time aimed at semi-documentary, hortatory, educational theatre, rather than at a realistic picture of private life and character drama. In order to achieve his "epic" (disjunctive, chronicle or episodic) style, however, Piscator resorted to many other effects, disregarding both realistic illusion and symbolist unity of style and mood. He employed slogans, platforms, tread-mills for traveling scenes, and motion pictures; in short, everything that would bring facts and attitudes to the attention of the public. (See pages 492–93). The German poet Bertolt Brecht, who translated this style of theatre into provocative drama, also amplified "epic" staging and acting style in directing his own plays.

Fire in a Tenement looks like a naturalistic setting *par excellence.* This scene, however, was only one of many in *One-third of a nation,* a documentary "epic" drama or "living newspaper," dealing with the housing problem and the "New Deal's" slum clearance program in 1938. Other scenes were more distinctly stylized. The characters watching the fire in this scene had previously debated and demonstrated various economic and social questions, sometimes on the bare forestage. The "epic" style of this "living newspaper" mingled various styles of presentation. This naturalistic conflagration scene — and *only partially naturalistic,* since, for example, the wall and windows are removed from the second story room in the center — was preceded by entirely non-realistic stage effects, as when the stage floor was imaginatively divided into city blocks in order to relate real-estate interests to the problem of providing adequate housing for the underprivileged. The tenement façade, however, remained as a permanent, symbolic background.

Next, in *scene from Alexis Tolstoy's "Revolt of the Machines,"* we see modern industrialism reflected in a style of scenery and stage production called Constructivism, which became fashionable, especially in Russia, during the nineteen-twenties. Meyerhold became the leader of this type of staging on ramps and cat-walks which required athletic agility from actors and discouraged character or "inner" acting. (See pages 539–40.) More or less moderate applications of constructivism were frequent after 1920. Thus constructivism was designed by Lee Simonson in designing an important power-plant scene in the New York Theatre Guild production of O'Neill's *Dynamo.* A moderate constructivism was also used to represent modernist, functional interiors, as in Simonson's hotel setting for Robert Sherwood's *Idiot's Delight.*

Also, the theatre after World War I adopted a style of "theatricalism," by means of which the theatricality of stage production was stressed. In other words, staging was playfully stylized and artificial (see page 423) in order to make the reader aware that he was watching theatre, not "real life." For this purpose, long discarded painted settings were reintroduced and employed with striking decorative effect. (This tendency started most strikingly with the advent of Diaghilev's Russian Ballet and Leon Bakst's designs for Diaghilev.)

Theatricalism is shown here by the *Scene from "Pickwick Club,"* a dramatization of *The Pickwick Papers.* Here, both constructed and painted scenery, and both living actors and painted figures, were used.

Finally, the *Setting for "Processional"* shows theatricalism clearly associated in the American idiom as this Theatre Guild production was intended to present a "jazz symphony" of American life in the nineteen-twenties. The setting provides of an extravagantly festive and garish background.

PLATE 1. The Theatre at Epidaurus. Best Preserved Greek Theatre.
Note the circular area or "orchestra," and the ruins of the "scene building"
behind it.

PLATE 2. Comedy Scene, showing Cheery and Testy Old Men, Flute-Player, Youth and Servant. (From *The Development of the Theatre* by Allardyce Nicoll)

PLATE 3, above.   Reconstruction of the *Frons Scenae* at Aspendos.
Stage façade or back wall of a Roman Stage, highly decorated.
below.   View of the Japanese Nō Stage.

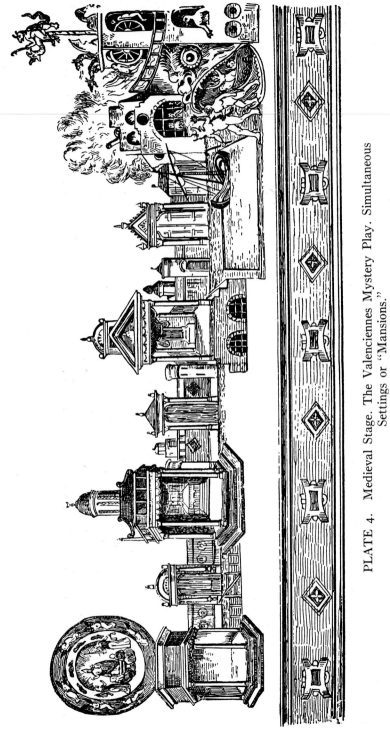

PLATE 4. Medieval Stage. The Valenciennes Mystery Play. Simultaneous Settings or "Mansions."

(From *A History of Theatrical Art in Ancient and Modern Times* by Karl Mantzius)

PLATE 5. Architectural Scenes for Comedy (*above*) and Tragedy (*below*)
as Prescribed by Serlio in 1545.

PLATE 6, *above*. Interior of the Globe Theatre.
A reconstruction by John C. Adams now on display in the Folger Library, Washington, D. C. The outer stage and the "tiring house" are shown with the two inner-stage curtains closed. Photo by Wendell Kilmer. Courtesy of John C. Adams.
below. An exterior setting by Giovanni Maria Galli-Bibbiena.

PLATE 7. Versailles Gardens 1673 production of Molière's *Imaginary Invalid.*

PLATE 8, *above*. Interior of Drury Lane Theatre, London, 1808.
below. Romantic Setting in Germany for 1817 production of Friedrich
von Schiller's romantic drama *The Maid of Orleans*.

PLATE 9. Realistic Scene from the Moscow Art Theatre's Production of
The Lower Depths. Naturalism.
(From *My Life in the Russian Theatre* by Vladimir Nemirovitch-Dantchenko)

PLATE 10. Design by Gordon Craig for Sophocles' *Electra*.

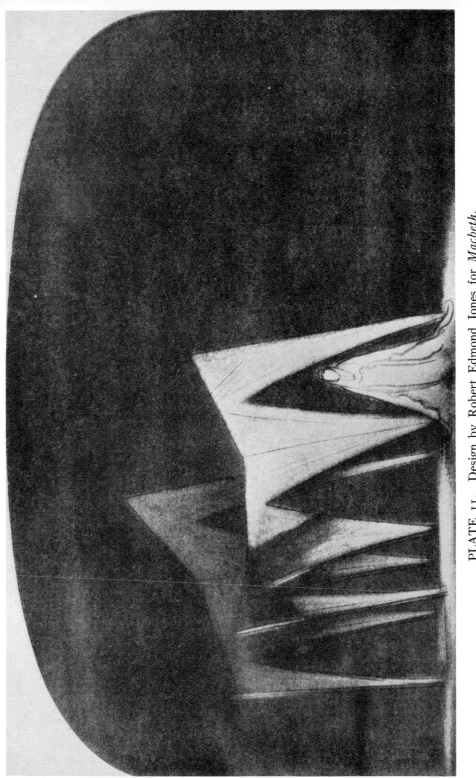

PLATE 11. Design by Robert Edmond Jones for *Macbeth*.
A Symbolist setting. Photo by Peter Juley.

PLATE 12. Setting by Lee Simonson for Jean Giraudoux' *Amphitryon 38.*

PLATE 13. *above*. Design by Emil Pirchan for the expressionist Leopold
Jessner's Production of *Richard III*.
On these blood-red steps (the *Jessnertreppen*), Richard III has been crowned, with
all his courtiers, clad in scarlet, kneeling on both sides of the steps. In the later
scene represented here we see the Duke of Richmond, later Henry VII, in a white
robe at the head of his army, also in white. From *Continental Stagecraft* (1922)
by Kenneth Macgowan and Robert Edmond Jones. Courtesy of the publishers,
Harcourt, Brace & Co.
below.   Scene Designed by Georg Grosz for Piscator's "Epic Style"
Production in Berlin of *Das trunkene Schiff*.

PLATE 14. Fire in a Tenement, Scene from *One-Third of a Nation.*
A setting by Howard Bay for Lem Ward's Federal Theatre production, 1938.
Federal Theatre Photo by Edward Waterbury and Arthur Steiner.

PLATE 15, *above.* Scene from Alexis Tolstoy's *Revolt of the Machines.*
A Constructivist setting in the Russian theatre under the influence of Meyerhold.
below. Setting by Williams for Moscow Art Theatre Production of
Pickwick Papers.
Theatricalism, with emphasis on painting.

PLATE 16. Setting for *Processional* by Mordecai Gorelik. Satirical
Theatricalism.

crude audience. He had coped with it in the Roman farces of his early acting days, and he could cope with it again even if this time he was employing the highly literate art of Greece.

The theatre of Rome which he improved was a rough and ready type of folk farce. Much of it had come from the Romans' neighbors the Etruscans, whom they finally overthrew and subjugated. Etruria had followed the usual course from ritual to art, converting its vegetation and fertility rites into dramatic performances by means of improvisations, and by the specialization of the rustic performers into full-fledged actors. Known as the Fescennine Verses (probably from the town of Fescennium or from the Latin word for phallus, from which we derive the word "fascinate"), and performed chiefly at marriage celebrations, this form penetrated into Rome. And although its obscenities in time led to its suppression, it left an impression, along with that related but somewhat later Etruscan form of comedy, the *saturae*. Brought to Rome in 364 and added to the city games or *ludi* (from which our word "ludicrous" is derived), the *saturae* pleased the popular palate and became fused with other imported forms like the Atellan farces of Campagnia, which were full of stock characters, and with the travesties of the Greek colonies in southern Italy and Sicily.

When he began to compose his comedies some time before 204, Greek influence was already strong. However, it is possible to exaggerate Plautus' debt to Greece, for his style is not Greek but Roman. Rome was beginning its triumphal conquest of the world, and the vigor of his work is Roman vigor just as his crudities are those of a nation that put warfare and political power above culture. His dialogue was no mere translation of the polished Menander but the rough-and-tumble colloquy of the military camp and the market place. His zest, which far exceeds Menander's, springs from the martial age of an expanding empire.

His output began to mount until it reached a total of one hundred thirty pieces, of which twenty-one are extant, and his popularity may be gauged from the fact that no other classic playwright has survived to such a degree. Respectability also came to the seasoned adventurer who was long known only by his nickname of Plautus or "Splay-foot" and later called himself Maccus ("Clown") Titus. He was granted citizenship, and soon he was given permission to assume three names like a true-born Roman. Displaying his inveterate sense of humor, he chose the name of Titus Maccus Plautus!

Always quick to take the pulse of his audience, he kept his comedies not only diversified and native but topical. His *Miles Gloriosus* referred to the imprisonment of the poet Naevius for satirizing the aristocracy; *Cistellaria* alluded to the conflict with Carthage; *Epidicius* and *Aulularia* touched upon the repeal of the puritanic Oppian Laws; and *Cap-*

tivi and *Bacchides* mentioned the wars in Greece and Magnesia. In this way Plautus continued to some moderate degree the social interest of Aristophanic comedy. He died in 184 after having lived through one of the most momentous periods of history, for it was in his time that Rome destroyed Carthage, its only serious rival for hegemony in the Mediterranean world. Hannibal died three months after Plautus.

A few of the comedies are sufficient to describe all of them. To read them in bulk is to risk being surfeited. Nor are all of them in the best Plautine vein, for so voluminous a writer who was interested in hard cash rather than immaterial fame was inclined to write perfunctorily. Sometimes, moreover, he essayed a more temperate style which failed to exploit his robust talent; those of his works which he tempered too greatly are saved from the dust-bin of mediocrity only by one or more well-drawn Plautian rogues. *Aulularia* or *The Crock of Gold,* which served as Molière's model for *The Miser,* is a relatively tame story of how a young man seduces a miser's daughter and succeeds in marrying her despite the curmudgeon. But the skinflint Euclio, the kind of man who "when he goes to sleep, he'll tie the bellows round his throat . . . lest he should waste his breath," is a delightful caricature. And the common folk—the cooks, parasites, and flute-girls—bring a droll realism to the stage. The dialogue, as in all of his plays, resembles musical-comedy patter (and was in fact supplied with a musical accompaniment). It rattles along *con brio.* This is, to be sure, not great art such as the fifth-century Greeks gave us, but it provides rollicking entertainment. When one of the characters rails against women she says in equivalent English: "No woman can be picked out best; but A than B's the greater pest." The homespun *dramatis personae* of the comedies of Plautus can be best described by such close translation as Old Skinflint (*Euclio Senex*), Mother Bunch (*Staphyla Anus*), Mother Goodbody (*Eunomia Mulier*), and Whirl the Slave (*Strobilus Servus*).

A comparatively gentle comedy is *Amphitryo,* based on an early Greek example of the Middle Comedy, which dramatizes Jupiter's visit to Alcmena in the guise of her martial husband Amphitryon. In the delicate treatment of Amphitryon and the virtuous Alcmena Plautus is exercising a restraining hand on the hobbyhorse of adultery. At the same time, the fanciful commingling of gods and mortals, and the comic potentialities of the theme, possess a fascination which at least thirty-six later writers—if we are to believe Giraudoux, the author of the successful *Amphitryon 38*—found it impossible to resist.

A favorite with teachers and anthologists because of its unsalacious situation is *Captivi* or *The Captives,* in which a father recovers his two sons, one of whom was lost long ago while the other was captured in a local war. The absence of a love-intrigue reduces the humorist to resorting to unexpected discoveries; chiefly to a deception whereby a captive's slave enables him to escape from the custody of an old man by taking his place only to discover later that he, the slave, is the long-lost son of the man he had deluded. The principals of this senti-mental comedy are likable, but the play is most enlivened by the irre-pressible parasite Ergasilus, who says, in English paraphrase,

> Grace *is the name the boys have given me,*
> *Because I'm always found* before the meat!

When the person on whom he would foist himself tells him that his table is really coarse, Ergasilus refuses to be discouraged and replies: "Don't tell me you eat brambles." When his prospective host warns him that his dinner is "from the soil," the leech replies, "So is good pork."

Nevertheless, the play is mild and well-mannered compared with such works as the *Bacchides,* a lively story about two courtesans, the *Asinaria* or *Comedy of Asses,* in which an old man is caught caressing his son's mistress, and the somewhat inferior *Menaechmi* whose twin brothers experience the complications which served Shakespeare in *The Comedy of Errors.* The *Miles Gloriosus* or *The Braggart Soldier* belongs to the same category of prodigious buffoonery, largely by virtue of two of the most amusing of Plautian characters: a proto-Falstaffian soldier whose vaunts reach the sublime by way of the ridiculous and his hum-ble companion called Breadmuncher, who is an early Sancho Panza. Very much in the style of *The Merry Wives of Windsor,* the lecherous braggart is made to believe that his neighbor's wife has fallen in love with him and is consequently trapped into making a ninny of himself. *Persa* or *The Persian Stranger* is a classic *Beggar's Opera,* written with great gusto and enlivened by a vivid picture of the shady world of pro-curers, cheats, and courtesans.

To the *Pseudolus* or *The Trickster,* which is a play of the same feather, we owe the insufferable pander Ballio and the helpful slave Pseudolus who is an excellent model for the crafty servants of later European comedy. Ballio, who is on the verge of selling a slave girl to an officer is outwitted by Pseudolus who steals her for his young master. Per-haps the most amusing of the comedies, however, is *Rudens* or *The Slip-Knot,* adapted from a play by Menander's contemporary, Diphilus. Here a worthy gentleman whose daughter was kidnaped in childhood and sold to a procurer recovers her at last. The girl was to be sold by the procurer to a gentleman who fell in love with her, but inspired by greed her owner makes off with her. Fortunately, they are shipwrecked near the shore, the pander is put to rout, and all ends happily. The interest which lies in the variety of the intrigue and in the brashness of the rogues is well sustained, and riotous jollity pervades both the dialogue and the lyrics.

As in most of his extant work, Plautus who was not only the playwright but also the actor manager of his plays, gives evidence of enjoying himself in the *Rudens* as much as he hoped his audience would. He never seems to have grown up, and not even the success of his later years could turn him into a polished gentleman or *litterateur*. That distinction was left for his successor Terence, a man of entirely different tastes. Plautus was content to remain a man of the theatre, and it must be said that the stage amply repaid his loyalty by stimulating him to write living drama instead of anemic closet plays.

3 TERENCE AND THE GREEK REVIVAL

The three-quarters of a century which intervened between Plautus and the next important writer of Roman comedy produced a stratification of taste to which no artist could fail to respond. Drunk with conquest, the Roman populace developed an insatiable taste for rude farces and acrobatics, while the aristocracy was increasingly Hellenized much to the regret of such an unrelenting puritan as Cato the Censor who resented the relaxing influence of the Greeks. In other words, the taste of the lower orders became coarser while that of the upper classes became more refined, even to the point of attenuation.

Terence was not the people's poet but the darling of the aristocracy. He could never have written plays for the former, because he felt alien to them. Publius Terentius Afer was a Phoenician or Semite and a native of Carthage, where he was born about 190 B.C. Brought to Rome as a slave, he was carefully educated by a master who quickly recognized his talent and emancipated him. His personal grace, as well as his literary ability, made the young alien an amiable companion of the cosmopolitans of high society. He not only knew his limitations but gloried in them, declaring that it was his chief aim to please the *boni* or elect.

His output was meager not only because he was lost at sea when he was at about the age of thirty, but because he was such a scrupulous stylist. From his first play the *Andria*, written at the age of nineteen, to his last work the *Adelphi*, his development was primarily in the direction of polish and more polish. It is little wonder that the art of Greece was his sole interest and that he devoted himself to capturing the spirit of his originals with practically no concession to popular taste. He had gone to Greece, probably in order to be closer to the fountain of his inspiration, when he met his untimely death. Nor is it any wonder that his work continued to be considered a model of Latin purity of style, that he won the admiration of Cicero and Horace, and that he was the only classic playwright whom the medieval churchmen of Western Europe could tolerate.

Taking for his springboard the comedies of Menander, who was with a single exception his life-long model, Terence felt free to adapt them as he pleased, thereby courting the charge of *contaminatio* although he justified his practice by pointing to the work of his predecessors as Ennius, Naevius, and Plautus. He was, he claimed, a creative writer in the freedom with which he used his material instead of following the *obscura diligentia* of some of his plodding contemporaries and of one of his detractors. Still he not only confined himself to the *palliatae* or dramas of Greek subjects and backgrounds, but tried to equal the delicacy of the works he revered, cultivating their refinement of sentiment to the point of depriving most of his comedies of vigor and movement.*

Terence does not laugh as much as smile, and instead of ridicule he employs irony. Among the Roman playwrights he is perhaps the only one who aimed at perfection rather than at instant pleasure. His characterization is relatively subtle, and his dialogue combines grace with economy. For colloquial speech he who wrote under the patronage of the aristocracy reveals no taste. But his diction and syntax have a fascination and poetry of their own, a limber and yet restrained beauty which can hardly be conveyed in translation. It is instructive to compare such translated lines as "When you link a son to you by kindness, there is sincerity in all his acts; he sets himself to make a return, and will be the same behind your back as to your face" with the spare original:

> *ille quem beneficio adiungas ex animo facit,*
> *studet par referre, praesens absenque idem erit.*

The gulf that yawns between such art and the taste of the impatient Roman populace was, of course, too wide to allow him much popularity. Time and again in his prologues Terence complains that "the uproar drove our company from the stage" (Phormio); that "I have never been allowed a silent hearing . . . in flocked the people with uproar and clamor and a struggle for seats with the result that I could not hold my ground," and that "the people's thoughts were preoccupied by a rope-dancer" (*Hecyra* or *The Mother-in-Law*).

As in the case of Plautus, it is unnecessary to review all his plays to observe the quality of the dramatic output. *The Eunuch* (*Eunuchus*), for instance, tells the story of Thais, a courtesan who takes a girl

---

* A play based on Greek New Comedy was called *fabula palliata* and was distinguished from a *fabula togata,* in which Italian manners were treated and the characters wore Roman togas.

under her wing while she herself is in love with a young man of good family. She receives the girl as a gift from an admirer Thraso, a bragging and fatuous old soldier. At the same time she takes into her house a eunuch presented to her by her lover Phaedria. But the latter's younger brother, having fallen in love with her young charge, takes the place of the eunuch and seduces the girl, a serious misdemeanor when she is discovered to be free-born. All ends well, of course; Phaedria drives off the boastful soldier and his retinue, and wins Thais for himself, while her protégée marries the younger brother. The humor derives largely from the discomfiture of the *miles gloriosus,* the vainglorious but essentially cowardly soldier who has so many counterparts in Elizabethan drama. Sentiment, however, is the predominant note of the comedy. Thais is a very worthy person despite her station, her charge is a delightful girl, Phaedria is a spirited and well-intentioned lover, and his younger brother has the excuse of youth and infatuation for the ruse by which he enters the house and wins the *ingenue.*

In *The Mother-in-Law,* which recalls *The Arbitration* of Menander, a husband suspects his wife of gross misconduct when she gives birth to a child during his absence, but discovers in the end that his wife was the girl he had assaulted earlier and that he is actually the father of the presumably illegitimate infant. The play is light and genial; even the courtesan Bacchis, who says of her profession that "it is not in our interest to have marriages happy," is not without saving grace when she enables the man who has been visiting her to discover his wife's innocence. As usual, the action is carefully developed and the audience is kept in suspense.

Perhaps the most delightful of Terence's works, however, is *Phormio,* named after the parasite who advances the action and supplies much of the comic effect. This, the only comedy not adapted by Terence from Menander but from the other New Comedy playwright Apollodorus, is the liveliest of his plays. Phormio is supplemented by the intriguing slave Geta, another ancestor of Molière's resourceful servants and Beaumarchais' Figaro. Molière, in fact, utilized *Phormio* in one of his earliest works *Les Fourberies de Scapin,* just as Terence's *Andria* was used by Molière's successor Baron in *Adrienne* and by Richard Steele in *The Conscious Lovers.* The bigamous old man of *Phormio,* Chremes, had a wife in Lemnos who came to Athens and died there, leaving her young daughter helpless. The girl attracts Antipho, Chremes' brother's son, who falls in love with her and marries her with the assistance of Phormio and a servant. Both his father and his uncle Chremes are highly indignant, until the latter learns that the girl is his daughter. Complications are added by a parallel love affair on the part of Chremes' son who is restrained by his father with doubtful consistency. The old men, especially the susceptible Chremes, are amusing portraits, and Phormio is truly memorable.

Phormio's insolence and resourcefulness are equaled only by his love of sponging on others: "Think of it!" the parasite declares. "You come scot free to your patron's dinner, all perfumed and shining from the bath, with a heart free from care, when he's drowned with worry and eaten up with expenses. While everything's done to your liking, he's snarling. You can laugh, drink your wine before him, take the higher seat; and then a puzzling banquet's set spread." Asked what a puzzling banquet is, he replies, "That's when you're puzzled what to help yourself to first." After having exposed Chremes to his wife, Phormio who has thus paid him in good coin for mistreating him congratulates himself, "Now she's got something to din into his ears just as long as he lives." He is also richer by thirty pieces of gold at the end for having consented to marry Antipho's girl whom the lad's father had tried to remove from the field. Moreover, in winning the favor of Chremes' wife, Phormio now has another place where he can always get a free dinner. . . .

After Terence's death the Roman drama deteriorated rapidly. Neither Plautus nor Terence had a permanent theatre in which to present their plays: they wrote for a platform stage. Theatrical display now became the rage, especially when Rome became a monarchy and a rapidly decaying one after the death of Julius Caesar, who was himself a discriminating critic and was not even satisfied with Terence whom he called a "half-Menander." The engineering genius of Rome expressed itself in marble theatres and an abundance of stage machinery. The populace had little regard for the drama itself, vastly preferring elaborate shows, gaudy processions of captives and slaves, circuses, and mimic sea-fights in Naumachiae so elaborate that they defy description. True drama no longer flourished in a nation whose economic and political policies had impoverished the people to the point of pauperism and dependence on a dole, while the ruling classes frittered away their energy in debauchery and the struggle for tyrannical power. Opium is what the masses needed to forget their condition, and it is opium they received in the spectacle of gladiators slashing each other to death. Butchery took the place of comedy.

By the time the Roman empire collapsed under the weight of its economic contradictions and its glories crumbled away in corruption, only pantomimists and jugglers or acrobats, known as *mimes,* were left. Little better than vagabonds, they satisfied a crude desire for entertainment during the Dark Ages but remained beyond the pale of respectability. The theatre in Europe had to be built anew, out of fresh material and with new forces, and it was ironically the historic task of the Catholic Church to foster beginnings in an art which it was the first to despise but which it could not ultimately resist. Once more, as in Greece, Rome, and almost everywhere on man's planet, the drama had to be cradled anew in the rites of religion.

Part III

EAST AND WEST

As IF it were ordained that the drama should never entirely hide its light under a bushel, the East filled the gap of darkness between the classic age and the next bright noon of European theatre. There is a divergence of taste and tradition between East and West not always bridged for us. Nevertheless, the adage that all men are brothers is perhaps nowhere so pertinent as in the history of the theatre. If the Orient employed a variety of stage conventions that seem strange to many of us, the difficulty can be greatly exaggerated. This is readily shown by the ease with which we adapted ourselves to such Oriental stylization as appeared on the American stage in the Chinese *Lady Precious Stream* and in Thornton Wilder's *Our Town*. The common sense approach to Oriental drama would seem to be the simple one of discarding recondite, hyperesthetic considerations, and evaluating it as one would any Occidental play. It is to be noted only that in the most characteristic works of the East, the emphasis is on the spiritual and sensuous possibilities of the art.

VII

THE PLAYWRIGHTS OF THE NEAR EAST

I HEBREW LITERARY DRAMA

THE TRADITIONAL VIEW which assigns no theatre to the ancient Hebrews calls for modification with reference to the Jewish settlements in Greek territory. There was a body of drama in the Alexandrian third-century community based on two independent sources of inspiration, the Old Testament and the Athenian drama, particularly on the tragedies of Euripides which had been transplanted to Egypt and imitated there. The Jews of Alexandria, who assimilated Hellenic culture to such a degree that the Old Testament had to be translated for them from Hebrew into Greek, readily turned to the drama. Although the full extent of their theatrical activity cannot be gauged for want of surviving texts, their leading spirit is known to us through several fragments.

Ezekiel, "the poet of Jewish tragedies," wrote, in the Greek language and style, an *Exodus* based on the Old Testament account, and its fragments enable us to reconstruct the play. It apparently opened with an extant monologue in which Moses, having fled to Midian after killing the Egyptian taskmaster, recited the story of his life. Next came the incident of his meeting with the Midianite priest's daughters and his marriage to one of them. Later Moses has a dream which his father-in-law interprets as presaging a high destiny for him, and it is not long before the voice in the burning bush orders him back to Egypt to deliver his people from bondage. Then came the escape of the Hebrews and the drowning of their pursuers in the Red Sea. Finally, the chosen people were seen in the wilderness, and a Messenger informed Moses that there was an oasis near by with palm trees and numerous springs of water. The verse of the fragments is, however, undistinguished, and the conventional estimate of Hebrew dramatic talent cannot be greatly modified by this play.

It is in the Old Testament that any ponderable dramatic power is to be discovered, although the absence of any suggestion of a real theatre among the people steeps the subject in controversy. That the Israelites' aversion to the polytheism and to the anthropomorphization of God out of which the drama arose was not sufficiently consistent is attested by the anti-pagan diatribes of the prophets. Nevertheless, the paganism which lay like a sea around Judea never gained a strong foot hold and was untiringly repelled by the prophets and priests. The worship of the Golden Calf, the touch of witchcraft in Endor, the annual lamentation for Tammuz in Syria, the sporadic polytheism of the kings, and the trace of phallic worship in Solomon's two pillars Jachin and Boaz (signifying potency), never won sufficient acceptance. Judea could not develop a theatre in which gods and mortals exhibited their Passion.

Nevertheless, the dramatic genius of the Hebrews is indisputably attested by the manner in which the dramatic spirit enters Hebraic literature and culture. Miriam the prophetess of the exodus led a dance with timbrels in honor of the Lord, David danced before the holy ark, and dancing was also one of the functions of the Levites in the temple. Like Dionysus, Jehovah had his dithyramb, and like his Greek counterpart he was celebrated for his benevolence and his potency. In this rudimentary form of drama, which was supplied with music and may have been acted out by the Levites in honor of the one God in forms possibly more vividly theatrical than we know, the Hebrews were in fact past masters. Their dithyrambs, the Psalms, are tense with the spirit of a passionate race, rich in the imagery of a pastoral and agricultural people, forceful with martial reminiscence, highly personal at times, and permeated with faith in a ruling spirit. Moreover, the Hebrew super-Dionysus, who succors the downtrodden and is the fountainhead of justice, surpasses any of his prototypes in nobility and justice.

The dramatic talent of the ancient Hebrew also made itself felt in the histrionic methods of the prophets, who appear to have been past masters of the art of agitation. Time and again they act out their warning to their fellow-men, in addition to clothing it in magnificent poetry. (See, for example, the nineteenth chapter of *Jeremiah*.)

The closest approach to the drama, however, is to be found in those two major pieces of Hebrew literature, *The Song of Songs* and *Job*. Even if one rejects the theory that the former is a play, there is little doubt that it is highly dramatic in content and form. Properly arranged, that sensuous work *The Song of Songs* even lends itself to production like a play specially written for the theatre.[1] If there is no evidence that it was produced in a theatre (there were no theatres in Judea), it was probably often performed in part or whole at wedding celebrations as an epithalamion, thus having a kinship with the popular Fescennine Verses performed in Italy. That it was suitable for production in this manner is evident when the work is read in a later arrangement like Moulton's *Modern Reader's Bible*.

Whether we call *The Song of Songs* an idyl or a collection of wedding songs, it remains a lovely romance with a dramatically cohesive action and story. True, this story shifts back and forth like a shuttle: it is constantly turning from present fact to tender, passionate or playful reminiscence. But the realistic, persistently forward-moving convention of play structure is not the only possible one.

Professor Moulton's fairly unforced summary of the plot [2] suffices to reveal the dramatic quality of the whole. King Solomon while visiting the vineyards of Mount Lebanon with his followers discovers a beautiful Shulamite girl. She flees from him, but the monarch returns to the scene in the guise of a shepherd and wins her love. After this he comes to her again, this time in state, and makes her his queen. The play begins with the wedding, in the course of which these events are brought out, being retold haphazardly, as is natural when a happy bride and bridegroom recall the first wonder of courtship. In the second of the seven songs, the bride recalls the king's wooing; and in the third, she remembers how he visited her in state and became betrothed to her. In the fourth section, she dreams of losing him; in the fifth, the king remembers his courtship and enlarges on the beauty of his bride. In the sixth, the bride longs for her former haunts and asks her husband to revisit them with her; in the seventh, the two of them take the journey, find the spot of their first meeting, and finally depart.

If there is any fault to be found with this rare rhapsody it is in the confusion of incidents, which may conceivably be the fault of transcribers. But the glorious poetry and dialogue would salvage an even vastly faultier work. Except in *Romeo and Juliet* and *Antony and Cleopatra*, it is difficult to find words more evocative of passion and lines more complimentary to womanly beauty. The greatest exultation alternates with the infinite tenderness of such similitudes as "Thy teeth are like a flock of ewes, which are come up from the washing; whereof every one hath twins, and none is bereaved among them," and of banter like "We have a little sister, and she hath no breasts."

A work which celebrates physical passion with such uninhibited paganism could not have escaped suppression unless it could be turned to allegorical uses. Interpreted as an allegory representing the love of Israel and God and, later, the love of Christ and the Church, *The Song of Songs* continued to enjoy a strained respectability. Of the real author, who may have merely amalgamated a number of old wedding songs, nothing is known. But he was assuredly a poet who lived close to nature and possessed a cheerful understanding of the human heart.

Even this splendid idyl must, however, take second place by comparison with that monument among literary masterpieces, the dramatic symposium of *Job*. It is, in fact, a conclusive proof of the natural bent of the ancient Hebrew spirit that its greatest literary work should also be its most dramatic.

Although *Job* was not written to be performed, and was never acted in an ancient theatre, it needs only some arrangement (even less than that so ingeniously provided by Horace M. Kallen in *The Book of Job as a Greek Tragedy*) to reveal its essentially dramatic character and structure. Kallen's version of *Job* was successfully produced by at least two dramatic groups. *Job* was, in fact, arranged as a drama as early as 1587 by the famous Theodore Beza, and continued to be regarded as such in the eighteenth century. Whether it is drama by intention or accident is a moot question that need not actually be settled for our purpose. It may have been written merely as a symposium on the subject of divine justice and been instinctively permeated with a dramatic *élan* or later recast under the influence of the Greek theatre prevalent among the Hellenic colonists of Asia Minor. Or *Job* may have been written even at first, in the fifth century, with the Greek drama in mind, in which case it could have owed something to Aeschylus whose justification of God is paralleled in the Hebrew work. It may have then been reworked by later writers of the third century or even somewhat later, in which case it owed much to Euripides whose formal structure, as well as skepticism, is duplicated in *Job*. But drama *Job* is, even if it will not prove outwardly packed with excitement in the theatre. Its spirit, like its dramatic struggle, is inward, and as closet drama it is unsurpassed by any work in existence. "Closet drama," however, has an unpleasant ring and this description implies a futility and pretentiousness that cannot be attributed to so great and genuine a work. *Job* may be more justly classified as miracle play (in the medieval sense) which the lack of a theatre in Judea left in the library.

The climax of various currents of Hebrew thought, the work addresses itself with typically Hebraic earnestness to the problem of human calamity and divine justice. At the time of its original composition in the fifth century a great wave of questioning had risen in the Near East, particularly in the Persian Empire which had absorbed the Jews. This was the age of the Persian reformer Zoroaster who explained the existence of evil by dividing the sovereignty of the world between Ahuramazda, the god of light who was all-good but not all-powerful, and Ahriman, the independent power of darkness and prototype of Satan "the Adversary." But whatever disillusionment adhered to Zoroastrianism, then the religion of a dominant nation, could only be mild in comparison with that of the Hebrews. Collapse of their state and exile had been their lot in 586 B.C., but for a long time they could take their prophets' word for it that the catastrophe was condign punishment for sins committed against Jehovah. In the fifth century, however, this explanation was open to question. The Jews had rebuilt their state and social order along lines which accorded with the prescriptions of their ethical monotheistic religion, and yet, no matter where they looked, evil and suffering still prevailed. The remote consolation of an inferno for the wicked had not yet been discovered, and the explanation of original sin, subsequently revived by Christianity, was no longer a salve. Had not the advanced prophets of the new age been most explicit in discarding the theory that the sins of the fathers were visited upon their children for a thousand generations! Ezekiel, the leader of the post-exilic moralists, had already announced the "new covenant" that the children would suffer only for their own sins. But if they had *not* sinned, the disillusioned could ask, why did they suffer? Where was divine justice then? And what policy should a man follow if the wicked prospered?

The skeptics, all the more profoundly disheartened because they had been taught to center the universe and the moral order in a providential and righteous God, had much food for thought. It was at this juncture that one of them (if there was only one original author of the *Book of Job*) found in the legendary story of the patient man already mentioned by Isaiah a serviceable springboard for his questionings. Job, the prosperous just man who has lost his property, his children and the soundness of his body in a succession of arbitrary disasters, ceases to be patient in this redaction of the legend. He begins to question the justice of God with the extreme passion of one who has been wounded in his faith, and his friends give him the most indigestible crumbs of consolation. In three rounds of argument, their bromides leave Job exactly where he was at the beginning. In the first debate, Eliphaz advises him to be patient on the ground that suffering is the lot of man and that God will reward him in the end; Bildad seconds Eliphaz; Zophar, repeating the tenuous formula of the older prophets, even suggests that Job has no right to call himself righteous since all suffering is an expiation of sinfulness. In the second round of the debate, all three friends seize upon this explanation. In the third, hard pressed by Job's asseveration of his innocence, Bildad begs the question by making the commonplace assertion that God is too great to be questioned, while the other friends obstinately hold to the theory of Job's guilt until they become pathetically wearisome. Their arguments are as unavailing as their intended consolations, and they have actually only incited their friend to a stronger statement of the skeptical position: namely, that God heaps misfortune on the just, favors the wicked, and that if He is beyond human interest and cannot be reached he is useless to man. "Lo here is my signature—let God reply," Job declares.

Thus far in this disturbing work skepticism has the advantage, and it may well be that the author was inclined to rest his case at this unresolved point. Still, what follows is a rhapsodic vindication of God without which the book would no doubt have fallen afoul of the Argus-eyed guardians of orthodoxy. It is not necessary, however, to see in the justification of Providence a practical compromise. Whoever completed the symposium could not lightly renounce the faith in which he had been reared; it was the one staff that little Israel could lean on without renouncing the whole sorry business of living. And the answer that reaches us is infinitely deeper than any conventional explanation. When the friends have been effectively silenced, a young enthusiast, Elihu, appears as if from nowhere and implies that they are all wrong. But Job too is mistaken in being so sure of himself. Why is he so certain that God owes him anything for his righteousness? Elihu has faith in a divinity that will somehow justify itself, and no sooner has he expressed his credo than God answers Job out of the whirlwind of his majesty.

The divine self-justification is susceptible of a variety of interpretations, but its general line of thought is clearly Spinozistic. God's answer is simply that his benevolence is not to be sought in the particular, but in the general; and that man, who is not the whole of creation, must not exaggerate his personal problem. Jehovah, whose anthropomorphic features were constantly being reduced by the more philosophical members of the Hebrew community, describes himself as the generative and living force in nature. It is in the contemplation of the universe as a whole, with its wonders and multiplicity of forms, that Job loses his sense of personal suffering and injustice. This pantheistic experience is a poetic and mystic one close to the later Jewish philosopher's *amor intellectualis dei,* the intellectual love of a god who comprises all nature. It is as if God said, "I guarantee the life of all phenomena, I am in fact that very life, and the rest is not my concern but yours."

If this solution, however, is not wholly satisfactory or understandable to the orthodox and the unimaginative, there is another one made comprehensible by the conventional prologue and epilogue, which may have been taken literally from the old legend that served as a basis for the work. In the prologue, God had allowed the Adversary to test the most righteous man he could find; in the epilogue, the just man is rewarded. *Job,* in brief, has, like many a Euripidean tragedy, *two* endings—a conventional one for the average man, and an unconventional one for the thinker.

The power of the work does not, however, come solely from the profundity of the solution. *Job* provides a catharsis as dramatic as any to be found in Sophocles or Shakespeare; man's tussle with the problems of evil, injustice, and death, here expressed in the greatest poetry, reaches the highest pitch of agony and despair. There is infinite pathos in the physical and mental plight of Job, splendor in the epiphany, and variety of characterization in Eliphaz the Polonius who counsels patience, Bildad the pompous proponent of convention, Zophar the dogmatist, and Elihu the impetuous young poet. There is also a dramatic pattern in the manner in which the tension mounts from Job's lamentations to the heat of the argument, which later reaches a stalemate and is resolved by God's voice out of the whirlwind.

Now and then, it is true, the work suffers from contradictions, but these can be discounted when we remember that the orthodox scribes entrusted with the preservation of the Old Testament endeavored to lessen the thrust of Job's arraignment of God by putting into his mouth incongruous pieties.* These are mostly in prose and are not found in the second-century Greek translation of the Septuagint. The orthodox redaction of *Job,* however encompassed, provides it with some of its highest attributes: the rounding out of the symposium, which would have otherwise left the work in a state of uncertain suspension, and the remarkable nature poetry of the epiphany.

It remained for the dramatic promptings of the Jews to express themselves only once again—this time in the Gospels, which are rich in dialogue and characterization, possess a supremely dramatic hero, and surge forward toward a tragic conclusion. Although the theatre was of course far from the mind of the authors of the Gospels, they created what is unquestionably the greatest of the Passion Plays devoted to the many vegetation and ancestral gods who die and are resurrected for the benefit of mankind. The materialistic objective of the Egyptian and Syrian Passion Plays here becomes a spiritual one, and the god who suffers in the Gospels has lost his clay feet without abating, but actually increasing, his reality as a man. If structurally the Gospels are narratives, their pattern and effect are unmistakably dramatic. They were found so by the numerous playwrights who created the drama of the Middle Ages.

2 KALIDASA AND THE INDIAN THEATRE

The Hindus saw a living theatre slowly growing out of their ritual. For a time closely associated with rites of religion, their drama was finally emancipated as a lay form of entertainment which was only now and then pressed into service by the Buddhists. Unhampered by prohibitions against magic-making and polytheism, India followed the same course as early Greece. The process of anthropomorphization by means of which natural forces and divinities can become *dramatis personae* began possibly as early as 1000 B.C., when the Hindus composed the beautiful hymns known as the Vedas which were sung and acted out to some degree by the Brahman priests. The Rig-Veda extols and personalizes the

---

* The King James version collaborates with the scribes in reading, for example, "Though he slay me, yet will I trust in Him" and "I know that my Redeemer liveth" for "Aye, though He slay me, I tremble not", which Job follows with "For all that, I will maintain His course to His face" and "Then I will know that my defender [a human vindicator] will arise."

gods, and the Atharva-Veda provides numerous magical spells which would have been anathema to the Hebrews. Moreover, at least fifteen of the Vedic hymns employ dialogue in a dramatic manner, some of them calling for as many as three speakers.

Legend sanctified the drama by attributing it to the desire of Indra, India's colorful national god, who requested a dramatic spectacle of the All-father Brahma and was granted his wish in the form of the Natya-Veda (*natya* meant dancing, hence "nautch" girls). A divinely appointed legendary architect designed the first theatre, and the mythical sage Bharata was made the director of the celestial stage. So seriously did the Hindus take their drama that they composed textbooks like the Natya-shastra early in their history, and their far-flung primitive theatre could be found wherever a good Brahman expounded his teachings by means of a half-extemporized play. Greek culture, introduced by the conquests of Alexander the Great and his generals, may have also contributed an influence, and Buddhism too encouraged the theatre. Fragments of three Buddhist plays written by the romantic poet Ashvaghesha in the second century A.D. already reveal marked development. One of the plays, the *Shariputra-prakarana* in nine acts represents the conversion of the Hindus by Buddha. Another is a religious allegory like the medieval morality plays, and employs such abstract characters as Wisdom, Glory, and Firmness. The third play, more secular in character, has a courtesan for its heroine, as well as a rogue who supplied some undoubtedly well-appreciated humor.

But the great age of Hindu drama first began more than a century later in 320 A.D. when, after a period of chaos resembling the Dark Ages of Europe, the capable rajah Chandragupta established a hegemony over the most fertile and populous parts of Northern India. These possessions were subsequently extended by his soldierly son Samudragupta, and when this Indian Napoleon died in 375 his son Chandragupta II, known as *Vikramaditya* or "Sun of Power," inaugurated an epoch of cultural development which was never again approached in a country which later fell afoul of a host of conquerors. At his court lived India's ablest writers, known as the "Nine Gems" in the extravagantly complimentary language of the East. Fortunately, moreover, in such an unstable region as India, the Chandragupta or Gupta Renaissance continued for another half century after this *Roi Soleil's* death in 413, long enough to assure the theatre a healthy growth before India fell into the hands of the conquering Huns about 500 A.D.

The theatre which flourished under these royal auspices was a leisure-class product which could not have been understood by the lower orders. These spoke dialects whereas the dominant language of the plays was

Sanskrit. An optimistic outlook, naturally prevalent at the luxurious court, favored romantic material, artificial plots, and a happy conclusion. The writers fluttered pleasantly and wittily over the surface of life while the underdog, whose lot could not have been enviable even under a benevolent Oriental monarchy, remained inarticulate. He was allowed to make an appearance only as an amusing foil for the princely heroes. This, in short, was a theatre of artifice, and the Hindu writers were masters of that art.

Dhanamjaya's tenth-century *Dasharupa* or *Ten Forms,* which based its precepts on the practices of the earlier classic age, bristles with artificial laws. An example is the eight-fold classification of heroines, among whom are "the one who is enraged at discovering her lover having relations with another woman," "the one who is separated from her lover by a quarrel," and "the one who has her husband in subjection." In every case, the noble ladies are engrossed in sentimental affairs of the heart without treading upon the precarious heights of a great passion, while the gentlemen are susceptible, sometimes volatile, and never seriously engaged in the world's business or travail. The rogues and commoners also are expected to have specific attributes even to the point of speaking more or less rigidly prescribed dialects—the Avanti dialect for the rogues and gamblers, a corrupt argot for barbarians, and so on. The elaborations of euphuism, familiar to us from Elizabethan, Spanish and Italian literatures, are favored in the dialogue. As in Shakespearean drama, both prose and verse are permitted within the same play but their use is carefully prescribed; and ordinary women, villains and members of the lower castes must not speak except in prose. Each princely hero has his appointed followers who set off the jewel of his personality. He has his *vidushaka* or sportive servant who corresponds to the court jesters of European comedy and supplies the low comedy, and his *vita,* a more dignified personage who plays Kent or Horatio to royalty.

After a benediction or prayer, which disposes of the religious debt of the drama, the play proceeds to a prologue between the stage director and the chief actress (a device imitated by Kalidasa's great admirer Goethe in his *Vorspiel* to *Faust*). This serves to remind the audience that the play is only an entertainment. Since the nobles have all the time in the world, the comedy can run on to as many as ten acts, a fact which need not, however, dismay the Occidental playgoer familiar with *Back to Methuselah, Strange Interlude,* and *Mourning Becomes Electra.* By the time the play was over, the court had had a variegated and playful celebration and could disband in the best of humor.

The background and staging of the piece, which did not depart from the studied charm of the composition, could only add to the amenities. Performed on a simple platform in the hall or courtyard of the royal palace amid sumptuous hangings and impressive architecture, the play made no pretense to realism. The actors made no great attempt to create the illusion of reality. A curtain sufficed to conceal them as they dressed for their parts, waited for their cues, and supplied the appropriate sound effects. There was no proper scenery, except for decorations and "props" like seats, thrones, and chariots. The one concession to realistic staging appears to have been the employment of real animals for drawing a chariot across the platform. Ordinarily, however, the entrance of a horse was simulated by the actors, whose movements were fairly conventional and could be foreshortened when the action required considerable travel between their lines. Certain it is that the burden of the staging devolved upon the actor, who was required to be infinitely resourceful and suggestive. Female roles were generally assigned to women, there being no prohibition against actresses in India, but boys and young men would substitute in parts which required too much exertion.

When Kalidasa began to write he had reason to feel a certain humility and apprehension. Can the audience feel any respect for him, he asks in the prologue to his first play, coming as he does after such illustrious authors ás Bhasa, Saumilla, and Kaviputra. Thirteen plays discovered in 1910 and attributed to Bhasa, although some of them may be by several other hands, justify the modesty of the young playwright. Possibly written about 350 A.D., some fifty years before Kalidasa turned to the stage, they are largely romances taken from the famous epics the *Mahabharata* and the *Ramayana* which influenced the course of Hindu drama from the beginning. All of the plays are admired by the Hindus, but perhaps the best of them is *Svapnavasavadatta*. In it the minister of a state tries to strengthen his lord's power by arranging a marriage with the daughter of an important ruler. But the King is too devoted to his wife to consent, even when the Queen is ready to sacrifice herself to his interests. Consequently the Queen and the minister escape to a hermitage, arranging their flight in such a way that the King believes that they died in a palace fire. Then the former wife reappears in order to wait upon the new queen and is recovered by her husband.

The most notable of the plays that preceded Kalidasa's, however, is the ten-act romance *Mricchakatika* or *The Little Clay Cart,* which was based upon Bhasa's older *Daridracharudatta* or *The Poor Charudatta,* of which four acts have survived. Although traditionally attributed to King Shudraka, a versatile genius described as a long-lived mathematician as well as an amorist and an expert on elephants, the play is probably by some less royal hand. *The Little Clay Cart* contains romance and politics, adventure and social idealism, and humor and pathos.

If it possesses less charm than the *Shakuntala,* not having been nourished at the peak of the cultured age, it has considerably more force
and depth, and may be preferred on these counts.

In bald outline it is the story of the love of a beautiful and noble
courtesan Vasantasena for the impoverished Brahman Charudatta,
whose wife does not appear to resent the liaison. Nor does his extra-
marital relationship in a less monogamous period than our own detract
from his piety, to which he actually owed his impoverishment. The
Brahman, who had become poor because of his inexhaustible liberality,
is lauded as "A tree of life to them whose sorrows grow. . . . The Mirror of the learned; and the sea where all the tides of character unite.
. . ." Complications arise only when his mistress becomes the object of
the wicked prince Sansthanaka's attentions, and is compelled to conceal
her jewels in the Brahman's home. Additional difficulties appear when
the gems are stolen by a burglar who proves to be her maid's lover,
whereupon the Brahman's wife, concerned for her husband's honor,
forces him to accept her own string of diamonds in order that he may
compensate his mistress. Fortunately, the thief soon restores the jewels
at the insistence of the courtesan's maid. Meanwhile, in another episode
Vasantasena is seen in the noble role of trying to save the cowherd
Aryaka (the legitimate claimant to the throne) from imprisonment
by the prince's brother-in-law. It is the jewels, however, that indirectly
produce the catastrophe, for coming to the Brahman's house to inform
him that they have been recovered she is forced by the weather to spend
the night there. Impulsively she fills his little son's cart with diamonds
when he weeps that it is only made of clay (hence the title of the play).
But since her good deed, which augurs well for her love, makes her too
happy for caution she commits the mistake of entering the bullock-
drawn wagon of her princely persecutor. Rejecting his wooing, she
arouses his fury to such a pitch that he strangles her and then charges
the Brahman with the deed. The judge who tries him suspects that a
villain like Sansthanaka is not above incriminating a just man, but he
is intimidated by his dread of this prince. The innocent Brahman is
therefore convicted and brought out to be executed. But the villain's
machinations are finally exposed when the driver of the bullock wagon
accuses the prince of deposing falsely against the accused; and Vasantasena, who survived unknown to the villain, herself appears and points
out the real criminal. This victory for righteousness is followed by another gratifying climax when the cowherd she had tried to save escapes
from prison, overthrows the old rajah and seizes his throne. He makes
the Brahman governor of a province and allows him to marry the exemplary courtesan.

Although this intricate fabrication is overlong and episodic, its strings are ultimately tied together for those who have the requisite patience. Moreover, one is rewarded for such perseverance with shrewd observations on life, and with a group of charmingly drawn characters, among whom the Brahman's comic servant Maitreya is easily the most delightful. The villainous prince, who reveals his ignorance by misquoting the Hindu epics, is another well-drawn character, as is the king who distrusts his brother-in-law's allegations but is willing to countenance injustice in order to protect his unsteady throne. Ingenuity, vigorous verse, and a wealth of incident add to the amenities while the note of social criticism is sounded in the exposure of political corruption and in the climactic revolution. Of the court which tries the Brahman the playwright declares that it looks like a sea: "its tossing waves are wrangling advocates; its brood of monsters are these wild animals—death's ministers; attorneys skim like wily snakes the surface; spies are the shellfish cowering amidst its weeds, and vile informers, like the hovering curlew, hang fluttering over, then pounce upon their prey. The beach that should be justice is unsafe, rough, rude and broken by oppression's storms." In abbreviated form, the play proved engaging when produced by the Neighborhood Playhouse of New York in the early nineteen-twenties.

Social criticism, however, was left in abeyance by the writers of the Golden Age. The man who was affectionately called the "Bridegroom of Poetry" by the Hindus and wrote their most famous play was of a different mold from that of the unknown author of *The Little Clay Cart*. The darker side of the world seemingly escaped Kalidasa's attention, and he was content to sport on the foam of life with charm, if not without some of the irony generally picked up in polite society. He was a poet, too, the finest among the Hindus barring the unidentified authors of the epics, as gifted in the art of description as he was in the more dramatic one of comic intrigue and portraiture. His two poems, *Ritusamhara* or *The Seasons* and *Meghaduta* or *Cloud Messenger* are as descriptive as Shelley's *The Cloud*. An unverifiable story spoke of Kalidasa's grace and handsomeness which brought him to the attention of a princess who married him. Legend also had him involved in the perilous business of keeping a jealous mistress who finally murdered him. It is only too conceivable that the author of the *Shakuntala* was an accomplished gallant. The three plays of his which have survived obviously do not stem from a hermitage even if their author was apparently a Brahman by birth.

The earliest of them, *Malavikagnimitra* or *Malavika and Agnimitra* has King Agnimitra falling in love with the picture of an exiled servant girl. The King's jocose attendant, always ready to oblige, forms a plan whereby his master may get sight of the maiden, who is the pupil of a notable dancing master. The latter is ordered to exhibit his talent at court, and Malavika is naturally brought along by him. The Queen, infuriated by her husband's passion for the girl, imprisons her in a cellar. Ultimately, however, the girl proves to be a true-born princess, and this legitimizes the affair. Also reconciled to the marriage is another of the susceptible rajah's wives, whose nose had been put slightly out of joint by Malavika. The humor of this romance may easily be gathered from even so bare an outline as this. Taken with the grain of gentle cynicism which Kalidasa drops into each of his comic sauces, it makes adult entertainment.

Richer in poetic beauty and more fanciful is Kalidasa's third play *Vikramorvashe* or *Urvashi Conquered by Valor,* which dramatizes the love of the mortal king Pururavas for the celestial nymph Urvashi. His wife and his comic servant, puzzled by this infatuation for a strange maiden, soon discover his secret, which the King also confesses in the invisible presence of the nymph herself. He is so ardent that Urvashi cannot resist him. She writes him a love letter on a birch leaf and reveals herself to him before returning to heaven to perform in a celestial play. But the nymph's infatuation gets her into trouble when she misses her cue and pronounces her lover's name during the performance. For this mishap she is banished from heaven with a curse to the effect that she will be forced to return the moment her lover sees the child which she will bear him. A minor catastrophe occurs when she is transformed into a vine for inadvertently invading a sacred grove, and her lover succeeds in recovering her with the aid of a "gem of reunion" only after an extended search! Thereafter the happiness of the lovers is troubled only by the King's longing for a child, but he learns in time that they have a child which Urvashi had concealed from him in order to escape the curse. Ultimately, the celestial powers relent in deference to true love and the nymph is allowed to remain with her husband until death. A touch of passion and some latent tragedy do not prevent the fantasy from remaining a perfumed fairy tale on the order of *A Midsummer Night's Dream.*

In the Kalidasa canon it is the *Shakuntala,* however, that claims first place by virtue of its lovely poetry, shrewd playfulness, and almost uninterrupted humor. King Dushyanta who enters the wooded hermitage of a saint while hunting wild animals meets the ascetic's ward, the lovely Shakuntala. She is instantly attracted to him and finds various excuses for lingering behind her companions. An obliging bee which pursues her enables the King to come to her rescue, and thereafter the course of true love leads to marriage. But it is not long before the royal husband, who is called back to court by some pressing business, leaves the hermitage, promising to send his retinue for her. Unintentionally offending a saint, however, Shakuntala is cursed to the effect that her husband will forget her, and the sole concession made by the ruffled holy man after he has been properly appeased is that the King's memory will be restored when she presents him with the ring he gave her. Naturally, as destiny and dramaturgy would have it, she loses the ring while bathing, and the king's memory is a long time in abeyance. Repulsed at the court, she is miraculously transported to the mountain hermitage of a great sage where she gives birth to her son Bharata, the "All-Tamer," who is destined to become a famous leader of his people. Ultimately, of course, the ring is recovered. A fisherman finds it, the King's aberrant memory returns, and husband and wife are happily reunited.

The abundant humor of the play is particularly evident in the wooing scenes, in the bluff behavior of the King's charioteer, in the antics of an official who proves himself a veritable Dogberry while examining the fisherman, and in the sophisticated implications of the royal husband's lapse of memory. Well spiced with delicate and descriptive poetry, the comedy is a delightful amalgam of all the resources of a courtly playwright who makes artifice look natural and nature seem artifice.[3]

Kalidasa's successors lived in troubled times, and no Hindu playwright could quite recapture his grace of expression and unfailing cheerfulness, qualities without which romance limps instead of flying. The last native king of India to enjoy importance, Harsha, a noteworthy general and patron of the arts, achieved distinction as a playwright with three plays ascribed to him. One, *Priyadarshika,* describes the vicissitudes of a princess, and is distinguished by the familiar introduction of a play within a play; another, *Ratnavali* or *Pearl Necklace,* presents the romance of a king and a princess in disguise, and employs the ingenious device of having a parrot repeat the heroine's confession of love for her royal suitor; and the third and best known of Harsha's works, *Nagananda,* is a miracle play revolving around a Buddhist saint who allows himself to be devoured by a monster in order to save the Naga race. Conveniently, the monster relents at the end and the saintlike hero is restored to life along with all the Nagas who were destroyed by the creature. The play is notable for its simple descriptiveness and for its Buddhist lesson to refrain from destroying life and make good will prevail among men. Harsha, who reigned from 607 to 647, was succeeded in the next century by another royal author bearing the formidable name of Mahendravikramavarman; but if one may draw conclusions from the single farce of his which has survived, the scepter suited him better than the pen. To come to a dramatist whose stature is in any way comparable to Kalidasa's we must skip another century, to the beginning of the eighth, a fact that illustrates the progressive decline of the Hindu theatre. Even this playwright Bhavabhuti is, however, only remotely related to his illustrious predecessor.

A Brahman who won fame slowly, Bhavabhuti was weighed down by a depressing outlook on life. Although his three plays are strongly poetic and are steeped in romance, they do not trip lightly, and one cannot call them particularly amusing. His departure from Kalidasa lies in a stronger sense of reality and a stronger emotionalism. Quite in accordance with his temperament he favored poetic grandeur and dispensed with the buffoon who furnishes so much entertainment in the older writer's work. His best known play *Malatimadhava* or *The Stolen Marriage* is the Hindu *Romeo and Juliet*. Two young people who are brought together by a nun fall in love; but when a favorite of the king asks for the girl's love and her father is afraid to refuse him, their happiness seems blasted. The nun who had promoted their affair, however, acts as their intermediary and enables them to elope. At the wedding between the courtier and the girl, a friend of hers is substituted and the suitor is frustrated in an amusing scene. The weird background, peopled with ghosts and permeated with demon worship, intensifies the romance and provides the poetry with a *frisson* or two not unwelcome in a romance that lacks Kalidasa's comic legerdemain. Bhavabhuti's other plays, however, are in the main inferior as drama and owe their chief interest to their poetry.

Still, he was the last of the classic Hindu playwrights. He is hardly approached by the later Vishakhadatta, who wrote a drama of political intrigue in *The Signet of Rakshasa*, and by Bhatta Narayana, whose *Binding of the Braid of Hair* is highly regarded by the Hindus for its regular construction. Still later interest attaches only to the eleventh century Krishna Mishra's *Rise of the Moon*, a morality play resembling pre-Elizabethan works of the same class with such allegorical characters as King Error and King Reason. Of still later works even mention would be an extravagance; the author, who has dipped into some of them, confesses himself beaten by their formidable length and dullness.

Not until the late nineteenth century, with the advent of the Bengali poet Rabindranath Tagore, did the Hindu theatre experience a revival. Although his reputation has declined considerably in the West ever since neo-romanticism retreated into its pearly shell, Tagore, who won the Nobel Prize in 1913, became one of the leading writers of modern poetic drama. For those who are not driven to impatience by the luxuriance of Hindu mysticism and romance (Kalidasa's *Shakuntala* is another matter, since Kalidasa does not take romance too seriously), Tagore's *Chitra* and *The King of the Dark Chamber* are works of some distinction. At least the latter, which describes how the people failed to appreciate the king who moved among them invisibly, compares more than favorably with the best plays of Maeterlinck. Tagore was the ideal writer to mediate between the East and the West.

VIII

THE PLAYWRIGHTS OF THE FAR EAST

I THE HUMBLE CHINESE DRAMA

ALTHOUGH older than Hindu culture by far, Chinese civilization began to make its contributions to the theatre after Hindu drama had passed its peak. The beginnings of Chinese drama were, needless to say, ancient enough, although it is difficult to speak here with any show of authority. During that hoary "Golden Age," the second dynasty which lasted from 2205 to 1766 B.C., there were already ceremonial dances representing various occupations and sensations. Already, too, the stylization which characterizes the Chinese theatre was manifesting itself in a variety of regulations, such as those calling for vermilion shields and jade-embossed battle-axes in military celebrations, the jade signifying "virtue and the shields benevolence, to inculcate clemency to those defeated." [1] By the eighth century B.C., the drama had even gained a sufficient foothold for a theatre to be established under royal patronage; and for a school of acting or College of the Pear Orchard to be founded by the emperor Ming Huang to whom incense is still being burned in Chinese greenrooms.

But it was only two thousand years later, during the Yüan dynasty established in 1280 A.D. by the storied Kublai Khan, that the Chinese theatre began to achieve literary significance. And it is easy to read into this belated development that long-standing reluctance of Chinese writers to lend their skill to the theatre which seems partly responsible for its low estate. The traditional view is expressed by Cheney who writes that the "Chinese drama has no literary values for us," [2] and the Chinese themselves have been extremely modest in their claims for the art. The vitality of their theatre is gauged by the animation of the performances, and it is customary to describe these with that esoteric air of rapture which is more often than not a symptom of lack of understanding.

Why a stage convention should be elevated to a mystery simply because it does not happen to be our own eludes this writer. It is sufficient to note that Chinese actors employ highly stylized movements, dispense in the main with scenery, and frankly avow the fact that they are play-acting by employing a property-man who supplies the necessary furniture in full sight of the public. Naturally, the expertness demanded of the actor within such a convention provides an additional fillip to play-going, which is no mystery since good acting has proved as attractive to Occidental audiences as to Oriental ones. That stylization with musical accompaniment by an orchestra at the back of the stage should give the Chinese plays a greater amplitude or distinction than is afforded by the mere text is also no mystery. Why writers should be led to speak affectionately of the "naïveté" of the Chinese stage is likewise unclear, since all theatre depends on a suspension of disbelief. And lest we maintain an exaggerated notion of the barrenness of the Chinese stage, it is also worth remarking that a single beautiful piece of furniture can fill the scene tastefully, there being no scenic gain in a cluttered-up platform, that the costuming of Chinese plays is resplendent and in fact so costly that clothes are usually rented rather than bought, and that color is further supplied by the custom of painting the face with red, black, green, white, and gold. The seeming difficulty of plays that last from afternoon to midnight or sometimes contain as many as *forty-eight* acts is also easily removed by the knowledge that printed plays are not necessarily acted without considerable abbreviation (just as Shakespearean drama is frequently abbreviated), and that what those insatiable playgoers the Chinese see during so long a session in the theatre is not a single play but a whole series.

Moreover, if prescribed action often creates scenery in the sense that an actor pretends to climb an imaginary hill, if the delivery of the actors in the form of a chant is remote from realism, and if their symbolic posturings give the outsider the impression of a cryptogram (which is only an added delight to the Chinese connoisseur), the plays themselves submit their meaning without the slightest need of esoteric explications.

In fact, the examples with which we are familiar are exceptionally clear and forthright. It is to their lack of intense passion, to their relatively uncomplicated characterization, and to the fact that the mandarin poets disdained so popular a medium as the theatre that we must attribute a want of greatness to the Chinese drama. Even with this concession, however, the customary funeral oration on the Chinese plays is somewhat inappropriate. At least a number of them compare favorably with great stretches of the European drama. The law of averages itself might make this inevitable if we remember that in the ninety years of the Yüan dynasty alone some five hundred plays of known authorship were written by eighty-five playwrights.

The plays afford such variety that it has been customary among the Chinese to classify them, the groups ranging from civil to military ones, from historical to ethical ones, from romance to crime, from pleasant fantasy to social problems. Tragedy does not figure prominently on the stage, although it is not absent in so mournful a work as *The Sorrows of Han,* which laments the misery of an infatuated ruler who lost his empire, or *Beauty,* the heroine of which is taken from her home by marauders and dies patriotically. Satire, however, is rarely absent in a nation which has had so many and such long-standing reasons for disillusionment. Love, in particular, is treated with the irony characteristic of a race that regards it as a form of childishness and banishes actresses from the stage, leaving most feminine roles to highly paid masculine specialists like the famous Mei Lan Fang.

A number of the plays which have had the good fortune to be translated into European tongues won appreciation, if not enthusiasm, in the West. The thirteenth century *Romance of the Western Pavilion* (*Hsi-siang-chi* to the Chinese), apparently the first to be translated, relates the adventures of a scholar who is separated from his love by the necessity of going to the capital to take civil service examinations. (It was recently adapted for the London stage by S. I. Hsiung, who was responsible earlier for *Lady Precious Stream.*) Another adventure play, *The Chinese Orphan,* won Voltaire's approbation. *The Intrigues of a Soubrette,* also liked by the French, dramatizes a love story. *Leaving a Son in a Mulberry Orchard* deals with a father's sacrifice for his child. *The Empty City Trap,* .one of the numerous military plays of China, describes the escape of a beleaguered city when its commander opens the city gates and, disguising his handful of soldiers as streetcleaners, instructs them to sing of the fabulous strength of his army, until the enemy is frightened away. *The Sorrows of Han,* which has considerable literary merit and is affecting, sounds a warning against decadent luxury and irresponsible government which leads to national disaster.

Perhaps, however, the most interesting product of the Chinese theatre for us is the thirteenth- or fourteenth-century *The Circle of Chalk* (*Hoei-Lan-Kin*), variously translated and adapted (among others, by the German poet Klabund). By means of abundant comedy and intrigue, the play succeeds in presenting a sharp satire on corruption in official circles. But if it is the Confucian doctrine of upright government or social justice that gives the play its vigor, it is its graceful dialogue and shrewd characterization that make it a fairly charming comedy of manners. Its sharply defined situations though basically serious are sometimes broadly humorous, and a number of the lines afford amusement by their ironic elaborateness as when a character declares: "I fear to approach the Excellent One, as he augustly permits himself to be in a new fit of rage."

The story revolves around an illicit affair between a law clerk and a married woman who poisons her husband, lays the blame on his innocent second wife, and claims the latter's child to whom the inheritance must go. The victimized second wife is condemned by the governor of the province with the connivance of the clerk and is acquitted by a higher judge only after enduring many torments. This worthy, whose wit is equal to his integrity, uses Solomon's tactics in discovering the real mother of the child. Drawing a supposedly magic circle of chalk around the lad, the judge declares that only the real parent will be able to draw him out of it. Since the woman who has falsely claimed him as her own does not even make a move in his direction, while the real mother takes her child by the hand at once, the judge succeeds in exposing the culprits.

Plays continued to be composed after the high-water mark of the Yüan dynasty, and the subjects and backgrounds were frequently amplified, even if no genius arose to lift the drama to new heights. *Lady Precious Stream,* one of a number of adaptations by the living writer S. I. Hsiung, recently found favor in the English-speaking world, but can hardly be reckoned among works of importance. What new developments may arise cannot be foretold at this distance, but it is possible that the reawakening of the Chinese people will provide a fresh incentive to significant dramatic composition.

2 THE LAMA-PLAYWRIGHTS OF TIBET

If the mellow culture of China has not shown itself at its best in the drama, it is not surprising that other stretches of the Far East have been even less productive. Java has its threefold theatre, one devoted to the unique practice of shadow-plays, one to puppets, and one to dance-drama whose literary import, so far as we know, is nil. Burma has a variety of drama which has attracted some attention but without arousing marked enthusiasm. Impassable and geographically vague Tibet alone enjoys not only a host of dramatic spectacles under priestly supervision but some drama of a recognizable quality.[3]

Its Shakespeare is the unpronounceable Sixth Tale-lama Tsongsbdyangs-rgyam-thso of the seventh century A.D. A "delicate poet, in love with the arts and with beauty in all its forms, the feminine principally," he was also the author of some highly seasoned erotic poems which could hardly have been consonant with his sacred office.

His plays, as well as those of his anonymous colleagues, are more indebted to the Hindu theatre than to the Chinese, which is only a natural consequence of the spread of Buddhism to Tibet in the seventh century. The romances and Buddhist mysteries which flourished so abundantly in India are paralleled in Tibet by a number of religious plays founded on legend partly indigenous and partly taken from the Hindu fables or *jatakas* dealing with the multiple existences of Buddha. Played only at set times of the year in or near monasteries by the monks, with the support of lay professionals who assume the female roles, the dramas are highly formal in both composition and performance. The narrative portions are extensive, and are assigned to a Brahman in pieces drawn from Indian matter and to a special actor called *hunter* when the subjects are Tibetan. The *hunters* also comprise the chorus which supplies the accompanying ballet and uses a variety of masks suggestive of primitive totemism. Both the narrative, which is in prose, and the dialogue in verse are danced and sung, a slower tempo being reserved for the indispensable royal character whose sentences are enthusiastically picked up on the last word by the whole court. As there is much improvisation in the long plays, and since parts of them are merely acted out instead of being spoken, publication cannot do complete justice to the drama of Tibet. But the plots are colorful and attractive in the extravagant manner of romance.

Three familiar plays are those entitled *Tchrimekundan, Djroazanmo*, and *Nansal*,[4] the first an account of the penultimate earthly existence of Buddha or Shakyamuni, the second a fairy tale of lost children in the Hansel and Gretel tradition, the third a drama of Tibetan manners, as well as a philosophical lesson. In perhaps the most representative of the trio the *Tchrimekundan*, a princely St. Francis (of course, an incarnation of Buddha) who bears infinite love for all creatures and cannot resist a request, gives away a jewel which enables its possessor to realize all desires. Thereupon the prince's father, grieved at a loss which threatens his kingdom since the jewel was given to an enemy, exiles his son to a wild mountain for twelve years. But the exile's charitable disposition remains undiminished. After he has given away all his provisions and elephants to three poor Brahmans, he travels painfully on foot with his family. The demands on his charity are seemingly inexhaustible, and in time he also gives away his children and his wife, who are however returned to him by the god Indra who had disguised himself as a beggar in order to test the saint. After the term of his exile expires, while he is returning to his kingdom, the prince climaxes his saintly behavior by giving both his eyes to a blind man, a deed so noble that his admiring father bequeaths the kingdom to him.

Such superhuman charity unfortunately does not commend itself to the Western reader, even if it is a "weeping success" in Tibet. But the passion for the absolute spills over as an infectious poetic experience, and the prince's adventures possess the fascination of a dramatized fairy tale. The very extravagance of Tibetan humanitarianism becomes a poetic virtue. Here, in short, is the theatre of idealism in its most unalloyed form.

3 MASTERS OF THE JAPANESE DRAMA

It was in Japan, however, that the Far-Eastern drama celebrated a genuine triumph, providing an original and fascinating form in the Noh play whose authors proved themselves masters of the exquisite.

Not all of Japan's drama shares this quality, which the sentimental like to associate with Japanese gardens and their stunted flora. The same Oriental class stratification that kept the Chinese mandarins from contributing their great poetry to the theatre, produced two sharply differentiated stages in Japan: the Noh for the élite, and the theatre of the *Kabuki* with its related forms, as well as the puppet or "Doll" theatre, for the populace.

For the commoners' stage, which developed after the Noh drama, the popular playwrights supplied numerous plays of unconfined sensationalism. *Kabuki* (a term loosely applied here to the entire popular theatre) grew out of public recitations called the *taiheiki*. These developed into dramatized accounts of stories recited by a single actor to the accompaniment of music supplied by a three-stringed guitar and rhythmic tappings with a fan. The earliest works in this vein were plays relating the adventures of a nine-foot hero with the reddest face in creation and a noble passion for destroying demons and beasts. The first regular *Kabuki* theatre came early in the seventeenth century when O-Kuni, at first only a renegade priestess, collected a number of dancing girls into a theatrical troupe and gave public performances. In time, stories from common life were added to those borrowed from legend and the plays became increasingly plebeian in their melodramatic style and in their length. (Performances may last some eight hours, from early morning to the late afternoon, although some of the plays can be quite short.) The masks of the early Noh plays were discarded, the flowery runway from the back of the audience to the stage later popularized by Max Reinhardt's *Sumurun* and our more pretentious burlesque houses came into use, and even a revolving platform was employed to enliven the proceedings long before Europe adopted it.

The playwrights of the popular drama were shrewd carpenters who hammered out elaborate plots that submitted their meaning to the last melodramatic detail, and greatest among them was Chikamatsu who was born in 1653 and died in 1724. His work may be taken as representative of the best that they can offer.

Chikamatsu Monzayemon, a Samurai originally prepared for the priesthood and later a retainer of various noble houses, became an outlaw or *ronin* who shared the desperate deeds celebrated in so many popular legends and plays. No one was more qualified to titillate the taste of the populace than this Robin Hood of the stage to whom no less than a hundred plays are attributed, fifty-one of them being printed as unquestionably his. Nor are they short works like the Noh plays or even the Greek tragedies, but more than full length. His facility was truly remarkable if we are to credit the story that he wrote one of his plays in a single night, and unbounded admiration has been his in Japan which has doubtfully compared him to Shakespeare.

His works combine comedy and tragedy, with prose and poetry allo-cated to the characters in accordance with their social standing. Fierce combats, wantonly cruel deeds, scenes of torture and suicide, all luxuri-antly blended, provide many a *frisson*. A fairly charming romance by this obliging writer is his *Fair Ladies at a Game of Poem-Cards* which contains an amusing caricature of a villainous minister and an elaborate intrigue arising from his jealous passion for a court lady. Ultimately this hypocrite who conceals his lubricity behind a mask of righteous-ness is exposed and killed, and his victims are reinstated at court. Al-though beheadings and murders are not wanting in this Japanese ro-mance, the benevolence of the Empress who favors the love-lorn maid and the formal playfulness of the piece make an entertaining play. But this comedy does not convey the full extent of Chikamatsu's wrestlings with melodrama. *Divertimenti* could not entirely satisfy the jaded pal-ate of the lower orders for which he wrote.

As sheer entertainment, incidentally, the *Fair Ladies* is not the best example of Japanese drama. It is excelled by more economical and less high-flown comedies like the anonymous fourteenth- or fifteenth-century *Abstraction,* in which a husband in search of extra-marital pleas-ures prevails upon his servant to take his place under an "abstraction" or prayer blanket in order to deceive his wife. Upon discovering the servant under it, she takes his place and hears her husband, when he returns, confessing his amour much to his subsequent discomfiture.

Chikamatsu's most famous play, the *Kikusenya Kassen* or *Battles of Kikusenya,* composed in 1715, runs the full gamut of melodrama and is most representative of his normally turgid muse. To use the utmost economy in initiating the Western reader into its colossal elaborations, be it said that a Tartar king demands a Ming emperor's favorite con-cubine as the price of friendship. This is merely a pretext for an inva-sion of China, the signal for which is given by a traitorous minister when he stabs out his own eye with a dagger. After sundry events in which the Emperor is deluded by his minister, the Tartars appear at the gates millions strong and are routed by the Chinese general Go San-kei with a mere handful of soldiers. While he is engaged in this stu-pendous feat, however, the evil minister's younger brother cuts off the

Emperor's head and binds his concubine. Go Sankei thereupon decapitates the murderer and releases the concubine. She is, however, killed by a bullet later on, and Go Sankei saves the child she is bearing by performing a Caesarean operation in full sight of the audience. To deceive the enemy, which is bent upon seizing the imperial heir, he then kills his own child, which has been lashed to his spear throughout the engagement, and substitutes it for the recently delivered prince. Meanwhile the Emperor's daughter and the general's wife escape to Japan where they win the assistance of a great Japanese hero. On the way, while bearing his old mother on his back, this hero tames a tiger, and the beast subsequently assists him in routing the huntsmen of the evil minister. Finally, he comes to the aid of the loyal general Go Sankei who is keeping the royal prince in hiding, and what gargantuan battles ensue can easily be imagined.

A greater contrast to this super-film than that provided by the earlier Noh plays can scarcely be imagined, and it is only natural that this should occur in a land where differences in social position still remain distinctly feudal. The taste of the Japanese plebeian was nowise shared by the cultivated nobility which held the popular theatre in utter contempt. The aristocracy's theatre is remarkably restrained and subtle. Its own blemish is the expected one of preciosity.

Born of the pantomimic dance or *Kagura,* performed in connection with Shinto worship and reminiscent of the Greek dithyramb, the Noh play has a sacred origin. Legend sanctified it as early as the eighth century A.D. in an account of how the Sun Goddess, upon being disgusted by the unseemly behavior of her brother, shut herself up in a cave and deprived the world of light until she was lured out of her retreat by another goddess who performed a mimic dance on a resonant tub. Supplemented with rustic exhibitions of acrobatics and a species of elementary opera called *Dengaku,* as well as with recitations and Chinese dances, the Noh play took shape gradually, until in the fourteenth century it achieved literary status in the work of two talented aristocrats, Kwanami Kiyotsugu and his son Seami Motokiyo.

The drama they served, and to the staging of which they greatly contributed, was performed on a rectangular platform open on two or three sides to the audience, with the chorus squatting in one of the wings and the musicians playing backstage. Eight to twelve persons in native dress comprised a chorus which sang the actor's words for him when his dance-movements interfered with his delivery and commented on the action. The musicians employed a stick-drum, a hand-drum played with a thimbled finger or with the bare hand, and a flute reserved for special intervals such as the beginning and the climax of the play. The actors, generally sparingly used, were rigidly divided in function. The principal actor or *shite* danced the important business of the play while the secondary actor or *waki* engaged him in dialogue and introduced or explained the story; a variable number of *tsure* or assistants to both the *shite* and the *waki* facilitated the proceedings. Rigidly set movements, slow and solemn, characterized the dancing of each of the gorgeously costumed and masked performers. Their stylized gestures, the subtlety of their delivery, and the insinuating rhythm of their dance tapped out on the wooden platform produced the effect of a rite. The stage itself, although it dispensed with illusive scenery, was well appointed with conventionalized properties, an open framework representing a boat or a chariot, four posts covered with a board serving as a palace or house. These conventions have been carefully preserved up to the present time.

Suiting the text to the stage, the dramatists created a pattern which must be considered the epitome of compression and delicacy. The actual action was reduced to a minimum but was transfigured by the graceful poetry in which a large part of the play was written. The verse, embellished with parallelism and "pivot words" (words used in two senses) was chanted, while the prose passages gradually rose in exaltation until they turned into poetry. But the most unique device of all was the reminiscent or retrogressive form in which the story was generally cast.

First came an opening couplet, in most instances a dignified philosophical statement like

> *Life is a lying dream, he only wakens*
> *Who casts the World aside.*
> *We who on shallow hills have built our home*
> *In the heart's deep recess seek solitude.*[5]

Then the *waki* appeared and named himself, announced his destination as well as his purpose, and traveled long distances during the course of a brief travel song. In time this personage would meet a strange character who behaved mysteriously and turned out to be the hero of the play, frequently the ghost of the departed to whose shrine the traveler had repaired. And at this point the drama reached its most dramatic section, for the strange character, alive or dead, remembered his past and the earthly climax which had ended in exile or death. He remembered his final struggle with intense feeling, rapture and grief, acting out his reminiscence in a dance until, spent with passion, he disappeared.

Here was largely ghostly drama recalling the primitive theatre when the actor merely reincarnated the spirit of a heroic ancestor. On a higher plane, however, here was also the deeply troubling yet assuaging drama of reminiscence; it suggested the brevity and vanity of human existence. Delicate as a Japanese drawing, full of grace and individuality, and exuding the *Weltschmerz* of the Buddhist belief that all life was illusion, the plays commended themselves to the aristocracy by their charm. The plays, moreover, pleased the nobility by recalling the heroic feudal age of Japan. The nobles were not even above acting in the Noh along with professionals and favorite passages were recited by them at private entertainments. By this means a vital relation was established between the drama and the upper classes.

First to give the Noh its artistic form was Kwanami Kiyotsugu, a priest associated with temple theatricals, who was born in 1333 and died in 1384 after composing fifteen plays. The famous Shogun Yoshimitsu, after watching him perform an early Noh, took him into his service and so established the tradition of aristocratic patronage for the theatre. Yoshimitsu's favor extended to Kiyotsugu's talented son Seami Motokiyo and was apparently so marked as to arouse the envy of members of the court. One of them recorded surprise in his diary that the Shogun and the boy should share the same meat and eat from the same vessels. Basking in this friendship, Kwanami Kiyotsugu, who may have contributed the music and staging and merely adapted older texts, established the high estate of the Noh in a number of excellent pieces.

Of these his *Sotoba Komachi* is perhaps the best and certainly the most affecting for the Western reader: Komachi was supremely beautiful in her youth, and beauty bred pride when many lovers courted her. Among them was Shii no Shosho who traveled long distances to win her. But she stipulated that she would listen to his entreaties only after he had visited her for a hundred nights. Braving the elements he made the long journey ninety-nine times but at last died of exhaustion on the hundredth night. Great suffering followed her cruelty, for the former beauty became old and unsightly, friends and fortune forsook her, and she was left a tattered beggar-woman bereft of her senses and possessed by her lover in a manner familiar to us from *The Dybbuk*. Her story is revealed by her to a priest who has come to visit the shrines of the capital, and the ghost of her lover retraces the fatal wooing until he finally leaves the woman's spent body. Not only is the play rich in pathos, but its characters are vividly realized, and the tellingly simple poetry harmonizes with the story. An example of Kwanami's style is to be found in Shosho's miming of his night-journey:

> *Pulling down over my ears the tall, nodding hat,*
> *Tying over my head the long sleeves of my hunting cloak,*
> *Hidden from the eyes of men,*
> *In moonlight, in darkness,*
> *On rainy nights I traveled; on windy nights,*
> *Under a shower of leaves; when the snow was deep.*

This playwright's forte appears to have been just this evocation of the gentler emotions and their tragic consequences. It makes itself felt in another famous play, *The Maiden's Tomb*, whose beautiful heroine is punished for the rivalry of her lovers which resulted in their killing a mandarin duck—a fowl renowned for its loyalty to its mate. In grief she drowned herself, thus burdening her soul with another sin. Consequently, she has to endure the torments of the eightfold Buddhist hell, although the priest in the play declares that her infernal existence is actually *illusion*, like all other things.

Kiyotsugu's son, however, wrote some of his best work in the stronger vein of heroic drama, reviving the events of the eleventh-century "Wars of the Roses" between the powerful Taira and Minamoto tribes; Seami was fascinated by the heroic spirit. *Kagekiyo* is perhaps the most powerful of his pieces with its story of the downfall of the great Taira hero Kagekiyo. When the Minamoto triumphed, this intrepid soldier was exiled to a distant place where he became a blind beggar. In the play he is being sought out by his daughter who has grown up into a young woman during his exile. After an arduous journey she finally arrives at his retreat and meets the blind man (not a ghost in this play) who is ashamed to be seen by her. He sends her away after recounting some of the heroic deeds for which he became known as "Kagekiyo the Passionate."

The tone of reminiscence is established at the beginning with the lovely epigram

> *Late dewdrops are our lives that only wait*
> *Till the wind blows, the wind of morning blows,*

and the pathos of the old hero's plight is nowhere so vividly realized as in his story of how he stopped the rout of his soldiers by engaging the enemy's leader Mionoya in a duel and putting him to flight. Admiring each other, the two opponents exchanged banter and went their respective ways, his foe exclaiming:

> *O mighty Kagekiyo, how terrible the strength of your arm—*
> *And the other called back to him, "Nay, say rather How strong the shaft*
> *Of Mionoya's neck!" So laughed they across the battle,*
> *And went off each his way.*

This bitter-sweet reminiscence ended, Kagekiyo forgets the rest, the "things unforgettable"; remembering only that he is old, he bids his child, "the candle in his darkness," a sad farewell.

In another of Seami's short historical plays the *Atsumori*, Buddhist idealism is satisfied when the rival heroes of the clans become reconciled. The priest Rensei, formerly the warrior Kumagai, having repented of sinful warfare seeks out the tomb of Atsumori, whom he had slain in battle. The ghost of his enemy appears to him in the guise of a reaper and re-enacts his last fight when he was left behind while his fleet sailed away. But just as he is about to hurl himself at his slayer he becomes reconciled with him, since

> *the other is grown gentle*
> *And calling on Buddha's name*
> *Has obtained salvation for his foe. . . .*

In a related play *Tsunemasa,* as well as in other Noh plays, the Buddhist hatred of bloodshed is expressed by the unqualified manner in which the greatly admired national heroes are nevertheless consigned to the Japanese inferno because they lived and died by the sword or were guilty of the passion of hatred. The priests of Buddha may not have succeeded in stamping out the military spirit so strongly rooted in the warrior caste, but they expressed their disapproval of bloodshed as best they could in the works which they influenced. It remained for the nomadic Arabs and the piratical European Nordics to first supply a heaven instead of an inferno for military heroes.

Seami, and not Chikamatsu, was the real Shakespeare of his people, and he left behind him not only ninety-three of these playlets (they are no longer than short one-acters) but a number of treatises on his art. He formulated the laws of acting and went to the heart of the Noh with his concept of *Yugen* which is to the Japanese what Aristotle's catharsis is to the Western World. *Yugen,* as Arthur Waley declares, means "what lies beneath the surface; the subtle as opposed to the obvious; the hint, as opposed to the statement." [6] The extent of this Japanese master's talent is further shown by the fact that he composed both the music and libretti of his various pieces.

The art that the father and son perfected remained associated with their descendants, who continued to be favored by the shoguns. Seami's son-in-law in the fifteenth century wrote twenty-two plays, and the Indian summer of the Noh play lasted for about a century and a half after Seami died in 1444 at the ripe old age of eighty-three. The complete collection of Noh drama contains more than two hundred and thirty individual pieces, several of which are produced on the same program with comic interludes of slight distinction known as *kyogen,* very much as the Greek tragedies were followed by satyr-plays.

The Noh has had a guarded reception in the West, where some writers have considered it inferior literature because it foregoes the minuscule perfection of Japanese poetry. A few writers like W. G. Aston, who see the drama only in terms of conventional European patterns and are sorely troubled by violations of the unities, have considered the plays of little dramatic value. Others have described Noh drama as something so esoteric that it is allegedly beyond the comprehension of the West, and poor translations have added to our difficulties. We owe a great debt, therefore, to ·Arthur Waley who has translated the plays with poetic feeling and straightforwardness. A common-sense attitude toward the flexible nature of dramatic action, combined with some imaginativeness and sensibility, will find these little dance-dramas a vivid condensation or sublimation of experience.

The only other works of the Japanese theatre worthy of notice arose from the meeting of Eastern and Western culture in the nineteenth century. Shakespeare won favor with the Japanese, and all of his plays were translated in our time by the scholar Tsubouchi. A museum ·is maintained in his honor at Waseda University, in Tokyo. However, the tenor of Japanese censorship was amusingly illustrated when in December 1938 the police of Osaka forbade a performance of *Hamlet* because it might be "injurious to public morals." The British-owned *Japanese Chronicle* of Kobe countered with the quotation: "There are more things in heaven and earth, Horatio, than are dreamt of in your philosophy." [7]

Tolstoy, Ibsen, Strindberg, Shaw, and O'Neill exerted a powerful influence on the later Japanese writers. Among the best known of these have been the Tolstoyan Takeo Arishima who divided his property among his tenants two years before his death in 1923, Saneatsu Mushakoji, and Senzaburo Sudzuki. *Burning Her Alive,* a one-act play by Sudzuki, is a particularly effective Strindbergian treatment of an artist's jealousy.

Still the glory of the Japanese stage remains the Noh play to which little was contributed after the beginning of the modern drama in Europe. Kiyotsugu was Chaucer's contemporary and Seami's works were written more than fifty years before *Everyman* was produced in England. It is logical, therefore, to take up the survey of European drama at the point when it began to live again, at first unevenly but vividly in the medieval religious plays and later with the splendor that made it a worthy successor to the theatre of Greece.

Before his death in 1939, Sidney Howard, in collaboration with Will Irwin, helped to call attention to another Chinese classic, and one of the most affecting, *Pi-pa-ki* (*The Story of the Lute*) which stems from the 14th century and continued to retain its popularity on the Chinese stage. The provincial hero, who loves his wife and his parents devotedly, goes to the capital in pursuance with his father's injunctions to seek fame and fortune at court. Winning great honors in a public examination, he is compelled to marry a princess, whose father prevents him from communicating with his family. A famine reduces the family to beggary and his parents, tended with extreme self-sacrifice by their daughter-in-law, die. His desolate wife goes to the capital to seek him out and forgives her husband after learning that he was not entirely guilty.

Part IV

THE MEDIEVAL COMMUNION

In that curiously remote age which lives for us mainly as a memory of armored knights and cowled priests one comes upon a drama that is a medley of austere piety and observant humanity. The most striking feature of the medieval theatre is that it began as a communion in church and ended as a communal festa. Once again humanity, emerging with the aid of religion from a new tidal wave of barbarism, found the drama a potent organ for both common reality and aspiration. Once again the stage demonstrated its suitability as a meeting-ground for God and man. God was, in fact, the visible and invisible protagonist of medieval plays. At the same time the theatre once more afforded society an opportunity to assert an essential spiritual unity, giving the individual an indispensable but relatively unregimented sense of belonging to something larger than himself. Out of this, in the Middle Ages, arose that mixture of reverence and joy or of bondage and release which is so often the very soul of the drama.

IX

PLAYWRIGHTS OF THE CHURCH AND THE GUILD

I THE PLAYWRIGHT IN THE CHURCH

TIME and again conditions arise in society which seem to spell the death of the theatre, but the desire to dramatize never disappears. Rudimentary drama appears in the community and ultimately flowers as some important dramatic form the moment men develop cohesion in some point of view or aim.

The dark ages of medieval Europe from the fifth to the tenth century were barren of important drama, and for six centuries the theatre was, so to speak, padlocked. When Europe was parceled out into small communities and men led an uncertain existence in them, the Roman theatres were abandoned to decay and it seemed that the Church had completely displaced the temple of Dionysus. Nevertheless, the theatre was dormant rather than dead, and even this statement is an exaggeration with respect to anything but the written drama. Even the early Middle Ages are found teeming with theatrical and semi-theatrical activity, for in addition to itinerant troupes of mimes and acrobats who survived the collapse of the Roman empire Europe was experiencing new developments.

Primitive Teutonic rites foreshadow the drama. In the countryside, the half-converted and the intractable heathen or people of the heath perform agricultural magic dealing with the death and resurrection of the vegetation. Unable to stamp out these vestiges of paganism, the highly politic Church associates them with the festivals of Christmas and Easter. This is the origin of the Christmas mummings, Maypole celebrations, dances, and St. George plays which survived well into modern times. Among examples of this curious form of drama are the sword dances which were recorded at Revesby Abbey in Lincolnshire and taken down by Sir Walter Scott in the Shetland Islands,[1] and such extravaganzas as the St. George plays. Thomas Hardy was to remember one of the latter when he came to write *The Return of the Native*. Verily St. George and his dragon, Old King Cole, Father Christmas, the Turkish champion, Giant Blunderbore, and the doctor who revives ("resurrects") the combatants after they are all slain were characters

139

too close to childhood fantasy and magical thinking to be easily forgotten.

Poets—the scops or bards—embody dramatic elements in their recitations. Minstrels recite poems with appropriate pantomime or romantic tales like *Aucussin and Nicolette* and farcical ones like the *fabliaux.* Many early ballads are charged with drama and are dramatic in structure, since they tell their story by means of dialogue and observe the principle of dramatic progression. Some of them, the Robin Hood ballads, actually develop into short plays in which the romantic brigand challenges the regime of the Norman conquerors of England. Tournaments, public executions, state and religious processions, marionette players and jongleurs or acrobats supply the color and mass excitement of theatre, without crystallizing into plays.

It is the Church, however, that provides the greatest ferment for the rising drama. At first the Churchmen who despised the popular theatre were content with pious efforts in the monasteries where classical learning had not been completely destroyed by the crumbling of the Roman state. We are familiar with the work of a determined nun in the Benedictine Gandersheim Abbey in Saxony, Hrosvitha, variously acclaimed as "the Christian Sappho" and "the loud voice from Gandersheim," who glorified martyrdom and chastity in pieces modeled after the refined comedies of Terence.* These exercises in the Benedictine Cloisters were addressed to a small circle of the learned, and the spirit of this theatrical activity, which may well have advanced the histrionic talent

---

* Hrosvitha's life reflects a minor renascence in Germany during the reign of the Saxon Ottos. Otto the Great was a patron of the convent of Gandersheim, which became a center of cultured womanhood. Hrosvitha's six comedies (*Gallicanus, Dulcitius, Sapientia, Abraham, Callimachus,* and *Paphnutius*) are written in wretched Latin. Although they are called "comedies" and were written to supplant the plays of Terence, which she deprecated, they lack humor. Only the *Dulcitius,* in which a lustful pagan governor embraces sooty pots in the illusion that he is courting three Christian virgins, contains comic elements. These comedies belong to medieval martyrology, and are graced with the title "comedy" only in the medieval sense, as in Dante's *Divine Comedy*—that is, because they end happily with the salvation of their heroines when these are martyred. Nevertheless, Hrosvitha is important because she anticipated the later development of the miracle play and the "moralities." The *Dulcitius,* for example, deals with three saintly maidens and contains two miracles: one when two of the virgins cheat the stake by dying before they are cast into the flames and their bodies remain untouched by the fire; another, when the third martyr is transported to a mountain by two supernatural figures and can be slain only when the soldiers shoot arrows into her. The *Sapientia* is an allegory like *Everyman* with such abstract characters as Wisdom, Faith, Hope, and Charity. In addition, the learned nun composed a number of Latin poems commemorating the reign of Otto and the history of her convent. One of them tells the Faustian story of Theophilus who sold his soul to the devil. An ardent feminist would find much comfort in the career of this tenth-century lady who may be described as a saintly George Sand.

of the clergy who later performed for *hoi polloi,* lacked the popular elements so necessary for the creation of vital drama.

Still the Church was bound to create more popular plays. It had the richest resources for the drama by virtue of its pre-eminent position in Europe. This haven of most of the lettered and gifted people of the dark ages could provide its own playwrights, and as the spiritual center of Europe it had an outlook upon life many degrees above that which prevailed among the barons and serfs. Church ritual, moreover, revolved around that death and resurrection of a God which proved so fruitful in the primitive history of theatre. Christianity's entire creed and literature was one great drama. "Do you sigh for the sordid shows of the theatre?" wrote Tertullian whose assault on the stage in his *De Spectaculis* may have given the old Roman theatre its *coup de grâce*. Behold is there a greater show than that of our faith, "the coming of the Lord . . . the glory of the rising saints . . . and that last and eternal day of judgment!"

Tertullian, who would have no traffic with the blasphemous breed of actors, was of course speaking only metaphorically when he glorified the drama that could be extracted from religion, and the theologian Arius, who dared to suggest the establishment of a Christian theatre to combat the pagan one, was naturally not heeded after his teachings were pronounced heretical. But Christian drama came inevitably as a response to the practical problem of bringing religion to an unlettered populace unable to understand the Latin responses and St. Jerome's Latin Bible.

The priesthood began to employ living tableaux like those described in connection with the Syrian worship of Tammuz, and added symbolic pantomime when it solemnly lowered the crucifix on Good Friday, hid it under the altar, and then raised it again with appropriate jubilation on Easter Day. Permanent sepulchres were soon erected for this purpose in the choir area, the spectacle became increasingly elaborate, and the dramatic representations began to acquire chanted dialogue preceded and followed by the great Latin hymns, for again as in Greece and the East the early medieval theatre was inseparable from music and lyric poetry. Thus the ocular translation of the Gospels which had begun in the plastic arts (in sculpture, painting, and stained glass) reached its climax in the drama.

By the ninth century a chanted dialogue or trope was inserted into the wordless sequences of the Easter morning mass. The chorus was divided into two antiphonal groups, with the white-winged angels standing guard over Christ's sepulchre on one side and the women who came seeking Christ's body on the other. The angels chanted: "Whom

seek ye in the sepulchre, O followers of Christ?" and the women or
Marys responded that they had come in search of "Jesus of Nazareth,
who was crucified." Thereupon the angels informed them that he was
not here but had risen as he had foretold, and commanded them to "Go
and announce that he is risen from the sepulchre." The news was greeted
with inexpressible joy, and the entire congregation rang out with the
glorious *Te Deum* that followed. This is the content of the earliest preserved text, the *Quem-quaeritis* trope found at St. Gall. In another version additional visual detail was furnished when the Marys, stooping
over the sepulchre, drew forth from it the Saviour's muslin wrappings
and, lifting them in full sight of the congregation, provided indisputable
evidence that Christ had risen. Slight as this playlet may seem to us,
it possessed highly dramatic values when augmented by the colored vest-
ments of the monks, the festive dress of the people, the imposing background of the church or cathedral, and the emotional state of the believers.

Moreover, this little scene was the epitome and climax of the whole
drama of Christianity and served as a foundation for the more developed plays of later times. From this dramatic rite, and from others
associated with Christmas containing representations of the child in
the manger (the trope known variously as *Tres Reges, the Magi,* and
Stella), the next step was elaboration of related material from the Bible
and even from the Apocrypha. Soon short plays in Latin were supplied by talented priests and were presented—at first in the choir, then
in the larger space of the nave—with music now specially composed for
the dialogue. The effect was consequently greatly heightened, as when
the words for God were set for tenor, bass and alto. By the thirteenth
century the evolution of the trope into what may be called drama was
complete. Even comedy began to enter into the ecclesiastical theatre
when, for example, much was made in the early thirteenth-century Sienna
Passion Play of Mary Magdalene's purchase of cosmetics from a merchant.

The Easter trope grew into a liturgical play (variously known as
representatio, representatio miraculi, and simply *miraculum* or miracle
play) like the *Sepulchrum* of Orléans, which consists of three episodes
—the visit of the three Marys, their imparting of the news to Peter
and John that Christ has risen, whereupon the two saints race to the
tomb, and the appearance of Christ to Mary Magdalene just as she
cries out "My heart is burning with desire to see my Lord." For Mon-
day of the Passion Week there was such a play as the twelfth-century
Peregrini or *Wayfarers* of the Cathedral of Rouen, in which the travelers on the road to Emmaus meet Christ and fail to recognize him
until seated at the table he breaks bread "unto them" and disappears.

For Christmas there were plays like the *Pastores* or *Shepherds* of Rouen. Twelve days later came the *Magi,* in which the three foreign kings appear resplendent in their robes and bringing rare gifts, and a related play like the *Herodes* of Orléans in which, upon learning that the king of the world has been born, Herod comports himself like the ranting hero referred to by Shakespeare. Historically even more important, although far less effective, is the *Prophetae* or *Prophets* in which the liturgical drama is already acquiring material from the Old Testament and preparing the way for such charming plays in the vernacular as the Brome *Abraham and Isaac.* Among the characters of the Prophets are Isaiah, John the Baptist with his long hair, and even Balaam upon his articulate ass; and their prophecies are supported eclectically, in characteristic medieval fashion, by Virgil with his ink-horn and quill pen, the Roman Sibyl, and Nebuchadnezzar. . . .

Still another step was the use of the hagiology of the Church as a source for additional story material. Saint plays began to be composed in connection with saints' days and church processions, the most elaborate of them being associated with the spring festival of Corpus Christi founded by Pope Urban IV in 1264 in honor of the Sacred Host. Corpus Christi became, in fact, the chief occasion for the presentation of the miracle or so-called "mystery" plays, as well as of the saint plays. The two English plays in the vernacular, *The Conversion of St. Paul* and *Saint Mary Magdalen,* are within the biblical canon and are not greatly embellished, but the moment the latter-day saints became dramatic characters the medieval penchant for martyrology and miracles ran riot in the theatre. St. George has his dragon in plays composed in his honor, and Saint Nicholas becomes the subject of fanciful elaborations suitable to this prototype of Santa Claus. In one of the plays, produced probably between matins and vespers on St. Nicholas Day, he provides the daughters of a ruined nobleman with gold and husbands. In another play, the *Adeodatus,* he is faithful to his vocation as protector of children when he solves a kidnaping case and restores an abducted son to his father. Numerous miracles attributed to the Virgin, whose cult flourished mightily in France, were likewise celebrated.

As there were many saints and saint days, the number of these plays was considerable, especially among the French, and the authors who supplied them evidently enjoyed sufficient popularity to be remembered, an unusual distinction in the Middle Ages. The Norman scholar Geoffrey came to England after being associated with the University of Paris. His *Ludus de S. Katharina* apparently contained some secular details that troubled his conscience so greatly that he took religious orders.

Hilarius, an Englishman who spent much of his life in France and followed the great Abelard, dramatized the stories of Daniel and Lazarus but was perhaps best known for the St. Nicholas play. Although these dramatized legends were inferior to the strictly biblical drama, they marked an advance in the free handling of material and the introduction of secondary characters. With the saint plays, the churchly drama written in Latin and enacted in the Church reached the limit of its potentialities, and the drama could move forward only by employing vernacular dialogue and by providing free play for the common tastes and interests. But once the drama acquired a rounded subject in the biblical narratives and became pliable, as well as understandable to those who knew no Latin, it could be taken over by the active middle classes in the towns. Performances, moreover, outgrew the physical bounds of the cathedrals and had to be played in the churchyard; finally, they were transferred to the streets and public squares. Once more, as in Greece, the drama left the church.

2 THE PLAYWRIGHT OUT OF THE CHURCH

It cannot be said that ecclesiastic officialdom was sorry to see it go, for the momentum of dramatic development made the theatre a somewhat dubious ally of religion. Its spirit was becoming rebellious, and its excrescences in the church proper became increasingly offensive. The lower clergy, consisting of sub-deacons, clerical students and other unchastened members of the younger generation, was enlivening the austerities of ecclesiastic discipline with increasingly ribald displays. It was even venting resentment against episcopal authority in the Feast of Fools or Feast of Asses. In this "shindig" of the lower clergy, which originated in the Feast of Circumcision and contained more than one suggestion of vestigial fertility rites, a stench was used as incense, a real ass was brought into the Church, the responses were brayed, dice were cast on the altar, a mock bishop was elected, mock sermons were preached, and obscene words were sung to the sacred tunes. The burlesque was then concluded with a riotous procession through the town, sometimes being received as it deserved when virtuous matrons poured slops on the revelers. Here was a typical form of release in the medieval church, which had its counterpart in the non-dramatic antics of the wandering scholars or *Goliardi* (all of them loosely attached to the church) and of clerics like the irrepressible poet Villon who was not above robbing the church treasury. The Feast of Fools (later paralleled in England by a Feast of Boys ruled by a "Boy Bishop") contributed comic elements to the medieval theatre. But these revels, whose literary value does not rise above the Beauvais Cathedral's text of the *Festa Asinaria* and is at its best mere parody, could only offend the upper clergy. The bishops prayed earnestly against the "execrable custom . . . by which the Feast of Circumcision is defiled" and finally took action to expel the entire drama.

The expulsion was not thorough and the theatre did not follow the same development in every country, but the trend was in every case toward secular drama, and may be most clearly described by confining the picture to its most significant portions. In France, the religious plays become the property of the towns. Mons, for example, devoted four days to the presentation of successive episodes of the Old and New Testaments, and spent huge sums to defray the expenses of productions which despite their crudity were colorful, realistic to the point of naïveté, and ingenious enough to employ pulleys, platforms, trapdoors for the devils, fake bodies for the martyrdom of the saints, and mechanical animals. Productions like this *Mystery of the Passion* at Mons in 1501, regarding which there are full particulars in a recently discovered prompt book, give evidence of a tremendous theatrical development in all departments.

The setting consisted of numerous mansions or "stations" arranged in a semi-circle (there were sixty-seven of them in Mons), or in a straight line as at Valenciennes, each being decorated for a different episode. Most exalted was of course the "station" of Heaven where God the Father appeared, and most vivid was the booth called Hell-mouth, shaped to resemble a dragon's mouth and amply supplied with devils in disguise. Live animals such as rabbits, horses, birds and lambs were employed on this multiple stage, much use was made of lighting effects to irradiate the nativity or give a realistic representation of Hell. Color was used not only lavishly but suggestively, as when the archangel Raphael's face was painted red. Costuming was also not only gorgeous but imaginative; the Apostles, for example, wore white robes, and the devils were grotesquely arrayed and masked as in the fantastic paintings of Hieronymus Bosch. The cast was enormous; three hundred and seventeen actors were used at Mons for about three times as many roles and were rehearsed for forty-eight days.

Here, in other words, was theatre running riot and engaging the entire community instead of being confined to a dozen or so city blocks in Manhattan and a select theatre-going public. All over Europe these spectacles were duplicated with great vividness.

In various English towns each trade guild assumed responsibility for a single play to be presented (except in a few cities where stationary stages were used) on wagons, high two-story scaffolds on wheels with the lower story reserved as a kind of dressing room. Except where two pageant wagons were used together, each perambulating stage appeared at a stated time at a stated place, presented its play, and moved on to succeed another play at some other street or square. Each place was visited by a succession of pageant wagons until the complete story from the Creation of the World to the Second Judgment had been enacted. In other particulars, however, the productions resembled those of the Mons or Valenciennes Passion Play, their spectacular character being proportionate to the ostentation of the respective craft or trade guilds.

The actors in these plays—which came to be known as "mysteries," not because their content was mystic but because they were produced under the auspices of the masters of the guilds—were in some instances professional minstrels or mimes and members of the lower clergy like Chaucer's Jolly Absalon who "plaieth Herod on a scaffold hie." The latter even became a chartered company in London in 1233 and are known to have been playing before royalty as late as 1409. But for the most part the performers were amateur members of the trade guilds who possessed some talent. The plays would be parceled out among the crafts with some propriety; the plasterers were assigned the creation of the world, the fishmongers and mariners chose Noah and his ark for their subject, and the bakers presented the Last Supper in the city of York. The expense list of one production included such items as "a pair of gloves for God . . . four pair of angels' wings . . . a pound of hemp to mend the angels' heads . . . and a link for setting the world on fire." [2]

Who wrote most of the mystery plays we do not know, as they are subject to the same anonymity which covers much of the art and literature of the Middle Ages. In England only the redactor or possible author of the Chester cycle is known by name—Ralph Higden, poet of the *Polychronicon*. Clearly the plays were founded on the Latin liturgical drama and must be attributed in the first instance to talented members of the priesthood. But the evidence of folk authorship is marked in the mystery plays, and it is more than likely that these playlets were refashioned and elaborated by the members of the guilds in England and by miscellaneous laymen elsewhere. The plays are often crude in structure, style and versification, their action lags, their characterization is conventional, and their content is slight. Yet taken as a whole, and we must remember that they were in the main regarded as merely episodes of a single drama that might last several days, they possess the sweep and excitement of great drama to such an extent that we forget their imperfections. England, for example, had many cycles; and in France there were three groups of plays, dealing respectively with the Old Testament, the New Testament, and the Acts of the Apostles, to which may be added another, independent cycle, the *Miracles de Nostre Dame* in honor of the Virgin.

In Central Europe, the cycles developed in the same manner and were equally numerous. Christmas plays appeared in Germany by the eleventh or twelfth century, Easter or Passion Plays were developed by the thirteenth century, and complete cycles amalgamating both Christmas and Easter pieces reached their zenith in the fifteenth century. Augsburg, Freiburg, Heidelberg and other cities played host to the multiple stages on which the drama was enacted by hundreds of men, women, and children while the rest of the population provided the audience. Seats were supplied for the nobility, and unruly spectators were likely to be pulled by the actor-devils into their mimic Hell-mouth. Here, too, the staging of the religious drama made abundant use of machines and fireworks, and intermissions were filled with choral singing by the guild of mastersingers. The German translations and adaptations of the Bible in the short rhymed lines of the plays gave the common man his only inkling of the words of the Bible, and undoubtedly helped to sow the seeds of the Reformation which made such a point of acquainting the people with the holy book. For saint plays Germany showed less taste than France; but the nation was hospitable to miracles of the Virgin like Theodor Schernberg's *Play of Frau Jutten* (1480) in which the Devil leads Lady Jutten to pursue learning in male attire until she becomes Pope. She is dragged away to the infernal regions after giving birth to a child, but is saved by the intercession of Christ's Mother.

Strange things happened to this Catholic body of drama in Germany when Protestantism filled the land with religious contentions between the followers of Luther and the papists. The former frowned on the miracle plays. They tried pruning them of irreverent humor or seeming idolatry and forbidding the appearance of Christ on the stage. Efforts were also made to inject the Reformation into the cycles, and a certain Bartholomäus Krüger in the sixteenth century even introduced Luther into the miracle plays. The theatre veered with the wind of social and political change.

Still the medieval drama was not sufficiently altered to suit the Lutheran faith, and it died out in the Protestant principalities. Its ultimate substitute in those regions was the dramatic chanting of the gospels in the oratorio form, which represents in fact a return to the early tropes or chanted dialogues. In the oratorios of Johann Sebastian Bach one may well find the highest transformation of the Catholic miracle plays into Protestant drama refined of any suspicion of "idolatry" and irreverence. The characters of the oratorio are not mimed, and no histrionic or scenic devices detract from the spirituality and universality of the performance. That this sublimation of the theatre should have resulted in such flights of human genius as Bach's early eighteenth-century *St. John's Passion* and the great *St. Matthew's Passion* more than compensates one for the decline of the regular religious drama in Protestant Germany.

To some extent the Reformation actually helped to preserve the miracle plays here and there. The Catholic counter-reformation of the seventeenth century saw in the plays an effective instrument of faith and encouraged their survival into our own day. To this reanimation of the failing medieval drama we owe the present Passion Plays in the Tyrol, Bavaria, and Switzerland. The most famous survival, the Oberammergau play, was created in 1662 by combining two Augsburg cycles of the fifteenth and sixteenth centuries. Performed once in every ten years by the townspeople, who ply their humble trades during the long interval, this Bavarian Passion Play still supplies a good inkling of what the religious drama of the Middle Ages was like.

Individual plays of merit, belonging to the cyclic type of drama, abounded on the continent, one of the most important being the transitional *Adam*, written in French and Latin probably about the middle of the twelfth century and performed in the vicinity of a church, since the stage-directions have "God" moving into and coming out of the house of worship. The plot is the familiar one of the first couple and the serpent and the death of Abel at the hands of his brother Cain, followed by a brief epilogue in which the patriarchs and prophets (including the indispensable Nebuchadnezzar) foretell the coming of the Saviour. The charm of the play lies in the dialogue which possesses many lines of genuine dramatic poetry, as when Eve, regretting her sin, declares, "The rib the body hath betrayed" [3] and Adam complains, " 'Twas corn we sowed—thistles spring up instead." Adam is a typical husband who reproaches Eve vigorously, Eve an inquisitive but repentant female, Abel a prig, and Cain a skeptic as well as a miser. The prophets are, alas, dull gentlemen, although their words are frequently winged. A Provençal play, which begins with the marriage of the Virgin and concludes with the Nativity is notable for its characterization of Joseph as a perturbed old husband married to the young virgin who conceives so strangely—the Gallic touch, no doubt; a *Nativity* is the work of the fifteenth-century nun Katherine Bourlet.[4] Germany boasts a fine—if characteristically anti-Semitic—sample in the Redentin play.

To capture the quality of medieval drama at its best it is necessary, however, to turn to the cycles written in England possibly with the aid of French originals, as well as to the best individual pieces of the English school.

The old town of Wakefield in Yorkshire had such a cycle, the manuscript of which was preserved in the library of the Towneley family in

Lancashire. It consists of thirty-two plays distinguished for their vivacity, familiar treatment of sacred matter, and flavorsome dialect. Here the rough and ready English spirit asserts itself in distinctly native form, undiluted by the literature of chivalry or the refinements of feudal upper-class culture. The fourteenth-century Wakefield drama festival, which lasted three days during the feast of Corpus Christi,* began in Heaven with God on his throne creating the world with the aid of lanterns, bushes, and wooden birds and beasts. The cherubim who are quiring the Creator are particularly impressed with his creation of the dazzlingly bright angel Lucifer, and their lovely hymn to the archangel fills Lucifer with fatal pride. He therefore tries to occupy God's throne during his absence and is cast into Hell along with his followers. God resumes his throne and calmly proceeds to complete his work, molding Adam out of clay and Eve out of the first man's rib, and warning both against the tree of life. But Adam, like any farmer eager to explore the terrain, goes away and leaves Eve exposed to the wiles of the serpent.

The next playlet, presented by the glovers of Wakefield on a second pageant wagon, enacts the death of Abel. This piece is a farce, supplied with a saucy plowboy Garcio who badgers the spectators as well as his master Cain. Indulging in one of his pranks he weights the plow with stones and Cain, irritated by the contrary behavior of his beasts of burden, deals him a blow in the face which is promptly returned. Cain is a typical Yorkshire farmer, gruff, surly, and close-fisted. Unlike his gentle brother Abel he addresses God with a blunt prayer, and grudges him the few sheaves of thanks-offering which he is urged to give. Irritated when his sacrifice fails to burn and fills his lungs with smoke, Cain quarrels with his officious brother and kills him. Blasphemer that he is, he has no respect for God's warning voice—"Why," he asks gruffly, "Who is that Hob over the wall?" But the play is not allowed to end on a tragic note, and Abel's murder is followed by an anti-climactic scene of excessive buffoonery.

The Noah play that follows is written in the same vein when Noah the pious patriarch is saddled with a termagant who delays his departure in the ark and is received with a flogging by the harassed husband. She is not, however, easily tamed, refuses to sue for mercy, and returns his blows efficiently. Next come the pageants of the sacrifice of Isaac, in which the relationship between father and son is effectively, if discursively, dramatized; Jacob's victory over Esau; the former's wrestling-bout with the Angel; Moses' presentation of the ten

* At first the cycles were divided between Christmas and Easter, each feast having its appropriate plays; then the two cycles were combined and performed on Corpus Christi day, the principal holiday of the fourteenth century.

commandments, along with sundry prophecies; and Moses' triumph over Pharaoh.

These plays are followed by a New Testament series, beginning with a burlesque in which Caesar Augustus, represented as a fatuous bully who swears by Mahomet (an anomalous detail which shows the extent to which the crusades affected the popular imagination) is enraged to discover that Christ is about to be born. The next pageant is the Annunciation, and here in a lovely scene tidings are brought to Mary; and simple old Joseph is perturbed no end by his virgin wife's condition. Then follow two pageants representing the night watch and adoration of the shepherds, farcical in tone and characterization. The shepherds of the first piece are Yorkshire boors who quarrel with each other and make a ludicrous attempt to imitate the "Gloria" of the angels that startles them during their vigil. But they are touchingly devout in the presence of the Christ child in the manger, and the play rises to heights of tenderness when these simple men offer the infant their humble gifts—a little wooden coffer, a bottle, and a ball.

The second piece generally known as the *Second Shepherds' Play* is even better. The best farce among the mystery plays and a perfect product of popular humor, it is a little masterpiece of realism. A northern winter provides the setting, and the inadequately clothed and nourished shepherds are cold. The note of social protest is struck immediately by the first shepherd, and we know at once that the common people are introducing their travail into the religious drama when he declares:

> *We're so burdened and banned,*
> *Overtaxed and unmanned.*
> *We're made tame to the hand*
> *   Of these gentry men.*
> *Thus they rob us of our rest, our Lady them harry!*
> *These men bound to their lords' behest they make the plow tarry.*
> *What men say is for the best, we find the contrary. . . .*[5]

This protest is amplified with feeling, and it is perhaps all the more pertinent since it precedes the birth of the Saviour who comes to establish justice and charity on earth. The third shepherd, who is a servant to the first and shows that he too is disgruntled with his lot, suggests that he has done some tall thinking lately:

> *That such servants as I, that sweat and swink,*
> *Eat our bread full dry gives me reason to think.*
> *Wet and weary we sigh while our masters wink. . . .*
> *But hear my oath, master, since you are at fault this way,*
> *I shall do this hereafter—work to fit my pay.*

In other words, he threatens some new-fashioned I.W.W. sabotage. . . .

We know nothing definitive about the author of this curiously modern work, but we may be sure that he was a writer of uncommon ability who had brooded somewhat upon the plight of the common people. He may well have been in sympathy with the popular Peasants' Revolt of the second half of the fourteenth century under Wat Tyler and the "mad priest" John Ball. The slogan of these revolutionists,

> *When Adam delved and Eve span,*
> *Who was then the gentleman!*

and the idealism of England's first proletarian (not revolutionary but Tolstoyan) poem *The Vision of Piers Plowman*, in which social injustice is indicted in the name of Christ the worker, lives again in this play. In the light of so much injustice in the world the brief conclusion in which the infant Saviour of mankind is acclaimed has a profoundly dramatic connection with the rest of the work instead of being an unrelated episode. The middle section of the piece, comprising the glorious farce of the sheep-stealer Mak who hides the sheep he has pilfered in his wife's bed, is also relevant. Mak's behavior and the picaresque farce of his wife's pretense that she has given birth to a child exemplify the sinfulness of man, even if the episode is sufficiently justified as simple humor.

Next in the York cycle comes the noisy pageant of the *Magi* in which Herod swaggers mightily, no doubt greatly elating his audience which could see him as a typical swashbuckling nobleman. This episode is followed by the Flight into Egypt, in which the old carpenter Joseph is aroused from his sleep and told to flee with Mary and the infant. In this domestic drama the emphasis is on characterization, especially that of the elderly husband. Then the sound and fury reassert themselves in *The Massacre of the Innocents,* in which Herod's soldiers are stoutly resisted by the mothers whose children they have come to slay. Several other plays succeed this early pogrom, among which the *Pagina Doctorum* or Doctors' Play provides a charming picture of the child Jesus impressing the Rabbis in the temple with his learning. The cycle ends with the Last Supper, the betrayal of Christ, the trial scene, the Crucifixion with all its brutality, the colorful and grotesque Harrowing of Hell, the glorious resurrection, and finally Doomsday. In these climactic pageants, the bubbling folk-humor is kept in check by the solemnity of the matter; and the drama, rough-hewn though it be, glows with the dark splendor of a Rembrandt painting.

The same story was told in numerous other cycles, sometimes more briefly and sometimes at greater length, for in the heyday of the "mysteries" there was hardly an important English city that lacked a series of biblical plays. London even had two, one lasting a week and a day, and a shorter series requiring three days. Many of them, like the London cycle, are lost, or survive only in a few individual pageants, the most famous of which is undoubtedly the tender and beautiful *Sacrifice of Isaac* (also known as *Abraham and Isaac*) preserved at Brome Manor in Suffolk. (It may, however, have been designed for independent production.) This best English mystery play of a serious nature, which has its counterpart in an independent Dublin version as well as in the pageants of several cycles, is uncommonly rich in poetry and possesses abundant suspense, economy, and pathos. Abraham's disinclination to sacrifice his son and Isaac's oscillation between fear and courage are admirably realized. The boy, upon learning that he is about to be killed, declares with simple pathos, "Now I would to God my mother were here on this hill." His tenderest thoughts are for his mother: "But, good father, tell ye my mother nothing. Say that I am in another country dwelling." When he is saved by the timely intervention of an angel, he is a trifle wary as he assists his father in preparing the fire for the sheep that takes his place on the altar. "But, father, if I stoop down low, Ye will not kill me with your sword, I trow?" And as they turn homeward, he remarks with a retrospective shudder, "I will nevermore come there, Except it be against my will!"

Among the cycles that have survived, the York pageants are notable for their relatively graceful poetry, which possesses variety of meter and cadence. The tone of this collection is dignified and devout, and the legendary material taken from the apocryphal gospels lends a touch of fantasy to the otherwise painfully realistic details of the Passion. The Roman standards bow in homage of Christ despite the standard-bearers' efforts to hold them upright, and Christ's cross is fashioned from a mystic wood—the "King's tree." There is also much gentleness in the York drama: Noah's home-life is properly spiritual, and the Joseph and Mary scenes are models of domestic tenderness. The Nativity in this series is a particularly beautiful little play permeated with simple but imaginative piety. It takes place on a bitter cold night; "the fellest freeze that ever I felt," says Joseph before he goes out for fuel. During his absence Mary gives birth to the Child and is transported with an ecstasy that destroys all consciousness of pain until she can declare, "I am all clad in comfort clear." When Joseph returns he is astonished at the sight that greets him: "O Mary! what sweet thing is that on thy knee?" He joins Mary in adoration, and the cattle low so eagerly for the infant that the parents lay it gently in the manger and let the beasts warm it with their breath. This pageant of the York thatchers epitomizes the devotional spirit of the entire series.

The twenty-five plays of the Chester cycle have been associated with the name of a local monk Ralph Higden, although he probably had a Latin and possibly a French source. But if Higden was responsible for the *élan* of the pageants he must have been a fun-loving cleric. As in the Wakefield cycle, a fine example of folk humor is the Noah play, in which the patriarch's obstreperous wife has to be carried into the ark by her sons and, resenting the suggestive tone of his "Welcome wife into this boat," greets her husband with a stout blow. Her gossiping friends are delightful characters when they console themselves with a bottle of malmsey wine and sing their tipsy song. Even the Nativity play of this series contains elements of fun. The shepherds who drink and eat heartily, quite unlike their humble counterparts in the Wakefield cycle, enjoy a wrestling bout and sing lustily. The Chester playwright was capable of devotion for all his hearty jests and earthly realism, but even then he does not altogether restrain his youthful vivacity; in the Doomsday pageant the author has the audacity to consign a pope to perdition, along with a queen and a loquacious Chester woman who may have been accorded this fate for adulterating her ale. Perhaps, too, the Chester players were also ingenious mechanics, for the Ascension play calls for spirits suspended in mid-air and the Emission of the Holy Ghost has angels in the upper air sprinkling flames over the Apostles' heads as in the famous El Greco painting.

Of the English cycles only one other has survived, the so-called N. town plays which were probably performed at Northampton, but they need not detain us with their relatively dull and undistinguished pageants. Although they were once called the Coventry plays, the real Coventry cycle is lost except for two surviving pageants best remembered for their lyrics—the Shepherd's Song, "As I rode out this enderes night" and the Song of the Bethlehem Mothers, "O sisters two, how may we do For the preserve this day. . . ." It is to the Celtic regions of Cornwall that one must go for another and really charming cycle, and the difference between it and the English pageants is a striking illustration of the folk-nature of the mystery plays despite their common liturgical origin.

The realistic tendency of a hard-headed middle-class unconcerned with the romanticism of the feudal barons is most marked in England. In the Cornwall cycle realism is less in evidence, and robust comedy is likewise absent. Instead, Celtic fantasy runs riot and symbolism is employed wherever possible. Here, more than in any series elsewhere in Europe, the mystery plays are close to medieval religious romance, bearing an affinity to Wolfram von Eschenbach's *Parzival* and other versions of the Holy Grail story. As in that product of the Celtic imagination the Welsh *Mabinogion,* life in the Cornish plays is full of mystery and wonder. As the cursed and exiled Adam tries to dig the ground for the first time the earth cries out and resists him until God comes down from heaven to rebuke it. When Adam is about to die, Seth journeys to Paradise and brings back three seeds of the apple Adam bit before his expulsion and places them on his dead father's tongue, whereupon three rods spring from his grave. These figure prominently in later episodes as symbols of salvation, for they are ultimately used for Christ's cross. Fantastic legends relating to Pontius Pilate follow the Crucifixion. He cannot be executed because Christ's seamless vesture is now in his possession, and when he stabs himself in desperation the earth bounds up and rejects his body. Thrown into the Tiber, he stains the river black until a rock is split asunder and devils, emerging therefrom, take the sinner away. With the Cornish plays we reach the furthest use of fabulous material and imaginative artistry in the "mystery" drama.

3 THE MORALISTS AND THE TUDOR PROPAGANDA PLAY

In the sixteenth century, Protestantism and Renaissance worldliness provided an inhospitable environment for the mystery plays associated with medieval Catholicism. Although they continued to be produced in England even as late as Shakespeare's boyhood, they were gradually eased out of the theatre. The Corpus Christi theatre festival was abandoned, the "vexillatores" or banner-bearers no longer sounded the "banns" advertising the performances, and the pageant wagons stood cracked and warped in the weather.

Other forms of drama which began to develop later in the Middle Ages, however, held their own more tenaciously. Of these the morality plays, didactic exercises inculcating the avoidance of vice and the observance of virtue by means of allegorical characters, were in vogue in England from the second quarter of the fifteenth century to the beginning of Elizabeth's reign in the second half of the sixteenth. The plays arose as a natural development from medieval allegories like the famous *Roman de la Rose* which Chaucer translated, as well as from popular homilies, moralizing passages in the miracle plays, and hortatory pieces like the fourteenth-century Paternoster or Lord's Prayer plays of York, Beverly and Lincoln regarding which only scattered records are available. France seems to have developed the morality form even earlier, and traces of it are to be found elsewhere on the Continent.

The moralities which, like the saint plays, were not produced on pageant wagons even in England but on stationary scaffolds arranged around a *platea* or place, were less spectacular than the mysteries. Although they provided entertainment by means of such figures as the Devil and the so-called Vice, a "flippant and persistent elf of evil" who appears under many names, they aimed at instruction and tended to be desiccated. They marked an advance in playwriting, it is true, in being longer, reaching out beyond strictly religious material, and requiring the author to invent his plot instead of taking it from scripture. Still they were, with the one glorious exception of *Everyman,* uninspired moralizations devoid of the pathos, humanity and exaltation of the mystery plays.

The one masterpiece among the moralities is the famous late fifteenth-century *Everyman* which may have been derived from the earlier Dutch morality *Elckerlijk* or from a common Latin source. It owes its power to the winning simplicity of its fable of how Everyman on his way to the grave is abandoned by everyone but Good-Deeds, who alone will accompany him to the judgment seat of God and plead for him. The ominous figure of Death, who comes straight from the *danse macabre* of medieval imagination and who attained such effective picturization in the work of Holbein and Dürer, wafts solemnity on the scene. The satire is homespun and trenchant when Fellowship leaves the dying man, when Cousin complains of a cramp in the toe which prevents him from accompanying Everyman on his last journey, and when Goods, a character shown on the stage surrounded by chests and bags, explains:

> *I lie here in corners trussed and piled so high,*
> *And in chests I am locked so fast,*
> *Also sacked in bags, thou mayest see with thine eye*
> *I cannot stir.*

The tragedy deepens when Strength, Discretion, Beauty, Five Wits and even Knowledge also leave him as they must leave every man. They have promised not to forsake him, but one by one they sing a different tune when Everyman declares that he is too faint to stand and must "turn to the earth, and there sleep." The pathos of such human details as Everyman's dread, his realization of failure, and his loneliness is too overwhelming to be lessened by the persistently moral tone of the play. It would be difficult to find a sermon so simple and yet so true and— *final.*

If the other moral plays had half the merit of *Everyman,* it would be worth stopping to examine them, since they are historically valuable. But when Miss Katharine Lee Bates writes of the moralities that "the very word is like a yawn" she is, in the main, distressingly close to the truth. The playwrights of the Church and the trade guild were followed by pedagogues and uninspired propagandists. *The Castle of Perseverance* owes its chief interest to the fact that it is the earliest and most primitive example of the *genre.* The second of the so-called Macro Moralities (so named because they were once in the possession of a certain Mr. Macro) is entitled *Mind, Will and Understanding,* attributes which are conspicuously absent in the play. The third Macro morality called *Mankind* shows Mercy and Mischief struggling for the soul of Mankind with somewhat better results.

Still later moralities are historically interesting when they enter the field of religious controversy. The embattled Protestant Bishop John Bale of Ossory thunders volubly against the Church of Rome in *The Treachery of Papists, The Three Laws of Christ* and in *King Johan*, an early historical play which presents King John as a noble king maligned and persecuted by the Church. In R. Wever's *Lusty Juventus* the hero is ultimately converted to the Reformed faith. The Scottish poet Sir David Lyndsay's *Satire of the Three Estates* calls for reformation of the church, as well as for social justice when "Pauper" bewails the tyranny of "Landlord" and "Clergy." The moralities of the early sixteenth century, moreover, became instruments of propaganda for Catholics as well as Protestants, and the Catholics had their *Hycke-Scorner* and *Interlude of Youth*.

Even the dangerous subject of politics entered the theatre—a rather remarkable advent in the absolutist period of the Tudors. The poet John Skelton's *Magnificence,* written about 1516, is a sermon against extravagance intended for Henry VIII whose tutor he had been. *Lord Governance,* acted before Cardinal Wolsey by the young lawyers of Gray's Inn, was so barbed that the wrathful Lord Chancellor sent its author John Roo and some of the performers to Fleet prison.

Still other moralities make an ardent plea for humanism or progressive education, and Sir Thomas More's circle of intellectuals appears to have been particularly impressed with the pedagogic possibilities of the theatre. In 1517 John Rastell, More's brother-in-law, wrote *The Four Elements* in advocacy of learning and filled his play with scientific matters including the once startling conclusion that the earth is round. Henry Medwall, who grew up with the author of the *Utopia* in the humanist Cardinal Morton's household, writes a similar eulogy on enlightenment in his otherwise desiccated *Nature. The Four Elements,* in 1519, also alludes to the discoveries of Amerigo Vespucci and maintains that theology must make way for science. The school teacher John Redmond, master of the choir boys of St. Paul's Cathedral, celebrated the romance between a student and Lady Science and satirized Ignorance and his mother Idleness or the older educational methods of scholasticism in *Wit and Science,* written in the fourth decade of the century.

The English moralities, in other words, adjusted themselves to the conditions of the Renaissance and Reformation. They remind one of the much shorter, and therefore occasionally more exciting, skits of the young revolutionary theatre of the early 1930's in America when stereotyped representations of Capital and Labor held forth on economic problems from many an improvised platform while the unemployed sold apples on the street-corners. Moralities continued to be written even after the dawn of the Elizabethan period and overlapped the radically different work of Shakespeare and his contemporaries. Throughout this later period, however, they remained anomalies, and these vestiges of medievalism in the Renaissance were no better than they could be. That they should have had an audience at all was due no doubt to the favor of the Puritans whose ability to take punishment in the form of sermons is not the least evidence of their sturdy character.

4 JOHN HEYWOOD AND THE FARCEURS.

Fortunately, there is no need for so sober a leave-taking from the medieval drama as the moralities would provide. The reign of a new and vivacious drama was being ushered in even while the moralities aired their righteousness. In France, among numerous *soties* or clown plays of no particular distinction, we find the delightful anonymous *Farce of the Worthy Master Pierre Patelin,*[6] in which a poor lawyer gets out of paying a draper's bill by pretending madness and then wins a shepherd's case by instructing him to behave like an innocent by answering "Bah" to all questions. Then, when the successful advocate tries to collect his fee, he is treated to the same medicine by his client, who has profited too well from Patelin's instructions. This farce also appeared in Germany, where the vogue for comedy was equally strong.

In sixteenth-century Germany the irrepressible Nuremberg master-singer Hans Sachs, who is endeared to us by Richard Wagner's opera, wrote in addition to some forty-four hundred poems over two hundred short plays, many of them farces notable for their vivid folk pictures and homespun humor. Sachs was keenly aware of the progressive forces of his times, but his best work in the drama belongs to the folk-spirit of the Middle Ages. *The Wandering Scholar from Paradise* is representative of the German *divertimenti.* Here an itinerant scholar who pretends that he is but newly arrived from Paradise prevails upon a dull-witted peasant woman to load him with gifts for her deceased first husband, whom the student has described as living in dire need among the saints. When her close-fisted second husband, who considers himself less gullible than she, tracks him down he too is properly fleeced.

Unhappily, Germany was not destined to develop its rich comic resources. Already in Sachs' time, the theatre was becoming increasingly polemical. The Reformation was absorbing the energies of the nation, and Sachs, himself, gave liberally of his talent to the utilitarian art of Protestant satire. One of the first poets of his day to support Martin

Luther, he honored him with the title of "the nightingale of Wittenberg" in a famous epigram. The exigencies of the Reformation and the devastating effects of thirty years of relentless civil war stalemated the German theatre at the very moment when it was beginning the same ascent as the theatre in England, Spain and France. Sachs died in 1576, and two centuries were to elapse before Germany could again make a valid contribution to the drama. In the third quarter of the sixteenth century the populace became almost wholly dependent upon English and Italian touring companies for entertainment and edification.

In England, medieval farce found one of its most entertaining forms in the so-called "interludes" or dramatic debates, of which the instructor of the singing and acting boys of St. Paul's Cathedral John Heywood was a past master. Although the interludes were static conversations, they could bubble with wit and humor, and they even reflected the critical bias of a new age. Gone was all pretense to allegory and moral exhortation, for the prime object of an interlude was to entertain. In the halls in which they were performed on platforms, laughter—sometimes good-natured, sometimes derisive—resounded. John Heywood, who had been born in 1497, was himself as much a product of the transitional period as was the literary form he adopted. His orthodox piety, which resulted in his exile from England, reflects the Middle Ages, and his humor is allied to the spirit of the medieval *fabliaux*. Nevertheless, he is also close to the Renaissance by virtue of his secular conception of the drama, and to the Reformation in his unsparing satirization of corruption within the Church.

His interlude *The Play of the Weather,* in which he returned to the trappings of the morality play, revolves around that highly debatable topic. His masterpiece, the earlier *Four PP,* however, seasons its folk humor with satire and includes some characterization reminiscent of Chaucer's *The Canterbury Tales.* It employs three Chaucerian characters, a Palmer or pilgrim, a Pardoner, and a Pothecary. The Palmer who self-righteously believes that he has earned salvation by tramping from shrine to shrine, the pardoner who peddles his "great toe of Trinity" and "buttock-bone of Pentecost," and the apothecary who cheats the populace with macaronic remedies like "blanka manna" are delightfully realized characters. Each "P" displays his skill as liar, and a Pedler, a prime prevaricator in his own right, is appointed judge of the ensuing lying contest which scales Rabelaisian altitudes. The pharmacist describes his rare cure of the falling sickness, and the pardoner recounts how he rescued his crony Margery Corson from hell. The latter prides himself especially on his acquaintance with the Devil, having known him often "in the play of Corpus Christi," for it was not long before Satan agreed to release Margery Corson. This is a tall tale, to be sure, but the stout Palmer can top it by simply declaring that

> *Not one good city, or borough*
> *In Christendom but I have been thorough,*
> *And this I would ye should understand:*
> *I have seen women five hundred thousand*
> *Wives and widows, maids and married,*
> *And oft with them have long time tarried,*
> *Yet in all places where I have been*
> *I never saw, nor knew, in my conscience,*
> *Any one woman out of patience.*

This whopper wins the prize. Even more vivacious and decidedly more dramatic is Heywood's salacious *Merry Play of John, Tyb, and Sir John*,[7] in which a priest comports himself in a manner hardly consistent with his tonsure.

Heywood's six interludes are indeed far removed from the moral and religious drama of medieval times. With Heywood, however, we are in the midst of a new age; when he died abroad at the patriarchal age of eighty-three, its choicest flower Shakespeare was already in the bud.

I. THE FOUR ENGLISH CYCLES: 1) THE YORK CYCLE, of which 48 complete plays are extant, existed as early as 1378, probably earlier. 2) THE TOWNELEY CYCLE, later in origin, with 32 plays extant, performed probably on fixed stages rather than pageant wagons in the town of Wakefield. 3) THE CHESTER CYCLE, with 25 plays extant, probably early 14th century, nearer in sobriety of spirit to the early liturgical plays. 4) N. TOWN PLAYS (N. probably standing for *nomen*, so that the name of the town where they were performed could be filled in), with 42 plays extant. Also known as *Hegge Plays*, from the name of the owner of the 15th century manuscript. Formerly called the Coventry Plays, *Ludus Coventriae*, erroneously. Later than other cycles, probably performed by strolling players, not by the Guilds, on fixed stages. Contains more theology and some allegorical characters (probably owing to the influence of the Morality Plays).

II. MORALITY PLAYS: These owe their origin to the prevalence of sermons and literary allegories such as the 5th century *Psychomachia*, a poem dealing with the battle of the Virtues and Vices, by Prudentius; the *Roman de la Rose*, and the popular 14th century Tolstoyan poem *Piers Plowman*. The first mention of a Morality Play is *circa* 1378 by Wyclif. The earliest form is the *Pater Noster* type of play, of which there are no examples extant. The "moralities" probably came at first in the form of cycles like the mystery plays, and may have been played on pageant wagons, but only single plays, written for performance on fixed stages, have been preserved. A complete "morality" had three themes: The Coming of Death; The Debate of the Heavenly Virtues, in which Mercy and Peace intervened with Justice and Truth on behalf of the man's soul after death; and the Conflict of the Vices and the Virtues for his soul. All three themes appear in *The Castle of Perseverance* (about 1450); only the first theme appears in the much shorter *Everyman*, more correctly entitled *The Summoning of Everyman*.

III. INTERLUDES: The earliest extant interlude is *Fulgens and Lucres* (about 1497), by Henry Medwall, dealing with the rivalry of a nobleman and a plebeian over a Roman senator's daughter.

PART V

THE THEATRE OF SELF-ASSERTION

EUROPE bursts the shackles of the medieval spirit in the fifteenth and sixteenth centuries. The old feudal aristocracy falls into decay and gradually makes way for the middle classes. Economic activity reaches a state of genuine fermentation, and voyages of discovery and conquest in the new world open up new horizons. The growth of national unity, especially in Spain and England, releases new national energies that enrich and inspirit the individual. The pursuit of happiness, the acquisition of comfort and pleasure, and the assertion of the personal will become fine arts. A new principle of self-realization and a passion for power and glory animate European man, and he supports his right to self-development with the example of the newly recovered culture of the classic world.

The theatre responds by expressing the sensuousness and joyfulness of the age, and by exalting or examining the human will. After a period given over to imitation of the classics, the drama becomes gloriously intoxicated. It is slipshod, extravagant, and frequently chaotic. But it recovers its most valuable stock-in-trade—the ecstasy of release and passion. The Renaissance masters and journeymen create a drama devoted to the intensities of human experience and human personality, and in this teeming market place and temple of aggressive humanity Shakespeare is, of course, both chief merchant and high priest.

X

THE JOURNEYMEN OF THE RENAISSANCE

I THE HUMANISTS AND THE DRAMA

"Encrease hath a time," wrote the learned Ascham who was one of the strongest proponents of the new dawn in Europe. In a time of "encrease" like the Renaissance, the theatre naturally displayed mounting energies and shared the transition from the Middle Ages to the modern world with other cultural and social activities. A mere procession of dates is no blueprint for an epoch that begins at first imperceptibly, does not assume definite form in different countries simultaneously, undergoes transformations without preconceived plan, and concludes with something less than the precision of a stop-watch. It can only be said that the Renaissance becomes full grown in the sixteenth century, blossoms first and most completely in Italy, and spreads northward in a widening arc of classic culture and modern thought. It can also be noted that in the theatre the movement is one of overlapping trends of classicism, surviving medieval tendencies, national expression, experiment in dramatic forms, and enriched stagecraft.

The strictly transitional stage of Renaissance drama discovers no masterpieces, and its "humanist" playwrights are journeymen rather than masters of their trade. When the "revival of learning" movement recovers Europe's classic heritage, it encourages imitation of Roman drama and sends authors to the great plays of Athens which were practically unknown to Western Europe before the fifteenth century. Had not one Roman Catholic dignitary declared that "It's Greek; we don't read it"—"*graecum est, non legitur*"?

A major problem for the early Renaissance period, therefore, is to edit and publish the Athenian drama. The manuscripts reach the West through Greek scholars who are attracted by the wealth and patronage of the Italian principalities or are driven into exile when the Turks finally conquer Constantinople in 1452. In 1502 the seven extant plays of Sophocles are published by the famous Venetian printer Aldus. A year later Euripides is accorded the same honor, and in 1518 Aeschylus, whose older Greek was more difficult to decipher, is printed by the same press. For years the task of editing and translating the Greek drama absorbs the energies of scholars and poets to the exclusion of genuinely creative work.

Some advance was registered earlier when poets turned to Latin drama, which was so much more familiar to the West. A tragedy of tyranny like Mussato's *Eccerinis,* written in Latin as early as 1315, may be regarded as the first full-length secular play of modern European drama. But Mussato's and his successors' model was Seneca, that decayed limb of classic greatness who encouraged rant and frightfulness at the expense of both characterization and action. Further progress is made by the imitation of Greek models, such as the erudite poet Trissino's *Sofonisba,* the first classic tragedy in Italian, composed in 1515. Genuine passion appears again on the boards of the theatre. Sofonisba, daughter of the Carthaginian general Hasdrubal, is betrothed to the East Numidian prince Masinissa. But she is given instead to the king of Western Numidia and is later brought to Rome. Thereupon Sofonisba drains a cup of poison sent to her by her lover and dies. Trissino, who avoids the excesses of Senecan melodrama, also takes a step toward the liberation of the drama from classic prosody by employing blank verse for the first time, the play being written in Italian rhymeless hendecasyllables. Still, most of the action is relegated to five messengers, who relate the events that the modern drama would present visibly on the stage, and the chorus reduces any active drama that the messengers might have left untransformed into narration. Trissino's tragedy is characterized by good taste and simplicity, but it is woefully deficient in movement.

His friend, Giovanni Rucellai, writes a *Rosmunda,* which is even more static, although its story of a tyrant's vengefulness contains the elements of tragedy. Another of the latter's plays, *Orestes,* is based on Euripides' *Iphigenia in Tauris* without, however, marking any advance in the direction of modern drama. Lodovico Dolce adapts Euripides' tragedy of the fratricidal conflict between the sons of Oedipus (*The Phoenissae*) in his *Giocasta.* Later, in 1533, another compatriot, the Florentine Martelli, writes a *Tullia* based on Sophocles' *Electra,* which concludes with an antique *deus ex machina* when the deified hero Romulus appears on the scene to cut the crudely tied dramatic knot. Lodovico Dolce's *Marianna,* a tragedy of jealousy, is a comparatively dynamic work: Herod, the tyrant who appeared so often in medieval drama, becomes inordinately jealous of his wife Marianna and successively murders her supposed lover, Marianna herself, his two sons by her, and her mother. But Dolce's attachment to Senecan horrors results in wild extravagance.

The work of the translators also continues elsewhere on the continent and likewise moves from scholarship to a semblance of creativeness. An inspired French poet like Jodelle creates something living in his translation of *Antigone,* and also composes in 1552 the first original classic drama in the French language, *Cléopatre Captive.* His associates in the poetic and humanistic circle known as the *Pléiade* (the Pleiades, a properly classic designation!) are so overjoyed that they present him in Greek fashion with an ivy-garlanded goat, causing a scandal by their pagan behavior.

In Germany Luther's friend Melanchthon and his pupils translate the Greek plays into Latin and perform them, along with the tragedies of Seneca, untroubled by the patent inferiority of the latter. The Protestant humanists justify their attachment to pagan drama on moral grounds, proclaiming that "To a corrupt and gluttonous age, Greek tragedy still preaches Virgil's lesson." Particularly active is the theatre at Strasbourg, the center of German humanism, which becomes a public institution about 1580. And every effort is made to make the plays comprehensible and immediate to their new public. A prologue to *Prometheus Bound,* in 1601, explains the story; added scenes amplify the action, an epilogue sums up the moral, and a partial German translation—a "book of words"—is provided for the audience. Prometheus is identified with the spirit of the Renaissance; and God, the public is assured, has given Germany her own Prometheus in the person of the inventor of the printing press! Adaptations of the classics are also performed; that versatile writer Hans Sachs even writes an original *Alcestis* in 1555. The humanists of Holland, led by the poet Vondel who inspired Milton, are also not remiss in the propagation of the classics, although the emphasis here is on Terentian comedy saddled with homiletics. Crossing the English channel, the movement transplants itself into England with results that no humanist could have anticipated when the Elizabethan drama reached maturity.

One might expect that a period as distinctly alive as the continental Renaissance would have quickly flowered into one of the great ages of the drama. Yet the record is distressingly uninspiring, and the age that produced a Dürer, a Michelangelo and a Leonardo da Vinci on the continent rose to no altitudes in the literature of the theatre. The period of assimilation in letters was unduly long, and not before men could be released from the task of digesting the contributions of Greece and Rome could they turn to the popular art of the drama.

The Renaissance first released the energies of European man in the direction of intellectual and sensuous activity. Of brilliant thinkers and of masters of the sensuous like the great painters there was certainly no dearth. But great drama is never wholly committed to the intellect or to the senses; it pays tribute to both, but owes prime allegiance to the claims of emotional conflict. Although the Italian Renaissance was remarkably passionate and active, it found only incomplete expression in the drama; its active life could not be safely poured into the serious drama. In dramatizing political conflicts the drama would have had to cope with the Machiavellian princes of Italy who would not have relished seeing their criminal acts exposed. It is significant that such topics were dramatized not in the country of their greatest diffusion, but in distant England. Great drama, moreover, is national drama, and Italy was a patchwork of rival principalities. It is significant that the theatre's golden age both in England and Spain followed the unification and stabilization of these nations.

Still, if the art of tragedy merely broke the shell of medieval homiletics and acquired some literary polish, comedy rose to an appreciably higher estate. It became limber and it gained satiric force. And in the field of theatrical production Italy reveled so freely that it gave birth to the modern physical theatre.

2 THE ITALIAN THEATRE

Because the art of stage production titillated the spectacle-loving aristocracy and enjoyed the services of the great painters and architects of the age, it suffered no inhibition. Italy's achievements may be summarized briefly under the twin headings of magnificence and experimentation. It is hardly necessary to dwell on the former, except in the reflection that plays were smothered by the splendors of the physical production. Almost anywhere a play could be interrupted to make way for a splendid spectacle; every drama became, in Lee Simonson's phrase, a "painter's holiday."

The experiments in architecture and scenic design are, however, of extreme importance. The application of the principles of perspective to scenery, the astute use of vistas on the stage, and the gradual separation of the auditorium from the playing area set the drama behind a frame which it has rarely broken even in our own day. Behind the proscenium the romantic play could be furnished with every inch of color and invested with an aura of distance and elegance. Pushed behind the proscenium arch, the play became in time a picture to be watched by the public, as it is generally today, rather than an action communicated by direct intercourse between the actor and the spectator, as it was during the Middle Ages. This was not the case, for the most part, during the late sixteenth and early seventeenth centuries in England and Spain, for the technical developments of the Italians were only gradually absorbed elsewhere. It was not long, however, before the formal theatre of the Italian Renaissance prevailed in Europe.

The new theatre began largely as an adaptation or amplification of classic scenic art and architecture based on the rediscovered, if not too well understood, text of Vitruvius' *De Architectura*. In the Roman times described by Vitruvius (*fl.* 70–15 B.C.; his *Ms.* printed. 1511), the stage wall had been highly decorated and the periacti [1] — those painted prisms used for scene changes—had been in use. Humanist Italy believed that these devices were equivalent to full-stage scenery; and following Vitruvius' statement that the permanent front of the Roman stage was furnished with three doors, architects pierced the stage wall and filled the arch-ways with vistas worked out in perspective by means of painted flats. (In time the stage was arranged to provide a single vista, as in the theatre of the present.) Three types of scenes to be used as vistas were elaborated from Vitruvius' descriptions of classic scenery. When in 1545, about seventy years after the Roman treatise had been published in Italy, Sebastanio Serlio wrote his famous *Architettura,* he prescribed fixed scenery for tragedy, comedy, and pastoral or "satyric" drama after the Roman model: a severe street perspective for the first, a more decorative or rococo one for the second, and a perspective of trees and cottages for the third. Further elaborated by means of the architectural constructions of the Bibbienas, the perspectives became huge affairs of arches and columns. The Renaissance closed its chapter in theatre history with the creation of a theatre primarily adapted for pomp, color, and sensational stage effects.

3 TASSO AND THE PASTORAL DRAMA

The drama written for this stage is a curious amalgam of classicism and romanticism. Tragedy, as already noted, remains cold and formal; it does not go much beyond the *Sofonisba* in freedom of treatment. The elements of a serious national drama contained in Italy's medieval religious plays or *sacre rappresentazioni* bore no fruit, since they were neither entertaining enough to please the pagan taste of the Renaissance nor sufficiently rooted in national life to survive. But the masque and the pastoral drama flourish exceedingly in sixteenth-century Italy. Invariably an artificial society toys with the idea of returning to nature, and a delicately contrived wildness is cultivated by courtiers and court ladies who posture as shepherds and shepherdesses. What that mordant economic philosopher Thorstein Veblen would have called a variant of "leisure-class art" is born.

Taking a leaf out of the classic idyls of Theocritus and his successors, the Italians turned to pastoral drama. Its results cannot, of course, be classified as great literature, but fortunately the purveyors of this form of entertainment were not necessarily mediocrities. They counted among their number no less a poet than Torquato Tasso, celebrated author of *Jerusalem Delivered.* In the days of his happiness, before his mind was clouded with paranoia, Tasso brought the idyllic form to its peak. His *Aminta,* performed at the court of Ferrara in 1573, told the graceful story of the shepherd Aminta's love for the beautiful Sylvia who has devoted herself to the worship of Diana, chaste goddess of the hunt. Pursued by a designing satyr and tied to a tree, she is rescued by Aminta and his friends. Aminta, driven to despair by her indifference, tries to kill himself, but this drastic conclusion is not consummated and love wins the day.

This sentimental tale is managed delicately. It is replete with the morning freshness of natural haunts and pristine poetry. A nostalgic sweetness, perfumed by a trace of disillusionment, only enriches the sentiment. Tasso is singing of an early, Golden Age, for—as one of his characters says—the world has grown old, and growing old has grown sad. The enormous success of the play, which had more than two hundred printings and was translated into many languages, attests the fashionableness of pastoral literature. It was the fashion that Shakespeare himself did not scorn when he wrote *As You Like It*.

After Battista Guarini's *Il Pastor Fido* or *The Faithful Shepherd*, a longer and almost equally beautiful work, in 1585, the high noon of the pastoral drama declines in Italy. It is not difficult to sneer at its sentimentalities, but the work of Tasso and Guarini goes beyond mere effervescence. As in all compositions that bear the stamp of genius there is a concealed maturity and "criticism of life" in them. Both Tasso and Guarini were sensitive spirits who saw the Renaissance falling into corruption. Their evocation of an older age of bucolic beauty and simple desire is all the more glowing because it is born of dissatisfaction. Tasso went mad and Guarini retired from the world.

4 GIOVANNI BARDI'S CIRCLE AND THE OPERA

Related to the pastoral drama, another soaring flight from the common light of day and another peg for theatrical luxuriance, was the new art of opera. Natural development and one signal experiment inspired by the classical bias of the age favored its genesis.

The liturgical plays of the Middle Ages had anticipated opera by employing a chanting delivery of lines. As early as 1422, the humanist Angelo Poliziano had written a dramatic poem *La Favola di Orfeo, The Fable of Orpheus*, revolving around Orpheus' search for his lost Euridice in the infernal regions. Poliziano's libretto was set to music, with solos, dialogues, and choruses derived from the carnival and dance songs of Italy. Thereafter it was not unusual to supply court plays with songs and musical interludes or *intermezzi*.

The main impetus to the creation of opera came, however, from the humanist studies of the age. The Florentine nobleman Giovanni Bardi had gathered a circle of poets and musicans at his *palazzo* for the promotion of classic studies. In the course of its investigations this informal academy—which included the three musicians Jacopo Peri, Giulio Caccini, and Galileo's father Vincenzo Galilei—hit upon one aspect of Greek drama that had been hitherto neglected; they discovered its musical character. Proceeding from the assumption that the dialogue of Greek tragedy had been declaimed or sung, they soon created a form of music-drama. Their first important effort, the *Dafne* for which the poet Ottario Rinuccini wrote the words and Peri the music, was first performed in 1597. It was followed by other "works (i.e., *opera*) in music" like the *Euridice* of Peri and Caccini, for which Rinuccini again supplied the libretto, and other pieces with music by the noted composer Claudio Monteverdi.

Bardi's dilettantes had not intended to subordinate the dramatic text to its musical accompaniment. But the momentum of the times and the genius of Monteverdi was unfavorable to a proper balance between drama and music, and the latter prevailed. The libretti which continued to be turned out in abundance by various poets, of whom the eighteenth-century Metastasio was the most adept as well as the most prolific, possessed no remarkable merits with which to command priority; but the music, amplified and more richly orchestrated, did. With Monteverdi's pieces—a *Dafne,* an *Arianna* and an *Orfeo,* performed at Mantua in 1607 and 1608—began the opera as we know it. The declamatory style of the Florentine amateurs was supplanted by the operatic one, in which the words of the libretti were of secondary importance. Arias became increasingly important, and vocal acrobatics like roulades and trills came into vogue. Moreover, any importance that might have been left to the dramatist was thrust into the shade by the claims of the scenic designer and stage architect. Exceptionally large theatres were built for opera after 1637, and this type of construction is the "Italian style" that prevailed in Western Europe for over two and a half centuries and made every theatre an opera house in effect. A performance in which the scenery included landscapes, harbors, the open sea "with tritons," the underworld, and the "heavens" [2] was not unusual. By marrying its drama to music during the Renaissance the theatre gave Europe a new and vastly popular art. But it had to renounce importance in its own right before it could become hybrid. The energies of many dramatists were drained off or inhibited by the new form. Librettists, among whom the eighteenth-century Metastasio was pre-eminent, could write with facility and feeling but they could hardly achieve significance as playwrights.

Two centuries later, opera began to return its debt to the theatre. Casting aside its pomp, ceasing to be "grand," it began to augment the drama with musical comedies. Offenbach's pieces enlivened the Parisian stage at a time when its regular plays were of minor importance, and Gilbert and Sullivan made the Victorian theatre tolerable. In America nearly every theatrical season is enriched by musical comedies like *Of Thee I Sing* and *Leave It To Me* which are frequently more entertaining or incisive than many comedies that are not supported by a score.

5 THE ACTOR-PLAYWRIGHTS OF THE COMMEDIA DELL' ARTE

Comparing the plays of Italy with those of his native England, a patriotic Elizabethan called them "rather jigs than plays." But one aspect of the Italian theatre, comedy, could not be so cavalierly dismissed. It flourished naturally in the joyous or at least morally relaxed period. It even came close to comprising a people's theatre in Italy.

It had a dual origin—in the art of the mime, who, stemming no doubt from the folk-farceurs of Roman times, became the strolling players of the Middle Ages; and in the formal comedies of Plautus and Terence. Imitations of the latter provided humanist comedy of known authorship and fixed text. Elaborations of the Atellan or Roman farces resulted in the so-called *commedia dell' arte*.

The greatest vitality and dispersion were enjoyed by these improvisations. The players assumed their parts for a lifetime, enabled to do so by the fact that the characters in the plays were types bearing stock names like the familiar Dottore or Doctor of Bologna, Pantalone, Arlecchino (Harlequin), Brighella, and the Capitano. Inventing their own lines, they needed nothing more than an outline of the play they were to perform; consequently *commedia dell' arte* plays are nothing more than synopses. Here were, in brief, actor-playwrights whose comedies cannot be divorced from spontaneous presentation on quickly improvised stages.

The quality of the plays is, however, no mystery. They are vivid descriptions of character types and contemporary manners suspended on plots of farcical intrigue. Old men are satirized as fools, and endless changes are rung on the theme of cuckoldry. Unlike the comedies of Terence which were imitated by the humanists, these plays pay scant attention to long-lost relatives, and the humor is far less kindly and conventional.

The fifty synopses of the actor-playwright Flaminio Scala, collected in his *Theatre for Fifty Days* which served that most famous of *commedia dell'arte* companies *I Gelosi,* exemplify a drama that frolicked mischievously. *The Portrait,* which stems from the third quarter of the sixteenth century, is a representative synopsis. Here Isabella, the wife of the rich merchant Pantalone, enjoys a liaison with a cavalier Oratio and gives him her portrait, which he places in a locket. The actress Vittoria, whom the young man visits, removes the portrait, and Pantalone, also calling upon her, is surprised to find his wife's portrait in her possession. Upon being upbraided by her good husband, Isabella quarrels with Oratio and demands the return of the portrait. Oratio's attempt to recover it from the actress, the wooing of the latter by Pantalone and by another old man Gratiano, the betrayal of Gratiano by his wife Flaminia with another cavalier Flavio, the romantic attachment of young Silvia to the braggart Captain—these, as well as subordinate intrigues maintained by the servants Arlecchino and Petrolino, provide a story that bubbles with action, surprise, and salacious humor.

Pantalone, the gulled old man who appears sometimes as husband and sometimes as father, could be endowed with a variety of characteristics descriptive of grasping or doting old age. The Dottore, sometimes given a personal name like Gratiano in *The Portrait,* exemplified pedantry in its various guises. Arlecchino was the servant who invariably got his orders confused, and variants of this type could be presented as buffoons and as shrewd satirists of their time. Brighella, another servant, who had a close cousin in Scapino, was generally distinguished by his roguery. The Capitano, descended from the *miles gloriosus* or vainglorious soldier of Roman comedy, was satirically suggestive of the condottiere of Italy or of Spanish bravos in the Spanish-owned parts of Italy. Pulcinella—the Punch of our puppet shows—was an older, more sophisticated, and more pugnacious Brighella. Cruel, malicious and egotistic, he represented the sinister element in life.

These fellows, the none too scrupulous lovers and their ladies, who were rarely encumbered with virtue, comprised a rogues' gallery of considerable dimensions. Masked and typed though they were, they were nevertheless strongly individualized as to speech and dialect. Taken together they comprised a cross-section of middle- and lower-class society the like of which is found only in early "picaresque" or rogue novels like *Lazarillo de Tormes* and Nashe's *Unfortunate Traveler.* A "slice of life" on a figured platter, the plays are in many respects close to the realistic drama of the nineteenth century.

It is not surprising that the *commedia dell'arte* enjoyed great popularity and exerted a marked influence on later playwrights, especially on Molière. Performing in hundreds of market places on crudely constructed platforms representing the conventional street scene described by Serlio, using curtains for backgrounds and as few props as possible until they received a permanent theatre, the troupers supplied standardized amusement for the masses. Since, moreover, they counted many accomplished performers and beautiful actresses among their number, they also attracted the favor of the nobility, even when the Church thundered against them. Nor were they wholly committed to playmaking and buffoonery. The famous and beautiful star actress of the *Gelosi* troupe Isabella Andreini and her husband Francesco had enough learning to put a scholar to shame. They knew several languages and were accomplished musicians. They, too, were in a sense humanists.

Still it is not for their learning that the Italian comedians are to be remembered. They created the first popular theatre on the continent that could supplant the religious theatre of the Middle Ages, and if we are in no position to gauge their stature as playwrights, it is not difficult to imagine the wit and pungency of the dialogue that kept Europe laughing and applauding.

6 ARIOSTO, ARETINO, AND MACHIAVELLI

The men of the Renaissance did not, however, rely solely upon the actor for their supply of comedy. After much fumbling that promised little more than humanist redactions of Plautus and Terence, comedy began to claim writers of unquestioned talent who came from other pursuits to enlist under the irreverent Muse.

Known as erudite comedy—*comedia erudate*—classic imitations consisted largely of intrigues, kidnapings, and recognition (*anagnorsis*) scenes in which long-lost relatives were joyfully recovered in the last act. Il Lasca, a contemporary critic of comedy, complained bitterly that the "comedy of *anagnorisis*" was dated. "We have other manners, another religion, another way of life. . . . There are no slaves here; it is not customary to adopt children; our pimps do not put up girls for sale at auction; nor do the soldiers of the present century carry long-clothed babies off in the sack of cities, to educate them as their own daughters and give them dowries; nowadays they take as much booty as they can, and should girls or married women fall into their hands they either look for a large ransom or rob them of their maidenhood and honour." [3] It was some time before Il Lasca's polemic became inapplicable to Italian comedy.

The high-water mark of this neo-classic comedy was reached by the poet Lodovico Ariosto (1474-1533) whose full-blown romance *Orlando Furioso* was the most fashionable poem of its time. This elegant and well-born poet had a keen eye for the manners of his time. Taking for his frame the comedies of the Romans, he was therefore able to invest them with the itching flesh of the Italian Renaissance. His *Cassaria* told the familiar story of two young men who fall in love with two girls owned by a white-slaver and free them with the aid of resourceful valets. His *Suppositi* or *Pretenders* relates the intrigues of a young man who disguises himself as a servant in order to seduce a maiden. This salacious comedy won the approval of the Pope himself when it was performed in his theatre with settings by Raphael. More original was *Negromante,* which revolves around the paradoxical plight of a young man who keeps his wife in concealment but lives openly with his mistress. To rid himself of the latter he is compelled to feign certain physical shortcomings with the assistance of an intriguing astrologer who mulcts everyone, including the unmarried woman's parents who are eager to have their "son-in-law" healed.

Best among Ariosto's pieces, because of their vivid pictures of life in Ferrara, are his *Lena* and *Scolastica*. *Scolastica,* completed after Ariosto's death by his brother Gabrielle, deals with the complications arising from the love of two students for two girls. How they override opposition with the assistance of a clever servant Accursio and of a kind-hearted keeper of lodgings furnishes most of the humor. In this comedy, Ariosto does not, however, confine himself to the mere invention of situations; and his characters bear the unmistakable stamp of individuality. Moreover, for all his gambolings and his ventures into polished obscenity, Ariosto discharges some well-directed satire. Bureaucracy, court favoritism, and judicial corruption are his butts, and in *Scolastica* he even ventures to satirize the church in the person of an avaricious friar. The friar makes it clear to his client that there is nothing in the world so serious that it cannot be overcome by *l'elemosine* or "charity," which is in his case unvarnished bribery. Ariosto knew too much of life to remain a mere purveyor of gay nonsense, even though he was too greatly attached to classic formulae and no master of vernacular composition.

Most thoroughly vernacular and most completely disengaged from Roman comedy are the comedies of Pietro Aretino (1492-1556), that phenomenal adventurer of the Renaissance. Princes who feared his stinging pen, which seemed to them dipped in venom instead of ink, paid generously for his silence. Equally at home in the courts of the aristocracy and the brothels of the commonest people, he who began as a lackey acquired a first-hand knowledge of the corruption of the times. But his gusto and his amusement at life's antics far exceeded any righteous anger. It is not for nothing that legend had him dying of excessive laughter. Perhaps the best commentary on the easy morals of his day is the fact that this diligent roué and assassin of reputations came close to being made a Cardinal.

His *Cortiagana* has a provincial gentleman arriving at Rome in order to make his fortune and falling prey to a rogue who introduces him to the demimonde under the pretext of turning him into an accomplished courtier. Where else can he learn so much about the court and its ways as in the stews! His mentor then lectures him lengthily on the vices that will ensure his success in the precincts of aristocracy. Above all he must avoid speaking "badly." What is speaking badly? asks the bumpkin. To tell the truth, replies the voice of experience. This acid satire, sharpened with pictures of courtesans and tavern life, makes a pungent realistic comedy that is closer to a product of nineteenth-century naturalism like Hauptmann's *The Beaver Coat* [4] than it is to most of the comedies that succeeded it for three centuries. The Renaissance educator Castiglione had drawn an ideal portrait of a courtier in *Il Cortigiano;* Aretino drew an actual one in the *Cortiagana.*

Aretino returned to the assault on polite society with lessened virulence but increased vivacity in *Marescalco,* in which a wealthy fool and pederast who is prevailed upon to take a wife is mulcted and then deceived into marrying a boy in disguise. It is possible that Ben Jonson was indebted to Aretino for this comic situation, which reappears in *Epicene or The Silent Woman.* Aretino's intimate acquaintance with the lower depths also resulted in a comedy of courtesan life, *Talanta,* and several less renowned comedies supplied his rogues' gallery with portraits of a religious hypocrite and a variety of numskulls. Had Aretino mastered the difficult craft of dramaturgy and had his plays not been overblown with undigested material, he would now be celebrated among the masters of realistic comedy.

He would not, however, have been a lone pine among the humanist chrysanthemums, since Machiavelli (1469-1527) lent a fraction of his redoubtable intellect to the theatre. As one of the most experienced men of his time, chancellor of the Florentine republic at thirty and ambassador to various Italian states, he too had ample opportunity to observe the realities of his time. His close association with Italy's leading politician Cesare Borgia, and his analysis of the technique of power politics in *The Prince,* made him eminently fit to lead comedy into the fertile field of satire. A patriot and a visionary who dreamed of a united Italy some four centuries before the event, he was susceptible to promptings that Aretino could not even remotely entertain. Unhappily married, persecuted when the Medici merchant-princes returned to power in Florence, and forced to spend his best years in retirement, he understood his times better than most men and was consumed with bitterness. The exactions of a busy career and the impossibility of composing political comedy in the age of petty tyrants alone prevented Machiavelli from making a major contribution to the theatre.

However, he managed to compose two (possibly four) comedies, and to make one translation from the Latin. His *Clizia* is a vivid and unconventional study of a Florentine household, spoiled only by that incubus of Renaissance comedy, the "recognition" scene, in which the father of the heroine appears to claim her as his own. The intrigue revolves around an elderly gentleman who tries to marry his ward to his servant with the intention of using the latter as a screen for an illicit affair. He is opposed by his wife, who tries to marry the girl to a sober bailiff, and he is exposed by the girl herself, with the aid of her pursuer's son, when they substitute a page for her on the night of the wedding. The hero of these adventures is not an ordinary fool but a roundly characterized respectable merchant who has temporarily taken leave of his senses. The humor of the dialogue is particularly notable, for Machiavelli proves himself a master of irony.

It is in *Mandragola,* however, that Machiavelli put forth all his strength and struck the same vein of objective cynicism that distinguishes his devastating manual for princes. Again the background is the middle class which had attained such affluence in sixteenth-century Italy and so won a place in its theatre earlier than elsewhere. A young flame Callimaco, becoming infatuated with Lucrezia, the conventionally moral and contrary wife of a worthy but fatuous doctor of laws Nicia, enlists the aid of a depraved parasite Ligurio. Nicia, who has an inordinate desire for a child which his wife seems unable to give him, is prevailed upon to employ the services of a physician, who is no other than the young lover in disguise. The latter prescribes the mandragola or mandrake plant as a means of inducing fertility, but warns him that the first person who cohabits with the patient will die of the effects of the drug. It becomes necessary, therefore, to find someone to take the husband's place. After prevailing upon her mother and her unscrupulous father-confessor to win her consent to the substitution, the disguised Callimaco allows himself to be hustled away to her room. Callimaco then reappears in his medical robes and Nicia is so grateful that he invites him to become a frequent visitor at his home. Machiavelli's unsavory exposure of the vices of his day is to continental drama what *Volpone* is to English comedy. Sparing neither fool nor rogue, even if it draws no moral, *Mandragola* has the solidity of granite.

Like *Clizia, Mandragola* is written in sharp and precise prose, with generally mordant verses between the acts. The comedy, written about 1514, probably owes its mood to Machiavelli's state of mind at the time of its completion. He had retired to his farm near San Casciano after losing political influence with the restoration of the Medici and being treated to "four turns of the rack" [5] before he was released by a papal amnesty. He was in the proper frame of mind for dividing the world into fools and rogues.

Those who like to picture the Renaissance as sipping blissfully at the innocent flower of pagan beauty will find no comfort in *Mandragola.* The age did experience a notable release from the cathedral gloom of medievalism, but the new freedom proved a very mixed blessing. It unleashed much conscienceless rapacity and allowed individualism to run riot at the expense of humanity. Tyrants established petty dictatorships and sought to secure and extend them by means of perfidy, force, and poisonings. The middle class developed a voracious appetite for profit which was to become cumulative in the next four centuries. It is no wonder that Machiavelli called his Italy "the corruption of the world." Its artists exhibited the flowers of the Renaissance. Machiavelli and Aretino photographed the weeds.

XI

LOPE DE VEGA AND CALDERÓN

ONE ASPECT of the Renaissance, the growth of nationalism, proved a progressive step insofar as it unified large geographical areas under one law, gave them a common purpose, and provided security for the development of commerce and industry. The Renaissance theatre needed only this galvanizing factor to reach maturity. The medieval stage had owed its triumphs to the spiritual and cultural unity of Europe under the one Church and to the energy of the towns made prosperous by the local middle class. The Renaissance stage beyond Italy was indebted to the unification of individual nations that released national, rather than municipal, energies and ferments.

Spain and England came to the fore at approximately the same time. But it was sixteenth-century Spain that first attained prosperity and hegemony. The nation, which already throve on the sound economic base that was supplied by the Moors and the Jews, added a new source of income as riches poured into its coffers from Mexico and Peru. Hardened by centuries of struggle with the Moors, who at one time held most of the country, the Spaniards of the sixteenth century were a race of soldiers and adventurers whose faculties were invigorated a second time in the conquest of America. The country that had once produced the Cid and later the soldiers of Ferdinand and Isabella who reduced the last strongholds of the Moors continued under Charles V and Philip II to produce conquerors and adventurers. Even the Church, inimical as its instrument the Inquisition may have been to religious liberty, was energetic, militant, and adventurous. The state, although equally intolerant toward other races and religions, as well as resolutely autocratic, was likewise vibrant with energy. For the Spaniards, who had never known political liberty, autocracy was not particularly irksome. In curbing the feudal aristocracy it even became the temporary ally of the middle class and the peasantry. Moreover, all the regimentation of priest and king could not prevail at first against the ferment of an age of conquest and adventure.

It was out of this intensification of national life that Spanish literature and the Spanish theatre rose to those heights which it was never again to see. "*El Siglo de Oro*" or the Golden Age, as the Spaniards call the period, witnessed tremendous developments in poetry, prose, and drama, and it culminated in two giants—Cervantes in the field of fiction, and Lope de Vega in the drama.

I THE MONSTER OF NATURE

In a period of striking personalities one of the most colorful was the master of the Spanish theatre who is a veritable epitome of the nation's energies, accomplishments, and limitations. Born on November 25th, 1562, about two years before Marlowe and Shakespeare, he outlived them both. Marlowe was a naughty youngster and Shakespeare a sedate bourgeois by comparison with the flamboyant lover, soldier, careerist, and author of approximately 2,200 short and long plays, over five hundred of which have survived. All this, in addition to numerous lyrics, fulsome epics, an autobiography, and miscellaneous religious writings! He was a greater romanticist than Cortez, a more impressive—and a more fortunate—phenomenon than the Spanish Armada. Cervantes rightly referred to him as the "Monster of Nature."

It is typical of the age of adventurers that Lope Félix de Vega Carpio (a name also typical of Spanish aplomb) should have been the son of Asturian peasants living in Madrid. In our day he would have been a Harvard prodigy, for at the age of five he could already read Latin, as well as Spanish, and wrote poetry. At the age of fourteen he was a student at the Imperial College at Madrid, probably owing to the influence of his uncle the Inquisitor Don Miguel de Carpio, since his own father was now dead and the family was scattered by poverty. At this tender age he became adept at fencing, dancing, and music, as well as literature and "ethics." Possessed by the same urge that sent his elders on the high seas, he ran away from college at this time and traversed northwestern Spain with a classmate. At fifteen, by his own account, he was a soldier in an expedition against Portugal, and weathered one battle. Shortly thereafter the Bishop of Avila took Lope under his wing and sent him to the University of Alcalá, where he took his bachelor's degree and was on the verge of also taking the tonsure. But by then, at the age of seventeen, Lope's heart had become inflammable in a manner which may be mildly described as chronic. "I was even," he writes in a letter, "on the point of becoming a priest; but I fell blindly in love, God forgive it; I am married now, and he that is so ill off fears nothing." [1]

From Alcalá he went to the Azores on a successful naval expedition and then to Madrid, where he began to make his mark in the theatre and rapidly gained a reputation for wit. Though his means were slender, his pretensions were great; he claimed to write only for pastime and he strutted with the best of the *hidalgos*. Soon he won a double conquest— over Jerónimo Velazquez, the producer who bought his plays, and over the latter's daughter Elena, who was married to an actor. He celebrated her under the name of Filis in many a ballad while she gave him her love and her jewels, and his devotion appears to have been longer than was usual with fine blades of his ilk—it lasted five years. But when it was terminated in 1587, it was done so with *éclat,* and a furious quarrel with her father, to whom he began to refuse his comedies and whom he lampooned mercilessly, resulted in a libel suit. He was imprisoned and then exiled from the kingdom of Castile for two years. Accompanied by a faithful friend, who had his own escapades and had to be rescued from prison by Lope, he went to Valencia, where he continued to practice his craft. Three months later, at the risk of being sent to the galleys, he returned to Madrid and eloped with Isabel de Urbina, a prominent courtier's daughter. He married her, but left her in Madrid and joined the Spanish Armada in 1588:

Fortunately for the theatre, he escaped the fate of many of his compatriots during the disastrous venture that made Britannia mistress of the seas. His galleon, the *San Juan,* was one of the few ships to return to Cadiz. It was a long six months' voyage, which included circumnavigation of the British Isles, but Lope was not to be disturbed by a few hazards; he spent the time composing the artificial romance *The Beauty of Angelica,* one of his several voluminous ventures in epic poetry. A month later he returned to Valencia and settled down to the serious business of earning his living in the theatre.

Plays followed in rapid succession, until more than one manager depended upon the supply. His young wife died after many a jealous hour and fretful memory of how he had abandoned her. A new love had appeared on his horizon, the actress Micaela de Luxon, who gave him four children and provided the occasion for many a sonnet. He remained constant to her in his fashion, which is equivalent to saying that she shared his devotion with several other Spanish ladies. In 1598 he also married the daughter of a successful pork merchant and enjoyed the comforts of a gratifying dowry. His versatile fatherhood was signalized in one year, 1605, by the successive birth of a son by his wife and a daughter by Micaela, who also gave him two years later the talented son Lopito (formally known as Lope Félix del Carpio y Luxon) who wrote some impressive poetry. Later, in 1610, after he had attained some degree of affluence from his earnings and from the patronage of a succession of noblemen among whom the young Duke of Lessa was the most generous, he established his family in Madrid, and when his wife died in 1613 the devoted, if indiscriminate, father brought his illegitimate children under the same roof.

Unconscious of any contradictions of principle, the great lover turned to the Church next year, took minor orders, and became a "familiar" of the Inquisition. But this step brought no interruption to his literary and amatory pursuits. Just as he had written numerous religious pieces during his unfrocked days, he continued to write secular plays during his priesthood. At least two other liaisons followed his assumption of piety—one with a wild actress Lucia de Salcedo whom he described as "the mad one" (*la loca*), and one with his "Amarilis." She was Doña Marta, a young married woman who was relieved of her husband three years later after increasing Lope's miscellaneous paternity at a time when he was approaching sixty. He lost Doña Marta in 1632, long after the flame of their love had guttered into friendship. Three years later he also lost his son Lopito, who died at sea, and his illegitimate daughter who eloped with a courtier. These calamities weighed heavily upon the seventy-three-year-old genius, and he died in the partial odor of sanctity on August 27, 1635. This complex individual (we shudder to think what a psychoanalyst would say about him) was in the habit of scourging himself for the good of his soul until the walls of his room were flecked with blood!

2 LOPE AND THE SPANISH THEATRE

The theatre to which Lope lent his phenomenal energies had been growing rapidly and fixing its conventions for some time. Emerging from the medieval miracle-play period, which continued to claim Lope and his colleagues when they composed their numerous *autos* or sacred one-acters, the Spanish theatre had followed the Renaissance pattern to some degree. Imitations of Roman comedy and even of Greek tragedy were composed by academicians. But it was as difficult to remain academic during the dynamic age of Spanish imperialism as it was during the Tudor period that paralleled it in England. Fifteenth-century comic interludes or *entremeses,* grew in popularity and were followed by miscellaneous transitional plays and playlets. Intrigues, largely drawn from the Italian *novelle,* began to fill the theatre with vigorous and flavorsome pieces until they attained the salacity of the famous *Calixto and Melibea* or *Celestina,* of uncertain authorship. The efforts of the early playwrights, among whom was "the father of Portuguese drama" Gil Vicente, were amalgamated in the first decades of the sixteenth century by Naharro, who developed characterization and unity of plot. Then Lope de Rueda, who started life as a goldsmith and became an actor, produced four vigorous comedies that anticipated Lope de Vega's. One of his pieces *Los engaños* bears a strong resemblance to Shakespeare's *Twelfth Night* and is derived from the same Italian source. He was not only witty and entertaining in his own right, but he wielded an influence on all his successors, who formed a school around him. One of these, Juan de la Cueva, who spent three years in Mexico, enlarged the resources of the craft by introducing varied meters into Spanish drama, began the custom of using historical subjects, and developed the romantic "cape and sword" (*capa y estapa*) plays which occupy so large a place in Lope's output. Still another playwright was none other than Cervantes himself, who was wise enough to bolster his fame with the far more enduring merits of *Don Quixote*.

For Spaniards some of the plays of this preparatory period are still pleasurable, and one must concede them some degree of theatrical ingenuity. But light drama of this order, which so frequently swamps the theatre and provides momentary gratification, is impressive only when it achieves the greatest zest. And it was by providing such zest, with the aid of the most abundant resources of theatricality, that Lope rose above his predecessors and contemporaries. Moreover, he forged far ahead in a number of works which, despite the limitations of his talents, achieve an emotional power and provocativeness. He is never better than when he can move freely; he is never less impressive than when he is following conventions like stilted dialogue.

The public theatres in Madrid and Valencia, like their Elizabethan counterparts, were large open-air structures modeled on the corrals which had housed entertainments before his time. A platform, provided with little scenery, jutted into the audience and allowed rapid continuity of action without interruption by falling curtains and laborious scene changes. On this stage he could allow full play to his fabulous inventiveness, to the duels and meetings, and the misunderstandings and complications, of his heroes and heroines. Here he could spin his complicated romantic plots without elaborate motivation and painstaking preparation. Lope had the advantage of being able to keep his invention limber enough to thumb its nose at ordinary reality and substitute for it the illusory reality of the theatre.

3 THE PLAYS OF LOPE

His sacred *autos,* spiced with robust introductions or *loas* and farcical *entremeses,* and his full-length *comedias de santos* or saint plays harked back to an earlier period. Only their resourcefulness and entertainment value distinguished them from medieval drama. He wrote them because they were close to the heart of his strongly Catholic country and because they satisfied the curious piety that ruled him side by side with impulses one does not ordinarily associate with piety.

Most of his plays founded on the melodramatic details of many Italian *novelle* dramatize crimes of ambition and passion. They are melodramas like those which delighted Elizabethan audiences and culminated in such sanguinary works as Webster's *The White Devil* and the *Duchess of Malfi*. But unlike these plays, Lope's efforts in this vein are devoid of the emotional depth and outcries against human corruption which raise Webster's work to the estate of tragedy; Lope had neither the taste nor the depth for this noble art. A typical novelesque play is his *Punishment Without Revenge* (*El castigo sin venganza*) which dramatizes the conflict between the duke of Ferrara and his illegitimate son who falls in love with his father's neglected wife. The duke, being informed of this affair on his return from a journey, induces his son to kill the erring wife unwittingly and then has him slain as a murderer. Here is the old Hippolytus theme of Greek tragedy and of Racine's *Phèdre* without the depth and humanity associated with it. The fine edge of Lope's strength is to be found elsewhere—in his comedies and histories. The former triumph through sheer ingenuity, the latter through a firm hold upon the realities of society.

His light plays, technically known as "cape and sword" comedies because they dealt with the flamboyant aristocracy, are whirling affairs of intrigue, love-making, and mistakes. Their variety can barely be suggested. Their quality may be conveyed by two of the better examples: *A Certainty for Doubt,* and *El acero de Madrid* or *Madrid Steel,* which served as a model for Molière's *Physician in Spite of Himself.*

A forceful representative of swaggering romance, *A Certainty for Doubt* describes the rivalry of Pedro the Cruel and his brother Don Enrique for the love of Doña Juana. Although Pedro has the advantage of power, which enables him to banish his brother, and Enrique the disadvantage of being troubled by two other women, Doña Juana favors the latter and rejects the king's advances. The king tries to have his brother assassinated and to marry the lady forcibly. Instead Enrique appears in disguise at the ceremony and becomes the bridegroom. Naturally, Pedro discloses a generous nature and pardons the lovers. It would be difficult to match Don Enrique's gallantry as he risks all for a sight of his lady, and the *brio* of his temperament is sufficient to captivate even the most phlegmatic of stage heroines, although Doña Juana surely belongs to a more spirited sorority.

Belisa, in *Madrid Steel,* falls in love with the young spark Lisardo, and being watched by an argus-eyed duenna Teodora pretends to be ill. A doctor is called in, who is none other than the young man in disguise, while Teodora is kept engaged in the park by his friend Riselo who pays court to the somewhat astonished but grateful lady. As this intrigue is prolonged for months, the lovers are in danger of losing each other. Riselo's lady-love frets at his neglect while he is distracting Teodora from her watch, and Belisa's father is laying plans for marrying her to someone else. In these straits, Belisa flees from her father's house to her lover's and a double wedding ends all complications.

How Lope keeps the fun jigging may be shown by the scene in which Belisa manages to meet her lover Lisardo. Accompanied by her duenna, she comes out of church and sees him. Her duenna upbraids her,

> *Show more of gentleness and modesty—*
> *Of gentleness in walking quietly,*
> *Of modesty in looking only down*
> *Upon the earth you tread.*

Belisa assures her that this is precisely what she is doing, and when the duenna says "What! When you're looking straight towards the man!" Belisa replies pertly,

> *Did you not bid me to look upon the earth*
> *And what is he but just a bit of it?*

She pretends to stumble, and is helped by the young man. She looks back as she leaves him, and the duenna remonstrates with her: "But why again do you turn your head?" Belisa replies blithely:

> *Why, sure you think it wise and wary*
> *To notice well the place I stumbled at,*
> *Lest I should stumble there when next I pass.*

Plays of this type are marvels of improvisation; they are limited only by an absence of that depth of characterization and that ability to leap from a slight comic situation to a startling vision of beauty which make Shakespeare Lope's superior even in romantic comedy. The same shortcomings are reflected in Lope's versification, which tumbles like a brook and is full of play and variety but never becomes a stately river of sound.

Lope's forte lies in a bustling vista of men grasping eagerly at physical gratifications. If his comic method deepens at all it is only in the more developed characterization of a work like *The Gardener's Dog,* in which Lope delineates the inner conflicts of a high-born lady struggling with a love that goes counter to her social code. Here the proud Countess Diana is loved by her secretary Teodoro and responds to him. But his humble rank proves a barrier to her affections, and she oscillates between love and scorn until a quick-witted *gracioso* or comic rogue invents a family tree for Teodoro. The conflict between love and social position and a certain mockery of rank by a playwright who had himself risen from the third estate provide overtones of a greater range than the conventional "cape and sword" comedies. Shrewd commoners are indeed a valuable addition to all of Lope's comedies, very much as they were to Shakespeare's. They bring the leaven of the soil to the artifices of the better situated characters. The humor of common sense and plebeian intelligence also enriches such a play as *Wise for Herself,* in which a girl educated as a shepherdess but brought to the court of Urbino as heir to the Duke puts her rusticity to good use and proves herself more than a match for her sophisticated enemies.

So energetic and fascinating a personality as Lope's was also naturally attracted to legendary and historical material. Here he could find those large events and heroic deeds that gratified his martial tastes. His *comedias heróicas* or *comedias historiáles* covered a wide field ranging all the way from conventional histories like *The Crown of Otun,* which dramatizes the downfall of the unfortunate king of Bohemia Ottokar, or *Rome in Ashes (Roma Abrasada),* a melodrama revolving around the character of Nero, to a few unexpectedly provocative social dramas. Even the weakest of his historical plays, however, possess considerable excitement, and are flavored by some delightful anti-heroic fooling on the part of a plebeian *gracioso* or clown. Lope had Shakespeare's penchant for adding comic relief to momentous events, and the rising middle class was beginning to move into the theatre through the servants' entrance.

Long acclaimed but now considered spurious, *The Star of Seville* is a drama of love and honor, and it approaches tragedy in its story of the Sevillian knight who is ordered by his sovereign to kill his friend. He obeys the royal order and is absolved of the crime by the king. But the judges, exhibiting an unusual degree of integrity, refuse to acquit him, and he is saved only by the king's confession of his part in the murder. Particularly powerful is the scene when the alcaldes refuse to acquit the hero. Lope's frivolity and flamboyance were frequently tempered by a rugged sense of justice and a respect for honest government not ordinarily asociated with a purveyor of fashionable trifles. This was a deeper facet of his character, although less unique than his curiously inconsistent pietism.

At least for twentieth-century tastes, however, Lope comes closest to eminence in those plays which dramatize the sturdy character and heroic struggles of the Spanish peasantry. Himself the son of peasant parents, he was never so vigorous and exciting as when he paid tribute to his ancestry. Out of a number of plays dealing with commoners, at least two— *The King the Greatest Alcalde* and *Fuente Ovejuna*—are of distinct value to the modern theatre.

In *The King the Greatest Alcalde,* which he based on the chronicles of Spain, Lope turned to the reign of Alfonso VII of Castile, who was renowned for his justice and could have served as a model for Lope's own rulers, the less admirable Philips II, III and IV. The peasant Sancho goes to his feudal lord Don Tello to obtain the customary permission to marry his beloved Elvira. But after granting the request, Don Tello abducts this girl because she won his fancy when her peasant lover brought her with him. Sancho, with the aid of his prospective father-in-law Nuño, makes every effort to retrieve his bride. But when he comes to plead with his master, he is driven away by the latter's servants. The resolute peasants then go to the king who orders the nobleman to relinquish the girl without avail. Considering himself the chief justice of the land—*el mejor alcalde*—Alfonso hastens to the seat of the trouble, releases Elvira, and has the refractory lord executed.

Sancho is a magnificent character, and it is to the credit of Lope that he could have turned from his ever-popular flamboyant gentlemen and comic plebeians to the portrait of a peasant hero. This was even more than Shakespeare ever did. Only in the long formal speeches which lack the magic of Shakespeare's poetry does Lope fall short of the possibilities of his strongest themes. Even Lope's glorification of the ideal of Spanish monarchy is progressive rather than retrogressive. The centralized state was a progressive principle in the sixteenth century, and the people could only consider it a vast improvement on the arbitrary rule of their feudal overlords.

Still more effective, and far more original, is the *Fuente Ovejuna* or *The Sheep Well,* in which the struggle of the peasantry against its feudal overlords assumes the proportions of a mass drama. Here there is no single hero, even though the play contains several vivid portraits; *Fuente Ovejuna* has a collective hero—the community of peasants in Fuente Ovejuna. Lope had found their story in the chronicles of Spain for the year 1476 but changed its details to suit his purpose.

The Commander who lords it over the village is a high-handed and corrupt nobleman, but the peasantry is more than a match for him. It is the same stock that fought the Moorish hordes for centuries, that made Spain great on two continents, that later fought Napoleon to a standstill, and recently offered the same stubborn resistance to native fascism supported by foreign troops and war planes. The feudal lord, who has hitherto possessed himself of the village maidens at will, is temporarily routed when he lays siege to the spirited Laurencia. When he seizes the peasant girl he is driven off by her dependable rustic lover Frondoso. Undaunted by such ominous signs of resistance, the Commander, however, sends an armed force to seize another girl Jacinta, and when the peasants plead for her their spokesman Mengo is taken away to be flogged. Soon the people have fresh grievances when their tyrant, resenting the marriage of Frondoso and Laurencia, arrests the couple and has the girl's father, who is an alcalde or justice of the peace, beaten for insubordination. The aroused peasants assemble, and are driven by the disheveled and wronged Laurencia to such a pitch of fury that they swear to stand by each other and destroy the Commander who now also intends to hang Frondoso.

Forcing their way into the castle, they kill the Commander and his minions and place his head on a pike. When judges arrive from the royal court to try them for murder, they meet a united people. Not even tor-ture can compel the villagers to divulge the names of their ringleaders; although three hundred of them are tortured on the rack, including boys of ten, they reply as one man that Fuente Ovejuna (the name of the village, which also means "the sheep well") killed the Commander. The judges report to King Ferdinand that he must either pardon the uniden-tified murderers or wipe out the village to the last man. Filled with ad-miration for his heroic peasants, the sovereign pardons them and takes them under his special protection.

Fuente Ovejuna is a long-neglected classic. It was hailed in Soviet Russia as the first proletarian drama, and the Russians should be au-thorities on this question. But this remarkable work has such a plenitude of passion, characterization, and local color that it has been acclaimed with equal enthusiasm by the London *Times* and the Moscow *News*.

The play makes one regret that Lope did not write more frequently in this vein. It is evident that his addiction to light comedy won him temporary success at the expense of the more enduring fame that his talent could have assured him. The contradictions to be found in his work are, however, too ingrained in his character and in his times to en-courage the hope that he might have applied himself more consistently to drama of genuine passion and broad significance. A man who could write a furiously chauvinistic epic like the *Dragontea*, which painted Sir Francis Drake as an incredible monster, and who could preside at the execution of a Franciscan monk burnt at the stake for heresy, lacked the steady humanity of Shakespeare and the Greek tragedians. Lope plumbed the depths and scaled the heights only too rarely for one endowed with his genius for the theatre. Still, his accomplishment is no mean one.

4 CALDERÓN DE LA BARCA

Lope, like Shakespeare, was no lone figure. His junior by nine years, Guillén de Castro y Bellvis wrote many plays in the same style, one of which *Las Mocedades del Cid,* dealing with the life of Spain's greatest national hero, was the original of Corneille's better known *Cid*. Inferior to the French tragedy in diction and depth, it is nevertheless superior in dramatic movement, which was less restricted on the Spanish stage than it became in the classic age of France. More important than Castro, was Tirso de Molina whose *Burlador de Sevilla* or *The Deceiver of Se-ville* brought the immoderate Don Juan into the theatre. In reality Don Juan was killed by the friars of a Franciscan monastery who pretended that, having insulted the statue of the man he had murdered, he was re-moved to the underworld by supernatural means. Tirso's fanciful embroidery of this story gave rise to a body of literature which includes Molière's comedy on the same theme, Byron's poem *Don Juan,* and Rostand's brilliant play, *Last Night of Don Juan,* as well as to Mozart's great opera *Don Giovanni.* Tirso's other and occasionally better but less renowned plays were also in Lope's vein, and like the older man who undoubtedly influenced his work Tirso died in the bosom of the Church at the ripe age of seventy-seven. Another distinguished practitioner of the school, Juan Ruiz de Alarcon, who was born in Mexico in 1580, divided his attention between the law and the stage, and wrote only thirty plays —a small number for his prolific contemporaries. He is best known for his firm characterization and for supplying a model for Corneille's *Le Menteur* in *La verdad sospechosa* or *Truth Itself Suspected,* a comedy in which a chronic prevaricator becomes entangled in his own lies. His romantic play *The Weaver of Segovia* deals with a Robin Hood character who joins a band of brigands when he is mistreated by his king and is justified only after heroic exploits. One may find echoes of this drama in Schiller's *Robbers.*

Lope's colleagues were indeed numerous; Underhill mentions sixty-six in Castile alone, and Lope's successors were also numerous. To his incredibly large output, they added so many plays that by 1700, according to one account, the Spanish drama reached the staggering total of thirty thousand works.[2] Whatever reservations one makes regarding the quality of this collection, the mere quantity gives impressive testimony to the Spanish theatre's prosperous state. It is not surprising that the Spanish stage should have wielded such an influence on later continental and English writers. It was at least numerically too overwhelming to be disregarded.

Moreover, at least one of its later figures, Calderón de la Barca, who was born in 1600 nearly forty years after Lope and died in 1681, left his mark on the European drama through his merit. Although he, too, had military inclinations and took part in campaigns in Italy and Flanders, as well as in the suppression of a Catalonian revolt, his disposition was philosophical. He was given to greater refinements of thought and sensibility than his swaggering predecessor. He was attached to various noble households and won such favor at court that he was knighted. The last thirty years of his life were spent in holy orders, which he respected with greater consistency than Lope.

Of his hundred and twenty surviving pieces, about eighty are *autos* celebrating the mystery of the eucharist on Corpus Christi day and are generally allegorical in the manner of the English "moralities." Whatever merits may be attributed to them by his Spanish admirers, and one such virtue is their competent lyricism, they are unimpressive as drama. However, they were not the only works of Calderón to be covered with a religious and reflective patina. The famous *Magicc prodigioso* or *The Wonder-Working Magician* is a thoughtful work bearing a resemblance to Marlowe's earlier *Dr. Faustus* and even more to the many analogous stories current during the Middle Ages. The devil tempts the pagan philosopher Cipriano with a Christian beauty appropriately named Justina. When the virtuous maiden rejects the scholar, he is driven to such extremes of despair that he renounces his studies and signs his soul away in exchange for victory over Justina. But the devil has no power over her pure soul, and the savant is so enlightened by the experience that he turns Christian and seeks martyrdom. Justina and he are united in death when they are martyred together by the Roman governor of Antioch. Considerable intrigue rounds out this pious exercise, which once enjoyed a far greater reputation than our contemporary theatre would grant it even in a benign mood.

Calderón varied his style with the composition of a number of "cape and sword" plays considered by some authorities more brilliant than Lope's.[3] The highly esteemed *La dama duende* or *The Fairy Lady* is an ingenious comedy of love. A lover's passion, crossed by the maiden's family, finally prevails against all odds. One or two other plays of similar quality can be mentioned without either decreasing or increasing their author's reputation. But Calderón, who is decidedly pleasing in his comedies, is most impressive in his graver moods, for which he possessed a rare gift of sonorous and yet sensitive and fluent poetry.

Least suited to our twentieth-century taste among the serious plays are the tragedies of jealousy and marital honor. They are written with marked power but with an obtuseness to moderation and humanity which again enforces the distinction between the Spanish masters and a universal genius like Euripides or Shakespeare. The former rarely could lift themselves above the Spain they knew, and its conventions too often counted more with them than the claims of reasonableness and compassion.

A comparison between *Othello* and Calderón's *Physician of His Own Honor* (*El medico de su honra*) is not favorable to the Spanish dramatist. Othello's unreasonable jealousy is grounded not only in his impetuous and honorable character but in the circumstances of his marriage. Before jealousy makes its appearance Shakespeare has shown us Othello's romance with Desdemona, their elopement, and the barrier of race which the two have overleaped. For Desdemona to prove seemingly unfaithful to Othello after such a sealing of the bonds of passion is a blow which the noble Moor could not bear without losing all moderation. Moreover, this jealousy does not rise from a conventional code of marriage as in the Spanish drama, but from the machinations of the villain Iago. Othello is not a conventionally jealous *hidalgo*, he is not even jealous by disposition—his infirmity is artificially induced by a Machiavellian enemy. Moreover, once the unhappy man has murdered his wife he does not sit back complacently and spout about his vindicated honor.

Othello is not Shakespeare's best tragedy, but it is immeasurably superior to a work like *The Physician of His Own Honor.* In Calderón's play a husband believes that his wife, who is actually above reproach, is in love with his brother Prince Enrique, who leaves his dagger accidentally in her room. After prevailing upon the king to banish the Prince, the husband deals with his wife. He brings a surgeon to his home and forces him to bleed his wife to death. Then he tells the king of his wife's death, which being unwilling to admit that his wife had so dishonored him he claims was accidental. But although the sovereign is aware of the situation, he respects the husband's attitude. Then, by some logic that passes comprehension, the king orders him to marry Leonora, a lady whom he had been in honor bound to marry long ago. This act will clear him of the murder for which the king can punish him if he chooses. The hero consents with the proviso that his future wife realize the punishment which will be hers if she proves unfaithful. "Mark me," he tells the happy bride, referring to his murder of his first wife, "if already once unto my honor I have proved a leech, I do not mean to lose my skill."

But Calderón approaches international importance in two widely recognized dramas. One, *The Alcalde* [or Mayor] *of Zalamea* (*El alcalde de Zalamea*), is a social drama. The other, *Life Is a Dream* (*La vida es sueño*), sublimates this playwright's love for dialectics, which he acquired from the Jesuits who supervised his early education, into a thoughtful and original philosophical drama.

The Alcalde of Zalamea follows the pattern of Lope's peasant dramas. The Spaniards have always insisted on applying the principle of "honor" among all social classes; the pride, independence, and rebelliousness of the Spanish people are inseparable from it. Lope dramatized it in *Fuente Ovejuna* and created an epic of the people. Calderón followed suit in his drama of the villagers of Zalamea, although his play lacks some of the breadth and vigor of Lope's. The captain of a troop of soldiers quartered in the village abducts his host's daughter, violates her, and ties her father to a tree in the woods. These people, he considers, are commoners and one can treat them as one pleases. Her father Crespo, who has been meanwhile elected *alcalde* or chief magistrate and mayor, however, has a different conception of the people's rights. He has him captured and tries him himself. The culprit's superior officer Don Lope de Figueroa, learning of his capture, demands his freedom in the king's name, and the king himself, who has arrived at the village, requests his officer's liberty. But Crespo delivers only the captain's corpse to the sovereign, since he has already had him executed. Impressed with the courage and justice of his alcalde's behavior, the king appoints him *alcalde* for life instead of punishing him. The play is generally considered Calderon's greatest work. For once Calderón placed the theme of honor on a broad folk basis, and his spirited evocation of common Spanish life is a welcome relief from the artificialities of his usual manner.

Life Is a Dream alone can be mentioned in the same breath with this social drama. It is, in fact, not so radically different from *The Alcalde of Zalamea* since its theme is closely related to the problem of good government. King Basilio, having been warned by a prophecy that his heir Segismundo would work much evil, keeps his child confined in a tower. After many years, his father decides to give the young man a trial. He has him drugged and spirited to his palace, and gives him an opportunity to reveal his character. Here, however, the young prince behaves so abominably that his father realizes the impossibility of ever entrusting the crown to him. He has him drugged and returned to the tower, and when the prince awakens he is persuaded that he had never left the place and had been merely dreaming. A popular rising liberates him later and makes him king. But now he is so fearful that his new-won royalty will prove to be only another dream that he conducts himself with discretion and humanity. Consequently he overcomes the curse that rested on him until then. To realize that life is only a dream, Calderón seems to say, is perhaps the most effective means of neutralizing one's lust for power.

If *Life Is a Dream* seems too given to moralizing and is not wholly convincing in its psychology, it is nevertheless to be accounted an ingeniously contrived fantasy which follows a logic of its own. Its subdued speculation is even supported by modern psychiatry; a dream, psychoanalysts assure us, can provide a discharge for destructive impulses. Segismundo's drama, moreover, is to be gauged not by its adherence to strict probability and psychological motivation, but by its power of suggestion and its reflective fantasy. Calderón's verse, besides, is altogether equal to the demands of this philosophical fable; it is marred only by passages that followed the fashionable affectations of language known as euphuism in England and Gongorism in Spain.

Calderón's influence on European drama was tremendous, and it was not always good. If it encouraged thoughtfulness, it also propagated artifice. He lacked the breezy health and the rich theatricality of his great predecessor and his character drawing was vitiated by the growing artificiality of Spanish life during the seventeenth century.

He was a true son of Spain's rapid decline. Empire was passing from the Iberian peninsula. Its economic life, deprived of the artificial stimulus of gold from America, was beginning to feel the effect of the expulsion of the Moors and the Jews who had promoted the nation's commerce and industries. The lessened energy of the times is reflected in

Calderón's generally tame plays, and the decadence observable in his own works grows apace in that of his successors Zorilla, Moreto, and others. Even historians partial to Spanish literature concede the twilight of the drama after his death. The theatre closed another cycle after having given birth to a vast body of ingenious romantic comedies and tragedies, to several provocative social dramas, to Lope's one important mass drama, and to a philosophical play distinguished by originality of form and beautiful versification.

A still more significant cycle which began about the same time had closed about half a century earlier. Before it was brought to a close in England, however, the drama had achieved its second great age. The Spanish Renaissance was, in effect, merely a prelude to it.

A NOTE ON JESUIT DRAMA

The energetic Jesuit leaders of the Counter-Reformation fostered the theatre in their schools, and also wrote numerous plays in Latin from the late sixteenth century to the latter part of the eighteenth century. Much attention was lavished by them on the art of production. Performances were open to the public, which was supplied with synopses in the vernacular languages. The subjects of the plays were mainly historical figures, saints' lives, and allegories. It was in the Jesuit schools, we may note, that Corneille, Molière, Le Sage, Diderot, and Voltaire got their early training in theatre, and the influence of the Jesuit order was, naturally, especially strong in Spain and the New World colonized by the Spaniards and Portuguese. The Jesuits, indeed, supplied the only truly international theatre the world possessed after the Middle Ages. They were especially energetic in Central and Eastern Europe. (A short survey will be found on pages 240–44 of Allardyce Nicoll's *World Drama*, 1950). The Jesuits also employed non-literary theatrical means for providing moral and religious instruction — outdoor theatricals, such as processions and *tableaux vivants*. These had been, indeed, popular before, during the Middle Ages. The Elizabethan period had also favored lavishly staged "royal entries," processions, and pageants, many of them allegorical. The *tableaux vivants* were often explained to the public by an expositor.

XII

CHRISTOPHER MARLOWE

I THE LAUREATE OF MAGNIFICENCE

CHRISTOPHER MARLOWE stands as a symbol of the theatre's second great age, not merely because he is its first major playwright but because he expressed its romantic strivings more directly and singularly than any of his predecessors or successors. He had in him, as the friendly poet Drayton noted, "brave translunary things," "raptures all air and fire," and an abundance of "fine madness." "Man of the Renaissance" is a title which belongs to him more than to any other European playwright, since no one cherished the epoch's strivings for magnificence—in its thought, action, and enjoyment—with the same glorious drunkenness.

This Elizabethan Icarus emerged from a still partly medieval chrysalis. Canterbury is the Vatican city of England, and it was here, in the shadow of the great cathedral, that the son of the shoemaker John Marlowe was christened on February 26, 1564. Its bells must have lulled the child to sleep, wakened him, and called him to prayer. Its peace was redolent of an age of faith, which he was later to renounce, and the gargoyles that leered at him from the cathedral were visible representations of the terrors that awaited sinners and unbelievers.

But a new age was already jostling the old one during Marlowe's childhood. Worldliness was having its way as England became a commercial nation and as the love of magnificence increased at court and in the towns of the prosperous middle class. Gorgeous spectacles and processions attested the new reign of splendor, and one of these occurred during Queen Elizabeth's visit to Canterbury during Marlowe's youth.

The lad also grew up in an environment which respected the strong successful individual above all men. The medieval worship of the saints was being supplanted by worship of those super-entrepreneurs the heroic freebooters, conquerors and merchants of the age. Long before becoming familiar with Machiavelli's teachings in *The Prince,* which was little more than a manual for the enterprising Renaissance individual who happened to be a ruler, Marlowe could have imbibed the philosophy of power from the common air of England. His art, which turned so eagerly toward the sun of personal glory, did not need a foreign stimulus even if "Machiavellism" was a convenient label for the superman dream. The worldly outlook was, moreover, closely related to the resurgence of classic culture and to the sensuousness and intellectual curiosity of the age.

The new learning of the Renaissance already commanded respect in the land, having been zealously promoted by eight decades of scholarly endeavor by leaders like Sir Thomas More, the author of *Utopia*, Sir Thomas Elyot, whose book *The Governour* was a manual of the new humanist education, and Roger Ascham, whose *Schoolmaster* was another. They had promoted the study of Greek and promulgated the ideals of a rounded education which would put the scholar in touch with the world and the world in touch with scholarship. If Marlowe's early education in Canterbury was dominated by the clergy, it was nevertheless pursued under the aegis of an archbishop who was a scholar and an ardent book-collector. A point was stretched to allow the apparently bright youngster to enter King's School, and he was favored again when he was awarded one of Archbishop Parker's scholarships at Corpus Christi College, Cambridge, in December 1580.

This scholarship was indeed intended for lads who were expected to enter the church, and Cambridge, too, still cast a backward glance at the Middle Ages. But here were the treasures of classic culture and modern thought for those who had an aptitude for them such as Marlowe began to display. Francis Kett, the unitarian who was burned at the stake as a freethinker four years before Marlowe's death, had been a fellow at the University half a year before the young scholar matriculated there. Another prominent skeptic Thomas Fineux joined the College shortly before Marlowe left in 1587. The new modernistic *Logic* of Peter Ramus was taught side by side with Aristotle's *Analytics*, and astronomy was assiduously studied. Above all, Marlowe could graze in the University's excellent library, and here he found many a book that fired his imagination and provided him with material for the plays he was to write not many years later.

Nor was the theatre neglected at Cambridge, for the Universities had become the first important theatres of the English Renaissance. Roman comedies, imitations of the classics, didactic pieces, and plays brought to the scholars from London by troupes like the Queen's Players and Lord Rich's Players filled the halls of the venerable institution. That early chronicle play in Latin, Thomas Legge's *Richardus Tertius*, was produced at the University when Marlowe was a freshman, and other "school plays" followed. Performances were prescribed by the University statutes, and students who refused to take part could be summarily expelled.

If these exercises were labored and were inferior to the new free romantic drama which was soon to prevail in England, the productions were nevertheless not lacking in excitement. Trinity College had to put in new windows "after the plays" in 1583 and thereafter found it advisable to remove them during the theatrical season. Students who kept order at the performances wisely carried drawn daggers and swords, and took the added precaution of wearing "visors and steel caps." [2]

Marlowe's role in these demonstrations is unknown, but he was certainly not the kind of scholar who could be repressed by an academic atmosphere. It is true that he took his bachelor's degree in 1584 and stayed for the coveted master's degree, which he received three years later. But a more unconventional scholar could hardly be imagined. According to the university records, he disappears frequently during his last years in Cambridge, exceeding the number of absences permitted by statute. No sooner had he received his bachelor's degree than he was to be found less and less at the University, and part of his time was spent in Rheims among the Catholics who were plotting against Queen Elizabeth's Protestant regime across the channel. The University did not know the reason for these absences, suspected him of papism, and refused him a degree. The Privy Council however, interfered and ordered the dons to grant him the master's degree, testifying that he had comported himself discreetly "whereby he had done her Majesty good service, and deserved to be rewarded for his faithful dealing." [3] His patron and friend Thomas Walsingham was closely related to Sir Francis Walsingham, head of Her Majesty's secret service; Robert Poley, one of the latter's agents, was Marlowe's companion and was present at the poet's strange death. It is characteristic of his impassioned character that he should have thrown himself into the thick of Elizabethan politics and intrigue while still attending the University. The Renaissance had exploded the notion that a scholar must lead a retired existence; his learning was in fact a recommendation for public activity. There was, moreover, enough adventure and excitement in Marlowe's hazardous assignment to attract a young romanticist.

In July 1587 Marlowe, now a master of arts, settled in London and began his career as writer and bohemian, though he was probably still in the secret service. In the capital he plunged into the social life of the poets and playwrights, and associated with colorful literary aristocrats like Sir Philip Sidney and Sir Walter Raleigh, with whom he discussed philosophy and shared dreams of glory and adventure. If Marlowe's station precluded a public career like Raleigh's, he could at least realize his dreams vicariously in the characters he created; Tamburlaine, the hero of his first successful play, was a super-Raleigh and a super-Essex.

When, moreover, the intoxication of his dreams was insufficient he could lose himself in the bohemian life of his fellow-writers. He shared rooms with Thomas Kyd, his equal in popularity in the early Elizabethan theatre, and led a dissolute life with such shady playwrights and pamphleteers as Robert Greene and Thomas Nashe. Possibly he also acted for a while, and certainly he was in touch with the famous actors of his day, especially the enlightened and impressive Edward Alleyn who contributed so greatly to the success of his plays. An "atheistical" society or "School of the Night," frequented by Raleigh and intellectuals like the noted mathematician and astronomer Thomas Harriot, provided him with further stimulation. The taverns of London must also have resounded with his bold speculations, and doubtless he delighted in shocking his hearers with talk that often struck them as rankly heretical. Brawls, too, were not unknown to a poet who had to be "bound over to keep the peace."

Oscillating between the fashionable households of Walsingham and Sidney's sister the Countess of Pembroke, and the seedy life of the plebeian intelligentsia, Marlowe felt the pulse of the entire age. And no matter who his companions were, they lived and thought boldly and sometimes recklessly. His friend Raleigh's exploits against Spain, political rivalry with Lord Essex for the Queen's favor, settlement of Virginia, and reputation for heretical speculation have gone down in history. His magnificent appearance, impulsiveness, and his bejeweled costumes were the talk of the town. His fellow-"atheist" Thomas Harriot joined Raleigh on his expeditions to America and his scientific genius led him to experiment with inventions and make astronomical predictions that earned him a dangerous reputation for black magic. Marlowe's wonder-working Dr. Faustus had a living model in that intrepid mathematician. The scientific progress of the Renaissance, which was paralleled on the continent by Galileo and Kepler, touched Marlowe directly, and it is not surprising that his plays should contain numerous allusions to astronomy, that they should be full of the wonder of an expanding universe.

Sidney's pre-eminence at court and heroic death in the Netherlands, and Walsingham's vigorous career in the service of the Queen as her indispensable Secretary further represented the active life which the poet glorified so consistently. The writers and actors of the lower strata were not timid recluses either. They were uprooted no doubt, in the London underworld, but colorful personalities like Greene, Peele and Nashe wallowed in the muck with a certain magnificence. Even the spies, swindlers and murderers of the demimonde like Ingram Frizer, Robert Poley, and Nicholas Skeres with whom he associated played some part in taking the classics-loving poet out of the library.

That Marlowe moved through this welter of Elizabethan life with the intoxication of a wonder-loving boy is abundantly evident. He became the poet of magnificence, of physical and mental splendor and adventure. He remains to this day the greatest romanticist of the theatre.

It is necessary only to complete this portrait with a few darker colors than are usually employed, for he was not so intoxicated that he remained entirely star-dazzled. He had wakeful, sobering moments. He never married and he appears to have become increasingly irritable and quarrelsome until even his friends lost patience with him; his companions Greene and Nashe spoke disparagingly of him and his roommate Kyd complained of his pugnacity. Irked by the disparity between his dreams and the realities of his situation, for he had neither wealth nor position, he felt bitter and frustrated. He was aware of the evil and hate of the world, of corruption, political intrigue, and injustice. Even the ultimate futility of all aspiration was present to his mind. How else could he have written tragedy, and it is after all tragedy, not romance, that he created. For comedy he displayed practically no talent; his was never an easy-going or even well-tempered personality. Much villainy is recorded in his plays, much frustration, and much embitterment.

His opinions, too, seemed to become increasingly pronounced. His assertions, recorded no doubt with some exaggeration by the scapegrace Richard Baines who informed against him, referred to the contradictions of the Bible very much in the vein of Thomas Paine's *Age of Reason*. For the apostles he evinced scant respect; among them "Paul only had wit," Marlowe was said to have maintained, but "he was a timorous fellow in bidding men to be subject to magistrates against his conscience." Moses was able to perform miracles because he had learned the "arts of the Egyptians"; he was but a "juggler" and kept the Jews in the wilderness for forty years "to the intent that those who were privy to most of his subtleties (tricks) might perish, and so an everlasting superstition remain in the hearts of the people." He appears to have doubted the legitimacy of Christ. All Protestants were "hypocritical asses" and "the beginning of religion was only to keep men in awe." [4]

Marlowe fell under suspicion of heresy, his friend Kyd was tortured into giving evidence against him, and a warrant for his arrest was signed. But before he could be found and brought before the Privy Council the twenty-nine-year-old poet was dead. On May 30th, 1593, in Dame Eleanore Bull's tavern, in the little village of Deptford hard by London, Marlowe, Frizer, Poley, and Skeres asked for a private room. They dined and supped there, the wine flowed freely, and suddenly Marlowe, probably intoxicated, fell to quarreling with Frizer over the bill. He seized Frizer's dagger and attacked him with it, but Frizer defended himself, caught Marlowe's arm, and drove the weapon back into his assailant's right eye, giving him a mortal wound. This at least is the deposition of the witnesses. It has been conjectured with good reason that the affair was not as accidental as it appears, and it is more than possible that Marlowe was deliberately provoked and killed to prevent his arrest. Had he been put to torture by the Privy Council he might have implicated men of importance, possibly Raleigh. In any case, the poet's words at the conclusion of *Doctor Faustus,*

> *Cut is the branch that might have grown full straight,*

proved prophetic of his own fate. His violent and untimely death, seven years after his appearance in London, closed a meteoric career that began and ended very much like one of those tragedies with which he had ushered in the great febrile age of the English drama.

2 MARLOWE AND THE DAWN OF THE ELIZABETHAN THEATRE

Had Marlowe never written a play, he would still be remembered as a poet. He was an inspired lyricist, and the author of one of the most beautiful poems in the English language *Hero and Leander,* completed by his friend Chapman, the translator of Homer. It was, however, the drama that attracted the dynamic young writer. Like so many other Elizabethan scholars who found themselves propelled into a precarious literary career, he settled down to the business of supplying plays for the theatre.

It would have been like Marlowe to apply Augustus Caesar's boast to himself, to have claimed that he found the theatre made of brick and left it made of gold. He was conscious of a mission when the Prologue of *Tamburlaine* announced his intention of leading audiences away

> *From jigging veins of rhyming mother wits*
> *And such conceits as clownage keeps in pay.*

In the "jigging veins of rhyming mother wits" we have long recognized an allusion to the unnatural rhymed verse employed by his predecessors. But Marlowe is objecting to something more fundamental—namely, the want of greatness in English drama until then. With the "conceits" of "clownage" he has only impatience; pre-Shakespearean comedy was devoid of high poetry, and he seems to have lacked a genuine sense of humor in what Shaw has harshly called his "clumsy horseplay." (If indeed it was his.) The full significance of his departure from his predecessors cannot, however, be comprehended without some knowledge of the five decades of theatrical activity which preceded his own, decades that laid out the brick foundation to which he added his gold and gilt.

Like the Italian drama, the Elizabethan began with revivals and imitations of classic comedy and tragedy. The learned Scot, George Buchanan, for example, translated Euripides' *Medea* and *Alcestis* into Latin for performance by his students at Bordeaux, and dramatized biblical material in the Greek manner in his *Baptistes*. The more familiar Latin drama wielded a still greater influence, and Terence, who was specially favored in the schools, inspired didactic pieces closely related to the old morality plays; many of these came from France and Holland. One of these pieces, the Dutch scholar Gnaphaeus' *Acolastus* even became a textbook in England. In the first English novel, *The Unfortunate Traveler,* Marlowe's companion and collaborator Thomas Nashe recalled one of the crude university performances of the *Acolastus:* "One as if he had been playing a clay floor, trod the stage so hard with his feet that I thought verily he had resolved to do the carpenter that set it up some utter shame. Another flung his arms like cudgels at a pear tree, insomuch as it was mightily dreaded that he would strike the candles that hung above their heads out of their sockets and leave them all in darkness."

More enlivening were the English imitations of Plautus which began as early as 1533, with Nicholas Udall's *Ralph Roister Doister*. Although Udall was successively headmaster of Eton and Westminster, he found in Plautus a model who encouraged sprightly humor rather than dull didacticism. Udall's object may have been the pedagogic one of providing his pupils with an exercise. But he conceived the idea of giving them an English counterpart of Roman comedy, from which he borrowed its type-characters of fool, braggart, and parasitic rogue.[5] His comic hero Ralph, an affluent fool infatuated with the worthy English matron Dame Constance, is led by the parasite Matthew Merrygreek to woo her with an ardor and resolution that annoy her exceedingly and imperil her betrothal to the respectable merchant Gawain Goodluck. Acting on the principle that "Mirth prolongeth life, and causeth health" provided it is mixed with "decent comeliness," the learned playwright created a series of complications that result in a pitched battle between Ralph's retinue and Dame Constance's household, which contains some robust housemaids. Since they have a way of turning a frying-pan into an instrument of destruction, the impetuous lover is routed with trusty blows. "Ralph Roister will no more wooing begin," and Dame Constance and her respectable fiancé are reconciled. By virtue of its native humor, its salty vernacular, and its middle-class background, *Ralph Roister Doister* became the first English comedy of the Renaissance. Ralph may be romantic in a fashion, but he has the English faculty of calculation when he appraises Dame Constance's dowry, and Merrygreek for all his mischief is capable of such practical observations as that

> *An hundred pound of marriage-money, doubtless,*
> *Is ever thirty pound sterling, or somewhat less.*

English saws keep the comedy close to the soil, as when the lady's maid Tibet Talkapace remarks that

Old brown bread crusts must have good mumbling
But good ale down your throat hath good easy tumbling.

Hearty English songs like "Whoso to marry a minion wife" and "I mun be married a Sunday" enliven the episodes. Udall's schoolboys must have had robust inclinations, and *Ralph Roister Doister* is an earthy comedy that can still be revived to advantage.

It was followed shortly by the famous *Gammer Gurton's Needle,* a village comedy of uncertain date and authorship (it may have been written by the John Bridges who later became Bishop of Oxford),[6] which has even greater gusto. This comedy, too, was of academic origin and was first acted at Christ's College, Cambridge, although no comedy could be more remote from the midnight oil of scholarship. The old crone Gammer Gurton loses her greatly prized needle and is prevailed upon by the mischief-loving Diccon to suspect her neighbor Dame Chat of the theft. The *affaire Gurton* reaches mock-heroic proportions, and the entire village is set agog. The tippling parish priest Doctor Rot interferes with lamentable results and the tolerant village official Master Bayly vainly tries his hand at pacification, until the needle is ultimately found in the breeches of Gammer's manservant Hodge. The robustness of the humor is particularly marked in the tenor of the dialogue and in the Rabelaisian climax, which locates the lost article somewhat painfully for Hodge "in the exact place on which Gammer Gurton's industry had been employed."[7] Again, too, this second play is the richer for a splendid song in honor of English ale, "Back and side go bare, go cold."

The style of these pieces was, however, too plebeian for a man of Marlowe's acquired aristocratic tastes; and their meter, with its "doggerel couplet of twelve syllables or thereabouts" in the case of the first comedy and couplets of fourteen or even sixteen syllables in the second instance, could only strike him as pedestrian. It remained for the more versatile genius of Shakespeare to incorporate their folk humor in his famous passages devoted to bumpkins, rogues, clowns, and comic policemen. Nor could Marlowe have had much regard for the comedies of the court which succeeded those of the school, tepid pieces written in the classically inspired Italian manner first domesticated by the minor playwright George Gascoigne in his prose adaptation of Ariosto's comedy of mistaken identities *The Supposes,* presented by the budding lawyers of Gray's Inn in 1566.

For the court which favored the spectacles, revels, pastoral plays and fragile fantasies so much in vogue in Italy another university graduate John Lyly, born a decade before Marlowe in 1554, provided a series of better exercises. He had made his mark with the fashionable novel *Euphues* which popularized the affected language subsequently known as "euphuism." His prose, which went into arpeggios of alliteration and allusions to pseudo-scientific curiosities, titillated the taste of the aristocracy. Although he never acquired the position of Master of Revels which he coveted, Lyly became the darling of the court, and the disappointed but persistent courtier whom Marlowe knew well continued to woo Queen Elizabeth's favor with a series of cultivated comedies. The first *Campaspe*, acted before her in 1581, celebrated the perfervid love of Alexander for his Theban captive Campaspe who in turn loved the painter Apelles. Commissioned by the conqueror to paint the beautiful lady, Apelles falls in love with her, too, and Alexander is noble enough in the end to sanction the marriage of the two lovers. Duels of wit, particularly when the crusty philosopher Diogenes is on the stage, and sentimental passages adorned the piece.

Lyly's next effort *Sappho and Phaon* was another love story—that of Sappho's passion, inflamed by the capricious Venus, for the handsome boatman Phaon. Here the allegorical flattery of Queen Elizabeth was continued with mythological trimmings, and these features reached the acme of their tinsel perfection in his *Endimion,* produced a year or so before Marlowe made his mark in the theatre. Here Elizabeth is Cynthia, the chaste lunar goddess, and falls in love with the beautiful youth Endimion (the Duke d'Alençon who courted Elizabeth at this time), who has been put to sleep for forty years by a witch because she is enamored of him and is jealous of the goddess. His later efforts gave a satirical twist to his fantastic art in *Midas* and *The Woman in the Moon,* a cynical exposé of womanhood which may have been inspired by his disappointment in the Queen because she showed no inclination to reward him for his flattery. He also attempted pastoral drama in *Love's Metamorphosis,* and Italian comedy of intrigue in *Mother Bombie* during the years 1587-1589.

Except in *The Woman in the Moon* Lyly wrote his plays in pleasantly mannered prose, interspersed with lovely lyrics like the well-known "Campaspe's Song," and it must be conceded that he had a "pretty talent." Shakespeare was indebted to him, not always to advantage, in his romantic comedies for suggestions and style. Full-blooded and intolerant Marlowe, however, could have little respect for work that wanted vigor and passion. Nor could he have cared for Lyly's actors, the boy players attached to St. Paul's church. Marlowe's plays were staged by full-chested men like the seven-foot, majestic Edward Alleyn who alone could do justice to his vigorous heroes. Lyly's vein, which was also tapped by other writers, added at most a number of divertissements to the theatre.

It was in early Elizabethan tragedy that English drama began its triumphal march. Between 1559 and 1566 were published five of Seneca's tragedies, and the whole body of work attributed to him appeared in 1581 in the historic volume *Ten Tragedies*. Moreover, Seneca was familiar to the Elizabethans in Latin long before that time. His strong rhetorical style plentifully charged with blood and thunder, his high seriousness, and his melodramatic plots provided the first model for exalted drama, although medieval influences dominated the stage more than is often realized and the Elizabethans did not slavishly imitate him for long.

The earliest notable "Senecan" drama *Gorboduc* by the poet Thomas Sackville and Thomas Norton told a typically Senecan story of fratricide. Gorboduc divides his kingdom between his two sons Ferrex and Porrex. But evil counselors egg them on to attack each other, and Ferrex is killed by his brother, who is in turn murdered by his mother who always favored Ferrex. The people arise and put both the King and Queen to death. Following the Senecan formula, Sackville and Norton relegated these melodramatic events entirely to obliging messengers. The Elizabethan love of stage action, partly inherited from the medieval theatre, was, however, met with a series of "dumb shows" or pantomimes that supplied the visible events merely reported in the play proper. The authors made the departure of turning from classic subjects to English history and paid less attention to the unities of time and place than was required by their model. Above all, they cast their play not in classic prosody but in its native equivalent, the "blank verse" of unrhymed pentameters which had already proved somewhat effective in English poetry.

Their play even introduces that topical interest in problems of good government, civil discord and succession to the throne which occupied every intelligent Englishman and made many an Elizabethan historical drama a veiled lesson for the times. To be concerned with these subjects and to illuminate them was equivalent to touching upon the most vital topic of the day—namely, the preservation of the strong centralized government which England had finally obtained under Elizabeth after much civil war and political discord. *Gorboduc* inveighed against "the lust of kingdom" that "knows no sacred faith, no rule of reason, no regard of right."

Its most immediate effect was, however, chiefly an extension of melodrama. Followed in the sixties by other Senecan tragedies like Gascoigne's *Jocasta, Tancred and Gismunda* (by five collaborators in the well-tried Hollywood manner) and Thomas Hughes' *Misfortunes of Arthur*, *Gorboduc* set the pace for the drama of unbridled horror which characterized the first period of the Elizabethan theatre and continued to vitiate it to the end. Still other efforts extended the field, exploring romantic themes in a tragedy like *Appius and Virginia,* staging the action instead of reporting it (as in Thomas Preston's otherwise execrable *Cambyses*) or introducing tragi-comedy as in the *Damon and Pythias* exercise which ushered in the typically Elizabethan commingling of tragedy and humor. Neither Marlowe nor Shakespeare was always free from the bombast and bad taste exhibited by these early writers.

Still, for better as well as for worse, they gave the later Elizabethan dramatists their cue for emotionalism and violence. Moreover, tragedy was beginning to make new strides at the very time when Marlowe was completing his education and beginning his career. It was tapping a new poetic vein, a veritable *dolce stil nuovo,* in his friend George Peele's work. This "university wit" or bohemian, famed for his recklessness and the subject of the largely apocryphal "Merry Jests" which had him stealing a pair of trousers out of dire necessity, followed Lyly in composing refined comedy like *The Arraignment of Paris* and satirical fantasy like his *Old Wives' Tale.* The same refined talent went into his biblical tragedy *David and Bethsabe,* produced about the same time as Marlowe's first play. Although awkward in construction, *David and Bethsabe* was marked by that poetic genius which, to a far greater degree, is Marlowe's prime contribution to the drama. It is not difficult to find in it cadences like

> *God, in the whizzing of a pleasant wind,*
> *Shall march upon the tops of mulberry-trees,*
> *To cool all breasts that burn with grief*

and

> *Then let them toss my broken lute to heaven,*
> *Even to his hands that beats me with the strings.*

If no one had to teach Marlowe to sing, it is nevertheless true that his work was preceded and paralleled by the growth of genuinely poetic drama in the work of his colleagues.

Melodramatic treatment was also beginning to turn from a mere reporting of events to vivid stage presentations, most strikingly so in the work of Thomas Kyd, who wrote in the same room with Marlowe and was accused of the same heresies. Less brilliant and less poetic than Marlowe, Kyd nevertheless possessed tremendous vigor, and he understood the requirements of the stage even better than his friend; moreover, despite the punning of Ben Jonson who called him "sportive Kyd," he had a natural bent for tragedy. Although he does not appear to have come from one of the two universities, he possessed at least the superficies of a good education and was accepted by the "university wits" or college-bred bohemians of his time as one of their colleagues. This was also his misfortune, for he was arrested on the same charge of atheism as Marlowe in 1593. He seems to have been broken by imprisonment, torture, and disgrace, and died a year later. The long arm of the Elizabethan law claimed another victim in the playwright who alone equaled and perhaps even surpassed Marlowe's popularity in his own day.

Kyd translated Garnier's French Senecan drama *Cornelia* while moving in the classical circle of the learned Countess of Pembroke and her brother Sidney. He appears to have written by 1589 a lost *Hamlet* which was the original of Shakespeare's tragedy, and his hand has been traced in the latter's *Titus Andronicus* and *Henry VI*. The one extant play which can be ascribed to him with certainty is *The Spanish Tragedy*, the most successful work of his day. Although it was acted by 1588, this dramatic *tour de force* continued to be popular throughout the Elizabethan period. A notable feature of Senecan drama was its employment of the revenge motive. Kyd's tragedy, which dramatized the revenge of a grief-stricken father, brought this type of drama to its highest peak before Shakespeare.

Horatio, the only son of the marshal of Spain Hieronimo, wins the love of the beautiful Belimperia, but is murdered by the Prince of Portugal and by her brother Lorenzo who wants her to marry the Prince. Belimperia is spirited away to prevent her from bearing witness against them, but she succeeds in sending Hieronimo a letter written with her blood for ink. The grief-stricken father discovers the murderers, demands justice from the king in vain, loses his wife who dies of grief, and hesitates long, sick in mind and feigning like Hamlet even more madness to avoid suspicion. Finally while Belimperia is being married to the Portuguese prince against her will, he stages a tragedy for the wedding which is so literally performed that the miscreants are killed. Belimperia ends her own life, and Hieronimo, who bites out his tongue to prevent the king from forcing him to reveal his confederates, stabs himself. Powerful situations and highly affecting lines make *The Spanish Tragedy* an overwhelming melodrama despite its obvious puerilities. Marlowe could not have been impervious to Kyd's influence when he wrote his own revenge play *The Jew of Malta*.

If Kyd, moreover, was the author of *Arden of Feversham*, acted between 1586 and 1592, he was the founder of middle-class tragedy, a *genre* approached by neither Marlowe nor Shakespeare. This rare dramatization of a recent crime reported in that inexhaustible source book of Elizabethan playwrights Holinshed's *Chronicles* is a masterful and surprisingly modern work. Alice, the wife of the worthy gentleman Arden, betrays him with a common fellow Mosbie and prevails upon the latter to rid her of her husband. After much intrigue and many failures they succeed in murdering him but fail to cover their tracks and are executed for their crime. The agonizing suspense of the action is equaled only by the tortured and subtle characterizations of the protagonists. Alice is the victim of an overpowering infatuation, Mosbie is dominated less by passion than by greed and even hates her, and Arden is heavy of heart, alternately weak and strong, suspicious and overconfident. Nor is he entirely blameless in his life, which he would not perhaps have lost if he had not succumbed to the growing middle-class vice of avariciousness which made him enemies. The noblest character in the play is the Franklin or freeholder, who remains loyal to him but sententiously comments that

> *Arden lay murdered in that plot of ground*
> *Which he by force and violence held from Reede.'*

The dramatist errs only in making Arden too gullible in his attitude toward Mosbie and his wife, whom he trusts at times to a degree which exceeds credibility.

In this dark drama of criminal passion no one is happy or exalted, and the realism of the work foreshadows the middle-class' drama of a much later age even if it was followed by a few Elizabethan imitations like *A Warning for Fair Women* (1599) and *A Yorkshire Tragedy* (1608), another powerful play. The author of *Arden of Feversham* realized that he was writing against the grain of his time when he concluded defiantly that

> *. . . . simple truth is gracious enough,*
> *And needs no other points of glosing stuff.*

Elizabethan drama had, in short, reached the foothills and was beginning its final ascent when Marlowe appeared on the scene. All that was needed was a bold leap such as no one had yet dared or been able to make. The honor of making it, which was tantamount to enthroning the great poetry on the stage that distinguishes Elizabethan drama and counteracts its besetting error of tearing a passion to tatters, was reserved for a great poet. In the difficult department of dramatic construction Marlowe was not progressive; in such works as *Tamburlaine* and *Dr. Faustus* he was even retrogressive, and he never built as carefully as the author of *Arden of Feversham*. But he had the rarer qualities of poetic inspiration, far-flung vision, and intense perceptions.

By 1587, moreover, the Elizabethan stage was ready to receive his genius. It had begun to flourish half a century before his birth, in academic and private halls; it had moved during his childhood into the open inn-yards which were galleried within; and it had settled during his youth in specially constructed playhouses, modeled after the inn-yards and situated just outside the jurisdiction of the puritanical Lord Mayor of London. Eleven years before *Tamburlaine* was performed, a joiner by trade James Burbage who had been a member of the Earl of Leicester's company conceived the idea of building a playhouse, The Theatre, near Shoreditch north of the Thames. In time on the low marshy region of Southwark known as the Bankside—a red-light district that accommodated taverns, gambling-resorts and stews occupied by ladies euphemistically called "Winchester Geese" because the land was owned by the good Bishop of Winchester—the public could visit the Rose. the Swan, the Globe, and the Hope theatres. By the close of the century there were eight playhouses on the north and south banks of the Thames.

Into the fascinating story of these enterprises we cannot enter here. E. K. Chambers' four-volume history, *The Elizabethan Stage,* and other scholarly studies do ample justice to the subject. Even if our records are not always definitive, it is clear that the public theatres were round or hexagonal structures capable of housing large audiences. Courtyards open to the sky and surrounded by two or three galleries reserved for gentlemen and ladies, they lacked artificial means of lighting, so that performances had to be given in the afternoon. There were no seats in the orchestra or pit where the groundlings jostled each other and wore out their patience when they were not regaled with an abundance of spectacle, costuming, jigging, bawdry, high-astounding words, and rapid-fire action.*

The stage was a platform jutting into the audience and surrounded on three sides by the audience; in Alleyn's theatre, the Fortune, "the thrust was forty-three feet in a building along fifty-five feet square within."[8] The artificial division between the audience and the stage which prevails in our theatre was absent in such a structure, and that the more forward gallants should have even sat on the stage is merely another sign of "audience participation." The tiring house or property and dressing room which backed the platform provided a permanent background. Its doors served for entrances and exits, and a gallery provided a setting for such episodes as the balcony scene in *Romeo and Juliet,* while a false ceiling known as "the heavens" gave the impression of a strip of sky. A curtain that could be drawn when necessary divided the stage into fore and aft. The latter portion and the permanent background with its gallery served for specified localities, while the fore-stage was used for general and unlocalized action sometimes even crudely identified by placards.

---

* The informal frame of mind in which audiences patronized the Elizabethan drama is unintentionally indicated by Sir Henry Wotton's account of the fire that destroyed Shakespeare's Globe Theatre during a performance on June 29, 1613. The audience escaped injury—"only one man had his breeches set on fire, that would perhaps have broiled him, if he had not by the benefit of a provident wit, put it out with a bottle of ale."

The primitiveness of this stage has been, however, exaggerated. A permanent setting can be a very effective one, as Copeau has demonstrated in our own time. The drama needs suggestion and playing space far more than it needs close approximations to actual rooms and buildings. Moreover, the Elizabethans made use of flats, arras and painted cloth stretched on wooden frames, and these could represent houses with actual doors, pastoral scenes, and a great variety of furniture. Rapid changes were managed behind curtains when, for example, small interiors were set on a portion of the stage. So long as continuity of action could be maintained the Elizabethan public theatre progressed toward representation of backgrounds, while trapdoors facilitated apparitions and numerous devices provided spectacular effects such as lightning and fireworks. Aided by the property man, the scenic designer, and the actors who became increasingly proficient in their art, even if they rarely dispensed with declamatory mannerisms, an Elizabethan playwright could feel that his lucubrations were receiving a good measure of justice. Only one thing was tacitly understood—namely, that the flow of the action must remain unimpeded, since the dramatists remained free to roam through time and place without having to worry over time-consuming changes of realistic settings. In so active an age as the Elizabethan, action rather than localization of the action was the prime consideration.

This commercial theatre had begun a flourishing existence by the time Marlowe lent his genius to playwriting. Puritans might chafe at its existence, plagues might close its doors and send the actors touring the provinces, and the competition of the boy players of the Chapel, Blackfriars and Paul's might reduce box-office receipts. But the taste of a vigorous population avid for dramatic action ensured adult playing companies like the Lord Chamberlain's, the Lord Admiral's, the Queen's, and the Earl of Worcester's players a steady patronage. Only playwrights fared poorly unless like Shakespeare they owned shares in their company; and it was no doubt for this reason that they wrote voluminously, coveted the patronage of the nobility, tried their hand at other tasks like pamphleteering, and often led a Grub Street existence. Marlowe's plays enjoyed the advantage of being presented by the successful Lord Admiral's company under Alleyn, who acquired enough money to be able to endow a college in Dulwych twenty years after the death of his unfortunate playwright.

3. MARLOWE'S "MIGHTY LINE" AND THE NEW DRAMA

In the "wooden O" of the elder Burbage's Theatre and Rose buildings, owned by Alleyn's father-in-law and the theatre's most famous broker Philip Henslowe, the Elizabethan public saw during the years 1587-1593 a series of plays by a young poet that differed in quality from

every earlier product. The groundlings were stirred by him with tragedies of ambition and passion that flamed to the skies. No playwright had
hitherto invoked the world, the flesh, and the devil so magnificently, or
had employed such vigorous yet cadenced verse in his incantations. The
blank verse of *Gorboduc* and *The Spanish Tragedy* was at best adequate,
but Marlowe's was lambent. The satirist Nashe might refer to the "swelling bombast of a bragging blank verse," but posterity gratefully remembers it as Marlowe's "mighty line."

Marlowe may have begun to write in Cambridge when he composed
an indifferent tragedy of unhappy love, *Dido, Queen of Carthage,* in collaboration with Nashe. But his entry into the professional theatre was
effected with pyrotechnics. Although long-winded, tedious, and shapeless,
the tragedy of *Tamburlaine* was too overwhelming a panorama of colossal aspiration and breath-taking conquest to be gauged by a foot-rule.
If Marlowe neglected every other principle of sound dramaturgy, he observed the ultimate one of providing excitement and magic. In the presence of the superman Tamburlaine, audiences could forget everything
but the pageant of power. For all its defects, the play possessed an element of greatness hitherto wanting in their theatre, and its reception encouraged the young playwright to give an encore in a Second Part of the
tragedy.

Fashioned out of youthful dreams of glory, *Tamburlaine* crystallized
an age, as well as a personality. The Renaissance or Elizabethan passion
for power and glory found its fulfillment in the Scythian conqueror who
rises from a shepherd and highwayman to a dozen thrones, all won by
dint of courage and unflagging confidence. Marlowe's Tamburlaine is a
poet who expresses himself in action. He clothes his dreams of conquest
in language as magnificent as his deeds. He not only overthrows king
after king in his quest for "the sweet fruition of an earthly crown," but
can win Theridamas, who is leading an overwhelming force against him,
through the sheer magic of his tongue. He is also a lover of beauty who
sees the unattainable beckoning to him and insists that

> *Our souls, whose faculties can comprehend*
> *The wondrous architecture of the world,*
> *And measure every wandering planet's course,*
> *Still climbing after knowledge infinite,*
> *And always moving as the restless spheres,*
> *Will us to wear ourselves, and never rest. . . .*

"If all the pens that poets ever held" combined to express beauty, he
adds, yet should there remain something still unexpressed and unattained,

> *One thought, one grace, one wonder, at least*
> *Which into words no virtue can digest.*

The personality of Tamburlaine, combined with the crowded action and barbaric splendor of his battles and triumphs, provided a memorable experience to which no summary can do justice. It may be added only that the somewhat overlooked elements of incidental compassion in the play deepened it. The conquered Bajazeth, Emperor of the Turks, and his Queen become pathetic figures when, unable to bear their cruel humiliations any longer, they kill themselves against the cages in which they are kept by the conqueror. Zenocrate, Tamburlaine's wife, also sounds the note of pity, and there is much that is moving in the plight of the Damascan maidens who plead for the termination of the siege. Such details help to counteract to some degree the bloodshed and bombast in which the poet reveled often at the risk of ludicrous extravagance.

The deeper note is also sounded by the second part of the tragedy which recounts Tamburlaine's disappointments, sorrows, and end. One of his sons proves such a coward that he kills him, he loses his beloved Zenocrate who precedes him to the grave, and although he remains undefeated by man, "death cuts off the progress of his pomp." The unmartial son, a character compounded of sensitivity as well as cowardice, is a sore trial to the conqueror, and the loss of Zenocrate overwhelms him with despair. "Black is the beauty of the brightest day," he cries, and his rage against a power superior to his own expends itself only after he has burnt down the city in which she has died. Henceforth he carries her embalmed body with him wherever he marches. Marlowe, moreover, does not miss an opportunity to inject a stinging criticism of Christian conduct in the episode of Sigismund's violation of his pact with his Mohammedan allies. Although the Second Part is less splendid and more hastily written than its predecessor, it actually marks a deepening of Marlowe's artistry.

A series of second-rate imitations like Robert Greene's *Alphonsus of Arragon* and Peele's *Battle of Alcazar* followed *Tamburlaine,* but Marlowe had meanwhile moved ahead. When next he turned to the drama of ambition a year or so later, his battlefield was the intellect. Many of the triumphs of the Renaissance had been won in the conquering mind, and Marlowe, the intellectual and friend of intellectuals like Harriot, found an excellent theme in the medieval story of the magician Dr. Faustus. A German folk-book published in Frankfurt in 1587 had told his deeds at length, a ballad on Faust was popular in England although it may have appeared after the play, and other lost versions may have been current. These could have been merely sensational tales of magic. For Marlowe, however, their unhappy hero who sealed a pact with the devil in exchange for supernatural powers and pleasures became a symbol of the tragedy of intellectual aspiration. In Dr. Faustus he created a man of learning and daring who is consumed by a passion for power that can only be attained with the aid of extraordinary agencies. The mind is its own enemy, and Faustus is assailed by his conscience which takes the shape of a good angel. He is often on the verge of remorse, and only the weakness of his character and the threats of his darksome ally prevent him from saving his soul. After tasting power and attaining one tall spire of ecstasy in the Helena episode, when the ineffably beautiful Helen of Troy appears before his eyes, Faustus is seized by the infernal agents.

In the mutilated text which has come down to us, *Dr. Faustus* is an extremely uneven play. Structurally close to the moralities of the Middle Ages with its struggle between good and evil and its retailing of the Seven Deadly Sins, the tragedy poured the new wine of Renaissance aspiration into an old bottle. Nevertheless, the play is consistently exciting, rising to one of the great climaxes of the world's drama as Faustus counts his last hour by the striking of the clock. His torment produces those unforgettable lines in which he pleads with time to stand still, and those in which he cries,

> *O, I'll leap up to my God! Who pulls me down?*
> *See, see where Christ's blood streams in the firmament!*
> *One drop would save my soul—half a drop: ah, my Christ.*

Dreading eternal suffering as the demons approach, he longs for the dissolution of his immortal soul:

> *O soul, be changed into little water-drops,*
> *And fall into the ocean—ne'er be found.*

His last pathetic outcry is the extraordinarily dramatic line, "I'll burn my books." Without yet mastering the architectonics of drama, Marlowe achieved mastery over two of its inestimable elements—stirring episodes and dramatic poetry.

The tragedy, moreover, doubles its stature when it is regarded imaginatively rather than literally. Every particle of information concerning Marlowe cries out against the possibility that he took his story at face value. Like the classic Greeks before him and like Goethe after him, Marlowe retained the antique outlines and background of a legend without accepting its conventional meaning. Long before the end of the tragedy, he has allowed the infernal Mephistopheles to express such heterodox views on hell as

> *Hell hath no limits, nor is circumscribed*
> *In one self place, for where we are is hell,*
> *And where hell is there must we ever be.*

Hell is, in other words, presented as a state of mind or a lack of grace, and the visible presence of the devils at the end merely serves the requirements of theatrical representation. The popular form of the play dictates the supposition that Marlowe's prime intention was to write a "good show," but our knowledge of Marlowe assures us that his own conception of *Dr. Faustus* may have been close to symbolism. Faustus' tragedy is the plight of the aspiring intellect that seeks what is beyond human ken and experiences rare ecstasies and delusions during the quest but is doomed to final frustration and defeat. The mind that oversteps the bounds of human power finally becomes its own victim and suffers the atavistic terrors and regrets from which only few intellects, if any, are completely emancipated. It is in some such conception of this play that we can capture its proper dignity and depth, even if its execrable humor—possibly by another hand—remains an obstacle. If the groundlings did not need this interpretation and the "show" can do without it, it is nonetheless true that Marlowe's heterodox intellect must have viewed this fable like a true rationalist. He probably also understood it autobiographically, for Faustus' drama was in a sense Marlowe's drama. Like his hero he was too daring for his peace of mind. We may even agree that "The very vehemence of his professions of impiety was a sign that his emancipation was incomplete." [9]

Marlowe, however, had no particular love for symbolism and fantasy, which he was likely to associate with the anemic trifles of Lyly. After this attempt to inject Renaissance aims and ideology into medieval legend, he returned to less winged and more literal material. His remaining work was for better and worse almost wholly devoted to objective historical material. He may well have had a hand in the composition of the *Henry VI* trilogy, and in his unfinished and poorly written *Massacre of Paris* he dramatized, with patent disapproval of intolerance, the religious struggles of France that culminated in the massacre of the Huguenots on St. Bartholomew's Day. In *The Jew of Malta,* which followed *Dr. Faustus* about 1592, he wrote a revenge drama founded on a jumble of historic details. Barabas, a wealthy Jew, is unjustly deprived of half his goods by the Christians of Malta, and when he voices a manly protest all his goods are confiscated. An inordinate thirst for revenge overcomes him and he becomes guilty of horrible crimes executed with the diabolic skill which Elizabethans described by the term "Machiavellism." In time he delivers Malta to the Turks and then the Turks to the Christians before he falls into the caldron of boiling water he had prepared for the former.

The Jew of Malta possesses moments of greatness of which few playwrights have been capable. Barabas is a magnificent figure at the beginning of the play, as distinctly a poet of riches as Tamburlaine was of military prowess. Even when he becomes a monomaniac raging for revenge he exercises the fascination of a powerful personality. Nor is there any lack of intellectual fire in the play. Marlowe again seizes an opportunity to castigate "Christian" conduct, and he throws the weight of sympathy on his hero's side until the latter's revenge exceeds all bounds. He makes Barabas reflect on the difference between Christian professions and behavior:

> *For I can see no fruits in all their faith,*
> *But malice, falsehood, and excessive pride,*
> *Which methinks fits not their profession.*
> *Haply some helpless man hath conscience,*
> *And for this conscience lives in beggary.*

For all the increased pliability of his dramatic verse and the power of isolated details Marlowe failed to overcome the limitations of the revenge play. *The Jew of Malta* has come down to us only in the botched adaptation of Thomas Heywood, as played before Charles I. If the shapelessness of this edition of 1633 must not be laid at Marlowe's door, he is nevertheless responsible for the tenor and tone of the text. Marlowe's Barabas becomes a monster and the tragedy is allowed to walk the treadmill of successive revenges that fail to illuminate man and circumstance. It remained for Shakespeare in *Hamlet* to transform revenge drama into the tragedy of man, thus renewing the accomplishments of Aeschylus and Euripides in their treatment of the Orestes-Electra story.

Still, Marlowe was wisely taking steps toward sublimating Elizabethan popular forms, and in the famous *Edward II*, acted in 1592 about a year before his death, Marlowe achieved a sublimation of the historical drama which only Shakespeare could refine further. This time, moreover, perhaps because he was sampling native historical material of great national interest, he achieved the balance and objectivity that had been absent in his earlier work. Edward II alienates his nobles and his Queen by successive infatuations with the upstart male favorites Gaveston and Young Spenser. He is so self-willed and extravagant while his opponents are so irritatingly arrogant that intermittent civil war ensues. They murder Gaveston, and then when the wheel of fortune turns against them, they forfeit their lives to the King while his Queen Isabella flees to France for protection and aid. But her lover Mortimer and she return with an army and Edward is defeated, imprisoned, and murdered in his cell by Mortimer's agent. Then Mortimer is himself executed by the young king Edward III and the Queen is committed to the Tower.

As a chronicle play *Edward II* is ranked as high as Shakespeare's *Richard II* and *Richard III*, if not higher. Although this opinion is open to question, especially with respect to *Richard II*, the effectiveness and distinction of Marlowe's tragedy cannot be denied. The tragic pathology of Edward may become a trifle wearisome, but is daringly penetrative and its effect on the kingdom comprises a vividly dramatized, if somewhat repetitious, picture of civil war. Edward's death, moreover, is one of the great scenes of the world's drama and its pathos alleviates the effect of a character who has been in no way admirable. (Unless one approves him for his democratic choice of favorites.) Marlowe discovered the power of compassion in his last play. For the first time in his career as a writer he took a weakling for his hero, and pity and understanding also appear in the characterization of the unhappy Isabella, who becomes unfaithful to Edward only after long neglect and humiliation. A deepening of characterization is further present in the portraits of the unhappy wife, her psychologically singular husband, and his vacillating brother Kent. The murderers and the nobles are English types hitherto absent in his plays, and the young Edward III is one of the better realized children of Elizabethan drama. Marlowe's verse, moreover, is by now wholly freed from extravagance; it has become the perfect instrument, and the lines are as close to natural speech as blank verse would allow.*

John Mason Brown makes Marlowe say of himself, "I was more self-contained than the very nature of the playwright's task permits him to be." [10] Truer words were never said about the bulk of his work. In *Edward II* fortunately he was beginning to be less *self-contained*.

It is disturbing only to realize that Marlowe did not achieve the comparative perfection of *Edward II* without some sacrifice of greatness. The intoxicating splendors of *Tamburlaine* and the fiery imaginativeness of *Dr. Faustus* are absent here. Shakespeare learned to regulate and humanize his talent without planing it down. Marlowe apparently could not, although he might have learned in time. The theatre, however, is a cruel taskmaster. It cannot live on anything less than accomplishments, and it is idle to speculate on what Marlowe might have accomplished if he had been spared the dagger thrust that ended his life in his twenty-ninth year.

His special contribution was actually finished. He had enthroned poetry in the theatre, he had filled it with powerful personalities, and had expressed their travail in striking scenes. More than any of Shakespeare's predecessors he had made the Elizabethan stage the theatre of romantic individualism, and Elizabethan tragedy the drama of the will rampant. No other kind of dramatic art could have expressed this era of national expansion in its first flush of power and expectation. Of this age, while it retained its early magnificence, Marlowe was the undisputed laureate. His very immaturity as a man and an artist made him that.

---

* Marlowe's contribution to the development of the Elizabethan "chronicle" or historical play may, indeed, be even greater—if, as is believed, he had a hand in the composition of parts 2 and 3 of *Henry VI* and *Richard III*.

XIII

WILLIAM SHAKESPEARE

I THE MAN OF STRATFORD

IF THE classically minded Marlowe would have preferred to go down to posterity as another Icarus who flew too near the sun and fell, the historian must also consider him as a slightly sodden John the Baptist. He heralded one greater than himself, though undoubtedly without knowing who it would be, or greatly caring. Approximately two months after Marlowe's birth, in the town of Stratford-on-Avon, was born another son of the middle class, the second child of the freeholder, glover and tanner John Shakespeare who had married the daughter of the ancient house of the Ardens.

William Shakespeare's early years were spent in an atmosphere of comfort and prosperity while his father acquired position after position until he reached the high municipal offices of alderman and bailiff of Stratford. The lad received the usual elementary education and attended a grammar school where he acquired the "small Latin," if not "the less Greek," with which Ben Jonson later credited him. But there was to be no university career for him. When he was thirteen or fourteen his father's fortunes began to wane, and by 1577 when William was thirteen the family was actually impoverished. William left school and worked for his father, relieving the tedium of a workaday life with occasional prankishness and a little innocent poaching on Sir Thomas Luce's preserves, if common report is to be credited. His clash with the poaching laws—which may not have included the whipping mentioned in Rowe's account—at least appears to have remained in his memory at the writing of *The Merry Wives of Windsor* in the reference to Justice Shallow who bears "a dozen white luces" in his coat and is the subject of the same pun on "louses" which appears in the ballad on "lousie Lucy" attributed to Shakespeare. The young man appears to have been something of a wit, and he was probably acquainted with the rude performances of the strolling players who visited Stratford from time to time. It is clear that he was leading a scrambled kind of existence, and in his restlessness he appears to have run away from his father's tannery, which included a little old-fashioned butchering.

The blunderings and trials of a young man are even more apparent in the indiscretion that compels him to marry at the age of eighteen, and well it is that the marriage is hurried because the bride is already with child. Less than six months after the license is issued for the marriage on November 27, 1582 (while Marlowe is still a college sophomore), Shakespeare becomes a parent. Three years after the birth of this daughter Susanna, he is also the father of the twins Hamnet (or Hamlet) and Judith. His wife Anne Hathaway is eight years his senior, and perhaps for this reason alone the poet's domestic relations do not appear to have been as ideal as his Victorian admirers could have desired. It is not impossible that Shakespeare was drawing on his experience when he made the Duke in *Twelfth Night* sound a warning against a marriage in which the groom is younger than the bride:

> *Let still the woman take*
> *An elder than herself; so wears she to him,*
> *So sways she level in her husband's heart.*

His memory serves him as late as the composition of *The Tempest* where prenuptial relations are said to breed "barren hate, sour-eyed disdain, and discord."

After 1584 there is no record of his staying with his wife or visiting her until his only son Hamnet dies at the age of eleven and is buried on August 11, 1596. Between 1584 and 1592 Shakespeare may have been teaching school in the country, though the record of these years is nebulous. But by 1592 he is certainly in London, already an actor, a play-doctor, and a playwright.

Plunged into the roaring caldron of London by unrecorded circumstances, he is by September, 1592, actively associated with the Lord Strange's company which became the Chamberlain's. His association with this successful group, which included the great tragic actor Richard Burbage and the accomplished comedian Will Kempe, probably began in 1591 when he wrote or adapted the second and third parts of *Henry VI*. Next year he is already sufficiently successful in his craft to excite the envy and wrath of the university man Robert Greene, who speaking not only for himself but for Marlowe and the other educated playwrights calls him an "upstart crow, beautified with our feathers, that . . . supposes he is as well able to bombast out a blank verse as the best of you; and being an absolute *Johannes fac totum,* is in his own conceit the only Shake-scene in a country." Moreover, the young man, who a few years before was probably only an unknown hanger-on of the theatres, even if the report that he held horses at the playhouse door is apocryphal, already commands some measure of respect. Henry Chettle, the publisher of Greene's scurrilous pamphlet *Groat's Worth of Wit,* apologizes for the slur on Shakespeare; "Myself have seen," he declares, "his demeanor no less civil than he excellent in the quality he professes. Besides, divers of worship have reported his uprightness of dealing, which argues his honesty, and his facetious grace in writing, that approves his art." [1]

During the next two years Shakespeare continues his literary labors for several companies. He writes *Richard III*, which is a continuation of *Henry VI*, the revenge play of the Senecan-Kyd tradition *Titus Andronicus*, which he probably touched up rather than created, and his *Comedy of Errors*, a free adaptation of the *Menaechmi* of Plautus and a tribute to the earlier humanist tradition of Italian comedy.

Even these early works disclose more progress than could be expected of a half-educated yokel under ordinary circumstances. But the circumstances were far from ordinary. Poets are born, if they are also made, and the Stratford lad appears to have had the most natural gift for verbal music and imagery ever entrusted to a human creature. His knowledge of the English landscape, of flowers and birds, could have been easily acquired during his peregrinations in the countryside. An understanding of the human heart and of human behavior must have come easily to an observant youth who shared his family's vicissitudes, had considerable business experience at an early age instead of being cloistered in a university, and became a father at eighteen and a roving man at twenty-two. Then coming to metropolitan London he had found a new world opening before him. "In Shakespeare's time every influence of the old and the new world met and parleyed," and "the complete eclecticism and confusion of his time gave him that universality" which he shared with so many Elizabethans.

He had experienced the life of a wealthy burgher during his childhood and the poverty of a commoner during his youth. He also had a link with the gentry through his mother and through the very life of a period during which the lower classes were achieving independence and men could make their way in the world. Mentally he belonged to both the middle class and the aristocracy at a time when the frontiers of both groups were decidedly elastic. Add to this the fact that in the demimonde of actors and bohemian writers he could also acquire some familiarity with the "proletarians" and the rogues of his day, and it is clear that Shakespeare soon commanded a very wide acquaintance indeed.

If his formal education was negligible, his age and his circumstances could make up the deficiency to a remarkable degree. The classics were becoming available in English through an increasing number of splendid translations like North's version of Plutarch's *Lives*, which appeared as early as 1579, and various renditions of Ovid, Seneca, Virgil, and other staples of a humanist education. Later, in 1598, he could also acquaint himself with Chapman's *Homer* and Florio's translation of Montaigne's provocative essays. A knowledge of foreign languages is a desideratum but not an indispensable condition for a creative talent. Moreover, much knowledge could be acquired from conversations with actors and bohemians, as well as from the numerous older plays which he read or adapted. Shakespeare became a child of humanist learning by adoption.

Material for a professional playwright was available everywhere. Shakespeare found it in numerous older plays, many of which served as a basis for his own; in Holinshed's *Chronicles* of England, in other histories, and Plutarch's *Lives;* in English romantic tales like Sidney's *Arcadia* and Greene's *Rosalind;* and in the *novelle* or short stories of Italy so often exploited by the Elizabethans. Technique could likewise be easily acquired. Invaluable to a budding playwright was the experience of acting in plays, and Shakespeare was a recognized actor of his day even if he did not achieve the eminence of an Alleyn or Burbage. Collaboration with other writers and revamping older works also provided invaluable training. From Kyd he could learn methods of filling the stage with striking actions, from Marlowe he could derive the example of transfiguring action through poetry and capturing the imagination with heroic personalities. The trick of classical allusion he could acquire from any number of plays, while the refined rhetoric of Lyly was a model for purple patches and courtly dialogue in fashionable comedy.

Intellectual content could be drawn from the very air of Elizabethan society by an intellect as keen as his. Problems of government; the triumphs and failures of historic characters; the divine right of kings, the right of rebellion, and the rights of individuals; religious questions, national aspirations, foreign politics, humanist philosophy, scientific inquiries, and metaphysical speculations—these and other matters occupied every intelligent subject of Queen Bess. When Shakespeare alludes to them or delves into them he is merely on common ground with numerous minor writers of his epoch. Shakespeare is singular only in his enormous faculty for assimilating the intellectual ferment of his times, in associating it convincingly and appropriately with living characters, and in fixing it in the matrix of his dramatic situations with a considerable effect of rightness and dramatic inevitability. And because these thoughts are captured with the intensity of something newly discovered, because everything is sensed by him with wonder, passion and singularity, Shakespeare seems a more comprehensive dramatist than anyone who has followed him. He assimilates the Elizabethan Renaissance as if by osmosis. This does not make him a social or philosophical thinker, but it does make him a playwright of almost infinite scope.

Hardly less striking is the personality of the man who levies this tribute upon the rich resources of this age. His poetic gift is obviously developed under the influence of an age in which lyric and blank verse are increasingly perfected even before he is ready to contribute to their progress. His unparalleled mastery of language is achieved in a period when words have not yet become hardened and stamped like a coin but are still plastic, and when sentences are still comparatively free from schoolmaster's grammar. Still, Shakespeare's uncanny gift for cadences and for a pregnant vocabulary is also an essentially personal endowment. If, with respect to his poetic and verbal gifts, he does not differ from other Elizabethan masters in kind, he differs from them in degree—and the secret of human superiority is, after all, a matter of degree.

Mental alertness and balance form the arch of his personality. His alertness promotes such keen observation and such plasticity of the intellect that every experience or mood leaves its mark upon him—he absorbs everything, he rejects nothing. His comparatively balanced soul saves him in his maturity from the excesses to which Elizabethan playwrights were partial. This endowment he owes, however, not only to the sweetness of temper attributed to him by all his contemporaries and not only to the extreme refinement of his intellect. Shakespeare differs from his fellow-geniuses in possessing a simple humanity, an abundant supply of common sense, a sizable portion of earth in his fire.

Thomas Mann has remarked in one of his essays that the greatest genius always contains an element of the commonplace and is the better for possessing it. This residue of earth serves as a link between a man's genius and common reality; between extraordinary humanity, which can only too easily lose itself in the clouds, and the ordinary humanity which is the basic material of creative effort. This point is especially well illustrated by Shakespeare, who is a typical bourgeois in his pursuit of wealth and quest for a patent of gentility. Like Balzac, who lived in a similar period of commercial expansion, Shakespeare is constantly making financial investments. The same practicality makes him the expert showman who knows all the stops of the audience on which he is playing and veers with the tide of fashion in the theatre, turning to whatever kind of drama—comedy, history, tragedy, and romance or so-called tragi-comedy —is temporarily in demand. As an actor, playwright, and shareholder in his company he could not, indeed, remain above practical considerations. The effect of such eclecticism on his art cannot be overestimated; his work almost contains a whole world, captures numerous aspects of humanity, and projects reality to a greater extent than any other writer with the possible exception of the novelists Balzac and Tolstoy.

Even Shakespeare did not, of course, surmount all the limitations of his particular milieu in London. He did not capture all the phenomena presented by Renaissance Europe; no single individual could. The revolutionary promptings that produced the revolt of the Netherlands and the socialist uprising of the Anabaptists in Germany did not come within his horizon. The struggle for religious liberty in Europe affected him only slightly; if he does not appear to have been as intolerant toward Catholicism as many of his colleagues,* still he enunciated no broad principle of religious tolerance, and toward the Puritans or Protestant Dissenters he maintained an attitude of unrelenting hostility.

Renaissance science found expression in some of his allusions, and in his attitude toward the after-life and divine justice. The dying Hamlet is only concerned about his posthumous reputation or "wounded name," which he entrusts to his friend Horatio—"the rest is silence." "A divinity shapes our ends;" on what principle we are not told. Gloucester sees a malignant waywardness in the operation of the universe—

> As flies to wanton boys are we to the gods;
> They kill us for their sport.

And there is no one in the tragedy to contradict him! If evil is often punished in Shakespeare's plays, the triumph of moral principle rights no wrong and heals no heart except in the comedies and romances in which life is not treated seriously. Moreover, the villain suffers defeat because he has sown the seeds of his own destruction rather than because a god has intervened. To this extent Shakespeare reflects the mundane outlook of the Renaissance. But Bacon's dream of perfecting scientific methods and using them to win control over nature does not find expression in Shakespeare's work. Nor is this generally modern playwright free from a lingering supernaturalism shared by most of his contemporaries, although he makes excellent use of his witches and ghosts.

In the realm of politics he is insular: even his Italian characters are Englishmen, England's weal or glory is his sole concern, and he is sometimes inclined to chauvinism. He also does not see beyond a benevolent autocracy, even if, contrary to the assumptions of certain scholars, he is not a hidebound reactionary indulging an illimitable contempt for the common people. He merely does not consider them a reliable agency of government: except in his Roman tragedies, where he is dealing with given material, he simply does not represent them as a major political force for either good or evil. In the matter of social justice, he is typically oblivious to the plight of the expropriated English peasantry when "enclosures" for sheep-grazing (for the growing wool industry) reduced a considerable portion of the population to the status of vagrants who were ultimately to comprise the wage-earning proletariat of modern capitalism. He is critical toward feudalism, setting down its failure in *Henry VI, Henry IV,* and *Henry V,* and toward irresponsible or incompetent monarchy as exemplified by a wavering King John and a blundering Richard

* It is even contended that he died in the old faith. See Clara Longworth de Chambrun's *Shakespeare Rediscovered,* Scribners, 1938.

II. But in this he is merely beating a dead dog, unless his criticism is to be construed positively as a glorification of the anti-feudal and responsible Elizabethan monarchy.

His most positive reaction to the social scene is indeed this concern for stable government, associated with which is his interest in the welfare of the common people that depends upon such a regime. In tragedies of civil discord like *Macbeth* and *King Lear,* caused by usurpations and corruptions of royalty, it is the whole nation that suffers. That the stable monarchy he celebrates is an absolutist one does not trouble him greatly; his middle-class characters manage to thrive under it, as they actually did until the late years of Elizabeth when they began to feel the effects of monopolism. He notes the self-assertiveness and independence of this class in many plays and records their jollity. The cure for an irresponsible autocracy in his plays is rebellion, to which he opposes the divine rights of the ruler in question. (Without, however, denouncing those who violate it, provided of course they are of royal blood.)

It is in the general outlook and content of Shakespeare's work that one will find that summation of a great epoch and that broad relevance to humanity which, for want of a stricter word, men call "universality." The key to life is for Shakespeare, as it is for his age, the assertion of individuality. He creates highly individualized characters more abundantly than any other dramatist, and the conflicts in his plays are invariably produced by the exertions of the human will. Man struggles against man, and not against Fate, god, heredity or glands. Shakespearean drama is drama of the individual will.

That a theatre of this nature is gloriously active and exciting, that it can plumb many depths of the human personality, and that it is capable of great definiteness and clarity, is self-evident. And since man exists and exerts his will in every age, the supreme master of the "theatre of the individual" is inevitably universal, even if his characters bear the stamp of their own times. Moreover, in a period when class differentiations are becoming flexible, Shakespeare gives his attention to representatives of nearly every level of society. The same hand that draws princes and nobles also delineates merchants, petty officials, common soldiers, rogues, and vagabonds. The same individualization extends to both sexes and some of the greatest triumphs of his art are to be found in his women.

The zest for life so abundantly felt in a dynamic age pulsates in every page of his work. Laughter and tears, concentrated ambition and wasted motion, serious employment and the blithe pursuit of pleasure, jostle each other in the same work. Intensity is all! His characters are nearly all active personalities, from the heroes who win crowns or glory to the vagrants who cut purses or revel in the stews, from passionate queens to promiscuous "queans" and nubile girls who dress in boys' clothes to follow the men of their desire.

What is more, his characters frequently triumph even over their deficiencies. They wrest new intensities from their defeats whether these arise from bodily impediments, in the case of Richard III, or from external failure produced by their own error or evil. When Richard II, for example, is dethroned, he reveals new resources of strength in an intensified and dignified sensibility which invests this irresponsible weakling with nobility and fresh interest. Lear is never beaten down; he is never so impressively positive as when he is cast out by his daughters, and he is not only emotionally enhanced by his sufferings but intellectually enlarged, since he gains a fresh understanding of life. Othello reasserts his dignity after his long siege of fatuous jealousy when he stabs himself. Macbeth is never so great as when he rises from his sordid, blood-stained usurpation of the throne to a realization that "all our yesterdays have lighted fools the way to dusty death" and goes out bravely to meet inevitable death on the battlefield. Richard III refuses to accept the limitations of his crippled body, compensating for it with a ruthless mind and an undaunted spirit which do not fail him even in his last hour. The characters have, in short, the right tragic stature.

Even his comic characters—low or high—possess an exalting self-assurance. Perhaps the greatest triumph of any character in the theatre is Falstaff's. John Palmer has aptly called Shakespeare's tun-bellied knight "the most vital expression in literature of man's determination to triumph over the vile body." In his quick resource of wit and spirit we have "the image of all mankind as a creature of divine intelligence tied to a belly that has to be fed"—and lubricated.

Intellectual activity, enjoyed for its own sake, also supplements the struggle for self-assertion. One finds it in the brilliant verbal play assigned to all strata of society, in numerous allusions and reflections, and in the inquiries and doubts of a multitude of characters. Mercutio, Jaques, Lear, and Hamlet—princes, and fools—all are inquirers. Even Romeo, absorbed in his youthful passion, is not incapable of reflecting on the lot of a poor apothecary and on the curse of gold as he pays him for his drugs: "I sell thee poison; thou has sold me none." The passion for inquiry that dominates the modern world finds its epitome in the constant mental alertness of Shakespeare's characters.

Finally—insofar as one can write *finis* to so limited an analysis—the keystone of Shakespearean drama is its humanitarianism, which stands in such marked contrast to the will-to-power "Machiavellian" philosophy of the age which Marlowe glorified. Without beating the drum for a non-existent democracy or championing the disinherited Elizabethan peasantry and crying out against the outrages of the Queen's barbaric penal laws, Shakespeare is the greatest humanitarian who ever wrote for the theatre. Such resolute reformers as Ibsen and Shaw cannot approach him in this respect. Shakespeare's ability to create infinitely human characters stems from a pervasive love of man which no degree of pessimism in his climactic period can obliterate. He is not such an invertebrate philanthropist as to spare the lash of satire, and he could strip the mask from corrupt humanity as ruthlessly as Jonathan Swift did later. Gloom overcomes him during the period when he composes *King Lear* and *Timon*. But he is not so Calvinistically upright as to condemn mankind in general or for long. After his dark tragedies, in which there are always such noble creatures as Kent and Cordelia, comes the sunlit procession of his romances. Of real grossness there is little or none in his plays; and, except possibly in *Timon* and *Troilus and Cressida*, he is never the cold cynic even when he takes the world apart.

Except in the early *Titus Andronicus*, he never condones wanton violence, wrong, or injustice, and he is immune to that poetic intoxication with the magnificence of power which dominates most of Marlowe's work. His rulers and conquerors are but flesh, and all flesh, no matter how glorious, is ultimately inglorious grass. Those who live by the sword —his usurpers, tyrants and murderers—die by the sword. Shakespeare is as great a poet of *Hubris* or pride as Aeschylus. His analysis of crime-stained greatness is always a high point in his craftsmanship, and his favorite historical figure Henry V is a humane and democratic ruler who mingles with all classes.

The great tragic or historical characters all learn, in one degree or another, the vanity of power. The greatest of them, however, go even one long step further; they become oracles of humanitarian pity. Hamlet is painfully aware of

> *The oppressor's wrong, the proud man's contumely,*
> *The pangs of disprized love, the law's delay,*
> *The insolence of office, and the spurns*
> *That patient merit of the unworthy takes.*

King Lear, standing in the great storm, takes heed of all the miseries that had eluded him when he ruled his kingdom—

> *Poor naked wretches, whereso'er you are,*
> *That bide the pelting of this pitiless storm,*
> *How shall your houseless heads and unfed sides,*
> *Your loop'd and window'd raggedness, defend you*
> *From seasons such as these? O! I have ta'en*
> *Too little care of this. Take physic, pomp:*

Expose thyself to feel what wretches feel,
That thou mayst shake the superflux to them,
And show the heavens more just.

No comparable cry had resounded in the theatre since Euripides troubled the conscience of his Athenian public two thousand years before. And even the Attic humanitarian had not employed such a frontal assault on corruption in a dozen consecutive lines as Lear's second outcry, in the sixth scene of the fourth act, which begins with the prose assertion, "There thou mightst behold the great image of authority; a dog's obey'd in office" and concludes:

Through tatter'd clothes small vices do appear;
Robes and furr'd gowns hide all. Plate sin with gold,
And the strong lance of justice hurtless breaks;
Arm it in rags, a pigmy's straw doth pierce it."

Without succumbing to what Shaw has called "bardolatry," it cannot be denied that Shakespeare's accomplishments prove him to have been one of the truly great spirits of the world. To content oneself with a description of him as a consummate showman—which he indubitably was—. is to be guilty of crass philistinism. The romantic critics, Coleridge and his followers, may have fallen into the opposite error of claiming every conceivable virtue for Shakespeare, but they were closer to a just appreciation of his greatness than the narrow constructionists who would judge him with the same yardstick they apply to a Molnar or a Noel Coward. In time the apotheosis of Shakespeare grew sickening, and the only way to escape nausea was to point to his feet of clay. But to forget that he was a great man expressing a great age, as well as, in Ben Jonson's memorable line, "not of an age but for all time," is to embrace the asinine in preference to the divine.

2 SHAKESPEARE'S CAREER IN THE THEATRE

It is impossible to attempt any detailed analysis of Shakespeare's work in a single chapter. It would also be supererogatory in anything except a book solely devoted to the subject and provided with new information or interpretation like Mark Van Doren's book on Shakespeare. If any attempt to speak of his work is being made here, it is undertaken solely in preference to leaving a glaring gap in our survey of the drama. Fortunately, however, the reader is in a position to fill in the details of the outline, and if he is interested in matters of interpretation, which are always also matters of controversy, there are entire libraries at his disposal. It is Shakespeare's career as a dramatist that can be most easily sketched in a dozen pages, and such an outline serves a purpose if it reveals him assimilating the advances made by the Renaissance theatre, enriching this theatre, giving it greater scope and depth, and making it a mirror of an era in particular and of humanity in general.[2]

Up to 1594, the year at which we left him, he has written the following authentic plays: *Henry VI*, parts two and three (1590-91), sequels to an early play by a different author or authors; *Henry VI*, part one (1591-92); *Richard III* and *The Comedy of Errors* (1592-93); *Titus Andronicus*, and probably *The Taming of the Shrew*. It will be seen, then, that he has already applied himself to English history, farce, and revenge melodrama.

In the last-mentioned department he has made no advance. Even if we concede that he has invented few of the execrable details of *Titus Andronicus*, he has certainly not improved upon his material. Incredible as it seems that Shakespeare should have written this Grand Guignol, it is only too credible that a self-confident young showman should have tried to exploit a fashion by going to its extremes.

The *Henry VI* trilogy, based on older plays, portions of which are retained unchanged, is scrambled and frequently repetitious, as well as awkwardly versified. There is a touch of Greene in the work, and Marlowe's hand can be traced in many passages which were either written by him or composed under his influence. But Shakespeare's style is beginning to take shape here, many passages are felicitous and fine touches of characterization abound. A deep disapproval of civil discord permeates this work in which most of the tragic events that bleed England white are seen to be the direct outcome of feudal anarchy. One compassionate passage speaks for common humanity; a father discovers that he has killed his son and a son discovers he has slain his father, both in a cause that was not their own. They fought simply because they belonged to different nobles, and the king who watches both tragedies cries out:

> *While lions roar and battle for their dens,*
> *Poor harmless lambs abide their enmity.*

Moreover, this trilogy of the Wars of the Roses, of the fiery crucible out of which emerged modern England, is packed with excitement and possesses much narrative value. Stirring, in the first part, is the second scene of Act II where the white and red roses are plucked as emblems of the rival factions, and if the exploits of Joan of Arc are treated crudely and unsympathetically, they at least contain a great deal of movement and tension. "Brave Talbot," the English general, is a dashing character, and the weight of emphasis is on the jeopardy of a nation at war when its leaders engage in private ambitions. In the second part, the rebellion of Jack Cade, however unsympathetically treated, is a realistic picture of how anarchy in the upper reaches of society is inevitably duplicated in the lower depths. The final section of the trilogy, which deals with the continuance of the civil war, is filled with pity and terror. Henry VI, the irresolute monarch, is a pathetic character, and the sinister figure of Richard of Gloucester, who is soon to become Richard III, looms over the scenes as a portent of further barbarism.

In the trilogy, however, Shakespeare is still greatly dependent upon other writers; more than 3200 lines of *Henry VI, two and three,* are taken bodily from two older plays, *The First Part of the Contention* and *The True Tragedy of Richard Duke of York.*

In *Richard III,* which carries on the story begun in the third part of *Henry VI,* he creates a unified effect and settles down to the rounded characterization of a dynamic personality. Like Marlowe, he has turned to the study of a Machiavellian figure, and the humpbacked Richard is almost sublime in his demoniac force and inhuman energy. He is the product of a sense of physical inferiority seeking a compensation in a sense of superiority. He is also the bitter fruit of civil dissension, the super-tyrant who supplants the petty tyrannies of a disorganized upper class with the terrible efficiency of a single concentrated will. He is finally overthrown by the hatred he has harvested, and he fails at last both as a ruler and as a man who is condemned to suffer the torment of loveless isolation. "The lust for power is an inward agony to him." [3]

In this work Shakespeare is already forging ahead of Marlowe by virtue of his deeper sense of reality, his surer understanding of character, and his more even-tempered soul. This drama of power-politics and of a superman has none of the naïve adulation of *Tamburlaine.* Only in the dearth of overtones and in a relative neglect of minor characters is *Richard III* inferior to Shakespeare's ultimate triumphs. What the play gains in concentrated power it loses in broad humanity. Moreover, the young playwright has not yet mastered the art of subtlety, and the characters explain themselves self-consciously in soliloquies; "the time is yet to come when Shakespeare no longer dreams of making his characters formally hand over to spectators the key to their mystery." [4]

The Comedy of Errors is Shakespeare's first venture in humor and pleasantry. He composes a silly farce of mistaken identities and relies on one of the oldest and most obvious devices of the comic theatre. In *The Comedy of Errors* the sources of laughter lie wholly in situations based on an extravagant hypothesis. Only Adriana, the jealous wife, possesses a shade of reality. But it is something for Shakespeare to have discovered one of the main resources of a practical playwright—namely, the trick of managing a plot and keeping it moving, which is simply the indispensable art of dramatic invention. And in *The Taming of the Shrew,* in which collaboration is sometimes traced, he manipulates this gift with considerably more probability, while at the same time he moves into the higher realm of comedy. He has discovered the art of extracting humor out of character rather than out of mere fabrication and incident. His shrew Katherine and her tamer Petruchio are vivid personalities and enact the duel of the sexes with a wealth of amusement. Laughter is becoming one of their creator's major accomplishments.

An interruption occurs about this time, and the theatres are closed by the plague in the city. Shakespeare turns to more purely literary efforts, composing his two erotic narrative poems *Venus and Adonis* in 1593 and *The Rape of Lucrece* in 1594, each dedicated to the young Earl of Southampton. Some monetary reward is involved in Southampton's patronage, even if Rowe's account that Shakespeare received a thousand pounds certainly erred on the side of exaggeration. Shakespeare appears to have invested the Earl's gift in the newly formed company patronized by the Lord Chamberlain, Henry Hunsdon. The playwright thus lays the foundations of his later fortune by becoming a shareholder in that eminently successful company—the Chamberlain's and later the King's—which ultimately operated the Globe and the Blackfriars theatres. Shakespeare then gains the advantage of writing for a company of which he is a part owner, instead of having to peddle his work, a necessity which is the bane of all playwrights in modern times. He can compose his work with his finger on the pulse of the public and with a sure knowledge of the capacities of his actors.

He also achieves some standing in society, and is not unknown even at Elizabeth's court, where the company performed from time to time. Since the patron of the Chamberlain's troupe was Elizabeth's nearest cousin and closest adherent, Shakespeare was assured the favor of royalty. The Queen appears to have liked, as well as admired, him, and the report that she asked him to revive the fat knight Falstaff in *The Merry Wives of Windsor* is not unfounded.

His relations with the nobility become cordial. He knows the Pembrokes and through Southampton he may have become intimate with the Earl of Essex, whose execution was followed by Shakespeare's darkest tragedies. It is significant that the Essex conspirators prevailed upon the Chamberlain's men to revive *Richard II* on the eve of the uprising of February 8, 1601. The parallel that could be drawn between the king who was overthrown by his subjects and the Queen who, it was hoped, would soon be supplanted by Essex was the motive of the performance. To her Keeper of the Records of the Tower, Elizabeth confided: "I am Richard the Second, know ye not that?" [5]

Throughout his career, moreover, he is a man of the world who is keenly aware of the intrigues of the court, the problem of the succession to the throne, and the political conflicts with France and Spain. Of direct allusions in his work there are few, but of larger topical significances there are many in the work of a playwright who was close to the sources of English government. That the same man should also have commanded the attention and respect of the literary world is understandable. Jonson and Francis Beaumont had a high regard for him, even if they considered him deficient in scholarship, and the learned Chapman may have been the rival poet mentioned in the *Sonnets.* By 1596 Shakespeare is a "gentleman"; he has received a coat of arms from the Herald's Office— "Or on a bend sable a spear of the first steeled argent," as the quaint formula reads, with the crest showing a falcon bearing a spear.

 · In 1594-95 he begins his career as a purveyor of romantic comedy with *Two Gentlemen of Verona* and *Love's Labour's Lost,* and as a tragedian with *Romeo and Juliet.* In the first-mentioned work he is essentially a romancer and creates the first of his charming young women in the characters of the tender Julia and the astute Sylvia. Robert Greene, hopelessly debauched though he was, had brought lovable English womanhood on the stage in his two romantic comedies *Friar Bacon and Friar Bungay* and *James the Fourth,* probably as a peace-offering to a conscience that must have reproached him often for abandoning his good wife for a gross attachment in London's underworld. Dorothea, the heroine of the second play, was a patient Griselda who remained true to her husband even when he drove her from court and tried to kill her: she wandered disguised as a page; she was loved by a woman who judged her sex by her clothes; and ultimately she was reunited to her antipathetic spouse. There is something invincibly silly in these sentimental meanderings, but Dorothea is infinitely more real and appealing than her devotion to her lord would warrant. Shakespeare's first comedy of faithless and faithful love is written in the same vein when Julia follows her lover in male attire, and it would be poor stuff indeed if his humor had not somewhat cracked the shell of mannered romance. The playwright's fine faculty of criticism through laughter begins to assert itself in his plebeians, and the balloon of inflated sentiment shrivels whenever that clod Launce walks across the stage with his cur Crab and travesties his social superiors.

Love's Labour's Lost goes one step further and is directly critical of the artifices it creates with such abandon. To the bubble of polite affectation it applies the pin of common sense, and the comedy concludes as a plea in behalf of natural behavior. The King of Navarre and his courtiers who have vowed themselves to a life of study, fasting and seclusion cannot hold out against the French girls who turn their heads and their hearts. Smaller bubbles are also pricked in the persons of the braggart soldier Don Adriano de Armado, Sir Nathaniel the curate, and the pedantic schoolmaster Holofernes. Literary satire also makes its appearance in some comment on the linguistic refinements of euphuism,

on "taffeta phrases, silken terms precise" and "three-pil'd hyperboles."
Still it cannot be said that Shakespeare's progress in comedy is anything phenomenal. *Two Gentlemen of Verona* is a generally uninspired piece of stage trumpery, and *Love's Labour's Lost* is, in the main, a lagging and wordy affair. It is in the tragedy of *Romeo and Juliet* that Shakespeare first makes an inspired leap.

Like all of his major works it is too well known to require any discussion in this chapter. As Dowden says, *Romeo and Juliet* is "a young man's tragedy," and it is perfect in its kind. Its author is already a great poet, a master of verbal music, rhapsody, and lyric compassion. At the same time, he is already a sufficiently mature person to set off the jewels of young passion with the plain metal of Mercutio's mockery and the Nurse's vulgarity. He has in this tragedy translated the voluptuousness of his two erotic poems into the language of living theatre, and he has achieved this in terms of valid characterization. Particularly notable is the growth of the lovers from mere children of the senses to tragically troubled, painfully maturing individuals. To allow characters to develop during the course of a play and to enable their centripetal passions to become centrifugal until their private sufferings embrace the whole world of man, as in *Hamlet* and *King Lear,* is no easy achievement.

In *Romeo and Juliet* he may be seen ascending the heights of tragic art; and his feet are already past the foothills. If he is not yet completely the master dramatist this is largely owing to the comparative stiffness or rather the formal symmetry of his construction[6]; and to his retention of rhymed couplets and the use of stanzaic forms and conceits, a case in point being Romeo's tender lines,

> *If I profane with my unworthiest hand*
> *This holy shrine, the gentle fine is this;*
> *My lips,* two blushing pilgrims, *ready stand*
> *To smooth that rough touch with a tender kiss.*

Romeo and Juliet is his great lyric drama; the most dynamic examples of his tragic art are still to come.

Next year, in 1595-96, he applies the same lyric gift to the fantasy of *Midsummer Night's Dream.* Coupled with the earthy fooling of Bottom and his fellow artisans, and with delightful folklore, the lyric element provides a dual world of fancy and reality. If a deeper note is struck at all, it is to be found in the lightly suggested thought that love is a dream and an illusion. But thought is not the province of the play. Shakespeare has merely taken the fantastic embroidery of Lyly for his model and woven a many-colored web of his own. Nothing world-shaking has been accomplished, but one entertaining form of dramatic art has achieved its proper perfection.

The same year, however, the playwright returns to the mundane field of history with which he had busied himself before. Marlowe's *Edward II* has often been coupled with *Richard II,* but there can be no doubt regarding the superiority of the latter. Edward's vice is comparatively simple and his pathologic infatuation with two upstart courtiers is elementary and repetitious. *Richard II* has for its subject a remarkably complex character. A certain femininity has survived in the genes that gave him his personality, but this does not explain all of Richard's behavior. He is willful, sensitive, reckless, and self-pitying; he is, above all, an irresponsible esthete who loves pleasure and finery and turns every event, except his death, into an embroidered work of art. He has a "rhetorical imagination" rather than any consistency of feeling and action. One also finds a paradoxical profundity in this unstable manic-depressive or at least "cyclothymic" personality who oscillates between the highest exaltation and the deepest depression. If anything, Richard II is too complex a characterization to provide unity of effect. By now, moreover, Shakespeare is writing numerous memorable lines, even if his blank verse is still frequently end-stopped or rhymed and consequently lacks the maximum fluidity and naturalness of his greatest poetry.

Nor does he remain on the pinnacle he has attained, as if he were not yet completely sure of his craft. *King John,* which comes next year (1596-97), contains a sensitive and pathetic portrait of the unhappy Prince Arthur who is victimized by his uncle. He is the first moving portrait of a child in Shakespeare's gallery (unless we consider Romeo and Juliet children), and it may well be that Shakespeare drew in Arthur an image of the little son he lost that year. But King John is a weak character who, unlike Richard II, has no compensating complexities or depths. A defense of England's independence in John's defiance of the papacy and some patriotic fervor inspirit the tragedy. But its chief claim to merit must remain its distinct superiority to an older play upon which it is based.

In the same year, however, Shakespeare achieves stature again in the well-known drama *The Merchant of Venice,* notable for its poetry, its sympathetic understanding of Shylock (even if he could only be a comic drudge for the Elizabethan public), and its portrait of that intelligent and modern character Portia. To interpret this comedy as a problem play having racial tolerance for its thesis is a patent falsification. But it is, of course, no more so than to consider it a glorification of racial persecution, not only because Shylock's vindictiveness is psychologically justified by the treatment he has received from Antonio but because one of its romantic plots revolves around the lyrically entrancing love of the Jew's daughter Jessica and the Christian youth Lorenzo. *The Merchant of Venice* is simply a romance, and only as such does it maintain a unity of tone and point of view. It has, however, one distinction which becomes increasingly characteristic of Shakespeare's broad creativeness: it holds many elements of experience and thought, of sentiment and laughter, in solution. Romance in this play is not a single hot-house flower, but a garden open to the sky.

This comprehensive quality of his art, already apparent in *Romeo and Juliet,* henceforth becomes the very kernel of Shakespearean drama. It appears next year (1597-98) in the two parts of *Henry IV* and in *Henry V* a year later. The wealth of life, both heroic and comically anti-heroic, packed into those chronicles is remarkable. The mere mention of Falstaff, his boon companions, Prince Hal, and Hotspur is sufficient to prove the point. Moreover, Shakespeare is no longer overwhelmed as he was in *Henry VI* by the vastness of his canvas; his composition is clear and finished—a point worth stressing equally because of the progress he is making in his craft and the tendency to regard the play as unwieldy and scattered. Episodes may jostle each other in the chronicle, as they must, but they are tied together.

The main thread is the making of a great English king who overcomes the romantic feudalism of which Percy Hotspur is the representative. Sir John Falstaff, with his extraordinary common sense and unmartial virtues, is the antithesis to feudal heroics. Prince Hal, who has come into contact with everyday characters and has felt the pulse of national life, supplants feudalism with a centralized government. Hotspur, the glorious adolescent of chivalry, is supporting an anomalous and anarchic world in which each baron strives to rule independently. His place must be taken by a prince who is in a sense classless and will promote the interests of a united nation. Since Falstaff is, in one respect, merely the comic counterpart of the Hotspur and represents the same ultra-individualistic, irresponsible principle, he too must be removed. Prince Hal, who has seen Falstaff playing havoc with order and filling the royal army with cripples because the able-bodied paid him discharge-money, banishes the genial colossus from his presence.

In *Henry V,* the young king has succeeded, very much like Queen Elizabeth, in organizing the nation into a powerful instrument. He now defeats flamboyant feudalism in France, just as he cropped its head in England when he slew Hotspur. He has coalesced his nation into a spearhead of united action for conquest; he is the first imperialist of the English theatre, and a practical John Bullish one, as his blunt courting of a French princess accustomed to Gallic refinement indicates. To balk at Shakespeare's rather narrow nationalism is possible but not feasible. England was his world, and when he looked at the rest of Europe, as we in America do today, his own relatively democratic country seemed a rather enviable plot of ground. If *Henry V* does not rank with his greatest work, it is because his hero is at times a glorified boy scout and because the playwright has depended upon the device of explanatory choruses to supply the continuity of the action. With *Henry V,* however, Shakespeare comes to the end of his career as a chronicler of England. He has brought his country's history up to that point of unification and national triumph which he sees repeated and amplified in the reign of Elizabeth.

When Shakespeare again turns to history in *Julius Caesar, Coriolanus,* and *Antony and Cleopatra* his matter is Roman. Although it parallels his English chronicle plays, it introduces a different world to his audiences. He returns to purely English history only at the end of his career, in *Henry VIII,* and here he is only a collaborator. As a matter of fact, the Roman period begins in the very next year (1599-1600) with *Julius Caesar,* the familiar drama of tyrannicide and civil war which has been left to the untender mercies of schoolboys although it is one of the most vital political plays of the world. By going back in time Shakespeare actually achieved universality in this drama, which provides one of the noblest characters of the drama in that eternal liberal Brutus and one of the great mob scenes of the theatre in the lynching of the politically innocent Cinna the poet, a telling lesson on mob hysteria which the world has yet to take to heart.

The years which saw *Henry V* and *Julius Caesar* are, however, by no means confined to history. *Much Ado About Nothing, As You Like It,* and *Twelfth Night* mark the climax of his efforts in the field of romantic comedy. The first and weakest of the trio is marred by the unpleasant and rather stupid love affair between Hero and Claudio. But its pair of sophisticated lovers Beatrice and Benedick have irradiated this comedy for nearly everyone but G. B. Shaw, and the immortal Dogberry who is the very incarnation of blundering officialdom counteracts much romantic posturing. *As You Like It* and *Twelfth Night,* of course, need no introduction to anyone who can read English. It is worth repeating only that *As You Like It* brings the pastoral form of drama to its highest perfection, and again by virtue of the triple Shakespearean gift of glorious poetry, brilliant characterization, and ingenious mingling of common reality with idyllic grace. *As You Like It,* naturally, does not call for any exertion on the part of the reader or spectator, and apparently it called for very little from its author; he wrote it with gay abandon.

Twelfth Night, with the comic Malvolio, Sir Toby Belch, Sir Andrew Aguecheek, Feste, and the sharp waiting-maid Maria, has also added considerably to the gaiety of mankind. Its moral may well be found in its clown's words: "foolery, sir, does walk about the orb like the sun; it shines everywhere." In both plays, as in a number of other works from *Two Gentlemen of Verona* to *Cymbeline,* much of the action hinges on a girl who appears disguised as a young man. The device was undoubtedly encouraged by the interdict against actresses, for whenever this disguise was employed it must have concealed the deficiencies of the squeaking boys who impersonated women. It was indeed responsible for much absurdity, and when Bernard Shaw was a dramatic critic he denounced Shakespeare for it. It is manifestly ludicrous to assume that the disguise could be carried off very successfully. In *As You Like It* and *Twelfth Night,* however, one would have to be hopelessly dyspeptic to resist the comic verve which suspends all disbelief. One would also have to be impervious to two of the most charming young women who ever trod the boards: Rosalind and the Viola of *Twelfth Night,* who combine a conspicuously modern resolution and freedom from inhibitions with basic femininity in that oldest of feminine occupations which Shaw himself recognized—namely, the pursuit of a mate. No kindlier spirit ever breathed than the creator of Viola, who is the epitome of delicate womanliness without surrendering an iota of her right to either intelligence or matrimony.

With *Twelfth Night* Shakespeare approaches the end of his unclouded period. Arthur Symons called this comedy Shakespeare's "farewell to mirth." It is perhaps, however, followed by that hilarious farce *The Merry Wives of Windsor.** Apparently complying with a royal request, Shakespeare revived Falstaff and forced the muse of laughter to work overtime. If Falstaff is not at his best in this comedy, it is because here his sublime impertinence is secondary to his folly. Whereas he had always been the master of any situation in *Henry IV,* he is now a continually duped victim. The fat knight has fallen ignominiously; he is no longer the imposthume of wit but the twenty-stone incarnation of fatuousness. The amenities are, however, served admirably by the middle-class women Mistress Ford and Mistress Page, who prove more than a match for their knightly suitor. Without making a mountain of a mole-hill by claiming that Shakespeare made a butt of Sir John Falstaff in order to assert the "revolutionary" claims of the middle class, as does a Soviet critic,[7] it is interesting to watch the playwright turning to middle-class comedy. In creating the spirited characters of Mrs. Ford and Mrs. Page, who are in no way impressed by the fact that Falstaff is a knight and are never intimidated by his position when they plague him with their pranks, Shakespeare caught the spirit of independence that animated the Elizabethan third estate. Tudor playwrights had occasionally favored middle-class life ever since Ralph Roister went a-wooing and Gammer Gurton lost her needle in her manservant's breeches. A year or so before *The Merry Wives,* Thomas Dekker had produced a spirited celebration of the burghers of London in *The Shoemakers' Holiday.* Shakespeare merely followed the fashion.

* Unless Leslie Hotson's argument for an earlier date for this play is accepted.

With the year of *The Merry Wives,* 1600, begins the tragic and cynical decade of his career which gives us his greatest work, and this farce is as much of a "farewell to mirth" as any showman can allow himself. Shakespeare continued to write comedies, since no showman can nurse his private sorrows for long; but the tragic note predominated. Much speculation has been expended upon the causes of his sable period, but it is probable that more than one factor combined to produce it.

The showman responded to a revival of the "blood-and-thunder" tragedy which had been prevalent in the heyday of Senecan imitations a decade or so earlier in the theatre. Revenge plays, seasoned with characters portrayed as malcontents and cynics, were again becoming popular. John Marston's tragedies *Antonio and Mellida* and *Antonio's Revenge* had already reached the stage by 1599; and the latter play, in fact, contains the Hamlet-like figure of Antonio, a scholar and a melancholic who is saddled with the burden of having to avenge his father's death. No radical departures were made from the drama of the eighties and early nineties by such work, and the main external features of the new plays were the same madness or pretended madness of the protagonist, the same horrors, ghosts, love interests, murders, and discoveries that characterized the earlier *Spanish Tragedy.* It is, in fact, significant that Kyd's tragedy was revived in 1601 and 1602, with "additions" by Shakespeare's greatest contemporary Ben Jonson. A jaded public was to be won by this return to tragedy, and the chief playwright of the Chamberlain's company could be depended upon to do his part.

Moreover, a pall was beginning to fall on the age. Elizabeth, now approaching old age, was becoming increasingly irascible and tyrannical. She was sixty-seven in 1600, and was desperately concerned with concealing the ravages of time. Her most unselfish counselors were passing on or losing favor, and the court was teeming with intrigue and self-seeking. Francis Bacon, who veered with the wind and betrayed his friend Essex to the executioner's axe, was typical of the age. "Love as if you should hereafter hate, and hate as if you should hereafter love," his favorite maxim, could have served many of England's new leaders.

The religious conflicts of the age were being exacerbated by the rising militancy of the puritanic factions and the growing intolerance of the Queen. The Queen's encouragement of monopolies also gave rise to keen dissatisfaction, and the pursuit of private wealth by the merchant class was darkening the national idealism of earlier years. Wherever a sensitive soul turned, it was confronted by evidences of growing corruption. The climax came after two years of surging conflicts and intrigues when Essex, who had supplanted Elizabeth in the favor of many Elizabethans and had finally revolted against her, faced the headsman's block on the twenty-fifth of February, 1601. Shakespeare's former patron Southampton was at the same time imprisoned in the Tower for life on the same accusation of conspiracy.

The charged atmosphere evidently affected so keen an observer of his age as Shakespeare as early as 1600 when he turned to the old tragedy of *Hamlet* and made it the sounding-board of his disillusionment. When the head of Essex was severed by three blows of the axe next year, Shakespeare—who had apparently been on intimate terms with the unhappy lord and his friend—wrote that bitterest of comedies *Troilus and Cressida*. The play is a snarling attack on fickle womanhood, and it may well have had Elizabeth for a model or an incentive. A Queen who had sentenced her lover to death at least qualified for this portrait. The court, which had indulged in the most arrant plotting against Essex, may have likewise been present in Shakespeare's mind as he drew his picture of the time-serving and corrupt leaders of the Trojan War. The memory of the conduct of the courtiers may have rankled and may have been revived by fresh examples of outrageous villainy when he created the sinister figure of Iago two years later in *Othello*, whose Essex-like hero is another victim of rampant Machiavellism. The ravages of unscrupulous ambition, moral corruption, and growing civil discord could find expression again, one year later, in *Macbeth* and *King Lear*, as well as two years later in the final vitriolic outbursts of *Coriolanus* and *Timon of Athens*. The two comedies he wrote during this period, *All's Well That Ends Well*, in which Helena's love is compelled to cope with much meanness and pain, and *Measure for Measure* are no longer in the vein of unalloyed laughter. Dark shadows move across his comic stage. *Measure for Measure*, the most painful of the comedies, is Shakespeare's *Tartuffe*, an excoriation of hypocrisy and social corruption.

These perturbations of the political observer and friend of the nobility appear to be tinged also by private disappointments which have been made the subject of many speculations. Disappointment in love is the general tenor of most hypotheses, and the possibility of an unruly passion cannot be disregarded in the case of a hale man of thirty-six who was to all intents and purposes separated from his aging wife. Moreover, the famous sonnets unmistakably refer to a passion that could not have been wholly literary. Whether or not the "dark lady" or brunette was the Queen's maid-of-honor Mary Fitton, her effect on Shakespeare, whom she appears to have betrayed, is unmistakable. His love is "as a fever, longing still for that which no longer nurseth the disease," "desire is death," and even her betrayal cannot end it:

> *When my love swears that she is made of truth,*
> *I do believe her, though I know she lies.*

The literary products of this concatenation of private and public disturbances cannot be analyzed here. It is imperative only to observe that Shakespeare remains the master of his depression rather than its victim. His craftsmanship is not destroyed by his mood; at worst it is somewhat jarred, while at its best it is firmer than ever.

Troilus and Cressida suffers from diffusion, and it lacks the nobility that transfigures its author's most characteristic work. But, within the limits of cynical realistic comedy, *Troilus and Cressida* exploits a negativistic, anti-heroic mood and outlook as completely as is humanly possible. The Greeks of the Trojan War, idealized by Homer, are divested of every vestige of decency; they are more stupid and vicious than even Euripides dared to make them. Hector, the one gentleman in the play, is a Trojan or enemy of the chief characters, and he is not overthrown in glorious combat with Achilles but practically murdered by three Greek "heroes" while he is unarmed. The war is a senseless blood-bath fought over a Helen who is a harlot, in defense of a Menelaus who is a plainly denominated "cuckold"; the young heroine Cressida is also contemptible. If it is not easy to enjoy this play, it is even more difficult not to respect it as a searing comment on the failings of humanity. Shakespeare is here addressing that small portion of mankind that can give itself to the intellectual enjoyment of an undiluted caustic. *Troilus and Cressida,* along with Ben Jonson's contemporaneous *Volpone,* is a special type of comedy; it should be labeled "Poison" and taken from the shelf only when the rats of the world are on the march.

The other comedies of the dark period, *All's Well That Ends Well* and *Measure for Measure,* are unfortunately divided in mood, as if their author were torn between bitter truth-telling and the demands of comic showmanship. But his tragedies are, with the exception of *Timon of Athens,* among his best constructed plays because their author has a single vision in them and does not allow it to move out of focus.

Shakespeare still manages to relieve his picture with humor and to supplement villainy with glimpses of uncorrupted humanity. Those dreadful women of *King Lear,* Goneril and Regan, are balanced by their sister Cordelia; and their husbands, servitors and Edmund by the worthy Kent and the loyal inimitable Fool. The innocent Ophelia and that even-tempered friend Horatio flourish in the debauched court of Hamlet's uncle. Even in *Timon of Athens* there is a noble steward to remind us, however slightly, that mankind is not entirely hopeless. Nor does Shakespeare withhold his sympathetic understanding and unsentimental compassion from his major villains. Although Claudius and Hamlet's mother are steeped in guilt, they are both recognizable human beings. Macbeth and his wife, both of them blood-stained, become recognizable creatures.

Antony's and Cleopatra's adulterous love is transfigured by the nobility of their passion. Coriolanus, the betrayer of his country, is a tragically bewildered young man, even if he is a prig and fool most of the time. Only such personifications of natural evil as Goneril and Regan are almost wholly outside the pale of humanity, as is Othello's demon Iago, whom Hazlitt[8] has aptly described as a representative of "diseased intellectual activity," of a kind that was not absent in Renaissance Italy.

Noteworthy, too, is the fact that Shakespeare does not renounce the right of critical evaluation even when the sufferings of his characters justify their bitterness; Hamlet and Lear are in part the authors of their own suffering because they swerved from some principle of reasonable conduct. Hamlet's procrastinations and Lear's gift of his kingdom to his two hypocritical daughters, whom a father should have known better than he did, are both regarded as aberrations from sound policy.

It is also worth observing that throughout his greatest work Shakespeare achieves a remarkable unity of tone, so that the language of his play—with its imagery and cadences—is a symphonic evocation of the dramatic content. Each play has its appropriate music. Finally, it is to be noted how the overtones of these plays—their philosophical meaning, so to speak, and the many reflections with which they are studded—grow out of the matrix of the dramatic action. Hamlet's sharp questioning of man and society emanates from the dramatic shock of discovering the murder of his father and his mother's infidelity. Lear's bitter social critique, as he reflects upon the lot of those former subjects of his whose very existence had escaped him before, comes when he is himself an outcast wandering on a storm-filled heath.

In his great tragedies Shakespeare is indeed grappling with the whole world on a scale approximated only by the profound tragedians of Greece. Tragedy in his work goes beyond individual failure and becomes *Weltuntergang*—a cosmic collapse. Nations crumble, and ambition, lust, and ingratitude sear the earth. Sensitive souls shudder at the scene. They question the chimeras of man and fate, receiving dusty answers. Love for them turns to mockery, common decency becomes a jest; they see blood flowing like a torrent; conscience gnaws at the marrow of their being; self-disgust and a general disgust with mankind ravage many of them. Much is involved, even if this war with the world grows out of the specific personal situations of the characters.

Moreover, even the anarchy of the larger picture is held together by the logic of dramatic structure. Anyone can marvel at the purple passages and striking situations in these works and imagine that he has caught their worth. Any romanticist can pay rapturous tribute to them. But only the careful scrutiny of a man of the theatre can disclose the wonderful architecture of these works. J. Dover Wilson's *The Meaning of Hamlet* and H. Granville-Barker's *Prefaces to Shakespeare* are excellent examples of the specific method that approaches each Shakespearean play as an organic whole. *"Disjecta membra,"* wrote Thomas Carlyle, "are all that we find of any poet." But no playwright can be a master of his craft until his work consists of something more than scattered elements or *disjecta membra,* and the greatness of the plays in which Shakespeare is in complete command of his art cannot be comprehended by a collection of wonderful speeches and episodes.

The fragmentary approach, however, becomes regrettably necessary when having rounded the stormy capes of the great plays, Shakespeare arrived at the shallow places—namely, when he wrote the romances of *Pericles, Cymbeline,* and *The Winter's Tale* in (1610–1611). It is conjectured that Shakespeare suffered a nervous breakdown after *Timon of Athens,* in which he had already begun to flounder, and that the new romantic style is the effect of convalescence and recovery. Even without this hypothesis, however, it is evident that the poet who had reached the ultima Thule of tragedy had to turn back; he had nothing further to express or express after *Timon* without becoming mad as a man and chaotic as an artist. Besides, he was still a showman. He had ventilated a mood perhaps even longer than he could afford to, and a new fashion of romance was beginning to claim the London stage.

In all but the last of his new series of plays, *The Tempest,* it is only the *disjecta membra* that attract attention, and the superiority of Shakespeare is seen only in the glowing quality of many fragments. The pseudoclassical romance *Pericles,* in which he appears to have collaborated with another writer, has indeed "the slightness of a preliminary sketch." But the character of Marina, the sea-born child, is drawn by the same sure hand that delineated Viola, and the shipwreck music of the play belongs to the greatest poetry of the sea. Imogen in *Cymbeline* is one of Shakespeare's loveliest creatures and her lost brothers in their idyllic background are charming creatures even if the romance that contains them is a rather inept play. *The Winter's Tale* suffers from a stuffy and unconvincing treatment of jealousy in the person of Leontes ("a blood-pressure case," Ivor Brown calls him), but Perdita is another of Shakespeare's exquisite girls, and the light-fingered vagabond Autolycus is a supreme creation. No one who is not close to the fountainhead of joy and laughter could have created this nimble thief who leaps over the laws of property like the ethereal Puck. One would be hard put to it to find his counterpart anywhere except in that Homeric hymn on Hermes, the god of all thieves, which belongs to the morning freshness of the world. Shakespeare must have been healed of all sorrows when he conceived this irrepressible jack-of-all-trades and "snapper-up of unconsidered articles." And in his last testament *The Tempest* there is not even a sign of the old distemper.

The poet of this superb romance, which surely needs no description here, expresses—whether or not he feels it—complete peace with the world. He has, moreover, mastered the art of romance, and this work again is a rounded whole rather than a collection of fragments.

Although Shakespeare performs some theatrical chores for another year (1612-13), collaborating indifferently in *Henry VIII* and *The Two Noble Kinsmen* with a younger man, and perhaps touches up another piece of work now and then, he follows Prospero's example and renounces his magic. After 1613 he writes no more, having returned a little earlier to Stratford as a prosperous citizen who had fully effaced the social disgrace of his father's poverty. He is now comfortably ensconced in the largest house in the town. A country gentleman, he travels to London only occasionally to settle some business matter or to make an investment. He plants mulberry trees and, like all wise men who are able to afford it, he cultivates his garden. Being wiser than most men, he owns, in fact, *two* gardens.

What troubles he has now are minor, domestic ones. His married daughter Susanna brings action against some slander of her character; her sister Judith marries in a season prohibited by canon law. His joys are the simple ones of the countryside, supplemented at most by an occasional visit by his colleagues from London. One of these convivial reunions probably cost him his life. According to a reliable source,[9] "Shakespeare, Drayton and Ben Jonson had a merry meeting, and it seems drank too hard, for Shakespeare died of a fever there contracted." On the twenty-fifth of March, 1616, apparently some premonition led him to complete his will; less than a month later, on April 23rd, he was dead.

A large number of plays were published individually in quarto volumes, known as the Quartos. The first collection (36 plays), in a folio volume now called The First Folio, was published after Shakespeare's death by his fellow players John Heminge (or Heminges) and Henry Condell in 1623. It contained twenty plays never before printed. Other folio editions followed. The first edited collection of Shakespeare's work was made in 1709 by the playwright Nicholas Rowe, who provided a list of characters, gave the locale of different scenes, added stage directions, and was the first editor to consistently divide the plays into the conventional five acts, whereas there is no evidence at all that Elizabethan drama was performed with more than one intermission. Here it is impossible, of course, to supply even a fraction of the scholarly material that has accumulated over the years, and the reader must be referred to the anything but exhaustive bibliography in the appendix.

XIV

BEN JONSON AND THE "NOBLE BROOD"

WE HAVE long outgrown the notion that Shakespeare was an isolated genius. In the very heyday of "Shakespearolatry," the great critic Hazlitt already made it plain that he considered him not "something sacred and aloof"; Shakespeare "was one of a race of giants—the tallest, the strongest, the most graceful and beautiful of them; but it was a noble brood." [1]

"The Genius of our life is jealous, and will not have any individual great, except through the general." Emerson's words are applicable not only, as he intended, to the social sources of Shakespeare's strength, but to his community of spirit with his fellow-artists. They rise from the same soil and put forth their branches in a common growth. Moreover, Shakespeare, whom Emerson rightly called "the most indebted man," borrows from many of them, and in turn influences his creditors and his successors. They, in turn, not only parallel but supplement his revelation of the age and complete his expression of the first epoch of the modern world.

That many of them were men of extraordinary talent no one can deny. But it is equally undeniable that most of them were sloppy craftsmen whose slipshod ways were encouraged by the lack of literary and theatrical discipline in their time. A dual attitude has, therefore, characterized their reception by posterity. The romantic school of the early nineteenth century and that incorrigible rhapsodist Algernon Swinburne, finding gorgeous flashes of poetic or dramatic genius in their work, sometimes overrated them. The romanticists, who had no sound theatre of their own, often judged the so-called minor Elizabethans with slight reference to the requirements of completeness and logic in the theatre. In the extravagant efforts of the "noble brood," moreover, they found justification for their own unrestrained imaginative flights. The inevitable reaction, toward the end of the nineteenth century, to such indiscriminate idealization went to the other extreme of denying many of Shakespeare's confrères or successors any merit whatsoever. Shaw, who dubbed John Webster a "Tussaud laureate" and baited the whole brotherhood mercilessly, was the bell-wether of this reaction.

Our own day, however, is sufficiently remote from the heat of controversy to arrive at more equitable conclusions. We can dismiss much of the "minor" work of the period as rubbish without denying credit to fragments of superlative writing or acknowledging a number of plays as flawed but genuine masterpieces. What the "minor Elizabethans" had in common with the president of all playwrights cannot be prized too highly. They possessed a capacity for dramatic intensification and poetic expression which has been granted only sparingly to the playwrights of later, tamer periods. If they lacked the workmanlike perfection of many modern writers, they possessed something infinitely precious—inexhaustible passion and vigor.

About one of their number there has, however, been no serious controversy; he has been admired even when disliked. Ben Jonson, the boon companion and discriminating critic of Shakespeare, retains his position as a master satirist.

I THE BRICKLAYER OF THE DRAMA

Among personalities in the theatre none is more immediately striking than the robust man who held his own with Shakespeare—so much so, in fact, that "critics call him by his first name upon very slight acquaintance." [2] Born in London in 1573 of tough-fibred, puritanic North Country stock, he received the Old Testament name of Benjamin, which was to be permanently abbreviated to Ben by his colleagues. His Protestant father, who had been imprisoned and deprived of his estate during the Catholic reign of Mary Tudor and subsequently became a preacher, died in the winter of 1572-73 bequeathing nothing more to his son than a penchant for excoriating vice in the theatre instead of the pulpit. His heir was born a month later. Left without means of support, the widow married a master-bricklayer whose enthusiasm for learning could not have been remarkable. But the intervention of the generous scholar Camden, second master at Westminster school, saved the lad from the fate of "small Latin and less Greek" which Jonson deprecated in Shakespeare's case. Camden, who must have noticed exceptional abilities in him, took him under his tutelage, which was evidently worth more than a university education. Jonson became one of the most learned men of his time and the recipient of honorary degrees from both Universities.

From school the young man appears to have graduated into his step-father's bricklaying business, a profession he was to pursue on a more sublimated plane in the laborious composition of his plays. He was to be often twitted in later years for his slow and lumbering ways with the pen. Nor can one resist the frivolity of remarking that Jonson the irrepressible satirist was more proficient in brick-heaving. Be that as it may, the young man displayed little patience with the bricklaying business, just as little as his step-father did with Jonson's literary inclinations. In the Netherlands the embattled Protestant burghers were defending their religious and political liberties against Catholicism and Spanish rule. Fired by both idealism and love of adventure, Jonson enlisted with the English supporters of the Hollanders. A stubborn and a doughty man, as formidable an enemy with the sword as with the pen, Jonson fought with the best of them, capping his soldiering days with a characteristic act of valor and classic bravura. Advancing before the English volunteers, he challenged a Spaniard to single combat, slew him, and then stripped the corpse of its armor in the best Homeric tradition.

About 1592 he is reported to be back in London, plying his literary labors, and marrying a woman whom he subsequently described as "a shrew yet honest" and whom he abandoned for five years. He also became, in 1596, a father to a son whom he called his "best piece of poetry" and mourned deeply when the plague struck him down at the age of seven. He steeped himself in the bohemian life of the city, carried more than the normal quantity of liquor, acted on the stage, doctored the old *Spanish Tragedy* for the theatrical manager Philip Henslowe, and wrote an imitation of two Roman comedies in *The Case Is Altered*. Finally, in 1598, he emerged from the limbo of unrecognized playwrights with an eminently successful play *Every Man in His Humour,* dedicated not to some pretty lord but to Master Camden, "the most learned, and my honored friend." It is a singular piece for its time, as Jonson himself realized when he added a Prologue to it which reads like a manifesto. He will give the groundlings no romantic shudders—no fights between the houses of York and Lancaster or fireworks to please boys and frighten gentlewomen, "but deeds, and language, such as men do use." He will "show an image of his times," and will write a comedy, "such today as other plays should be."

Although *Every Man in His Humour* is loosely constructed, held together only by old Edward Kno'well's attempt to follow his son's questionable meanderings in London and by the various disguises of their servant Brainworm, this play is a masterpiece of its kind. Jonson here anticipated Charles Dickens in the art of achieving comic realism by means of accentuating idiosyncrasies. The trick of extracting humor out of some eccentricity, as in the portraits of Pistol, Nym, and, in a broader sense, Malvolio, had been employed by Shakespeare frequently enough. But it was not applied to principal characters. Jonson who was familiar with the exaggerations of Roman comedy, however, deliberately made a fetish of eccentricity, which he called a "humour" because the primitive physiology of his day attributed behavior to certain bodily secretions (not so primitive at that when one considers the theories of some of our own endocrinologists!). That such resolute classification of human oddities should produce a veritable whirligig of farcical humor is understandable. It is particularly vivid when so acute an observer as Jonson, who knew every nook and cranny of London, as well as every shade of the rich common speech to be heard there, called the tune. Every character except young Kno'well, who is merely busy sowing wild oats in the usual manner, is hag-ridden by his "humour;" nowadays we call it a "complex." Old Know'ell is the victim of a ludicrous anxiety concerning his son; a merchant gives a fantastic exhibition of jealousy; Justice Clement has a fixation on a cup of sack; two gulls, one from the town and one from the country, have a pathologic gift for being duped; and Captain Bobadill elevates blustering to a fine art with his decorous manners and the deadly calm with which he utters his lies. Jonson's caricatures, however, serve a larger purpose. Placed side by side, they form a composite picture of the foibles of mankind and the follies of the time. *Every Man in His Humour* is one huge canvas of the Elizabethan age drawn in screaming colors.

In a self-congratulatory mood, which was not infrequent in his case, Jonson now carries himself like the very button on fortune's cap. But disaster follows quickly. Quarreling with the actor Gabriel Spencer, Jonson kills his opponent in a duel with a blade ten inches shorter than Spencer's. Imprisoned and brought within the shadow of the gallows, he escapes execution only by reading his "neck verse" of Latin, which entitles him to "benefit of clergy" and a mild sentence. His property is confiscated and he is branded on the thumb, but he is released. In prison he secretly embraces Catholicism while under the influence of a priest, taking his first sacrament in prison bread. Since his "recusancy," as such a perilous relapse into the older faith was called, did not greatly affect his behavior or his work, there is no need to investigate the matter further.

Jonson's release in 1599 was celebrated by the performance of his new play *Every Man Out of His Humour,* a companion piece to his first work in which his talent for caricature goes completely berserk. Less amusing and coherent than its predecessor, this comedy nevertheless reveals a sharpening of his style. He is no longer merely drawing an amusing picture of London life but flatly assailing the morals of the age. In the person of Asper he announces his intention to expose "the time's deformity," and recounts in telling lines the fripperies and corruptions he is going to scorn. This Induction concluded, the playwright proceeds to ferret out as mad a collection of rogues and fools as any to be found in creation. Here are upstarts like Sogliardo, threadbare sharks like Shift, a fantastically doting husband Deliro, an affected courtier Fastidius Brisk, and a gross profiteer Sordido. These and other characters arouse the hatred of Macilente, an accomplished scholar who chafes to see wickedness and stupidity thriving while honest merit walks on crutches. His chagrin becomes a consuming passion or "humour," and with malevolent ingenuity he manages to avenge himself on all of them.

There is considerable amusement in the law-student Fungoso's efforts to keep up with the fashion in clothes, only to find that his new suit is always obsolete by the time it is finished, as well as in Puntavolo's attempt to relive the age of chivalry by entering his own house with the punctilio of a knight arriving at a medieval castle. But the dominant mood of this comedy is anger. The same disillusionment with a great age going to seed produced both Shakespeare's tragedies and Jonson's comedies. *Every Man Out of His Humour* strikes us as a rather heavy exercise in vindictiveness, but it was a potent piece of criticism in its own day, and Jonson scored a second success with it.

Henceforth he is in great demand. In the same year, 1599, he is collaborating on two other plays, both lost like so many other Elizabethan works for the stage. Two years later, his battering-ram is again in action in *Cynthia's Revels,* a comedy supplied with the brilliant Aristophanic conception of a Fountain of Self-Love from which courtiers draw their folly. The rift between the middle class and the aristocracy was growing wider, and Jonson, although in no way entranced with the former, was swimming with the tide in satirizing the latter. Unfortunately the execution of Jonson's original comic device leaves much to be desired. But here again his contemporaries differed with us by giving the play their favor.

The play was a *succés de scandale* because by now its author was in the thick of a war with his fellow-playwrights and caricatured prominent personalities. The "war of the theatres" started when Jonson took offense at the satirist John Marston's portrait of him in the *Histriomastix* as a pedantic scholar. He countered by burlesquing Marston's fustian in *Every Man Out of His Humour,* and was summarily punished in his opponent's *Jack Drum's Entertainment.* Jonson countered in *Cynthia's Revels,* in which he also attacked his former collaborator Dekker; he received an answer in Marston's *What You Will,* replied with a new and better play *The Poetaster,* and was in turn raked over the coals in Dekker's *Satiro-mastix.* Even "gentle" Shakespeare, who is said to have given Jonson a purging pill, was apparently involved in the controversy; the burly figure of Ajax in *Troilus and Cressida* was said to have reference to Jonson. Undoubtedly there was some bad blood between the choleric playwright and his colleagues, and Jonson later declared that he beat Marston and took his pistol from him. But much of this imbroglio may be set down as a pre-American publicity stunt. When the hostilities had served their purpose, they were laid aside, and within three years Jonson was collaborating with Marston (and Chapman) on that excellent comedy *Eastward Ho!*

Able as he always was to put anger and irascibility to good uses, Jonson wrote an impressive play as his parting shot in *The Poetaster.* Although his constant self-inflation is irritating enough, he makes affectionate use of the classical poet Horace who is saddled with an unsympathetic father and a pack of foppish rivals among whom Marston and Dekker appear under classic names. The play becomes another thinly veiled satire on the Elizabethan age and essentially another "comedy of humours," which is here, however, dignified with noble rhetoric. In effect *The Poetaster* is equally an exposure of artistic pretensions and a glorification of genuine art. Horace, conscious of the dignity of letters, is not afraid to chastise the Emperor Augustus for a passing reference to his straitened circumstances.

The Emperor's daughter Julia bestows her affections on the poet Ovid, respecting his plebeian worth, and the Emperor himself knows how to honor a great poet like Virgil. Conscious of the *noblesse oblige* of letters, moreover, Jonson announces his withdrawal from petty disputations; something, he declares, comes into his thought

> *That must, and shall be sung, high and aloof,*
> *Safe from the wolf's black jaw and the dull ass's hoof.*

He is as good as his word. He goes into seclusion and does not emerge from it, despite the calumnies of his detractors, until he has completed the high-minded, meticulously written Roman tragedy *Sejanus* that addresses itself indirectly to the growing disintegration of English government. Essex has been executed and Elizabeth's rule is maggot-eaten with growing tyranny and corruption. Elizabeth's popularity had, in fact, waned so greatly that Jonson found it necessary to apologize for his eulogy of the Queen in the epilogue to *Every Man Out of His Humour*.

Jonson recounts the career of Sejanus, the Machiavellian upstart who makes himself the favorite of the dissolute Emperor Tiberius and begins to grasp at the throne. Sejanus removes the latter's son Drusus with poison after debauching his wife Livia, causes the downfall of the next heirs to the crown, and destroys the civil liberties of the Romans. He is consequently making himself virtual dictator of Rome. But Tiberius is a bird of the same feather and equally adept at stratagems. His suspicions aroused, Tiberius has Sejanus shadowed, separated from his military guard, exposed in the Senate, and killed by the people.

Although Jonson was incapable of plumbing the depths of human psychology, *Sejanus* is a provocative drama. Despite his affectation of neo-classical rules, Jonson does not hamper himself with them and employs many scenes to describe the moldering, vice-ridden empire. *Sejanus* is an authentic picture of an age, consisting of a carefully assembled mosaic of facts and quotations from classic authors. But even more effective is Jonson's excoriation of degenerate rulers and of upstart dictators whose efficiency is even more destructive than the inefficiency they are supplanting.

Powerful strokes abound in this remarkably modern play. Livia plots

her husband's death while busying herself with cosmetics. Sejanus removes a high-minded opponent by hiring an *agent provocateur* to incite
him to treasonable utterances while soldiers are hiding behind a door to
seize him. Such are the ways of political tyranny, Jonson says; and his
veiled diatribe is as relevant to our own day as it was to the author's.
Even book burnings and the persecution of liberal-minded men of letters
belong to his picture. Cordus, the historian, is accused of having treated
the dead Brutus and Cassius respectfully in his "Annals." Since these
noble Romans had defended the Republic, they are not proper objects
of praise in a time of dictatorship. Cordus is therefore arrested, and his
books are burned. The tragedy comes to a strong close with the well-
deserved fall of the upstart. Nevertheless, Jonson makes no concession
to optimism in destroying Sejanus, since Tiberius who has triumphed
over his sinuous rival is certainly no savior of mankind. An old tyrant
has overcome a young one—that is all; and the poison of corruption continues to eat its way into the heart of an empire.

Although Jonson is a stiff and unsympathetic tragedian who makes
slight use of pathos, he triumphs in this unsubtle play through the sheer
power of his exposition, and *Sejanus* deserves greater admiration than
it has often received. Still its author must have realized that his strong
point was comedy. *Sejanus* is not followed by a series of noble tragedies,
but by a number of remarkable comedies. First comes *Eastward Ho!*, in
which he collaborates with his erstwhile enemy Marston and his close
friend Chapman; the next year he produces his most powerfully constructed comedy *Volpone*, four years later the hilarious *Epicene or The
Silent Woman*, in 1610 *The Alchemist*, and in 1614 *Bartholomew Fair*.

Eastward Ho!, a vivid comedy of London life, becomes a *cause célèbre*.
For an inadvertent insult to Scottish royalty, which the new king James
I, Mary Stuart's son, had reason to resent, Chapman and Marston are
cast into prison. With characteristic bravura Jonson voluntarily joins
them in prison, claiming equal responsibility for the play, and all three
are in imminent danger of having their noses and ears clipped. High connections and undoubtedly the favor Jonson was winning as a writer of
masques for the court save them from the barbarities of the penal code.
Their release from prison is celebrated by a banquet given in their honor
by writers and scholars. The climax of the celebration comes when Jonson's mother exhibits the "paper full of lusty poison" which she intended
to give her son if execution of the sentence had not been averted; and
to show "that she was no churl," she "minded first to have drunk of it
herself." Jonson becomes a hero to the intelligentsia.

In *Volpone* Jonson dispenses with the "humours" in favor of the downright vices and composes a highly concentrated satire on the greed which
was becoming a formidable feature of the economic system ushered in by

the Renaissance. The glorious age of individual enterprise was rooted in commerce; the Italian patrons of the arts were actually merchant princes; accumulation of power through wealth became the ruling passion of the age. Jonson was not the only humanist and man of letters to regard the phenomenon with dismay and disgust. But no one created such an epitome of its sinister and vulgar nature as the author of *Volpone*. His villain is the rich merchant Volpone, in whom acquisitiveness has become a primary passion and the dominant intellectual pursuit. With diabolic ingenuity he hits upon the scheme of pretending that he is dying and of prevailing upon an assortment of characters not less rapacious than himself to swell his coffers with gifts in the hope of being made heirs to his fortune. Each of these gulls is portrayed with the aid of a scalpel rather than a brush. The merchant Corvino or Little Crow even offers him his innocent wife Celia and drags her to Volpone with threats and violence. Corbaccio, or Old Crow, comes sniffing at Volpone's body to make certain that he is dead. Voltore or Vulture, the lawyer, is equally venal and unscrupulous. Each of them is appropriately named after some beast of prey and illustrates Mosca's pronouncement that almost

> *All the wise world is little else, in nature,*
> *But parasites or sub-parasites.*

But rogue breeds greater rogue, and the tables are turned on Volpone by his accomplice Mosca or Fly who makes himself heir to his fortune and tries to keep him legally dead. Complications ensue, and all the villains and gulls are exposed and punished.

Laughter so savage and pursued with such concentration of purpose is rarely to be found elsewhere in the annals of the theatre; it was conceived in prison and written under the same cloud of disillusionment that hovered over Shakespeare's tragic period. In outlook *Volpone* is not basically a comedy but a lacerating morality play, and it is fortunate only that Jonson is capable of extracting a fantastic kind of mirth from the materials of his indignation. Although it is incredible that so brutal an exposure of the cupidity of man should be amusing, the fact remains that it is vastly entertaining; the sinister elements of the comedy are too egregious not to be ridiculous. Moreover, Jonson had the wisdom to dilute his acid with the milder humor of a subordinate story in which Sir Politick and Lady Would-be, "my madame with the everlasting voice," are representatives of folly rather than of vice.

Perhaps sensing that he had reached the limits of didactic comedy, Jonson returned to the art of unadulterated entertainment in *Epicene*, another comedy of humours that revolves around the figure of Morose, a hypochondriac who has a fantastic abhorrence of any kind of noise.

His servants may address him only in sign-language, his staircase is quilted, his shutters are closed; and when he resolves to marry, the bride must be dumb. How he is saddled with a boy in disguise furnishes most of the humor. No sooner has the supposed bride been married than she becomes as talkative as a dozen fishwives, and pandemonium breaks loose as Morose is visited by a band of revelers. From this plague Morose is released by his nephew, who was responsible for all the complications, only after the latter receives a substantial gift of money from his miserly uncle.

Epicene is a heavy enough frolic, but it is a frolic nonetheless, and its style reappears in Jonson's next two satirical comedies, both of which are the better and the gayer for it. In the first, *The Alchemist,* the sharper Subtle poses as an alchemist, and the philosopher's stone which is to transmute base metal into gold proves an irresistible attraction to a lawyer's clerk, a tobacconist, the distinguished gentleman Sir Epicure Mammon, and the two pious puritans from the congregation of Amsterdam—Parson Tribulation Wholesome, who holds that the end justifies the means, and Deacon Ananias who concurs after some hesitancy. *The Alchemist,* composed in vigorously comic verse, satirizes gullibility and greed without lapsing into bitterness, and its successor *Bartholomew Fair* repeats the performance with equal zest but with an even richer folk picture. Elizabethan life bustles and capers at the fair which is the scene of the comedy, and pious hypocrisy was never to be more gaily unmasked in the theatre except in Molière's *Tartuffe.* Jonson's puritan "of a most lunatic conscience," Rabbi Zeal-of-the-Land Busy who has acquired a reputation for piety and has forced himself into the puritanical household of Mistress Purecraft, is a veritable oracle. When her daughter "Win-the-Fight," who is *enceinte,* develops an insatiable craving for pork, it is Busy who must first be consulted. This diet is forbidden by his sect, which affects the observation of Old Testament regulations. But there is a time for everything, and when Mistress Purecraft pleads "Think to make it as lawful as possible," the pious opportunist gives his consent, provided her daughter eats the tidbit with "a reformed mouth!" At the fair, after imbibing more liquor than is seemly he becomes such an interfering nuisance that he is put in the stocks. These adventures, well supported by those concerning the whole crew of merrymakers, produce one of the most riotous satiric farces of the theatre.

This is a far cry from the noble art of tragedy with which he sought to strengthen his claim upon posterity. Jonson, therefore, interposed another Roman drama *Catiline* between the two last-mentioned comedies. Catiline's conspiracy against the Roman republic is the theme. Again the classic background is captured with great fidelity, and one excellent scene, in which the plot is revealed by an offended courtesan, is a brilliantly satiric commentary on how small and private an event can affect the course of history. *Catiline* is, nevertheless, a second-rate effort, and thereafter Jonson contents himself with exercising his gift for satire. But the gift proves less pliable than hitherto, and although his later work continues to be inventive or boisterous, it becomes progressively weaker. *The Devil Is an Ass* is perhaps the best of these efforts; it at least contains the sharply satirical idea that Satan is an amateur demon in comparison with humanity. Only the beautifully written but unfinished pastoral drama *The Sad Shepherd* and his poetic but inconsequential masques, written as entertainment for the court and serving as occasions for the engineering and pictorial feats of England's greatest scenic designer Inigo Jones, continue Jonson's more exalted vein.

He lives on long after Shakespeare, and piles comedy on comedy. He becomes a victim of illness and obesity, weighing nearly twenty stone and acquiring a "mountain belly." But the years also bring much compensation. The aristocracy continues to favor him with presents and invitations, and his conversational gifts, not to speak of his overpowering personality and convivial habits, make him the literary dictator of England until his death on August 6, 1637. This Grand Cham of the Mermaid and other taverns attracts a brilliant circle of writers and wits who are proud to call themselves "the sons of Ben." To them he dispenses the mortal part of his talent—namely, those verbal fireworks of which only a few sparks are retained in the *Discoveries* and in the *Conversations* recorded by his Scottish host William Drummond.

So ends a career of another typical Elizabethan who fought and reveled but retained withal a high respect for the dignity of letters. Equally admirable are his excellent lyrics (the well-known "Still to be neat, still to be dressed," "Drink to me only with thine eyes," and the marvelous *Dirge for Narcissus*), and his forceful colloquial dialogue. Marriage is "the wedlock noose," Morose wants to see her "whom I shall choose for my heifer" and sells "my liberty to a distaff"; men "should love wisely, and all women"; revelers returning from another bout of conviviality will "pluck a hair o' the same wolf today." His talent for delineating the life of his time was of the highest order, and his greatest deficiency, apart from his general want of joyful laughter, was an inability to create rounded or self-contained personalities on the stage—perhaps because he was himself a self-contained personality rather than a *tabula rasa* like the Stratford poet he admired so greatly.

Later generations were to do him the disservice of praising him formidably rather than invitingly. T. S. Eliot, who has a talent for recovering overshadowed reputations, states the case with his usual precision: "To be universally accepted; to be damned by the praise that quenches all desire to read the book; to be afflicted by the imputations of the virtues which excite the least pleasure . . . —this is the most perfect conspiracy of approval."

Our own age is in a position to restore him to his position as the master of English comedy who has only one equal—Shaw. In comparison with Jonson's comedies, the work of most of his more frequently revived successors is anemic and trivial. He had a typically Elizabethan capacity for encompassing experience and mirroring it with gusto and intensity; his laughter does not cackle, it roars; he does not play with comic material, he grapples with it. These qualities are far more important than the academic fact that he championed classic principles of dramaturgy in a romantic age and that his work is studded with examples of his great learning. Although he is rarely as nimble as a comedian must be in our own day, he has the impressiveness of a panoplied war-horse in action. His singular virtue, and perhaps the only one that really matters in the theatre, is that he is gloriously alive. If he was often inebriated with alcohol, he was also continuously and immoderately intoxicated with life.

2 BEAUMONT AND FLETCHER

Jonson was the "John Bull" among the playwrights. But the age was not wanting in gentlemen who comported themselves with elegance. And none of them was so elegant in style and gleaned the harvest of artificial refinement in the courtly atmosphere of James I's reign to such a degree as Francis Beaumont and John Fletcher. Fletcher, born some fifteen years after Shakespeare in 1579, was the son of a man who became bishop of London. Consequently he moved in the most refined circles until his father died and left him in financial straits. Beaumont, his junior by five years, was the son of a prosperous judge and was slated for the law until he fell under Jonson's influence and joined the bohemian writing fraternity. The two gentlemen's sons became fast friends, occupied the same quarters near the Globe Theatre, and shared their property. The relationship lasted until 1613 when Beaumont married and returned to the bosom of respectability. He died three years later, leaving his friend to serve the theatre alone and in collaboration with other men for another nine years.

At first they also wrote separately, Beaumont turning out a mock-heroic play *The Woman-Hater* in 1609, and Fletcher a beautifully written imitation of Guarini's *Pastor Fido* entitled *The Faithful Shepherdess* in 1610. But it was in collaboration that they shone best. In 1609 they composed that brilliant burlesque of the Elizabethan stage *The Knight of the Burning Pestle,* and a year or so later they practically started the fashion of tragi-comedy in *Philaster,* which bears the alternative appropriate title "Love Lies A-Bleeding." The play amply fulfills their definition of the *genre* of tragi-comedy, regarding which they wrote that it "wants deaths, which is enough to make it no tragedy; yet brings some near it, which is enough to make it no comedy." *Philaster* developed the rivalry of a noble and an ignoble person who fall in love with the same maiden. She employs the time-honored disguise of male attire in order to have access to her idol Philaster. Tragedy is imminent, but love wins the day and an audience that has been worked up to a pitch of suspense is sent home reassured and happy. This florid play, which is said to have been directly responsible for Shakespeare's *Cymbeline,* has the same lack of plausibility and coherence but little of the poetic charm of the elder playwright's romance.

About a year later came their most highly regarded play *The Maid's Tragedy.* It is, technically, far closer to tragedy than *Philaster* and it discloses some unwonted independence of thought. Here Evadne, the King's mistress, is married to an honorable but unimpressive gentleman. On the night of the wedding, however, Evadne informs the bridegroom that she cannot actually be his wife, and when he insists on pretending to the court that the marriage has been consummated the king makes it clear to him that Evadne is royal property. The husband thereupon betrays his distress to her martial brother Melantius, who is also his good friend. Outraged by such behavior, Melantius reproves Evadne and tells her to murder the king. Evadne—whose change of heart is never made plausible—binds the king in his bed and stabs him to death. She also turns the knife against herself when her horrified husband Amintor spurns her love. To make matters more cheerful for late Elizabethan playgoers, Aspatia, the girl who had been abandoned by Amintor in favor of Evadne, disguises herself as a page, provokes him to a quarrel, and gets herself mortally wounded by his hand.

To reveal the insipidity of the plot, its execrable motivation or the want of it, and the tastelessness of many of the lines one would have to reprint the play. It is incredible that *The Maid's Tragedy* should be ranked among the best Elizabethan tragedies by many writers. (Distressed by the unorthodoxy of his private opinion, the present writer reread the play twice before writing this chapter, in the hope of being able to revise his judgment.) Here, as in so much of Beaumont and Fletcher's work, shallow showmanship usurps the place of honest craftsmanship. Only the vivid picture of courtly corruption and the partial justification of regicide distinguish the play from more commonplace efforts by the same and other hands.

Fletcher's unaided tragedies and tragi-comedies, as well as most of his collaborations with others, are even less impressive, and no great purpose would be served by discussing them here. Beaumont appears to have been the more talented and critical of the friends, and if he did not wholly succeed in lifting Fletcherian drama out of the slush of artificial composition, no one could. Perhaps it may be conceded that Fletcher's collaboration with Shakespeare in *Henry VIII* after Beaumont's marriage was more fruitful, but the merits of the play are decidedly scattered; when Fletcher's hand alone is visible, the work is facile and hollow. *The Two Noble Kinsmen*, in which again Shakespeare's hand is seen (especially in the first scenes of the first and fifth acts), is chiefly notable for the master's passages which compare favorably with many of his best. Founded on a poem by Boccaccio and Chaucer's *Knight's Tale*, the play dramatizes the rivalry of two kinsmen for the hand of Emilia, sister of King Theseus. It ends in a duel and a fatal accident for the victor. Fletcher's contribution to the play, which owes its plan to him, is as contrived and hollow a piece of stage machinery as Shakespeare's poetry is excellent.

The easy versification and superficial theatricality of Fletcher alone or in collaboration made him the most prominent and successful writer of his day. Even Shakespeare was temporarily overshadowed by him. But it is only in isolated poetic passages and in the boisterous burlesque of *The Knight of the Burning Pestle* that his greatest strength is put forth. Fletcher can hardly be blamed for reflecting a period of decadence, even if he did not have to pander to it, and his showmanship is a valuable accomplishment in the theatre. But his influence may well have been partially responsible for the decline of the Elizabethan stage.

3 THE LAST OF THE GIANT RACE

Beaumont and Fletcher, for all their tragic pretensions in *The Maid's Tragedy,* belong to the bright and tidy little men of a decadent age. But there are a number of twisted and ungainly giants who walk among them like survivors of the age "before the Flood," as Dryden quaintly put it. A hasty review of their work discloses flashes of genius, of rare dramatic passion and illumination.

George Chapman, the oldest of the brotherhood, lumbers on the stage with an air of top-heavy greatness. His learning was at least equal to Ben Jonson's. His fame rests securely on his compelling, if faulty and exaggerated, translation of the *Iliad* and the *Odyssey* to which Keats later paid the tribute of his famous sonnet. His life spanned Elizabethan theatre from its beginnings to its senility. Born about 1559, he reached manhood nearly a decade before Marlowe wrote *Tamburlaine,* but he stood more or less aloof from the theatre until about 1596 and his first ventures in playwriting were interrupted by the labors of his mighty translation.

He found time in 1605 to write the intelligent and entertaining comedy *All Fools,* which recalls Terence by its satirization of an unduly severe father who discovers that the paragon he thought he was rearing has married under his nose. He essayed romantic comedy in *The Gentleman Usher* next year, with indifferent success, and character comedy of considerable merit in *Monsieur D'Olive*. His major, if more uneven, efforts, are however those in which he wrestled with tragedy.

In 1607 came his *Bussy d'Ambois*. It is notable for its treatment of contemporary continental material; Chapman, who had traveled extensively and was far less provincial than his fellow-writers, followed the troubled history of France with keen interest. The play, which treats the reign of the French Henry III and revolves around a colorful bully and great lover, is written in Marlowe's vein; Bussy is a minor and Gallic Tamburlaine. Incredibly turgid because Chapman was intoxicated with language and dearly loved complexities of thought, the play nevertheless possesses a majestic sweep. It was followed by the weaker *Revenge of Bussy d'Ambois*, which bears more than one resemblance to *Hamlet*. Custom requires Clermont de Bussy to avenge his swaggering brother who was treacherously killed, and the revenger is another Hamlet in his procrastination, since he, too, is a reflective character. Reflectiveness is, in fact, the essence of Chapman's serious work in the theatre. Without this quality, which is frequently as sententious as it is at other times incisive, the Bussy plays would be undistinguished continuations of blood-and-thunder melodrama. Lines like "Kings punish subjects' errors with their own" or "Kings are like archers, and their subjects shafts" and the passage in which Clermont anatomizes married love and proves it to be logically impossible are characteristic of Chapman's tedious greatness.

Most strikingly effective in their crabbed magnificence are the two plays *The Conspiracy of Charles, Duke of Byron* and *The Tragedy of Charles, Duke of Byron,* both dealing with a notorious conspiracy against Henry IV of France. The character of the unstable feudal nobleman is effectively contrasted with the king's shrewdness. The growth of rebellious thoughts in Byron, the temptations to which he is exposed, the manner in which he is lured to Henry's court by a traitor, and his downfall comprise a frequently moving psychological history. If only Chapman had possessed greater talent for casting his material into dramatically effective situations, the two Byron plays would be memorable. They possess essential tragedy of plot and characterization, as well as a greater number of memorable lines than we now expect even of our best contemporary playwrights. Like other Elizabethans he is particularly forceful when his mood is funereal and is tinged with philosophical dialectics. Byron cries out,

> . . . *wretched world,*
> *Consisting most of parts that fly each other;*
> *A firmness breeding all inconstancy,*

A bond of all disjunction; like a man
Long buried is a man that long hath lived;
Touch him, he falls to ashes.

Sharp dramatic utterance is also his. As Byron is blindfolded by the hangman, the Archbishop comforts him,

My lord, now you are blind to this world's sight,
Look upward to a world of endless light.

But the words are flung back in his teeth:

Ay, ay, you talk of upward still to others,
And downwards look with headlong eyes, yourselves.

To another character who admonishes him for not allowing the hangman to cut his hair,

My lord, you make too much of this your body
Which is no more your own,

Byron retorts: "Nor is it yours." He dies bitterly resenting the mortality of man:

Such is the endless exile of dead men.
Summer succeeds the spring; autumn the summer;
The frosts of winter, the fall'n leaves of autumn:
All these, and all fruits in them yearly fade,
And every year return: but cursed man
Shall never more renew his vanquish'd face.

The great wind of drama, it will be seen, blows moodily through the crannies of this passionate scholar's intellect.

Chapman continued to write for the stage until 1612, the year of *The Widow's Tears*, a forceful if ill-sustained ironic comedy. But after 1613 his plays became extremely few in number and undistinguished in quality. He who had not turned to the theatre until he was approaching forty practically abandoned it during the last twenty-one years of his life. In an age less completely wedded to the theatre, Chapman might indeed never have written a play. But the Elizabethan stage was a powerful magnet that drew nearly all talents to it. Such is always the attraction of a vigorous theatre, and few imaginative people can resist it.

The same half-hearted attachment to the stage is apparent in the career of the scurrilous satirist John Marston (1575-1634) who devoted only some nine years to the stage. He wrote the blood-soaked melodramas *Antonio and Mellida* and *Antonio's Revenge* which revived revenge tragedy before the production of *Hamlet,* as well as mordant comedies like *The Malcontent.* After these loosely constructed but frequently powerful works, Marston abandoned playwriting and spent the rest of his life, a full quarter of a century, in the bosom of the Church. His *Parasitaster or the Fawn* possesses many a bold comic stroke at the expense of courtly life, *The Dutch Courtesan* is a strong if unpleasant study of physical passion, and his collaboration *The Insatiate Courtesan* contains a powerful portrait of a woman who is sufficiently described by the detailed title. To the still more notable collaboration *Eastward Ho!,* famous for its vivid picture of London life, Marston contributed other excellent characters—rogues and fools who are singularly alive because they are not saddled with Jonsonian "humours."

Invariably Marston's power arises from his fiery negativism and impassioned cynicism. His *Malcontent,* the drama of a duke who loses his duchy and learns to hold humanity in contempt, anticipated Molière's *Misanthrope* and Wycherley's *Plain Dealer.* Its cynic's words, "This earth is the only grave and Golgotha wherein all things that live must rot; 'tis but the draught wherein all heavenly bodies discharge their corruption; the very muck-hill on which the sublunary orbs cast their excrements," express an anguish that man is not yet able to exorcise. In such a world, thought is futile, and the vanity of striving for knowledge has rarely been put into such felicitous lines as the passage in *What You Will* which concludes with

> *I staggered, knew not which was the firmer part;*
> *But thought, quoted, read, observed and pried,*
> *Stuffed noting-books, and still my spaniel slept.*
> *At length he waked and yawned, and by yon sky,*
> *For aught I know he knew as much as I.*

The same sense of futility is indicated in Marston's withdrawal from the theatre while he was still at the peak of his powers.

Most Elizabethan playwrights, however, could not afford to abandon the stage, even if they had been so disposed; and a good many of them were not. They wrote copiously, collaborated frequently, turned out a great deal of insignificant trash, and occasionally wrote something memorable.

Perhaps the most talented, as he was certainly the most sunny, of the hacks was Thomas Dekker, who was born as early as 1570 and died only a year or so before the closing of the theatres by the successful Puritan Revolution in 1642. Like Robert Greene earlier, he tried to augment his slender means by writing realistic satirical books like his cyclopaedia of thieving and vagabondage *The Bellman of London* and the delightful *Gull's Hornbook* which is replete with intimate details of London life.

He collaborated so extensively with both his equals and his third-rate inferiors in the theatre that he had little time for independent work; only eight or nine extant plays are his alone. But even this furious scribbling did not improve his finances sufficiently to keep him out of debtor's prison on several occasions; and one of these lasted three years.

His genial spirit was not soured by these experiences. His was a sanguine nature, not greatly burdened by learning or the power of reflection. He could, however, sing beautifully and laugh robustly, and he had keen powers of observation. His fantasy *Old Fortunatus*, a blundering and occasionally absurd play, is richly imaginative and poetic. The verse

> *Tomorrow, Shadow, will I give thee gold,*
> *Tomorrow, pride goes bare, and lust a-cold,*
> *Tomorrow will the rich man feed the poor,*
> *And vice tomorrow virtue will adore,*
> *Tomorrow beggars shall be crownéd Kings.*
> *This no-time, morrow's time, no sweetness sings*

needs no commendation. Fortune's excellent monologues in the first act contain lines like

> *This world is Fortune's ball, wherewith she sports,*
> *Sometimes I strike it up into the air,*
> *And then create I emperors and kings:*
> *Sometimes I spurn it, at which spurn crawls out*
> *The wild beast Multitude. . . .*

A collaboration with Middleton, *The Roaring Girl*, is a vigorous picture of low life and contains the vivid figure of Moll Cutpurse who may be taken as the original "moll" of the American vernacular. This girl in breeches is the opposite of the numerous Elizabethan maidens who sport their innocence in male attire; she is an expert highwayman and even her rehabilitation at the end does not lessen her robust geniality. This frequently entertaining if somewhat sentimentally contrived comedy is, however, more Middleton's than Dekker's.

His basic tender-mindedness stood Dekker in good stead when he wrote the two parts of *The Honest Whore*, a diffuse comedy of manners and intrigue which contains excellent characterizations of the reclaimed prostitute Bellafront and of her watchful father Friscobaldo. But it is in the frolicsome kindliness displayed in his masterpiece *The Shoemakers' Holiday* that one finds his sunny genius at its zenith. Here Dekker is one of several Elizabethans to celebrate the middle class that is rising both politically and socially in some proportion to its growing prosperity. Thomas Deloney, the novelist who had traced this development in his short novels, provided the subject, and Dekker turned his story of Simon Eyre, the shoemaker who became Lord Mayor in the reign of Henry VI, into an endearing romantic comedy. *The Shoemakers' Holiday* combines a "success story" that must have pleased the groundlings with a general picture of artisan life and a romance in which the nephew of an earl disguises himself as a Flemish shoemaker in order to win Eyre's daughter Rose. Democracy gains a victory when this unequal match is sanctioned by the king, and it also prevails when the apprentice Ralph, returning from the wars, recovers his wife from a well-to-do gentleman who is about to marry her. Glorious humor and vigor are supplied by the genial self-reliance of Simon Eyre and by the antics of his mettlesome apprentices who stage the first labor strike in the drama and enable Ralph to win back his wife by flourishing their cudgels. The gaiety of the piece is, moreover, not as "unthinking" as some authorities hold. It is the best social comedy of the age, and its democratic humor has commended it to our own time.

The same sympathy with common life was displayed by that other fertile playwright Thomas Heywood, whose *Woman Killed with Kindness,* written in 1603, is a tribute to the common sense and humanity of the third estate. In a simple and moving play Heywood told the story of the solid citizen Master Frankford who learns that his wife Anne is betraying him with a poor gentleman Wendoll whom he has been sheltering. Instead of giving vent to the customary heroics and killing the lovers, he maintains a becoming dignity. He separates from his wife but provides for her, and his pity is far greater than his pride. She dies heartbroken by the remorse that his kindness has evoked in her, though not before he has forgiven her. The unconventionality of his conduct is commented on by a neighboring nobleman who declares he would have killed both the woman and her lover. Despite some weakness of motivation in the wife's behavior and notwithstanding the presence of a secondary plot, *A Woman Killed With Kindness* retains its flavor of genuine pathos and humanity.

Heywood's loyalty to the burgher class appears in a number of other plays like *King Edward IV,* which celebrates the siege of London and the spirited behavior of its citizens who rout the enemy, and in *The Four Prentices of London,* in which the four sons of the medieval crusader Godfrey of Bouillon who are apprenticed to different trades cover themselves with glory through exploits in the Holy Land. Heywood's picture of seafaring life in *The Fair Maid of the West* and the homespun materials of *The English Traveler* and *The Fair Maid of the West* possess the breath of life and reality. Heywood, however, pandered to every conceivable taste of the times and the great bulk of his work is negligible.

The middle class was also treated by the anonymous authors of *Warning for Fair Women* (1599), dealing realistically with the murder of a London merchant, and of the excellent *Yorkshire Tragedy* (1608), a portrait of a debauchee who becomes a murderer and is consumed with remorse. More middle-class drama was supplied by the talented, if extremely uneven, playwrights Middleton and Massinger. The former, who served as chronologer of the city of London and was in charge of many a civic masque or pageant, wrote a glorious comedy of English sharpers in *Michaelmas Term*. The manner in which an innocent from the country is ensnared by a usurer's assistant and the vivid description of shady business practices make this comedy a minor triumph of realism. The same author's *Trick to Catch an Old One* is a pungent farce in which a thriftless nephew imposes on his grasping old uncle. The play is alternately salacious and satirical, and it owes a great deal of its interest to that gusto for creative colloquial speech which is presented in the work of most Elizabethans but which strikes us as so remarkable whenever we come across it in the plays of our own time. Old man Hoard, believing himself to have been deprived of a business deal, exclaims that it was unfair for his rival "to come in the evening of the bargain, and glean all my hopes in a minute; to enter, as it were, at the back door of the purchase." When a character separates the bellicose old men, he declares regarding them that "when the fire grows too unreasonably hot, there's no better way than to take off the *wood*."

It would also be difficult to find an Elizabethan play so breezy, ribald and steeped in common life as Thomas Middleton's *Chaste Maid in Cheapside*. T. S. Eliot, in his admirable essay on Middleton, makes a precise estimate when he writes: "As a social document the comedy of Middleton illustrates the transition from government by a landed aristocracy to government by a city aristocracy (*i.e.*, the bourgeoisie) gradually engrossing the land." But Middleton wisely concentrates on vivid personalities instead of economic abstractions.

The style of middle-class comedy was also continued in the next generation by Philip Massinger, who was born fourteen years after Middleton in 1584. The younger man's *New Way to Pay Old Debts,* written in 1625, is one of the theatre's most amusing satires on the acquisitive instinct. Its seventeenth-century representative, Sir Giles Overreach, who cheats his nephew Wellborn, hopes to cozen a widow of her estate, and tries to elevate his social position by marrying his daughter to a peer of the land, is one of the memorable portraits of the age. When his daughter elopes with a lover and Wellborn recovers some of his wealth, the old sinner goes mad; he is patently insane, since he is giving money away to everyone he meets!

Still, the last flashes of greatness in the period of decline come from the typically Elizabethan gift for keeping emotion at white heat. Sparks continue to fly, and the great age sputters out—even as it began—in a passion.

Middleton begins to tap the usual vein of pathos in *Women Beware Women*, in 1612, when he describes the affectionate domesticity of a young married couple. But it is not long before the milk of the story curdles, and the play becomes an accumulation of human depravities. This work is followed by a series of intense tragedies, in which Middleton collaborates with the actor-playwright William Rowley. Among them is the frequently powerful drama *A Fair Quarrel*, which makes strong use of the anguish of a son whose mother has pretended dishonesty in order to save him from a duel, and one outstanding work *The Changeling*. This tragedy, produced about 1622, has the true Elizabethan flame that flares even if it smokes. The beautiful Beatrice who is in love with Alsemero is compelled by her father to marry the nobleman Alonso. In despair she accepts the services of her father's resolute servant De Flores, whose silent passion she has hitherto scorned. He is a desperate man who has experienced much suffering and has looked deeply into the abysses of human injustice. Murdering her suitor for her, he claims her virtue as his reward, and soon her loathing for him is changed into a perverse kind of love which he compels by the strength of his nature. After having experienced De Flores' passion she can only find her husband Alsemero a faint taper; at least, as T. S. Eliot suggests, she has become "habituated" to the agent of her crime. Ultimately the criminals are unmasked, but De Flores cheats justice and escapes the humiliations of punishment by stabbing her and himself. *The Changeling* is a powerful psychological drama, and although it is tinged with reflection and is full of the pity of human frustration it moves with breathless intensity.

"Our audiences," wrote Lamb, "come to the theatre to be complimented on their goodness." This was in 1820, and the statement is more or less applicable to long stretches of the English theatre. Elizabethan audiences, on the contrary, came for the intensification of experience and were grateful to the playwright who could show them the vertiginous depths and heights of passion. *The Changeling* was one of the later plays that met this challenge to playwrights. This was not, moreover, (nor could it be) accomplished without that poetic gift which

some of the Elizabethan playwrights retained to the end. Dramatic lines
like De Flores'

> *Can you weep Fate from its determined purpose?*
> *So soon may you weep me,*

and Beatrice's words, explaining her perverse tie to the man she detested,

> *Beneath the stars, upon yon meteor*
> *Ever hung my fate, 'mongst things corruptible,*
> *I ne'er could pluck it from him; my loathing*
> *Was prophet to the rest, but ne'er believed.*

are worthy of Shakespeare, whom the minor Elizabethans always touch
in their moments of genuine exaltation. These moments are fairly frequent in *The Changeling*.

Powerful poetry appears again in the generally shoddy but sometimes
extremely stirring work of Cyril Tourneur; in his two somber plays *The
Revenger's Tragedy** and *The Atheist's Tragedy,* which appeared in
1607 and 1611 respectively. Both tragedies swelled the blood-and-thunder revenge literature of the day. But the second one made the departure
of dramatizing the *refusal* to revenge private injuries. Charlemont, who
is deprived of his inheritance and whose father is murdered by his cynical ("atheistic") uncle, refrains from the shedding of blood. Instead
he leaves the villain to the justice of providence, which obligingly destroys him. The passion for wealth dominates the "atheist" so completely that the play becomes another Elizabethan critique of the passion for riches. It is well to remember that the Elizabethan playwrights
saw the rise of middle-class enterprise before it became a social norm;
they had not yet learned to accept a commercial society as the fixed order
of things and therefore observed its rise with unhabituated—marveling
or horror-fixed—eyes. For those who cannot stomach the continuous villainies of the plot of *The Atheist's Tragedy,* Tourneur's other play, *The
Revenger's Tragedy,* with its picture of corruption at court, is more impressive. Time and again, its characters, speaking under the compulsion
of some wrong, burst out into stinging lines like those of Vendice, the
brother who is trying to save his sister's and his mother's honor:

> *Were't not for gold and women, there would be no damnation.*
> *Hell would look like a lord's great kitchen without fire in't . . .*
> *Does the silkworm expend her yellow labours*

---

* On some extremely tenuous evidence this play is sometimes assigned to Middleton; see *The Authorship of the Revenger's Tragedy* by Wilbur D. Dunkel, PMLA,
Sept., 1931.

For thee? For thee does she undo herself?
Are lordships sold to maintain ladyships,
For the poor benefit of a bewildering minute?

It is regrettable only that Tourneur, about whom we know little more than that he devoted himself only casually to the theatre, should have allowed the machinery of his plays to creak so audibly.

4 JOHN WEBSTER, THE FINAL ELIZABETHAN

Even Tourneur, however, is a mild playwright by comparison with John Webster, who is truly the last of the great Elizabethans.

Webster also overshadows the prolific Philip Massinger who survived until 1639, and wrote many romantic dramas and tragedies like *The Duke of Milan*, *The Maid of Honor*, *The Bondman* and *The Roman Actor*, a glorification of the acting profession. For all their emotionalism and their comparatively careful structure, Massinger's serious plays are stiff and monotonous. The dignity of his work is the product of a meticulous rather than dramatic talent. The greatly praised playwright John Ford is also Webster's inferior. Ford travailed like a volcano in an effort to arouse the jaded appetites of his public. He piled sorrow upon sorrow and assaulted the tear-glands with a battering ram in his perfervid love tragedy *The Broken Heart* which has been accorded a reputation far beyond its deserts. Its story is a lush canticle of a woman Panthea who dies of a broken heart when, being compelled by her brother to marry a rich man, she finds herself torn between her longing for her lover and her dread of adultery. Her heartbreak is paralleled by that of the princess who becomes betrothed to Panthea's brother only to lose him when he is stabbed by Panthea's lover. The title of the play is indeed too modest, as there are two broken hearts in the story. In his other, and more powerful, work *'Tis Pity She's a Whore* Ford also spared no means in his striving for sensationalism. Giovanni and his sister Annabella fall in love with each other and are guilty of incest. Annabella marries another man and, having developed scruples, denies herself to Giovanni. Thereupon he kills her and carries her heart on the point of his dagger! There are, it is true, moments when the play is nearly great. The growth of the incestuous passion against which the characters struggle in vain and Annabella's final change of heart are powerfully realized. And an atmosphere of fatality emanates from the somber poetry of this dramatist about whom we know practically nothing except the contemporary comment that

Deep in a dump John Ford was alone got,
With folded arms and melancholy hat.

Still, Ford's plays lack the vision and ecstasy that alone could justify his sensationalism. Consequently they fall short of Webster's tragedies. Naturally, too, these could not be approached by the work of James Shirley, chronologically the last of the Elizabethans since he died in the reign of Charles II. Shirley constructed his comedies and tragedies carefully but borrowed liberally from his contemporaries, as well as from the Spanish playwrights, and he lacked true fire. Webster's came from a temperament that is not given to common men.

Webster is another of those shadowy Elizabethans about whom little is known. He may have been born as early as 1570, but he first appeared in the theatre at the beginning of the new century. The first record of him again reminds us that Hollywood factory methods of collaboration have not been confined to the modern machine age. In 1602 Philip Henslowe lends the Admiral's Company five pounds with which to pay Anthony Munday, Thomas Middleton, Michael Drayton, John Webster, "and the rest" for a play entitled *Caesar's Fall*. By then, therefore, this son of a member of the Merchant Tailors' Guild must have left his studies at the Middle Temple law school to engage in literary pursuits. For the next dozen years the record has him collaborating with Dekker, Heywood, and others, writing a prologue to Marston's *Malcontent,* and composing his two masterpieces *The White Devil* and *The Duchess of Malfi,* in 1611-12 and 1613-14 respectively. Suddenly in these two works a genius comes to the fore as if from nowhere. Then his star falls from the heavens and dissipates its light in several undistinguished comedies and in a well-constructed but largely uninspired tragedy. A year after his second major work he contributes some new character sketches to the sixth edition of Overbury's *Characters.* In 1619-20 he writes his comedy *The Devil's Law Case,* which is followed next year by a collaboration with Middleton, *Anything For a Quiet Life.* About 1625 he collaborates with Massinger and Ford on *The Fair Maid of the Inn,* and on *A Cure for a Cuckold* with Rowley and possibly Heywood; and some time before his death he writes the Roman tragedy *Appius and Virginia,* in which Heywood's hand is traced.

Little more is told about him except that he is a slow writer who torments himself as he writes his greatest work.

> *See how he draws his mouth awry of late,*
> *How he scrubs, wrings his wrists, scratches his pate.*
> *A midwife, help! By his brain's coitus,*
> *Some centaur strange, some huge Bucephalus,*
> *Or Pallas, sure, is engendered in his brain*

writes a contemporary satirist and lawyer. While most of his fellow-writers are being influenced by facile Spanish heroic drama and tragi-comedy, Webster remains true to the demoniac, tragic outlook of the earlier Elizabethan drama. He is an easily aroused person, and is nettled by the imputation of slowness. He expresses scorn for the public and for the very patrons whose favor he is seeking, declares that he does not "look up to titles," and is defiantly conscious of his merits. His contemporaries refer to him as "crabbed Websterio."

Turning to two Italian themes, he writes unmitigated tragedies in which, for all his slipshod workmanship, he sometimes approximates Shakespeare's greatest work. His characters are dynamic and alive with passion, their pathos is never sentimental, their evil is unconventional and reaches sublimity. His verse is poetry of the highest order and equals the best of Marlowe and Shakespeare, while his prose crackles with satire. The spirit of greatness hovers over the stormy waters of his invention.

His genius, it is true, is narrow, since he knows nothing of the genial laughter, the tenderness, and the pleasant fantasy of Shakespeare. It is humanity's anguish and evil alone that capture his interest. He is the elegist of a dying age.

Others sang the same dirge—Shakespeare in his tragic period, Marston in his satires, Tourneur in his evocations of evil, the poet Donne, and the prose masters Burton of *The Anatomy of Melancholy* and Sir Thomas Browne of *Urn Burial*. But Webster was an infinitely better playwright than Marston or Tourneur and, unlike Shakespeare, he approximated greatness only as a desperate tragedian. His fame rests almost entirely upon the two pillars of despair he erected as the world's epitaphist. Rupert Brooke recognized him as "the last of Earth, looking over a sea of saccharine," T. S. Eliot as the poet who was "much possessed by death, and saw the skull beneath the skin."

This estimate of him, however, borders on sentimental exaggeration, despite the fact that his mortuary lines are the most quotable and that he makes much of the villainy of mankind. Not all of mankind is corrupt in his tragedies, and his portrait gallery contains such moving characters as the lovable duchess of Malfi and the noble steward on whom she bestowed her love with tragic results. Brachiano's duchess in *The White Devil* is an affectionate wife cruelly done to death, and the same play contains one of the most appealing children of the Elizabethan stage. In the final analysis, Webster is, like Shakespeare, simply a master of pity and terror—in brief, a true tragedian.

In *The White Devil*, Vittoria, a beautiful and spirited woman married to a dolt who happens to be the nephew of a Roman cardinal, falls under the spell of the dashing Renaissance prince and soldier Duke Brachiano. At first their love is clandestine. But it is threatened on all sides—by the fatuous but suspicious husband Camillo, by this fool's uncle the

Cardinal, and by Brachiano's brother-in-law the Duke of Florence. Once at bay, the lovers, prompted and aided by Vittoria's brother Flamineo, get rid of Camillo and of Brachiano's duchess. Brought to trial for the murder of Camillo, Vittoria defends herself splendidly and the charge is dropped. Nevertheless, she is committed to a reformatory or House of Convertites as an immoral woman. The Duke of Florence, however, is not content with this mild punishment. Bent upon exposing the illicit lovers and destroying Brachiano, whom he fears to attack directly, he sends a love letter to Vittoria which arouses Brachiano's jealousy. A furious lovers' quarrel ensues, and it has the desired result of making Brachiano steal his mistress out of the House of Convertites and bring her to his court. Since they are now flaunting their passion to the world, they draw down the Pope's excommunication and give the Duke of Florence all the justification he needs before destroying them. Appearing at Brachiano's court in disguise, Florence and his hired assassins poison Brachiano and stab Vittoria, as well as her brother and her Moorish servant.

A great deal has been made of the melodramatic nature of the plot, but it is no more melodramatic than the external plot of Shakespeare's greatest tragedies. Webster's horrors have been made an excuse for severe indictments. But there is as much horror in *King Lear*. The plot is complicated by many threads, but again no more so than in *Lear*. *The White Devil* only wobbles somewhat when Webster presents the murder of Camillo and Brachiano's duchess in dumb-show through an illusionist's magic. This is doubtless a careless device, but Webster is guilty only of relying too heavily on Elizabethan showmanship, and both scenes can be omitted without seriously violating the continuity of the story. Moreover, Webster compensates us amply for his deficiencies.

Vittoria is a remarkable woman, all fire and spirit. That she should turn from a tepid marriage to a clandestine love is inevitable. She is not a cheap murderess, even if she countenances the death of those who stand in the way of her passion. When Vittoria is brought to trial, she makes her defense with all the resourcefulness of a woman who is fighting for her love and her self-respect. In the jealous quarrel with Brachiano she is not a passive mistress; sure of her love and unbowed in spirit she gives him strong words and creates perhaps the most exciting lovers' quarrel in all dramatic literature. She also dies uncowed, troubled only by the reflection that her love had to be stained with crime. To her murderer she says scornfully,

> *'Twas a manly blow;*
> *The next thou giv'st, murder some sucking infant,*
> *And then thou wilt be famous.*

Brachiano's personality is almost equally splendid. Although he allows the officious Flamineo to rid him of Vittoria's husband and of the Duchess, he is neither a tyrant nor a lecher but a passion-swept man. The corruption is not in him but in the age, and it is far more apparent in Florence's diabolical plot against him and in the cynical behavior of Vittoria's brother. But even the latter is not a stock character. He was a scholar who discovered that innocent intelligence and decent behavior left men out in the cold. He therefore applies his intellect to the profitable employment of pandering to his sister and the Duke. However, he never represses his individuality or his mordant satire of the society that has warped his talents. He also says the final word on his sister's stained passion or violation of man-made morality in an age in which adultery took the place of divorce:

> *Know many glorious women that are famed*
> *For masculine virtue have been vicious.*
> *Only a happier silence did betide them.*
> *She hath no faults, who hath the art to hide them.*

The innumerable telling moments of the play, its passion and anguish, its exposure of men's depravity and society's hypocrisy, the explosiveness of the dialogue, and the sense of the horror of life and its end that reaches its climax in the famous dirge "Call for the robin-red-breast and the wren" and in the death of the lovers—these qualities belong to the highest reaches of tragedy.

The Duchess of Malfi, which is sometimes preferred to *The White Devil,* has the advantage of greater pathos, since its principal characters are innocent and lovable. The evil of the world stages a macabre dance in the behavior of those who persecute them to the last extremity before being themselves destroyed. The widowed Duchess of Malfi is forbidden to marry again by her brothers Duke Ferdinand and the Cardinal because they covet her estate. But she falls in love with her steward Antonio, wooes him charmingly since he is too lowly to woo her himself, and marries him secretly. They live happily, and she gives birth to three children. But the marriage is discovered by her brothers' spy and murderous agent Bosola and the lovers are forced to flee. She is captured, imprisoned, tormented with representations of her supposedly dead husband and children, and finally strangled along with her children and servant woman. The crime is followed, in quick and incredible succession, by the madness of Ferdinand and the death of the Cardinal. Antonio—whom the relenting Bosola had hoped to save—is also killed, as is Bosola himself.

In this tragedy reality is exceeded, as it is not in *The White Devil,* which is the superior play. Judged objectively, it deserves something less than the highest praise that has been lavished on it. It is redeemed, however, by moments of pity and terror worthy of Shakespeare. Moreover, even if it goes counter to modern taste, *The Duchess of Malfi* is a splendid nightmare, and is to be evaluated as such. It is a last testament of the horror and despair that overwhelms a sensitive spirit. And who, in the last analysis, shall say that it exaggerates when the facts of history, even in our own day, disclose exhibitions even more horrible?

After this second visit to the charnel house of humanity, Webster makes the best of what there is to life. He lapses into fairly amiable second-rate work, and speaks out only in the contemptuous cynicism of his *Devil's Law Case* and in casual passages in his collaborations. He can still snarl in a few lines that equal Flamineo's in *The White Devil*,

> *O men*
> *That lie upon your death-beds and are haunted*
> *With howling wives. Ne'er trust them! they'll remarry*
> *Ere the worm pierce your winding sheet; ere the spider*
> *Make a thin curtain for your epitaphs.*

The rest, however, is mediocrity and silence.

In this decline the age follows him. Mediocrity gluts the stage as numerous writers like Glapthorne, Brome, Armin, Barnes, Markham, Day, Randolph, Field, Suckling, Davenport and D'Avenant, reputed to be Shakespeare's illegitimate son, continue to pour out native comedies, imitations of Lope de Vega, and a host of miscellaneous pieces. Now and then a tragedy like the anonymous *Nero* (1633) and a mild but charming fantasy like John Day's *Parliament of Bees* reveal poetic power. Now and then a comedy like Suckling's *Goblins* proves sufficiently amusing. But brightness is falling from the air. Finally, in 1642, when the Puritans close the public theatres, there is darkness.

SOME ADDITIONAL PLAYS

By Ben Jonson: *The Staple of News,* 1626, satire on avarice and credulity; *A Tale of a Tub,* 1633, a fresh, realistic comedy.

By Beaumont and Fletcher: *A King and No King,* 1611, romance and satire.

By John Fletcher: (probably alone): *Wit Without Money,* c.614, a good comedy; *The Loyal Subject,* 1618, another good comedy; *The Wild-Goose Chase,* 1621, romantic comedy; *The Woman's Prize,* before 1625, a comedy in which Petruccio is tamed; *Rule A Wife, Have A Wife,* 1624, his most highly regarded comedy.

By Philip Massinger: *The City Madam,* 1632, a realistic comedy of manners; *The Great Duke of Florence,* 1627, genial romantic comedy.

By John Ford: *The Chronicle History of Perkin Warbeck,* 1634, considered the best Elizabethan historical play after Shakespeare; *The Witch of Edmonton,* after 1621, in collaboration with Dekker and Rowley, an effective domestic drama.

By James Shirley (1596-1666): *Hyde Park,* 1632, a comedy of fashionable London; *The Gamester,* 1633, a realistic, bawdy comedy; *The Lady of Pleasure,* 1635, a comedy of intrigue with effective satire; *The Cardinal,* 1641, a well written tragedy.

PART VI

THE POLITE PLAYWRIGHTS

EUROPE had liberated itself from medievalism by means of a tremendous upsurge of creative energies during the Renaissance. The next step was to consolidate the victories of the Renaissance, and this involved the stabilization of culture, especially in France and England. Literature became less entranced with buccaneering individuals and more interested in characters who were expected to accommodate themselves to prevailing standards of conduct. The drama, too, expressed the new outlook.

In the main, playwrights made heroism or individual desire subservient to duty, and passion subordinate to sensibility. Comedy likewise fell under the new dispensation. Since Shakespeare's romantic comedies had celebrated triumphant individuality and Jonson had thundered violently in the theatre, their art did not seem sufficiently housebroken for the new age which flattered its formalism by calling it classic and by citing ancient authority in its favor. With few exceptions, the writers of comedy in the new age accommodated themselves to an urbane view of life, avoiding exhibitions of anger and mocking all departures from either reasonable conduct or fashion. The theatre, in short, exalted the civilized qualities of refinement and order.

A less sympathetic view of neo-classicism is Irving Babbitt's description of it as "a mixture of Aristotle and the dancing master." But the attempt to create "a tragedy of reason," to use Francis Fergusson's phrase, was nonetheless a noble enterprise, especially in the case of Jean Racine; and Molière's contribution to the art of comedy was a major achievement in world drama. Nor was dramatic excitement necessarily absent, in spite of formalism in tragic composition when even Racine exemplified the conflict between reason and irrational passion.

XV

CORNEILLE AND RACINE: POLITE TRAGEDY

I THE HEROIC DRAMA OF CORNEILLE

WHEN Pierre Corneille, barrister and author of a number of comedies, startled the French theatre with his magnum opus *The Cid* late in 1636, England was approaching an upheaval that would strike the death-blow to absolute monarchy in Shakespeare's island. In France, on the contrary, monarchy was first approaching its peak. When the French Henry IV bought Paris with a mass in 1593 he gave his country its greatly needed unity and enabled his sagacious minister Sully to lay the economic foundations of its greatness. The assassination of the king by a Catholic fanatic when Corneille was still in his infancy did not stem the tide of national progress. Under the astute statesmanship of Louis XIII's minister Cardinal Richelieu, the feudal nobility shrank appreciably but the middle class grew by cubits, and the Cardinal's "intendants" or middle-class appointees took over the government of the provinces. The dual process of the centralization of government and of economic progress continued under Louis XIV and his able ministers Mazarin and Colbert. These commonplace facts are indispensable to an understanding of the formal nature and philosophy of French neo-classicism—although, naturally, they do not explain the personal artistry of Corneille and his chief successor Racine.

Corneille, born of the middle class in 1606, was an up and coming bourgeois dedicated to the law, the profession pursued by his father who was the king's advocate in Rouen. Practice and promotion came to him easily, and he was not inclined to dismiss the value of money; if anything, he had a reputation for parsimony. But he was also endowed with a strong literary gift and a love of the theatre. A strolling troupe headed by the successful actor Mondori appeared at Rouen, and Corneille added the comedy *Mélite* to its repertory.

He knew little about writing for the stage, but he allowed common sense and the popular theatre to guide him. The French theatre was moving away from the stilted humanist drama of Jodelle, Garnier and Montchrestien. But a popular art of comedy derived from native farces and Italian *commedia dell'arte,* as well as much loosely written tragedy and romance, was flourishing mightily under the leadership of the unclassical showman Alexandre Hardi. Theatrical companies were arising in the first three decades of the sixteenth century. By 1610 Paris had a permanent company in the King's Players, with Alexandre Hardi as its director, and by 1629 arose the Prince of Orange's company with headquarters at the converted tennis court, the *Marais*.

It was the second organization that first acquired Corneille, who thus set up shop in competition with a number of writers, among whom Rotrou (author of a clever version of the Amphitryon story) and Mairet, as well as Hardi, are still remembered in a fashion. *Mélite* was successfully revived in Paris and was followed by *Clitandre*, written in a spirit of bravado characteristic of the pugnacious playwright. He had been told that his first comedy was not in accordance with the highly touted classic rules that a play must transpire within twenty-four hours and must be noble in style. Resenting the censure of fellow-playwrights, Corneille resolved to write something that would conform to the rules and be "generally worthless." He succeeded only too well.

Corneille then added four other comedies to his belt and became a recognized master of the craft. Even his rivals did not stint their praise, and soon the playwright became a member of the staff of writers whom Richelieu hired to assist him in the composition of a comedy. Completing his assignment, as well as composing independently another comedy and his first tragedy, the classic imitation *Médée*, Corneille retired to Rouen and resumed his legal practice. But he did not remain in retirement for long. Stimulated by his acquaintance with a former Secretary of Queen Marie de Medici who urged him to write something worthy of his talents, Corneille applied himself to the study of the Spanish theatre which was already at its zenith. One of its products, Guillen de Castro's *Las Mocedades del Cid*, attracted him with its exciting account of the exploits of Spain's most popular hero. The result was the tragi-comedy *The Cid*, one of the masterpieces of French drama.

Since Mondori's theatre was occupied for the season with the biblical drama *Marianne* by a new luminary François Tristran, Corneille gave his play to its rivals at the Hôtel de Bourgogne, and the close of the season of 1636-37 proved memorable for both the author and the rival company. "Beautiful as *Le Cid*" became a proverbial expression. Town and court alike acclaimed the play, the author, and Richelieu's niece to whom he had dedicated it. Louis XIII and his queen complimented Corneille and granted his father a patent of nobility ostensibly as a reward for his services but actually as a compliment to the son.

No play bears the stamp of Corneille as distinctly as *The Cid*. To understand its significance fully one must regard it as a transitional work, for Corneille was a transitional figure. Although he respected the new autocratic France, he was an independent spirit and not yet the complete courtier who became the ideal of the age. His *Cid* paid tribute to the ideals of "honor" or duty, and to this extent it reflected the new age which set social responsibility above personal impulses. The individual personality glorified by the Renaissance was now required to submit its ego to "law," and Corneille found this law in the strict requirements of honor. Nevertheless, the play also celebrated the claims of individuality by the intensely heroic quality of its leading characters and the strength of their emotions. In structure and style the play was likewise something less than a rigid observance of the regulations that were now being imposed on the drama by scholars and critics in the name of Aristotle. True, he paid lip-service to the principle that the action of drama must take place in a single locality during a single day. But the stormy events of *The Cid* violate the spirit of these laws, and the action of the play is more suitable to the diffuse Elizabethan stage. In twenty-four hours, "Roderick declares his love, fights his first duel, kills his sweetheart's father, repels in a tremendous battle a national invasion, wins a trial by combat, and in the course of all this loses and regains favor of his king and the lady of his heart." [1] Even unity of action is imperiled in a story that embraces so many events, although the play successfully avoids the secondary plots that so frequently clutter up the work of the Elizabethans.

In vigorous, exalted dramatic verse, unequaled by anything hitherto written in the French language, the play told a storm-swept tale in which love and honor contended for victory. Since they are dominated by the Spanish code of honor, the characters must strike a later age as somewhat stilted, argumentative, extravagant. Nevertheless, the emotion that courses through their veins is genuine, and its eddies are traced faithfully and with notable sensitivity.

Rodrique and Chimène are well-bred young lovers and her father, the hardy warrior Don Gomez, approves the match. Chimène is as happy in her love as the Infanta of Spain, who had promoted the courtship in order to still her own politically impossible love for Rodrique, is unhappy. But at the height of the lovers' joy, jealousy prompts Don Gomez to insult and strike Rodrique's old father. It is incumbent upon Rodrique, who had never fought before, to avenge his father, and in the ensuing duel he slays Don Gomez. Between the young lovers rises an almost insuperable barrier, and the situation is aggravated by the code of honor or of vendetta which forces the girl to demand her lover's death. Rodrique resolves to die by his own hand, but persuaded by his father to seek death honorably on the battlefield he puts himself at the head of a small band which is trying to stem a Moorish invasion. The invaders, however, are routed and Rodrique returns a national hero. Nevertheless, Chimène continues to demand his death; the Infanta's and the King's pleas and her own yearning for the young soldier—she fainted when she thought he was dead!—cannot prevail against her sense of duty. A duel is arranged between him and her champion and suitor Don Sanche, and the wise monarch stipulates that she must marry the victor. In a moving scene Rodrique visits her and informs her of his resolve to lose his life in the duel—"I go to punishment not to a combat. . . . I cannot strike the arm that fights for you." All her love for him and all her distaste for marrying Don Sanche, should he be victorious, well up in her. She appeals to Rodrique to defend himself and to win her hand. In fact, she has already tried to ensure his victory in a typically feminine way when she selected the inexperienced Don Sanche to be her champion. Rodrique is naturally the victor and becomes betrothed to her with the understanding that she will have a year in which to forget her father's death.

Much of the bright cynicism of our own day would be wasted on this play. The lovers are pathetically young and live in a feudal and warlike world. The code of honor that dominates them is intensely real in its own day, and if our own is inclined to sneer at it we should not forget that at heart Chimène also revolts against it. Moreover, the barrier of a father's death at the hands of a girl's lover is valid enough in any age. Nor, in the last analysis, is the principle of "honor" that prevails in this play and in Corneille's other tragedies as extravagant as it seems. Translate it into modern circumstances and it proves a force that has lost none of its potency and tragic possibilities. It reappears in our own day, for example, in Maxwell Anderson's *Winterset* when Mio tries to vindicate his unjustly executed father and finds that he is in love with the sister of the man who could have saved him with a word at the trial. Another contemporary treatment of duty is present in Hemingway's *Fifth Column*.

The Cid was Corneille's last tribute to individuality. His age demanded something else. A cabal against him, inspired by Richelieu, caused his temporary retirement, and when he emerged from seclusion he appeared with his wings somewhat clipped. His next play accepted a stricter definition of the dramatic unities than his spirit could endure, and his work became increasingly strait-laced.

A rugged power pervades his *Horace*, which dramatizes the conflict between love and patriotic duty. The ancient Romans and their Alban neighbors are at war. But Sabina, an Alban by birth, is married to the Roman Horatius, and the latter's sister Camilla is in love with an Alban soldier Curiatius. National rivalry thus crosses the grain of natural affection and it tears lovers and families apart. The crisis comes when Horatius and his two brothers are selected to do battle with Curiatius and his two brothers. Horatius is victorious at the expense of his wife's brothers who are all killed, and among them is Curiatius, his sister's lover. Another tragedy ensues when this sister, distracted by her loss, goads

Horatius into killing her—a rather forced situation which blemishes the play.

Here again Corneille is not a moss-backed playwright: his theme is relived whenever nations are at war; it was felt keenly by German-Americans during the World War, and it was represented recently in one of the strongest scenes of the popular Broadway spectacle *The American Way*. Corneille's real deficiency is the increasingly rigid technique imposed on him by the literary fashion of French classicism, since the principle of "order" in all things had by now invaded dramatic construction. He was at his best when he could fill his stage with action and excitement; and this Elizabethan at heart was unhappily caged in the age of Louis XIV.

His next work, *Cinna,* which revolves around a conspiracy against Augustus Caesar, shows the sad effects of this imprisonment. Although its theme of royal clemency and generosity strikes a sage and humane note, the play is more exalted as poetry than interesting as drama. However, its relevance to the internal struggles of the country—which had witnessed the revolt of the "Fronde" against royal authority during the minority of Louis XIV—ensured it such a notable success that even Richelieu renounced his animosity toward the author. The Cardinal and prime minister even enabled him to marry a lady of high station.

Corneille, in turn, was quick to cement his reputation with what he expected to be an even more appealing play, *Polyeucte,* the drama of a Christian convert married to the daughter of a Roman governor, who is in love with another gentleman. Nevertheless, she is such a stickler for wifely duty that she makes every effort to gain her husband's freedom when he is condemned to death for overturning the idols in the temple. Hoping to share his fate when he is executed, she becomes a Christian, too, and is followed by her father. After some vicissitudes, *Polyeucte* became another tremendous success, and took its place as his masterpiece. This verdict is, however, debatable. For all its nobility, the play may well strike us as a strained work sadly in need of the sense of humor which the French tragedians were forbidden to indulge in serious drama. In fact, Corneille, who may have himself felt the need of relief, turned to comedy in his next work *Le Menteur* (*The Liar*), an amusing adaptation from Alarçon's Spanish *La Verdad sospechosa* which revolves around the mendacities of its hero.

By 1642, the date of *Le Menteur,* Corneille, however, had also passed the peak of his talent. He continued to produce numerous plays of indifferent quality which reaped scant success. "Am I not always Corneille?" he complained bitterly. Although Corneille died more than forty years later, in 1684, his fame rested largely on the work of some six years before he had turned middle-aged.

He spent the second half of his life in a world that respected him but had little use for his impassioned and moralistic work. His splendid "crash of sound" and his strident affirmations of the heroic spirit seemed wearisome or a trifle barbaric. The age called for a tamer genius. Under Louis XIV, who assumed full control of France in 1661, Corneille's countrymen were more interested in refinement and sensibility than in major crises and larger-than-life characters. Beyond the borders of the country, wars were constantly raging. But within France, society was given over to the social whirl of a contented middle class and an affected and effete aristocracy. In order to hamstring the obstreperous nobility the king had built the stately pleasure grounds of Versailles, a dozen miles from Paris. Here all nobles who hoped for advancement, many of whom had had their strongholds razed to the ground, led a life of leisure, intrigue and subservience to the monarch. The erstwhile warriors were proud to be allowed to dry the king after his bath or assist him to the lavatory.

Anyone who hoped to win a public of sedate burghers and gallivanting courtiers with serious plays would now have to address himself to the refinements of love and gallantry. He would have to deal with private emotions. He would have to achieve the utmost polish of literary style. Greatness of character, high-mindedness, and major conflicts were consonant with neither the principle of subservience to the state nor the scrupulously cultivated taste of the court.

The only art that could possibly succeed was that which entertained polite society. This was accomplished by the neatly turned fables of La Fontaine, the pleasant character sketches of La Bruyère, the worldly epigrams of La Rochefoucauld, the precious conversations of the fashionable *salons,* and the polished skeins of romance provided by novelists like Madeleine de Scudéry in *Le Grand Cyrus* and Mme. de la Fayette in *La Princesse de Clèves.* The theatre favored spectacles, pageants, opera and comedies, particularly when these were light and avoided social criticism. In order to succeed, tragedy had to entertain not by exciting the passions, but by framing them delicately.*

Moreover, the frame would have to exhibit certain formal features that are *prima facie* inimical to naturalness. Poetic practice and dramatic theory conspired to make French tragedy as artificial as possible. Blank verse is practically impossible in French, and rhyme virtually indispen-

---

* The contemporary critic Saint-Evremond, writing in 1672, summarized the requirements of polite society when he assailed Aristotle's theory to the effect that tragedy must arouse pity and terror. Both emotions were too intense and anarchic to be tolerated. Had they not interfered with the orderly processes of Athenian society! Saint-Evremond wanted nothing more of tragedy than "a greatness of soul well expressed," something to excite in the audience, which was not to be unduly disturbed, "a tender admiration." [6]

sable. The plays had to be written in rhymed hexameters (the Alexandrine), with every four lines exhibiting a fixed difference between the first and second couplet. The first, called "masculine," had to end in a full vowel sound which counts in the twelve syllables of the line; the second, called "feminine," had to close with a mute *e, es, ent,* etc. The one effort to create plausibility in plays was the insistence on the unities of time, place, and action that the critics had derived from Renaissance dramatic theory in the writings of Italian theoreticians like Vida, Cinthio, Castelvetro, and Vettori. In rationalizing their adherence to these rules, which were actually accepted because they appeared to be classical and because they introduced order into the drama, the French claimed they were making the theatre credible. A play, in other words, would become more believable if its action transpired within a day or preferably less than a day, and if the scene remained unchanged.

Our own Samuel Johnson dismissed the whole question with characteristic dispatch when he wrote that these rules gave more trouble to the poet than pleasure to the auditor: "The truth is, that the spectators are always in their senses, and know, from the first act to the last, that the stage is only a stage, and that the players are only players. . . . The delight of tragedy proceeds from our consciousness of fiction; if we thought murders and treasons real, they would please no more." But the claim of credibility was an evasion; the French critics were essentially interested in keeping a tight rein on the impetuous art of the drama. They did not want it to be too comprehensive or disturbing.

Drama was to possess the formal beauty of a jeweled cameo. The play was to exhibit as little action as possible; events were to be reported by messengers; characters were to reveal their emotions by conversing with those nuisances of the French theatre the *confidantes;* and drama was to be confined to a central situation. No formal regulations hampered the choice of content, but it was more or less understood that love between the sexes was the chief wonder of the stage. Contemporary themes were excluded and lowly individuals were of course strictly barred from the tragic stage. Characters, moreover, were expected to be types rather than distinct personalities.

2 ORDER AND SENSIBILITY: RACINE

Many playwrights undertook the assignment, and oblivion was their reward. To create something that suits the requirements of polite society and yet possesses enduring qualities requires a special genius rare among tragedians. By its very nature, tragedy is antipathetic to *politesse.* An age, however, often creates its special genius, and such was the case when the youthful Racine entered the lists of the many who are called and the few who are chosen by the tragic theatre. Men like Quinault, the composer Lulli's librettist who enjoyed a brief triumph, were adept at softening the drama to meet the new requirements of the stage. Only Racine was capable of turning pseudo-classic restrictions into an advantage. This was partly because his gift for refinement produced a wonderful verbal music granted only to genuine poets, and partly because his insight into the feminine heart was so natural and deep. He belongs to that species of genius which embraces femininity without foregoing masculinity or a masculine response to the other sex. The emotional bisexuality which Havelock Ellis and others have noted in the artistic temperament was clearly his. It is not without reason that so many of his tragedies are named after female characters whereas the rugged and only half-polished Corneille gave masculine titles to his plays— *The Cid, Cinna, Horace, Polyeucte,* and so on.

Still these qualities alone are not sufficient to make an important playwright. Racine was fortunate in possessing two indispensable qualifications for tragedy: he possessed a dramatic temperament and a strange perturbation of the spirit. His talent may be likened to a small volcano covered with a patch of flowers. His polished lines are more dramatic than a casual reading, particularly in their inadequate English translations, would reveal. Recited by a competent artist, not to speak of a Rachel or a Sarah Bernhardt, the precise phrases rise and fall with emotion. Lines like Hermione's cry in the *Andromaque,* after she has ordered the assassination of the man she loves, are typical:

> *Où suis-je? Qu' ai je fait? Que dois-je faire encore? . . .*
> *Errante et sans dessein, je cours dans ce palais.*
> *Ah! ne puis-je savoir si j'aime ou si je hais?* *

Such lines are not merely plentiful in Racine's work but preponderant.

Nor are the passions he describes dammed up by victorious reason or morality, as in Corneille's plays. They are too strong to be restrained even when their danger is apparent to the individual himself, and from his characters' inability to liberate themselves from an obsession arise inner conflicts that are little short of infernal in their agony. It is, indeed, customary for English readers to condemn Racine as undramatic on very insufficient grounds. He has held the French stage for more than two and a half centuries and his heroines have been played by nearly every self-respecting French actress.

His life reflects his talents. It oscillates between the attractions of polished society and the somber call of a calvinistic religion. He is torn between high ideals and pettiness; he is alternately noble and irascible,

---

* "Where am I? What have I done? What must I do now? Wandering and without a plan I wander through this palace. Oh! I am unable to know whether I love or hate."—The inadequacy of translation is apparent.

rancorous and ungrateful. He wavers between an inflammable heart and a strong sense of guilt. He loves the court and yet is not insensible to the miseries of the lowest orders which did not share the prosperity of the urban middle classes during the reign of the "Sun-King."

Born in 1639 of a well-to-do family, he was orphaned at the age of four, educated by fanatical relatives, and finally sent to the monastery of Port Royal, the seat of the Jansenist sect which held that all but a few individuals favored with divine grace were doomed to perdition. He steeped himself in Greek and Latin for four years, poring over Sophocles and particularly Euripides, but he also lost himself in romances which were thoroughly condemned by his instructors. When the Hellenistic romance *Aethiopica* was cast into the fire by his mentors, he simply procured another copy, memorized its contents, and then gave it to the sacristan to burn it if he wished. From Port Royal he went to the college d'Harcourt to study philosophy, and then wavered between law and theology, finally choosing the latter. But even then he could not resist the attractions of a literary career. He established himself in Paris, gave himself up to the pleasures of the capital, fell into dissolute company, and ridiculed the Port Royalists who were deeply distressed by their protégé's behavior. An ode won him the patronage of the critic Chapdelaine who recommended him to the King and procured Racine a hundred louis d'or from the royal treasury. After writing another poem, he won the fruitful and lasting friendship of the leading critic of his day, Boileau.

His first tragedy *Amasie* was bought but not produced by the Bourgogne company. Fortune smiled on him, however, when Molière befriended him and produced his second play *Thebaide* in 1664. It proved successful and was followed by another treatment of Greek material— a study of Alexander the Great, *Alexandre le Grand*. Ungratefully, Racine gave the play to Molière's rivals at the Hôtel de Bourgogne shortly after it was produced by his benefactor's company. The Bourgogne players being more adept at tragedy than Molière's Comédiens du Roi, the comparison of the two productions was unfavorable to the latter. Molière, who had lent Racine money and continued the run of *La Thebaide* at a loss, was deeply hurt and never spoke to Racine again.

Racine, however, was pleased to find the excellent Bourgogne company at his service, and soon, in 1667, gave them his first memorable tragedy, *Andromaque* or *Andromache*. The play is a powerful study of character and passion. Andromache, Hector's widow, is loved by her conqueror Pyrrhus, the son of Achilles who had slain her husband at Troy. The memory of the hero she had loved is too great for her to bear the thought of a second love. But bear it she must because only by marrying Pyrrhus can she save her infant son from destruction by the Greeks who are eager to remove the seed of Hector. She agrees, therefore, to marry Pyrrhus after exacting from him a promise to protect her son and resolving to kill herself after the marriage ceremony. The tragedy comes to a climax when the Greek princess Hermione, whose love for Pyrrhus is a consuming obsession, has him assassinated by her lover Orestes and then stabs herself.

Although the theme is remote, Racine succeeds in giving emotional reality to the inner conflicts of a woman who is loyal to her first love but must accommodate herself to circumstance and of a girl whose passion drives her to destroy the man she loves. The subtleties of Racine's dramatic method are exemplified by such a detail as Hermione's exclamation concerning Pyrrhus,

> And do not trust my anger's wavering
> Till death removes this monster; for unless
> He dies today, tomorrow I may love him.

Only the wooden behavior of Orestes reduces the potency of this play. Of course, too, the whole situation may easily strike us as narrow. It is never so when treated by Euripides who knew how to make his tragedies a criticism of life because he had the gift of seeing mankind in the large whereas Racine rarely rose above the immediate situation of his play. But Racine's tragedy also has its validity—as a psychological drama. It is a moving elaboration of human passion.

Racine next turned to comedy with an amusing and mordant adaptation of Aristophanes' *Wasps* entitled *Les Plaideurs* or *The Litigants*. He wrote most of the piece in a fashionable tavern as an exercise of wit, not putting much stock in the piece. But this did not prevent him from extracting considerable comic vitality out of his judge who is so enamored of his calling that he sleeps in his judicial robes and out of the overzealous lawyer who opens his plea with an account of the Creation of the World. Moreover, after this casual excursion into foreign territory, Racine returned to his own domain in *Britannicus*, a powerful representation of Nero and his court.

Racine could not write a chronicle of Nero's life within the confines of the unities of time, place, and action. He could only concentrate on one situation which ushered in this tyrant's career. Nero's ambitious mother Agrippina, who has made him king, soon has reason to regard his future course with misgivings. He is unscrupulous in his passions and allows himself to be guided by an evil counselor Narcissus. Being infatuated with Junia, who is betrothed to the legitimate heir to the throne Britannicus, he seizes her and poisons Britannicus while pledging friendship to him. Junia flees to the vestals and dedicates herself to the gods and Narcissus is killed by an outraged populace when he tries to drag her from the altar. Nero is overcome with helpless rage, and his mother and tutor can only hope that this crime will be his last. Nero is thus left at a critical point in the development of his character. What the Elizabethans would have made merely the beginning of a tragedy here becomes the complete play. Nevertheless, Racine makes the crisis which dominates the entire play exciting and fraught with psychological and dramatic portent.

Mithridate, written in rivalry with the aging Corneille, was another effective drama of a man's passion for a woman, even if it lacked the scope and depth of *Britannicus.* Its superiority over Corneille's work was patent and its success considerable. About this time, too, Racine won the signal honor of being elected to the French Academy which chose him instead of Molière when the latter refused to abandon the humble acting profession.

Racine had begun to make enemies with his sharp tongue and haughty behavior, and the friends of Corneille hated him wholeheartedly. One of those literary cabals which keep the French at boiling point was organized against him, and the new playwright Pradon was trotted out and pushed into eminence. Racine, however, countered with his *Iphigénie,* a version of the sacrifice of Iphigenia at Aulis that was full of gratifying sensibility. Racine triumphed again, even if his new tragedy was not for the ages. Nor could there be any dispute about the distinction of his next depredation on Euripidean drama, *Phèdre.*

In Euripides' *Hippolytus,* Racine found a theme of love-passion which called forth his greatest powers. When it is compared with the Greek tragedy, Racine's drama is only a minor triumph. Gone in the French tragedy is the provocative symbolic conflict between the two human instincts respectively represented by Artemis and Aphrodite. Gone, too, is the deep psychological symbolism of a young man destroyed by the love instinct or the Aphrodite he has denied in himself. Here, instead, is a neatly composed obbligato played on the one string of a woman's consuming passion for her stepson Hippolytus. The latter is even supplied with a sweetheart, since Louis XIV's bright courtiers would have found the chaste young man of the Greek story an object of ridicule. There is consequently much "prettification" and sentimentalization in *Phèdre.* Still, within the limits of French classicism, the play could only appear as a tremendous *tour de force,* since it is remarkable for its exploration of the recesses of a passion-obsessed mind.

The growth of Phèdre's passion for her husband's son and her struggle against her infatuation, which is making her pine away, are vividly realized. She has rejected food for three days. Finally, Oenone, her nurse, discovers the source of her malady and devotedly proposes to heal it. Since, in particular, Theseus is reported to have been killed during his travels, she argues that Phèdre's passion is no longer criminal. In an anguished scene Phèdre, therefore, reveals her passion to Hippolytus. But she is rebuffed by him, and overwhelmed with shame she hurries away. Suddenly Theseus returns and fearing that Hippolytus will accuse her mistress to his father, the devoted nurse resolves to accuse him first. Hippolytus, too honorable to cast shame upon his mother by justifying himself, allows himself to be cursed by his father. The curse destroys him, and Phèdre, overwhelmed with grief, kills herself.

The elaborate and sensitive presentation of Phèdre's passion, shame, and grief requires a more extended analysis than can be given in a synopsis. No one can question its effectiveness, and the role of Phèdre is so magnificent that it became the *pièce de resistance* of every French tragedienne. The famous Rachel and Sarah Bernhardt won no laurels more honorable than their triumphs in the part.

By now, however, the cabal was up in arms against Racine and hit upon the expedient of getting another *Phèdre* by Pradon produced two days after the premiere. Buying seats for Racine's opening they left them unoccupied, casting a chill over the performance. Instead they repaired to Pradon's play and made it a signal success. The *affaire Phèdre* was such a conspicuous example of viciousness and Racine was so deeply wounded by it that he retired from the stage. Sick at heart he returned at the end of 1677 to Port Royal, which eagerly took its prodigal son back into the fold. Theologically, they could argue, his last play had been sound Jansenism; was it not the tragedy of a woman who possessed every quality but the grace of God without which there can be no salvation! Dominated by her *flamme funeste*, and supremely conscious of her guilt and damnation, Phèdre was a heroine decidedly acceptable to the Jansenists. Port Royal won its author back completely, and gave the erstwhile lover of popular actresses a pious wife who never read a line of his plays. Racine himself began to regard them as a crime against the true religion.

Racine, it is true, did not wholly give up the world and remained a courtier to the last. He resumed residence in Paris and continued his literary labors as historiographer to the king, a position which he owed to the favor of Louis XIV's Madame de Montespan. But he returned to playwriting only on two occasions, both sacerdotal, when the King's pietistic new love Madame de Maintenon requested him to write two biblical plays for her girls' school at St. Cyr. *Esther*, the first of them, retold the familiar story of Haman and the Jewish queen who saved her people from an early pogrom. Written in excellent verse and supplied with choruses of great beauty, the piece was received enthusiastically when it was produced in 1689 before an audience which included the King and Mme. de Maintenon. It was particularly appreciated for its allusiveness; Ahasuerus was Louis XIV, Madame de Maintenon was the pious Esther, and the discarded first queen Vashti was none other than Madame de Montespan who had recently suffered a similar débacle. The analogy between Queen Esther and Madame de Maintenon, who had belonged to the Huguenot Protestant sect which was being oppressed by Louis, who revoked the Edict of Nantes, was strained, since the new French Queen had been too discreet to intervene in behalf of her former co-religionists. But the discrepancy between Esther and de Maintenon was not regarded as a criticism of the latter. Nor was the suggestion in the play that a king could be misled in signing a decree prejudicial to religious liberty considered an allusion to Louis XIV who had signed the Edict of Nantes only four years before. That indefatigable letter-writer Madame de Sévigné echoed the opinion of the literati concerning Racine: "He now loves God as he used to love his mistresses." *Esther*, which strikes this reader as only a cut above a beautiful academic exercise, won the admiration of the court.

Although Racine refused to countenance its presentation in the public theatre, he turned to the drama again with renewed enthusiasm, and within a year he produced the second St.-Cyr tragedy *Athalie* or *Athaliah* which many consider his greatest work. The tragedy met Madame de Maintenon's request for a loveless drama to perfection and none of her tender charges had their innocence tempted by so much as a word. Nevertheless, *Athaliah* is a stirring work. Nowhere is Racine's lyric power greater and nowhere did he fill his severely limited stage with so much movement and excitement. The idol-worshiping queen Athaliah who had assumed power by murdering the royal family is troubled by a dream that warns her that an heir to the throne still lives. He does in the person of young Joash who had been rescued by the high priest and brought up in the temple. Athaliah enters the temple, interviews Joash without learning who he is, and is singularly moved by affection for him. But the time has come to enthrone the young prince, who will observe the true Hebrew religion faithfully. The high priest, therefore, arms the Levites, separates Athaliah from her guards, and has her slain. The play concludes with a rhapsodic hymn of triumph.

The powerful characterization of the guilt-laden Queen and of the sweet-tempered lad, the effective dialogue, and the magnificent lyrics of this tragedy create an impression of rare majesty. If some of us must find its labors academic, it is difficult to withhold one's admiration for Racine's virtuosity or deny this work the right to be considered the greatest of all biblical plays.

Although again withheld from the public stage, *Athaliah* was produced with resounding success in 1691 at both St. Cyr and Versailles. Nevertheless, Racine's last days were clouded by disgrace at court. He had ventured to draw up a plan for the amelioration of the poor, who were increasing in number while Louis XIV bled his people white with his extravagance and his imperialistic wars. The autocratic ruler was angered when he found Madame de Maintenon reading Racine's proposal. "Racine must not imagine that because he is a great poet he ought to be a minister of state," the king declared. Virtually expelled from court, Racine grew ill with vexation. His pious aunt prayed daily that God should humiliate him for the good of his soul. He was not one to take the decline of his fortunes lightly. He worried himself into an illness and died on April 21st, 1699, in extreme pain.

Racine left a heritage in his collected works which gave expression to some of the most typical elements of French genius. Its sensibility and converse with the passion of love live splendidly in his plays, but the national talent for order, cerebration and analysis is likewise present in them. The famous critic Jules Lemaître has put this more precisely when he declared that Racine expressed *"la génie de notre race— ordre, raison, sentiment mesuré, et force sous la grâce"*—order, reason, measured sentiment and force underlying gracefulness. Racine substituted character analysis and emotionalism for the major Corneillian motives of moralization and "admiration"—that idealization of human behavior which is supposed to evoke admiration for the protagonists. Except indirectly in his biblical plays, Racine wrote drama of "admiration" only in *Berenice,* in which Titus denies his love in deference to the Roman custom which forbade an emperor to marry foreign royalty.

Passion was the proper province of the playwright of whom it has been said that his female characters were "fair women full of Attic grace but who lack the grace of God." Whereas Corneille celebrated man's strength, Racine, always a partial Calvinist, dramatized man's weakness, and the tragic failure of his characters in most of his plays represents the victory of the passions over reason. It is in this manner that Racine paid dual tribute to the "sensibility" prevalent in the courtly life of his times and to the rationalism that dominated both political theory and philosophy. And the same dualism appears in his technique, which is more orderly than Corneille's. Concentration on the crucial moment in the lives of the characters rather than on the developments that led to the crisis makes for a compact, rationally ordered dramatic form. Action, moreover, is relegated to off-stage events, reported by messengers, and becomes secondary to analysis in works of this order; "what happens is of less importance than the mental reactions of the characters . . . action is practically confined to the mind." [2] Nevertheless, his compression of passion into one major crisis generally provided the greatest intensification of feeling.

To the Anglo-Saxon reader such compactness seems the acme of literary constipation, and the analytic approach to the emotions strikes him as a form of pernicious anemia or atrophy of emotion. There is, indeed, little doubt that Corneille and especially Racine made a contribution to the drama and humane letters that does not meet the modern demand for action. Nevertheless, their real limitation is not structural. If one can be irritated by Corneille, it is because he is so highflown and sententious. If one can dislike Racine it is because one can become sick of the passions, the *"soupirs et flammes,"* of his heroines; one tires so easily of torrid femininity. In introducing order into playwriting, Racine, as a matter of fact, made an important advance which was to serve the realistic drama greatly. The later drama of prose and of ordinary life could not afford the diffuseness of Elizabethan or later romantic tragedies. Plays like *Ghosts* or *Hedda Gabler,* no matter how greatly they may depart from Louis Quatorze taste in other respects, possess a compactness of structure without which they would lose most of their power.

3 THE AFTERMATH

Still the dangers of Racine's formalism were great, and frigidity became the bane of his contemporaries and successors. Pradon, Thomas Corneille (Pierre's brother), Campistron, La Fosse and others are mere names now. Paul Scarron is remembered for his pranks, unbecoming in an abbé, or for his beautiful wife who became Madame de Maintenon, and not for his prose tragedy *Zénobie* or even for his broad comedy *Jodelet* which anticipated Molière's witty dialogue. Only Crébillon the Elder and Lamotte-Houdart at the beginning of the eighteenth century still retain some slim claim to attention—the former with *Rhadamiste and Zénobie,* the latter with *Inés de Castro.*

Voltaire's fame as an essayist and as a public figure makes us remember the eighteenth-century tragedies *Oedipe (Oedipus)*, *Brutus, The Death of Caesar, Zaïre, Mahomet,* and *Mérope.* These tragedies, written between 1718 and 1732, reveal considerable showmanship, and some of them contain challenging touches of free thought and satire characteristic of Voltaire the liberal philosopher, as well as of the general ferment which culminated in the French Revolution. "Priests are only what stupid people make them; our credulity comprises all their knowledge (*notre crédulité fait tout leur science*)" in the *Oedipe* is a typical eighteenth-century "philosophical" line. Voltaire's *Brutus* glorifies a republican hero and his *Mahomet* is such a vigorous attack on religious bigotry that one of its characters Séide passed into the French language as a synonym for the word fanatic. But Voltaire's dramaturgy remains,

in the main, forced and cold. He who called Shakespeare a splendid barbarian could have used some Elizabethan barbarism himself.

The French were themselves becoming dissatisfied with their dramatic
conventions. Voltaire cast a longing glance at Shakespeare, and later the
playwright Ducis, who was born in 1733 and died in 1816, even went
so far as to adapt the English tragedies. It is unfortunate only that in
tightening them he was not above making Ophelia the daughter of Hamlet's uncle and that in moralizing them he lapsed into inevitable banality.
Even earlier, Lamotte-Houdart protested against the "unities" and agi-
tated without any avail for prose drama, while the prolific playwright
and novelist Marivaux (1688-1763) struggled against formalism with all
the resources of romanticism and sentimentality.

An important theoretical advance in French drama came mainly from
that progressive thinker the encyclopaedist Denis Diderot who called
for a new kind of tragedy; for *drame bourgeois* or a middle-class tragedy
that would deal with common people and consider the influence of their
economic activity or social position on their character. He became, in
effect, the philosopher of modern realism and social drama, and his principles, which he applied unsuccessfully in his own plays *Le Fils Naturel*
and *Le Père de Famille* (1757-58), are common practice today.

It was a long time, however, before his dream could be effectively
realized on the French stage. Revolutionary idealism fired the content
of plays like Saurin's *Spartacus* and Lemiérre's *Guillaume Tell* devoted
to champions of liberty, but the treatment remained formal and high-
flown. The theatre of the French Revolution and the Napoleonic period,
although it ensured the triumph of the middle class, was still favorable
only to inflated oratory. At most, an able poet like Maria-Joseph Chénier
produced a protest against the religious bigotry of St. Bartholomew's
Massacre in *Charles IX* on the eve of the Revolution in 1789. His
democratic sentiments aroused a storm of enthusiasm despite the tedious
formalism of the work. One cannot report a dearth of theatrical activity
in a period which gave birth to the great actor Talma. But playwriting was in a decline, and the new social forces made a slight impression
on it; "the revolutionaries who fought for and in the great French
revolution remained literary conservatives."[3] This phenomenon was
duplicated in the art of painting which was affected by the same factor
of continued classicism now sanctified by the fact that the original classi-
cists were the republicans of Athens and Rome.

The aftermath in the rest of Europe was likewise unimpressive.
French classicism rested like a dead hand on the German theatre, which
had no creative energies of its own, and it perverted the English theatre.
It is true that John Milton, who had already composed the greatest
masque of all time in his *Comus,* wrote a magnificent biblical tragedy

Samson Agonistes during the zenith of the Restoration period. If it is not particularly actable, it is nevertheless a monument to the spirit of struggling humanity, all the more stirring because Milton, the die-hard republican blind among aristocratic enemies, saw himself in the figure of Samson blind among the exulting Philistines. The learned poet, however, went back to the Athenian drama, whereas the Restoration playwrights patterned their work after French classicism when they wanted to write tragedy. England borrowed its worst features when it combined the example of Corneille and the romantic tradition of Beaumont and Fletcher in a special form of so-called "heroic tragedy" written in rhymed couplets. The artificial courtly society that returned to power when Charles II was restored to the English throne broke out into a rash of inflated heroics with the great essayist and able poet John Dryden as its theoretician as well as its chief practitioner.

By 1656 the Puritans had relaxed their severity toward the drama sufficiently to allow William D'Avenant to regale the public with "an allegorical entertainment by declamation and music." It was followed in the same year by his *Siege of Rhodes* based on Corneille's conception of love and honor and on the French romances—a worthless piece except for its lyric quality but important as the germ of both English opera and "heroic tragedy." With the return of Charles II the theatres became feverishly active. Two theatres—the King's and the Duke of York's—were given letters patent. D'Avenant and the famous Thomas Killigrew became active producers. Talented actors with Betterton at their head won popularity, and actresses like the notorious Nell Gwyn, admitted to the stage for the first time, won the public fancy with their amours. D'Avenant's *Love and Honor* in 1642 (the title supplies all the description that is needed), Killigrew's *The Prisoners* and *The Princess,* revivals, imitations of Beaumont and Fletcher drama, and perversions of Shakespeare* captured the stage.

Then the pent-up romanticism of the cavaliers flared up in the most furious conflagrations of the short-lived "heroic tragedy," and Dryden produced his perfervid *Indian Empress, The Conquest of Granada* and *Aureng-Zebe,* all replete with characters whose blood has been described as only "electrified sawdust." Typical of the entire group is *The Con-*

---

* Although Shakespeare was not given his due in the early years of the Restoration, it is a mistake to assume that he was ever entirely neglected. One of the greatest roles of the low-voiced, bulky Thomas Betterton, who shone in contemporary plays, was Falstaff. He also played Hamlet, Othello, and Mercutio in the doctored versions which were then popular. The films, by the way, are not the only culprits when it comes to saddling tragedies (see the film versions of *Winterset* and *The Plough and the Stars*) with happy endings. The *Romeo and Juliet* in which Betterton played Mercutio ended happily for Shakespeare's star-crossed lovers.

quest of Granada, the ten acts of which contain three love plots, a siege, a civil war, a hero Almanzor so valorous that the fortunes of a nation depend upon him, and a heroine Almahide so pure that only this soldier can win her. It is no wonder that "heroic tragedy" died of sheer exhaustion and that the Duke of Buckingham's clever burlesque *The Rehearsal* [4] gave the style its greatly needed coup de grâce so quickly in 1671.

Dryden himself came to recognize its worthlessness, paid tribute to Shakespeare in his *Essay of Dramatic Poesy,* and turned to Shakespearean drama in the well-known *All For Love,* his classicized version of *Antony and Cleopatra.* Nothing indeed illustrates the difference between Elizabethan and pseudo-classic drama better than Dryden's compact tragedy which reduces the world struggle between Antony and Octavius to a mere love affair occurring in one locality within a single day. Still, Dryden's conversion to blank verse resulted in a noble and respectable drama of classic distillation, and considerable excellence appeared again in his *Don Sebastian* and *Cleomenes,* serious plays that were no longer subservient to the principle of magniloquence. But these works were also more respectable than stirring, and of their characters Saintsbury wisely declares that "we, as it were, leave cards of sympathy on them in the correctest manner." [5]

It is, in fact, now only in throwbacks to Elizabethan tragedy, never entirely discarded, that the pulse of drama beats audibly. An awakening of national consciousness and some weariness of courtly and foreign models usher in a brief return to Elizabethan drama in the last quarter of the century. The short career of the mentally disturbed actor Nathaniel Lee produces frenzied plays like *The Rival Queens* and *Mithridates* in the Elizabethan manner, recalling the sensuousness and verbal intensity of the great age. Although these pieces were sufficiently successful in their day, they now commend themselves to psychoanalysts rather than to the plain laity of the reading and playgoing public.

Finally, another unhappy talent creates something fairly memorable in *Venice Preserved.* Its author Thomas Otway, another actor who was plagued not only by his poverty but by his infatuation with the popular actress Mrs. Barry, turned from heroic tragedies like *Don Carlos* to blank verse drama in *The Orphan* in 1680. Out of the feverish complications of two brothers' passion for their father's orphaned ward Otway created a play of considerable passion and pathos, although we must now regard it as an exaggerated, second-rate effort. Moreover, the piece served as a finger exercise for his flawed but powerful *Venice Preserved,* written two years later. A weak-willed lover Jaffier joins a conspiracy against the state when a Venetian senator denies him his daughter Belvidera. The latter, however, persuades him to renounce and reveal the plot, which is led by his close friend Pierre; and both his love for her and his realization of the slaughter that must ensue from the revolt make him a traitor. He is confronted by the conspirators in a moving scene and realizes the full enormity of his deed when the Senate refuses to pardon them and they refuse to accept their lives on terms of bondage. He stabs his friend at the latter's request, in order to save him from an ignominious execution, and then kills himself, while Belvidera's mind becomes distracted.

For more than a century there was nothing in English drama within striking distance of Otway's troubled and bitter tragedy. Rowe's plays *The Fair Penitent* and *Jane Shore,* in 1703 and 1714, were pale shadows of Elizabethanism, and their author is now best remembered for his compilation of unverifiable anecdotes regarding Shakespeare's life. Edward Young's tragedies were pure bombast, and Addison's frigidly recitative *Cato,* a great favorite in its day, was an impossible classic exercise. The middle class expressed itself several decades later in the work of George Lillo, whose moral tragedy *The London Merchant or The History of George Barnwell* (1731) dramatizes the fate of an apprentice driven to crime by his wayward affair with a prostitute. For all its influence on continental, chiefly German, drama, this piece is claptrap. Its successor *The Gamester,* written a quarter of a century later by the cloth merchant Edward Moore, is only slightly better.

For genuine tragedy eighteenth-century England had to rely entirely on mutilated versions of Shakespeare's works, enhanced by the performances of the great Garrick whose acting was a major advance over the stilted style of his predecessors.* In fact the entire period has gone down in history as the golden age of English acting. The line of notable actors from Betterton to Garrick included the notable Mrs. Barry, Anne Oldfield, Peg Woffington, Colley Cibber, James Quin, and Charles Macklin. They outshone the dim constellation of playwrights and gave further evidence of the truism that the theatre does not necessarily go bankrupt when the drama defaults.

This unedifying situation was not appreciably different anywhere else in Europe until tragedy found a new foothold in a nation long deprived of genuine drama. This occurred in Germany toward the close of the century.

---

* Garrick's reverence for Shakespeare appears to have been so great that he used a volume of his plays instead of a Bible whenever he administered an oath to a friend. This did not, however, prevent the actor from committing mayhem on the author's text. He omitted the Grave-diggers from *Hamlet* and the Fool from *King Lear* — no doubt to ensure "unity" of action and mood. He gave *Romeo and Juliet* a scene in the tomb. He changed and added lines freely. Garrick himself wrote twenty-one plays between 1740 and 1745. One of these, *The Clandestine Marriage* (1766), was a lively collaboration with George Colman the Elder (1732–94). David Garrick (1717–79) was the greatest figure of the age.

XVI

MOLIÈRE AND THE COMEDY OF SOCIETY

IT IS a curious indication of the complexity of man and his world that the age of Corneille and Racine should also have been the age of Molière. For while tragedy was erecting a tower of ponderous dignity, comedy was busy tearing it down. While tragedy invested aristocratic and upper middle-class society with jeweled robes, comedy stripped it clean to the motley underneath—and what society does not wear motley underneath! And here again seventeenth-century France assumed the leadership. From the conjunction of an age and a genius arose one great figure that cast its ample shade over the entire European theatre, and it requires no sagacity to recognize in this description Molière, the comic master of the modern drama, until the advent of Shaw.

I THE COMIC GENIUS OF MOLIÈRE

Of comedy, its expert practitioner George Meredith wrote: "Its common aspect is one of unsolicitous observation, as if surveying a full field and having leisure to dart on its chosen morsels, without any fluttering eagerness. Men's future upon earth does not attract it; their honesty and shapeliness in the present does; and whenever they wax out of proportion, overblown, affected, pretentious, bombastical, hypocritical, pedantic, fantastically delicate; whenever it sees them self-deceived or hoodwinked, given to run riot in idolatries, drifting into vanities, congregating in absurdities, planning short-sightedly, plotting dementedly; whenever they are at variance with their professions, and violate the unwritten but perceptible laws binding them in consideration one to another; whenever they offend sound reason, fair justice; are false in humility or mined with conceit, individually, or in the bulk; the Spirit overhead will look humanely malign, and cast an oblique light on them, followed by volleys of silvery laughter. That is the Comic Spirit." [1] No description of seventeenth-century French society is more apt. When the aristocracy began to cultivate the graces instead of the art of war, and when the upper middle class began to ape its superiors, the time was ripe for the complete flowering of the Comic Spirit with which no nation is as richly endowed as the French.

This was the era of "conspicuous waste," with the gentlemen and ladies of the court making a virtue of extravagance in dress, speech and behavior, with the *salons* buzzing with artificial love-making and even more artificial speech. This was the heyday of philandering or of less innocent encounters between ladies and gentlemen, and the high noon of idealization of the sexes which covered a multitude of sins. The peasantry was hungry and oppressed, foreign wars were exhausting the finances of the nation, autocracy was riding roughshod over the people, and Jesuitism wielded such control over intellectual inquiry that it forced thinkers like Descartes into exile. But the nobility took no heed of this situation, while the nabobs of the middle class waxed fat with profits from corrupt practices and made a passion of the acquisitive instinct.

Molière was no reformer of the militant stamp; although he was the intellectual superior of most men of his generation, he was a true son of the age. Indignation was not in good taste when the predominant ideal of French society was reasonableness. Moreover, a display of bad temper in the theatre would not have been consonant with the viewpoint of a man who made irrationality and excess the butt of his wit. He never roared like Jonson; he simply laughed.

His comic method was accordingly sure and neat. Most of his plays were written in the formal Alexandrine couplets with general adherence to the unities, of time, place, and action. Even when he had more than one plot in hand, his story remained lucid and its events were scrupulously balanced. His style was playful even when most terse, and restrained even when most playful, for his laughter at its best was, without ceasing to be laughter, "nearer a smile"; it was, in short, "humor of the mind." [2] A unique talent for grace and flexibility, for the deft use of the fencer's foils, is a prerequisite for this kind of humor, and it is little wonder that Molière seems rather commonplace and vacuous when his glinting lines are dulled in English translations. As Joseph Wood Krutch has astutely remarked, "Put any of his verse into the heavy-footed prose of the pedant, and little remains except the substratum of now platitudinous *bon sens*." Rarely is his limber and pirouetting, yet direct and manly, manner captured in English, as it was to some degree in Arthur Guiterman and Lawrence Langner's adaptation of *The School for Husbands*. Underlying this style is a culture or a refinement of manners not equally dispensed to every creature, and a "gaiety of disposition" which Voltaire rightly attributed to all masters of laughter. (Even if, being human, they too must on occasion experience anger and despair.) There is something rare in such a disposition, despite the assumption that any fool can laugh. As a matter of fact, fools can't; they can only guffaw.

It is a mistake to believe that such a style is an easy accomplishment; actually, in Molière's case, it was the product of a process of refinement and it was attained only after many essays in the more easily acquired art of horseplay. It is equally a mistake to imagine that it is synonymous with superficiality. Actually the smile of the truly civilized artist is "something overcome"—a triumph of spirit over error or failure. And this was particularly true of Molière whose private life was unhappy and whose personal outlook was distinctly critical. Nor is his smile at all reminiscent of the frozen expression of some pre-Attic statue. It was instinct with tenderness for natural people, young lovers, and sensible persons of all classes. He had real humanity—he had feeling without sentimentality. Molière succeeded, both as a dramatist and as a showman, by astutely combining wit, criticism, and appealing characterization.

Only in never sentimentalizing the latter and in retaining his equanimity when his characters are calculating or stupid did he maintain that intellectual flavor which gives high comedy its clean sharpness. He possessed a fundamental humanity, but he expressed it best in comedy that is as "pure" or "high" as it can be made without approaching inhumanity. He was rarely neutral in issues involving hypocrisy, unreason or denial of healthy instinct; he is not found neutral in his comedies when Tartuffe is triumphing and when miserly or fatuous old men strive to frustrate youthful love. That is the basis of such a neat judgment as John Palmer's that "Justice in the comedies of Molière is always done. There is no intrusion of the man of feeling or prejudice to mar the even tenor of his comic way." [3] Only with respect to this balanced approach to humanity are Bergson's words that "laughter is incompatible with emotion" true of Molière.

Horace Walpole's definition, "Life is a comedy to the man who thinks and a tragedy to the man who feels" is a brilliant epigram on comic effect rather than a complete truth about any important comic writer's life. That many great men have wrested laughter out of suffering and feeling is well known. Was Jonathan Swift without feeling, was Aristophanes, was any comedian of real magnitude? Disconcerting as it may be to those who favor pat definitions, the fact remains that far from being content with unmoved contemplation, Molière essayed tragedy and tragic acting and would have liked to succeed in these departments. His life and career reveal a rounded personality and not a disembodied intellect. Surely, the modern theatre's second universal genius is not the cerebral wart that some of his admirers discover in their eulogies. He merely allowed intelligence to dominate the emotions.

2 THE "HUMAN COMEDY" OF MOLIÈRE

Midway in the absolutist era, fourteen years after Corneille but seventeen before Racine, on January 15, 1622, was born Jean Baptiste Poquelin (Molière). Reared in the household of his father, a rising upholsterer, the lad received every advantage without being spoiled by extravagance. Soon, moreover, his father became attached to the court as one of the king's eight *valets de chambre tapissiers* who took charge of the royal upholstery and furniture. The title gave old Poquelin some social standing, and attendance on the king's household for three months every year was sufficient entrée to the inner circle that his son, who later accompanied him in the execution of his duties, was to satirize so intimately. The lad soon began to display a gift for mimicry, much to the distress of his pious mother when he began to mimic her priest. She was a persistent woman and might have cured him of his disturbing talent. But she died when he was eleven, and any restraint that his step-mother might have been tempted to impose on him was cut short when she too died about four years later. At fifteen he was left with his father to whose trade he was probably apprenticed at this time, although not too strictly. In 1636, the year of *The Cid* and of Descartes' famous essay on the processes of reason, the *Discourse on Method*, he entered the best school in Paris, the Collège de Clermont.

Instructed by the Jesuits, who reaped so many freethinkers with their excellent curriculum, Molière acquired a firm command of logic and rhetoric. Here he also became acquainted with Roman comedy, and his histrionic gifts were stimulated by teachers who not only stressed pub-lic declamation but required their pupils to perform Latin plays written by the professors of poetry and rhetoric. Here, moreover, he formed valuable friendships with the young Prince de Condé and Chapelle, the illegitimate son of the financier Lullier who encouraged his guest the famous Gassendi to give the lads private instruction in modern scientific thought. Molière the future skeptic probably owed a great deal to the informal instruction he received from that brilliant man who knew every branch of science, corresponded with Kepler and Galileo, and was an admirer of Lucretius. It is not without significance that Molière's first literary effort should have been a translation of Lucretius' poetic treatise on epicureanism and the atomic theory, *De Rerum Natura*.

It soon became necessary for the young man to choose a career. He could follow his father's trade or he could enter the law. He chose the latter. But the claims of the theatre were too strong for one who was a natural actor and had long been attracted by the Italian comedians who were performing in Paris. In July 1643 he enrolled in an amateur com-pany situated in a racket court and enjoying the magniloquent name of the *Illustre Théâtre*. Rashly it moved to a large tennis court and began to charge admission and the results proved disastrous. But the company, in which he was becoming a leading figure, refused to give up the ghost. Reorganized, it now contained the buffoon Duparc known as Gros-René and the red-headed and accomplished Madéline Béjart who won Molière's heart. Probably in order to spare his father the embarrass-ment of having an actor in the family, young Poquelin now changed his name to Molière and quickly devoted himself to the enterprise. In 1644, full of high hopes, the company made a formal début in a good location. But still to no avail, and Molière not only acquired onerous debts but found himself jailed by his creditors for a week.

Undaunted, however, the little troupe sallied into the provinces and, matured by three years of struggle in Paris, Molière settled down at the age of twenty-five to the serious business of creating a successful touring company. He became a shrewd showman whose edge was naturally sharpened by twelve years of touring. Since there were from twelve to fifteen such companies, the competition was keen; and the privations and humiliations were many since the actors had no social standing and were forced to cope with a variety of blue laws. But the experience was invaluable and the troupe became the most accomplished comedians of the kingdom.

Crucial was their stay at Lyons where they settled for a time. The inhabitants had a typically southern relish for the theatre. They had enjoyed the antics of the *commedia dell' arte* with its masked stereotypes, the comic servants, pedants, love-sick youths and impressionable girls who bore the stock names of Sganarelle, Mascarille, Lélie and Harlequin. The people of the Midi expected similar entertainment from Molière's comedians. Here Molière, with his wide-set eyes, his long legs appended to a short trunk, and his swarthy complexion, became an accomplished actor. His gestures were mobile, his power of suggestion was keen; moreover, he was an excellent informal speaker, notably successful in disarming an audience with his preliminary addresses. Here also he mastered the craft of playwriting, combining the tricks and character types of Italian comedy with shrewd observation of French life.

It was at Lyons that he produced, among a dozen plays, his first important work *L'Étourdi* or *The Blunderer*. A five-act piece in rhymed Alexandrines, it followed the escapades of a shrewd servant Mascarille who designs many schemes for furthering his master Lélie's love affair only to have the lover ruin them by his blundering interference. The piece proved eminently successful and the company gained new members, among them the accomplished Lagrange and Mademoiselle Debrie who supplanted the apparently unresponsive Madéline Béjart in Molière's affections.

Difficulties arose when the civil war of the Fronde devastated the provinces. Molière, however, weathered those trying times, his uncertain health improved in the warm climate, and his career as an author was now fully launched. *Étourdi* was followed by another entertaining piece *Le Dépit Amoureux* or *The Love Tiff*, which retained its popularity long after his death and became the subject of several imitations like Dryden's play of the same name and Vanbrugh's *Mistake*.

Friends having advised the successful troupe to settle near Paris, Molière brought his actors to Rouen. Here Louis XIV's younger brother, the Duke of Anjou, took them under his patronage, and on October 24, 1658 they finally made their bow before the King in the guard hall of the old Louvre. Unaware of their limitations in the tragic field, they committed the mistake of presenting Corneille's second-rate *Nicoméde*. But realizing their danger in the nick of time, Molière came forward at the conclusion of the tragedy and asked permission of the King to present one of his seasoned interludes. His offering was only the slight farce *Le Docteur Amoureux* or *The Love-Sick Doctor*, but it won such favor that the company was accorded the use of a Petit-Bourbon theatre on the alternate days when the building was not occupied by the Italian comedians.

There on a shallow platform about one hundred by forty feet, facing an orchestra filled with standing commoners and overlooked by galleries divided into boxes for the ladies, Molière had an almost Elizabethan stage. The scenery was not ample, the stage of the fully enclosed house in which plays were produced in the late afternoon was poorly lighted with candles, and the actors were jostled by gallants who sat on the platform. Except when he staged a scenically ingenious ballet-drama at court, Molière had to cope with inadequate and difficult physical conditions. His humor had to be continuous and vigorous if it was to overcome these limitations. Moreover, in Paris he had a public that had learned to expect not only the prankish contrivances of Italian farce but the more refined entertainment of such pieces as Corneille's *Le Menteur*. Molière's work had to combine polish with liveliness, *commedia dell' arte* with high comedy.

He continued to produce tragedies or heroic plays by Corneille and even attempted to write one himself, the lamentable *Don Garcie*. But it became increasingly apparent that the company would have to rely chiefly on farce and comedy. Molière began to win the town with those early *pièces de resistance* of his touring days *Étourdi* and *Le Dépit Amoureux*, and followed them with the brilliant satire on the manners of the capital the *Précieuses Ridicules* or, as it is known in one translation, *The High-Brow Ladies*. The fashion of precious speech and romantic love-making sponsored by blue-stockings like the famous Madame de Rambouillet and encouraged by popular romances like *Cyrus* had gone to ridiculous extremes. Its proponents were the *précieuses* who called a chair "a commodity of conversation" and expected love to move by degrees from Indifference to Disinterested Pleasure, Respect, Assiduity, Inclination, the City of Tenderness, and the Dangerous Sea.

Ridiculing the *précieuses*, Molière invented the story of two bourgeois daughters Madelon and Cathos who, aping their social superiors of the *salons,* call themselves Polixene and Aminte, name their maid Al-manzor, and expect the utmost refinements of speech and gallantry from anyone who can hope to win them. Their lovers therefore decide to teach them a wholesome lesson by dressing their valets Mascarille and Jodelet as noblemen and sending them to woo the affected misses. Consulting their mirror or "the Counselor of Graces," the girls prepare to meet their new suitors, who appear with the proper éclat when Mascarille insists on being carried into the house in order not to soil his shoes. Their wooing has the required *bon ton* when upon meeting Cathos, Mascarille insists that he fears "some larceny of my heart, some massacre of liberty" from her eyes. Cathos asks him to be seated in her politest manner, "Pray, sir, be not inexorable to the easy chair, which, for this last quarter of an hour, has held out its arms towards you; yield to its desire of embracing you." Mascarille recites an execrable poem in honor of the girls, who are particularly fond of the opening exclamation "Oh! oh!" which Mascarille commends to them. He even sings the lines; of course he has not studied music, but, he assures them, "People of rank know everything without ever having learned anything." In time the original suitors arrive, unmask their servants, and prepare to gloat.

This comedy sounded the death-knell of the most fashionable cult of the court. Its proponents were still sufficiently powerful to make their wrath felt, and Molière placated them somewhat by declaring that he had not aimed his barbs at them but at their bourgeois imitators. Nevertheless, Madame de Rambouillet's devotees began to resume their baptismal names and to speak intelligibly. The play became so popular that Molière doubled the price of admission and was invited to give a performance before the king. Molière, therefore, had no reason to renounce his censorship of society.

In his next piece, the one-acter *Sganarelle* or *The Imaginary Cuckold,* he turned to the middle class with a portrait of a vulgar citizen who believes himself to be betrayed by his wife. Played by Molière himself, Sganarelle was a comparatively new figure on the French stage—a realistically drawn burgher who combines self-deception with cunning. This slight piece was followed by a failure in tragedy, by command performances of earlier farces that won him the favor of the powerful prime minister Mazarin, and finally by his first full-length composition in Paris *The School for Husbands.* Based on the *Adelphi* of Plautus and on a comedy by Lope de Vega, this three-act play revolves around two brothers who desire to marry their respective wards. Ariste, who has confidence in his ward, gives her the utmost freedom, whereas Sganarelle, racked by jealousy and tyrannical by nature, keeps her sister in seclusion. But the lass has the natural cunning of Eve and makes a fool of him until he even becomes her messenger to her lover. A piquant comedy, full of sound sense and good spirits, *The School for Husbands* was a triumph in the capital and had the desirable effect of cementing the King's favor.

Molière's next effort was far less innocent, although even *The School for Husbands* could not be agreeable to some moralists. Fouquet, the financier who hoped to win the King's favor, commissioned him to write an entertainment for the gardens of Vaux that could be tricked out with pageantry. Molière obliged with *Les Fâcheux* or *The Bores* which caricatured various courtiers who could only squirm as the satirist's pencil drew their faces. La Grange the lover (it was customary to give characters the names of popular actors like Molière's popular associate) is intent upon making a declaration of love to a suitable lady. But each of his efforts is interrupted by the appearance of a courtly bore who talks at great length. A gallant who imagines himself to be a composer insists upon singing his song, and a gaming courtier breaks out into a passionate description of piquet. *Précieuses* debates the question of whether jealousy is permitted in a lover; a duelist displays his skill by defending his friends from imaginary assailants; and a bore caps the agony by recounting how someone bored him. . . . The indignation of the satirized nobles was, however, no greater than the pleasure of the King, who liked to see others annoyed. Louis XIV even suggested the inclusion of a hunting bore, quickly supplied by Molière who now had the double satisfaction of having produced another success and having extended the boundaries of his comic art. In *Les Fâcheux* he virtually created a *comédie-ballet* of social criticism.

Molière was forty now, a dangerous age for an inflammable bachelor, and the same year 1662 marked the beginning of his private misfortunes. Madéline Béjart had a young sister Armande who had grown to womanhood under his very eyes. He had given her a leading part in his *School for Husbands* and she had proved herself adept at coquetry on the stage. He had found the theatre a lucrative business, enjoyed excellent connections and many distinguished friends, and entertained visitors lavishly. He was ready for the luxury of a new romance. Besides, Mademoiselle Debrie, his mistress and loyal friend, was nearer to his own age than the fascinating young actress. Against his better judgment Molière wooed Armande and was—unfortunately—accepted.

Under his surveillance she became an accomplished artist who was equally effective in delicate and indelicate roles, so that henceforth he wrote his plays with the intent of displaying her talents. She also bore him three children, only one of whom survived him. But he was, after all, twenty years her senior, and so the master satirist of jealous and betrayed husbands became, ironically enough, a proper subject for his own plays. She was a vain, giddy and cold-hearted opportunist who made her curiously infatuated husband as miserable in private as he seemed light-hearted in public. Thereafter, his laughter was indeed "something overcome," and it is from this unhappy time that his genius dates its deepening thought and observation.

His first post-marital play *The School for Wives*, written in 1662, still bore an aura of happiness. Full of sympathy for young love and natural gaiety, the play is one of Molière's most zestful and unreflective exercises. Again a jealous guardian, Arnolphe, is the butt of the jest. A young man Horace, taking him for a friend, confides to him that he is in love with a girl who is carefully guarded by a tyrannical old man. Arnolphe, recognizing himself and his ward in that description, makes every effort to rout him from the innocent Agnes whose native intelligence begins to bud simultaneously with her love. When Arnolphe orders her to throw a stone at her lover the next time he appears under her window, she obeys the command literally but attaches a letter to the missile. Horace, still taking Arnolphe for someone other than Agnes' guardian, tells him about the progress he is making with Agnes, and the complications become fast and furious as Arnolphe resolves to marry the girl immediately and as Horace, stealing her from her house, trustingly leaves her in his care. Finally, Horace's father arrives and puts an end to the complications by enabling him to marry the girl.

Much humanity permeates this unpretentious comedy. Agnes is a charming innocent, and even Arnolphe is a sympathetic figure whose débacle comes when he desires something contrary to nature and common sense. Curiously enough, this sympathetic play was denounced as immoral because Molière had cast doubt on the law that gave guardians of minors absolute authority over them. But the urbane playwright dispersed his critics with a brilliant literary satire, the brief *Critique de l'École des Femmes,* and royal favor was more bountiful than ever. He was granted a pension of a thousand livres and his troupe was invited to court more frequently than before.

Louis, who was avid for amusement, considered Molière a mere entertainer and was surprised when Boileau told him that the comedian was a great man. But even though Molière sensibly continued to regard entertainment as his chief business, his art was developing in scope and seriousness. Significantly, his contribution to the festive *Pleasures of the Enchanted Island* at Versailles in 1664 was not a customary trifle but a three-act version of the great satire on religious hypocrisy *Tartuffe*. And even Louis had to recognize the fact that his court jester had exceeded his license. The king forbade him to produce it in public, and five years elapsed before the commoners could see the play on the stage in its rewritten and final form.

A reaction against the rising tide of religious and scientific skepticism was sweeping France. Liberal thought was being denounced by the religious sects, among which the Jesuits and the Jansenists[4] were most active. Pietism was becoming fashionable, and not all of its manifestations were disinterested and sincere. Tartuffe was the incarnation of self-seeking and dishonest pietism, and the drama which showed him worming himself into an honorable household and setting it agog with his intrigues was a telling satire. It caused the playwright to be cried down as an atheist by those whose sensibilities were hurt. Molière, however, had nothing but a sneer for his detractors and referred sardonically to egotists who consider an insult to themselves an insult to God. *"Suivant leur louable coutume,"* he wrote in his preface to the published play, *"ils ont couvert leurs intérêts de la cause de Dieu."* He had not attacked religion, he insisted, but the manner in which it can be used to conceal self-interest.

Molière, moreover, had the wisdom to remember that the object of comedy is laughter and entertainment. Tartuffe is a ridiculous as well as a sinister force. Although his hold upon his credulous host Orgon becomes so tenacious that only the king's intervention can break his grip, Tartuffe meets his match in Orgon's young second wife, her stepdaughter, and their pert servant girl. Orgon may be a dupe, but the female members of his family are too intelligent and spirited to be taken in. How they expose Tartuffe, how they lead him on to a declaration of love to Orgon's wife while the husband is peeping and how they strip him of his mask produces as amusing a series of complications as any that Molière concocted in his earlier and more carefree plays. Only the ruthlessness of his hypocrite and the suggestion that pietism can become a dangerous instrument when the unscrupulous employ it against the credulous can dampen the exuberance of the work.

Tartuffe is a supreme example of Molière's "thoughtful laughter." There is, besides, a fundamental critique in the play in so far as it refers to the contradiction between men's professions and deeds. It is not surprising, therefore, that variants of the Tartuffe *motif* should appear in a multitude of plays. One of the most recent of them, S. N. Behrman's *End of Summer,* in which a scheming psychoanalyst took the place of the religious hypocrite, illustrates the latitude with which the theme can be treated.

Undaunted by the difficulties he encountered with his *chef d'oeuvre,* Molière stuck to his heavy artillery in *Don Juan,* composed in 1661 while *Tartuffe* was still banned. Molière was in an embattled mood during this period, and his new comedy, written in prose and more loosely constructed than most of his works, turned the conventional moralistic treatment of the Don Juan legend into a brilliant portrait of a skeptic and epicurean. In a comic scene, Don Juan is dragged away to the underworld with appropriate fireworks while his servant Sganarelle cries out, "Oh, my wages! My wages! His death is a reparation to all. Heaven offended, laws violated, families dishonored, girls ruined, husbands driven to despair, everybody is satisfied. I am the only one to suffer. My wages, my wages, my wages!" If the demands of morality are formally satisfied in this scene, it is surely difficult to take the conclusion seriously.

Molière found an occasion to satirize the arrogance of the nobility in Don Juan's uninhibited behavior toward men and women. The aristocrats of the age and of the next century were guilty of many atrocities and were not above having a commoner waylaid, beaten and even murdered—as, for example, Voltaire was to learn in the next century from sad experience when he offended a nobleman. But the playwright, who was pleased to be able to score this point against the courtiers, does not appear to have been troubled by his character's offenses against convention. Don Juan's cynicism was illuminated with brilliant flashes of wit. In comparison with his clever sallies, his servants' commonplace precepts sound like parodies on conventional morality. Nor could Molière forego the opportunity of covertly sounding the message of *Tartuffe* in the new work. His Don Juan resolves to play the role of a reformed roué, and he is so nauseatingly sanctimonious in the part that even Sganarelle is disgusted. Even the latter prefers frank cynicism to unctuous pietism.

Moreover, it is not difficult to see in the immoral hidalgo a perverse idealist who tilts at the windmills of convention and lacks the ability to adjust himself to a humdrum life. At the heart of all his depredations on female virtue is a desire for perfect ecstasy, and this he can only find in the exhilaration of the chase. "Once we have succeeded," he declares, "there is nothing more to wish for. All the attraction of love is over, and we should fall asleep in the tameness of such a passion."

It is not surprising that *Don Juan,* which ranks with the greatest of Molière's plays, was also severely denounced as licentious and atheistic. But still the developing playwright refused to be swayed from his purpose. Although his next work, in 1665, the comedy-ballet *L'Amour Médecin* or *Love Is the Best Doctor,* was a minor piece intended to amuse the king, it directed some stinging barbs at the pretentious medical profession of the day. The physicians formed a powerful and jealous guild that could only squirm when Molière exposed their pseudo-scientific jargon and carefully concealed incompetence. A love-lorn girl pretends that she is ill, and her servant Sganarelle calls in four physicians who disagree violently. A little later the lover appears disguised as a fifth physician and cures the patient by marrying her under the very nose of her parent. *L'Amour Médecin* was quickly followed by that superb social satire *The Misanthrope* which many of Molière's admirers rightly prize above all his other plays.

Brought out in 1666 at the Palais-Royal theatre, *The Misanthrope* did not prove immediately popular. It dispensed with vigorous or spectacular action, and appealed to the intelligence. It is, in fact, the coolest and most Olympian of his comedies. It is an exposé pure and simple; the action is left scrupulously unresolved at the end and the characters remain pretty much as they were at the beginning. The play simply revolves around Alceste, an upright man whose disgust with the follies, affectations, and corruption of his times, amounts to an obsession. The social world that buzzes around him is a collection of fops, bootlickers, intriguers, and philanderers. With them he finds it impossible to compromise even though his loyal friend Philinthe counsels caution. He would rather lose his law case than bribe the court, and he would rather make enemies of the courtiers than flatter their stupidity. The weak point in his armor is his love for an incurably flirtatious woman, whom—like Molière himself—he loves against his better reason. But in spite of his infatuation with her, he cannot bring himself to accept the world of intrigue which is her natural habitat. When she refuses to leave it for a life of retirement with him, he renounces her too.

It has been held that Molière maintained equal objectivity toward Alceste and the butterflies of the world which the latter contemned, and it is beyond dispute that he conceived Alceste as a comic character. To ram one's head against the inert wall of society could only appear ludicrous during the seemingly stable age of Louis XIV. Alceste is guilty before the immutable law of the comic spirit which regards all excess as ludicrous. To pursue integrity without regard for social realities and to demand the impossible from a shallow woman could only lead to personal disaster. And since Alceste could not hope to budge society his behavior could only be pettish and excessive. His honesty, however admirable, is heroism misapplied.

Nevertheless, regardless of the easy construction put upon Alceste in his own day, there is nothing basically comforting in *The Misanthrope*. Not only is the satirization of the "social set" merciless but it is permeated with a misanthropy that is particularly telling because it is presented as the only attitude a reasonable person can hold. Society, as he describes it, cannot be reformed because mankind is fundamentally corrupt. Molière, one recalls, was living before the heyday of the eighteenth-century philosophical movement which proclaimed the doctrine of the perfectibility of man and regarded man's future with optimism. He did not particularly fancy the life of his times but he could not envisage a new society that would supplant it with something more tolerable. He could not see the crumbling cement behind the façade of Louis Quatorze society.

When Alceste's "reasonable" friend Philinthe declares, "My mind is no more shocked at seeing a man a rogue, unjust or selfish, than at seeing vultures eager for prey, mischievous apes, or fury-lashed wolves," he announces a philosophy of pessimism which is supported by nearly every event of the comedy. Alceste can only have the satisfaction of having his worst fears confirmed. "I shall see by this trial," he declares, "whether men have sufficient impudence . . . to do me this injustice in the face of the whole world." And, of course, they have. Only a general conviction, somewhat nebulously supported by the data of the play, reasserts Molière's customary reasonableness and sense of balance. Philinthe pleads for leniency for human nature; men must be taken "quietly just as they are." And yet there is no joy in the thought. In no play did Molière come so close to the sullen laughter of Ben Jonson. Nowhere does he give such support to Ludovici's theory that laughter is a baring of the teeth. To found a philosophy of comedy on the hopelessness of the human species is scant consolation. That the effect is nevertheless distinctly comic is a superb achievement of wit and delicacy.

With this beautifully written and magnificently constructed comedy Molière had reached the limits to which a showman of the age of Louis XIV could go. The play must have effected a catharsis in Molière, as well as reminded him that he was pursuing a track that would get him nowhere with his contemporaries. He returned to showmanship and to a more innocuous censorship of his age.

Showmanship, pure and simple, reappeared in his *Médecin malgrè lui* or *Physician Against His Will,* which came two months after *The Misanthrope.* When Sganarelle, formerly employed as a servant to a physician, becomes dissipated and beats his wife, she avenges herself by palming him off as a physician. In this compulsory role, he becomes an intermediary between a girl and her lover, and he enables them to outwit an obstinate father. Moreover, Sganarelle finds medical quackery so profitable that he resolves to ply this trade henceforth. This joyous comedy, which is satirical only in its random thrusts at the medical profession, was rewarded with immediate success. It was followed by several minor efforts, by his polished reworking of Plautus' celestial bedroom comedy *Amphitryon,* and by the more acerb *Georges Dandin* which revolves around the marriage of a rich peasant to a down-at-heels daughter of the aristocracy who deludes and betrays him. No doubt the public saw in this comedy only another jest at the expense of a cuckolded husband and a stupid bourgeois. But the aristocracy almost comes off just as poorly in Molière's portrait of a needy and unscrupulous nobility.

This play in fact marked a return to satire, and his next work *L'Avare* or *The Miser,* based on Plautus' *Aulularia,* is a caricature of miserliness and covetousness that bears some kinship to Jonson's *Volpone.* The repellent miser Harpagon is finally routed when the girl he has desired is married to the son he has mistreated, although his grief is lightened by the reflection that his other child, an eloping daughter, will be married "without a dowry." Harpagon is not, indeed, a sinister figure like Jonson's Volpone; he is too easily outwitted by the pleasant lovers and he is genuinely amusing when he steals oats from his horses or when his constitutional aversion to the word "give" compels him to use the salutation "I lend you good day." A few months later *Tartuffe* received its long-awaited regular run, so that the years 1668-69 must be reckoned as a return engagement for Molière's heavy bombardment.

He was forty-seven at the time, and had only four more years to live. His health was poor and his domestic life still left much to be desired. But the years worked no decline in his talents. His comedy-ballet *Monsieur de Pourceaugnac,* which played havoc with a provincial who finds himself at sea in the capital, proved to be one of his broadest farces and capped his experiments in what would now be called "musical comedy." His pleasant comedy *Le Bourgeois Gentilhomme* or *The Would-Be Gentleman* travestied the social ambitions of the wealthy middle class in the person of the inimitable Monsieur Jourdain who discovers that he has been speaking prose all his life and essays the social graces with the agility of an elephant dancing the rumba. Then after a number of perfunctory gambols, among which *Les Fourberies de Scapin* or *The Tricks of Scapin* is the best, even if it returns to the farcical methods of his early period, Molière created a final masterpiece in his *Femmes Savantes* or *The Learned Women.*

He had at last become reconciled with his wife who had suffered a severe illness, and an aura of happiness pervaded this new work. In *Femmes Savantes* he wrote one of his serenest high comedies. Returning to his early satirization of the précieuses, Molière created a household of women who pursue learning with the fluttering ardor of a flock of cackling geese. The fashion of preciosity among blue-stocking ladies had been cropping up again in the form of pretentious dabblings in the sciences and classics, and it was time to weed it out again. How the new précieuses are told off by a winsome daughter of the house whose happiness is being threatened by their pedantry is the gist of this finely cut comedy of character. Again the *bas-bleu* Madame de Rambouillet and her cohorts were indignant. But Trissotin, the inflated darling of the *salons,* was completely routed from Paris after the caricature Molière drew of him in the person of Tricotin. He became the laughingstock of the capital and retired from the pulpit which he had graced.

Molière's health was, however, failing; he had suffered most of his life from tuberculosis and the disease was now gaining rapidly. He had time only to write one more play, appropriately a satire on the medical profession of his day which could not do anything for him. *Le Malade Imaginaire* or *The Imaginary Invalid,* early in 1673, proved to be a rollicking extravaganza. A hypochondriac becomes the prey of quacks who give him drugs and purges when he actually needs mental healing. He is delighted with the inordinate attention he is receiving, for even the bills he gets are calculated to coddle his ego, as when his apothecary charges him thirty sous for the "refreshment of his intestines"—*pour refraichir les entrailles de Monsieur.* However, Monsieur Argan entertains a passion for frugality as well as for therapeutics. He therefore makes an effort to get a doctor into the family by marrying his daughter to a quack and finally resolves to join the medical fraternity himself when his brother tells him that he is hardly more ignorant than members of the profession. In a burlesque ceremony smothered in pidgin Latin he is made a doctor—that is, he is given the right to purge, bleed, and kill people at will.

Molière played Argan himself, and his physical appearance could only enhance the realism of the performance. Unwilling to cause any financial loss to his faithful company, he disregarded the advice of his friends and appeared at the fourth performance of the play in a critical condition. He was seized with convulsions and died some four hours later, on February 17th, 1673, in the arms of a sister of mercy while two parish priests denied him extreme unction because he had been a player. The Church approved their conduct and refused his body burial in the parish cemetery. The funeral was delayed four days and the king's intercession was needed before the greatest man of his day could be buried with a simple ceremony from which the solemn service was omitted.

3 AFTER MOLIÈRE: BEAUMARCHAIS

Opera under Lulli had become a powerful rival even during Molière's last years. Molière's company, led after his death by the actor La Grange, held its own for a time largely with Molière's plays. Seven years later the troupe was fused with the actors of the Hôtel de Bourgogne and became that still flourishing subsidized theatre the *Comédie Française.* Known at first as the *Théâtre Française,* the company produced both comedy and tragedy, and its greatest artistic triumph in the eighteenth century was, in fact, the acting of the famous tragedienne Adrienne Lecouvreur whose tragic passion for a nobleman was common talk in Paris and became the subject of the successful nineteenth-century play that bears her name.

Molière's mantle first fell on Regnard, whose *Residuary Legatee* (1708) satirized avarice and *Démocrite* resembled *The Misanthrope.* Then it rested more worthily on the brilliant novelist Alain René Le Sage whose picaresque novel *Gil Blas* is a classic and whose *Devil on Two Sticks* is almost as memorable. When Le Sage turned to the theatre, he brought to it much of Molière's ingenuity and satirical power. His farce *Crispin* continued the tradition of *commedia dell' arte* with the intrigues of the roguish servant Crispin, who tries to marry his master's lady-love. His excellent comedy *Turcaret*, which appeared in 1709, introduced a direct kind of social satire into the eighteenth-century theatre. Here Le Sage aimed his darts at the long-standing abuse of farming out the provinces to financiers who collected revenue for the government at a profit. *Turcaret* is a satirical portrait of one of these cordially detested *traitants* or "farmers of revenue" who waxed rich at the expense of the state and the people. Poetic justice overtakes him when he is duped by his valet, who is an even greater rogue than his master and at last acquires his wealth and power. The reign of Monsieur Turcaret is over, he exults, and his own is now beginning.

During the regency which followed the death of Louis XIV the Italian comedians, who had excellent actors in their midst, gained ascendancy once they discarded their own language and produced French comedies largely supplied by the sentimental Marivaux, whose preciosity and lack of satirical power ushered in a reaction to the high comedy of his great predecessor. The reign of sentiment in eighteenth-century France as practised by Marivaux, Destouches, La Chaussée and others, in fact nearly eclipsed the pointed art of Molière. But high comedy is in the last analysis imperishable, either because society sooner or later creates its own purges or because this art is the ultimate in civilized laughter and cannot long be resisted. In spite of the popularity of second-rate opera, of vaudeville which began at this time in France, and of "sentimental comedy" which the French aptly called *comédie larmoyante*— tearful comedy, the spirit of Molière was reincarnated on the eve of the French Revolution in Pierre-Augustin Beaumarchais, adventurer extraordinary to the French nation.

He began with a romantic comedy *Eugénie*, which he intended to be a *"drame bourgeois"* in the manner of Diderot, without accomplishing this purpose. His second effort *The Two Friends* dealt with business and the workaday world; it was written, he declared, "in honor of the Third Estate." Beaumarchais, who had moved up from the middle class to considerable favor in aristocratic circles, was indeed a militant bourgeois and quickly began to assert with his pen those claims to power which the lower orders were soon to assert with gunpowder and the equally efficacious guillotine. However, the unconscious revolutionary fermentation of his brain could not yet produce in *The Two Friends* anything better than a tepid tribute to honest businessmen.

It was in uninhibited comedy that Beaumarchais made his mark. He had no notion that he would win immortality when he tossed off *The Barber of Seville* to escape from the grief that overwhelmed him when his beloved Geneviève died in childbirth. All the amusing complications of mistaken identities and love intrigue went into this comedy. That the aristocratic lover Count Almaviva wins Rosine from her jealous guardian Dr. Bartholo with the aid of the infinitely resourceful Sevillian barber Figaro is not *prima facie* a remarkable plot. But the robust intrigues and characterizations of the comedy would be sufficient to turn the most hackneyed of themes into a *tour de force,* and Figaro, "innocent of cash" but irrepressibly self-assured, is the epitome of self-confident plebeianism. He expresses his philosophy trenchantly when he asks the Count, "In comparison with the virtues demanded of a domestic, does your excellency know of many masters worthy of being valets?" When the Count, who requires his assistance in furthering his love affair treats him civilly, Figaro exclaims, "The plague! How soon has my usefulness shortened the distance between us!"

Beaumarchais' subsequent encounters with the high-handed aristocracy, which resulted in his banishment and imprisonment, only sharpened the edge of his satire. In that scintillating sequel *The Marriage of Figaro,* he "contributed more to the French Revolution than he would have done had he organized a revolt in 1774."[5] Into the irrepressibly amusing tale of how the Spanish count tries to seduce a lady's maid who is affianced to his lackey Figaro, Beaumarchais poured all his scorn for the arrogant nobility of the dying years of the Bourbon monarchy. The redoubtably ingenious and self-assured servant holds up a mirror to the aristocracy in no uncertain terms when he declares, "Because you are a fine gentleman you think you are a genius? . . . What have you done to merit this splendor? You made the effort to be born, and that is all. You are a very ordinary fellow, while I, an obscure man in the crowd, required more wit and knowledge to rise in the world than has been invested in recent years in the government of all the Spanish provinces."

No wonder that the play was suppressed by Louis XVI and that its public premiere at the Théâtre Française in 1784 resulted in a riot on the part of the delighted third estate. Beaumarchais lived to see the monarchy overthrown only five years later. He who had delivered arms under the monarchy to Washington during the American revolution now became an army contractor for the republic in his country. Since revolutions have a saturnine way of consuming their own children, Beaumarchais himself fell afoul of the revolutionaries and awaited the guillotine in the company of the nobles he had fought most of his life. But the author of *The Marriage of Figaro* was not wholly forgotten by the Republic. While his fellow-prisoners were wheeled away in the tumbrils to their last public appearance, Beaumarchais was released. He was again in danger when he was included in the list of exiles while he was at the border trying to procure rifles for the nation on behalf of the Committee of Public Safety. He returned to Paris, to die there in May, 1799, after a vain attempt to prevail upon Talleyrand to send him as ambassador to the United States which owed him uncollected millions for armaments. He was clearly more fortunate as a playwright than as a man of affairs. His two masterpieces have lost none of their glitter, and they hold the international stage more frequently than Molière's pieces—at least in the operas of Rossini and Mozart.

Molière's influence on European comedy was widespread. It reached as far north as Scandinavia where Ludwig Holberg, his Danish disciple, born in Norway in 1684, was active until his death in 1754. A widely traveled man who departed from the Scandinavian practice of writing learned studies in Latin, he produced important historical works in the Danish language. Then upon being made manager of a new theatre in Copenhagen he turned to playwriting in order to provide his public with plays in Danish. The theatre was consequently responsible, to a large degree, for the birth of at least one modern European literature.

Thirty-three plays, most of them comedies, made him the northern Molière, and although they have left only a slight impression on the rest of the world, at least one of them, *Rasmus Montanus,* possesses a measure of incisive humor which entitles it to respect. It is a witty, if somewhat laborious, satirization of pedantry, as well as of rustic conservatism. The provincials are bewildered by Montanus, who trumpets his learning in their ears and spouts Latin phrases at the slightest provocation. In practical life he proves an arrant ass, and everyone is relieved when he is impressed into the army. Military discipline cures him of his philosophizing, and he is even willing to return to pre-Columban geography. "Mr. Lieutenant," his father-in-law insists, "let him be made a soldier again until the earth becomes flat." Montanus, who had earlier made a nuisance of himself by proclaiming the roundness of the earth to the rustics, finally yields a point: "My dear father-in-law, the earth is as flat as a pancake. Now are you satisfied?" It is not difficult to find echoes of Molière's satirization of preciosity and pedantry in the play.

At the other extremity of Europe, Carlo Goldoni made himself the Italian Molière after a session with strolling players. Incredibly prolific, he became the purveyor of numerous comedies, as well as of some tragedies, for the Venetian theatre. He labored mightily to establish comedy of average life and speech in Italy, and he succeeded for a time even if the resolute opposition of the critic Gozzi caused him considerable difficulty.

Molière's capacity for satirizing society was given to Goldoni only to a slight degree. He was more facile than incisive, and it is perhaps largely the comparative poverty of the Italian drama that won him the high esteem in which he has sometimes been held. William Dean Howells became his American champion, but as that wit of the theatre Lee Simonson once remarked, we are now off the Goldoni standard. Still, the liveliness and naturalness of *La Locàndiera* or *The Mistress of the Inn,* in which four men of different station are shrewdly managed by a vivacious woman, produce a radiant little piece. If no one endowed with a sense of proportion is likely to rank it with masterpieces of the drama, it is still sufficiently permeated with Molière's comprehension of humanity to be generally liked. There is also good featherweight humor in other Goldoni items: *The Curious Mishap* revolves around a clever daughter who outwits her father by pretending that her lover is interested in one of her neighbors, and *The Ostentatious Miser* transforms an avaricious nobleman into a spendthrift in the course of an unsuccessful courtship. Another comic contrivance, *The Fan,* weaves gossamer complications out of the loss of a fan and the courting of a spirited girl.

Still, Goldoni's realistic touches, slight as they were, had to retire to the background when his foe Gozzi turned from criticism to playwriting. With his fairy tales, among which *The Three Oranges* and *Zobeide* are the most reputable, he routed Goldoni from the stage. Goldoni went to France, received a pension from the king, wrote many of his plays in French, and died in poverty in 1793 after the Revolution had ended the royal subsidy. Gozzi, who in addition to his fantasies turned out one mild but charming feminist comedy *Turandot,* and several other playwrights who are merely names to the English reader, supplemented Goldoni's contributions to the Italian theatre. Nothing of moment, however, can be reported from this quarter. It is chiefly in England that comedy of manners proves itself not unworthy of Molière. who is one of the sources of its inspiration.

4 FROM ETHEREGE TO SHERIDAN

Before the Puritan revolution England had possessed realistic pictures of common life and romantic ones of upper-class society. When in 1660 the aristocracy returned from its exile in France, it ran riot. The social whirl began in earnest, and cynicism and debauchery became the rage. During this reaction to Puritanism and to the middle-class decencies at a time when the republican bourgeoisie seemed crushed, unconventionality became conventional and only disreputable conduct was reputable. The more innocent side of the picture is illustrated by the anecdote that a certain fashionable preacher pleaded with a nobleman not to snore so loudly at chapel service lest he awaken the king. Affectation, rakishness, and a generous interpretation of marriage became fashionable; in fact, marriage was considered a bondage that could lose a man his reputation for intelligence. When a character in Vanbrugh's *The Provoked Wife* declares, "I could love you even to matrimony itself, almost, egad," he is going far indeed.

Since the honest burghers held themselves scrupulously aloof from the theatre which they had kept padlocked as long as they were able, the stage became a leisure-class institution. It confined itself solely to the life of the drinking and philandering gentry. If most of the plays are mediocre and some of them are downright wretched, it must be conceded that the best Restoration pieces have at least one virtue which is not always observable in much of the more moral literature that passes for comedy; they are genuinely amusing. George Jean Nathan's generalization is distinctly apropos: "Sound and charming sentiment is impossible to a dramatist who does not constitutionally and philosophically view sex as either a humorous or a transient thing." The true Restorationists could not imagine any other attitude for a *"civilisé."* [6] The valid indictment that can be brought against these playwrights is the fact that they repeat themselves and are sometimes so persistently bawdy as to become wearying, for the adage that brevity is the soul of wit is nowhere so pertinent as with respect to pornography. The Restoration playwrights are also for the most part patently inferior to Molière as world figures; Molière, after all, saw the world as something more than one huge erotogenic zone.

Nevertheless, there is something invincible even in the elementary Pullman joke—perhaps, if we are to be solemn about it, because it discharges a basic instinct that keeps man rather occupied. And the playwrights of the restored monarchy possessed much resourcefulness for ringing changes on the familiar theme while maintaining the utmost unity of structure in accordance with the strictest classical comedies. Good *risqué* comedy requires as much craftsmanship as the most solemn tragedy or problem play—perhaps even more. The salacity of Restoration comedy often becomes a verbal or "absolute" experience like first-rate prose written about an inconsequential subject. Charles Lamb saw in the plays of the period a jest played for its own sake.

Lamb, however, went further in his frequently quoted defense of Restoration comedy. He could "never connect those sports of a witty fancy in any shape with any result to be drawn from them to imitation in real life." He added, "They are a world of themselves, almost as much as fairy-land." Its characters, according to him, live in a "Utopia of gallantry," in "a speculative scene of things which has no reference whatever to the world that is." This explanation is ingenious, even if it could hardly soothe the moral susceptibilities of the dawning Victorian age. Nevertheless, it is wide of the mark in contending that Restoration comedy has no reference to reality. The Restoration playwrights described a real, if narrow, world, and one of their claims to attention is the fact that they created a vivid picture of sophisticated society. Its authors who were true "sons of Belial," as Milton, then occupied with his *Paradise Lost,* sulkingly called them, knew whereof they wrote; and one of them, Wycherley, even ventured to be critical toward his times.

Upper-class society became the subject of comedy of manners even before the Restoration, particularly in such pieces as Shirley's *Hyde Park* and *The Gamester.* But some pretense to virtue is still present in them. The works that appear shortly after the reopening of the theatres, on the contrary, play havoc with morality. John Wilson's *The Cheats* in 1662 ribs the defeated Puritans unmercifully, and a year later Dryden's *The Wild Gallant* fully captures the spirit of ribaldry. Its character Lovely is a typical spark and the pursuit of women becomes a major occupation for a gentleman of his breed.

The following season marks the début of the first important practitioner of the new art, the fast-living George Etherege, whose *Comical Revenge, or Love in a Tub* captivates the town in the midsummer of 1664. Its Sir Frederick Frolick is the first well-realized gallant of the Restoration stage. Four years later comes the same author's *She Would If She Could,* an amusing picture of gay blades and equally skittish ingénues whom an admiring horseman in the play aptly describes as "country fillies that have breathed a course." In 1676, when the fashion is in full swing, Etherege produces his happiest work *The Man of Mode or Sir Fopling Flutter,* a veritable monument to frivolity. Its hero Dorimant is an erotic who is as witty as he is unscrupulous; Sir Fopling Flutter, newly come from France, is the *dernier cri* of fashionableness; and the women carry no impedimenta of modesty. Even the charming Harriet who wears down the resistance of her Dorimant to the point of marriage is an unconventional heroine.

Still Etherege, who retired to Paris and died in that haven for Belial's brood in 1691, is a tame gallant by contrast with his successors. In 1671 William Wycherley, educated in France and a wit in the *salon* of Madame de Rambouillet's daughter before his return to England, follows Etherege's first comedies with his *Love in a Wood.* It wins him the favor of Charles II's mistress, the Duchess of Cleveland, who leans out of her carriage affectionately and calls him by a name which according to Macaulay might "more justly have been applied to her own children." Out of the mummings of its Addlepot, Dapperwit, Lady Flippant, Ranger, and his mistress Lydia only one moral could emerge:

> *The end of marriage now is liberty.*
> *And two are bound—to set each other free.*

A year later appears *The Gentleman Dancing Master,* the witty piece in which a gallant disguises himself as a dancing master in order to carry on a secret flirtation.

After this apprenticeship came his *Country Wife* and *The Plain Dealer,* two genuinely distinguished works within the limitations of their *genre.* The first paints a vivid picture of the philandering world, satirizes jealousy in a manner worthy of Molière, and employs one of the master's most amusing characters—that of the awakening ingenue —Mrs. Margery Pinchwife, a bundle of "self-will, curiosity, art, and ignorance," to use Hazlitt's description. Transplanted from the country, she quickly takes root in the foppish world and becomes one of its hardy perennials—that is, she betrays her husband in the most fashionable city manner. In the indelicate device, borrowed from Terence's *Eunuchus,* of Horner's pretending impotence in order to gratify his lusts, Wycherley makes a virtue of indelicacy. But it cannot be denied that *The Country Wife* is a finished and keen piece of fooling, if just a trifle tiresome unless it is creatively revived and elaborated.

Wycherley's last work *The Plain Dealer* before he retired to matrimony, lawsuits, and seven lean years of imprisonment for debt is a monument to his mordant vein. Borrowing more than a hint from Molière's *Misanthrope,* without, however, assimilating his model's urbanity, he wrote a crabbed and rather splendid valedictory in *The Plain Dealer.* Here he paints a merciless picture of the world he knew. His acidulous but upright hero Manly is almost driven to distraction by the frivolity and dishonesty of the town. Not only the fashionable world comes under the lash; concerning lawyers, for example, his lieutenant remarks that "a man without money needs no more fear a crowd of lawyers than a crowd of pickpockets." The chronically litigious Widow Blackacre is a masterly portrait. Regarding friendship Manly says he knows "that generally no man can be a great enemy but under the name of friend." The play concludes with the disillusioned, betrayed Manly winning back some of his regard for mankind through the love of Fidelia who has followed him disguised as a boy in the well-tried *Twelfth Night* manner. But the acerbity of Wycherley's humor is not appreciably softened by this conclusion. Largely on the strength of *The Plain Dealer,* Wycherley holds an important position in the progress of Restoration comedy, since he showed "how the familiar material could be treated with a withering scorn in place of cynical indifference or approval." [7] After him only one more step could be taken in the field without retrogression. It was made by William Congreve, the supreme genius of English comic dialogue who added the alembic of subtle characterization and verbal power to the picture of upper-class manners.

Other practitioners merely glutted the stage with duplicate copies of

Restoration comedy. Mrs. Aphra Behn, the first professional female author of the English stage, rang changes on flirtation with liveliness but without manifest distinction; Dryden followed the fashion with his customary flexibility; Charles Sedley, the chief rake of his day, the droll and politically interested John Crowne, and Shadwell, who was unfairly designated by Dryden as the prodigy who never deviates into sense, added mediocre items to the supply. Sir John Vanbrugh, the architect of Blenheim and other "Brobdingnagian mansions," composed a number of comedies among which *The Relapse* and *The Provoked Wife* contain vital characterization and vivid situations. Lord and Lady Brute in the latter play are an amusing couple at variance with each other. Vanbrugh's dialogue displays a bluff vigor that can be distinctly entertaining, as when the neglected wife of Lord Brute wonders "Perhaps a good part of what I suffer from my husband may be a judgment upon me for my cruelty to my lover." When Lady Brute declares, "I wish I did but know how I might please you," her husband, who became a favorite part with Garrick, responds, "Ay, but that sort of knowledge is not a wife's talent." A coarseness of effect, however, vitiates Vanbrugh's humor.

In Congreve's mature work, on the contrary, everything is as light as a feather and as polished as a gem. This "Phoebus Apollo of the Mall" was born in the heyday of artificial comedy, in 1670, and was practically brought up on its graces. After acquiring an excellent education and becoming Dryden's protégé, Congreve won an encouraging success in 1693 with his first play *The Old Bachelor*. His second amusing play *The Double-Dealer,* produced in the same year, was, on the contrary, coldly received, and Congreve, irritated with the obtuseness of the public, wrote only three more plays.

He possessed an indispensable talent for gaiety, being uninhibited by any misgivings concerning the society of gallants, fools, scandal-mongers, and flirtatious women which he described. Thackeray[8] paid homage to him above all Restorationists when he wrote, with some exaggeration of the French influence, that "She was a disreputable, daring, laughing, painted French baggage, that Comic Muse . . . a wild, disheveled Lais with eyes bright with wit and wine." And yet decorous in her best moments, Thackeray might have added; decorous, that is, in its insistence upon a scrupulously polished style and upon grace in misbehavior.

Congreve, who had not the slightest interest in reforming what he saw, who was devoid of "the spirit of meliorism" which seeks to convert that which it ridicules, was content to be a laughing recording angel. If some of his notations can be collected as a bill of indictment against the age of Charles II, and even against other periods in which the social set runs riot, it is his laughter that is of primary purpose and interest. And this laughter is as swift as it is observant, as daring as it is sometimes sensitive.

These qualities, which already appear in *The Double-Dealer*, dominate his maturest plays *Love for Love* and *The Way of the World* before he retires from the theatre to lead a leisurely existence on fat sinecures and to enjoy the friendship of such luminaries as Pope, Swift, Gay, Addison, Steele, and Arbuthnot; before he becomes, as he insisted much to the irritation of his visitor Voltaire, a "gentleman" rather than a literary man. For twenty-nine years he lives on his reputation, which earns him Pope's dedication of his *Iliad*, for which many a peer of the realm would have given his eyeteeth. He dies in the full blaze of the great age of wit, on January 19, 1729, with his glories still intact and the loss of his social charm deeply regretted. He is buried in Westminster Abbey, and the Duchess of Marlborough erected a monument over his grave.

The advance in Congreve's technique is marked by a simplification and unification of his plots. He kept several lines of action concerning credulity whirling in *The Old Bachelor*, and he snarled the intrigues of a false friend Maskwell, who deceives everyone with the simple device of telling the plain truth, in *The Double-Dealer*. In *Love for Love*, however, Congreve keeps the humor revolving around a few more or less simply related matters. Valentine is such a prodigal son that his father disowns him and brings back his sea-faring son Ben with the intention of marrying this young hopeful to a friend's naïve daughter Prue. Ben's affair, however, does not prosper; he is too straightforward to tolerate the mincings and intrigues of polite society, while Prue's innocence is so sublime that it is quickly lost to a gallant. Valentine pretends madness in order to nullify his father's efforts to disinherit him and sends his lawyer packing, and all ends well when the clever Angelica, who has seemingly consented to marry his father, marries him instead upon proof of real devotion on the part of this indefatigable wit.

The odd fashionable set, the bluff tar Ben with his salty speech, the intelligent Angelica, and the brazen prodigal Valentine comprise a delightful portrait gallery. And even more delightful is the running fire of wit that blazes through the dialogue, to which only substantial quotation could do justice. Valentine pretending madness and calling himself Truth prophesies to old Foresight who has a passion for casting horoscopes. He will tell him what will happen tomorrow: "Tomorrow knaves will thrive through craft, and fools through fortune; honesty will go as it did, frost-nipt in a summer suit. . . . Oh, prayers will be said in empty churches at the usual hour. . . . Husbands and wives will drive distinct trades. . . . There are two things you will see very strange; which are, wanton wives with their legs at liberty, and tame cuckolds with chains around their necks." Ben, the sailor, does not fancy matrimony; "I could never abide to be port-bound;" a man that's married, according to him, resembles a galley-slave—"he is chained to an oar all his life; and mayhap forced to tug a leaky vessel to the bargain."

Even *Love for Love,* however, is not as abundantly supplied with verbal fireworks as Congreve's valedictory work *The Way of the World,* which revolves around the slender plot of a lovers' intrigue which enables them to marry in spite of Millamant's aunt Lady Wishfort, who is rightly resentful because the lover Mirabell pretended a passion for her. The pursuit and the surrender of the heroine Millamant is perhaps the most brilliant sophisticated romance in the drama. It is genuine high-comedy since the humor springs from characters who are irresistibly scintillating. It is difficult not to be infected with a liking for the lovers when the rakish Mirabell, upon observing his Millamant surrounded by two of her fatuous admirers, remarks: "Here she comes i' faith, full sail, with her fan spread and her streamers out, and a shoal of fools for her tenders;" or when Millamant excuses her tardiness to Mrs. Fainall: "Lord, have I not made violent haste: I have asked every living thing I met for you; I have inquired after you as after a new fashion." When Witwoud asks her why she did not ask Mrs. Fainall's husband for his wife, Millamant is astounded! "By your leave, Witwoud, that were like inquiring after an *old* fashion, to ask a husband for his wife."

Mirabell and Millamant are the lineal descendants of Benedick and Beatrice. Even when they are genuinely in love with each other these masters of verbal bravura know how to wear the protective armor of humor becomingly. Their story is, as noted, a love affair in which they overcome the impediment of a disapproving aunt who controls the purse strings. But far from becoming—as it easily might—a lush romance, the play remains a collation for the intellect and a feast of spiced insouciance. In their love scene Millamant's banter brooks no romantic nonsense and asserts woman's liberty of action in the same breath that suggests some sound, if comically draped, foundations for a happy marriage. She will not be called silly endearments, that "nauseous cant in which men and their wives are so fulsomely familiar." She will not have him kiss her before others, "nor go to Hyde-park together the first Sunday in a new chariot, to provoke eyes and whispers, and then never to be seen together again." Let them keep some distance between them: "let us be as strange as if we had been married a great while; and as well bred as if we were not married at all." She must have liberty to pay and receive calls and write letters as she pleases, and he must always knock at her room before entering. These articles subscribed to, she may by degrees "dwindle into a wife." Mirabell agrees, provided she in turn respects his freedom and sensibilities, for when she dwindles into a wife he does not wish to be "beyond measure enlarged into a husband."

Congreve, however, was singular in his day. Moreover, the temper of the age was changing. In the bloodless revolution of 1688 which brought constitutional monarchy to the fore the middle classes returned to power, and the excesses of the Restoration aroused a sharp reaction which culminated in a Society for the Reformation of Manners and in the fulminations of the High Churchman Jeremy Collier against comedy. The latter's polemic *A Short View of the Immorality and Profaneness of the English Stage* which appeared in 1698, two years before the production of Congreve's last play, took effect. In vain did Congreve, Vanbrugh and the rest of the wits indite replies. The fig leaves which they pasted on their comedies simply would not stick. The wits of the Restoration theatre were silenced and the literary leader of the day John Dryden even kissed the Reverend Collier's rod in an orgy of self-abasement.

George Farquhar, the last of the Restoration celebrities whose first plays were licentious enough, became moderate and comparatively pure in spirit. His merit lay in his introduction of some new types of characters in *The Recruiting Officer* and in *The Beaux' Stratagem,* in abandoning London backgrounds in favor of the countryside, and in the easy progress of his comic matter. Soon, moreover, the stage became glutted with sentimental and moralistic plays. The transition was begun as early as 1696 by the actor-playwright Colley Cibber in *Love's Last Shift,* a comedy dealing with the reformation of a roving husband which evoked Vanbrugh's realistic *Relapse,* and was continued in the next century. Then that lovable essayist Richard Steele saw fit to bolster his own unsteady behavior with full-blown sentimental comedies like *The Tender Husband* and *The Conscious Lovers* which are about as amusing as a Good Friday sermon. They commend themselves most to the historian who sees in them further proofs that the middle class was shaping public taste in the era of the Industrial Revolution that began in England. The new style evoked a literary controversy, in which the critic Dennis vainly maintained that a comedy without ridicule is unthinkable and that obviously comedy must concern itself with follies and vices if it is to be amusing.

Only the irrepressible John Gay managed to squirm out of the moral straitjacket of the new fashion during the first part of the century. Acting on a suggestion made by Dean Swift that he write a "Newgate [Prison] Pastoral," Gay enriched the world with his *Beggar's Opera* in 1728 and with its sequel *Polly,* as well as with a few minor items like *Achilles* and *The Distressed Wife.* In the rollicking ballad-opera *Beggar's Opera,* compounded of the trials of the polygamous bandit Macheath, Gay wrote a satire of the underworld which was only too applicable to the corrupt administration of England's first prime minister, Robert Walpole. Most of the complications arise from the fact that Peachum, who plies the double trade of spy and receiver of stolen goods, resents his daughter's marriage to Macheath. This is disadvantageous since such a son-in-law could easily inform against him; certainly a marriage would be inadvisable. An affair with Macheath would be in perfect taste; it is marriage "that makes it a blemish." Peachum, therefore, tries to get Polly's husband hung, and nearly succeeds. In *Polly*, the heroine ventures into the distant world for her husband, who has now turned pirate, and his adventures in the new profession again bear a parallel to the greater depredations of high office. Spiced with wonderful lyrics written to old tunes, Gay's operas were a welcome relief from the solemnities of Steele and his school.

But Gay did not operate in the regular channels of comedy of manners. Nor did England's master novelist Henry Fielding when he wrote such riotous pieces as his burlesque on heroic tragedy *Tom Thumb the Great*, a glorious bit of fooling with mock-heroic lines like Doodle's opening speech,

> *Sure such a day as this was never seen!*
> *The sun himself, on this auspicious day,*
> *Shines like a beau in a new birth-day suit. . . .*
> *All nature wears one universal grin.*

Only a number of mediocre pieces and his clever adaptations of Molière's comedies, *The Miser* and *The Mock-Doctor* (*Le Médecin malgré lui*) held the fort for regular comedy; unless one adds that competent midway piece Garrick's and Colman's *The Clandestine Marriage*.

Only in the last quarter of the century did comedy of manners temporarily recover some of its vigor. In 1773, the same year that Foote produced a timely burlesque on sentimental comedy *The Handsome Housemaid*, appeared Goldsmith's *She Stoops to Conquer* which needs no introduction to anyone who has passed grammar school. Goldsmith's first and weaker play *The Good-Natured Man* made a departure from genteel and righteous comedy as early as 1768, distressing members of the audience who greeted his amusing bailiff scene with cries of "Low! Low!" until the poor author felt compelled to complain that "humor seems to be departing from the stage." Despite the authority of the schoolmasters, *She Stoops to Conquer*, with its farrago of pleasant nonsense arising from young Marlow's delusion that he is stopping at an inn when he is actually in his fiancée's house, is only a mild farce. It strains the bounds of plausibility and wears thinly. But it is at least moderately amusing in an age of paradoxically solemn comedy.

Moreover, the next few years were enlivened with the last splutter of the comic spirit of the Restoration in the English theatre. Richard Brinsley Sheridan, who was responsible for the phenomenon, cannot be said to have completely emancipated himself from the sentimental style, even if he mocked it with notable liveliness in his short literary satire *The Critic*. But his two major comedies *The Rivals* and *The School for Scandal*, given in 1775 and 1777 respectively, recaptured much of the humor of the Restoration without its obscenity. Sheridan, who had a decided talent for comic situation and dialogue, knew how to draw upon his intimate observation of polite society in Bath and London.

The Rivals revolves substantially around the hero's attempts to marry the heroine without losing the money she will forfeit if she does not win her aunt's consent. The play, it is true, is not devoid of high-flown sentiment. Yet its Bob Acres, Lucius O'Trigger, and the inimitable Mrs. Malaprop who commits mayhem on the King's English have become household figures, and Sheridan here, as elsewhere, displayed a rich capacity for epigram and liveliness. The superior *School for Scandal* likewise atones with abundant humor for its sentimental vindication of the prodigal Charles Surface who wins his uncle's heart by cherishing the family portraits. His hypocritical brother Joseph is unmasked and the good-hearted Charles is rewarded with the lady of his heart. If the formula smacks of syrup, the play possesses a welcome tang. Its satirization of sanctimonious hypocrisy and scandalmongering has made the play a minor classic of the English stage. Its Joseph Surface, Sir Peter and Lady Teazle, Backbite, Snake, and Lady Sneerwell have worn remarkably well through a century and a half.

Although he had a managerial interest in the theatre, as part owner of Drury Lane, Sheridan wrote only a few plays, and most of them are unimportant. His *Trip to Scarborough* is an amusing adaptation of Vanbrugh's *Relapse,* and *The Critic* is a charming little literary satire. But *St. Patrick's Day, or The Scheming Lieutenant* is only a trifle, *The Duenna* is an undistinguished operetta, and *Pizarro* is an adaptation of a German melodrama. Sheridan's attention to the theatre was deflected by Parliament, where he made brilliant speeches which were overshadowed only by Edmund Burke's.

Sheridan's work did not inaugurate a new reign of high comedy. When he died in 1816 he had no progeny in the theatre; nor was he to have any for many decades. He was not an innovator but an epigone. The age was unfavorable to the cold splendors of the most intellectual of the arts.

Sentimental comedy continued to gratify the complacent businessmen of the ensuing decades. Even the revolutionaries, who responded to the overthrow of the monarchy in France, had no reason to despise the consolations of plays that dispensed with an ironic or negative attitude toward humanity. Friends of social reform like Miss Hannah More and Mrs. Inchbald wrote idealistic problem plays. Lachrymose comedy—a contradiction in terms, a fact which was not apparent to its proponents! —won acceptance by its optimistic view of mankind in an era which swore by the principle of the "perfectibility of man." To businessmen this meant an increase of material prosperity, to idealists a perfection of society and of man's intellect. Neither group could encourage irony in the theatre.

Not before a century had elapsed did the taste for sentimental drama actually recede. The favor of the middle-class and the promptings of humanitarianism, intensified by the influence of Rousseau, merely strengthened at the end a tendency that had started at the beginning of the century. Actually it was not an English playwright but a French one who most thoroughly advanced and best exemplified sentimental comedy. He was Pierre Marivaux (1688–1763), master of the style of paradox and preciosity that came to be known in France as *marivaudage*. Writing chiefly for the Comédie-Italienne in Paris but also for the Comédie-Francaise, he became known for his pictures of cultivated society, for his tasteful study of sentiments, and for his attention to women's feelings and interests. He reduced intrigue and action in favor of the emotions and "psychology" of his characters, though there was also no want of mere polish and refined wit in his work. The most charming of his comedies, *The Game of Love and Chance* (*Le Jeu de l'amour, et du hasard, 1730*), can still delight French audiences. Much insight and humor emanate here from the disguises and consequent misunderstandings between a young nobleman who pretends to be his valet's valet and of a young girl who masquerades as her maid's servant in order to test each other before they accede to a marriage arranged by their parents.

Significantly, the term *marivaudage*, at first applied contemptuously, became a complimentary expression. In France, the influence of Marivaux grew instead of diminishing as the century's theatre continued to reflect both aristocratic and upper middle-class taste before the Parisian masses began to dance their revolutionary *carmagnole* and beheaded Marie-Antoinette and Louis the Sixteenth. In Germany, even that incisive intellectual and rationalist Gotthold Ephraim Lessing (1729–81) wrote sentimental comedy, though rather refreshingly, when he composed his most successful play *Minna von Barnhelm*, a duel of sentiments between a Prussian officer and a young Bavarian gentlewoman, in 1767. In Italy, Carlo Gozzi (1720–1805) varied his improvisatory *commedia dell'arte* Venetian pieces, such as *The Love of the Three Oranges* (1761), with *fiabe* or fairy-tales, such as *Turandot* (1762), and routed Carlo Goldoni (1707–93), the Italian Molière.

Part VII

THE "MODERN" DRAMA

THE main body of "modern drama" begins as a response to the revolutionary speculations and promptings of the second half of the eighteenth century. An idealistic school arises that acclaims aspiration, the principle of liberty, and its associated ideals. It goes under the name of "romanticism," and its essential promptings continue to prevail in the theatre long after the specific romantic technique and style have changed substantially. As Western Europe, however, becomes a predominantly middle-class world that busies itself with practical matters and commonplace interests, its playwrights begin to grapple with realities instead of favoring romantic dreams. They not only accept their environment as a subject for study and improvement but derive from it a new, comparatively literal, style and approach.

The result is the realism—whether reportorial or critical—that distinguishes a major portion of the drama from the beginning of the eighties to the present day. A variously modified approach arises from the conditions of modern life and a variety of generally new conceptions of man and society appears on the stage. A vast and troubled life, inseparable from the travails and aspirations of modernity, unfolds before the dramatists of Europe and America. Many of them try to face it bravely and intelligently. In trying to project it effectively from the stage, moreover, the playwrights experiment with styles that carry them well beyond realism, too.

Modern theatre, of which Romanticism is the seedbed, becomes, then, a richly varied enterprise of realism, on one hand, and of numerous departures from it, on the other. It becomes a theatre for the dramatist with the microscope and the portfolio of case histories, for the dramatist with the scalpel, and for the dramatist with the trumpet who leads assaults on the walled cities of vested interests. And in the rear of the procession come the poets and pseudo-poets of theatrical art who push their way to the vanguard. Some of them even try to fly above the common scene — often, but fortunately not always, with "inept Icarian wings."

XVII

GOETHE AND THE ROMANTIC SPIRIT

I A LYRIC POET IN THE THEATRE

THE stalemate of the European theatre produced by decrepit classic tragedy and decayed comedy was first broken in Germany. This was not accomplished in a single move, but the one literary master associated with the victory is Johann Wolfgang von Goethe. In Germany's greatest writer were combined all the promptings of the age. His career spanned the eighteenth and nineteenth centuries, and his rare capacity for growth enabled him to absorb and then reflect the successive radiations of a changing world. His intellect was sufficiently broad to comprehend the modern world and his poetic faculty sufficiently intuitive to convey that world's strainings.

What had to be expressed was a ferment or an aspiration. Simplified formulas such as economists in the field of criticism favor cannot convey the living spirit of the times and of the romantic theatre. Undoubtedly the years 1780-1830 marked the destruction of the last important vestiges of feudalism in Western Europe, the middle class won a final victory, and capitalism forced itself into the seats of the mighty. But the process that overthrew monarchical government violently in both America and France and shook the thrones of absolutism elsewhere was obviously not a simple business transaction. It was a gripping human experience full of exaltation, disappointment, and renewed hope. In the realm of ideas, too, there was a considerable transfiguration of economic fact. Every age carries a knapsack full of ideals for spiritual nourishment. The middle classes might have wanted only to do business at the old counter without being annoyed by monarchical regulations, to have a voice in legislation affecting their interests, and to enjoy the social position that their wealth enabled them to afford. But once men are aroused, ideas and passions have a way of developing their own momentum.

The second half of the eighteenth century, recalling the dreams of the Renaissance, was the age of the *philosophes* and of revolutionary ideals without respect for mere business considerations. It was the age of Rousseau and his followers who, opposing the claims of nature to those of a frozen, polished society, acclaimed the equality of man and his essential goodness and perfectibility. It was the age of Voltaire who

applied the dynamite of rationalism to the concrete of established religion and government, and of Montesquieu, Diderot, Condorcet, Jefferson, and Washington. It was an age of bold dreamers who believed in
the imminence of the millennium, provided man struggled for it with
good will and right reason. In the American Revolution and in the
French Revolution of 1789 the common people saw the beginning of a
democratic dispensation. The masses were fired by the ideals of "liberty,
equality, and fraternity," and there were even leaders like Babeuf
among them who wanted to extend the revolution to basic property
relations. The revolutionists, we recall, also tried to enthrone the Goddess of Reason in place of the old god of Christianity and renamed the
months of the year in an effort to make the break with the past a clean
one.

The excesses of the upheaval, the depredations of the corrupt speculators, and the triumph of Napoleon, who turned the republic into a
monarchy, substituted unpleasant fact for high ideals. But the European
dream of a noble and progressive world was never entirely relinquished.
It moved in many shapes even in the darkest prisons of the post-Napoleonic reactions, even as it lived in the concentration camps of our own
day.

It is this dream that hovered in the wings and moved across the
boards of the romantic drama; sometimes visibly, sometimes invisibly,
and sometimes in almost unrecognizably distorted shapes. Romantic
drama is at its best the embodiment of aspiration. It is essentially, therefore, a poetic flight; and its greatest playwright, however unsatisfactory
he may be purely as a playwright, is very appropriately the lyric poet
Goethe.

2 LESSING AND THE RELIGION OF REASON

Goethe's life was a constant oscillation between anarchic emotion and
rational thought, even if they both sprang from the same afflatus. He
applied himself with equal zest to the adolescent sorrows of Werther who
died of *Weltschmerz* and the evolutionary significance of the inter-
maxillary bone in man. The same poet who made Faust a symbol of
man's yearnings for the infinite also allowed him in the end to content
himself with the amelioration of mankind by commonplace measures.

The simplest manifestations of the parallel currents of rationalism and
romanticism are to be found in two other playwrights: in Gotthold
Ephraim Lessing the rationalist, who preceded Goethe in the theatre, and
in Friedrich von Schiller, the romanticist, who followed Goethe but died
more than a quarter of a century before him.

Lessing, moreover, made the flight of the romantic playwrights possible by destroying the shackles of French classicism and setting the

drama a high goal of freedom and liberal idealism. Although his own stature as a playwright is modest, he is a major figure in the drama by virtue of his polemic activity and the example he set to his creative superiors.

The theatre which this son of a clergyman, born in 1729, knew in his student days at Leipzig was the spawn of decadent French drama, a stiff and lifeless exercise in classic heroics and recitation. Even this was, in fact, an improvement, from a *literary* standpoint, over the long reign of undistinguished farces that had kept the populace edified with the clownings of Harlequin, Germanicised as Pickelherring. To such a pass had Germany come owing to the ravages of the Thirty Years' War. It is true that native seventeenth-century writers like Gryphius, Rist and Lohenstein produced historical plays, classic exercises, moralities, and comedies of a sort. But these were crude affairs and Germany's literary dictator Gottsched saw only one solution for the low estate of the theatre; namely, to import French tragedies like Pradon's *Regulus,* adapt other items of the Louis Quatorze repertory, and launch imitations like his own *Dying Cato.* Only in the field of acting did the theatre awaken to some semblance of modernity owing to the efforts of the noble Caroline Neuber and her company.

Lessing's battles with the German pontiff of classicism were at first informal and tentative. It was not as a critic and reformer of the stage that he sought to shine at first. Instead he dreamed of becoming a comedian and playwright like Molière; he took lessons in elocution from an actor and progressed rapidly. Still, his ambitions as a playwright were aroused as early as 1748 by the success of his first play *The Young Savant,* a satire on a pretentious student written by Lessing to prove that he could surpass the French school. Six slight pieces followed this initial effort without marking any development in content or treatment. But in his twenty-sixth year came *Miss Sara Sampson* which for all its faults is superior to the models of "bourgeois tragedy" provided by Diderot and Lillo. This tragedy of a middle-class heroine was the first modern German drama to be taken from actual life and to be written in natural dialogue.

Literary criticism, which he enriched with his excellent *Literary Letters,* took him from the theatre for a time. Then came years of secretarial work in the service of the governor of Breslau, General Tauentzien, which removed him entirely from the battlefront of letters between 1760 and 1765. But in 1766 Lessing was back in harness with the publication of his brilliant study *Laocoon* limiting the fields of poetry and painting; and a year later he gave the German stage its best comedy for many a decade, *Minna von Barnhelm.*

If Lessing still harbored the hope of becoming a German Molière, candor compels one to admit that he had far to go. Too much saccharine went into the composition of the piece, and, as Brander Matthews has noted, "*Minna* is less comic than Molière's lighter plays and it is less weighty than Molière's major masterpieces." Still, Lessing's effort is not entirely negligible. Besides being historically important as one of the earliest plays in any language to change sets for every act, *Minna* provides an appealing romance in the behavior of the spirited heroine who woos her lover when his loss of position and lack of means prevent him from taking the initiative. Moreover, the comedy was intended to heal the wounds of the Seven Years' War with its celebration of the hero's humanitarianism. Frederick the Great's officer Tellheim having been ordered to collect a fine from the conquered Thuringians, advanced the sum himself and was dismissed from the service on the suspicion of having compromised with the enemy. Living in extreme poverty, helped only by his faithful comic servant, Tellheim nurses his wounded honor in a tavern. But Minna, the Thuringian girl who learned to love him for his generous behavior toward her people, has no difficulty in finding him and overcoming his scruples. The winning characterization of Tellheim, Minna and their servants produces a pleasant comedy. It has long held the German stage in lieu of something better—which the Germans, who have not been remarkable for their sense of humor, have not supplied with much frequency.

Still plying his dual functions of critic and playwright, Lessing soon repaired to Hamburg to assume the position of "critic of plays and actors" or adviser at the newly founded first German National Theatre. The noble enterprise failed ignominiously. However, the criticisms Lessing wrote for it between April 1767 and November 1768, collected under the title of *Hamburg Dramaturgy* (*Hamburgische Dramaturgie*), were epoch-making. With this work he became the second great critic of the drama, if Aristotle is to be denominated the first. He not only demolished the stilted French school in Germany but established the critical basis of the whole romantic revolt by his exaltation of Shakespeare as the king of dramatists and by his insistence upon a dramatist's right to create as he pleased without wearing the fashionable straitjacket of the "unities." His statement that "the only unpardonable fault of a tragic poet is this, that he leaves us cold; if he interests us he may do as he likes with the little mechanical rules" is now one of the commonplaces of dramatic criticism.

Lessing was nearly turned against the theatre by the unfortunate complications that ruined the Hamburg experiment. He was oppressed by debts contracted in connection with it, his health began to fail him, and his wife died in childbirth one year after their marriage. Only his post as librarian to the Duke of Brunswick at Wolfenbüttel made life tolerable for him. Nevertheless his embattled intellect lost none of its resolution. The "Reimarus" controversy which he waged against orthodox theologians was one of the most exciting battles of the "rationalists," and his last two plays *Emilia Galotti* and *Nathan the Wise* were his most ambitious works for the theatre. Both were charged with thunder against the prevailing state of affairs. *Emilia Galotti*, published in 1772, pointed to the petty despotisms of Germany; *Nathan the Wise*, published in 1779, while the American colonies were fighting valorously to erect a state that would not discriminate against any creed, celebrated religious tolerance.

In *Emilia Galotti* Lessing adapted the classic story of Virginia, the Roman maiden who was slain by her father when her virtue was threatened by a tyrant. The classic Virginia became the middle-class Emilia (a *bürgerliche Virginia* the author called her), and the Roman deceiver became an Italian princeling. Avoiding melodramatic partisanship, Lessing made Emilia susceptible to the charming but dissolute prince. Only when she realizes the hopelessness of the situation of becoming the despot's mistress, when her fiancé has been assassinated and she has been abducted does Emilia prevail upon her upright father to kill her. There is something forbidding in the theme despite Lessing's careful motivation of the behavior of the principals, and *Emilia Galotti* is deficient in breadth and sympathy. Nevertheless, this "bourgeois tragedy" is a modern drama, and it was sufficiently relevant to conditions in Germany to strike home. The year of its publication heard the firing of the first gun of the romantic revolt in Goethe's *Goetz von Berlichingen*. But the credit for anticipating the barrage belongs to Lessing who conceived *Emilia Galotti* twelve years earlier.

An even more explicit expression of the eighteenth-century "Enlightenment" is to be found in *Nathan the Wise*. This play is to be regarded as Lessing's last testament not only because he died two years later without leaving another play except a provocative fragment of a projected Faust drama but because it is the most spirited and the noblest of his works. He came to it after having concluded a bitter theological battle in favor of rational religion, and it is even possible that *Nathan* would never have been written if the authorities had not forbidden the publication of further pamphlets on his "Reimarus case." No European play gave such direct and elevated expression to the ideals of religious tolerance.

In Nathan, modeled after his Jewish friend the philosopher and reformer Moses Mendelssohn, Lessing not only challenged racial prejudice by portraying one of the noblest characters in literature but presented an example of a man who lives by "natural religion." He is no more an orthodox Jew than he is a Christian or Mohammedan. In opposition to the strident claims of every religion, which insists that it alone has a monopoly on the true faith, Lessing showed Nathan leading a life of impeccable morality without supporting any creed, even if he retains his forefathers' simply because he was born in it. Nathan is more Christian than the followers of Jesus in the play. Having lost his wife and children in a Crusaders' pogrom, Nathan follows the precepts of Christ by saving and rearing the orphaned Rebecca, the daughter of a Crusader.

The story acquires a romantic twist when Rebecca and the Templar fall in love only to learn that they are brother and sister; they are discovered to be the children of the Sultan Saladin's dead brother, who embraced Christianity before his death. The idealization of Nathan also goes to romantic extremes. But the play borrows its thesis and its essential tone, which is cool and reasoned, from the rationalistic liberalism of Voltaire and the Encyclopaedists. Its high point is the indisputably great speech of Nathan when Saladin tries to trap him into forfeiting his goods by asking him which is the true faith.

Nathan replies with the famous Parable of the Rings, adapted from the *Decameron* and the earlier *Gesta Romanorum*. A father possesses a ring which has the virtue of making its owner beloved of God and man, as well as lord of the household. Since the father loves his three sons (Judaism, Christianity, and Mohammedanism) equally well, he promises the ring to each of them. Being unwilling to disappoint any of his sons, the father therefore has two other identical rings made. Then he bestows "his blessing and his ring on each—and dies." Immediately each son, without knowing that the others also possess a ring, claims priority in the house. A quarrel ensues, and a judge is consulted.

Saladin upbraids Nathan for evading the question, but Nathan replies that the three religions, however disparate they may seem now, "differ not in their foundation." The judge is unable to render a verdict. The possessor of the true ring would have to be beloved by all, which is obviously not the case when the young men are bringing each other to court instead of yielding gladly to one brother. "Who of the three is loved best by his brethren?" the judge asks.

> *Does each one love himself alone? You're all*
> *Deceived deceivers. All your rings are false.*
> *The real ring, perchance, has disappeared.*

His judgment, therefore, is that they give their rings a long trial. He who succeeds in making himself most worthy of love will be the true heir. The religion that does the most good or reaps the greatest harvest of love through the ages by its active humanitarianism will prove to be the true faith. Here is the essence of eighteenth-century liberalism, if not of all liberalism in religious matters. To it, moreover, is added a philosophy of freedom:

> *Your father, possibly, desired to free*
> *His power from one ring's tyrannous control.*
> *He loves you all with an impartial love*
> *And equally, and had no inward wish*
> *To prove the measure of his love for one*
> *By pressing heavily upon the rest.*

If Lessing's poetic powers had been equal to his material, *Nathan the Wise* would probably have ranked with the great plays of the world, instead of being a comparatively poor one. Still its intellectual fire and impassioned modern idealism crack the cold shell of Lessing's didacticism. For all its faults as a play, *Nathan the Wise* is, next to *Faust,* perhaps the noblest expression of Western idealism.

The men of whom civilized Germany has been proudest have all paid their homage to Lessing freely and generously. Heine perhaps worded the tribute most eloquently when he wrote that in all of Lessing's works "breathes the same grand social idea, the same progressive humanity, the same *religion of reason,* whose John he was, and whose Messiah we still await." And it was Goethe and Schiller in 1801 who gave *Nathan the Wise* its first successful production, in a somewhat modified version prepared by the latter. Lessing died without seeing his last testament on the German stage; he had himself noted that no place was sufficiently enlightened to receive *Nathan,* adding, "But all hail to the place where this may first be done!" Two years after his death in 1783, the play was presented at Berlin, and understandably with scant success. It remained for that little Athens of Germany, Goethe's Weimar, to give *Nathan* due honor. Thereafter it was translated into nearly every European language and its vogue in Germany, although clearly dependent upon local weather conditions, has until recently been notable. Thus the season of 1900-01 recorded forty-five productions; the season of 1938-39 none, of course.

3 SCHILLER AND THE ROMANTIC AFFLATUS

Lessing would probably have scorned to translate his humanitarianism into the language of the young Schiller, and it is known that he was disturbed by the emotional pyrotechnics of the younger generation. But moderation was no way to popularize the drama of the European "Enlightenment." This popularization was most successfully accomplished by the diametrically different playwright Schiller. This rapt lyricist caught fire from the young Goethe in the company of other young men like Friedrich Maximilian Klinger whose extravagant play *Storm and Stress* (*Sturm und Drang*) in the year of our Declaration of Independence lent its name to the entire first stage of the German romantic movement.

Schiller's emotional liberalism was heightened by his early experiences. Born in 1759 in the little duchy of Würtemberg, he tasted the irksomeness of parental discipline from a father who served as a captain in the Duke's two-by-four army. Since he inherited his mother's sensitivity along with her blue eyes and blond hair, he was first intended for the clergy. Nevertheless, he soon entered a Prussianized military academy at the Duke's command. At sixteen he was allowed to substitute medicine for military science; only, however, to become a regimental surgeon at Stuttgart in 1780.

The caged youth began to flutter his wings in morbidly sentimental and pessimistic poems, and a year after his appointment to the army appeared his first play *The Robbers*. Full of romantic rebellion and gloom, it contrasted the extreme nobility of the wronged Karl Moor with the utter villainy of his designing brother who piles evil upon evil in a world which favors hypocrisy. The wronged hero of this energetic but adolescent tragedy takes to the forests where he plays Robin Hood to a band of outlaws whose morals are superior to those of the philistines who hug their pelf under the protection of the law. When the play was produced at Mannheim in January 1782, its effect was electrifying. Years later the French Republic made the author an honorary citizen in recognition of his services to the revolutionary cause, although his own ardor had somewhat cooled by then.

Defying his Duke's order to write no more without ducal permission and to correspond with no one abroad, Schiller escaped from Würtemberg in a closed carriage, spent some time in Mannheim under a false name, and found himself without means when the intimidated director of its theatre rejected his new work *Fiesco*. This play, another and somewhat better constructed paean to rebellion set in Italy, was published by a courageous bookseller. A noble lady Frau von Wolzogen gave the refugee shelter in her country house near Meiningen where he spent half a year until the middle of 1783. Here he prepared his next bombshell *Intrigue and Love* (*Kabale und Liebe*), a bourgeois tragedy patterned after *Emilia Galotti*. Like Lessing's play, *Intrigue and Love* exposed corruption in the courts of Germany's petty autocracies and described the victimization of a heroine of the people who is loved by a scion of the nobility in defiance of his father.

Fortunately Schiller was soon able to overcome the scruples of the Mannheim director Dalberg and became his "theatre poet." *Fiesco* was produced next year and *Intrigue and Love* followed soon after. Here

Schiller also founded a literary journal, wrote criticism, and published the first act of his next play *Don Carlos* with which he won the favor of the "German Maecenas" Duke Karl August of Weimar.

Removing to Leipsic and living happily among generous literary friends, Schiller became a calmer spirit. Here he wrote lyrics like the famous *Hymn to Joy,* engaged in historical studies, and completed the play *Don Carlos* which was based on them. It was his first drama in verse, and despite its zealous liberalism it revealed the poet turning from revolution to evolution. On the negative side, it described the corruption of the Spanish court of Philip II and honored the revolutionary idealism of the ill-starred Don Carlos. But the moral emphasis was on the noble figure of the latter's friend Posa who held that man could be redeemed by sweet reasonableness and proved the point by converting Philip, although not soon enough to save Don Carlos. This play, which for all its sprawling propensities has been a favorite in Schiller's homeland, is in fact an epitome of Schilleresque romanticism. At this time, too, Schiller contracted a happy marriage with his devoted Charlotte, in whose home he had met Goethe.

Through the latter's official influence, he soon received a professorship in history at the famous University of Jena, and it was in connection with this position that he completed his book *The Revolt of the Netherlands* and turned out his popular *History of the Thirty Years' War* which gave him material for his next play, the trilogy of *Wallenstein.* After traveling for his health, he finally settled in Weimar, basked in the friendship of Goethe, and was further steadied by him. Here he wrote his final chapter in the German theatre, along with his best poems.

Wallenstein's Camp (Lager), a vivid picture of military life, appeared in 1788, and eleven years later came its sequels *The Piccolimini* and *Wallenstein's Death* generally considered his best work and accorded the accolade of an impressive translation by Coleridge. The trilogy dramatizes in human terms the tragedy of the Catholic generalissimo of the Thirty Years' War who, upon losing favor with the Emperor and developing doubts concerning the righteousness of the war, plans to make peace with the Protestants and establish an independent kingdom in Bohemia. He is assassinated before he can do so, having been betrayed by his closest friend Piccolimini, whose idealistic son is betrothed to Wallenstein's daughter. *The Piccolimini* is wearying, but *Wallenstein's Death,* except for its characteristic over-idealization of the lovers, is a painstaking tragedy of noble proportions.

Schiller, however, lapsed into intellectual mush in the works that followed. He chose sentimental themes, idealized his characters, and substituted heat for thought. His *Maria Stuart* in 1800 still disclosed some grasp of the realities in presenting Mary as a crime-stained, if exalted, heroine who, in addition, loses her temper in the crucial scene with Elizabeth. Leicester, the vacillating lover, and Queen Elizabeth also possess some gristle. Only Schiller's easy forgiveness of Mary, a characteristic fault of the author, keeps the well-constructed tragedy in a romantic quicksand. But *The Maid of Orleans* (*Die Jungfrau von Orleans*) in 1801, for all its noble sentiment which gave it much popularity, often wallows in slush. Joan of Arc escapes from prison miraculously, and everything is pretty and flamboyant. Set beside Shaw's *St. Joan* it rouses more than a suspicion that Schiller, for all his dabblings in history, philosophy and esthetic theory, possessed a diluted intellect.

In his pseudo-classic *Bride of Messina* (*Die Braut von Messina*), supplied with beautifully written choruses and rhymed dialogue, he tried to pull himself together. But the fratricidal rivalry of two brothers over a girl who turns out to be their sister produces a remote "fate" drama and Schiller's customary romanticization of life is present behind the classic façade. Schiller's last play, the familiar *Wilhelm Tell,* written in 1804, is an epitome of its author's virtues and faults. It is a stirring evocation of the liberty-loving Swiss who rise up against their oppressor, and it revels in an unforced lyric splendor. Yet its elementary division of goats from sheep, of the perfect Tell from the melodramatic Austrian tyrant Gessler, produces Schiller's characteristic defects.

On the ninth of May, 1805, Schiller succumbed to his tuberculosis in the forty-sixth year of his life. Racing against time, he wrote at night, immersing his feet in cold water in order to stay awake. He died, mourned by everyone who knew him, for he was one of those lovable poets who win every heart with their unassuming spirituality. Madame de Staël's impression, when she visited Weimar, of "his sweet and gentle character," his tall, slender figure, and his "exquisitely chiseled" mouth and Roman nose is the picture of a matinee idol and makes a suitably romantic symbol. His idealizing imagination and dream of the good and the beautiful, combined with a showman's instinctive feeling for theatre, kept him the favorite playwright of the German people for more than a century.

4 GOETHE, THE LAST OF THE UNIVERSAL MINDS

If Schiller, for all his ventures in philosophy, remained a simple and naïve poet to the end of his days, Goethe's excursions are the history of a constantly deepening mind. This mind is, moreover, continually stopping to examine itself as if it were the center of the universe.

It is a characteristic of romanticism that it made a fetish of self-expression. The revolt against a society hedged about by conventions led to an idealization of man as a being whose primal right was to coddle his emotions and realize his individuality privately. Santayana has noted that "the zest of romanticism consists in taking what you know is an independent and ancient world as if it were material for your private emotions." Goethe is an ideal example; he lived and wrote as if he created "a new heaven and a new earth with each revolution in his moods or in his purposes." [1] It is fortunate, therefore, that his moods and purposes were so comprehensive. Consequently, he became a breathing and working epitome of the nineteenth century for which nothing seemed impossible.

We see him at first as the son of a well-to-do Frankfort lawyer, highly educated, full of sensibility, and moving from university to university. He disappoints his father by failing to settle down to a profession and by falling in love almost chronically. His father resolves that Goethe is to study law and the lad is duly packed off to Leipzig in 1765, in his sixteenth year. At first he attends classes faithfully, but he soon falls into a dejected state of mind, devotes himself to the study of art, studies Lessing's critical work, and participates in private theatricals. He falls in love again, is disappointed, leads an irregular life, suffers a severe hemorrhage, and is forced to return to Frankfort. His convalescence is interrupted by new maladies, he falls under the spell of mysticism fostered by his mother's friend Susanna von Klettenberg, works out an elaborate theological system, and dabbles in alchemy. Like his character Faust, young Goethe is completely at odds with the world.

As soon as his health is somewhat improved, the twenty-one-year-old poet obeys his father's wishes and goes to Strassburg to resume his legal studies. Here, however, he falls under the spell of the critic and philosopher Herder who awakens his interest in folk poetry, nature, Rousseau, Shakespeare, and the sentimentalists Laurence Sterne and Goldsmith. The whole field of romantic poetry becomes his province. And again it is a love affair that holds him in its grip. Its object is the simple daughter of a Protestant pastor Friederika Brion, the Gretchen of his Faust and the inspiration of many of his matchless lyrics.

The thought of marriage was repugnant to Goethe who could not imagine himself living contentedly in the narrow sphere of a clerical family and who felt that there was still so much for him to experience and learn. At the price of much suffering and many pangs of conscience he abandoned Friederika and thereafter spent a large portion of his life making literary amends to her while she remained faithful to his memory by never marrying. Although he began to practise law in Frankfort in the fall of 1771, his experience made a poet and playwright of him. The medieval tragedy *Goetz von Berlichingen* was the first fruit of his novitiate, which also included some magnificent lyrics. By no means a faultless work, woefully diffuse and poorly focused, *Goetz* became the spearhead of the early romantic revolt. Its hero Goetz is presented as struggling tragically against the pettifogging absolutism of the Holy Roman Empire. Historically considered, he was actually trying to perpetuate the feudal age. But Goetz, the honest and plain-spoken soldier, was a vehicle for Goethe's revolt against a philistine society. And the result was indisputably stirring. Goetz is a vigorous and noble character, and his sister's tragic betrayal by the statesman Weislingen is abundantly supplied with pathos. The play, Shakespearean in structure and the most stageworthy of Goethe's dramatic works, made him become a literary lion. A whole school of dramatists, with Kinger, Lenz and Schiller at its head, was born of this effort to express an inchoate revolt against the workaday world.

The play did not purge the young poet completely. He suffered from another depression, which was probably aggravated by a hopeless love for a friend's fiancée. Suicide seemed to him the only solution, and he slept with a dagger by his side. Out of this relapse was born the woeful short novel *The Sorrows of Werther* which, appearing in 1774, became the bible of the romantic school. It possessed all the requisite ingredients of abandonment to the spell of nature-love, infinite restlessness and self-pity, and a pathetic love affair. Nevertheless, Goethe's next plays are more objective. *Clavigo* is a well-constructed if insignificant study of a weak character. *Stella,* written in 1775, provides a typically romantic solution when its hero Ferdinand, who is in love with two women at the same time, settles the problem by living with both of them. Even this, however, is an improvement over stewing in one's juices *à la* Werther, although it discloses a very feeble hold on reality until Goethe changed the conclusion thirty years later and allowed Ferdinand and Stella to commit suicide.

It was at this time, moreover, that Goethe began to conceive the drama *Faust.* The 1774 draft contains practically everything that is essential in the First Part of the completed tragedy. Faust is already something more than the vulgar magician of the old Folk-book from which the story was taken. He is already a seeker after infinite knowledge and an affirmer of the questing human spirit which is denied by the Adversary who cannot comprehend the soul's aspirations.

The year 1775, which was punctuated by another love affair, with the fashionable beauty Lili Schönemann, was Goethe's last in Frankfort. The young romanticist found a kindred soul in the young Duke of Weimar, threw up his repugnant profession, and became attached to the court which he made the most civilized in Europe. And it was here that he laid the foundations for his diverse intellect, making scientific investigations, serving in many official capacities and applying himself to problems of finance, transportation, and government. The sensible and sympathetic matron Frau von Stein became his Pallas Athene for ten years, and under her aegis he learned moderation and practical wisdom. It was in this spirit of inquiry and self-education that he began to write his long "educational" novels *Wilhelm Meister's Apprenticeship* and its sequel *Wilhelm Meister's Travels,* in which he traced the career of an autobiographical hero from his first romantic strivings to his final reconciliation with the limitations of mundane existence. It was in this spirit, too, after his travels in Italy which brought him closer to the classic world, that Goethe wrote his two thoughtful plays *Iphigenia in Tauris* and *Torquato Tasso.*

Iphigenia, conceived in 1779, is Goethe's testament to the new dispensation. Taking the Euripidean story of Orestes' escape with his sister from primitive Tauris (where he is about to be sacrificed to the goddess Artemis), Goethe infused it with a high moral purpose. Iphigenia refuses to deceive even a barbarian like the Scythian king and successfully appeals to his humanity after confessing that Orestes is her brother and that he must bring back the statue of Artemis if he is to be cured of his madness. In Iphigenia's moral victory Goethe solemnizes his new-won principle that man can win salvation only through self-renunciation and justice. The ancient curse that rested on the house of Atreus is at last removed by *"reine Menschlichkeit,"* by pure humanity; as Goethe expressed it in a later poem,

> *For each human fault and failure*
> *Pure humanity atones.*

Iphigenia is enriched by a keen psychological analysis of mental perturbation as it appears in the fury-driven Orestes, and Goethe's exalted thought is supported by some of the finest writing in the German language. The play is not simply another pseudo-classical exercise, but a modern "morality." It is regrettable only that Goethe wrote it less as a play to be acted than as a dramatic poem to be read.

Torquato Tasso is an even deeper psychological study, with the Italian poet Tasso supplying the data from his tragically troubled life. Tasso is a morbidly sensitive character who is driven to distraction by the fact that a sensible statesman refuses to coddle his ego. Tasso becomes furiously jealous of him, challenges him to duel, expresses an extravagant passion for his patron's foster-sister, and is on the verge of madness before he is finally appeased. The play is resolved too suddenly and easily; a character as far advanced in paranoia as Tasso cannot cure himself with a stroke of common sense. And again the play is more dramatic in the parlor than in the theatre. Nevertheless, *Tasso* too is a distinguished literary drama, and its understanding of neurotic temperament leads to a wholesome affirmation of the anti-romantic principle that a good poet is by no means more important than a wise statesman. Moreover, according to Goethe now, the great poet is he who rises above self-absorption and knows his place in the scheme of things.

Goethe had learned this lesson personally, even if his first ten years at

Weimar finally became so irksome that he escaped to Italy. *Tasso* expressed a solid truth of which he never lost sight again. Even the somewhat earlier *Egmont,* which dramatizes the revolt of the Netherlands and closes with a rapturous vision of triumphant freedom, reflects a sober outlook. Egmont fails as a revolutionary because he lacks the qualities of a statesman and man of the world. His trusting and love-absorbed nature results in his arrest and execution by the Spaniards. This study is a far cry from the flamboyance of Goethe's first treatment of a rebellious hero in *Goetz.* It lags here and there, and the vacillations of the unfortunate Count become wearisome. And yet *Egmont* is a provocative drama on the subject of the eternal liberal who fails, even if he honors his cause, by his nobility.

Goethe's major forays in the theatre ended with *Egmont, Iphigenia,* and *Tasso;* there is a long gap between them and *Faust,* on which he worked throughout his life until it became the compendium of a lifetime and of fifty years of European history. The completed First Part as we now possess it appeared in 1808; the Second Part was finished on his last birthday, shortly before his death in 1832.

Nothing is more misleading than the custom of separating the two parts by considering Part One as a complete drama and dismissing Part Two as a jumble of fugitive scenes. Although *Faust* grew by accretion, the play is a complete entity and the summation of a vision. It is a mosaic whose pattern is man's blundering search for the meaning and purpose of life. *Faust,* in other words, is a history of man judged by the metaphysics of human aspiration. It is not a pat play but a record; it does not fit any more neatly into the theatre than does life itself.

It begins in Heaven where God pronounces the key to the drama by his benediction on man the eternal seeker: *"Es irrt der Mensch so lang er strebt"*—man errs as long as he strives. But this very striving will save him in the end, and the rest of the play simply demonstrates the truth of this proposition.

Faust, the object of the experiment, having tired of the piddling efforts of medieval science which do not satisfy his yearning for "knowledge infinite," resorts unsuccessfully to magic. He is ready to renounce the whole sorry business of life when Mephistopheles, the skeptical Devil, promises him the fulfillment of every desire. Scornful of this promise and certain that this negative, superficial spirit can never satisfy his questing spirit, Faust signs a compact with him. The wording is significant:

> *When on an idler's bed I stretch myself in quiet,*
> *There let, at once, my record end!*
> *Canst thou with lying flattery rule me,*

> *Until, self-pleased, myself I see,—*
> *Canst thou with rich employment fool me,*
> *Let that day be the last for me. . . .*

He is willing to let the Devil take his soul if ever he finds a moment of satisfaction sufficient unto his infinite desire:

> *When thus I hail the Moment flying:*
> *"Ah, still delay—thou art so fair!"*
> *Then bind me in thy bonds undying,*
> *My final ruin then declare!*

Mockingly, since he is certain that Mephistopheles can never create such a Moment, Faust goes through the mumbo-jumbo of the medieval blood-compact. Mephistopheles, who has no comprehension for man's quest, then proceeds to gratify his charge as best he can. He renews Faust's youth, plunges him into grotesque dissipation, and leads him to ruin the innocent Gretchen, who is executed after killing her illegitimate child. Still, the very fact that Faust is seized with remorse confounds the Devil's designs; Faust emerges from the depths of this experience as a passionate human spirit and not as an inveterate debauchee. The first part of the play leaves Mephistopheles morally, if only tentatively, defeated.

Still, man's odyssey has only barely begun. Freed from remorse, which can only imprison an aspiring spirit, Faust plunges into the great world and makes Mephistopheles an instrument of his insatiable search and later of his creative will. His adventures lead him to the court of the Emperor where he struggles fantastically with the financial problems of the empire. Amid much hocus-pocus his next quest is for classic beauty, and it is realized in the beautiful Helena episodes. Then follows the symbolic Euphorion episode in which the catastrophic behavior of the child born to Faust and Helena demonstrates the dangers of disembodied aspiration. Euphorion, who also represents rootless romantic art and in whom there is more than a suggestion of Byron, is shattered by one precipitous leap into the void.

Finally—and this is the modern philosophy propounded by Goethe—Faust who has by now exhausted every poetic flight settles down to practical activity in line with Goethe's pragmatic pronouncements that "only that which is fruitful is true," and that "if you want to reach the infinite, traverse the finite to all sides." Just as the aspirations of the French Revolution were canalized into the economic and scientific activities of the nineteenth century, just as the lyricist Goethe himself became a government official and a scientist, Faust now grapples with the actual world. He applies himself to cultivating a strip of land, to draining swamps, and to establishing a prosperous society.

Faust's strivings, like those of all practical builders, cause pain to others; it is not only the destroyers who hurt the world's gentle people. One of his last acts sanctions the expropriation of an innocent old couple. This leads to their death when they refuse to leave their home to make way for "progress," and Faust reflects bitterly on the pain he has caused. But he is not to be stayed by remorse, a virtue that Goethe considered dangerous when it led to a cessation of human effort. Although blinded by "Care," Faust still calls for "quick diligence" and "severest ordering." Only by this means will his vision be realized, and glorying in the ultimate fruition of his efforts, he suspects that they will bring him as close to inner gratification as anything can.

Millions will live happily in freedom, united by common activity, for

> *He only earns his freedom and existence,*
> *Who daily conquers them anew.*

He foresees a "free people" standing on a "free soil," and on that great day he could "hail the Moment fleeting" with those words which he never thought he would be able to say—

> *Ah, still delay—thou art so fair!*
> *(Verweile doch, du bist so schön)*

He goes even further:

> *In proud fore-feeling of such lofty bliss,*
> *I now enjoy the highest Moment—this!*

Still the uncomprehending Nay-saying spirit, Mephistopheles laughs at Faust as he sinks back and dies, laughs at him for desiring this

> *latest, poorest, emptiest Moment,*

and wonders at the purposelessness of life:

> *What good for us, this endlessly creating?*

But he receives his answer when Faust's soul is saved from his clutches and is borne away by the Heavenly Host. A spirit as aspiring as Faust's is made for eternity, and it is received as a "chrysalis" for a new birth. The "eternal feminine" or the creative principle draws Faust up to the highest heaven, to the realm of the Absolute where alone there is complete fulfillment. For his earthly struggle was only a symbol of the eternal aspiration and unceasing creativeness that characterizes the universe. In short, Faust's struggle was a cosmic symbol, for

> All things transitory
> But as symbols are sent.

Out of the multiplicity of suggestive situations and lines in *Faust* comes a vision of creative evolution. It is only to be borne in mind that Goethe the philosopher was also Goethe the poet and the fragmentary playwright. There are scenes in which Goethe is only playing with his theme and enjoying a bout with the world of nonsense. In fact, much of *Faust* is written whimsically. How else could Goethe present his philosophy of the indomitable will without succumbing to puerile flamboyance, inflated rhetoric and pulpit solemnities? If Dante wrote a "Divine Comedy," Goethe created a Divine Whimsy.

It would be futile to defend the whole of *Faust* as a simple stage play, although it has been successfully staged in its entirety from time to time in Europe. But it is equally futile to complain because Goethe did not choose to turn out a neat drama. He had other aims, and in realizing them he created something else—an "epic drama" or dramatic pageant. *Faust* is, in short, a poem of "experience." It is the testament of a poet who believed that man was capable of every achievement and set out to prove the proposition by devoting himself to most of the arts (poetry, fiction, drama, the essay, painting, music), to philosophy, government, botany, biology, anatomy, geology, and the theory of colors. Obviously, he could not excel in all these departments, and sometimes he was grossly in error since his method in science was largely intuitive. Like Leonardo da Vinci he failed at much, but he did not fail at experience. Therein lies his unassailable modernity. Therein, moreover, is to be found his ultra-modern principle of balance, which may be defined as repose in movement.

Gretchen is as excellent a stage character as any to be found in more perfect plays, Dr. Faust is one of the great figures of the theatre, and individual scenes like the prison scene of the First Part and the blinding of Faust in the Second Part provide great drama under any classification. But the work in its entirety defies definition. In its purposeful chaos we find the logical termination of romanticism. "To be miscellaneous, to be indefinite, to be unfinished," is as Santayana noted, "essential to the romantic life." Only the last part of Santayana's statement—namely, that romanticism is "obstinately empirical, and *will never learn anything from experience*"—is not justly applicable to Goethe. Goethe learned from experience as much as any classicist or realist.

The proper charge against *Faust* is that it becomes blatantly operatic here and there,* and that it often indulges in more nonsense than it can carry off with good effect. Goethe was not a narrow nationalist, and he prided himself on being a cosmopolitan or a "good European." But he could not overcome the Germanic inclination toward elephantiasis. There is little pleasure in watching an elephant become skittish.

Fortunately, however, Goethe's divagations from good taste are compensated by superlative lyricism, intellectual vigor, and a serenity born of respect for the dignity of man—which included a generous supply of self-respect. The symbol of a pachyderm for this "poet of pure experience" falls short of justice. For it may be substituted Heine's half-mocking, half-reverential picture of an Olympian Zeus which Goethe's majestic figure and steadfast eyes suggested. "When I visited him," Heine reported, "I involuntarily glanced around to see if I might not behold at his side the eagle with the thunderbolt in its beak. I was about to address him in Greek. But, as I noticed that he understood German, I told him in the latter language that the plums along the roadside were excellent. . . . And Goethe smiled. He smiled with the same lips with which he had once kissed the beautiful Leda, Europa, Danae, Semele, and many other princess or ordinary nymph"—including the housekeeper Christiane who finally became his wife.

* It is not surprising that it was turned into an opera by Berlioz, Gounod, and Boito, not to mention nearly a dozen less-important efforts.

XVIII

ROMANTICISM OVER EUROPE

GOETHE illustrates the well-known tendency of the major writers of drama to project the promptings of dynamic periods of human history. Eighteenth-century protests against social stagnation and dreams of an enriched humanity meet in his bloodstream with the nineteenth century's faith in man's ability to subjugate nature by means of practical activity. But Goethe was one of those rare writers who contain in themselves whole worlds which less comprehensive personalities can capture only in fragments. During his lifetime, while he outgrew the extravagances of *Sturm und Drang* so that he could at last announce his conviction that "the classical is health; and the romantic disease," and several decades after he died, the lesser luminaries of the theatre struggled with the changing world in dubious battle, sometimes retreating into private shelters and sometimes attacking recklessly.

Some of them coddled the ego which the romantic movement had overrated and aired their soul-sickness. Others returned to the revolutionary attitudinizing of the earlier period, and still others sought to express their rebellion in new dramatic forms. Finally romanticism began to make way for tentative realism in playwriting.

Few of the plays of these romanticists and of the practical showmen who grew up in their midst rank high. But some of their efforts comprise a chapter in the transition from romanticism to realism in the theatre; and other works—in the main, highly extravagant ones—indicate a trend toward genuinely modern psychological drama.

I THE GERMAN ROMANTICS—DEBIT AND CREDIT

Set beside Goethe, the other romanticists of the German school look like so many weak sisters, and the temptation to dismiss them with a casual reference is strong. They were all failures because they possessed Goethe's sensibility without the strong intelligence which enabled him to look at the world without blinking. Frightened by the march of events in Europe, by the blazing star of Napoleon and by the rise of an industrial society, they withdrew into the snail-shell of frantic inversion. A Kotzebue or an Iffland in Germany and a Nestroy in Austria * could

* Kotzebue, who exceeded Schiller's popularity, became the source of many adaptations, among which we find Sheridan's *Pizarro* (a "hack Bucephalus," if one

turn out third-rate trash for the edification of the multitude. But the convinced romanticists who were active in the last three decades of Goethe's long life would have no traffic with the actual or even superficially romanticized world. They drifted into a mystic or flabby kind of Catholicism, and espoused a morbid and sensational medievalism. To Goethe, who never departed from his antipathy to the Middle Ages, which he considered the era of intellectual darkness, they seemed puerile. They, in turn, considered him unfeeling and superficial.

Ludwig Tieck, although a leader of this second and largely reactionary romantic movement, showed a grain of common sense. He composed an able Aristophanic satire in his *Puss in Boots,* he encouraged the cult of Shakespeare, and lent his name to the most famous German translation of the bard's works. Tieck's play *Genoveva,* the legend of a saint, is reasonably rational, and his versions of Ben Jonson's *Volpone* and *The Silent Woman* are excellent.

Karl Gutzkow, who was born in 1811, belonged to a third period of German romanticism which returned to liberal idealism. The new group, which called itself "Young Germany," had only contempt for the reactionary romanticists who aired their soul-sickness during the Napoleonic period. It will be remembered that liberals like Bruno Bauer and revolutionists like Karl Marx sprang from the new movement. Gutzkow's work is therefore free from morbidity and is fired by zeal for a liberal Germany. His best known play *Uriel Acosta,* the tragedy of a Jewish heretic, is a searching picture of the struggle for intellectual freedom.

The young genius Georg Büchner, Gutzkow's protégé who died in his twenty-fourth year after being hounded by the police during the revolutionary years of the eighteen-thirties, belonged to the same dispensation. Born on October 17, 1813 near Darmstadt and saddled with a tyrannical father who was unsympathetic to his son's literary efforts, he reached maturity during revolutionary rumblings of the thirties in Germany. He studied the natural sciences and philosophy at Strassburg and Giessen, where he became an active conspirator in his student days. Here in 1834 he published and distributed his revolutionary pamphlet *The Hessian Courtier,* later considered one of the most brilliant brochures in the German language and hailed as one of the notable pre-Marxist pronouncements on socialism. Forced to flee the Duchy of Hesse-Darmstadt, he went to Strassburg. In the remaining two years of his short life—he died on February 19, 1837—he became disillusioned regarding all dreams of revolution, which had cost his associate three years of imprisonment, and devoted himself to notable scientific studies

may use the adapter's own apt phrasing). Nestroy was long popular in Central Europe, and one of his farces supplied the incentive for Thornton Wilder's failure of the 1938-39 season *The Merchant of Yonkers.*

that earned him a doctorate and lectureship in comparative anatomy at the University of Zurich.

His literary work included, in addition to the above-mentioned pamphlet and an unfinished novel *Lenz,* translations of two of Victor Hugo's plays, a play *Pietro Aretino* destroyed because of its unorthodoxies by the woman he loved, one short comedy, one full-length tragedy, and one great fragment. His short play *Leonce and Lena* was a clever romantic whimsy, as well as a satire on the aristocracy. The fragment *Woyzeck,* which was turned into an opera in our day by the modernist Alban Berg, is the gripping tragedy of a Slavic soldier who is persecuted by Prussian superiors who stretch his nerves on a rack and betray him with his wife, until he kills her and drowns himself.

In 1835, the young playwright became manifestly disheartened. Revolution had lost its glamour for him, and his hero Danton in *Danton's Death (Dantons Tod),* written in 1835, goes to his death as a disillusioned liberal who is sick of the bloodshed he had started. *Danton's Death* is an overrated drama; its structure is disjointed and its terse style easily becomes gnomic. But it has flashes of unquestionable genius in the breathless pace of the events, the picture of mob hysteria, and the characterization of Danton and of Robespierre, the ruthless instrument of self-righteousness.

Büchner was a forerunner of both naturalism and expressionism in the drama, although his life was cut short before he could develop the possibilities of either style. He had the naturalist's "despair over life's uncleanliness" and the expressionist's technique of substituting psychologically suggestive brief scenes for elaborately developed situations. He was, in effect, an anti-romanticist in his romantic milieu. His philosophy of character, which stemmed from the outlook of nineteenth-century mechanistic science, is a distinct departure from "storm and stress" heroics. *Danton's Death,* with its portraits of Danton and Robespierre, who are both caught in the swirl of an unleashed revolution, exemplifies his deterministic outlook. "Individuals," he wrote, explaining himself, "are so much surf on a wave, greatness the sheerest accident, the strength of genius a puppet play—a child's struggle against an iron law."

The romanticists of the Napoleonic era, however, were birds of an altogether different feather, combining extravagant theatricality with fuliginous mysticism; most of them were ruffled peacocks pretending that they were phoenixes. The fiction writers, Fouqué and Brentano, and the lyric poets Körner and Uhland turned out rickety medieval plays. But the prize goes to the playwrights Werner, Klingemann and Müllner, who beat the air with frenetic inspiration.

As a clinical exhibit, and a sufficient contrast to Goethe's treatment, one may offer the conclusion of Klingemann's *Faust.* Faust in this play was allowed four sins before the Devil could seize him. When he exhausts three chances in causing the death of his wife, his child, and his father, the Devil or Stranger comes to seize him. Faust protests: "Accursed! Ha! I am! I am! Down at my feet! I am thy master!" When the Stranger says "No more," Faust inquires "More? Ha! My Bargain!" The Stranger tells him that it is concluded, since he also committed the *fourth* sin by concluding the pact with the Devil: "This signature— was thy most damning sin." Faust rages, "Hamspirit of lies!" But the Stranger "in highest fury" [*sic*], thunders "Down, thou accursed!" and drags him away by the hair. The scene changes to "a horrid wilderness," fire rains down on all sides, and Faust descends into the appropriate regions, "huzzaing" in wild defiance, "Ha, down! Down!"

This demonstration removes the necessity of continuing the record, unless one takes note of Müllner who swelled the list of eccentric masterpieces with a proper regard for incest and mystic fate in his *Twenty-ninth of February;* this is the date when the progeny of an incestuous woodcutter must be visited by a catastrophe every fourth year until they are all murdered—to the great relief of the reader. All these works are equivalents of the so-called Gothic romances of which there are such familiar English examples as Walpole's *Castle of Otranto* and Mrs. Radcliffe's *Mysteries of Udolpho*.

Such was the upshot of the straining for the marvelous, the flight into the blue, and the escape into subjectivism sanctioned by the philosophy of the regressive or decadent period of romanticism. Its theory and practice were both effects of the sentimental overvaluation of personal uniqueness, the keynote of which is sounded by Rousseau in the naïve opening lines of his *Confessions:* "I am different from all men I have seen. If I am not better, at least I am different."

Beginning as a revolt against a decrepit aristocratic regime and a staid pre-revolutionary middle class, the cult of "uniqueness" later became the defense mechanism of an intelligentsia that was disheartened by the excesses of the Revolution and its sequels—Napoleonism, war; and the grasping, materialistic society so vividly described by Balzac. Among critics, Goethe's early mentor Herder, who did not altogether lose sight of objective realities, stressed the fact that genius was intuitive. But Schelling, coming somewhat later, already went further and announced that the activity of the mind was mystic.[1] And the theoretician of decadent romanticism August Wilhelm Schlegel, pontificated in the first decade of the nineteenth century that the "fancy" of the moderns must be "incorporeal," that writers must deal with "higher feelings" to the neglect of concrete realities, and that the "finite and mortal" must be "lost in the contemplation of *infinity*."

It is only fair, however, to record the fact that the insanity of the period was relieved by a glimmer of intelligence and talented playwriting in Heinrich von Kleist who wrote one healthy comedy of some distinction *The Broken Pitcher* (*Der zerbrochene Krug*), in 1808, one clearly realized historical drama *Die Hermannschlacht,* dealing with the defeat of the Romans by the Germans under Arminius and alluding to the possibility of an uprising against Napoleon in 1809, and one solid psychological study of a military hero who goes to pieces before his decreed execution, *The Prince of Homburg.* There is considerable Prussianism in this piece and some chauvinism pervades the *Hermannschlacht,* for Kleist was fired by a passionate desire to see Napoleon routed from Germany. The apathetic state of his divided nation darkened Kleist's mind before he ended his life at the age of thirty-four, in 1811, in a suicide pact with his beloved.

Kleist also wrote two morbid psychological dramas: *Das Käthchen von Heilbronn,* a study of the Griselda complex in which a masochistic maiden endures every humiliation from the man she loves and follows; and *Penthesilea,* in which the Amazon Queen's love for Achilles takes the form of a sadistic murder of the hero for whom she is tempted to violate the laws of the Amazon world. He also essayed an unfinished fusion of all the arts—a romantic *mélange des genres!*—in his *Robert Guiscard;* only a beautifully written fragment survives, as Kleist burned his manuscript in an access of despair.

Kleist is a fascinating dramatist who still waits for an effective interpreter to the English-reading public. He is the unrecognized father of modern psychological drama, the forerunner of Strindberg and O'Neill. It is, in fact, not surprising that the morbid introspection of the romanticists should have given birth to the psychological literature that is a major achievement of the late nineteenth and the twentieth centuries which produced Dostoyevsky, Proust, and Joyce. It is unfortunate only that his most ambitious efforts are tantalizing, painful, and confusing. Out of his morbidity he wove a world of the deepest psychiatric observations. But he made the mistake of confusing the theatre with a clinic. Only a great genius could cope with his material, and Kleist died before he could prove whether he qualified for the title.

The only other dramatist of note, the popular Austrian Franz Grillparzer, was an eclectic and synthetic dramatist who outlived his school, dying in 1872 at the age of eighty-one. His *Ahnfrau* or *Ancestress,* written in 1817 while the temperature of German romanticism was still at boiling point, has all the *frissons·* of Gothic romance. His *Jewess of Toledo,* a repugnant but intense work, resembles Kleist's psychological dramas; an infatuated king realizes the worthlessness of his mistress and the grossness of his passion for her only when he is shown her dead body. *King Ottokar's Fortune and End* is an inflated attempt at Schilleresque historical drama that is not without pathos in the characterization of the ill-fated Bohemian ruler who realizes at last the vanity of imperial power. A philosophical comedy, *The Dream Is a Life* (*Der Traum ein Leben*), influenced by Calderón, preaches quiescence but makes original use of the dream technique in drama, and *Woe to Him Who Lies* (*Weh' dem der lügt*) is fairly entertaining, although it is to be better remembered for the fact that its suppression at the *Burgtheater* in 1838 because of the author's alleged liberal sentiments caused his permanent retirement from the stage. *Sappho,* a treatment of the love-tragedy of the Greek poetess, is a tender and limpidly written drama of no great consequence, as is another love-drama concerning Hero and Leander. But his *Golden Fleece* trilogy, which treats the Medea story from a modern historical and psychological viewpoint, is for all its verbosity and length a work of depth and power that has yet to find effective champions in the English-speaking world. Medea's plight is that of a foreigner in a world which does not countenance the elementary standards of love and hate to which Medea was accustomed in her homeland before she followed Jason to Greece. She loses his love by clinging to the former adventurer with an intensity that is off pitch in his own humdrum world. The legendary catastrophe, her murder of her children, is an inevitable and carefully mitigated circumstance. Only the reflection that Euripides said almost as much in less time and space diminishes one's enthusiasm for Grillparzer's *magnum opus.*

It is, in fact, only in the related field of the opera that post-Goethean romantic drama in Germany achieved a measure of greatness. Richard Wagner's music-dramas, which cannot be discussed here, attack their romantic material of medieval knights and Germanic warriors and deities with the dual resources of jingling poetic libretti and magnificent music, both composed by himself. Considered purely as dramas most of Wagner's operas are hopelessly verbose and extravagant. It would be, in fact, unfair to judge them as plays if Wagner had not tried to stress dramatic values, and if he did not believe he was the direct successor to Shakespeare. Wagner believed he was creating super-theatre, and even refused to be called a musician. He also believed he was giving the world a great vision. Actually, however, his operas are simply musical expressions of extreme romantic matter, ranging from the idealizations of love one finds in *Tannhäuser* and *Lohengrin* to the far-flung cosmic symbolism of the "Ring" cycle. Of Wagner's original intention to show the old gods destroyed by their greed and failure to order the world, very little remained in the final version. Wagner, who began as a persecuted "Young Germany" man, ended in the bosom of Schopenhauerian philosophy, writing off the world as illusion; then taking the final viaticum in *Parsifal*, much to his friend Nietzsche's disgust, he became a Christian mystic.

It is incontestable that the grandiose efforts of the romantics found their proper transubstantiation in Wagnerian opera. Most of the playwrights had an operatic imagination without a musical talent; Wagner combined both. Moreover, he was able to give concrete realization to the romantic dream of a fusion or *mélange* of the arts which alone would attain a complete magic and expressiveness.

2 THE DIFFUSION OF ROMANTICISM

Although the rest of Europe does not reveal the accomplishments and extravagances of romantic drama to the same degree as Germany, the stream wound through the Western World without respect for boundaries. From France to Russia, from Scandinavia to Italy runs the current, and insular England is girt by it. Everywhere, however, the main achievement of the romantic movement is to be found in poetry, and most of the plays are shoddy as drama.

In brief review we note the dramas of Adam Oehlenschläger; his *Correggio*, his historical tragedy *Hakon Jarl*, and other plays drawn from the romantic age of medieval Scandinavia. Born in 1779 he lived until 1849 and was acclaimed as the "Scandinavian King of Song." His influence on the young Ibsen should not be minimized. Italy vibrated to the tremor of romanticism in the work of several undistinguished playwrights of whom Pindemonti with his sentimental *Ginevra of Scotland* is the best remembered along with the tragedies of the exalted poet Vittorio Alfieri. Alfieri observed the "unities" scrupulously, so that the mold of his monotonous dramas was strictly classic. But their patriotic and liberal idealism was romantic. His *Philip II*, which employs the same subject as Schiller's *Don Carlos*, painted its subject as a darksome tyrant and glorified his liberal son Don Carlos; his *Virginius* treated the same material that Lessing converted into middle-class drama in *Emilia Galotti*.

In Russia, the liberal romantic movement flowered as "Byronism," tussled with the autocracy of Alexander II, and exploded toward the end of the year 1825 in the conspiracy of the "Decembrists." It found its major expression in the poetry and fiction of the two geniuses of first rank Pushkin and Lermontov. Pushkin also revealed a notable dramatic talent. His short pieces *The Miser Knight, The Feast During the Plague, Don Juan* and *Mozart and Salieri* are minor efforts, although the two last mentioned miniatures are decidedly interesting. Some critics regard these "miniature plays," as Pushkin called them, as distinct innovations, since they are not, strictly speaking, one-acters but nervous dramatiza-

tions of the crisis or climax in a character's life. Moreover, Pushkin's
major contribution *Boris Godunov,* written in verse and prose under
Shakespearean influence, is a powerful chronicle play. The tragedy of
the usurper Boris, who removed Ivan the Terrible's heir Dmitry or Demetrius in order to make himself Tsar of Russia, is permeated with
anguish born of a sense of guilt. The portrait of the ambitious monk who
pretends to be Demetrius is vividly executed, and powerful mob scenes
bring the masses into the historical picture. *Boris Godunov,* for all its
structural flaws, is a vivid evocation of seventeenth-century Russia and
a well-realized study of criminal ambition. Pushkin, living in exile in
Southern Russia, had overcome his subjective Byronism when he began
to compose the tragedy in 1824, and the exigencies of dramatic construction further encouraged the lyric poet to adopt historical objectivity.

The bulk of non-Germanic drama in the romantic vein is to be found,
however, in England and France, where non-dramatic literature was
most notably active. By their influence on European culture England
and France, next to Germany, left the greatest impression on the drama
that preceded the advent of realism.

3 THE POETS IN THE ENGLISH THEATRE

As the best stabilized country in Europe, Britain was not at first a
fertile soil for the revolutionary excrescences of "storm and stress."
The French Revolution in 1789 did, of course, find supporters in England, particularly among the young poets Coleridge, Wordsworth, and
Southey. Coleridge, in addition to composing a sentimental tragedy *Remorse* and an imitation of Shakespeare's *Winter's Tale* in his *Zapolya,*
translated Schiller's *Wallenstein.* But the excesses of the upheaval across
the Channel aroused a reaction that discouraged revolutionary romantic
drama. Many a young firebrand became a middle-aged conservative like
Wordsworth, and Coleridge celebrated the end of the Terror in the short
and exciting but hopelessly rhetorical play *The Fall of Robespierre.*
England, therefore, remained satisfied with mystery melodramas, theatrical versions of the Gothic romance of vengeful ghosts, and artificial horrors like Matthew Gregory Lewis' *The Castle Spectre* and *Rugantino.*
The work of Lewis is historically important for its favoring of "melodrama," which is literally drama supported by "melody" or music. Owing to the fact that the plays of Lewis and his school used every resource
of horror, the form became synonymous with violent superficial action
even without musical accompaniment; it survives as the modern murder
mystery and thriller. These exercises debased the English theatre for
many decades. Only the performances of such famous actors as Macready
and Kean kept the stage from complete destruction.

Acting, in fact, was an important concomitant of the romantic movement in Europe. The German stage owed a great deal to Ekhof, who was called "the German Garrick" for his development of restraint in the art, and to Friedrich Ludwig Schröder who as actor-manager struggled to revive the Hamburg National Theatre and promoted ensemble acting long before it triumphed in the Moscow Art Theatre. Later, Ludwig Devrient developed emotionalism to accord with the decadent romanticists' worship of feeling, and his followers appropriately favored a pale and emaciated appearance with sorrowful eyes and an ineffably melancholy spirit. In France Talma, squirming in the conventional straitjacket, managed to infuse stilted pseudo-classic drama with unusual energy and emotion, and his successor Frédéric Lemaître met the most extravagant demands of Victor Hugo's dramas with notable passionateness. Rachel Felix, the first Semitic queen of French tragedy, made the works of Racine a vehicle for stormy emotionalism, thereby again turning dramatic classicism into theatrical romanticism.

In England the great eighteenth-century age of acting continued into the nineteenth century. The virtuous and stately Sarah Siddons, who made a successful début at the Drury Lane Theatre in 1782, transformed the "noble" classic style into a personal experience, and her less inspired brother John Philip Kemble, the actual director of Drury Lane while Sheridan remained its nominal head, galvanized restrained acting and production into an effective theatrical experience. Surviving into the next century, Kemble supervised the transition of the English stage to the age of romantic acting which was epitomized by Edmund Kean. Kean, who made his début at Drury Lane in 1814, met all the requirements of the romantics with his heightened emotionalism and wild appearance. In Shakespearean roles like Richard III and Othello he gave his contemporaries a taste, for better and worse, of what acting must have been like when Alleyn and Burbage trod the boards of the great "O" of the Elizabethan public theatres. Coleridge paid him the supreme tribute of the Romantics when he declared that to watch Kean was "like reading Shakespeare by flashes of lightning." Even when the English drama was torpid, the English theatre breathed intensely, thanks to its actors.

Still, the reactionary regime of Castlereagh and the promptings of the French Revolution (distant enough by 1820 to cause no alarm to the new generation of writers) aroused a second wave of liberal romanticism. Although the commercial theatre was largely averse to the new stream, the drama received some of the overflow. John Sheridan Knowles' theatrical but largely vapid verse plays *Virginius* in 1820 and *William Tell* in 1825 reflected the new spirit, and genuine poets invested it with distinction in their plays.

Byron's *Sardanapalus* is mere flamboyant orientalism, *The Deformed Transformed* and *Heaven and Earth* are negligible, and *Werner* possesses dramatic power without much interest for us. But his Venetian tragedies *Marino Faliero* and *The Two Foscari* honor the spirit of rebellion in a sometimes effective, if largely pseudo-classical and congested, manner. It is a mistake to consider Byron deficient in dramatic ability; he certainly had the right temperament. *Manfred* with its coddling of soul-sickness, its mumbo-jumbo about inexpressible guilt, and its sentimentalization of the "unique soul," dramatizes the romantics' defiance of convention. Although this dramatic poem, written in 1817, is intellectually contemptible by the side of *Faust*, which it resembles, it is not without a perverse kind of power. There is, moreover, unmistakable force and pathos in *Cain*, which celebrates the first murderer as the first rebel against authority. Cain rages against a God who condemns beings to Hell, loves blood and desires the sacrifice of innocent animals on his altars. Nor will he worship Jehovah for doubtful benefits:

> *For what must I be grateful?*
> *For being dust, and groveling in the dust,*
> *Till I return to dust? If I am nothing—*
> *For nothing shall I be an hypocrite. . . .*

Cain, entitled a "mystery drama," is an intransigent version of the medieval Cain plays. The fourteenth century would have considered it the work of the Devil.

An even greater poet, Shelley, wrote the decidedly better play *The Cenci*, which is in fact the only English tragedy between the Elizabethan age and the twentieth century that possesses some genuine greatness. The poet was in virtual exile in Italy in 1819 when he received a copy of the old manuscript which recounted the tyranny and incest of Count Francesco Cenci who oppressed his immediate family, as well as his subjects, and assaulted his own daughter Beatrice. Fired by this sixteenth-century story of oppression—and tyranny always sent Shelley into a frenzy of anger and made him cry out with all the pathos of a wounded spirit!—the young poet wrote memorable, if somewhat verbose, tragedy in *The Cenci*.

Beatrice is a magnificent heroine, worthy of Webster, if not of Shakespeare; her equally unhappy stepmother Lucretia is a deeply realized portrait of a helpless victim; and several of the other characters are etched with remarkable precision. Although Count Cenci is a melodramatic villain, he is also more than that. He is the product of unchecked power and social corruption which is condoned by the Church, then in its moral nadir. He has always been able to buy off the guardians of justice with a slice of his property, and he can think of no crime that he cannot commit with impunity. His victims, led by the wronged Beatrice, can find no alternative to having him murdered. And such is the state of society and of the Church (which is not, however, without one noble representative) that it is only when the victims have risen up to defend themselves that the long arm of justice intervenes. Suddenly it is discovered that "law and order" have been violated, and Beatrice and her associates are executed! Beatrice, condemned by her papal judges, goes to her death unbroken in spirit and triumphant in her tragically won knowledge of "what a world we make, the oppressor and the oppressed"—a vision worthy of Euripides.

Shelley, who always surprises the "Ariel" school of his biographers whenever he exhibits some sense of reality, maintained a common-sense attitude toward the drama. He intended the play not for the pages of a book but for the stage of the Covent Garden Theatre and made an attempt to interest the capable Miss O'Neill and Edmund Kean. The subject of incest was, however, considered objectionable and the play did not receive a public performance in England until November 13, 1922, during the centenary celebrations of the poet's death. Apparently in the hope of seeing the tragedy performed on the American stage, and "out of an overmastering desire to present this great drama in a form as simple and as direct as itself," Robert Edmond Jones made six suggestive drawings in 1912. But the Broadway theatre remained oblivious to the hint. (The first private performance in England was by the Shelley Society in 1886.)

In spite of speeches of greater length than is feasible in the non-classic theatre, Shelley also respected the requirements of the drama more than most of the other romantic poets. He kept his action simple and direct even when he delved into psychological subtleties worthy of the twentieth century. *The Cenci,* he declared, "is not colored by my feelings nor obscured by my metaphysics."

Shelley's successors, however, did not improve upon his example, or even equal it. The unique poet Thomas Lovell Beddoes wrote two scattered romantic exercises, *The Bride's Tragedy* and the morbid *Death's Jest-Book,* both under the influence of the German school and of native products like Maturin's feverish *Bertram.* His plays give off sparks from the Elizabethan smithy like

> *Nature's polluted,*
> *There's man in every secret corner of her. . . .*

but they completely defy stage production.

Keats wrote uninspired and lagging plays, Matthew Arnold later tried classic drama, Swinburne classic and romantic pieces—all negligible as theatre. Tennyson in *Harold, The Cup, Becket* and other efforts revealed a minor talent for the poetic drama, and his *Becket,* as late as 1884 even proved, after sufficient pruning, a vehicle for Sir Henry Irving. Although Robert Browning's poetic plays *Strafford, A Blot on the 'Scutcheon,* and *Colombe's Birthday* were once also found stageworthy, they reveal his considerable dramatic talent far less than do his famous dramatic monologues. Between tenuous literary drama and worthless popular plays like Bulwer-Lytton's *The Lady of Lyons* there was a wide gap that no one in England filled to any extent until the last decade of the century.

4 VICTOR HUGO AND THE FRENCH ROMANTICS

France, where romantic literature had prospered since Rousseau and was further emotionalized by Madame de Staël and Chateaubriand, held on to pseudo-classical drama until about 1830 for reasons already noted. Then when the theatre finally felt the romantic afflatus it accepted the bravura of Victor Hugo and of the fabulous Alexandre Dumas.

Dumas' *Henry III and his Court,* first acted in 1829, was a romantic historical drama in which the king's mother tries to cement her control over him by setting her possible rivals St. Mégrim and the Duke of Guise at loggerheads. She incites the former to make love to the latter's wife and so encompasses St. Mégrim's destruction. As a drama of intrigue, which is strengthened by several well-executed characterizations, the play possesses some power and interest. Although Dumas, the Autolycus of literature, snatched some scenes from Schiller, it is his best drama. His *Antony, Tour de Nesle, Caligula* and other efforts also display ably written scenes, but their tempo, content, and bombast belong to the indiscretions of French romanticism.

Dumas belongs largely to the field of fiction. The other playwrights of the period were in the main lyricists, although Hugo was equally adept at fiction. The passionate poet Alfred de Musset wrote a historical drama *Lorenzaccio* in the proper hypomanic mood, as well as some very graceful comedies, among which his "comediettas"—entertaining one-acters built around old saws—can still be enjoyed. One of these, *A Door Must Be Either Open or Shut,* in which a Count's sentimental love-making is accepted unceremoniously by a Marquise, is neat and witty in a manner which is, in fact, anti-romantic. (See page 353 for De Musset's modernism.)

The excellent poet Alfred de Vigny created dignified tragedy in *Chatterton,* a play dealing with the sufferings and death of the unhappy young English poet who had long been cited as an example of how the Philistines mistreat poetic genius. Although written with more than customary restraint, it is a typical example of romantic sentimentality. To the bread-and-butter bourgeois world of the post-Napoleonic Era the French romanticists liked to oppose the aristocracy of the artist class.

However, the honor of actually tearing down the tenaciously defended classic portals was reserved for that juggernaut of French letters Victor Hugo. He announced his program of doing away with the "unities" (about half a century after Lessing!) in the preface to his unproduced historical drama *Cromwell,* which failed to observe unity of action and was full of riotous stage movement even if it never got anywhere. The play was written in 1824 for the great French actor Talma, who was prevented by death from appearing in it. In 1829 came his *Marion Delorme,* perhaps the first sentimentalization in the French theatre of the eternal courtesan. Then in 1830 the main assault started with his *Hernani,* a wildly romantic treatment of love and honor in the Spanish manner. Hernani the outlaw and Don Carlos the heir-apparent are rivals for the ward of an old Spanish nobleman who intends to marry her himself. Hernani joins a conspiracy against Don Carlos who is now the king of Spain, but the latter having been elected emperor of the Holy Roman Empire exercises regal magnanimity. He restores Hernani to his title and lands and bestows the heroine upon him. Then at the height of the lover's ecstasy the old Count asserts a claim upon his life and Hernani honorably follows the Count's horn which calls him to death. The play is of the right operatic vintage (it survives now chiefly in opera), and it is difficult to see eye to eye with the period that hailed it as a masterpiece even if it still makes exciting theatre. But *Hernani* was not only a play but a cause, and literary causes raise the temperature more appreciably in France than anywhere on the planet—except perhaps in Ireland! *Hernani* became the occasion of a pitched battle between the conservative literati and the romanticists, who went forth dressed in full regalia to do battle in the pit. The play won the day, and its services in clearing the way for modern French realism cannot be dismissed lightly.

Hugo's later plays followed the same pyrotechnic formula. *The King Amuses Himself* (*Le Roi s'Amuse*) in 1832 dramatized the vengeance of the king's jester against the profligate master who has seduced his daughter. Although the play, which was prohibited by the government for daring to bespatter royalty, simply revels in excitement, it can now be endured only in a suitable reincarnation—in Verdi's *Rigoletto.* Then Hugo, who had given these works the benefit of his genuine though overblown poetic gifts, took another step toward liberating French tragedy by writing the prose dramas *Lucrèce Borgia* (turned into an opera by Donizetti), *Mary Tudor,* and *Angélo.* Finally, he returned to the grand style with *Ruy Blas,* another Spanish tragedy even more poetical than *Hernani,* likewise converted into an opera, and with a trilogic fiasco entitled *The Burgraves.*

Hugo labored like a mountain, and since such thumping birth pangs are theatrically impressive, he remains a ponderable figure in the theatre's annals. But the dramatic work of this poet who has been aptly called a "Michelangelo in *terra cotta*" is more grandiose than substantial. He dissipated, it is true, the slow-motion, recitative technique of

French classicism, and he helped to prepare the theatre for the reception of any kind of experiment on the principle that there should be "no more formulas, no standards of any sort." But the uses to which he put the new freedom were themselves artificial, and his exotic art was, therefore, a quickly extinguished blaze. Even in the heyday of his success, in fact, he shared his popularity with one who wooed the large prosaic world of the middle classes, and the march of the drama was to leave the gargantuan romanticist far behind.

5 SCRIBE AND SARDOU

The general direction of the drama was largely traced by the practical playwright Eugène Scribe, who wrote nearly five hundred plays for popular consumption. Scribe, who was born on the twenty-first of December, 1791, was a perfect Christmas gift to the entertainment-seeking bourgeoisie of Paris. He began the successful part of his prolific career in 1816 with the composition of a one-act vaudeville and thereafter turned out every kind of play—comedies, tragedies, and vaudeville farces, as well as libretti for Meyerbeer like the successful *Robert le Diable* (1831) in which the Devil is suitably sentimentalized into a tender father. He became a veritable factory, paying royalties for other men's ideas; theatre for this paragon of middle-class efficiency was a business, and he made it a profitable one.

Scribe's plays presented elaborate, carefully contrived and neatly resolved plots in which an intrigue clicked smoothly like a well-oiled machine. Letters were planted and discovered at the appropriate moment, suspense was maintained at any cost, and in the conclusion of the piece all knots were tied together, leaving nothing that the intellect would have to examine or ponder. Even when he deals with contemporary heiresses, flighty wives, shopgirls, millionaires, and careerists who use adultery as a stepping-stone to fortune, Scribe is chiefly occupied with making his plot leap through the hoops without a mishap. A typical Scribe play like his *Verre d'Eau* or *A Glass of Water* provides a perfect example of his technique. It revolves around intrigues at the court of Queen Anne of England. The Whigs led by the mettlesome Duchess of Marlborough are at odds with the Tory opposition under Bolingbroke which seeks to terminate the costly war with France. Bolingbroke uses a pair of lovers, Masham and Abigail, to further his intrigue against the Duchess who dominates the Queen. Since the latter is in love with Masham, Bolingbroke effects a rupture between Anne and the Duchess by hinting that the handsome young officer has become Marlborough property.

Scribe's name has become synonymous with trashy playwriting. Such is time's revenge on the mechanic who dominated the French theatre for half a century. And, as usual, time is a trifle unfair to his mediocrity. He set an example of closely knit dramaturgy which proved helpful to Ibsen and others who needed a neat edifice for the realities that could not be scattered over the stage in Shakespearean or romantic fashion. The "well-made play" or *pièce-bien-faite* which he favored is not theoretically a felony. It is artificial, of course; but then the theatre is artificial, too. A convention is not objectionable; only its results can be so. The completely valid objection to Scribe, the real reason for his obsolescence, is the superficiality with which he treated his material. Whatever his subject might be—whether he accepted romantic or everyday material that might pass for realism—Scribe wrote without distinction, vision, or depth. At most in *Verre d'Eau* he intimated that history often depended on petty details, since the important course of English politics in the play is affected by Queen Anne's infatuation. Scribe, in short, was too exclusively the showman to become a dramatist. And he was content to remain simply a showman. Only in the vastly popular collaboration with Ernest Legouvé, *Adrienne Lecouvreur,* the tragedy of the great eighteenth-century actress who was allegedly poisoned by her aristocratic rival, did he aspire to a niche in literature.

Scribe's mantle fell on Sardou, who was forty years his junior. Like his master, Sardou tried everything that would meet the popular interests of his day without evaluating them or seeking to probe any possible depths either in general problems or in characterization. It was immaterial to him whether he wrote realistic or romantic drama so long as it "clicked." On the one hand, he could turn out a piece like *Divorçons* in response to a law legalizing divorce in France. The husband in the play encourages his wife's lover to visit her at home so often that she tires of him. On the other hand, he could parade in Hugo's feathers—without Hugo's wings, of course, since he was no poet. The romantic *élan* spawns a *Tosca* (the source of Puccini's opera) in which the passionate heroine avenges her lover when a villainous official condemns him to death for trying to save a political offender. Romance also palpitates like an artificially made heart in the vastly popular *Fedora* in which a Russian princess ruins her fiancé's murderer, falls in love with him, and finally kills herself when he is about to be imprisoned in Siberia on the strength of information against him which she herself supplied before becoming infatuated with him. Fortunately Sardou had the great actress Sarah Bernhardt to impart the illusion of reality to these trumperies. He was sufficiently theatre-wise to keep her in mind when he wrote this kind of claptrap, and to restrain his grand manner when she was no longer young enough to sustain new parts.

He has been contemptuously called a "barometer playwright" and a "journalist-playwright." But there is nothing particularly contemptible in keeping a weather eye on one's milieu; and in this tendency he was actually a forerunner of realistic drama. The real trouble with Sardou was that he saw only surfaces and that he was not even interested in regarding surfaces too closely so long as he could piece out a play. On the rare occasions when he did become intellectually involved in a contemporary situation he thought like a butter-and-egg man, with that worthy's superficial and property-conditioned mentality. He primed his satirical comedy *Rabagas* in 1872 against Gambetta and the French liberals, his picture of the Reign of Terror *Thermidor* against French republicanism, and his *Uncle Sam* against the United States, which he accused of favoring Germany in the Franco-Prussian War. His idealism at its highest produced a smooth historical melodrama like *Patrie,* in which heroic self-sacrifice for one's country overshadows any analysis of characters and issues. Normally, he celebrated the decencies of married love in French households and earned a pretty penny by coming out for morality. When he turned to larger domestic problems as in the conflict between a scientist and his wife in *Daniel Rochat,* Sardou made sure that the scientist and unbeliever would be properly punished; his freethinker cannot seduce the woman from her faith and the marriage ends in a separation.

To dramatists of a higher order Sardou is, moreover, an irritant on technical and artistic grounds. He described his method as one of finding a situation and fitting character to it. His characters consequently lack the breath of life. For this mechanical art, successful though it proved, Shaw—who fought it to the bitter end in his critical essays—found the only proper term, "Sardoodledom."

Scribe and Sardou signalize the recession of dreams and the triumph of the commonplace. The drama which had started out as a fiery Pegasus increasingly became an ordinary drayhorse, and it was naturally called upon to drag around the lumber of the common world.

6 DUMAS FILS AND AUGIER: THE END OF ROMANTICISM

There was one alternative to bearing the harness of the commonplace patiently. It was—to upset the cart! This was the method of critical or honest realism which is associated with the name of Ibsen. It was even to some small degree already beginning to be practised during the reign of Sardou. Both Alexandre Dumas *fils,* the illegitimate son of the facile romanticist, and Émile Augier moved in the direction of critical realism.

The younger Dumas made his first mark in the theatre in that sentimental vehicle *La Dame aux Camélias, The Lady of the Camellias,* in which a prostitute is ennobled by suffering and self-sacrifice. He had already told her story in a novel, but it was in the theatre that he emptied

TEXT CONTINUES ON PAGE 351 FOLLOWING THE PICTURE SECTION

PLAYWRIGHTS

PLATE 1. AESCHYLUS (525–456 B.C.) Museum of the Capitole.

PLATE 2. SOPHOCLES (496–406 B.C.) Statue in the Lateran Museum, Rome. Photo Anderson.

PLATE 3. EURIPIDES (484–406/7 B.C.) The Louvre.

PLATE 4. ARISTOPHANES (c. 448–380 B.C.) Offices Museum, Naples.
Photo Brogi.

PLATE 5. LOPE DE VEGA (1562–1635) Portrait by Carreño.

PLATE 6. WILLIAM SHAKESPEARE (1564–1616) First Folio Engraving.

BEN JONSON (1572–1637).

PIERRE CORNEILLE (1606–1684).

PLATE 7.

JEAN RACINE (1639–1699).
Theatre Collection, N. Y. Public Library.

PLATE 8.   MOLIÈRE (1622–1673). Attributed to Roland Lefebvre.
Photo Hehog Chauvet.

ROBERT BRINSLEY SHERIDAN (1751–1816).
Theatre Collection, N. Y. Public Library.

PLATE 9. WILLIAM CONGREVE (1670–1729).
From a painting by Sir Godfrey Kneller.
Photo Emery Walker.

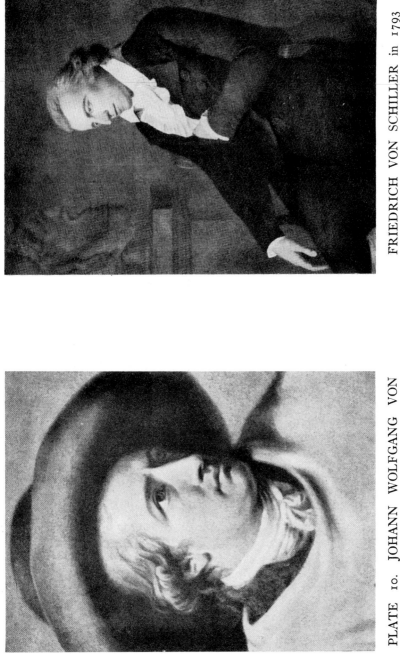

FRIEDRICH VON SCHILLER in 1793
(1759–1805). Painting by Von Simanovitz.
Schiller National Museum.

PLATE 10. JOHANN WOLFGANG VON
GOETHE (1749–1832). Goethe in Italy.
Painting by Tischbein. Goethe National Museum.

AUGUST STRINDBERG (1849–1912)
Theatre Arts.

PLATE 11. HENRIK IBSEN in 1878 (1828–1906)
Photo Franz Haufstaengel.
Courtesy of Gyldendal Norsk Forlag.

PLATE 12. (From right to left) LEO TOLSTOY (1828–1910) and
ANTON CHEKHOV (1860–1904).

PLATE 13. MAXIM GORKY (1868–1936).

PLATE 14. GERHART HAUPTMANN (1862–1946) Theatre
Collection, N. Y. Public Library.

PLATE 15.   FERENC MOLNAR (1878–1952).
Courtesy of M. Molnar.

EDMOND ROSTAND (1868–1918) Theatre
Collection, N. Y. Public Library.

PLATE 16. BERNARD SHAW (1856–1950).

SEAN O'CASEY (1884–) Photo Ben Pinchot. Courtesy of Macmillan Co.

PLATE 17. JEAN-PAUL SARTRE (1905–) Photo Roger Parry. Courtesy of Alfred A. Knopf, Inc.

T. S. ELIOT (1888–) Photo Elliott & Fry.
Courtesy of Harcourt, Brace.

PLATE 18. WILLIAM BUTLER YEATS (1865–
1939) Photo Martin Vos. Courtesy of Macmillan Co.

PLATE 19. EUGENE O'NEILL (1888–1953) Photo Cecil Thorne. Theatre Arts.

S. N. BEHRMAN (1893–) Photo Lotte Jacobi.
Courtesy of S. N. Behrman.

PLATE 20. MAXWELL ANDERSON (1888–)
Photo Karch. Courtesy of The Playwrights Company,
William Fields, press representative.

PLATE 21. ROBERT E. SHERWOOD (1896–)
Courtesy of The Playwrights Company, William
Fields, press representative.

CLIFFORD ODETS (1906–) Photo Ruth Sondak,
Keystone Pictures, Inc. Courtesy of Clifford Odets.

PLATE 22. LILLIAN HELLMAN (1905–) Photo Bender.
Courtesy of Lillian Hellman.

PLATE 23. TENNESSEE WILLIAMS (1914–) Courtesy of Audrey Wood and Tennessee Williams.

PLATE 24. ARTHUR MILLER (1916–) Photo Esther Handler.
Courtesy of James Proctor, press representative for Arthur Miller.

every tear-duct with a representation of the beautiful girl who preserves a longing for a purer life throughout her sinful career and is wasted by disease before she can be completely reclaimed. Produced after considerable delay in 1852, the tragedy proved highly successful and eased its author's financial situation considerably. That it is a romantic concoction—and a good brew solely for a certain type of actress—is only too obvious. Nevertheless, its evocation of a sordid life introduced more descriptive realism than the theatre was expected to contain. No one, in fact, dared to produce the play until Napoleon III's minister, the Duke de Morny, thought it would be a good idea to divert attention from Louis Bonaparte's *coup d'état* (which made him Emperor of France) by giving the Parisians a sensation.

Following this triumph, Dumas *fils* began to add social criticism to descriptive realism, without of course departing from the conventional dramaturgy of intrigue. His best-written play, the *Demi-Monde* or *The Outer Edge of Society,* criticized a contemporary situation—the infiltration of courtesans into respectable society. Its astute heroine Suzanne d'Ange fastens herself upon the gallant soldier de Nanjac and almost attains to the state of marriage when she is exposed and routed by his friend de Jalin. In 1855 the play seemed important and represented much application to the realities of society—to the superficial ones at least.

Two years later, moreover, Dumas turned to the more important subject of business enterprise. *La Question d'Argent* or *The Money Question* provided a fairly sharp portrait of a representative self-made man Jean Giraud who elevates profit-making to a fine art; this unscrupulous speculator could have walked out of one of Balzac's realistic novels. Thereafter, Dumas took up a variety of topical matters, concerning himself in *Le Fils Naturel* or *The Natural Son* with the problem of illegitimacy—a subject on which he could claim considerable authority, and with the woman question. In the *Idées de Madame Aubray* he even wrote a tract in favor of the rehabilitation of fallen women, although he swerved from consistency in still later plays. Consistency was, in fact, the least of his virtues, and when he retired from the stage in 1887—eight years before his death—he could gaze back upon a career that looked like a patchwork of assorted principles and ideas.

For a stricter application to realities and a firmer technique the French had to rely on his fellow-playwright Augier who began his work in 1844 during the reign of Scribe and closed his shop in 1878 shortly before the rule of Ibsen. Augier, who wrote only when he had an idea which he wished to present, was by descent half-aristocrat, half-bourgeois. Born in 1820, he grew up in the romantic movement, but evinced little taste for its flamboyance. After a brief apprenticeship with two plays, he turned to serious domestic drama with *Gabrielle.* Adultery is here represented as anything but seductive, and the husband who lost his wife by too much absorption in his business reclaims her by setting forth the disadvantages of becoming someone's mistress. Stuffy as the play must seem to us today, *Gabrielle* in 1849 represented the claims of common sense in the theatre. Augier, in fact, felt that he was divinely chosen to preserve the domestic virtues of the French, and his best serious play *The Marriage of Olympia* is a vitriolic exposé of a designing courtesan who takes advantage of a young man's inexperience. She marries him but soon tires of respectability and intends to return to the muck to which she is accustomed. Her final act is to blackmail him and his family, and only a bullet can end her depredations. Olympia and her mother are splendid portraits of gross characters, and numerous other touches provide a realistic picture of society uncommon in the French theatre. Olympia is, as Brieux noted, "the exact counterpart of Marguerite Gautier in *La Dame aux Camélias*," a completely unsentimental study. If the play in which she plies her trade seems dated today, it is because the action is so close to melodramatic villainy and intrigue.

Augier reveled in his mission and used the stage as an agency of reform—a tiresome thing unless the playwright possesses the gift of creating dynamic characters or unless he is dominated by powerful drives that keep him from droning. In *Lionnes pauvres*, a collaboration, he again warned society against domestic laxity; in *La Jeunesse* or *Youth* he called attention to the dangers of greed; in *Les Effrontés* he attacked the unscrupulous press which dominated public opinion; in *Contagion* he opposed religious skepticism. The list of his plays reads like a list of Dr. Frank Crane's admonitions.

Augier was fortunately able at times to hammer out a forceful indictment or create a powerfully realized character; in *Les Effrontés*, for example, one finds a vivid picture of society and a vigorous portrait of the upstart Vernouillet who controls public opinion because he possesses, as he says, "money and the press." And, fortunately, Augier possessed a talent for comedy; *Les Effrontés* is a satiric comedy of character and mores, and his best known play *Le Gendre de M. Poirier* or *Monsieur Poirier's Son-in-Law*, written with Jules Sandeau, is for the most part delightfully entertaining. It suffers from an easy conclusion which is tainted with sentimentality, but its portrait of a socially ambitious bourgeois and an aristocratic son-in-law who considers work beneath his dignity entitles the play to its niche in the comic theatre of the French.

Nevertheless, European realism would have been a rotarian exercise if it had remained in the hands of writers like Dumas *fils* and Augier. These writers lacked the ability to touch the emotions or to measure man in society with anything larger than a foot-rule. They possessed no aim beyond correcting misbehavior in the manner of the Society for the

Suppression of Vice, and their horizon did not extend beyond the bourgeois virtues and commonplaces. Even when they assailed the power of money in society, they were merely objecting to the enterprise of capitalists who were making life uncomfortable for the less resourceful middle classes; they rarely challenged money standards *per se*.

Brieux's tribute to Augier unintentionally points to the great gulf that separates the latter's light housecleaning from Ibsen's summary slumclearance. "Émile Augier," Brieux wrote, "has always stood for the great middle classes. Its ideals are order and regularity, justice, the family and the fireside." [2]

Mélange des genres. Lessing may have thought that he had delimited the various arts in his famous essay *Laocoon,* but the romanticists refused to accept limits to expressiveness and let reason dictate to art. They sought to express the ineffable, to evoke rare and commingled sensation, to weave a spell and produce magic. In the field of lyric poetry the results were frequently superb; such poems as *Kublai Khan, The Eve of St. Agnes,* and *The Witch of Atlas* evoked a rare visitation of sensations, so that it is impossible to separate verbal meaning, painting, and music in them. In the drama, the results were often chaotic, but not without enhancement of theatre magic, a synthesis of all the arts—as must have been the case in 5th century Athenian productions, and as it still is in the Chinese theatre and such contemporary American productions as *Oklahoma.* The most idealistic romanticists were not troubled by charges of ambiguity· and indefiniteness. They freely confessed to the intent, and Friedrich Schlegel, their critical bellwether, wrote explicitly: "It is the beginning of all poetry to abolish the laws and methods of the rationally proceeding reason, and to plunge us once more into the ravishing confusions of fantasy, the original chaos of human nature." And the romanticists' confidence that they had planted a seminal idea into the womb of all future art has been borne out in twentieth century "expressionism," "futurism," "vorticism," "surrealism," etc. We may not approve, but we cannot deny their existence and place in the history of the arts. Novalis expressed the desire for "poems which are melodious and full of beautiful words but destitute of meaning or connection" and "having an indirect effect like music." His hopes were realized, for better or worse, in Gertrude Stein's *Four Saints in Three Acts,* produced in 1934. The play made absolutely no sense, but the New York performance was hauntingly beautiful theatre.

Alfred de Musset (1810–57): The modernity of de Musset as a playwright is a surprising aspect of his romantic talent, and stands in sharp contrast to his poetry. His *Fantasio* (1833), in which a disenchanted young man saves a princess from an unhappy state marriage with pranks performed in the guise of a clown, employs romantic grotesquerie *à la* Hugo, but has incisive irony and an anti-romantic conclusion. The comic presentation of amorous bickerings in the remarkable *On ne badine pas avec l'amour* (published in 1834), translated as *No Trifling with Love,* culminates tragically; here an exquisite comedy of sentiment and manners becomes transmuted into bitter wisdom when the innocent peasant victim of the aristocratic lovers' caprices kills herself. Another play, *The Follies of Marianne* (1833), blends romantic sentiment with an anti romantic conclusion, and *The Chandler* (1935) is an ultra-sophisticated lark, not without penetration, which surpasses anything Noel Coward has written in that *genre.* (See John Gassner's *Treasury of the Theatre,* 1951, volume 1, pp. 551–60.)

* * * * *

Note: For a new translation of Buechner's memorable *Woyzeck,* made by Henry Schnitzler and Seth Ulman, see New Directions XII, 1950; here, see also Karl Viëtor's introduction, pp. 405–14.

XIX

IBSEN, THE VIKING OF THE DRAMA

I THE LONG VOYAGE

A HAND wielding a hammer—this is the symbol that appears on Ibsen's grave. It is generally considered an inspired sculptural idea, and it undoubtedly conveys the conventional view that so often describes his contribution to the theatre and to society in terms of utility. According to this opinion, which is based on that small portion of his work which is called realistic, Ibsen wore overalls; sometimes he was part of a wrecking crew methodically dismantling ramshackle edifices and at other times he was just as methodically driving bolts into a rising skyscraper. This designation is partly valid, and it covers some of his activities, particularly with respect to the laborious manner in which he constructed his plays, tore down old façades, and created new mansions for the spirit.

There is still another view, favored by some theoreticians of the proletariat, which, on the contrary, denies him a union card. According to them, he worked for a brief period, but only as a dilettante. They see him lending a hand to both the wrecking crew and the construction gang, but only as a means of self-expression and with only a vague notion of why he was banging àt the timbers and of what kind of building was to be constructed in place of the old one. No! he was only a gentleman worker or, to use a more recent cant phrase, a fellow-traveler, deserving signal honors for deserting the Park Avenue district but still not to be listed among the men with the hammer. Ibsen's assault on society and his constructive ideas tend indeed to be wayward, so that the socialist scholar Plekhanov could produce strong arguments for calling him a "petty bourgeois revolutionist." [1]

Still, if symbols are useful in helping us to grasp the character of this prolific father of the modern drama, neither the man with the hammer nor the man with the silk hat will do. Perhaps the only image which would cover the whole range of his career is that of a viking standing at the prow of his tilted boat with the sea widening before him. The cynic might like to clap a top hat on this figure, add some convexity to the visceral regions, and hang an umbrella on one of its arms. And it must be conceded that the temptation to accept the caricature is strong at times. But under the impedimenta of his exterior Ibsen is a viking nonetheless. One sees him brushing the soil off his feet, setting his face toward distant shores, stopping at times to ravage some sedate settlement with fire, and finally plunging into the uncharted Atlantic with only a hazy notion of where he would come to rest, if ever. His work is precisely such a voyage of adventures, depredations, and explorations. Perhaps those admirers who refer to him as a poet come closest to defining him. Even in his realistic middle period, if we look closely enough, he remains essentially a poet, just as realism at its best is a kind of poetry.

At first we find him in his native Norway, his blood boiling with desire for the open sea as he moves among the solid burghers of his family and their neighbors, pursues a profession, studies at the university, and enters the narrow theatre of his day. This is the period of his mild romantic plays which are supplemented by radical journalism and lyricism. Soon, after much provocation and growling, he takes a long journey— geographically only to Southern Europe but spiritually to the far corners of the world. In *Brand* he announces his departure from the congregation of landlubbers with a fanfare; and in *Peer Gynt* he adds the brash taunt of laughter.

Then suddenly he swoops down upon the settlements of the slumbering bourgeoisie. He burns their "doll's houses" amid loud outcries from those whom he has so rudely evicted. This is the period of his *Pillars of Society, League of Youth, Doll's House, Ghosts,* and *Enemy of the People.*

But he is himself a portion of the humanity which he has scorned. Pity overcomes him, doubt reduces his self-assurance, and he begins to look tolerantly upon human frailty. He writes works like *The Wild Duck* and *Rosmersholm.* Yet he cannot endure the placid habitations of men very long. He discovers how easily the rust of compromise and complacency eats its way to the core. Returning to his former scornful manner, he rebukes the weaklings and gives warning examples of their compromises in plays like *Little Eyolf* and *When We Dead Awaken.* Back in his longbeaked boat, he sails out again, his destination vague, his heart a trifle troubled, and his aging eyes a shade dim but still resolute.

Whether one takes this chronicle to mean that Ibsen was a "petit bourgeois" in the uneven and sometimes ambiguous course of his revolt or that Ibsen was simply a necessarily limited human being who could waver and ask more questions than he could answer, the effect of his work is essentially the same. Like all great writers he was a warrior and a voyager, and the upshot of his struggle is an unavoidably flawed but noble body of drama which expresses modern man.

In the course of both grappling with realities and sometimes evading them in his own peculiar way, Ibsen inaugurated important modifications in modern dramatic practice. More than any of his immediate predecessors, he discarded at long last the "well-made play" of graduated intrigue and obvious plotting which Scribe and his followers had put on the market in the nineteenth century. He built a number of plays that gave the illusion of undistorted reality, enabling the playgoer to observe the characters and ponder the ideas or implications of a drama instead of watching the gyrations of the plot. And although contrary to some glib generalizations that neglect the great Athenians, Shakespeare, Goethe, and others, Ibsen did not actually invent the drama of ideas, he ensured its triumph in the modern world. He did this by applying himself boldly to ideas of broad relevance to man and society and by projecting them in defiance of conventional taboos. His was no timid, comparatively philistine intellect like the younger Dumas' and Augier's who believed they were dealing with great problems when they were actually conventional meliorists, and his ideas were no driblets of warmed-over concepts.

For all his superficially provincial tendencies and despite the small-town backgrounds of many of his plays, he possessed something of the largeness of spirit that is to be found among the Greeks and the Elizabethans as well as among the greatest romanticists. The bold creativeness of Shakespeare and Goethe is sporadically present in· the totality of his output, echoes of *Faust* resound in *Brand* and *Peer Gynt*, and Euripides' frontal attack on convention, as well as the Euripidean retrospective technique, pulsates in Ibsen's work. Even a brief summary of his life and work discloses the essential largeness of his mind and spirit.

2 THE ROMANTIC BEGINNINGS

Skien was a small shipping town, one of the many that dot the Norwegian coast-line. It was close enough to the sea for its citizens to feel the salt tang in the air but it was sufficiently engrossed in commerce and puritanic morals to represent Scandinavian life almost anywhere. Wherever, in fact, the middle-class world plied its trade without feeling the stirrings of cosmopolitan culture, one could find a Skien like the one that nourished Ibsen's restlessness and indignation; Shaw once remarked that one needed only to take the train out of London to find communities like Ibsen's.

The family into which Ibsen was born on the twentieth of March, 1828, in a house owned by the merchant Stockman, was likewise typical of the confining little world, and it is noteworthy that once Ibsen left his home he practically severed all connections with it. His mother may have had artistic inclinations in her youth, but she soon became a depleted parent of six children. His father's family on the male side favored the amenities, and the father himself possessed a fund of wit which sometimes offended people. But his immersion in business and speculation and his subsequent bankruptcy were sufficient to wreck the liveliest humor.

The youthful Ibsen did not see his family in all its glory of prosperity and social success since its fortunes vanished irretrievably by the time he was eight. Of all its wealth only a small farm a few miles north of Skien remained, and it was there that the family lived for about eight years, neglected by former acquaintances and distinctly *déclassé*. The ground was thus prepared for the future writer who was to castigate the false respectability and complacency of the middle classes. The family did not return to town until he was fifteen, and even then its means remained meager. Ibsen in 1844 consequently apprenticed himself to a chemist—perhaps too dignified a word for a humble druggist—in Grimstadt. The family, which needed assistance from him that he could not give for many years, in time came to regard him as a freethinker and lost soul; and attempts on its part to convert him to piety could only intensify his estrangement.

The small shipowners' town of Grimstadt, where he spent the next six years, was for a long time no improvement over the outskirts of Skien. With the aristocracy of well-to-do merchants and politicians the thin and pale drudge of a seedy druggist could have no contact. Underpaid, lacking good clothes, and sharing his bedroom with his employer's little sons, the growing lad brooded alone. Only the sea gave him comfort as he gazed out at its expanse with longings that may well be imagined. He was painfully alone, as he could hardly communicate his mental gropings to the few people he knew, and in his loneliness he turned to one of the servant girls of the household who was ten years his senior. She bore him a child when he was only eighteen, and this relationship which he could not forget during the fourteen years that he supported its fruit remained an unpleasant memory of which he discharged himself in one of the best scenes of *Peer Gynt*.

The last three years of his captivity were, however, more tolerable. His shop, which acquired a new owner, was moved into more congenial quarters, Ibsen became an assistant chemist, and he earned more money. He made friends with whom he discussed the world of affairs during the revolutionary period of 1848. He wrote poems discharging his feelings, satirized conservative leadership, and championed liberty in heated conversations, gaining a reputation for radicalism which attracted the younger members of the local aristocracy. It was at this time, too, influenced by his reading of Cicero's orations while preparing for matriculation at the University, that he composed his first tragedy *Catiline*, in iambic pentameters. Attracted on general principles to this character who had tried to destroy the *status quo* of Roman government, Ibsen nevertheless dramatized Catiline's errors and hesitations like a budding psychological playwright. This did not, however, prevent him from composing a romantic melodrama in which a vengeful vestal Furia, sister to another vestal who had been raped by Catiline, misleads him, turns his allies against him, and sends him hurtling to his ruin.

Unimportant as this play is in effect, it nevertheless "contains much that was to become true Ibsenism." [2] When it appeared in 1850 it was, in fact, the first Norwegian play to be published in seven years. But Ibsen's ammunition was not exhausted by this initial effort; no sooner was *Catiline* completed early in 1849 than Ibsen turned to political sonneteering, urging Sweden and Norway to support Denmark in the war over Schleswig with Prussia. The poetry was poor but the spirit was willing. It even held out the hope of ultimate victory for the Hungarians whose revolution was crushed that year, and there is significance in the fact that the young playwright was beginning to fling himself into the stream of European life.

Catiline was also followed by the indifferent one-act play *The Normans* (later entitled *The Warrior's Barrow*), and Ibsen now felt himself a full-fledged literary figure. Less than three weeks later he arrived at Christiania to take examinations for matriculation at the University. Here he quickly renounced his medical ambitions, attended lectures on philosophy and literature, and sold the publication rights to his one-acter and to one of his poems. And once more he espoused the cause of liberty, then associated with the demands of the working-class for protection against the rising capitalism of the period. [3]

The young provincial was becoming, in fact, a thorough student of social questions. In 1851 he was an active journalist, associating himself first with the socialist labor-union organ the *Arbeider-Foreningernes Blad* which was suppressed by the government after six months, and then with a more eclectic liberal journal *The Man* which also gave up the ghost after half a year. To the last-mentioned publication he contributed poetry, dramatic criticism, and political articles.

Nevertheless, he was already in those days expressing a deep distrust for politics and politicians of any shade. It was not, therefore, difficult for him to throw in his lot with Ole Bull, the progressive theatre manager who gave him a position in the little theatre of Bergen. Soon the management also gave him a stipend for travel in Denmark and Germany where he was expected to prepare himself for the post of stage manager and instructor. But it was not only the mere mechanics of stagecraft at the Copenhagen Royal Theatre and the Dresden Court Opera that attracted his attention; in Germany he came across a short critique by the scholar Hermann Hettner, *Das Moderne Drama,* which admonished playwrights to introduce psychological analysis into their historical plays. Ibsen took the lesson to heart and applied it in his next work.

When he returned to Bergen and was made official playwright of the theatre toward the end of 1851, he set himself the task of creating a national drama by celebrating the early history and heroic spirit of his nation. With this in mind he wrote a fairy comedy *St. John's Night* in 1852 built around Scandinavian folk songs; and although it was a romantic play with some resemblance to *A Midsummer Night's Dream,* it contained the promise of critical intelligence in its caricature of a poet who poses as a nationalist. This play, as well as a revision of *The Warrior's Barrow,* failed but could not dishearten its author. After an interruption caused by an affair with a girl whose well-to-do father objected to a match with an impecunious writer, Ibsen composed a new historical drama. In this play, *Lady Inger of Östråt,* Ibsen added character analysis to the story of a daughter's love for a warrior who opposes her patriotic aspirations, since he is intent upon keeping Norway under Denmark's yoke. Although the liberation of medieval Norway is the keynote of the drama, the mother Lady Inger is prevented by her doubts and attachments from giving herself unreservedly to her ideal. The national conflict was in this way transferred to the inner man, so that Hettner's prescription of psychological drama was in some measure filled.

Ibsen, it is true, was still far from mastery of an independent technique; Scribe's influence is evident in the intrigue that keeps the play jogging in the customary manner. But in the fact that the intrigue involves a major antithesis—that between an awakening Norway and an oppressive Denmark—one can already detect the Ibsen of the later dramas. Perhaps for this reason, and because he had succeeded to some degree in penetrating to the heart of his characters, Ibsen was in a confident mood even though the 1855 production of the play was unsuccessful. In the summer of the same year, possibly in imitation of a popular piece by the Danish playwright Henrik Hertz, he wrote a new play *The Feast at Solhoug* based not on the old sagas but on the later balladry of medieval Norway. The dramatic core, still highly romantic in treatment, was furnished by the heroine whose repressed love for the man she failed to marry drives her to crime. Here the author already dispenses with the romantic impedimenta of supernatural characters. Scribean intrigue is also absent in this drama, although the central story is not in any way superior to any of the situations favored by Ibsen's French master. And this time Ibsen was rewarded with signal success when the play was produced by the Bergen Theatre and subsequently by the theatre in Christiania.

However, a second ballad drama *Olaf Lilyekrans,* revolving around a knight who is deluded by a mysterious woman into forgetting his fiancée, proved to be such a mishap that it wrote *finis* to this phase of Ibsen's romanticism. In his next play *The Vikings of Helgeland* Ibsen, therefore, returned to the material and spirit of the Norse sagas. The great *Volsunga Saga* furnished the subject of the heroine Hiördis who kills her lover and then herself. Sigurd, the lover, had taken another to wife, and the larger-than-life Hiördis who recalls the Brynhild of the old Norse story becomes his nemesis. There is nothing picayune about *The Vikings;* it wrestles with elemental passion, and Björnson, Scandinavia's leading literary figure at the time, rightly considered it the strongest Norwegian drama that had yet appeared.

3 THE FIRST VOYAGES

Ibsen, however, had to cut his romantic moorings more completely before he could usher in the modern drama. He was, he realized, making little headway as a successful dramatist and he failed to receive subsidies for the Christiania Norwegian Theatre, to which he was now attached, or for himself when he asked the state for a traveling stipend. Like any other writer, he began to be tormented with self-doubt, and the poetry he composed at this time is bitter with disillusionment. In this manner he floundered for several years, planning and finally completing in 1862 the poetic but satiric *Love's Comedy* which is distinctly the child of his anger and frustration. Out of this upheaval of the spirit Ibsen first embarked upon that investigation of modern man and society which stamps his major contributions to the theatre.

Conventional love and marriage became the subject of this loaded satire. The high-spirited heroine Svanhild is defeated in the play, and the poet Falk, who like Ibsen himself tires of pure estheticism and attempts to come to grips with reality, can save himself from the cheap world only by escaping to the mountains. Here already Ibsen branded society as a house of lies and called for liberation by learning and applying the truth regardless of conventions. There was even a strong trace —and a confusing one—of an implication that love and marriage are incompatible. Much vigor went into the composition of the piece and it is not surprising that it should have been immediately set down as an attack on the sanctity of married life. His critics warned him that skepticism was not a poetic mood. Ibsen's intention, however, was more moderate than they thought; he had aimed his barbs at superficial abuses rather than at the whole structure of society. The truth of the matter is that he had not yet developed a definite critique of society, and that his material and his characters asserted themselves independently. One of his characters, the merchant Guldstad, actually presents a very solid argument for marriages of convenience. The result of Ibsen's lack of a single direction, as well as his use of poetry for a prosaic social problem, caused Ibsen's most important effort thus far to fall between two stools.

The reception of the play did not encourage him to resume the same vein in his next work, just as it could not encourage the aged Minister

Kiddervold and the Norwegian parliament to grant a new request for a stipend to a man who had scoffed at the holy state of matrimony. In his disappointment, Ibsen returned to the saga material of his earlier plays. The result was *The Pretenders*, a nearly great historical drama of the Norwegian civil wars which should be better appreciated than it is at present. Out of the conflict between Earl Skule, a dreamer who lacks a central vision, and Hakon, a great and single-minded ruler who conquers him both physically and spiritually, Ibsen created a deeply reasoned and deeply felt tragedy. Hakon triumphs because he has a "king's thought" which could not occur independently to a pathetically limited individual like Skule in the thirteenth century—"Norway has been a kingdom; it shall become a people!" But Skule, who ultimately realizes his inner failure when he refers to himself as "God's stepchild on earth," can only regard Hakon with embittered rivalry. At most, he can *steal* "the king's thought" and when he at last understands the truth of life's law that a man's supremacy or genius lies in his ability to conceive a great act, he can only sacrifice his life for his rival's idea. For, as Skule's bard had once told him, "A man can die for another's life-work, but if he go on living he must live for his own!"

Here for the first time Ibsen completely realized Hettner's principle that any historical play worth the paper on which it is written must be a psychological drama. *The Pretenders*, moreover, holds in solution the essential philosophy of Ibsen's later works in which an individual loses happiness and self-respect unless he can acquire creative freedom of thought and action. In the matter of style, too, the play marks a great advance in Ibsen's artistry; his prose dialogue in crisp phrases has become an instrument for sharp thinking and intense feeling. That it was written in white heat is shown by the fact that the play was composed within two months in the fall of 1863.

The play is not wholly satisfactory because it makes cumbersome theatre. It is too long, and one also tires of Earl Skule as one tires of all weaklings in the drama unless they are transfigured by some compensatory depth or by some perversion of strength, as in *Hedda Gabler*. But its power could not be denied even in Ibsen's day; it became his greatest early triumph.

Aided by a government stipend and by private contributions collected by his friend and admirer Björnson, Ibsen left Norway in the spring of 1864. This trip, ostensibly intended for quiet study, became of momentous consequence; it precipitated him into the larger European world. In Copenhagen he was deeply affected by the defeat of Denmark by Prussia and Austria, and he protested passionately against another "Prussian misdeed," as well as against his country's failure to assist the Danes. In Germany, he saw the conquerors rejoicing; he left Berlin quickly when he saw the populace spitting into a captured cannon, a sight which he never forgot. Prussia he never could endure, and it was only in the more congenial principalities of a still uncentralized Germany, Vienna, Switzerland, and Italy that Ibsen found himself at ease.

Like many a northern visitor he felt a new burgeoning in himself in the colorful, sun-lit South. The classic world and the artistic wonders of the Renaissance also unrolled before him in Rome, and Norway, which had filled him with so much disappointment, now seemed only a narrow and unpleasant memory. Impressed by a Danish narrative, and perhaps more profoundly influenced by the majestic memories of the Renaissance, his mind took hold of the sweeping dramatic idea of *Brand,* the most heroic and affirmative of his plays. He was distressed by the European situation, but he was happy in the consciousness of new poetic powers within himself. Never before, moreover, had he found such potent means of discharging his pent-up dissatisfactions with the commonplace middle-class world he had known in Norway.

His starting-point in *Brand* was well expressed by the unorthodox preacher Sören Kierkegaard, who may well have served as Brand's prototype for Ibsen. Kierkegaard refused to concern himself with the petty vices which are normally assailed in sermons; the trouble with his times, he declared, was not that they were evil, but that they were mean-spirited and contemptible. Brand's complaint is likewise against the lukewarmness of the age: the Devil, says Brand, is compromise! Today the play is somewhat wearying with its solemn reiteration of the "be yourself" formula, and even when it calls men to heroic action it seems inadequate from a positive viewpoint since action without specific aim or direction is futile. When Ibsen blows his trumpet here, he sometimes sounds like a boy scout; the poet had not yet acquired the human purposefulness of a realist. Brand's sacrifice of his child and his wife would be more tolerable if it were made inevitable by some recognizable necessity. As things stand in the play, Brand at times becomes an insufferable prig or a madman. Ibsen was still intoxicated by the sagas and was still deluded by romantic poetry into believing that a symbol is deeper than the symbolization provided by forceful reality.

Nevertheless, the warm reception of *Brand* when it appeared in 1866 is understandable, and the play has more power than might be expected. In the embattled parson Brand, Ibsen created the most audible protest against the complacencies of the average citizen and his world at a time when both were permeated by commercial philistinism. *Brand* is effective when its author is satirizing the petty world in portraits of a mayor who is a perfect political Babbitt, of an artist who leaps from the timidities of conventional art to those of conventional religion, and of a populace that instantly renounces idealism when a safe way of making profits presents itself. Moreover, the stridencies of the tragedy are mitigated by Brand's moments of doubt and by the somewhat confusing but poignant conclusion when Brand appeals to heaven to vindicate his behavior. Having sacrificed others as well as himself to the principle of "all or nothing," he is overcome with doubt. "Cannot the uncompromising assertion of man's will merit redemption?" Brand cries as the avalanche rushes down upon him. To this question the divine voice, speaking through the thunder, replies *"deus caritatis"*—"God is Love." If one is to postulate consistency for the play, one must take the last words to mean simply that, unlike Brand, God is forgiving. He will forgive this unforgiving idealist. "Brand," as Shaw noted, "dies a saint, having caused more intense suffering by his saintliness than the most talented sinner could possibly have done with twice his opportunities." [4] He needs precisely the kind of tolerance which he himself never extended to anyone.

Basically, then, *Brand* is not only a challenge hurled in the teeth of the world's philistines but also a human document describing an inspired and unconventional parson's struggle against the spiritual poverty of his people. Brand's disgust with the common ways began when he saw his mother, who had denied her heart and married for money, greedily rummaging among her dying husband's effects. Thereafter the young cleric pursues the opposite course of complete self-abnegation, fearlessly bringing comfort to a dying girl over wastes of snow which her own father does not care to traverse and risking his life in a storm. Conversely he does not spare those who are closest to him, rejecting his own mother when she holds on to her possessions and refusing to take his ailing child south because this would be construed as desertion of his parishioners. In other words, the personal drama of an idealist supports the preachment and humanizes its absoluteness. Moreover, a certain quality of genius fires many of his categorical imperatives. Religion is not a convenience, he holds, but an aspiration that challenges every petty element in the human soul. He does not consider himself a parson of the pragmatic Church, he is not even sure that he is a Christian; but, he declares, "I am certain of *this*, I am a Man." The Catholic, he finds, "converts the Hero of the Redemption into a suckling," while the Protestants "turn the Lord into a decrepit old man. . . ." Everyone narrows the Lord's kingdom and wants a "God who'll peep through his fingers," while Brand's own God is a storm. Brand's complaint, which Ibsen's later plays were to echo time and again, is basically that the individualistic middle-class society in which he lives actually weakens individuality. That was to be Ibsen's later protest against the family and its conventions as well, and in fact he already had ringing words against this institution. "You look upon a child," Brand says to his mother, "as a steward of the posthumous family rags" thinking that by "tying up your property to your family . . . you can produce eternity."

Brand made a deep impression upon the consciousness of the liberal sixties, which teemed with ideas of liberation and witnessed the abolition of serfdom in Russia and of slavery in America. Ibsen became the trumpet of the time-spirit, and it was unlikely that he would be contented with one blast. Fortified by substantial royalties, by a pension from the government, and by general acclaim, Ibsen turned out another and more brilliant version of his challenge within a year.

Brand had declared, "If you cannot be what you *ought,* then be thoroughly what you *can.*" In the new play *Peer Gynt* Ibsen created a character who was the antithesis of the mountain-climbing cleric of the previous play. Peer is the incarnation of everything that is vacillating and unstable in man, and appropriately his story is told in the spirit of picaresque fantasy. No matter how much weight of thought one finds in this symbolic exercise, it will never yield its charm to anyone who does not respond to its playfulness.

Its didactic content is easily summarized. Peer considers himself a distinct personality because he has traveled and experienced much. Society, he thinks, has never fettered him, since he has coddled his wayward desires and has evaded every responsibility. Here Ibsen hit upon one of the verities; for this is precisely the popular definition of a free personality. But Peer, like his countless cousins, made one error in his calculations. He forgot that he really had no personality, that he had merely been a hit-and-run driver on life's parkway. He had been a coward and an opportunist; he had mistaken willfulness for will, impulse for resolution. In short, he was merely a romantic edition of Mr. Zero the average man, and it was inevitable that the Devil who battens on human frailty should appear to Peer as a button-molder who threatens to melt his soul with other base metal. Peer's protests are futile; he cannot even prove that he was a personality in evil, since all his sins were such mean-spirited ones. Only in Solveig's loving memory had he existed as a real personality, and this alone may save him from the casting-ladle.

It is not, however, the bare idea but the amusing fantasy and occasionally touching reality of Ibsen's play that ensured its triumph. Basing his work on an old legend, Ibsen created a human Puck in the lad who upsets the neighborhood with his pranks and grows up into a typical careerist with a good deal of resemblance to the masters of modern business enterprise. He is almost as rich and permanent a character of the world's literature as Don Quixote and Falstaff. A more amiable rascal never haunted the theatre than this modern Eulenspiegel of the first three acts of the play; for all his failings, as Shaw observed, it was better to be Peer's mother or sweetheart than Brand's.

Peer appears first as an incorrigible liar and fantasist, the very "devil's storyteller." He goes awooing with blithe insouciance, after perching his protesting mother Ase on the roof of their cottage. He steals another man's bride under his very nose, takes her up a mountain path, and then abandons her. Pursued by the villagers, he takes time off to engage in more amatory details, dancing off with three girls toward the mountain tops. Next he courts the gross daughter of the supernatural troll-king and almost becomes the latter's son-in-law but for his refusal to renounce his greatly treasured human personality. A specialist in self-delusion, he has no difficulty in accepting the ugly creature as a beauty and in idealizing the unsavory habits and food of the trolls, but he balks at having his eyes permanently distorted in deference to the troll-king's wishes. An encounter with the great Boyg, a supernatural incarnation of public inertia, teaches the youth a lesson that he hardly needed to learn—namely, to *"go roundabout;"* Peer pressing against the Boyg overcomes him only because "there were women behind him"—a detail that anticipates Ibsen's great faith in the liberation of mankind by the other sex. Real love comes to him only when he meets Solveig, who has cast off her parents for him. But again Peer proves that he lacks the stamina to hold on to what he desires; being confronted by the troll-king's daughter who has by now borne him an unwanted child (even as Ibsen became the father of an illegitimate child), fearing to be plagued by responsibility for it, and feeling that he is too sullied for his pure new love, he abandons the cottage where Solveig and he were making their stay. He comes home only to find his mother dying and to comfort her poignantly with his irrepressible fantasies.

When next we meet him he has degenerated in accordance with his weak nature. He is an ex-slave trader who prospered in America and is now yachting on the coast of Morocco. It is true that he had found the business "on the outer verge of the allowable," but it was hard to break away from it. Then he hit upon a suitable substitute in the best traditions of laissez-faire business when he shipped idols to China every spring and missionaries every autumn! He could salve his conscience at the same time that he made a substantial profit: for every idol that he sold a missionary got a coolie baptized—"So the effect was neutralized." Now he is planning to become Emperor of the world, and since he needs additional gold with which to realize his ambition he is turning to international finance. Greece has revolted against Turkey; therefore, in accordance with good business practice, his partners are to go to Greece where they are to fan the flames of revolution while he lends money to the Turks! His partners being men of the "Gyntish" stamp themselves, however, rob him of his pelf and abscond, leaving him stranded. The next adventure displays him as a middle-aged, fatuous roué, and all his

subsequent experiences underscore his spiritual bankruptcy. Cheated by
the Mohammedan beauty Anitra, trapped in an insane asylum, nearly
drowned on the voyage to his homeland, and saving himself only at the
expense of another drowning person, Peer returns as a greatly cheapened
egotist. The law of deterioration is inherent in the world's weaklings!
Then comes retribution in the shape of the button-molder, and Peer the
individualist learns much to his distress that he has been a very ordinary
person, fit to be "merged in the mass." A Babbitt on horseback, he has
ridden hard and fast—without getting to either heaven or hell.

A brilliant satire on second-rateness, with incidental thrusts at pedantry and business ethics, *Peer Gynt* at once took its place as the most
daring extravaganza of the modern theatre. Here was an essentially
realistic critique couched in terms of mock-heroic fantasy which managed to be as entertaining as it was sound. The diffuseness of the piece,
especially marked after the third act, the inconsequentialities of portions
of the fourth act, and considerable lagging throughout the work weaken
it. Ibsen's habit of publishing his plays before they were produced made
him an undisciplined playwright in those days. But although *Peer Gynt*
is an uneven play, it is so distinguished a *tour de force* that it overshadows the trim accomplishments of average playwrights. Moreover, Ase's
death scene in the third act and Peer's last-minute realization of failure
in the closing scenes would be high points in any drama.

Ibsen never quite overcame either his taste for symbolism or his
search for broad dramatic concepts. But in *Peer Gynt* he had moved to
the farthest reaches of his fantasy, he had discharged himself of his
poetic impulse, and he had announced his general philosophy for the
second time, having now expressed it both positively and negatively in
Brand and *Peer Gynt* respectively. It remained now to embody both his
protest against the narrow life and his vision of a liberated humanity in
concrete social studies. These were to be written in everyday prose and
were to deal with situations, as well as characters, that were rooted in
the ordinary world. Realistic writing was by then making its appearance
in the drama, and no one was more fitted to bring to the new style the
mental and emotional vigor without which it could only remain a very
drab kind of photography.

4 THE REALISTIC ASSAULT

The first fruits of the new style appeared in *The League of Youth*
that he began to write in 1868. Here was no fantastication on the subject of compromise, but a realistic exposure of local politics. Its hero, the
pettifogging and opportunistic politician Stensgard, was none other than
Peer Gynt in mufti. The play is a drama of intrigue, but the conven-
tionalities of his technique do not greatly matter, since gyrations of plot

only enhance a farce. Björnson called the play an "assassination in the sacrificial grove of poetry," and the premiere in the fall of 1869 was generously hissed by the liberals in the audience. But *The League of Youth* rises above partisanship, since the conservatives fare almost as badly and since true liberalism is nowhere assailed. Socialist critics may complain as bitterly as they please that Ibsen was a dreadful bourgeois and denied the possibilities of group action. The fact remains—and it was the only one to be observed by the playwright—that politics does not normally smell like a rose. Ibsen, moreover, hung a collection of delightful caricatures in his local gallery, in addition to the more rounded portrait of Stensgard whose impoverished home life has conditioned him to opportunism without let or scruple.

Still, the Ibsen of masterful realism is only fitfully present in this superficial comedy, and its author was not yet in the mood for consolidating his gains. As a matter of fact, he had one more comprehensive philosophical inquiry or statement which he felt compelled to discharge in the drama. He had pondered the question of Christianity versus paganism for a long time. Now he came to the conclusion that what was needed was a "Third Empire" representing a synthesis of paganism and Christianity, a combination of the joy of life or freedom for the individual with the ethical claims of the spirit. His idealistic character Julian the Apostate in the two formidable parts of *Emperor and Galilean* tries to re-establish paganism and fails. The battle is between the "First Empire" of pagan sensuality, and the "Second Empire" of self-denial; the one is outworn since our first innocence cannot be recaptured, the other is unnatural since it suppresses individuality and happiness. The victory falls to "the Galilean," and the day when the genuine values in Julian's faith will be fused with those of Christianity, when both "Emperor" and "Galilean" will disappear in the new synthesis, is still to come. Maximos the philosopher proclaims this unity, but only the future will give it realization.

There is a breath of greatness in this last of Ibsen's cyclopean creations; the vision possesses magnitude and the background has something of magnificence in it. It is unfortunate only that Ibsen did not achieve the same integration in his play that he envisaged in the world of the future. Emperor Julian is unevenly characterized, and his tragedy becomes extraordinarily long-winded. For one who was soon to compose some of the most economical works of the stage Ibsen displayed a curious prolixity in this play.

The years 1870-73 during which he wrote *Emperor and Galilean* were, however, not wholly devoted to philosophy or historical investigation. Society had been becoming an ever-pressing problem for him since the days when he had composed *Love's Comedy;* and the radical spirit of his journalistic comments, of his poem "The Assassination of Abraham Lincoln" in which he assaulted the corruption of the prevailing order, and of his recent plays could only be exacerbated as he continued his observations. At this time, moreover, he came face to face with an event that made him wonder presciently whether European civilization was not heading for destruction. He had only recently returned from Egypt where he had seen relics of another extinct civilization. Now he saw the rise of German militarism with its concomitant mechanization of the individual into a state-controlled robot. At Dresden during the Franco-Prussian War of 1870 he was given the benefit of a lesson that he could not easily forget. He heard the iron heel resounding on the streets of a city normally devoted to culture, and his little son Sigurd felt its pressure at school where his classmates beat him regularly because he did not conform to their chauvinism. He protested against the suppression of freedom in some trenchant verses and give himself to serious speculations on the conflict between the state and the individual. He began to dread the state and to maintain that it would have to be undermined completely.

Out of this conviction came first *The Pillars of Society,* in which he harnessed the Scribean technique to the idea that society was founded on corruptions and lies. In the person of Consul Bernick, whose reputation is based on two base deceptions, all society is indicted. One by one the rotten props of his reputation collapse as his success is discovered to be based on his desertion of the woman he loved, on a friend's assumption of responsibility for his misconduct with an actress, and on a dishonest stroke of business for which the same man suffered the blame. Consul Bernick even allows a rotten ship to leave his yards in order to rid himself of his scapegoat, and only the promptings of his former fiancée and the imminent death of his stowaway son awaken him to the enormity of his behavior. Then he makes full confession acknowledging that the real pillars of society are Truth and Freedom.

The happy conclusion is as jerry-built as are the revelations, and *Pillars of Society* does not by any means rank with the masterpieces. But progress is already noticeable in the concreteness of Ibsen's critique. The rotten ships sent out to sea by venal shipowners created a major scandal in Europe, and financial manipulations were well-known facts. Ibsen also created the first of his modern women in Lona Hessel who does not require the protection of a male and has a mind of her own.

Ibsen was indeed becoming increasingly convinced that civilization could not be free while one half of the race was still in legal bondage—a state of affairs particularly applicable to the provincial society which he was exploring. Moreover, it seemed to him that civilization could only be saved by women; they were less directly attached to the world of venal enterprise, and it was from mothers that man first received his training. Women, in short, were to become the "pillars of society."

When he regarded the actual scene—and if it was a provincial one it nevertheless covered the greatest areas—Ibsen noted the bondage of women. Therefore in *A Doll's House* he addressed himself to woman's place in the home, to which he attributed all her limitations. According to her creator, Nora was a failure as a personality because she had never been allowed to develop one. First her father sheltered her, then her husband; and neither of these men had allowed her any opportunities to acquire a broad education or even to master the elementary realities of the social world. No wonder she had blithely committed forgery in order to acquire a loan with which to save her husband's life. Then suddenly the complications that ensued from her ignorance awakened her to the necessity of learning something about the world at large. This she could only do if she left her husband who had locked her in a "doll's house" where she was expected to be pretty and playful, submissive and mindless. It would have been surprising indeed if a writer who responded so keenly to the currents of his day should not have been touched by the movement for the emancipation of women. John Stuart Mill had published his *Subjection of Women* in 1869, Georg Brandes had translated it into Danish, and several Scandinavian women had taken up the struggle by establishing a "reading society," writing pamphlets, and delivering lectures. One of these women had served as a model for Lona in *Pillars of Society,* the first draft of which had contained a great deal more feminism than the final version. Conversations with another of these feminists, the brilliant Camilla Collett, were partly responsible for *A Doll's House.*

Today the issue is unlikely to cause any excitement, unless the merry-go-round of history brought the world back again to the *"Kirche, Küche, Kinder"* formula from which another revolt would be necessary. Ibsen's story, moreover, suffers from transparent improbabilities. Would even a sheltered woman like Nora lack the elementary knowledge that forgery was illegal? Given the character of a dependent wife, would she have failed to confess to her husband? Given this character, moreover, it is also extremely improbable that she would have left him and, above all, her innocent children. Finally, it is by no means clear that Nora is going to learn anything by leaving her husband that she could not have learned in her own household; she is without any inkling of a plan for self-education, she is going back to a house inherited from her father, and does she not herself declare, "I have no idea of what is going to become of me." Today the propaganda in the play can only strike most of us as a small flash in a very small pan.

Yet it is undeniable that *A Doll's House* became a burning issue, for here was Ibsen calling upon women to come out into the world. More-over, despite some Scribean tricks and the unconvincing change-of-heart in the man Krogstadt who is threatening to expose the forgery, Ibsen infused the play with more power than is sometimes realized in our impatience. In terms of simple human drama Helmer's attitude to-ward his wife's error is real and Nora's shock at his stuffy and selfish behavior is genuine. It might not have led her to desert her children, but it could have certainly killed her love for him. There is also con-siderable poignancy in her inability to ask their family friend Dr. Rank for assistance when she learns that his fondness for her borders on pas-sion. Then, too, Ibsen—unlike his most recent American Nora, Miss Ruth Gordon—was at pains to stress Nora's native intelligence and energy. She resolutely acquires money in order to save her husband's health and life, at the same time shielding his pride which would not allow him to borrow; then, she works secretly in her own room in order to pay off the debt. A woman of this order, no matter how inexperienced, may easily possess the spirit to realize that her marriage is unsound and to assert her independence. The woman in the doll's house was not in-trinsically a doll; barring the initial forgery, she only pretended to be one, because this was expected of her.

Perhaps, too, Nora's leaving house and children is not so outrageously incredible as it seems at first sight, Ibsen having very astutely planted an extenuating circumstance. Like so many of her comfortable sisters, Nora has had very little function in her own household; servants had managed everything, including the children, and they can continue to do so. "The maids know all about everything—better than I do," says Nora. Finally, Ibsen did not close the door to a reconciliation. Perhaps Helmer will become something other than the self-centered demigod of the home—now that his doll is taken away from him! If this miracle takes place, Nora and her husband may re-establish their marriage—on a sound basis. This is not a divorce but a separation.

A careful examination of this old warhorse of the realistic problem drama, foaled in 1879, will show that it still has some teeth left. It is sometimes poignant, the exposure of Helmer is well established, Nora is more appealing than irritating, and some of the realities of middle-class society are well observed. Besides, the world has not yet been changed to such a degree—except in the cosmopolitan sophisticated circles to which critics usually belong—that Nora's domestic problem has completely vanished. Certainly at the heart of many men there is still the desire to own a doll's house and, if department-store sales and observable behavior are any indication, there are still many women who are not averse to leading or accepting a doll's existence.

The one quality least evident in the play is some peak of greatness.

But the intensification of Ibsen's grappling with realities was soon to reach that elevation. In *Ghosts,* which came two years later, in 1881, he discarded the pretty little devices of *A Doll's House* and increased the reality of his dialogue and dramatic development, until the play could become an example to every writer who sought to create naturalness in the theatre. Henceforth a playwright was not to expect honor for merely cooking up a stew of a plot; and although many a practitioner has continued to acquire riches and a pretty reputation by no other means, a new standard of excellence was established. Content, meaning, and reality comprised the new dispensation.

Ghosts, the tragedy of Mrs. Alving whose observance of the conventions of marriage bound her to a wayward and syphilitic husband, startled the world by introducing the subjects of heredity and venereal disease into the theatre. And again Ibsen was only responding to the ferment of the age of Darwin and the naturalism of Emile Zola's Rougon-Macquart novels. In fact, Ibsen had already suggested the problem of the hereditary taint in *A Doll's House,* when Helmer warned Nora against the heritage of dishonesty which she may pass on to her children; and according to his preliminary draft of the same play, he had even intended to treat the subject at greater length. The diseased Dr. Rank, moreover, is only an elderly Oswald, for he too is paying for his father's misconduct.

Nevertheless, the content of *Ghosts* is larger than the "hospital literature" to which it was consigned by the mild-mannered German novelist Heyse. Otherwise the play would be deadwood in our age of prophylactics, mercury compounds, and fever treatment, although statistics might indicate that the disease has been far from eradicated. Not even the question of mercy-killing which confronts Mrs. Alving after she has promised Oswald to end his life the moment he loses his mind would be a sufficient basis for the play's longevity. The fact is that Ibsen created a taut human drama and at the same time, without violating its naturalness, infused it with the comprehensive thought that man was ghost-ridden by the dead conventions to which he adhered and that, in the words of Shaw, "every step of progress means a duty repudiated." Heredity itself is conceived in a manner that suggests the Greek idea of fate and retribution rather than the dull pronunciamentos of a eugenics forum; Oswald's hereditary disease is virtually the domestic *Até* of the Alvings.

Broadly conceived, then, *Ghosts* combines the bleakest realism with an intense protest against everything that shackles the individual in his pursuit of happiness and integrity. Ibsen followed this track to a point at which he could even pity Mrs. Alving's husband. Despite her bitterness against him, Mrs. Alving notes that the conventions of early training, which made a frigid woman of her, were responsible for his looking for love beyond matrimony. He, too, was frustrated! The same line of reasoning also leads Ibsen to deplore Mrs. Alving's sacrifice of her happiness for the sake of family respectability when she failed to leave her husband; and by the same token the author approves the healthy-minded girl Regina's refusal to stay with Oswald and minister to his ailing body. Ibsen would have agreed with his champion Shaw that there is nothing in society so mean as "forcing self-sacrifice on a woman under pretence that she likes it." Had *Ghosts* been no more than a prosaic statement on the dangers of inherited diseases, it would hardly have outlived its age; and if, in fact, its status is a trifle doubtful at present it is only because the venereal-heredity problem is too obtrusive.

It has long been a popular game to describe the horrified outcries that greeted *Ghosts* and the ensuing battle between the Ibsenites and the die-hards. But it is necessary to refer only to Ibsen's *Enemy of the People* to sense the provocation to which he was treated by the unco guid. The worthy Dr. Stockman who runs amok and berates the "compact majority" that feeds on lies and protects its trough with swinish ferocity is Ibsen himself. Instead of apologizing for his temerity in representing paresis on the stage and for casting doubt on the sanctity of the family n matter how corrupt, Ibsen defied his enemies in Stockman's own ringing words to the effect that the majority is always wrong.

The pugnacity of the play has endeared it to many people, and no one in the theatre, it is true, had struck society so flatly in the face before; whenever a modern play like Galsworthy's *Mob* opposes an idealist to a misguided or frenzied majority it is not difficult to descry the ghost of Ibsen in the wings. Others have found the play fairly tiresome. At a distance the issue of the infected municipal baths of a small Norwegian town resembles a tempest in a half-pint teapot, and Stockman looks somewhat ridiculous as he hits out at the whole world. *An Enemy of the People,* however, is telling in its mockery of the complacencies and hypocrisies of respectable society which is willing to countenance anything for the sake of a profit, as well as in its exposure of the spinelessness of so-called liberals of the press. And if, more often than not, Stockman behaves like an irate gentleman in the process of wielding an umbrella, this can only enhance the play because *An Enemy of the People* is intrinsically a comedy. It is distinctly a mistake to play it with the solemnity of a sermon. Before the curtain falls the good doctor has seen his supporters desert him when he tried to have the baths condemned; and he has made a fool of himself in trusting the careerists and householders of the towns. But he has given them an enormous piece of his truly ponderous mind, and he will continue his defiance. Moreover, he is going to take ragamuffins off the street and try to turn them into

idealists by educating them in his home. Stockman is assuredly Don
Quixote in a frock-coat! His story, for all its assault on society and its
call to arms, remains on a high comic plane, almost like *The Misanthrope*.
Ibsen could not treat the conflict between his shifty provincials and his
naïve idealist on the heroic plane of tragedy for the simple reason that it
is impossible to execute a flock of sheep in a dignified fashion.

The worthy Stockman has troubled some critics[5] because he attacked
the majority and glorified the strong idealist who stands alone. Obviously, Stockman's quarrel was basically with the powerful rich and
the press which they controlled. His condemnation of the people at large
is, therefore, somewhat illogical. But one does not expect scrupulous
reasoning from the ruffled doctor. He may have served as Ibsen's mouthpiece for the moment; but in the dramatic setting of the play, Stockman's words are partly truth and partly persiflage, having a touch of
comedy such as comes from excessive pugnacity. The gist of this argument is that there is more fun than thunder in the pyrotechnics of *An
Enemy of the People,* despite a fundamental earnestness of purpose in
Ibsen's assault on calculating respectability.

5 THE LULL IN BATTLE

Years later Ibsen himself confessed to a German admirer that Stockman was partly a grotesque adolescent and a hot-head—*"ein grotesker
Bursche und ein Strudelkopf";* and even when he completed the play in
September 1882 he told his publisher that, although the doctor and he
agreed in many respects, the former was the more muddle-headed of
the two.[6] Not only, then, was Ibsen dramatist enough even in his berserk
period to allow his characters to become independent personalities, but
he possessed some saving grace of objectivity and humor.

His extreme enemies who called him a "crazy fanatic" and a "ghoul"
would not of course grant him these qualities; and the worthy William
Winter, who possessed a talent for keeping his ideas in cold storage, held
on as late as 1913[7] to the notion that the stock playwright had a "dis-
ordered brain." Ibsen, however, was to confute his critics beyond doubt
a year later in *The Wild Duck.* At Gossensass in Tyrol he found
himself remarkably relaxed, and the "integrity fever" in him went down
many points as he worked away at the play until its completion in 1884.

It is true that his contempt for emotional bankrupts did not leave him
when he drew the second-rate egotist Hjalmar Ekdal who lacks character enough either to resist the crackpot idealist Gregers Werle or to convert idealism into something ponderable. But Ibsen was ready to acknowledge the fact that the little people of the world are better off with
their illusions, and there was more pity for them than the author of
Brand had entertained at any time before. Nor was his new attitude

confined to pity, which is directed only at the broken-down divinity student Molvik and Hjalmar's superannuated father. For such realists as Werle's housekeeper and Hjalmar's wife Gina there is respect because they live their compromises without illusion, while for Hedwig, the dreamful young daughter of the Ekdals, there is nothing less than love in Ibsen's heart. People could discover at last that the viking of the modern drama had a heart after all.

The Wild Duck is notable for its combination of reality and poetry. Against its realities of characterization and family life shimmers the lovely, slightly heartbreaking, illusory world of Hedwig and her grandfather who plays Nimrod in a garret. The latter is, in a sense, all humanity when he is content to let four or five withered Christmas trees make his forest. The pity of life is present in these characters, as well as in the inebriated theological student Molvik who dreams that he is "daemonic"; and it is cardinal in Dr. Relling's philosophy that the average man cannot exist without "life-illusions." The understanding which is the basis of all true compassion is not withheld even from Gregers Werle whose preoccupation with the "call of the ideal" grows out of his conditioning by a sick mother. One can only pity his warped personality further when his ideal of truth-telling shatters in his hands, even while one despises him for destroying the happiness of the Ekdals and the life of little Hedwig by revealing Gina Ekdal's past affair with his father.

There is, besides, considerable astuteness in Ibsen's choice of an idealist whose failure is so deeply rooted in psychopathology; this lessens the importance of the play as an anti-idealist tract and allows it to materialize as a tragedy of human frailty. Ibsen never came closer to Chekhov than in this drama which can only be spoiled for us when an interpreter refers to Ibsen's "disappointment and hopelessness over humanity." The lovely glow of *The Wild Duck* could not come from disappointment and hopelessness; it emanates instead from a realization of how delicate is the thread of human happiness. Besides, what was there to be disappointed about and how can one denounce all idealism through Gregers Werle when this idealist is such a mess to begin with? The world's ethical leaders, barring some ultra-purists perhaps, are not to be measured by a provincial neurotic. In fact, Werle is not a leader at all, since he merely busies himself discovering new individuals or "phoenixes," as Dr. Relling calls them, and attributing extraordinary qualities to them. Similarly when the excellent biographer Koht writes that in this play "Ibsen had lost faith in that people could bear the full truth" [8] we can afford to be unconcerned; the "truth" that the Ekdals couldn't bear is decidedly small-town stuff not remote from the cackling of a brace of lantern-jawed gossips. This is true regardless of Ibsen's intentions, which greatly perplexed his admirers. Whether he strained a point in seeking to prove that ideals and illusions are the same* or put a parochial construction upon idealism, his real triumph lay in character drawing, imagination, and compassionateness.

It is also significant that despite the explicit philosophy of *The Wild Duck* Ibsen had not foresworn agitation by any means. In the spring of 1885 Ibsen left Rome for his homeland. In Trondheim he addressed the Labor Union, which celebrated his arrival with a procession, and he announced his dissatisfaction with the progress of liberty under the new state administration. He also called upon the working class to erect a new society and infuse it with a nobility of spirit. In Copenhagen he attacked the conservative leadership of the Norwegian Students' Union, and two months later he became an honorary member of its radical wing the Liberal Students' Society.

Still, his recognition of human frailty was not diminished by these scuffles with the old order. His new play *Rosmersholm* reflects the Norwegian struggle but is darkened by a realization of defeat. His hero Rosmer, who represents the liberal clergy, is galvanized into action by one of Ibsen's "new women," Rebecca. But he cannot stand alone. When he learns that his sibyl Rebecca was responsible for his wife's suicide by suggesting it, he loses his power to oppose the forces of conservatism represented by the shrewd and self-assured Rector Kroll. Rosmer is, in short, a failure no less than his former mentor, the quondam idealist and present vagabond Ulric Bendel. Victory falls to His Excellency the ecclesiast Peter Mortengard, who "never wills more than he can do" and is "capable of living his life without ideals."

But the trouble is much more deeply rooted. Ibsen was already treading the path of qualified disillusionment with the "new women" he had chosen to save the world. Rebecca, the new woman, came to Rosmer with the intention of expressing herself through him and making him the instrument of her will. For this purpose she was so completely "emancipated" that she was not burdened with love or a tender heart. "I knew no scruples," she confesses. "I stood in awe of no human tie." Having concluded that Rosmer's ailing, gentle wife Beata was an impediment to his liberation, she simply got rid of her. Her subtly poisoned suggestions worked, and Beata effaced herself by going to her death. The failure of the "new woman" lies in the fact that she is all "will" and no heart.

Nevertheless, Rebecca could not emancipate Rosmer. Moreover, having gone to these extremes she could not remain on her frozen elevation. Being human and a woman, she fell in love with Rosmer. Nor

* When Dr. Relling declares, "While I think of it, Mr. Werle junior, don't use that foreign word: ideals. We have the excellent native word: lies."

could she withstand her conscience any more than could Dostoyevsky's Raskolnikov whose superman complex fails him so miserably after he has murdered a wretched money-lender. The "Rosmersholm spirit" creeps into her bones and saps her strength; "the Rosmer view of life ennobles," she cries. "But it . . . kills happiness." She can, therefore, only restore his faith in her and expiate her crime by hurling herself into the mill-race in the company of the spiritually liquidated Rosmer who has succumbed to "the old fatal ideal of expiation by sacrifice." [9]

This conflict between the old conscience and the free spirit produces an occasionally haunting tragedy in *Rosmersholm*. The play falls short, however, of *The Wild Duck* to which it is so closely related, by its comparative stiffness of characterization. The pulsation of nature in Rebecca's blood—the sea in her soul and the famous hallucinatory "white horses of Rosmersholm"—do indeed permeate the play with a dissolving poetry. But this also produces some mystification that does not benefit the drama, with the result that it does not translate itself as satisfactorily on the stage as *The Wild Duck*.

Still *Rosmersholm* again marked an advance in a new direction, for Ibsen's grasp upon the complexities of the unconscious was increasing at the same time that his evangelical anger was abating. In his next play *The Lady from the Sea,* completed two years later, he still insisted on the gospel of individual liberty and oversimplified matters when Ellida overcomes her fascination for a mysterious sailor the moment her understanding husband allows her perfect liberty of action. "Freedom under responsibility" is the basic vision of *The Lady from the Sea*. Ellida, however, is most interesting as a battleground between conscious adjustment to life and unconscious drives as represented by her dreamy attachment to the only half-real sailor with the fish-eyes. Psychologists can make as much of her hallucinatory disturbance as moralists can make of her liberation the moment her husband allows her to leave him if she wishes; perhaps Ibsen was only reflecting the new trend toward the psychology of the unconscious which became especially marked in the nineties with Janet's investigations.

As an imaginative psychological drama, this study is not unworthy of Ibsen the voyager across troubled waters. Ellida's subjection to the pull of the sea and the tug of mysterious freedom represented by the man with the fish-eyes is motivated by her sheltered marriage to a middle-aged physician. Until Dr. Wangel fortifies her self-respect by allowing her freedom to choose between himself and her dream, until she achieves individuality and a sense of responsibility in remaining with him, she is herself only half-real. She is an idle, dependent woman; even her housekeeping is done by someone else—by her stepdaughter.

She is also childless. Restlessness—not to mention the more serious matter of neurosis—is frequent among her kind. *The Lady from the Sea* therefore possesses much solidity of characterization, as Duse must have shown when she played Ellida. The real misfortune of the play is only that it is not worthy of Ibsen the craftsman. Like so many other playwrights before and especially since his time, he proved himself a poor arbiter between the rival claims of symbolism and reality. The body of the play is confusing because it is too elusive.

Fortunately, however, Ibsen's blunderings were not wasted and his delvings into human complexity soon produced a drama in which he plumbed the depths with the calculated precision of a deep-sea diver. Foregoing symbolism and concentrating directly on human character as it reveals itself in recognizable action, Ibsen created a masterpiece in *Hedda Gabler*. Here explanations are unnecessary, Hedda being a crystal-clear example of a maladjusted woman. She has sisters in every city, for she belongs to the widely dispersed sorority of moderately comfortable women whose restlessness and envy arise from their false standards of happiness, as well as from their egotism and uselessness. No doubt she existed in the past, but her specific type is undeniably modern. Unlike the women of the older middle class who had their noses to the grindstone of the hearth, who reared children and ran their home, the Heddas described by Ibsen are rootless. Ibsen had envisaged emancipated women who could erect the home on new foundations, who would rear a generation of broad-minded individuals, and who would achieve economic independence if necessary. Hedda and her kind were of a different breed, since they were relieved of the old responsibilities without assuming new ones and were endowed with desires for a richer life without having learned that it must be won strenuously. In creating Hedda, Ibsen was, then, moving further along the road of qualified disillusionment, and he was making further strides toward realism; for it must be remembered that Hedda is a remarkably real person regardless of any reference to conditions in Zenith or Middletown.

Hedda, the daughter of General Gabler, belongs to the aristocracy by birth, but hers is no aristocracy of the spirit. Vague aspirations agitate her, but these are sterile and lead to no valid course of action. At the same time, like so many of her sisters, she is basically a philistine; wanting comfort and security, she plays safe. She marries the plodding scholar Tesman and covets a university position for him even while she resents the narrow professional world in which she finds herself. She dreams of a gloriously intoxicated life but cannot venture the experience; she likes a garland of "vine-leaves," so long as someone else wears it and pays the price for it. Lacking courage for experience and being too much the egotist and frigid woman to give herself to love, she naturally feels frustrated. Pregnancy, which she detests, only exacerbates her sense of frustration.

Envy consumes her when she sees that her former schoolmate Mrs. Elvsted whom she had despised is endowed with the courage of love and labor. Since Mrs. Elvsted is helping Hedda's former admirer Lövborg to realize his talents, Hedda discovers gratification only in spoiling the other woman's creation. Lövborg, who has overcome his inner chaos and dipsomania and is now forging ahead in the literary world, must be undone. She therefore causes him to relapse into his old ways and drives him to suicide. Then when the consequences of her action become serious and she must endure a humiliating liaison with the roué Judge Brack as the price of his silence she can find no alternative to shooting herself. The revolver she employs is her father's, the one relic of her shoddy and useless aristocracy.*

Hedda, the type of woman who so often finds her way to a psycho-analyst's door nowadays, is a supreme creation. Ibsen the portrait artist is both analytical and compassionate, mercilessly objective and yet by no means exultant over his subject's shortcomings. Combined with vivid portraits of the pedant Tesman, the daemonic Lövborg, and the complete woman Mrs. Elvsted, *Hedda Gabler* is a masterful character drama. Ibsen wrote much that was more ambitious but nothing greater.

6 JOURNEY'S END

Ibsen did not remain content with the powerful objectivity to which he had finally attained. Being at heart a poet, he lacked the capacity for permanent adjustment to realism. Once more he turned to the open sea of poetic adventure and his last works are, with one exception, permeated with longing for a life of courageous freedom and revolt against compromise. Perhaps the fear of old age overcame him and sharpened his thirst for self-realization. He had come down with acute influenza in 1890 and thoughts of death invaded his mind. Perhaps, too, his final resettlement in Norway in 1891 irritated him at least as much as it satisfied him. If he could now live comfortably with his devoted wife on the fortune he had accumulated from his work, he was no doubt also aware of the fact that he was distinctly rusticated. It was perhaps this unendurable thought, too, that brought him back to the lyric aspiration of his earlier years.

* It is perhaps worth observing that in her suicide, as in so many of Ibsen's catastrophes, Ibsen is still relying somewhat on the older dramaturgy, no matter how scrupulously he uses it. Women like Hedda fail even more completely by simply hanging on to life and by continuing to make everyone, including themselves, miserable. Shaw astutely remarked that the "tragedy of Hedda in real life is not that she commits suicide, but that she continues to live." [10]

At the same time, moreover, a sense of weariness and failure is never absent in his last works. In each instance, his characters look back upon an aborted or wasted life. When they win their way to the heights, it is almost too late or the defeat looms at least as large as the victory. Defeat is also his portion in his own creative work, and he is no longer a sure and dynamic craftsman; his plays become obscure or thin out, and the decline is, in the main, progressive.

In the best of latter-day works, *The Master Builder,* he still commands pathos and excitement. His failure is due to an attenuation of his material and a readiness to use a symbolic situation where an actual one would be more immediate and effective. Still he does not give up easily, and there is much provocativeness and color in his portraits. Although Hilda no doubt symbolizes the eager new generation that calls upon its elders to climb heights which the latter's blood pressure no longer allows, she is a vividly realized, if irritating, young person. She was, in fact, based upon observation, for Hilda resembles one of the many young women who had pursued Ibsen ever since he became an apostle of feminism. An additional model is probably a young woman he met in Tyrol who confessed a penchant for luring other women's husbands away from them. And the architect Solness is another product of direct observation with the author himself as the model; Ibsen was in those days himself a master builder who was torn between conservatism and liberalism, being hailed as their own by representatives of both factions and sensing no doubt some insufficiency in himself.

Solness is a memorable character who embodies all the qualities of an aging man and artist. Memories weigh him down, and he is tied to his frustrated wife who never used her talent for "building up the souls of little children" after her little twins died. Then, too, their death is on his conscience, since he had willed the fire that was indirectly responsible for their illness. The master builder has a sick conscience. He is, moreover, terrified of the younger generation when there is any likelihood of its competing with him; he fears that his young assistant Rognar Brovik is going to supplant him by conceiving new styles of architecture—"Not the old-fashioned stuff that *I* am in the habit of turning out!" At the same time he still dreams of doing great, bold things, of building "houses with steeples." He is therefore also irresistibly attracted to this new generation as represented by Hilda, and he would like to meet her expectations of him. Naturally, this leads to a catastrophe: although he fears high places, he ascends a tower at her request, and crashes to the ground.

It is one of life's ironies, if not laws, that he should try to reassert his youth only by undertaking something that he cannot perform because he suffers from dizziness. And there is even more irony as well as pathos in the fact that he should respond only to that element in the new generation which is least wholesome. He does not favor the honest and constructive young artist Brovik but the girl Ibsen himself described as a "bird of prey," for Hilda only covers her own insufficiency by seeking thrills. Actually, the only edifices Solness can now build are "castles in the air," though he still realizes that they ought to have a "firm foundation."

The Master Builder again dramatizes aspiration or the exertion of the will in defiance of inhibiting circumstances. Only, as we noted, it is heavy with a realization of the defeat of life. It contains great beauty and is richly suggestive. But like Master Solness it possesses an only partially realized life, and it suffers a catastrophe when it climbs the heights of symbolism.

The deterioration in Ibsen's craftsmanship became symptomatically even more marked in his next play completed two years later, in 1894. The symbolism of *The Master Builder* was continued in *Little Eyolf,* and the new play was in a sense a sequel. Loath to accept the closing defeatism of *The Master Builder* and inspired by one of his several friendships with young women (the accomplished pianist Hildur Anderson, the daughter of an old friend), he sounded a new hope. Whereas Solness and his wife fail to surmount the defeat of their lives, Alfred and Rita Allmers overcome their painful past. Their unconscious desire to get rid of their child "Little Eyolf," whom they considered an impediment to their freedom, had resulted in his death. This is a tenuous idea, eked out by the even thinner symbolism of the "Rat-Wife." But Alfred Allmers learns the truth of Brand's statement that "to live is an art"; he renounces his dreams of literary eminence to devote himself to the advancement of mankind. A powerful theme was lost in *Little Eyolf* when Ibsen immersed himself in mystifications and failed to endow the play with dramatic action.

He was more successful in *John Gabriel Borkman,* written in 1896 with greater intensity than the aging playwright had experienced for some years. He returned in this play to the betrayal of love or the sacrifice of love for material advantage which he had treated in *Pillars of Society.* Borkman renounced his love for Ella Rentheim in order to make his way in the financial world when the man who could ensure his success, who also happened to be in love with her, insisted upon the sacrifice. Instead Borkman married her cold-hearted sister, and lacking love for the latter he allowed his already egregious passion for power to intoxicate him. It led him up the vertiginous heights of financial speculation until he fell; he ruined hundreds of investors, big and small, and himself with them. He emerged from five years of prison life a broken man and added eight years of voluntary imprisonment in his room. He finds freedom and courage through Ella Rentheim only when it is too late; as he leaves his house "the cold" kills him. He meets his death from the same element that had killed him spiritually long ago.

The tragedy of this man who failed because he renounced every normal gratification is, however, only one facet of this provocative and deeply felt, if far too statically executed, tragedy. Even while his technical skill was failing him, Ibsen added a new tragic character to the drama. Borkman is a curious amalgam of a materialist and a poet. He serves his acquisitive instinct ruthlessly, but he is also intoxicated with the dream of conquering nature and increasing man's resources by means of his transactions. If he has ruined everyone, including himself, his motives were not mean-spirited. What he wanted was not merely "the kingdom—and the power—and the glory" in a literal sense. The kingdom included the wonders of modern industry; he wanted to see things wrested from the earth and shaped by man for human use. The tragedy, as Ella Rentheim declares, lies only in the fact that "there comes an icy blast from that kingdom." Borkman is Marlowe's Jew of Malta reincarnated after the Industrial Revolution. He is as contemporary as Insull, and writers like George Middleton who commemorated the latter in *Hiss, Boom, Blah* and S. N. Behrman who dissected the type in *Meteor* still portray the Borkmans of the modern world.

The firmly drawn Mrs. Borkman, who while hating her husband is fanatically bent upon twisting her son into a super-financier who will make it his mission to rehabilitate the Borkman name, is the feminine component in this tragedy of an entrepreneur. With additional effective characterizations of Mrs. Borkman's frustrated sister and of the pathetic clerk Foldal who wanted to be a writer, the play hammers at the emotions. Here again Ibsen conveys defeat more powerfully than liberation; although Erhart, the Borkmans' son, rejects his mother's mission and goes away with Mrs. Fanny Wilton claiming his right to happiness, it is the painful features of the play that leave the deepest impression. The depression is in fact so ingrained that it burdens *John Gabriel Borkman* with an almost insupportable heaviness.

The mood spread even into the valedictory *When We Dead Awaken,* which he completed in the fall of 1899. Only the conclusion sounds a note of venturesome triumph. The sculptor Rubek cheated Irene of life by using her only as a model for his art instead of giving her his love; and by the same token he cheated himself, too. The time came when he realized that there is no substitute for a rich emotional life, that "all the talk about the artist's vocation and the artist's mission" is "very empty, and hollow, and meaningless at bottom." But Rubek was the slave of art as much as Borkman was of finance. There is, then, a bitter protest in the play against everything—no matter how exalted—that deprives men of happiness. And no commodity seemed more precious to

Ibsen when life began to slip away from him. It seemed to him that everyone was cheated or cheated himself of it. "When we dead awaken, what do we really see then?" he asked in the play. "We see that we have never lived."

Ibsen suffered a paralytic stroke in the spring of 1900. A year later a second stroke deprived him of the use of his legs. Soon his hands failed him, and then the old fighter who had continued to plan new assaults upon the public was completely caged. Finally, his mind became clouded and he lingered in a twilight world until his death on the twenty-third of May 1906. What remained of the life-long viking was buried with official pomp by the government, an ironic conclusion that did not escape a German critic[11] who reported: "The ruling men in Norway had a daemon among them, and they buried a grandee."

When We Dead Awaken, although a weak and tenuous drama, was a suitable conclusion to his testament. He ended, as he began, a champion of individual happiness in the modern world which for all its worldliness was constantly denying personal happiness, which for all its philosophy of individualism in economic enterprise hampered the development of free and rich personalities. He had fought a half-century battle against every convention and tendency that impoverished the individual; whether he employed the most microscopic methods of realism or the most telescopic means of symbolism, his purpose remained the same. "No man," he declared in his sixties, "is ever free of responsibility for the society to which he belongs or without a share in its guilt."

When We Dead Awaken closes with a song of triumph: Rubek and Irene rise above their earth-bound failure, fearing neither the "powers of light" nor the "powers of darkness." They move up in search of spiritual peace "through all the mists and then right up to the summit of the tower that shines in the sunrise," and as they are engulfed by the murderous ice of the mountain peak, Irene's nurse—a Sister of Mercy—pronounces the benediction: *"Pax vobiscum."* Meanwhile Arnold Rubek's young wife, the sensuous pleasure-loving Maia who represents the vernal earth-spirit that Arnold had killed in himself and in Irene, sings in the valley below. For life is continuous and somehow invincible!

The conclusion of *When We Dead Awaken* is a last reminder that Ibsen struck for victory to the end, and also that for all his limitations or lapses into provincialism he was not a prosaic realist. Shaw who originally admired his Norwegian master for his assiduity in posing problems in the theatre, later recognized his superiority to the mere practitioner of the problem play and honored him because he "was to the last fascinating and full of a strange moving beauty." [12] This could only be because Ibsen was, for all his frequent gloom and anger, an apostle of Nietzsche's *gay saber.* His prime concern in the realistic and symbolic plays was with the "gay science" of human happiness for the sake of which he felt the necessity of destroying or remolding old foundations in man's spirit and society. Hence, for example, his dynamiting of old concepts of duty, to which he opposed the concept of self-realization, "the last step in the evolution of the conception of duty." [13]

That he did not always give due recognition to the fact that happiness and even self-realization are not entirely private achievements may have resulted, as some critics claim, from his egocentric outlook regarding society. Since Ibsen was a child of the individualistic middle class and since the working-class movement was still in its infancy, particularly in Norway—say these socialist critics[14]—he could not envisage the creation of a new society. Consequently he relied almost entirely on the individual. Actually, of course, Ibsen did envision a new social order. He merely differed from the socialists in the manner in which he expected it to be created—in relying upon individuals, in underestimating the relation between happiness and economic security, and in the vagueness of his ideas respecting the *modus operandi* of the new society.* These are his shortcomings in the opinion of the socialist critics who nevertheless admire him for his critique of the *status quo*. And for a related reason he is likewise troublesome to those who care little for either economics or socialism but believe that the rounded individual, far from being a rampant bull in a china shop, is a well-adjusted member of society or the partaker of a particular culture. A devotee of culture like Stark Young[15] could only consider Ibsen somewhat barbaric.

There is some truth in both these charges, and indeed no one is expected to find either a blueprint for effective social action or a serene Sophoclean spirit in his work. But by the same token he was a poet capturing resplendent half-truths through characters who move in "mental air" as well as in social surroundings. Did he not sense his attributes himself, as well as pay respect to the fluidity of dramatic creation, when he declared that he did not provide answers but only asked questions! His quintessence, as even Shaw conceded, is "that there is no formula."

* Even in this respect, however, he may tantalize these critics when he writes of the Paris Commune in 1871 that although its excessess have ruined the socialist idea for many a year "Yet it has a sound kernel . . . and some day it will be put into practice without any caricature." Even his belief that the state must be abolished—an anarchist idea—is not inconsonant with the socialist idea of the "withering away" of the state.

XX

THE SCANDINAVIAN SUCCESSION AND STRINDBERG

I IBSEN OVER EUROPE

IBSEN's spirit brooded upon the theatre and brought forth a progeny that multiplied itself prodigiously. It exhibited, and continues to exhibit, much variety and inequality of talent, and it is not easy to put the post-Ibsen playwrights into well-labeled pigeonholes, which is no doubt a good thing. One Ibsenite, that Aristophanes of modernity whom no one will fail to identify as Bernard Shaw, equaled his master's stature, and one antagonistic Scandinavian—Strindberg—was his equal in genius, if not in execution. Many of them were timid, cautious, or greatly limited men like Pinero and Sudermann. These writers marketed sugar-coated capsules of realism and throve exceedingly well. Others like Brieux and Hauptmann sometimes inflated themselves and have been for some time deflated. Some playwrights like Schnitzler, Synge and Chekhov made no effort to storm heaven and hell, but attained much sweetness and light. Also among the highly respected laborers in the vineyards of the bacchic lord were the associated artists of the theatre Antoine, Brahm, and Stanislavsky, who translated the new texts into stage movement.

The controversy that raged over Ibsen throughout Europe and in America has lost its interest because it was so thoroughly decided in Ibsen's favor. The *Schimpflexicon* in which H. L. Mencken commemorated his own notoriety during the nineteen-twenties would have to be turned into a Yearbook if Ibsen's voluble opponents were to be properly dishonored. This would serve no purpose, however, except to remind us that the world does not take lightly to innovators. Far more important is the fact that advanced spirits everywhere rallied to Ibsen's defense; that he found formidable champions in men of the stamp of Georg Brandes, Björnson, Shaw, William Archer, Edmund Gosse, Hermann Bahr, Ludwig Fulda, Leo Berg, Otto Brahm, and Emile Zola.

Although his work was occasionally suppressed in Germany and he was forced to placate respectability by adding a happy ending to *A Doll's House,* Ibsen won his first important victories in that country. Wherever the insurgent German theatre raised its head it bristled with Ibsen, and the greatest stage directors and actors presented his plays

384

during the eighties. No important German playwright could afford to neglect his example.

In France his triumph was limited by the French temperament and by the inadequacy of his translator Count Moritz Prozor, a Lithuanian by birth who knew German better than French. But the great critic Jules Lemaître noticed Ibsen with interest, and Emile Zola recommended his work to the enterprising young producer André Antoine. Antoine presented *Ghosts* in 1890 and played Oswald himself. The battle ended only in a draw, and conservative critics continued to disparage Ibsen. But Lugné-Poë kept him alive with pedestrian productions, and the great actress Réjane scored a signal success in 1894 with her Nora. In the other Latin countries Ibsen's example proved less galvanic. Yet he did not lack followers even in Spain and Italy, and Eleanora Duse's luminous acting furthered his reputation wherever she appeared.

Skirmishes in the eighties made him known in England largely owing to the interest of William Archer, the Scottish critic who had Scandinavian relatives and had learned Norwegian in childhood. Archer, who met Ibsen in Rome in 1881 and in Scandinavia in 1887, translated his *Pillars of Society* as early as 1880 and printed it in 1888. Mrs. Eleanor Marx-Aveling, Karl Marx's gifted daughter, followed suit with translations of *Ghosts* and *An Enemy of the People*. A volume containing the three translations in 1888 won many adherents. Next year *A Doll's House* was produced in another Archer translation, and a year later J. T. Grein defied the censor by giving a single performance of *Ghosts* at his Independent Theatre. Both plays aroused spirited controversies that brought Ibsen to the foreground. Archer wrote in his defense, and Shaw contributed the heavy artillery of his *Quintessence of Ibsenism* to the cause. By 1900 Ibsen was already so completely accepted as the father of the modern drama that he was actually being regarded as a moderate. Today he is not only taken for granted but considered somewhat antiquated by many critics.

It remains to be noted, however, that the dispersion of Ibsen's realism over Europe was a process rather than a static *fait accompli,* and most new playwrights did not follow a straight line. As a matter of fact, the drama traced a triple course in their work: at first it still worked in the romantic tradition, then it adopted realism, and finally it swung away from literal realism and turned to imaginative or "symbolic" drama. Some of the oldest of the playwrights went through all three stages, as was the case with Ibsen and Strindberg; or through the first two, as did Björnson. Younger men like Hauptmann and Wedekind (after insignificant romantic efforts which are the privilege of every nascent writer) often first made their mark in realism and then graduated to symbolism or "neo-romanticism."

Still in most instances, their lasting work belongs to the realistic theatre, since it was through realism that they were most closely allied with the promptings of their age and achieved the broadest intensities of experience and illumination. Moreover, their art was most communicable when they submitted to the demands of clarity or definiteness which symbolism could rarely meet.

2 BJÖRNSON AND STRINDBERG

In his own country Ibsen did not labor in a vacuum. He had co-workers, champions, and successors who furthered his efforts to create a new dispensation in the theatre. Although he often met with misunderstanding or vituperation in Scandinavia, and although he was surrounded by playwrights who did not share his interests, Ibsen found a brother in Björnstjerne Björnson, his friend and rival. The two men differed radically in temperament. Whereas Ibsen was seclusive and complicated, Björnson was sociable, given to exuberance, and superficial. But they had this in common—they were keenly concerned with the problems of their day and wanted to enlighten their compatriots. Moreover, the two men supplemented each other; Ibsen supplied the depth and intensity, Björnson the persuasiveness that ensured the success of realism in the North.

Persuasiveness came easily to Björnson. From his father, who was a Lutheran pastor of some standing, he seems to have acquired a talent for making sermons palatable. His enthusiasm, which was not overshadowed by introspection, led him into politics as well as literature, and for forty years he was an influential leader of Norway's Liberal Party. It was therefore Björnson, and not Ibsen, who won the greatest success in the Norwegian theatre. His superficiality irritated Ibsen, and their friendship was interrupted for a time. But it was precisely Björnson's popularity in politics and literature that enabled him to champion his friend's work with the greatest effect.

One who could ride the two horses of politics and letters with such ease had no difficulty in displaying the greatest versatility as a writer. Poems, essays, novels and plays flowed from his pen in almost equal profusion. Although born four years later than Ibsen, in 1832, he arrived at literary fame more quickly because he wasted no time in rounding out his education. At the age of twenty-six he published his first play, a one-acter *Between the Battles,* and in the same year he became a director of the Bergen theatre.

Like Ibsen he was first a romanticist with dramas like *Sigurd the Bad,* a saga play, and *Mary Stuart in Scotland,* a thin historical romance which appeared in 1864, the year of Ibsen's *Pretenders.* But by 1874, five years after the latter's social satire *The League of Youth,* Björnson was already writing realism in his drama *The Editor;* and a year later *A Bankruptcy* anticipated *Pillars of Society* in portraying a dishonest provincial business man. Tjaelda, an affluent merchant and brewer, discovers that his business is badly rocked by his friend's bankruptcy. In danger of becoming bankrupt himself, this "pillar of society" doctors his accounts in order to get a loan from a Christiania bank. His trick is discovered, and he is declared insolvent. However, the experience effects a spiritual awakening in his household; his family acquires new values and, like Consul Bernick, Tjaelda himself substitutes inner integrity for the money standard.

The double standard which Ibsen had attacked in *A Doll's House* evoked Björnson's problem play *The Gauntlet* four years later. A young couple comes to the parting of the ways when it is discovered that the man has had a mistress. Alfred Christensen pleads that this does not prevent him from now loving Svava deeply and faithfully. But, asks her mother, would Svava have been believed by him if the tables were reversed? The point of the argument is that a woman has the right to require of a fiancé the same prenuptial innocence that a man demands of his bride. Here, in fact, is a typical problem play such as Ibsen never quite wrote; the problem is everything instead of being incarnated in well-realized human characters. Needless to say it is satisfactorily settled when the estranged couple is reunited, solutions being easier for lesser men like Björnson than for Ibsen.

The Gauntlet was one of the first of the didactic pieces of the realistic theatre that challenged a convention in terms of a discussion. Nor was it the last to be written by Björnson, who never doubted that the theatre was the best Sunday school for the people. Once, however, in *Beyond Our Strength,* written during the same year as *The Gauntlet,* this good man discovered the flesh and the devil. Probably drawing upon his early pastoral environment, he created a fairly poignant tragedy of a clerical family. Pastor Sang is a courageous and devoted servant of God, but his wife is an unbeliever who sacrifices her health for his faith only because she is devoted to him. She has worked hard to protect the family while he was impoverishing it with his benefactions, and she has sent their son and daughter into the outside world in order to free them from their unhealthy environment. Meanwhile, however, she becomes more ill and her husband decides to heal her by prayer. He seems to cure her, even as he works cures among the rest of the people. In fact, he becomes a serious problem to the Church, which does not know what stand to take toward miracles; of course, its credo includes faith in miracles, but it is another thing to be confronted with them in one's own backyard. The bewilderment of the ecclesiastics produces a comic scene full of sly thrusts. But this drama is, in the last analysis, personal rather than philosophic.

It is clear that Pastor Sang's cures have been unintentionally effected by suggestion. His wife, who has at first responded to his faith-healing by exerting her will, he cannot cure; she dies when she attempts to leave her bed in order to give him the miracle in which he believes. And one astutely introduced detail even goes deeper into the recesses of the human soul. Cryptically, he cries out that perhaps God actually answered him and granted him his real, if unspoken, prayer; perhaps he secretly wanted his bedridden wife to die. . . .

Björnson never again reached the summits of this tragedy. A second play with the same title, written years later, dealt superficially with the capital-labor problem; and in other exercises he continued to examine phases of society as if in a test tube. He survived until 1910 without deepening his talent but also without losing the respect of his world, which rewarded him with the Nobel Prize in 1903—while Ibsen, to whom no such honor came, was still alive.

Even more overshadowed for a time, was the one writer who attained still greater intensities than Ibsen and carried his realistic art further than anyone in the North. August Strindberg, who was born in 1849 in Sweden, twenty-one years after Ibsen and seventeen after Björnson, was Saturday's child. In the first of his several memorable autobiographical novels, Strindberg called himself "the bondwoman's son," and he had many valid reasons. This Ishmael also set himself down as a "scoffer" and "a wild man," and if he had at the same time called himself a keen and compassionate observer of man and society he would have drawn a complete self-portrait. Elsewhere, in his play *The Great Highway*, he did add the final touches to the picture when in reply to the question "You do not love your fellowmen?" his autobiographical character says, "Yes, far too much."

His mother was indeed a "bondwoman," a barmaid in Stockholm. His father, a businessman who contracted the *mésalliance* much to the distress of his family, married her only a few months before August's birth—after two other children had been born. Strindberg was cradled in poverty, and the family was harassed by many births and deaths as long as the bondwoman lived; there was a time when the household crowded ten people into its three rooms. Home and school were equally uncongenial to the sensitive lad who was plagued by his older brothers and resented discipline of any kind. He became inordinately sensitive, suspicious, and irritable—traits that were exacerbated by his mother's death when he was thirteen and by his father's second marriage within a year. Nor was there much relief for Strindberg when he entered the University of Uppsala at eighteen only to freeze and go hungry in a garret. Unable to continue his studies after the first semester, he found himself constrained to teach in the same public school where he had suffered as a child. Whatever he did, he always seemed trapped; and given a proud and intense nature, it was inevitable that he would become "a wild man," a near paranoiac, and an overwrought pessimist.

Out of his despair arose a desire to express himself in literature. After attempting to write poetry he began to compose short plays, one of which was produced by the Royal Theatre with moderate success. Then another romantic piece, *The Outlaw* set in ancient Iceland, won him a stipend from Charles XV of Sweden which enabled him to return to the University. But he soon quarreled with the professors and neglected his studies in favor of literary pursuits, and he lost his stipend when the genial old king died about this time. Cutting loose again, he studied medicine, became an actor, and plied the trade of journalism, until finding all his efforts fruitless he retired to an island and gave himself wholly to writing. But the failure of *Master Olaf,* the full-length romantic historical drama which he completed there, was a keen disappointment and almost led him to abandon writing.

Having luckily found employment in the Royal Library he browsed and brooded, studied philosophy, tried to master Chinese, and wrote a learned monograph. Then he fell in love with a married woman, the Baroness Wrangel who divorced her husband for his sake, and under her influence he returned to literature, winning his first success with a novel. It was followed by a history *The Swedish People* which soon became the most popular book in Sweden next to the Bible, by a series of historical short stories, and by a volume of essays that turned from the past to the present and hammered away at social conditions.

Finally, after a successful revival of *Master Olaf* he returned to the theatre with a number of romantic plays, as well as with a satirical fairy tale *Lucky Pehr.* Ibsen's influence may be traced in this Swedish *Peer Gynt* although it ranks far below the Norwegian dramatic poem. In *Lucky Pehr,* for all its amateurish fiddle-faddle about elves and fairies, Strindberg opened a vein of social satire in the Swedish drama. It makes ingenious use of the speaking statue of a mayor, and its political satire is particularly incisive when Pehr is placed in the pillory after a vain attempt to introduce a few innocuous civic reforms.

Confident that he could now earn his living by writing, he resigned from the Royal Library and retired to Switzerland. Here he wrote a striking series of short stories on modern matrimony entitled *Married,* outraging respectability and causing his publisher to be arraigned in court. Although the book was confiscated, the episode only increased his popularity with the younger generation, particularly when he hastened home and, taking the publisher's place, won the case. A second volume of *Married* in 1886 was an even more uncompromising exposure of marriage, and with its publication Strindberg laid the groundwork for his major contribution to the theatre. Here were all the familiar elements of Strindbergian drama: ultra-realistic observation, psychological excoriation, and anti-feminism aimed at the cult that found comfort in *A Doll's House*. The latter element in his stories proved particularly important, since for reasons which had best be left to psychoanalysts Strindberg had begun to dread and resent women. The gist of his thesis was that between man and woman there exists a constant and consuming struggle for power. Moreover, this conflict is only exacerbated by the emancipation of women, which intensifies their will to power and actually makes them stronger than man because they are more unscrupulous. Like D. H. Lawrence, Strindberg maintained that someone must be the master in marriage, and that the power was far less likely to be abused by men than by women.

Whatever one may think of Strindberg's inordinate suspicion of the other sex and his angry protest against feminism, there is no disputing that he became an extaordinarily analytical and intense dramatist. Out of his private experience, both normal and pathological, he dredged up many pertinent observations on human beings and became the master of the psychological drama. In the Anglo-Saxon countries his plays are more frequently respected than produced—one reason perhaps being the importance of women as customers of the theatre, another being his extremely analytical style. But the Anglo-Saxon theatre has accepted him indirectly through O'Neill; Strindberg the realist is not distant in *Before Breakfast, All God's Chillun Got Wings,* and *Strange Interlude,* while the later "symbolist" Strindberg breathes in such work as *The Great God Brown.*

One year after *Marriage,* in 1887, appeared *The Father,* one of the most gripping psychological dramas of the modern theatre. A cavalry Captain and his wife Laura have been struggling for supremacy during the twenty years of their marriage, and she has worn him down in countless ways. Interfering in his management of the estate, she has nearly ruined him; and disliking his preoccupation with valuable researches in meteorology, because they involved expense and threatened to make him too famous for her, she has tampered with his correspondence. Moreover, he finds himself living in a matriarchy, since his home is ruled by his wife, her mother, and his old nurse, all of whom control his seventeen-year-old daughter. The crisis comes to a head when he tries to send her to a boarding school where she will be free of their pietistic influences. The issue, however is basically one of possession; and woman being the most possessive of all animals, the wife gives no quarter in this unequal battle. Laying her plans with ruthless cleverness—first getting rid of the old doctor who was friendly with the Captain, then driving the latter to distraction with the lie that he has no right to Bertha because she is not really his daughter—she finally has him declared insane. He cheats her of this final triumph only by dying in the straitjacket which his devoted old nurse has slipped on him.

On the surface the play suffers from melodramatic action, and obviously it drives its point too hard. But the intensely unfolding plot, the gradual exacerbation of the man until he is broken in spirit, and the subtle characterization of the wife produce a searing impression. How remarkable an analyst Strindberg could be at his best is to be seen in the character of the wife Laura, who combines shrewdness with ignorance, orthodoxy with a complete lack of morals, and kindness toward others with absolute diabolism toward the man she married. Moreover, it is only too clear that she is as much of a failure as the husband she has destroyed; she may not realize it, but she is an emotionally shipwrecked woman.

Strindberg was so obsessed with her personality that *Comrades,* which followed *The Father* in 1888, revolves around another Laura. The heroine Berta, an artist by profession but a parasite by nature, sucks her fill of her husband's superior talent and forces him to do hack work while she pursues her art. She gloats over his failure to win a prize that she actually gained only because he had without her knowledge signed her name to his own painting; she even tries to rid herself of him now that she considers herself superior. But when the rejected picture turns out to be her own, she is taken down a peg. Her husband Axel at last wakes up to the fact that a marriage cannot survive when wife and husband are competitors. Moreover, this vastly overrated modern marriage of "comradeship" is merely a means of serving the woman's interests, since she invariably advances herself at the expense of her mate's talent and freedom. Axel, therefore, is going to take a "sweetheart" and he leaves, declaring, "I like to meet a comrade at an inn; at home I want a wife."

Creditors, two years later, was likewise devoted to the danger of allowing a woman to deplete a man's strength. Here the literary wife, who exploited her first husband and libeled him in a novel, is now sapping her second husband's strength. Actually she is a weakling and a debtor to both her husbands. This long one-acter is a triumph of precision; it is a long mental duel between the wife and the ex-husband who disillusions his miserable successor.

A far more elaborate study of the duel of sex, the double drama *The Dance of Death,* written many years later (in 1901), revealed no falling off in Strindberg's analytical powers. Here, however, it is the husband, a morbid artillery captain, who is the tormentor. His wife is freed from his reign of terror only after he suffers a second stroke of apoplexy. This egotist and sadist dies fully convinced that he is righteous and has much to forgive his wife. She, who is also far from guiltless because she has provoked and betrayed him, strikes him and pulls his beard when his condition leaves him helpless. Hatred has bound them together as strongly as if they had loved each other, and their perverse relationship produces two of the most demonic characters of all literature.

Strindberg, it must be conceded, was always on the verge of becoming repetitive in his animadversions against predatory females. But his variations on the theme remained fresh and original, so that they possess reality even now when militant feminism is no longer an issue. In both his full-length plays and one-acters, Strindberg proved himself a master of psychological conflict, as well as an unflinching painter of the realities which the extreme realists or so-called naturalists often confined to the surface of life. He possessed, above all, a talent for avoiding the commonplace in reality. True dramatic naturalism, he contended, "loves to see that which cannot be seen every day," and his characters, as Storm Jameson has written, are "exceptional people in conflict with exceptional circumstance." It was the same talent for piercing the surface of things that led him to look askance at facile solutions of the sexual problem like those proposed by the feminist writers. It is not too much to rank him with such master psychologists of modern literature as Tolstoy, Dostoyevsky, Proust, and D. H. Lawrence. If he lacked Ibsen's largeness of spirit, he possessed more depth and intensity. It was his misfortune only that the depths often proved marshes which held him fast and finally swallowed him up.

Between *The Comrades* and *Creditors* came the remarkable *Miss Julia*, a work of such resolute realism that only a strong stomach can endure it. This short drama, for which the *motif* was supplied by a story he had heard a few years before, fuses two major observations into one powerful, compact plot—the duel of the sexes and the duel of the upper and lower classes. Miss Julia having been brought up by a rabidly feminist mother, alternately detests men and desires them nymphomaniacally. But invariably it is her hatred that gains the victory. Sadistically, she cuts her upper-class fiancé with her whip and loses him when he rebels. Her libido overwhelming her repugnance, she dances with the menservants and throws herself into the arms of her father's lackey. She almost runs away with him in order to avoid the inevitable scandal; but her repugnance prevailing again, she goes out to kill herself. This tense drama, suggestively strengthened by contrasts between the servants and their mistress, between upper- and lower-class viewpoints, belongs to the finest works of "naturalism." Zola had announced a naturalist program of observing the beast in man very much as a biologist would. Strindberg made no formal pronunciamento, although he did defend himself in a preface to the play, but the net effect was the same.

After these symptomatic works, no one could be surprised when in 1891 Strindberg's marriage ended in a divorce under highly unpleasant circumstances. The unsavory affair left a deep impression on him; six years later he wrote a strong drama about divorce in which the effect upon children is the prime consideration. In *The Link* two people are bound together by their child even while they sue each other with all the animosity customary in such proceedings. The earlier but decidedly powerful one-acter *Mother-Love* likewise pertains to the plight of children, with the added uncomplimentary detail of a girl's frustration by a divorced and prostituted mother. In 1893 he married an Austrian writer and became a father. But this second marriage also ended after a few years, as his overclouded mental state was not conducive to marital happiness. Strindberg began to engage in fantastic chemical experiments, became a Swedenborgian mystic, and experienced curious psychic reactions that could lead to only one conclusion. He found it expedient to enter a private sanatorium, and the timely precaution resulted in a quick recovery.

The shock to his nerves could not, however, be entirely erased. His mental seizure had opened doors which are usually closed to the normal person. Thereafter he saw experience as composed of continual recurrences and regarded the human personality as something that divides itself mysteriously. To the psychiatrist Strindberg's new outlook manifests the curious phenomena of *déjà vu*. depersonalization. and schizophrenia. Concurrently the character of his work underwent a marked change. His work became kinder and more pitiful. perhaps because his religious mysticism tempered his anger : "One gets more and more humble," he wrote. "and in the shadow of death many things look different." But his plays also became decidedly subjective and elusive.

One portion of his creative personality apparently retained complete normality, for he wrote a round dozen lucid historical plays. Among these *Queen Christina* contains a remarkable study of the sexually maladjusted, unstable woman who was finally compelled to abdicate when her subjects rebelled against her irresponsible management of the kingdom. Here Strindberg displayed his previous ability to probe feminine character with a scalpel, and the play won esteem abroad—notably in Germany where Elisabeth Bergner played the queen. *Gustavus Vasa,* the drama of a forceful ruler, is greatly admired in Scandinavia, and companion pieces enjoy comparative esteem in their native land even if most of them are too remote in historical interest to make much impression beyond Swedish territory. In the main, however, Strindberg is least impressive during this last period when he is most normal.

The other half of Strindberg's mentality moved in a subjective world. It expended itself in fairy-tale dramas of slight importance (although

The Bridal Crown is a charming folk story), and it seethed in unique symbolic plays that are of the highest importance. These works are not simply symbolic and suggestive like Ibsen's last efforts but dissociated, schizophrenic products combining the most scrupulous realism of detail with the most evanescent plots and characters.

Only the most hardy adherent of "experimental drama" will claim plays like *To Damascus, The Dream Play, The Great Highway,* and *The Spook Sonata* for the unspecialized theatre. Strindberg failed to become a completely communicable master when his mental crisis sent him to the sanatorium. Nevertheless, one cannot write *finis* to this verdict without important qualifications. The truth is that these symbolic works, which are full of compassion for bedeviled mankind, exercise a curious fascination. They provide a *surréaliste* experience that perturbs the soul and opens windows in it without quite communicating with the mind. Taken together, the plays may also be read with interest as chapters of a unique autobiography. In the theatre, moreover, they make Strindberg the forerunner of the expressionistic stage which widened dramatic horizons without exactly littering the stage with masterpieces.

But even these works have intrinsic merits because they are born of a probing, intense intellect and an infinite sensitivity to the pain of existence. His expressionist plays possess numerous incisive symbolizations of both the external and inner world of modern man. Provocative in *The Dream Play* are such details as the lawyer whose hands are too black ever to be made clean, and the lovers who stop at "Foulstrand" while *en route* to "Fairhaven." . . . The conflict of the social classes is suggested when coal-heavers exclaim that they are in "hell" while the rich in the Casino declare smugly that they are in "heaven." All the works of man are shown to be hollow in this strangely disturbing work. Earthly life is a nightmare, since it is the product of a fall. The feminine principle triumphed when the pure idea (of Buddhism and Swedenborgian mysticism) fell and was wedded to procreative matter. The human beings born of the union long for freedom from their flesh, and only their suffering can cleanse them.

All roads lead to Damascus (in the three parts of *To Damascus*) if the traveler is "sincere"; and all characters split, multiply and vanish in the infinite flux which is life. Life is full of the weeds of corruption in the *Spook Sonata*. The hell into which Christ descended was the hell of this world, and only faith and patience can end the tragic cycle of illusion, guilt and suffering. Anticipating both the subcutaneous explorations of psychoanalysis and the nightmares of the post-war expressionists who saw modern mankind in all its war-maddened horror, Strindberg belonged in spirit to the painfully parturient twentieth century. By comparison with him Ibsen is essentially an optimist and a naïve child of the nineteenth century which reposed such infinite faith in evolutionary progress.

After a third, also short-lived, marriage in 1901 with a young actress who performed in his symbolic drama *Easter* and after producing a continuous harvest of work which cannot be viewed without wonder as well as irritation, Strindberg finally found the only quietus that was possible for him. He died on May 14, 1912, leaving behind him a group of plays that can never command much popularity in the world at large and yet entitles him to a place among the leaders of the modern drama.

Like Ibsen and other masters of the new school, he had devoted a lifetime of study to problems of adjustment, and his twin themes of injustice in the home and in society provide both dramatic experience and illumination. He was a master of both naturalism and symbolism, and a forerunner of the "expressionism" of the post-war theatre. For it could be said that the sun never set on his influence; it extended from Japan to America. Strindberg lacked only one attribute that belongs to the greatest dramatists; he was deficient in balance and consistent rationality. Yet it must be conceded that without the unwholesome quirks in his constitution he would probably have failed to fathom the horrible depths. If Ibsen was the theatre's viking, Strindberg was its deep-sea diver.

He was also the last of the Scandinavian universal masters. The example of Ibsen, Björnson and Strindberg was indeed too potent to allow the Northern drama to lapse into cheapness, and it has remained eminently thoughtful. Idealism, too, has never been abandoned by this theatre. The critic Bjorkman has summarized the Scandinavian heritage, which stems from the ancient sagas, in two conclusive sentences: "Back of all recording of sordid deeds lies the desire to set examples for the making of men as they should be. And the old Scandinavian ideal of a man was that he should never let himself be daunted by either men or facts."[1]

Problem plays continued to flourish abundantly, and they naturally also spread to the related nation of Finland where its Helen Wuolijoki celebrated feminism and social justice in works like *The Women of Niskavuori, Justine* and *Hulda, Daughter of Parliament*. Hjalmar Bergström, the best known of the Danish playwrights, wrote social plays like *Karen Bornemann*, a drama of feminine emancipation, and *Lynggard & Co.*, a picture of the class struggle in which the good intentions of kindly capitalists prove futile. The eminent novelist Knut Hamsun, J. Anker Larsen, Paul Knudson, Gunnar Heiberg, known for his deflation of passion in *Balcony* and *Tragedy of Love*, Gustave Wied who was admired in Germany — these and many others turned out adequate some work. In distant Iceland Johann Sigurjonsson, born in 1880, conveyed a rich and novel background of primitive life in *The Hraun Farm* and in the adventurous and highly poetic *Eyvind of the Hills* (1911).

Most notably, the Swedish playwright Pär Lagerkvist (1891–   ), responding to the influence of Maeterlinck and the Strindberg of the dream plays, wrote some original and misty symbolist pieces, among which *The Hangman*, written in 1934 with obvious reference to Hitler, was the most vigorous. It showed the fear and fascination that evil can exert on people. The idealistic Danish clergyman Kaj Munk (1898–1944), assassinated by a pro-Nazi band in his own country, tried to recover the grand manner banished by Ibsen. Although capable of writing with strong realism, he relied on passion, violent action bordering on melodrama, and rather old-fashioned poetical fervor to support his nobly intended didacticism. His religious drama *The Word* (1932) and his patriotic last play *Niels Ebbesen* (1943) made the strongest impression in a body of work that included a number of historical plays. An impression, too, was created by the younger Danish dramatist Kjeld Abell (1902–   ) who created odd fantasies in the nineteen-thirties such as *The Melody That Got Lost* and *Eve*, the latter a comedy in which pictures in a museum come alive to impress the moral that since life is not a museum new values must be sought in the world. Although Abell's work was tenuous, its clever, more or less expressionist, stylization attracted attention.

Nevertheless, regardless of realistic, romantic, or expressionist style, Scandinavian drama failed to cast a second spell over the international theatre after the labors of Ibsen and Strindberg. The later playwrights were tamer men. They were epigones in spirit, as well as by birth, under the huge shadows cast by two men who in their different ways had more kinship with the heroes of the *Eddas* and *sagas* than with the tailored realists and fantasists of literary circles.

XXI

THE JOURNEYMEN OF THE FRENCH SUCCESSION

No COUNTRY in the world is so passionately enamored of literary and art movements as France, and no nation is so partial to labels. Nowhere was classicism a more rigid formula; romanticism burst upon France in a welter of pronunciamentos; and the formulations of Parnassians, realists, naturalists, symbolists, impressionists, cubists, unanimists, and surrealists—to select only a few—are enough to keep historians in a perpetual whirl. It is not surprising, therefore, that when the French theatre finally turned to modernist realism the transformation was managed with the greatest tub-thumping.

At the same time, however, few nations are so gifted with rationality, and the citadel of *bon sens* was never completely captured. Even during the flamboyant age of romantic drama Alfred de Vigny adhered to a classic style. In the same period, Alfred de Musset wrote his delightful curtain raisers *Comédies et Proverbes* (*Comedies and Proverbs*) in the style of Molière or balanced the stormy glorification of his passion for George Sand in *On ne badine pas avec l'amour* (*One Does Not Trifle with Love*) with humor; rarely did this violent romantic fail to apply some Gallic salt to the wounds of Eros.

Similarly, when realism was becoming a dominant factor in the theatre, a semi-classicist like Bornier could still find a place on the stage with a *Fille de Roland* (*Roland's Daughter*) in 1875 and with a *Fils de l'Aretin (Aretino's Son)* as late as 1895. Francois Coppée could still uphold the romantic tradition with historical plays like *The Jacobites* in 1885 and Jean Richepin could score a success with an idyllic poetic drama like *Le Chemineau* (*The Road*) in 1897. Pure humor has also jostled the most sober exercises of the French theatre. While Augier and Dumas *fils* were turning out their problem plays Eugène Labiche marketed his hundred and fifty-odd workaday farces for appreciative audiences between 1845 and 1875. These ranged from pure *Room Service* type of harum-scarum amenities like *Le Chapeau de Paille d'Italie,* produced in New York under the title of *Horse Eats Hat,* to more thoughtful farces like *Le Voyage de M. Perrichon* based on the theory that we are fonder of those whom we help than of those who help us. Even when extreme realism or naturalism was finding a foothold with the work of Henri Becque, Edward Pailleron did not feel any hesitation about continuing his humorous vein in a number of pieces and capped them with his famous satire on respectability *La Monde où l'on s'ennuie*, known in English as *The Art of Being Bored*. And it may be conceded that this old-fashioned comedy of the fashionable world "where one is bored" is more readable than some more modern and serious efforts.

Both the strength and the weakness of the French drama after 1880 come from this chronic inability to surrender completely to some aim. Decidedly more entranced with sheer theatre than with the high art of drama, the French did not encourage the birth of a single playwright of distinct eminence; and their contributions to realism—no matter how well supported with pronunciamentos—have been wayward. They attempted to create realistic and naturalistic plays, but only rarely did they seek or accomplish drama of significance. The major accomplishment of the French theatre was, for the most part, a sharpening and intensification in the presentation of human relationships in love and marriage rather than a probing of ideas and social conditions which gave realism its chief importance in the work of Ibsen, Strindberg, Hauptmann and Shaw French drama has lived by its gaiety, its wit and its civilized comprehension of ordinary human problems.

I ZOLA AND NATURALISM

Impatience with the theatricalism of the French theatre and the call for "a slice of life" came from the novelists. Balzac had completed a large part of his document of French life in the novels of his Human Comedy by 1839 when he turned to playwriting. But plays like *Vautrin* and *Le Faiseur* (*The Swindler*) were unsuitable for their day, and would have been dismissed even if they had been better than they were. Flaubert stood despairingly aloof from the theatre, complaining that all his efforts at playwriting ended in "perfect vaudeville" and giving only the novel the benefit of his masterful realistic art. The de Goncourt brothers, adopting the opposite policy of ardently patronizing the stage after 1851, made vain demands upon it. Clamoring for the same naturalism that they were applying to fiction, they announced a program: "Ordinary speech would replace high-flown periods, scenery would have some connection with the action, actors were to speak their lines like humans . . . and, most daring, the play was to have an idea, political or otherwise." [1] This at a time when the fastidious Gautier was not above declaring that Molière's plays were vulgar rubbish! But when they tried their hand at filling their own prescription with *Henriette Maréchal* in 1865, they were greeted with catcalls and were so belabored as offensive vulgarians that they were routed from the stage.

Edmond de Goncourt, however, lived long enough to see their innovations become solid conventions largely because another and more embattled novelist, none other than Emile Zola, manned the naturalist guns between 1873 and 1878. Like Edmond de Goncourt who complained that there was hardly a dénouement that was not brought about by someone overhearing a conversation or intercepting a letter, Zola began by protesting against the reign of intrigue in the theatre. The prevailing drama, in his opinion, was nothing more than "a mere game of patience." Hugo had stormed the classic stage by protesting against the "vice that kills it—the commonplace." [2] Zola, in turn, enthroned the commonplace in the name of truth. Opposing the whole concept of art as an "arrangement" of reality, he called for a "large and simple delineation of men and things," and for characters who "do not *play* but *live* before the public." [3]

Even the realistic problem play, the *pièce à thèse,* of Dumas *fils* and Augier seemed to him an arrangement of life and consequently a violation of reality. Not preachment but the application of the methods of the natural sciences—in short, "naturalism"—would serve his purpose. Zola's aim of submitting humanity to "a system of precise analysis, taking into account all circumstances, environment, and organic cases" was a large order which even a sequence of novels like his Rougon-Macquart series could not completely fill. But at least dramatists might discipline themselves with making each play a *lambeau d'existence* or fragment of real life. Consequently the "fragment"—or, to use a more familiar term, the "slice of life" (*tranche de vie*)—became the new ideal of the drama. It was with such precepts that Zola ushered in a phase of realism that went beyond the most realistic works that Ibsen was yet to write. For Ibsen never attempted a mere "slice of life," whereas Zola refused to be content with anything short of an objective case history reported in the manner of the natural sciences.

Zola put his theories into practice in the drama as well as in the novel. In spite of their theories, the de Goncourt brothers had not been above using accidents and coincidences in *Henriette Maréchal;* a shot kills the wrong person and the defender of an unknown woman is accidentally brought into her house when he is wounded. Zola, too, wandered from the straight and narrow path of naturalism, but his dramatization of the novel *Thérèse Raquin* in 1873 was the first conscientiously written naturalist drama. Thérèse and her lover, living only in their senses, drown her husband and are at last free to marry, but they are so overwhelmed with remorse and superstitious fear that they take poison on the night of their marriage. Carefully located in a petty bourgeois background and well supplied with commonplace realities, which are intensified by the horrors of crime and remorse, *Thérèse Raquin* was precisely the slice of life which Zola wanted to substitute for the neat artifices of the theatre. There was ruthless realism, even at the risk of horrifying his audience, in a work regarding which he wrote: "Given a strong man and an unsatisfied woman, to seek in them the beast, to see nothing but the beast, to throw them into a violent drama and note scrupulously the sensations and acts of these creatures. . . . I have simply done on two living bodies the work which surgeons do on corpses." [4] *Thérèse Raquin*, however, was hissed off the stage, and the influential critic Francisque Sarcey left this "somber and stifling tragedy" [5] complaining "This fellow, Zola, makes me a little sick."

Hugo had used the "grotesque," creating curiously ugly or weird characters like his vengeful court jester or the unfortunate whose features express laughter even when his heart is breaking ("The Man Who Laughs"), in order to intensify feeling. Zola, on the contrary, employed ugliness in order to convey the realities of commonplace society. Moreover, influenced by Claude Bernard's psychology of the nervous system, as well as constitutionally addicted to unsavory details (he had, for example, a penchant for foul odors), Zola was led to reduce emotion to the lowest common denominator of physical sensation. It is not surprising that this assiduous presentation of ugliness should have been found offensive. Even his subsequent tragi-comedy *Les Héritiers Rabourdin* (*The Rabourdin Heirs*) was set down as "dull, repulsive, and immoral." In 1874 Zola qualified completely for a monthly "Dinner of Hissed Authors" attended by Flaubert, Turgenev and Edmond de Goncourt, all of whom had met reverses in the world of letters.

Failure did not, however, prevent Zola from crystallizing the fundamentals of extreme realism or naturalism as it appears in much of the work of Strindberg, Hauptmann, O'Neill and others. In varying proportions the same elements are found in many of their plays: pictures of drab or commonplace life interrupted by sudden flashes of violence, overpowering sexual drives, and fatalism stemming from the belief that man cannot overcome heredity, environment, and lust.

Since it was from the novel that the drama was acquiring its naturalist technique, Zola was followed into the theatre by his fellow-novelists. Alphonse Daudet contributed diluted realism with his *L'Arlésienne*, and Maupassant infused his trenchant realism into two unsuccessful plays. But the triumph of the new drama could only be ensured by leaders who were something more than novelists vacationing in the theatre. A born playwright and a courageous theatrical producer were needed, and France soon found the former in Henry Becque and the latter in André Antoine.

2 BECQUE AND ANTOINE

Becque had the right disposition for naturalism. He was a misanthrope who considered men capable of the utmost baseness, accused them of persecuting him, and even brought suit against a manager for refusing a play of his. He also found sufficient provocation in a life of poverty and failure. Born in 1837, he began to write tentatively in the sixties, although his first substantial work *L'Enfant prodigue* (*The Prodigal Son*) in 1868 already revealed a talent for mordant comedy. After a few crude efforts, he achieved objective characterization in a one-acter *Les Honnêtes Femmes* (*The Honest Women*) in 1880, and finally by 1882 when his *Les Corbeaux* (*The Vultures*) appeared he was a highly potent naturalist.

Nothing so uncompromising had appeared on the French stage as this picture of the despoiling of a wealthy industrialist's family by his dishonest partner Teissier, by a ravenous notary, and by other vultures. M. Vigneron leaves his wife and three daughters helpless in their clutches when he dies. Knowing nothing about business, they are preyed upon until they are practically ruined. In this critical situation, with one sister losing her fiancé and another faced with no alternative but a life of shame, the third and most clear-minded of the daughters Marie consents to marry the rapacious old partner. Now that he is in the family he routs the other birds of prey and the women are saved—at the expense of Marie's happiness.

Lacking a historical perspective, its pessimism is more prominent than its critique of society, and its long speeches, soliloquies and asides make the play somewhat old-fashioned. Yet a more powerful exposé of the rapacity of middle-class life can hardly be conceived than this "Bible of naturalism," and the ghost of Becque hovers in the wings whenever a contemporary playwright addresses himself to the laissez-faire spirit in our civilization. One can imagine Becque rubbing his hands in delight when the curtain rose in 1939 on the vultures of American industrialism who appear in Lillian Hellman's *The Little Foxes*.

Three years after *Les Corbeaux,* Becque tightened his method, concentrating his focus on a single unpleasant character in *La Parisienne* or *The Parisian Woman*. Superficially a triangle play, it is actually a merciless anatomy of a conscienceless woman. Clotilde is a perfect wife. In order to advance her husband's interests she dismisses one lover and turns to another. The same practicality finally makes her return to her first lover, because a *ménage á trois* for her must be a settled and respectable affair! The bitter irony of such a "slice of life" is a more effective exposure of baseness than any number of moralizing denunciations, and the playwright's objectivity possesses the sharpness of a scalpel. Clotilde is perfectly unconscious of her vileness; she even complains to her lover that he does not care enough for her husband, although actually the two men are on excellent terms with each other. She declares herself a "downright conservative" and a believer in "sound principles." Upbraiding her lover she says in perfect innocence, "You are a freethinker! I believe you would even get along with a mistress who had no religion."

In these *comédies rosses,* as they were called, characters are capable of anything without being aware of their degradation or failing to maintain a façade of respectability. Becque's objectivity, moreover, makes him leave conclusions to the audience instead of winding up his play in the neat manner of the *pièce bien faite* or commenting on his picture by means of some *raisonneur* or omniscient mouthpiece. The picture, the slice of life, is sufficient for this naturalist; he would no more think of moralizing on his discoveries of human baseness than would a physiologist lecturing on the diseases of the liver. Becque continued to write in this vein, although he never again approximated the importance of *Les Corbeaux* and *La Parisienne,* until his death in 1899.*

Two years after the last-mentioned play, the foundations of naturalism were completed by the creation of a theatre largely devoted to its principles. An employee of the Paris Gas Company André Antoine had found himself attracted to the stage. At first he hired himself out as a *claqueur* at the *Comédie Française,* leading the applause at the old house for a price and for the opportunity to watch its performances. Later he trained himself as an actor and became a member of an amateur company, the *Cercle Gaulois.*

In 1887 he still had only a vague aspiration for success in the theatre, and he had as yet no program. He was merely interested in excelling a rival amateur group. But to do so he needed new authors, and being a dogged individual he was soon discovering fresh talent. His big moment came when Leon Hennique, a member of Zola's literary circle, gave him a one-acter based on a story by the master. It nearly wrecked the *Cercle Gaulois* because conservative members forbade Antoine to use the

---

* Becque had a number of followers like Henry Céard, Romain Coolus, Jean Jullien and Georges Ancey who wrote acrid comedies or so-called *comédies rosses* in the manner of *The Vultures.* In Ancey's *School of Widowers* a father and a son share the same woman's favors and in *The Inseparables* two friends have a like arrangement; in Jullien's *l'Echéance* or *Day of Reckoning* a husband condones his wife's relationship with a benefactor. Zola's descriptions of common brutality also won adherents among a number of playwrights who debased the high intent of naturalism with melodramas of the grand guignol variety or wrote peasant plays like Jullien's *Master.*

name of the club for any such departure from conventional drama. Antoine consequently hit upon a new name *Le Théâtre Libre* or The Free
Theatre. His first bill of one-acters, given on May 30, 1887 after much
grubbing for funds and subscriptions, enjoyed the support of Zola,
Daudet and the rest of the naturalists. And it was through their interest
that the *Théâtre Libre* became the organ of naturalism.

Two months later a second bill in Antoine's improvised playhouse
won enough public recognition to encourage the amateur director to resign from the gas company and give himself professionally to the stage.
Henceforth he devoted himself to uncovering playwrights, and to introducing the work of Ibsen, Strindberg, Tolstoy, Hauptmann and others
who were bringing new life into the theatre. Curel, Porto-Riche, Brieux
and numerous other authors owed their first opportunity to him; no one
who strove for realistic expression found this intrepid director wholly indifferent. For seven years the *Théâtre Libre* became the fortress of the
new drama, and its example was followed throughout the Western World.

Nor was the *Théâtre Libre's* function merely that of a repository for
the realistic drama. For realism or naturalism to be successfully transferred to the stage, a new style of acting and production was imperative,
and here again Antoine was in the van. French acting was rooted in classic and romantic traditions, and naturalness could hardly be conspicuous
in a theatre that still loves the kind of inflated oratory that "lifts a
Frenchman out of his seat and makes an American wish to crawl under
his. . . ." [6] Antoine replaced the conventions of "theatricality" with
those of "naturalness"; his actors "talked into the fire," turned their
backs on the audience, and spoke in natural accents which were sometimes barely heard. In his little theatre in the Passage de l'Elysee Beaux
Arts, moreover, realistic drama received a realistic setting or *mise en
scène*.

Antoine's subscription theatre declined after four or five years and he
resigned from it in 1894. He became a celebrated actor later on, established another group, and was for several years director of the National
Theatre at the Odeon.

In time, naturalism began to wane in France. French drama returned
to polite humor and extravaganza, to light "boulevard" comedies of
adultery like the clever contraptions of Sacha Guitry, and to melodramas and sentimental exercises like many of the plays of Henri Bernstein. Even romanticism came back, both in its old form and in the new
incarnation of symbolism; the author of *Cyrano de Bergerac* made his
debut in the same year that marked Antoine's resignation from the
Théâtre Libre. The conditions of the French theatre and the nature of
French naturalism lacked the requisites of great realistic drama.

3 THE DILUTION OF NATURALISM

Only Eugène Brieux, the son of a carpenter and a dramatist who was close to the miseries of common humanity, made some effort to preserve naturalism by finding a justification for it. Born in 1858 in Paris, he reached maturity during the Zola-Becque period, and his first acts are generally masterly examples of naturalist exposition. But Brieux was fired by deep convictions and stirred by pity for humanity. In play after play, beginning with *Blanchette* in 1892, he addressed himself to the conditions which produced misery and injustice in the modern world, and his long list of plays reads like a social service catalogue. *Blanchette* attacks society for not giving young women an opportunity to find an outlet in the teaching profession; *The Philanthropists* describes the shortcomings of philanthropy; *The Three Daughters of M. Dupont* represents the calamitous effects of marriages of convenience; *Maternity* presents the sufferings and dangers entailed by the absence of legalized birth control; *The Red Robe* exposes abuses in the administration of justice; *Les Avariés* or *Damaged Goods* discusses the ravages of venereal disease. These are only a few of the numerous problems which he set on the stage. It was a consuming pity, moreover, that drove Brieux to strive for the reformation of society.

Brieux almost moved away from the gelid, unemotional methods of naturalism, employing its formidable objectivity only when he introduced his situations and characters and minced no words in describing unsavory realities. Unfortunately, however, he lacked the poetry and subtlety of a great playwright. He did not fail precisely because he presented problems in the theatre. He fell by the wayside because of his journalistic and didactic intellect. No sooner has he presented a situation than he resolves it with arguments, preachments, harangues, and platitudes. "It is my nature to preach" Brieux admitted with obtuse pride: "The theatre is what attracts the people; there you can get them." The reaction against his problem plays was bound to be violent; when he died in 1932 few people were inclined to feel the loss.

Nevertheless, Brieux did not always forget that the theatre is not a Russell Sage Foundation. Even a problem play like *The Three Daughters of M. Dupont* strikes fire with a mordant satire on mendacity and greed in conventional marriage agreements. There is rich humor, worthy of Molière, in the description of the Dupont and Mairaut families when each party tries to fool the other with promises of wealth; and there is considerable pathos in the unhappy marriage that they have arranged between their children. Brieux is particularly effective in his "happy endings," in which a conventionally happy solution is basically tragic, as when the young wife in the Dupont play returns to a life of misery and deception with her husband.

His domestic tragedy of selfish mother-love *La Couvée* or *The Brood*, written as early as 1893, contains much understanding pathos, and *La petite Amie* (*The Little Friend*), in 1902, provides a fairly moving picture of two gentle people who are made miserable by the ruthless ambition of the father of the family. Finally, *Les Hannetons* (*The June Bugs*), with its sardonic point that free love can become an even greater bondage than marriage and its powerful picture of the lover Pierre who cannot shake off the woman who preys on his weakness, is an incisive comedy. What it lacks in finish it makes up in sharpness. Despite his many irritating lapses into mere didacticism, Brieux had the potentialities of a powerful, if never of a first-rank, dramatist; his first acts attest this. When he was defeated by his pedestrian rationalism, French realism lost one of its most ambitious exponents.*

What emanated from the movement started by Zola, Becque, and Antoine was a highly intelligent and reasoned drama which at its best interests us by its intelligence and neatness, occasionally stirs us with its insight into character, and often amuses by the brilliance with which it flickers on the surface of human behavior. Indisputably, men like Porto-Riche, Lavedan, and Hervieu—the first ponderable playwrights of the new dispensation—diluted naturalism. But each of them contributed drama that one can at least approach with some respect and pleasure because they were urbane and fairly finished writers.

Georges de Porto-Riche, Brieux's senior by nine years, began his career by writing poetry, and the same delicacy permeated his plays without detracting from their vigor. To the ancient subject of the battle of the sexes he brought a rare intelligence which gave the French theatre in 1891 one of its minor masterpieces—*Amoureuse* or *A Loving Wife*. This comedy, which he had anticipated three years before with a one-acter *La Chance de François*, reverses the triangle and balances it on its point. Here domestic unhappiness and adultery are caused not by a woman's

---

* It should be noted that Brieux did not lack followers. The reformist drama had among its devotees Emile Fabre, noted for his numerous attacks on the unscrupulous pursuit of wealth, stockmarket manipulations, imperialistic exploitation, and so on. (*Money*, performed by the *Théâtre Libre*, *Gilded Stomachs*, *The Locusts*). Another foe of predatory wealth, Octave Mirbeau, expressed sympathy for labor's struggle against capital in *The Bad Shepherds* and composed an incisive portrait of a financier who worships the power of money in *Business Is Business*. Numerous other playwrights including Curel, Lavedan, Donnay, Lemaître, and Bernstein, occasionally added their mite. Bernstein, in fact, turned from melodrama to problem plays that are painfully slow and dull. Brieux made a brave effort to wean the French theatre from frivolity, but the *ersatz* article which he provided was inadequate.

inability to love her husband but by the latter's inability to endure her extreme affectionateness. A prominent scientist, Dr. Etienne Feriaud, finds that his energies are too greatly taxed by his doting wife Germaine. She is interfering with his medical researches, and he even gives up an important scientific congress because her love prevents him from leaving her. Having sowed a peck of wild oats previously, he does not want love but a peaceful arrangement that will enable him to ply his researches without hindrance, and his irritation is so great that he drives his wife into the arms of a family friend. Written with enough wit to float a fleet of second-rate comedies, with shrewd insight expressed pithily in such sentences as Etienne's statement, "To me, a mistress had meant a regular life, my wife made my life irregular," *Amoureuse* belongs among the pointed high comedies of the modern stage. It is unfortunate only that Porto-Riche had only one string to his lyre; moreover, he not only repeated himself in his best work but lost his economical style. The more painstaking he became in such works as *Le Passé* (*The Past*) and the tragic *Le Vieil Homme* (*The Old Man*) the less he succeeded in conveying the neat effects appropriate to the Gallic analysis of domestic relationships. Only in the spare comic art of *Amoureuse* did he find a proper instrument.

Fortunately for the amenities, however, the French theatre has never been devoid of playwrights who can extract intelligent humor from domestic situations. A decline in his powers was, then, hardly a catastrophe. Moreover, the drama needed and received more deepening than Porto-Riche could provide. His juniors by a number of years, de Curel, Lavedan and Hervieu all developed new resources of psychological and social analysis.

Viscount François de Curel, a reserved aristocrat who could afford to brood over his plays and limit his output, was constitutionally qualified for dissecting curious emotions. Trained in the sciences, he developed a cold, precise style. Reared in a wealthy industrial family, he acquired a knowledge of the world of affairs. Consequently he brought to the theatre a dual aptitude: he created psychological drama and "drama of ideas."

In 1891 Curel submitted three plays to Antoine under different pseudonyms, and when all were accepted he was encouraged to devote himself to the stage. The first of them to be produced, in 1892, was *L'Envers d'une Sainte* (*A False Saint*), the tragedy of a woman who retired to a convent after trying to kill her rival. After eighteen years she learns that she renounced life in vain, since her behavior had not been kept secret by the other woman. A year later, appeared Curel's *L'Invitée* (*The Guest*), another psychological study in which a woman who left her husband and her children because of his infidelity allows herself to be maligned for sixteen years. Finally, she returns, vindicates herself in the eyes of her neglected daughters, and removes them from their father's influence. Still another analytical piece *La Figurante* (*The Dancer*) describes a young woman's successful effort to win her husband's love after she marries him with the understanding that he is to retain his mistress. In these plays, Curel was essentially a psychologist.

In other works, however, this probing playwright addressed himself to larger problems. As early as 1892 he proved himself a keen social diagnostician in *Les Fossiles* (*The Fossils*), a powerful study of the decayed aristocracy which sacrifices everything for its family name. The Duke de Chantenelles and his family are leading a life of embittered seclusion, since they are without any function in the French Republic. When his dying son Robert, the last of the line, requests the presence of a girl who was his mistress the Duke allows them to marry. He does this despite the fact that the girl was also his own mistress, because any outrage is permissible so long as the family name will be preserved; and preserved it will be since she has borne a son to the Chantenelles family. Robert learns the truth at last from his sister Claire, and deliberately shortens his life, first enabling his wife and child to leave the decayed household in order that the latter may live in the real world where nobility is not a patent but an active pursuit.

Curel's inquiring intellect carried him even further into the theatre of ideas. In *Le Repas du Lion* or *The Lion's Feast* he followed his young nobleman into the modern world of socialism, trade-unionism, and social problems. Curel's absorption in the struggle between aristocracy and socialism was, in fact, so great that he returned to this play, which he had written in 1897, and revised it in 1920. His inquiring intellect also made him project the modern conflict between science and faith through the inner struggle of his Dr. Donnat in *La nouvelle Idole* (*The New Idol*). The same questions in *La Fille Sauvage* or *The Savage Girl*, written eight years later, in 1902, even forced him to crack the mold of his realistic technique and adopt symbolism in an overambitious effort to convey the conflict between instinct and religion in the human soul.

Struggling with difficult material and writing his plays without an easy correspondence to the demands of the practical theatre, Curel never became a popular playwright. When he died in 1929 France lost a playwright of the highest integrity, an austere and yet intense artist, and a superb diagnostician of tortured souls. He stands at some distance from his easy-going fellow-playwrights and is decidedly out of place on the boulevards. It must be conceded only that he was an uneven playwright and thinker whose situations were often exaggerated and unconvincing.

When he plunged into the depths he was sometimes lost; when he soared toward a vision he was often grounded. His colleagues often excelled him by being less nobly encumbered with substance.

Thus Henri Lavedan's realism was free of the torments that made Curel both moving and formidable, both astute and wearisome. He, too, addressed himself to such social phenomena as the decay of the aristocracy. In *Le Prince d'Aurec* the family is ruined by the decadent young prince who is addicted to gambling, and the family honor is saved only by his mother who is not an aristocrat at all but only the daughter of a merchant! In a sequel *Les deux Noblesses* or *The Two Nobilities*, Lavedan carries his point further by allowing a d'Aurec to restore the family fortune by becoming a businessman and adopting a plebeian *nom de guerre*. Lavedan, however, lacked depth and distinction of either thought or characterization, and his limited talent was shown to greater advantage whenever his aim was moderate. When he confined himself to comedy of manners he came closest to both naturalism and compelling drama with vivid and somewhat scandalous exhibitions of corruption that entitle him to the position of a French Noel Coward. His *Viveurs,* in 1895, was a telling picture of "high life" with its endless round of trivialities and vices, and the same unmoralizing anatomy of "sophistication" gives *Le nouveau Jeu* (*The New Fad*), *Le vieux Marcheur* (*The Old Sport*) and *Le Goût du Vice* (*The Taste for Vice*) a breezy vigor that is absent in their author's more ambitious undertakings. In the last analysis, Lavedan's real talent was for the boulevards.

For a dramatist of ideas who approached Curel one turns to another playwright, to the scrupulous artist Paul Hervieu (1857-1915). Serious and moralistic in his outlook, as well as somewhat deficient in humor, he might have become another Brieux if he had not avoided preachments. He was at his best a psychologist applying his methods to case histories which more often than not verged on a thesis. His ability at suggesting a topical problem first appeared in *Les Tenailles* or *The Nippers,* the tragedy of a married couple. When the wife wants a divorce the husband refuses it; but when several years later the husband is willing to grant it, after she has told him in the course of a quarrel that he is not the father of her child, it is the woman who is adamant, because she now has a son to protect. In *La Loi de l'Homme,* written two years later, a deceived wife is unable to secure a divorce, the terms of the separation which she is granted are severe, and later she even finds herself forced to return to her husband in order to assure a happy marriage for her daughter. Here a thesis *à la* Brieux was more prominent than in the first-mentioned play.

But his work generally had a broader scope. *Les Paroles restent* (*Words Remain*) traced the destructive course of a slander that ruins many lives, and *Connais-toi* (*Know Thyself*) provided a studied plea for tolerance, as well as a vivid contrast between the convention that requires a betrayed husband to divorce his wife and his natural impulse to forgive her. Frequently, too, Hervieu's protests against the legal advantages enjoyed by men are decidedly secondary to his humane consideration for children who can only be painfully affected by divorce; this is the basis of that frequently moving tragedy of a mother and child *Le Dédale* (*The Labyrinth*). He can be even broader, however, and a fairly powerful drama is precipitated in *La Course du Flambeau* (*The Passing of the Torch*) out of a woman's self-sacrificing bondage to her maternal instinct. For her daughter's sake she dismisses the man she loves only to find that the girl is getting married. But this vain sacrifice is merely followed by other demands upon her maternal love when her son-in-law's fortunes wane. Ultimately this greatly tried mother, who has not hesitated to risk her own mother for her daughter's happiness, is left alone depleted of her life. Here it is no legal problem like divorce that commands Hervieu's interest. His *chef d'oeuvre* exemplifies a larger issue and one that cannot be resolved by legislation—namely, the fact that mother love is stronger than filial affection or gratitude.

Hervieu's analytic skill in the dissection of human problems has been a very general commodity in Paris, even if his style and occasional depth are peculiar to himself. A Maurice Donnay could wax tragic and lyrical in his *Amants* or *Lovers,* in which two lovers are separated by social barriers. But the general trend of the best French drama continued to be relatively cool and analytical. Jules Lemaître, the famous critic, wrote another *Connais-toi* in his *La Française,* and added other fine, if not particularly dramatic, studies of infidelity, political opportunism, invalidism, and old age, most notable in *L'Age difficile* or *The Difficult Age.* Henri Bataille (1872-1922) approached Donnay at times but was at his best when he was analyzing the libido in such pieces as *Maman Colibri* and *L'Amazone.*

In fact, the number of French writers who have combined psychological drama with comedy of manners is legion. Nor has the output suffered any decrease in the post-war period, as may be seen in the work of such practitioners as Paul Géraldy (*Aimer, Christine,* etc.), Jean-Jacques Bernard (*Martine,* a touching story of a farm girl deserted by her upper-class lover), Denys Amiel (*M. et Mme. Un Tel* or *Mr. and Mrs. So and So,* in which an intelligent husband treats his erring wife with understanding forbearance), Steve Passeur (*Les tricheurs* or *The Cheats,* an analysis that resembles Ben Hecht's *A Jew in Love*), and Jacques Deval (*Étienne,* a sensitive study of adolescence, and *Mademoiselle,* a portrait of a spinster). To these writers may be added François Mauriac, whose *Asmodée* dramatizes a middle-aged woman's love for her children's tutor and her final renunciation in favor of her daughter, and André Birabeau, a master psychologist of childhood and adolescence in *Dame Nature, Pamplemousse* or *Grapefruit,* and other plays. And light comedies of love intrigue have of course continued to be a staple of French playgoers in superabundance, providing pleasure sufficient unto itself in the work of Guitry, Savoir, Achard and a host of other stage carpenters.

Sometimes, moreover, this professional concern with the anatomy of love which becomes so tiresome to transatlantic citizens, has led the French dramatists into the distinctly clinical field. This has produced a psychopathic study like Steve Passeur's *L'Acheteuse* or *The Woman Buys,* which reports the sadistic perversions of an old maid who has "bought" a nauseated husband. If work of this kind is as repulsive as a case report at the American Psychoanalytic Association, it is nevertheless a welcome relief after an overdose of triangle plays. And in one instance, Edouard Bourdet's penetrative treatment of Lesbianism in *La prisonnière* (*The Captive*) in 1926, the psychiatric approach has produced notable drama. Despite the fact that this tabooed subject gave the play a reputation for sensationalism which made its suppression in New York a censorship issue, *The Captive* is exemplary for its delicacy, sound and mature, and moving. Irene de Montcel, the perverse heroine who wages a losing battle against her abnormality, is a tragic figure, for homosexuality in her case is only a psychiatric edition of Fate in human tragedy.

Finally, it is unfair to cast the horoscope of latter-day French drama solely under the planet Venus. The playwrights of Paris may not have proved themselves mental giants, but they have continued to be eminently alert and civilized gentlemen. A darling of the boulevard like Sacha Guitry could write a loveless biographical play like *Pasteur* which records the asexual struggles and progress of the great scientist. A Jacques Deval can play lightly with the contrast between bolshevism and capitalism and poke delightful fun at the servant-master relationship in *Tovarich*—which still does not, of course, make the play more than froth. Marcel Pagnol, who added only a variant of local color to his love stories in *Marius* and *Fanny,* could write a *Merchants of Glory* (*Les marchands de glorie*) with Paul Nivoix in 1924, dramatizing the painful exploitation of the soldiers of the World War by civilians. Four years later, in *Topaze,* moreover, Pagnol built a memorable social satire around the figure of an obscure professor who wins fame and honors when he becomes a sharper. The voluminous novelist Jules Romains has also contributed clever social satires like *Dr. Knock* and *Donogoo.* Another novelist Jean Giraudoux has not only written a clever variant on bedroom farce in *Amphitryon 38,* which is more replete with brilliant ideas than the abbreviated American adaptation by S. N. Behrman, but he has grappled unevenly with difficult social problems in *Siegfried,* a study of post-war Germany and France, and in *The Trojan War Will Not Take Place,* a shrewd satire on the eternal recurrence of war. Romain Rolland, the author of *Jean-Christophe,* turned out a number of serious historical dramas steeped in liberal idealism. Paul Raynal has written a number of elevated tragedies, one of which, *Le tombeau sous l'Arc de Triomphe,* moves from personal drama to the larger issue of war and social chaos. In *La chapelle ardente* Gabriel Marcel wrote an intense drama about a mother who is driven to vengefulness by the death of a son killed in the World War. Charles Vildrac has added several gentle —and it must be confessed, tepid—dramas of disillusionment; in that tender and sad little play *Paquebot Tenacity* (*S.S. Tenacity*) the separation of two friends bound for Canada is more important than the actual love story that causes it. Jean-Jacques Bernard's reaction to theatricality took him even further; he espoused static drama and called the theatre "the art of the unexpressed," although his practice in *The Invitation to Travel* and other works could hardly be considered inspired.

The French theatre, in short, has struggled unequally to assimilate modern realism, achieving penetrative psychological plays, comedy of manners, and drama of ideas. Its abundant harvest leaves a reporter in a whirl, and the idealist who wants the theatre to harbor great masters is bound to be depressed by the sight of so much talent and so little genius. Nevertheless, one can only conclude that the embattled realists and naturalists who captured the French theatre about the same time that Ibsen started his revolution in the northern regions were far from fruitless. If they did not exactly achieve their aims, they at least made the French drama a flexible instrument of reason.

4 MAETERLINCK, ROSTAND, AND THE DEPARTURE FROM REALISM

Reason, however, is an irritant. Man may pride himself on being *homo sapiens*—man, the knower!—but there are moments when he realizes with relief and pleasure that there is more in life than the mathematical eye can see. That which flies in the face of fact often seems to him just as actual or real, and there comes a time when he frets at the bar which holds him in the narrow prison of measurable truth. And, undeniably, there is both self-delusion and philistinism in abiding by merely measurable truth. When Zola declared that naturalism in literature had the "exactness, the solidity, and the practical applications of science" he was obviously deluding himself, since the emotions defy scientific exactitude. If scientists cannot discover the chemical composition of protoplasm until it is dead and static, how much more difficult must it be for the artist to create a science of the human emotions. Moreover, no matter how objective his approach may be, he is still approaching reality through a temperament. He would have to know his own temperament with scientific exactitude—which is an impossibility—before he could discount the personal element in his observations. Zola—who was as capable of romantic idealism and passion as any crusader, when for example he defended Dreyfus, and who had an abnormal fondness for ordure which present-day psychiatrists might diagnose as coprophilia— also colored reality.

A wave of reaction against naturalism was inevitable. In France it arose when neo-romantic poets reacted against the cold, formal poetry of Parnassians like Leconte de Lisle and declared themselves "symbolists." They sought to convey the fluidity of emotions and perceptions, and found life full of fugitive impressions and sensations that meant nothing to sociology or science and yet were symbolic of existence and were immediate to the spirit. With the Irish poet Yeats they strove for the "expression of moods by the vehicle of symbol and incident." With Anatole France, who maintained [7] that writers "who flatter themselves that they are putting anything but their own selves into their works are dupes of the most fallacious delusion," they prided themselves upon being personal and subjective.

Playwrights throughout Europe joined the revolt. They reasserted the artist's right to haunt the misty mid-regions of Weir, to recognize the unknowable as a part of experience, to convert concrete occurrences into symbols or moods, and to tell fables whenever he pleased. They counted among their brethren a few writers who had never completely renounced the romanticism of the elder Dumas and Hugo, but they also went further. They were interested in the symbol behind the strange; they were concerned with the soul of man and the universe rather than with external adventures. If, with the exception of Rostand, they bore any resemblance to the older school, it was actually to the subjective and psychological German romanticists, to Kleist and E. T. A. Hoffmann.

A new planet seemed to rise in the Belgian poet and playwright Maurice Maeterlinck. Born in 1862 in the old Flemish city of Ghent, where he imbibed the miasmic medieval world, he was constitutionally qualified to bring wonder and dreamfulness back into the theatre. After some dabbling in a legal career, he went to France in 1886 and fell under the influence of the symbolist poets headed by the "Afternoon of a Faun" apostle, Mallarmé, and the great lyricist Paul Verlaine. Two volumes of poetry announced Maeterlinck's adherence to the school. Then in 1889 he turned to the drama with *La Princesse Madeleine*, an inconsequential pseudo-Shakespearean imitation that won him inordinate praise. In the next five years, however, he developed a style of his own which made him the Messiah of a new type of drama devoted to mystery and "the interior life."

Being an essayist as well as dramatist—a better essayist than play-wright, in fact—he set down a program which was at once greeted as a new revelation. In a series of volumes, the first of which appeared in 1896 under the title of *The Treasure of the Humble*, he called for a drama that concerns itself solely with the inner life. With the natural-ists he maintained that every-day tragedy is more real and more in keep-ing with our true existence than the tragedy of great adventures. But he added that normally tragedy was interior and almost completely without external movement. A motionless old man seated in his arm-chair but sensing the world around him seemed to him living "a deeper, more human and more general life than the lover who strangles his mis-tress . . . or the husband who avenges his honor." There is undoubtedly much truth in this asseveration, and a Chekhov who dramatizes inner incidents in very minor lives gives Maeterlinck's theory a lasting dra-matic reality. Maeterlinck, however, wanted a *motionless* drama—a seeming contradiction in terms, but a contradiction which he refused to acknowledge. "I do not know," he maintained, "if it is true that a static theatre is impossible. It seems to me, even, that it exists."

Adding to this theory of drama a philosophy of fatalism, he wrote his series of "static dramas" in which a brooding sense of futility supplants visible action. The first of these, *L'Intruse* or *The Intruder* shows a fam-ily at night sitting around a table while the sick mother is dying in the next room. Nothing occurs in the scene, there is only the suggestion that the "intruder" Death is coming. In *Intérieur* the event has already hap-pened; a young girl has been drowned and the dialogue is maintained by a number of people standing outside her house and hesitating to in-form her family. The people who will be affected by the tragedy do not appear at all; only their shadows are seen by the spectators outside, and their emotions are conveyed solely through the anticipatory comments of the people who are bringing the news. More suggestive still is *Les Aveugles* or *The Blind,* in which a number of blind old people are sud-denly left alone when the priest who has led them out for a walk through the forest falls dead. Unaware of what has happened and groping help-lessly before an approaching storm, they make a highly pathetic appear-ance.

Interpreted as a symbolization of humanity wandering in darkness now that its guide the Church is dead, *Les Aveugles* proves to be some-thing more than an evanescent mood and commands greater intellectual interest than most of Maeterlinck's static pieces. But in these and other early efforts so reminiscent of Edgar Allan Poe the suggestion of feel-ings and moods is everything. Only the general idea of fate gives them a uniformly larger content. "You never can tell if you have made a move-ment for yourself, or if it be chance that has met with you," declares a character in *Alladine et Palomides*. It is not surprising, therefore, that the title of Maeterlinck's early volume was *Three Plays for Marionettes*, and that Maeterlinck seriously considered the possibility of banishing living actors from the theatre because these brought their own private personality to their roles. In this effort to exorcise the creative part of the actor in the theatre, Maeterlinck anticipated Gordon Craig's ambiguous dream of employing mechanical actors completely dominated by a creative super-director.

Maeterlinck filled the theatre with many anti-realistic promptings that undeniably widened horizons. But his essentially undramatic efforts could only lead into a pseudo-poetic morass. Probably under the influence of the actress Georgette Leblanc whom he married, he himself came to realize the unfeasibility of the static drama. In a letter to Barrett H. Clark[8] years later, he asked his correspondent not to attach too much importance to the word "static," claiming that the whole idea had only been "a theory of my youth, worth what most literary theories are worth —that is, almost nothing." Beginning with *Pelléas et Mélisande* in 1892 he used visible action in his plays, and in *Monna Vanna*, eleven years later, he wrote an orthodox romantic play. Even his philosophy underwent modification, and when he came to write his *Ariane et Barbe-Bleu* or *Ariane and Bluebeard* in 1901 he also retreated somewhat from his fatalistic position. With his heroine who breaks Bluebeard's windows and lets in the light, he practically restored the importance of the human will, although he continued to insist that we can have little influence over external events.

Nevertheless the incubus of tenuous fantastication and obscurantism was never shaken off by Maeterlinck, not even in his occasionally poignant *Pelléas et Mélisande*. In this retelling of the Paolo and Francesca theme, the uncanny setting and the even more mysterious figure of the fey child-wife Mélisande create a tragic atmosphere. And this atmosphere is frequently more prominent than the visible tragedy that ensues when the jealous elder brother Golaud kills his wife and his brother Pelléas. In a variety of less effective later plays, moreover, this playwright still coddled his moods in cadenced or poetic prose. In the vastly popular *Blue Bird* (*L'Oiseau bleu*) which took the world by storm in 1908, he brought his work to its logical conclusion in a fairy tale and allegory devoted to such bromides as the view that the dead live in our memory and that happiness can be found at home. It is unhappily one of life's ironies that the poet who began by denying the theatre became an addict of claptrap theatricality. The hierarch of the steely goddess of Fate found himself at last at the altar of Pollyanna.

Only a more robust talent than his could grow to some stature in the hard soil of European realities, and that talent belonged quite appropriately to Edmond Rostand, a flamboyant poet of the Provence. Maeter-linck's colors were subdued to the point of invisibility, but Rostand's blazoned like the Southern sun that flares on Van Gogh's canvases. Born in Marseilles in 1868, he was heir to the tropical love poetry and dash-ing self-assurance of the troubadours. He is the chief poet of thermo-dynamics in the modern theatre. Moreover, his bravura belonged emi-nently to the theatre and a saving grace of humor softened his funda-mental sentimentality.

After a brief session with jurisprudence and an inevitable volume of poetry, he appeared in the theatre—at the *Comédie Française* in 1894—with his first play *Les Romanesques* or *The Romancers*. Its young lovers discover the primary emotion while reading *Romeo and Juliet,* and if the results are negligible the play is nevertheless casually captivating by vir-tue of its lyricism. Frankly and refreshingly theatrical, it concludes with the actors facing the audience and singing a rondel in defense of the play since it provides "rest for our nerves from all these bitter plays."

Les Romanesques was followed in 1895 by another tender but fulsome romance *La Princesse lointaine* or *The Far-Away Princess,* and here Ros-tand celebrates the romantic passion of the troubadour Rudel who fell in love with the Countess of Tripoli whom he had never seen and met only when he was dying. Both these efforts were, however, extremely mild, and the next play, the biblical *La Samaritaine* or *The Woman of Samaria* proved a complete mishap. But in *Cyrano de Bergerac,* written for the spirited, declaiming actor Coquelin, Rostand successfully tapped all his resources—his bravura, his wit, and his idealism. His reward was instantaneous and the story of the swashbuckling Cyrano whose spirit is as beautiful as his nose is unprepossessing became one of the staples of the theatre because it was wholly of the theatre.

Judged by the standards one reserves for masterpieces, *Cyrano* shrivels considerably; even if Cyrano the duelist, wit, and self-sacrificing lover is a magnificently living character, the play is essentially a contrived stage-piece. Rostand is, moreover, only a junior member of the fraternity of poets; set beside Racine's noble architecture, most of his verse looks like a gaudy circus tent. Nevertheless, he proved himself an infectious playwright with *Cyrano,* which will probably outlast many sounder works because the theatre thrives on instantaneous effects. Moreover, the manipulated plot that makes Cyrano conceal his passion for the fair Roxane and write love-letters for the handsome young nonentity whom she fancies is enriched with a vivid seventeenth-century back-ground.

Rostand's galvanic dramaturgy was not sustained in his next effort, *L'Aiglon.* Sarah Bernhardt in the role of Napoleon's dreamy and inef-fectual young son imparted great pathos to the play, and there is some genuine feeling in the frustrations of the eaglet who found his wings clipped by Napoleon's enemies when his father was no longer there to teach him how to fly. But here Rostand's besetting sin of sentimentality is not alleviated by either wit or bravura. This imaginative Southerner's art reached a second peak only in his beast-fable of modern life, the widely appreciated *Chantecler*. Enlivened with some of its author's best lyric verse, this allegory is eminently engaging. His animal world is simultaneously human and animal; the blackbird may be a cynic but he is also a bird, the golden pheasant is both the "eternal feminine" and a fowl, and Chantecler remains a rooster even when he is clearly a human idealist. The story, in short, unfolds lucidly on both the animal and human levels. Finally, Rostand succeeded in spinning a yarn that was both amusing and touching, and his rooster belongs to the theatre's immortals. Chantecler, the idealist who believes that his crowing makes the sun rise, learns that he is not indispensable to the universe. But after his initial heart-break he rallies his spirits; if he cannot make the sun rise, he can nevertheless do valiant service in his own barnyard. . . . It is this resilience which enables him to defeat the trained fighting cock by dint of superior courage. If *Chantecler* is not a profound drama (it is difficult to understand how any beast-fable *can* be even when one is not forced to balk at seeing a company of grown-up actors pretending that they are animals), it remains a generally charming novelty.*

Rostand's poor health which made him retire to the Pyrenees and cut his life short in his forty-ninth year did not allow him to extend the triumphs of *Cyrano* and *Chantecler*. His *Sacred Wood* is a trifle, and his last play *Don Juan's Last Night* was left somewhat uncompleted. Fortunately, this work, which first appeared posthumously in 1922, is sufficiently complete to indicate a capacity for growth which might have increased Rostand's stature by cubits. Difference of opinion concerning *Don Juan's Last Night* is possible. It contains many of its author's characteristic faults, including a touch of preciosity that is least objectionable in *Cyrano* because that play is set in the golden age of the *precieuses*. Nevertheless, this subtle drama, in which Don Juan is granted a respite from the grave only to discover how fugitive and illusory his love affairs were, is memorable. In short, beautifully conceived scenes full of irony and tenderness Rostand captured the tragi-comedy of self-delusion as no other modern playwright except perhaps Pirandello has done.

Rostand was only a sport in the latter-day French theatre and left no school. As heedless of his example as it was of Maeterlinck's, the thea-

---

* Unhappily the English translation, with its colorless prose and tawdry colloquialism, is no more adequate than a performance of Beethoven's *Eroica* on a steam calliope.

tre in France continued to obey the dictates of *bon sens*. Nevertheless it has hardly remained unchallenged, and there have been various efforts to crack the shell of realism which has imprisoned so many French writers who are incapable of evoking more than chamber realities within its confines.

Mystic and idealistic dreams have appeared sporadically. Among them are Boursac de Saint Marc's *Le loup de Gabbio* or *The Wolf of Gabbio*, which dramatizes the reformation of a bandit by a pietistic, saintlike girl who enters a convent once her work is completed. That excellent poet but slow dramatist Paul Claudel's *The Tidings Brought to Mary* is laved in religious ecstacy (see p.709) a program note in Germany announced that "This piece is not to be played, it is to be celebrated." Paul Demassy's biblical plays *Jésus de Nazareth* and *Delilah*, as well as his *Faust*, are conceived in a similar spirit; and his *La tragédie d'Alexandre* has retrieved the style of Corneille and Racine in somber colors. André Obey's *Noah* has combined tender common sense, in its portrait of the patriarch, with much philosophical delectation; and like Demassy, Obey has also attempted classicism with his *Rape of Lucrece*, another variant on the old Roman story which served Shakespeare and other dramatists. Still more recently, Gaston Baty's *Dulcinée*, adapted from the story of Dulcinea in *Don Quixote*, pays poignant homage to idealism. Dulcinea the promiscuous barmaid is so moved by Don Quixote's noble love-letter which was forwarded to her through a prank that she devotes herself to pious deeds. She becomes known as a witch, and goes out to her death at the hands of a superstitious mob, invincible in her faith, even though every effort has been made to disabuse her of the belief that the Knight of the Woeful Countenance chose her among all women.

Other writers have uncovered modern symbolism in Greek legend. Jean Giraudoux, whose *Amphitryon 38* is mainly a philosophical boulevard piece with Zeus supplying the third side of a triangle, has turned the Electra story into a haunting, if overcomplicated, tragedy of Fate (*Electre*). That versatile genius Jean Cocteau, who has also proved his ability to treat domestic situations with analytic realism in *Les parents terrible* or *The Terrible Parents*, has reworked Greek matter with a fugitive imaginativeness that recalls his autobiographical account of drug addiction, *Opium*. His elusive Orpheus drama *Orphée* has led Cocteau's translator Carl Wildman to declare that it "works on people like music" and that "those who wish to understand, instead of believe, stand outside Cocteau's world. . . ."[9] His *Antigone* was similarly intended to address the "unconscious" and was suitably supplied with scenery by the cubist Picasso, music by the unconventional Honegger, and masks by the author himself. An opera-oratorio *Oedipus Rex* involved collaboration with no less a modernist than Igor Stravinsky. *The Infernal Machine,* an even more thorough reworking of the Oedipus tragedy, is another Cocteau fantasy on an ancient theme. Its characters are deeply alive but are laved in symbolism; the gods who spin the dreadful web of Oedipus' incest unintentionally make a hero of him because he has endured and faced so much.

Turning to Arthurian romance, and again giving symbolic interpretation to legendary material, Cocteau has written a *Chevaliers de la table ronde* or *Knights of the Round Table.* Other work by this restive writer like *Parade* in 1917 found its fitting *mise en scène* in cubism and employed symbolic characters; and his collaborations with the ballet, as well as the circus, have likewise broken with the realistic theatre in favor of *surréaliste* fantasy.

Expressionism, with its technique of dissociated scenes and its exploration of unconscious drives, has also made a few invasions into the French theatre. It appeared to some degree in such work as Gantillon's *Maya* which combined a naturalist picture of prostitution with a sentimental symbolization of the harlot as the haven of men's various dreams. A baffling shifting of scenes and tone also appears in the work of Crommelynck (*Carine* and *La femme qui a le coeur trop petit*). The moving picture technique in Jules Romains' *Donogoo* likewise falls within the classification of efforts to depart from realism. The French apostle of expressionism, however, is H. R. Lenormand.

Born in 1882 and author of two ordinary plays between 1909 and 1914, Lenormand first made his mark in the theatre in 1919 with *Les ratés* or *The Failures,* a sketchy clinical study of the deterioration of a dramatist and a comedienne. After *The Failures* his interest in the subconscious deepened and his passion for the outlandish in human behavior made him write complex exotic works rooted in psychoanalysis and even in "relativity." His *Time is a Dream* (*Le temps est un songe*) presents a miserable character who commits suicide upon failing to unravel the meaning of human existence; his death, moreover, is anticipated by his fiancée in a hallucination! Time, in other words, has no extension; past, present, and future are seen as essentially simultaneous even if the normal mind must differentiate them.

The Dream Doctor (*Le Mangeur de Rêves*), produced in 1922, dissects the character of an amateur psychoanalyst who is obsessed with ferreting secrets out of the souls of others because his own psyche is diseased. Unable to cure, he can only cause destruction when he dredges up secrets which his victims should forget. His therapeutic meddling turns one girl into a pathological sadist or criminal and is responsible for his latest patient's suicide *Man and his Phantoms* (*L'homme et ses Fantômes*), which appeared two years later, is a painful analysis of morbid love set down in scenes as disjointed as the pathological "mother-fixated" hero whom Lenormand is eviscerating. The patient is a Don Juan who has been driven to seek satisfaction from different women because he is actually seeking his mother. As he is about to die he comes to the end of his search, and his mother's phantom brings him solace!

In addition to further explorations of the psychoanalytic field, Lenormand wrote *The Coward* (*Le Lâche*) in 1925, a frequently powerful but strained diagnosis of an artist who evades service in the World War. At first he is shamming illness with an untroubled conscience, since his mind and his creative temperament tell him that nothing but life matters. Merely "to breathe, to look at the sky, the horizon, streets" is infinitely precious. Gradually, however, he begins to suffer inner torments and falls prey to both German and French spies. Consenting to engage in espionage for his country as an alternative to returning to the front, he makes a mess of things, causes two French agents to be captured, and is finally executed.

A number of exotic but not particularly incisive plays, a satire on the commercial theatre, and a modern version of the Medea legend *Asie* complete the inventory of Lenormand's work. Throughout his career, which closed in 1938, he made every effort to abandon the surfaces of the Parisian drama and to plunge into the abysses. If he brought up more slime than pearls one must still grant him some credit for having dared to plunge.

Despite all these efforts, however, the fact remains that the various attempts to find a substitute for French realism have been more fascinating than successful. Preciosity and incomplete communicability have vitiated Cocteau's efforts, and symbolist drama continued to be tenuous; religiousness in Claudel proved too verbose; Lenormand's efforts to externalize the unconscious merely outlined the dynamics of human character instead of filling the stage with living personalities.

5 ADOLPHE APPIA AND THE SCENIC MOVEMENT

The most lasting triumphs of the movement against literal realism were accomplished in the arts of production and scenic design, and not in the drama.

During the greater part of the nineteenth century only slight progress had been made in scenic art. Romanticism had at most generated a spectacular antiquarian movement which strove to give the produced play the scope of a spectacle with some fidelity to the costuming and setting of the period in which the action was laid. Thus after 1823, when the Kemble production of *King John* presented the first completely "historical" setting of a Shakespearean drama,[10] it became customary in England to bill Shakespearean revivals as historically correct. Gas was substituted for candlelight, providing greater and more easily varied illumination, and electricity soon served the same purpose even more effectively. These improvements proved valuable without, however, materially affecting the style of the productions. The settings remained painted flimsy flats arranged in perspective so that the nearer the actor came to them the more disproportionately large he seemed.

The new realists of the third quarter of the century could hardly be satisfied by an art of theatre that was so patently artificial. The movement toward realism could, however, benefit by the gradual removal of the apron and the proscenium doors that had survived since the Renaissance days of Palladio. The proscenium arch now completely separated the play from the audience. Moreover, the eighteenth-century custom of representing a room by means of a backdrop and side-wings was in time supplanted by flats forming three sides of an interior, covered by a ceiling. As a result of these changes, the spectator became fully conscious of a "fourth wall" in front of him. Through this wall, which was generously left invisible, he was privileged to see the actors comporting themselves as if they were unobserved by a thousand or more Peeping Toms seated in the auditorium.

To accentuate the illusion of reality, which became the prime ideal of realistic production, flimsy frameworks of lath covered by painted canvas were generally discarded in favor of solid scenery. Doors were henceforth to be real doors opened and closed by turning real door knobs. Audiences that had acquired an increasing interest in tangible reality in all the arts, were pleased with familiar objects and were titillated by their presence in the unfamiliar environment of the theatre. The modicum of realism which some romanticists had attained in "accurate" antique or bucolic backgrounds was now extended. Pictorial realism was now applied to the commonplace, frequently ugly, life which the dramatists were favoring. The famous royal innovator of the stage George II, Duke of Saxe-Meiningen, even used a stuffed dead horse in a death scene in order to convey greater reality, and Antoine in 1888 included real meat on the stage in a butcher-shop scene. (Real beer was still being served in the saloon scenes of the 1939 production of Saroyan's *Time of Your Life.*) Transported to America, literal realism found its high-priest in David Belasco who treated the gaping audience to replicas of real bars, telephones, linotype machines, and escalators.

It was not long, however, before men became aware of the illogicality and wastefulness of too much literal procedure in a medium that is essentially make-believe. After all, the "fourth wall" is only empty space; foreign characters in a play do not speak their own tongue but that of the country in which the production takes place; and even the most natural acting—like the most "natural" drama—violates actual reality in order to convey an *impression* of reality. In time, therefore, naturalism was supplanted by a "selective realism" which employed real objects only insofar as they might provide the illusion of reality, and this is the prevailing style today.

The reaction to naturalism in the nineties went much further than mere selective realism. The word "theatricality" which had been buried with so much opprobrium by the naturalists was restored to good standing. Working hand in hand with the neo-romantic and symbolist playwrights, producers began to restore imagination and poetry to the art of theatre. Opposed to Antoine's *Théâtre Libre* there arose little "art" theatres which strove to swing the tide back to theatricalism in the name of beauty and spiritual truth. As early as 1890 the poet Paul Fort established his *Théâtre Mixte,* later known as the *Théâtre des Arts,* and dedicated it to the discovery of "the miracle of daily life, the sense of the mysterious." Two years later, Lugné-Poë's *Théâtre de l'Oeuvre* opened with Maeterlinck's penumbral *Pelléas et Mélisande.* The "little theatres" soon spread over Europe, sometimes being founded by the playwrights themselves; by Strindberg (in his mystical, "expressionist" period), by Benavente and by the anti-realist Pirandello.

Efforts to depart from realism led to simplifications of the stage, even to a return to Elizabethan structure in the case of Jocza Savits' Shakespeare Theatre in Munich and William Poel's Elizabethan Stage Society in England. Perhaps the most notable simplifications were achieved by Jacques Copeau in his *Théâtre du Vieux Colombier,* established in 1913. Here the forestage was lengthened into an "apron" in the Elizabethan manner and the practically bare stage was backed by a permanent set. This theatre's successor the *Compagnie des Quinze* followed very much the same principle by using an austere setting that consisted almost solely of pillars. Here was the ideal of an architectural stage that would lend itself to suggestion rather than a duplication of actual rooms. Other departures brought the non-realistic painter into the theatre; just as the Duke of Meiningen had used settings by the realistic painters Israels and Liebermann, French producers employed Picasso, Matisse, Derain, Braque, and Fernand Léger.

These and many other efforts to "retheatricalize the theatre" were directly or indirectly inspired by the work of the two poets of the physical theatre Adolphe Appia and Gordon Craig. And significantly the first impetus came from music, the least representational of the arts.

Early nineteenth-century romanticists had long ago held the doctrine that music was the source of all the arts and that the theatre could reach its apotheosis only in music. The philosopher Nietzsche stressed the same doctrine in *The Birth of Tragedy,* and his friend Wagner's significant innovations in opera served the romantic ideal of fusing the arts into a single overwhelming theatrical experience. His formula "Music is the soul of drama, drama is the body of music" announced a synthesis or *mélange des genres* to which all his operas were devoted. The great composer regarded himself as primarily a theatrician.

His far-flung dreams were translated to the theatre proper by his French-speaking Swiss disciple Adolphe Appia who had worked with him in Bayreuth. In 1895 appeared Appia's *La mise en scène de drame Wagnérien,* with eighteen settings for the Wagnerian operas; in 1899 appeared *Die Musik und die Inscenierung* (translated from a French text), and this was followed by a series of shorter studies. Remote from the naturalism that had gained a foothold in Paris, Appia wanted to endow scenic representation with the fluid and suggestive quality of music—that "loftiest expression of the eternal in art." [11] The elements of scenic design were to be the scenery, the floor, the moving actor, and the lighted space. The theatre that gives life to the dramatist's script was to present a perfect synthesis or a single effect. And the unifying element was to be light, which was no longer to provide a blank visibility but was to mold and blend the scene and actors, thereby creating a unified mood and conveying the essence of a dramatic production. Only light, Appia declared, can express "the inner nature of all appearance." Light, with its "infinite capacity for varying nuance" is the "counterpart of a musical score," [12] and it must play as directly upon the emotions as music.

Appia's temperament was anti-realistic, and his identification of the drama with something so indefinite as music denied the basic principle of the naturalist theatre, which demanded duplication of concrete realities. Ellen Terry's erratic son Gordon Craig was his spiritual heir, and being a much more popular and strident pamphleteer than Appia, he became an even more prominent apostle of the doctrine of theatricality. He, too, considered the ideal production of a play to be a single effect that would touch all the senses simultaneously and would address itself directly to the spirit. Throughout all the inconsistency of his preachments and despite his failure as a practical scene designer, he maintained a steady gospel to the effect that suggestion is the supreme law of the theatre. "Actuality, accuracy of detail, is useless upon the stage," he declared. But by means of suggestion "you may bring to the stage a sense of all things."

The main instrument of suggestion, moreover, is organization or *design,* and every production needs a pattern. So concerned was Craig with the inviolability of "design" that at one time he even wanted to banish the actor from the theatre as an unreliable agent easily disturbed by accidental factors like the emotions; the "ideal and tentative solution" [13] proposed by Craig was a "super-marionette." With his magazine *The Mask* and a series of pamphlets and books, the first of which, *The*

Art of the Theatre, appeared in 1905, Craig took the theatre by storm. His ideas were provocative and his drawings beautiful, even if his own efforts to apply them misfired.[14]

Maeterlinck and Rostand left no school, and failed to steer the drama away from realism to any extent because events between 1910 and our own day have made romanticism and the coddling of spiritual nuances largely impossible. One cannot expect a living theatre subjected to the hammering immediacy of disturbed private relationships, economic problems, war and class struggle to play much with moods, brood in dank castles, follow little Tyltyl's peregrinations, and woo the Princess Far-Away in troubadour accents. But the revolution in theatrical art promulgated by Appia and Craig was another matter. If Craig was impractical, he nevertheless set up an ideal of production and scenic design. The practical directors and designers who followed parallel paths or caught fire from his ideas at least discarded literal realism.

In numerous instances, they created imaginative theatre which revivified the classics, or they responded to the expressionistic subjectivism and the revolutionary dynamics of post-war playwrights. Most frequently, however, they were called upon to project realistic plays for which ultra-simplification or ultra-idealization was unfeasible and would have seemed ludicrous. But they could always bring expressive design into the theatre. This is the history of many contemporary designers like the Americans Lee Simonson, Robert Edmond Jones, Jo Mielziner and Mordecai Gorelik, and of numerous directors like Max Reinhardt, Vakhtangov, Jessner, Jouvet, Arthur Hopkins, Philip Moeller, Guthrie McClintic, and Lee Strasberg. In Appia, moreover, the scenic artists found the basic principle of their art—namely, the use of light as an expressive medium. If Appia the Wagnerian romanticist touched them only slightly, Appia the practical forerunner of contemporary lighting technique still dominates the theatre, even when this theatre continues to express realism.

Georges Courteline (1861–1929). In the history of modern French drama, Courteline occupies a unique place because he combined the usual light "boulevard" spirit of the popular Parisian theatre with a salty naturalism that commended his work to Antoine at the Théâtre Libre. Ultimately winning a place at the Comédie Française, his plays gained much popularity. Especially successful was his *Boubouroche* (1893), a comedy of common life.

XXII

LATIN POSTSCRIPTS—BENAVENTE AND PIRANDELLO

THERE is an anecdote to the effect that when our transcendental Margaret Fuller told Thomas Carlyle that she accepted the universe, the dour Scotsman exploded, "By gad, she'd better." Something in the Latin temperament, however, finds that such acceptance goes against its grain. A glance at the French drama has indicated that despite the highly touted *clarté française* the French theatre did not relish the idea of bowing before hard facts. But if naturalism soon gave way to modified realism on the stage, along with a good deal that was distinctly theatrical and nonrealistic, this is even more strongly the case in the South European countries. France had at least gone through a period of intensive industrialization, whereas the Spanish and Italian peninsulas underwent comparatively minor economic changes. Tradition—especially theatrical tradition—was, moreover, stronger in these nations and did not lightly make way for the new realities of modern Europe.

Although both countries felt the influence of Ibsen and harbored a realistic movement, they welcomed the new dispensation with only moderate enthusiasm. When realism was adopted in these countries it stormed no citadels of convention, contenting itself with minor forays into social criticism. Trenchant drama, it is true, was not absent on the peninsulas, as may be seen in the work of Pirandello and his school. But this was drama of a different color—it was the very antithesis of realism. Whatever power and significance may be found in Pirandello come from other, though by no means less modern, sources.

I BENAVENTE AND THE UNDYNAMIC SPANISH DRAMA

Spain, with its large agricultural society, its dominant priesthood and its moribund aristocracy, made only a half-hearted effort to face the new world. The romantic movement had to some extent revived dramatic talent on the peninsula after a long dark period. If the Duque de Rivas (*Don Alvaro* in 1835), Hartzenbusch (*The Lovers of Teruel* in 1835, etc.) and Zorrilla (*Don Juan Tenorio* in 1844) were insignificant figures in the world's theatre, they at least brought some vitality to the Spanish stage. They were followed by writers like Lopez de Ayala and

Tamayo y Baus who attempted to introduce the kind of half-hearted, contrived social homilies that Augier and Dumas *fils* were developing north of the Pyrenees. But the transition from romanticism to realism was most marked in the work of José Echegeray.

Writing in verse about legendary subjects, Echegeray was essentially a romanticist whose "favorite formula was to spin a romantic intrigue on the warp of a social or ethical thesis, embellishing his work with the conventional sure-fire tricks and melodramatic effects." [1] But his vigor helped to resuscitate the Spanish theatre, and he was new-fashioned in some respects. Not always adhering to rhetoric or concerning himself with the threadbare theme of Spanish "honor," he felt the influence of Ibsen. In his best-known work *The Great Galeoto* he treated "honor" originally. A woman wrongly accused of adultery with a poet finally turns to him, feeling herself forced to accept him by so much unfounded scandal. Honor, then, is something that exists only in opinion—a view which carries us far beyond Lope de Vega and Calderón. In *The Son of Don Juan*, Echegeray paid an even more literal tribute to the great Norwegian and to the realistic interest in heredity by attributing the philanderer's downfall to natural law rather than supernatural vengeance. The latter's promising son Lazarus succumbs to Oswald's disease! He collapses calling like Oswald for "the sun," and to stress the moral Echegeray reminds us that the young man's father had once also asked for the sun after awaking from a debauch. The law of heredity is further substantiated when the heroine of the same play pays for her father's sins by succumbing to tuberculosis.

A theme that Ibsen had utilized in *Ghosts* for a challenging call for moral freedom, becomes in Echegeray's drama a literal demonstration of heredity supplemented by conventional ethics. The parents are punished for having violated the taboo against profligacy instead of suffering for accepting the conventions of marriage as denounced by Ibsen. Although Echegeray furthered the cause of realism, he first whittled it down by a few cubits.

In this he set an example to the entire Spanish school which even Galdós, a realist of integrity, could not eradicate. Benito Pérez Galdós (1843-1920) turned from the composition of serious novels in order to fill the theatre with their spirit of truthfulness. In *Will* he described a middle-class bankruptcy in the manner of Björnson and showed a sensible girl taking her muddling family in hand. In *The Duchess of San Quintín* the impoverished young aristocratic widow rejects a safe and idle marriage in favor of a poor young plebeian and socialist; the lovers will go to America to lead a useful existence. To his advocacy of an *honest democratic life*, Galdós, moreover, added a blast against clericalism in a number of pieces, maintaining in *Electra* (which was severe-

ly assailed for its liberalism) that life in a convent is not the only kind
of sanctity possible for a woman. Galdós, in short, was moving toward a
vigorous theatre of modern ideas and spoke for the modern orientation.
But Galdós was essentially a novelist and lacked complete mastery of
the theatre. His example was consequently insufficiently impressive. If
he did leave an impression, he was aided by the shock of the Spanish-
American War in which long slumbering Spain proved herself such a
poor match for a modern nation and came to the realization that it was
time to grapple with realities.

Modernity also entered the theatre of Catalonia, the most progressive
Spanish province. The best known of its playwrights Angel Guimerá
drew pictures of modern life in *Aurora,* which dramatized the love of a
factory girl and a young scientist, and attacked the arrogance of wealth
and position in *Terra Baixa* (*The Wolf*). Guimerá, however, had no
vital vision or analysis to contribute to the modern drama. Moreover,
Galdós and the Spanish free theatre movement were minority voices.
The ideas and problems of modern Europe were insufficiently rooted in
Spain except in the syndicalist working-class movement which was intellectually too far in advance of the bourgeois Galdós to find a satisfactory gospel in his writings. The revolutionary ferment in Spain later
found poets in the brilliant Rafael Alberti, who was born in 1902, and
in the poet-playwright Federico Lorca, who was executed by the Franco
regime during the Civil War. During this critical time, too, a working-
class theatre was beginning to make headway. But this development
came to an abrupt end when the Loyalist government collapsed in 1939.

The Spanish theatre between 1890 and 1935 contented itself with
extracting sense, moderation, and realistic background from European
realism, and with adopting a moderately liberal attitude toward morality. Reality and romanticism had always waged a struggle in the life
and arts of Spain. The modern Spanish drama merely effected a compromise between the two forces. The result was at its best an attractive
kind of drama pleasantly sentimental when written by the Quintero
brothers and by Martinez Sierra, intelligent and subtle when written
by the Nobel-prize winner Benavente.

The Andalusian Quinteros (Serafin, born in 1871, and Joaquin Alva-
rez, born in 1873) proved themselves colorful and genial playwrights.
The warm Southern blood was in their veins, and their art favored relaxation both in numerous *sainetes* or little folk farces and in more serious plays. Tolerance and kindliness suffuse their abundant work, and
life in their hundred or more plays is simple and humane. *A Sunny
Morning,* for example, is a charming picture of two elderly people who
had once been lovers. They meet on a park bench after many years
and quarrel. When they recognize each other they try to conceal their

identity and elaborate a fiction to explain their separation. Another play *A Hundred Years Old* is a pleasing but unexciting portrait of an old man who is more understanding and liberal on his hundredth birthday than his ultra-respectful descendants who oppose his great-granddaughter's marriage to her poor cousin. The Quinteros also composed high-spirited farces like *The Women's Town,* in which the inhabitants of an undermanned village contrive a marriage between two young people who had no intention of marrying. A kindred piece is the amusing *Lady from Alfaqueque* with its ingenious rogue who worms himself into favor with gifts which have to be paid ultimately by the recipients. His defense, even after his hostess discovers that he has compromised two girls, is that he is a poet!

Sometimes, moreover, these genial collaborators deepened their note with a piece like *Malvaloca*. Here a young man marries the social outcast who had been seduced by his brother, and his tolerance toward her error, as well as the simple character of the girl Malvaloca, create a touching little play. In lieu of great drama, which no one could reasonably expect from the Quinteros, they provided gentle humane drama. They have been properly labeled "professors of happiness."

A spirit of quiet longing and frustration broods in the work of Gregorio Martinez Sierra, who was born in 1881 and was young enough to be affected by Maeterlinck. The quietism of Maeterlinck never left him. He has been well described as "an intellectual by temperament;" [2] he deepened as he matured, grew interested in social reform, and, stimulated by a progressive wife, he even became a feminist. Nevertheless, he was content to convey only those situations which reveal humanity reaching delicately and privately for life rather than battling for it. His characters illustrate nothing more than a quiet persistence in love, desire or simple service.

Playwrights like Sierra are bound to store up riches on earth, and—if kindness is celestially rewarded—also riches in heaven. His light pieces make sentiment all prevailing as when the oleomargarine maker of *The Lover* madly follows the Queen wherever she goes, treasuring every object she drops, saving her in a carriage accident at last but demanding no other reward than a railroad pass in order to be able to continue his devoted peregrinations. His deeper work often celebrates altruism or purity of heart in a hard and troubled world. In *The Kingdom of God,* which was graced in New York by Ethel Barrymore, a girl enters a religious order, much to the distress of her family, and ministers to paupers in an old men's home. Ten years later we see her expending her love and care on fallen women in a maternity hospital and rejecting a proposal of marriage from a physician because the world's unfortunates need her services. Old age finds her supervising an orphanage, too busy to converse with God except through her charitable work but enjoying a moment of pleasure when one of her young charges brings her the ear of the first bull he has conquered. In *The Two Shepherds,* an old physician and an old priest, both out of step with modern requirements in medicine and theology, are displaced by better trained men. But they do not pass from the scene without first reaffirming the power of simple faith and intelligence. In Sierra's best known play *The Cradle Song,* written in 1911, the nuns of a convent expend their frustrated maternal feelings upon a prostitute's foundling until she is ready to leave them for marriage. This infinitely human picture, full of glinting insights into the insignificant peccadilloes of the Sisters, marks the peak of its author's work.

Nevertheless, sentimentality exacts a heavy price from a dramatist, and Sierra lacks the qualities of passion and excitement. Despite theories of a "silent drama" or a "theatre of kindliness" (a phrase which was used to describe the art of the Quinteros), the drama is a thing of passion and struggle; it is the poetry of human crises. As Joseph Wood Krutch wrote in connection with the Quinteros,[3] "There are only two ways of dealing with life—the way of passion and the way of intellect. Either one can accept reality and master it after a fashion, but sentiment refuses to play the game at all unless it can do so with loaded dice." It is significant that Sierra should have devoted himself to the films after 1925.

After Galdós the completely European note was sounded only by Jacinto Benavente, who was born in 1866 and was therefore closer to the realistic program than Sierra. It is true that as a man of the theatre he did not disdain any kind of play that would prove marketable; in fact, he displayed remarkable versatility and fecundity. The miraculous Lope de Vega was not an isolated case in Spain. (Most Spanish playwrights have been prolific, and the Spanish theatre has used a profusion of writers because the people have an insatiable appetite for amusement. Moreover, this appetite demands constant variety!) Nor can it be said that, except in the case of *The Passion Flower,* Benavente revealed any inclination or ability to draw man or society relentlessly; his affinity to Zola, Becque, Shaw or the young Hauptmann always remained somewhat remote. But Benavente proved himself an intelligent and shrewd observer, and he belongs to the strong intellectual current that gave Spain its great novelist Pio Baroja, its eminent critic Azorin, and its philosophers Unamuno and Salvatore de Madariaga.

There are abstruse or philosophical overtones in many of his plays. Sometimes the treatment is light, as in the one-acters *Teatro fantástico,* published in 1892. An example is *The Magic of an Hour,* in which porcelain statuettes in a room come to life and enact the whole tragi-comedy of ephemeral desire and passion. Their yearnings are quickly ended after passion causes the "Incroyable" to chip a piece out of the "Merveilleuse's" cheek with a kiss, and the statuettes—like human puppets —freeze back into immobility! More elaborated is *The Bonds of Interest,* written in 1907. In this piece Benavente appends a philosophy of society and sentiment to a *commedia dell' arte* plot. Here two indigent young men, chancing upon a great city, plan a campaign for making their fortune there. For this is not really *one* city, they realize, but *two* cities—"one for people who arrive with money, and the other for people who arrive like us." Then the rascally worldling Crispin, posing as his friend Leander's servant, proceeds to further the latter's courtship of an heiress.

His efforts, he is certain, will be successful, for has he not discovered the secret that "men are like merchandise; they are worth more or less according to the skill of the salesman who markets them." When, moreover, his salesmanship encounters difficulties, Crispin puts into practice the even more pragmatic principle that men in society are bound together by the "bonds of interests," and that "this is a world of giving and taking, a shop, a mart, a place of exchange, and before you can ask you have to offer." He avoids exposure of his own and Leander's pretensions by proving to people that it is to their advantage to allow Leander to marry the girl.

Genuine love flowers in the end when Leander is redeemed by his affection for Sylvia, and now the lovers refute Crispin's contention that "the ties of love are as nothing to the bonds of interest." To this the invincible pragmatist replies, "And is love a slight interest?" Significantly, nine years later Benavente reveals Leander as a debauchee in *The Glad and Confident City.* Although Benavente's frankly contrived morality play (he acknowledged his situation as improbable and called his characters puppets) did not attract the American public, *The Bonds of Interest* is a brilliant trifle about matters that are not trifles.

The same symbolization appeared in some of the author's weightier plays and with greater straining for profundity. This was notably the case in the early *Saturday Night* (1903) which lacks the clarity and tidiness of *The Bonds of Interest.* Considered a profound drama by some champions, it must leave most of us sadly bewildered. Something to the effect that ambition or the will must sacrifice the joy of youth before it masters the world does emerge from the chaos of events. But profundity gained at the expense of a rationality or credibility of dramatic plot is normally not worth the effort.

Wisely, however, Benavente did not remain addicted to the dubious art of carrying champagne in a sieve. Nor could Benavente oppose the demands that realism was making upon his observant intelligence. He responded with a long series of plays which satirize realistic situations, study character, or describe passion with a touch of pungent naturalism. The satires *His Widow's Husband* and *The Governor's Wife* prod the shallow world of high society and politics. Without leaving any mark on the theatre of the world, they are at least relevant and pointed. In another age like seventeenth-century France, when he would have operated within a convention of poetic artifice, Benavente might have become a comic poet like Molière; in their modern investiture Benavente's realistic satires are clever but mild.

Liberal sentiment also entered into his realistic efforts. The best example of this vein is *The Field of Ermine* (1916) which expresses the democratic view that character and love are more important than noble birth. Here an unmarried duchess adopts a lad who is alleged to be her deceased brother's illegitimate son but returns him to his conniving plebeian mother upon discovering that she has been deluded. Nevertheless, her love for the admirable boy leads her to overcome the "chill of justice." She destroys all evidence against his birth and takes him for her own. "Upon the ermine of my field," Irene declares, "I shall place a lily as a new charge, whiter than ermine."

This sentiment is not the best recommendation one can give to the play. Far more impressive are the sharply drawn portraits of two groups of connivers, one in the plebeian circle and another in the patrician one which opposes the adoption of the child. Even this play, however, is not a major export, and its welcome in New York left something to be desired; the reality of the picture loses its immediacy on foreign soil, while its one transmissible attribute—its mild equalitarian gospel—could have no striking features for us. Weaker efforts like *The School of Princesses*, which stresses the importance of personal sacrifice as the main duty of royalty, are even less exportable.

Benavente also attempted to convey quiet effects or drama of attrition resembling Chekhov's vein. Such a reserved tragedy of poverty and loneliness as *A Lady* is an example of this striving for everyday reality. A woman who sacrificed everything for her lover and lost every penny lives alone and refuses to be helped. Women's sufferings and fortitude are indeed a favorite theme in this writer's work. Unfortunately, in spite of the opinion of so able a champion as John Garrett Underhill, Benavente is no Chekhov.

Benavente was better advised when in 1913 he made one powerful experiment in naturalist drama with *La Malquerida* or *The Passion Flower*, a Freudian drama of repression and passion. A peasant girl Acacia who seemingly hates her stepfather Esteban for taking her father's place unconsciously loves him, and her stepfather is equally in love with her. Thereupon his servant, who reads his master's thoughts, murders her suitor. Ultimately the girl and the stepfather confess the desire that has been secretly racking them. Her mother flings herself in his way to prevent his yielding to his incestuous passion, and is happy when he wounds her mortally since henceforth her death will be an impassable barrier between the lovers. Love in this drama is a force that overrides the conventions, and the slow progression of the passion which takes Esteban and Acacia by surprise and overwhelms their reason removes the stigma of deliberate sensationalism from the play.

With enough virtuosity and intelligence to furnish a dozen playwrights, Benavente, the author of about one hundred fifty plays, kept the Spanish theatre alive with the variety of his resources and with his sharp insights. Where the Spanish stage failed most signally was in its inability to discover a dynamic modern drive. Numerous playwrights did not even approach Benavente's concern with ponderable mental or emotional experience. Only the excellent folk poet Federico Garcia Lorca loomed large among Benavente's successors, and unfortunately his tense life was cut short, and even his memorable *Blood Wedding* cannot receive its due on the English-speaking stage because it is distinctly Spanish and subordinates action to lyricism.[4] Nor did the civil war of 1936-39 further the growth of the drama. Perhaps, however, the memory of this sanguinary struggle will give birth to searing drama—if Spain recovers from the wreckage and the theatre regains the freedom it cannot possess under the present fascist regime. (See p. 703 for more on Lorca.)

2 PIRANDELLO AND THE ILLUSIONISM OF THE ITALIAN STAGE

The same want of realistic dynamics characterizes the Italian theatre. Modern Italian drama responded for a while to European realism with Giacosa and others, lapsed into inflated romanticism with D'Annunzio, and then reached a point of disillusionment which nearly denied the validity of all objective reality. The Italian people, by nature and tradition, have always prized theatricality above drama. Flamboyant Italian nationalism was more conducive to romanticism than to realism and postwar fascism could not readily tolerate any direct grappling with problems of society or of individual development.

The realistic movement in Italy, which followed much unimpressive early romanticism, found a suitable slogan in "Verism." It found little else. Its proponents Giacosa, Verga, Rovetta, Praga and Bracco made careful transcriptions of local life and recorded the animal passions disclosed there. But their insight into human nature remained too elementary to add any vision or comprehensive criticism of life to the drama. The most important of them, Giuseppe Giacosa, born in 1841, came significantly from the industrial northern part of the country. After early verse plays in the romantic key which gave him a marketable reputation for comedy, he wrote pedestrian problem plays. For Italy his *Unhappy Love* treated marital infidelity with sensible restraint—that is, without rhetoric, teeth gnashing, and murders. In *Like Falling Leaves* (*Come la foglie*), written in 1900 and once greatly admired in France, Giacosa turned to the realities of the business world. In this unexciting but solid picture of a business man's home which recalls Björnson's *Bankruptcy* he conveyed the life of a family which is incapable of coping with realities when the father becomes bankrupt. In this crisis only the serious-minded girl Nennele keeps her wits about her; the rest are driven helter-skelter by the wind of adversity "like falling leaves." Finally, five years later in *The Stronger* (*Il più forte*) Giacosa presented a sharp picture of the commercial world with a portrait of a man who triumphs through his knowledge of the business game and his readiness to play it without a scruple. Giacosa remained a very moderate realist and dramatist. Today he is paradoxically known to most people as the librettist of Puccini's *La Bohème, Tosca,* and *Madama Butterfly*.

His confederates in realism have even less to offer. The vivid Sicilian novelist Giovanni Verga is best known for his peasant story *Cavalleria Rusticana* (1884), which he dramatized for Mascagni's opera. His other plays like *At the Porter's Lodge,* in which a brutish character favors a slut in order to torment her honest and loving sister, and *The She-Wolf,* a drama of animal infatuation, are naturalistic documents. His object was Zola's—to represent the brute in man. He succeeded only too well, with much melodramatic straining and with little point that would commend his dramatic work to the world beyond.

Marco Praga, a younger writer, defied the tropical Italian code that demands vengeance for adultery in *The Friend.* He came still closer to naturalism and treated the domestic triangle cynically like Becque in *The Ideal Wife* when he made a woman simultaneously satisfactory as one man's wife and another man's mistress. One of his pictures of shabby society, *The Closed Door* even possesses some immortality because it served Eleonora Duse as an adequate vehicle. Still, Praga remained a monotonous playwright and was incapable of uncovering any observations that are not within reach of the average practitioner.

Roberto Bracco's realism was a finer commodity when he wrote the vivid dramas of Neapolitan low life *Don Pietro Caruso* and *Lost in Darkness,* although they have only surface values. In *The Right to Live,* in 1900, he even attempted a picture of social injustice but without giving it more than pedestrian treatment. It is indeed significant of the power of religious and racial tradition in Italy that those writers who responded to Ibsen and his theatre of ideas either wrote tepidly or reacted negatively to the ideas themselves. When, for example, Enrico Butti turned to the problem of feminism in *The End of the Ideal* he maintained that woman must be dependent upon a lord and master. In *Utopia* the same author assailed the rationalism inherent in science and eugenics.

Lacking any extraordinary accomplishments, the realists naturally failed to hold a public that was in any case disposed to be resistant to prosaic drama. The great Eleonora Duse may have given, as it is claimed, the best performances of Ibsen roles, but Ibsen found no peer in Italy. It was, therefore, relatively easy for Gabriele d'Annunzio to capture the Italian theatre. He possessed everything this public favored —melodrama, sensationalism, rhetoric, and intense theatricality. His passion was a blaze of fireworks. His intellect was showy and for all his undisputed verbal magnificence he only repeated the platitudes of early nineteenth-century romanticism. As Huneker noted, "His art, despite exquisite workmanship, is still a gallery of echoes." [5] This dashing playwright, who held the public ear with his exhibitionistic estheticism and with his well-aired love affair with Eleonora Duse, was an accomplished publicity agent for himself. He retained this talent even in his later years when he seized Fiume for Italy with an easy *coup d'état* from the air after the collapse of Austria, and he concluded a career that Casanova might have envied by becoming a monk.

D'Annunzio had a talent for lyricism which could produce a colorful folk drama like *The Daughter of Jorio*. His concern with morbidity entailed the modern theatre's study of psychopathology, and his ability to depict violent emotions against vivid backgrounds produced affecting moments. All concessions in his favor are, however, insignificant beside the fact that he was a self-hypnotized *fakir* and sensationalist devoid of ideas and genuine emotions. Artiness, superman-worship and violence for the sake of violence mar his plays, or "word operas," as Ralph Roeder calls them.

His first important play *The Dead City* (*La Citta Morta*), written in 1898, is a typical example of his strained passion. Here an archaeologist excavating the tomb of Agamemnon falls in love with his own sister and frees himself of incest by drowning her. The deed is also motivated by his desire to preserve his friendship with her lover, since now he will no longer have reason to be jealous of this man! *Francesca da Rimini* treats the familiar Paolo and Francesco story with equivalent sound and fury. *The Daughter of Jorio,* set among the pagan peasants of Abruzzi, makes primitive folk melodrama of considerable power out of the story of a sorcerer's child who is protected by a shepherd. She, in turn, assumes his guilt when he is about to be executed as a parricide. *Fedra* makes the heroine of Euripides' *Hippolytus* and Racine's *Phédre* a nymphomaniac and has her killed by a ray of moonlight sent by the goddess Diana who favors the chaste Hippolytus.

In the comparatively restrained *Gioconda,* d'Annunzio propounds an idea at last. A sculptor torn between his wife and his mistress-model wounds himself, tries to remain faithful to the former after she has nursed him back to health, but finally deserts her for the beautiful model. Since she alone can inspire his work, he must abide with her. His wife, who sacrificed her beautiful hands to save his statue, must make way for his urge to create "beauty." Although d'Annunzio wrote many other plays and spectacles after *Gioconda,* he did not advance beyond its principle of "life for art's sake" and "art for art's sake." To the end of his days he remained a furious egoist and esthete. Oscar Wilde might have given birth to him—by palingenesis.

In time even Italy refused to follow the d'Annunzian orbit, and among his satellites only Sem Benelli possessed some distinction. The latter, who is known to us for that melodrama of Renaissance jealousy, vengeance and fratricide *The Jest,* infused some psychological analysis into his work. In *The Jest* he wrote, in fact, a much better play than d'Annunzio would have composed. But Benelli, too, only demonstrated the hopelessness of hitching the drama to a golliwog tricked out as a fire-dragon.

A complete denial of the past—of its conventions, its stability and its certainties—soon began to appear in Italian literature. This reaction began a few years before the World War and found its strongest roots in the plastic arts. The new theorists and artists led by Marinetti would have nothing to do with conventional beauty, melodious verse, and all the trappings of romanticism. "Futurism," as the movement was called, was in a sense the climax of romanticism because it was pursued with furious flamboyance. But the futurists' aversion to idealization of women and love and their eagerness to celebrate the machine age (no matter how romantic such worship may be, in the last analysis!) called for a new and modern art.

After the War, futurism became deepened by disillusionment and pessimism. The Italian drama became bitter, querulous, and completely skeptical. It flowered like a pungent weed in a movement that called itself "grotesque" and strove to be extravagantly mocking. The initial proponent of the so-called *Teatro del Grottesco,* Luigi Chiarelli, assaulted the conventions. Something might have come of his satirical work if the decried conventions had possessed any large significance. In Chiarelli's *Mask and the Face,* written in 1914, all that was exploded was the Italianate code requiring a man to avenge his wife's infidelity. The hero of this piece mouths the ancient canon more furiously than any of his friends before he learns that he is betrayed. But he soon discovers that he cannot bring himself to kill his wife, and spiriting her away because he is too proud to admit any contradiction between his theory and practice, he gives out that he has killed her. Brought back after his acquittal in great triumph, he arranges a mock funeral and then runs away with the supposedly dead woman. The grotesquerie of the funeral and the dénouement is highly original. But the convention of marital vengeance that is exploded here lacks importance for most of us, and the humor belongs in the last analysis to the puerile Grand Guignol variety.

Grotesquerie deepened in Chiarelli's other plays as his bitterness increased. In *The Silken Ladder,* written in 1917, he created a lurid picture of social corruption, expressing disillusionment with the world of success which remains closed to honest men but is wide open to every rascal and pretender. Four years later came his *Chimere* or *Chimeras,* an exposé of idealists who prove themselves to be vulgar opportunists, and in 1923 his *Death of the Lovers,* a caricature of the "grand passion" which in the present world can be produced only artificially and ludicrously. Chiarelli had one dominant idea in his satirical plays— "that this world is nothing but sound and fury signifying nothing." [6]

Italian negativism went to even greater lengths. In Luigi Antonelli it became fantastic. Even an enchanted island cannot bring happiness to man in *The Man Who Met Himself;* fairy-land is only "a replica of our own dull vesture of decay," and animals become corrupt the moment they adopt human civilization in *The Island of Monkeys.*[7] Another playwright Ernesto Cavacchioli considered life to be mere illusion, and the most gifted of the minor "grotesques" Rosso di San Secondo saw human beings as puppets living a nightmare of longing and suicidal thoughts (*What Passion, ye Marionettes*). He described life as something as unsubstantial as color in *The Sleeping Beauty,* and in *The Terrestrial Adventure* his pessimism even maintained that we cannot know anything. Man disappears as an entity in the chaotic post-war scene viewed by Italy's most sensitive spirits. Nor could this pessimism and puppetry be lifted by fascism which converted a land of intense individualists into cogs of a totalitarian machine.

Such was the milieu of Luigi Pirandello who became an important figure in the modern drama by dint of applying a fine intellect to the negativism of his colleagues. His was a highly modern mind replete with the relativistic philosophy and psychiatric science of the twentieth century. In addition, he possessed an original inquiring spirit which after pondering acutely on the relation between the drama and subjective life did not hesitate to break down the last formalities of dramatic structure. The social and political realities which had forced themselves into the modern theatre received scant attention from him, and the situations which he most favored are remote from the cardinal conflicts of the age.

Nevertheless, both his disillusionment and his psychology stamp him as an ultra-modern.

Pirandello achieved stature because his temperament, training and private life blended so completely with the "grotesque" dispensation. Born in 1867, in Girgenti, he was a native son of Sicily, the homeland of irascible temperaments and animal passions. Even his able apologist Domenico Vittorini [7] declares, "I should not say that Pirandello is a kindly person." Naturalism flourished on Sicilian soil when Verga and others set down its primitive life. A streak of naturalism appeared in Pirandello in his early works and it is present even in many of his most cerebral efforts, since these also present sordid situations and deal with elemental passions. Incest, prostitution, and suicide appear liberally in *Six Characters in Search of an Author*, for example. Early in life he became violently anti-d'Annunzian. Living in a land of simple peasants over whom hung a "pall of inertia broken by sudden outbursts of jealousy and crime," he could have little patience with d'Annunzio's rococo sentiments and superman-worship. For Pirandello, as for the naturalists, all men were little specks of sensitive flesh, and these specks lived passively in a world over which they could exercise little authority.

In the preparatory years of his life, Pirandello was not yet completely devoted to the non-political contemplative life. His early poems were filled with optimism and political idealism. He was a liberal in politics, a realist in literature, and a champion of the Sicilian people. He was stirred in 1898 when the impoverished Sicilian peasantry in Palermo seized the lands belonging to the crown and suffered many deaths in an encounter with the militia. Earlier he had been strongly affected by the scandalous failure of the Roman Bank in 1894. His first disillusionment with society came when he grew tired of political corruption and social hypocrisy. Thereafter he came to regard the state with those anarchistic suspicions which colored many of his statements and determined his continual satirization of social conventions, especially of so-called respectability.

Perhaps it was this loss of faith in the state that led him to avoid all programs of reform. Possibly, too, it was his disillusionment with man as a social animal which enabled him to accept Mussolini's fascism until he scandalized American opinion in 1935 by defending the seizure of Ethiopia. From a cynical viewpoint fascist practices are hardly disturbing! Yet the man who referred to society as a "league of brigands against men of good will" [8] could never have been a fascist at heart. He was essentially an anarchist who had no use for society, and above all a pessimist.

He sometimes denied that he was one. But his explanations were exceedingly tenuous.[9] Although he struck a comic note in most of his plays, and called them comedies, his vision was fundamentally tragic. He himself once stated, "I see life as tragedy," and it is not only the tragic content of such plays as *Six Characters in Search of an Author* that confirms this admission. In a foreword to a book about himself [10] he wrote: "I have tried to tell something to other men, without any ambition, except perhaps that of avenging myself for having been born."

His humor throughout is ironic and saturnine; its brilliance owes everything to these attributes. It might be argued that anyone as cerebral as Pirandello, whose plays are full of logistic contortions, is essentially anti-tragic. His characters are the puppets of perverse syllogisms and Stark Young has rightly stressed the fact that they are theatrical abstractions. According to the latter, Pirandello has "transferred to the mind the legs and antics and the inexhaustible vivacity and loneliness and abstraction of the *commedia dell' arte*." A writer who plays with such abstractions would indeed seem to be far removed from the field of tragedy. But had not Pirandello's spiritual parent Chiarelli already made a distinction between "the mask and the face"? Behind Pirandello's defensive *commedia dell' arte* mask it is easy to detect a face contorted with pain and a sense of futility. Did he not himself write in his thirty-fifth year: "Ask the poet what is the saddest sight and he will reply 'It is laughter on the face of a man.' " [11] Did he not add, "Who laughs does not know."

Pirandello is, however, an exception to his own axiom: He laughed because he "knew." He "knew" that life is absurd. If, like a Talmudist or a medieval theologian, he took delight in subtle dialectics for its own sake (in Rome and Milan people rioted and fought duels over him on this score), he was also expressing a conviction that nothing in life is certain except its uncertainty. Life possesses only the reality that the mind creates for itself; and the mind creates this reality—a man, to use his phrase, "builds himself up"—in order to defend itself against personal defeat.

This attitude—his pessimism and the relativist view that considers reality an opinion or belief—was not, however, a merely philosophical conviction, and it was never a pose although it hardened into a formula and made him repeat himself unconscionably. It was burned into his soul by a tragic private experience as fantastic as any of his situations. In his youth he married a girl he had never seen before, the marriage having been arranged by his parents in accordance with custom. She was his father's partner's daughter, whose mother had died in childbirth because her husband was too insanely jealous to make the attendance of a doctor feasible. At first the young couple was happy and there were three children from the union. (One son—Stefano Landi—is now a writer, and another is an artist.) Then came the loss of the family fortune when his father's mines were ruined by a flood, and Pirandello was forced to take a teaching position in a normal school for girls in Rome. His wife Antonietta lost her dowry in the catastrophe, and this event, coupled with a painful delivery when the third child was born, unsettled her reason. She became psychotically jealous, caused frightful scenes, and left him for several months. Pirandello tried in vain to allay her suspicions by staying at home and giving her every penny of his earnings. This situation alone could have impressed upon him the observation that a person is what others believe him to be and that, moreover, reality is a different thing to different people—to the observer and to the individual himself.

Donna Antonietta became so violent after a while that she should have been confined to a sanitarium. Instead, Pirandello kept her at home for seventeen years while she made life miserable for him and his children. His daughter, whom the mother persecuted with particular venom, tried to kill herself with a revolver which was fortunately too old to be serviceable. Pirandello's teacher's salary was meager, and only when his plays finally proved profitable was he able to send her to a private sanitarium. Pirandello's laughter under these circumstances was as heroic as it was bound to be hollow.

He first entered the theatre in middle age, shortly before the World War, having previously written numerous short stories and novels. His late devotion to the stage was, however, as intense as a middle-aged passion and he wrote with an eager absorption in the new medium that enabled him to turn out as many as nine plays in one year. And the theatre proved a gratifying mistress. It gave him fresh interests, including the pleasure of organizing a company in the Odescalchi Theatre in Rome where Podrecca had first won fame with his marionettes, and of staging his own plays. Mussolini took Pirandello's troupe under his wing, the famous Ruggiero Ruggeri joined the group, and an extensive tour to England, France and Germany brought "Pirandelismo" to the attention of Europe. In the theatre the dramatist also found an understanding friendship with that superb actress Marta Abba (seen here in *Tovarich*) who played the leading feminine role in most of his plays. Finally, it is to the stage that he owed the greatest portion of the immortality that may be his reward.

Among his early naturalistic sketches is the folk comedy *In a Sanctuary* revolving around a rustic quarrel concerning the intelligence of pigs, and *The Other Son* represents the heartache of a destitute old mother whose son has emigrated from Sicily. *The Patent* is a delightful farce about a poor fellow who is harassed by his neighbors because they consider him a sorcerer. He sues for libel and refuses to be placated by a patient, Pirandellian judge. An accident to the judge's goldfish in open court, however, confirms his reputation as a sorcerer. And by then the desperate and pathetic victim of rumor has decided to capitalize his notoriety. He will make the townspeople pay him to plague their competitors or to ward off evil from themselves by removing himself from their presence. *Sicilian Limes,* written in 1910, is a tender little play. A humble piccolo player who enabled a poor rustic girl to achieve fame as a concert singer visits her in northern Italy in the hope of winning her love. But he departs a painfully disillusioned man when he finds her morally corrupted by her sophisticated circle. A number of other effective pieces in Pirandello's early vein mark him a near master of the one-act form.

However, Pirandello achieved his mark in radically different work, which he anticipated in 1904 with his novel *The Late Mattia Pascal,* the story of a librarian who escapes an unpleasant domestic life by pretending death by drowning and assumes a burdensome new personality. True to his custom of dramatizing his short stories, he wrote *Pensaci Giacomino* (*Think of It, Giacomino*) in 1914, and many characteristics of his art first came to the fore in this play. It possesses saturnine humor, a perverse character, and logic defensively pursued to extravagant lengths by this person. Old Professor Toti revenges himself upon the school system by marrying a pregnant young girl; now the authorities will have to pay a pension to his widow long after his death! He remains a husband only in appearance, however, while she enjoys the boyish love of young Giacomino. In fact, the husband expects to be betrayed since this marriage is unnatural—"Otherwise, how could I, poor old man that I am, have any peace." He does not mind the gossip of the town, is fond of her lover, and actually forces him to remain true to her. And he is satisfied, despite the laughter of the multitude, since he has saved a girl from prostitution and misery by his behavior. Here already we have Pirandello turning the conventions topsy-turvy, and proving that the socially incorrect view may be the better and more humane one.

The Pleasure of Honesty, in the same year, is another sardonic chuckle. A woman who is distressed by her daughter's unmarried state sanctions her liaison with a Marquis. But Agata becomes pregnant and needs the cloak of honesty which only a husband can supply. A husband is found for her in the person of a lonely and strange individual who agrees to screen the lovers for a consideration because he has no illusions regarding honesty. Yet once the mask of honesty is assumed, he insists that the mummers wear it forever. He insists on the utmost honesty after the marriage, and this cynic succeeds so well in upholding the principle of "honor" that he wins his wife's love and society's esteem.

Cap and Bells in 1915 marked a further step in Pirandellian satire. Men "build themselves up," says Pirandello, and cannot forgive anyone who destroys the role they are playing. "We are all puppets," one of the characters declares, but "we all add another puppet to that one; the puppet that each of us believes himself to be." And everyone wants that second puppet to be inviolable—that is, he wants everyone to respect it. In *Cap and Bells,* the grotesquely ugly bookkeeper Ciampa is not troubled by the knowledge that his wife is betraying him with his employer; why shouldn't she, since he is so ugly, so long as others do not suspect the situation and laugh at him! But when the employer's jealous wife exposes the intrigue and has her husband arrested at Ciampa's house, the situation is impossible not only for this woman who will now have to leave her husband but for Ciampa who is furious at having his "puppet" destroyed. Thereupon he hits upon a solution:—the jealous woman, who is already repenting her hasty deed, must allow herself to be declared insane. Then when the case against her husband is dismissed and Ciampa's honor is saved, she can return from the asylum —"cured." She doesn't fancy the idea, but Ciampa gets his way, and she is carried out of the house shrieking while Ciampa grins contentedly.

From *Cap and Bells* to *Right You Are if You Think You Are* the way leads to the meaning of truth. After having maintained in *Cap and Bells* that each man creates a suitable mask for himself, Pirandello declared in his new play that we are incapable of penetrating the mystery of another person's identity. This means that we must exercise tolerance toward others; that is, we must respect their deepest fabrications because we cannot really know the truth about them. Suppose that all records were destroyed by an accident like the earthquake referred to in *Right You Are,* we would then have no way of verifying that people are what they claim to be. To demonstrate this point Pirandello concocted an extravaganza in which the élite of a provincial town are set at loggerheads because Signor Prola does not allow his wife's supposed mother to see her. He claims that the old woman is his mother-in-law only by a first marriage and that she is laboring under the illusion that her daughter is still alive. She, in turn, claims that Signor Prola is suffering from the delusion that his wife died and that the woman he is living with now is his second wife. Prola and his mother-in-law are, however, kind to each other and comparatively happy until the town begins to buzz with scandal. Nor can the town discover the truth since Signora Prola is willing to be a second wife to her husband and a daughter to the old lady. The point is not only that we cannot discover the identity of Signora Prola, but that it is unnecessary to do so. Illusion is a bitter necessity to at least one of the principals of this play, and it must be respected. The town is consequently satirized for its idle curiosity. Judged by realistic standards, *Right You Are* is of course preposterous, but accepted as a philosophical extravaganza it is neatly pointed, and it comes close to Aristophanic humor. Its real shortcoming is the thinness of the plot.

Thereafter many of Pirandello's plays were only comic or serious variations on the relativity of reality or the "drama of being and seeming," as Vittorini calls it. Dual personality is the theme of *Signora Morli One and Two,* in which a woman reveals different features to the gay husband who abandoned her and to the grave lawyer who protected and made her his wife in all but name. Dualism also appears in *As You Desire Me.* Here the characters alternately defend and accuse a woman who was responsible for a friend's suicide, and since each disputant wins his opponent over to the opposite position the woman's guilt can never be determined. Such is the value of men's opinions of each other or even of themselves.

In *Naked,* a pathetic creature clothes herself with illusions in the hope of concealing her frustrations and inner poverty. The nurse Ersilia who has made what she believes to be a successful attempt at suicide tells a newspaper reporter that she is dying for love because she wants to be interesting to herself before the end. She recovers, however, and upon being wooed by the repentant lover who had abandoned her she confesses that he means nothing to her; she did not try to commit suicide for him and she will have nothing to do with him. These and other revelations culminate in everybody attacking her. She had only wished to die clothed in a beautiful romance which had been beyond her reach in life, but now she is accused of immorality and imposture. Stripped "naked" by others who fail to comprehend the complexity of human motives and finding herself forced back into the colorless reality from which she had tried to escape, she attempts suicide for a second time and dies.

The ultimate in self-delusion, however, is insanity, and it is with good reason that Pirandello put much of his best dramatic talent into his treatment of that theme. *Henry IV* is the tragedy of a complex and painful character who lost his mind after falling from his horse at the conclusion of a masquerade. A wealthy relative coddles his illusion that he is the medieval German emperor Henry IV and surrounds him with a grotesque retinue. After twelve years he recovers sanity but pretends insanity because the real world, in which he found so much perfidy and lost the woman he loved, is a poor substitute for the illusory one. When this woman and his rival, who had caused his fall out of jealousy, appear together, "Henry IV" wounds him mortally. Now, however, the pretence of madness is more imperative than ever if he is to escape the legal consequences of his vengeance, and he must remain Henry IV for the rest of his life. The challenge of the play lies in its hero's deliberate renunciation of reality as something too painful to bear. Without this

nihilistic animus, *Henry IV* would be an inexcusably contrived melodrama. With it, the play is still contrived—but for a purpose. This is
hardly sufficient to place it among the world's major plays, but owing to
its bitter intensity and unique background it is one of the most powerful
of Pirandello's work.

Finally, Pirandello's foray into mirrors through which even Carroll's
Alice did not venture also led him to question the adequacy of art. He
devoted several plays to the problem and provided contradictory answers. *When One Is Somebody* is the tragedy of a famous writer who is
compelled to remain in the mold which he created for himself by his
works. Although a noble love rejuvenates him to the extent of giving
him a new literary style and a fresh vitality which no one would have
associated with him, society will not allow him to leave the prison walls
of his fame. He must not violate the style which made him famous! In
Trovarsi a famous actress cannot surrender her stage personality; she
loses her lover, who resents the similarity between her public and her
intimate behavior, but gains the seemingly greater gratification of remaining an artist.

As a rule, moreover, Pirandello expressed a strong dissatisfaction with
art, complaining that it fell so short of the truth. In this he was not,
however, echoing the complaint of the naturalists against those writers
who failed to photograph factual reality. He was indeed genuinely displeased with conventional theatricality and satirized it mercilessly. But
his basic disaffection arose from the fact that life, which is constantly
changing, is invariably distorted or killed when presented on the stage.
Human motives, too, are multifarious and cannot be reduced to a simple
formula for a public impatient with subtleties. Pirandello, therefore,
either denies the validity of all drama or calls upon it to become as fragmentary, relative and fluid as life itself.

In *Tonight We Improvise,* which describes a play in the making, he
contrasts the intense aliveness of the characters with the artificiality to
which the stage reduces them. Here the actors lose themselves in their
role so completely that they crack the mold into which a fussy stage
director tries to place them. Pirandello, who had a penchant for unconventional dramatic devices and prided himself on the ingenuity of his
plots, found ample opportunity to exercise this talent in his critiques of
the drama. He reached the peak of dramatic originality and critical profundity in the well-known *Six Characters in Search of an Author.*

Here the characters lead an independent life because their author
failed to complete their story. They invade a rehearsal of another Pirandellian play and insist upon playing out the life that is theirs. Constantly
interrupting the stage manager and the actors, disapproving narrow
stage interpretations and insisting upon explaining themselves, they

break down the structure of the play until it becomes a series of alternately comic and tragic fragments. Here Pirandello has, so to speak,
written a play to end all plays. And all this comes from the fact that life,
with its subjective complexity and irrationality, defies the glib interpretations of the stage and its actors.

One character protests to the director and the actors: "Of my nausea,
of all the reasons, one crueler and viler than another, which have made
this of me, have made me just as I am, you would like to make a sentimental, romantic concoction." No naturalist could have made a severer
charge against formal dramaturgy. Moreover, the *dramatis personae* are
"characters"—that is, they are stamped with certain characteristics
which create their own situations regardless of the intentions of their
creator: When a character is born he acquires immediately such an independence from his author that we can all imagine him in situations in
which the author never thought of placing him, and he assumes of his
own initiative a significance that his author never dreamt of lending him.

The drama which the six characters insist upon acting out in defiance
of all the contrivances favored by the ordinary theatre is a nightmare of
sordid situations and self-torment. The Father, who came to believe
that his gentle wife was more in rapport with his humble secretary than
with himself, set up a home for them. The family does not credit this
motive and suspects that he wanted to rid himself of his wife; and no
doubt his motivation was more complex than he can possibly understand
or acknowledge. He kept the Son for himself, and the latter grew up
into a lonely, embittered youth. After the clerk's death the Mother, who
bore him three children, disappeared with her new family, and the
Father met his Stepdaughter only years later in a disreputable establishment. He was prevented from committing incest only because his
wife who saw the Father and the Stepdaughter together warned them.
The Father took the family back with him, but since then their hearts
have been consumed with shame, sorrow, and exasperation. The legitimate Son resents the presence of the Mother's illegitimate children, the
Mother is passively miserable, her adolescent Boy broods upon suicide,
the Father is constantly apologizing, and the Stepdaughter cannot ever
forgive him or overcome her disgust. Ultimately the Mother's youngest
child is drowned, the Boy shoots himself, and the characters run off the
stage in confusion.

Try and make a neat little play out of all this, Pirandello seems to
say! This is life! The tragedy of the six characters can never be completely dramatized because their motives are so mixed; because some
of them—the Mother and the Son—do not explain themselves sufficiently; because others—the youngest child and the Boy—are inarticulate. Moreover, some of them are too passionately eager to justify them-

selves and are too bedeviled to stay within the playwright's frame. Many of the tendencies of the twentieth century—its impatience with formal art, its investigation of the nebulous but explosive unconscious, and its relativist philosophy—are caught in this work. *Six Characters in Search of an Author* is as important as a monument to the intellectual activity of an age as it is original and harrowing. And it is harrowing despite comic details because Pirandello's puppets are intensely, if fragmentarily, alive. Only in some unnecessarily metaphysical passages which produce more confusion than profundity can the play be said to fall short of complete realization.

Pirandello reached his high point with this work, written in 1921. Numerous other variations on his favorite themes merely displayed his ingenuity, and a few full-length dramas of womanhood (*As Well as Before, Either of One or of No One, Other People's Point of View,* and *The Wives' Friend*) are in the main only conventionally affecting. He repeated himself, lapsed into sterile cerebration, and generally missed the attribute of living characterization which distinguishes the work of most masters of the drama. His sardonic viewpoint too often evoked puppets and snarled his plots until both became mere contrivances. Only the power of his intellect set him above the mere artificers of the theatre.

He continued to write until his death in 1936, winning the Nobel Prize in 1934. That year the inevitable happened and this intellectual anarchist found himself in difficulties with the fascist regime. His libretto *The Fable of the Exchanged Sons,* the comedy of a prince who decides to let an idiot who had been exchanged for him at birth "run the king business," was booed as anti-fascist and suppressed. The cynic in Pirandello might have reflected that all men were brothers under the skin, since *Six Characters* had been banned in London for a while as "unsuitable to the British people." His work was condemned by the Italian government for "moral incongruity," and his doctrine that "nothing is true" was declared to be at variance with fascist principles. Pirandello was consequently held guilty of creating "bad art." But his cynicism or at least his mask of cynicism prevented him from open defiance of the ruling powers, and he made his peace with Mussolini by defending the Italo-Ethiopian war during his American visit in 1935. When asked by reporters why Italy should appropriate Ethiopia, he replied, "Well, you took America from the Indians, didn't you?" When an American delegation of writers led by Clifford Odets interviewed him, he gave no comfort to their outraged sensibilities. But his answers were all equivocal. His explanation, "I am a Fascist because I am an Italian," resembled another skeptic's defense of conformity: Montaigne, we recall, declared that he was a Christian because he was born one.

His work remains a monument to the questioning and self-tormenting human intellect which is at war not only with the world, the flesh and the devil but with its own limitations. Once the intellect has conquered problem after problem without solving the greatest question of all—namely, whether it is real itself rather than illusory—it reaches an impasse. Pirandello is the poet of that impasse. He is also the culmination of centuries of intellectual progress which have failed to make life basically more reasonable or satisfactory. He ends with a question mark. He should come at the end of this history of the drama's interpretation of man and his world—if art were a syllogism.

The drama, which is perhaps the oldest of the arts, began with the question "How shall we exist?" Logically—after three thousand years of human effort to solve this first problem—it might therefore end with the question "Do we exist at all?" But the drama has always been a faith rather than an argument, and it has sought to provide an answer that would strengthen the spirit for its continual battle with the "Everlasting Nay" that grins at us in a thousand shapes. The first answer came when primitive drama strove to conquer the world with witch-doctor's magic. The last and perfect answer has always come when dramatists have tried to overcome the world with the strength of the human will and spirit.

Pirandello's viewpoint which led him to much repetition, statics and tenuousness was the consequence of a triple defeat. He was defeated in his private life, in the war which refuted the optimism of the nineteenth century, and in fascism which denied humanitarianism even in theory. Only the élan of his whimsy and humor made his acceptance of defeat tolerable—and in a sense, even contradicted it. The stream of modern drama, however, dispensed with the inexorable logic of his negations before and after his appearance in the theatre. In Germany, in the eighties, arose a vigorous theatre that carried Ibsen's affirmation of reality further. From Russia and Ireland came a deeply humane drama, from England Shaw's mental fight, from America O'Neill's grappling with the world and the varied affirmativeness of his successors.

XXIII

GERHART HAUPTMANN AND THE MODERN NATURALISM

I THE GERMAN BATTLEFIELD

NOWHERE did the modern spirit rumble so violently as in the modern German theatre. Both realism and the expressionist reaction to it later were carried to their extremes there, and the heaviest artillery was characteristically fired from the stage. A viewpoint is a passionate affair in Germany, and not a flirtation.

Realism began to emerge in the middle forties. The most considerable mid-century playwright Friedrich Hebbel was the son of a North German mason and carried his father's profession into the theatre. Born in 1813 and dead in 1863, he grew up in the declining years of romanticism. Inevitably, therefore, he wrote a number of romantic plays like *Judith, Herod and Mariamne, Gyges and his Ring* and a *Nibelungen* trilogy. Even in these works, however, he created much solid masonry. They are written in severe verse and are devoid of romantic grace. Their biblical, oriental and medieval scenes are bulky psychological and philosophical structures. *Herod and Mariamne,* for example, is a massive tragedy of abnormal jealousy. *Gyges and his Ring* turns Herodotus' ancient story of a Lydian queen's vengeance upon the husband who allowed her to be seen disrobed into a philosophical fable; the vengeful Queen who later kills herself is Nature, and Nature punishes all those who unveil her.

As early as 1844, moreover, Hebbel anticipated the drama of naturalism with a powerful middle-class tragedy *Maria Magdalena.* Its tragic events transpire because the local bourgeois standards make them inevitable. A rigorously honest and puritanic joiner Anthony is driven frantic when his impulsive son Karl is innocently arrested for theft. Deeply wounded in his self-respect, he threatens to cut his throat if additional disgrace should ever be heaped upon him by his daughter Clara. But it so happens that the latter has yielded to her fiancé Leonard who insisted on prenuptial intimacies because he was jealous of her secret love for a university graduate. Bourgeois to his fingertips, Leonard, however, abandons her when her father uses up her dowry in order to save an old friend from death and when the family name is disgraced by Karl's arrest. Knowing herself to be with child and fearing that her father will kill himself when he discovers her condition, she drowns herself in a well. Although its soliloquies stamp *Maria Magdalena* as some-what old-fashioned, this taut play anticipated Ibsen and German natu-ralism by more than thirty years.

Hebbel's oscillations between romanticism and realism also appeared in the work of Otto Ludwig whose *Erbförster* or *The Forester* in 1853 provided much painful realism. Imitations of French problem plays also appeared now and then.[1] Finally, German peasant drama or "folk pieces" used realistic backgrounds and dialect to advantage. The Vien-nese Ludwig Anzengruber wrote peasant plays in Austrian dialect with distinct vigor and reality. His *Double Suicide* (*Der Doppelselbstmord*), for example, is a rustic version of the Romeo and Juliet story. Accus-tomed to realism by his experience with dialect drama, Anzengruber also proved himself a rugged realist when he turned to city life in his bleak *Fourth Command* (*Das vierte Gebot*).[2]

The stage also began to favor the realities. In the seventies the Duke of Meiningen's famous company began a revolution in the art of theatre. By stressing authenticity of costuming and settings, artistic unity, ef-fective mob scenes and ensemble acting, the company anticipated the basic ideal of realism—namely, the creation of perfect illusion. For seventeen seasons between 1874 and 1890, the "Meiningers" spread the new gospel of realistic production, even while they were still producing only Shakespearean and romantic plays. Antoine and Stanislavsky were among those to be directly fired by the Meininger troupe's memorable travels through Europe.

More potent than any individual efforts, however, were the general trends of German history and thought. First to be noted is the tre-mendous upsurge of the German states, united by Bismarck in 1870 into a nation powerful enough to defeat the French empire. Thereafter Ger-many became the most dynamic and progressive country in Europe, and it was inevitable that the drama should respond to the new age of Prus-sian hegemony. Such a response, moreover, could only stimulate a new realistic outlook. The Germans did not have to look to Zola or Ibsen for an example, although in their new frame of mind they naturally wel-comed the realistic drama of other countries and were the first to accord Ibsen a place in the theatre.

Romanticists and their apologists were, of course, far from absent in a nation that had accepted romanticism more completely than any other people. Conservatives naturally favored the older drama because it did not disturb the *status quo*. In 1863 the critic Gustav Freytag even created a hard and fast theory of playwriting in his *Technique of the Drama*, in the hope of stabilizing the stage. He labored mightily to establish a formula for "well-built" plays which would serve up the old passions and interests in the most easily digestible manner. The drama was to avoid "painful discord," retain its spirituality, and refrain from representing "the social perversions of real life, the despotism of the rich, the torments of the oppressed." * It was sufficient to achieve theatrical effect, and Freytag created his system of play construction to ensure this effect. Belated romanticists like the capable Ernst von Wildenbruch and Adolph von Wilbrandt even found a romantic stimulus in the new realities of the empire. Had not united Germany proved herself mighty and glorious under the Hohenzollerns! Consequently Wildenbruch paid tribute to Germany's heroic past and to the ideal of national unity in several historical plays. His *Carolingians* honored this ideal and his *Quitzows* represented the Hohenzollerns' services to the country. Kaiser Wilhelm I had good reason to compliment him. "Dear Wildenbruch," he wrote: "Such pieces as these are what we want just now. Thank you for making my task easier." [3]

But there were deeper realities in the Kaiser's bailiwick even if he could only look askance at them. The scientific attitude toward life was taking hold in Germany, and it was calling not only for a careful recording of facts but for a mechanistic philosophy. The biologist Haeckel, who tried to unriddle the universe by explaining its operation mechanically in *The Riddle of the Universe,* was leading the German intelligentsia away from mysticism. The idealists of German philosophy who maintained that the world was the "idea" of God were being supplanted by the rationalistic and materialistic thinkers. "Idealism" was even becoming a boomerang in the hands of its younger German disciples. It had been doing so, in fact, for a long time—ever since followers of the pontiff of German philosophy Hegel put a new construction upon his theory that the world moved forward by a conflict between opposite principles. Hegel saw the processes of historical change coming to an end and reaching stability in the Prussian state. His followers, the so-called "young Hegelians" among whom Karl Marx was outstanding, considered the process as continuous. Moreover, they interpreted his "dialectics" (or theory of change by means of conflicting principles) materialistically. Hence arose the concept of class conflict, according to which material interests determined the battle between different classes—the final conflict being waged by capital and labor.

Marx and his followers focused attention on the realities of society, and the socialist or "Social-democratic" movement created by Marx even waxed strong enough to convert theory into practice. Social reforms, labor-union activity, and political battles waged in the name of

---

* To this end Freytag even revised the Aristotelian theory of purgation. In order to banish everything that is of immediate interest or is painful in the theatre, Freytag maintained that the spectator of a play was purified, not, as Aristotle held by direct contact with *pity* and *terror* but by release from pity and terror— that is, by *"a feeling of security."*

Socialism filled the consciousness of the German playwrights. Even when they did not accept the tenets of the *Communist Manifesto* and did not enroll in any political party they could no longer neglect the ponderable realities of society. And Marxism reminded them in theory, as Ibsen did in practice, that no artist's consciousness could escape these realities.

The drama that arose in Germany and adopted the slogan of "naturalism" thus acquired roots in modern thought and fact. Marx and the socialist movement, which even the iron Chancellor Bismarck could not suppress, impressed upon the playwrights the importance of describing *environment* scrupulously and of representing behavior in relation to social conditioning.* At the same time, the new dramatists bowed to the even more pronounced dicta of mechanistic science which maintained that man was a product of heredity and a helpless victim of physiological promptings.

Truthfulness at all costs was the slogan—the truthfulness of science and sociology, in so far as art could approach it. (And the naturalists believed that it could.) A new conception of tragedy came to the fore— that of Fate inherent in heredity, instinct, and environment. A new technique was also sought—namely, a type of drama which would not manipulate reality for the sake of theatrical effect but would simply reproduce reality. Zola had, in fact, already acclaimed the "slice of life" treatment, just as Ibsen had already dropped intrigue from the playwright's bag of tricks. But the German playwrights resolved to better the example.

A concerted literary movement soon enthroned the new orientation in the theatre. Writers banded together to publish polemical magazines, and artists of the theatre organized themselves into stage societies. The literary movement, with centers in Munich and Berlin, grew apace, and finally it prevailed. In Berlin a literary club *Durch* ("Through") proved especially potent. Its membership list included a scientist like the well-

---

* Marxism, however, went further by its sympathy for the proletariat, and the note of social pity soon pervaded many of the observations of the naturalists. Such humanitarianism ran counter to the professions of strict naturalism, which strove to banish emotion as something inimical to scientific objectivity. But the gain frequently exceeded the loss, as in *The Weavers,* in which naturalism became tinged with emotional appeal. Marxism, it must be recognized, also modified the fatalism of the strict naturalists by emphasizing the role of active will in society, since there were loopholes in its concept of the determinism of economics. It held that "men make their own history;" that history is the resultant of "many wills operating in different directions," even if these wills do not exist in a vacuum but are the result of specific social conditions. One should not forget that "circumstances are changed precisely by men!" (*Feuerbach* by Engels, and *Theses on Feuerbach* by Marx). Unfortunately, however, scant attention was paid to qualifications of determinism. Brunetière's sound principle that the drama represents the will of man in conflict with the powers that limit it was insufficiently observed by the naturalists. Neglect of this principle, without which there can be no exaltation and very little excitement on the stage, was in fact a major limitation of the new drama.

known Wilhelm Bölsche, a liberal theologian and precursor of the present Ethical Culture movement like Bruno Wille, and the nascent playwright Gerhart Hauptmann. A number of them formed an artists' colony
in a suburb of Berlin where Hauptmann and his brother Carl had already settled. Strindberg visited the colony, and other German writers,
including the excellent poet Richard Dehmel and the playwrights Wedekind and Halbe joined it in time.

Fortunately, too, a leader arose among them· in the person of the
hypnotic windbag Arno Holz who possessed a talent for making more
gifted people than himself toe the line of his theories, as well as for
setting them pregnant examples. Turning first to lyric poetry Holz legis-
lated against the use of stanzas, rhyme and regular meter, and acclaimed
Walt Whitman. The novel next attracted Holz, and here he set his
cohorts an example under a Norwegian pseudonym by writing the photographic sketches *Papa Hamlet* with the aid of his more talented friend
Johannes Schlaf. Finally he engaged the drama, and again enlisting the
creative Schlaf, composed the lengthy and labored *Family Selicke* (*Die
Familie Selicke*) in 1890 as a lesson for naturalists.

It proved to be a pungent picture of lower middle-class life. The father
is an alcoholic bookseller, the mother struggles to make ends meet, and
one of their children dies of tuberculosis. The elder daughter alone
possesses the stamina to hold the family together, and to this end she
sacrifices her single opportunity to escape from the morass. The effect of
the sordid setting, against which the lowly characters suffered and hoped,
and the avoidance of theatrical contrivances were momentous. Years
later, without benefit of Schlaf, Holz wrote impossible plays, proving
that his personal endowment was slight. Shortly after *Die Familie Selicke*
Schlaf, without benefit of Holz, however, added new dimensions to the
naturalist drama with *Master Ölze,* a Dostoyevskian psychological character study of a murderer. It is only one of Nature's Aristophanic jests
that the super-realist Schlaf should have ended as a theosophist who
went so far as to deny the spherical shape of the earth.

Equally important, moreover, was the rise of a new naturalist theatre
which could accommodate the new drama without violating its character. Ten progressives, taking a cue from Antoine's *Théâtre Libre* which
had visited Germany, founded the *Freie Bühne* or Free Stage with Paul
Schlenther and Otto Brahm as directors. In the latter, besides, the
theatre found an artist of the highest integrity. Otto Brahm (born Otto
Abrahamsohn, in 1856) worked as a clerk, studied extensively at four
universities, and took a doctor's degree in 1879 before turning to a literary career. During the next ten years he became one of the most eminent
dramatic critics of his day and proved himself a staunch defender of
Anzengruber, Björnson and Ibsen. At the same time he laid the founda-

tions of his realistic stage technique with critical comments on acting, from which he demanded naturalness, immersion in the role, and consciousness of the ensemble. When, therefore, he became affiliated with the *Freie Bühne* Brahm, who considered himself a "fighting person by nature," girded himself to make his theories prevail.[4]

Fortunately his work was made easier by the progressive writers in Europe, by the example of Balzac, Flaubert, the de Goncourt brothers, the plays of Ibsen and Tolstoy, and the new native drama. He opened his theatre appropriately with Ibsen's *Ghosts*. *Die Familie Selicke* was by now ready to be performed and struck sympathetic critics as the most momentous production of the *Freie Bühne*. In the same season appeared Anzengruber's *Fourth Command*, a first play *Before Sunrise* by a young writer who was soon to outdistance all local competitors, and translations of the de Goncourts' *Henriette Maréchal*, Björnson's *Gauntlet*, and Tolstoy's peasant tragedy *The Power of Darkness*. In the second season came several new plays uncovered by Brahm; in the third, Strindberg's ultra-naturalistic *Miss Julie* with its kitchen setting and its repulsive characters.

The problem of getting naturalistic performances was, strangely, a more difficult matter. Actors, trained in the conventional style, tended to follow individual styles and to prime their acting for "big scenes." It is to be noted that even the Meiningen company favored broad gestures and declamation. But as the leading actor of the new dispensation Emanuel Reicher, wrote, naturalism demanded a "simple, natural voice" and natural behavior "regardless of whether the accompanying gesture is gracious or not, and regardless of whether it fits in with the conception of stock types." The problem was "to adapt the representation to the simplicity of nature" and to reveal "a complete human being." [5] Brahm consequently realized that he would have to organize a permanent company; and this being difficult when his most adaptable actors tended to leave the *Freie Bühne* because of infrequent employment, Brahm joined the older and larger *Deutsches Theater* or German Theatre in 1894. Here, holding an acting group together for a decade, he continued to employ the naturalist style, failing only when he applied it incongruously to Shakespearean and romantic classics and faltering only in allowing insufficient scope for passion and exaltation on the stage. Despite his limitations, moreover, he outdistanced every other director outside of Russia in creating a style capable of translating the naturalist drama into stage action. According to one anecdote, he once asked an actor whether a particular bit of business would achieve a "grand effect." When the latter proudly declared that it would, Brahm promptly ordered him to discard it.

Ultimately, however, the naturalist method could be justified only through the work of its playwrights, and Brahm unintentionally demonstrated this fact whenever his efforts to revive older plays met with failure. Only as long as he could draw fresh realistic writing talent into the theatre could the "Brahm style" prevail. Fortunately, a number of writers arose to supply him with the necessary scripts, and among them were men of considerable talent, the greatest of them being the young Hauptmann whose *Before Sunrise* appeared in the *Freie Bühne's* first season.

2 GERHART HAUPTMANN

Hauptmann, who was born in the Silesian village of Obersalzbrunn on November 15, 1862, was still in his twenties when he fell under the influence of Arno Holz. But he had meandered a long way before he found a focus for his talents. First he shook off the bondage of business, for his father did not envisage an artistic career for his son. This prosperous innkeeper sent him to a *Realschule* at Breslau, where science was taught, and then to an uncle's estate to study agronomy. Hauptmann, however, felt himself strongly drawn to the arts. After attending an Art School at Breslau, he determined upon sculpture and went to Rome. Shortly thereafter he turned seriously to poetry, which he had been writing since boyhood, and being delicate in health, an esthete to his fingertips, and the inheritor of mystical pietism from his grandfather and mother, he naturally favored romanticism at first. His marriage at the age of twenty-three was likewise a fragile romance; his wife was one of three rich sisters living exquisitely in a lovely retreat in Saxony.

Nevertheless, so impressionable a youth could not resist the call of the new movement and he soon proved himself capable of adopting its scientific realism with greater rigor than any of his associates. Ashley Dukes has accused Hauptmann of possessing the inconstancy of a weather-vane, and the charge is confirmed by the facts of his life. However, inconstancy at the age of twenty-three is not only natural but salutary. As was to be seen later, Hauptmann never lost his romantic disposition, and it could in fact expend itself for a time even on the naturalist movement, which was young and truculent. But the fact remains that Hauptmann's literary romanticism was not only successfully repressed in the early nineties but that it was supplanted by its extreme opposite. And the transition was not altogether miraculous or artificial. To his early enforced study of practical matters and scientific farming he had added a course of lectures at the University of Jena given by none other than Haeckel, the persuasive philosopher of a mechanistic universe. Gerhart's elder brother Carl, who took him to Jena after expulsion from the Breslau art school for disciplinary reasons, was a confirmed student of science and philosophy, and he no doubt also contributed an influence.

Hauptmann first accepted naturalism with short fiction, in *Bahnwärter Thiel (Wayman Thiel)* and *Fasching* or *Carnival,* both studies of humble people and passive victims of circumstance. He turned to the drama under the influence of Holz, who offered to collaborate with him on his first play, inspired its conclusion which resembles that of *The Family Selicke,* and supplied the title *Vor Sonnenaufgang (Before Sunrise).* The play was immediately admired by critics sympathetic to naturalism and was commended to Otto Brahm for the *Freie Bühne.* Its fame preceded its production in 1889, and among the anticipated sensations was the picture of a' woman in the process of giving birth.

Even without this clinical detail, which was prudently omitted by the management, *Before Sunrise* became a sensation. Fulfilling the requirements of naturalism, the dialogue was phonetically correct; the educated people spoke high German, one character who had come from the capital used the Berlin dialect, and the rest employed the Silesian patois. The environment was a scrupulously photographed decaying farm in a Silesian coalfield, and the characters were for the most part degenerate peasants ruined by drink, immorality, and sudden wealth. The action was likewise rendered with a relish for unsavory realities. The sodden father Krause assaults his own daughter while his second wife is betraying him with his future son-in-law. One sister is a dipsomaniac whose first child died of alcoholism and whose second child is stillborn. Her husband, to spice the situation, is making advances to his sister-in-law. In this inferno only the latter, Helene, who had been reared in a convent, retains her purity. Alfred Loth, the socialist idealist who has come down to investigate economic conditions, falls in love with her, and for a time there is a strong possibility that she may escape from her brutal home. But warned by a physician against the dangers of hereditary alcoholism, Loth deserts her. Finding herself trapped again, the lovely girl stabs herself while her lascivious father reels into the house singing a bawdy song.

Adolescent doctrinairism on the subject of heredity vitiates this *Tobacco Road* play, and Hauptmann's approval of Loth's conduct smacks of smugness. Although the naturalists insisted upon the avoidance of all contrivance, upon absolute adherence to a "slice of life technique," the young author was actually writing with a program in mind. He was bent upon proving the fatality of heredity and upon demonstrating that one cannot escape from its grip any more than one could the *Ananke* of the Greeks. To this end he piled on every enormity, closed every avenue of escape, and justified Loth who acknowledged the futility of opposing the dreaded genes of the Krause family even though Helene is untainted. Nevertheless, the power of this tragedy was unmistakable, and its enthusiastic reception fixed its author to the lode-star of naturalism.*

The same gloom and darkness appeared a year later in his next work *Das Friedensfest* or *The Feast of Reconciliation*, although the general effect was somewhat diffuse and tepid. It was again a family picture but on a somewhat higher social level. The father torments his wife in an unhappy marriage and becomes estranged from his son after being struck by him. Father and son, who have wandered miserably alone, meet and are reconciled on Christmas Eve. But the wretched family starts another quarrel, and the inebriated father, fancying that another son is about to assault him, has a stroke. He dies and the family reunion ends in bitter recriminations. Ibsen's example in dragging skeletons out of family closets and revealing the corruptions of a sacrosanct institution proved so potent that Hauptmann and other naturalists tried to better his example.

The family was again the center in Hauptmann's third tragedy *Lonely Lives* (*Einsame Menschen*) which has echoes of *Rosmersholm*. Here, moreover, he was treading on personal ground, since Hauptmann had begun to chafe at the marital bit. Feeling that his wife was not a sufficiently understanding companion, he soon separated from her. Both the husband and wife of this family portrait are lonely and miserable because they have nothing in common. The scholarly Johannes Vockerat, passive but aspiring, feels himself caught in a morass of mediocrity. And his situation is such that he cannot even revolt against it with a clear conscience, since his wife Käthe is a kind soul and his conservative parents, who dread his lapsing into free thought, are lovable within their limits. At last he finds a friend in an intelligent, emancipated woman, the student Anna Mahr. The relationship is platonic, but this makes little difference to his neglected wife and his narrowly moral parents. Anna is forced to leave him, and her departure signalizes the complete collapse of his will. Unable to endure life without her, and too passive to separate from his family, he drowns himself in the Müggelsee. The hand of fate hangs heavily upon this group of unfortunates, all of them well-intentioned but incapable of meeting on common ground.

The net effect of the play is rather tepid. Yet, except for the unconvincing and unnecessary suicide (since it would be more natural to leave the weak-willed Johannes Vockerat stewing in his juices), *Lonely*

---

* A technical detail in naturalistic dramaturgy, which Hauptmann began to observe in his first play, was the use of elaborately descriptive stage directions. Since the background of every play was an important element in dramas that strove for the utmost fidelity to life, the playwrights took pains to describe the setting of the play with as much factual reality as they could muster.

Lives was an outstanding example of naturalism. Not only did Hauptmann dispense here with the supernaturalism or symbolism of Ibsen's *Rosmersholm,* but the whole point of the play is that many lives are destroyed by mere attrition. There are no major conflicts or actions in the play, barring the aforementioned ending; the struggle is merely an inner state of tension for which no one is willfully responsible. Anna Mahr realizes this when she leaves Vockerat; she comprehends the fact that they lack the ability to bear the burden of suffering that would ensue if they went away together. The integrity of the naturalist method was nobly exemplified in this pathetic drama, even if it was maintained at the expense of dramatic movement and was spoiled by inconsistency at the end owing to an impulse to conclude the tragic situation with a strong climax.

Hauptmann's next effort, in 1892, was the realistic comedy *Colleague Crampton,* a portrait of a seedy and dissipated painter who loses his professorship and his wife. He becomes dependent upon his daughter and her lover, whom he instructs in art and despises as incompetent. But this play proved only faintly comic, and its failure must have convinced its author that he would have to plunge into a really stirring situation if the ways of naturalism were to be justified by his work. When in the same year he solved the problem of making naturalism exciting he had reason to feel that his preparatory period had come to an end. In *The Weavers* (*Die Weber*) Hauptmann created a timeless work. Radicals may complain, as they do, that the play does not outline an acceptable course of action, and their opponents may dislike its painful picture or its social implications. But *The Weavers* lives by its vivid evocation of realities and by its tight-lipped compassion. The most vigorous tendencies of the age were welded into drama when Hauptmann combined naturalist observation with social-democratic sympathies in this history of the revolt of the Silesian weavers in 1844.

First comes the exposition: The weavers, who operate under the domestic system and work at home, are being cheated of their wages, and these are being lowered further by competition. Becker who protests against these conditions is summarily dismissed. Old Baumert has had to kill a little dog to get "a bite in the house;" a sickly child of eight faints with hunger. This last incident arouses the weavers, they air their grievances, and even humble old Baumert declares that Becker was right in speaking up. Meanwhile their employer Dreissiger merely blames the parents, justifies himself on the ground that business is bad, and threatens to shut down his plant. Hauptmann then takes us to the Baumert home, where hunger stalks visibly; old Baumert cannot even keep down the miserable dog's-meat that he has eaten since his stomach is no longer accustomed to meat.

Into this household comes Mother Baumert's spirited nephew, the recently discharged reserve soldier Moritz Jaeger. He has already spoken with the malcontent Becker and gone with him to Dreissiger's home to sing the derisive ballad "Bloody Justice" under the latter's window. As he repeats it to the Baumerts, they are stirred by their wrongs and are ready for action. When we see the weavers again (after further exposition that draws the class lines firmly) they are banded together under Jaeger. Joined by the old smith Wittig, the village radical who is blackballed for his opinions, they defy the police order forbidding them to sing "Bloody Justice." Soon they rush out to wreak vengeance on Dreissiger, who is about to take on two hundred new weavers. They storm his house, where he is entertaining his supine parson and dismissing the liberal family tutor. Dreissiger and his family flee, but the weavers invade his home and destroy every stick of furniture in it. Then, after having ruined his textile stock as well, they march off to destroy the steam looms in the neighboring village of Bielau which have depressed their wages. Here they call out the Bielau weavers, terrorize the local employer, and drive off the soldiery with stones after fusillades by the latter kill the local patriarch Hilse who has piously refused to join the revolt.

The Weavers was epoch-making. Never before had naturalism been linked so plainly with direct social issues, and with this drama Hauptmann cemented a new bond between the realistic theatre and the masses. Ibsen's plays, like those of the French school, had been directly relevant only to the middle classes. With *The Weavers* the theatre became aligned with the common people and with the social-democratic movement. Nor was the play close to the working class merely because it gave an historical account of their early struggles or because it could be construed as a reminder that they might revolt again and this time in a better organized manner. The folk flavor of this play written in the Silesian dialect and filled with vividly realized common people raises this work above the level of the average propaganda piece. But the same quality conveyed a reality of detail with which a proletarian audience could identify himself. For the first time, moreover, the hero of a play was not an individual but a group.

It is true, of course, that historical plays like the *Henry VI* trilogy and *Wallenstein's Camp* were mass dramas. But these were military plays, and elsewhere too it was crowded military action or regal pomp that produced mass effects. A new factor made itself felt once the drama of the closing decades of the nineteenth century assumed the task of reproducing common life faithfully. Characters who are nearly equal in importance owing to the leveling process of economics were henceforth to be frequently grouped together as a single dramatic subject. The individual shrank in importance as the group or class came to the foreground, for it was the group that seemed most important to playwrights who focused attention on common humanity. The possibilities of "mass treatment" were to be well realized in plays like *The Lower Depths, The Plough and the Stars, Street Scene* and *Stevedore,* as well as in many notable examples of the expressionistic drama like *Gas, Masses and Man,* and *Processional.* Hauptmann's dreary collective hero consists of "flat-chested, short-winded, sallow and ill-looking creatures of the loom," women who look "overdriven, worried, restless," and young girls whose charm consists in "a wax-like pallor, a slender figure and large projecting melancholy eyes."

Hauptmann was in the first flush of idealism when he composed *The Weavers,* and his sympathy with the underdog tempered the clinical harshness that proved to be the severest limitation of naturalism. It is true that the play is by no means perfect; the exposition repeats itself thrice (in the first, second, and fifth acts, which describe the miseries of the people), and the weavers' revolt is likewise repeated. Nevertheless, compassion and excitement galvanized him to a greatness which he never attained to the same degree in his other realistic works. Huneker expressed the majority opinion when, describing this "symphony in five movements, with one grim, leading motive—hunger," he wrote, "If Hauptmann had died after writing *Die Weber,* he would have been acclaimed a great dramatist." [6] Staged by the *Freie Bühne* on February 26th, 1893, after a year's litigation with the authorities, the play took its place immediately as a modern masterpiece. Both the *Freie Bühne* and its offspring the *Neue Freie Volksbühne* almost doubled their membership after their productions of the piece. Shortly thereafter the *Deutsches Theater* signalized its conversion to naturalism under Brahm by reviving Hauptmann's drama with a notable ensemble that included Emanuel Reicher and the young Reinhardt. Kaiser Wilhelm II, who was never able to forgive Hauptmann, removed the imperial coat-of-arms from the house in protest. But the loss was not felt at an opening night which was signalized by one of the greatest demonstrations ever staged in the auditorium of a theatre. Led by the inflammable veteran socialist August Bebel, the audience which had been incessantly cheering from the galleries and booing from the orchestra, interrupted the performance by singing the stanzas of the weavers' song which ran like a *leitmotif* through the play.[7]

Hauptmann, however, was a pacific person with very moderate political convictions. He did not, therefore, return to the theme of social conflict except in a remote historical play. Instead he pursued the more conventional naturalistic exercise of simply capturing unpleasant realities in the service of scientific truth. His next step led him to the virgin field of naturalistic comedy.

His new play *Der Biberpelz* or *The Beaver Coat* was a mordant comedy, differing from the standard variety in evoking a background as low as any to be found in the theatre. American comedies of seedy life like *Tobacco Road* and *The Primrose Path* belong to the same genre, and it is not too much to say that the credit for developing naturalistic comedy of low life belongs largely to Hauptmann. His thieving washerwoman Mrs. Wolff, who is the wife of a poacher, is a magnificent character, and the impudence with which she hoodwinks the bewhiskered police-superintendent Werhahn after she has stolen a beaver coat is conducive to rich earthy laughter. Werhahn is a perfect caricature of an officious incompetent, and much irony is achieved when this Dogberry who suspects a red network in every corner proclaims the amoral Mrs. Wolff the most upright woman in the village. She takes the compliment gracefully and improves upon it by declaring that the place is becoming positively too immoral for her! Hauptmann was indeed so delighted with his heroine that he revived her later, in 1901, in *Der rote Hahn* (*The Red Cock,* translated as *The Conflagration*). Here Mrs. Wolff, now epic in her sordidness and cunning, has not lost her fine Italian hand. Taking a cue from some of her neighbors, she sets fire to her house, collects the insurance money, and then commissions her son-in-law, an architect, to build her a better one. A neighbor's half-witted son is accused of the crime, and Mrs. Wolff's villainy is not detected until she has been gathered to her ancestors—Falstaff and Autolycus.

Both plays suffer from static dramaturgy, but they are memorable examples of the new kind of "low comedy" which was created by naturalism and is still with us. That these pieces should have been written by a playwright who was at heart an esthete is abundant evidence of his flexibility. This quality later led Hauptmann into dubious, romantic channels, and it ultimately destroyed his integrity both as an artist and as a man. But his flexibility also served him well. His ability to accommodate himself to different styles enabled him to add much territory to the naïve initial naturalism of *Before Sunrise*.

Flexibility and vague social-democratic idealism also led Hauptmann, in 1896, into the field of historical drama with *Florian Geyer*. And here again he marked out relatively new territory for naturalism. This picture of the Peasants' War of the time of Martin Luther was in most respects a complete departure from the romanticism which had hitherto held a virtual monopoly on the historical drama. The new historical method is vividly illustrated by Goethe's and Hauptmann's respective portraits of the freebooter Goetz von Berlichingen. In the drama of the same name by Goethe, Goetz was a flagrantly misunderstood idealist butting his head against the rising materialism and cupidity of the world. But in *Florian Geyer* he joins the peasants for selfish motives and then betrays them to their masters. Hauptmann, moreover, concentrates upon a wronged peasantry and upon a nobleman who identifies himself with the common people and dies waving their banner in the face of the feudal knights. The background is vividly realized and the early sixteenth century is represented by conscientiously archaic speech. *Florian Geyer* was a failure on the stage, although it was later acclaimed as a noble proletarian drama during the early years of the Weimar republic. It suffers from diffuseness and confusion, and is weighed down by labored discussions of political and religious problems. Nevertheless, Hauptmann's effort to compose historical drama without the trappings of romanticism which are still fashionable was notable.

Hauptmann was deeply chagrined by the unfavorable reception of his ambitious flight in *Florian Geyer*. But he had no reason to believe that his public would not follow him in even bolder experiments when these were skillfully managed. Earlier, in 1893, responding to a rising reaction against naturalism, he succeeded in dissolving the rigors of his realistic style. *Hannele's Himmelfahrt* (*The Assumption of Hannele*, or known simply as *Hannele*) achieved a brilliant, if oversentimental, synthesis of naturalism and fantasy. This play begins as Inferno and ends as Paradiso without doing violence to either outer or inner reality.

Into an almshouse peopled by quarreling paupers, prostitutes and thieves, the schoolmaster Gottwald brings a dying waif. She is the fourteen-year-old orphaned Hannele Mattern who tried to drown herself after continual mistreatment by her drunken stepfather. Despite the ministering efforts of the kind teacher and of a deaconess, Hannele is manifestly dying, and her delirium runs the gamut from extreme terror to euphoria. Her fantasy, which occupies the major part of the play, transforms real characters into fictitious ones who bear the stamp of the fairy tales and religious teachings with which she is familiar. Her cruel stepfather is summarily punished, but she is rewarded and taken to the bosom of the Lord. She is now Princess Hannele or Cinderella, and the village tailor who arrays her for heaven brings her "the smallest slippers in the land." As she lies in her coffin, flowers are heaped upon her, everybody mourns her, and people remark upon her beauty. A crystal coffin is being brought for her, and an angel has come for her. This Stranger, who bears the features of the good schoolmaster, is soon transformed into Christ. He fills her with everlasting light and takes her to heaven amid the quiring of angels whose song becomes a lullaby. Then it grows fainter and ceases.

Hannele is a memorable fusion of realism and fantasy in the modern theatre. The imaginativeness of the delirium is as free as the almshouse frame is fettered to the most repulsive reality. If the former is generously sentimental and confused, it does not go counter to inner reality, since it arises from a much-suffering child's mind; Huneker rightly described the play as "the history of a child's soul." Moreover, fact and fancy are admirably unified, since the naturalistic framework is a tangible link between Hannele's frustrations in the real world and her compensatory dreams. Hauptmann's first departure from strict realism was nothing short of a triumph. This much can be conceded even by acidulous critics like the present author who hold that pathos is a poor substitute for tragedy.

Hannele awoke in Hauptmann the romanticist he had so long repressed in his plays. Although he had held to realism more tenaciously than many of his fellow-writers, the reaction to naturalism was becoming a veritable avalanche, and Hauptmann was not the man to resist a new fashion for long. The new movement of symbolism which Maeterlinck had launched in 1890 spread rapidly in Germany, formerly the happy hunting grounds of romantics. Here Nietzsche was now decrying factual observation and altruism, setting an example of daring imaginativeness in *Thus Spake Zarathustra*. A signal success was scored in 1892 by the wavering realist Ludwig Fulda with the verse drama *The Talisman*, a satiric fantastication based on Hans Christian Andersen's story of the emperor who had no clothes. And in neighboring Austria, ever since 1891, the fine poet Hugo von Hofmannsthal was blowing a retreat from naturalism with stirring words on the importance of poetic vision, as well as with numerous symbolic verse plays like *The Death of Titian* and *Der Tor und der Tod* or *The Fool and Death*. These works were exceedingly tenuous, and Hofmannsthal, who will be remembered longest as Richard Strauss's librettist, never became a substantial playwright; not even in his pseudo-primitive and torrid version of *Electra*. But his work possessed poetic distinction and pointed to an escape from the rigors of factual observation that many people found comforting.

By 1896 the symbolists were also enlisting the hesitant Hauptmann in their ranks, and the results for Germany's greatest playwright were as dubious as the entire movement, which was too obviously out of step with the spirit of the age to supplant realism for long. Under the "blue flower" dispensation he wrote one near-masterpiece, *Die versunkene Glocke* or *The Sunken Bell,* one noble failure *Der arme Heinrich* (*Poor Henry*), and a great deal of unmistakable tripe.

If he did not altogether fail when he adopted symbolism, the reason lies in his poetic faculties, and if he very nearly triumphed in *The Sunken Bell,* it is because he was personally involved in its subject. His first marriage had failed and he had turned to another companion who had greater sympathy with his creative spirit. As an artist, moreover, he found himself wavering between two worlds; between the romantic heights to which he had aspired in the first flush of his youth and the severely circumscribed lowlands of naturalism which he had explored thoroughly. The pity that the bleak realistic scene had mobilized within him was not an exalted emotion, for Hauptmann was no Dostoyevsky or Tolstoy; and the call of social justice implicit in *The Weavers* had proved as fugitive as smoke, for Hauptmann was miles removed from active social agitation. Naturalism could not, therefore, afford him complete gratification. Heinrich, the bell-founder of *The Sunken Bell* who abandons his wife for the pagan mountain sprite Rautendelein and is torn between ethereal heights and his common soil, was a projection of the author's ego. Although *The Sunken Bell* has faded considerably owing to overelaboration of fairy-tale material and obscurity in some points, it remains a fundamentally engrossing play.

A synopsis of the gossamer plot is the worst way in which to support this contention. The bedtime story, with its synthetic mythology, holds its interest because Hauptmann's fantastication is sufficiently delicate and atmospheric to maintain the illusion. It commands a certain respect because it is so obviously an adult allegory of humane and artistic aspiration. Heinrich cannot remain with Rautendelein, for the pull of the earth or of common humanity is too strong. Heinrich is drawn back to the valley by despair when his wife drowns herself and her dead hand tolls the sunken bell in the mere. By then, however, he is unsuited to either the heights or the lowlands and must die:

> He who has flown so high
> Into the very Light, as thou hast flown,
> Must perish, if he once fall back to Earth!

Hauptmann intended to give the final victory to romantic aspiration, and Heinrich dies ecstatically in Rautendelein's arms. German actors, however, have favored a pessimistic treatment of the conclusion. They have added a bit of pantomime showing Rautendelein turning away sorrowfully from the dead Heinrich and re-entering the well where the unpleasant water-spirit Nickelmann now holds her in thrall. This anticlimax—from the romantic standpoint—was omitted by E. H. Sothern after a few performances with gratifying results—to wit, five curtain calls.[8]

The German theatre's insistence upon ending the play on a note of defeat displays the strength of the realistic movement, which refused to be downed for long. For Hauptmann, moreover, the pessimistic conclusion was peculiarly relevant. When, like his Heinrich, he left common humanity he doomed himself to failure. Whatever subtleties or noble moments may be found in this or that romantic play, the net result is abortive.

In *Schluck and Jau,* in 1899, Hauptmann used a hint from the Induction to *The Taming of the Shrew* with good effect. Two tramps—the bully Jau and his passive companion, the genial buffoon Schluck—are picked up by a royal hunting party. Jau is put to bed and led to believe that he is a prince, while Schluck is disguised as his "princess." But Jau, whose character remains unchanged behaves so truculently that he is put to sleep and then restored to beggarhood. A metaphysics of character and station is erected on this jest, and the symbolism is further intensified by the "Life Is a Dream" philosophy of Calderón. Here, however, the most gratifying portions of the play owe nothing to symbolism but draw their strength from the gross vitality of Jau and the infectious geniality of Schluck.

In *Poor Heinrich* there is verse of a high order, and the medieval fable of the knight who was cured of leprosy by a maiden's willingness to shed her blood for him receives a provocative twist. Heinrich is healed by a miracle precisely because he refuses her sacrifice at the zero hour. There is painstaking psychological motivation in the girl's growing passion for sacrifice and in the knight's progressive degradation until he is willing to allow her to die for him. But Hauptmann's craftsmanship deteriorates in this work. Much of the vital action is relegated to report and one wearies of so much morbidezza.

And Pippa Dances signalizes a further deterioration. The play has an excellent first act, giving a realistic picture of tavern life in a glass-works district, but it soon degenerates into a hodgepodge of symbolism. The dancing Pippa is the ideal that constantly flickers before man and eludes him; lust personified in the giant Huhn abducts but cannot hold her and Capital, in the person of the glass-works owner, cannot buy her. Only the poet can love her even after she has expired. If this play of 1906 vintage has any status today it is that of another forerunner of expressionism. *Griselda,* three years later, scarcely improves upon the legend of the long-suffering lower-class wife of a nobleman retold by Boccaccio, Chaucer and Kleist, among others. The motives are realistic but the setting is tiresomely romantic, and the hypothesis of a woman's willingness to suffer every humiliation at the hands of a lordly husband tastes stale on the modern palate.

Of Hauptmann's latest romantic emanations the less said the better. Only *Der weisse Heiland* or *The White Redeemer,* a picture of the conquest of Mexico by Cortez, achieved some eminence; and this was because the aging Hauptmann recovered in 1920 a grain of his former vigor in a protest against the cruelties of the Spanish *conquistadores.* Cortez and his minions carry the "White Man's Burden" in the time-honored manner—that is, they transfer it to the backs of a subject people. Considerable pathos is also engendered by the Aztec emperor Montezuma, whose mystic belief in the coming of a "white savior" as foretold in the solar cult of Quetzalcoatl led him to surrender his power to the white-skinned Spaniards. Unfortunately, however, this tragedy is too declamatory and static in execution for the exigencies of the modern theatre. And with *The White Redeemer* died the last glimmer of a nearly great man's genius. His quixotic reworking of *Hamlet* and such a feeble exercise as *The Golden Harp* in 1933 may be discreetly wrapped in silence. These last works were paralleled in the political sphere by the aged Hauptmann's capitulation to the National Socialist regime.

Fortunately, however, one cannot leave Hauptmann without noting a sporadic renascence of his greatest style between 1898 and 1912. Two years after *The Sunken Bell* Hauptmann returned to naturalism with *Drayman (Fuhrmann) Henschel,* one of the most powerful works to flow from his pen. Its account of the destruction of Henschel by a ruthless harlot recalls Strindberg's *Father* both in theme and intensity. Hanne Schäl, the Henschel maid, wins him after his wife's death in spite of his promise to the dying woman not to marry her. Once in the saddle, Hanne neglects his child, for whose sake he had married her, until it dies. Then she betrays him with a waiter and drives him to frenzied jealousy until, overcome by remorse for having broken his oath to his first wife, he hangs himself. The lumbering drayman's gruff loyalty to his first wife; his subjection to Hanne's wiles; his kindness to his neighbors and to her illegitimate child, which he totes with him when Hanne resents the presence of this memento of a former lapse; his growing jealousy and morbidity—all this is human drama. Written with restraint and fluidity, and transfigured by a deep compassion for bedeviled common humanity without violation of reality, *Drayman Henschel* proves how superlative was Hauptmann's real endowment. The author of this book is surely not alone in ranking the play next to *The Weavers* in the Hauptmann canon.

Michael Kramer, in 1900, was a pathetic study of a misunderstanding father and a promising son whose sensitivity drives him to suicide. Rebuked by his father for falling in love with a café owner's daughter, rejected by her, and subjected to mockery from an insensitive circle of bar-flies, poor Arnold Kramer sees no alternative to doing away with himself. The father's high hopes for his son are blasted, and he feels that the future can hold no further joys or terrors for him. For the tragedy is also the father's since he failed to understand the son he had loved and tried to turn into an artist who would realize his own frustrated dreams. There is something Chekhovian in this play.

Three years later, this affecting, if somewhat drawn-out, drama was followed by another impressive naturalist work, the peasant tragedy *Rose Bernd*. It was all the more remarkable, coming as it did one year after the sentimentally romantic and miracle-mongering *Poor Heinrich*. (This in turn had been preceded by the pungent peasant comedy *The Red Cock* or *The Conflagration*. Such were Hauptmann's waverings between two styles.) Against a vividly realistic background and amid characters as real as the soil, Hauptmann placed a robust girl who is hounded to death by lustful men. Debauched by the likable but frivolous squire Flamm whose healthy sexuality is frustrated by an ailing elderly wife, Rose delays her marriage to a pietist favored by her father. She consents at last when she finds herself carrying a child. With the best intentions she severs her relations with Flamm—only, however, to fall prey to the contemptible machinist Streckmann and to be forced to buy his silence with her body. But in a drunken brawl, in the course of which the latter knocks out her fiancé's eye, he betrays her secret. Thereupon her irreproachably moral father takes the fatal step of suing Streckmann for libel. Soon the litigation begins to divulge her guilt, and Flamm upon discovering her submission to Streckmann complacently washes his hands of the affair. The desperate girl gives birth to a child on her way from Flamm's house and strangles it. She is found in an unconscious condition by a neighbor, and brought home. Then she confesses her crime to the police.

Although *Rose Bernd* suffers from a plot that is too melodramatic and contrived, the reality of the principals gives it abundant life, and the effect of reality is amply reinforced by the inarticulate and fumbling pathos of the peasant girl. It is her tragedy that she draws upon herself the lust of men whom she cannot resist for one reason or another, and that she can hope for no understanding from her pious father. Rose is another Gretchen, but one that only a naturalist could draw. There is no mystical chiaroscuro in the portrait and the background is unrelieved by any glimpses of a divine plan. Fate resides in the libido of the victim and of those who persecute her.

That Hauptmann did not lightly relinquish the naturalist credo was again, and more formally, demonstrated eight years later in that curious amalgam *The Rats*. There are two lines of action—Mrs. John's devious way of procuring a child to satisfy her maternal cravings, and the theatrical manager Harro Hassenreuter's efforts to return to the stage. The second line serves as a commentary on the first, so that the play actually becomes a deliberate demonstration of the validity of naturalism. An old-style theatrician Hassenreuter abides by romantic notions of the drama. But his involuntary involvement in the tragedy of the seedy woman who, pretending to her husband that she has given birth, buys a child from a ruined girl and has her murdered, convinces the stage manager that tragedy may be found in the most sordid circumstances. The Hassenreuter episodes are jumbled and the play fails to fuse its two plots into a complete unit. Yet even as late as 1911 Hauptmann was master enough of the school that regarded him as its high priest to turn out a picture of life in a tenement that can vie with Elmer Rice's related exhibit in *Street Scene*. Alternately grotesque and tragic, facetiously humorous in the Hassenreuter scenes and uncompromisingly sordid in the Mrs. John imbroglio, *The Rats* might have seemed a promise of further extensions of Hauptmann's brand of realism. Actually, however, it proved to be a belated effervescence of naturalism and became its swan song with respect to the author.

Gabriel Schilling's Flight next year (1912) was a pulpy realistic psychological effort revolving around an artist who is driven to suicide by the rival claims of his wife and his mistress, both equally possessive. Schilling is a neurotic whose psychology is well observed. But the Strindbergian echoes in the play lend it only a specious depth, and a mountain is made of a situation that is merely an inconspicuous molehill. A much later attempt in *Dorothea Angermann* to revive the Rose Bernd theme on a higher social level also proved abortive.

Hauptmann, as noted, was not content to rest his claims of permanence upon his two great naturalistic spurts but thought to improve his fame with many later attempts which ranged from one honorable failure in *The White Redeemer* to at least half a dozen puerile fiascos. These were insufficiently redeemed by a few interesting ventures into fiction like the interesting mystical novel *Der Narr in Christo Emanuel Quint* (*The Fool in Christ, Emanuel Quint*).

It is unfortunately only too easy to be irritated with this weather-cock genius. But a rereading of Hauptmann's output, which does not seem to occur to many who dismiss him airily, reveals him as one of the permanent figures of the modern drama. His greatest loyalty was, after all, to realism, and his best work lives by its fidelity to life and character, as well as by the restrained compassion that he often infused into his work.

There has been, except for a brief early period, too deep a gulf between the best German drama and our own. A difference in national temperaments is partly responsible for this, although the gulf may some day be bridged again by a venturesome and astute director. There is, of course, an inherent difficulty in transplanting naturalist drama from its native habitat; what is so faithful to local reality in work like Hauptmann's does not easily communicate the same effect on the American stage. Yet truth about common things is universal, and time (and, let us not forget, circumstance) may yet vindicate Huneker's generous estimate of Hauptmann: "He began his artistic life as a poet-sculptor, and he has been modeling human souls ever since. Perhaps they may be as imperishable as if they had been carved in marble." [9] It remains only to be added that the permanence of his modeling arose solely in conjunction with the growing enlightenment of Europe. For, be it repeated, naturalism at its best borrowed objectivity from the scientific progress and democratic humanitarianism of Western European culture before its bankruptcy in the World War and its aftermath.

XXIV

HAUPTMANN'S FELLOW-TRAVELERS AND THE EXPRESSIONIST ERUPTION

TIME and distance have dealt more harshly with the Central European writers who grew up with Hauptmann and more or less followed his course. That there has been considerable justice in their fate is undeniable. Taken as a whole, the naturalists, however, comprised an honorable and vital movement. Without, in the main, extending the frontiers that Hauptmann explored, the naturalist group helped to establish them. The best of them are not undeserving of a salvo as artists and as men who enriched the humanity they took for their field of vision. Some of them, moreover, set the dynamite for a second explosion—that fascinating expressionism which rocked the European theatre for more than a decade and caused reverberations even across the Atlantic.

I HEIJERMANS AND THE PROBLEM PLAY

The purest spirit of them all came from Holland, which had cultivated the drama with honor, although without exceptional distinction, ever since the Middle Ages. Having a strong affinity to realism, which has been well exemplified by the Dutch painters from Frans Hals to Israels, Holland uncovered a worthy body of drama at last in the realistic movement. If the modern Dutch drama is known to us largely by a few examples like Van Eeden's *Ysbrand* and Roelvink's *Stormbird* (translated respectively by the poets Harry Kemp and Arthur Davison Ficke), this is due to the linguistic barrier, and to the fact that most of these works do not supply anything which cannot be provided by native products. But naturalism struck real fire in one compassionate Hollander, Herman Heijermans.

Born in 1864 in Rotterdam he was in his twenties when the naturalist movement spread over Europe. After a first abortive venture, Heijermans scored a sensational success in 1893 with *Ahasverus*, a play that was said to have been written with tears and to have been "lived" rather than written. Turning socialist in politics and anti-authoritarian in religion, Heijermans launched into a series of naturalist dramas that explored the miseries and struggles of common life.

A high-water mark was *The Ghetto* in 1898, a vivid and intensely real picture of Jewish life in Amsterdam revolving around a rebellious son's war with orthodoxy. Unfortunately, the youth is inadequately realized and his conflict is superficial, so that only the milieu is triumphantly executed. *The Machine,* in 1899, dealt with the industrial problem, and *The Seventh Commandment,* a challenging play of the same year, treated middle class hypocrisy and fear of scandal. Championing the poor and the downtrodden, he also turned out a "Hannele" in *Uitkomst,* which dramatizes the delirium of a poverty-stricken child.

Women's tragedies also interested Heijermans greatly. *The Maid* (1905), analyzed the corruption of character that ensues from the miseries and injustices of the social order. The loveless servant girl in this play being frustrated in her desire for tenderness, avenges herself by torturing her mistress with an incriminating letter that she has stolen from her. Even more compassion entered into *Eva Bonheur,* written in 1916 in the midst of the World War which sounded the knell of so many of Heijermans' hopes for mankind. In this uneven work, too, a woman is malignant; a tragedy is averted only by a kind and philosophical father who forgives his daughter's misstep with the words "There is only one kind of disfigurement, the disfigurement of the soul." Heijermans' best days were, however, over by then. His fortune was destroyed by an unsuccessful theatrical venture, and soon his health was undermined by disease. He died in 1924 shortly before his sixtieth birthday, an event that his country had planned to celebrate with befitting honor.

It is, indeed, characteristic of the power inherent in naturalism whenever it rose above the level of a slumming party that his greatest work, and the only one for which he is internationally known, is *The Good Hope.* In this drama of fishermen sent out in a leaky vessel by the cupidity of a capitalist, Heijermans is not writing case histories with the cold Zolaesque detachment that was required by naturalist theory. Nor, on the other hand, does he divert his humanitarianism into the usual Brieux problem play where the living creature disappears and his place is taken by a puppet. This triumph of protoplasm over mere sociology is, moreover, all the more remarkable since *The Good Hope* is a mass drama like *The Weavers.* Heijermans' reward was ample. Not only was this play, written in 1900, performed more than a thousand times in Holland but, except for some local and topical details, it showed no signs of wear a quarter of a century later when revived by Miss Eva LeGallienne's New York Civic Repertory Theatre.

Heijermans, who was a master of characterization, drew his fisher-folk as people who possess personal complications and lead a vivid life bound up with the sea. Some of them are passive and humble; others, like Geert, are passionate and turbulent. Economic duress is not the only force that drives them to the sea; there is custom, and there is pride in one's profession. The tragedy which befalls all the families that suffer when the rotten ship sinks is deepened by the woman who forces her timid son to sign up for the voyage. The note of bereavement and the foreshadowing of further suffering for the mourners, sharply underscored by the ironic face-saving of the shipowner who has profited by the catastrophe, bring the play to a moving and provocative conclusion.

2 SUDERMANN AND COMPANY

In Germany, other theatres than the *Freie Bühne* and the *Deutsches Theater* accepted and encouraged the new realistic drama. Notable was the *Lessingtheater* founded in 1888 by Oskar Blumenthal. Here, however, the drama was pursued with less naturalism. Its chief playwright was the East Prussian Hermann Sudermann who rose from a childhood of poverty to a lucrative career as Germany's most popular dramatist. Born in 1857, he first made his mark at the *Lessingtheater* with *Die Ehre* or *Honor* in the same year that Hauptmann made his debut with *Before Sunrise*. Here Sudermann, who combined the technique of Augier with a naturalist picture of the lower middle class, described the different concepts of honor that prevail in aristocratic and commercial circles. A rich young man has an affair with a poor girl across the street. Her brother, who is in love with the seducer's sister, proposes to fight a duel with him. But his code of honor, picked up during his absence from his home, means nothing to his lowly family and he is compelled to abandon his revenge. Thereupon he leaves his circle, marries his upper-class girl, and resolves to build himself a "new home, a new duty, and a new honor." With this facile conclusion, so far removed from Hauptmann's uncompromising naturalism, Sudermann won fame and set the seal of opportunism on his work.

His second play expressed his liberalism, for Sudermann long retained the amorphous democratic idealism of 1848 and of the student movement of those days. *Sodom's Ende (The Destruction of Sodom)* exposed corruptions in the upper levels of society. A young painter, patronized and corrupted by a banker's wife, becomes her lover. About to marry her niece for better concealment of the intrigue, he drives his foster-sister, whom he has ruined and abandoned, to suicide. There is considerable vigor in the exposé, although it is discreetly moderated by the artist's remorse, confession, and death after a providential hemorrhage. Then, with a bow to Ibsen, Sudermann turned to the conflict between old morals and new. *Die Heimat*, known to the English-speaking world as *Magda*, won wide-spread attention as a significant social drama. The daughter who leaves her old-fashioned father when he tries to marry her off to a parson becomes a concert singer in Berlin, leads a bohemian life, and bears an illegitimate daughter. But returning home years later for a festive occasion, Magda resumes the struggle with her father and her childhood environment. Her father learns that she has borne a child to the local councilor von Keller who had been her lover, and insists that they repair their error by marrying. When the latter is willing to comply only on condition that the child is not brought home, since this would reflect upon his reputation, Magda rejects him scornfully, and the shock kills the old colonel after he has tried to shoot his disobedient daughter. This dated drama (though not so dated as to be inapplicable to more communities than a cosmopolitan critic is likely to realize) is manifestly contrived. But its good old Scribe technique ensured it much theatrical effect, and there is solid, not impermanent characterization in the upright father, the "new woman" Magda, and the hypocritical von Keller.

After *Heimat* Sudermann favored social satire in a variety of tepid plays, among which *Storm Brother Socrates* is the most entertaining. Much humor is extracted from the idiosyncrasies of veterans of the 1848 liberal movement who remain formally hostile to the new Reich and imagine that they have retained the radicalism of their youth. The old men, who have a Club in which their children are forcibly enrolled, are horrified when one of the sons co-operates with the government by performing an extraction on the police commissioner's dog. But an iron cross placates and converts the young dentist's father! Sudermann also added to his repertory a number of serious personal dramas like *The Fires of St. John* and *Das Glück in Winkel* or *The Vale of Content* which has some touching details and recalls Ibsen's *Lady from the Sea* when a husband wins his wife back by his tolerance. Romanticism tempted the opportunist into a field (A John the Baptist play *Johannes, The Three Heron Feathers* reminiscent of Rostand's *Princesse lointaine*, etc.) in which his mediocrity became pronounced. A second wave of realism resulted in a few respectable war plays between 1914 and 1918. In the main, Sudermann, whose novels *Dame Care* and *The Mad Professor* enhanced his reputation, remained only an accessory to the fact of naturalism.

Still, he added some intelligence and sound observation to the drama, and this is something after all. If his characters are only "born to the boards," this merely marks the difference between the journeymen and the masters of the drama. On his grave (he died in 1932) may be inscribed the only tribute to which he is entitled: He made German naturalism palatable to the million.

The large company of his less successful and less prolific peers sometimes improved upon his work, sometimes fell short of it. All of them, however, explored environment with valid results and drew characters whose reality is not invalidated by the fact that they are no longer close to us after four or five decades across an ocean for which Americans can often be religiously grateful.

A close cousin to Sudermann, Ludwig Fulda tried many styles in response to many fashions. And lacking stamina, he has not weathered the decades. His early comedies and later romantic dramas are of no consequence, unless generosity honors the success of *The Talisman,* notable for its satire on monarchy. He paid a passing tribute to Barrie in pieces like *Comrades,* which good-naturedly ribs the "new woman" of the feminist era, and *Robinson's Island* which exhibits an *Admirable Crichton* situation when a nonentity in Berlin becomes a leader of men on a desert island. In his middle period, Fulda enrolled under the naturalist banner, and produced a drama of class conflict, *The Lost Paradise* and an attack on the single-standard, *The Female Slave.*

Naturalism paid substantial dividends to Georg Hirschfeld, who proved himself an uncompromising reporter of current realities before he attempted romanticism and folk comedy. His early works possessed a quiet but compelling power because he was content to record common life without comment or embellishment and rejected thumping conflicts where they seemed inappropriate. His one-acter *At Home* is simply a vivid report on a trapped life; a hard-working man comes home to a joyless house where his daughter is ill, his son shiftless, and his wife frivolous. Only his eldest son who, upon returning after a long trip, deplores this situation gives the breadwinner a new lease on hope. *The Mothers* is a carefully drawn full-length picture of a Jewish middle-class family such as the author knew by experience. The drama resembles Ibsen's work in being retrospective, but unlike Ibsen Hirschfeld seeks no conversion and sounds no call from the heights of idealism. There are only plateaus in average life, and such a plateau is photographed when a musician, who was driven away by his father's opposition to an artistic career, returns after the latter's death bringing with him his lower-class mistress. No major conflicts ensue, yet it becomes clear to her that she is out of her element and would only hinder his career if she married him. She departs, therefore, without informing him that she is bearing his child. In *Agnes Jordan,* Hirschfeld's last important work, this devotee of naturalism extended its frontiers by spanning an era in the manner of *Milestones* and *Cavalcade.* Although each separate background is realistically rendered, the eye focuses on a historic process —namely, the change in the life and outlook of different generations of a Jewish-German family.

Max Halbe also enriched naturalism, in 1893, with the highly lauded *Jugend* or *Youth* which describes racial antagonisms between Poles and Germans in Prussia and dramatizes the tragic awakening of two youngsters who fall in love only to have their happiness destroyed. As in Hauptmann's work, heredity is the invisible protagonist of the play. The girl Annchen. born out of wedlock, has inherited her mother's passionate disposition; the half-wit brother, who kills her accidentally, was crippled by his mother's frantic worry concerning her daughter's illegitimacy. Humanizing the rigors of naturalism with much tenderness, Halbe won an honorable place in the theatre. His specific contribution, the study of adolescence, introduced a rewarding subject to realists.

A sequel *Mutter Erde* (*Mother Earth*) revives the tragic lovers as grown-up people who have found only unhappiness in their marriage and finally drown themselves. Although the romantic conclusion in which they are borne away by phantom steeds is no credit to Halbe's naturalism, his appraisal of the sorry fruition of romantic love is decidedly trenchant. An early work *Der Eisgang* (*The Ice Drift*) contributed another run-of-the-mill study of class conflict to the naturalist theatre of Germany. The rest of Halbe's work, except for some romantic pieces, treated with variable results the unedifying passion for property which naturalism frequently noticed, the feminist question, and similar agenda.

The north Germans Max Dreyer and Otto Ernst, both former teachers, extended the field with plays devoted to education. The former contributed *The Teacher in Training* (*Der Probekandidat*), which dealt with a progressive young instructor who is forced to submit to his anti-Darwinian superiors, and Otto Ernst wrote the popular *Master Flachsmann* (*Flachsmann als Erzieher*), a satire on educators. The domineering ignorant pedagogue Flachsmann represents in fact the worst features of Prussianism in education. His assistant Flemming, a disciple of Pestalozzi's progressive ideas, comes into conflict with him and is swamped by the conservative opposition until his superior is exposed as an ignoramus and a fraud. The play struck a blow for progressive education and, despite a shallow contrivance which makes Flachsmann an impersonator, it still possesses a modicum of vitality.

The school play still occupies a place in the theatre of democratic Europe and America, although it is often sentimentalized as in Ian Hay's *Bachelor Born* or made palatably farcical in such a characteristic George Abbott comedy as *What a Life*. (Its counterpart the college play, which can be just as replete with familiar problems, has fared less well, probably because it provides less colorful and appealing characters.) Even in Germany, in fact, there was no dearth of sentimental and romantic variants on Ernst's theme, as a hasty recollection of Meyer-Förster's frequently regurgitated *Old Heidelberg* will show. Ernst, however, was an embattled writer, and his other works included attacks on various other abuses and conventions.

Finally, the naturalist drama acquired a number of humorists who have dated less severely than writers of problem plays. Otto Erich Hartleben mingled humor with serious considerations in palatable compounds like *Education for Marriage* and *The Moral Demand*. The Bavarian Ludwig Thoma turned out amusing, ironic pieces like *The Local Railway,* a farcical picture of small-town life which is disturbed by the coming of the railroads. Thoma's *Moral* is, moreover, a well seasoned satire on Comstockian vigilantism. This comedy about reformers who try to expel the local Mrs. Warren only to find themselves registered in her diary was a variant of the realistic theatre's frequent encounters with puritanism. Its contrivances may seem hackneyed today, but its irony still bubbles and its matter reappears in the theatre from time to time.

The ablest master of comedy, however, was the younger man Carl Sternheim (born in 1881) who although—or perhaps because—he was a banker's son, had an invincible detestation for bourgeois society. In satire after satire he excoriated respectability, snobbism, social climbing, and the go-getting Babbittism to which our own Sinclair Lewis later erected a familiar monument. First Sternheim deflated the romanticism of gallantry in *The Trousers,* a ribald farce revolving around a married woman's loss of her unmentionables. The ensuing complications reveal the pettiness of the mercenary middle-class soul.

Social climbing was caricatured in *Burgher Schippel* whose proletarian hero gets into the middle class by several flukes—by a vacancy in the town quartet, by a widow's need for a husband to conceal a misstep, and by a duel in which this coward accidentally wounds his antagonist and becomes a hero. Now at last he is a gentleman and a burgher!

The making of a millionaire is the burden of *The Snob,* a laconic satire which traces the social success of the son of the heroine of *The Trousers* in the earlier comedy. The remarkable Christian Maske acquires wealth and social position by progressive steps of calculated intrigue and pretension. He reaches the pinnacle of success when he marries an aristocrat's daughter and breaks down her resistance to him after the marriage by declaring himself an illegitimate son of a nobleman. Maske reappears in a less scintillating sequel *1913,* this time as an ennobled nabob and industrialist who is disappointed in his dissipated son. To cap the satire, his Socialist secretary sheds his principles and wins the upstart's daughter immediately after Maske's death.

Other climbers were satirized by Sternheim in *Tabula Rasa* and *Der Nebbich,* for which *The Weakling* is as good a translation as any. This German Molière lacked breadth and warmth, and the telegraphic style that links him with the post-war expressionists made his boldest imaginative flights prosaic. His mordant humor was, nevertheless, an original acquisition. His resemblance to George Kelly is striking, his tempo is modern, and his satire is unrelenting. If his cynicism is often unbearable, it has the virtue of integrity to a far greater degree than the George S. Kaufman school in America. When the world is more removed from the immediacy of his pictures, it will perhaps enjoy him only as a fantasist. He belongs, however, to a very sturdy tribe—to the brotherhood of Aristophanes, Ben Jonson, and Wycherley.

3 SCHNITZLER AND THE AUSTRIAN THEATRE

A transformation of naturalism was inevitable, and it was natural that it should occur in the more congenial Central European monarchy which had Vienna for its center. In the hands of Arthur Schnitzler, it became, as Lewisohn has called it, an "exquisite transformation."

Naturalism was championed in Austria by Hermann Bahr. But it is symptomatic of the Southern atmosphere in which he operated that his best work should have been the pleasant comedy *The Concert,* a familiar triangle based on the incurable infidelity of a musician who loves his wife but seeks insurance against old age. The ensuing complications with female admirers and with the wife, who teaches him a traditional lesson by philandering in turn, could hardly have met the requirements of Hauptmann before his grand climacteric. Bahr's *Mongrel,* the tragedy of a lonely roadmender who is driven frantic when his dog is killed by a forester, conforms more nearly—but not wholly—to the principles he espoused in his numerous essays.

More consistently a naturalist, the physician Karl Schönherr responded to the new drama by introducing realistic problems into the traditional Austrian folk play. His first contribution, *Sonnwendtag* or *The Solstice* dramatized the struggle against Catholic clericalism in his country, and his best work *Erde* or *Earth* uncovered cupidity and tenacious possessiveness in the peasantry. An old peasant retrieves the property which has already been divided among his descendants and recovers his strength while the family is hypocritically mourning his death. Schönherr's one-acters were silent tragedies of the people; in *Caravan Folk,* for example, a lad is tempted to betray his father to the police when he is offered a loaf of bread. In *The She-Devil* Schönherr created a powerful Strindbergian tragedy centering around an invalid smuggler's wife who philanders with a customs inspector in order to put him off the scent but soon betrays her husband in earnest. Then when her lover wants to leave her she is filled with such hatred for both men that she foments a domestic quarrel that ends with the inspector stabbing her husband. Another play *The Children's Tragedy,* which sets forth the miseries of three children when their mother has an amour, also attested Schönherr's single-minded devotion to naturalism before he came to write inconsequential romantic pieces. But Schönherr, who came from the Tyrol although he practised medicine in Vienna for a decade, was exceptional. His blood did not course in waltz time.

Schnitzler, the master of Austrian drama, was Viennese to the bone. Born in Vienna in 1862 and, like so many Central European writers, of Jewish descent, he was a cosmopolitan and an urbane man of letters. The Viennese pursuit of pleasure entered his blood much to the disappointment of his father who wanted him to embrace the medical profession whole-heartedly. At the same time the son of a famous throat specialist could not easily renounce his heritage. Dutifully he pursued the study of medicine, got his M.D. in 1885, served two years on a hospital staff, and contributed to his father's medical journal. Psychiatry, then making great strides which were to establish Vienna as the center of psychoanalysis, also attracted him, and he published a monograph on hypnotism in 1889. Later, after a professional trip to London, he started a practice of his own and collaborated on his father's exhaustive *Clinical Atlas of Laryngology and Rhinology*. Meanwhile he was also writing literary sketches and plays.

This oscillation between science and letters left its mark on his subsequent literary career. Occasionally his scientific training led him into the hard naturalism of *Reigen* or *Hands Around,* and it filled him with an unmoralistic attitude toward sexuality in his plays and fiction. Medicine also gave him a bedside manner in the theatre, and he approached his characters with an unruffled temperament. But the dancing spirit of Vienna, which he registered like a blood chart, also claimed the urbane young physician. He was, it is true, a more consistent naturalist than most of his northern brethren. But he applied himself mainly to sophisticated society, observed its elegancies and flirtations, and conveyed its follies and failures with deft mockery or subdued regret. His art possesses superlative refinement and a civilized comprehension of the human soul. It misses only the terror and the exaltation of the greatest drama.

His first dramatic work, written in 1893 while he was still immersed in medical studies, consisted of the seven scenes of *Anatol,* brief episodes in the life of a mercurial gallant. Although this play established its author's reputation and was long identified with it in the popular mind, it was a maiden effort. It must now be regarded as an overrated essay on the mutability of love. When serious it is sentimental, when frivolous it is only moderately amusing. Only its flickering style remains a pleasure and reveals a master of letters. But his numerous later variations on the Anatol theme overcame the monotony of the subject by the mental and emotional finesse of the execution. After some retrogression in his next work and in a slight verse play, Schnitzler forged ahead in that moving tragedy *Liebelei* or *Light-o'-Love.* It is the reverse of the gay picture of *Anatol,* contrasting the philanderings of a young spark with the emotional depth of the lower-class girl to whom a friend introduces him in the hope of curing a *grand amour* with a married upper-class woman. The plebeian girl takes her love seriously enough to commit suicide upon learning that her lover died in a duel with the husband of the other woman.

After a play about the Central European custom of dueling, which is necessarily a special subject, Schnitzler paid his ultimate homage to naturalism in *Reigen,* an interlocking series of sexual episodes treated with the sure hand of a surgeon exploring the human viscera. So clinical indeed were these scenes of the "round dance" which begins with flirtation and culminates in physical consummation followed by emotional depletion that they were only printed privately years later in 1909. Even the Hauptmann of *Before Sunrise* would have been satisfied with these sketches. But for Schnitzler *Reigen* was merely a medical excursion and most of his remaining work presented only the veiled surface of the prime emotion. At most we find Schnitzler plunging into the depths of a philosophy of frustration or wistfully remarking that men cheat themselves in the race for life.

This half-world was most beautifully explored in *The Lonely Way* (*Der einsame Weg*), a poignant play which proved too delicate for American taste. A wonderfully balanced work, it contrasts the urge to experience life with the loneliness that lies at the end of the shining road that is traveled by aristocratic or artistic hedonists. As Sala remarks, "The process of aging must needs be a lonely one to our kind." And as he realizes, "To love is to live for someone else"—which Schnitzler's fastidious gentlemen of Austria are rarely able to do.

Being a physician, Schnitzler was almost professionally interested in ensuring the patients in his plays a fruitful life. That was the purport of his paganism in *The Call of Life* (*Der Ruf des Lebens*), written two years later, in 1905. The heroine Marie, hearkening to the call of life outside her door, kills her monstrous father and goes out to rejoin her lover. To her physician she confesses her self-torment: "What a creature can I be to emerge out of such an experience as out of a bad dream— awake—and living—and wanting to live!" To which Schnitzler's *alter ego,* the physician of the play, replies with a serenity that must terrify moralists, "You are alive—and the rest *has been.* . . ."

The right to live, which is now being denied in Central Europe more cavalierly than Schnitzler ever dreamt it could be, is indeed an ever-recurring *motif* in his work. In *Liebelei,* the kind old musician who is the heroine's father, devotedly shielded a sister until she became a frustrated old maid. He had been less kind than he had thought; when he saw her resigned expression, old Vyring regretfully exclaims, "I could have gladly gone down on my knees to her and begged forgiveness that I had guarded her so well against all dangers—and all happiness!" Poor Johanna in

The Lonely Way expresses the same thought with her outcry: "I want a time to come when I must shudder at myself—shudder as deeply as you can only when nothing is left untried." *Countess Mizzi,* the long one-acter Schnitzler wrote in 1909, also played a sensitive variation on this life-*motif.* A father and a daughter lead separate amicable lives, each having a tasteful amour without believing that it is known to the other. Tolerance, unmarred by vulgarity or brash affirmativeness such as is only too conceivable beyond Schnitzler's native haunts, laves the play in beauty and irony. "The soul is a vast country, where many different things find place side by side," writes the brilliant Viennese psychoanalyst Theodor Reik, commenting on Schnitzler's connection with the psychoanalytic movement inaugurated by his contemporary fellow-citizen Sigmund Freud. It is that indeed in Schnitzler's work, even if he generally avoids the wonderland of psychopathology. He even devoted a long play to this subject *Das weite Land* or *The Vast Country,* a loose series of character studies.

Thus Schnitzler rang changes on the life-force, seeing it alternately with the eyes of a scientist, a family physician, and an urbane philosopher. He departed from his natural field only in some poor romantic excursions, and in his single problem play *Professor Bernhardi,* an exposé of anti-Semitism which presents a powerful picture of calculated injustice and is weakened only by a dubious initial cause and a faint conclusion. (It is also more than a little dated by the harsher realities of the present Central European situation.) One can, however, wish that Schnitzler's departure from waltz-time civilization had been more frequent, and more effective. As Ashley Dukes says apropos Schnitzler, "One can have too much of the twilight mood . . . , the melancholy and the grace." [1]

In the annals of the theatre he remains an exquisite artist who transferred the objectivity of the naturalist method to the romantic field. Thereby his work suffered dilution, and consequently (and because of his restricted subject matter) he remains a minor dramatist. Thereby, also, he cultivated a technique that verges on the static and does not reveal its special excellence to nations that follow a more rapid tempo. To them he is, therefore, best recommended by his short pieces like the finely written series entitled *Living Hours.* In the one-act form his static treatment is less trying, and it is perhaps in many of these fugitive pieces that he is most surely a modern master. One who is sensitive to Schnitzler's artistry leaves his work with regret as if for a vanished world—which is, as a matter of historic fact, the case. . . . He is supreme only among "the dramatists of the half-world." Moreover, it became impossible to find any refuge in this penumbral region even before his death in 1931.

4 MOLNAR AND THE HUNGARIANS

By comparison with Schnitzler's work the successful purveyors of Hungarian drama, which is so closely related to the Viennese spirit, were artificers. Even in Budapest, however, the theatre moved beyond the romantic period. The chief product of the latter was the Faust-like chronicle *The Tragedy of Man* of 1862 vintage. Its greatly harassed aristocratic author Madách, who lived through the revolution of 1848 and suffered a year's imprisonment for sheltering a rebel, was an out-and-out romantic poet—and an able one. His dramatic poem, modeled after *Faust* and Byron's *Cain*, traces the history of bedeviled mankind from the Creation to the second fall when mankind supposedly succumbs to complete collectivization. After this picture of the final era of scientific regimentation which anticipates *R.U.R.* and Aldous Huxley's *Brave New World* by more than half a century, civilized mankind comes to an end and only a few degenerate Eskimos remain on earth. But Lucifer, who has presented this pageant of the ages to Adam in the hope of leading him to self-destroying negation, is defeated in the end by the yea-saying first man. Pessimism and courage are combined in *The Tragedy of Man* into a far-flung vision that exceeds the scope and depth of any imaginative product of European romanticism except *Faust*. However, this noble rhetorical work can be admired in our own time and place only as literature.

The stirrings of the realistic drama in Europe effected external transformations in the Budapest theatre. The romantic spirit so ingrained in Hungarian nationalism was superficially democratized and transferred into the homes of the bourgeoisie and the hovels of the proletariat. Romance instead of stalking on the fields of honor or storming high heaven wore less braid; fashionable clothes and rags served equally to cover its palpitating ventricles. Moreover, the Hungarian playwrights at their best began to adopt a playful objectivity toward the exacerbations of romance; and their leader Molnar, in particular, concealed his sentimentalism behind a mask of *mondaine* cynicism. Hungarian life was dominated by a landowning aristocracy grudgingly co-operating with a mercantile upper middle-class. These classes patronized the arts with unstinted enthusiasm, but tolerated only a pleasant evening in the theatre. Entertainment, spiced with urban sophistication, became the criterion of modernity in the Hungarian theatre.

Of the host of writers who purveyed this entertainment—Lengyel, Biro, Fodor, Zilahy, Földes, etc.—a survey that writes so to speak *sub specie aeternitatis* can say nothing more. At most there may be a passing bow to Ernst Vajda for his *Fata Morgana*, where the meeting of an adolescent lad and a sophisticated married woman produces an understanding psychological observation or two in addition to clever entertainment. •That the episode is quickly put to rest and is somewhat dipped in saccharine does not invalidate our moderate satisfaction with it.

Hungary's leading playwright Ferenc Molnar, moreover, epitomizes all the virtues and defects of the school. His life and work reveal everything that is characteristic of a theatre that won wide acceptance abroad and belongs to dramatic history as one popular way of coping with life —that is, by sugar-coating it. (Legitimate or otherwise, it *is* one way; and if people avail themselves of it, this is a significant fact, and we must reckon with it. The sugar-coating did not, of course, prevent a short-lived Bolshevist revolution in Hungary and later the partial Nazification of that proud country. And that, too, is to be reckoned with!)

Molnar, born in 1878 to a Jewish mercantile family, studied law, succeeded in journalism, and wrote fiction before turning to the theatre in which he became an accomplished playwright and director. His aptitude proved both technical, as his showmanship proved, and temperamental, as many a charming lady has known by experience and many a friend by conversation. His has been a dramatic personality, inflammable in its many courtships and hedonistic in its tastes for feminine charm, food, plum brandy, and music. (Molnar plays several instruments and is reputed to possess a fine voice.) As a dramatist he revealed in addition to gifts of facile showmanship and ready wit considerable imagination and a fund of compassion.

After a first farce *The Attorney-at-Law* in 1912, in which a thief commits numerous burglaries in order to help his lawyer friend, Molnar struck a favorite vein with *Jozsi* (1904). He has always been fond of children, writing an engaging novel about them in *The Paul Street Boys,* and indeed even his adults often trail the proverbial clouds of glory. But the psychologist largely overruled the sentimentalist in him in *Jozsi,* which dissected the spoiled children of the comfortable classes. *The Devil,* three years later, was a fashionable variation on the Faust theme, with Mephistopheles employing suggestion to facilitate adultery. Although amusing, the play is the thinnest of triangular exercises. But its resounding success apparently incited Molnar to another bout with fantasy, and the ensuing marriage of imagination and compassion in *Liliom* produced a play of rare beauty.

This tale of an amusement-park barker and bouncer who mistreats his wife, who idles while she works, and who tries to rob a cashier when he needs money for the baby she is expecting is a tragi-comic tribute to the nobility that exists in everybody. Behind Liliom's worthless behavior and loafer's bravura hides an affectionate human being; the trouble is only that his good angel is *gauche* and inarticulate. He is destined to repeat the pattern of his life even in his ghostly existence after he has stabbed himself to avoid arrest for the intended robbery. From the early scenes which bear the stamp of the naturalist school the scene shifts to the only kind of heaven that Liliom could have imagined—a celestial police court. Fifteen years later he is paroled for a day to visit his family, and to redeem himself by a good deed. But Liliom, the useless "lily," is unchanged. Eager to bring his daughter a gift, he can think of nothing better than to steal a star for her during his descent. Hungering for affection in his gruff way, he slaps her when she shrinks from him, and the Heavenly Police, shaking their heads deploringly, take him back as a hopeless case. But his inchoate love remains a fact that his simple wife—and perhaps heaven, too!—understands fully.

A failure when first presented in Budapest in 1909, *Liliom* was successfully revived ten years later and became the Hungarian Theatre's principal export. For once Molnar created such a synthesis of his defects of sentimentality and contrivance that they became a virtue and made *Liliom* one of the most gratifying romantic plays of the twentieth century. Subsequently Molnar produced a long series of comedies and fantasies possessing variable merits and limitations. *The Guardsman* was a clever variant on the ancient triangle; *The Swan* revived the princess-meets-commoner theme with sly satire, as well as with the usual ingredient of saccharine; *The Glass Slipper* combined a naturalistic background of low life with romance, retelling the Cinderella story with gentle irony since the prince of the fable is only a middle-aged cabinet maker. About a dozen and a half other pieces have attested Molnar's facility, and most of them have held their own on the Hungarian stage. That they will receive short shrift from the higher court of dramatic criticism is, however, a safe prediction.

The Hungarian theatre has been active and colorful for many decades. But Molnar has only repeated himself for many years and his followers have been small fry. Attempts in a different vein have not been absent; a Sigmund Moricz employed plain realism for his studies of peasant life, an Alexander Brody for his social plays. Franz Herczeg, who indulged in successful romantic farce, sometimes waxed satirical and attained some stature with historical pieces commemorating Hungary's heroic past and struggle for independence. These playwrights have not been without well-intentioned followers.[2]

All Hungarian drama has not been froth. But it has reached no international heights in any field other than that cultivated by Molnar. With the decline in the harvest of polite drama (a decline of which the American public is keenly aware when treated to such tripe as Fodor's *I Love an Actress* and *Jewel Robbery* or Bus-Fekete's *The Lady Has a Heart*).

the Hungarian contribution has become as bankrupt as the Hungarian constitution. And possibly even for related reasons.

5 WEDEKIND AND THE EXPRESSIONISTS

That volcano which we call Central Europe did not, however, reach a state of benign inactivity once the naturalist eruption came to an end. Austrian and Hungarian drama was essentially quiet because it was "old world." Not so the German drama. Its temporary quiescence in romantic symbolism was soon interrupted by various rumbles followed by some distinct explosions. A restless, challenging quality entered into the romantic work of Herbert Eulenberg, who declared "war on the Philistines" in *Alles um Geld* or *All for Money*. The psychological phenomenon of dual personality, which belongs to the most modern psychiatric vein of the drama, as seen in the work of Pirandello and the "expressionists," occupied the romanticist Wilhelm von Scholz in *Der Wettlauf mit dem Schatten* or *The Race with the Shadow*. Romanticism in Fritz von Unruh became allied to anti-romantic, ultra-modern clipped speech in the manner of Georg Büchner and Carl Sternheim. The historical pieces in which this "Junker" celebrated Prussia's past were, moreover, followed during the war by nightmare visions of a destroyed world (*Opfergang* or *The Way of Sacrifice*, and *Ein Geschlecht* or *A Family*) that have nothing in common with the medieval atmosphere of such romantic pieces as Karl Vollmöller's rehash and Reinhardt's production of the Sister Beatrice legend in *The Miracle*.

The seething time-spirit demanded more immediate and less assuaging content than that provided by Vollmöller's renegade nun and the Virgin who took her place at the altar. And in production, too, romanticism could not long remain content with the gilded past. Unlike Otto Brahm, who accepted the Indian Summer of romanticism with the greatest reluctance, Max Reinhardt reveled in it for a long time. This imaginative stage director added the alembic of poetic production to the poetic plays that were supplanting naturalism. In addition to giving all the modern poets a hearing by staging the most full-blown works of Maeterlinck, Hofmannsthal and Vollmöller, he dusted off Goethe's and Schiller's youthful plays in some spectacular productions. Seeking scope for Dionysiac exaltation, he renewed the connection between the audience and the stage by demolishing the peephole theatre of realism. To him we owe the ramp that bridged the stage and the audience in *Sumurun* (that hallowed platform of present burlesque houses), the removal of footlights and curtains, and the staging of plays in circus arenas, cathedrals, and in the immense Theatre of the Five Thousand. Nevertheless, he could not destroy realism, and Reinhardt's flexible sensationalism actually became a stepping-stone to the theatre that was soon to leave the romantic woods. The social struggles of the post-war period needed a broad arena for mass effects, a theatre that would burst four-wall interiors and spill over into an audience which was to be propagandized. Reinhardt's fulsome romantic stage, denuded of its velvet trappings, could be appropriated—or, as the post-war revolutionaries would have said, "expropriated"—for incendiary purposes. Reinhardt's principle of imaginativeness, divested of archaic fairy-tale elements, could serve the bold flights of the new playwrights which were challenging the world of war, authority, profits and industrialism.

Naturalism was likewise pregnant with the drama of insurgency that exploded in the early years of the post-war period. There was only a short distance between the potential insurgency of the naturalists so vividly realized in *The Weavers* and Toller's idealism in *Masses and Man* or *The Machine-Wreckers*. The difference between the generations of 1880 and 1918 was one of intensified revolt and an appropriate technique of rapidly diversified scenes, impassioned speech, and mechanized stylization. Moreover, the naturalists themselves were not so hidebound in their program that they would hesitate to modify the slowly elaborated unity of their plays. Hauptmann exhibited considerable flexibility when he wrote *The Weavers* in a nervous tempo, when he filled *Florian Geyer* with mass action and rhetoric, and when he mingled realistic with dream scenes in *Hannele*. Schnitzler used episodic brief scenes in *Reigen* to demonstrate the "irrationality of animal impulse," [3] and occasionally shifted from present fact to dream fantasy, as in *The Lady with the Dagger* where a woman whose virtue is in danger in a picture gallery dreams of an identical situation during the Renaissance.

In fact, the first step toward the nervous, half-realistic, half-fantastic drama that went under the name of "expressionism" during the first post-war decade was taken by an ultra-naturalist. Frank Wedekind, who was born in 1864, belonged to Hauptmann's generation and adopted its program with greater vehemence than Hauptmann himself. In order to describe the tabooed realities of sexuality and bring to this subject all the apparatus of medical and psychological science, Wedekind wrote a number of plays which even exceeded the candid camera shots of his contemporaries. After a negligible first comedy, he turned to his proper métier in 1890 with *Die junge Welt* or *The World of Youth*, which described conditions in a girls' boarding school. Although here he aimed a blow at naturalism in his ridicule of a character who resembles Hauptmann, Wedekind's picture revealed the girls as troubled by the libido and repressed by their instructors. A year later, moreover, came his *Frühlings Erwachen* or *The Awakening of Spring*, an unvarnished diagnosis of adolescence and a fierce attack on the educational system's obliviousness to the sexual problems that bedevil schoolchildren.

Like Ibsen, whom he long admired and recited professionally at public readings, Wedekind proved himself a bitter enemy of social hypocrisy, and he found the most injurious hypocrisies in the manner in which society denied or warped the sexual instinct. In this "children's tragedy," as he called his play, a group of adolescent boys and girls between the ages of fourteen and seventeen are variously preoccupied with the libido. But they receive no enlightenment or guidance from their parents and teachers. Fourteen-year-old Wendla, whose mother refuses to help her in the crisis that impends when she falls in love with the schoolboy Melchior, becomes pregnant. Her mother, who dreads scandal more than the loss of her child, engages a bungling midwife because one can count on her silence. Melchior, the culprit, is an earnest and brilliant student who would have behaved more discreetly if he had been better instructed. In his *gauche* manner he also figures in a second catastrophe when, imparting sexual information to his hypersensitive schoolmate Moritz, he drives him to suicide. Only Melchior refuses to be completely engulfed by the difficulties of adolescence. Expelled from school and sent to a reformatory, he is troubled by his conscience and entertains suicidal thoughts, only to reject them.

The Awakening of Spring exploded in the theatre like a bombshell. But what shall be said about Wedekind's reprise in *Erdgeist* or *Earth Spirit* and its sequel *The Box of Pandora!* In the former the woman Lulu, blithely unaware of her own evil, is a demoniac incarnation of the primal instinct and lover after lover is destroyed by this succubus. Her perfidy gives her first husband a stroke, and drives a second one to cut his throat; the third she kills herself after he has caught her intriguing with numerous men, including his own son, and boasting that she poisoned his first wife. In *The Box of Pandora* she reappears after escaping from prison. But she is no longer a triumphant demon and becomes the sordid victim of the same erotic force that led her to destroy her husbands. After murdering a blackmailer, she flees to London, starves in its streets, and is finally slashed to bits by one of her clients who proves to be a Jack the Ripper. The cycle of elemental lust thus comes to an end when the sadism of the female encounters the rawer sadism of the male. Here Zola's formula for naturalism—"to see the beast in man, and only the beast"—is carried to a more than logical conclusion. Ringing further changes on his primal theme, and writing penetratingly in *The Marquis of Keith, The Tenor,* and other works, Wedekind carved out the most pungent "slices of life" in the German theatre.

But Wedekind was an unstable personality who refused to be confined to any school even before he turned to manifestly romantic, symbolic material. He had begun his career by appearing in a cabaret where he recited grisly ballads, and his taste for the macabre remained with him even when he explored the same field as the naturalists. This taste, as well as his love of sensationalism and his impatience with organized artistry, led him to clap a fantastic ending to *The Awakening of Spring*. When Melchior, escaping from prison, visits the graves of his fellow-students, Moritz comes to life and insists that he join him in death. But a "Masked Man" appears and dissuades Melchior from suicide, whereupon Moritz returns to his grave. The same tendencies led Wedekind in *Earth Spirit* and *The Box of Pandora* to create situations and characters that exist only partially in the real world. In the main, they are symbols of Eros, and Lulu is less of a real person than an allegorical representation of the sexual instinct. Thereafter Wedekind became increasingly inchoate and a late contribution by this anarchic genius like *Such Is Life* is a curious stew of philosophy and melodrama.

Wedekind, sex-obsessed and hopelessly neurotic, was shipwrecked by his morbid personality, and for all their dynamic quality his plays remain in the limbo of half-realized efforts. But his deficiencies and experiments were straws in the wind. When the German nation began teetering on the edge of war, precipitated itself into the cataclysm, and emerged from it wrecked in body and soul, dramatic violence like his found strong incentives. The provocation to storm high heaven and thresh one's arms against a mad world with commensurate madness was too strong to be resisted. This began to be the case some years before he died in 1918.

Out of this turmoil came the work of Walter Hasenclever. His febrile talent, expressing itself in staccato dialogue and rapidly shifting extravagant situations, engaged such issues as the clash of generations, the evil of the war-making state, and the violence that arises in a maddened world. In *The Son*, completed in 1914, a young man resents his father's tyranny with such intensity that he would kill his parents. He is incited to the deed by a friend who declaims: "Destroy the tyranny of the family, the medieval blood-bath. . . . Do away with laws! Restore freedom. . . ." This adolescent fanfare was followed by two comparatively reasoned pieces: *The Savior*, in which a poet tries to stop the war at the risk of his life, and an adaptation of Sophocles' *Antigone* which Hasenclever turned into a pacifist drama. Since these plays were written in 1915 and 1917 respectively they were naturally suppressed. But when the lid was lifted from the insurgent drama, nothing short of exhaustion could stop the young writers.

Hasenclever's *Men*, in 1918, proved a veritable nightmare; the hero is a corpse who returns to life and sees the whole madness of the world unrolling before him until he finds peace in the grave. (Corpses or ghosts, not to speak of half-corpses, were particularly favored by the post-war playwrights, and the habit is still with us in such recent products as Rice's *American Landscape* and Capek's *The Mother*.) A corpse was again the center of attention in *Jenseits* or *Beyond,* written in 1920. Here a husband who was killed in an explosion constantly interposes himself between his wife and her lover until in despair the latter stabs her and kills himself. The dead man's presence makes itself felt throughout when doors open and close by themselves, when the fire assumes the shape of his face, and when the house is at last demolished by invisible hands. Uprisings and chaos also reappeared in *Decision,* and this bitter satire on the failure of revolution was amply supported by the betrayal of the 1918 revolt by pussyfooting and smug Social Democrats like Scheidemann and Ebert.

Hasenclever continued to capitalize his fantastic and bitter vein to the end. In 1930, shortly before the collapse of the Weimar Republic, he brought Napoleon back to life in *Napoleon Enters the Scene.* Napoleon struts again, but it is not long before he is committed to an asylum because his dictatorial ambitions are too romantic for the modern practical world. As events were soon to show, Hasenclever proved himself more Shavian than prophetic. When a Napoleon reappeared in Germany in 1933 he succeeded so well that it was Hasenclever, a half-Jewish descendant of Goethe, who was forced into retirement.

Hasenclever's brothers-in-arms were numerous, and although it is difficult to find a definition which would cover all their work they discovered a slogan in the term "expressionism." All the arts shared the new viewpoint, and the very term first came to the fore when the new painters looked for an antonym that would express their divergence from the "impressionism" of Monet and Manet. Painting, sculpture and architecture were to turn from the duplication of nature to the "expression" of inner experience. It is not surprising to find in the ranks of the expressionist playwrights a painter like Kokoschka and a sculptor like Barlach.

Expressionism called for the presentation of inner states rather than outer reality, as well as for the distortion of the latter by the inner eye. This type of drama was in the first instance defiantly and flagrantly subjective, and it capitalized personal disillusionment and revolt. In more objective forms it could also be imaginative rather than completely distorted by the creator's ego, as in the case of *The Goat Song* and *R.U.R.* But even the more objective approach called for stylization of one kind or another and frequently strove to represent the anarchic state of the world by a corresponding anarchy of rapidly shifting elusive scenes, by an alternation of fantasy and reality, and by characters who are fantastic either in themselves or in their visions or moods. To use an elementary example, if a woman clapped into prison for revolutionary activity in *Masses and Man* mulls over the struggles in which she has just engaged, the playwright visualizes her thoughts in stylized, fantastic scenes. If the great world is essentially unreal to a character, as it is to the embezzling cashier of Kaiser's *From Morn to Midnight,* the play makes the world look commensurately unreal by means of extravagant and fugitive scenes. If a character himself is unreal or only half-alive the author may give him a mechanical appearance and supply him with a number instead of a name, as was the case in Elmer Rice's *Adding Machine.* As might be expected, work of this kind afforded a golden opportunity for modern theatrical art and designers, directors and actors met the requirements of the young playwrights with notable ingenuity. In fact, many directors like Leopold Jessner, and Jürgen Fehling, along with scenic designers and actors like the elastic Fritz Kortner, were frequently far more successful in justifying expressionism than were the playwrights.

No single formula can, however, cover the multifarious puerile aberrations and noble endeavors of this volcanic school. The plays ranged all the way from the most furious melodramas and fantasies to carefully conceived dramas of social protest written in a more or less expressionistic style. At the beginning especially one finds such exhibits as Reinhardt Sorge's early *Mendicant* (*Der Bettler,* in 1912), Arnoldt Bronnen's *Parricide,* and Hanns Henny Jahn's sanguinary *Medea* and *The Coronation of Richard III.* The recently discovered Oedipus complex and a natural revolt against a war-mongering state were represented by plays in which a son is invariably flying at his father's throat in the name of freedom.

The horror of the World War could not lightly be forgotten, and the love of blood-letting appeared to have become a habit. Alfred Kerr, the eminent German critic who defended the new drama as long as it retained a grain of sanity, describing Jahn's *Richard III* in which "people were continuously being slaughtered, tortured and buried alive" ("on one occasion a gentleman's liver was cut out and eaten"), exclaimed sadly, "They actually produced that in the theatre. Oh, you know too little of this era of the German drama. . . ."

Paul Kornfeld, another disciple of the new "storm and stress" movement, honored his hero in *The Seduction* for strangling a bridegroom simply because he had found the latter's philistinism offensive. A girl admires him for the deed, her brother poisons him, and he in turn induces his murderer to commit suicide! A grocer's dozen of murders, all in the name of "love" is likewise glorified in Kornfeld's *Heaven and Hell.* Unquestionably taste had been debauched by four years of blood-lust and starvation.

However, this turbulent period was not entirely devoid of controlled direction. Expressionism had its moderates like Anton Wildgans whose *Poverty* is a powerful picture of a middle-class family embittered by destitution and whose *Love* mourns the attrition of happiness in marriage. Only by his combination of sordid reality with intense lyricism in these painful plays did Wildgans reflect the expressionist movement, although elsewhere (in *Dies Irae* and *Cain*) he shared the excesses of his compatriots.

The provocations of militarism, social injustice, and revolution, moreover, soon brought thoughtful and poignant works. Whatever sanity or nobility can be ascribed to the post-war German drama came largely from those writers who rejected adolescent posturings and addressed themselves to tangible realities in society or in the human spirit. No matter how febrile or mechanical their style, writers like Kaiser, Werfel, the Czech Capek brothers and Toller made some honorable contributions to the modern theatre because they navigated in the great stream of dramatic humanism.

Most open to suspicion was the talent of Georg Kaiser, who often proved himself an opportunist and a sensationalist. Kaiser, however, reached his maturity, not in his numerous easy concessions to the public among which the melodramatic *Fire in the Opera House* is one of the most pretentious, but in broadly relevant works. In his *Gas* trilogy, he created a symbolic history of modern civilization rushing headlong toward destruction by profit-motivated industrialism. In *From Morn to Midnight,* he satirized the cheapness and futility of this civilization, as well as the inability of its robots to recover their freedom and individuality. A robot-like cashier embezzles his bank's funds in order that he may court an exotic foreign lady, but she turns out to be a respectable woman. Since he has already crossed the Rubicon by stealing the money, he resolves to make the best of the situation and tries to capture the fullness of the great world beyond his cashier's cage. In successive nightmarish episodes, however, he finds this world deceitful and illusory. The pleasure-seeking crowds are automata and the girl who entertains him proves to be a pasteboard beauty with a wooden leg! Soon the jig is up and he can only kill himself to avoid capture when the Salvation Army lassie who pretended an interest in his soul informs the police. So ends the tragedy of a white-collar slave who tried to live like a man! So, too, ends the crucifixion of one who represents the masses, and Kaiser took pains to impress the symbolic nature of his hero's Passion with a variety of details. In one weird and lonely scene when the cashier spreads out his arms he looks as if he were nailed to a cross, and in this portentous moment he has premonitions of the end that bear a fugitive resemblance to the Agony in the Garden nineteen hundred years before. In this bitter summary of a soul's defeat and in the stenographic world-vision of the

Gas trilogy, Kaiser wrote memorable, if by no means great, drama. His inability to create full-blooded characters and his chronic sensationalism would have relegated him to a speedy oblivion but for the fact that he put his shortcomings to effective use when he conveyed the hollowness and mechanization of the post-war era.

Franz Werfel, who also attained distinction as a poet and novelist, lost himself in confusion and metaphysics when he dramatized the conflict between the social and the anti-social self in his elaborate *Mirror Man* and in the psychiatric *Schweiger* which makes much of hypnotism and insanity. His non-expressionistic plays (*Juarez and Maximilian* and *Paul among the Jews*) have not been particularly effective; and his chronicle of the Jews *The Eternal Road*, although it was effectively staged by Max Reinhardt, was little more than a good pageant. But *The Goat Song* is, despite some tantalizing confusions, a memorable fantasy. Its story of an eighteenth-century insurrection on the part of the homeless drew a provocative parallel to the revolutions that followed the World War. Werfel, who has always distrusted the beast in man, symbolized the dangers inherent in such an upheaval when his revolutionists put an escaped monster at their head and make him the symbol of their revolt. They are crushed by the army, the monster is destroyed, and the old order is restored. But the masters, whose actions gave birth to both the revolt and the monsters, will not remain unchallenged. A woman is bearing the monster's seed in her womb. The cycle of oppression and revolution will not easily come to an end! Lacking the optimism of the true revolutionist who expects a triumphant new order, as well as the optimism of the reactionary who believes that he can stamp out the revolutionary spirit without eradicating the provocations he himself is supplying, Werfel could not gratify either camp. But despite some confusion, *The Goat Song* is replete with dramatic excitement, and its overtones are stimulating. The embattled twentieth century has found few symbols in the theatre as comprehensive as this work. Werfel's pessimism was proved to have been prescient when the advent of a new monster—a monster of reaction—drove him into exile.

Prescience was also an attribute of his countrymen the Capek brothers who gave the Czechoslovak theatre its masterpieces. (Werfel who was born in Prague in 1891 was technically a Czechoslovak after the Treaty of Versailles, although he continued to write in German.) The liberal Czech republic established by the Treaty of Versailles counted among its many achievements a progressive stage distinguished by brilliant productions. The Czech drama was, however, too young to develop much individuality except for some patriotic plays. When Czech playwrights did not favor the light Austrian-Hungarian drama (sometimes with a Shavian touch) as in the work of Frantisek Langer, whose *Camel*

Through the Eye of the Needle is known to the American public, they were attracted to expressionism.

Stirred by the German movement in 1921, Karel Capek wrote a memorable play in *R.U.R.* (Rossum's Universal Robots). Observing the growing mechanization of men by mass-production industry, Capek conceived a future in which all the workers would be automata or "robots." Their ultimate revolt when they acquire souls and the ensuing catastrophe comprise an exciting and vivid experience in the theatre. Here Capek succeeded in conveying a contemporary phenomenon in robustly melodramatic but imaginative and provocative terms. Although this fable suffers from Wellsian superficiality and didactic obviousness, it employed expressionism with more than ordinary force and intelligence.

Capek next addressed himself to the problem of longevity and spun out a thin fantasy in *The Macropoulos Affair* to prove the banal point that old age is not a blessing. Feeling the pressure of the horrible thirties, however, he retrieved his hold upon contemporary realities in two earnest and deeply troubled plays: *The White Plague* or *The Power and Glory*, a taut anti-fascist fantasy; and *The Mother*, a lament for the European mothers who lose their husbands and sons in its wars and discords, written shortly before the nearly simultaneous death of the author and his country. Although both plays won esteem in England, Capek was unable to recapture the dramatic power of *R.U.R. The White Plague* was too obviously contrived, and *The Mother* proved static and repetitious. However, *The Insect Comedy* or *The World We Live In,* a collaboration with his brother Josef, must also be listed among the assets of Central European expressionism. This pessimistic allegory of man's rapaciousness and stupidity, as duplicated in the insect world, is as neatly contrived as it is uncomfortably true. Josef Capek's independently written *Adam the Creator,* was another but inferior pessimistic document, expressing the hopelessness of ever weaning mankind from its lust for property and power.

Pessimism was, in truth, the dominant note of those expressionists who revealed any maturity as artists. Kaiser, Werfel and the Capeks, all of them seated on the Central European volcano, looked out upon a crumbling world, and one can hardly be surprised if their writing hand shook with anxiety. To be a serene and rounded artist under the circumstances was impossible; to have tried to be one would have argued superhuman power or a dubious talent for shutting both eyes. Only one writer, Ernst Toller, the noblest and most dramatic of all the expressionists, commandeered faith in a new world at least for a time. Like several other expressionists (among whom the Austrian Hans von Chlumberg contributed the occasionally effective, if operatic, *Miracle at Verdun*), Toller turned first to the tragedy of war. With Shelley-like confidence in man

Toller celebrated a spirited conversion to pacifism in his immature *Transfiguration,* written in 1918 while he was in prison for supporting an anti-war demonstration. In both realistic and dream pictures a sculptor, who enlisted for foreign service, becomes a pacifist. Toller here envisaged a revolution without bloodletting—a conversion to reason and love that would make the soldiers beat their swords into plowshares.

Soon enough, however, Toller came up against the material reality of revolution and counter-revolution. After his release from prison for pacifist agitation, he was elected to the Bavarian National Congress and became a member of the Bavarian Soviet, although he deplored the untimeliness of the uprising. His five years' imprisonment in the fortress Niederschönenfeld after the collapse of the revolution could not crush his spirit. In prison he wrote the two noblest plays of the post-war German theatre *Masses and Man (Masse-Mensch)* and *The Machine-Wreckers,* as well as the beautiful and more consistently satisfactory poems of *The Swallow Book.* Neither play relinquished any faith in the ultimate triumph of humanity or countenanced violence. Both works expressed the idealism of communism without countenancing sanguinary methods. Both were consequently poems of suffering and aspiration rather than mere appraisals of reality.

In *Masses and Man* an upper-class woman deserts her husband and supports the common people in an anti-war strike. But when the masses get out of hand and commit violence she makes an impassioned effort to restrain them. She is mocked and overruled, and the resulting revolt is crushed. But it is she who is dragged to prison and forced to suffer for the people. Refusing to be saved by the nameless proponent of mob-violence and awaiting execution, she endures visions in her cell that fortify her instead of crushing her spirit. Memorable was Toller's fine presentation of the great dilemma of all idealists. "The Nameless," as the leader of the mob is called, insists that evil can be destroyed only by violence because the intractable masters cannot be overthrown by any other means. But Sonia cannot countenance murder from any source and in any cause: the masses, who have been poisoned by oppression and made murderous by their wrongs, must not build a new world of hatred. To the tactician of revolution poor Sonia (and, with her, Toller) is hopelessly "confused." But, like Toller, she is the incarnation of all the dreams of all the lovers of humanity. "You live too soon," says her antagonist.

Similarly in *The Machine-Wreckers,* a horrible picture of the first phase of English industrialism which led to the Luddite riots in 1815, it is an idealist who opposes violence. The enlightened worker Jim Cobbett calls upon the desperate weavers to desist from destroying the machines to which they attribute their plight. The machine can become the slave of humanity; and it can be turned into a blessing if the workers will only organize themselves into an effective body. The maddened and misled mob, braving the power of the English government, disregards his plea and kills him. But the ultimate effect of *The Machine-Wreckers* is far from dispiriting, for Cobbett—according to Toller—was only anticipating the day when the desperate mob would become an organized and intelligent working-class.

Even Toller's nerves, however, were affected by the war in which he had served as a student officer. In *Hinkemann* or *Broken-brow,* the morbid domestic tragedy of a soldier who is unsexed in the war, bitterness overwhelmed the artist in Toller. Dismay also struck his heart as he watched the growing flabbiness of the opportunistic German Social-Democratic Party. The idealist in one of Toller's last plays *Hoppla* leaves an asylum only to discover that his erstwhile socialist comrades have become liberal time-servers and to be made responsible for the assassination of one of their number by a Nazi—a deed which he planned to commit himself for precisely opposite reasons. He is ultimately exonerated, but it is too late; he hangs himself in his cell.

Toller's later plays could not recapture the hopeful passion and superb lyricism of his youth, and his despair grew deeper until his sensitive soul could bear it no longer. After years of exile in England and America while his relatives suffered in German concentration camps, this Christ-like poet, whose last act was a single-handed effort to bring relief to the starving children of Spain, hanged himself in his New York hotel. Perhaps his private demons were seconded by some vague belief that his death would shake the world and awaken its conscience. Perhaps he thought that his sacrifice would cleanse the world. Toller was one of those sons of man who cannot sacrifice others—they can only sacrifice themselves. Had he not written in *Masses and Man:* "Who acts may only sacrifice himself."

Only the playwrights of the ultra-left persuasion, supported by the certainty of ultimate victory for the proletariat, and a few congenial playwrights, among whom Carl Zuckmayer was the most talented, revealed genuine vigor. Zuckmayer, who started out as an expressionist of the Wedekind variety, began to write pungent folk comedy in 1926 with *The Happy Vineyard.* Then he turned to fantastications, the most notable being his *Captain von Koepenick* founded on a popular story in which a shoemaker disguises himself as a captain, arrests the mayor of the city, and confiscates the local treasury. This fable is sharpened by an implied satire on Prussianism, for the "Captain" accomplishes his object solely because the Germans obey a uniform! Other plays by Zuckmayer dramatized Germanic legends with fewer implications and greater *insouciance,* as in *The Rogue of Bergen.*[4] Considerable solidity also appeared in the work of the noted sculptor Ernst Barlach who confined a personally reassuring mysticism with a vivid evocation of common South German life in such plays as *The Blue Boll* and *The Genuine Sedemunds*. Reality is spiritualized in his plays, but it remains reality too.

The more rigorously social-minded playwrights wrote realistic plays like the physician Friedrich Wolf's stirring and provocative account of a mutiny in the Austrian fleet shortly before the close of the war, *The Sailors of Cattaro*. Or, led by the poet Bertolt Brecht and the original director Piscator, who was a broad-minded creative artist of the first rank with a main allegiance to critical modern interpretation, they adapted expressionism to the requirements of forthright exposition. Except in a few unimportant realistic plays Toller, along with minor expressionists, had treated social subjects spiritually; the others treated them intellectually and with documentation.

Brecht's prize-winning *Trommeln in der Nacht* or *Drums in the Night* dramatized the fury of a returned soldier when he finds that profiteers are preying on the people. After his *Three-Penny Opera* which expressed a similar detestation of venality in satirical lyricism, Brecht began to write "epic drama" or "learning plays" like *Die Massnahme* or *The Expedient* in which several revolutionists justify their execution of a comrade before a large chorus by evoking vivid scenes that demonstrate the necessity of their course of action. Here personal expressionism was supplanted by "realistic" social analysis and explanation even if the dramatic structure was expressionistic instead of unfolding a tightly knit realistic sequence of events and character development. Brecht and his proponents made much of the "social realism" of his kind of epic theatre, claiming that it strove for the enlightenment or education of the audience instead of appealing to the emotions which they regarded as an unreliable social agency. It is the present writer's belief that an unemotional theatre is as intangible as the Cheshire cat's grin. Nevertheless, an expository theatre is far from impossible or worthless. This was sufficiently demonstrated by the American Federal Theatre's "living newspapers" which presented relevant economic and social facts without pretending to tell a continuous personal story. Plays like *Power* and *One-Third of a Nation* merely happened to be both instructive and stirring, and the instruction was accepted all the more readily because it was fortified by an appeal to the emotions. Moreover, thought is also charged with emotion.

Erwin Piscator whose view of epic theatre differed from Brecht's in some respects did not, however, seek to banish emotion from the stage. He strove to correlate the dramatic story with the world in which it transpired, surrounding it by various boldly original means like slides, films, treadmills and commentators with relevant facts of a statistical, explanatory, and representational nature. This was demonstrated by Piscator's productions of a classic like Schiller's *Robbers* and of current plays like *Hoppla,* the anti-militarist satire *The Good Soldier Schweik,* and the dramatization of Dreiser's *American Tragedy.* In most cases, moreover, the director was a creative playwright who adapted the texts to his purposes, as did Meyerhold in Russia and Orson Welles in his notable New York productions of *Julius Caesar* and *The Shoemakers' Holiday*—in a more limited way. Piscator strove to enlarge the scope or meaning of the drama, to put modern technical inventions at the disposal of the theatre, and to supplant the nebulous emotionalism of both latter-day realism and expressionism with intellectual clarity. This was germane both to contemporary sociological thinking and the hard-headedness of the long line of Lutheran clergymen from whom he descended. Champions of his style like Mordecai Gorelik called it the most important and promising advance in modern stagecraft.

These innovations, variously justified and variously assailed, were the last experiments of the German theatre. Upon seizing power the National Socialist Party quickly placed the theatre under its boot, and most prominent playwrights, actors, and producers either went into exile or were silenced. The theatre that had been for decades the most independent, humanitarian, and boldly experimental in Western Europe for nearly half a century bowed to totalitarianism.

It then had to content itself, in the main, with farces, musical comedies, a few historical pieces, and generally undistinguished revivals acceptable to the totalitarian government or, in the case of Goethe's and Shakespeare's plays, too firmly rooted to be dislodged. The best new plays were now simple peasant or "folk" dramas. The sprinkling of literate political plays by Hans Johst, Richard Euringer and others were rabidly chauvinistic and partisan, and they were all patently unworthy of the drama's traditional humanitarianism.

One playwright of the fascist dispensation, Richard Euringer, gave evidence of genuine talent. His *Deutsche Passion: 1933* (*The German Passion Play: 1933*) contains effective verse. A lambent imagination colors his picture of the so-called redemption of Germany by an Unknown Warrior who rises from the dead wearing a crown of barbed wire. He calls the people to arms in vain, and comes into conflict with Satan. He apparently redeems Germany through his death. (Since this scene, with its Christian martyrology, was apparently too unpalatable to the German state to remain intact it is not quite intelligible.) Satan cannot of course claim the dead Leader, and the latter goes to Heaven. However, Euringer could not be accepted *in toto* by the ruling powers because his fantasy is so full of Christian overtones (his suggestion that the Leader must die is also a *faux pas*), and he cannot be regarded as more than a promise blighted by fanaticism. His play oscillates between the sublime and the ridiculous. He is at his best when he is lyrical and imaginative—that is, when he feels no compulsion to vent orthodox puerilities. (According to the author the German army was never defeated by the Allies but was stabbed in the back by "dreamers, writers, criminals, Democrats, Jews, pacifists, Marxists, and raspberry-Christians"—a somewhat inclusive classification.)

Across the border, in Switzerland, there still lived a free German-language stage which still put on Lessing's *Nathan the Wise* and Schiller's *Wilhelm Tell*. But the great German theatre had vanished from the earth. It lived only in the memory of mankind and in the influence which it had exerted and might still be exert on the theatre of the world.*

* The fascinating history of the post-war German theatre would require much fuller treatment than can be given in the present survey. It should also be borne in mind that it is difficult to gauge the merits of the drama apart from the brilliant work of the stage directors, scenic designers, and actors who used the plays as *libretti* for a synthesis of the arts.[5] For additional treatment of Zuckmayer, Brecht, and others see pages 695-696 and 705-707

XXV

CHEKHOV AND THE RUSSIAN REALISTS

As TIME PASSES, one name among the post-Ibsen dramatists leads all the rest. This modern Abou-ben-Adhem is Anton Chekhov, and he was quite simply a good man! All his work is an emanation of a personality so simple, humane, and honest that a biographer would be stumped if he tried to exploit it in the market place.

Yet the question arises whether a writer like Chekhov would have turned playwright in any other country than Russia; whether he would not have crawled into the privacy of a shell and left the theatre to more spectacular people. Chekhov, it must be noted, worked in a national tradition which allowed him to realize in the drama what was best in himself. No matter how personal his art may be, it drew nourishment from the great stream of nineteenth-century Russian realism. He was one writer among many who were realists because they could not be anything else and still remain true to the spirit of a nation that, except at court, wore none of the tinsel of European "culture." Nowhere was life so elemental and so rough hewn.

Russian writers needed no high-sounding program to announce their loyalty to realism. Once they shook off foreign classical and romantic influences and attempted to create a national literature, the Russian writers became the ablest realists of Europe by a process as natural as breathing. Masters like Gogol, Turgenev, Tolstoy, Dostoyevsky, Chekhov, Bunin and Gorky are second to none in the art of revealing life instead of sugar-coating or gilding it. From the beginning, their revelations were completely devoid of sensationalism. The well-spring of their art was humaneness. Realism in Flaubert and Maupassant had a brain, but realism in the Russian masters had a heart. Nowhere, moreover, did it need one so badly as in that vast country of Tsarist absolutism, bureaucratic cruelty, and cankerous slavery.

It was a stout heart. The Russian people, tempered in the fire of centuries of Mongolian invasions and barbaric oppression, developed a stubborn strength. There is only one metaphor for this people, that of a harassed giant—alternately gentle and fierce—who stumbled heavily and blindly but somehow always picked himself up. Whether this tall fellow stumbled and roared or merely bowed his head and stood still, he was infinitely alive, and strong in pain and hope. We have heard a great deal about the plotlessness and irresolution of Chekhov's work.

495

But we have not heard enough about the secret strength and drive, the portentous hunger for life and positiveness, in his plays. We hear a great deal about Chekhov's simplicity but overlook the terrible power that often resides in such simplicity. Without it, Chekhov would have been a tame writer. His compatriots Gogol, Tolstoy and Gorky, all "good" men in their respective ways, could explode disconcertingly when the fuse was lighted. The Russian people were, in short, the terrible meek.

Naturally, in speaking of Russian literature, we refer to something larger than the drama. In fact, until the rise of the Soviet regime, the drama was only a minor portion of the literary life of the nation. The most serviceable medium for the inclusiveness and humanitarianism of this literature was the novel. It is truly significant that with one exception the chief Russian dramatists invariably had achievements in fiction to their credit before they entered the theatre. Their preparation in a medium that does not generally make a virtue of condensation no doubt explains the characteristic looseness and apparent rambling of the most important Russian plays.

The theatre enjoyed so little freedom that significant plays could be produced only after countless difficulties with the authorities. Although Russia evinced a passionate love of the theatre, its profoundest dramatists considered the stage an uncongenial medium. Turgenev never expected his plays to be produced, Tolstoy remained aloof from the theatre for a long time because he resented Tsarist censorship, Dostoyevsky reserved his great dramatic talent solely for his novels, and Chekhov constantly railed at the popular stage that flourished under the Tsars. When the short-story writer Chekhov turned to playwriting he could have justifiably maintained that his predecessors were primarily novelists.

I THE RUSSIAN DRAMATISTS

When Dostoyevsky once declared that all Russian novelists emerged from Gogol's cloak, he was facetiously referring to the latter's tragic-comic short story *The Cloak,* the first important piece of realistic Russian fiction. The same might be said of the Russian dramatists, despite the fact that the Russian stage—such as it was—had always tended toward realism.

Simple folk drama of a religious nature had been present in Russia since the sixteenth century. In Kiev, students added comic interludes to the religious plays and introduced vigorously drawn Ukrainian characters. These were later incorporated in puppet-shows that lasted well into Gogol's day and were recollected by him in his early tales. Realism also appeared in the more literary work of the seventeenth century, chiefly in the plays of the unworldly St. Demetrius of Rostov. Even the classical eighteenth century refused to endure the bit of French formalism.

Tragedy, it is true, remained strait-laced despite some revolutionary thinking attributed to the tragedian Knyazhnin. But the comic poet Fonvízin dispensed home-made vinegar. *The Brigadier General* satirized the superficial polish of fashionable French education and exposed the barbaric country squires of Russia. Although Fonvízin wrote in the Molière tradition, he created folk comedy. In the last-mentioned play, the gross Madam Prostakov, her fatuous husband, her brutish brother with his extravagant fondness for pigs, and her idiotic sixteen-year-old son Mitrophan provide lively realism. And the same realistic, earthy qualities are to be found in Fonvízin's contemporaries Knyazhnin, Matinsky and Kapnist whenever they satirized serfdom and bureaucracy. The keynote to their satire is sounded by the chorus in Kapnist's *Chicane* when the magistrates explain, "What are our hands attached for, but to grab, grab, grab?" [1]

Realism also appeared in the first decades of the next century in the midst of the romantic movement. The prose parts of Pushkin's historical drama *Boris Godunov* are the best in the play, and its great mob scene anticipates the later realistic mass drama. Moreover, Pushkin's character drawing is executed with sharp and precise realism.[2] The same period also produced one notable realistic comedy, *Woe from Wit,* by the talented dilettante Griboyédov. Alexander Sergeyevich Griboyédov, born in 1795, led an active military and political life; he narrowly escaped summary punishment for complicity in the Decembrist uprising against the monarchy, and he distinguished himself by important diplomatic work in Persia which ultimately cost him his life. His numerous, and mostly insignificant comedies, were consequently tossed off in moments of leisure. *Woe from Wit* was conceived in the classic French tradition and owed its popularity to scintillating epigrams. But Griboyédov placed the stamp of reality on his characters. Typical is his portrait of Repetilov who mouths liberal platitudes in clubs and coffee-houses but reeks of alcohol and fawns on his superiors. Famous, too, are the complacent head of the family, his shifty and hypocritical secretary, the sensible daughter Sophia, and the infectiously eloquent lover Chatsky.

Despite these anticipations of Russian realism, however, it was Gogol in the thirties and forties who stamped it upon the theatre. The great Ukrainian, who was wholly of the nineteenth century (he was born in 1809), was a broad humorist like Dickens. But at the heart of much of his laughter lay disillusionment and disgust. As he looked around him, he saw a vast and potentially great nation sunk in the mire of listlessness. He described its natural wonders in beautiful tales and celebrated its heroic past in the stirring prose epic *Taras Bulba.* He laughed at its idiocies in that delightful short masterpiece *The Story of How Ivan Ivanovich Quarreled with Ivan Nikiforovich,* and he expressed his pity for its humble stepchildren in the famous short story of a poor government clerk's misadventures, *The Cloak*. Then, mustering all his powers, he painted that great realistic canvas *Dead Souls* in which bitterness and despair vied with humor. His rogue Chichikov covers large stretches of the Russian land in an ingenious effort to collect collateral for a loan by buying up "dead souls"—that is, serfs who have died since the last census. The picture is terrifying: most of the people are virtual slaves bound to their masters' estates and can be bought and sold. The rural gentry consists of downright boors, sharp horse-traders like the woman who complains that she is not getting enough for her "dead souls," refined people like the couple that procrastinates for years over covering a chair, and intelligent men who are steeped in despair. It is slight wonder that the author of such an indictment in pre-revolutionary Russia should have found reality unendurable in the end. He sought an escape in religious mysticism and died under a cloud of melancholy in 1852 after having destroyed most of the second part of his great novel. To the drama he gave only a small portion of his time and talent, but this was sufficient.

Gogol's first play was the genial comedy *Marriage,* begun in 1832 and completed ten years later. Jogged out of his indifference to marriage by a female matchmaker, the bachelor Podkolyossin consents to propose to an eligible merchant's daughter. After a spirited quarrel with the matchmaker, an officious friend takes matters in his own hand and drags the bridegroom to the girl's home. Then just when everything seems settled and after three insipid rivals have been routed, Podkolyossin takes mortal fright, jumps out of the window, and takes a cab home. *Marriage* is, however, a mere soufflé by comparison with Gogol's later plays. The hardest strokes of the realist's brush appear in his last comedy, a long one-acter, *The Gamblers,* begun in 1836 and finished in 1842; the broadest and boldest are to be found in his masterpiece *The Inspector General*.

The Gamblers is a naturalistic picture of a group of sharpers and a relentless exposé of middle-class life. The cocky gambler Iharev, having just won eighty thousand rubles with a pack of marked cards to which he has affectionately given the name of Adelaïda Ivanovna, hopes to double his winnings. But he is properly fleeced by superior scoundrels who let him win, hold out the hope of fresh gains elsewhere, and then take his eighty thousand in exchange for a worthless I.O.U. This rogues gallery provides a masterpiece of satire and caricature.

It was neither *Marriage* nor *The Gamblers* that gave Gogol his reputation as the first modern Russian dramatist. He owes this distinction to *The Revizor* or *The Inspector General* * which came between these plays, having been begun by Gogol in 1834 and produced in 1836. In-

---

* Also translated under the title of *The Government Inspector*.

ferior to them in continuity and surprise, *The Inspector General* overshadows them by virtue of its larger theme and greater implications.
The old Russian theatre never revealed so sharp a satire on official corruption. The Tsar, who was then favoring a more stringent regulation of
municipal affairs in his far-flung empire and was amused by Gogol's
piece, interceded in its behalf. Otherwise it would never have been seen
on the stage; Gogol discarded another satire on bureaucracy *The Vladimir Order* in 1833 because he never expected it to weather the Tsarist
censorship.

Relying on his remarkable gift of observation and mimicry in *The
Revizor*, Gogol created a *Dead Souls* in miniature, and its hero Khlestakov is another Chichikov. This young adventurer, who finds himself
penniless in a provincial city, does not forego his aplomb. On the contrary, he comports himself so arrogantly that he is taken for an inspector
from the capital. The community is an urban edition of the village visited by Chichikov and is run by a pack of easy-going, bribe-taking,
ignorant officials. The Mayor, who has been winking at his colleagues'
negligence and peculations, is aroused only when he learns from an obliging friend that they are to be investigated by a special commissioner. The
friend had written: "As I know that you have your little failings like
everybody else, for you are a sensible man and don't like to let things
slip through your fingers, I advise you to take steps in time." In turn
the Mayor warns his subordinates.

The Charity Commissioner Artemy Filoppovitch, for example, has
been cheating his patients. He and the German doctor "came to the
conclusion a long time ago that the nearer to nature the better." No med-
icines, therefore, for his charges! "They are simple people: if they die,
they'll die anyhow; if they recover, they recover anyhow." Besides the
doctor couldn't interview them, even if he wanted to, since he doesn't
understand a word of Russian. The Judge, Ammos Fyodorvitch, admits
that he takes bribes but "there are sins and sins;" he takes only wolf-
hound puppies, and "that's a very different matter." The Mayor has even
more cause for alarm since the aroused shopkeepers and townspeople
insist that he is the plague of their lives, though "God is my witness,"
he declares, "if I have taken something here and there, it has been with
no ill-feeling." He consequently orders the postmaster to unseal all letters to see whether there is any tale-bearing correspondence. And needless
to say, the postmaster has anticipated the order.

When they take Khlestakov for the inspector general and realize that
he has been in town for a fortnight, they are desperate. "Within this
fortnight the sergeant's wife has been flogged! The prisoners have not
had their rations! The streets . . . like a regular pothouse! and the
filth!" The patients at the municipal hospital have been fed nothing but

cabbage, the local soldiers march through the streets with their coats "over their shirts and nothing on their legs," the local policeman is drunk, and the Judge hasn't looked into the statement of a case for fifteen years. Naturally the bureaucrats must ingratiate themselves with the supposed inspector, and he in turn is not loath to avail himself of their generosity. But when he has had his fill of them he disappears, and it is only after his departure that the officials discover that they have been duped.

This classic exposure of old Russia, executed with broad but supple characterizations and with rich dialogue for which every Russian-speaking critic vouches, made *The Revizor* a landmark of the Russian stage. The road to which it pointed was realistic social drama, and it was followed variously by nearly every Russian playwright.

Equally noteworthy was the contribution of Turgenev, Gogol's peer in the novel a generation later. His work in the drama nearly escaped attention because it was so delicate and quiet. Turgenev was an aristocrat and a Westerner who spent a large part of his life abroad. Since the bulk of his work dealt with the landed upper classes and the intelligentsia, his picture of life was comparatively pleasant. And, unlike Gogol, he was a serene and well-tempered person, less inclined to snarl than to observe; he was a physical giant with the manners of a lamb. Yet he was a true realist—an inner realist; explaining himself, he said, "What do I care whether a woman sweats in the middle of her back or under her arms? I do not care how or where she sweats; I want to know how she thinks." [3]

Nor did he remove himself from the social scene while observing the inner man. In his novels *Rudin* and *Virgin Soil* he exposed the failure of the intelligentsia to overcome its natural sloth and waywardness. The most famous novel *Fathers and Sons,* as well as *On the Eve* and *Virgin Soil,* sketched a new and vigorous generation that would grapple with the old order by means of scientific intelligence, revolutionary action, or reform. His picture of his times was consequently comprehensive and provocative.

Turgenev's outlook in his plays is, regrettably, narrower because he had no confidence in his dramatic talent. At most he hoped that the plays "though not entirely satisfactory for the stage, may afford an interest in reading"—a judgment that was reversed years later on both sides of the Atlantic when the Moscow Art Theatre and the Theatre Guild of New York produced *A Month in the Country.* The larger issues of his novels appear at least in solution, although they are easily overshadowed by his insight into the realities of character.[4]

A delightful satire on the shiftless upper class is the one-acter *Broke,*

in which the young squire Zhazikov hides from his creditors and seriously thinks of returning to the country only to forget his resolve the moment a friend lends him two hundred rubles. A typical detail occurs
after a dunning shoemaker is sent away by Matvei, the old servant.
Turning to the latter, Zhazikov declares: "Matvei, I want to order a
livery for you. . . . I want to order a livery of the very latest style for
you, a purple-gray, with blue shoulder knots. . . ." Hardly has he uttered the thought than he has to hide behind a screen when another creditor rings the bell. Turgenev's remarkable ability to describe commoners
is also present here, as it was in his famous short stories in the *Sports-
man's Sketches*. The patiently disapproving Matvei is excellently delineated, and it would be hard to equal his conversation with a persistent
merchant anywhere except in the Irish theatre. *A Conversation on the
Highway* is another authentic picture of Russian society compressed into
nothing more than a spat in an old coach rolling along a country road. A
quarrel between country squires over a piece of land in *An Amicable
Settlement* also suffices to reveal a facet of Russian society.

In another one-acter *Where It Is Thin, There It Breaks* Turgenev's
social and the individual analysis meet most effectively. Gorski is a
typical Turgenev hero—introspective, complex and irresolute; and Viera
is one of this author's typical heroines—a sensitive but sensible and resolute girl. Gorski loses her to a friend whom he himself introduced into
the family. His hesitant wooing of her, caused by congenital irresolute-
ness, strains her long forbearance and insults her so deeply that she
throws herself into the friend's arms. Gorski, in short, is one of Turgenev's Russian Hamlets.

The Bachelor, a full-length work, is a delicate and touching comedy
about the middle-aged "collegiate assessor" Moshkin who tries to marry
his nineteen-year-old ward Maria to a weak-willed young subordinate
but wins her himself on the rebound when the latter abandons her. A
characteristic Russian touch is the fact that Moshkin adopted her after
an accidental and slight acquaintance with her mother because the girl
had nowhere to go. Petrusha, the fiancé, is another well-drawn character; this weakling deserts Maria when a pedantic Russified German
tells him that she isn't "cultured" enough. And as usual Turgenev is
most successful when he draws his heroine; Maria is a masterly portrait
of a sensitive but courageous and practical girl. In order to avoid misunderstandings after her rejection by Petrusha, she is ready to leave
Moshkin's house and is willing to brave poverty in the home of a poor
aunt. Moshkin wants only to protect her by marriage, having no illusions
about his attractiveness to a young girl. But Maria is grateful and sensible enough to want to give him her love, and she is unassuming enough
to be as good as her word.

This play is inferior only to Turgenev's masterpiece, *A Month in the Country,* which possesses greater scope.and complexity. A youthful and energetic tutor Bieliaev attracts the mistress of the estate Natalia, who pays scant attention to her industrious husband Islaev. Her young ward also falls in love with him while the object of so much adoration is quite unconscious of attracting either woman. Natalia becomes jealous of the young girl and tries to marry her off to a stupid and absurd neighbor, deceiving herself into believing that she is only helping her ward. The latter, however, senses that Natalia is her rival and confesses her love to the tutor, and Natalia follows suit. Her husband discovers her weeping on the shoulder of Rakitin, her platonic admirer and confidant, because of her frustrated love. Rakitin, in an embittered mood, confesses to him that he loves Natalia and prepares to leave. Finally Bieliaev also departs. The girl, who now hates Natalia decides to marry the fatuous neighbor as a means of escape, and Natalia remains alone and frustrated. The play thus ends in a stalemate with the characters fading out and their frustration deepening.

In these works one already finds intimations of Chekhov's art. They are distinguished by the same kind of psychological penetration and sensitivity, as well as by the same sense of an unhappy life seething beneath the quiet surface. Finally, they possess the same fugitive quality, for which one may borrow a term from the English critic and translator George Calderon. The ordinary Western play, Calderon declared, is "centripetal"; that is, the attention of the spectator is drawn to the group of people immediately before him in the play. The characteristic Russian drama of the nineteenth century is, on the contrary, "centrifugal"; that is, the group of characters who are on the stage draw attention to humanity at large.

This is not true of every Russian playwright; nor can the Western playwrights be set down as exclusively "centripetal" when one notes such exceptions as Shakespeare, Webster, Racine, Molière, Ibsen, and Strindberg. But Calderon not only described an attribute of many Russian plays but hit upon a word that denotes another quality possibly unnoticed by him. Russian drama is frequently "centrifugal" in the sense that the action frequently draws away from the core of the plot, that life defies the rounded contrivances of theatricality and flows away, that characters fade away or are left stranded. This is not, as a rule, the method of the greatest drama, and it has distinct shortcomings because it can cause flabbiness and tepidity. But this procedure creates a highly poetic and yet realistic way of depicting common humanity. Here are no well-made plays, "no heroes, no heroines, no villains . . . no fantastic adventures," [5] and the result is truthfulness. Here the ebb and flow of emotion create a haunting sadness, and the result is a poetry of the commonplace. In an age when the poetry of rhetoric seems incongruous such poetry is frequently irresistible.

Nevertheless the progress of Russian drama in the living theatre could be ensured only by writers who modified Turgenev's oversubtle centrifugal tendency. There is also justice in Prince Mirsky's judgment that "what Turgenev was in touch with were not the raw realities of Russian life but only their reflection in the minds of his generation of Russian intellectuals." [6] The writers who supplied what was wanting in Turgenev's artistry were the somewhat younger men of his generation, Ostrovsky and Tolstoy. (Turgenev was born in 1818, Ostrovsky in 1823, Tolstoy in 1828.) Both, it is true, compensated his deficiencies at some cost: Ostrovsky, who was Russia's most important professional playwright, achieved power and comprehensiveness at the expense of such depth and subtlety as will be found in Turgenev; and Tolstoy did so at the risk of some distinctly labored didacticism. But both extended the scope of the Russian drama and invigorated it considerably.

Alexander Nikolaevich Ostrovsky was the Balzac of the Muscovite merchant class. He commemorated—and sometimes pilloried—one of the most conservative elements of old Russia, a smug group that oppressed its women-folk and children and throve by the most brazen kind of chicanery. It was the kind of life that this robust son of a lawyer and clerk of the Moscow Commercial Court knew only too well. And although he wrote unevenly and carelessly, so that many of his forty-eight plays have fallen by the wayside, he could be equally effective in satirizing this class or discovering tragedy in its midst.

Enough Stupidity in Every Wise Man, made famous by the Moscow Art Theatre production, reveals Ostrovsky's realistic comic vein at its best. Here an ambitious rascal Glumov sizes up his smug and hypocritical environment and advances his fortunes by playing upon its weaknesses. By judicious flattery of influential people, including an eccentric uncle, and by carefully planned romances with a benefactor's wife and an eligible widow, he almost attains his ends. He is finally exposed by a blackmailing journalist who sends the young man's uncomplimentary diary to the uncle. But Glumov rallies his powers and bluntly assures his victims that they need not take too much umbrage at his unpleasant remarks about them; after all, each of them would approve his comments on the others. Moreover, they need him, for who would supply them with clever phrases for their speeches, who would gratify their vanity by listening to their inanities, and would keep their wives occupied! In plays of this type Ostrovsky proved himself a master of comedy of manners. In a somewhat more somber mood he also reverted to Gogol and satirized Russia's bureaucracy. Particularly effective was *The Poor Bride,* which anticipated

Becque's *Vultures* by three decades. In the milieu of minor officialdom, a family is on the verge of ruin and is saved only when a strong-minded daughter sacrifices herself by marrying a ruthless suitor.

Ostrovsky proved most incisive when he compiled his "natural history of the Russian merchant class," as Edward Garnett calls his work. His very first play *The Bankrupt*, in 1850, called the tune. In this comedy, which recalls the satires of both Ben Jonson and Henri Becque, Ostrovsky exposed the raw laissez-faire philosophy of the merchant class with such results that there is not a single tolerable character in the play. Its hero is a merchant's clerk who wins his employer's daughter and a fortune by dint of sheer chicanery and then lets his father-in-law languish in prison instead of paying his creditors. He is equally ruthless toward the lawyer and matchmaker who furthered his schemes, while his wife—who had once entertained high-flown romantic notions—complacently approves his conduct.

This writer's insight into the mercantile world (which, however, he sometimes glorified with some inconsistency) also led him into the field of tragedy. His tragic masterpiece *The Thunderstorm* (1860) uses the same ingredients as his comedies; here, too, the world is predatory, callous, and narrow-minded. Tragedy arises from the ruin of a dreamy young wife who is misunderstood, persecuted, and driven to desperation. Much poetry emanates from the woman's yearnings which find a response in nature, and the play is highly atmospheric. It has been aptly called "a poem of love and death." [7] Yet it is also an unvarnished picture of the despotic domestic life of the old Russian merchant class.

When Ostrovsky died in 1886 he had an impressive body of work to his credit, and he could rightly claim that he had advanced the Russian drama on all fronts. He reduced the aimless theatricality of conventional comedy and like the later naturalists of Western Europe he intensified the art of representing unsavory middle-class realities. The bulk of his work is too local and too devoid of spiritual or intellectual values to rank him with the major dramatists of the modern world. But his plays remained the most important contribution to the active Russian theatre until the advent of Chekhov.

His two contemporaries Sukhovo-Kobylin and Pisemsky swelled the contribution of the mid-century. The former wrote an amusing comedy of intrigue *The Marriage of Krechinsky*, which became a favorite with the Russians after its premiere in 1855, and his *Death of Tarelkin* proved another sharp satire in the manner of Ostrovsky's *Bankrupt*. In addition to farces in the Gogol manner, the novelist Pisemsky wrote one powerful naturalistic tragedy *A Hard Lot*, in which a landowner seduces his serf's wife. Although the former is the master and therefore commands obedience, the serf insists upon his rights as a man and as master of his

own household. There is no villainy on anyone's part since the landowner and the serf's wife are genuinely in love and the husband possesses
dignity even after he murders her and confesses his crime to the police.
The tragedy is inevitable and unsensational, and so expert a critic as
Prince Mirsky sets this peasant play above Tolstoy's more famous *Power
of Darkness*.

It may also be noted that the sixties and seventies enjoyed a revival
and extension of poetic and historical drama. Ostrovsky himself contributed to this stream, in a number of mediocre historical plays and in the
charming legend *The Snow Maiden* (*Snegurotchka*) which Rimsky-
Korsakoff used for his well-known opera. The work of one practitioner,
Alexey Tolstoy (not the great novelist), was brought to the attention of
the world by the Moscow Art Theatre when it produced his trilogy *The
Death of Ivan the Terrible, Tsar Fyodor* and *Tsar Boris*. Vivid and full
of vigorous characterization, these plays written between 1866 and 1870
are powerful examples of the modern historical drama. Particularly fine
is the study of Tsar Fyodor, a weak but well-intentioned ruler who is
ruined by an evil minister. Much power is also achieved by the tumul-
tuous mob scenes and the semi-oriental color of these works.

Despite the interest of these plays, however, the next advance in the
Russian theatre was characteristically made by another realist and novelist, none other than the great Leo Tolstoy. His dramatic realism was
of a different order from that developed by Gogol, Turgenev and Ostrovsky respectively. Like Gogol he proved himself a potent satirist, but his
Fruits of Enlightenment is less important for its satire than for its representation of a class in the process of decay. Like Turgenev he was a master of characterization, but his characters possess power as well as complexity. Like Ostrovsky he painted the social scene, but his object was
not that of representing society but of reforming it. In fact, Tolstoy was
intentionally didactic in both comedy and tragedy, and only his great talent and his vigorous personality enabled him to surmount the level to
which didacticism is so frequently relegated in the realistic theatre.

He delayed making his contributions to the theatre until he had
passed the peak of his genius. He had both *War and Peace* and *Anna
Karenina* behind him when he wrote the first of his important plays *The
Power of Darkness* in 1887. Tolstoy had by then undergone his unorthodox conversion to Christianity and had come to regard his earlier un-
didactic work as wasteful. In his greatest work, despite his talent for
capturing exterior reality, he had concentrated on the inner world of his
characters. Now he was convinced that his art could be justified only if
he tried to reform this inner world and helped to rid society of corruption and injustice.

In his zeal to improve the peasantry, from which this aristocrat expected the millennium, he wrote a charming trifle *The First Distiller,* an attack on the chronic alcoholism of the common people. He followed this folk-play with the famous *Power of Darkness,* a stark naturalistic document; for in turning to the realities of peasant life in the interest of moral regeneration Tolstoy arrived, inevitably and independently, at the naturalism which the West was developing about the same time. *The Power of Darkness* is perhaps the most powerful peasant tragedy of the world. When a young laborer Nikita has an intrigue with his master's wife, the youth's grasping mother prevails upon the woman to poison her husband. But once Nikita is safely married to the murderess he begins to seduce her half-witted stepdaughter, and when the girl becomes pregnant it is necessary to marry her off. This, however, would be impossible if her indiscretion were known to the prospective bridegroom. Consequently Nikita's mother urges him to crush the baby under a board and to bury it in the cellar. Unable to resist his mother's promptings, and further incited to the crime by his wife (because she wants him to be as guilty as herself), the weak-willed Nikita commits the murder. But Tolstoy was not content to describe horror for its own sake or for the sake of the literary method of naturalism; with few exceptions, Russian realism never wallowed in the mire without a purpose, and in Tolstoy that purpose was moral regeneration. Nikita is ultimately overwhelmed with remorse and confesses his crime at the wedding of the girl whose child he destroyed.

If the play derives its strength from the marvelous naturalistic portrayal of the culprits, it is the totality of effect that is important. The play is a tragedy of sin and expiation, and it takes the Russian drama beyond Ostrovsky in one important respect: it adds the dimension of humanitarianism to the stark photography of life. As Arthur Symons wrote, Tolstoy created his tragedy "out of some abundance which has taken the dregs of human life up into itself and transfigured them by that pity which is understanding." [8] A humane spirit distinguishes this work from the mere muckraking that appears in much of Zola's work.

Tolstoy's conversion naturally set him at loggerheads with the upper classes, and it was at them that he aimed his robust comedy of intrigue *The Fruits of Enlightenment.* It is a devastating, if contrived, satire on the shallowness and credulity of the rich and idle who dabble in spiritualism while squeezing their peasants dry. The intrigue begins when a landowner's muzhiks try to purchase a piece of land on the instalment plan. They are refused until a clever chambermaid poses as a spiritualistic medium and extorts the master's signature to the bill of sale. This satire is liberally interspersed with amusing details concerning the fatuous behavior of the upper classes and the shrewd earthy ways of the peasantry. The comedy also has serious implications when the muzhiks observe the tremendous waste of time, money, and food in the homes of the élite, and when the latter are revealed as sufficiently decayed to be ripe for the tumbrils. Bernard Shaw paid this comedy high tribute by listing it, along with *The Cherry Orchard,* as one of the forerunners of his *Heartbreak House.* He called *The Fruits of Enlightenment* "the first of the Heartbreak Houses and the most blighting." In point of fact, it is *not* the most blighting (Shaw's is), but it was probably the first in the theatre.

During his apostolic career Tolstoy found himself in opposition to the state, as well as to the Greek Orthodox Church which excommunicated him for applying the Sermon on the Mount too literally. In fact, only his international reputation and his social station saved him from prosecution. His opposition to military service gave rise to the Dukhobor sect which suffered persecution for its pacifism and finally found a haven in Canada. Supporting his gospel of passive resistance (later applied by Gandhi) with notable pamphlets, letters, short stories, fables, and novels, he became a latter-day prophet and the grand old man of Europe. His last two plays, *The Living Corpse* and *The Light That Shines in Darkness,* were devoted to expressing the same views in the theatre.

In *The Living Corpse* or *Redemption,* he combined an attack on Russian marriage laws with his Christian gospel of self-sacrifice. Fedya upon realizing his own unworthiness and his wife's love for his friend, disappears in order to give them their freedom. Believing him to be dead when he deliberately leaves his coat on the bank of a river, they marry and enjoy unwonted happiness. But his identity is revealed to the police by a blackmailer and the lovers are accused of having connived with him in order to commit bigamy. Since, divorce being impossible, the happily married couple is about to be separated and punished, Fedya sees no alternative to killing himself. Supplied with excellent dialogue and a provocative and tense situation, *Redemption* made a strong impression in the European theatre. It is frankly a problem play, but despite its contrived and melodramatic plot it is superior to the theses composed by Brieux and the French school.

Even more powerful is *The Light That Shines in Darkness.* Although Tolstoy left this work unfinished' (the last act exists only in outline), it is a fascinating exhibition of the inner struggles and shortcomings of an idealist like himself. Here an aristocrat who is trying to practise literally the teachings of Christ comes into conflict with his wife. When she refuses to let him impoverish his family by renouncing his possessions, he transfers the estate to her. But this compromise torments his spirit and he tries to leave her. Moreover, his pacifistic influence on a young nobleman turns out tragically for his disciple. Doubts overwhelm the idealist, and death comes to him when the young man's outraged mother shoots him down. Declaring that he shot himself accidentally, he dies peacefully, averring that evidently God did not want his service.

With this play, begun in the eighties and worked on as late as 1902, ends Tolstoy's testament in so far as he gave it to the theatre. The well-aired domestic struggle that embittered his last years and culminated in his fatal flight from his home in 1910 is here commemorated with psychological power and spiritual depth; and here, as well as in his other plays, Tolstoy left the imprint of a great personality on the drama. In him, fragmentarily, realism found an affirmative elevation and the poetry of a questing spirit.

2 CHEKHOV AND THE SUBLIMATION OF REALISM

If Tolstoy by virtue of his heroic and moral spirit might have become modern Europe's Aeschylus, Chekhov was surely its Sophocles. In an oppressive world he retained a lovable simplicity and sweetness of temper. Both as a person and writer he possessed the ancient Sophoclean balance—the "even-tempered soul"—without relinquishing an iota of truth about the realities that faced him from without and clawed at him from within.

Without there was the Russia of the old regime: the dispirited and listless pre-revolutionary intelligentsia, the ignorant and hardened peasantry which he described in many short stories, and the barbaric penal system which he studied at first hand in a special trip to Sanghalien, Russia's Botany Bay, in 1890. *Within* was the pained consciousness of these realities and the lack of progress in his country, and within too was the disease of tuberculosis that ravaged him for years and cut his life short in 1904 at the age of forty-four. But as long as his health permitted, he worked valiantly to alleviate suffering as a country doctor, frequently taking no fee from his destitute patients and braving the cholera epidemic of 1892-93 in his district. His sense of humor never failed him, and not only did he find people lovably amusing but he had a childish love of pranks, as when he pretended to be passing out bombs to policemen during a red scare. Gorky said of him, that in his presence, "everyone felt in himself a desire to be simpler, more beautiful, more oneself. . . . All his life Chekhov lived in his own soul; he was always himself, inwardly free." [9]

Never, moreover, did he lose his inner optimism—that faith in man which is the essence of optimism. For him there were no failures, even if few of his characters succeed in the world or integrate themselves. Although he diagnosed their complaints with the objectivity of a physician, for him there were no completely hopeless cases. In each of his characters he discerned longings that revealed a hidden power to beautify and ennoble life. Each of them is a seeker and dreamer within the limits of his personality and *beyond* the limits of his environment. Stanislavsky, having staged the plays, understood them better than anyone else. And it is Stanislavsky, the alleged proponent of penumbral Russian art, who wrote that it is possible to "feel in the everyday plots of his plays the eternal longings of man for happiness, his strivings upward. . . ." [10] Both Astrov and Uncle Vanya, in *Uncle Vanya,* struck Stanislavsky as "not simple and small men, but ideal fighters against the terrible realities of the Russia of his time."

It is not difficult to discover why the world has been deceived by Chekhov's characters. He did not find any revolutionists in the superficially quiet world which he knew best, and he was too scrupulous a writer to drag them in by the hair. Nor did he like to underscore an idea or point a moral, preferring to leave the spectator to draw his own conclusions. (Perhaps, like most quiet thinkers in the theatre, he overestimated the intelligence and sensitivity of an audience!) Referring to one of his famous stories *The Horse-Thieves,* he once wrote to a friend: "You scold me for my objectivity, calling it indifference to good and evil, lack of ideas, and so on. When I describe horse-thieves you would have me say: 'Stealing horses is evil.' But that was known long ago without me." [11] Moreover, his characters are always alone. It was his belief that essentially all men are lonely; in spite of many friendships there is deep sincerity in his complaint, "As I shall lie alone in the grave, so, indeed, do I live alone."

Still his sense of unity with mankind glows in the understanding which he brought to every character and in the wry pity which he felt for the victims of social decay. He watched the stalemate of the isolated Russian intellectuals with keen sympathy and was overwhelmed by the ignorance and barbarism of the backward world in which they led a wasted existence. Still, his frustrated and fumbling dreamers have moments when they envisage men joining hands to create a better world. They have more than a glimpse of a truth that Chekhov often repeated and practised as long as his health permitted—namely, that each man must work for mankind. The frustrated women of *The Three Sisters* know that they must leave their Heartbreak House and instruct the new generation. (And in old Russia, with its high percentage of illiteracy, the profession of an elementary teacher had an evangelical connotation.)

Anton Chekhov came to the theatre by a thorny path. His grandfather had been one of Russia's stepchildren. He was a serf who ultimately acquired some money by trading and purchased freedom for himself, his children, and his grandchildren. Anton himself was a serf until the age of nine; the Russian Sophocles sprang from the commonest soil. His father enjoyed a period of prosperity which enabled him to give all his children a liberal education. Yet Anton's childhood was made unhappy by his hard-driving father who kept him behind the counter of his shop despite the lad's delicate health. He never forgave his father for beating him. "In my childhood," he wrote later, "I had no childhood," and the unhappiness of children often appears in his short stories.

In time, too, the family fortune dwindled and disappeared while Anton was receiving his secondary schooling. He was forced to help himself through the medical school from which he was graduated in 1884 at the age of twenty-four. But by then he was already contributing to comic journals and he soon became sufficiently successful in the field to be the mainstay of his family. Signing his work with such facetious pseudonyms as Blockhead, Man Without Spleen, My Brother's Brother, and Chekhonte, he turned out farcical stories prolifically. He said later that he wrote them "as a bird sings"—they came so easily to him.

Two years after receiving his degree, while he was still refraining from medical practice because it was bound to be less lucrative, he collected his tales in a book which won immediate success. It was followed by other collections and these at last enabled him to break with his original publishers; Chekhov abandoned the comic vein and began to compose the great stories which made him the world's foremost master of short fiction. Confident, moreover, of his ripening talent at this time, he also turned to the drama.

The theatre had long attracted him. At first like most mortals, he sought only amusement and forgetfulness from the stage. At school he had been especially fond of vaudevilles and French farces. Nor did he forget his first love in later years when he tossed off his hilarious one-acters. *The Bear* or *The Boor,* produced in 1888, is only a delightful little vaudeville. It revolves around a boorish creditor who bullies a woman vowed to perpetual widowhood and ends by proposing to her after she has given him a taste of her spirit by consenting to fight a duel with him. Its successor *The Proposal* extracts a wealth of farcical amusement from a landowner and from the girl he has come to woo. Instead, they engage in a violent quarrel over a piece of land until the suitor makes his escape. When the girl learns that he actually came to propose to her she sends for him in haste, but again they bicker. The suitor swoons, he is revived and betrothed, and then the quarrel is resumed. In *The Wedding,* written in 1889, the bridegroom insists upon having a general to grace the wedding and the bride's family tries to oblige. But the general turns out to be a retired naval captain "of the second rank" who bores the guests to extinction with his nautical verbiage. In *The Anniversary* the starch is taken out of a credit banker's plans for a shareholders' celebration by an altercation with a peasant woman. According to Chekhov's brother Michael, he loved these farces, and he never considered it undignified to write them. To a friend he wrote, "Don't give up the vaudeville. Believe me, it is the noblest work and not everyone is called to it."

Still he felt the call of the depths in his plays just as distinctly as in his short stories. In 1884, while his contact with the drama had not yet graduated from the vaudeville stage, he wrote that somber one-acter *On the High Road* which remains his greatest short play. "Chekhov," his publisher Suvorin recollected, "was interested in graveyards and circuses with clowns—thus illustrating the two sides of his talent." [12] The leading characters are poor pilgrims, an innkeeper, a thieving tramp, and a ruined landowner who is consumed by alcoholism. Both the tramp Merik and the landowner Bortsov owe their deterioration to betrayal by women. Bortsov took to drink after his wife ran away with a lawyer immediately after the wedding. A coincidence brings this woman, richly dressed, to this inn of derelicts, and Merik nearly kills her with an axe in a blind effort to avenge his own betrayal by another girl. The power of the play exceeds the effectiveness of the story. The atmosphere might have been painted by Israels, Bortsov's quest for a drink of vodka is pathetic, and Merik's and the innkeeper's gruff sympathy for him when they ply him with drink and the thief lets him sleep on his bench is as moving as it is simple and natural. Nowhere in his plays did Chekhov reveal the heart and the manners of the common people as fully as in this early work.

There is much affinity to Gorky in Chekhov's sketches of the vagabond, the pilgrims, the factory-hand Fedya, and the bank cashier Kuzma who identifies Bortsov. Typical of the common man's viewpoint is Kuzma's comment on Bortsov's wife: "Not one of these low-class women or anything in that way, but just . . . giddy . . . trailing her petticoats and making eyes! And always laughing and laughing! No sense. . . . The gentry like that; they think it's clever. But we peasants would have turned a giddy-pate like that out of the house." But more important than the Gorky touch is the fact that the play contains strong intimations of Chekhov's later manner which has been aptly described as a "matchless combination of pity and elliptical humor, of light-flecks amidst the darkness. . . ." [13]

As if to mark out the difficult terrain which Chekhov was to traverse in the theatre, *On the High Road* was suppressed in 1885 by the censor who condemned it as "gloomy and filthy" presumably because it presented a *barin* or landowner as a drunkard. His first serious full-length effort *Ivanov,* written in 1887, suffered an even worse fate. It came to grief when it was produced at a private theatre, and one critic went so far as to say that Chekhov could not be "a poet" because he was a physician. Even his great admirer and patron in the theatre Nemirovitch-Dantchenko, coming across the play in a monthly magazine, considered it as "merely a rough draft for an excellent play." [14] The criticism is, moreover, not unwarranted, for *Ivanov* is plainly a maiden effort. It is an unpleasant anatomy of a Russian Hamlet who marries a frail Jewess. Her wealthy family disowns her and she succumbs to tuberculosis. Meanwhile Ivanov's affection for her cools, he neglects her, and he falls in love with a friend's daughter. His wife finds them together and infuriates him with her justified but venomous jealousy to such a degree that he callously betrays the fact that she is dying. A year later, after her death, he is about to marry the girl when an interfering family doctor threatens to denounce him for his brutality to his first wife. Having suffered many pangs of conscience before that, and being stung by the doctor's threats, Ivanov shoots himself.

Although the plot is melodramatic and one tires of Ivanov, Chekhov nevertheless was already revealing his characteristic power in this play. It contains some powerful characterization in the poor Jewess, whose illness alienates her husband and sharpens her tongue. Ivanov is also a well-realized character; depressed by poverty and frustrated love, and tormented by his conscience, he recognizes himself as a failure. In his discouragement one finds the seeds of later Chekhovian characters, most of them stalemated souls and intellects. The drama as a whole, moreover, conveys the true Chekhovian principle of tragedy, for Ivanov is destroyed slowly; without pitting his will against another character's, he is defeated by the inner conflicts which gnaw at him.

More than any other dramatist Chekhov departs from the classic and romantic concepts of tragedy. Tragedy, he says in effect, is not the result of a clash between individuals but of attrition. What is most tragic about any ordinary life is that it is gradually worn away and impoverished. The will is atrophied, the nerves are jangled, the mind is befuddled, and life simply wears thinner and thinner. To many, this concept of tragedy must appear aimless and undramatic. To the proponents of old-fashioned theatre it always seems so. Moreover, a play that observes this principle requires the utmost subtlety; it must contain a clear direction in its seeming indirection. (That is the secret of the success of such Chekhovian dramas as *Heartbreak House* and *Awake and Sing*.) Finally, this type of drama requires a type of ensemble acting which the old-fashioned theatre of grandiose effects and flubdubbery cannot supply.

Ivanov scored a success later when it was repeated at the St. Petersburg Imperial Theatre, but as Nemirovitch-Dantchenko recalls [15] there was nothing strictly "Chekhovian" about the production and it was essentially a triumph for a popular actor, Davidov. Chekhov still had to develop a style that could sufficiently uphold this theory of tragedy and he had yet to find an acting company that could translate it on the stage. His next attempt *The Forest Spirit* also proved unsatisfactory, and after showing it to some unimpressed friends he laid it aside. Resolving to abandon serious dramaturgy, he wrote instead the aforementioned series of one-acters or "vaudevilles." These were favorably received and long retained their popularity in the provincial and "little" theatres. Only in 1896 did he venture to pick up the threads he had left dangling in *Ivanov*.

The new play was *The Sea Gull*, and in it he took two significant steps. This time he dramatized a group rather than an individual, giving, it is true, individuality to each of his characters but making them part of a compact environment—namely, provincial Russia. By this means Chekhov added both dimension and purpose to his dramas. *The Sea Gull* represents not only the misunderstandings that exist among people but their inability to realize themselves in a static environment that encourages both self-absorption and escape.

To this, moreover, Chekhov adds an *active* principle which thereafter appeared in all his plays, for, although the characters are submerged, they are not necessarily passive. They dream, they rebel, and they reach out for what they want. The young man Treplev tries to create a new, imaginative art; the girl Nina pursues her dream of a rich life by following a successful novelist and sacrificing her palling security. Characters like these attract us by their aliveness, and life is justified and exalted by them. In this way Chekhov aligns himself with the masters of tragedy who have known how to transform defeat into spiritual triumph.

Finally, Chekhov achieves a poetry of emotions and environment which the greatest realists and naturalists have rarely failed to instill into their work. This poetry abounds in the best work of Ibsen, Schnitzler, Synge, and O'Neill. Chekhov creates it by means of a mood that consists of alternate shadings of despair and hope, tears and laughter. Like Ibsen, moreover, he begins to employ symbolism in his work; this he does discreetly by introducing some suggestive detail which somehow epitomizes the pattern or meaning of the play. In *The Three Sisters* the sisters' desire to go to Moscow represents all the frustrations and yearnings that pervade that drama, and in *The Cherry Orchard* the orchard is the ever-present symbol. In *The Sea Gull* the tragedy of young people cut off in their prime is represented by the sea gull which the young poet Treplev shot down without rhyme or reason.

Against a background of dormant life on the Sorin estate, in the midst of people immersed in their respective frustrations, transpires the tragedy of Treplev and his beloved Nina. Treplev writes a symbolic play with cosmic overtones only to be laughed at by his mother, a celebrated actress. His effort to soar above arid mediocrity fails ignominiously and he even loses Nina who is attracted to his mother's lover, the popular novelist Trigorin who knows himself to be a failure in the light of eternity but incarnates for Nina the great world for which she has been longing. She becomes his mistress and bears him a child, while Treplev tries unsuccessfully to commit suicide. Cast off by Trigorin and by her outraged father, and losing her child, she becomes a third-rate provincial actress, but not without discovering that it does not matter whether she succeeds or fails so long as her acting gives her an inner satisfaction. Treplev, who had railed against conventional realism and had tried to create new forms, also grows up when he realizes that "it's a matter not of old forms and not of new forms, but that a man writes, not thinking at all of what form to choose, writes because it comes pouring from his soul." [16] Nevertheless, he is still weaker than Nina; although he has achieved a reputation in Petersburg and Moscow, he still has no definite purpose, and is still chaotic and sunk in gloom. She departs unbroken by her sufferings and dreaming of the time when she will be a great actress. He, having no such faith, having never thrown himself into the arduous but bracing world outside, and losing her again, shoots himself.*

Stanislavsky admitted that at first he did not understand "the essence, the aroma, the beauty" of *The Sea Gull*. How much less, therefore, could it be understood by others. Chekhov was doomed to another keen disappointment when it was first presented in 1896 by the Imperial Theatre in St. Petersburg; the play failed miserably and critics called it not only bad but absurd. "Never will I write these plays or try to produce them, not if I live to be 700 years old" was Chekhov's comment.[17]

Fortunately, however, there arose a new organization a year later which could make him reconsider his decision. On June 21, 1897, there occurred a historic eighteen-hour conversation between two lovers of the theatre who wanted to reform it. They were the critic and playwright Nemirovitch-Dantchenko and the amateur actor Constantin Stanislavsky. The result of these conversations was the greatest theatre of modern times, the Moscow Art Theatre. Meticulousness in the preparation of a production, even if this required months of rehearsal, was the first principle to be agreed upon. Dantchenko notes that there had been no dress rehearsals in the Russian Theatre until three years before his conversation with Stanislavsky; whereas Dantchenko and Stanislavsky were to insist on as many as five or six dress rehearsals. They proceeded cautiously, spending an entire year on preparations, unifying their respective theatrical companies, and laying down principles.

They soon arrived at the core of the art for which they became famous by defining the function of the stage director, in relation to the actor.

---

* How strongly Chekhov believed in affirmativeness, while sympathizing with those who lacked it, is shown by the comic lines he omitted from this play. When the schoolmaster Medvenko declares "The earth is round," Doctor Dorn asks him, "Then why do you say it so unconvincedly?" See Notes for Actors, p. 120, in Stark Young's translation of *The Sea Gull*, Scribner's, 1939.

The director was to be a *regisseur-mirror* who reflects "the individual qualities of the actor" and a *regisseur-organizer* who supervises the entire production. Above all, however, they insisted upon "the necessity of the *death* of the *regisseur* in the actor's creativeness." [18] For the Moscow Art Theatre was not merely the last word in superficial realism— that is, in the faithful rendition of the background of a play. As a matter of fact the Moscow Art Theatre attempted to produce a number of non-realistic plays like Maeterlinck's *Blue Bird,* even if it owed its greatest triumphs to realistic works. The secret of its mastery of theatre lay in the discovery of an essential principle of creative realistic production —namely, the ability of the actor to submerge his individuality in his role. Acting must follow "the law of inner justification" and the actor must create his role as if it were at one with his personality. In no sense must the director impose the role on the actor; he must evoke it instead out of the actor's inner self. The founders of the Moscow Art Theatre wanted a realistic theatre which would go beyond their scrupulous attempt to photograph externals. Rightly they called their enterprise "a theatre of inner feeling."

Thus was born the so-called Stanislavsky system of acting. It has always been more or less used by good actors, even if it is the Moscow Art Theatre that has given them the greatest opportunity to put it into practice by means of long rehearsal periods and a repertory system of long standing. Nor is Stanislavsky's "system" a rigid formula guaranteed to create inspiration whenever it is applied. No procedure has ever done this or is ever likely to. Stanislavsky himself declared in his *Life in Art* that he did not intend to inculcate inspiration by artificial means: "What I wanted to learn was how to create a favorable condition for the appearance of inspiration by means of the will, that condition in the presence of which inspiration was most likely to descend into the actor's soul." The careful observer Norris Houghton [19] has, however, set down ten points in the actor's preparation: 1. physical development or flexible body movement; 2. personal psychology—that is, the actor must place himself "in a circle" in order not to be distracted or must shut out the audience by means of a "fourth wall"; 3. imagination, whereby the actor recreates the situation in terms of his impressions, memories and associations; 4. mastery of the play's situations to such a degree that if "the actor is required to write a love letter, he must not convey to the audience that he is writing a business letter, or that he is writing just any kind of letter;" 5. "naïveté"—or capacity to believe in what he is saying or doing ("the magical, creative IF"); 6. contact with other actors—"talk to your partner-actor's eyes, not to his ears," or produce "rays" to be absorbed by the other person; 7. memorization of emotions in order to recreate them in any role that requires them; 8. rhythm—

each circumstance calling for a different rhythm in addition to the general rhythm of the production; 9. mastery of the "kernel" or personality of the role; 10. consciousness of the *aim* of the role, the actor answering by his performance the cardinal question "What do I want and why?"

Given a group of talented actors trained on these principles, a production of a Chekhov play was bound to do justice to its symphony of characters, desires, and moods. And conversely it is Chekhov's work that could enable the Moscow Art Theatre to display its procedure to the greatest advantage. Although the Art Theatre's first production *Tsar Fyodor* in October 1898 was successful, its second offering *The Merchant of Venice* proved a fiasco and nearly wrecked the organization Fortunately, however, Dantchenko succeeded in overcoming Chekhov's objections to a revival of *The Sea Gull,* and this production saved the Art Theatre. "The fact is," writes Dantchenko, "our theatre was on the verge of complete collapse," and only when the ovations of the premiere had ended could it be said that "the New Theatre was born." Chekhov was also vindicated, and the effect of his first real success as a playwright was as salutary as it was encouraging. With renewed energy he returned to his scrapped play *The Forest Demon* and turned it into the beautiful *Uncle Vanya* which consolidated his alliance with the Art Theatre in 1899.

Here, too, the atmosphere is charged with passion and frustration. On the estate of the retired Professor Serebyakov, his daughter by a first marriage Sonia and his brother-in-law Uncle Vanya wear themselves out for him. The futility of their lives strikes them, however, only when the Professor returns with a charming young wife. Vanya, falling in love with her, becomes jealous of the professor and for the first time realizes that he had been sacrificing himself for a fussy mediocrity. Sonia, too, feels the impact of the new situation when her admirer, the district doctor Astrov, also falls in love with the professor's wife. The crisis is aggravated when Vanya learns that his brother-in-law intends to oust him from the estate by selling it. In despair Vanya tries to shoot him, but—as may be readily expected from Vanya—the shots go wild. The professor leaves after forgiving him, and life settles in the old rut for Vanya and Sonia.

Life in this tragedy simply rusts away. And, what is truly important, these lives did not deserve to rust away, because they are rich with sensitivity and with the capacity for service. Vanya, who might have gone out into the world and advanced himself, fixed his life to the false star of a pedantic brother-in-law from whom he expected great things. Unhappily, he is too gentle and too isolated in the provinces to start a new life once he realizes that he was not serving humanity by relieving the professor of economic burdens. He is left with nothing except his fierce longing:

"If only one could live the remnant of one's life in some new way." He knows only that "we must make haste and work, make haste and do something" if life is not to become unbearable. It was this desire and realization that sent the intelligentsia of Chekhov's generation "down to the people" and led it to throw itself into revolutionary work against the Tsarist regime. And Vanya's dream is expressed even more strongly by the district doctor Astrov who is in despair because in the whole district there are only two decent, well-educated people, himself and Uncle Vanya, both of whom have been swamped by "the common round of trivial life . . . with its putrid vapors." Astrov cannot even do justice to his profession, fighting as he does alone and without adequate means and preparation against a typhus epidemic. "Those who will live a hundred or two hundred years after us, for whom we are struggling now to beat out a road," he wonders, "will they remember and say a good word for us?" The play is thus both a personal tragedy (or tragi-comedy perhaps) and the drama of a shipwrecked generation. Nor is it confined to Chekhov's generation, as the cycle of man's history reveals; an eternal verity resides in the play—a verity as eternal as human waste.

Chekhov was not spared long enough to write more than two plays after *Uncle Vanya*, but these were those notable masterpieces *The Three Sisters* and *The Cherry Orchard*. They are not radically different from *The Sea Gull* and *Uncle Vanya* in form and style, although they are more finished in this respect. But they are richer in content, more distinct in outline, and more vigorous. His creative spirit was becoming stronger and his confidence was waxing even while his health was failing him. He was at last succeeding in the theatre, and he was finding new friends among the artists of the Moscow Art Theatre who were making tangible progress in decadent Russia. He was also enjoying the friendship of writers of great vitality; of Tolstoy, who was still hurling his giant strength against the world, and of the newcomer Gorky, who stemmed from the raw and restive masses. Above all, the great actress Olga Knipper of the Art Theatre became his friend and finally married him. Without losing his awareness of the comic and tragic frustrations for which he had so much understanding, he began to feel the surge of new powers within himself.

The Three Sisters, which appeared in 1901 and remained according to Dantchenko "the best production of the Art Theatre," is again the familiar picture of lives that seek but do not find fruition. Three sisters and a brother are stranded in a provincial town after the death of their father. Their one hope of escape from the tedium of their exile is this brother Andrei who has prospects of a professorship in the capital. But he deteriorates after marrying a shallow woman who betrays him; he will never be anything but a petty bureaucrat, and he will never take them to Moscow. Olga remains wedded to her commonplace schoolteaching job, while Masha is dismally united to a fatuous pedagogue. If normally we would not be concerned about their frustrations, Chekhov endows his characters with so much life that even their minutest problems possess vitality. These women and their younger sister are literally quivering with desire and energy.

Olga keeps herself discreetly in the background, heartening her sisters, and advancing herself in the position to which she is tied. Masha becomes the mistress of a friend of her father's, the garrison commander Vershinin who is married to a shrew and cannot leave her because of his children. The youngest sister Irina, who is energetic enough to take a job in a telegraph office and later to become a teacher, longs for a richer life. And it seems possible that she will at last leave the province with the lieutenant Baron Tusenbach who resigns his commission for a business career. But Vershinin must depart with his regiment and the Baron is killed in a duel with an eccentric rival. Both Masha and Irina are left stranded again.

To the end, however, the three sisters remain vital personalities instead of jaded provincial women. Although there is undoubtedly much heartbreak in their resolution, it is impossible to relegate them to the dustbin reserved for those weak spirits that allow themselves to be discarded. "We've got to live," cries Masha. "Time will pass . . . and we shall be forgotten," says Olga, "but our sufferings will pass into joy for those who live after us . . . it seems as though a little more and we shall know what we are living for." She adds, "If only we knew—if only we knew," but vaguely they already know. Irina, who is the most hard hit of the sisters, declares that she knows how they can serve the future: "We have got to work, only to work. . . . I shall teach in the school, and I will give all my life to those to whom it may be of use. Now it's autumn; soon winter will come and cover us with snow, and I will work, I will work."

Moreover, their words are not confined to their private, if wholly sufficient, drama. They represent a general impulse. As if to convey the tremendous energies that longed for release in old Russia, Chekhov placed the same thoughts in the mouths of the departed lovers who are members of the military class and of the aristocracy. Vershinin avows his trust in progress and the Baron, who renounces an idle military life in favor of a more active world declares: "Something formidable is threatening us, a strong cleansing storm is gathering us. . . . It will soon sweep our world clean of laziness, indifference, prejudice against work, and wretched boredom. . . . I shall soon work, and within twenty-five or thirty years everyone will work—everyone." These words were written seventeen years before the revolution that transformed Russia into a hustling nation of workers—a fact that may well be conceded without commitment to any political philosophy or practice. *Per aspera ad astra* would be a fitting slogan for this beautiful play which is one more refutation of such time-honored bromides as "the inconclusiveness of Chekhov's plays" and the allegedly aimless and listless "Russian soul." Certain it is that Stanislavsky, who would be expected to know something about his chief playwright's work, protested vigorously against this superficial interpretation of Chekhov's characters: "Just the opposite," he wrote, "they, like Chekhov, seek life, joy, laughter, courage. . . . They are active and surge to overcome the hard and unbearable impasses into which life has plunged them."

An impasse is partly overcome in actuality and wholly overcome symbolically in his crowning work *The Cherry Orchard,* produced in 1904. Chekhov, whose health was declining rapidly, wrote his masterpiece slowly and painstakingly, crying out against the fate that made him a writer. But he was straining toward a masterpiece, and perhaps, being a physician himself, he knew that it was to be his last work. Here both the causes and consequences of the drama are active and distinct. The three sisters could hardly avoid their fate and did not cause their own defeat; moreover, their struggle closed with a hope rather than with the actual presentation of a new way of life. In *The Cherry Orchard* the chief character Madame Ranevsky, who with her ineffectual brother Gaev represents the upper classes, brings on her calamities (like so many Russian aristocrats) by leading a spendthrift life abroad and by refusing to make the necessary adjustment of converting her estate into a summer colony. The practical economies of her adopted daughter Varya who manages the household are insufficient to save the situation and are being constantly counteracted by Madame Ranevsky's extravagances; accustomed to a life of pleasure and liberality, she simply cannot stop them. Possessing no understanding for the practical world and having an insurmountable repugnance for business owing to her background, she spurns the merchant Lopahin's endeavors to save the estate; she simply cannot consent to raze her ancestral home, and to cut down her beloved cherry orchard is out of the question. Nevertheless, the cherry orchard is a useless luxury that can no longer be afforded. It must go. And the aristocrats must go with it. The estate is auctioned off; and since classes come and go, it is bought by the former serf and present merchant Lopahin. A lovely but useless world comes to an end, and those who helped to support it are also doomed. Varya, who might have married Lopahin if he had not been too busy for love, will have to find employment somewhere, and the octogenarian family butler Firs is forgotten in the haste of the departure. He is left alone in the old house, which is to be dismantled in the spring; locked in, he will no doubt die, thus sharing the fortunes of the society he had served.

Chekhov regrets the passing of a way of life that had much charm and beauty, a world which moreover consisted of affecting human beings; and he is equally mindful of the fact that the new dispensation is hard and pragmatic. Nevertheless, he recognizes the fact that life must move on and that there is a cleansing power in its unavoidable abrasiveness; the productive world of tomorrow is being born with every stroke of the axes that are felling the trees of the cherry orchard. How often has this been the case! How often will it continue to be the case! Out of "the reticences, nuances, and little moments" of Chekhov's art, as Oliver Sayler calls them, emerges a radically different order.*

3 AFTER CHEKHOV: ANDREYEV AND EVREINOV

When Chekhov died in 1904, Russia was on the eve of the abortive revolution of 1905. This dress rehearsal for the Bolshevist upheaval of 1918 was followed by a dozen years of progressive decay and smoldering revolt climaxed by nearly four years of slaughter and starvation during the World War. Under these circumstances, it could not be expected that the theatre would be replenished by another genius of Chekhov's basic serenity and quiet humility. Only one major writer, not primarily a dramatist, succeeded him—Maxim Gorky. And Gorky, for all his benevolence, was of a different temper, benevolent but not benign. Bearing the tempest in his heart, he belonged to a more vigorous and embattled age. Significantly, he survived into the Soviet era, and his contribution belongs to another chapter of history.

The dramatists who filled the interim were minor writers, poorly oriented toward reality, and exotic. In them, understandably, it is the credo of negativism or subjective retreat that predominates. The broad humanitarian stream of Russian literature either ceases to flow, as was the case with Artzybashev, or it froths and becomes murky in Andreyev. The others need not even detain the general historian.

Reflecting the art for art's sake movement of Western Europe, Fyodor Sologub, author of that remarkable psychological novel *The Little De-*

---

* Chekhov admirers will be interested in his early full-length play *That Worthless Fellow Platonov*, written in 1889 and recovered only during the Soviet period. It contains much the same material that appears in his later plays. The chief character is an irresolute young Don Juan who tries to remain faithful to four women. Everybody had expected great things from Platonov, who is now embittered and misanthropic, offending everyone. After betraying his wife, who poisons herself, and philandering with a middle-aged widow, with her daughter-in-law, and with another young woman, he is shot by one of them. The play possesses good characterization, but it is too wordy and melodramatic to receive more than a secondary place in Chekhov's legacy.

mon, wrote a number of fantastic or symbolic plays for the greater glory of "Beauty." One may draw a merciful veil over his adolescent moonings while recording the fact that these represented the tendency of the post-1905 intelligentsia to seek a bomb-proof shelter while the explosives were flying. The two extremes of the theatre in those days were best represented by the sensational naturalist Artzybashev and the feverish symbolist Andreyev.

As a reaction to the dispiriting failure of the 1905 uprising, Michael Petrovich Artzybashev contributed the novel *Sanine,* the most famous work of its day which is now generally forgotten except by publishers who make a specialty of reprinting erotica. This writer's complete abandonment to the physiology of sex and glorification of the ruthless superman assuaged the frustrations of the intelligentsia which had merely philandered with revolution and now retired to lick its imaginary wounds while Lenin was slowly rebuilding his party. Turning to the theatre, Artzybashev composed a drama *Jealousy,* which the author himself defined as "a concert of amorous tomcats." Another work, *Enemies,* described "the barnyard world of sex," as Granville Barker called it, by recounting the marital difficulties of a professor's family; his son is physically inadequate for his wife, while his daughter is married to a polygamous man who insists that his practice is in harmony with "nature." In *The Law of the Savage* a man who remains faithful to a single woman is set down as a curiosity. Here the double standard so flattering to masculine vanity is rigidly enforced, and the libertine who has seduced his wife's sister kills the man whom his wife has designated as her lover merely to arouse his jealousy. Artzybashev even introduced his erotic naturalism into a field where other writers have found more immediate problems; his play *War,* in 1914, centers attention on women whose sole reaction to the holocaust is to adopt other lovers in the place of their dead or maimed companions. Artzybashev was the only Russian playwright of any moment who adopted crass naturalism, and he travestied it almost beyond recall.

Leonid Andreyev expressed the deterioration and bitterness of the period more honestly and more effectively in his largely symbolic works. He was not, indeed, above sensationalism and posturing, but whatever he undertook was the product of an intensely morbid and moderately talented personality. As a realist he was negligible except perhaps in *To the Stars* and *Savva.* The former, written in 1905, was an attempt to salve the wounds of the disheartened intelligentsia. Here an astronomer assuages his grief over the execution of his revolutionary son by pointing to the infinity of the universe. What do our personal griefs matter in the light of eternity! *Savva,* another tragedy of revolution, dramatizes the struggle against the Russian church, one of the chief pillars of Tsarist absolutism. Savva tries to expose its miracles as impossible and false, but is overreached by the priests and killed by their flock. Other realistic works by Andreyev were equally melodramatic but with considerably less effect. *The Waltz of the Dogs* described the deterioration of a man who is overwhelmed by his fiancée's treason and by his worthless brother's effort to kill him for his insurance money. The somewhat deeper *Yekaterina Ivanovna* is the tragedy of a woman who loses her self-respect when she is innocently suspected by her husband. Thereafter she lives the role that her husband's imagination foisted upon her. All told, Andreyev's once considerable reputation had scant justification.

If he was more effective in his symbolic plays, he was never more than a second-rate dramatist who seemed a first-rate one because he gave his audience an extra *frisson*. *The Life a Man* (1906) is a Poësque chronicle of man's struggle against Fate personified by the "Being in Grey." Since it is replete with theatrical effects, it gave its public an illusion of profundity. Although the Moscow Art Theatre gave the play a notable production, it remains a mass of platitudes and adolescent clichés. Also overrated but theatrically effective and occasionally incisive is the only slightly symbolic *He Who Gets Slapped* in which an intelligent and sensitive man who has been betrayed by his wife joins a circus. As the clown who gets slapped he derives a double satisfaction: his mortification intensifies his negation of life, and his antics enable him to fling unpleasant truths at the spectators. When his repentant friend, who seduced his wife, visits him at the circus, he does not have to fear that "He" will return to the world and expose him as the thief who stole and vulgarized his ideas, for by then "He" is beyond any interest in a world that deserves only to be despised. Yet "He" had also hoped that the slaps he received would reawaken love in his frozen heart, and it is reawakened by the young bareback rider Consuelo whom he vainly tries to save from being sold to a nobleman by her supposed father. As a last resort he poisons her and himself.

There is a certain perverse power in Andreyev's negativism, and the picture of circus life possesses novelty and color. Nevertheless, *He Who Gets Slapped* is a *tour de force* rather than a great play. His other and more symbolic work is likewise novel but artificial: *Anathema*, one of the world's numerous Faust versions, is full of platitudinous pity for mankind. Here a sentimentalized Mephistopheles sympathizes with man but is doomed to see him defeated. Man, or the Faustian spirit, is defeated in the person of a philanthropic Jew who gives away the fortune he won at a lottery only to find that it is insufficient to feed and heal humanity. He dies a victim of the endless stream of sufferers who came at his call and found themselves cheated. Divine assurance to the effect that all this frustration or failure has a purpose and that the "cosmic

will" cannot be appraised by the logic of Man or Devil does not assuage
the disillusionment expressed by the play.

The failure of the humanitarian cause is also the theme of *King Hunger,* a poignant symbolization of the revolt of the masses. They are led
by "King Hunger," and he is temporarily a potent ally. But all the
technological resources of their masters are mustered against them, and
in the end even "King Hunger," who is after all the slave of their rulers,
betrays the downtrodden! Andreyev was most masterful, however, in
dramatizing morbid psychology. *The Black Maskers,* the most original
of Andreyev's symbolizations, is an internal drama full of schizophrenic
intimations. Here a soul is destroyed by corruption, disruption, and doubt
of its origin and nature. Duke Lorenzo is terrified when uncanny mummers representing his lusts and falsehoods invade his castle in grotesque
animal shapes. All his glory and all his aspirations become a mockery
and soon his double arrives to plague him with self-doubt by accusing
him of illegitimacy. Lorenzo slays his double to no avail since he remains
in doubt of his identity. Only when his faithful court jester fires "the
castle of his soul" does the Duke expire in the flames triumphant over
evil and self-doubt. Unfortunately, the fascination and provocativeness
of this work are only too frequently nullified by its tortured and esoteric
symbolism. Only once, in his objective satire on political compromise
The Sabine Women, did Andreyev succeed in creating symbolism that
was not at least partly banal or mystifying.

There is no obscurity in the picture of the Sabine men who try to recover their wives from the rapacious Romans by supporting their case
with law-books and marching two steps forward and one step backward
—to ensure moderation. Although intended to refer to the vacillations
of the Constitutional Democrats in Russia, this delightful Shavian
broadside is applicable to other occasions and countries without loss of
effect. Elsewhere Andreyev was enmeshed by his subjectivity. In exploring the Sargasso Sea of abnormality Andreyev emerged with many a
rare find but also with a good deal of common mud; sometimes, moreover, he brought up misshapen objects that tax our understanding. After
1914, when *He Who Gets Slapped* appeared, Andreyev's output became
negligible. The war turned him into a ranting chauvinist and he died in
exile, railing to the end at the Bolsheviks for having signed the Treaty
of Brest-Litovsk.

Nor did the other symbolists possess any power to keep the Russian
drama from becoming moribund. The most talented poet among them
Alexander Blok, who won fame with his poem of the Bolshevist revolution *The Twelve,* composed beautiful but only half-dramatic ironic pieces
like *The Puppet Show* and *The Stranger* between 1906 and 1907. The
cultured and liberal Lunacharsky, who became the Soviet's first Com-

missar of Education, wrote a series of symbolic pieces embodying the socialist ideal. Of these *Faust and the City,* rewritten after the revolution, modernized Goethe's poem. Here Faust is faced with a revolt of the people, who are led by his daughter's lover. Stubbornly, he abdicates rather than grant them an equal voice in the government. But he finally becomes reconciled to the new order, and beholding the happiness of the masses he experiences the perfect moment which Mephistopheles had been unable to provide. There is considerable nobility in this poetic drama, and it was superior to the early agitational plays of the Soviet. Yet the bulk of Lunacharsky's dramatic work is negligible, and he will be remembered longest for his moderating influence on the literary zealots of the Soviet's first years.

Even the most talented dramatist among Andreyev's co-symbolists Nikolai Nikolaevich Evreinov, his junior by eight years (he was born in 1879), was more original than effective. He proved himself an able exponent of non-realistic stagecraft or "theatricality," and like Andreyev he stressed the importance of inner drama or "theatre of the soul." Every drama, Evreinov held, should be a "monodrama" or a projection of the inner self. This theory, to which he devoted a polemical book "The Theatre for Oneself," was exemplified in a short play *The Theatre of the Soul.* In this "monodrama" the same person appears in three representations: M_1—the rational self, M_2—the emotional self, and M_3—the "subliminal" self. As the lecturing professor declares, M or the "great integral self" is the sum of M_1, M_2 and M_3! M_1 and M_2 quarrel with each other over M_1's readiness to betray his wife with a dancer. Since M_1 and M_2 have different conceptions of the wife and the dancer, each of these characters appears in two radically different forms on the stage. The wife seems glamorously loyal and noble to M_1 and appears shrewish and sluttish to M_2, whereas the dancer is repulsive when seen through the eyes of M_1 but desirable to M_2. The latter, disregarding the warnings of M_1, abandons his wife, is quickly disillusioned by the dancer, and commits suicide. Abruptly at this point M_3—the eternal self— wakes up, puts on his hat, takes his bag, and follows the "Porter," declaring "I have to change here."

Evreinov's interest in bizarre representations of personality led him to still more developed Pirandellian experiments. The most notable of these *The Chief Thing* affirmed the healing power of illusion. Anomalously, it was written in 1919 and produced in Petrograd in 1921 after the triumphant Bolsheviks had established a new order officially opposed to illusion. Here the "Paraclete" or divine Comforter appears in numerous guises and even hires actors to play selected roles with a view toward creating comforting illusions for a number of miserable people. Despite a certain intentional artificiality and some thinness, *The Chief*

Thing possesses novelty and interest. Evreinov's later work never approximated its engaging theatricality.

But even Evreinov's best work was quickly dated. After indulging in fantasies of world revolution which extended even to Mars, the Soviet playwrights understandably settled back to realism. And just as the earlier Russian realists had not been content with realism for its own sake but spiritualized it, so the new writers adapted realism to the spiritual and practical aims of a collectivist social order, creating so-called "socialist realism."

In this new order of things most of the older playwrights who survived into the Soviet age could have no place. Fortunately, however, Gorky was spared for many years, and it is in his work that the pre-revolutionary and post-revolutionary drama found an impressive bridge. It is significant that his two outstanding plays belong respectively to the Tsarist and the Soviet eras: *The Lower Depths* appeared in 1902, *Yegor Bulichov* in 1932. Until his death in 1936, Gorky was the grand old man of Soviet literature, and the new regime went so far as to rename the city of his birth, Nizhni-Novgorod, in his honor.

XXVI

MAXIM GORKY AND THE SOVIET DRAMA

"THE DEATH of Chekhov tore out a large part of the heart of our theatre," wrote Stanislavsky. That it was only a part, however, was fortunate, and for this too the credit belongs largely to Chekhov. He had not seen Stanislavsky's productions of *The Sea Gull* and *Uncle Vanya;* he had not seen the Moscow Art Theatre at all, because his physicians forbade him to leave his retreat in the Crimea. The company therefore decided to visit him at Yalta, playing *en route* in Sebastopol to defray expenses. As they were looking for the country house which Chekhov had lately erected they were met by a man "above average height, lean but strongly built, with a markedly duck-like nose, and thick reddish moustaches" dressed in high top-boots and a sailor's cloak.[1] He directed them to the villa and then disappeared. When they arrived at their destination Chekhov's first words were: "Gorky has only just left. He waited for you. He wanted to make your acquaintance."

I MAXIM THE BITTER

To the members of the Moscow Art Theatre this information was not particularly startling, since all they had heard were rumors of "a tramp from the Volga with an enormous writing talent." But Gorky came back and, encouraged by Chekhov, the actors soon busied themselves with the difficult task of prevailing upon him to give them a play. As they spoke to him of their efforts to create a new theatre the rough-hewn son of the people attired in his Russian peasant blouse sat "intently listening, captivatingly smiling or narrating, deftly choosing picturesque bold, characteristic expressions." Between the Chekhov-Art Theatre coalition and Gorky there was at first a chasm, for they were "middle class" while he was a charter member of the proletariat. Gorky had no love for the "bourgeois" amenities, as he was to show during the winter following the Crimean visit when he came to Moscow to see one of the Art Theatre's performances. The well-dressed spectators stormed Dantchenko's study which Gorky had entered. They were so persistent that Gorky at last came out. His face was clouded with anger as he sent them packing. "Well, why do you want to see me?" he said to them. "I'm neither a drowned man nor a ballet girl, and when you consider what a remarkable play is being given, your idle curiosity is simply disgusting!" The Moscow Art Theatre, however, respected his integrity and Chekhov did not fail to recognize in his protégé a cleansing power. "Gorky," he said, "is a destroyer who must destroy all that deserves destruction. In this lies his whole strength and it is for this that life has called him."

He was the people's angry man, and when Alexei Maximovich Pyesh-kov adopted the *nom de plume* or *nom de guerre* of Maxim Gorky— Maxim the Bitter—he did so with good reason. He had come up from the same "lower depths" that he later represented in his dramatic mas-terpiece. The orphaned son of a dyer at an early age, bullied by his grandfather, and apprenticed to many trades, he tasted bitterness at the fountain. Running away from his employer, he joined the caravan of tramps and pilgrims with which the steppes of Russia were littered. In-termittent employment was his lot for a long time; one critical period found him serving as a cook's helper on a Volga steamboat and learning his letters by painful application. Everywhere he came upon inhuman brutality that made his blood boil.

It was during this infernal itinerary that he shared an overturned boat during a storm with the bruised and embittered street-woman he described in his famous story *One Autumn Night*. Somewhere on this journey through the Russian land he also met the half-wit Igosha who was hungrier and "more hunted than an animal," Panashkina the de-cayed and wall-eyed blueblood who dreamed of "an affair with an officer not lower in rank than a lieutenant," and the mad "Mother Kem-skikh" with her seven subnormal children. Everywhere he saw women abused, overworked, and beaten, his first memory being the childhood one of seeing his stepfather striking his consumptive mother who had fallen on her knees, her back arched with pain. He was only eight years old at the time, but he hurled himself against her tormentor with a bread knife in his hand. It became the pattern of his life to pit himself henceforth against every tormentor regardless of the risk. Once he hur-ried to the defense of a peasant woman in a little village through which he passed; he received a beating for his pains, and was saved only when a pedestrian found him in the bushes and took him to a hospital.[2]

All this and more he was to remember when, after educating himself, he was encouraged by the novelist Korolenko to write stories. His nu-merous tales, novels, autobiographies (they are his greatest work), and plays became one long series of protests against inhumanity. Becoming the literary champion of the "creatures that had once been men," he fought the Tsarist government until he became one of the most sus-pected men of his day and suffered imprisonment and banishment. The Gorky archives also contain twenty-two cases of "persecution by the tsarist censorship." Nor was he content with blind anger and revolt, just as he soon went beyond the youthful despair that made him send a bullet through his chest, weakening his lungs permanently. Slowly he developed a firm faith in social revolution and became a convert to socialism.

When the Bolshevik revolution occurred he gave it his support. He did not like everything that he saw during the first years and tried to mitigate the rigors of the revolution, speaking out boldly to Lenin himself. (Lenin, it is reported, was patient with the great man and explained that one could not make "an omelet without breaking eggs.") But when Russia entered upon the constructive era of the five-year plans Gorky gave the new regime unqualified support and made himself invaluable by championing broad principles of tolerance and humanity in the Soviet literary world. Characteristic was his warning in an article "About Plays": "We should not paste the class label on a person as we are used to doing."

If he was a realist, even a naturalist, in his pictures of life as it was, he remained an unabashed romanticist in his fidelity to the dream of liberation and brotherly love. Under the Tsar he had proclaimed that the "Holy of Holies"—"the true Shekhina"—is Man. Under the Soviet he fixed his hope in the natural goodness of childhood. "A new life is being born," he wrote, "thanks to the children's ardent love toward the entire world. And who shall extinguish this love? . . . The earth gave birth to it, and all life wants its victory—all life." Just and proper is Romain Rolland's tribute when he called him "the man who, like Dante, emerged from hell, but not alone, who brought with him his companions in torment, his comrades in salvation."

When he entered the ranks of the dramatists in 1900 he was, however, less sanguine and serene; anger and desperation crackled in his lines. Since the meeting with the Art Theatre in the spring of 1900 Gorky had spent nearly two years on two plays. The first to appear was *The Smug Citizen,* a picture of middle-class family life which was in effect a miniature of Russian society. A complacent Babbitt rules his household with an iron hand; the wife is a browbeaten creature, and the daughter Tatiana is a frustrated girl who takes poison when her foster-brother Nil does not return her love. This young man also feels the "smug citizen's" wrath because he rejects a rich girl in order to marry a poor seamstress. The worst offender, however, is the son Peter who is suspended from the university for radicalism and scorns the bourgeois pettiness of his parents' home and society. Peter leaves home with the widow of a prison official who found the company of the prisoners preferable to that of the respectable citizenry. Ultimately Tatiana is left alone, heartbroken and despairing, in this citadel of respectability.

This blast was produced by the Moscow Art Theatre in the fall of 1902, but only in an emasculated version. Since the Tsarist police now had a file on Gorky, his election to the Imperial Academy of Russian artists was annulled at this time, drawing a spirited protest even from the mild-mannered Chekhov. The premiere, therefore, was a tense affair and a squadron of mounted Cossacks was drawn around the theatre to guard against an expected public demonstration. Meanwhile, however, the censor had done his bit of snipping. Among the deleted passages were Nil's statement, "He who works is the master," Peter's lines, "Your truth is too narrow for us. . . . Your order of life is no use to us," and a drunkard's apology, "In Russia it is more comfortable to be a drunkard or a tramp than to be a sober and hard-working man. It is better to drink vodka than to drink the blood of the people—especially since the blood of people today is thin and tasteless and all their healthy blood has been sucked out." [3]

If Gorky's first play was a minor explosion, his second work, which had been rehearsed during the run of *The Smug Citizen,* was an artistically executed bombardment. In *The Lower Depths,* which appeared in the same season, Gorky expressed a substantial portion of the experiences of his *Wanderjahre* and of the vision he had gathered on the way. The inscription James Huneker proposed for this play is entirely appropriate—*De profundis ad te clamavi,* for here Gorky was literally crying "out of the depths."

About these depths, moreover, Gorky knew the alpha and omega. Huneker rightly noted that although Zola posed all his lifetime as the father of naturalism, "he might have gone to school to learn the alphabet of his art at the knees of the young man from Nizhni-Novgorod." And the Art Theatre took pains to reproduce his picture faithfully on the stage with Gorky's expert co-operation. He taught Olga Knipper, who played Nastya the streetwalker, how such women rolled their cigarettes and naïvely offered to bring one of them to stay with her in order to give her "a deeper insight into the psychology of an empty soul." [4] Madame Chekhov discreetly declined the experience, but Gorky did take a number of the actors to the underground dens of the Khitrov Market, and the sight seared Stanislavsky's memory. "The excursion," he wrote in *My Life in Art* two decades later, "more than any discussion or analysis of the play, awoke my fantasy and my creative mood." The play came to mean "Freedom at any cost" to Gorky's great *regisseur,* and with these words Stanislavsky illuminates the nature of this masterpiece more than any number of paeans to Gorky's "naturalism." Even in this gruesome picture of the underworld, Russian realism sublimated reality into a passion for humanity.

As a dramatist Gorky touched fingertips with the masters only twice—once in *The Lower Depths* and once in *Yegor Bulychov.* But that is sufficient to give him an honorable place among them. His technique in

The Lower Depths resembles Chekhov's more than may be generally realized. Oliver Sayler, the Moscow Art Theatre's able American publicist, describes it well when he writes that *"The Lower Depths* is not so much a matter of utterable line and recountable gesture as it is of the intangible flow of human souls in endlessly shifting contact with one another." At the same time, as in Chekhov's work, the play brings its shifting lines into a definite focus, and its conclusion has a classic firmness.

Huddled in a "cellar resembling a cave" are a number of outcasts who pay rent to the contemptible receiver of stolen goods Kostilyoff and his lustful wife Vassilisa. With them are Vassilisa's victimized sister Natasha and their lodgers. Here are the Baron, of dubious ancestry, and the romantic streetwalker Nastya who supports him and is scorned for her pains; the saturnine Satine, the actor whose lungs have been worn to shreds by alcoholism, Kvayshnya the shrewd pie-vendor, the unemployed locksmith Kleshtch and his dying wife Anna, Vaska Pepel the resolute young thief, and sundry other creatures. Into this dive enters the pilgrim Luka, bringing with him his gospel of kindness and the solvent of the useful lie or illusion recommended by Ibsen's Dr. Relling and Evreinov's Paraclete. He does not understand the social and psychological causes of the misery that he finds here and elsewhere, and he has no political plan for eradicating them. But the old man knows that all men —good and bad—belong to the same species. "For my part," he declares, "there's no bad flea—they're all black—and they all jump." And the characters bear him out, for behind their hardened exterior they all cherish dreams and want what all men desire. He also has a glimpse of the main source of evil when he says that "Everybody is trying to be boss—and is threatening everybody else with all kinds of punishment— and still there's no order in life—and no cleanliness." He tries to alleviate suffering by inculcating and practising kindness, by fanning the spark of humanity that he finds among men, and by instilling delusory hopes into those of them who are too far gone to be saved. (It is a mistake to assume that Luka believes only in the ameliorative lie.)

The dying Anna is unable to remember a single day when she was not hungry or when she did not tremble waking, eating, and sleeping lest she should not get another bite. To her the pilgrim brings the hope of another and kinder world. To the actor who was told that his "organism" is poisoned with alcohol, he extends the hope that he can be cured, that there is a hospital for drunkards somewhere. Not a lie after all, but an illusion with respect to Tsarist Russia and its underdogs! Pepel is a fatalist: "My father spent all his life in prison, and I inherited the trait. Even when I was a small child, they called me thief—thief's son." But Luka encourages Pepel to break with the proprietor's wife, marry her sister, and find honest employment. And Pepel listens to Luka. "A woman," he reflects, "must have a soul. We men are beasts—we must be taught."

Still, illusions are not enough, philanthropy is not enough, and good will is ineffective when life is so involved and diseased. The proprietor's wife, who had hoped that Pepel would take her "out of this swamp" and free her from her contemptible husband, assaults her sister when she discovers Pepel's intention to leave with Natasha. In the scuffle the proprietor is killed and Pepel, who struck in defense of Natasha with no intention of murdering him, is taken away to prison. Luka disappears quietly, and the disillusioned actor hangs himself. Satine, the mordant skeptic, touches upon the futility of individual and undirected pity when he says to the locksmith, "What good can I do you by pitying you?"

However, Gorky does not end on a note of fatalism, and the stagnant pools of the lower depths have been stirred. The locksmith declares that one cannot live without the truth. And Satine, moved by the tragedies that have transpired in the cellar, thunders: "The weakling and the one who is a parasite through his very weakness—they both need lies— lies are their support, their shield, their armor! But the man who is strong, who is free and does not have to suck his neighbor's blood—he needs no lies! . . . Truth is the religion of the free man." "Each individual," he adds, "thinks that he's living for his own self, but in reality he lives for something better." We must respect every person, because we do not know whether he may not do something to lead humanity out of the depths. Especially must we respect children, for out of them may rise the new humanity—the thought that Gorky was to reaffirm in winged words after the revolution.

The Lower Depths became one of the signal triumphs of the Moscow Art Theatre. It was followed, however, by a decline in Gorky's dramatic power. *Summer Folk,* a satire on the futile intelligentsia (1903), the tragi-comedy of the same class *Children of the Sun* (1904), *The Barbarians* (1905) in which a group of engineers debase the common people, and a drama of the class struggle *Enemies* (1906) fell far short of his masterpiece. None of these plays, it is true, were devoid of power. *Summer Folk,* with its satire on complacent and futile intellectuals, was sufficiently caustic to evoke hisses from some of the spectators when Gorky came out to receive the applause at the final curtain. They resented especially one character's indictment of them "You are simply summer visitors in your own country." (Needless to say, Gorky, who never gave quarter, hissed back vigorously.) *Children of the Sun* made a trenchant reference to the massacre of the people in 1905 through the heroine Lisa who saw the blood on the street and was unnerved forever. *Enemies* is a relentless strike play in which the presence of a normally sympathetic factory owner does not alleviate the rigors of the struggle when capital and labor lock horns. The workers are led off to prison and death after his harsh partner has been killed. "Master" and "man"— between the two there is a chasm, and according to this play all the conflict arises from this relation. *The Judge* (1918), in which one ex-convict presumes to judge another and drives him to suicide, attacks the custom of setting oneself up as a judge over one's neighbor without realizing one's own abasement. These plays rise above the level of most Russian plays of the period; they merely lack dramatic distinction.

But the revolution fanned his dramatic fire once more before he died or was allegedly murdered by an anti-Stalinite physician who treated him for pneumonia.[5] He began a trilogy on the decay of the Russian bourgeoisie, completing the two parts *Yegor Bulychov and Others* and *Dostigaev and Others* in 1932 and 1933 respectively. The latter, a picture of post-revolutionary times during which the middle class was trying to regain its foothold in the national economy, is more effective as a historical document than as a drama, although it is notable for its humor. *Yegor Bulychov*, however, is a stark near-masterpiece, a tragedy of the inner failure of the merchant class. Although its representative and symbol Yegor has acquired wealth, he is alone and futile. He is dying of cancer and the humanity that surrounds him is even more corrupted than his body. The priest has been mulcting him for years and is only waiting for a legacy; Yegor's sister-in-law, the abbess, is another harpy who quarrels with the priest in the hope of getting money for her order; his daughters are quarrelsome and contemptible and his son-in-law is a cheap intriguer. Ignorance and superstition permeate the background. To cure Yegor or alleviate his sufferings the crassly ignorant Bulychovs resort to a female charlatan, a faith healer, and later to a trombone player who is supposed to blow the noxious air out of his system. Only his illegitimate daughter Shura loves him and is not tainted by sordid greed.

Yegor, who amassed wealth by riding rough-shod over people and yet commands a certain respect for his strength, dies bitterly disillusioned. He is magnificent when he sees through other people's hypocrisies and stupidity. Moreover, trying to be just to his character, Gorky presented him as a product of a predatory society—"man does not thieve; the ruble thieves, money is the arch thief." Significantly, Yegor dies while the masses are gathering for the last assault on the old order in which he flourished. As the singing in the street comes nearer, Shura, who is alone with him, goes to the window. She waves to the demonstrators, and the last flicker of Yegor's consciousness hears in that music "the burial service—singing me out of the world." This play is a triumph of both symbolism and characterization, of both generalization and dramatic individualization. Here Gorky conveys a historic event in terms of well-realized and, in the case of Yegor and Shura, powerfully drawn characters. Without inflammatory rhetoric and without didactic comment he makes his meaning clear in terms of a human tragedy as vivid as Tolstoy's famous story *The Death of Ivan Ilytch.*

2 DRAMATISTS OF REVOLUTION AND RECONSTRUCTION

Gorky, who watched over the younger Soviet playwrights like an eagle, did not live to find any eaglets among them. Despite much official encouragement, the first two decades of the Soviet era were not conducive to the leisurely development of dramatic genius. Playwrights were subjected to shifting party programs and some of them were no doubt fearful lest their work be construed as inimical to the aims of the Soviet. They were also understandably eager to serve the immediate needs of a nation of one hundred and sixty million people in the throes of building an industrial nation on the shambles of old war-destroyed Russia. Many of them therefore devoted themselves to literal utilitarian drama. They inculcated the virtues of collective work and efficiency, or they dramatized immediate problems of adjustment which possess a topical and practical interest for the most part. These plays, and there have been scores of them, are not necessarily devoid of some dramatic effectiveness. But they are mainly interesting only as fragments of social history.

Among them may be mentioned Nikolai Pogodin's *Tempo,* which describes the transformation of shiftless and inefficient peasants into intelligent and responsible industrial workers. Another example is Vladimir Kirshon's *Bread,* a description of the Soviet's efforts to collectivize the farms. Plays of this type generally fail to illuminate human personality beyond a certain obvious descriptiveness, and they divide characters into black and white sheep much too arbitrarily. However, even in this highly utilitarian department of the Soviet drama there has been one unexpected exception, Pogodin's play *Aristocrats.* A striking picture of the re-education of prisoners on the Baltic-White Sea Canal project, it is not only a provocative study of criminology but a richly humane document. The carefully developed reformation of the prostitute Sonia and the bandit Kostya adds credibility, as well as pathos and humor, to the drama. In this account of the completion of the famous canal by criminals and "ex-wreckers" Soviet Russia was obviously putting its best foot forward, but the idealism of the author's case report is exemplary for any nation. Moreover, Pogodin personalized this story, and if the solution seems too pat for general application it may well be valid for the author's selected characters.

The play, moreover, is an interesting reflection of a basic hypothesis of Marxist philosophy that links it with the optimism of the eighteenth-century rationalists. The generation of Voltaire, Diderot and Condorcet affirmed the perfectibility of man; it saw infinite possibilities in that perverse biped and believed that these could be realized by the application of reason to education and society. Marxism, which is the child of eighteenth-century rationalism, revived faith in this premise. All that is necessary to reclaim the individual is a confluence of favorable social conditions, and *Aristocrats* postulates their existence in contemporary Russia. The point may be debatable, but there is a noble aspiration in Pogodin's play.

Considerable interest also attaches to studies of adjustment to the Soviet regime. Sometimes the problem revolves around loyal communists who are bedeviled by personal problems. In Anatole Glebov's *Inga* a woman who becomes the manager of a factory is beset by emotional conflicts when she falls in love with a married man and encounters his wife's jealousy. The assistant director, who resents the fact that his superior is a woman, harasses and humiliates Inga, and she is further troubled by the fact that her emotional difficulties impair her usefulness. In a manner which seems too facile owing to the author's desire to convey a lesson, the sage chairman of the factory committee prevails upon the jealous wife, who nearly commits suicide, to start a new life. But still the personal equation is unsolved, for Inga finds her lover Dmitri jealously interfering in her work and lessening her authority. The personal problem is becoming a social one and must be solved for the greater good; Inga, again with somewhat questionable credibility, therefore separates from Dmitri.

This problem of "credibility" is, of course, less simple than we care to think. Identical behavior may be less credible in one social *milieu* and more credible in another, since we are products of conditioning. Properly conditioned in a world in which everyone emphasizes social utility, Inga might conceivably separate from Dmitri. The mote may, therefore, be in our eye and not in the author's although this may still reduce the effectiveness of the play for us so long as we are differently conditioned. And it is to the playwright's credit that he represents Inga's personal conflicts and the envy of her assistant instead of describing both characters as shining examples from the beginning. A similar qualification pertains to the question of topicality. Regarded in the light of faith in a happy collective world which the characters are allegedly building the topical details of many Soviet plays have a larger or more universal point of reference. Only insofar as we rightly or wrongly reject the hypothesis that collectivism is desirable does the topical aspect of the plays remain merely local and topical. However, even if these concessions are granted, works like *Inga* lack the depth of characterization and feeling and the overtones that persist in the unmistakably distinguished dramas of the world.

More personal are the complications of Kirshon's and Ouspensky's *Rust*, produced in Russia in 1926 and later by the New York Theatre Guild under the title of *Red Rust*. Here representative young people are trying to adjust themselves to the new life and to contribute to it. Particularly difficult is their encounter with the primal urge. Interpreting the early sexual code of the Soviets more liberally than is feasible, they fall into many errors, and the revolutionary libertine Terekhin takes advantage of the new freedom to gratify his lust and egotism. Terekhin's wife Nina, however, places a more exalted construction upon love and marriage and is attacked as a hopeless bourgeois. Only Fedor, who is in love with Nina, insists that the abolition of the old code is intended to promote a nobler love relation rather than to sanction a reversion to animality. At the conclusion of a scene in which she is humiliated by Terekhin she runs out of the room and allegedly commits suicide. Thereupon he is tried by his circle and expelled from the party for libertinism, and later, he is also exposed as Nina's murderer. *Red Rust* is an interesting and colorful picture of a transitional period, but it is a discursive and melodramatic play.

More successful is a farce like Valentine Katayev's *Squaring the Circle*. Too thin to rank high, it is nevertheless not only amusing but rather penetrative. Two couples marry simultaneously and try to share a single room owing to the congested condition of Soviet cities. The intellectual worker Vasya marries the wholly feminine Ludmilla who has a passion for prettifying her nest and likes to prepare good food. Conversely, the light-minded Abram acquires the intellectual Tonya who cares more for the communist cause than for the household amenities. After an inevitable accumulation of irritations, therefore, the men exchange partners. Considerable humor arises from the fact that most of these young people are so earnestly trying to remain good communists, and practical wisdom wins the day when an older party leader assures them that their private peccadilloes "won't hurt the revolution." "It won't hurt the revolution" is in fact the *leitmotif* of gay reason and tolerance that pervades this piece, which is perhaps the most pleasantly humane of the Soviet plays. Katayev's *Last of the Equipajevs*, a genial exposure of an inveterate bourgeois, is written in the same spirit.

A deeper note was struck when the Soviet playwrights began to dramatize the relation of the pre-revolutionary intelligentsia to the new social order. Yuri Olesha's melodramatic *List of Advantages*, written in 1931, revolves around the experiences of a rebellious actress who flees to Paris but is converted when she becomes disgusted with the machinations of the Russian emigrés and is disillusioned with Western Europe. Although the play has been highly touted, it is a shoddy piece of dramaturgy; it is most satisfactorily written when its author confines himself to exposition in pictures of an artist's life in the Soviet and of the behavior of expatriated "white Russians." An earlier play, Alexis Faiko's *Man with the Portfolio,* describes the counter-revolutionary behavior of a scientist whose father had been a general under the old system. Escaping detection, the former saboteur or "wrecker" Gratanov achieves a position of prominence in the Soviets until the esteem with which he is regarded by his students and the realization that he can find new roots in his country produce a change of heart. But his past tracks him down when he meets a former associate who may incriminate him, and in his desperation he throws the man off a moving train. Hardly, however, has he freed himself from this incubus than his aristocratic wife, who had fled from the country, returns. He sends her away and conceals his anxiety by pretending to be even more fanatical than genuine communists. Finally, after having driven his wife to commit suicide and having caused his old professor to die of heart failure by accusing him of political heresy, Granatov is exposed as a murderer. He makes a public confession and then shoots himself. Although the tragedy of a man who is caught in the net of his past possesses considerable pathos the play cannot be exempted from the charge of contrivance and melodrama. *The Man with the Portfolio* is at its best when it provides a simple analysis of anxiety.

A related work, Alexander Afinogenyev's *Fear,* is for the most part a work of greater integrity both as art and social history. It is largely free from melodrama, and it treats the intellectual's maladjustment with understanding when it criticizes the intolerance and suspicion to which he is exposed. Anxiety, in other words, is perfectly comprehensible when society insists on too much conformity and when heresy is suspected everywhere, as is too often the case in periods of extreme tension. An unconverted and irritable psychologist contends that fear has become a conditioned reflex in Russia. However, although his irritations are not presented as without foundation, he is finally proved wrong, and his ultimate conversion, in a didactic and facile conclusion, pours oil on the troubled waters.

Still, there is enough criticism in the play to create an impression that contradicts the solution. Its author, in fact, appears to have had serious differences with the ruling powers. Whether he was simply too outspoken or whether he actually engaged in conspiratorial work, as was charged, Afinogenyev fell afoul of the government in 1938 or 1939.[6] This is regrettable since his later play *Dalekoe* or *Distant Point* was a beautiful, if static, character study of a Far-Eastern general *en route* to Western Russia who stops at a remote Siberian community and gives it a touching lesson in unselfish behavior.

Another group of Soviet plays has reflected the struggles and ardors of the revolution and of the civil war that followed it. Some of the early works like the polyphonic poet Mayakovsky's *Mystery-Bouffe,* in which revolution floods the whole world, and Alexei Tolstoy's *Aelita,* in which it reaches Mars (!), were puerile. They are now apparently dated even in Russia. Other dramatists, however, substituted history for fantasy with better results. These works, among which Michael Bulgakov's *Days of the Turbins,* Leo Slavin's *Intervention,* Vsevolod Ivanov's *Armored Train,* and Sergei Tretyakov's *Roar China* are the most familiar to us, are—with the exception of Bulgakov's drama—simple plays. Their psychology is elementary, their plots melodramatic, and their viewpoint intensely partisan. Nevertheless, they all capture the excitement of the Soviet's first critical years and they are frequently vivid and impassioned.

The exception, *The Last of the Turbins,* describes the Civil War when the Ukraine was the battlefield of "white guard" (Tsarist) forces, bandit generals, German armies, and communists. Here, however, the emphasis is on the personal conflicts and problems of a group of Russian aristocrats who find the reins slipping from their hands. They are not villains but confused and troubled human beings with an ache in their hearts. They are characters such as Chekhov might have drawn; the difference between Bulgakov's play and Chekhov's masterpiece resides chiefly in the altered circumstances—the aristocrats are summarily blasted out of their cherry orchard. By virtue of its delicacy and insight *The Last of the Turbins* became the best Soviet play to date. This touching tragedy (adapted for England by Rodney Ackland) could have made a strong impression in America were it not that its reference to the contending forces in the Ukraine is too snarled for anyone who is unfamiliar with Soviet history.

By comparison with its symphonic qualities the other plays are Sousa marches, stirring but obvious.* *Intervention* tells the story of Anglo-French intervention in Odessa during the Russian revolution. Its high point is the desertion of several Allied soldiers who ascend the towering steps of the quay to join the Bolsheviks. *Armored Train* is a revo-

---

* It is not surprising that *The Last of the Turbins* should have had a checkered history in Russia. Its sympathetic treatment of the aristocracy at a time when the revolutionary spirit would concede no virtues to the liquidated upper classes was regarded with suspicion, and the play was suppressed for a long period, until its matter was no longer considered prejudicial to Soviet ideology. The most gifted of the new playwrights, Bulgakov had the least talent or inclination to regulate his writing, with the result that several of his other plays have been suppressed. Nevertheless, this did not prevent him from scoring a signal success with his dramatization of *Dead Souls,* one of the triumphs of the Moscow Art Theatre.

lutionary melodrama of the Far East culminating in the capture of a
military train owing to the self-sacrifice of a Soviet hero. The best of
these elementary pieces, *Roar China,* presents an encounter between
Chinese coolies and foreign imperialists with thumping effect. Written
in the heat of conviction with intense pity and anger, this anti-imperialist blast may be said to transcend the limitations of political melodrama,
but even *Roar China* remains essentially external drama.

To become enthusiastic about the Soviet drama is to substitute wishful thinking for criticism, a charge that applies to some apologists although it cannot be leveled against its most informed friend Professor
H. W. L. Dana. The plays have been too didactic in many instances,
too heavy-handed, and too unilateral. The Soviet playwright has certainly not spoken out with the creative abandon of great dramatists. He
has not soared sufficiently, nor has he conveyed the rich inner life of
man; there has been altogether too much elementary extroversion in his
playwriting. Contrary to the general assumption, the limitations of Soviet drama have not, however, been purely the result of state control,
although this did not make life easy for Bulgakov, Afinogenyev and
others. The frequent shift in party programs alone would have precluded
the triumph of a completely rigid formula for playwrights. Moreover,
state absolutism has by itself never prevented the flowering of the drama.
Racine and Molière lived under the absolute monarchy of Louis XIV;
obviously, too, Shakespeare did not live under a democracy, and we
know of cases where playwrights and actors were censored and punished
by the Elizabethan authorities. An important deterrent in Russia has
been the playwrights' understandable immersion in immediate problems
like the five-year plan; another has been a philosophy of art that stresses
direct utility. Besides, there may also have been an undersecretion of
talent in the practitioners of Russian drama between 1905 and the present period. If a man of Gorky's stamp could find some genuine satisfaction in Soviet drama it is because much of it was so earnestly concerned
with social welfare.

However, Gorky or any observer could have few reservations concerning the Soviet theatre. It is even possible that a reason for the Soviet
playwrights' defective or scrappy dramaturgy has been the fact that
they have relied too heavily on the frequently brilliant collaboration of
the theatre arts in that country. Two examples come to mind: whereas
the productions of *Anna Karenina* and *The Human Comedy* have been
generally acclaimed as remarkable, an examination of the texts discloses
nothing to warrant such enthusiasm. The reservations would mostly refer
to the early and more experimental examples of futurist or constructivist
stagecraft and to related excesses produced by a combination of youthful exuberance, contempt for bourgeois achievements, and artiness or

sensationalism inherited from the pre-revolutionary symbolist decade. Most of these excesses were later eradicated, and even that theatrical genius Meyerhold ultimately suffered severe reproof and demotion for overreaching himself. And a sign of returning sanity appeared early when the Moscow Art Theatre came back into favor.

No other country in our epoch gave the stage so much scope. In 1938 there were theatres in thirty-one languages throughout Soviet Russia,[7] one thousand regular theatres and five thousand theatres run by collective farms, workers' clubs and factories, in addition to smaller and more special enterprises. In 1936 or 1937 Russia had 22,500 regularly employed actors.[8] The theatres, moreover, were at once opened to the Soviet's millions and were avidly patronized by them. In addition to native plays, the classics from every language were regularly performed on the Soviet stage, and taste in foreign drama appeared extremely catholic —more so, surprisingly, than perhaps in any other country. The one fly in the ointment is the fact that many of these plays had been more or less adapted to Soviet requirements—not so cardinal a sin as it may appear, however, since many older plays require at least some adaptation. Moreover, less tinkering with them became countenanced in Russia after the passing of Meyerhold's supremacy. Furthermore, nowhere in our century has the theatre been so replete with color and vivacity; for every serious production there have been numerous folk-pieces, festive, splashed with oriental color and choreographic. And nowhere were the theatrical arts practised with such daring and vigorous creativity as in the nineteen-twenties.

The Moscow Art Theatre, renamed The Gorky, has continued to function in its time-honored fashion. It weathered the difficult first years of the Soviets when it was dismissed as "bourgeois" and later its prestige remained unimpaired. But it shared honors with other theatres which favored other new technical and interpretive principles. Although many of the experimentalists began their innovations before 1918 under the blue flower of symbolism, they flourished and came to fruition under the red poppy of Sovietism. Evreinov moved from a theatre of "illusionism" to a theatre of mass spectacle, staging the celebrated pageant of the storming of the Winter Palace in 1920. Vsevolod Meyerhold, who left Stanislavsky's company many years before the revolution to direct for the celebrated actress Kommisarjevskaya, became a master of the art of rehabilitating older plays and giving them fresh and contemporary interpretations. In this field he displayed a rare comic and satiric gift and an unmistakable talent for creative theatricality. First he ran riot with "constructivism," adopting the sensational, frequently puerile use of bare scaffoldings recalling the skeletons of skyscrapers and factories as acting areas; then he employed a "static" style of symbolization effected by conventionalized postures. In contrast to Stanislavsky's principle of making the actor pre-eminent and leading him to create the inner reality of a role, Meyerhold used the actor as a puppet to convey the play's idea and viewpoint. His technique was particularly suited to the requirements of older plays which had to be given contemporary or topical significance and of purposeful new plays in which the immediate message was primary.

Alexander Tairov, the director of the Kamerny Theatre which he founded in 1914, also made the theatre "theatrical" instead of trying to reproduce reality. His method was at first primarily "esthetic" and favored formalism. In his later modified realistic style he retained stylization up to a point, and achieved it with the aid of actors from whom he demanded the abilities of a dancer, singer, and acrobat. Tairov, however, was overshadowed by the genius of Eugene Vakhtangov. Dead at an early age in 1923, Vakhtangov has remained a living memory and an invaluable example to Soviet directors. His practice of "controlled spontaneity," decorativeness, and illuminating fantasy was not only theatrically beautiful but notably interpretive and creative; his production of *Princess Turandot* was acclaimed as one of the loveliest creations of the twentieth-century stage.

Regarding his approach he wrote, "Stanislavsky could find harmony only in the moods of the society of his day. Not everything of the times is eternal, but the eternal is always of the times. Meyerhold cannot feel tomorrow; he can feel only today. But one should be able to feel today in tomorrow and tomorrow in today." [9] It is because he strove to make this principle prevail, and because he exercised his imagination freely without hardening into formalism or abiding by one inflexible style that the few productions Vakhtangov lived to direct are listed among the greatest triumphs of the Soviet theatre. His influence, next to Stanislavsky's, has been the most consistently fruitful. The theatre which is named in his honor gave masterly productions such as *Yegor Bulychov* and *Intervention*. The great artistry of the Habima Theatre, which staged the famous *Dybbuk* in the Hebrew language, was also directed by Vakhtangov for a time, and owes its reputation to his methods.*

But the work of these and other directors, as well as of brilliant scenic designers like I. Rabinovich, cannot be conveyed by a cursory and theoretical summary. Only detailed descriptions like Norris Houghton's *Moscow Rehearsals* can outline the protean shapes of the Soviet theatre, and of course only intimate firsthand knowledge can arrive at a sound evaluation of its individual accomplishments. No doubt such criticism would reveal shortcomings and strayings that eluded present

---

* See appendix for comment on the Jewish and Polish theatre and drama.

enthusiasts from abroad, and the Russians themselves can be sharply critical of their theatre. But the Soviet stage was a stupendous phenomenon for two decades.

Periods when the theatre outdistances the drama have been frequent indeed. And the Soviet republics provided the twentieth century with the greatest example of a communal theatre since medieval times when the culture of Western Europe was federated by the Universal Church. Perhaps when—and if—the strains and stresses of the present age disappear or are reduced, and when a greater freedom from utilitarian demands and conformity prevails, the Russian drama will rise to new heights. Certainly it would be a regrettable expense of spirit if this theatre failed to discover a drama worthy of its immense resources.

XXVII

JOHN MILLINGTON SYNGE AND THE IRISH MUSE

THE THEATRE being generically a democratic institution, it is seldom that dramatic history is made in one man's brain, especially when that man is not himself a major dramatist. Ireland being "different" (so its sons believe), *two* historic moments emerged from the parturient mind of William Butler Yeats, poet, incipient dramatist, and man of affairs. It occurred to him in 1899 that Ireland ought to have a national theatre, and the Irish Literary Theatre was born. In the same year, while staying at a students' rooming house in the Latin Quarter of Paris, it occurred to him that a frail young Irishman was a genius who needed only to be unfolded. The bud in question was John Millington Synge. Born in County Dublin in 1871, graduated from its university and like so many Irishmen quickly expatriated, he had been earning a modest living by fiddling in an orchestra and writing reviews on French literature for English and French publications. "You will never create anything by reading Racine, and Arthur Symons will always be a better critic of French literature," Yeats told him. He urged him to go to the Aran Islands in the extreme Western part of both Ireland and Europe, to live among the most Irish of the Irish people, and to "express a life that has never found expression." Synge heeded him and headed for these barren islands "where men reap with knives because of the stones," but where he reaped so abundantly.

It is not mere chronology that places Synge and his fellow-playwrights in the immediate proximity of Chekhov and Gorky. In Russia at the extreme East and Ireland at the extreme West the drama became an instrument of national resurgence. Both countries felt the rumblings of discontent and experienced successive explosions; widespread poverty and impotence, conspiracies, assassinations, terror from the "left" and the "right," and revolutions checkered the life of both peoples. Both the Russian and the Irish dramatists came close to the common man, and parallels may be found in their respective pictures of frustrated and dreamy country gentlemen, restless commoners who are or become vagrants, and embattled proletarians. St. John Ervine, who speaks from experience, has declared, for example, that "Few Irishmen have any difficulty in perceiving the point of Chekhovian plays; they have only to look around them to see it sticking out yards and yards." [1] Finally, each country produced a superlative dramatist—Chekhov and Synge respectively—who remained an objective artist and yet transfigured realism until it became a commingling of reality and poetry.

I WILLIAM BUTLER YEATS AND LADY GREGORY: "THE CELTIC RENAISSANCE"

That the nation which gave the English theatre Farquhar, Goldsmith, Sheridan, Wilde and Shaw should not have developed a national drama before the closing years of the past century is a telling symptom of the depressed condition of this long-suffering country. The beginnings of the drama were undoubtedly present in early druidic worship, and the "mystery plays" appeared in Dublin during the Middle Ages. They did not, however, find strong roots in Ireland because they were "foreign importations." The Church was never friendly to the theatre, and both the bards of the upper class and the "shanachies" or story-tellers of the masses contented themselves with mere recitation. The trade guilds under which the medieval drama normally flourished lacked an adequate economic basis in Ireland and moreover became Protestant during the reign of Henry VIII. Later, the secular theatre developed only under Protestant and English control and patronage, and both the Catholic Church and the patriots remained aloof from it. The only imported plays that commanded a large interest came from the pen of the American-Irish Dion Boucicault whose romantic and high-flown melodramas, with their Irish patriots and virtuous heroines, flattered local self-esteem. The low estate of the Irish theatre was paralleled in literature, and no Irishman who had arrived at the age of literary discretion could take pride in his fellow-writers' accomplishments. Owing to poverty, isolationism, and political chaos Ireland had simply skipped the European Renaissance and its sequels.

In the eighties, however, Ireland achieved a Renaissance in the teeth of despair or because of it. Never had there been such high hopes in their hearts as when Parnell was bringing home rule nearer day by day by means of strategic parliamentary action. Parnell's fall from power in consequence of his unfortunate love affair was, therefore, an intolerable blow to the nation. But when despair overwhelmed the land that had lacked sufficient tolerance to divorce his public from his private life, a few courageous citizens felt the necessity of turning the political struggle into a cultural one. The nation was first reminded of its noble, legendary past, by Standish O'Grady's *History of Ireland* (written between 1878 and 1880), and in time such organizations as the Gaelic League, founded in 1893, and the Irish Literary Society arose to teach the people that they were a nation with an independent language. Scholars like Douglas

Hyde reminded them that they had a native medium for literature until even the expatriated George Moore toyed with the idea of writing in Gaelic. It was this movement, which was dignified by Douglas Hyde's *Love Songs of Connacht* and *Religious Songs of Connacht* (in Gaelic and in English translation), that inspired the young poet Yeats. Along with "A.E." (George W. Russell) and lesser writers, he felt the call to mine the rich ore of Irish legend and to shape it into a symbol of national aspiration. Since, moreover, the drama throughout Europe was beginning to pulse with the new blood injected into its veins by Ibsen, by the founders of the art theatres, and by latter-day romantics like Maeterlinck, it was naturally this medium that Yeats and his colleagues favored particularly.

Yeats was in his early thirties (he was born near Dublin in 1865) when he joined the Irish dramatic movement. As became the son of the well-known painter John Butler Yeats, he had oscillated for a time between art and literature. In London he became associated with the luminaries of the mauve nineties, founding the Rhyming Club with William Morris, Henley, Symons and Lionel Johnson, and supporting the Yellow Book. Oscar Wilde, Maeterlinck and Verlaine, whom he visited in 1894, also provided their inspiration to the young litterateur. At first he was not a nationalist; he was not a Catholic but a Church of Ireland man, and his primary allegiance was to art instead of politics. He was an esthete among esthetes, and no one could mistake his vocation who saw him wearing his long black cloak drooping from the shoulders, his soft black sombrero and his voluminous black silk tie. His early work was not Irish in setting or theme; in fact, as a steady adherent to the "art for art's sake" formula he even went so far as to attack Irish patriotic verse.

His conversion to nationalism came in the main through his estheticism. In Ireland he found a largely untapped source of romanticism and a crepuscular vision of remote and intangible beauty. The theatre interested him not as a forum or platform but as a temple for mystic beauty and an auditorium for spoken poetry. Years later his penchant for mysticism was to become an obsession which limited his communicability as a writer, and already he was evincing an interest in spiritualism and Oriental philosophy that brought him close to that greatest mystic of them all "A.E." As for spoken verse, the dream of hearing poems "spoken to a harp" before an audience "for it is not natural to enjoy an art only when one is by oneself," had been with him since boyhood.[2] And here again Ireland, the traditional home of fine speech and recitation, endeared itself to him. Finally, he found in his native country the primitivism he considered essential to poetic emotion. Although the drama thrives in cities, where alone it can find a sufficient audience, he feared that emotion could not thrive there. Only "when the emotions of cities still remember the emotions of sailors and husbandmen and shepherds and users of the spear and the bow" does the drama reach greatness.[3]

He had already written *The Land of Heart's Desire* and had seen it produced by the London Independent Theatre in 1894 when his famous conversations with Lady Gregory occurred. She had had only a casual interest in the theatre up to this time. But married to Sir William Gregory, a political leader and an Irish member of Parliament, this witty and beautiful woman was an ardent, if largely unpolitical, nationalist. In close touch with the peasants of County Galway for the greater part of her life, despite her English descent and Protestant faith, she was attracted to their customs and folklore until she thought and spoke like them. Malicious people put an unpleasant construction upon her traffic with the peasants, calling her a "souper" or proselytizing Protestant. Undeterred by slander, however, this resolute woman continued her visits, collecting folk-tales and aligning herself with Douglas Hyde and the Gaelic League. Therefore when Yeats won her to the cause of an Irish theatre, Lady Gregory quickly became its *sage femme*. It was she who insisted that the theatre be located in Ireland rather than in England and ensured it the support of powerful patrons.

Support also came from her well-to-do neighbor Edward Martyn. One of the most retiring of men, he had nevertheless distinguished himself by active opposition to the recruiting of Irish volunteers for the Boer War and assumed the presidency of the Sinn Fein nationalist party for a brief period. Although a devout Catholic, he had also been one of the first Irishmen to discover and acclaim Ibsen. Attracted to the theatre project by his political interests and by his distaste for materialism, he gave the literary movement the benefit of a rare intelligence. A fourth associate was none other than George Moore, and both his social prominence and his fame as a novelist were tangible assets to the struggling organization.

Martyn differed with Yeats and Lady Gregory on the question of repertory because he favored Ibsen and the continental drama, and his devotion to Catholicism ultimately led to his estrangement from the new theatre. And George Moore, always more English and French than Irish, soon lost his interest in the venture and later affronted his former associates with some caustic recollections of this formative period in *Hail and Farewell*. Fortunately, however, the four champions co-operated long enough under Lady Gregory's guidance to ensure the project some greatly needed financial support, and the Irish Literary Theatre was able to open its doors on May 8, 1899 in the Ancient Concert Rooms of Dublin.

Like all important events in the Irish theatre the premiere received its appropriate baptism of fire when Yeats' play *The Countess Cathleen* was denounced for daring to suggest that an Irishwoman might sell her soul to the devil and that heaven might condone the deed. Only the presence of police prevented unruly members of the audience from avenging the insult to the Faith. Since nothing of importance in Ireland was said to transpire without a riot, and since visiting London reviewers were favorable, the venture could be set down as a success. Next year the theatre brought over an English company to present three plays. There were no riots this time; George Moore's insignificant *The Bending of the Bough* was received without disturbance despite its political allusiveness, and Martyn's fantasy *Maeve* even captivated the audience. The third season, in 1901, saw a collaboration by Moore and Yeats *Diarmuid and Grania* which the authors discreetly left unpublished. But the performance was memorable as the last one to be presented by actors imported from England, and in the same season appeared the first effort to produce Irish plays with Irish casts, the event being Douglas Hyde's *Twisting of the Rope* played in Gaelic by the author in association with a group of Dublin amateurs.

The fourth season proved the most momentous. The brothers Frank and William G. Fay, who had been touring plays with a brilliant small company, had approached "A.E." with the request that he write a play for them. He gave them his *Deirdre* and brought Yeats to a rehearsal, with the result that Yeats gave the group his *Kathleen ni Houlihan*. On April 2, 1902, with P. J. Kelly and Dudley Digges in their ranks, they presented both plays before a wildly enthusiastic audience. Encouraged by their triumph they formed the National Dramatic Society with Yeats as president and concluded the season with four additional productions. In 1903 the company revealed two pieces by Yeats, *The Hour Glass* and *The King's Threshold*, Lady Gregory's *Twenty-Five*, Padraic Colum's *Broken Soil*, and the first of Synge's great one-acters, *In the Shadow of the Glen*. In the same year the actors repeated their success in London when the plays and the unaffected performances captivated the jaded English public. As W. G. Fay later noted in his memoirs *The Fays of the Abbey Theatre*, the year 1903 was truly their *annus mirabilis*. They had begun in dire poverty as "the laughing-stocks of Dublin," yet within six months they were being acclaimed as masters of their art. They revealed Synge to the world, acquired a remarkable actress in Sara Allgood, and found in Miss A. E. F. Horniman the generous patron who soon made the Abbey Theatre possible.

In 1904 the company suffered a severe loss when the Irish section of the St. Louis Exposition invited it to perform in America. A few members accepted the invitation, with the result that P. J. Kelly and Dudley

Digges never returned. Difficulties were also encountered when the Sinn Feiners, led by Arthur Griffith, assailed the group for not presenting patriotic political plays and rioted at the premiere of Synge's one-acter on the grounds that its tale of a woman who leaves home with a tramp maligned Irish womanhood. But if Arthur Griffith proved a devil's advocate in those critical years, Miss Horniman remained its good angel. After having watched the actors at work and helped them considerably by designing and supplying their costumes, she offered to provide and equip a small theatre and run it at her expense for a period of years. An old theatre in Abbey Street was reconstructed at a cost of thirteen thousand pounds and a patent to the Abbey theatre was granted in 1904 over the violent protests of the superpatriots. The latter, who had been routed by Lady Gregory's influence, could comfort themselves only with the fact that the license limited the attractiveness of her little theatre (it seats less than six hundred) by forbidding the sale of spirits. Thus was born the latest of the leading European theatres, a fitting companion to the *Théâtre Libre* of France, the *Freie Bühne* of Germany, the Moscow Art Theatre, and the Independent Theatre of J. T. Grein in London.

Although its stage technique always remained somewhat humdrum, the Abbey triumphed by dint of superbly musical, simple, and singularly honest acting. Despite defections in the ranks when the Fays quarreled with the management, and when the lure of higher salaries in other parts of the English-speaking world proved too attractive, the Abbey has enjoyed a gallant company of artists. Today, for all its technical shortcomings, this company holds a position in the theatre. Moreover, no other twentieth-century theatre has justified itself so richly through its playwrights. In America, the Provincetown Theatre brought forth O'Neill, the Theatre Guild Behrman, the Group Theatre Odets. But the Abbey's honor roll includes Synge, O'Casey, Carroll, as well as a host of respectable practitioners like Lady Gregory, Edward Martyn, Padraic Colum, T. C. Murray, William Boyle, and Lennox Robinson.

2 THE FIRST GALAXY

The first galaxy of Irish playwrights possessed stellar attributes in an almost literal sense: each dramatist possessed a highly personal fire, each radiated a light peculiarly his own, and each moved in a private orbit much of the time. Yet a larger orbit held all their motion in one closely related movement. The same impulse of national awakening bound romanticists and realists together, so that such diverse characters as Yeats, Lady Gregory, Synge, Martyn, and "A.E." grouped themselves naturally around the Irish National Theatre.

Yeats, who began with a private impulse to make the poetry of noble dreams prevail regardless of national origins, realized them most richly when he struck national roots. For his fairy drama *The Land of Heart's Desire* (1894) the Celtic twilight world provided a rich texture of folk-lore; Maire the bride who hearkens to the call of the elfin world "where nobody gets old and godly and grave" expresses a universal longing but is distinctly Irish in her dreamfulness. This poet's dream of high deeds unfettered to the everyday world found an eloquent voice in *The Countess Cathleen* (1892, produced in 1899), the Faust-like poetic drama of a woman's sacrifice of her soul to save the Irish people from starvation and perdition; and the call of the absolute that ultimately led Yeats to Oriental mysticism, received an Irish legendary setting in *The Shadowy Waters* (1900).

National idealism was only a facet of a more abstract idealism for Yeats, but it made him a literary nationalist. In his play *Kathleen ni Houlihan* (1902) the ideal is Ireland. First she appears in the guise of an old woman as the wizened reality. But even her haggard ugliness ex-erts an attraction that Michael Gillane, who is about to marry a young girl in order to assure his parents' security, cannot resist. Fired by her tale of how "strangers in the house" robbed her of her "four beautiful fields" (the four provinces of Ireland), Michael leaves his home to right her wrongs. His sacrifice, moreover, renews her youth, and his brother sees her going down the path with Michael as a young girl—"and she had the walk of a queen." Yeats the Maeterlinckian symbolist found Yeats the patriot when he sought roots for his poetry, and *Kathleen ni Houlihan* became the noblest patriotic play of Ireland.

Yeats created another spirited Irish tale with *The King's Threshold* in 1903 when he proclaimed his faith in the supremacy of poetry. This doc-trine, so distinctly the credo of the esthetic nineties, is sanctified by the voluntary martyrdom of the poet Seanchan who prefers to starve at King Guaire's threshold rather than take an inferior seat at the royal table. The romantic battle for the "right of poets" would have seemed far more adolescent if Yeats had not linked it with his country's past. Ideal love, another tenuous romantic theme which has produced so many puerilities, found noble expression in his nationalistic *Deirdre,* taken from the treasury of Irish legend which O'Grady, Hyde and Lady Greg-ory had been collecting for the greater glory of Ireland.

After the first flush of the literary movement, however, Yeats be-came an almost dual personality. As a man of affairs he became in-creasingly associated with the practical destinies of his country, and he closed a career that had been originally devoid of all political interest by becoming a senator of the Irish Republic. As a poet and dramatist, at the same time, he returned to the insubstantial and ideal world from which he had been deflected only by the momentum of the Irish movement. He became increasingly the mystic and the only half-communicable dramatist of symbols or abstractions. Significantly, one of his last works, *The Words Upon the Window Pane,* in 1934, affirmed his faith in spiritualism, evoking the astral body of Dean Swift in a biographical one-acter that is far more convincing as character analysis than as spiritualist drama. His last plays confirmed his specialness as a dramatist, and most of them are rarefied even in the narrow compass of the one-act form which he generally employed. The bulk of his work, too, is less memorable for its dramatic power than for the fact that he put better verse into the drama than any writer in English after Shelley and that he was the moving spirit of the Irish theatre.

The movement that he helped to inaugurate followed its own momentum in response to cultural and social pressures which he himself (and that other excellent poet "A.E.") could not heed sufficiently in his dramatic work. Edward Martyn responded to them far better when, in addition to the romantic *Maeve,* he wrote *The Heather-Field* for the first bill of the Irish Literary Theatre in 1899. His symbolism was that of the realistic Ibsen and not of Yeats—that is, it remained free of supernaturalism. The symbol of a man's or Ireland's struggle for a fruitful life was embodied in a realistic tale on which both Ibsen and Chekhov could have collaborated. Carden Tyrrell, a landlord of west Ireland, is obsessed with his project of reclaiming a wind-swept heather field into pasture land until it becomes an all-consuming ideal for him. Into this futile endeavor he puts all the passion and longing that Chekhov's "sisters" put into their longing for Moscow. In order to drain the swamps and remove the barren rocks he mortgages his estate and is ever ready to make further sacrifices when the soil resists him. To prevent him from mortgaging his remaining possessions his wife finally tries to have him declared incompetent. But she is foiled by a friend who fears that this will drive Tyrrell truly insane, and the obsessed man pursues his plan so persistently that he alienates his tenants until he is in danger of being shot down by them. Compelled to remain within doors for fear of them, he becomes so increasingly strained that his mind gives way completely when his little son brings him a handful of heather buds from the field which has refused to renounce its primeval wildness. He dies in an ecstasy of faith in the beauty of the world and in his own power to master it.

With *The Heather-Field,* unfortunately, Martyn shot his bolt. His later plays were inferior, he lacked a true dramatist's stamina, and he failed to match his thought with sufficiently powerful dialogue. *Maeve,* the most popular of his works, was least representative of his aim to create a thoughtful, intellectual drama in the Ibsen manner. Although

Martyn called *Maeve* a psychological drama, there is nothing but national romanticism in its attenuated story of a girl who climbs the mountains, identifies herself there with a legendary heroine on the eve of her marriage to a rich Englishman, and dies ecstatically. If, according to Yeats, the play symbolizes "Ireland's choice between English materialism and her own natural idealism," it still remains a romantic conception which fell short of Martyn's professed Ibsenism. In *A Tale of the Town* he came closer to his aims by presenting the problem of a political leader, Jasper Dean, who is torn between the rival claims of his Irish following and of a fiancée whose uncle is the mayor of the English town which Dean is opposing. But even here Martyn lacked the power and subtlety that alone could sustain a problem play and his later work proved even more feeble.

Martyn's championship of the continental drama of ideas conflicted with the insular aims of the Irish revival, and except for George Moore's social play *The Strike at Arlingford* it was only later that the drama of Ireland adopted a continental outlook. Still it was Martyn rather than Yeats who won the ultimate victory. His recognition of the fact that the Irish drama could not afford to remain a conglomeration of Yeatsian pixies and primordial heroes was eminently sound, even if it remained for abler dramatists to justify him.

The most ponderable reality in Martyn's Ireland was the agricultural character of Irish life. Even Yeats, who had envisaged a theatre for the select few, later conceded that the Abbey became a "folk theatre, a playhouse of the people." [4] It became that because a truly national movement could not ignore the masses, and its playwrights turned increasingly to the peasant drama because the peasantry was then the masses. Without entirely renouncing the afflatus of romanticism or ever dispensing with the Irish gift for humor, moreover, this drama became inevitably realistic. Sometimes almost naturalistic in background, realistic in characterization, and indeterminately romantic in spirit, the Irish peasant stage became a unique department of the European realistic theatre. Yeats, who had hoped to transplant Maeterlinck to Ireland, soon discovered that his theatre had transferred its allegiance to commonplace material—though without leaving it commonplace.

It was his closest associate and the co-founder of the Abbey, Lady Gregory, who betrayed him thus without any deliberateness on her part. Lady Gregory had begun her literary career in the romantic tradition when she made her famous collections of folklore. But when she found the national theatre deficient in comedy and resolved to supply the need, she turned naturally to the peasantry she knew so well. Adopting the language of her people instead of the formal, poetic dialogue of Yeats, she wrote those folk comedies which constitute her claim to eminence as a dramatist. They opened the rich vein of peasant drama which quickly became the chief glory of the first phase of the Irish theatre. Henceforth great Yeatsian verse like

> *The years like great black oxen tread the world,*
> *And God the herdsman goads them on behind,*
> *And I am broken by their passing feet* [5]

was to be heard less and less in the Abbey. But against this loss must be set many gains. Henceforth the drama was to lose itself less and less in abstractions. It acquired the flavor of the rich colloquial speech of Ireland, characters who were flesh rather than transcendental shadow, and situations more relevant to modern life than the heroics of any number of Cuchulains.

Lady Gregory created, in the main, slender but delightful farces. The first of them, *Spreading the News,* squeezes humor out of the stale lime of gossip. A slightly deaf market woman misunderstands a statement to the effect that Bartley Fallon is bringing a hayfork to Jack Smith. She spreads the news that the former is following his neighbor with a hayfork with murderous intent, and before long everyone has Jack Smith dead in consequence of a love triangle. The avalanche of misstatements rolls merrily on and no one can foretell what the upshot will be. In *Hyacinth Halvey* a young man, who comes to town with a host of indirectly acquired recommendations and is about to be shanghaied into all kinds of wearisome obligations because of them, strives desperately to prove that he is not a paragon of virtue. But he succeeds only in confirming the town's uncomfortably high regard for him, such being the power of reputation and circumstance. When he lifts a sheep from a butcher's counter, he earns the latter's undying gratitude because he has just saved him from arrest for selling diseased meat. When the lad robs the poor box and proclaims himself the culprit he is complimented upon taking the blame for another's crime upon himself. Nothing poor Hyacinth does can destroy the reputation that has been foisted upon him.

From such contrived little farces, so shrewd and vivid and yet so superficial, Lady Gregory, however, moved to the high estate of comedy with one short masterpiece. In *The Workhouse Ward,* written in 1907, her preoccupation with common folk produced two remarkably vivid and charming characters. The two old paupers Mike McInnerney and Michael Miskill are so attached to each other by their pungent life-long quarreling that they cannot bear to separate. When Mike's widowed sister comes to fetch him to her farm, he tries to take his companion along, and failing to prevail upon her with his highly ingenious arguments he chooses to remain in the workhouse. She leaves, and the cronies resume their quarreling.

In satire Lady Gregory revealed an incisive talent and in her three-act comedy *The Image* in 1909 she achieved a critique of Irish character that goes far beyond the scope of genre painting. Here villagers on the West coast are so busy arguing about what they will do with the oil of two whales that have been washed ashore that they lose both of them. The exposé of Irish impracticality is shrewd and vivid, even if it is too thin for a full-length comedy. *The Canavans* is a cutting exposure of political opportunism, and only the bitterness of her attack on Parnell's enemies weakens her third satire, *The Deliverer*.

Lady Gregory also gave expression to the national struggle of the people from whom she was separated by religion and English affiliations. Many of her patriotic pieces were melodramatic or pedestrian, and even the well-known *Rising of the Moon,* in which a police sergeant connives in the escape of a revolutionist who has moved his spirit, is a very modest accomplishment; the sergeant's conversion is an affair of sentiment rather than a result of characterization, although the effect is tense and poetic. But for once, when her patriotism found roots in peasant life, Lady Gregory created a second short masterpiece, *The Gaol Gate.* The play conveys a tragedy through its effect upon the old mother Mary Cabel and her daughter-in-law who visit an Irish lad in prison expecting to find him safe because he was reported to have betrayed his comrades. They learn that he was hanged because he refused to inform against his people. The emotions of the women who alternate at first between satisfaction that he is safe and regret that he proved a traitor are depicted with magnificent realism. Their triumph over their grief when they learn that "Denis Cabel died for his neighbor" brings the play to a poignant and noble conclusion.

Irish peasant realism found its first effective realization in the work of Lady Gregory, and her best plays, however slight, are exquisite. There has been much praise for her full-length legendary tragedy, *Grania,* and there is indeed much beauty in this story of the energetic Grania, who rejects the legendary hero Finn for his youthful follower who dies in battle to prove his love for her. Still, the interest of *Grania* remains relatively remote and Lady Gregory never wrote anything more representative of the deep sympathies and abounding energy of a long life that ended in 1932 than her folk pieces.[6]

Her example assured the triumph of peasant drama and was followed by a number of younger writers. When George Fitzmaurice was not writing merely pleasant folk fantasy like *The Dandy Dolls,* he could create amusing realism like *The Country Dressmaker,* a comedy of a pathetic silly woman who feeds on cheap romances, as well as fine tragedy like the one-acter *The Pie-Dish,* the story of a peasant artist who devotes his whole life to making a wonderful pie-dish which he is unable to complete. And Padraic Colum proved himself a powerful play-wright before migrating to America. He was only twenty-two when the national theatre produced his *Broken Soil* in 1903, later revised and re-named *The Fiddler's House*. This affecting play revolves around the restlessness of a natural-born fiddler and wanderer. His elder daughter strives in vain to keep him tethered to his farm, but realizing the useless-ness of the struggle she lets him go and sacrifices her personal happiness in order to be able to watch over him. Colum's bitter comedy *The Land* describes the conflict between the older generation which clings to its little strips of land and the children who are attracted to the great world beyond. *Thomas Muskerry,* produced by the Abbey in 1910, however, revealed a falling off in power; its story of Muskerry's deterioration until he dies a pauper in the workhouse which he had once supervised was replete with drab pathos but proved too static. Colum withdrew from the Abbey in protest against *The Playboy of the Western World*. He re-joined the National Theatre later, but without bringing his great promise to fruition and devoted himself to the composition of children's books in America. In a lighter vein, William Boyle revealed a fine talent for homely humor in *The Building Fund,* a picture of grasping farmers out-witted by a dying old woman who is their match in every respect. A year later, in 1906, he drew sharp portraits of farmers in *The Mine Workers,* and then extended, but also cheapened, his realism with a satire on a shifty local politician *The Eloquent Dempsey*. Thereafter his work be-came paltry enough to classify him with purveyors of minor entertain-ment who have been as numerous in Ireland as elsewhere.

3 THE GENIUS OF SYNGE

It was Synge who held most of the elements of the dramatic Renais-sance in one sparkling solution. His genius was unique not because it was different from anything else produced by his contemporaries but because he alone fused their attributes into something rare and perfect. Like the romanticist Yeats he recognized the importance of instilling poetry into the modern drama which realism was threatening to make flat and pallid, but like a true realist he shaped his poetry out of col-loquial speech. He adopted Celtic romanticism, but he invigorated it with reality and he spiced it with humor, and even his treatment of the remote Deirdre legend is always close to psychological truth and never abstruse. The folk comedy of Lady Gregory became in his hands some-thing just as real and yet more poetic. The restlessness that Colum dis-covered in Irish life and the sordidness that Boyle found in it were like-wise conveyed in Synge's plays but in a manner that transformed both elements into rare delicacy and beauty. Even Irish fantasy became something profoundly original when Synge wrote *The Well of Saints* with bitter mockery of reality and man's efforts to circumvent and deny it.

His manifold genius, so native in its volatility, was the product of normally conflicting talents or interests. Synge, we know, had no respect for Ibsen the realist and Zola the naturalist, and he was grateful for Ireland where one could find "for a few years more . . . a popular imagination that is fiery and magnificent, and tender." And throughout his work (except possibly in *The Tinker's Wedding*) he strove to make that imagination prevail. Nevertheless, this was the same man who in the same apologia spoke for realism when he deplored the literature of the towns because it was "so far away from the profound and common interests of life." In the same breath, Synge also prided himself on his realistic dialogue; "I have used," he wrote in the preface to *The Playboy of the Western World,* "only one or two words that I have not heard among the country people of Ireland, or spoken in my own nursery before I could read the newspapers." An ultra-realist like Hauptmann could not have proclaimed his fidelity to the Silesian dialect of *The Weavers* with such satisfaction as did Synge when he pointed to the phrases he had taken from "herds and fishermen along the coast from Kerry to Mayo, or from beggar-women and ballad-singers near Dublin." No realist could have been more outspoken on the subject of a playwright's affinity to realities than Synge when he stated a few lines further in his preface that "All art is a collaboration," and when he wrote that in the writing of *In the Shadow of the Glen* he got more aid than any learning could have given him from a chink in the floor of the old Wicklow house which enabled him to hear "what was being said by the servant girls in the kitchen." [7]

No professional realist, moreover, could have prepared himself more conscientiously for his task than Synge when he went to the Aran Islands in 1898 and steeped himself in local life for a period of three years. Of prime importance was the local idiom that he absorbed there, for Synge wisely set great store by language and, like Shakespeare and the minor Elizabethans, he owes much of his distinction to his superb dialogue. His quarrel with Zola and Ibsen, according to the preface of *The Playboy,* was basically that they dealt with reality "in joyless and pallid words." *
Here, moreover, he came across the anecdotes and manners which he was later to transcribe, and his close observation of common life is attested by his vivid book *The Aran Islands.*

He was not even remotely a "social playwright," as that term is commonly and superficially understood. Yet this former esthete of the "Left

---

* With respect to Ibsen, it is to be remembered that Synge could have been familiar only with the Victorian Archer's colorless phrases and Prozor's flavorless French translation.

Bank," as chauvinist enemies called him, occupied no ivory tower when
he attained his majority. To dispel this notion it is necessary only to
read his sympathetic and practical account of the economic problems of
the Irish in his excellent report, *In the Congested Districts*.[8] In his plays
he extracted much pungent humor from his vagrants, tinkers, and beggars; yet he was far from oblivious to their less exhilarating realities of
hunger and homelessness. Moreover, the hard and precarious struggle
for existence which is the common man's lot is rarely set forth with such
pity and truthfulness as in *Riders to the Sea;* even if the adversary is
the sea and not a social system or a villainous capitalism, the reality of
work and occupational disaster remains undiminished in this picture.
Synge lacked only the comprehensiveness of a great dramatist of ideas,
and this is his greatest limitation. Instead he remained, superbly, an
ironist and an objective observer of men's peccadilloes, difficulties, and
passions.

A stylist *par excellence,* he laved his work in glorious speech. This he
did without destroying its naturalness and fumbling only in some over-
elaborated sentences that the actors, according to Fay, found too difficult to manage.[9] The distillation of poetry out of common speech was
uniquely his accomplishment among the masters of the modern drama.
Equally a lover of common ways and of uncommon intensities he combined both in one rare synthesis. "On the stage," he wrote, "one must
have reality, and one must have joy." [10] He conveyed both (by "joy"
he no doubt meant exhilaration and exaltation, as well as fun), thereby
creating a *poetry of realism*. And Synge was, as he was himself the first
to realize, singularly fortunate, for in another Western European country he might have had to forego either the "reality" as did Maeterlinck,
or the "joy" as did most of the naturalists. It is true that in Ireland at
the turn of the century the reality of impoverishment, parochialism, and
political stagnation was pressing indeed. But the magnificence of nature,
the fiery abandon of unmechanized life, and the local color of communities long isolated and still in the main unindustrialized were equally
present. He was grateful when he wrote that "those of us [in Ireland]
who wish to write start with a chance that is not given to writers in
places where the springtime of the local life has been forgotten, and the
harvest is a memory only, and the straw has been turned into bricks."
Each of his plays recovers this springtime even when the "reality" recalls a winter that has left permanent ravages and when the "joy" has
intimations of unavoidable autumn.

His first one-acter *In the Shadow of the Glen,* produced in 1903, is a
peasant drama. Already a perfect work of art, it conveys the lonely and
difficult life of peasant women with a few broad, yet delicate, strokes.
Nora Burke's elderly husband, who has apparently long suspected her

restlessness in the narrow sphere of a County Wicklow cottage ("the last cottage at the head of a long glen"), pretends that he is dead in order to catch her in *flagrante delicto*. To a tramp who is sheltered by her she confesses that she had been in love with the deceased Patch Davey, and to make matters worse she goes off in search of a friendly young neighbor Michael Dara to tell him that her husband is dead. During her absence the corpse sits up, demands a drop of whisky because he is "destroyed with the drouth," and complains that he has "a bad wife in the house." When Nora returns with Michael, her husband slips under the covers to watch the proceedings. She confesses that she married Dan Burke as a hard alternative to remaining poor, "for a bit of a farm, and cows on it, and sheep on the back hills." It was not a pleasant marriage, and her only reason for rejecting the businesslike Michael's proposal to her right there and then is her fear that in a little while he will be just as repulsive as her husband "with a shake in your face, and your teeth falling out, and the white hair sticking out round you like an old bush where sheep do be leaping a gap." This insult, coupled with her complaint that he always had "a rough word in mouth, and his chin the way it would take the bark off an oak board" is too much; Dan Burke jumps out of bed and drives her out of doors. Then the suitor Michael, who is afraid of Dan and has no intention of becoming involved in an affair with a married woman, sits down to a glass of whisky with Dan— such being the ironist's view of peasant romance. Synge's Nora goes out into the world with the tramp who alone sympathizes with her and promises to provide her with "half of a dry bed."

The tragic implications of this delightful play are concealed by its fresh humor. But Synge's next one-acter *Riders to the Sea,* staged in 1904, was unrelieved by anything other than the nobility that mankind reveals in suffering and defeat. This tragedy of an Aran mother who has given all but the youngest of her five sons to the sea and now loses him is too uneventful, as well as too well known, to be summarized; for all its descriptiveness and realism, it lives most fully as music and might well be defined as a tone-poem. Nothing happens in Maurya's cottage, very much as in Maeterlinck's "static" one-acters which Synge may have seen on the continent.

There is a note of anguish at the beginning, in Maurya's premonitions born of past experience as she tries anxiously to keep her last son Bartley from the sea. Like other Aran Islanders, he must take the risk, and he will return, he assures her, "in two days, or in three days, or maybe in four days if the wind is bad." But this is not the way on the islands, old Maurya knows, for the sea is merciless and the young men who live by it also die of it. "In the big world," she knows, "the old people do be leaving things after them for their sons and children, but in this place it is the young men do be leaving things behind for them that do be old." A little later the islanders carry in Bartley's body on a plank with a bit of sail on it and the dark music ends with a resonant coda. Sentimentality is out of order among these hard-working people who are too familiar with disasters at sea to be unnerved by another accident. Maurya has boards in readiness for a coffin, and her neighbor complains only because she has forgotten the nails: "It's a great wonder she wouldn't think of the nails, and all the coffins she's seen already." For Maurya, moreover, the disaster ushers in a terrible calm, as she reflects that "They're all gone now, and there isn't anything more the sea can do to me." Now at last she will be free from anxiety—"It's a great rest I'll have now, and great sleeping in the long nights after Samhain, if it's only a bit of wet flour we do have to eat, and maybe a fish that would be stinking."

Although very little else transpires in *Riders to the Sea,* this short play lives richly and dramatically. Not only is the interest sustained by the magic of the mood, not only is the spirit moved by the stark pathos of Maurya, but the imagination is stirred by the unseen sea and by the lightly suggested yet intensely present epic of a people struggling with an implacable natural force. Synge was clearly not interested in promoting Maeterlinckian "static drama," although no other play could justify this *genre* so completely.

As if to disclaim any affiliation with Maeterlinck, although none need ever have been suspected, his next play treats the theme of blindness in a manner which is radically different from the Belgian playwright's one-acter *The Blind,* for *The Well of the Saints* is a thoroughly active and vigorous comedy, despite its symbolism. The two beggars Martin and Mary Doul, who are miraculously cured of blindness by a saint, discover that the real world contradicts the ideal one which they have imagined for themselves. Whereas they had deluded themselves into believing that they had retained their youth, they are actually old and repulsive. Mutually disappointed, they quarrel acrimoniously and part ways. Then Martin Doul, the more intractable of the two, finds his work for the hard-mannered smith Timmy irksome and actually less lucrative than beggary. Moreover, his resolute wooing of the fine-looking girl Byrne makes him such a confounded nuisance that the smith, who is going to marry her, drives him off. Martin and Mary meet on the road, disillusioned and weary of the blessing of eyesight. Fortunately, however, their eyes begin to dim again, and this time nothing can persuade them to accept a second miracle from the obliging saint. In total blindness, they at last recover their confidence and begin, like the rest of mankind, to erect new illusions—for as Pirandello was to note later, men must "build themselves up" if they are to endure their limitations and those of the world. She will have beautiful white hair soon, "the way when I'm an old woman there won't be the likes of me surely in the seven counties of the East." He, in turn, will be letting his beard grow, "a beautiful, long, white, silken, streaming beard you wouldn't see the like of in the Eastern world."

Some writers believe that Synge was laughing "at those of his countrymen who would prefer the dream to the reality," [11] and even Fay who directed the play, feared that Synge expressed "too much bad temper," surely a narrow nationalist interpretation when there is all life to resent, laugh at, and also pity in this play. What Maxim Gorky said of Synge's next work *The Playboy of the Western World* is even more applicable to *The Well of the Saints:* "the comical side passes quite naturally into the terrible, while the terrible becomes comical just as easily." [12]

The charge that Synge was satirizing Ireland could be, and was, leveled more confidently at the new play, and the indignation with which *The Playboy* was received by Dublin patriots at the premiere on January 26, 1907, is now inscribed in Irish history. The audience which had already had an encounter with Synge about *The Shadow of the Glen* became increasingly resentful as they heard the oaths multiplying and saw Irish vestals fluttering around a professed parricide with unconcealed admiration. Pandemonium broke loose, the audience stamped, booed, swore in Gaelic, sang "God Save Ireland" and shouted with unconscious self-criticism that "what would be tolerated in America will not be allowed here." The bedlam continued on successive nights, until on the fifth night police were placed in the Abbey to maintain order. But the presence of the "Saxon myrmidons" struck patriots as only another example of unparalleled treason to Eire by those "degraded Yahoos" Yeats and his co-directors. The latter also took the unkind precaution of padding the floor with felt to absorb the stamping, and this combination of law and upholstery at last enabled the actors to make themselves heard.

Amusing, but at the time tragic, exhibitions of indignation on the part of normally intelligent artists were provided by two of the Abbey's own playwrights Padraic Colum and William Boyle. Others described the Abbey as an anti-Irish institution financed with English gold. But the cream of the sour jest was the anger caused by Synge's alleged immorality because he dared to use the word "shift" on the stage when Christy says "It's Pegeen I'm seeking only, and what'd I care if you brought me a drift of chosen females standing in their shifts itself, maybe." A clever versifier suspected to have been "A.E.'s" secretary found inspiration in this scandal for a delightful poem "The Blushes of Ireland" which told Yeats

You're quite too dense to understand
The chill—the thrill—of modest loathing
With which one hears on Irish land
Of underclothing. . . .

And look, sir, do not sh-ft your scenes—
There's scandal aided and abetted.
Let them, now virtue interferes,
Be chemisetted. . . .[13]

How far the patriots misunderstood Synge, whom they pictured as a foreigner consumed with hatred for all humanity and particularly for the Irish, is attested by the many intimate portraits which present him as a shy, pacific, and good-natured person. But it is idle to expect fairness or reason from a harassed or embattled people.[14] Even if the Abbey's performance had not been mistakenly too literal and had interpreted the play more fantastically, as it should be, *The Playboy* could not have escaped abuse in 1907. But it has weathered three decades and will probably weather many more as one of the masterpieces of the modern drama.

Actually the play is a folk tale spiced with some sly digs at hero-worship and the making of reputations. Chapter and line can be cited from Synge's book *The Aran Islands* to prove that Synge took his plot from an anecdote told to him by an old islander about a Connaught man who fled to the island after killing his father with the blow of a spade and was kept hidden by the natives for three weeks in a hole before being shipped to America. The one criticism that might perhaps be leveled at Synge is that he failed to stress sufficiently the wonderful tolerance of these provincial Irishmen who, according to his own report, had a feeling "that a man will not do wrong unless he is under the influence of a passion," and put the delightful question, "Would any one kill his father if he was able to help it?"[15]

Synge's treatment of the story is more mordant. When Christy Mahon arrives footsore and exhausted at a public-house on the wild coast of Mayo and explains that he has killed his father with a single blow, he horrifies no one. On the contrary, the presence of a parricide is such a novelty in this remote community that Christy's strength is acclaimed by the women who are attracted by his youthful figure and his fiery tongue. Especially titillated are a persistent widow and the publican's peppery daughter Pegeen. The admiration in which he is held, moreover, transforms the shy and dreamy lad into a self-confident extrovert with the result that he wins every athletic prize and becomes a veritable "playboy of the Western World." But his heavily bandaged father tracks him down and deflates him in the eyes of Pegeen, who is disappointed now that Christy's boast is disproved by his victim's presence. Made desperate by his father, Christy knocks him down again and leaves him for dead. This time, however, murder has occurred in their own backyard. The peasants therefore tie Christy up in order to turn him over to the law, and the enraged Pegeen even scorches his feet with a bit of burning turf, formulating the reversal of public opinion accurately when she declares that "there's a great gap between a gallous story and a dirty deed." Fortunately, however, staunch Irishmen do not die easily from a blow on the skull, and the father returns to take the culprit away. Moreover, he departs with head unbowed though slightly broken, sniffing at "the villainy of Mayo" for having mistreated his son and at "the fools is here" for having been taken in by him; it's a fine reputation that Mayo will get from his report!

Thus ends the making of a hero who is glorious only when he commits his crimes out of sight. Thus also ends the self-delusion of young Christy, who learns like other "heroes" how quickly admirers become enemies in foul weather. His education completed, he discards his dreamful passiveness and becomes an aggressive lad who will henceforth take no nonsense even from his parent. Having struck him down twice, Christy is "master of all from now." Astounded and gratified to find such mettle in his son at last, old Mahon exclaims "Glory be to God" and goes out with a broad smile. The only political implication that could properly be deduced from this extravaganza was that the Irish were mercurial in love and hate and dearly loved a "hero." But there was more amusement and universal irony than malice in this innuendo.

Its language "fully flavored as a nut or an apple" (Synge's ideal for dialogue), its fable richly imaginative and yet realistically set off, the characters vivid and yet earthy, and the situation both exuberant and provocative, *The Playboy of the Western World* marked the peak of Synge's talent. He was spared only for two more spurts during his brief race for the poet's bays that had for a second time proved to be poison oak in Kathleen ni Houlihan's "four fair fields." Each of these plays —*The Tinker's Wedding*, written in 1909, and *Deirdre*, staged the following year after his death—was, however, a masterpiece in its own class.

Far from being intimidated by the reception of his previous extravaganza, Synge proceeded in *The Tinker's Wedding* to give his humor even freer rein. "Of things which nourish the imagination," he wrote in the preface to this comedy, "humor is one of the most needful, and it is dangerous to limit or destroy it." Answering the critics of *The Playboy* and anticipating those of the new play, who might put a political construction on it, he also insisted, "The drama, like the symphony, does not teach or prove anything." And pleading with his public, he concluded that he did not believe his countrymen, from the vagrom tinkers to the dignified clergy, "who have so much humor themselves," would mind "being laughed at without malice, as the people in every country have been laughed at in their own comedies." [16] But again neither explanations nor apologies could prevail, and even the Abbey did not dare to stage this delightful *fabliau*. The National Theatre must have feared it would be only too easy to attribute to Synge, the "foreigner" and "bohemian," the dire intention of satirizing the clergy and condoning immorality. Although *The Tinker's Wedding* is the most joyous, pungent modern low comedy in the English language, a conspiracy of stupidity and cowardice has practically kept it off the stage to this day.

Its two acts dramatize a moral moment in the lives of two vagrant tinkers. Michael Byrne and Sarah Casey, who have been living together without benefit of clergy, resolve to marry. Michael anticipates the happy prospect rather grimly, and his tippling old mother shares his qualms. But since Sarah is insistent, he makes a ring with her, and after some stout bargaining with the village priest the marriage is arranged at a cost of "a crown along with ten shillings" and a "gallon can." Unfortunately Michael's insatiable mother steals the can and exchanges it for a spot of whisky. When the priest returns for the ceremony he is outraged to find three empty bottles in the bundle instead of the can. His Irish temper boils over, he refuses to marry the couple, and the ensuing recriminations end with his being bundled into a sack and thrown into a ditch.

It is perhaps the unsuitability of this comedy for the Abbey that induced Synge to return to tragedy, which he had not attempted since *Riders to the Sea*. He had waved a farewell to the Irish twilight school in one of his poems "The Passing of the Shee," writing

> *Adieu, sweet Angus, Maeve, and Fand,*
> *Ye plumed yet skinny Shee. . . .*

Perhaps, therefore, he turned to the long-exploited legend of Deirdre with the faintly malicious intention of showing the Abbey's directors and public that he too could play the game of Celtic revivalism, and that he could in fact play it better. Whether or not this was his intention, he must have quickly become entranced with his subject, with the result that his *Deirdre,* even in the unrevised state in which he left it, is unquestionably the masterpiece of Irish romanticism.

Returning "to the frank materialism of the original story," he blended realistic primitivism with the romantic story of how Deirdre and her lover Naisi met their death in ancient Ireland. The protagonists of this love drama, the greatest in English since the Elizabethan age, have been hiding for seven years from the jealous passion of Conchubor, king of Ulster. But time has not diminished Conchubor's longing for the ineffable Deirdre, and he sends his unsuspecting friend Fergus with offers of reconciliation to the lovers. Deirdre suspects treachery but consents to return to the court with Naisi when she discovers her lover's restiveness, for love has ceased to be sufficient for Naisi and he longs for the life that should be his at the court. Perhaps it is better so, she reflects; if they die now, they will at least escape old age and the fading of their love. Naisi and his loyal brothers are killed treacherously and Deirdre, cheating Conchubor of his prize, joins Naisi in the grave by stabbing herself.

Synge did not live long enough to polish *Deirdre*, although it seems polished enough in the version he left. Nor did he live to write the next play which he contemplated, a drama of slum life that might have revealed a new facet of his talent; the Abbey had to wait fifteen years before Sean O'Casey supplied such a picture with *Juno and the Paycock*. Synge, in fact, was still forging ahead when he died of cancer in his thirty-ninth year on March 24, 1909. But death did not come before this descendant of Cheshire Englishmen had made himself the master dramatist of Ireland, and before this protégé of a romantic national revival had given fresh power to the realistic drama which he had once dismissed as too anemic.

4 AFTER SYNGE

Synge's death was a blow to the Abbey, which like all theatres was destined to have severe trials and was soon to be accused of failure to move with the times. As Burns Mantle has written, "He was one who could have stood between the poets and realists and composed their inharmonies." [17] Genius was absent for fifteen years in the Irish theatre which had not only revealed fresh and original plays but had given the one-act form its highest estate since the Middle Ages. (Between 1904 and 1908 twenty-two of the Abbey's thirty-six plays were one-acters.) Nevertheless respectable talent remained abundant, and in the nick of time genius also appeared. When it arose in Sean O'Casey, moreover, he followed Synge's example of combining salty comedy with irony and he took up the work of Synge at the point at which death had interrupted it—namely, the drama of the cities and their proletariat.

Seumas O'Kelly whose *Shuiler's Child*, produced in the year of Synge's death, is the poignant tragedy of a vagrant woman who gives up her child in order to place it in a respectable household, revealed a genuine but narrow talent. O'Kelly also turned to Ibsenism in an attack on nepotism *The Bribe* (1913) and in *The Parnellite* (1917). But, like his problems, his dialogue and outlook remained halting when he left the apron strings of folk drama. T. C. Murray, whost first play *Birthright* appeared in the same year as Synge's *Deirdre,* was another solid but distinctly limited realist. The two-act *Birthright* is a peasant variant of the Cain and Abel story. A crusty farmer Bat Morrissey has no understanding for his imaginative elder son Hugh whose energies flow into other channels than agriculture. He therefore packs him off to America, retaining contrary to custom his younger and more practical son Shane; thereupon the boys quarrel and in the ensuing scuffle Hugh is killed by Shane. Murray's second work, *Maurice Harte,* in 1912, is a poignant study of the Harte family which, like so many humble folk in Ireland, sacrifices everything in order to prepare its favorite son Maurice for the priesthood. The lad unwillingly proceeds with his training but breaks down and is verging on insanity on the eve of his ordination. This play is unfortunately saddled with an insufficiently prepared climax, and it treats the principal character Maurice less effectively than it treats his family. *Autumn Fire* in 1924 is a strong Irish variant of the *Desire Under the Elms* theme—a triangle of an old father, a young second wife, and a son who loves her. But again the play ends inconclusively with the lovers resigning themselves to awaiting the invalided husband's death. Later plays marked a further decline in Murray's power.

More effective has been Lennox Robinson, the one-time Abbey stage director. Beginning with a grim little melodrama *The Clancy Family* in 1909, he marked time with a problem play (marriage for patriotic reasons) *The Crossroads,* and with the better realized thesis of *Harvest* which deplored the false education that deprived Irish farms of their immaturely sophisticated young people. With tragic irony in *Patriots,* in 1912, Robinson also described the disappointment of a political prisoner who finds the people indifferent to his resumption of insurgency after he has been freed. This thesis to the effect that parliamentarianism had replaced revolution, surely a hasty conclusion on the part of the author when the Easter Rebellion was only four years in the offing, was followed by a Robert Emmet play *The Dreamers,* one year before that event. In time, however, Robinson found his true calling with the charming comedy *The White-headed Boy* for which he is best known. Despite the author's assurance that the play is "political from beginning to end," it is a pleasant trifle compounded of scatterbrained likable people and a good-humored satire on Irish manners. Robinson followed this engaging comedy with another political satire *The Last Leader,* in which Parnell seemingly returns to life only to be struck dead in a riot by a blind man. a sharp reflection of the bitterness over the betrayal of the Victorian liberator which still rankled. Then Robinson returned to simple humor in the charming one-acter *Crabbed Youth and Age,* in which an intelligent mother proves more fascinating to young men than the daughters they should be courting, and he scored a full-length triumph in the gay domestic comedy *The Far-Off Hills.* Notable is its shrewd characterization of the domineering elder daughter Marian, the lugubrious Dickensian suitor Harold who imagines himself to be in love with her only so long as his passion is hopeless, and the young "go-getter" who wins her with the promise of new opportunities for running things now that her father has eluded her management by remarrying. Robinson favored topical matters again in a sympathetic picture of the struggles of the landowning class to orient itself toward Irish life, *The Big House.* And being an eclectic, he later concocted Pirandellian porridge in the thin comedy *Is Life Worth Living* which ascribes domestic disturbances in a remote Irish resort to the performance of continental problem plays by a high-minded troupe; the inhabitants adopt new and "frustrated" personalities much to the distress of everyone in sight. Both as a director and as a playwright, Lennox Robinson was a tower of strength to the Abbey over many difficult years. If he was a frequently pedestrian writer he was nearly always a reliable one; if he was often too facile or superficial, he rarely failed to be interesting or entertaining.

St. John Ervine, also for a time—and a very stormy one it was for him and the Irish acting company—a director of the Abbey, revealed a much sturdier talent. In 1911 he delivered the powerful problem play *Mixed Marriage,* a study of religious conflict in Ireland. There had been religious riots in Belfast during which a girl was killed by a shot while standing at her door; Ervine, however, gave this incident a larger significance by setting her tragedy against a labor background. For the workers to win, it becomes imperative for Catholics and Protestants to shelve their differences. But John Rainey, whose influence over the Protestant workers makes him an important figure, opposes a united front upon learning that his son intends to marry a Catholic girl. The consequences are tragic for both the labor movement and the girl. Faced with the catastrophes he has caused, the old man can only mutter with stubborn defensiveness "A wuz right. A knew a wuz right." In this play, which contains impressive character drawing, Ervine gave the Irish theatre a more modern problem play than it had yet presented; it was the first frontal attack on bigotry and representation of the rising class struggle in Ireland.

Ervine seemed ideally chosen for the task of modernizing the Irish theatre. As a Belfast native (he was born there in 1883), he escaped the irresistible charm of Celtic folklore and manners. Moreover, he had gone at an early age to London where he fell under the influence of Shaw and the socialist Fabian Society. He invoked the shade of Ibsen in his next problem play *The Magnanimous Lover,* which proved unsuccessful in 1912 partly because of its unconventional story of Maggie who refuses to be made "an honest woman" by a repentant but smug lover. Ervine's next work, *Jane Clegg,* followed the road of modernity even further and revealed a strong continental, naturalistic influence. It is a stark domestic tragedy of corrosion and rebellion in an urban middle-class environment. Jane Clegg, saddled with a weak-willed husband who cannot resist the influence of the "bookie" Munce, struggles for a decent life against great odds, and in creating Jane Ervine again exhibited his talent for using a strong and dignified character as the pivot of his play. When Jane Clegg finally recognizes the weakness and pettiness of her husband who has betrayed her, she simply sends him packing despite his cringing and pleading. Her standards of "decency" are painfully beyond his understanding; he could understand it if Jane would "tear Kitty to bits" but not her sending him to Kitty. "You're condoning the offense," he cries.

Being more English than Irish by inclination, and seemingly regarding the Abbey as just another repertory company rather than as a national institution, Ervine gave *Jane Clegg* to the Manchester Gaiety Theatre in 1913. But he returned to the fold with his greatest play *John Ferguson* in 1915. This was another middle-class tragedy, but set on a farm. The doldrums of its Ulster Protestant family are described with severe realism unrelieved by poetic transubstantiation as in Synge's work. Old John Ferguson, whose son Andrew is unfit to manage the farm, finds it hard to make ends meet and writes his brother in America for money. Meanwhile his farm is mortgaged to the brutal and high-handed miller Henry Witherow who threatens to foreclose. Ferguson, who can save it only by marrying his daughter Hannah to the obnoxious village grocer Jimmy Caesar, is too upright to take advantage of Hannah. There is, however, no reward for his virtue from the god he serves so scrupulously; Hannah is raped by Henry Witherow, then the latter is found dead, and finally Hannah's brother delivers himself up to the police as his murderer. Except for the melodrama of the rape and for some coincidences like the arrival of money from America just when it is too late, *John Ferguson* is a near masterpiece. The granite figure of the afflicted old man, an Irish Job who keeps a bridle on his tongue, cancels whatever flaws may be found in this tragedy. Moreover, Ferguson sublimates the potentially depressing matter of the play into something ineffably noble. In this the author merely followed his own excellent prescription that "an audience should leave a theatre, after seeing a tragedy, in a state of pride."

After a tart farewell in the one-acter *The Island of Saints, and the*

Way to Get Out of It, St. John Ervine shook the dust of Ireland off his feet and transplanted himself permanently to England. Since then he has written some eight plays, all neatly constructed, penetrative, and flavored with sharp common sense. But none of them—not even the amusing *First Mrs. Frazer* (1930) and the successful *Robert's Wife* (1937)—have equaled the strength he displayed in his Irish period. Patriots might suggest that the British climate softened his spirit, but this would have to be taken with more than a grain of reservation. As dramatic critic for the *London Observer* he has revealed such unabated vigor that his numerous victims probably shudder at the mere mention of his name.

For more than a decade the absence of his rugged power was a severe loss to the Abbey, which was not repaired by the work of earnest writers like Rutherford Mayne and other "social-minded playwrights." [18] Nor did that talented *frisson*-monger Lord Dunsany relieve the situation with his numerous thrillers in the style of his early *Gods of the Mountain,* in which some unfortunate merry-makers are frozen to statues. For sheer "thrill" it would be hard to equal *A Night at an Inn* with its familiar Hindu idol that hunts down the Englishmen who have stolen the jewel from its forehead. For its author one may, however, paraphrase Tolstoy's famous remark about Andreyev: Dunsany says "Booh!" but I refuse to be frightened.

5 THE SECOND COMING: SEAN O'CASEY AND PAUL VINCENT CARROLL

In this general drought, which the Abbey failed to end with a few foreign imports by Shaw and Evreinov and with a belated production of *A Doll's House* (in 1923!), it suddenly discovered a potent rain-maker, and a veritable man of thunder. And significantly, it found him where the Abbey's directors had been least inclined to look, among the urban proletariat.

Sean O'Casey, whose first work *The Shadow of a Gunman* was staged a week after Ibsen's play, came from the slums of Dublin. He has described his boyhood with characteristic fire in the autobiography *I Knock at the Door* (1939), the opening salvo of his projected autobiography *Swift Glances Back at the Things that Made Me.* It is the story of an ailing, half-blind, imaginative Protestant lad guided and cured by a courageous poor mother who recalls the heroine of *Juno and the Paycock.* His meager education by a clergyman has merely rated bitter words from O'Casey about "being lugged off along at the backside of this soft-hatted, stiff-collared, egg-headed oul' henchman of heaven, to be added to the swarm of urchins cowering and groping about in the rag-and-bone education provided by the church and state for the children of those who hadn't the wherewithal to do any better." He left school at an early age after an unfortunate encounter with his teacher, he learned "poethry," and "kissed a girl." Prematurely out in the world and insufficiently educated, he began to "knock at the door" of literature with clumsy but powerful hands.

He was fated to continue knocking at doors for many years. Meanwhile there was a hard bread-and-butter road ahead of him. In the half-industrialized seaport of Dublin where casual work was far more abundant than regular employment, he moved from job to job; dock-worker, hodcarrier, and stone-breaker on roads, his record of employment reads like one of Whitman's polyphonic paeans to labor. Bitterness and pugnacity were aroused in him as he was pushed from pillar to post: He was dismissed from his first real job at the age of fifteen for refusing to take off his cap while receiving his pay; he fought through the fierce transport strike of 1913; he joined the Citizen Army, and did not participate in the Easter insurrection of 1916 only because he was at that time a prisoner of the English government.

O'Casey has always been a nonconformist and a plain-spoken, embattled man who never shrinks from a fight. He quarreled with the Abbey when it rejected *The Silver Tassie,* and he lambasted the English critics in a truculent book *The Flying Wasp* for failing to appreciate his symbolic social drama *Within the Gates* while reserving their generosity for Noel Coward's cream-puffs. He left Ireland and settled in England, but without surrendering to the spell of English country-house complacency. Today he is still Ireland's and the underdog's angry man. His 1940 play (unpublished and unproduced at this writing) proclaims the struggle against fascism and the dawn of a working-class republic in spite of politicians, corrupt labor leaders, and princes of the Church.

His genius is a compound of anger and pity, and of laughter and sorrow. It puzzles his critics because it avoids easy formulations; thus he can convey the courage of the Easter rebels and yet scorn their unthinking and wasteful self-intoxication in *The Plough and the Stars;* thus he can mingle comedy and tragedy in *Juno and the Paycock* without separating them in convenient compartments. Reading Shakespeare voraciously in his youth, and going without food to buy books, he educated himself without benefit of school and college. He also studied old Irish literature, acquiring its heady eloquence and bravura. O'Casey made his first effort in the drama at the age of seventeen, and about a year later he had the mortification of having another maiden effort *Frost in the Flower* rejected by a "little theatre" group because the play satirized its members. But the Abbey, which also rejected it, sent him detailed criticism and encouraged him to write.

After turning down two other plays by him, it finally staged *The*

Shadow of a Gunman in 1923. Although O'Casey is said to prefer it to *Juno and the Paycock,* this relatively short, two-act play moves slowly toward its painful climax. Nevertheless, it already embodied his characteristically pungent artistry. In a rooming house one inmate speaks so eloquently of Irish emancipation that everybody regards him as a heroic revolutionist and a young girl is fired by his words. But another fellow quietly disappears one day and it turns out that he is the real man of action. Before his fellow roomers can dispose of the explosives he has left behind in his luggage, English soldiers are at the door. Thereupon the simple girl takes the dynamite up to her room and sacrifices her life. The point of view is ironic since it is loud-mouthed romanticists like the windbag in the play who cause such tragic waste of life while hugging their self-esteem; his words sent the girl to her useless death.

Here O'Casey's characterization is already vivid and his dialogue is passionately alive. Only his story is somewhat meager and unnecessarily elusive. But in the next work *Juno and the Paycock* O'Casey is singularly definite despite its ambling technique and mingling of humor and tragedy. The play is a picture of a down-at-heels family kept together by a sharp-tongued but courageous wife and mother while her husband, "Captain" Boyle the "paycock," idles with his drinking companion Joxer. The daughter Mary is on strike against the mistreatment of a fellow-worker, and the son Johnny who was "only a chiselur of a Boy Scout in Easter Week" got shot in the hip and later lost his arm in an explosion. A streak of unexpected luck comes to the family in the form of a supposed bequest, and the Boyles begin to refurnish their home on credit; Jack Boyle gets a new suit, the family buys a gramophone "on tick," and Mary acquires a suitor in a schoolteacher and budding lawyer. But the bequest proves to be a mistake, Mary is abandoned by her suitor and becomes pregnant, and Johnny, who has betrayed one of his revolutionary comrades, is executed by them as a spy. Juno is left alone with the wreckage of the lives that have been dear to her. "Sacred Heart of Jesus," she cries, "take away our hearts of stone and give us hearts o' flesh! Take away this murdherin' hate an' give us Thine own eternal love." As if in answer to her prayer Jack Boyle returns home roaring drunk, "talking patriotic nonsense," and repeating his usual ineffectual complaint to the effect that the whole world's in a "terrible state of chassis."

The point of view is, despite criticism to the contrary, quite clear. Not only are O'Casey's poor Irish afflicted by circumstances in general, but they are making a frightful mess of their lives by their perversities, while innocent people like Mary and her long-suffering and understandably tart mother are the greatest victims. Related to this theme is the tragi-comedy of lowly folk who almost emerge from the cellar of poverty but are quickly thrust back by circumstance, and O'Casey's specific criticism of the Irish is likewise fine and deeply considered. The English critic Ivor Brown's judgment cannot be improved when he writes, "Mr. O'Casey has set down once and for all the weakness of a nation which has been cosseted with the idea that its members are all saints and martyrs. So Captain Boyle can stop in his tippling to boom away about the glories of Irish history . . . while his fellow-soak 'Joxer' is never able to pay for a drink but always able to fetch up a quotation from the poets. His English parallel would find his pence for a pint, but would be totally incapable of citing a verse. . . ." [19] *Juno and the Paycock* suffers from some gratuitous melodrama in Mary's betrayal and from some lagging and diffusion. Moreover, as George Jean Nathan has pointed out (with some exaggeration, in my opinion), O'Casey "so segregates comedy and tragedy that one kills the effect of the other." Still, this intensely realized chiaroscuro evokes a passionate poetry of the sordid, and *Juno and the Paycock* may rightly be considered the masterpiece of modern urban realism. When the first-night curtain fell on March 3, 1924, it was evident that the mantle of Synge had at last found a shoulder that could wear it with honor.

However, O'Casey had to wait for an "Irish success" until the Abbey presented his tragedy of the Easter Rebellion *The Plough and the Stars* on February 8, 1926. Only murmurs had greeted its predecessor, but this time the audience rioted and exchanged blows. Yeats, ever loyal to the Abbey even when it continued to scuttle his poetic theatre for the chosen few, told the mob from the stage that they had "once more rocked the cradle of a reputation."

The profound critic of *The Nation*, Mr. Joseph Wood Krutch, has complained that he has never discovered "just where the author's sympathies lie." This confusion exists because of O'Casey's fairness, although the Abbey's audience had no doubt that his sympathies were anti-Irish. He recognizes the nobility and courage of the rebels, but he resents their intoxication with romantic and superficial objectives. Through the class-conscious Covey, in fact, he presents the trenchant criticism that the patriots who fought for political independence neglected the far more immediate problem of eradicating the pressing problems of poverty and social evil that are so vividly realized in this slum tragedy. But beyond this pertinent criticism is the immediate tragedy of women who lose their men for causes that do not touch the direct and ever-present realities of eating, home building, love, and childbearing.

"The women live and die for the realities." [20] Jack Clitheroe goes out to fight and die while Nora, who clings to him, is pregnant and is crazy with anxiety. Pathetically she has pleaded with him at a time when she needs him most, "They are all afraid, don't you be afraid to be afraid."

She gives birth to a dead child as a result of her anxiety and becomes demented. Other tragedies transpire while the men are bleeding for something that seems abstract and remote by comparison. There is, for example, the poverty that makes termagants of some of the women; there is the shiftlessness of men like the remarkable Fluther Good and old Peter, both flamboyant patriots who talk well and drink better; there is the ailing and neglected child that dies in the tenement; there is the crowded tenement itself. Here in the slums, O'Casey seems to imply, is the real evil that men must conquer, and every other cause should be secondary to this problem.

"His clinical portrait," George Jean Nathan has written, "is the most vicious thing in modern dramatic literature, but the viciousness is that of a deep understanding." O'Casey never lets us forget the essential unity of the underdog whether he be Irish or English, Catholic or Protestant, Home-ruler or Unionist; the fellowship of suffering and the reality of natural sympathy that exist, for example, in the heart of the Anglophile virago. She nurses Nora with whom she has constantly quarreled and dies from a stray bullet while leading her away from the window. O'Casey exhibits no sympathy for the English government and its soldiers, but his deepest concern is for the contradictions and realities that strike closest to everyday life. His is the critique of a son of the slums who reflects international European socialism and clothes the problems of ordinary people with eloquent flesh that is closer to both reality and drama than any flurry of romantic nationalism.

Restive as ever, O'Casey turned next to expressionism when nothing else could express his all-embracing indignation at that other nationalistic flare-up the World War. *The Silver Tassie* mingles powerful realism in the figure of an incapacitated ex-soldier and athlete with a febrile phantasmagoria of the horrors of modern warfare. The Abbey rejected the play and was promptly flagellated by O'Casey, and the reception in London was mixed. But it found such discriminating friends as Shaw who acclaimed the piece rhapsodically. "The hitting gets harder and harder right through to the end," Shaw wrote. This is certainly true, and *The Silver Tassie* is one of the most trenchant pacifist protests of the generation. Nevertheless, O'Casey was fumbling in his effort to develop a new medium for his genius, and one misses in this play the vivid characterization and consistency of its author's masterpieces.

Tenaciously O'Casey continued on the path of expressionism in *Within the Gates,* staged before World War II. Here with lines of searing eloquence and beauty he dramatized the misery of the world's outcasts in the person of The Young Whore, the hypocrisy of the master classes and the Church in the character of the Bishop who fathered and forgot her, the impoverished spirit of the people in the chorus of Down-

and-Outs, and the upsurge of the human will in the Dreamer. The author's own explanations of his allegory are abstruse and the precise meaning of his symbolism is open to discussion. Also controversial are the dramatic merits of the work, and the New York production, except for the performance of Miss Lillian Gish, did little to present them advantageously. One also misses in this play O'Casey's robust characterization, a clear crystallization of conflict, and a conclusiveness which is particularly indispensable in a morality play.

The play is, nevertheless, a powerful example of expressionism, and if its effects are scattered, this i. the intrinsic fault of the expressionist medium about which, it seems, nothing much can be done even by the greatest dramatists. O'Casey's humanity, biting irony and purple patches of indignation and hope make this at the very least a noble failure. There are never enough of those in the theatre at any time, and failures have a way of looming larger than most successes with the passing of time. What may still come from the impassioned spirit of O'Casey cannot of course be predicted, but that it will never be complacent or mediocre seems certain.

After 1926, however, the Abbey no longer enjoyed the support of O'Casey, and for a decade it revealed no stronger talent than that of George Shiels, whose *New Gossoon* is nevertheless a charming peasant comedy graced by one of the most delightful rogues of the stage—Rabit Hamil, a very Autolycus of a poacher. The talk went round that the Abbey was dying, and the absence of new playwrights of stature, as well as the Abbey's conservative stage technique, paved the way for a rival organization. In 1928 was founded the Dublin Gate Theatre, notable for original and brilliant productions of foreign works from Aeschylus' Oresteian trilogy to Ibsen's *Peer Gynt* and Shaw's *Back to Methuselah*. The very size, not to speak of the quality of these plays, is an indication of the scope of the younger theatre, which has also distinguished itself with highly praised Shakespearean productions. Only its native playwrights have been thus far less arresting. Mary Manning displays a satirical art without modifying or improving upon previous efforts in her field. Denis Johnston becomes bogged in esoteric expressionism which makes pieces like *The Old Lady Says 'No!'* fit only for Irish consumption and the *A Bride for the Unicorn* which defies comprehension by the present writer, although the Harvard Dramatic Club seems to have understood it by some special dispensation. His realistic plays *Storm Song* or *Letters in Lights* is merely another satire on the films, and only *The Moon in the Yellow River* (1931), produced by the Abbey, revealed a powerful and communicable talent. The failure of the last-mentioned play in New York is indeed no criterion. It is a caustic but affecting and enchanting picture of Irish incompetence and idealism facing the new mechanical age. It is deficient only in integration and unfortunate only in being too elusive for those of us who have problems enough at home to familiarize ourselves with Ireland's.

Just as the Abbey, however, seemed to have sunk into a slough from which there was to be no escape, it uncovered a new dramatist strong enough to extricate that venerable institution. This savior was not, as some of its directors believed, Miss Teresa Deevy whose much lauded *Katie Roche* is in the main negligible, but Paul Vincent Carroll, who quickly proved descent from the Irish masters.

Born in 1900, the son of a teacher and himself a schoolmaster, he was, he claims, a dramatist by observation. Leaning against Nelson's Pillar in Dublin, he saw Padraic Pearse storm the General Post Office at the point of the bayonet in the Easter Rebellion. He saw the tanks crawling down the streets and the sharp-shooting, and he lived through English martial law and the "Black and Tan" terror before leaving Ireland in 1920. Returning later, he felt his blood boiling as he observed the merchants and the clergy waxing rich on the results of civil war and national independence, and he was particularly perturbed by the sad state of education, "completely in clerical hands." Becoming a teacher in one of the priest-dominated schools, he did not like the experience any more than his rebellious father had. A year later, therefore, he left for Glasgow where the Catholic schools are controlled by the non-religious county councils and he has been a fairly satisfied instructor of the young ever since.

Seeing Ireland in perspective there, he began bombarding the Abbey with plays, and finally in 1932 shared its prize with Teresa Deevy for *Things That Are Caesar's.* He first reached his maturity, however, in *Shadow and Substance,* introduced to the Dublin public in 1934. Combining Celtic legend with the experiences of his Irish schoolteaching days, he invigorated this magnificent play with a stinging exposé of the school system revolving around the conflict between the liberal teacher O'Flingsley and his superior Canon Skerritt. Going much further at the same time, he created a portentous picture of bigotry and of the fascist-minded mob spirit which it can let loose and laved his critique in poetry and personal tragedy. His plea for a humane and truly Christian religion, as practised by his simple servant-girl heroine Brigid and as neglected by the Canon whom she serves, rose far above the common levels of problem drama. Torn between her employer and the schoolteacher because she loves them equally, Brigid finally dies while protecting O'Flingsley from the mob that tries to lynch him for his authorship of an anti-clerical book. Giving his play the stamp of genuine talent, Carroll created glorious dialogue, a vivid background, several finely drawn characters, and two superlative ones. Brigid is not Pollyanna but a modest country girl who may owe her saintliness equally to her unspoiled young womanhood and the apparently congenital queerness which makes her see visions. And Canon Skerritt is a masterful portrait of a noble spirit hardened by his superior intellect and his frustrated estheticism into a domineering priest for whom religion is an aristocratic intellectual exercise, rather than the creed of Christ who mingled with lepers and vagrants and calloused his hands with humble carpentry.

Shadow and Substance is an imperfect play; it is diffuse when its author introduces too much low comedy into it and gives Brigid's visions too much space, and it is also a trifle sentimental and stereotyped. (As John Mason Brown observed, Kathleen ni Houlihan is not far off in the portrait of Brigid, especially when she regenerates the Canon by her death.) But Carroll gave the Abbey and the English-speaking world a play of noble proportions, fine feeling, and alternately scintillating and simply affecting speech.

In his next (and at this writing, last) play *The White Steed,* he made some progress by improving his dramaturgy. This simpler drama tells a well-knit story of fanatical reformism inaugurated by a priest who intimidates townspeople, breaks the spirit of a weak-willed young schoolmaster, and rallies vigilantism and the mob spirit to his Comstockian cause. The cause or its proponent, Father Shaughnessy, is defied by a plain Irishman, by a peppery lass who loves the teacher, and by a staunch constable who fought in the Irish rebellion and does not intend to let the priests take the place of the banished English masters. Bloodshed is imminent when the old and paralyzed but sensible Canon Lavelle for whom Father Shaughnessy is substituting takes the reins. His sharp tongue sends the rioters home with their tails between their legs. Sensible and undesigning citizens are safe again, the schoolmaster can at last breathe freely, and his girl may possibly make a man of him by marriage.

The Canon's more or less miraculaus release from paralysis strains credulity, and it is sometimes difficult to understand why the refractory heroine doesn't break a saucer over the sniveling schoolmaster's pate instead of taking him under her wing. Nevertheless, *The White Steed* proved to be a comedy of extraordinary vigor and momentum. Again, although to a slighter degree, Carroll revealed an uncanny deftness both as a portraitist (the character of the salty Canon is delightful) and a caricaturist; and to an even greater degree than was the case in *Shadow and Substance,* Carroll presented the dangers of mass hysteria with striking effectiveness. Moreover, his assault on intolerance and Comstockism was augmented by a telling defense of the democratic policy of separating the

Church and the State. Carroll's name must be added to the honorable list of the theatre's liberal thinkers, although it is his spirited and poetic realism that recommends him as an artist.

The magnificence, the poetry, and the quality that Brooks Atkinson has described as "grandeur of emotion" of *Shadow and Substance* are less abundantly present in *The White Steed*. Nor does the play contain a character of such singular depth and dimension as Canon Skerritt. Nevertheless, its author's advance in dramaturgy, even if it should be temporarily halted, augurs well for the Irish drama which began with a magnificence of emotion and speech and seems destined to end with it —if end it must at some time which may be happily remote.

It is this magnificence, enriched but unfettered by realism, that comprises the Irish contribution to the modern drama. It makes itself felt even when the Abbey under its present directorate rejects a play like *The White Steed* and has to be taken to task by the fiery author in the *Irish Times*.* Romanticism was inherent in Irish nationalism, and realism was enforced upon playwrights by peasant life, economic distress, and the pressure of other national problems. The greatest Irish dramatists were able, however, to combine romanticism and realism successfully. Consequently, Irish drama has glowed with a spirit that the English-speaking theatre has rarely known since 1620.

* The Abbey, which included a physician and ex-finance minister in its apparently increasing timid management, may, however, deteriorate as it has been doing, and it may continue to be financially embarrassed, as it has been since 1932. It may even become more distinctly what George Jean Nathan once called it—a "caricature of its former self"—if it is further subjected to the microbe of censorship which the Irish State seems to have acquired along with its independence.

XXVIII

BERNARD SHAW AND THE
BRITISH COMPROMISE

According to tradition the first Christian missionary to set his feet on British soil came from Ireland. And St. Columba arrived with his gospel of Christ and civilization at a time when the fair-haired Anglo-Saxons were still a rabble of half-piratical barbarians who had knocked Celtic-Roman culture into a cocked hat by dint of brute force, rapacity and absolute lack of humor. A little over thirteen centuries later—when piracy had become imperialism, when rapacity was dignified as liberal laissez-faire philosophy, and when humorlessness had become decorum in England—there came a new mission from Ireland. But instead of settling on the west coast it headed straight for the theatres of London.

If the Irish dramatists had awakened only Ireland our debt to them would be sufficiently great. But they awakened England too, and this they did even before they aroused their own countrymen. Born in Dublin within two years of each other, in 1854 and 1856 respectively, Oscar Wilde and Bernard Shaw descended upon England when the British drama was a fen of philistine abominations. In their own land the case was even worse, for the Irish Renaissance had not yet taken place; England had at least some distinguished poets, novelists and belle-lettrists, if it could not yet boast a professional dramatist above the degree of literacy. But comparisons did not daunt these immigrants who had given up their own country as hopeless. They made themselves at home in the English theatre and began to move the furniture around. Better still, they began to make things lively for their self-satisfied host with devastating results to his aplomb and his clothes.

1 THE DANDIACAL BODY OR THE AUGEAN STABLES

"Clothes" is a particularly apt word, since England, to use the phrase of an earlier immigrant from Scotland, was "a dandiacal body." This critic, Thomas Carlyle, had defined a dandy as "a clothes-wearing Man, a Man whose trade, office and existence consists in the wearing of Clothes," adding that "every faculty of his soul, spirit, purse and person is heroically consecrated to this one object." He was thinking specifically of the English people. The process of bedecking and concealing oneself with an assortment of garments had been continuous in

English society ever since the steam engine and the spinning jenny made England the leading industrial and imperialistic nation of the world. But more than forty years of prosperity and of peace (except for minor or remote tempests) under the good queen Victoria fixed the clothes like a pigment into the English body.

Every contradiction in society was scrupulously covered with rationalizations. While the factory owners waxed wealthy an increasing number of workers were condemned to a life of poverty and incredibly long hours of labor for man, woman and child in unhygienic mills and mines. This condition was unctuously defended by a Manchester School of economics which contended that nothing must interfere with the divine right of competition. This passed for liberty and was the chief article of faith in the doctrine of Liberalism represented by a Whig or "Liberal" party which received its support from the thriving industrialists. At the same time, the Tories or Conservatives of the landed gentry were equally willing to thrive on the squalor of the rent-burdened countryside in the name of tradition, the Crown, the established Church, and the glorious Constitution. In the strictly political field, too, matters stood no better. Before the Reform Bill of 1832, British "democracy" in the opinion of so authoritative a historian as Carlton J. H. Hayes, surely no radical, had been "notoriously corrupt, absurdly unrepresentative, and hopelessly reactionary." When a large section of the middle class won the franchise in 1832, it was content to enjoy the spoils and make terms with the gentry. "From 1832 to 1867," writes Professor Hayes, "was the era of the bourgeois compromise—the 'Victorian Compromise'—between democracy and oligarchy, whereby the bourgeois enjoyed political rights and left the lower classes to shift for themselves. It was tacitly assumed that if a man was poor, it was due either to his own fault or to inexorable economic laws—and in either case he was unfit to vote." [1] Entranced with the political progress that had been achieved thus far and by the prospect of bigger factories and profits, apologists like Macaulay saw a golden age at the rainbow's end, while England's poet laureate Tennyson predicted the Parliament of man and the Federation of the world held in "fretful awe" by the "common sense of most."

In the related field of manners, morals, and religion the British compromise, moreover, manifested nothing less than genius. Science, which had made industrial civilization possible and was in turn stimulated by it, gathered momentum until it threatened the religious and moral assumptions of Victorian society. But the established religion and the domestic conventions were older than Darwinism, their usefulness in keeping the lid tightly sealed over the potentially unruly lower orders was manifest to all who enjoyed the benefits of the age, and a maximum of emotional stability was one way of keeping Britons free to carry on the exacting business of making money and dominating the world. Since it was inexpedient to kill the goose of science which was laying so many golden eggs, Victoria's subjects hit upon a double expedient: First of all, they made morals or conventions more rigid than ever in the name of good taste, as well as good citizenship, and so established that reputation for prudery which seems destined to be forever associated with the word Victorian. Then they bargained with science. Darwin's doctrine of biological evolution through the struggle for existence in nature was simply perverted into a social principle justifying the competitive, laissez-faire economic system, with its ruthlessness toward competitors and indifference to the conditions of the lower orders. Physical science subjected the world to mechanistic forces, it is true; but its conclusions must not be applied too broadly, said the Victorians. The mechanistic, materialistic principle was all right in the laboratory and in industrial processes. But surely the mechanical forces of the cosmos were merely the means by which God realized his intention, this intention having perfection as its aim.

Nothing, Tennyson assured his generation, "moves with aimless feet" and still more blithe was the assurance of Robert Browning, the robust son of a rich father, that "God's in his Heaven, All's right with the world." Among the major poets of the age only Matthew Arnold would go further and admit that he didn't know what to make of the new scientific dispensation, that he was "wandering between two worlds, one dead, the other powerless to be born." Only many years after the optimistic eulogy on the age in *Locksley Hall* did Tennyson venture to admit that something was wrong when he wrote the refrain of "Chaos! Cosmos!" in *Locksley Hall Sixty Years After.*

Moreover, for the average person there always remained the simple and prevalent alternative of remaining ignorant of scientific thought or ignoring it and holding stubbornly to conventional piety and hallowed decorum while pursuing the world's business. In this, Victoria Regina set the example. Prince Albert might have entertained doubts about the miracle of the Gadarene Swine or recommended in his memorandum on the education of the Prince of Wales that his son's religious training should exclude "the supernatural doctrines of Christianity." But the royal widow, "who gave her name to the Age of Mill and Darwin," remained to the end of her days attached to her spiritual advisers, forbade smoking in Windsor castle, and prescribed whipping for any advocate of "women's rights." In her, the middle classes, "firm in the triple brass of their respectability," found comfort and salvation, and the good Queen knew she could count on their support. "How kind they are to me!

How kind they are!" she cried during the Jubilee of 1897 when her grateful subjects thronged around her, and her final years, as Lytton Strachey wrote, "were years of apotheosis." [2]

Substantial qualifications to this idyllic picture are of course in order. Pressure from the lower classes, beginning with the Chartist Movement in 1848, produced another Reform Bill which extended the suffrage to them, without, however, making it universal even for men—such being the tenacity of the compromise habit; and more reforms followed in 1885, though relics of absolutism and feudalism were retained in the Crown and the House of Lords. In time, social legislation in the form of factory and mining acts ameliorated the most glaring abuses of laissez-faire industrialism, and the trade union movement wrested further concessions regarding wages, hours, and sanitation from employers. Living in exile, Karl Marx was quietly and laboriously sharpening his axe *Das Kapital* in the British Museum as he watched the flourishing bay tree of capitalism adding ring after ring. Socialist agitation made itself felt among the working-classes and found intellectual allies like William Morris and the members of the Fabian Society. Agnostic societies were formed, freethinkers published pamphlets and books (one of them by Inman even denouncing Christianity as phallic worship!), and a few scientists like Thomas Huxley refused to confine their opinions to the laboratory. Religious idealism, from the Christian Socialism of Kingsley to the neo-Catholicism of John Henry Newman, opposed materialism. And in the literary field discontent, criticism, and rebellion were becoming increasingly audible.

In the genial meadows of belles-lettres strange sounds could be heard. From his wife's home in Craigenputtock Thomas Carlyle roared like the bull of Bashan at the Dismal Science of economics which justified exploitation and materialism. Looking for a savior after this onslaught in *Sartor Resartus,* and distrusting a democracy that tolerated corruption, he called for heroic leaders who would redeem mankind by the force of their will. The gentle Ruskin turned from rapturous worship of Gothic and Renaissance art to the contemplation of the utilitarian ugliness of England's cities. Wealth was nothing unless it nourished "the greatest number of noble and happy human beings;" while the mass of people lived in squalor, indulgence in luxury was criminal; and it was impossible to create or enjoy beauty under these circumstances. Not content with mere preachment in florid essays and public addresses to the British working man, Ruskin spent nearly the whole of his fortune of two hundred thousand pounds on his model industrial community, the Guild of St. George. Matthew Arnold turned from the study of literature to the study of society in the name of humanism and culture, calling England's progress nothing but machinery, and dividing his fellow-citizens into aristocratic Barbarians, middle-class Philistines, and "Populace." The first two classes were condemned to failure because of their respective imperviousness to ideas and culture; and since the day of the Populace was approaching, civilization could be saved only by permeating the masses with tolerance and understanding. Culture, according to Arnold, could not flourish in an inequitable society since "our inequality materializes our upper class, vulgarizes our middle class, brutalizes our lower class;" culture therefore "seeks to do away with classes," and its proponents are "the true apostles of equality." [3] John Stuart Mill championed personal liberty, the emancipation of women, and a utilitarianism primed for "the greatest good of the greatest number." Walter Pater raised the slogan of art *versus* utility, and refined pleasure *versus* humdrum duty.

The poets also began to lock horns with industrialism and Victorian morality. The pre-Raphaelite Brotherhood, led by Dante Gabriel Rossetti, extolled estheticism and set art above business, beauty above pounds sterling. They were followed by Swinburne who added overtones of free-thinking and democratic romanticism to the main theme of estheticism. William Morris ·became an active Socialist and dreamed himself into Utopias with *The Dream of John Ball* and *News from Nowhere*. Matthew Arnold's brilliant friend Arthur Hugh Clough, son of a cotton merchant, lost his faith and separated from the Church but reinforced his spirit with apostrophes to courage like *Say Not the Struggle Nought Availeth*. Moreover, his mockery of the Victorian compromise in *The Latest Decalogue* is a veritable epitome of the entire Victorian rebellion:

> *Thou shallt have one God only: who*
> *Would be at the expense of two?*
> *No graven images may be*
> *Worshipped, except the currency. . . .*
> *Honor thy parents: that is, all*
> *From whom advancement may befall;*
> *Thou shallt not kill, but needst not strive*
> *Officiously to keep alive:*
> *Do not adultery commit—*
> *Advantage rarely comes of it.*
> *Thou shallt not steal—an empty feat,*
> *When it's so lucrative to cheat . . .*
> *Thou shallt not covet, but tradition*
> *Approves all forms of competition.*

This poem written in 1849 could have found a place in The Revolutionist's Handbook of Shaw's *Man and Superman*.

The novelists, too, behaved with an obstreperousness hardly tolerable at Windsor Castle. From Thackeray's cynical picture of the materialistic upper classes, sentimentalized for the most part only when he turned to characters remote from the contemporary scene, to Dickens' gallery of a dogmatic middle class and a brutalized populace, the Victorian novel at its best was abundantly critical. Dickens' exposure of conditions in British prisons, workhouses, and schools was, in fact, a powerful incentive to reform. George Eliot, freethinker and humanitarian, reproved moral prejudice, moralized in turn, and gave prominence to social struggles in *Felix Holt* and *Daniel Deronda*. The Yorkshire riots appeared in Charlotte Brontë's *Shirley* and the independence of the "new woman" in the tentative *Jane Eyre*, while her sister Emily's *Wuthering Heights* presented a picture of incandescent passion that would have sent England's Queen into a seizure. Elizabeth Gaskell's *Mary Barton* and *Ruth* described the kind of life in the workers' quarters that Victorian gentlemen would have gladly left unnoticed. The Reverend Charles Kingsley added moral passion to his exposures of slum and factory conditions in *Alton Locke* and *Yeast* about the same time that he was writing romance like *Westward Ho!* for boys and *Water Babies* for younger children. Charles Reade supplemented his *Cloister and the Hearth* with stories of prison and factory life in *Never Too Late to Mend* and *Put Yourself in His Place*. George Meredith reviewed British society with considerable criticism and with particular scorn for the people who "fiddle harmonics on the strings of sentimentalism." To the proponents of false Victorian relations between men and women, he opposed independent women who demand equality with men. That unnatural morals must make way for naturalness was the burden of Meredith's paradoxically mannered novels *The Ordeal of Richard Feverel, Rhoda Fleming,* and *Diana of the Crossways*. Rejecting the Victorian compromise between science and religion, Thomas Hardy declared himself for scientific determinism, saw only "crass casualty" in the world, and assailed the crushing intolerance of society, sending shivers through the gentle protoplasm of his readers with *Tess of the D'Urbervilles*. Samuel Butler played havoc with the sacrosanct Victorian home in *The Way of All Flesh*.

Here, in short, was a body of literature that Shaw could respect, and it is not too much to say that he could have found much sustenance in it even if he had never read a line of Schopenhauer, Nietzsche, and Ibsen. He is in fact a lineal descendant of the Victorian writers to a greater degree than is generally suspected. His penchant for polemics, his belief in evolution, social reform, and the superman, his skepticism regarding middle-class democracy, his excoriation of respectability—all these elements of his dramatic work were clearly anticipated by them.

But Shaw was to fulfill himself in the drama, and in the British theatre until he spoke in it as both critic and dramatist there was hardly a whisper of the battle that was raging in the literary world.

As late as 1879, so scrupulous a critic as Arnold could declare with absolute literalness that "In England we have no modern drama at all." The theatre had been long held in contempt by the middle class as an ungodly institution, being tolerated only when it exhibited conventional heroism and sentiment. Melodrama requiring no mental exertion alone could command attention; hence the success of Bulwer-Lytton, H. J. Byron, Tom Taylor and Boucicault. When in 1832 Douglas Jerrold tried to introduce the miserable life of the peasantry into *The Rent Day,* he had to submerge his essential theme of an eviction in gallons of melodrama; and even this half-hearted effort was not repeated for decades. Comedy was a drug on the market, its place being taken by primitive farces and curtain raisers or after-pieces like John Madison Morton's *Box and Cox* of 1841 vintage. This, perhaps the best of them, later considered good enough to be turned into a one-act operetta by Gilbert and Sullivan, hammers symmetrical humor out of the identical reactions of a hatter and a printer to the unedifying prospect of marrying the rich widow Penelope Anne.

Only in the work of the mid-Victorian T. W. Robertson did the voice of reality rise above a stage whisper, and it was so unusual for a playwright to venture beyond polite sibilance that Robertson was something of a prodigy for his age. In 1865 came his comedy *Society,* notable for its comparatively witty dialogue but most memorable for its blunt satire on the materialism of the period. Lady Ptarmigan, urging her rebellious daughter Maud to marry a rich dolt, declares flatly that "Money can do everything," and the suitor Chodd Junior is equally confident that "Capital commands the world." "The capitalist commands capital, therefore the capitalist commands the world," and nothing—neither the House of Commons nor the most fashionable house—can resist the open sesame of his check book. Marriage he considers "a union mutually advantageous;" honor "means not being bankrupt." This satire is, however, properly laved in romance, and true love wins the day when Chodd's impoverished rival wins a fortune. Robertson's *School* troubled the domestic waters in 1869 with an assault on the doll's house convention, Lord Beaufoy shocking his interlocutor with the declaration that he does not want a regulation doll for a wife. But the Victorian compromise is carefully maintained in this play; as for suffrage, "if women were admitted to electoral privileges, they'd sell them for the price of a new chignon," declares another character, though he adds cynically that "man as a nobler animal has the exclusive right to sell his vote—for beer!"

Robertson clearly left the status quo alone. He was convinced that the stratification of the classes in England was sound and he reserved some of his sharpest satire for social upstarts.

Robertson's frequently impartial satire was, nevertheless, bracing for its time, and his tentative attempt to introduce realism into his stage pictures was sufficiently novel to give him a reputation as an innovator. This in spite of the fact that his plays were feeble in characterization and rode the conventional soliloquy and aside for all they were worth. *Caste,* despite its sentimental absurdities, was hailed in 1867 as the last word in truthfulness, and it is a sufficient comment on the state of the English drama that more than two decades later Shaw still could treat Robertson with respect. The theatre of the seventies and eighties retreated rather than advanced, being given over chiefly to vapid adaptations from the French at which Sydney Grundy was past master owing to his smart dialogue.

Only in the field of musical comedy did the seventies and eighties speak out boldly and freshly through the puckish genius of W. S. Gilbert whose gibes were properly palliated with charming lyrics and with Sir Arthur Sullivan's music. A professed conservative in politics, Gilbert had a genius for finding breaches in the Victorian barricade. It is hardly possible to better his travesties on the hereditary aristocracy of the House of Lords in *Iolanthe,* a member of which confesses "I don't want to disparage brains, I admire them; in fact, I often wish I had some myself," and he was equally disrespectful to the bench in *Trial by Jury,* to the British navy in *H.M.S. Pinafore,* or to the upper classes in general. Without a social or moral program or a capacity for indignation, he continually satirized his times "without for a moment ceasing to be a Victorian." [4] He was at heart an irrepressible poet-child who could treat the most fanciful things with the literalness of childhood and the most solemn facts with irreverent fantastication. He was, moreover, a born humorist whom the age kept well supplied with fuel for his fire. Little wonder that the good Queen was "not amused." But Gilbert-and-Sullivan musical comedy was a special department, requiring an almost freakish talent and a rare genius for poetic nonsense. The future of the English theatre could not be determined by the Savoy operas even if they left reverberations in the spacious brain of Shaw and in the smaller cranial compartments of Noel Coward and several Americans. Progress in the theatre had to come from other sources.

In the late eighties the French market practically disappeared, for English writers could not possibly adapt the pungent naturalistic pieces of Becque, Zola, and their followers for the Victorian market. At the same time, however, the developments across the Channel could not leave English playwrights unaffected. The drama of ideas and critical realism was also assailing them from other quarters, chiefly from Scandinavia where Ibsen was establishing a new dispensation. It was evident that the English stage would have to take account of the new phenomenon and that audiences reared on the British essayists and novelists required at least a portion of the stimulation to which their reading had accustomed them. And the playwrights responded as best they could—that is, by compromising. They forged nothing comparable to Ibsen's thunderbolts, but they produced imitations that were less dangerous than the real article and yet gave their public the illusion of danger.

After writing some trifles and a thumping melodrama, Henry Arthur Jones stepped into the breach between the English and the continental theatres. Having been born in 1851, he was still young enough and still insufficiently habituated to drivel to want to reorient himself. He even considered himself a pioneer, and in a sense he was that when he insisted upon treating stage pieces as literature. In 1884, moreover, he wrote what was for its day a slashing attack on commercial philistinism in *Saints and Sinners*. For all its sorry faults, it presented a slice of English life that only Robertson had placed on the counter. Stressing the fact that there was a wide discrepancy between the religious professions and practices of the age—a point that was still new in the theatre!—Jones described the persecution of a noble-minded pastor Jacob Fletcher by his deacons Hoggard and Prabble. Unable to resist the current fashion of melodrama Jones cooked up a melodramatic stew of seduction and exposure. He concluded with the punishment of his stage villains and the vindication of injured innocence, although the play closed without the conventional happy ending in the case of the parson's daughter. But the picture of drab and mercenary life and the scarification of religious hypocrisy marked an advance in dramatic realism. Satire predominated in the exposure of the deacons, Prabble stating bluntly that having observed members of the congregation going to the Co-operative stores he was asking the pastor to preach against them. He makes it all very plain to the pastor: "If I support your chapel, I expect you to get the congregation to support my shop. That's only fair."

Jones returned to this theme in *The Triumph of the Philistines* in 1895 and *The Middleman* in 1889, and he questioned the shams of marriage conventions five years later in *The Masqueraders*. Finally, a year later, he wrote a weighty analysis of religion in *Michael and His Lost Angel* which may be recognized today as one of the supreme examples of the British compromise.

This play, which was attacked in its own day as irreverent because it revealed a clergyman in the throes of illicit passion, begins as a preachment on the subject of not casting stones. The Reverend Michael Feversham who had compelled a girl in his congregation to confess her shame publicly in church soon commits the same sin himself. Moreover, he finds that he is not sorry in the least. At this point, however, Jones violated all semblance of dramatic unity and logic by bringing his audience back to righteousness, and the third act is consumed in repentance and expiation. Penitently Michael Feversham makes a public confession of his sin, leaves his congregation in disgrace, goes into seclusion, and never again sees Audrie Lesden until she is brought to him in a dying condition. There may be psychological truth in this conclusion, given the stiff character and training of the clergyman, and for this reason the play is not wholly devoid of power. Audrie is a charmingly if sketchily realized character who dies with a variation of Heine's cynical words on her lips, "Le bon Dieu nous pardonnera; c'est son métier"—God will forgive us; that is his business. *Michael and His Lost Angel* was, in fact, a vast improvement on the customary treatment of illicit passion in the Victorian theatre. But the fact remains that, as Shaw noted, Jones found it expedient to accept the conventional device of "a monastery for the man and death for the woman as the only possible stage ending—surely not so much an ending as a sopping up of the remains of the two poor creatures." Owing to his sense of obligation to convention, Jones remained a pseudo-Ibsenite, and since the formula of "all or nothing" is nowhere so imperative as in the drama of ideas his most ambitious efforts have lost most of their justification as dramatic literature.

The habit of making concessions to the public was in fact remarkably tenacious in this writer who set himself up as a champion of modernism. In a letter to Brander Matthews written late in life he admitted that although he had composed about ninety plays and believed he had helped to move things, he had been able to write only four or five times "the play I should have written if the conditions of the English theatre had been as easy for the dramatist as they are today." He probably would not have been able to write it under any circumstances, since despite much experience in the world which he entered at the age of twelve with little schooling he was essentially a simple-minded man.[5]

Ironically, in view of his ambitions, his most readable and actable plays today are slender comedies of manners like *The Liars* and *Dolly Reforming Herself*. The former is an amusing picture of smart manners in 1897 with friends and relatives wheedling a husband and his flirtatious wife into a reconciliation and packing her lover off to the colonies. Being a commoner by background and instinct, Jones could observe the upper brackets with detached amusement. It is unfortunate only that he found it necessary to abide by conventional ideas in a comedy that would profit from more boldness of thought. More consistently comic, *Dolly Reforming Herself* (written eleven years later) is an even more amusing, and more penetrating, concoction. The domestic squalls of a thriftless wife and the flirtations of her friend, who is married to a psychologist patterned after Herbert Spencer, are highly diverting, and some discreet cynicism at the expense of a clergyman who labors under the delusion that his sermons reform people adds a dash of lemon to the playwright's sauce. However, even in these pieces, as well as in *The Case of Rebellious Susan* whose heroine leaves her home (but returns to it, of course!) when her husband proves unfaithful, Jones appears to have believed that he was wrestling with modern problems. There was indeed much justice in Professor Gilbert Norwood's wholesale indictment of the Jones-Pinero school when he wrote that "Your pseudo-advanced writer invariably reveals his calibre by this assumption that the 'problem-play' must treat of marital infidelity; there is only one sin—the Decalogue has become a monologue." [6]

Even more willing to move with the tide so long as it did not sweep him out too far, Arthur Wing Pinero followed Jones' example. Better educated, having been trained for the law, and even more at home in the theatre owing to his five years' apprenticeship in Sir Henry Irving's company, Pinero brought much facile craftsmanship and specious progressivism to bear on the pseudo-Ibsen plays that he began to write so successfully after composing a number of superior Victorian farces like *The Magistrate*. In 1887 he produced a tragedy *The Profligate* in which he factitiously proved that character is destiny when the profligate Renshaw cannot make his marriage successful and finally takes his poison. This conclusion was quickly turned into a happy ending by the author out of deference to the public, so that his first effort to create realistic drama died aborning. Pinero, however, found his favorite pattern in this play, and the result was a series of labored domestic dramas with strong pretensions to realistic characterization and social analysis.

Discreetly he did not write the first of them until after England had had a taste of Ibsen, until after Shaw had written his *Widowers' Houses*, and until after J. T. Grein founded his Independent Theatre in 1891 for what Shaw described as the "apparently hopeless attempt to bring the English theatre into some sort of relation with contemporary life." [7] In 1893, however, the great English public was still innocent of any knowledge of the truly modern drama and Pinero's first "modern" tragedy *The Second Mrs. Tanqueray* was hailed as epoch-making. It made a woman with a past the heroine of a tragedy, and it even sympathized with her efforts to adjust herself to respectable society. At the same time, the play provided moments when Paula's vulgar past showed through her acquired veneer, and this had to be set down as realistic character drawing. Pinero also allowed much of her unhappiness and some of the play's complications to stem directly from her character, and this application of the formula that "character makes destiny" was a sign of realistic dramaturgy. Here was no sentimentalization about heaven rejoicing over one sinner saved.

By comparison with *Ghosts,* which the Independent Theatre had presented two years earlier, the play was, however, mild and dishonest, conventional morality being left untouched by investigation and winning the battle when Paula Tanqueray poisoned herself. Moreover, this conclusion was encompassed by the stage trick of a specious coincidence when Paula's former lover turns up as her stepdaughter's suitor and Paula finds it necessary to reveal his identity to her husband. This in turn leads to accusations of immorality on the part of the pure-minded stepdaughter who has suspected Paula all along (in a manner which leaves either the playwright's craftsmanship or the tiresome girl's purity open to doubt). Shaw was apparently the first to point out, in defiance of Pinero's admirers, that what they actually meant by praising their favorite author's craftsmanship was "recklessness in the substitution of dead machinery" for vital action. But "epoch-making" the play remained for them, and Pinero found it profitable to explore the vein further between essays in comedy of manners like *The Gay Lord Quex* which are perhaps less questionable today because they were less pretentious.

It may also be noted that he advanced in some directions. In *The Notorious Mrs. Ebbsmith* the following year he created a harassed but spirited character of some reality and force, even if her gesture of rebellion when she throws the Bible that is offered to her for consolation into the fire is hastily smoothed over when she retrieves it at once. *Iris,* written in 1901 (after Shaw's *Candida* and *Mrs. Warren's Profession,* be it noted!), contains a still more completely realized character in the weak woman Iris whose tragedy arises from her inability to stand a life of poverty after having enjoyed riches. Her irresolution culminates in her being driven out into the streets when her lover discovers her apparent treachery. However, Pinero's vaunted craftsmanship again relies upon adventitious occurrences to promote the supposedly inevitable sequence of events. Finally, *Mid-Channel,* in 1909 (after Shaw's *Man and Superman* and *Major Barbara*), added a touch of social investigation to the tragedy of another unfortunate woman whose marriage, as she admits, was doomed from the moment her husband and she agreed that they would never be encumbered in their career "with any—brats of children." Moreover, shifting fortunately to high comedy, Pinero wrote his most interesting play *The Thunderbolt* a year earlier. Although he availed himself of the device of a lost will, he managed to permeate his theme with tart satire on the cupidity of the philistines, so that the play was denounced as insulting "to the provinces." The vividly delineated respectable Mortimores, who had not been on speaking terms with a rich brother until the day of his death, are about to inherit his wealth. They are already laying plans for solidifying their business or social position when his daughter turns up and the wife of the poorest Mortimore confesses that she destroyed the will. She had done this in the hope of lifting her children out of the swamp of poverty, but now that she has discovered that the legitimate heir is a lovable girl she is repentant. After much conniving and many recriminations that tear the mask from her relatives' smug faces, the Mortimores effect a compromise. The ending is of no great consequence, and the play lives by its trenchant exposure of philistinism and its sharply etched characters.

Pinero's best plays, however, were not only overshadowed by the work of Shaw but were buried under an avalanche of rubbish like *Preserving Mr. Panmure* and *The 'Mind the Paint' Girl* which this pragmatic playwright turned out indefatigably. Moreover, he never ceased to employ stock devices, most of his characters were stage types, and his mind remained sealed to the mental or emotional storms·that make tragedy an energizing experience rather than an exhibition of simply regrettable events. As early as 1895, Shaw labeled him·"a humble and somewhat belated follower of the novelists of the middle of the nineteenth century." This judgment still seems valid.

Jones and Pinero lived on into the post-war period, dying in 1929 and 1934 respectively, and they might have been comforted by the reflection that many playwrights were still paying them the homage of imitation. But it was not for want of better examples that these epigoni hid in the greenrooms of their once venturesome elders. A veritable cleansing of the Augean stables—a more appropriate name for the greenrooms—took place in the nineties. If Jones and Pinero applied only a cautious hand to the broom, Wilde and Shaw never hesitated to make the dust fly. Both men evinced scant respect for conventional or "sound" dramaturgy, Wilde using claptrap plots as pegs for his irreverent epigrams and Shaw giving as much time to his polemical disquisitions as he found necessary while the plot was left cooling its heels in the wings. Both men took pleasure in the sheer exuberance of their impudence and enjoyed baiting respectability with the blithe sadism of born satirists. And both of them, though they were stigmatized as mere clowns, also entertained a serious destructive purpose.

Of the meteor which was Wilde's reputation actually only a little dust remains. Born of cultured parents and a brilliant student at Trinity and Oxford, the young writer descended upon London with an aplomb appropriate to the name Oscar O'Flahertie Fingal Wills Wilde. His comportment, which still fascinates biographers and literate stenographers (the knee-breeches, the flowing tie, and the lily in his hand or the sunflower in his lapel), invited percussion from satirists. However, "Punch" and Gilbert and Sullivan's *Patience* left him tolerably intact and disaster overtook him only when he courted it himself with his ill-advised libel suit against the Marquess of Queensberry. But although Wilde was destroyed by his two years' imprisonment in Reading Gaol for sexual inversion and was buried ingloriously in the cemetery of Père Lachaise in 1900, his career produced interesting fireworks.

The truth is that Wilde's career was a portent and a protest. His behavior, like his theory that life is the imitation of art, was in effect an affirmation of Arnold's battle against philistinism and of Ruskin's effort to bring beauty into the everyday life of industrial England. In his avidity for rare sensations, he was merely putting into practice Pater's theory of esthetic gratification; and if he succeeded only in travestying the latter's philosophical paganism, if he applied it coarsely like a salesman on a spree (for Wilde was more commonplace than he conceived), the revolt against Victorian smugness was apparent in his effort. He himself lapsed, it is true, into another kind of smugness—into the smugness of the snob, such being the ironic revenge of the age on one of its rebellious sons. Nevertheless, the immediate effect of his conduct was anti-philistine. Moreover, his keen intelligence made him a critic of society, and the pleasure he took in epigrams for their own sake did not preclude serious and sound observation. Certainly Wilde, the social lion with his "singular mixture of Balliol and brogue" did not live exclusively in the dream-world of estheticism. Ford Madox Ford even recalled that the bulky dandy whom he used to see at his uncle's home every Saturday evinced a strong concern for interest rates on Consols.[8] (Ford also recalled that the dreamful pre-Raphaelite poetess Christina Rossetti noted the fluctuations in the price of Consols on the back of the manuscript of her last poem. So much for the notion that poets are necessarily immune to the virus of their age!)

When Wilde turned to the drama early in his career with the puerile *Vera, or The Nihilists* in 1883 he merely paid his respects to Victorian melodrama. Eight years later the verse play *The Duchess of Padua* merely added Elizabethan trimmings to the thrillers of the day. His *tour de force, Salome,* in 1892 was another melodrama and a sufficiently operatic one to become the libretto of Strauss's well-known opera. This Grand Guignol of the beheading of John the Baptist at the instance of the love-mad daughter of Herodias had the merit of introducing the pungent element of sadism into the subject of passion which the Victorians had so liberally sprinkled with rose-water. Primarily, however, this one-acter was merely a decadent, hothouse hybrid of passion and neurosis. Wilde became a playwright of some importance only when he began his series of four comedies of manners with *Lady Windermere's Fan* in the same year.

Derivative in this piece, he harked back to the sentimental comedy of the eighteenth century. The plot of *Lady Windermere's Fan* is a saccharine concoction about the scandalous Mrs. Erlynne who saves her daughter Lady Windermere from committing adultery and suffering a fate like her own. The structure, trashy as in all of Wilde's plays, is the old-fashioned one of intrigue and misunderstandings: Lady Windermere suspects her husband of intriguing with Mrs. Erlynne, not knowing that Lord Windermere's friendship arises from his solicitude for her unrecognized mother. Seeking vengeance, Lady Windermere goes to an admirer's apartment and leaves her fan there, which is then claimed by Mrs. Erlynne at the sacrifice of her honor. After this noble gesture, Mrs. Erlynne retires from the scene still unrecognized by her daughter but taking with her a picture of the child whose equanimity must be left undisturbed by the truth about her mother's past. Since virtue is to be rewarded in this confection, however, Mrs. Erlynne marries the elderly Augustus. To these improbabilities Wilde appended the numerous coruscating epigrams which even frequent quotation has not quite reduced to platitudes. Some of them have a salutary anti-philistine objective, as when Wilde opposes the easy distinctions of Victorian prudery with the equally glib generalization that "Wicked women bother one. Good women bore one. That is the only difference between them." Hypocrisy is jarred by Mrs. Erlynne's observation that "if a woman really repents, she has to go to a bad dressmaker, otherwise no one believes her," and by Cecil Graham's assurance that "A man who moralizes is usually a hypocrite, and a woman who moralizes is invariably plain." Other generalizations, like the well-aired definition of a cynic as a man who knows the price of everything and the value of nothing give this Victorian comedy a fine varnish of ideas.

The logical apotheosis of the element of insouciance in *Lady Windermere's Fan* was farce, and Wilde made the most of it in *The Importance of Being Earnest*. Written in 1895, it was his last testament, and reverence for the stylist who tossed off lines like "Divorces are made in Heaven" and that "in married life three is company and two is none" has resulted in its being considered the best modern farce in the English language. Today there is humor but scant satire about its mistaken identities, its nonsensical young men who fool each other with a pretence of mourning, and its travesty on respectability when the rakish Ernest tries to keep his girlish ward pure-minded. Nor is there any remarkable satire in Aunt Bracknell's refusal to sanction Ernest's marriage until he finds some relatives, the infant Ernest having been lost in a hand-bag in which his absent-minded nurse had placed the manuscript of her novel. Satire effervesces very quickly when it is not mixed with the ingredients of poetic fantasy as in Aristophanes' work or with the cement of earthy characterization such as one finds in Shakespeare's clowning episodes. Wilde's farce being nonetheless full of mad brio was unfairly treated by the best critic of his day — who was Shaw, of course — as "stock mechanical fun." Surely, the epigrams gave a new fillip to the older farces of H. J. Byron, with which Shaw identified *The Importance of Being Earnest*. Wilde, however, had other resources than insouciance, and he wrote two clever if contrived, comedies of ideas in his earlier produced plays, *A Woman of No Importance* (1893) and *An Ideal Husband*.[9]

Anticipating Somerset Maugham's *Our Betters* in the first of these, Wilde centered part of the play around the experience of an American girl in sophisticated English society. Here he struck cleverly at the American habit of knocking at the portals of aristocracy with quips like Lord Illingworth's remark that "American women are wonderfully clever in concealing their parents." The cream of the jest, however, lies in the fact that highly touted British society is itself pinchbeck, a point that Wilde presses home not merely in so dazzling and Shavian an epigram as his definition of the British idea of health, "The English country gentleman galloping after a fox—the unspeakable in full pursuit of the uneatable" but in his entire gallery of hollow characters. They are emptily conventional like Lady Hunstanton, airily wasteful like Lord Alfred who can afford gold-tipped cigarettes only when he is "in debt," or flippant like Mrs. Allonby and Lord Illingworth who note that a "bad woman" is "the sort of woman a man never gets tired of." This is the world where one can live down "anything except a good reputation" and where simple pleasures are adored because they are the last refuge of the complex; this is the philandering world which holds that "the Book of Life begins with a man and a woman in a garden" and that "it ends with Revelations." Restoration comedy of manners is revived here to perfection until the plot thickens, and Congreve's ghost must have chuckled in the wings upon hearing Mrs. Allonby assure her female friends that her husband was a promissory note and that she was tired of meeting him.

Loosely related to this social satire is the assault on the double standard which makes Mrs. Arbuthnot a social outcast whereas Lord Illingworth who gave her an illegitimate son goes scot free. Wilde failed to realize the point that conventional morality has saddled Mrs. Arbuthnot with an insufferable, masochistic conscience; and that consequently she becomes a bore. Wilde did, however, explode her complaint by making Gerald tell his mother in all innocence that after all the blame for an illicit affair rests on both parties. And after the contrived climax when the truth about Lord Illingworth escapes her, Mrs. Arbuthnot does grow up sufficiently to be happy that she got a son even at the price of her innocence and to refuse Illingworth's offer of respectable marriage. The puritanic Hester and the prig Gerald, who ultimately become engaged despite the scandal of the latter's illegitimacy, also shed their armor of righteousness. On the strength of this comedy it is almost possible to call Wilde Shaw's comrade-in-arms. It is not surprising that casual epigrams like "All thought is immoral. Its very essence is destruction. If you think of anything, you kill it. Nothing survives being thought of" should also recall Shaw.

An Ideal Husband was another attempt at social satire, even broader in scope though only partially crystallized. Here the comic core is closely related to the exposure of a Cabinet member's past and it concludes with the deflation of his wife's smug morality. Sir Robert Chiltern founded his fortune on the sale of a state secret concerning the Suez Canal and his unsavory past enables the adventuress Mrs. Cheveley to blackmail him into supporting a wildcat scheme for a worthless Argentine canal. Wilde moderated the issue of political corruption by sentimentalizing his Under-Secretary into a repentant, high-minded gentleman who finally speaks against the scheme in Parliament at the risk of exposure. Similar sentimentalization occurs when the Wildean dandy Lord Goring neutralizes Mrs. Cheveley by discovering her theft of a bracelet and forcing her to burn the evidence against his friend. But the political satire is at least implicit in the theme, and the Victorian idealizations of the sheltered Lady Chiltern are shattered when she is forced to forgive her husband after realizing how easily she herself could have been embroiled in a scandal. For all its wit, *An Ideal Husband* is, in truth, a mess, but it is headed in the direction of comedy of ideas.

Wilde's contribution to the airing of the British theatre cannot be underestimated. It was his misfortune only that he was incorrigibly lazy and that his was not a mind of the first order. Both the energy and the mind for a fruitful encounter with the world were, however, quickly supplied by the second of the immigrants, by Shaw who brought to his laughter a great spirit and an intellect sharpened by deep application to both literary and social studies.

2 THE RESOURCES OF SHAW

No one has ever accused Shaw of want of humor or a dislike for sheer fun. To paraphrase his own comment on Wilde he has been the modern world's most thorough playwright since he has played with everything. He has been busy at the game of delighting himself and the world for the greater part of sixty years, and he proposes to enjoy himself, if nowadays less buoyantly, for another decade and a half—the "life force," his vegetable diet and German air squadrons willing. But he was equally addicted to working hard and earnestly. When he came to

London it was in a frame of mind radically different from that of his Dublin neighbor.

The "upstart son of a downstart," as he later described himself, he was forced to earn his living at an early age as a real-estate clerk,—a condition he must have felt all the more keenly because his family was well connected with the nobility. One grandfather, "a mighty procreator of children" St. John Ervine calls him, was Sir Robert Shaw of Bushey Park, and the family claimed Scottish descent from Macduff. "It was as good as being descended from Shakespeare," Shaw noted later. In Ireland the Protestant Shaws had been men of wealth and position ever since they arrived there shortly before the Battle of the Boyne and until the migratory instinct drove many of them to Australia where a Shaw River and a Shaw Mountain are part of the topography.[10] But the corn dealer George Carr Shaw, the playwright's father, became an alcoholic and went downgrade, and it is more than probable that Shaw's temperate habits and teetotalism, not to speak of his unorthodox views on home and hearth, date from this catastrophe. The humiliation of being declassed and of being regarded as such by his relatives must have been keenly felt by the youth who was later to play havoc with aristocratic pretensions without being immune to them himself.

If Shaw became a democrat after a fashion (for all his Social-Democratic leanings he was never without reservations regarding democracy), he was one by compulsion rather than conviction. Shaw has told the sorry story himself, and it explains the man, the philosopher and dramatist more than he probably realized. His father, whom he approvingly credits with a "humorous sense of anticlimax or a penchant for pricking conventions with laughter," was "racked with shame and remorse even in his cups;" consequently he was "a miserable drunkard and unbearable." He adds, "We were finally dropped socially. After my childhood I can never remember paying a visit at a relative's house." [11]

Fortunately left to his devices by a musically talented mother who had her hands full and believed "that correct behavior was inborn," the son led a free life, enjoyed a sea-faring uncle's profanity, and learned nothing at school. Much more instructive were the musical inclinations of the family; for his mother was a singer, an aunt played the harp, and an alcoholic uncle favored an ophicleide or primitive tuba. (It cured the latter of alcoholism until, after renouncing it for matrimony, he ended his days in an asylum believing that he was the Holy Ghost.) The taste he absorbed at home made him a music critic and a "perfect Wagnerite" in the nineties, and there was to be much musical feeling in the great prose of his prefaces and plays, as well as in their structure.

It is worth observing that Shaw has been partial to musical form in his plays, and it is noteworthy that the great scientist-artist Einstein should have likened Shaw's plays to Mozart's music, a point that Shaw has made himself. *Getting Married,* for example, is almost a fugue, variation upon variation flowing from his pen; and *Back to Methuselah* is a theme with variations. *The Apple Cart* employs an "Overture" consisting of the conversation between the King's secretaries, is followed by development of the theme in the King's banter with his Cabinet (the music "being tossed from one instrument to another," as Edmund Wilson observes),[12] and the act concludes after a climactic confession of faith by the monarch with the playful talk of the secretaries. One may also observe the varied use of the coda in the final scenes of *The Doctor's Dilemma* and *Saint Joan.* Rarely, moreover, has he departed from his habit of carrying an argument forward with a proper balance between warmth and formality, with suggestiveness and yet with remarkable precision. The "music of ideas" or moralities, to use another of Edmund Wilson's happy phrases, is the chief feature of Shaw's artistry, and it may explain much of the insinuating charm and force of Shaw's plays. Even when he has written a poor play, he has composed a notable symposium that recalls Plato's equally musical dialogues. He has himself declared that we must not suppose that he learnt his art from English writers but from "the masters of a universal language—Bach, Handel, Mozart [whom he has set above all composers], Beethoven and Wagner." This statement requires only the qualification that as both a moralist and stylist he also owes a great deal to the translators of the King James Bible and John Bunyan who have made more English writers than all the schoolmasters of Great Britain and America.

Still the lad who emulated his relatives by composing his own prayers "in three movements like a sonata" until his "conscience" obliged him to renounce "superstitious practices" soon found himself more immediately concerned with economic facts. Finding his clerkship too confining in 1876 despite the fact that after five years of application he was already at the age of nineteen an excellent bookkeeper with accountancy at the rainbow's end, he left for London where his mother had preceded him to teach music for a living. Here, working at first for a telephone company but soon subsisting on an allowance from his mother and on the meager pay of a literary hack, he devoted himself to private study in lieu of a university education.

Having come to London, as he said, because he was "not enamored of poverty, of ostracism, of contempt which these imply," he naturally turned to social philosophy. But after listening to Henry George's lecture on nationalizing the land he discovered that everything that he was mulling over—the Victorian conflict between religion and science, the education of women, "Mill on Liberty," the controversies over Darwinism, and the philosophy of Spencer—was not fundamental. It

was all "mere middle-class business," and the importance of "the economic basis" which he was later to introduce as a major contribution
to the content of modern English drama suddenly dawned on him. This
occurred in 1882 in a period of economic crisis which created a revival
of interest in Socialism. Shaw therefore studied socialist literature and
allowed Marx to make "a man" of him, as he declared in later years.

He became a founder, and in 1906-7 head, of the evolutionary socialist
Fabian Society in the company of such redoubtable students as Wells
and the Webbs. He acquired notable gifts as a Hyde Park orator and
as a public-hall lecturer, speaking as often as three times on Sundays
until he was prostrated. He even entered politics to the extent of becoming a vestryman and a borough councilor for St. Pancras district in
London from 1897 to 1903, being defeated only in 1904 when he outraged his free-thinking constituency by paradoxically advocating the
improvement of religious schools. The political habit has persisted with
him, and his pronouncements at the age of eighty-four are still good
newspaper copy. Moreover, although he has fathered nonsense from
time to time, his utterances still make better sense than those of England's official spokesmen; for the most part, his comment on Chamberlain policies in the year 1939 [13] does not leave much to be desired from
a free-lance and an honest man—two apparent disqualifications for
diplomacy. Perhaps he should have been England's Prime Minister, and
it is the English people's loss that he became a man of letters instead!
It is noteworthy, however, that the Fabianism he propounded in numerous tracts and in his bulky *Intelligent Woman's Guide to Socialism and
Capitalism,* scrapped Marxism of the class war theory and expected a
socialism run by experts and effected by non-revolutionary gradualism.
It was in this dilution of Marxism by the concept of change by gentle
reform and government by the élite that the British habit of compromise
caught up with Shaw. It was modified only by his continuous insistence
on equality of income.

Unfortunately, moreover, for those who deplore the absence of a perfect and exclusively socialist thinker in Shaw, the struggling young
writer also hearkened to other voices. He acquired a conglomeration
of viewpoints as confusing to smaller intellects (and to a lesser degree
to Shaw himself) as they are enriching to his cerebral comedies. Shavian
comedy, as has been proved, can in many instances dispense with almost
anything that has been regarded indispensable to a play—plot, development, characterization, and consistency. But one thing Shavian comedy
cannot dispense with—namely, the interplay of ideas. Moreover, the
interplay must be deft and precise and the ideas must be abounding;
when either quality is absent as in *The Simpleton of the Unexpected*

Isles or *The Millionairess* Shaw is a lost man. And these qualities require an eclectic mastery of ideas which must send a writer foraging
over the earth. In one of his masterful cartoons, Max Beerbohm represents the critic Brandes as a merchant to whom the playwright has
brought a parcel of clothes. Brandes asks the playwright what he will
take for the lot. "Immortality," replies Shaw with characteristic modesty. "Come," ejaculates the *marchand d'idées,* "I've handled these goods
before! Coat, Mr. Schopenhauer's; waistcoat, Mr. Ibsen's; Mr.
Nietzsche's trousers. . ." "Ah," replies Shaw, "but look at the patches."

The claims are indeed well divided. The goods had been handled before, for Shaw did not really forswear non-economic English thought
as "mere middle-class business" after hearing Henry George. Instead he
even added to his cloth Schopenhauer's concept of the world as "will,"
Nietzsche's faith in the evolution of man into superman, Lamarck's and
Bergson's theories of evolution, Ibsen's plea for uninhibited self-realization, and various other continental fabrics. Nor may one overlook Shaw's
respect for the pre-Victorian poets Blake and Shelley, both mystics and
social critics simultaneously. Still, the "patches" were Shaw's, and what
really mattered is that both the original cloth and the patches enabled
him to dress the drama in such an array of motley as it had never worn
before. In short, he gave the world of modern science and sociology a
comedy commensurate with its intellectual scope.

Profundity is not, however, a mere matter of intellect. Although as
George Jean Nathan remarked, some of Shaw's plays are as "unemotional as a mushroom" [14] his work is rooted in feeling. It reflects a humanitarianism that is as emotional as anything in the drama, and there
is a noble passion in it. And for all his so-called clowning, his writings
are permeated with a dignity that stems equally from an unintimidated
mind and a noble spirit. That dignity, which is equally a matter of style
and basic content, is a unique quality, and few of his imitators have
equaled it; some have not even approximated it.

A writer does not have to drool in order to convince us of his humanity; it is in fact the droolers whose humanitarianism is most suspect.
Shaw, the arch-enemy of sentimentality, betrays a private core of sentimentality only in his vegetarian detestation of "slaughter in the butcher's
yard." Despite his opposition to war (he was the only English dramatist
of prominence to raise his voice against the World War from the beginning), he has, it is true, been less tender-minded toward mankind. He
has not been averse to the liquidation of parasitic or idiotic members of
the race by the wholesale methods of dictatorship, and he has always
felt that mankind must be bullied into sanity and humanity. His has
been in some respects a calloused heart, as the rich and mighty and the

poor and stupid have often discovered. But no one can legitimately deny the presence of that potent organ in Shaw, and it has made itself known in many ways to both the wise and the innocent.

He has detested brutality in sports, and his hatred for competitive, dog-eat-dog society has been unlimited. He has even invented a special kind of lawn tennis for himself in which the object is to keep the ball in play, with penalties for the player who drives it too hard to be returned![15] In private life he has been one of the most generous of men, and his generosity has extended to his fellow-writers, a trait that is not conspicuous in the literary world. Although Shaw first made his reputation as a fearless drama and music critic, he has been unstinted in his praise not only for giants like Ibsen and Wagner but for younger contemporaries like O'Casey and for less worthy comrades of the pen. For the underdog he has evinced an impassioned concern that has led him to expose social injustice mercilessly. Never an esthete of the art-for-art's-sake variety, which he has regarded as both senseless and inhuman, he has had an almost esthetic aversion for the existence of poverty. If he has refused to sentimentalize the poor, this is only because he has been realist enough to know that poverty does not prettify people, and because he has been sensitive enough to be irritated by their blindness and submission. Toward woman as bride, wife and mother-image, he has maintained a wealth of unsentimental tenderness such as appears in his fine treatment of Candida and of Mrs. Dudebat in *The Doctor's Dilemma*. His own relations with women appear to have been impeccable, and his friendship with Ellen Terry would be a noble chapter in any man's life. His partiality for genius in either sex has amounted to nothing short of love, whether the character happened to be a bounder, conventionally speaking, like Dudebat or a saint like Joan of Arc. He has even manifested a fine understanding for economic villains like the munitions manufacturer Undershaft in *Major Barbara*. Only poltroons and hypocrites have been barred from his respect or kindliness, unless they happened to be sufficiently brash and amusing. Actually, Shaw has been one of the most humane playwrights of the world.

Surprising as it may seem, he loves real people. It has been often maintained that Shaw has been incapable of creating living characters. But though it is true that his *dramatis personae* frequently speak like their author, that he has not conveyed the passion of sexual love, and that he has been himself his greatest character (why shouldn't he be since he is the greatest personality in the field of modern letters), he has actually been a master of characterization whenever that art was called for by the nature of his play. Where in the modern English drama will one find characters better realized than his Candida, Dudebat, Julius Caesar, and Joan of Arc?

The old rationalist has also been a man of faith. His belief in the progressive purpose of the Life Force (only another name for God) is downright mystical. He has, in fact, always been a believer, beginning less remotely with faith in the power of reason to save mankind, in man's perfectibility, and in his ability to create a just and rationally ordered society. Shaw, the hard thinker, has been a dreamer of dreams, most of them unfulfilled. He has been, moreover, a special kind of dreamer and pietist. His kinship is with John Bunyan and the genuine Puritan spirit.

Like Bunyan's Christian, he has known that the road to salvation is a perilous one which requires unfailing exertion and faith. His alleged want of sexual passion and his abstemiousness may be nothing more than evidences of good habits and solid burgher virtues, from which other geniuses like Shakespeare and Thomas Mann have likewise not been exempt—and perhaps fortunately so. These traits are inconsequential beside his larger and splendid puritanism, which he has allowed Tanner to explain in *Man and Superman* when the latter declares that according to his experience "moral passion [Shaw has never been afraid of the word moral] is the only real passion" and when he exclaims, "Is the devil to have all the passions as well as all the good tunes?" Tanner adds that "It is the birth of that passion that turns a child a man." It turned Shaw into a man.

To this inventory of Shaw's resources it is necessary only to add— and to add emphatically—the components of playfulness, zest, and refined hedonism. Without these qualities Shaw might have been a great essayist or tragedian but hardly a master of comedy. An inner gaiety, recalling the music of Mozart and the essays of the eighteenth century, has pervaded his spirit. He has played with ideas like a juggler and he has immensely enjoyed his Irish gift of interminable speech. For all his solid reasoning he has not been a systematic philosopher or consistent thinker. If he had been more consistent it is even possible that he would have been less provocative and entertaining. Blueprints of this dramatist are worthless, and to expect them is the well-intended folly of pedestrian critics who should apply themselves to other fields than literature.

The elements of surprise and contradiction are part of the joy of receiving Shaw's work. His zest for controversial conversation, like his "moral passion," has often led him into garrulity and static dramaturgy; his love of fantastication for the sheer joy of being skittish or mischievous has caused him to write a number of inconsequential farces like *The Admirable Bashville* and it has worked havoc with the plots of several of his last plays. But, in the main, his playfulness has been an inestimable attribute of his creativeness, especially when the moral passion held it in check in about a dozen plays which belong to the finest work of the modern European drama. Moreover, combined with his prefaces, his plays (good, bad, and indifferent) comprise a body of literature greater perhaps than any that has appeared in English since Shakespeare.

3 SHAW AS CRITIC AND PLAYWRIGHT

Once Shaw resolved to become a writer, after a characteristic inaugural appearance in print when he announced himself as atheist in a letter to the journal *Public Opinion,* his first thought was the novel. The English theatre was still contemptible in 1879, whereas Victorian fiction had been replete for many years with intelligence, reality, and moral passion. But his own efforts resulted only in five poor novels, all written between 1879 and 1883. Even as vehicles for his ideas they were sufficient only unto the needs of the socialist publications in which they first appeared.

The first to be published, *The Irrational Knot,* was a tract on marriage and class relations which set up an exemplary worker Edward Connolly as a Shavian hero. Connolly refuses to take back his erring upper-class wife because she has failed to acquire a sound plebeian mode of living. (Since she dies of too many bouts with the champagne bottle, the novel also ventilates its author's detestation of liquor.) In 1881 came *Love among the Artists,* which separated the real artists from the false and displayed its author's intellectual wares without much order or reality. *Cashel Byron's Profession,* next year, was better because its burlesque character justified a certain degree of structural looseness. Here the Victorian world is turned topsy-turvy when a cultivated girl of the classes marries a pugilist because he would make a better husband and father than the gentlemen of her circle. Finally in 1884 appeared *An Unsocial Socialist,* a clever book that must not be considered as a novel but as a peg for Shavian ideas.

Obviously defeated by the novel, Shaw finally beat a retreat. It proved to be a strategic one, for it led him into the field of criticism where he was a natural-born master. His fiction had been most readable when he had scrapped all pretense of narration and appeared frankly as a critic of ideas and society. Now he took arts and letters for the subject of his criticism. In 1885 his friend William Archer got him a position as book reviewer for the *Pall Mall Magazine,* from 1888 to 1890 he reviewed music for *The Star,* and from 1895 to 1898 he wrote the famous examples of dramatic criticism for *The Saturday Review* which appear in his *Dramatic Opinions and Essays.* Independent volumes supplemented Shaw's journalism; in 1891 came his lectures (amplified in 1913) *The Quintessence of Ibsen,* in 1895 *The Sanity of Art,* and in 1898 *The Per-*

fect Wagnerite. This body of work, to which portions of his numerous prefaces to the plays must be added, is undoubtedly one of the greatest collections of criticism in the English language.

Shaw's views on any particular work are as open to criticism as any man's, although his opinions of Pinero, Wilde and other English contemporaries are now accepted for the most part as nearly perfect. With respect to Ibsen and Wagner, he was even more vulnerable than more humdrum critics because he was more polemical; and Shaw's yardstick of social criticism was sometimes too inflexible to measure the curvatures of great art when he underestimated Shakespeare and overrated Brieux.[16] Shaw, nevertheless, was not only a remarkably fresh but a frequently salutary critic. When he assailed bardolatry, he was actually fighting the unquestioning worship of Shakespeare that stood in the way of a new and modern English drama while permitting Sir Henry Irving to garble the bard's texts most outrageously. If, moreover, he overrated the problem play he was at least sound in prescribing a diet of ideas for modern dramatists. His criticism was, besides, eminently right for himself, and since his plays have been for half a century a very considerable portion of the theatre he was right for the drama too.

With scant respect for the drama of his day and with a philosophy of art already contained in the proposition that art is "the subtlest, the most seductive, the most effective means of propagandism in the world," Shaw in time sallied into the theatre. The "new theatre," founded by Antoine in France and Brahm in Germany, was at last becoming naturalized in England largely owing to the progressive work of J. T. Grein who founded the Independent Theatre in 1891. Everything, as Shaw later declared, followed from Grein's momentous decision—the Manchester Repertory Company, the Abbey Theatre in Dublin, the Court Theatre, the Stage Society, and the whole repertory chain of England. Unwilling to confine himself to continental drama, Grein began a search for native plays that had proved too trenchant for the commercial managers. He found only two acts of an unfinished play which the critic Shaw had cast aside seven years before owing to differences with his collaborator William Archer. As Shaw later reported, "Laying violent hands on his [Archer's] thoroughly planned scheme for a sympathetically romantic 'well-made play' of the Parisian type then in vogue," he had "perversely distorted it into a grotesque realistic exposure of slum landlordism, municipal jobbery, and the pecuniary and matrimonial ties between them and the pleasant people with 'independent' incomes who imagine that such sordid matters do not touch their own lives."[17] This is an excellent summary of *Widower's Houses*, and it was this play that he completed in 1892. The production that year at once made him "infamous as a playwright;" at the premiere socialists applauded him on principle, the rest of the audience hooted him also on principle, and Shaw being by now an expert "mob orator" made a resounding speech to the house. The newspapers treated the play in full and it ultimately appeared in the volume which he forthrightly entitled "Unpleasant," [18] since, as he explained, "all plays which deal sincerely with humanity must wound the monstrous conceit which it is the business of romance to flatter." [19]

Showing how the middle class and the gentry batten on slum rentals "as flies fatten on filth," Shaw wrote the first naturalist English play. It proved so shocking an exposure of the drainpipes of society that it wrung an anguished cry from his hedonistic admirer Huneker who asked, "How could Shaw be so philistine, so much like a vestryman interested in pauper lodgings?" Shaw replied that it was merely a transcript of reality. Huneker and Shaw notwithstanding, however, *Widower's Houses* is not a slum-clearance report but an ironic comedy of the profit system, and if its shortcomings are easily apparent its Jonsonian humor possesses a bouncing vitality rare in modern English drama.

Sartorius, the owner of miserable tenements, has educated and refined his daughter Blanche on his income—such being the irony inherent in the profit system that "culture" thrives on other peoples' dunghills. Blanche—and here is the first of Shaw's subtle characterizations—is a vital and energetic girl with spirit enough to resent the source of her income. But she conveniently transfers her anger to her father's victims, hating "those dirty, drunken, disreputable people who live like pigs," and not being above attacking her maid in an access of inherited brutality. Although her humanity is revolted by the effects of her father's exploitation, she overlooks the causes and, being only too human, she defends herself against this knowledge with loathing and misdirected hatred. Her idealistic fiancé Trench is cut from the same cloth. He objects to receiving a dowry derived from such a source, but his pride is quickly laid low when he discovers that his own fortune is founded on an identical dunghill, such being the complex basis of wealth under the present dispensation. And later when the dismissed rent collector Lickcheese acquires a fortune by imitating his employer Sartorius and becomes his partner, Trench is not above joining both of them in a plan to extort money from the municipality when it wants to build a street in the slums. Capping the irony, Trench marries Blanche!

After this socialist *Volpone*, which Jonson might have written himself if he had been Shaw's contemporary, Shaw left the naturalist mode. He returned to an old master, W. S. Gilbert, for a different type of comedy. Prior to the Savoy operas, Gilbert had extracted a good deal of humor in plays like *Engaged* (1877) from the contradictions between the romantic façade of society and its pound-sterling basis; this was precisely the theme that Shaw put to more serious use, with the aid of Ibsen's example, in *Widower's Houses*. In the Savoy operas, Gilbert gave him a second and more successful lesson the art of deflating solemn nonsense by means of imaginative farce.

It was to a Gilbertian theme and mode that Shaw resorted when he wrote *Arms and the Man* in 1894, a work so intrinsically operatic that it found reincarnation in *The Chocolate Soldier* of Oscar Straus. Behind its humor lay the serious purpose of stripping war of its glamour, but it is the humor that actually matters. It bubbles when the antiheroic Swiss officer of the routed Serbian army, Captain Bluntschli appears on the scene with his preference for chocolates instead of bullets and his theory that a soldier's first duty is to save his own skin. Romanticism is deflated in the person of the Bulgarian hero Sergius whose cavalry charge would have been fatal if the enemy's artillery had not been supplied with the wrong ammunition, as well as in the character of his fiancée Raina who adopts romantic verbiage because it is supposed to be proper. Ultimately they both shed their nonsense and let their natural instinct lead them where it will, Raina into the arms of her pragmatic chocolate soldier and Sergius into the claws of her maid Louka who is the first of Shaw's mighty huntresses. The play, then, pricks two bubbles simultaneously—the "romance" of arms and the "romance" of love. The second theme became, in fact, one of his favorite subjects and his treatment was to vary greatly in every respect except in its antiromantic, commonsense bias. In fact, he started reconnoitering the field about a year before *Arms and the Man,* writing that shrewd comedy *The Philanderer* in 1893 but throwing it aside because he did not believe that the acting of the Independent Theatre would be up to it. It was a double-barreled satire on the woman question, leveled at both the Ibsenites and their opponents.

The comedy bristled with sheer ridicule of the fashionable new woman of the "Ibsen Club"; his Sylvia, for example, is indifferent to the fact that her father is dying because "no woman is the property of a man." There is also good fun in the pretentious rationalism of the lover Dr. Paramore and in the plight of Sylvia's feminine sister Julia who realizes at last that she prefers the old-fashioned physician to a new-fangled "philanderer." Despite its slipshod dramaturgy and exaggerated characters, *The Philanderer,* in fact, marked an advance in Shaw's work; it revealed the true flexibility of a writer of comedy who can laugh at his own convictions when they become ludicrous through excess.

Leaving it unfinished, however, Shaw resumed his best apostolic manner in a new socialist drama, written in the same year that saw the production of *Arms and the Man*. The new play *Mrs. Warren's Profession* proved in effect so disturbing to the equanimity of the censor that it could not be produced for a number of years. In this drama of prostitution Shaw moved up his heaviest artillery; here was economic determinism, compact as a cannon ball, in the un-Victorian assumption that prostitution is caused by the poverty rather than the lust of the daughters of joy. Shaw even amplified this broadside by the suggestion that respectable citizens like Sir George Crofts were not averse to extracting profits from the sorry industry. When Mrs. Warren faced the alternative of grinding labor, she chose the easier way and ultimately graduated as a wealthy procuress of a chain of "houses." Her two moral half-sisters had had a miserable life, one of them dying in the odor of sanctity from lead poisoning in a factory where she worked twelve hours a day for nine shillings a week. Resolving not to be "such fools as to let other people trade in our good looks by employing us as shopgirls, or barmaids, or waitresses," Mrs. Warren and her sister Liz decided to trade in themselves directly, and got "all the profits instead of starvation wages." Mrs. Warren, however, is hardly a sympathetic person, especially since she is now engaged in exploiting other girls' "good looks" (a point that the author might have hit harder than he did). Consequently, her horrified daughter Vivie separates from her and renounces all love in favor of an independent life as a statistician.

In principle, *Mrs. Warren's Profession* releases a powerful barrage, its larger purpose being defined by Shaw in his 1898 Preface with customary precision: "I believe that any society which desires to found itself on a high standard of integrity of character in its units should organize itself in such a fashion as to make it possible for all men and all women to maintain themselves in reasonable comfort by their industry without selling their affections and their convictions." If the narrower idea of the play is less than startling today, this is partly the result of the finality with which Shaw himself made the economic interpretation of prostitution a common thought.

More serious is the dubious artistry of the piece; once Mrs. Warren has made her forceful confession to her daughter, the action is whipped up into hopelessly thin lather concerning Vivie Warren's decisions respecting her own life, and despite affirmations of feminine independence (the New Woman!) she becomes a tiresome and chilly subject. There could be no caviling, however, about Shaw's next play *Candida,* written in the same year. It came as a welcome surprise from any viewpoint. Having already revealed his uncanny ability to propel ideas from the stage, he now confounded his critics by showing them how well he could create character when he had a mind to.

Reducing socialist agenda to mere casual conversation in connection with Candida's father who calls himself an ideal employer now that the law has made him pay his workers a living wage, Shaw turned his attention to marriage. But this time he had no direct intention of exposing or reforming it, and the only unconventional fillip to the situation appears in the fact that Candida's reasons for remaining with her husband have nothing to do with the sanctity of marriage or with woman's dependence upon her husband for protection and strength. This, of course, introduces the so-called modern note, as does *The Lady of the Sea* motif of allowing a married woman to choose between her husband and another man, and this alone might have been sufficient for a play of "ideas." Shaw was willing enough to make use of the idea, just as he was not above concocting a delightful *opera bouffe* episode out of the rivalry of Candida's husband and the adolescent poet Marchbanks. Still, his primary interest remained characterization, chiefly that of the complete woman Candida who knows that all men are children and that happy women are mothers to them.

Everything that Ibsen's Nora had to acquire through the painful process of disillusionment is simply Candida's birthright. Candida is certainly the New Woman in the home, and she is so "new" that she is really "old" and "eternal" even to the point of slicing onions and staying with her husband, although her reasons are unconventionally stated. She settles the issue by deciding that it is the successful preacher Morell who needs her most and that she is too old for Marchbanks. A very easy decision, it must be said, since her virtue is hardly in danger; but it is no simple-minded woman who would voice the instinctive fact that wifehood is a form of motherhood and that the best guarantee of happiness is to be needed. And only an uncommon intelligence could discern in the physically fragile and cowardly eighteen-year-old Marchbanks a tower of strength and a paragon of self-sufficiency because he is a poet. Another excellently realized character, he moreover confirms her opinion by admitting that she cannot be everything to him and by exclaiming, "I no longer desire happiness: life is nobler than that." Being a woman, Candida lets him down gently, asking him to make a poem out of the sentences, "When I am thirty, she will be forty-five. When I am sixty, she will be seventy-five." Being a poet he refuses this consolation; in a hundred years, he replies, they shall be the same age, but he has a "better secret" in his heart. Shaw adds that the Reverend Morell and his wife do not know the secret in the poet's heart, but it is probably not far removed from the secret of self-sufficiency Candida divined in Marchbanks when she made her decision.

Candida reminds us that Shaw has never been an iconoclast for the mere pleasure of being one. Nor has he ever avoided a conclusion as patently Victorian as the safeguarding of Candida's virtue merely because it agreed with convention, just as he has never tried any of the experiments in marriage that he broached in his discussions of the subject simply because he did not feel he needed them personally. He has been too great a man to be a chronic *enfant terrible*. It is notable only that Shaw arrives at the conventions unconventionally and makes the journey with more *brio* than piety. He makes even conformity delightful.

Candida, moreover, was a portent. It ushered in two decades of magnificent creation during which he produced *The Devil's Disciple, Caesar and Cleopatra, Man and Superman, Major Barbara, The Doctor's Dilemma, Androcles and the Lion,* and *Pygmalion* among other works that would have alone made the reputation of a minor dramatist. Space limitations alone would defeat any effort to deal adequately with this literature. But his development is easily traceable if one follows the zigzag line that he very characteristically followed during these years.

After the slight comedy *The Man of Destiny* which portrays Napoleon as an essentially commonplace man who merely employed more common sense and ruthlessness than his opponents, Shaw focused in 1897 on the conventionally obscured question of sainthood and deviltry in *The Devil's Disciple.* His reprobate Dick Dudgeon proves himself a saint much to his own surprise when he takes the worthy Parson Anderson's place at the foot of the gallows. When Burgoyne's soldiers, who have been terrorizing the colonists by hanging their best citizens, find him in the parson's house, Richard allows a mistake to stand. Perhaps it is he who should really be the preacher, as his subsequent conduct as well as his earlier kindness to an orphan would indicate. And all this happens to Dick without his understanding how he could have behaved so decently! On the other hand, the parson discovers that he is really a man of action when he instinctively musters an armed band, helps to surround Burgoyne's army, and effects Richard's release. It is, in other words, convention or circumstance that fixes people in their respective grooves, and in a crisis they are apt to make startling discoveries about themselves. The "idea" of the play thus works havoc with conventional notions of character. Fortunately, however, Shaw did not stop with the ideas; he wrote an exciting and brilliant melodrama, spicing it with delightful digs at the military and with a subtle characterization of young and sentimental Mrs. Anderson whose hero-worship leads her to the threshold of adultery. It would seem impossible to write a comedy, a philosophy, and a melodrama all in one and all good; but this is precisely what Shaw achieved in *The Devil's Disciple.*

After these conventionally constructed iconoclastic plays, Shaw's next step was to treat dramatic structure as cavalierly as any other convention. Having already explored two types of drama—economic satire in *Widower's Houses* and comedy of character in *Candida*—Shaw began to create comedy of sheer mental play. The process culminated in *Getting Married* in 1908 and *Misalliance* in 1910, and was resumed in *The*

TEXT CONTINUES ON PAGE 605 FOLLOWING THE PICTURE SECTION

In providing this third photographic section, I have aimed at nothing more than some visual representation of the modern drama as it appeared on the stage. The productions are not necessarily the first that were given of the plays represented here. As for the style of presentation, no effort has been made, as in the first section of photographs to exemplify any sequence of theatrical convention and form. In a few instances, however, a special type of scenic design or staging is shown more for its own sake than for the purpose of "visualizing an important play." In all other instances, the reader who is familiar with the play that is represented will be able to draw his own conclusions concerning the style of presentation and the reason for it.

I trust that this section, too, will supplement the literary consideration of the drama in the pages of the book, even if it has been impractical to include more photographs and my choice has been dictated partly by the availability of good pictures. I should also note that chronology has had to be violated in a number of instances for mechanical reasons.

PLATE 1. A scene from Henrik Ibsen's *Ghosts* in a New York production, with Alla Nazimova as Mrs. Alving. The Sunrise Scene of Act III as lit by A. Feder.

PLATE 2. A scene from a New York production of Anton Chekhov's *The Cherry Orchard*, with Alla Nazimova playing Madame Ranevsky. Photo by

PLATE 3. A scene from the August Strindberg's *The Father*. Robert L. Joseph's New York production in the 1949-50 season, with Mady Christians as Laura and Raymond Massey as the Captain. Photo by George Kargel. Courtesy of Robert L. Joseph.

PLATE 4, *above.* The cottage scene from the Moscow Art Theatre's production in 1908 of Maurice Maeterlinck's fantasy *The Blue Bird*, an example of the Art Theatre's later interest in other than realistic theatre style. Sketch by V. E. Yegoroff.

      below. A scene from Jacques Copeau's production of *The Brothers Karamazov*, Copeau's own dramatization of Dostoevsky's novel, staged by Louis Jouvet, at the Théâtre du Vieux Colombier. Note the formalism of the permanent skeleton-set. The Gypsy Inn setting here represented is formed by means of an arrangement of paneled screens within the larger permanent setting. From *Continental Stagecraft* (1922), by Kenneth Macgowan and Robert Edmond Jones. Courtesy of the publishers, Harcourt, Brace and Co.

PLATE 5. The final scene from the 1946 José Ferrer production of Edmond Rostand's *Cyrano de Bergerac*, as staged by Melchior G. Ferrer and designed by Lemuel Ayers, with Ferrer as Cyrano and Patricia Reid as Roxanne in the center. Photo Talbot. Courtesy of José Ferrer.

PLATE 6. The amusement park prologue from the Theatre Guild (and first successful) production of Ferenc Molnar's *Liliom*, as staged by Frank Reicher and designed by Lee Simonson on April 20, 1921, with Joseph Schildkraut as the

PLATE 7, *above*. The expressionistic courtroom scene (note that the entire setting is askew) from the Theatre Guild production of Elmer Rice's *The Adding Machine*, staged by Philip Moeller and designed by Lee Simonson in 1923. Courtesy of the Theatre Guild.

below. Scene of the robots demanding the secret of life from a scientist in the Theatre Guild production of Karel Capek's *R.U.R.*, staged by Philip Moeller and designed by Lee Simonson in 1922. Photo Vandamm. Courtesy of the Theatre Guild.

PLATE 8, *above.* The setting by "Motley" of the revival of Wilde's *The Importance of Being Earnest,* directed by John Gielgud for H. M. Tennent in London and the Theatre Guild and John C. Wilson in New York (1947). Photo Vandamm. Courtesy of Joseph Heidt for the Theatre Guild.

below. Scene from the Gilbert Miller New York production of R. C. Sherriff's *Journey's End* (1929), staged by James Whale, with Derek Williams as Raleigh and Colin Keith-Johnston as Captain Stanhope in the center. Photo Vandamm. Courtesy of Gilbert Miller.

PLATE 9, *above.* The funeral scene on the bare stage from the Jed Harris production of Thornton Wilder's *Our Town* (1938), staged by Jed Harris. Photo Vandamm. Courtesy of Jed Harris.

    below. Scene from the Michael Meyerberg production of Thornton Wilder's *The Skin of Our Teeth* (1942), staged by Elia Kazan and designed by Albert Johnson, costumes by Mary Percy Schenck; with Frederic March as Mr. Antrobus (*i.e.,* Anthropus or Man). Photo Vandamm. **Courtesy of Michael Meyerberg.**

PLATE 10. The tent scene from the Theatre Guild production of Maxwell Anderson's *Elizabeth the Queen* (1931), staged by Philip Moeller and designed by Lee Simonson, with Alfred Lunt as Lord Essex. Photo Vandamm. Courtesy of the Theatre Guild.

PLATE 11. Scene from the Eddie Dowling production of *The Glass Menagerie* (1945), designed by Jo Mielziner, with Laurette Taylor and Eddie Dowling. Courtesy of Eddie Dowling.

PLATE 12, *above.* Scene from the Theatre Guild production of Eugene O'Neill's *The Iceman Cometh* (1946), designed by Robert Edmond Jones; from left to right, Carl Benton Reid, James Barton, Dudley Digges and Nicholas Joy. Photo Vandamm. Courtesy of Joseph Heidt for the Theatre Guild.

     below. The last scene from the New Stages production of Lorca's *Blood Wedding* (1949), directed by Boris Tumarin and designed by Ralph Alswang. Photo Fritz Hock. Courtesy of Boris Tumarin and New Stages.

PLATE 13. Scene from Erwin Piscator's Dramatic Workshop production of Sartre's *The Flies* at the President Theatre in New York (1947), directed by Paul Ransom, setting by Willis Knighton. Photo Alfred J. Balcombe. Courtesy of Erwin Piscator and the New School.

PLATE 14. Scene from the Robert Whitehead and Oliver Rea production of Robinson Jeffers' *Medea* (1947), staged by John Gielgud and designed by Ben Edwards. Lighting by Peggy Clark. Photo Alfredo Valente. Courtesy of Robert Whitehead.

PLATE 15. Scene from the Elia Kazan production of Arthur Miller's *Death of a Salesman* (1949), designed by Jo Mielziner with Lee Cobb as Willy Loman and Mildred Dunnock as Willy's wife. Photo Eileen Darby. Courtesy of James Proctor for Walter Fried and Kermit Bloomgarden, producers.

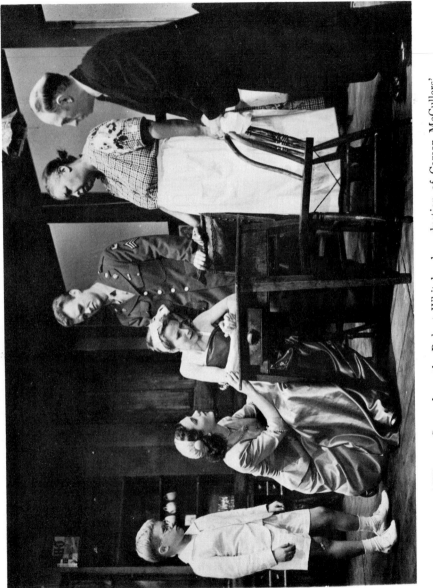

PLATE 16. Scene from the Robert Whitehead production of Carson McCullers' *Member of the Wedding*, staged by Harold Clurman and designed by Lester Polakov with Julie Harris weeping at the table and Ethel Waters observing her. Photo Alfredo Valente. Courtesy of Robert Whitehead.

Apple Cart, in 1930. Laxity of structure, however, began to appear at once in the play that succeeded *The Devil's Disciple* in 1898, and as in Shakespeare's case it occurred in a historical drama; *Caesar and Cleopatra* is a chronicle of political intrigue in ancient Egypt tied together by the personality of Caesar. The abundant but loosely related action—the conflicts between Caesar and Pompey, between Cleopatra and her brother, between their partisans, between nationalism and imperialism—creates a panoramic effect. It provides, above all, a peg for Shavian conceptions, chief of which is another unconventional portrait of a hero. Caesar is presented without an iota of fustian and braid; a middle-aged man keenly sensible of his advancing years and baldness, his strength lies in his sense of reality and his nobility in such complete freedom from sentimentality that he can be tolerant and magnanimous. He is a natural hero or, more accurately, a representative of a concept of heroism that Shaw has never tired of upholding—the heroism of triumphant Reason. The consequence is that *Caesar and Cleopatra* is the most completely anti-heroic play in existence that manages at the same time to be heroic.

This Shavian concept of heroism was, moreover, supplemented in *Caesar and Cleopatra* by numerous squibs—on "art for art's sake" as exemplified by Apollodorus, on insularism and English character as represented by Caesar's English secretary Brittanus, on the human petulance of royalty, and on sundry other matters. So determined was Shaw to give his critical faculty free play that he used any number of anachronisms without the least hesitation, a liberty that not even Shakespeare had exceeded at a time when historical accuracy was less expected.

Carefree treatment of structure reappeared in next year's *Captain Brassbound's Conversion,* in which Shaw did not hesitate to cook up a mess of pottage compounded of Moroccan romance and the United States navy in order to drive another wedge into the convention of heroism. The posturing hero Captain Brassbound learns to renounce his flamboyant righteousness. The bubble is pricked by a woman's common sense, and as the gas escapes the hero vanishes and the man appears. Brassbound took his intelligent uncle Sir Hallam, one of his Majesty's judges, for a villain from a story book and himself for a hero from the same source. Consequently, he assumed the role of a romantic outcast like Schiller's Karl Moor; now he realizes at last that "it was vulgar—*vulgar.*"

Still this play and its short successor, the finger exercise in the free form of burlesque *The Admirable Bashville* which Shaw based on one of his novels, were only overtures to something important. The increasingly buoyant dramatist was merely collecting his energy for one of his boldest excursions into theatre and social criticism.

Already a year before *Caesar and Cleopatra* he had returned to the theme of love and sex in the long comedy of *You Never Can Tell*. To the general idea that youth must cut the parental apron-strings and make its own discoveries of life no matter how grotesquely, he added a new treatment of the sex duel. Since love is a biological reality, Valentine's coolness toward Gloria is of no avail; she is the mother-goddess and huntress, and to the "life force" a mere man can offer little resistance. This is a fine, comic perception, although *You Never Can Tell* is not a fine play. Shakespeare, to whom its author has been constantly indebted, had anticipated him with many a huntress virgin like Viola, but Shaw called attention to the point directly instead of laving it in poetic romance. In his next important play in 1903, *Man and Superman*, he even went further—he inflated the point into an explicit philosophy.

Deflated to its proper size, which means deprived of its preface and the Don Juan episode in the third act, *Man and Superman* is merely a delightful comedy of the pursuit of the male by the female. The delight lies in the fencing of Tanner and Ann who astutely got him appointed her guardian, in Tanner's precipitous flight from her sexual magic to the Sierra Nevadas, in her pursuit, and in the characters. Tanner, at first supremely confident and rational but soon disconcerted and hunted down, and Ann, modest and pure-hearted yet unswerving in her purpose because the mating instinct is in her blood-stream, are two of the most ingratiating personalities in modern drama.

But *Man and Superman* is more comprehensive than this central situation, and the glistening surface of its comedy of the sex duel is supplemented by the deeper comedy of man the thinker. Tanner, who has acquired "moral passion," reveals man as independent thinker. Domestic love may be the core of Ann's being, but it fills only a small part of Tanner's nature; in fact, it is a disturbing intrusion into his revolutionary purpose of awakening society and making reason prevail. He is borne down, though by no means destroyed, by the sublime unreason of Ann's mating instinct. Moreover, this seeming defeat of reason is actually the work of the higher reason of the life force that ensures propagation. What is Tanner's dilettante, revolutionary work against the evolutionary force of nature? By himself he could hardly make the world move—this task requires the continuation of the race and the strivings of more than one generation. (Shaw, we recall, was a Fabian, and there is nothing so fabian as the slow strategy of time.)

Man and Superman is, then, a philosophy as well as a love story. Moreover, Shaw was not going to be prevented by conventional dramaturgy from developing his blend of ideas for all it was worth. Not only did he supply the long preface and the "Revolutionist's Handbook" to drive his points home in a blaze of verbal fireworks, but he invaded the play itself with his third-act Don Juan fantasy. And although it is so detachable that it has been omitted in performances and has been played separately, it constitutes a priceless conversation. If it slows up the drama to a point that may be unbearable for playgoers, it makes rewarding reading and must be set down as a distinguished contribution to the literature of the drama. It contains two comic reversals of conventional thought; the values of heaven and hell are reversed, and Don Juan is proved to have been the very opposite of a great, real lover. "Hell is the home of honor, duty, justice, and the rest of the seven deadly virtues," because "all the wickedness on earth is done in their name." Hell, however, has become insufferable for Don Juan because it is devoted to the continuous pursuit of happiness. Of course Heaven is equally boring with its rows of grave people sitting in glory not because they are happy there "but because they think they owe it to their position to be in heaven"; in fact, only the English find the place tolerable because "An Englishman thinks he is moral when he is only uncomfortable." But, tired of the "poetically nonsensical" in hell, Don Juan pictures the other region as a place where people live and work—some more of Shaw's puritanic theology. Don Juan is not, and had never been, a Don Juan at all, but another Tanner or devotee of "moral passion," which is only dramatically proper since the ghostly Spaniard is a figment of Tanner's dream in the Sierra Nevadas. Never having entertained any romantic respect for man's function as woman's partner in procreation, Don Juan acquired a lurid reputation for the reason that he ran away from possessive love. He evaded women because in seeking a husband she is the most unscrupulous beast of prey and because marriage is "a mantrap baited with simulated accomplishments and delusive idealizations." Thus he offended "morality," which is invariably identified with marriage when actually "the confusion of marriage with morality has done more to destroy the conscience of the human race than any other single error." The brilliance of this symposium in the nether world cannot, however, be conveyed by any summary of its drift; it is safe to say that it is one of the most dazzling examples of conversational dialogue in any language.

After *Man and Superman* almost anything Shaw could have written was bound to seem anticlimactic, and it is not surprising, therefore, that he marked time for a while with a trifle like *How He Lied to Her Husband,* a piece of trash *Passion, Poison and Petrifaction,* and *John Bull's Other Island,* a clever enough discussion of the Irish question full of incisive criticism sounder than many tracts on the subject but topical and in the main dated. *Major Barbara,* however, in 1905 again revealed the master of social comedy, even if it marked no advance in content over *Widower's Houses* with its point that tainted money is so widespread that it cannot be escaped anywhere. In a corrupted social order everything is defiled by the same pitch, and there is no chance for individual salvation except in the cleansing of society. Cheap and easy philanthropy is as effective as painting cancer with mercurochrome. Major Barbara of the Salvation Army approaches this conclusion when she discovers that her benevolent organization receives money from distillers and munitions-makers like her father—in other words, from the very industries that produce more evil than a thousand Salvation Armies can ever cancel. Sufficiently honest to recognize a truth when she meets it, unhappy Barbara Undershaft cries out, "My God, why hast Thou forsaken me," and takes off her uniform. If the play marks an improvement over Shaw's first drama, this is because Barbara is an affecting person and because the munitions-maker Andrew Undershaft is a superb character.

Only in *The Doctor's Dilemma* the next year (1906) did Shaw mark out new territory on anything that could be described as an altitude. It has probably suffered from its Preface which overstresses the playwright's animus against the medical profession. The satire on physicians in the play itself is an uncertain asset; despite many clever sallies and the implicit recommendation of socialized medicine, Shaw strained his criticism of the profession. Nor is the main problem—whether it is better to save a mediocre good man than a rascally genius like Dubedat— particularly interesting by itself, since the cards are stacked and there is nothing grossly villainous about the latter. But Shaw's humor when he draws his physicians is lively, the characterization of this painter and his wife becomes increasingly affecting, and the death scene in which the artist reveals the luminous spirit that hides behind his smoke is one of the great scenes of the modern drama.

Six years were to elapse before Shaw wrote anything of equal magnitude. *Getting Married* in 1908, a full-length play in one act, is a conversation, the debate being left airily unresolved and the *casus belli* fizzling out when the young couple that dislikes the antiquated British marriage contract signs it—with insurance against one of its antiquated provisions. Humor is added by an older divorced couple and by abortive proposals for new contracts, but the upshot of the play is fascinatingly nil. This *conversazione* was followed by *Misalliance,* another diffuse discussion on themes ranging from the tyranny of the family to anarchism and the educational value of the empire to Englishmen—"Opens our mind. Knocks the Bible out of us." More brilliant dialogue and more epigrams like "Common people do not pray, my lord: they only beg" and "Nothing is worth doing unless the consequences may be serious" enlivened the farce. Still, the characters were merely Jonsonian humors and the story was inconsequential. *The Shewing Up of Blanco*

Posnet was merely an abbreviated recapitulation of *The Devil's Disciple,* a thumping one-acter in which the socialist playwright was reaffirming the essential goodness of man in a crisis, even in the wild West. Fortunately, however, Shaw said nothing so favorable about another essential—the *intelligence* of man, and so he escaped contradicting himself when he gave mankind up as hopeless in *Too True to Be Good.* Pleasant trivia followed (*Press Cuttings, The Dark Lady of the Sonnets*). Then in 1910 came that ingenious satire on family life, respectability, and dramatic criticism *Fanny's First Play.* Shaw himself called it a pot-boiler, and rightly so because its parallel and simultaneous plots of a middle-class boy and girl spending a term in jail and marrying beyond the pale are thin and contrived. The most creative touches are to be found in the characterization of a secondary figure, Mrs. Knox. *Overruled,* a second-rate farce about marital infidelity with some first-rate lines, followed in 1912 and left Shaw's stalemate unchanged. Shaw's disregard for tried dramaturgy had merely proved that even he could not disregard its discipline in high comedy without, for the most part, courting defeat.

In 1912, however, the deadlock was finally broken with *Pygmalion* and *Androcles and the Lion.* In *Pygmalion* Shaw fused satire on society with comedy of sex, and improved both by the simple expedient of creating a plot. How the phonetician Henry Higgins takes up a bet and proceeds to transform the cockney flower-girl Liza into a lady who can pass for a duchess is equally good matter for the fabulist and the social satirist. The point that social distinctions are only skin deep after all and that "the difference between a lady and a flower-girl is not how she behaves but how she's treated" is brilliantly driven home by the action, and it is firmly held in place by the complementary idea that the social graces have to be supported on a comfortable economic base. Related ideas on marriage, middle-class morality, and happiness are bound together in *Pygmalion* like so many jewels in the satirist's crown.

Shaw chuckled over the success of his play, writing, "It is so intensely and deliberately didactic, and its subject so dry, that I delight in throwing it at the heads of the wiseacres who repeat the parrot cry that art should never be didactic. It goes to prove my contention that art should never be anything else." He might have noted, however, that the didacticism was largely imbedded in the Dickensian characterization of that proletarian philosopher Doolittle and in his daughter Liza herself when she emerges in her Pygmalion's studio not only as a pseudo-duchess but as a living woman. In fact, this Galatea becomes so completely alive that she disturbs the scientific equanimity of her sculptor, who is himself a vivid personality despite the mother-fixation that deprives Higgins of the conventional qualification of sexual passion. *Pygmalion* is a triumph for the preacher in Shaw because it is a triumph for the play-wright in him. Without condescending to wind up his story, relegating the conventionally required ending to a novelistic epilogue, Shaw spun out a delightful comedy of social experiment, impostures and personal relations.*

Androcles and the Lion was another carefully assembled play. If the transformation of Eliza Doolittle is hypothetical, although Shaw insisted in no uncertain terms that it was happening all the time, the history of Androcles and his lion was fantastic. This, however, only increased the witchery of Shaw's beautiful comedy of saintliness.

The theme was of course not new in the Shavian canon. Sainthood always interested Shaw, partly because he found so much pleasure in stripping this subject of its greasepaint and partly because he has always been partial to extraordinary characters. Real saints are supermen, and probably Shaw has imagined himself playing the role to perfection. In fact, he is one himself, as his purity of conduct and his moral passion would indicate, and the Middle Ages would have either canonized him or burnt him at the stake—probably the latter.

Fortunately, moreover, Shaw presented his hagiology not by conversation but by means of a story that assembles various types of would-be saints and martyrs from the coward Spintho to the saintly fighting-man Ferrovius who learns that he mistook his vocation after he has made mincemeat of the gladiators; from the intelligent martyr Lavinia who knows that sainthood has its interruptions but is ready to die for her beliefs to the sublimely innocent Androcles who is saved in the arena by the lion he had befriended in the jungle. Saints differ as much as other men, for saintliness can be sought by both the weak and the courageous, by the most intelligent thinkers and the most innocent of heart. And out of this rational and lucid analysis emerges a deeply sympathetic drama since Shaw knew that the world needs its saint-supermen. It is possible for British citizens and statesmen, he commented in his 1915 Preface, "to follow Jesus, though they could not possibly follow either Tweedledum or Tweedledee without bringing the empire down with a crash on their heads."

Native and foreign statesmen followed Tweedledee and Tweedledum and precipitated the world into the most costly war in human history. This also cost Shaw several years of comparative silence. He lay fallow in 1913 with nothing more fruitful than that bustling one-acter *The Great Catherine,* and from 1914 to 1917 he composed inconsequential short plays. In 1916, however, he began to apply himself to the problem of describing the vacillations and rapacities that brought the world to

---

* For a London revival in the spring of 1938 Shaw added a line that suggests the possibility that Galatea dragged Pygmalion to the altar.

the brink of ruin, a subject he had presciently started three years before. The result was the weighty extravaganza *Heartbreak House,* a verbose play no doubt but also a magnificent comedy of humors and a powerful symbol wrapped in whimsy.

Captain Shotover's house is a Noah's ark where the characters gather before the flood. They and the classes they represent have been making a hopeless muddle of both society and themselves. The only half-rational Hector Hushabye and his wife display the futility of the upper classes; a British aristocrat exemplifies the bankruptcy of Britain's rulers; the capitalist Mangan represents the predatory force of Mammon. All are equally blind to the wrath of God and to the storm they have been raising unknowingly. The innocents are helpless or they must compromise like the hard-headed poor girl who is willing to marry the capitalist for his money, and the one knowing person among them, Captain Shotover, has taken refuge in eccentricity. Then the storm breaks loose and death comes raining from the skies in an air raid. The despair in the play is manifest, for Shaw's pity and moral earnestness did not decrease with age; the harlequinade of *Heartbreak House* is a Dance of Death.

Still, Shaw the Fabian and one-time agitator was loath to renounce all expectation of salvation through a new order. Hope was implicit in the death of the thieves of the play who are blown to pieces by the bombardment; did not many socialists believe that predatory capitalism was finished by the war just as the capitalist Mangan was finished by a bomb! Amid the wreckage Shaw's remaining characters try to pull themselves together. The call for courage is sounded resonantly with Shaw's customary eloquence, as is the call for action when the antagonists of society's malefactors declare "We must win powers of life and death over them. . . . They believe in themselves. When we believe in ourselves, we shall kill them." *Heartbreak House* is, therefore, as highhearted as it is depressed.

The same vision of evil triumphant but of spirit unbroken pervaded *Saint Joan,* a sparer and more burnished drama. Unified by the dramatic struggle of Joan, this was his greatest play as a whole, although one may find greater flashes of genius in portions of his other work. Illuminated by her intelligent spirit, the drama became a phosphorescent thing of beauty. And this was a particularly notable achievement since Shaw employed cold historical analysis in explaining the causes of Joan's trial and death. Unconsciously, when Joan insisted upon her possession of private inspiration from Heaven and when she raised the slogan of "France for the French" she was guilty of a double heresy in the Middle Ages—she anticipated Protestantism and nationalism. The Church burned her for the first, the British invaders for the second. Only Shaw with his mastery of dialectical conversation, of pro and con, could have presented the alignment of forces and ideologies so vividly; only he could have brought to conscious and lucid statement what the principals could have only sensed dimly. Then moving from the debate of Warwick and Cauchon (of feudalism and Church) to Joan's trial scene, Shaw represented through dramatic action the situation which he had already expressed through considered analysis. This stroke of superlative dramaturgy was alone sufficient to dispel any doubts respecting his power to create genuine drama and to confound the tiresome complainers who had been willing to grant him everything but a claim to the title of dramatist.

But *Saint Joan* was his Indian Summer, and was followed by the winter of his discontent. The play, which was written in 1923, ended on the sorrowing note of the Epilogue. King Charles, whom Joan had enthroned in France, dreams of a time when the gallant heretic is canonized by the Church only to find that among all her voluble adorers only the profane common soldier who had held a cross up for her at the stake is willing to let her rise from the dead. One by one, for reasons of policy or fear, they shrink from encouraging the resurrection of a saint. "O God that madest this beautiful earth," cries Joan, "when will it be ready to receive Thy saints? How long, O Lord, how long?" The answer, however, was not forthcoming as Shaw observed the aftermath of the war eight years after the Versailles Treaty. He began to look for new redeemers, and he began to find them, with some reservations, in the dictators—those caricatures of his superman—who were beginning to master the world. Having always expected much from strong, uninhibited leaders, he gave the new Napoleons greater benefit of doubt than became him either as a thinker or as a humanitarian.

In extreme irritation with him, most of his liberal and radical critics refused to accept any explanation other than that of senility or plain middle-class treason, and Shaw, it is true, gave them indications of declining power which could after all be expected from a playwright in his seventies and eighties. Moreover, he was undoubtedly provoking in his ex-cathedra pontifications when he praised Hitler and Mussolini on little acquaintance with basic facts and condoned all their acts except their antisemitism. But his provocation was great, too, when Europe began moving toward new catastrophes owing to its inability to resolve any of its social contradictions.

What little faith he had left in the labor and socialist movement after its behavior in the World War evaporated when he saw the Labor Party government of Great Britain in 1924 fumble disgracefully under Ramsay Macdonald, the inheritor of Shaw's own temporizing Fabian Society

—a fact that the dramatist elided. Here was its great opportunity, and it failed miserably. Shaw reacted to this situation with *The Apple Cart* in 1930, a fantasia about the sagacious King Magnus who seized power (not as King, however, but as a talented and disinterested politician) and tried to make sense of the shoddy business of governing. A disjointed but charming play full of bubbling humor, *The Apple Cart* was also a devastating satire, its butt being a government that is led by the Labor Prime Minister Proteus but is actually controlled by Breakages Limited. Shaw's monarchical solution was patently untenable, so that the resolution of the drama was left hanging in mid-air. But the play was not essentially a solution but an exposition of a problem in the form of a fable. If the prescription was nebulous, the diagnosis was brilliant. It was also frightening: "Money talks; money prints; money reigns. . . . Ministers who are socialists to the backbone are as helpless in the grip of Breakages Limited as its acknowledged henchmen," as Shaw explained.[20]

Deprived of his long-cherished faith in Fabian progress, Shaw was, moreover, soon left with nothing but despair, and his next play *Too True to Be Good* in 1932 was very logically a funeral dirge. It began as a poor enough medley about a war-shocked clergyman who has turned thief and a wealthy invalid girl who escapes to an island with him stealing her own jewelry and pretending to be held for ransom in order to extort more money from her mother. Then the play employed random variations on several themes, the most interesting one occurring when by coincidence the clergyman Aubrey meets his father there leading the life of an expatriate from a dying civilization. Yet this improvisation was infinitely more impressive than a host of more carefully or convincingly constructed plays. Its satire on the suicidal folly of Europe was excellent, and the final act was eloquent with terror and tears. All attempts to lead mankind into the paths of reason have failed, Shaw declared, and his mouthpiece, the clergyman whose nerves were shattered when he bombed the enemy in the World War, admits that he is a preacher who has lost his faith and has no longer anything to say. "The Western world is damned beyond the possibility of salvation," and he knows only that he must continue to preach and preach even if he has "nothing to say." The critic John Anderson has rightly called this confession on the part of the Promethean, hitherto confidently superior, Shaw the "abdication of one of the tallest personal thrones in the world." It is truly "heart-breaking." [21]

Shaw, too, continued to preach and preach, and his more solidly organized *On the Rocks* of the year 1933, brought the lesson home to England in the story of a liberal Prime Minister who having read Marx tries to save the nation by socializing the country. The procedure smacks of both fascism and Fabianism, since the statesman leaves the owners in possession of their property and tries to ride many white horses simultaneously by satisfying every social stratum with partial concessions. But his solution, which in the last analysis cannot satisfy these conflicting groups, is not accepted from the Minister's gentle hand. He is defeated by withdrawal of support from the different quarters, and since he is deficient in ruthlessness he does not press the issue further and resigns himself to inaction. Fabianism, as Shaw admits, has failed again; the only compromise that Shaw ever accepted intellectually has failed. At this point the unemployed begin to riot in the street singing Edward Carpenter's song "England, arise." The minister is tempted for a moment to set himself at the head of the revolt, if only he were "the man for the job," and Shaw allows Sir Arthur to wonder, "Suppose England really did arise."

Still Shaw's hold on this expectation was slim. One of Sir Arthur's last remarks about the rioters was "Yes; they always break the wrong windows, poor devils," and the author's footnote adds that unemployed England does nothing more than "sing" to a "percussion accompaniment" of policemen's clubs. The train of Shaw's thought and of the world's behavior in the thirties did not encourage much faith in the initiative of the masses or in their ability to make right reason prevail, and Shaw completed his abdication by crawling into the miasma of *The Simpleton of the Unexpected Isles*. Already in the ponderous *Back to Methuselah* in 1921 the evangelical playwright had succumbed to "faith" rather than immediate "works." It is true that he promulgated an ambiguous "willing" process and eugenic action on the part of mankind which would result in longevity, and that he also showed the long-lived and therefore increasingly wise supermen of the future creating a scientifically conducted society. But not only was this based on a mystic belief in Lamarckism and nature, but on an equally tenuous faith in the fruits of this evolutionary process. The flower of ages of selection and of "willing" turns out to be a race of eternally alive beings who have ceased to be human. They know everything but seemingly feel nothing; ultimately they will leave the flesh entirely and emerge as disembodied spirit or energy. The long-livers are not improved human beings but something else, and society has been saved but not for people. Without Shaw having realized it, this is not only a horrible prospect but a completely negative one, since it means killing the patient in order to cure him. Dull and barely actable in long stretches, *Back to Methuselah* was at least an intellectual feat and a *tour de force* of sheer fantasy. It also possessed a brilliant comic idea in the suggestion that human beings do not live long enough to acquire maturity or wisdom; what can one expect from mere babes of sixty!

In the later hodge-podge of *The Simpleton of the Unexpected Isles* Shaw postulated an act of God by means of which all the useless people of the world, having been judged in Heaven, are mysteriously removed from the planet. This was a clever invention, diverting as fantasy and welcome after many warmed-over Shavianisms in the earlier portions of the play. The point was also deepened by the disappearance of the beautiful but vapid children who represent the worthless conventionalized ideals of civilization—Love, Pride, Heroism, and Empire. Obviously, however, this contrived act of God begged the question of what man could effect through his own action, and it left no hope for humanity. Shaw was merely talking in a fog by the side of his clergyman Aubrey, and the only rational meaning of the supernatural event was simply the negativistic one that "Civilizations live by their valuations. If the valuations are false, the civilization perishes as all the ancient ones we know of did . . . we are being valued." He continued merely talking, too, though with some eloquence, when his priestess Prola, harking back to the good old Life Force solution, concludes that "Women will never let go their hold on life. We are not here to fulfill prophecies and fit ourselves into puzzles, but to wrestle with life as it comes. And it never comes as we expect it to come."

Trying not to stop talking, Shaw composed two slim one-acters and in 1936 the knockdown farce *The Millionairess*. It proved amusing in moments but boring as a whole and was flagrantly insufficient as a demonstration of its beautifully written Preface on Bosses. The preface had posed the question of what was to be done with natural-born "dominators and deciders," who are valuable but dangerous since, as one of Shaw's masters William Morris had written, "no man is good enough to be another man's master." It also warned that "Uncommon people . . . are by no means wholly exempt from megalomania" when placed in authority. But the playwright's habit of becoming "waywardly facetious," as Ivor Brown has noted, overran *The Millionairess* with such details as the heroine's marriage to a prize fighter, her acquisition of an Egyptian philosopher-physician, and her display of the manly art of fisticuffs. Shaw's Epifania may be a born boss but she is also a natural bore. After introducing this representative of irresponsible plutocracy who dominates everything she touches, the play dribbles out in a series of inconsequential situations. In its successor *Geneva*, written in 1938, Shaw set himself the simpler task of satirizing the League of Nations, Hitlerism, and racialism. He succeeded in this but without plumbing any depth or rising to any altitudes. His latest play, on Charles II,

In Good King Charles's Golden Days, is an ingratiating but static piece of no great moment, somewhat vitiated by a garrulity that is perhaps pardonable in a gentleman who has reached the ripe age of eighty-three.*

Sophocles did better than that at the age of ninety if the Greek calendar was accurate; but that, one might argue, was in the Golden Age — so golden, the cynic would add, that Athens collapsed as Europe seems to be doing. That Shaw is still talking is, however, something to be grateful for. Nor is he always garrulous. Within a few days after Britain's decision to tour his *Geneva* in Canada as anti-German propaganda in the 1939 war, Shaw delivered himself of an article on the mistakes of British diplomacy and the real nature of its vaunted democracy; and there is nary a wasted word in that pronunciamento! The truth is that Shaw has been not only a man but a phenomenon. We shall probably not see his like in a century.

4 SHAW'S FELLOW-TRAVELERS

It is one of the disadvantages of listening to Shaw, which is like hearing the whole world since 1880, that he leaves one with little patience to listen to anyone else. He had several powerful companion playwrights in England until about 1920, but their voices were far less audible. Two of them—John Galsworthy, born in 1867, and James Barrie, born in 1860—were more consistently technicians, but they were mere mortals. They contributed interest, charm, and power to the theatre but they did not rock it to its foundations.

Galsworthy took the problem play, divested it for the most part of preachment, strengthened it with objectivity, and steeped it in gentle irony. An old-world gentleman with new-world ideas, he constructed dramas that were simultaneously restrained and provocative as became a legally trained mind at once graceful and firm. A novelist of parts, he rarely allowed the leisurely technique of fiction to intrude into his playwriting. But though his plays will long be revered for these merits, and though schoolrooms will long honor them as models in dramaturgy, the gentle do not have their full reward on earth. "Nothing succeeds like excess," noted Shaw. Galsworthy's talent was, in short, too temperate and circumspect to rank him with the giants of the drama. He was deficient in the heat of passion on the one hand, and in the cold fire of intellectual display on the other.

While some older writers like C. Haddon Chambers wrote like Pinero, with perhaps a fresh touch or two as in that tale of how a husband may be dominated by a loving mate *The Tyranny of Tears,* Galsworthy

---

* A revised and possibly improved version of *Geneva* is scheduled for production in New York as this book goes to press.

plunged into the drama of socially pertinent ideas in his very first play *The Silver Box*. By then Shaw had already paved the way for him while Galsworthy, under no necessity to earn a livelihood, was traveling abroad after the completion of an Oxford education and a bout with the legal profession. *The Silver Box*, written in 1906, dealt with the upper-class basis of justice which simultaneously frees a scion of wealth and imprisons a proletarian although both are equally guilty of theft. Affecting details of the poor family's plight gave force to the thesis, and some firm character drawing and cockney dialogue infused it with life. Regarding dialogue this playwright set down the rule that it is an austere art, "denying itself all license, grudging every sentence devoted to the mere machinery of the play . . . relying for fun and pathos on the fun and tears of life." [22] Although hardly one of the best of his plays, *The Silver Box* revealed the technique which subsequently distinguished his most important work—the presentation of a problem through characterization and vivid naturalistic dialogue, and the ironic exposition of a social situation ending with a question rather than a pat answer.

Having struck this vein, he analyzed the capital-labor conflict objectively in *Strife* but with the bias of a gentleman who deplores extreme actions regardless of the provocation, even when he understands the full extent of the provocation. Untold misery results from the fact that the irresistible force of the embittered labor radical meets the immovable object of the die-hard old capitalist. Ultimately both antagonists are removed and a compromise that could have been effected from the beginning is reached. A powerful picture of a strike, full of atmosphere, pathos, and character drawing, *Strife* marked a high point in its author's career. *Justice*, which followed it a year later in 1910, was a tragic exposition of how a well-intentioned forger is trapped by his sympathy for an unhappily married woman, how his venial sin is treated without understanding by the law, and how a prison record ruins his life in spite of his good intentions and those of his employers. Although it is now and then open to the charge of sentimentality, the play is relentless in its progress, sober in its characterization, and poignantly ironic towards fumbling humanity.

A long series of plays followed: *The Eldest Son*, with its ironic bow to double class standards which are differently applied to the same misstep when the culprits belong to different levels of society; *The Fugitive* with the old Woman Question in the foreground; *The Mob* written in 1914 and pertinently but schematically devoted to the tragedy of an idealistic statesman who is destroyed by a war-frenzied nation; *The Skin Game*, in 1920, which symbolized the inhumanity of the World War in the tragic rivalry of two English families who defile their essential humanity in an access of hatred for each other. These sober studies were followed by other weaker but equally earnest and ironic investigations of humanity in a crisis like *Escape* (1926), in which an absconding convict puts various representative citizens to the difficult task of sheltering him. Such plays as these added reality and feeling to the British stage without creating any remarkable intensification of the spirit and without greatly extending mental horizons. He was indeed most engaging in *The Pigeon,* written as early as 1912, which was essentially high comedy and was enlivened by unique characters. Here the central idea that people can only follow their strongest inclinations despite the guidance of friendly reformers was set forth by the delightful philosopher-vagabond Ferrand who wants no pity since "We wild ones—we know a thousand times more of life. . . ." In this play, which may be called Galsworthy's *Wild Duck,* it is admitted that even reform and philanthropy cannot solve the problems of those people who "cannot be made tame" and cannot avoid getting into trouble. Since the admission is both whimsical and wistful it is frequently captivating.

Success also attended Galsworthy's last important play *Loyalties* (in 1922) distinguished for its objective exposition of antisemitism in genteel English circles and of social alignments in general. The overscrupulous playwright left the issues too neatly balanced from the social standpoint but not from the psychological one owing to his firm characterization. In addition to his many novels, among which *The Forsyte Saga* is the most notable, Galsworthy left an impressive if hardly extraordinary collection of dramatic work when he died in 1933. His work was indeed most characteristic when he avoided anything extraordinary; and it was sometimes most dramatic when he avoided every semblance of dramatics. Galsworthy was so partial to "naturalness" that his curtains have been said to hesitate to come down on anything that could possibly be taken for a climax.

His co-workers in the field of social drama were numerous, and in a less notable period of dramatic history their achievements would have loomed larger than they do in this chapter. Some were Shavians like St. John Hankin and Granville Barker. Hankin, born in 1860 and a suicide in 1909 owing to his neurasthenia, pioneered without great power. One of a group of "uncommercial" writers whose plays were produced by Granville Barker's Court Theatre, he left five long and two short plays of uneven merit but of modern caliber. Of these *The Return of the Prodigal* (in 1904) satirized middle-class virtues and took delight in an unrepentant spendthrift. An earlier play, *The Two Mr. Wetherbys,* poked fun at sentimental codes of honor; the good Mr. Wetherby, James, has a miserable time of it because he honors the marriage that binds him to an unsympathetic wife whereas the "bad" Richard Wetherby is happily separated from his mate and even teaches James to assert his independence. In addition to some Nietzschean mockery of private philanthropy, *The Charity That Began at Home* contains some shrewd Shavian' humor, as when the cynic Verreker tells the woman he favors, "I love you as much as ever, more perhaps, now that I am going to lose you. But on every ground except love I'm quite unfit to marry you," adding, "Marriage isn't a thing to be romantic about. It *lasts* too long." An amusing point is scored in the once popular *Cassilis Engagement* when the astute Mrs. Cassilis saves her son from a designing girl by inviting her for a visit and allowing her to expose her vulgarity to him. Calculation on the part of both the mother and the girl and some trenchant lines add acid to the comedy, although it is pallid today. It is only in *The Last of the De Mullins* that Hankin actually approximated Shavian surgery when he eviscerated a quasi-feudal noble family which is shocked beyond endurance when one of its daughters, Janet, acquires an illegitimate child, refuses to marry its father who tries to live up to the code of "honor," and goes into the millinery business. Still Hankin was merely a diluted Shaw, and only his cynicism imparts a tang to his otherwise thin plays, as when Janet scorns the properly married Mrs. Bulstead who cannot overlook her conduct. "What right has *she* to look down that huge nose of hers at *me!* She's had *ten* children."

More interest attaches to Barker, his junior by seventeen years, who was always more weighty and sometimes peppered the drama of ideas with whimsy and imagination. After a mild, atmospheric play, he gave free rein to his didactic bent in *The Voysey Inheritance,* in which an idealistic son tries to clear up his domineering father's peculations by a public statement only to settle down to the less flamboyant and more difficult task of repairing them by hard application to the Voysey business. This extremely Shavian play was followed by *Waste.* a study of the ruin that can be caused by the "life force" when a promising politician's career is destroyed by scandal after the shallow object of his love dies from a wantonly undertaken abortion. A man who could have served mankind is thus stalemated by an irresponsible woman. Barker's plodding sobriety, unfortunately, gives this penetrative play an effect of stuffiness.

In *The Madras House,* however, this serious-minded playwright adopted a loose form that enabled him to play with problems like a master rather than a journeyman of the theatre of ideas. Clever satirization of a respectable draper's household and of another middle-class prison, a drapery establishment or "industrial seraglio" where the employees "live in" and must abstain from marriage, is supplemented by the pointed whimsy of the wife-deserting Constantine Madras who has become a Mohammedan. To the worthy *pater familias* Huxtable with his half-dozen cowed and unmarried daughters Constantine paints the advantages of polygamy; all the daughters could be taken care of by a single man! Moreover, the segregation of women would promote a rational life and society: "From seventeen to thirty-four—the years which a man should consecrate to the acquiring of political virtue—wherever he turns he is distracted, provoked, tantalized by the barefaced presence of women. How's he to keep a clear brain for the larger issues of life. . . . All politics, all religion, all economy is being brought down to the level of women's emotions." This is the bee in Constantine's turban, and it buzzes agreeably. Only his serious-minded son Philip, who concerns himself with human misery and fears that "we good and clever people are costing the world too much" is a proper foil to both the easy-going Constantine and the smug Huxtable. The drapery establishment of which he is part owner recalls both Carlyle's dour fulminations against the dandiacal English habit and Ruskin's views on art. Philip wants an "art and a culture that shan't be just a veneer on savagery," something that must come "from the happiness of a whole people." Therefore he is going into politics. Neither lightness of treatment nor weight of thought is absent in this rambling but fertile comedy of ideas. Nevertheless, Barker on the whole served the theatre better as stage director than as a dramatist.

Younger playwrights, who had an even greater opportunity to profit from Shaw's example, actually exhibited less effectiveness. The most accomplished of them, the short-lived Stanley Houghton, alone merits mention because his well-wrought comedy *Hindle Wakes* gave a new fillip to the usual "revolt of youth" theme by making the lower-class girl Fanny reject marriage to the rich weakling Alan Jeffcote because spending an illicit week-end with him is no indication of love for him. If men can enjoy a cursory passion, so can a woman, and the pained lad, who is being compelled to marry the "wronged" girl by his puritanic father, is left exclaiming, "But do you mean to say that you didn't care any more for me than a fellow cares for any girl he happens to pick up?" The Shavian point here is undoubtedly that what's sauce for the gander is also sauce for the goose in the case.

In the main, however, the most impressive social studies were conceived in the different vein of ordinary realism in which characterization and environment receive more attention than "ideas." Elizabeth Baker, a working girl familiar with "white-collar slave" life, created in 1909 a forceful naturalistic drama *Chains* in which a clerk who tries to escape the lower middle-class routine by shipping to Australia finds himself hopelessly trapped when his wife announces her pregnancy. *Chains* may be a slight play but it was a praiseworthy attempt to represent the "little man" who was so often neglected equally by the writer of "ideas" and the purveyors of popular entertainment. Like her contemporaries, Miss Baker had some sessions with puritanism and class conflict in her other pieces but she achieved greater distinction when her femininity led her to photograph ordinary life. Three years later, another talented woman Githa Sowerby burrowed into middle-class life in *Rutherford and Son,* a drama of domestic tyranny centering around the granite figure of the industrialist Rutherford whose children escape his tyranny only after being virtually broken by him. Dramatic power is also furnished by excellent characterizations of an old sister who fears him, a frustrated daughter who runs away with his foreman, and a weak-willed son who can only free himself by abandoning his wife and his child and breaking his father's cash box. Only the son's wife remains, and it is she alone who finally masters the hard old man now that he wants an heir to the house of Rutherford and is in need of such affection as he can find.

Rutherford and Son was, however, quite unique in the pre-war English theatre for its stark naturalism. The only other notable example, *The Tragedy of Nan,* was set far back in the early nineteenth century. Masefield's poetic naturalism—"Gothic" naturalism, one might call it— is a *tour de force* recalling *Wuthering Heights. The Tragedy of Nan* is not so much a modern play as a timeless evocation of brutality and poetry; the most sordid reality and a grisly nightmarish element were compounded in this peasant drama into something memorable. Only a poet like Masefield could have made such a departure from the norm in the English theatre in 1908.

Nan, the daughter of a man who was hanged for sheep-stealing, finds life in her uncle's home a constant torment owing to the persecution of his domineering and gross wife. Only when the grasping Dick Gurvil falls in love with her does the lovable and patient Nan breathe freely again. But her aunt Mrs. Pargetter wins him for her sneaky daughter Jenny after telling him that Nan is the daughter of a hanged man. Humiliated beyond endurance and at the end of her patience by now, the long-suffering girl stabs him to death immediately after her father's innocence is established and goes out to drown herself.

This story is simple enough and also somewhat melodramatic, but woven through its pattern run many threads of anguish and sordidness rare in the modern English drama. And one golden thread of beautiful poetry also runs through this play, which would otherwise be sickeningly oppressive. The sound of the river Severn brings the eternal note of sadness in, and the babblings of the almost clairvoyant old Gaffer, to whom Nan brings her sorrows, provide an eerie obbligato. The unearthly music of water and of Gaffer's unintelligible words blend with the harsher music of peasant dialect as spoken by the other characters into a majestic tone-poem. For one brief moment in the British theatre realism became sublimated into folk poetry and common speech acquired a golden tongue as in Ireland. There is piercing beauty in such speeches as the cracked old man's recollection of his wife's death fifty-nine years ago: "She looked out of the window, my white vlower done. She said, 'The tide. The tide. The tide coming up the river.' And a horn blew. The gold rider blew a 'orn. And she rose up, my white vlower done. And she burst out a-laughing, a-laughing. And 'er fell back, my white vlower done. Gold 'air on the pillow. And blood. Oh, blood. Blood of my girl. Blood of my vlower."

Still, Masefield's dramatic work left the stream of British drama unaffected. His long prose plays *Pompey the Great* and *The Faithful* were remote historical pieces, his one-acters *The Campden Wonder* and *Mrs. Harrison* were merely naturalistic melodramas, and verse plays like *Good Friday* were pedestrian. Even so vigorous a poet as Masefield did not succeed in bringing verse drama back into the theatre; nor did such fellow-poets as Gordon Bottomley or John Drinkwater, whose best full-length play *Abraham Lincoln* merely contained lyric interludes. It was Masefield himself who read the funeral oration on the poetic drama, which flared up only momentarily in the second-rate and derivative work of Stephen Phillips (*Paolo and Francesca, Ulysses, Herod*). In his 1911 preface to *The Tragedy of Nan* Masefield wrote: "Commonplace people dislike tragedy, because they dare not suffer and cannot exult. The poetic impulse of the Renaissance is now spent. The poetic drama, the fruit of that impulse, is now dead. . . . Our playwrights have all the powers except that power of exultation which comes from a delighted brooding on excessive, terrible things." The greatest poetic drama of the age, Thomas Hardy's Napoleonic epic *The Dynasts,* was not written for the theatre.

The British public preferred to get its poetry from the pulverized sugar of James M. Barrie's whimsies. He had, it is true, a great deal more to offer, for his insight into human nature was shrewd and no one had a keener eye for the starch in a stuffed shirt. His *Twelve-Pound Look* is a devastating satire on a pompous ass who is naturally a great success in British society; the hero's first wife left him to become a typist because he was such an egocentric bore, and his second wife also experiences a fugitive longing for a typewriter, although this hardly prevents him from being knighted. *The Admirable Crichton* frolicked with the pretensions of aristocracy, which are revealed to be a matter of pure convention; when a ship disaster compels a party of aristocrats to find shelter on a desert island, it is actually the imperturbable butler Crichton who proves himself the master. If the credit for resourcefulness is subsequently taken by his employer, the audience is certainly not fooled.

It is perhaps even noteworthy that Barrie, who was Shaw's junior by only four years, wrote *The Admirable Crichton* as early as 1902, about a decade before Shaw challenged the cultural prerogatives of the aristocracy with the accomplishments of his cockney Galatea, Liza. *What Every Woman Knows* also pricked a bubble or two—masculine vanity in the case of Maggie Wylie's husband whose political speeches have to be written by Maggie, and aristocratic shallowness in the case of her rival Sybil who proves herself a hopelessly useless companion to the rising politician. The ineffable Maggie, who is Barrie's most delightful character and a universal one, holds her husband because she makes herself quietly indispensable to him, and it would also be hard to improve upon her business-like brothers and father when they buy her a husband.

A capacity for shrewd observation made this writer a telling, if fugitive, realist. Moreover, a dour calvinistic temperament was not absent in this son of a Scottish weaver. Life, it is said, seemed quite intolerable to him; he led a retired life so that even his neighbor, Shaw, saw him only rarely. His large eyes were often sorrowful and, according to St. John Ervine, "his voice always sounded as if he were tired."

Peter Pan is perhaps the most "escapist" play ever written, and the reality that is so resolutely avoided in this charming fantasy is the entire adult world. But if this description of Barrie is true, it must be granted that he found other less admirable forms of escape. Sometimes he escaped into merely pleasurable artifice at the expense of power and profundity; sometimes he overcompensated both pain and cynicism with slush as in the ghost drama *Mary Rose, A Kiss for Cinderella,* and *The Old Lady Shows Her Medals,* written during the World War when his heart ached most acutely. As he grew older this charming playwright limped through the streets of the world on gilded crutches. Lovable he remained to the end, which came in 1937; and since he was an accomplished comforter, there was no dearth of voices to acclaim him Shaw's superior and the greatest modern British playwright. In America both William Lyon Phelps and Clayton Hamilton rose to the occasion and called him blest.

He was not always a comforter, of course, but his alleged cynicism could be accepted by the tender-minded because he exercised discretion and never left his audience with a feeling of discomfort or unhappiness. Even when he was not reuniting a ghostly mother with a stalwart soldier-boy as in *Mary Rose,* he was essentially a sedative. The social order is not changed by Crichton's supremacy on the distant island, for no sooner has Lord Loam's party returned to England than the aristocrats are back in their niches and Crichton is again a butler; Maggie forges ahead from victory to victory in her battle to keep her husband, and even if Barrie has to manipulate many strings to assure the triumph of

virtue, he does not hesitate an instant. Barrie never pressed his audience
to the wall, nor did he ever force a truth too far or too hard. After
Pinero, he was the British Compromise incarnate, and since he was a
canny dramatist he disarmed, entertained, and entranced all but the
most tough-minded members of the English-speaking world.

No great change in the alignment of forces took place in the English
theatre after the World War. There was the same conflict between the
tender-minded and the tough-minded, and at first it seemed that the
latter were winning. Their leader was that *enfant terrible* Noel Coward
whose laconic but very physical humor played havoc with respectability.
Very much of the younger generation, having been born in 1899, he first
attained recognition in 1924 with an exposé of neuroticism in fashionable
circles, *The Vortex*. A painful study of a woman, who tries desperately
not to grow old but is forced to resign herself to biological fact when
deserted by her gigolo, and of her son who is psychologically disqualified
for marriage, the play possessed pathos but attracted attention primarily
because of its audacious picture of decadence. Clearly this young man
knew the sophisticated post-war set, and he quickly made himself its
saturnine laureate. His ironic *Post Mortem* in 1930 was a didactic supplement to *The Vortex,* and the peace that followed the World War here
appeared as a sodden and revolting aftermath. His *Private Lives,* replete with the lunacies of the parasitic classes, transformed the same
picture into farce. Decadent melodramas like *Point Valaine* merely indicated that his conception of tragedy was limited by the very horizons
which he deprecated as a satirist, and his conception of fun was similarly
limited to the erotogenic zones slightly cerebralized, as the triangle
comedy *Design for Living* showed. But as a popular diagnostician he
had no peer among the younger playwrights. His numerous satirical
sketches in musical revues and several one-acters like the clever *Hands
Across the Sea* and *Ways and Means* from *Tonight at 8:30* presented an
upper class devoid of responsibility, aim and justification except insofar
as tinsel can be justified because it glitters. And Coward could be just
as savage when he cast a scornful glance at middle-class respectability
in such a piece as *Fumed Oak,* in which a harassed white-collar slave
casts off wife, mother-in-law and child, all of them equally impossible.

A dry and wry style, sometimes almost maddeningly monosyllabic, has
served this urbane nihilist efficiently. He has written with his nerves,
which have sometimes given way. Behind his facility lies a talent for
high comedy that he sometimes mistakenly forsakes for tragic banalities
and always frustrates with shallow theatricality. An unkind critic, St.
John Ervine, has accused him of a lack of intellectual resources, and it
must be confessed that these have not been greatly in evidence. Clifton

Fadiman has rightly noted that he is essentially an unreflective moralist, that when he faces a problem he becomes "a cross between a prep-school serious thinker and a concocter of Henri Bernstein melodrama."

More maturity entered into some of Somerset Maugham's comedies, as one might expect from the man who wrote *Of Human Bondage*. Feeling that he could not persuade himself "that the drama needs to be taken with the seriousness that is cultivated in certain quarters," he did not hesitate after some earlier serious plays to turn out unpretentious farces like *Home and Beauty,* produced in America under the title *Too Many Husbands*. This 1919 variant of the old "Box and Cox" story of two men equally anxious to rid themselves of a woman offered him relief when a tubercular condition compelled him to spend the last winter of the War in a Swiss sanatorium. But it was also during the War that his comedies began to grow sharper and more provocative. In 1917 came *Our Betters,* a devastating satire on the snobbery of American expatriates and their English set. The American girl Bessie Saunders is so aghast at the society into which she is being introduced by her titled sister that she takes a boat home. Here are noblemen like Lord Bleane who are eager to lay their coronets at the feet of every American heiress, duchesses like de Surennes whose maiden name in Chicago was Miss Hodgson and who favor good-looking boys less than half their age, and expatriated fops like Clay who speak condescendingly of "You Americans in America. . . ." A scintillating satire on the leisure class and on snobbishness or "the spirit of romance in a reach-me-down," *Our Betters* is one of the best comedies of manners since the Restoration. An even better play, *The Circle* in 1921 was far less exuberant but more clinical with its case history of what a great passion can culminate in—namely, false teeth and dyed hair and mutual boredom in the case of the elderly and futile Lady Kitty and Lord Porteous. Of course no two cases may be the same, and youth is not intimidated by what time and social prejudice have done to their elders; Lady Kitty's daughter-in-law Elizabeth therefore elopes like her mother-in-law with a high heart, and "the circle" is complete. Even *The Lady of the Sea* formula doesn't work; Elizabeth's husband takes his father's advice and offers his wife her freedom on the theory that if the bars and bolts are removed "the prisoner won't want to escape;" but she does.

Six years later the Shavian problem-play note was sounded with notable effectiveness by Maugham in *The Constant Wife*. When Constance discovers her husband's infidelity with her married friend Marie-Louise she prevents a scandal and then quietly goes into business. Soberly she asks herself the kind of question that Shaw would have raised —namely, what claim can she have upon her husband after fifteen years of marriage? Like other women of her class she has been, strictly speaking, a parasite, having rendered no services to her husband; once she possessed some physical usefulness, but the moment she ceases to please him as a woman she actually has no function and therefore no status in his house. Only by earning her livelihood can she recover her dignity, and then, at last, she also has the right to enjoy an old admirer's love. The justification for the double standard vanishes when its economic base disappears, as it did when women entered business during the World War. Recognizing, however, that man also had a legitimate complaint in the middle-class world, Maugham followed this charming comedy with the more humdrum one of *The Bread-Winner* in which a husband asserts his freedom from a family that expects him to slave for it without compensation. Thus Maugham, who expressed slight admiration for the "theatre of ideas," himself contributed some of its best examples.

He even went further when he responded to the disillusionment of the post-war period. *For Services Rendered,* in 1933, was a bitter drama of the aftermath, of a provincial household wrecked and stranded by the War. Earlier in 1920, he also concerned himself laboriously with the question of faith in *The Unknown,* the drama of a returned soldier who can no longer believe in the existence of God. And the same bitterness reappeared in 1933 when Maugham wrote his ironic tragedy *Sheppey* to prove that a follower of Jesus, like the sweepstakes winner Sheppey who distributes his gains to the poor, can only be adjudged mad. The world operates on the reverse principle expressed by Sheppey's alienist when that worthy declares that "It's quite obvious that a sane man is not going to give all his money away to the poor. A sane man *takes* money from the poor. . . ."

Maugham was not the only humorist to put bitters into his cocktail. The ingratiating Scot medical playwright Dr. Mavor writing under the pen name of James Bridie turned out dour and ironical, if unsustained, comedies like *The Black Eye* and *Storm Over Patsy* (based on a German play by Bruno Frank), as well as the pungent but spilled satire on eugenics *A Sleeping Clergyman.* C. K. Munro who could concoct so pleasant a trifle as *At Mrs. Beam's* also wrote the sharp, if obvious, satire on imperialism and militarism *The Rumor.* Even the laureate of Winnie-the-Pooh, A. A. Milne, grew sardonic in *The Truth About Blayds,* the story of a poet who became a national institution by stealing a friend's verses. The talented Rodney Ackland composed pictures of bankrupt intellectuals like his diffuse *Strange Orchestra* and dramas of middle-class decay like *Plot Twenty-One* and *After October.* J. B. Priestley sometimes waxed satirical before he took flight into the cumulus of time-relativity in *Time and the Conways* and *We Have Been Here Before.* But Maugham has remained the most trenchant of the mockers who sometimes turned mourners, and being a superlative craftsman and wit he has also been the most accomplished of these writers.

Sobriety celebrated victories in Robert Nichols' and Maurice Brown's *Wings Over Europe* (1928), an imaginative drama of a scientist's efforts to end European wars, and in the realistic work of R. C. Sherriff. The latter's *Journey's End* was a touching picture of the waste of human values incurred by a war that turns a fine schoolteacher like Osborne into an officer and sacrificial goat, that destroys the nerves of a spirited youth like Captain Stanhope, and that kills mere boys like Raleigh. Behind the restraint of this tragedy of English officers in a St. Quentin dugout there are evidences of anger and sorrow; there are such details as a suicidal raid insufficiently covered by artillery fire and a pointed anecdote about the English and German soldiers blowing each other's trenches to blazes after fraternizing. *Journey's End* was a trifle anemic; it lacked the abundance of life and movement of its American counterpart *What Price Glory?* and its criticism of war was deficient in passion and scope. Still Sherriff's play, written more than a decade after the Armistice, in 1929, differed radically from patriotic romance, and echoes of his realistic animus also appeared in his later collaboration with Jeanne de Casalis, *St. Helena,* a static anti-heroic picture of Napoleon's last years. The drama of Death, with which England had familiarized itself during the War, also found a corner in the theatre with Sutton Vane's affecting and theatrically sound *Outward Bound,* in 1923; conventional thinking did not lessen its persuasiveness. These serious works were supplemented by psychological studies of sexual maladjustment like Mordaunt Shairp's excellent tragedy of sybaritism *The Green Bay Tree,* Rudolf Besier's *The Barretts of Wimpole Street,* and Leslie and Sewell Stokes' *Oscar Wilde.* Historical pieces like Gordon Daviot's *Richard of Bordeaux,* and Laurence Housman's chronicle *Victoria Regina* also gave weight to the theatre.

In the thirties, moreover, the world depression made itself acutely felt and although London's commercial theatres ignored the situation young English playwrights noted it. Ronald Gow's and Walter Greenwood's *Love on the Dole* was one of several poignantly realistic plays that drew attention to the plight of the unemployed, and the imaginative satirical pieces *The Dog Beneath the Skin* and *The Ascent of F6* of the poet W. H. Auden and his collaborator Christopher Isherwood blazed away at capitalism and fascism. Although tiresomely rhetorical, as a rule, they occasionally achieved genuine eloquence, and *The Dog Beneath the Skin* won praise in England for injecting an astringent into British musical comedy. A "left" English theatre arose (an Experimental Theatre, a Unity Theatre, etc.), and although it made no deep impression on the thirties it was anything but tame or light-hearted except for the occasional expectation of a proletarian dawn. Its male Cassandras knew whereof they were speaking, and they were far more accurate in their prophecies as the second World War was to show in the fall of 1939 than their lofty critics. But accuracy and justified bitterness by themselves do not create masterpieces, and Auden, Isherwood, and Spender have yet to prove their mettle as bona fide playwrights. Their poetic efforts were, curiously enough, paralleled by writers of the extreme "right," by Anglo-Catholic mystics like the American-born T. S. Eliot, the converted detective-story writer Dorothy Sayers, and Christopher Hassall who also deprecated materialistic and individualistic society but saw hope only in the triumph of spiritual values. Eliot's *Murder in the Cathedral,* Mrs. Dorothy Sayers' *Zeal of Thy House* and *The Devil to Pay.* and Christopher Hassall's *Christ's Comet* possessed poetry of distinction. But their dramaturgy suffered various degrees of paresis, and their metaphysical ideas remained mournful echoes of the past.

Against the stream of incisive satire and noble grief, however, must be set the great tide of frivolity and sentimentality. It flooded the British Isles with the blithe operettas of Noel Coward; with the *Dear Octopus* benevolence of Dodie Smith and the pretty A. A. Milne whimsies of *Mr. Pim Passes By, The Dover Road,* and *Sarah Simple;* with the polished amenities of Frederick Lonsdale and the sentimentalities of John Van Druten whose boldest contributions (the school play *Young Woodley,* and the pacifistic *Flowers of the Forest*) were discreetly sugared; with the humors of Benn Levy, which were at their best in the amoral *Springtime for Henry,* and with popular lunacies like *George and Margaret* and *French Without Tears.*

For one who is so minded it would be child's play to detect evidences of shipwreck. That much was in fact confessed by the author of *French Without Tears,* Terence Rattigan, who justified his contribution about a year before the outbreak of the second World War on the grounds that "The dread of war, of civil strife, of national upheaval is far too real, far too intense in England at the present time to allow its audiences to listen with equanimity to gloomy reminders that our civilization is on the brink of destruction." It is true that the English Stage Society and various repertory companies continued to evince an interest in experiment.[23] Moreover, the spirit of Shaw was too formidable to be completely exorcised from the English theatre. But after World War I, leadership in the drama passed to a more fortunately situated English-speaking theatre, and America, which had the youngest drama of any importance, suddenly acquired supremacy.

XXIX

EUGENE O'NEILL AND THE AMERICAN SCENE

I DISCOVERING AMERICA

WHEN America discovered through O'Neill and his successors that the theatre was an art and not an industry, drama became one of its richest natural resources. That it should be properly tapped only in the past two decades was, however, surely no accident. This occurred at a time when America came of age, and the fact that maturity brought with it many painful problems after 1929 did not alter the situation materially since dramatists thrive on insecurity as well as security, on perturbations as well as certainties.

In both grief and gladness the American dramatist was distinctly vital and energetic. This vitality was in fact as natural as breathing to the writers of the new world. It was inherent in the great era of American expansion, and it could only find a proper stimulus when the nation found itself in a favored position between 1918 and 1929 as the creditor of the world and its citizens looked forward to unlimited material progress. Whether the playwright accepted or resented this development he shared its energy and exhibited it in his work.

Thirteen Atlantic seaboard colonies in the Western hemisphere had gradually pushed the frontier westward to the Pacific, conquering the wilderness, binding the vast territory together with railroads, and harnessing nature to the service of man through the extraction and conversion of raw materials. Opportunity seemed open to every man, riches were amassed by numerous individuals (legally and illegally), and a higher standard of living was established for a larger percentage of the populace than in any well-populated nation.

And with this advance in material benefits were associated qualities of mind and spirit that bespoke self-confidence, invincible optimism, and vigor. Even when Americans found the civilization they had created less than comforting, they loved its crudities—its machines entranced them, its factories gave them a sense of power, its crowded, smoky cities like "hog-butcher" Chicago filled them with self-assurance. *Homo Americanus,* as the American citizen was derogatorily named, struck foreign observers as almost a special creature. Through the successive pioneering

629

periods that opened up the frontiers, and owing to the abundant opportunities that were available to him, he had become rugged and independent. Tradition bound him less than his European cousins, the absence of a hereditary aristocracy left him largely unawed by coronets and fine manners, the existence of political democracy had inculcated in him a feeling of equality with any man. Moreover, he was a hybrid character—he was English, Scotch, Irish, Scandinavian, German, Italian, Jewish, Slavic, Magyar, and so forth; he was Episcopalian, Presbyterian, Catholic, Jew, Baptist, Lutheran, Mormon, Holy Roller, Greek Orthodox and what not. Despite some inevitable snobbery on the part of the longer settled families, which was generally overcome by the growing wealth or political power of the latest group of immigrants, America was the melting-pot of the nations. When America's poet laureate, Walt Whitman, looked at his miscellaneous fellow-citizens and loved them, he was drawing the whole world of man to his bosom.

Literature inevitably responded to this ferment. Although provincialism and the narrower brand of puritanism took its toll, and although academicism and the snobbery of some New England Brahmins resulted in effete imitation of European letters, American writers began to reflect the American scene even before the American Revolution. The spirit of enterprise and bluff common sense rang out lustily in the writings of that self-made American Benjamin Franklin. A brash Yankee Doodlism appeared in the satirical, anti-British broadsides of the 1776-83 period. The pioneer held his head high in James Fenimore Cooper's novels, and Whittier's Quaker gentleness savored of the soil rather than the library. Even the gentry of Massachusetts recognized the fact that it was living in a new world where the common man did not start life with a permanent stigma of inferiority and was not divinely destined for servility. The rounded periods of Emerson acclaimed a new heaven and a new earth, and when the thinker and naturalist Thoreau traveled "a good deal in Concord" he moved afoot as a self-sufficient plebeian and a man of independent conscience. Margaret Fuller, the blue-stocking, stood for the New Woman; Herman Melville, descended from the Gansevoort patroons, went to sea as a common sailor and brought back a feeling for the comradeship of races and men of brawn. And so the procession moved on to Bret Harte and Jack London who celebrated raw life in the West; to Mark Twain, the laureate of the Mississippi; to Vachel Lindsay, the troubadour of the Middle West and of the agrarian democracy of Populism; to Whitman singing of the open road but equally ready to herald America on the Brooklyn Ferry; to Sandburg reveling in the grime of Chicago; to Robert Frost wresting great song from common earth and common men.

Only the dramatists lagged behind, as they generally do, because a book can be composed independently but a play must be written for a theatre. As a public institution the theatre comes easily under the surveillance of the law (books can be distributed secretly and are never as conspicuous as plays), and it can affront the people more easily or flagrantly than almost anything in the world. It also requires a large and relatively homogeneous body of patrons, since as an expensive undertaking it depends so heavily on business considerations. Consequently, although a popular kind of theatre flourished mightily, the American drama remained feeble until after the World War. Even the kindest critics must concede its decided inferiority to European plays.

The American theatre's history is one of increasing productions starting with casual performances like that of the playlet *Ye Bare and Ye Cubb* in 1665 and with professional ones introduced by the Hallam Company which arrived from London in 1752 and gave *The Merchant of Venice* at its inaugural performance in Williamsburg. Progress was at first checkered owing to the animosity of the good citizens who shared a distrust of the theatre with those English Puritans who padlocked it during the Commonwealth. When in 1761 David Douglass led the reorganized Hallam troupe into Newport, Rhode Island, he had to advertise *Othello* as a "Series of Moral Dialogues." Even after the Revolutionary War it was necessary to call plays by the more innocent name of "operas" and to announce *The School for Scandal* as a "Comic Lecture in Five Parts on the Pernicious Vice of Scandal."

Nevertheless, the stage spread over the country—first on the Atlantic fringe, then into the Middle West by means of touring companies traveling in wagons and boats. No matter how far the covered wagons of the pioneers went the carts of Thespis were sure to follow; they even caught up with the Mormons in Utah and with the gold prospectors in the wild West. Great was the attraction of foreign stars like George Frederick Cooke, Edmund Kean, Junius Brutus Booth who journeyed as far as New Orleans in 1828, and William Charles Macready who reached St. Louis some fifteen years later. In time, American actors like Edwin Forrest and Joseph Jefferson arose to share and challenge the visitors' laurels, and resident stock companies served as supporting casts for the itinerant stars. The stock system fell on evil days owing to the exorbitant fees of the leading actors without whom it became impossible to attract an audience, and owing to their incompetence the resident companies became a vanishing quantity by 1860. But the theatre continued to thrive, and visiting actors began to take their own touring companies along now that the railroads provided adequate transportation facilities. In time, the task of directing some two hundred and fifty companies into about three thousand five hundred cities from a few centers, chief of which was New York's Union Square, became a mass production industry. A "Theatrical Syndicate" for this purpose was established in 1896 until the theatre became simply a monopolistic business like the trusts against which the Sherman Act was leveled. Revolts against this organization by independent actor-managers in 1898, 1902, and in later years proved futile. Nor did the long-drawn battle waged by the Shubert Brothers, which ended in the dissolution of the Syndicate in 1916, materially affect the quality of the plays and the productions. But there the theatre as "big business" ended! Owing to increasing railroad rates, wartime prices, and the rise of the films, which provided entertainment for a fraction of the price of theatre tickets, the tidal wave of stage entertainment receded. It receded further when the depression of 1929 began, until in 1934 there were only twenty-seven touring companies in the United States as compared with three hundred and thirty-seven in the same month of the year 1908. The commercial theatre became concentrated in New York, and even there it ceased to be a really large-sized enterprise.

The outlet for the American drama after 1915 became increasingly confined to a small number of commercial producers, a few art theatres, little theatres, college and labor stages, and a short-lived federal relief network for unemployed actors. But, ironically, it was only during this period, when the American stage was losing a great portion of its following, that the American drama became a genuine art.

For a century, American playwrights were of no importance whatsoever to the world, although they had the seeds of a vigorous democratic art in their matter and their bias. The very first (privately performed) play to be printed in the States, *Androboros* in 1714, sounded a sharp note of satire—at the expense of New York's Trinity Parish, no less. During the Revolutionary War the colonists squirted acid at the British and the native Royalists, leadership in this game being taken by General Warren's sharp-tongued wife, Mrs. Mercy Warren. Her play *The Group,* printed a day before the Battle of Lexington, hotly satirized the royalists as a "swarm of court sycophants, hungry harpies, and unprincipled danglers," and her burlesque *The Blockhead or the Affrighted Officers* badgered Burgoyne's officers ("the bastard sons of Mars") who were interrupted in their enjoyment of a play by news of the battle of Bunker Hill. It is to be noted, too, that Tory partisans replied to such attacks in the same uninhibited manner. American propaganda plays did not begin with the depression of 1929 but with the American Revolution!

Nor did social satire end with the attack on Trinity Church. In the best American play on an American subject, Royall Tyler's *The Contrast*

(1787), the satire was leveled at dandies like Dimple who return from Europe with a head full of fashionable villainies. Patterned after *The School for Scandal*, its feminine chatter may possess some old-world wit, but the play is on the side of the homespun virtues; Manly is the bluff and democratic—if, alas, boringly moralizing—American man, and he and his independent, practical-minded Yankee servant Jonathan affirm "the American Way." A host of later plays similarly delighted audiences with American characters or "stage Yankees" bearing such flavorsome names as Nathan Yank, Solomon Swap, Lot Sap Sago, and Deuteronomy Dutiful. Royall Tyler even went further and wrote direct social criticism in *The Georgia Spec, or Land in the Moon* (1797), a satire on land speculation. For a young nation, the drama began vigorously enough, and it is this penchant for realistic and forthright utterance that links the early nineteenth-century playwrights with many of their successors a century later.

The American dramatist, however, soon found himself enforced to depart from a genuinely national style and matter. Life was becoming tamer on the American seaboard, imitativeness took its toll, and the actors from England naturally increased the popularity of romantic drama. The trend of rank imitation began, in fact, with the very first play written by an American—that is, with Thomas Godfrey's neoclassic *Prince of Parthia* in 1736. It was carried further, in the romantic vein, by America's first professional dramatist William Dunlap who became a most prolific adapter of German and French plays, with the fulsome Kotzebue as his greatest creditor. American historical themes received the same kind of inflated treatment that prevailed abroad, and were supplemented by a series of "Indian" romances that had even less to offer to an adult intelligence.[1] Most romantic plays even in Europe tended strongly in the direction of melodrama, although the most distinguished of them had the intellectual force of *Cain* and *The Cenci*. American taste being in the main even simpler, audiences encouraged melodrama in its rankest forms, and except for some democratic fulminations against villainous aristocrats which naturally attracted the inheritors of the American revolution, the plays were devoid of thought. It was this appetite for contrived excitement that was fed most abundantly by Dunlap's most popular successor John Howard Payne of "Home, Sweet Home" fame, and by writers like the author of the rhetorical *Jack Cade* (Shakespeare's "pleb" villain here turned avenging hero), Judge Conrad. Even the finest taste for romantic tragedy could produce nothing more notable than George Henry Boker's *Francesca di Rimini*, a well written but derivative blank-verse piece. The climax of the less literary romantic drama appeared in a rash of Dion Boucicault melodramas possessing the merit of local color in such work as *The Octoroon,* with its picture of Negro slavery on the eve of the Civil War (December, 1859), but remaining claptrap nevertheless.

Both social drama like the lachrymose dramatization of *Uncle Tom's Cabin* in 1852 and efforts to capitalize on the Civil War in historical pieces like Boucicault's spy romance *Belle Lamar* and Bronson Howard's *Shenandoah,* written long after the event in 1888, were cut from the same cloth. And very much the same pattern prevailed in the still later and more compact *Secret Service* to which the actor-playwright William Gillette brought his persuasive personality. The tradition refused to die even in the twentieth century, which still paid attention to operatic sentiment such as was contained in Belasco's *Madame Butterfly* and in related pieces that ranged in location from the Far East to the setting of *The Rose of the Rancho.* The less exotic sentimental drama developed under the aegis of Augustin Daly was merely a Sears-Roebuck version of the same romanticism in the seventies of the last century. A costly civil war and the immediate rise of large-scale industrial capitalism left the theatre practically unstirred; audiences remained content with anything that merely titillated them. "It was this public," John Anderson notes, "that was daydreaming while the foundation of industrial feudalism was being laid under its nose. . . . Like the newly rich we were, we took our ease too soon—and for granted." [2]

The comic spirit was somewhat more vital, ranging from derivative remote comedy of manners like Payne's *Charles the Second,*[3] properly rounded out with the reformation of the rakish Duke of Rochester, to Anna Cora Mowatt Ritchie's more pertinent and thorough satire *Fashion* in 1845. Although this energetic and intelligent woman wound up her amusing comedy with the customary bouquets to virtue, she made the most of her brickbats at snobbism and the custom of aping the aristocracy. Nothing as good as her portraits of the fashionable Mrs. Tiffany, her circle, and the disguised chef Count Jolimaitre appeared in the series of social comedies that followed *Fashion.* But even these at least had some relevance and point, and later William Dean Howells, whose critical essays called for a discreet application of realism to the theatre, contributed gay farces in the manner of the Italian Goldoni whom he admired so extraordinarily. In the riotous Mulligan series, moreover, William Harrigan and his associate Hart, hammered together genial, unliterary farces of immigrant life that kept the public rolling with laughter at their ingenuity and verisimilitude.[4] With his successors in vaudeville and in lowbrow comedy, Harrigan brought into the theatre the robustness of the American spirit, and the result was actually far more exhilarating than anything that the literary theatre was producing. The farces and comedies of the American stage, from Winchell

Smith and Frank Bacon's *Lightnin'* in 1918 to the later Kaufman con-
coctions and the better musical comedies stem from the same native gift
for broad type characterizations and hearty laughter. It was the genteel
tradition that vanished like imprints on the Newport beach. Only in one
singular exception, Langdon Mitchell's bright treatment of divorce in
fashionable society *The New York Idea,* in 1906, did high comedy
bubble with continuous vigor.

Even that most successful writer Clyde Fitch proved himself a less
vital influence than the shrewd clowns in the field of comedy. Born in
1865 in Elmira, New York, of a cultured family, he was a child of the
genteel tradition. He might have become a master of comedy of manners by virtue of his knowledge of the upper reaches of society. His
portrait of a dandy in *Beau Brummell* at the beginning of the nineties
and the clever description of social foibles in *The Climbers* reveal this
playwright's potentialities for comedy; and these were considerably supported by the comparative stability of metropolitan upper-class society
in the "gay" nineties. He also had a sensitive camera eye for the color
and contour of these years in a number of plays like *Captain Jinks of
the Horse Marines.* In fact, he had all the superficial qualifications. All
he lacked were the basic ones that distinguish a master of high comedy
from a mere journeyman. His hold on his characters was slight and
nearly all of them were merely romantic sketches. He occasionally essayed an etching, as in *The Girl with the Green Eyes* in 1902, but his
analysis of jealousy in the case of its "Jinny Austin" merely nicked the
surface; when he created the heroine of the generally amusing comedy
The Truth he presented a crotchet—the habit of prevarication—rather
than a rounded character. Moreover, Fitch merely philandered with
ideas, playing with them in a few incidental speeches, and his statement
that "No one at present is getting the essence of his environment in
thought, word, and deed . . ." was only too applicable to himself.

It was not only, as Montrose Moses noted, that "in point of morality
Fitch was wholly conventional,"[5] but that Fitch lacked a vigorous
critical intelligence. If he had one, he frustrated it, or he had it frustrated for him by the requirements of the theatre for which he worked.
"What a state it is," he wrote in a letter, "when there is only *one man*
to whom one can offer a play and expect to have it in any half adequate
way presented," and this one manager demanded humdrum plots instead of incisive characterization and thought. Fitch submitted to the
status quo; he kept his comic spirit properly reined and satisfied his
public with any kind of play that would meet the market, including
conventional historical pieces like *Nathan Hale* and *Barbara Frietchie.*
Only in *The City,* which according to Professor Quinn he intended to be
his best work, did Fitch nearly carry his plot and characters to a sharp

conclusion, exposing corruption in public life quite relentlessly except for some romantic forgiveness on the part of George Rand's fiancée after he confesses his misconduct. When he died in Europe on September 4, 1909, Fitch had not succeeded—except perhaps in *The City*—in bringing America within striking distance of even Jones and Pinero at their best.

His more rugged fellow-citizens were likewise barred from more than a glimpse of the promised land. Bronson Howard, who in 1881 even anticipated some modern treatments of the class conflict between capital and labor in *Baron Rudolph,* could write forthrightly about Wall Street speculation in *The Henrietta* six years later. But his choice of topical themes was neutralized by enforced reliance on Sardoodledom, giving point to Brander Matthews' complaint that it was this author's tragedy that he was born too soon. Steele Mackaye, who tried to advance acting technique by promoting Delsarte training, observed the effects of predatory capitalism and warned against an uprising on the part of oppressed labor in *Paul Kauvar, or Anarchy* in 1887 without, however, plumbing any depths or reaching any distinction. Charles Klein, a prolific stage carpenter, could take a leaf from Ida Tarbell's history of the Standard Oil Company in writing *The Lion and the Mouse,* but he was content to turn out a facile play. Edward Sheldon could take note of political corruption in the states, but one of his two or three advanced plays *The Boss,* written as late as 1911, does not go beyond the mere portrait of a ruthless politician who is, moreover, safely reformed at the end and restored to domestic favor by his magnanimous wife. Turning more effectively to an important racial problem in *The Nigger,* in 1910, Sheldon could at best indulge in some tentative realism with his tale of a socially and politically ambitious Southerner who makes the catastrophic discovery that he has Negro blood in his veins, and the same writer's slumming expedition in *Salvation Nell* did not lead him further than a faithful description of the seedy side of American life.

The competent technician Augustus Thomas made preliminary efforts to dramatize new ideas and discoveries. But he could not venture much further than some tenuous experimentation with mental telepathy and psychological suggestion in *The Witching Hour,* written as late as 1907. Four years later more substance went into *As a Man Thinks* which added domestic relations and racial antagonism to the theme of suggestion, and Thomas made other bids for importance with pictures of the American hinterland in such plays as *In Mizzoura* and *Arizona.* Even in these relatively progressive undertakings, however, Thomas used pedestrian and rigid dialogue and failed to surround his matter with living characters. In *The Faith Healer* the poet William Vaughn Moody made one crude prose effort to create psychological drama in the portrait of a character whose hypnotic powers depend upon confident love, and he displayed admirable courage when he tried to treat puritanism and passion realistically in *The Great Divide*. Here he had the temerity to suggest that a woman could love a man who had violated her (a theme that Flaubert had treated with infinitely greater subtlety in the novel *Salammbo*), and he permeated the Western background and hero of the play with lusty life. But even here, Moody succumbed to stage machinery and sentimentalism.*

Realistic technique, however, could not by itself have lifted the American drama to any heights, just as "ideas" alone could not. As early as 1890 James A. Herne, having tired of romantic trivia and having struck up some acquaintance with Ibsen's work, had already gone further than the younger playwrights—which was quite remarkable in one who had been born in 1839. *Margaret Fleming*, the outstanding realistic play before the advent of O'Neill, revealed a well-intentioned weakling embroiled in an extra-marital affair, a girl dying in childbirth, and a hungry infant being suckled by his wife Margaret. In its revised form, which omitted a melodramatic kidnaping of Philip Fleming's legitimate child, the play even allowed Margaret to take the unconventional step of adopting the illegitimate infant. Other plays by Herne, like *Shore Acres*, and later Eugene Walter's sterner melodrama *The Easiest Way*, in which a well-intentioned but loose woman fails to reform herself, likewise heralded the rise of realism.

Still, something remained lacking—greatness of spirit, poetry of passion, and poetry of thought. Even when the American playwrights entertained a deep concern with dynamic issues—when Steele MacKaye and Howells championed justice in the Haymarket anarchist trials or when Herne interested himself in Henry George's single-tax doctrine— their plays continued to lack largeness of spirit. Similarly, in the domain of stage technique, Belasco could place all of Childs' restaurant on his platform without giving his picture the illuminating power that comes from interpretive and dynamic realism. And the poetic efforts of a Percy MacKaye in *The Scarecrow* or of a Josephine Preston Peabody in *The Piper* brought only tenuous, if rather charming, fancies or inventions to a theatre that needed the poetry of incandescent creation.†

* Moreover, the play was discreetly toned down by its producer Henry Miller; "we never got the true Moody play," writes the chronicler of the American drama, Montrose J. Moses.

† It is only fair to observe that the fine scholar Professor Arthur Hobson Quinn in his remarkably detailed and authoritative *History of the American Drama from the Civil War to the Present Day* treats the older American playwrights and plays with considerably more reverence than the present author. This is wholly proper when one is under no obligation to measure them by the yardstick of world drama. Moreover, since progress in the arts is anything but uniform, it is entirely

By 1914, however, a new order and a new state of mind was beginning to assert itself. It was not that a modern tone was beginning to assert itself in the comedies of Albert E. Thomas, Clare Kummer, and Jesse Lynch Williams—as in the latter's playful examination of the institution of marriage, *Why Marry?*—but that a different spirit began to permeate the American theatre. The contracted commercial stage found a cosmopolitan background in New York and was being supplemented by numerous campus and little theatres. Since the European theatre was making tremendous strides in stagecraft, American scenic designers and directors began embracing the art of Reinhardt, Gordon Craig and Appia with ardor. Huntley Carter's *The New Spirit in the Theatre,* Professor George Pierce Baker's slides of simplified settings by Craig, Appia and Ernst Stern collected by him during his trip to Europe, Reinhardt's exotic production of *Sumurun,* the Armory Show of modernistic painting in 1913,[7] and the ecstatic reports of travelers in foreign capitals—all this made the pulse beat faster. Americans had discovered the luxury of "art," and the discovery continued even after the World War. They had been restive in a world devoted to utility, and they continued to be dissatisfied even while recognizing the kinetic qualities of American life. Beauty, properly capitalized, became the fashion, and with it came a related passion for self-expression.

Too long had Americans been content with the growing wealth and enterprise of their country. The pioneering days were over, and now it was high time to make life more abundant with esthetic gratifications. The old forms had to be discarded, new forms had to be created, and the sons of Zenith returned to convert Philistia into Paradise. And since the old commercial theatre was unwilling to scrap tried methods of profit-making and was by now leaving large areas of the American landscape free from its dubious ministrations, its place could be taken by new groups unencumbered with the necessity or the desire to make money until Broadway also adopted the new methods.* Percy MacKaye, following in his father's footsteps, attempted to interest communities in pageants and spectacles. "Little theatres" sprang up mushroomlike wherever a small group of amateurs and an only slightly larger group of local patrons could be found. The great body of American citizens would ultimately perhaps leave their trough of dollar-mindedness; that is, if

true that many plays since 1918 have been patently inferior to some older plays. There is only one error that criticism may not make, and that is to set a perfect contrivance above an imperfect work that is permeated with inspiration. Even faulty work of O'Neill, Maxwell Anderson, S. N. Behrman, and Clifford Odets, for example, belongs to a higher level than more letter-perfect work by pedestrian predecessors like Fitch and Thomas.[6]

* Joseph Wood Krutch makes the point that the new art was not monopolized by the "art" theatres.

they were badgered long enough with bohemian satire, for the young Americans of Greenwich Village and tributary places had discovered the European game of baiting the bourgeoisie. Meanwhile, however, the art movement was to consist of an aristocracy of the spirit.

As early as 1911 a Drama League of America had begun to foster a literary drama of native and foreign origin. The Wisconsin Players at Madison and Milwaukee, the Chicago Little Theatre led by the Englishman Maurice Browne and Ellen Van Volkenburg, Professor Baker's 47 Workshop Theatre, the Carnegie Institute of Technology at Pittsburgh under Thomas Wood Stevens, Professor Frederick H. Koch's Dakota Playmakers and his Caroline Playmakers some years later, the little theatres in Cleveland, New Orleans and Pasadena—these and other organizations began to dot the country with oases of "culture." In time, their efforts were supported by books like Kenneth Macgowan's *Footlights Across America* and by the pioneering magazine *Theatre Arts* founded in 1918 and edited by Mrs. Edith J. R. Isaacs, Macgowan and Stark Young. Experiments in production, lighting, and scenic design were undertaken by such artists of the theatre as Robert Edmond Jones, Lee Simonson, Norman Bel Geddes, Irving Pichel, and Kenneth Macgowan. As one of the apostles of the movement Sheldon Cheney was to note later, "We were thinking of the theatre only on the esthetic side; thought to perfect it as a form of art expression." [8]

As early as 1914 and 1915, moreover, the movement reached a thumping climax. Naturally, this took place in New York's Greenwich Village which had become the Mecca to which every American devotee of art had to bring his oblations, unless he preferred the Medina of Harriet Monroe's poetry circle in Chicago. During the autumn of 1914 several enthusiasts—Robert Edmond Jones, Philip Moeller, Helen Westley, Lawrence Langner, Lee Simonson, Maurice Wertheim, Edward Goodman, and others built a stage in the rear part of a store in Washington Square. Calling themselves the Washington Square Players, they produced original one-act plays. Presently they moved into the little Bandbox Theatre, and after the War, in 1919, a number of them founded the Theatre Guild which became the longest-lived "art theatre" in America. It effected a characteristically American compromise with business, but it brought the progressive European drama to America with plays by Ibsen, Tolstoy, Strindberg, Ervine, Shaw, Molnar, Andreyev, Toller, Werfel, Kaiser and others, in addition to staging notable work by Rice, Barry, Howard, Anderson, Behrman, O'Neill, and other natives.

2 THE PROVINCETOWN'S PLAYWRIGHT

In 1915, another group from Greenwich Village, summering in the artists' colony of Provincetown, Mass., founded the Provincetown Players under the leadership of the adventurous "Jig" Cook, the playwright Susan Glaspell, Robert Edmond Jones, and others. Returning to New York, these zealous disciples converted a stable in MacDougal Street, named it The Provincetown Theatre, and made it the *Théâtre Libre* of the Village. Artists from all fields, supplemented by members of the Washington Square Players, joined them. Here the new native drama began to appear in America when one of their number, a gaunt young man by the name of Eugene Gladstone O'Neill, supplied them with several one-acters, short plays being in particular demand owing to the slim resources of the experimentalists. Although he was soon to be surrounded by a number of other original playwrights, his progress led him to altitudes reached thus far by no other American or European dramatist whose work lies wholly within the twentieth century.

O'Neill, like every significant writer, however, was not the product of merely theatrical developments or impulses. He was, above all, a unique personality; and despite the complacencies of those who see a playwright merely as an accessory to the fact of theatre or the fact of economics, a real dramatist is a real personality. He was, at the same time, a veritable seismograph of the ideas, viewpoints, and promptings of the new age. He reflected a general discontent with a materialistic America on the part of the younger creative sons of the age, a sense of frustration, a general straining for enriched experience, and an assimilation of European thought and dramatic art. He responded to these underground stirrings and rumblings with crude but impressive intensity. His impressiveness resides, in fact, not in the discovery of unique ideas but in his absorption of these ideas and even more importantly in the raw personal passionateness with which he employed them on the stage.

In him Europe and America interbred, the one providing the chromosomes of thought and experiment, the other the genes of grappling vitality. These were insufficiently matched or balanced, recalling in this respect the work of the minor Elizabethan dramatists who so often excelled in energy at the expense of form and even sense. O'Neill has been flatly called a "melodramatist" by one writer,[9] and the critic John Mason Brown has astutely sensed his kinship with that morning star of Shakespeare's Age, Christopher Marlowe.[10] They have both, as Mr. Brown has so beautifully put it, expressed hearts that were anvils unto sorrow, "borne desperate thoughts against Jove's deity," written "blood-drenched chronicles," prized "the passion that in passion burns," exceeded probability, and no stage could comfortably contain their thoughts. They were both titans of chaos rather than Olympian gods. They were both, at the same time, suspiciously youthful in their eagerness to make more of an intellectual discovery than balanced artistry can countenance.

O'Neill is one of the most imperfect of the theatre's great men. But it is folly to ignore his greatness because of its imperfection. The debit and credit of his contribution are interrelated; they are inherent in the struggle of a tormented noble spirit in an anarchic world. If there is anarchy in his work, it is derived from the larger anarchy of life in the early twentieth century which perhaps only a philosopher—of the "absolute" or of the "social" variety—could pretend to resolve. Certain it is that those who have supposedly resolved it in the theatre have been mediocre playwrights regardless of what one may think of their solutions, whether these be economic or religious; O'Neill himself wrote a mediocre play, *Days Without End*, when he thought he had found a solution. The chronicle of his career is one of as much failure as success. But he has both failed and succeeded greatly. Even the perspective of the future which some critics of O'Neill have forecast with an accuracy that has still to be tested [11] is likely to reveal this much.

The nature of this greatness cannot, however, be summarized coldly. It is a matter of his generally somber and sardonic tone, of his demoniac possession and writhings, and of reality honestly caught, intensely hated and passionately defied by him. His realism has indeed neglected reality as a phenomenon that might be clarified or ameliorated by social analysis and action. O'Neill has been extravagantly acclaimed as a mystic by the Catholic critic Richard Dana Skinner, when as a matter of fact many of his perceptions have caught and appraised reality realistically and psychologically while his visions have merely possessed that sense of eternity or kinship with nature which is any poet's prerogative. On the other hand, O'Neill has been severely criticized for treating the social realities of his time only tangentially or without awareness of their existence as a social problem.[12] The fact is that he has rarely regarded them as worth treating artistically except as manifestations of the struggle between man's will and fate, between passion and circumstance, and between forces of the inner self. This has resulted in much ambiguity, exaggerated ineffective emotionalism, and chafing against imponderables on his part. This has also disqualified him, for the most part, as a strictly "social dramatist" at a time when every playwright is expected to be one by the younger generation. But obviously there are many paths leading to a dramatist's heaven. Moreover, the common reality of society has a way of remaining under his feet even when he is ascending from private infernos toward the Empyrean and the Primum Mobile. Even in his metaphysical flight, O'Neill has caught the reality of common people living on sea or land; he has presented humanity struggling against inherited or acquired limitations and facing racial prejudice, poverty, the hardness of a stony soil, the frustrations of puritanism, and the effects of a materialistic world which thwarts or perverts the spirit.

Besides, it is precisely this urge to go beyond mere photography of the "surface of things"—though he proved himself an excellent photographer in the early plays—that enabled him to leave the commonplace theatre of his youth. Having, unlike Shaw, little concern for the dynamics of society, he could satisfy his aim of doing "big work" only by expressing inner conflicts. Being a frequently metaphysical thinker, he may leave one profoundly dissatisfied with his philosophy, and every formal statement of it in his plays or in his explanations may be either baffling or chaotic. But the necessity of expressing his thoughts in the theatre through actual characters and situations led him to create intense drama. Even if we accept one critic's charge that, with respect to his philosophy, he has been "forever arriving at the same comclusion and embarking anew on the same quest," [13] we must observe that many of his trips have been extended, intense, and remarkably exciting.

To qualities of the spirit O'Neill has fortunately been able to add qualities of dialogue, characterization, and dramatic construction that have given power to a considerable portion of his work. It is generally admitted that dialogue is the least of his merits. He has no magnificence of language with which to invest the magnificence of his matter, and he is often prolix and repetitious; sometimes he even descends to philosophical triteness caricatured in accounts of the sophomore who has just discovered "the facts of life." Although O'Neill has himself found that discovery a cause for patronizing laughter in *Ah, Wilderness!* (at a ripe age, be it noted), he continued to announce it for two decades. Nevertheless, there is a poetic quality even in the flat rhapsodies that he has discharged upon his audiences. Their repetitiousness evokes the surge of the sea, the ebb and flow of the tide, the weird monotony of unbroken horizons; there is a swelling music and a sense of distance and eternal recurrence in much of his dialogue. Moreover, he proved himself a master of American dialects in those plays which did not run their course in the parlor, and never before had the everyday speech of sailors, stokers and farmers of different races resounded in the American theatre with such vigor and color. His powers failed him only when his matter was too deep or too exalted for his verbal equipment; it was then that he came to rely too heavily on rhythm and too infrequently on creative imagery and concentrated phrasing.

The art of characterization has been more impressively, even if unevenly and schematically, practised by O'Neill. In externals it has been generally perfect; even if he achieved his greatest impression of reality in his common people (it was his unique contribution to bring most of them for the first time into the American theatre), it is not true that his later characters in the parlor are less clothed with flesh. But O'Neill, who has not been content with external portraiture, has used an X-ray machine as well as a painter's brush, and it is this method that has caused grave difficulties. It became his custom to turn a character into an attribute or a neurosis. Lavinia in *Mourning Becomes Electra,* for example, is for the most part a fixation. For closer inspection, he has also divided personality (as in the case of Dion and Anthony in *The Great God Brown,* and John and Loving in *Days Without End*); his method of characterization has consequently become a demonstration of ideas about character instead of individualization. Sometimes, moreover, his people have been symbols rather than identifiable persons. O'Neill has at different times been the Jack London, D. H. Lawrence, Freud, Maeterlinck, and Andreyev of the American theatre.

Nevertheless, his people have often made an insistent demand upon our attention by the intensity of their special attributes or by the singularity of their partial reality. Playgoers who have become accustomed to regarding human character as a series of psychic units—"id," "ego," "super-ego," the "conscious," and the "unconscious"—can find in the later O'Neill's work a new, dynamic concept of dramatic characterization. His accomplishment may often be irritatingly bald or schematic, but it has exerted a rare fascination. This is so not merely because his kind of characterization has been novel in the English-speaking theatre but because it actually affords the playgoer a new form of recognition; he recognizes in O'Neill's characters those attributes that psychoanalysis has directly or indirectly taught him to regard as the dynamics of character. Possibly, the individual's "unconscious" or simply his vaguely sensed self also recognizes itself in O'Neill's tormented half-personalities, so that the playgoer's recognition of their reality is not in the final analysis purely cerebral.

Moreover, O'Neill has found an excellent fixative for his characters in his dramatic structure. Robert Benchley approvingly noted the presence of the elder O'Neill's ghost in the wings of the Guild Theatre when *Mourning Becomes Electra* was performed, the point of the compliment lying in the fact that James O'Neill, star of the long popular melodrama *The Count of Monte Cristo,* would have enjoyed that "grand, stupendous thriller." With undue extremism, Virgil Geddes has likewise taken note of what he calls O'Neill's "melodramadness," and St. John Ervine has joined hands with Mr. Geddes across the sea.[14] Some evil certainly has come from this tendency; the plays often suffer from an "emotional orgy," from climaxes too final for psychological drama, contrivances, unconscious overvaluation, and overemphasis. (In *Beyond the Horizon,* for instance, the dreamer Robert Mayo's defeat, in his land-locked married life does not need, as Heywood Broun noted, the accessory facts of tuberculosis and death.) Nevertheless, it is precisely the quality of excitement and sheer theatre that O'Neill packs into his best plays that has most ensured his reputation.

Excitement neutralizes the otherwise static nature of his introspection, his schematization of people, and his poetic metaphysics. In other words, the activity of his characters produces the illusion of life. People who allow their neuroses or their abstruse quest to lead them into physical crime and violent expiation are too immediate to be dismissed as the automata they may be. A neurosis may be an abstraction, but a neurotic who commits a murder or becomes otherwise troublesome becomes a *reality;* he is too close to permit the comfort of merely rationalizing about him. O'Neill also knows how to play on the nerves, alternating settings astutely, grouping characters effectively, and allowing climaxes to explode at the most theatrical moment. Nor does he balk at any emphatic device, whether he employs the tom-toms of *Emperor Jones,* the masks of *The Great God Brown,* the asides of *Strange Interlude,* the Congo mask of *All God's Chillun Got Wings,* or the gorilla cage in *The Hairy Ape.* Invariably by action and other kinds of visualization, he succeeds in externalizing inner stresses, calling attention to them, and discharging them theatrically.

This is surely no crime; when one plays at theatre one might as well be effective, even if the apostles of restraint wince a little. Moreover, O'Neill parts company with the mere purveyors of melodrama by using these means for ends beyond themselves, as did Shakespeare who did not hesitate to strew his "wooden O" with corpses. The one possibly serious difference between his effects and those of the greatest tragedians (including Chekhov) is that O'Neill's characters are too often only pseudotragic, since they lack greatness of spirit and stamina. Their quest is too intangible, their discontent is too febrile, and their desire too introverted. They coddle their frustrations and submit too supinely to their disease or their defeat. O'Neill, in short, has performed too many symphonies on the sensory system. This creates greater "theatre" than "drama." It can be added, however, that since there is in effect no Mason and Dixon's line between the two, his "drama" benefits from his "theatre," just as his theatre sometimes suffers from his drama. Perhaps, too, our concept of tragedy needs modification.

Criticism is, in part, rationalization, and the above analysis may be suspected of seeking to vindicate O'Neill at any price. But the fact remains that he has produced a greater body of drama that has stimulated and stirred intelligent audiences in America and abroad than any playwright of his generation. This fact must be explained, since even O'Neill's severest critics cannot seriously deny it.

3 THE VOYAGES OF O'NEILL

The son who was born to the popular actor James O'Neill on October 16, 1888, proved himself an Ishmael like Herman Melville, but wholly by inner compulsion since the family was prosperous. It was to be a long time before he would strike roots anywhere, and even in his later years of discretion he has folded up his tent on occasion. His first seven years were spent all over the country while his father toured in *Monte Cristo* and other plays. Catholic boarding schools, an Academy at Stamford, Connecticut, and Princeton gave him a formal education which ended when after his suspension from college at the end of the freshman year he decided not to return. An avid reader of Jack London, Kipling and Conrad, he tired of a job in a mailing house in which his father was interested, and he also found himself restive during his first marriage, which began in 1909 and was terminated in 1912 two years after his son Eugene was born. In 1909 he left on a gold-prospecting voyage to Honduras, returned without other results than an intensified wanderlust, and made a vain attempt to settle down to the routine life of a stage manager in his father's show. About three months later he took to the sea again, landing at Buenos Aires and working there at odd jobs for which he was temperamentally unfitted.

It was the water front with its sailors, dock workers, and outcasts that attracted him, and it was here that he came in touch with the life that the American theatre had passed over in silence; this kind of existence actually submerged him and it made him one of the world's disinherited. He shipped again as an ordinary, and later as an able, seaman. Then he spent some time on the New York water front in the dive of "Jimmy the Priest's," returned to his father as a scapegrace, played a small part for him, and finally at the conclusion of the season held a job as a reporter and a columnist on the New London *Telegraph* for about a year. But his irregular life took its toll in December 1912, and he was forced to retire for five months to a sanatorium for tubercular patients. A year of rest and recuperation followed, and it was during this time that he began to write plays, turning out eleven one-acters and two full-length pieces, in addition to some verse.

His creative efforts on the *Telegraph* had been made in light verse, especially in parodies that revealed some shrewd political thinking and reflected Theodore Roosevelt's trust-busting activities. The tone became even sharper and more argumentative in verses contributed to the Socialist newspaper the New York *Call* and to the radical periodical *The Masses*. The poem "Fratricide" in the *Call* was an anti-imperialist, anti-capitalist broadside with references to "factory shambles." and "Standard Oil." [15] He had been reading Marx and Kropotkin. In the plays he was now writing he continued to express the life of the underdog, as well as the roaming instinct. But other interests were also asserting themselves in his work. His illness had brought him face to face with the terror of death, and death, in turn, raised the difficult problem of the meaning of life which became in his case something more than an academic question. His private disturbances also forced upon him an interest in sexual psychology and in inner stresses which the American theatre had conventionally evaded. During his convalescence he read not only the classic dramatists but Ibsen, Wedekind and Strindberg—"especially Strindberg," as he later confessed.

However, he studied them not only for their content but for their technique, and the ghost of Strindberg was to guide his pen later on several occasions. (O'Neill's representation of split personalities of *The Great God Brown* and *Days Without End* recalls the Scandinavian master's expressionist style, just as his use of masks harks back to the Greeks.) Moreover, feeling the need of further training, he joined Professor Baker's workshop at Harvard in 1914, contributing a full-length strike play to the course even if he learned little that he had not already mastered in his father's company. With experience and training behind him, he then joined the pilgrimage to Greenwich Village late in 1915, rubbing elbows with artists, radicals, and poor city people. A year later he became a produced playwright when the Provincetown Players performed his one-act play *Bound East for Cardiff* in Mary Heaton Vorse's Wharf Theatre at Provincetown. Other short pieces appeared in the playhouse on MacDougal Street until O'Neill became the mainstay of this experimental group, which he also served as an actor on three inconspicuous occasions and later as a director. Publication in the *Seven Arts Magazines* and in the *Smart Set* promoted his reputation; and soon that indefatigable discoverer of talent George Jean Nathan, then an editor of the *Smart Set,* helped him to secure productions for his later plays.

With the performance of *Beyond the Horizon* in 1920 O'Neill began a steady ascent to fame; his plays received countless productions in America and abroad. After the collapse of the Provincetown Playhouse and of the Greenwich Village Theatre, which he managed with Robert Edmond Jones and Kenneth Macgowan, he became the Theatre Guild's leading playwright and reached the great American public. Then the Nobel Prize in 1936 put an official seal on his international reputation, O'Neill being the only American dramatist to receive that honor. Finally, having made signal achievements in both tragedy and comedy, he retired in 1934 to write what promises to be the largest cycle of plays in any language. Typically American, O'Neill is resolved to build skyscrapers in the theatre and refuses to divulge portions of his new work until the flag-mast is secured to the roof of the edifice.

As restless within the theatre as beyond it, O'Neill has reversed Shakespeare's dictum that all the world's a stage and has treated the stage as a world where everything and anything can be found, if only one ventures far enough. His ship has never lain in dry dock, and his itinerary has taken him from the naturalism of some of his early work to the romanticism of *The Fountain;* from the symbolism of *The Hairy Ape* and *The Great God Brown* to the psychological stage novel *Strange Interlude.* There has been something heady in the experience of watching his travels through the theatre, and the mere review of his itinerary is exhilarating. Much has been made of O'Neill's gloom, but the total impression of his contribution to the theatre contradicts the charge. No man who has voyaged so frequently and so far could have lacked ecstasy. No dramatist of the century has been essentially so great-hearted and so resolute before the mast.

One sees him first moving from the shoals of many tentative one-act plays and heading for the horizon in *The Moon of the Caribbees and Six Other Plays of the Sea,* which he published in 1919. *Ile,* written in 1917, is a drama of a consuming passion or an *idée fixe* on the part of a sea captain who continues his search for whales even at the risk of a mutiny and of his wife's insanity. *The Rope* dramatizes a crasser form of greed ironically when the children of a miserly farmer by the sea try to locate his carefully hidden money and when their efforts are frustrated by a lad happily innocent of gold hunger who tosses the shining pieces into the sea "to watch the skip." But it is the cycle later known as the S.S. Glencairn series that leaves the deepest impression with its vivid portraits and poetically colored colloquial speech. The playlets are both descriptive of an occupation and poignantly human in their summation of the comradeship and loneliness of the common sailors who man the world's ships. Although one of these characters is a declassed gentleman who was ruined by drink and although their economic status is secondary to the sultry magic of the sea and to their personal bedevilment, the reality of O'Neill's picture is beyond cavil. There is considerable exaggeration in charging that they merely stress "the struggle of his own ego with the universe." [16]

The Moon of the Caribbees captures their chaotic, hard-drinking life and exotic compensations for the weary round of their labors. *Bound East for Cardiff* is a lyric picture of death coming to the common seaman Yank who is comforted in his last moments by the blustering Driscoll with whom he has fought and caroused. Yank's hankering for a home on dry land and Driscoll's ill-concealed tenderness laves the playlet in that beauty of common things which O'Neill was the first to discover for the American drama. *In the Zone,* a weaker and sentimental piece, reveals the private tragedy of the gentleman who went to sea after his alcoholism lost him the girl he loved. But both the comic naïveté and the fundamental decency of his companions in the fo'c'sle convey a gratifying feeling for humanity. The cycle is, moreover, concluded with that poignant one-acter *The Long Voyage Home,* in which the pathetic Swede Olson is shanghaied into a two years' voyage after making a valiant effort to remain sober in a London water-front dive. It teems with life, with pathos, and with something more than "fate" since the trick by which Olson is trapped was a common practice. It is not enough to hold with Barrett Clark that these pieces "were easily the most distinguished one-acters written in America up to their time;" taken together, they comprise the most trenchant "slice-of-life" collective drama written until Odets' *Waiting for Lefty* some fifteen years later.

Nevertheless, it is an error to romanticize the short plays out of all proportion as the best work O'Neill has done. O'Neill himself has regarded these and other short pieces like *Before Breakfast* and that intense evocation of gold-lust *Where the Cross Is Made*[17] as merely preliminary voyages. He proved this quickly enough with *Beyond the Horizon* in 1920 and revealed a decided talent for sustained drama. Moreover, the play was not merely an expanded one-acter; there were several facets to this tale of the Mayo brothers one of whom goes to sea while the other stays behind, marries, fails at farming, and dies.

Beyond the Horizon is one of the most ironic plays of the modern theatre. The dreamer Robert is trapped whereas the simple-minded farmer Andrew becomes an adventurer and reduces the former's quest to a sordid search for wealth. The destinies of both brothers are determined by irrational choices from which few people are free, choices of which tragedy is often compounded. To this *leit motif* O'Neill adds another and even more powerful one in the theme of a woman's unintentional destructiveness. Robert stays home and Andrew goes to sea because the girl Ruth chooses the former for her mate. But it is more than romance that she desires, and when he fails to make life tolerably comfortable for her love flies out of the window. They torment each other unwillingly until she wounds him to the quick with the confession that it is Andrew that she loves. Both man and wife have been tricked into an impossible relationship by the sexual impulse that made them see in each other the fulfillment of their dreams until these had to work themselves out in the commonplace world of earning a living. Naturally these trapped characters, who cannot understand what has happened, lay "some of the blame for our stumbling on God;" and this is inexcusable only if O'Neill shared their opinion, as he has given the impression of doing,[18] since the stumbling was caused by character, the blinding sexual urge, and the simple fact that a farm cannot be made to pay by a poet. Marred by Robert's fortuitous death that adds neither irony nor force to his frustration, and further weakened by the adolescent ambiguity of his quest, as well as by some lagging scenes, *Beyond the Horizon* is unmistakably an immature work. It is nevertheless a sardonic and poignant tragedy of attrition.

Pathos predominated in *The Straw,* written in 1918 and produced in 1921, a work steeped in the life of a sanatorium and more affecting than revealing. More concrete naturalism, however, immediately characterized the next important play *Anna Christie.*[19] Theodore Dreiser had already written the natural history of a prostitute in *Sister Carrie* as early as 1900. But the theatre had to wait for this theme until O'Neill invested it with humanity in 1921. Anna, sent to a farm by her sea-faring father to live with her cousins, became the object of their passions (so much for the legend of bucolic innocence!) and fled to the city only to be debauched there and to enter a house of prostitution. After an illness she returns to her father only to find him an embittered resident of a sailors' dive who blames the sea for his troubles. But life on his barge exerts a cleansing power on a woman who has sickened of the stench of the brothel, and in the burly young Irish stoker Mat Burke she finds a love that is as brisk and clean as the sea. Then her past destroys his confidence in her; Burke signs on a long voyage, and although they are united before he departs the future is dubious. As O'Neill has explained, "The happy ending is merely a comma at the end of a gaudy introductory clause, with the body of the sentence still unwritten."

Whether the ending is regarded as happy or unhappy, the play is, on the whole, steeped in reality—a poor word for the picture of the mess that Anna's father has made of his life and of the mire in which Anna has stumbled. Even a life redeemed by marriage cannot cancel her experience and the murk that befouls the world. It is true that the plight of Saturday's children has not been deeply investigated or resolved here and that causes and consequences have been skimmed over or blurred, as if the playwright had indulged in "a kind of flirtation"[20] with his matter. Consequently, *Anna Christie* is not a profound drama. But as a "slice of life" it is pungent and affecting, and Anna's sodden but childlike innocence is memorable.

O'Neill marked time in the other realistic plays of the period. *Diff'rent* concluded as mere melodrama, *"The First Man"* was stuffily contrived, and *Welded* allowed two married people to torment each other to no purpose. Still *Diff'rent,* written in 1920, revealed much insight into the psychology of puritanism and frustration with its story of Emma Crosby who once rejected a sea captain because he was not as sexually pure as she believed but finally falls an easy prey to the designing "doughboy" and "lady-killer" Benny thirty-three years later. *"The First Man"* is fugitively powerful with its domestic drama of a scientist who hates the prospect of having his work interrupted by the birth of a child. Pathos is not wanting in his wife's anguish and in his reaction to the mean-spirited relatives who sully the dead woman with suspicions of immo-rality because of his temporary antipathy for the child that cost its mother's life. Although *Welded* lacks the roundness of life, the sex duel between the characters who cannot leave each other alone possesses a Strindbergian intensity. O'Neill's failures were, then, essentially more incisive and ingrowingly provocative than other men's easy successes. Soon, moreover, he began to grip his themes with almost demoniacal fury and to wrest from them an anguish and a poetic intensity such as the American theatre has rarely known before.

In 1922 came *All God's Chillun Got Wings*, a tragedy of miscegena-tion that displeases critics who want him to treat the Negro problem with economic analysis and militancy but that possesses incalculable power as a psychological drama and not a little relevance to the actual social problem which he is accused of evading.[21] Essentially a naturalist tragedy of love and perverse passion, *All God's Chillun* could have tran-spired without the introduction of any race problem. Nevertheless, the play is thrice as intense and poignant, as well as provocative, because of it.

The tragedy begins on a deeply humane level in the picture of black and white youngsters who are drawn to each other by the unconscious democracy of childhood in the slums. Despite prejudices for which the children have no actual basis, the black boy Jim Harris and the white little girl Ella Downey love each other. Nine years later the age of in-nocence has receded, and Jim, now a sensitive and studious lad, is trying to become a lawyer while Ella has deteriorated into a gangster's mis-tress. Nevertheless, Ella who has been deserted by Mickey after she has given birth to an illegitimate child, clings to Jim and marries him. But by then her prejudices, which are intensified by her sense of in-feriority, poison their lives. She tries to drag him down to her level by preventing him from becoming a lawyer, a point which is valid psycho-logically since she is a woman, and socially since even white trash tries to salvage its ego by maintaining some semblance of racial superiority. Succumbing to a sense of inferiority himself—both because of his racial handicap and of his emotional dependence upon her—Jim becomes a failure. She, in turn, after a seizure of madness in the course of which she has tried to kill him, escapes her conflicts by regressing into child-hood; she is again little Ella, unsullied, uncomplicated, and in love with Jim who is henceforth tied to her diseased mind.

At the time of production in 1924, as O'Neill noted, he received "anonymous letters which ranged from those of infuriated Irish Catho-lics who threatened to pull my ears off as a disgrace to their race and religion, to those of equally infuriated Nordic Kluxers who knew I had negro blood, or else was a Jewish pervert masquerading under a Christian name in order to do subversive propaganda for the Pope." A decade or so later, the play also drew the fire of some "social" critics from the opposite camp because it did not settle the racial problem and concentrated its observation on special types. The fact is that he took both the social scene and human nature in his stride, subordinating the first to the second but conditioning his characters by their environment like a true naturalist.

He repeated this procedure, in fact, in the equally relentless but more integrated peasant tragedy of *Desire Under the Elms*. No firmer picture of the tenacious life of a New England farm could have been written. On the stony soil which old Ephraim Cabot subdued with his labor, men hunger for land and emotional release. Land is not easily available or fruitful; men therefore guard it greedily like Ephraim, desire it frantically like the youngest son Eben, or try to acquire it doggedly at the price of a loveless marriage like the orphaned Abbie Putnam who marries old Ephraim. But the land and a hard religion also play jangled tunes on the other passions. Ephraim was a hard husband to his gentle first wife whom he worked to death and whose child Eben he has hated for resembling her. This son actually avenges himself on him by possessing himself of his father's new wife Abbie. She, in turn, yields to Eben in order to secure her position by giving the old man a child. The birth of a child which the self-confident Ephraim believes to be his own leads to further complications. Eben, who is now loved by Abbie genuinely suspects her of yielding to him merely in order to strengthen her claim on the land, and only Abbie's frantic murder of the infant to prove that she no longer desires the farm for herself dispels his doubt. This is the end for what little happiness they wrested out of their land-locked and frustrated lives; overcome with remorse, Eben notifies the sheriff and announces himself as an accessory to the crime.

Powerful characterization and dialogue are combined here with a stark elemental theme and a sultry kind of nature poetry. Eben's Oedipus complex, the effects of farm life, and an inhibitive religion are fused into a tragic unit; they are so interrelated that it is difficult to isolate them, and the play is another example of how, intuitively, the creative artist can be in advance of the scientific thinker.[22] *Desire Under the Elms* is consequently the most consistently wrought of O'Neill's plays and marks the peak of his relatively naturalistic period. Moreover, this is true tragedy; the power of the passions, the impressiveness of the characters, and the timelessness of the inner struggle between a son and a father ensure tragic elevation.

O'Neill indeed practically created American naturalistic drama without actually confining himself to it in these plays, and such work as *Tobacco Road* and *Of Mice and Men* would possibly have remained unaccepted but for his potent example. Nevertheless, he was an eclectic theatrician and a poet who could not accept even the semblance of a straitjacket in naturalism. Four years before the production of *Desire Under the Elms* he wrote that simple expressionist study of a man's atavistic fears *Emperor Jones* which once rocked the theatre and is now curiously regarded by literal practitioners of social criticism as reactionary because it revealed a Negro retrogressing to "his aboriginal fears—as if regression were a stigma applicable to no other race." [23] As a matter of fact, this story of a Negro dictator's flight into the jungle from the natives he had oppressed during his reign was several things in one: It was a *tour de force* by virtue of its cumulative excitations, its amplification of the one-act form in eight short scenes, and its singular evocation of anxiety and terror; a psychological study was inherent in the account of Emperor Jones' atavistic fears; and a social panorama was provided by Jones' recapitulation of the experiences and sufferings of his race. Even so comparatively simple a play as *Emperor Jones,* written at the beginning of O'Neill's career in 1920, defies pigeonholing.

Even greater complexity characterized his second expressionist drama two years later. *The Hairy Ape* tells the story of the super-stoker Yank who discovers his shortcomings from a chance meeting with one of the passengers, cultured and wealthy Mildred. He has hitherto considered himself the Atlas of the world, but stung by Mildred's revulsion at his grimy appearance he throws up his job and goes forth to find a place where he can belong, as well as to avenge himself on those who have destroyed his self-confidence by their superiority. But Yank, the half-brute, cannot belong, and even his fellow-workers of the I.W.W., who are comparatively educated and realistically purposeful, will have none of him or of his plan to blow up the factories. His attempt to avenge himself on the rich also failing, he seeks the companionship of a gorilla in the zoo and discovers that he does not belong to the brute world either when the beast crushes him to death. In this schematic tragedy of the half-man, O'Neill dramatized, as it were, the theory of evolution.

The author's own explanation may seem metaphysical; he had tried, he declared, to create a "symbol of man, who has lost his old harmony with nature, the harmony which he used to have as an animal, and has not yet acquired in a spiritual way. . . . Yank can't go forward, so he tries to go back." This involves the problem of human happiness that D. H. Lawrence raised about the same time, as well as possibly society's plight, a society that has been catastrophically regressing to feral ways.

As a symbolization of this idea *The Hairy Ape* is singularly strained and barely acceptable. Perhaps, too, there is even more validity, regardless of O'Neill's approval, to any interpretation which regards Yank as the unenlightened worker who moronically exaggerates his physical power, easily loses his self-assurance, and strikes out blindly against forces he cannot comprehend. Even if, as one critic [24] has pointed out, there is no attempt to explain the real sources of Yank's brutishness and failure, O'Neill's tragic stoker is indeed more immediate as a moronic worker than as an intermediate stage in biological evolution. What nature, one might flatly ask, does Yank fail to harmonize with after his encounter with Mildred when his previous harmony was actually with his mechanical environment in the ship's hold—with the machinery that he served?

It would seem that the truest evaluation of *The Hairy Ape* must hold that it is a highly original and provocative but muddled work. O'Neill, who has rarely revealed any ability to cope consistently with either metaphysics or economic analysis in his work, is more suggestive than concrete. His metaphysics indeed generally becomes the mere repetition of some truism and his economic thinking is necessarily fugitive, incidental, or simply accidental. He is on safe ground only when he subordinates both metaphysical and social thought to a projection of the emotions, for he is the most emotional ranking dramatist of his age. Even the events of the extremely local *Desire Under the Elms,* as Joseph Wood Krutch noted, "really occur out of place and out of time." [25] In *The Hairy Ape* he composed a symbolic play that masters no problem but triumphs, to a degree, because it is evocative and headily stimulating.

The same uncertainty but provocativeness of effect appeared when, after the romantic Ponce de Leon search for youth in *The Fountain,* O'Neill began to schematize human personality in *The Great God Brown,* and when he repeated this thankless pursuit in *Days Without End.* Many deep perceptions appeared in the former play. It contains the finely realized inner torment of the artist Dion Anthony, whose extreme sensitivity in a materialistic world makes a neurotic and drunkard of him. His mother-fixation is only one factor in his bedevilment; he is, as his name (Dionysius St. Anthony) implies, the artist who is torn between pagan sensuousness and the flesh-denying Christian conscience that he imbibed in childhood. O'Neill describes him and others like him penetratively when he writes that Dion's torment is the result of "creative joy in life for life's sake frustrated, rendered abortive, distorted by morality from Pan into Satan, into a Mephistopheles mocking himself in order to feel alive. . . ." There are also fine perceptions in his wife's character, and in his successful friend and employer Brown's uncreative complacency which keeps the latter safe only so long as he does not acquire Dion's imaginative anarchism or sensibility. Unfortunately, how-

ever, O'Neill simultaneously schematized his characters so crassly and
endowed them with such complexity that the play is neither a clear
character sketch nor a rounded portrait of real people. Juggling masks
in a furor of melodramatic complications when Brown assumes Dion's
personality, O'Neill also failed to develop a coherent story. He paid the
penalty for trying to make a play perform the dual functions of an expressionist drama and a Dostoyevsky novel.

The fault in his procedure had its source in excessive cerebration,
and it came to the fore undisguisedly in his next abortive dramas, in
Lazarus Laughed, written in 1927, and in *Dynamo.* O'Neill was unsuccessful when he overstressed the idea of eternal life in the repetitiously
rapturous Lazarus story. Present in the play was a truly noble concept,
a more powerful thought than the merely banal poetic one of the continuity of life which is ordinarily stressed. Lazarus, who has risen from
the dead, refuses to be intimidated by death; and having overcome the
great dread that keeps men enslaved by oppressors he can defy the
world of the masters. The emperor Tiberius is entirely justified in his fear
that Lazarus' credo that there is no death will undermine his power,
since men are held in subjection by the dread of annihilation. Although
Lazarus' faith may seem too abstract for some social thinkers,[26] the belief in the eternity of life can be emotionally real, and its effect on the
conduct of men has been as potent at times as economic interest; Mo-
hammed's invincible hordes expected eternal sessions with the *houris,* and
the Teutonic warriors who destroyed Rome expected equally lasting
têtes-à-têtes with the Valkyries. Nevertheless, O'Neill's "idea" was re-
iterated in *Lazarus Laughed* at the expense of dramatic development
and characterization, and a lifeless and monotonous affirmation was the
result.

In *Dynamo,* two years later, O'Neill's trend toward intellectualiza-
tion reached its zenith. His Reuben Light emancipates himself from the
loveless faith of his fathers only to lapse into an equally sterile machine-
worship. But except for the injection of Freudian complications into
his character, Reuben remained an author's automaton and, what is
worse, an unmitigated bore. The failure of dynamo-worship was as incisive and contemporary a theme as any that a serious writer could have
chosen, particularly in the gilded twenties of American prosperity. But
O'Neill's habitual "subordination of the whole of life to a few parts"[27]
never appeared more apparent than in the case history of Reuben and
his Moloch the machine. O'Neill was one of the many writers of his
generation who deprecated the materialistic philosophy that dominated
the decade following the World War. But a bald symbolization was no
substitute for a living play.

Fortunately O'Neill did not remain wedded to any penchant for mere demonstration. Two years after *The Great God Brown*, and two years before *Dynamo*, he had proved his ability to wrap flesh around a skeletal idea. *Marco Millions* was his contribution to the anti-bourgeois barrage which was booming across the country. Sinclair Lewis, who had opened fire on philistinism with *Main Street*, continued his bombardment until he discharged *The Man Who Knew Coolidge;* the debunking biographers were busy making muck of the American hall of fame; and disgusted with the smug materialism of dollar democracy, numerous artists sought refuge abroad, though they were not so far removed from dollar-consciousness not to take account of the favorable foreign exchange rate. *Marco Millions,* which dispelled the notion that its author was incapable of humor, was in the first instance a sardonic travesty on "Babbitt" or the American rotarian ideal in the person of the thirteenth-century commercial traveler Marco Polo who traversed the fabulous lands of Kublai Khan without so much as noting a single pleasure-dome. The wonder of the East and the love of the Emperor's daughter Kuka-chin, who dies broken-hearted, leave him equally unmoved. Although O'Neill was guilty of sentimentalizing the ideality of the Orient, which after all employed slaves and was not free from business practices of its own, his satire was barbed, his story engaging, and his creation of character vivid, if generalized. It is also to O'Neill's credit that unlike Lewis and the other bourgeois-baiters he made his point imaginatively, musically, and poetically.

Moreover, his prior interest in inner states proved remarkably fruitful when he imbedded psychology in characterization rather than symbolization. His most ambitious and impressive plays, *Strange Interlude* and *Mourning Becomes Electra,* also schematized character but not abstrusely. In *Strange Interlude,* Nina reveals several facets of her character almost as if a human being consisted of disparate phrenological bumps. A bump for different kinds of affective relationships—one for the daughter, another for the wife, a third for the mistress, and a fourth for the mother in Nina—departmentalizes her character more rigidly than even authoritative psychoanalysis does. Obviously, too, the different men who know her in one relationship or another are primarily psychological attributes or stimuli to her different responses as daughter of a jealous father, as wife, mistress, and mother. This is, in fact, the main point of the play. Nina Leeds, who lost in Gordon the only man who could satisfy all her impulses, cannot find completion in any other man; since Charlie Marsden the family friend, Sam Evans her husband, and Darrell her lover gratify her only partially, she needs them all. Only in her son does she recapture the dead lover Gordon, and he, too, must leave her for a life of his own with the girl he loves. By then, however, she is middle-aged, and her quest for completion in love is brought to rest by sheer emotional exhaustion—the "strange interlude" of a woman's sexual life has reached its final phase and she can be content with the pallid friendship of Charlie the genteel novelist.

The indubitable fascination of this analysis, regardless of its scientific validity, would alone suffice to give *Strange Interlude* a unique position in the history of the drama. And some eminence would also be earned by its peculiar effect, for *Strange Interlude*, with its asides and lengthy progression, is nothing less than a stream-of-consciousness novel despite its dramatic structure. But above all qualifications for effectiveness must be set the simple fact that O'Neill succeeded in endowing his contemporary Hedda Gabler [28] with genuine life and passion; Nina Leeds is a memorable character because each of her emotional states is both vividly actual and psychologically complementary. A whole woman somehow emerges from the different elements of this chronicle of fixations and frustrations, and from their successive discharge in relation to a male character. Nor does Nina, who is an emancipated modern daughter of the middle class and therefore takes some daring steps where her emotions are involved, enter her relationships with cold deliberation. Even when deliberateness is present, as when she gives herself to Darrell in order to bear a child, her conduct is the result of her emotional need and of a dramatized situation—for example, from her intensely effective discovery that there is insanity in her husband's chromosomes. Nor are the men mere automata; the brilliant young physician Ned Darrell embittered by frustrated desire for Nina and for his unacknowledged son, Sam who grows from a weakling into a self-confident business man when he receives both financial backing and a son from his friends, Nina's son Gordon Evans with his boyish jealousy and intuitions, and even meek Charlie Marsden with his very active unconscious—all are vivid portraits. O'Neill was able to achieve this because with the expertness and daring of a technician he allowed his characters to express their unconscious thoughts verbally. The so-called aside in *Strange Interlude* is not so much related to the older conventions of the drama as to the stream-of-consciousness technique of Strindberg's expressionist plays and James Joyce's *Ulysses*. And this, too, was a notable innovation in the theatre, since in using this device with absolute lucidity he was the first dramatist to "make full use in the drama of that introspection without which it would be impossible to imagine the existence of a large part of modern literature." [29]

O'Neill, it is true, paid a heavy price for so ambitious an undertaking. The aside is sometimes overworked or obvious, and it becomes somewhat tiresome even when it is entirely appropriate. This nine-act play is too long by about two acts, if perhaps only because his invention was not strong enough to keep them pitched on a sufficiently high level of dramatic effectiveness. The play reaches no climax except that of exhaustion when it closes with the depletion of Nina's sexual energy or the termination of her strange interlude. The character of Nina also suffers from the extreme length of O'Neill's analysis; as revealed by her detailed inner life, she may strike an objective observer as too unlovable to be honored with so much attachment by her "three men." Tragic intensity is hers indeed by virtue of rebellion against frustration and her passionate search for fulfillment, but her resemblance to another well-known female insect known as the praying mantis is too uncomfortably close for genuinely tragic exaltation.[30] The playgoer must derive that exaltation in part from the joy of participating in O'Neill's brilliant analysis with his own mental activity. All told, however, *Strange Interlude* was a stunning performance.

If modern thought lacks a tragic outlook as Joseph Wood Krutch suspected (correctly at least with reference to sophisticated thinking),[31] this deficiency could not be charged against O'Neill's second endurance contest with the public, the thirteen-act trilogy of *Mourning Becomes Electra*. Some of its characters seem, indeed, almost archaic on their tragic pedestals. This is also true of the dramatic story itself, a primitive chronicle of Ezra Mannon murdered by his adulterous wife Christine, of her lover Adam Brant destroyed by her incestuous son Orin and her neurotically vengeful daughter Lavinia, and of Orin remorsefully committing suicide after confessing a passion for his sister. An incisive critic, Miss Charmion von Wiegand, can even object that in the Reconstruction Period of the play "more normal alternatives of action were open to all the characters than the one they chose of murder and blood or which their author chose for them, in mechanical imitation of the Attic pattern." [20] A retelling of the Oresteian trilogy of Aeschylus could hardly escape a suspicion of archaism, though it might be argued that the newspapers are full of the crimes of people who rejected "normal alternatives of action." Christine did not perhaps have to kill Ezra Mannon, and Lavinia and Orin did not have to murder their mother's lover and drive her to suicide. But the fact is that people behave precisely like that even in 1940. Only the concatenation of all these events in one work is extreme and therefore melodramatic.

Still, the characters acquire dimension through the intensity of their bedevilment, which O'Neill again explains for the most part in psychoanalytical fashion by means of fixations and complexes. These are, moreover, predicated on an ingrown life produced at least in part by social forces; the Mannons are New England aristocracy who keep aloof from their neighbors and are sealed up in themselves and in their family. Their stiff ancestors also retain a firm hold on the descendants. Their puritanic religion keeps the sexual instinct in close confinement, and when passion wells up from repression it is as raw as Ezra Mannon's brutish behavior on the bridal night or as horrible as the incestuous cravings of his children. In their narrow circle, these aristocrats are also capable of enduring hatreds like Abe Mannon's jealous persecution of his brother Dave, as well as of explosive deeds of violence. Finally, the older Mannons were hard-bitten merchants, acquisitive and possessive; and tenacity also appears in their progeny's libido. Indeed *Mourning Becomes Electra* is a remarkably scrupulous—deeply rooted and carefully explained—account of criminal passion. Therein alone it differs from mere melodrama, even as *Hamlet* departs from that classification despite many violently encompassed deaths.

Tragic stature is added by the pity that we must feel. Ironically, Ezra Mannon loses his paleolithic qualities and wins our sympathy just before he is removed by poison. He has returned from the Civil War a changed man who is eager to give and receive tenderness after having witnessed so much butchery on the battlefield. He will have no further traffic with the Mannon's traditional puritanism which is a denial of life and a kind of death. The Mannons, moreover, have had an appealing inclination, understandable in strong people, to seek release in their love for exotic women. Ezra's father Abe ruined his brother Dave out of desire for a French girl who preferred the latter; Dave's poetic son Adam Brant became a sea captain and adventured on the high seas; Abe's son Ezra married the foreign and exotic Christine who could never be happy with him, especially when he turned love into lust on the wedding night. Even the somber Lavinia, her daughter but a complete Mannon in nearly every characteristic, is attracted to the romantic sea captain who becomes her mother's lover, and she is nearly liberated from her hatred and her feeling of guilt after visiting the South Sea islands. Nor can pity be withheld from her brother Orin, the degenerate son of a strong stock who falls easily under the domination of Lavinia. After she has forced him to kill Adam Brant, he is instantly overwhelmed by remorse, very much like the original Orestes of the Greek plays. It is also, incidentally, worth noting that out of a deference for modern taste, O'Neill did not include the final touch of letting Lavinia and Orin commit the crime of murdering their mother, as the Greek pattern required, thereby ensuring some sympathy for them. Christine is a suicide after the slaying of her lover Adam.

Mourning Becomes Electra, finally, possesses the saving grace of purposefulness, for good art does not rack the emotions without purpose and it is the function of the noble art of tragedy to permeate human crises with a larger meaning than mere agony. Broadly considered, this trilogy serves a cleansing purpose: *consciously* that of exorcising violence, intolerance, and the possessive lust to which no people has ever been immune in history's terrible procession; *unconsciously,* perhaps, in discharging our own hidden complications. Narrowly considered, the purposefulness also takes the form of a social critique, even if it fails to conform to the requirements of O'Neill's Marxist critics. Long a critic of the allegedly life-denying puritanism of New England which he must have found antipathetic both as a Catholic and as an insurgent artist, O'Neill touched upon a major theme through his exhibition of the consequences of Mannon fixations or repressions. A good hater of the predatory aspects of society, he also allowed the tragic events of the play to emanate to some slight degree from the principle of "primary accumulation" that dominated the New England of the Mannons. Finally, and far more conspicuously, the play possessed a suggestive historical perspective in its picture of the disintegration of a puritanic aristocracy.

The valuable notes O'Neill kept of the work in progress do not, it is true, reveal a suspicion of any such intention to relate his psychological drama to the dynamic elements of its social setting, and such an intention may never have intruded itself into his consciousness. He selected the Civil War as background for a "drama of murderous love and hate" because this period possessed "a sufficient mask of time and space so that audience will unconsciously grasp at once it is primarily drama of hidden life forces. . . ." He noted even more emphatically that "No matter in what period of American history, play in hand must remain a modern psychological drama—nothing to do with period. . . ." [32] And O'Neill was right, since the basic substance of this trilogy is the agony of passion and desire. Still, the religious and social elements are present, in part explicitly and in part implicitly. And far from spoiling, they strengthen the work by giving the psychoanalytic drama an additional dimension and counteracting to some degree the repetitious effect of Freudian schematization.

Would that this had been counteracted much more conspicuously regardless of the means! For the chief flaw of this tragedy, besides its lack of a greatness of utterance commensurate with its overpowering dramatic drive, arises from O'Neill's immoderate piling up of complexes until we weary of them by the time the third part of the trilogy lumbers along. The English critic Charles Morgan has rightly complained that the story "ends, as it begins, in a condition of pathological neurosis," and that it is, therefore, "much narrower in its scope and of less spiritual force than the classical plays to which, in subject, it is related." [33] Even more accurate is Brooks Atkinson's estimate that *Mourning Becomes Electra* just misses greatness because "O'Neill's point of view has none of the breadth, richness, largeness of vision and natural understanding" that may be expected from the few great men of the world.

Still even to deplore the lack of so rare a concatenation of attributes is a compliment; one does not measure small men by the highest standards—and O'Neill indisputably deserved to be at least held to them after having labored so titanically. In fact, his creative explosion in 1931 had been so shattering even to himself that it was followed by an unusual calm. The poet of passion seemed spent and emotional anarchy was succeeded by reconciliation, as if he had at last purged himself of inner complications by the thoroughness with which he had projected them from the boards.

The first fruits of this peace, in 1934, was the benign laughter of *Ah, Wilderness!*, O'Neill's truest comedy. Significant for the psychoanalytically minded, and possibly also for others, is the fact that its leading adult character, the small-town editor Nat Miller, was the most generous portrait of a father to appear in O'Neill's work.[34] And O'Neill being no piddling painter executed the picture with a notable warmth of color and emotion. Moreover, *Ah, Wilderness!* was the dramatist's most idyllic picture of youth and its environment. Young Richard Miller's restiveness is set down genially as a transitory state of adolescence instead of being inflated into a cosmic philosophy or darkened into a neurosis and the merciful early nineteenth-century background bears no resemblance to the infernos O'Neill had previously favored. Even Main Street had lost its sting once regression to childhood bore no terrors for O'Neill. Consequently, *Ah, Wilderness!* was nothing more—and nothing *less*—than a sunny and uncomplicated comedy of adolescence and peaceful middle age. It is marred only by an occasional lapse into sentimentality, and it is limited only by that reduction of emotional power that occurs when one writes about sentiment rather than passion.

Reconciliation with faith also followed, but less successfully, when John, the hero of the psychological morality play *Days Without End*, rids himself of his Mephistophelian double, "Loving," at the foot of the cross. The implacable decrier of conventional religious consolation had at last written his farewell to skepticism and inner conflict. He rested comfortably (if perhaps only temporarily) in the bosom of the Catholic Church which has solaced so many spent or disheartened intellectuals from St. Augustine to Chateaubriand, Novalis, Huysmans, Sorel the father of syndicalism, and d'Annunzio the Dionysus of sensualism. By many this was regretted as the defeat of a gallant spirit, but it was a seemingly inevitable port for the wanderer between the two worlds of flesh and spirit, a conclusion for O'Neill's long voyage home. The only esthetic objection that could be raised was that when he docked his ship he whipped up a froth of religiosity, and that his abdication of independent inquiry was an anticlimax.

And at this point, in the year 1934, we must take leave of him for the present until his cycle of plays is completed. It appears that the new work will be a chronicle of American life and society, in which case the purgation of *Days Without End* may yet prove beneficial in objectifying his art. It remains only to be seen whether his greatness can flourish on something other than an inner volcano, and whether his new work will differ from the tragedies he has wrought from his and modern man's lack of fixity in either a comfortable cosmos or a spiritually acceptable society.

XXX

THE AMERICAN GALAXY

I TWO DECADES

O'NEILL was not a lone star in the firmament, although no other American playwright even approximated his magnitude. Spangled with a number of less luminous suns and a host of satellites, the theatre of the twenties and the thirties seemed a veritable galaxy. The effect of this splendid display cannot be described in anything short of a book devoted solely to it.

The causes of this sudden blaze in the American theatre were those operative in O'Neill's case supplemented by other factors that fired different temperaments. Inhibitions were removed to a great extent: the genteel tradition dwindled; censorship practically vanished in New York, though it cropped up from time to time in Boston and points west; and the comparative relaxation of conventions that resulted from the prosperity and cosmopolitanism of the twenties encouraged dramatists to write as they pleased. This situation prevailed even in the depressed thirties, owing to the example of the previous decade and to the tradition of political democracy which has made the American theatre of the past decade the freest in the world; nowhere else has it been possible to perform such incendiary drama as here or to travesty the ruler of a state as freely.

The stimulants and irritants that produced this drama were rooted in American life and to a smaller degree in the international situation. The stimulant of prosperity in the twenties enabled the theatre to flourish richly despite the comparative dwindling of the "road" and the competition of the cinema. In those years the Theatre Guild, now joined by the sage Theresa Helburn, became one of the foremost institutional theatres of the world. Notable experimentation in stage art also came from the Provincetown Players and the subsidized Neighborhood Playhouse, the New Playwrights' Group, Miss Eva Gallienne's Civic Repertory, and a number of Little Theatres, one of them thriving on Insull's money before that financier met his Waterloo. Excellent work by independent producers like Arthur Hopkins also appeared during that decade. The irritant of a straitened economy in the thirties, which left the Broadway theatre floundering for a time, resulted in the rise of uncommercial, socially critical, militant or ameliorative oganizations like the proletarian Theatre Union, the New Theatre League branches, the Group Theatre, and the relief project for the theatrical profession known as the Federal Theatre which became the first national institution of its kind in the United States.

The stage directors and scenic designers of the first decade who fought under the banner of "Art" reveled in creative forms of staging related to the work of Appia and Craig.[1] The theatricians of the thirties who followed the red flag or the pink or simply the less easily describable banner of social conscience expressed a purposeful virtuosity in the European forms of elementary "agit-prop," epic theatre of the Piscator manner, Orson Welles' revival style patterned after Meyerhold's work, and Moscow Art Theatre realism of the modified Group Theatre manner, as well as in the naturalized "living newspaper" technique of several Federal Theatre productions. There was, moreover, considerable overlapping. The twenties found room for militant staging like Lee Simonson's production of *Masses and Man* under "arty" Theatre Guild auspices whereas "esthetic," *surréaliste* technique appeared in Robert Lewis' production of Saroyan's *My Heart's in the Highlands* under the aegis of the socially purposeful Group Theatre of the next decade. In the thirties, moreover, several able independent producers like Guthrie McClintic in *Winterset* and *High Tor* and Jed Harris in *Our Town* produced in the stylized manner which employed only suggestive props, profited by the example that had been set by the art theatres of the previous decade. The interplay between drama and theatre, whereby each is enriched, was well maintained between 1920 and 1940.

It is true that the picture was less gratifying in its entirety than in some of its parts. Commercial considerations hampered the producers, who at best could experiment only occasionally, and the lack of well-trained repertory companies made many productions haphazard. The "art" directors, who had only a few root hairs in their native soil, were derivative, as were the later radical experimentalists. Nor did any director except Orson Welles attempt creative comprehensiveness such as distinguished a Meyerhold or a Piscator across the sea; and Welles himself has yet to achieve their scope. Still the art of theatre flourished better than could be expected under these difficult circumstances. Low comedy was invigorated by directors like Kaufman, Abbott, and Howard Lindsay; Guthrie McClintic excelled in imaginativeness; Philip Moeller perfected high-comedy style and illuminated O'Neill's tragedies with directorial genius; Lee Strasberg revealed creative fire; Harold Clurman proved himself a potent interpretive realist.

The public, which is an integral part of the theatre, was decidedly mixed, with middle-class elements inevitably preponderating, and its taste naturally favored entertainment and was least responsive to important experiments except when these possessed the lure of sensation-alism. Nevertheless, audiences were comparatively selective since the gratification of the lowest taste had become the virtual monopoly of the inexpensive and more accessible films and of radio drama. Moreover, some attempts were made to organize the public into a supporting unit for a particular kind of drama. In the twenties the Theatre Guild created an advance audience in New York for sophisticated or experimental pro-ductions and retained a variable portion of it in the next ten years while adding to it thousands of subscribers in many other cities. This assured a minimum four or five weeks' run for normally unsalable or quickly retired plays, a boon to impecunious playwrights and actors. In the thirties the Group Theatre developed a metropolitan clientele of some proportions. The Theatre Union had a subscription audience of prole-tarians and their friends for a few years. The New Theatre League educated a similar public in many localities with the aid of a generally excellent, though sometimes strident, magazine. The Federal Theatre drew thousands upon thousands into its fold until the Congressional axe fell upon the institution in the summer of 1939.

In the field of drama upon which all factors converged, the stimulants consisted in the twenties of improving stage practice, generously under-standing criticism, and singular national self-confidence and energy. The irritants were supplied by a dollar-minded complacency that aroused re-vulsion, anger, or derisive laughter in the playwrights; by contradic-tions between statistical prosperity and the lot of the underdog; by the juxtaposition of beauty and ugliness; and by a want of orientation on the part of a sophisticated generation that experienced extreme unhap-piness, verging on neurosis—despite its liquor-swilling bravado and pur-suit of self-expression. Both the health and the malaise of the period found expression in the twenties, and naturally there was considerable overlapping in the two decades.

In the next decade, the irritants preponderated. The balloon of pros-perity which burst in the stock-market crash of 1929 littered the nation with battered passengers. From ten to thirteen million unemployed clamored for food and work. Anger gripped the hearts of the sufferers and of their sympathizers among whom writers were naturally conspicu-ous since they are quick to respond to injustice or misery, and fascist rumblings put dramatists on their mettle or filled them with dread and despair. Naturally enough, many of them, especially the younger writers, grew somber or bitter, and their plays became didactic and hortatory. Seeking for some key to the distress which they observed, they accepted the Marxist explanation that capitalism was in the throes of death. Searching for some sign of hope, they listened readily to the prediction that a better society would arise from the agonies of the present. They dreamed of a world of collective effort undominated by the predatory and anarchic race for profits to which they attributed not only the sorry economic state of affairs but war, hatred, and the frustration of personality. Looking abroad, they saw a new nation arising in Russia, and despite the head-shaking and documentation of some disillusioned reporters the Soviets looked like the Promised Land to a number of the new and a few of the older playwrights. And out of these diagnoses and prognoses arose a new stimulus. The immediate battle between capital and labor, the coming struggle for power between the two classes, and the faith in the imminence of a new order made heady wine for the young men and women who organized new theatre units and wrote for them.

Many of these playwrights were immature and some were sociologists rather than artists. Their eagerness to convert the masses led them to neglect artistic finish, to wax rhetorical and demagogic, and to divide their characters into sheep and goats with scant respect for rounded characterization. The emphasis they placed on economic motivation and upon "dialectical materialism" tended to become literal, stereotyped and even naïve. (When, for example, they were prone to blame every intestinal disturbance on the big bad wolf "Capitalism" or on the "System.") They also tended to sentimentalize the worker as the Sir Galahad of the new grail, since Marxist history acclaimed him as the necessary builder of a collective society. Nevertheless, the ferment of anger and hope was not without beneficial results, and it is significant that every young serious writer of any power—Clifford Odets, Irwin Shaw, Sidney Kingsley, Lillian Hellman, John Wexley, Albert Maltz, and William Saroyan—was directly or indirectly affected by it. Nor was the enzyme of revolt present only in the content or viewpoint of the play. More significantly for an art, the effect appeared in style, which tended to be nervous and strident; and in form, which ranged from crisp exposition to thumping climaxes, from short montages and skits to elaborated expressionism or symbolism. It even made itself felt in the work of the older writers; not only in that of Elmer Rice and John Howard Lawson who had absorbed it earlier, but in that of Behrman, Anderson, Sherwood, Howard, and Kaufman who voiced interest, indignation, or anxiety. Moreover, the younger playwrights grew older, more discreet, and even less confident of immediate salvation. Consequently they began to rely on more oblique statements of their viewpoint and on more rounded characterization; they even smiled a little. And at this point of some temporary rapprochement between the veterans of the twenties and the recruits of the thirties this chronicle leaves them.

Since Burns Mantle's *Contemporary American Playwrights* lists some five hundred practitioners, it is patently impossible to review their work beyond this summary of main trends.[2] Nor is it necessary to present such a review here, since most of these works will no doubt be consigned to oblivion. Time, however, will probably be merciful to a number of them, even if they are certain to look smaller at a distance.

2 THE KAUFMAN CYCLE

Among the more significant writers, George S. Kaufman, with his numerous collaborators Marc Connelly, Edna Ferber, Moss Hart and others, achieved a veritable compendium of American trends. Since 1921 he has responded to nearly everything in American life, from its pleasant private vagaries to political mismanagement and the serious threat of fascism. His basic outlook has been, however, casually comedic and all interruptions of some serious critique like *Merrily We Roll Along* and *The American Way* have been hastily covered up by another rib-shaking extravaganza. His work has been one long cycle from comedy to comedy.

Since it provides, in the main, a very superficial *comédie humaine* the temptation to dismiss it has been strong. Kaufman himself has for the most part made no outrageous claims. Nevertheless, he has a right to some small niche. Energy and theatrical ingenuity are the pillars of his accomplishment, and since these have served as a base for many shrewd insights into character and manners Kaufman is a respectable dramatist. *Dulcy*, the witless busybody of the farce of the same name was so excellent a caricature of middle-class women that she became proverbial. *To the Ladies* was a charming comedy of home life with its queen-bee Elsie as the power behind the commonplace throne. *Merton of the Movies* was a hilarious but well-aimed travesty on mass-production in art, an exposé of Hollywood inanities emanating from the impossible effort to wed art to business on such a mammoth scale. Merton himself is one of those imperishable little men whose dreams transfigure them in the very teeth of reality, although his success story is a compound of paste and sugar. *The Good Fellow* brought the Babbitt theme into the theatre, naturally without the imaginative delicacy and poetry of O'Neill's *Marco Millions* but with robust satire at the American business man's passion for rotarian societies and their jollifications. His *Beggar on Horseback*, written with Marc Connelly and based on a German comedy by Paul Apel,[3] was a brilliant expressionist satire on big business projected by a young composer's dream of what would happen to him if he married successfully and became absorbed in mass production.

In addition to many amusing musical comedies, among which *Of Thee I Sing* was a pointed burlesque of American politics, Kaufman continued to tap the vein of genial satire on American art which he had opened with *Merton of the Movies*. In *The Royal Family* he conveyed the idiocies of a theatrical family with admirable delectation; *Once in a Life-*

time travestied Hollywood with unremitting sharpness at the time when the "talkies" introduced fresh confusion into the industry; *Stage Door* in the inclement year of 1936 took rather sentimental account of the tragi-comic struggles of young actresses in the legitimate but overstocked theatre. Larger segments of social life also claimed attention from this eclectic craftsman. Thus fashionable society was the anatomical subject of *Dinner at Eight,* which pointed to some diseased organs though without much effort to investigate causes. With some constructive desire that would have been more applicable to the gay twenties, Kaufman even wrote a prescription for happiness through carefreeness in *You Can't Take It With You,* a harum-scarum comedy-farce that managed to be warm amid its lunacies and that proves unsatisfactory only when one takes its authors for graduates of the Brookings Institute or for the philosophers they almost pretended to be. Certainly it failed to substantiate its point that "money isn't everything" since, as Clifton Fadiman pointed out, a steady income alone enables the characters to indulge themselves. Most recently, moreover, *The Man Who Came to Dinner* revealed an aptitude for character comedy, though it petered out—if pleasantly enough—as contrived farce.

Barring the pinchbeck *Weltschmerz* and lush masochism of *Merrily We Roll Along,* with its wail for artists who are ruined by money-consciousness, and that noble but glib paean to democracy *The American Way,* the Kaufman cycle is American humor at its most typical. It is remarkably shrewd but rarely thorough, generally smothering the satire in sentiment and skirting the issues it raises without sufficient inquiry. Its integument is hard but its core is soft. Regrettably, this work is not for the ages, but it has been amply sufficient unto the day. Fadiman has launched the most telling charge against the Kaufman clan when he wrote that when they put on their thinking caps, "the caps assume a vaguely conical shape." Perhaps they actually want this transformation for the "show business" to which they are unapologetically wedded.

Kaufman comedy found companion pieces in the amusing journalistic farce of Ben Hecht's and Mac Arthur's *Front Page,* in Louis Weizenkorn's *Five-Star Final,* and in Maurine Watkins' *Chicago,* the pungent comedy of a popular murder trial. It also served as a model for younger writers, who proved themselves quite adept at it—especially at its more obvious features; such examples as *Personal Appearance* and *Room Service* had deservedly their brief moments of triumph.

Close to the Kaufman vein lay the deeper resources of George Kelly, a tantalizingly uneven writer who at his best, however, created a dry kind of critical comedy. It was most effervescent when the theme was frothy, as in the amateur theatricals of *The Torchbearers* or in the extravagances of a typically brash American "go-getter" like the hero of

The Show-Off. There was a more subdued but telling humor in *Daisy Mayme,* with its satire on possessive females who mulct a bachelor brother and keep him from marriage until they meet their match in Daisy. The comedian and ex-vaudevillian Kelly, however, paradoxically attained the greatest power when he treated the sobering theme of middle-class womanhood in *Craig's Wife.* Here he set down an exposure of the "cash-nexus" in marriage through the excellent portrait of a calculating woman whose consuming passion for security proves catastrophic when she reveals her true nature to her husband by failing him in a crisis. Kelly, who was at heart a moralist, was not an incisive critic of the civilization that produced such types as his braggart and his acquisitive woman. But these and other characters were vividly drawn and spoke self-revelatory dialogue of rare reality. Kelly was also hampered by too great an immersion in the commonplace world, a danger that has limited a number of his colleagues. Yet his objectivity set him apart from those who were comfortable in it. Kelly, in short, made comedy a matrix of spiritual distempers but kept it on a level that precluded comic exaltation. This made him a sterling realist but only a journeyman in the buoyant trade of comedy.

More recently Miss Clare Boothe has revealed a talent that Kaufman himself might envy. *Kiss the Boys Good-bye,* an uneven and tenuous travesty on Hollywood stardom and on a variety of related matters, is written in his carefree manner. Her earlier satire on the shallow women of "the leisure class" (the leisure belongs entirely to the women) is as devastatingly amusing as anything he has written. *The Women* even goes far beyond comedy of feminine frailty, though as such it could be recommended to anyone preparing himself for professional misogyny. Were the term not too ponderous for *The Women,* one might describe it as social comedy, though its logic seems insufficiently comprehensive for this classification when one remembers the example of Shaw.

3 PHILIP BARRY'S COMEDY OF MANNERS

Polite comedy of manners, with its greater polish and restraint, nearly fell upon evil days in the contemporary American theatre. Even so consistent a practitioner as Miss Rachel Crothers, who had begun to write some years before the O'Neill renaissance, found it difficult to extract any remarkable wit from a world of shifting values. Miss Crothers was playful and intelligent but a pedestrian and admonishing mother-confessor of the naughty decades. Inevitably, by temperament and circumstance this genial writer became a purveyor of problem comedies like *He and She, Nice People,* and *Mary the Third.* Even *Expressing Willie* (in 1923), a satire on the pursuit of "self-expression," and *Susan and God* (1937) missed the high comedic virtue of relentless analysis. This genial author's procedure is well exemplified in *Susan and God;* it started as a delightful exposure of a sect-addicted egocentric woman, but Miss Crothers soon settled down to sentiment and closed with a pleasant domestic reconciliation. The problem that faced the professor of high comedy was what to do with a world in flux, since it is only a stable society (at least in the upper crust) that provides a sufficient basis for cool laughter.

The problem was not settled, but a suitable compromise was effected when Philip Barry found in the frustrations and petty rebellions of the children of the well-to-do a fertile theme. Against their divagations he opposed the conventional and materialistic world of their business-absorbed elders. The friction between the two groups produced a critical kind of humor, and Barry fought business-mindedness brightly and pleasantly (though none too incisively) in a number of plays.

The most explicit of these was *Holiday,* in which a rich man's rebellious daughter and her money-minded sister's fiancée go away together in common search for a rather ambiguous happiness beyond the barricade of a cotillion-leader's moneybags. *Holiday* came in 1928, at the peak of the Wall Street boom, after some delightful but sound flaunting of the conventions in *Paris Bound* (1927) with its warning against putting too much stress on an adulterous slip now and then, and in the comedy *In a Garden,* two years earlier, with its point that a woman always remains emotionally bound to the man who first awakened her sexually regardless of marital obligations. *Holiday* was, moreover, followed in 1932 by the equally unconventional comedy of *The Animal Kingdom* which showed an understanding mistress to be more truly a wife to a rich idealist than the parasitic woman of his set to whom he bound himself in the eyes of the law.

Yet Barry, who could describe people so deftly, could not fill the role of incisive critic which he appeared to claim as his own. He merely skimmed the surface with his anti-philistinism, and his revolt against convention was carefully circumscribed. When he took account of the wider scene in the bright and beautifully tailored comedy *The Philadelphia Story* in the lean spring of 1939, he added to his theme of the emotional awakening of a priggish society girl the sane but too easily compounded prescription that "with the rich and mighty always a little patience" is a good policy for the poor and weak. He was being less than either profound or scintillating when making some slight concession to economic realities or to the social insurgency of the era he indicated that radical intellectuals were also "nice people" underneath.

When nine years before, he settled down to a serious analysis of the neuroses of upper-class and intellectual individuals in the boldly original psychoanalytical drama *Hotel Universe,* he clarified less than he thought and solved much less than he intended through the cathartic confessions of his characters. The fact is that in his most serious grappling with ideas or problems he was at heart a conventional, if very humane, moralist of the Catholic persuasion, as was evidenced by *The Joyous Season* and other moralizing plays. When the thirties seemed headed in a nihilistic direction that outraged him, the times wrung from him that noble cry of God-seeking, despair, and faith in the light that burns in good men, *Here Come the Clowns.* Even this imaginative and profoundly suggestive play, however, lost itself in a mystic miasma and his quest was hampered by a circuitous approach. He has loved commiseration more than a master of high comedy can afford. He often came bearing not a scalpel but a Bible. The best that can be said of him is that as a comic writer he also carried a small glistening dagger for pricking and prodding his characters. Nevertheless he must be respected as an artist, since he proved himself a flashing humorist with a flair for the *mot juste*, as well as for the right juxtaposition of characters, and he was a provocative fantasticator in some of his somber moments.

4 BEHRMAN'S COMEDY OF IDEAS

S. N. Behrman coped with the difficult art of high comedy differently. As accomplished a portrait painter as Barry but a poorer manager of story elements, his superiority lies in his critical understanding and his capacity for harboring the dynamic trends or promptings of a turbulent period. The difference is indeed best indicated by the adjective "dynamic," for unlike Barry he delves beneath the surface of the turbulence as far as the comic temperament will allow; and he has also viewed the hurly-burly more comprehensively than his more genteel colleague, whose eye has so often settled on private distempers in the salons of the rich and sheltered. Behrman's faculty for capturing the driving forces of the contemporary scene is a multiple gift. He is a master of disputative or self-revealing conversation, and this in turn argues a marvelous mastery of phrasing. He is possessed of a fundamental earnestness and carries some curiously sensitive gray matter that takes an impression, even if sometimes a blurred one, of nearly every contemporary idea.

His mind is in continual suspension. He resolves nothing because that organ is too volatile and because his heart can give itself to no cause that may, as it seemingly must, realize itself at the expense of reasonableness and humane practice. This has troubled some of his younger critics a good deal, just as his inability to contrive a plot has worried their elders; he has even been troubled by his disposition himself. He has gone so far in *Wine of Choice* as to admit that he would regret the disappearance of the idlers of society because their charm is also something precious in the world. (To which the rebuttal might maintain that the world can pay too high a price for charm and that, besides, it is by no means the prerogative of the idlers!) And it may well be that his philosophical tentativeness provides an insufficient discharge for the weighty problems that he himself evokes in his picture of a world overburdened with social injustice, parasitism, and fascism. He is confronted by a dilemma: how can he function in a time in which nearly everyone seeks to destroy all principles but his own and still remain a writer of comedy? Yet he has found an answer; it consists of the essentially comic idea that there is something to be said for every viewpoint that is not patently mercenary or crassly complacent. Therein lies the humanism of Behrman comedy even if it solves no immediate problems, and even if this writer's frequently static dramaturgy may leave his point more devoid of theatrical interest than might be desired.

Behrman began his career more cautiously with *The Second Man,* a lightly executed but nearly perfect character comedy revolving around those basically meretricious well-to-do individuals who disarm one with their awareness of their own shortcomings. Its leading character Clark Storey starved through the idealistic stage of Socialism but became wealthy because he could write with facility, and he was prompted to do so at the cost of integrity because as he confesses there was "a second man—grinning, sophisticated, horrid" in him. He resembles the doctor of the later comedy *End of Summer* who became successful only when he discovered that while the poor had tonsils the rich had a more expensive superfluity of neuroses. In love Storey, who is likable because he is so coolly candid and therefore so right for comedy, is defeated because his "second man" will not allow him to receive or reciprocate it.

This critique, which arrived in 1927 on the crest of successful American materialism, was obviously derived from the trend of Mammon-worship. Behrman's next and less engaging play *Meteor,* written shortly before the collapse of the market in October 1929, was another but more concentrated portrait of a man of the twenties. The career of his 'financial wizard Raphael Lord was a superb example of the rise and emotional bankruptcy of an arrogant egotist. Lord's neglected wife leaves him when he becomes too obsessed with his thirst for power, friends abandon him, and failure threatens him. But he continues to ply his speculations, and at the end he is still resolutely pursuing his phantom of success.

A pleasant interlude in Behrman's ascent occurred in the romance of *Brief Moment,* in which an introspective scion of wealth marries a night-club singer because he believes her to be elemental. This proves to be the last of his illusions! The one glimmer of a typical post-1929 Behrman idea appeared in his subject Roderick's sense of futility with respect to himself and his milieu, of "things disintegrating. . . . some enormous transition—the final flicker of civilization"—an easy deduction in the fall of 1931. With his next play *Biography* in the following year Behrman, however, had become sufficiently acclimated to the stern thirties to describe the alignment of forces in those years. He did so in a manner which made the three-cornered battle of conservatives, liberals and radicals seem something more than a journalistic report. Each viewpoint was represented as a general attitude and a temperament rather than a political program, and it was wisely allocated to highly articulate characters. The fundamental issue between the liberal and the radical was feelingly realized in the persons of the lovers Marion Fronde, who is too easy-going to publish her sensational autobiography which would dispose of some stuffed shirts, and the journalist Richard Kurt, an embittered son of a murdered coal-miner who wants her to dynamite the capitalist foundations. When their differences prove too basic, they separate; Marion holds charmingly to her amused detachment while Kurt exclaims with equal, perhaps superior, justice that he now knows why social evil flourishes—that is, because people as they grow older lose the capacity for indignation and are merely amused by what they should hate.

In the essential matter of characterization and persuasiveness it is Marion who emerges victorious. The effect could therefore be stigmatized as an evasion of the moral issue, for it left the sorry state of the world (and it was Behrman who insisted that it was sorry) unchallenged in the mind of the playgoer. The latter could only be entranced with Marion while Kurt remained a secondary and rather futile fellow. Behrman concluded with a stalemate, as Molière had done in *The Misanthrope*, because he was on the side of the comic spirit. The play was, in other words, genuine high comedy. To justify Kurt completely was impossible in this form.

Behrman balanced matters in his next and most serious play, *Rain from Heaven* (1934), a comedy that frustrated its humor because it was darkened by a recognition of the fascist threat, anti-semitism, and the corruption of sound intellects and clean spirits by the poison of intolerance. That war against the powers of darkness is imperative is finally recognized by Behrman's exiled music critic Hugo Willens. After being insulted by an American aviator of the Lindbergh type, who proves himself a potential fascist and is being primed for a *putsch* by a reactionary capitalist, Hugo leaves the congenial home of the Englishwoman who loves him in order to join the underground anti-Nazi movement in his country. Although the humor of some entertaining situations was not too well fused with the gravities of this situation, and although the music critic's vague climactic resolution came only after much static and diffuse detail, *Rain from Heaven* was a noble and provocative play.

Its limitations were those of its mixed *genre*, since it is manifestly difficult to ride the two horses of comedy and tragedy at the same time unless one happens to possess Shakespearean vigor. Behrman, however, did not repeat this mistake in *End of Summer*, two years later, with the result that it became one of his most charming and successful comedies without foregoing incisiveness. Here he hit upon the comic point that even those who benefit materially by the unequal division of wealth are spiritually cheated. His rich woman Leonie Frothingham is lovable but so disoriented that she must hop from one delusory love affair into another. And no sooner has she extricated herself from her involvement with a designing psychoanalyst than a Machiavellian young radical Dennis catches her on the rebound because she simply cannot endure being alone. Ironically, Leonie will finance her young protégé's magazine, even though it would logically lay the axe to the foundations of her wealth and leisure. Contrasted with her, moreover, is rampant youth, either filled with vague idealism in the case of the penniless Will Dexter and Leonie's daughter or methodically militant—in an intellectual way—like Dennis. (He may be a caricature of professional revolutionists but he is surely an adequate portrait of some of their literary satellites.) Enlivened with brilliant dialogue and well-drawn comic characterization, *End of Summer* marked the peak of Behrman's dialectical comedy of manners.

Wine of Choice, two years later, was likewise filled with a consideration of conflicting viewpoints, and it concluded with an affirmation of the liberal spirit. Strengthened by the point that liberalism did not mean inaction but Fabian, practical tactics in preference to destructive ones, it possessed some fire, and there was depth in the characterization of the young woman Wilda whose efforts to acquire security are nullified by something in her nature that makes her respond invariably to the least practical kind of love. Unfortunately, however, the play was a thing of shreds and patches both in thought and situations, and its priggish radical loaded the argument for liberalism. Nor did Behrman's last contribution *No Time for Comedy*, a far more finished comedy, measure up to his previous work in scope or profundity. It enjoyed a genuine comic idea in the point that a man may feel an urge to traffic with the tragedies of his time or may be deluded into believing that the urge is present without actually being capable of anything other than the enjoyment or projection of life's minor and amusing complications. The dice, however, were loaded too heavily in favor of this viewpoint, and the play was most amusing as a clever, if somewhat laborious, triangle play. It might also be regarded as Behrman's apology for his ingrained inability to take a stand in a world in which most men of his intellectual caliber and sensibilities felt the compulsion to do so. As such it could be equally regarded as charmingly candid and disarming or as glibly evasive.

However, *No Time for Comedy* can hardly be expected to mark the end of this superbly literate observer's response to the conflicting ideologies of his day. The truth is that he is too fascinated by them to let them alone.

5 ROBERT SHERWOOD AND THE DECLINE OF THE WEST

Another expert writer of comedy found ideologies to his liking and advantage. An eclectic man of the theatre who has tried his hand at melodrama, comedy, and biographical drama, Robert Sherwood achieved a measure of prominence largely, though of course not exclusively, because of his strong historical interest.

This interest appeared in his very first play *The Road to Rome,* written in 1927. Rome facing destruction at the hands of the Carthaginian hero Hannibal is here saved, not by the worthy Fabius as history has it, but by his spirited and unconventional wife Amytis whose weapons are entirely feminine. Not standing in awe of conventional heroes and having no use for war, she visits Hannibal in his camp and takes his measure. Then her shrewd womanliness breaks down his resolve to become a great conqueror until he departs a wiser man but a smaller hero by his own standards. The comedy was in the main a clever duel of the sexes enlivened by the delightful characterization of Amytis. But it was evident that Sherwood's choice of a historical theme had its roots in a thoughtful disposition. An anti-heroic animus pervaded the comedy when Amytis blithely poked fun at the complacent fustian of the Romans, the pompousness of the great Fabius, and the self-hypnotic heroism of Hannibal. Her dislike for senseless slaughter rose to eloquence in her words to Hannibal: "I want you to believe that *every* sacrifice in the name of war is wasted. When you believe that you will be a great man."

Sherwood was a showman and therefore hid his light in some trivial comedies and obvious melodramas. But whenever the spirit moved him, and this, as might be expected, occurred with increasing frequency in the thirties, the three major serious *motifs* of *The Road to Rome* reappeared: He revealed a feeling for historical periods in *Reunion in Vienna, The Petrified Forest, Acropolis, Idiot's Delight,* and *Abe Lincoln in Illinois;* he deflated or humanized heroes and favored those characters who departed from traditional pomp, panache or heroism; and he revealed an antipathy for brutality and slaughter. In most cases he added a fourth dimension—namely, modern sex drama. It overshadowed his historical view delightfully in *Reunion in Vienna,* muddled it in *The Petrified Forest,* and diffused and interrupted it in *Idiot's Delight.* It proved both a boon and a bane—that is, it furthered his theatrical effect and made him turn out some successful "shows" but it diminished the provocativeness or integrity of his thought, as he himself confessed.

It proved an unqualified boon in *Reunion in Vienna,* one of the brightest comedies of the American stage, when he evoked shrewd humor from

Elena Krug's problem of choosing between the safe husband Anton and the totally irresponsible Archduke Rudolph who had been her lover in the old Hapsburg days. The contrast between the two men and the invincible femininity of Elena, who we presume gives Rudolph one night of love when he loses his overbearing aplomb and becomes an appealing child, combined modern sophistication and modern psychology with rare delicacy and humor. But historical perspective was an integral part of even this play. It appeared in the charmingly described post-Hapsburg and pre-Hitler Viennese background. The gay monarchy is passé, and its maudlin or helpless survivors can only mourn its passing; their pride and their hopes are both amusingly and pathetically incongruous. Their place is taken by the bourgeoisie, placid, respectable, and unexciting. Elena, who lives, so to speak, in two worlds, tries like a sensible woman to adapt herself to the new order by marrying a psychoanalyst. But the new rational outlook also has its *bravura*, and this appears in her otherwise stolid husband who believes that the emotions can be completely mastered by the scientific intellect. This sin against the comic spirit which regards life as too elusive for any science is amusingly rebuked when the superior Dr. Anton finds himself stripping off his coat to fight for Elena with the taxi-driving ex-Archduke. His philosophy is further contradicted when his "psychology" fails to prevent Elena and Rudolph from renewing their passion in defiance of logic and the code of honor. It is the comedy that matters, however, and it has well-tried ingredients that invariably gratify the adult intellect—the triumph of spirit over matter, of the emotions over staid self-assurance, of the incalculable over the calculable. In 1931 Hitler had not yet walked rough-shod over the amenities.

In *The Petrified Forest* and *Acropolis,* four and five years later, however, the solvent of humor was subordinated to some highly insoluble ingredients. Along with *Idiot's Delight,* in 1936, they might be described as Sherwood's tribute to Spengler and as his dirge for Western civilization; they were three chapters from a thoughtful playwright's *Decline of the West.* In the person of the disoriented vagabond poet Alan Squire, who seeks extinction and finds it at a gunman's hands, Sherwood represented the death of civilized values. Earlier, in *The Road to Rome,* Amytis had declared regarding herself and Varius that "We have the misfortune of being thoughtful people. . . . Thoughtful people are never very successful." Now in *The Petrified Forest,* the question was no longer one of success but of actual survival. Civilization is imperiled in this play by the confident and single-minded forces of destruction which materialism, economic collapse, and fascism have let loose upon the world. The men of good will are helpless, whereas the men of action are gangsters like Mantee. It could be argued that the dramatist and his representa-

tive Alan Squire gave up the struggle too easily, that Sherwood failed
to take account of the possibility that men of good will could also resort
to action. Moreover, Alan Squire was too shoddy a representative of
civilization; if there were no more to it than he exemplifies the loss would
not deserve much mourning. Consequently, real tragedy was absent in
The Petrified Forest. As a matter of fact, the play was a melodrama and
was completely successful only as such. Adept at dramatic manipulations Sherwood turned out a highly theatrical spectacle which could
gratify the groundlings with its sheer bustle while interesting, without
convincing, more serious dispositions with the suggestion of larger issues.

Evidently aware of this fact himself, Sherwood next attempted a re-
statement of his theme without the accessories of theatrical hocus-pocus
in *Acropolis.* The results were less gratifying as theatre, the London production was unsuccessful though it was respectfully received, and except
for a tentative showing at the little Heckscher Theatre it was not unfolded to the public in New York. But if it ever receives some necessary
revision and vitalization as theatre, it may prove a work of considerable
distinction. Sherwood drew in this drama a poignant parallel between
dying Athenian civilization and modern times: The Periclean Age is being destroyed by a protracted war and its concomitants—demagoguery,
political reaction, and intolerance of culture. Phidias, the great sculptor,
and Socrates no longer can be tolerated and even the once-popular statesman Pericles can no longer stem the rise of mass hypnosis. After them
the deluge.

In *Idiot's Delight,* moreover, this troubled dramatist no longer availed
himself of distant parallels too esoteric for the million. Sherwood chose
the next world war for an exemplification of the death of a civilization,
and prescience led him to his theme just three and a half years before
the new war actually started. Resolved to write a good "show," Sherwood filled the play with his bevy of chorus girls, "Les blondes." He also
kept the story bubbling with the American showman Harry Van's efforts to discover whether the pseudo-Russian mistress of a munitions
king in the Hotel Monte Gabriele is not the lady who shared his room in
an Omaha hostelry. These ingredients diluted the author's treatment of
the next Armageddon while ensuring the play a measure of success that
would have been absent if he had devoted himself more single-mindedly
to a thesis. Nevertheless, the failure of society and the destruction of
reason were more fully revealed than might be expected; they were
merely too submerged for definiteness. The thoughtful "hoofer" Harry
Van and the adventuress who loses her munitions magnate when she resents the source of his wealth are waifs of a futile and disorganized world.
They accept destruction in an air raid with bravura playing "Onward,
Christian Soldiers" because they have found nothing in their past worth

preserving. The abdication of reason is likewise stressed by the deliberate surrender of the enlightened Dr. Waldersee to jingoism; since his country requires his services he will lend his scientific efficiency to the furtherance of the slaughter which mankind richly deserves for its refusal to lead a rational existence. Even the radical French labor leader Quillery renounces his internationalism (a point that ardent young critics question with some obliviousness to historic fact) when he learns that his country has been bombed from the air; having patriotically defied the Italians, he is taken out and shot by them. War, an idiot's delight, takes its toll of everything that is noble and aspiring in humanity.

After a clever but insignificant adaptation of a French play, a "job" rather than an expression of personal interest, Sherwood capped his career with the biographical *Abe Lincoln in Illinois* in 1938. Again the familiar elements of a critical historical period and an anti-heroic conception of character gave his work extension and depth. The portentous years preceding the Civil War and Lincoln's critical election to the presidency provided the background. Moreover, the struggle between abolitionism and slavery served the author as a broad basis for thoughts about America in the thirties. The historical picture foreshadows the current conflict between capital and labor; it promulgates the defense of democracy and its extension into the fundamental social sphere. And out of this consonance between the past and the present arises a glowing affirmation of the American faith in the worth of the common man and in the value of a homespun conscience. All this is conveyed, not only in a number of highly stirring speeches condensed from Lincoln's own addresses, which include comments on the growing problems of industrialism, but in the figure of Lincoln himself. The picture of this man of the people is one of the noblest creations of the American theatre. It was not difficult to create since it was Lincoln who sat for the portrait. But the composition is Sherwood's. Here he was again utilizing his anti-heroic perspective: Lincoln is affecting precisely because he is so unpretentious, because he is so much like other men in his waverings, and because he shrinks from every course of action that might lead to bloodshed even when his anti-slavery sentiments would dictate another course of action. He is, moreover, like other historic figures *pushed* into prominence and a position of power.

Inevitably, Sherwood paid a penalty for this conception of Lincoln when he tried to set it down in scene after scene, for Lincoln's waverings are unexciting and, in the present writer's opinion, sometimes tiresome. Nor did the author successfully integrate the scenes in which this character vacillates or supply a sufficiently unified course of development toward his emergence as a national figure. Consequently, *Abe Lincoln in Illinois* is, for nearly two acts, a rather disjointed piece of dramaturgy consisting of fragmentary and undramatically related scenes. Still, there was enough suspension in this play to give it exceptional provocativeness, and the character of Lincoln suffused it with spiritual beauty. Here, at last, Sherwood affirmed the power of the new world on the Western hemisphere to survive the decline of the West. It is even more to his credit that he made this affirmation without pollyannic asseverations or neglect of the necessity of unremitting struggle with problems left unresolved by the Civil War. Since he accomplished this, in the main, through a character portrait, he invested history with palpitating and tragic flesh, so that Americans are right in treasuring this play despite its considerable shortcomings.

Although *Abe Lincoln in Illinois* is not a very good play, it possesses elements of greatness; and that is perhaps all (though not quite all) that matters. Sherwood himself has been brushed by the wings of a great spirit ever since he began to wonder at the world that men make and unmake in their procession through history.

6 MAXWELL ANDERSON, REALIST AND ROMANCER

This wonder is also at the heart of the best work of one who has been frequently named as O'Neill's successor. Maxwell Anderson's candidacy for this honor has been supported by his capacity for pungent prose and winged utterance. To these talents he has added not only a gift for humor and theatrical effect but a sensitive and questioning intellect. He has, moreover, revealed an ambition to move from immediate fact to altitudes of universal truth; almost alone in the American theatre since O'Neill, he has attempted to rise beyond the pedestrian realistic drama. He has tried to scale the forbidding peaks of poetic composition by means of a pliant and free blank verse, and he has even leaped into the stratosphere of fantasy. He has, above all, striven to make tragedy prevail in the modern theatre despite the untragic psychological and photographic viewpoints of the age.

Consequently he has been simultaneously the most gratifying and most disturbing playwright of any stature in America with the sole exception of O'Neill. Of his nobility of spirit there is no question, and it would be a sorry world indeed if that alone did not win the respect of his contemporaries. It is unnecessary to review his long-preserved independence which years ago cost him positions in college and in journalism, and which has more recently earned him the partly merited displeasure of younger men who would have liked nothing better than to have him as an ally; his work and life speak for themselves. But his flights have necessarily been circumscribed by unevenly distributed talents and by the ponderable facts of the modern theatre and of the contemporary world.

His prose is of sterling worth. But although he has been a practising lyricist whose verse was collected in a slender book, his efforts in dramatic poetry have been decidedly unequal. Much of his verse has been pedestrian; some of it has been loose and more of it overstrained, as if he were trying desperately to be poetic. (This was particularly the case in *The Wingless Victory*.) Too often, as the fine poet Archibald Mac-Leish noted, he has confused poetry with decorative rather than essential expression. Moreover, his realistic material has sometimes defied poetry. This was particularly evident in *Winterset,* where a gangster and some denizens of the slums speak blank verse with considerable incongruity before they have acquired sufficient intensification to take us out of the common light of actuality. (And even later the poetry sometimes sounds forced and decorative.)

The soaring of his thought and imagination has also been more tentative and uncertain than as continually gratifying as one could desire. He has jumbled themes and confounded council, as when he mingled a Hamlet theme and a Romeo and Juliet *motif* with the Sacco-Vanzetti problem of social justice set forth in the first two acts of *Winterset*. He has begged questions, as when that issue is left unresolved after the Judge's distinct confession of social bias in condemning a labor leader to death. The same elusiveness appears in *The Masque of Kings* when Crown Prince Rudolph's personal motives in staging and then renouncing a revolt against the Austrian monarchy are employed as a justification for the retention of the *status quo* in ante-bellum Central Europe which is earlier declared to be rotten with corruption. Anderson has also been guilty of dubious solutions as when young Van in *High Tor* leaves his mountain to find another retreat in the West, although there is actually no more frontier. Although as a private individual Van can perhaps settle on another mountain, he cannot as a representative of the idealists of our day unless the new peak is merely intended as a symbol of spiritual action —of which, however, there seems to be no indication in the play. Moreover, his flight from industrial civilization is totally divorced from the real problem of a generation that cannot scrap the industrial system but must strive to refine it and employ it for the greater benefit of all. A similar obfuscation of issues appeared in *Knickerbocker Holiday*. Here the author's spirited glorification of American man's independence and refusal to accept a master (which, it might be argued, he has actually accepted without much opposition in the economic sphere!) was set down as an argument against a more equitable distribution of the benefits of democracy among the American masses.

The truth seems to be that Anderson is at heart a romanticist who deals in generalities, valid for the spirit but not for the actual realities that he himself stresses by the choice of his themes and by his own utterances. Anderson flies high in his poetic style because he feels an impa-

tience with actual life. He flies equally high in his statement and resolution of dramatic themes because he wants the spirit to prevail at all
costs. Often, however, he flies too high, in the present writer's opinion
and therefore violates both the logic of his own situations and the logic
of common fact, which he must not violate if his intentional social comment is to be taken seriously. His efforts to embrace universals is highly
commendable; but, as he himself surely knows, they have an integument
wrapped around them by time and place which even a poet cannot juggle
too illogically. Shakespeare in *Macbeth, Hamlet,* and *Lear* put this
knowledge into magnificent practice; but when Anderson reaches the
heights, he sometimes allows the rarefied atmosphere to unsteady him.
It is then that he also becomes rhapsodically verbose.

Nevertheless, he has a right to climb or soar, and he is a more considerable artist for it. Moreover, even when he resolves his matter inconclusively, he often touches points of observation and insight that are
valid and effective independently. And if his idealism tends to be shroud-
ed in mist, he sometimes manages to punctuate his ascent triumphantly;
when he notes injustices and malignancies within the field of his observation, and when he strips them to the bone, he is magnificent. His irony
and his indignation are glowing coals, his dialogue catches fire, his portraits are lighted up brightly, and his situations become warm and finally
—for a brief moment—attain white heat. This may be seen, for example, when he observes the muck of war in *What Price Glory?*, the callous-
ness of power in *Elizabeth the Queen,* or the power-lust of Mary's local
enemies in *Mary of Scotland,* the cynicism of politicians in *Both Your
Houses* and *Valley Forge,* the corruption of justice in *Winterset,* hypocritical puritanism in *The Wingless Victory,* and the predatory materialism of the land speculators in *High Tor.* Anderson, moreover, can strike
fire from the gallantry of man whether it appears in the foul-mouthed
bluster of Captain Flagg and Sergeant Quirt in *What Price Glory?*, the
romantic headiness of Essex in *Elizabeth the Queen,* the nobility of victims like Mary Stuart, or the simple fortitude of Washington and his
ragged band in *Valley Forge.*

In each of Anderson's important plays, finally, there is a core of meaning to support his perceptions of character and mankind; he has never
cared for mere entertainment. In 1924, *What Price Glory?* raised the
question of the senselessness of slaughter and made the anti-romantic
point, in vivid speech and exposition, that modern war is not fought in
a blaze of idealistic glory. It unintentionally romanticized professional
soldiering, since Captain Flagg and Sergeant Quirt are such splendid
blusterers and since the war is overshadowed by their rivalry for the
favors of Mademoiselle Charmaine. Nor did the play investigate the
causes and consequences of war as much as some critics would desire.

But as a picture, rather than as an analysis, it was almost as decidedly pointed as it was richly human and vigorous. (Credit for this performance no doubt also goes to his collaborator, Laurence Stallings.) *Saturday's Children,* in 1927, centered pathetically and comically on the fact that the romance of youth is a frail reed in the bluff wind of economic circumstance. If this comedy resolved nothing (and its author had no such pretensions) and if the young couple did not examine their problem intelligently, the play was nevertheless warm and charming. *Both Your Houses,* written in 1933 when disaffection with politics was strong, was a trenchant but topical satire on Congressional logrolling and political apathy.

The core widened and deepened in Andersonian tragedy and fantasy. When he wrote that uneven protest *Gods of the Lightning* with Harold Hickerson in 1928, he struck at once upon the peculiar passion that has persisted throughout most of his major works. In this paraphrase of the Sacco-Vanzetti case, the disillusioned anarchist summarizes the dramatist's view of man as a private and political animal: "Man is old. You will not make it over. . . . The world is old and it is owned by men who are hard. . . . I tell you there is no government—only brigands in power who fight always for more power." Two innocent idealists are killed by the law in *Gods of the Lightning.* In *Elizabeth the Queen* the gallant Essex is destroyed by the small-minded conniving men who run Elizabeth's government; "those who are noble, free of soul, valiant and admirable—they go down in their prime, Always go down . . . the rats inherit the earth." A tragedy of the two conflicting lovers the Earl of Essex and Queen Elizabeth, this play is essentially a tragedy of character. But their love relationship and its tragic climax when Essex loses his handsome head on the block are embedded in the treacherous quicksands of politics and human evil.

The rats also inherit the earth in *Mary of Scotland* when the lovable queen is destroyed by the designing masculine woman who spins her web of intrigue from England. Elizabeth, now grown old and hard, is the very incarnation of the power of this world, of the ruthless nature of politics, of the fundamental sterility of calculation. So eager was Anderson to make this point that he oversimplified the conflict between Mary and Elizabeth and even romanticized his crowned victim out of all resemblance to historical fact. Anderson's historical analysis in *Mary of Scotland* is decidedly inferior to Shaw's *Saint Joan,* and Mary's and Bothwell's romance is so affectingly developed that the philosophy is further subordinated. Still the core of *Mary of Scotland* is the moral issue of innocence destroyed and evil fruitlessly triumphant in the feral race for Empire. The verse has a somber music appropriate to the theme.

In that spirited but discursive American declaration of independence.

Valley Forge, which followed in 1934, the rats did not inherit the earth. The men won out momentarily. They founded a Republic in this oft-told tale of the American Revolution which is here modified but also vastly strengthened by the invention of a significant episode. After having been disheartened by the political chicanery he sees sprouting around him, Washington rededicates himself to the democratic cause when his backwoods soldiers set him an example in fortitude and revive his faith in a cause that they have made their own. The American Revolution which began as a merchant's war "over subsidies or some such matter" is "taken over" by the common people, "an uncouth clan . . . but followers of dreams."

Winterset was, however, a wintry sequel to the springtime affirmations of *Valley Forge;* for here, in a play written only a year later, the democratic dream was being pushed to the wall and the rats were distinctly gaining ground. Nowhere in its author's work have his anger and grief been so glowing, his irony and laughter so bitter, his characters so tortured and anguished. Mio, the son of an idealistic father executed many years ago as a common criminal, embarks on a hunt for evidence that would clear his name. He discovers the truth from the remorseful and mentally disturbed Judge Gaunt and even meets the real criminal in the person of the gangster Trock. But like all children of the light he is too tender-minded to be able to cope with the powers of evil. Failing to expose the criminal because this would indirectly affect the beloved girl Miriamne, Mio is killed by Trock's henchmen.

As a discharge for the problem of social justice raised by Judge Gaunt's own words, the third-act conclusion of *Winterset* is patently inadequate; in fact, it is no discharge at all. Nor does the pseudo-rabbinical peroration make any sense as a commentary on that problem since it is pure rubbish for Esdras to say that Mio and Miriamne died unsubmitting when they actually went to their slaughter like lambs. This inconclusiveness cannot be concealed, in the final analysis, by a mass of verbiage and by the affecting Romeo-and-Juliet story of Mio and Miriamne who are divided by conflicting family interests. There is also much else to criticize in this play. Nevertheless, it stands at the peak of Maxwell Anderson's accomplishment. It is touched with greatness in language, characterization, and atmosphere. Moreover, it possesses consistency in two ways, both adequate by themselves: as a modern Hamlet story climaxed with a flat renunciation of vengeance that even the reflective hero of Shakespeare's tragedy could not arrive at in the Elizabethan age of vendetta philosophy (though Mio's quest is not rightly vengeance!); and as an exemplification of the Andersonian point that the rats conquer and that the men are destroyed but are transfigured by their heartening nobility.

A second devastating sequel to the American dream as enunciated by Washington appeared in *High Tor* in 1937. The burden of defeat was present here despite the light fantastications about Henrik Hudson's ghostly crew and the robust comedy of the land-speculators who spend the night in a steam-shovel, two somewhat insufficiently fused themes. Industrialism is destroying the landscape, factories enslave the young, the lust for profit corrupts the spirit, and the beauties of the past are phantoms. Van finds refuge on the mountain he has inherited, but everything conspires to deprive him of it and send him into the mills of Mammon. He can escape only by precipitate flight to another mountain, an indefinitely located one in a hypothetically open West. Consolation comes only from a dying Indian's assurance that this sorry civilization will also end since "nothing is made by man but makes, in the end, good ruins." And this is hardly any consolation for anyone who must breathe in the present world and has only one earthly existence. It is merely remote poetic justice, and that is cold porridge. Again there was a breath of greatness in an American play, even if its fantasy was tenuous and weakly nostalgic except for the robustly farcical speculator scenes.

In 1936 and 1937 derivativeness and overelaboration weakened the solidly constructed Mayerling tragedy of *The Masque of Kings* and the Medea-"Java Head" story of *The Wingless Victory* which was only slightly redeemed by some magnificent flashes of satirical indignation at a mercenary and hidebound world. Anderson's star dipped further in the Dear Brutus fantasy of *The Star Wagon* which owed its success to period humor, and even the distinguished libretto of *Knickerbocker Holiday* in 1938 fell short of this talented dramatist's best work. *Key Largo,* a noble paean to the human spirit, further exemplified this author's peculiar strength and limitations. Largely owing to its affirmativeness and realization that no escape from the necessity of making decisions is possible in this rodent world, this tragedy marks his closest acquaintance with greatness since the *Winterset-High Tor* period. No doubt, however, he has fresh strings to his bow, and wherever the arrows go they will fly high and the sun will flash on them from time to time. One wishes only that he would not send so many of them into the dark. for his aim is more indiscriminate than accurate.

7 AMERICAN SCENES: HOWARD, RICE, PAUL GREEN, AND OTHERS

As was to be expected, the number of writers who tried to paint American scenes without Andersonian sublimations but in subdued or heightened colors was legion; they were, after all, living in a world of realistic art and thought. Some of them were critical observers, and all of them had a keen eye for surfaces, regional or otherwise.

The most roving of them was Sidney Howard, who met an untimely death in 1939. A craftsman of the first order, his energies were often deflected into adaptations of plays, among which only *The Late Christopher Bean* was worthy of his talents by virtue of his masterly portrait of a tenacious New England woman. Little given to soaring, he was too often persistently pedestrian. But his fine ear for American dialect and his keen eye for local characters made him write *They Knew What They Wanted,* a delightfully humane comedy of the wine-producing regions of California. To this must be added the portrait of the self-made American business man of *The Lucky Sam McCarver,* an original series of tableaux, and the steady New England and brash or unreliable metropolitan types of *Ned McCobb's Daughter.* Small-town college life was the less successfully realized milieu of *Alien Corn.* Middle-class philanderings with supposed European culture, balanced by a hearty but uncaricatured American type of businessman, amplified his cross section of American life in *Dodsworth,* adapted from the Sinclair Lewis novel. Background was subordinated in the psychological drama *The Silver Cord,* a not too deep but wholly adequate and intelligent exposé of maternal possessiveness and mother-fixations intensified by excellent portraits of a possessive mother and a shrewd young modern wife. More background—that of a well-intentioned American upper-class family— enriched the otherwise static social drama *The Ghost of Yankee Doodle* which made the all too realistic point that economic factors both in the owning and working classes were stronger than basic decency and humane opposition to war. A sounder play could hardly have been written, and it was natural that it should have been composed by so honest a realist, even if the effect was decidedly unexciting. Finally, Howard must be credited with creating that highly original drama *Yellow Jack,* which celebrates the heroism of scientists and vividly drawn common soldiers in the fight against yellow fever. This fast-moving and noble one-act but full-length play excepted, Howard did not write anything particularly exciting. But his best work was as substantial as bread.

Elmer Rice gave the theatre metropolitan studies in the main. But he proved himself an excellent photographer of commonplace existence both in the expressionist and the realistic modes. *The Adding Machine,* written in the heyday of expressionism, in 1923, was one of the most original plays of the American stage. His stylized portrait of the morons produced by mechanization of culture and labor in the person of Mr. Zero, for whom Heaven is too immoral, was nothing short of brilliant. Here Rice triumphed as an ironist and as an observer. Observation, however, was his particular forte, and this was instantly substantiated by *Street Scene,* an effective photograph of teeming tenement life in New York. Observation also scored triumphs in *The Left Bank,* a picture of the pseudo-bohemianism popular among self-deluded Americans who coddled their second-rate talents on the *rive-gauche* of the Seine while despising their country for its raw strength, and *Counsellor-at-Law* provided a vivid character study of a former slum lad and present nabob of the legal profession.

Rice, nevertheless, was too intelligent a thinker and too sympathetic a person to be content with surfaces while the earth was shaking with disaffection. In 1933, at the height of the depression of the thirties, he created in *We the People* a veritable chart of the nation's rumblings. Nearly every line of the play recorded some injustice or contradiction—from racial prejudice to hunger and frustration in love, from the effects of the last war to labor trouble and legal frame-ups. In conclusion, he held his report angrily before the eyes of his audience and called for remedial action. It was a gallant effort, but one that was considerably weakened by diffusion and by a miscellaneous case history. *Judgment Day* was a superficial and melodramatic indictment of European fascism, and *Between Two Worlds* an intelligent but static discussion of social viewpoints. Finally, with *American Landscape* in 1938, Rice returned to the purposeful fantastication that had served him so well in *The Adding Machine*. It was a penetrative work owing to its implication that *homo Americanus* is too composite a person, compounded of ancestors from too many races and having too fine a tradition of liberalism, to indulge in prejudices without inconsistency. Moreover, the play was an explicit demonstration that American democracy is not only worth saving but extending in accordance with new requirements. Unfortunately, the imaginative device of bringing ancestral apparitions on the stage was not sufficiently primed for successful operation. With the single exception of *The Adding Machine,* Rice therefore remains in the honorable category of scene painters. But for this profession, he had not only every equipment but unusual penetrativeness.

Paul Green had an even stronger inclination toward provocative fantasy but justified it only in the pacifist extravaganza of *Johnny Johnson,* a deeply realized ironic drama of the plight of an honest man in an insane and corrupt world. Although the individual parts were not equal to the whole, it was an original experiment in the synthesis of music, mass chant, vaudeville skit, and straight drama. (Piscator's *pièce de résistance, The Good Soldier Schweik,* echoed through its story, but this does not detract from Green's originality of execution.)

Paul Green was too confirmed a poet not to emerge as one even in the realistic pictures of the South which he made his specialty. After the somewhat pedestrian didacticism of *In Abraham's Bosom,* a chronicle of the Negro's struggle for education and a place in the sun, he wrote the *Cherry Orchard* of the old South in *The House of Connelly.*

In addition, he composed numerous one-acters of Negro and Southern white life, many of them captivatingly charming and humane. Finally, in 1936, he capped his efforts in this field with the condensed chain-gang drama of *Hymn to the Rising Sun,* an ironic and agonizing study of a sadistic boss and general indictment of the Southern penal system through a vivid composite picture of its victims and their oppressor. Laved in the poetry of colloquial speech which rings out like music, this little tragedy is unquestionably one of the masterpieces of the short drama. His dramatization. *Native Son,* also had force and depth.

Marc Connelly, in addition to his collaborations with George S. Kaufman, revealed fine feeling for regional and folk drama ranging from that charming but unremarkable picture of life on the Erie Canal *The Farmer Takes a Wife* to that stunning adaptation of Roark Bradford's Negro rendition of the Bible, *The Green Pastures,* a pastiche of remarkable humor and nobility. It may be rightly regarded, despite some mixture of styles, as one of the outstanding chronicles in the history of the theatre. *Porgy* and *Mamba's Daughters* by the Heywards described the color and complications of Negro life in the South, as did William Jourdan Rapp's and Wallace Thurman's *Harlem* in the North.

John Steinbeck contributed a poignant and powerful drama of itinerant life in the profoundly human story of homelessness and simple comradeship which he lifted from his novel *Of Mice and Men.* The novelist Erskine Caldwell's horrible picture of Southern white-trash life rooting in personal and social decay made *Tobacco Road* a stark naturalist tragicomedy. A third eminent novelist Thornton Wilder graced the American theatre with an engaging reminiscence of the idyllic side of small-town life in the first two acts of *Our Town,* which affirmed the decency of common people while life is not too harassed. A third act in which some of the characters lead a ghostly existence took the play, at the price of some inconsistency, out of the category of *genre* painting and turned it into a classically poetic expression of the cycle of human existence from birth to death, even if the *genre* picture was more memorable.

More folk flavor emanated from Lynn Riggs' vigorously evoked life of the Southwest in *Green Grow the Lilacs, Cherokee Night,* and *Russet Mantle,* which added a tender regard for the disoriented younger generation; from Lulu Vollmer's *Sun-up* and other pieces; from Virgil Geddes' middle-western backgrounds (*The Earth Between* and *Native Ground*) with their excellently realized, tight-lipped but passionate and suddenly explosive natives; and from Emjo Basshe's and Arthur Kober's Jewish city types (*The Centuries* and *Having Wonderful Time*). Even Owen Davis stopped long enough in his profitable devotions to melodrama to depict New England in *The Detour, Icebound,* and the notable *Ethan Frome* adaptation, prepared in collaboration with his son. The spirit of

O'Neill rested like a fructifying cloud over most of the many efforts in this field when *Beyond the Horizon, All God's Chillun Got Wings* and *Desire Under the Elms* found such companion pieces.

8 CLIFFORD ODETS AND THE INSURGENTS

Disaffection with both the comparatively placid realism and the psychological upheavals of the twenties had flared up in the Coolidge-Hoover era. The neglect of the common worker and the conflict between capital and labor were felt to be more vital subjects for the theatre by a group of playwrights who banded themselves together under the label of the New Playwrights. Among them were Emjo Basshe, Michael Gold, the Siftons, and John Howard Lawson, and their work tried with variable results to convey this aspect of the social scene—as a rule expressionistically in the early Soviet manner. Among them Lawson alone emerged as a considerable dramatist, if not under their banner at least under the aegis of the more tranquil Theatre Guild in 1925. He merited attention with the striking "jazz-drama" of *Processional* which evoked the contradictions of American society with its labor struggles, its Ku Klux Klan antics, and its harebrained pursuit of excitement. Insurgency was already present in the gilded age.

In the depressed and shaken thirties disaffection, however, was supplanted by a veritable conflagration, and the number of playwrights who contributed fuel, sparks or dynamite comprised a legion of resolute hoplites.[4] In the inner circle of the Theatre Union the temperature was particularly intense, and out of it came the strident Paul Peters and George Sklar melodrama *Stevedore* devoted to the racial problem in the South and dedicated to the unity of the black and white worker. More impressive and far richer in characterization was Albert Maltz's picture of the mining areas and of the operation of the "blacklist" entitled *Black Pit*. Related to this theatre were also Albert Bein's affecting, if diffuse, folk drama of a textile mill strike *Let Freedom Ring*, enriched by mountaineer characters and flavorsome speech, and John Howard Lawson's diffusely poetic strike panorama *Marching Song*, written after two tentative social studies and one moderately incisive treatment of a business career in *Success Story*.

But the writers who were located on the periphery of this movement were even more effective. Some of them were actually produced under Broadway management without jeopardizing their integrity. Of these, easily the most effective and the best integrated was Lillian Hellman, whose masculine mind and vise-like grip on her characters produced two powerful plays. The first *The Children's Hour*, in 1934, was essentially a psychological tragedy caused by a neurotic brat and a homosexually inclined teacher; but associated with this theme was the related, if greatly subordinated, one of the destructive power of ready prejudice on the part of a well-to-do community. The second, *The Little Foxes,* written in 1938, drew an unmerciful picture of the rise of an American fortune, of the predatory nature of entrepreneurs who profited from industrial expansion in the nation, and of the warping of human nature produced by unlimited greed. Presented in terms of character rather than exhortation or diffuse exposition, this analysis was a notable encaustic. Even Miss Hellman's unsuccessful *Days to Come* possessed moments of astounding power.

Sidney Kingsley contributed a generally powerful picture of pungent slum life, of the making of gangsters, and of the juxtaposition of poverty and riches in *Dead End.* His dramatization *The World We Make* was an evocative and compassionate, if moderate, humanitarian drama. John Wexley, who had previously written a melodrama of prison life *The Last Mile* and a strike play *Steel* (later strengthened by revision), revealed a capacity for slashing indictment in his exposé of the Scottsboro Negro trial challengingly entitled *They Shall Not Die.* The Siftons wrote a diffuse but basically affecting case history of an unemployed worker, *1931.* George O'Neill brought poetic force to his one-act trilogy *American Dream,* a chronicle of the historic conflict between creative freedom and grasping Toryism in American life. Robert Ardrey satirized the submissive type of worker in *Casey Jones,* reflected obliquely and wryly on the struggles of the tender-minded in a dog-eat-dog world in *How to Get Tough About It,* and attempted to represent man's resources for the good life imaginatively in his *Thunder Rock.* Victor Wolfson's charming comedy *Excursion* conveyed the pressures of the day and impressed the futility of attempts to escape them by means of a tall tale about two old men who try to take their unseaworthy vessel into the South Seas. Its charm exceeded its social message by several leagues.

On the unpartisan but occasionally reformist and vitally important stage of the Federal Theatre arose a new form of expository drama, the so-called "living newspaper," exposing social problems schematically and statistically but nonetheless excitingly. The best examples were *Power* devoted to the utilities question, and the moving slum exposé *One-Third of a Nation.* The Group Theatre swinging into action in the fall of 1931 attempted anything from realism to expressionism, achieving distinction, if not mastery, in every form that could interpret contemporary forces. Potent or potentially powerful writers like Irwin Shaw, Clifford Odets, Robert Ardrey, and William Saroyan appeared under its banner. Another eclectic group, calling itself the Actor's Repertory Company, revealed Irwin Shaw's expressionistic and macabre anti-war play *Bury the Dead,* in which the dead leave the battlefield in order to win a better life in the world than had been their lot when they had been alive. This young writer revealed a fresh talent which was further attested by his full-length comedy *The Gentle People,* a symbolic representation of the revolt of the meek against their oppressors in terms of a vivid racketeer comedy which was unevenly constructed but combined humor with suggestiveness. The Repertory Company also enabled the middle-western folk painter E. P. Conkle, author of many charming little one-acters, to represent the struggle of dislocated farmers in Alaska (*Two Hundred Were Chosen*) with much color and feeling. The Mercury Theatre, essentially devoted to notable social interpretations of classics like *Julius Caesar* and *The Shoemakers' Holiday,* unfolded a highly original operetta by Marc Blitzstein, *The Cradle Will Rock*. It was the theatre that was rocked by Blitzstein's brilliantly and brashly scornful laughter at the expense of plutocracy's supporters and beneficiaries. Smaller and less expert groups, organized by the New Theatre League which had discovered Odets, Irwin Shaw, Blitzstein and other capable writers in quick succession, gave further incentives to fresh, if as yet insufficiently realized, talent.

Finally, the broadcasting field was invaded, especially Columbia's Workshop; and here two genuine triumphs of provocative imagination were scored by the excellent poet Archibald MacLeish. His *Fall of the City* presented a gripping symbolization of the coming of fascism when a city full of people capitulates to an armored figure that actually has no body in it. *Air Raid,* the second of these explosions of the ether, was a moving protest against the bombardment of civilians from the air by those who war on life itself. Both works displayed the wrought-iron poetry that MacLeish hammers out like a master.

Nevertheless, the foremost discovery of the thirties was Clifford Odets. His work began by being thoroughly inflammatory in *Waiting for Lefty* and then the fire went down appreciably later in the thirties in *Golden Boy* and *Rocket to the Moon*. But it continued to smolder, and the new pattern it wove remained the same regardless of how obliquely it reveals itself. No one gave himself to radical thought stemming from Marxist dialectics as wholeheartedly in the theatre as did Odets, just as no one succeeded in investing cold theory with so much palpitating and tormented flesh. Except perhaps in the throbbing but somewhat facilely melodramatic one-acter *Till the Day I Die* which dealt with the underground struggle against fascism in Germany against a background of unlimited terror and sadism, his diagnostic philosophy was simple enough. It consisted of two main principles: the increasing proletarianization or awakening of the middle class and the growing insurgency of the working classes. The first diagnosis appeared in his earliest play *Waiting for Lefty,* written in 1935; in those sections of this expressionistically condensed but realistically descriptive one-acter which represented professional men who had been forced into the ranks of the taxicab drivers by such factors as unemployment in the theatre, revulsion against serving munitions makers in the chemical field, or downright anti-semitism in the medical profession and discrimination against poor hospital patients. The theme reappeared in his and the present writer's favorite play *Paradise Lost* when a middle-class family loses its home in a bankruptcy and when its younger members fail to find a place in the world. The well-intentioned, humane father meets the catastrophe with a high-hearted faith in a new unmercenary world that will release the joy and greatness latent in men's hearts. *Golden Boy* called for an awakening from middle-class materialistic standards of success through a tragic demonstration of how the search for luxury warps the soul of a talented lad who becomes a pugilist. *Rocket to the Moon* (1938) showed the corrosion of life, the depletion of energy, and the frustration of love by absorption in the struggle for existence in the professions until its dentist hero Ben Stark utters a rather ambiguous, mystical faith in something better to come. In this play, the other characters are either totally warped like Mr. Prince who has acquired riches without happiness and the movie director Willy Wax who is frustrated and is apparently made neurotic by his devotion to commercialized art, or they are harassed to the point of desperation by lack of income like the other dentist Phil Cooper who becomes a blood donor. There can be no adequate lovers, Odets implied, unless men enjoy a rich inner life, which society fails to allow.

As for the playwright's account of the growing militancy of the working class, it is to be found in the general situation of *Waiting for Lefty* which reveals several workers driven to rebellion by an impoverished domestic life, by inability to find a sound economic basis for love, or by a general observation of the depressed condition of their world. The play closes with a fiery decision to strike against the taxicab owners and to make this demonstration a dress rehearsal for a general upheaval. The unproduced *Silent Partner* is another and more detailed description of a strike, and is vibrant with anger and energy. Odets' masterpiece in the opinion of most critics, *Awake and Sing*, reveals this awakening in the bosom of a seedy family. The mother has become calloused by the race with poverty, until she browbeats her ineffectual husband, forces her daughter into a loveless match, and scotches her son's budding romance with a poor orphan chiefly because marriage would stop his meager but badly needed contribution to the family's resources. In a fit of misdirected irritation she even drives her old but intelligent and sensitive father to suicide when she smashes his beloved Caruso records. But the boy who loses his girl and has been affected by his grandfather's spirit and tragic death resolves to come to grips with the world that cheats him of life even as it suppressed the old man's surging soul.

These themes are too close to the pulse of human life to be devoid of dramatic potentialities. And through Odets they find expression passionately and eagerly in nervous, poetic colloquialism. They cannot be wishfully eliminated from his special equipment for the theatre, though the validity of his thought does not necessarily bear a direct relation to the validity of his characters. Without his angry vision he, it would seem, would have been nothing. It had been fuel for his dramatic fire, and it had prompted him to searing stretches of realism and to glowing insights into character. His humor arises from his awareness of the contradictions between what the spirit desires and the flesh must deny itself in society. His eloquence is largely the product of his sympathies and indignations. His dramatic talent cannot be separated from his social animus, even when his thought is less than conclusive, in the plays written during the 'thirties.

His zeal has caused him much trouble, it is true; thus *Awake and Sing* does not really make out as good a case against the frustrations of capitalism as he thinks. The "singing and awakening" are pseudo-revolutionary pabulum when his promiscuous heroine elopes with the small-time racketeer for whom she abandons her infant without, moreover, the slightest certainty that she will find happiness with him. Her supposedly newly enlightened brother's approval of this step as an act of genuine liberation also casts suspicion on the nature of his own enlightenment. In *Golden Boy* the case history is wobbly because the tragedy of a promising violinist's success as a prize-fighter seems obviously contrived in order to prove a point. If his sacrifice of art to expediency is intended to be symbolic of capitalistic evil, it is too literal to serve as a symbol. In *Rocket to the Moon*, eagerness to combine various facets of the social stalemate caused the overzealous author to pack his play with ill-matched, if diagnostically related, case histories. Clifford Odets tended to blame too many psychic disturbances on the social system in the same play, causing him, for example, to overcrowd and weaken the analysis of middle-class bankruptcy in *Paradise Lost*. Not only does such diagnosis sometimes seem categorical and strained, although it gives his work an extension that carries him beyond literal realism (so much so, that *Paradise Lost* must not be construed as a family picture at all but as a suggestive condensation of a historic process), but it cannot be made wholly convincing in the theatre because three short acts are too skimpy for sufficient elaboration. Still, this playwright's zeal was a necessary ferment in his work; and to it were allied the intensity and compassion that so often won acclaim from even those critics who rejected his ideas.

It is certain that his analyses or ideas were frequently less overwhelming than his dramatic effects, and that the latter are ecompassed almost independently of his philosophy by his specific style and method. Critics have therefore found it quite easy to divorce his ideology from his dramatic impact. One notes the lambent dialogue so faithful to colloquialism and yet so essentially transubstantiated by a musician's poetry and imagery. (Odets is indeed an ardent if unprofessional musician.) At its worst his dialogue is mannered, gratuitously "wise-cracking," somewhat callow, and quite banally hortatory as when a striker cries out, "Put fruit trees where our ashes are." Odets can be considerably irritating in this respect. But when he is at his best, his words rise naturally from his characters and possess a highly dramatic, explosive quality. Moreover, he is an accomplished polyphonist; the characters speak at cross purposes, sometimes at the same time, and their lines match only polyphonically or contrapuntally.

His portraits are externally vivid and inwardly volcanic. The characters are not only as a rule people seen in the round but they are naturally dramatic personalities because they are treated with intense concern regardless of their contradictions and eccentricities, which may even give rise to slightly deprecatory laughter at their expense. *Awake and Sing* is more persuasive as a collection of characters than any philosophy they enunciate or any solution they determine upon, even if it could be granted that they find a solution. If, as Mrs. Isaacs maintains,[5] most of the characters "are clichés," they are clichés with a difference, for they have been projected through a temperament. They gain dimension, sometimes from an impression of significance provided by the fact that they represent a harassed world but mostly from their creator's highly personal—sometimes naïve—attitude toward them. He caresses his familiar stock figures with an impassioned belief in them until the spectator frequently also believes—at least at the performance—in their uniqueness even against his better judgment. There are times when one is inclined to believe that Odets could galvanize a corpse into providing an illusion of life. Whether this is invariably a virtue is, of course, another matter, since it is unfortunately too easy to question the author's rather undiscriminating evaluation of people. There is, for example, the case of the dentist's office girl in *Rocket to the Moon* who strikes us as too silly to command commiseration both for herself and her suitor when the dentist fails to take her for his own.

Finally, he often compels attention through his uneven but curiously forceful dramatic structure. It is sometimes loose and sometimes somewhat illogical, and yet it weaves a fine pattern in *Awake and Sing* or combines rapid and intense sequences as in *Waiting for Lefty, Till the Day I Die,* and *Golden Boy.* If, as Lawson declared, Odets is a scene-wright rather than a playwright (and this is true insofar as individual scenes are better than the play which contains them or are perfect gems when the play as a whole is decidedly imperfect!), it must be conceded that a man who creates scenes that can lift a spectator out of his seat is more valuable than a writer who can hammer a commonplace piece together without leaving any crevices. This, of course, does not wholly acquit him as a playwright. Yet it may explain the immediate dramatic impression Odets so frequently makes. His craftsmanship may be described as an electric spark that leaps the gaps in his structure and often gives a greater impression of unity than he actually provides; this is the case in *Waiting for Lefty, Awake and Sing,* and *Golden Boy.* It is after all one way, though not necessarily the best, of attaining an effect. He also favors symbolizations, and while this redounds to his credit as an aspiring dramatist it often proves tenuous or elusive; such was the case in the beautifully phantasmagoric *Paradise Lost* which fails when it is subjected to the test of plain realism. (A test that the author himself seemed but did not wish to invite.) This was also true of *Golden Boy.* Here the sheer melodrama of a bedeviled prizefighter's career made the symbolization of the social system, upon which both the author and his Group Theatre director Harold Clurman insisted, somewhat strained.

Odets, in spite of his errors in dramatic logic and lapses in taste, was nonetheless the major discovery of the social theatre of the nineteen-thirties. His flame leapt higher and burned more intensely than that of any of his emergent contemporaries. He was the natural lyricist of the common life. If his star declined in the nineteen-forties, it was not for want of talent. His major problem was one of orienting himself in a decade unfavorable to a writer of his volatile temperament and his tendency to join realism and social allegory with an imperfect marriage license.

At the end of the decade, the Group Theatre uncovered another vastly promising playwright who, however contained the seeds of disintegration in his indisicipline. He was the novelist and short-story writer William Saroyan (1908–   ), who first transferred his talent to the stage effectively with the long one-act play *My Hearts in the Highlands* a poignant caprice about an eccentric poet and his young son, produced in the spring of 1939. It was followed in the fall of that fateful year by *The Time of Your Life,* a compassionate extravaganza of life in a waterfront dive. Spontaneity and improvisation marked these plays, and his creative buoyancy kept much naive optimism and much sentimentality attractively afloat in his work. There could be little doubt that Saroyan had genius; it was less evident that he had talent and patience to meet the exactions of steady playwriting. Still, even his later work in the next decade — especially, the one-act realistic masterpiece *Hello, Out There* (1942) and the poetic, if disorderly, fugue *The Beautiful People* (1941) — refreshed the Broadway theatre. He was no thinker, and he held both logic and "play structure" in contempt. Yet even his dadaism or surrealism was freshened by a breezy American plebeianism.[6]

The times were not favorable to optimism. Yet partly owing to the brave spirit the theatre had manifested in the Depression period of the 'thirties, the present author was able to confront the dreaded 'forties with the following conclusion to the original 1940 edition of *Masters of the Drama:*

No *finis* can be written to the story of the drama, not even now that Europe is fighting its second great war since 1914. The theatre's search goes on, and its object is, as it has always been, Man. What will follow is far from certain. But what has already happened is evident. A great art has transcribed mankind's errors and aspirations for nearly three thousand years and has conveyed both its bestiality and divinity. This art has survived many catastrophes. It will no doubt survive the imminent ones of our times. And its three-thousand-year-old meaning, through what seems to be indomitable laughter and tragic bravery, is that man will somehow survive—probably to blunder but seek again and perhaps to find a way of life that the spirit can some day regard without a shudder. Over the entrance to every honorable theatre—whether it be devoted to laughter or suffering—one might confidently engrave two ancient and indispensable words: *Nil Desperandum*—Never Despair.   1940

SUPPLEMENT

1940-1945: THE TERRIBLE INTERIM

Hardly had the brave words of the conclusion to this volume gone to press in the spring of 1940 than the entire world seemed to be furiously bent upon tearing every shred of validity from them. Nation after nation, along with the culture vested in its theatre, was virtually expunged by the Teutonic hordes. The Dark Ages seemed to have descended again upon Western civilization, and it is only at the present writing—in the spring of 1945—that the darkness has begun to lift. Perhaps only a detached historian, for whom five years would be but a flicker in the general flux, could have concluded that the prophetic close of this book would not suffer the fate of most prognostications.

The few surviving national theatres of any consequence were variously constricted or paralyzed. In the first years of the war, the *blitz* closed the London houses, and the Soviet theatre moved beyond the Volga and behind the Urals. Even when, and where, the physical circumstances were more favorable, the creative climate was clouded. The English playwrights were, with very few exceptions, ineffectual; their response was limited to feeble expositions of the crisis and banal accounts of heroism; none of their stage plays came within hailing distance of Noel Coward's film *In Which We Serve,* perhaps because no neat little play could contain the epic of Britain's heroic stand. The Soviet writers understandably limited themselves to plays about the war, patriotic exhortations, and resuscitations of the past from which the Russian people might derive comfort and hope. Less understandably, perhaps, American dramatists were at first too paralyzed by the crisis to make a contribution worthy of the occasion; and again, because their medium had lost epic extension except in the biographical genre, their actual representations of the war were overshadowed by war films, especially documentaries.

Nevertheless, the stage held its ground, even if it provided no masterpieces. The Soviet theatre gave an unequalled account of itself as a morale-building force, and a glowing story remains to be written about its contribution to the Russian war-effort. The Red Army Theatre was playing *A Midsummer Night's Dream* when the German hordes crossed the Western borders. All theatres in the invasion area were removed intact and continued to function behind, and on many occasions at, the widening front. After Pearl Harbor, the American theatre roused itself to a splendid effort that carried volunteer troupes to all parts of the globe.

Finally, the dramatists, in both their few successes and many failures, accounted for themselves sufficiently to make a continuous record. Among the exiled German and Austrian writers, Georg Kaiser, located in Switzerland, where he died in 1945, acquitted himself of a penetrating and affecting play about the benighted soldiery of Japan, *The Soldier Tanaka,* which will probably be appreciated better when our passions give way to equable understanding. Franz Werfel turned out one of his finest plays, *Jacobowsky and the Colonel,* a comedy wrung out of the depths of defeat. There was a witty evocation of the conflict between two worlds—the feudal and the modern, the aristocrat's and the commoner's—in the story of the flight of a Polish Colonel and a Jew in the company of a French woman. Bert Brecht, the ablest German poet, reached the peak of his dramatic powers in a remarkably provocative fable set in China, *Der Gute Mensch von Setzuan* (The Good Woman of Setzuan), dedicated to the theme of how the people of good will must acquire the strength to cope with impositions upon them, and in *The Private Life of the Master Race* (published in English by New Directions), an epic chronicle of the corruption of the German populace. Ferdinand Bruckner, famous for his psychological *Sickness of Youth*, wrote several intelligent social dramas, including a profound play on Bolivar; adapted his psychological drama *Criminals* so that it became an illuminating study of moral disintegration in Germany on the eve of Hitler's triumph; and made a version of Lessing's *Nathan the Wise* which graced New York briefly with its gospel of tolerance. Erwin Piscator founded a Studio Theatre in New York which brought forth several valuable productions of foreign and American plays, among them Dan James' *Winter Soldiers*, the best treatment of the European underground. In short, the conscience of the German social theatre managed to persist in exile.

A new playwright of promise, the poet and able journalist Konstantin Simonov (*Fellow From Our Town* and *The Russian People*) won acclaim in Russia and gained some international recognition. Early in the war, the Russian stage lost one of its ablest men in Afinogenov during a bombardment, but not before he had produced the appealing war play *On The Eve* and a genial humanistic little comedy *Listen Professor*, in which an antiquarian leaves his shell to stand on common ground with the younger generation.

Noel Coward wrote his most imaginative and maturest play *Blithe Spirit*, the comedy of a husband who finds himself the object of contention between his ghostly first wife and his jealous second mate, during the darkest hours of England's history. The Welsh actor, Emlyn Williams, turned out a noble drama, *The Corn Is Green*, on the eve of the war. It would be difficult to find a better evocation of British idealism than this story of a spinsterly educator's work among the underprivileged children of Wales and her discovery of a rare talent in the environs of a colliery. In America, the play provided Ethel Barrymore with her greatest role. Rodney Ackland wrote a diagnosis of England's pre-war fumblings, *The Dark River*, a Chekhovian work of distinction that was too pessimistic for the contemporary scene. A new and rare, and as yet insufficiently recognized, talent appeared in the work of Vivian Connell, author of a searing drama of decadence in Ireland *Throng of Scarlet*, set among the fox-hunting and hard drinking gentry, and a terrifying forecast of disaster, *The Fourteenth Hole of Europe*. Living in voluntary exile from the Irish Free State and mingling realism and lyricism, Sean O'Casey turned out three challenging dramas, *The Star Turns Red, Red Roses For Me*, and *Purple Dust*, the first two devoted to revolutionary idealism, the third an extravagant satire on the English in Ireland. Although somewhat inchoate and produced only unprofessionally, each new O'Casey work nevertheless excelled in poetic inspiration and incisive satire. John Van Druten, who transplanted himself to America, amplified his talents to the point of turning out three distinguished comedies, *Old Acquaintance, The Damask Cheek*, and *The Voice of The Turtle*, and made a superb dramatization of life among the Scandinavian Americans, *I Remember Mama*.

Finally, among American playwrights, Maxwell Anderson treated the war in three plays, *Candle in the Wind*, which entailed noble utterance and some striking scenes; *The Eve of St. Mark*, a fairly effective, if uneven, account of a young American's emergence from the simplicities of farm life and romance to tragic heroism; and the largely unsuccessful *Storm Operation*. Paul Green made a vigorous dramatization of Richard Wright's *Native Son*, a realistic study of the effects of racial discrimination in the case of a bedevilled Negro. Clifford Odets wrote a parable for the times in *Clash By Night*, an ill-fated but by no means unworthy tragedy of the confusion and humiliations of the submerged little men of the world and their susceptibility to the poison of fascism. Lillian Hellman added a forceful, if insufficiently integrated, chronicle of the shameful decade of appeasements and evasions that led to the war, *The Searching Wind*. This was preceded by the moving drama *Watch on the Rhine*, in which a German underground worker and a decadent tool of the Nazis fought out their battle on American soil; the play presaged America's own involvement in the war. Sidney Kingsley recapitulated with some force the formative struggle of American democracy in *The Patriots*, in which Jefferson and Hamilton were the antagonists. Robert Sherwood turned to the current scene with *There Shall be No Night*, set first in Finland and later, for London production, in Greece. In essence, and quite apart from the originally pro-Finnish political setting (before Russia became an Ally), this play dramatized the transformation of a pacifist into a militant opponent of fascism. In *The Skin of Our Teeth*, a worthy successor to *Our Town*, Thornton Wilder wrote a fantastic parable of man's precarious struggle for civilization. Telescoping time and the problems of man's existence since the Ice Age, *The Skin of Our Teeth* was America's most original dramatic composition during the dark interim of the war.

The nimble wit and stylistic refinement of S. N. Behrman were fairly in evidence in the comedy of domestic tyranny *The Talley Method* and in his sprightly adaptations of *The Pirate* (based on a German play by Ludwig Fulda) and *Jacobowsky and the Colonel*. Moss Hart, without benefit of collaboration by George S. Kaufman, produced a theatrical *tour de force* in the psychoanalytical musical play *Lady in the Dark*, and wrote an ambitious chronicle of the air force in *Winged Victory*. Although William Saroyan's later work failed to match his first plays, he continued to contribute a quality of inspired, if half-realized, improvisation, and in the case of *The Beautiful People* created a mild but enchanting poetic play. In one singular instance, *Oklahoma*, an adaptation of Lynn Riggs' *Green Grow the Lilacs* by Richard Rodgers and Oscar Hammerstein II, the American theatre acquired a musical masterpiece that was utterly entrancing. It opened the sluices of invention in the musical genre, and introduced native ballet styles as an integral part of musical comedy.

As the darkness started to lift, the commercial stage in .America made a remarkable recovery. By the spring of 1945, there was a boom in the theatre that seemed well-nigh miraculous. The soaring national income was the ferment in Broadway's box-office receipts, but this was abetted by acceptable achievements in dramaturgy and stagecraft. Among these were the winningly human reminiscence, *I Remember Mama*, an enchanting comedy *Harvey* by Mary Ellen Chase, the astutely contrived dramatization *The Late George Apley* (by Kaufman out of the John Marquand novel), Paul Osborn's dramatization of *A Bell for Adano* which was a touching tribute to American idealism in international relations, and John Patrick's moving war play *The Hasty Heart*.

In this resurgent season, too, George Kelly returned to the *Craig's Wife* theme with a unique study of feminine egotism *The Deep Mrs. Sykes*, spare and static but distinguished in style, as well as incisive. And to climax the renascence, the American theatre brought forth *The Glass Menagerie*, a collective triumph for the producer Eddie Dowling, the notable actress Laurette Taylor, and a newly discovered dramatist Tennessee Williams, whose intense drama of small town frustration, *The Battle of Angels*, had been shelved several seasons earlier in Boston by the Theatre Guild, and whose distinguished one-acters were still unknown on Broadway. Imaginatively constructed, cast in the form and style of reminiscence, *The Glass Menagerie* translated a depression story into a sensitive character drama. It gave evocative realization to the ineffectual struggles of a small family—a seedy Southern woman who clung to the memory of better days, her painfully shy crippled daughter for whom the mother tried to find "a gentleman caller," and a restive poetic son who, tiring of perpetual nagging, ran away from home after the tragi-comic fiasco of bringing an already affianced young man for his sister.

It is only regrettable that the American war-time theatre was deprived of the services of several of its strongest dramatists. At the very beginning of the war the stage lost one of its ablest craftsmen and noblest spirits, Sidney Howard. After having contributed greatly to the progress of realism in the 'twenties, he had begun to experiment in more imaginative forms with his memorable *Yellow Jack* (see p. 684), and shortly before his untimely end he had turned out *Madam, Will You Walk*. This posthumous fantasy on the theme of Dionysian release, of the unshackling of the soul through zestful wooing of life's possibilities, awaits interesting materialization on the stage. Howard's second posthumous work *Lute Song*, an able and never esoteric adaptation of a Chinese classic with Will Irwin (see p. 135), was another challenge to creative stagecraft. Howard departed from the theatre when it had the most need of his unique combination of social vision and craftsmanship. His compeer Robert Sherwood directed his energies into the important channels of the war-effort. Eugene O'Neill continued with his mighty labors in seclusion.

XXXI

MIDCENTURY THEATRE AND DRAMA

I POST-WAR PLAYWRIGHTS AND REPUTATIONS

IN IMMEDIATE perspective, it did not appear that theatre after the Second World War was undergoing any particular transformation, or that any remarkable upsurge of dramatic writing was taking place. No millenial hopes were realized for either the drama or society. Reconstruction in war-shattered Europe was impeded or impaired by new political crises, as the Western democratic powers began to collide with the interests and designs of Soviet Russia.

If interest was warranted in the stage and in playwriting, this was due largely to the continuance of pre-war and war-time courses by a few new playwrights whose work was indicative of a mettlesome spirit or an adventurous mind, and by older practitioners of the drama, who traversed ground already more or less familiar to them. The only other important development in the international theatre came from the growing reputation of Paul Claudel, Jean Giraudoux, Federico Garcìa Lorca, and Henry de Montherlant, who had been previously favored only locally, or only by coteries and specialists. It is an important event when a distinguished dramatist of hitherto narrowly limited reputation has his plays read and performed outside his own group or country. His plays then enrich the world theatre and influence contemporary or future playwriting. A playwright belongs to two periods — that in which he wrote, and that in which his plays received public and, if possible, international recognition.

The few young playwrights of America and England who emerged or grew in stature during the 1945–50 period revealed talent without effecting any remarkable change in dramatic style and form except in departing from commonplace realism. The most important of these — Tennessee Williams, Arthur Miller, and Christopher Fry — had developed to a considerable degree under pre-war and war-time dispensations: Miller, for example, derived his art from the theatre of social consciousness that had flourished during the nineteen-thirties in America; Fry, from a turn toward verse drama in pre-war England. Tennessee Williams was discovered in 1940 and wrote one of his best plays before the surrender of Germany. The American and British

theatres, besides, continued to draw most of their literary sustenance
from men and women of earlier generations, such as O'Casey, O'Neill,
T. S. Eliot, Maxwell Anderson, Clifford Odets, Lillian Hellman, James
Bridie, J. B. Priestley. Only Eliot altered his dramatic form after
1945. The other writers had already solidified their art and craftsmanship.

The situation on the European continent was not conspicuously
different. The French theatre resumed its liveliness, but the most
impressive dramatic work came mostly from writers whose modes of
thinking and writing had been formed in previous decade; or, as in
the case of Jean-Paul Sartre, during the war period. After 1945, the
theatre in Austria and Germany showed signs of recovery from the
blight that Hitler had inflicted on the arts, but the men who contributed the most invigorating force, Carl Zuckmayer and Bertolt Brecht,
had won their reputations more than two decades earlier. In the
Scandinavian countries, the stage continued to have an honorable
position. Among the successors of Ibsen and Strindberg, however,
only the reflective Swedish novelist and playwright Pär Lagerkvist
(born in 1891) made some impression beyond Sweden, and only one
new Swedish writer, Stig Dagerman (born in 1923), revealed any
promise of distinction; mainly with his first play, *The Condemned*
(performed in 1947), an inquiry into the ironies of justice and fate.

In the other national theatres even less progress was evident. Even
when stage production attained proficiency, playwriting was at a low
ebb for one reason or another. The Russian theatre, largely given
over to "Socialist realism" except for folk art and musical productions, ceased to be on speaking terms with the West as a result of
growing international tensions. Apparently, all the Soviet playwrights, including the once promising journalist-dramatist Simonov,
subordinated their craft to the uses of propaganda, chiefly anti-
American, and flayed Western capitalism. Spain, still under the rule
of Franco, gave no evidence of any vital dramatic activity; and in
Latin America, where theatrical activity was abundant, the drama
remained only locally interesting, although there appeared to be some
possibility that the Mexican writers Rodolfo Usigli and Xavier Vil-
laurrutia, who had already made a start in the nineteen-thirties, would
become better known.

The Russian theatre's contribution to the Western world continued
to be largely its pre-Soviet drama, especially the plays of Chekhov.
His name continued to be invoked again and again, whenever new
works revealed some use of counterpoint. Italy's contribution to
modern drama continued to be associated almost entirely with the work

of Pirandello.* A hitherto unknown but extremely attractive, un-metaphysical comedy of his, *Liolà*, was staged in Italy during the 1950–51 season by Eric Bentley. The Spanish theatre derived international significance largely by virtue of the reputation of its distinguished poet-playwright Lorca, whose death in 1936 had been a prelude to the extinction of progressive theatre in Spain. Although productions of his plays failed to prove successful in the United States, his genius was freely acknowledged, and his work considered a landmark in the modern theatre's exploratory efforts to achieve poetic drama. His importance was likely to grow with the years. and his example could be studied instructively by aspiring playwrights. In any examination of the midcentury drama, Lorca may well figure prominently. The future of the modern theatre may depend largely on solutions of the problems of form and style suggested by his work, as well as by the previous experiments of Strindberg, O'Neill, and Pirandello and the continuing experiments of Eliot and Brecht.

2 LORCA AND POETIC DRAMA

It is generally held that Federico García Lorca (1899–1936) reached the peak of his dramatic art in his least stylized and most realistic prose drama. *The House of Bernarda Alba* (1936), written shortly before a Falangist band executed him. This sensitive and intense drama, which presents the frustration of the unmarried daughters of a proud Spanish matriarch, is a penetratingly candid study, and it mounts in tension as it moves toward the suicide of one daughter and the resigned anguish of her sisters. At the same time, Lorca made effective use of poetic overtones. The piece is drenched in an atmosphere of gloom lit up by flashes of rebellion in the case of the daughter who loves her elder sister's fiancé. For a playwright who was no more than thirty-seven at the time of his death, *Bernarda Alba*, subtitled "A Drama about Women in the Villages of Spain," was a remarkable achievement and a promise of masterpieces to come. This should be apparent even if the situation is too Spanish to communicate its passion to the American playgoer without some risk of seeming overstrained and redundant. Here Lorca created a naturalistic prose-poetry, combining realistic exposition with theatre of local color.

* That Pirandello's interest in metaphysical questions and unusual states of mind was still strong could be seen in such an operatic treatment of the quality of love and hate as Ugo Betti's fantasy *The Gambler*, presented in New York in 1952, and in the plays of Eduardo de Filippo, such as *The Big Magic* and *Fear Number One*, not yet produced in English (in 1953). See: *In Search of Theatre*, by Eric Bentley, 1953, pp. 281–95.

Nevertheless, Lorca may be regarded as more unique and exciting when he wrote stylized imaginative drama, rooted both in folk art and in the formalistic traditions of Spain's Golden Age of the late sixteenth and early seventeenth centuries. It was in these plays that this playwright, internationally celebrated for his lyrics and ballads, was most truly a poet in the theatre. His flame leaped highest in *Blood Wedding* (1933) and *Yerma* (1934), the former a fatalistic love story that attains the estate of high tragedy; the latter, a pulsating drama of a woman consumed with the craving for fertility while her husband persists in denying her a child. Passion flares up into violence in both dramas. In *Blood Wedding*, a bridegroom and his rival, a married man, slay each other in a knife-to-knife duel in a moonlit forest after the latter has abducted the bride. In *Yerma,* the desperate wife, whose yearnings are projected, atmospherically, in folk scenes and, symbolically, in the person of a lusty old Crone, strangles her husband.

In the more stylized of the two pieces, *Blood Wedding*, Lorca employed lyricism in a highly dramatic manner. He made powerful use of a wild and heart-breaking lullaby, of wedding songs that are intensely ironic since the bride loves another man, and of a choral dirge at the end that surpasses anything of its kind in dramatic literature after Euripides. These poems are written with the poignant simplicity of folk art. In intense situations, the dialogue becomes formal poetry; and even the prose passages are poetically charged. The variable atmosphere is always evocative and expresses the situation and the mood of the characters. In the forest scene, the lyricism of the hidden lovers attains the ecstasy of a "love-death," a *Liebestod*. In the same scene, while they are expecting the vengeance-bent bridegroom, the fateful atmosphere is intensified by the appearance of two allegorical figures: the Moon, which conceals them when it disappears and betrays them when it reappears, and a Beggar Woman who represents Death.

Blood Wedding is a work of poetic and theatrical genius, and its poetry and formalism dignify human passion. It is reported that Lorca found the germ of his play in a newspaper report, but waited many years before writing *Blood Wedding*. He was distancing and universalizing the original story, until he could transcend its commonplaceness and give it tragic significance. Lorca, here, as elsewhere, achieved a unique synthesis of folk art and highly sophisticated art. This was primarily the result of his possessing both poetic and dramatic genius. But he was spurred on by the responsiveness to folk theatre that led him to direct, from 1931 to 1934, the traveling company *La Baracca* that played in rural bull-rings and innyards.

In addition to the above-mentioned tragedies, Lorca also wrote a number of stylized farces, among which *The Love of Don Perlimpin and Belisa in the Garden* is the most poetic and *The Shoemaker's Wonderful Wife* the most vivacious. In these and other plays, his success lay in a bold theatricalization of the drama. Perhaps the most important task that faces the modern playwright is precisely this recovery of poetic and theatrical imagination after the long reign of realistic form and style. Although Lorca was not, of course, the first or only playwright to accept this assignment, his efforts remain memorable because they were so complete in artistry and so pure in spirit. His art was naturally passionate and naturally lyrical. There was neither intellectual pretentiousness nor straining for effect in it. His dramatic art was rooted in his instinct for life and in the impulses and traditions of the common man. His dramatic sophistication — that is, his stylization of the drama — was "unsophisticated." It had nothing in common with the *coterie* experimentation of Parisian dadaism and *surréalisme* (although he assimilated surrealism in his poetry), with the frenzy of German expressionism, or with the intellectualism of Pirandello. His reliance on folk art and the folk spirit was not condescension on his part. Lorca had a gift that has been especially rare in modern times — a born poet's power of achieving identity with nature, with his people, and with national tradition. Most modern artists have had a genius for disorientation; Lorca had a genius for orientation or integration — and this in spite of his awareness of the divisions and pressures of modern life.

3 POST-WAR GERMAN THEATRE: BRECHT AND ZUCKMAYER

In the German-speaking world, the most notable theatrical developments came from Bertolt Brecht (1898–), not only a distinguished poet and playwright but an original stage director. Applying his "epic theatre" philosophy, Brecht favored detached artistry as against a theatre of complete illusion and empathy; this, on the grounds that the stage should enlighten rather than induce emotional orgies. His productions, with only partial scenery and non-Stanislavskian acting, contributed a distinctive type of stylization. The presentation of plays by Brecht, plays that could not be shown in Germany from 1933 to 1945, was also an invigorating influence in a country that had been rampantly anti-intellectual for a dozen years under Hitler. Special attention was paid in Central Europe to his original and powerful chronicle of the Thirty Years' War in Germany, *Mother Courage*, which Brecht had written in exile at the beginning of the Second

World War. Interest was aroused not only in Germany but in Italy by his *Herr Puntila und sein Knecht Matti* (*Mr. Puntila and his Servant Matti*), a satirical extravaganza on the relations between master and man. His parables, *The Caucasian Circle of Chalk* and *The Good Woman of Setzuan*, written while Brecht had been in exile in the United States, were especially worth noting as examples of the wide range of his theatrical and poetic talent.

Brecht became the favorite son of the Eastern Zone, although he also managed to have his plays produced west of the "iron curtain." A conflict with censorious communism in eastern Berlin over an opera, for which he had written the libretto, did not seriously affect his status in 1951. The onus rested mainly on the music, and Brecht readily conceded ideological "errors" on his own part. In the United States, he remained a shadowy figure for the general public, but found a vigorous advocate, as well as translator, in the critic Eric Bentley. The stage director Joseph Losey also interested himself in Brecht, as did several other men and women of the theatre. Among these was Charles Laughton, who translated Brecht's biographical drama *Galileo* and played the role of the Renaissance scientist in a Broadway experimental production. Brecht brought inventive dramaturgy and pungent dialogue, as well as vigorous lyrics, to the theatre. He became an important figure in European drama and stage production as an opponent of the realistic convention and of the Aristotelian differentiation between dramatic and epic art. Although he revealed no inclination to accept Soviet-inspired "Socialist Realism" in his work, he was the foremost "anti-bourgeois" writer of the European theatre.

In the Western zone, Carl Zuckmayer (1896–   ) made a strong impression with two plays. He had been previously identified not only with delightful folk comedies but with the trenchant anti-militaristic satire *The Captain of Koepenick* (1930). His first new play to be produced after his repatriation, *Des Teufels General* (*The Devil's General*), became the most successful new drama to be seen in Germany. Written in America (original version, 1942; revised version, 1945; first published in Stockholm, 1946), *The Devil's General* had temporary interest as a tragedy of conscience. It revolves around a commander of Hitler's air-force who is torn between his professional pride and his contempt for the cause he is serving, once he realizes its baseness. Thematic interest, rich characterization, and immensely effective dialogue are here combined with a begging of the questions of guilt and expiation that exercised German intellectuals during and after the National Socialist terror. Zuckmayer published in 1951 a second — and fervidly "operatic" — study of guilt and conscience, *Der Gesang im Feuerofen*, which may be translated as *The Song in the Fiery Furnace.* Mingling realism with poetic allegory in this work, Zuckmayer dealt with the subject of hatred as the evil that destroys men and societies. *Der Gesang im Feuerofen* is a psychological story of a traitor to the resistance movement who was driven to treachery by his sense of inferiority and his consuming envy. Zuckmayer managed to convey a poet's and a humanist's view of the corruption of the German spirit with considerable dramatic effect.

4 POST-WAR FRENCH THEATRE: JOUVET AND BARRAULT

In France, theatrical art was somewhat haphazard and makeshift. Nevertheless, Paris remained a vital center of theatre. *The Comédie Française* acquired new polish and vivacity in both classic and modern repertory. The master of French theatrical art, Jacques Copeau (1878–1949), continued to exert an influence in spite of his retirement from the field of stage production. His former students and his disciples continued to be active in the Parisian theatre. Among these was Charles Dullin (1885–1949), who had toured unoccupied France during the war. Famous for his imaginative productions of Pirandello, Shakespeare and Ben Jonson, Dullin invigorated the Parisian stage until his death.

Copeau's distinguished disciple Louis Jouvet (1887–1951) was again active in the post-war period. He had his own theatrical company, and brought it to New York in the season of 1950–51 under the auspices of the American National Theatre and Academy. Here, his skill as an actor and his sense of stylization in stage production were still manifest when he presented Molière's *School for Wives*, a production for which he had been famous for some time. Neither in New York nor in France did Jouvet reveal any augmentation of his long recognized artistry. Jouvet, however, remained a force in the French theatre until his death. He gave Paris a memorable production of Jean Giraudoux' notable extravaganza *The Madwoman of Chaillot* and effective revivals of Molière's plays.

The setting for *The School for Wives*, replete with espaliered trees and artificial garden-beds, was a picturesque, mobile design by Christian Bérard that opened and closed like a toy. It gave visual realization to the grace and charm of baroque comedy in Louis XIV's time. Bérard, who had also created the internationally famous setting for *The Madwoman of Chaillot*, was France's most gifted stage designer. His influence on scenic art was one of the more gratifying features of the French theatre.

The freshest talent belonged to Dullin's pupil, Jean-Louis Barrault (1911–   ), best known in America for his memorable performance of the Harlequin or Pierrot in the French film *Children of Paradise*. Shortly after the war, Barrault established himself in the *Théâtre*

Marigny, where his mastery of style, especially his great art of panto-mime, was in evidence. Here, he gave notable productions of Paul Claudel's poetic tragedy *Partage de Midi* and of *The State of Siege,* a dramatization of Albert Camus' famous existentialist novel *The Plague.* In the early post-war period, Barrault also provided the *Comédie Française* with some noteworthy productions, the best of which was Claudel's *Le Soulier de Satin,* or *The Satin Slipper.* In the opinion of some observers, Barrault attained the peak of his artistry when he played Hamlet in a new French translation made by André Gide. In the summer of 1950, Barrault toured South America.

In the history of theatre and drama, Barrault became of prime importance because his art made a connection between modern stage production and the age-long vital tradition of the Roman mime and the Italian *Commedia dell'arte.* Although attentive to the demands of diction, maintaining that "the visual and auditory sensations must crystallize into a unity for the actor as well as the audience," he was unique in the emphasis he placed on "the art of gesture." He dedi-cated himself to "the recreation of life by gesture" neglected in the modern theatre. For this purpose, he returned to concepts af acting that the realistic theatre had gradually driven from the boards toward the end of the nineteenth century.

In a sense, Barrault also associated himself with the ideals of the art theatre promulgated many decades earlier by Gordon Craig and others in reaction to naturalistic or "photographic" theatre. He held that theatre is an artifice, like the wooden box we call a violin, and that the pleasure of art lies in instilling life into the artifice. One must proceed toward the imitation(recreation?) of life by artificial means. Consequently, the actor should have some quality of the robot in him — a view that reflects, if it does not entirely coincide with, Gordon Craig's dream of supplanting the erratic living actor with a *super-marionette.* (See Barrault's *Pantomime,* translated by Eric Bentley, in *Actors on Acting,* edited by Toby Cole and Helen Krich Chinoy, pp. 230–33, Crown Publishers, 1949, New York.) Since Barrault, nonetheless, was attentive to the *emotions* of the "mime," he also practiced the theatre of inner feeling that Stanislavsky had promoted — first by his work with the Moscow Art Theatre, and then by irradiation of stage art in the rest of the Western world.

Here we are most concerned, however, with the nature of the drama on the French stage. Parisian playwriting still favored the kind of fluffy, deftly composed, often risqué, boulevard fare upon which no important theatre can nourish itself. Nevertheless, an "existentialist" movement, started by Sartre during the war, proved invigorating, and more sustenance was at hand from several pre-war writers. A revival of interest in Paul Claudel (1868–   ), due in part to the resurgence of Catholicism in Europe, brought new recognition to a poet-playwright whose spiritual austerity had long lacked popularity. Considerable national and international renown came, in addition, to the established playwrights Jean Giraudoux, who died before the liberation of France, and Jean Anouilh, who had begun to attract attention in France during the decade of the 'thirties.

5 PAUL CLAUDEL

Claudel's plays are "cases of conscience" and, therefore, require elaborate exposition and expostulation. To the reader or playgoer accustomed to the pace of modern realistic drama, they must appear extremely static. His prolix dramas resemble a ship so ballasted down in dock that it remains stuck there. Yet in Claudel's case, the ship is constantly rocked by the tide of human passion. In his plays, as previously in Corneille's, drama consists, so an admirer noted, not of "things happening" but of "existence intensified by conflict."

The Satin Slipper derives its title from the action of an unhappy wife who takes off one of her satin slippers and puts it into the hands of a statue of the Virgin, in order that she may walk lamely toward the sin of adultery she is provoked to commit. This act is a fitting symbol of Claudelian drama, in which conflict emanates from the fact that passion is one pressing reality and that adherence to a moral and religious standard constitutes another inexorable reality. There would be less turbulence in the plays if there were less belief or religion in them. If one has any further doubts that Claudel can create dramatic intensity after reading *The Satin Slipper*, certainly a reading of that fierce, if verbose, drama of adultery and penitence *Partage de Midi* will dispel them.

The one, earlier expressed, doubt (p. 417) that the present author retains concerning Claudel is whether he actually belongs to the stream of modern theatre. *The Satin Slipper* was written in the period immediately after World War I, about 1921. It was first produced at the *Comédie Française* in 1943 when Occupied France needed whatever consolations of religion it could derive from this poet who, upon recovering his Catholic faith at Notre-Dame in Paris in 1886, became one of the most ardent of modern mystics, without, however, retreating from reality. Instead, he pursued a long and distinguished diplomatic career from 1893 to 1934, leaving no doubt as to his knowledge of the world, the flesh, and the Devil. (He was consul for France in the United States, China, Germany, and Italy, and ambassador to Japan, the United States, and Belgium). Yet, *The Satin Slipper* has slipped back into semi-obscurity, along with other Claudel plays, and it is unlikely to make any dent in the English-speaking professional theatre.

Claudel's work, nevertheless, is ultra-modern in some respects. His mysticism is not a fragile and delicately scented flower, blossoming in a herbarium. He mingles passion with devoutness, humor with tragedy, earth and heaven, darkness and sunlight. He is a sort of Walt Whitman or Victor Hugo of Catholicism, as his long and passion-charged lines of free verse and cadenced prose would indicate. *The Satin Slipper* is actually a panorama of history at the beginning of the great age of Spain. The action of *Partage de Midi*, which starts on a ship bound for the Far East, carries a man and a woman to the ends of the world for the consummation of their sin and their struggle for salvation. Spiritually, Claudel belongs even more to the decades of the 'forties and 'fifties than to the early decades of the century when he first made his contributions to poetry and drama. That is, he expresses a rejection of materialism and positivism that came into vogue in Western Europe (and, to some degree, in America) after 1945. His attitude is "anti-modern", if by "modern" we mean the world of relativistic morality and mundane liberalism.

His superabundant and surcharged theatre is actually less French than Spanish and recalls the theatre of Lope de Vega and Calderón. There is in his work, too, some of the extremism of the militant Spanish mystics and of the baroque Counter-Reformation. In the unhistorical drama *L'Otage* or *The Hostage* (1909, first produced by Lugné-Poë in 1914), a woman, to whom Napoleon has committed Pope Pius VII as a hostage, protects him by making the supreme sacrifice of renouncing the man she loves and marrying an egregious villain who murdered her parents. In *The Tidings Brought to Mary* (1910), the heroine contracts leprosy by kissing, out of pity and forgiveness, the face of the leprous cathedral architect who had previously tried to violate her, and she goes on to superhuman feats of self-sacrifice until she dies as a miracle-working saint. The devotional fervor of that play is at times extraordinarily flamboyant. Devotional writing such as Claudel's belongs to another age, and the English-speaking world has known it only twice — in the poetry of Donne and Gerald Manley Hopkins. T. S. Eliot is, by comparison, suave and worldly.

6 GIRAUDOUX AND ANOUILH

Jean Giraudoux (1882–1944), whose irony in *The Trojan War Will Not Take Place* (*La Guerre de Troie n'aura pas lieu, 1935*) was borne out when Europe plunged into war despite Prime Minister Chamberlain's "peace in our time" assurances, possessed a solvent of wit and fancy for the realities he knew so well as a man of the world and a career diplomat. The wit had been apparent in his brittle, boulevard comedy *Amphitryon 38* as early as 1929, and imagination had been present in his first, pacifist, play *Siegfried* written in 1928 and in his devastating tragedy of hatred, *Electra* (1937), a weird reworking of the classic revenge theme. His power of fantastication was especially marked in the romantic *Intermezzo*, in which the normal rule of mendacity and mediocrity in society is temporarily suspended to the utter confusion of its beneficiaries. (Written in 1933, this play was adapted for Broadway by Maurice Valency in 1948 under the title *The Enchanted*.) The less forceful *Ondine* (1939), a rueful romantic fable of the marriage of a knight to a mermaid or *ondine*, indicated that the tense European situation had not depleted Giraudoux of his poetic substance, and his talent for sparkling fantasy was triumphantly apparent in his last completed work *La Folle de Chaillot*, created in 1943.

Known to us under its English title *The Madwoman of Chaillot*, in the Valency translation made in 1947, this tour de force of theatricalized satire and fantasy was successfully produced on Broadway by Alfred de Liagre in the season of 1948–49, and gave the name of Giraudoux a renown in America it had never had even during the long run of the Lunts' production of *Amphitryon 38* more than a decade earlier. A mad countess resolves to rid the world of promoters, rapacious financiers, and other destroyers of happiness. Enticing them into the famed sewers of Paris with the promise of petroleum under the pavements, the countess saves humanity from its predatory exploiters and inaugurates a new reign of love and romance. A difficult piece to describe in terms of rational discourse, *The Madwoman* provided a poetry of theatre rare at any time, and especially rare during the continuing domination of realistic dramatic style. Although Giraudoux wrote *The Madwoman* before the conclusion of the war, it became, by virtue of its belated productions, a discovery of the postwar period. And it was a more significant play then than it would have been in 1943 when the paramount problem had been liberation from Hitler rather than from capitalists, real or fancied. It would be an error, however, to assume that the aristocratic and conservative Giraudoux wrote a Marxist tract. His play was essentially a romantic extravaganza confected by a man who loathed a dreary materialistic way of life, from which fantasy seemed to him the only possible avenue of escape.

Jean Anouilh (1910–) was the other major discovery, especially for the theatre in England. (None of his plays produced in America until 1952 made a favorable impression.) Like other French playwrights ever since the neo-classic period of Louis XIV, Anouilh treated classic themes in the spirit of his own age and temperament. His repertory of free adaptations included *Euridyce* (1941), *Antigone* (1944), and *Medea* (1946). The first of these adaptations was the somber *Eurydice*, in which Pluto is an interfering, sententious individual, Eurydice a morally weak actress, and Orpheus a poor violinist. — an accordion player in the English adaptation entitled *Legend of Lovers*. The best known of Anouilh's adaptations was *Antigone*, a veiled criticism of the Nazis, who must have permitted it to be produced in occupied Paris because Anouilh's pessimistic view of humanity made the play seem unpolitical. The ruler Creon was portrayed as a reasonable man. He forbids the burial of Antigone's brother solely for reasons of policy and demonstrates that Antigone's resistance to his authority is altogether perverse. It would be unfair to Anouilh to suggest that he was bent upon appeasing his country's oppressors, but his own attitude toward Antigone, the classic heroine of private conscience, was ambivalent at a time when ambivalence toward democracy was well marked in France He created an Antigone who violates Creon's edict against her brother's burial not so much because she loves the dead man but because she longs for death as a merciful release from a world filled with tawdry sentiments and cheap values.

The treatment coincided with the playwright's indured attitude toward life, and it reflected a general European disenchantment that was also present before and after the war. This did not, however, accord well with the American frame of mind, and the much heralded play failed to excite Broadway in spite of the personal popularity of Katherine Cornell, who played Antigone in the New York production. Like most adaptations of the classics, if unlike Sartre's *The Flies*, Anouilh's *Antigone* is an example of the anti-heroic disposition of much modern theatre. If there is heroism in the play, it is present there by a perversion of humanistic values; more specifically, in the perversity of the death-seeking, life-surrendering heroine. She represents the negativism and world-weariness of the harassed modern European intellectual, rather than the classic *arete,* or affirmative nobility, of the original character created by Sophocles. It was as difficult for Americans not to call Anouilh's play muddled as it was for social critics to refrain from denouncing it as decadent. It should be added that Anouilh's negativism was equally conspicuous in work not based on classic subjects, such as, *Le voyageur sans bagages* (*The Traveler Without Baggage, 1937*), a mordant amnesia drama about a soldier for whom recovery of memory is a painful and disenchanting experience. But *Antigone* has a sultry passion that flagellates the spirit.

Anouilh's reputation was also founded on sheer theatrical virtuosity, which is also not out of key with his philosophy, since an alternative to acceptance of reality is to alter it by means of "make-believe." The plays of his in which this was the case, in which some character invented an unreal situation and tried to make it prevail, Anouilh called *pièces roses* — "rosy-colored plays," so to speak, — while giving the published texts of his somber dramas the general name of *pièces noires* — "dark plays." Typical *pièces roses* were his *Thieves' Ball* (*Le bal des voleurs, 1938*), in which ingenious thieves masquerade as Spanish grandees in an Englishwoman's home; and the comedy *Le Rendez-vous de Senlis* (1941), in which the son of undistinguished parents, who would embarrass him before his lady-love, hires a pair of actors to impersonate them.

The culmination of Anouilh's English reputation in the immediate post-war world came with Christopher Fry's adaptation of the charade-comedy *L'Invitation au Château*. Under the title *Ring Round the Moon*, subtitled "A Charade with Music," the production staged by the brilliant young English director Peter Brook was the outstanding event of the London theatrical season of 1949–50. Although this success was not repeated in New York the next season, the play revealed the author as a resourceful theatrician who can put on a good face in the presence of life's futilities and frustrations. A rich young idler of brittle intellect and seemingly impenetrable heart hires a poor girl to deflect his sensitive twin-brother's infatuation with a heartless heiress. At a fancy ball, nearly all the characters, whether rich or poor, reveal abysses of disgruntlement with their lives, and the hired girl, instead of enchanting her quarry falls in love with her breezy young employer. After she has told him off roundly for treating her as a puppet and has attempted suicide, he succumbs to her, offstage, in a romantic conclusion sardonically noted by his dry-witted aunt. The play was patently tenuous, and it was possible to lose patience with the game of continual pretence. Nevertheless this comedy confirmed the author's reputation for both theatrical ingenuity and ultra-refined sensibility. The critic Louis Kronenberger cleverly described Anouilh as "the sort of man who could add *s'il vous plaît* to the Ten Commandments." Yet the *pièces noires* would indicate that overrefinement is balanced in Anouilh's case by other qualities — chiefly, by mordant disillusion and tragic atmosphere.

7 SARTRE, CAMUS, AND "EXISTENTIALIST" DRAMA

Other previously known writers contributed some work deserving of serious attention, and perhaps the ablest of these was Armand Salacrou (1900–   ), author of the ironical Renaissance drama *La terre est ronde* (*The Earth is Round, 1938*), *Atlas-Hotel, Frenzy*, and *The Unknown Woman of Arras*. Salacrou's *L'Archipel Lenoir* (*The Archipelago Lenoir, 1946*) proved to be a sardonic, if somewhat tricky, comedy. It revolved around the perturbation of self-interested members of a family when the grandfather, Paul-Albert Lenoir, is about to be arraigned in court for attempted rape. The frantic family considers the feasibility of killing him and later tries to induce him to commit suicide. The same playwright's resistance drama *Les nuits de colère* (*Nights of Wrath, 1947*) was an acute examination of the egocentricity of people even in times of national crisis. The play was both fascinating and confusing. The action moved from a realistic first scene, in which a number of characters are killed, to a fantasy in which these characters reenact scenes from life and hold conversation with still living characters.

The greatest stir in France and elsewhere was made, however, by Jean-Paul Sartre (1905–   ) who had begun to make an impression in Paris under German occupation with his reworking of the classic Oresteian legend *Les Mouches* (*The Flies, 1943*) and with his long one-acter *Huis Clos* (*No Exit*, in 1944). Novelist, essayist, and virtually the initiator of a new philosophical system, based on German thought and known as Existentialism, Sartre became the leader of French intellectual circles in the nineteen-forties. It has not been difficult to find gaps and contradictions in the philosophy he elaborated at greath length in the thesis *L'Être et le Néant* (*Being and Nothing, 1944*) and modified in numerous later tracts. Nevertheless, he expressed a strongly felt disorientation and distress in the Western European world, and he charged his plays with both passion and thought. In his dramatic work, as also in fiction and philosophy, Sartre tried to mediate between man's despairing sense of a void in the world and his need to recover some justification for remaining alive and respecting himself. Sartre took note of the opportunism and moral weakness of Western man and offered him a new gospel of courage and integrity.[1]

Before the war, Sartre had not been much more than a schoolmaster, with a degree in philosophy taken in 1929 and a career in various lycées during the nineteen-thirties. After 1936, he published several original studies in psychology. In 1938 also appeared his first novel *Nausea*, a "shocker" replete with a disgust at life on the part of his characters, and in 1939 a volume of short stories, *The Wall*, equally redolent of decadence and marked by desperation over the meaninglessness of existence. Along with other French works, among which Céline's novel *Death on the Instalment Plan* (1938) is the best known, Sartre's books reflected the state of mind of the French on the eve of the Second World War. It was a state of mind that had its correlates in the Munich Pact, the collapse of France after Dunkirk, and the Vichy regime under the former Verdun hero Petain.

Sartre, however, soon revealed the same resilience that the French nation manifested in its resistance movement and in the ultimate liberation of Paris by the valor of the Parisian people. Sartre's conduct and thinking during the war became charged with affirmativeness and courage. After serving in the French forces as an artillery observer in 1939–40, being captured in June 1940, and spending some nine months in a German prison camp, he made his escape to Paris and joined the French underground. Somehow, he also managed not only to write a book and two plays, but to get the latter produced in the occupied capital. Charles Dullin produced Sartre's *The Flies* at the *Théâtre de la Cité* in 1943, and a company using the once famous *Théâtre du Vieux-Colombier* produced *No Exit* in May 1944.

The two plays represented the negative and positive sides of Sartre's thinking. The less exciting of the two, *No Exit*, was a rather static representation of the view that average human beings tend to lack both integrity and self-knowledge. Two women, a demoniacal lesbian and a spoiled society woman, and a cowardly pseudo-idealistic journalist find themselves after their death in hell. They are held in a chamber in which they must always torment each other with awareness of their delusions or failure as human beings and with their dependency upon each other's opinion. Their dependency is the result of their lack of character and self-respect. Hell, therefore, as one of them remarks, is "other people."

In *The Flies*, Sartre presented the "existentialist" ideal of self-reliance. It is achieved by Sartre's hero Orestes, who acts as a free man and lives without emotional attachment to a world filled with foulness and delusions. Heroism consists of a sense of responsibility to one's own values. The play was a highly original reworking of the classic Oresteian theme within the framework of the author's existentialist philosophy. Its dramatic interest cannot, however, be subsumed wholly under any formula, since the work is dramatically and theatrically exciting as well as provocatively discursive. An extended discussion of its "ideas" would, indeed, have little meaning, unless the reader had the text before him. (See: *A Treasury of the Theatre*, ed by John Gassner.) The play revolves around the return of Orestes to his homeland, Argos, long after the murder of his father by his mother Clytemnestra and her lover Aegistheus. The latter are now the rulers of the city — its tyrants and deceivers, with the aid of the greatest of all tyrants and deceivers, the Olympian Zeus. Resisting their deceptions and rejecting their morbid moral values, Orestes kills Clytemnestra and Aegistheus and liberates Argos.

Paramount, since the free man takes full responsibility for his actions, is Orestes' rejection of the sense of guilt that the murderers foisted upon the people and established as a state of religion of self-abasement and masochistic penitence. Not even after killing his mother does Sartre's hero succumb to bad conscience, although his embittered sister Electra, who had thirsted for vengeance, is overwhelmed with remorse. He will carry the memory of the slaying with him always, and his mother's cries will rend his heart; but, knowing that his act was necessary, he will have no regrets. Indeed, he killed, not in order to wreak futile revenge for a father slain, but in order to put an end to the disgusting slavery of the city. By the sheer power of his independent spirit, he liberates the population from the degrading Furies or "flies" of guilt-feeling that had polluted the city ever since the murder of Agamemnon. Proudly announcing to the people of Argos that his crime is entirely his own, he discharges them of any responsibility for the death of its rulers Clytemnestra and Aegistheus. Nor will he rule over the people, as is his right. Being a totally free man, being a true "existentialist" who knows that a man must make his own life and be ruled only by his own values, he refuses to be any man's master. Nor is he dependent on any man; he can endure the anguish of loneliness and isolation — that is, the existentialist's special anguish. To his people he declares, as he bids them farewell to roam on the strange path of personal quest and destiny, "I wish to be a king without a kingdom, without subjects." He hopes that they, too, will achieve self-reliance: "Try to reshape your lives. All here is new, all must begin anew" — an admonition by Sartre to the France that would be liberated before long, and one that had still to be heeded in the post-war period. Then, playing the Pied Piper who made the rats of an infested city follow him out of its precincts, Orestes strides out of Argos, taking with him the shrieking insect-Furies who fling themselves after him.

In *The Flies*, then, Sartre conveyed his dual principle of existentialist "anguish" and "freedom." He expressed the suffering of the disillusioned man who is aware of the absurdity of the universe in which he tries to maintain his sense of self, and he announced a gospel of independence and of responsibility to oneself alone. Freedom in this sense isolates the individual, since he accepts no code except a self-made or self-chosen one and relies on no one's opinion. Yet, at the same time, the existentialist hero must "engage" himself, as Orestes did; to humanity and to social action, if he is to be truly tested as the possessor of a strong personality. Sartre's later formulation of his views in an essay written in 1946 was succinctly expressed by its title of *L'Existentialisme est un humanisme* — Existentialism is a form of Humanism!

It was to this theme that Sartre returned in his naturalistic yet philosophical Resistance drama *Morts sans sépulture*, produced at the *Théâtre Antoine* on November 8, 1946. (It was staged later in New York under the title of *The Victors*.) It is an almost unbearably gruesome story of the endurance of the patriots, and of the demoniacal self-torment of one of their Vichy-militia tormentors when faced with the invincible independence of the Resistance heroes. One of these, a woman of mettle, even consents to the murder of her weak-willed brother by her comrades when it is likely that he will betray the whereabouts of their leader.

Another existentialist hero in the person of a communist idealist was the subject of a still later play, *Les Mains sales*, seen in America in an unsatisfactory adaptation under the title of *Red Gloves*. A more tantalizing work than *The Victors, Red Gloves* proved quite confusing, and it is not at all certain that Sartre was not himself partly responsible for the confusion. Nevertheless, the play was far above the level of a drama of adultery and Graustark intrigue. Incidentally, Graustark drama of intrigues and murders in fictive Balkan countries does not seem quite so ineptly extravagant to the French — or even to the English — as it does to Americans, as Jean Cocteau's *The Eagle Has Two Heads* also exemplified during the post-war period. Intrigue of this sort is more "true to life" for nations close to the witches' cauldron of European politics. European playwrights have a way of taking such intrigue for granted, and do not consider it mere theatrical hocus-pocus. It is the *donné*, so to speak, upon which they graft ideas or embroider ironic commentary on human nature and behavior. *Les Mains sales* exposed the lack of integrity in political maneuvering, chiefly in the communistic movement, in spite of Sartre's disavowal of anti-communist intentions. Here, too, he was concerned with the paramount existentialist question of how the individual can remain true to himself; this time in a context of ideological conflict and political struggle intertwined with domestic complications.

Not without a discursiveness and ratiocination that impaired the dramatic effect of his plays, Sartre continued to engage difficult subjects on a level that may be considered philosophical as well as psychological, although fundamentally moralistic. Sartre's "existentialism" was aggressively atheistic, for life would not be absurd and man would not be lonely if God existed. Still, if atheists cannot rely on the divine spirit, they are forced to rely on man; and, if that is the case, man must be subjected to moral demands as excessive, considering human frailty, as the demands of faith. Actually more so! Hence, Sartre proved to be more of a Jansenist or Calvinist than he could possibly realize. Hence, too, his dramatic art was marred by an *ostinato* stridency and a haranguing, as well as twisting, discursiveness.

Sartre also impressed a good deal of irony into the service of his observations on human behavior. This was especially apparent in *La Putain respecteuse*, produced in Paris in 1946, which was also successfully staged under the title of *The Respectful Prostitute* in New York by Mary Hunter for a short-lived experimental theatre, *New Stages*. (The adaptation was made by a young American playwright,

Eva Wolas.) A flagrantly distorted picture of American manners, this sardonic piece about an attempted lynching in the South is not to be judged as realistic social drama, but as an existentialist extravaganza. Here, too, Sartre comments on the values to which men and women — whether Southern aristocrat or seedy harlot — conform. The prostitute heroine, who has insisted on protecting an innocent Negro from a Southern mob at considerable risk to herself, defers to the reasoning of a local "elder statesman" when he claims consideration for the family of the white gentleman who actually committed the act for which the Negro is expected to suffer. She succumbs to the appeal of social superiority. Fortunately, a different Negro has been mistakenly lynched in the meantime by the aroused mob, so that the Negro she has tried to protect is at last safe! The elder statesman's son, who tries to bully her into surrendering the Negro she is concealing, is motivated by a perverted sense of *noblesse oblige;* he believes it is moral to protect a friend at the cost of a Negro's life. The harlot's plucky resistance having won his questionable esteem, he generously proposes to make her his mistress. Moreover, the harlot, whose sense of values is also questionable, is quite sensible of the honor of rising in the social scale by becoming the mistress of a "gentleman"! Irony could hardly go further; and in once more demonstrating Sartre's contempt for moral flabbiness, *The Respectful Prostitute* bore a resemblance to his first play *No Exit.* It presented the obverse side of the existentialist heroism to be found in *The Flies* and *The Victors.*

In 1951, Sartre enjoyed another *succès de scandale* with a new, thoroughgoing existentialist play *Le Diable et le Bon Dieu (The Devil and the Good Lord,* or *God and the Devil),* lavishly staged by Louis Jouvet. (The production was an enormous undertaking, requiring the services of 104 technicians and 650 pounds of screws and nails, according to the *New York Times!)* It revolved around a heroic character, who, first tried to play devil and then god, only to arrive at the conclusion that there is no god because his efforts to do good have resulted in misery. (His good intentions give rise to a sanguinary peasants' revolt, the Peasants' War during the Reformation in Germany.) Although the play was pronounced a bore by several Parisian critics, it attracted a great deal of attention. It was considered an unwieldy "melodrama of ideas," but there was a possibility that the author could reshape it, if he were so inclined, into a powerful drama.

Whatever qualifications we may make concerning Sartre's plays, as well as essays and novels, we must respect him as a provocative dramatist in a period not conspicuously endowed with original playwrights. If he often overreached himself and twisted or thinned out human character in support of an idea or an ideology, he, nevertheless, commanded attention with his keen mind and lambent spirit. It is permissible to describe him as a modern and sceptical Corneille, although he was no poet and could never have become one.

His plays, moreover, were not the only more or less existentialist dramas, for Sartre found many associates in Paris, several of whom had literary, and even dramatic, talent. Existentialism became, indeed, ultra-fashionable in post-war Parisian circles, and the faithful made the "left-bank" Café de Flore their headquarters for a time. The movement even had its bohemian and frivolous aspects, as well as the moralistic side derived in part from the absolutist Scandinavian preacher Sören Kierkgaard, whose relentless "Either — or" principle Ibsen had long before incorporated in *Brand*.

In 1945, Sartre's friend, Simone de Beauvoir, dramatized the need of making decisions entirely upon one's own responsibility in *Les bouches inutiles* (*The Useless Mouths*), in which the mayor of a besieged city is called upon to sacrifice its "useless mouths" or noncombatants in order to keep the active defenders of the town alive. Later, Emannuel Robles explored a similar theme and dramatized the same torments of necessitous decision in *Montserrat*, a drama of the Spanish occupation of Venezuela in 1812, during the revolution under Bolivar that gave South America its independence. *Montserrat* was produced in New York in the fall of 1949, not quite successfully, in an adaptation written and staged by Lillian Hellman. The play was more successfully produced, however, in other countries, including Israel, where Harold Clurman supervised the staging. In this work, an idealistic Spanish officer risks the execution of innocent hostages in order to enable Bolivar to elude the Spaniards who are intent upon capturing him and scotching the revolution —a situation for which Robles could cite parallels during the French resistance. The idealist's anguish when the innocent must be sacrificed to the cause of freedom made gripping theatre, even if his having to face nearly the same problem with each hostage entailed considerable repetitiousness. In 1951, Robles also wrote a play *Juarez*, subtitled "The Truth Is Dead," dealing with the assumption of personal responsibility by the Mexican leader Juarez for abandoning a citadel and sacrificing his honor to what he knows to be sound military strategy.

Sartre's associate from Northern Africa, Albert Camus (1913–), also contributed more or less existentialist plays, although the author of two remarkable pieces of fiction, *The Stranger* and *The Plague*, proved to be a better novelist than playwright. Of his plays, *Caligula* (produced in 1945) was the most extravagantly existentialist treatment of the "absurdity" of life. Arriving at the conclusion that the world is a madhouse and that life is absurd, the young Roman em-

peror Caligula, who had started his rule humanely, exercises his royal
prerogatives to "show up" life by means of a succession of arbitrary
murders. Although the play frays the nerves, *Caligula* is a perversely
fascinating, psychological drama.

There is less to be said for Camus' earlier murder-play, *Le Malen-
tendu* (1944), translated as *Cross Purpose*. It was a "shocker", dependent on the ironic situation of a peasant mother and her sister,
who have been in the habit of murdering strangers, mistakenly killing
their own son and brother. Yet it is difficult to be chary in attributing
genius to an author who could create the character of the life-embit-
tered spinster-sister of *Cross Purpose*. In the season of 1940–50,
Camus' *Les Justes* (*The Just*) caused a controversy in Paris with its
exploration of the moral conflicts involved in arriving at revolutionary
decisions. The play revolves around the terrorist activities of the Social
Revolutionist party during the abortive Russian Revolution of 1905.
Since Camus' piece dealt with the making of decisions that involve
murder by sensitive and loquacious intellectuals, *Les Justes* was decidedly discursive. It was, nevertheless, a provocative play.

Although Camus disavowed adherence to existentialist dogma, his
plays, like his novels, had existentialist "anguish" and "freedom" at
the core of their dramatic substance. The dominant character of *Cross
Purpose*, Martha, the lonely old-maid sister who killed travelers in
order to be able to move to the sea-shore (in order to have the sunlight
"burn out" her sense of frustration), maintains that "one's gaze is
cramped on every side." She refuses to "bend the knee" to a universe
full of injustice. "Try to realize," she says to the wife of her murdered brother, "that no grief of yours can ever equal the injustice done
to man." Martha tells her to pray to God "to harden you to stone."
The one true happiness is to enter a hard, blind peace, since there is
for man only a choice between the mindless happiness of stones and
the peace of death. "Do as He does, be deaf to all appeals, and turn
your heart to stone while there is still time." Concerning the murder,
Martha has no remorse; there was "a misunderstanding" — and "if
you have any experience at all of the world, that won't surprise you."

As for the Mother, who had collaborated in the crime, she had been
"free" only so long as she had felt no attachment through love. Having
discovered from the visitor's effects, which included a passport, that
the man she killed was the son who had been absent for twenty years,
she knows she is undone. Not because she feels guilt, but because she
feels the pain of rekindling love — and that is too much for her to endure in a world that "doesn't make sense." She knows now that she can
no longer live without her son's love, and this craving for him destroys
her "existentialist" independence. "By one act," she explains some-

what too intellectually under the circumstances, "I have ruined everything. I have lost my freedom and my hell has begun." She goes out to drown herself in the stream into which Martha and she threw the son's drugged body.

The mad murder-lust of the "artistic" Roman emperor in *Caligula* is simply a more encompassing and diabolic exhibition of the same desperate "nausea" with existence. Caligula embarks upon mass-murder and sadism after the senseless death of his beloved sister Drusilla, in order to teach the world the truth about man's life — namely, that since men die and are unhappy, life is absurd. As he explains to his friend Helicon, "I wish men to live by the light of truth. And I've the power to make them do so." Camus presented this imperial monster as a life-wounded, world-wounded man, who has learned the full measure of human "anguish." Caligula is not oblivious to signs of nobility in others, but is suspicious of its authenticity. He is not incapable of generous action, but is obsessed with his passion for pressing home the horrible truth of Negation. He is gleefully eager to discover the cowardice of men : "No more masks," he declares.

Camus represents the Emperor's situation as a case of perverse idealism and logical madness. Caligula is striving for a freedom that has no bounds — freedom from all attachment, since attachment is pain. In his eyes the greatest crime is that of attributing importance "to people and things." The most understanding character in the play is Cherea, a man of letters who becomes the leader of the conspirators against Caligula. Cherea knows that hs is fighting "disinterested malice" in this man. He realizes that Caligula's "logic" must "founder in sheer lunacy." By killing Caligula, Cherea will have regained "some peace of mind in a world that has regained a meaning." What spurs Cherea on is his "very reasonable fear of that inhuman vision in which my life means no more than a speck of dust."

The historical significance of existentialism in the midcentury drama is as evident as the fact that it used much cumbersome melodrama of ideas. It gave considerable power and fascination to French playwriting — a fascination of ideas transformed into motivations and reactions unusual in Western theatre after the age of Jacobean drama in seventeenth century England. Melodramatic, horror-fascinated Jacobean drama had no future. It was open to question whether existentialist drama could have any. Negativism is subject to entropy. The energy of negation must lose its effectiveness because it logically contradicts the interest in life and characters that a play must exhibit. Sooner or later, too, the persistent Naysayers drive an audience to self-defensive irritation or apathy. Still, as a solvent for boulevard comedy and commonplace domestic drama, midcentury French existentialism was effective.

8 HENRY DE MONTHERLANT

One cannot, however, subsume the midcentury French drama under any single dispensation. Entertainment, sprinkled with the salt of Gallic humor, continued to be favored by playwrights, and this was abundantly present in such a play as Marcel Aymé's clever *Clérambard* (1950), a comedy in which the hero, an eccentric noble-man becomes far more troublesome after a visitation from St. Francis than he had been before his conversion into a lover of animals and a devotee of humility. Although faulty and non-exportable without thorough-going adaptation, *Clérambard*, with its amusing characters and hilarious scenes, provided intelligent relaxation from existential-ist rigors.[2] Moreover, the produced and published plays of Monther-lant indicated that even the ultra-serious French drama was not pre-empted by the Sartre-Camus school, the Anouilh of the *pièces noires*, and such occasional experiments as the dramatization of Franz Kafka's novel *The Trial* that André Gide made for a much disputed Paris production.

To Henry de Montherlant (1896–), indeed, belonged the most authentic genius for dramatic writing discoverable in France after 1940. He proved himself an original novelist and playwright, as well as a stimulating belle-lettrist. An independent aristocrat and a rest-less man given to athletics and bull-fighting, Montherlant belonged to no party and drew criticism from all quarters. His contempt for mediocrity and his extreme emphasis on personal pride as a sustain-ing force caused him to be identified with anti-democratic elements in France. He was, in fact, accused of collaborating with the enemy during the occupation of France, although the Germans suppressed one of his books in 1941, and although he ran afoul of the Gestapo in 1944. It does not appear to be true that he was actually a collabora-tionist, in the usual sense of the term. His dubious behavior was an esthetic aberration, and he expressed a perverse defeatism long before the fall of France. Neither was he by the remotest stretch of imagina-tion a liberal or a democrat. One might describe him as a disciple of Nietzsche in his detestation of average life and in his cult of superiority.

Montherlant, however, functioned in his plays as a dramatist whose first obligation is to submerge himself in his characters. No single character in the plays entirely speaks and acts for Montherlant. Although his work conveys a natural sympathy with characters who possess a large measure of self-esteem and self-reliance, he allows them their due portion of disenchantment, as in his portrait of King Ferrante in *Queen After Death*, and he does not spare them failure, as we see in *Malatesta* and *Tomorrow the Dawn*. He also enables us, in other instances, to judge them as they do not judge themselves. This is especially the case in *The Master of Santiago*, whose Spanish knight of the Order of Santiago deprives his daughter of happiness as a result of the austere idealism that rules his life and constitutes his self-esteem. Montherlant found in the drama a beneficial discipline, and his worst personal traits, his perverse egotism and sense of superiority, were sublimated in his plays.

First and best known for his novel-sequence *Les Jeunes Filles* (1935–40), translated in America under the title *Costals and The Hippogriff*, Montherlant first aroused attention as a playwright with the 1942 *Comédie Française* production of *La Reine Morte*, translated under the title *Queen after Death*. This was followed by *Fils de personne* or *No Man's Son* (first produced in 1943), *Malatesta* (published in 1946), *The Master of Santiago* (1947), which had over 500 performances in Paris, and *Demain il fera jour* or *Tomorrow the Dawn*, produced in 1949 along with *No Man's Son*, to which it is a sequel. In 1948, *La Reine Morte*, returned to the repertoire of the *Comédie Française* and won considerable attention. These plays finally reached American readers in an edition entitled *The Master of Santiago and Four Other Plays* (Alfred A. Knopf) in the summer of 1951.

Two of the plays, *Queen after Death* and *The Master of Santiago*, are dramas of pride, and are appropriately set in sixteenth century Portugal and Spain, where the cult of "honor" had been carried to heroic lengths. *Queen after Death* revolves around the Portuguese King Ferrante's conflict with his son Pedro over the latter's marriage to an illegitimate woman, Ines de Castro, and over Pedro's rejection of the Princess of Navarre whom the king had selected for him. When Pedro refuses to consider an annulment of his marriage, King Ferrante has Ines murdered, although he has grown fond of her and has previously resisted his counsellors' suggestion that he eliminate her. Ferrante has her destroyed against his better intentions for reasons of pride. He cannot bear the prospect of having her still unborn child a future member of his dynasty; and, above all, he is moved to destroy her because, in a moment of weakness, he had betrayed to her his extreme disillusion and world-weariness as a ruler. Ferrante, Ines, and the Princess of Navarre are such intensely realized characters, and the dialogue that reveals them is so remarkable, that *Queen after Death* cannot be dismissed as merely another pseudo-historical drama.

In *The Master of Santiago*, a father refuses to take any steps to secure his daughter's perfectly honorable marriage to a man she loves, because he rejects all compromise with life in complacently prosperous and power-minded Spain after the defeat of the Moors. His daughter, stirred by her father's extreme honorableness, puts an end to the hoax that would have secured him riches and that would have enabled her to marry. The father is a remarkably well-drawn Don Quixote (without any ludicrous attributes, however), and his aversion to the conniving world and the enslavement of the American Indians by Spain rises to truly heroic proportions. The flame of idealism in this drama is all-consuming. One could wish only that it also had more human warmth. The knight's almost superhuman purity of motivation is, no doubt, intended as a slap in the face of ordinary humanity — for which Montherlant had perhaps too much contempt to become a truly great dramatist.

A third drama in a historical setting, *Malatesta*, contains one of the most impressive exotic characterizations in modern drama. It is a superb study of a Renaissance freebooter who is both a murderer and an art-lover in the manner of Browning's Duke in *My Last Duchess*. The play does not impress the present writer as crystallizing into a sufficiently well shaped and integrated drama. There is enough insight and drama in *Malatesta*, however, to float several ordinary plays.

That Montherlant, moreover, could also be effective in treating contemporary subjects was shown by *No Man's Son* and even by its weaker sequel, *Tomorrow the Dawn*. In both plays, the main character is a prominent lawyer, Georges Carrion. In the first-mentioned play, set in unoccupied France in 1940, Georges rejects his fourteen-year-old illegitimate son "Gillou" because the uncompromising father detects a strain of mediocrity in the boy. Georges allows his son to leave for bomb-exposed Le Havre with the boy's restless mother, who hankers for a lover living in the north of France. What makes the play noteworthy is the acute conflict between the father, whose heart is torn by his desire for a son worthy of his exalted ideals, and his affectionate son, who is incapable of rising above natural limitations and is ground between the upper and nether millstones of an intellectual father and a foolish and flighty mother.

In the sequel *Tomorrow the Dawn*, we meet the characters of *No Man's Son* some three years later, during the period of the Normandy landings. They are now in Paris. Georges Carrion has settled there in order to be near "Gillou;" for the once obstinately uncompromising father has longed for his son. The lad, now seventeen, wants to join the Resistance movement in order to participate in the Liberation. The anxious father forbids the boy to risk his life in underground activity; and for once, the mother, who has grown less foolish since the failure of her love affair at Le Havre, sees eye to eye with the father. Georges himself, however, has lost the fine integrity that had made him reject his son on grounds of principle three years earlier. Having entered the Occupied Zone, he found himself under some compulsion to cooperate with the Germans. Overcome with anxiety for his own safety as the time of the Liberation approaches, and hoping to win acquittal through the merit of a son associated with the Resistance, he reverses his decision. He allows "Gillou" to join the Parisian underground, and the boy is killed. This is a tragic ending for Georges, who is overwhelmed by the realization of his weakness anod perfidy. Montherlant has provided an ironic ending for a man who had dreamed of raising a heroic new generation and who, when he felt disappointed in the boy, had once exclaimed (in *No Man's Son*), "To think that tomorrow the dawn will come, and with sons who won't be mine."

In *Tomorrow the Dawn,* the father's last line on his destroyed honor is the cry of a man whose almost intolerable, if intellectually heroic, pride in *No Man's Son* was later overwhelmed by the instinct of fatherhood: "It's because I loved him that I came back to Paris, and all that [his collaboration with the Germans] has happened." Earlier he had declared, "The old get away with it always, it's the sons who pay for them." It is apparent, then, that here, as in the other plays, Montherlant, the arrogant and perverse maverick of French literature, was not subservient, as existentialist authors were, to philosophical formulations. He remained an acute and sympathetic observer of human nature, in spite of his Nietzschean contempt for the common man.

Having suffered great trials during the war and strong perturbations for some years before 1939, France acquired a strong intellectual and artistic ferment. As is usual in France, the results were recorded in the theatre, as well as in fiction, poetry, and criticism. Playwrights of the calibre of Giraudoux, Anouilh, Sartre, Camus, and Montherlant made the mid-century French drama the most stimulating in the world. Since France somehow never changes, boulevardism remained intact in spite of the tensions of French society, but the acuteness of the creative French mind and spirit also remained unblunted.

9 POST-WAR ENGLISH THEATRE

In England, one major development galvanized the post-war theatre. Established during the war, in 1940, the Arts Council of Great Britian devoted itself to "increasing the availability of theatre

to the British people" and improving its "standard of execution." As
a result of assistance by the Arts Council, which amounted to a partial
subsidy in so far as approved acting groups were insured against a
deficit, theatrical production increased greatly in Britain. The possibilities of non-commercial and experimental stage production grew in
Britain in spite of the nation's economic difficulties and the tottering
condition of the British empire. Notable revivals and new plays resulted from the British people's revived interest in theatre. The work
of Christopher Fry, T. S. Eliot, and others received some form of
government sponsorship, which often proved to be the first step
toward a successful production in London's West End and also (in
the case of *The Lady's Not for Burning* and *The Cocktail Party*) on
Broadway. Theatre was now a nation-wide activity in England.
Provincial companies became associated with the Arts Council, and
such enterprises as The Theatre Royal in Bristol and the Arts Theatre
in Salisbury were operated by it. The remarkable "Old Vic" acting
company also shared in government assistance and became "a National
Theatre *de facto*," as Robert Speaight (*Drama Since 1939*) put it.
It was about to become more than that in 1948, when Parliament voted
a million pounds for a National Theatre building. (Difficulties and
conflicts within the organization began to mount, however, after 1950.)
In London, too, the Arts Theatre Club and the tiny Mercury Theatre
promoted poetic drama; and the leftward-leaning Unity Theatre, led
for a time by the energetic stage and film director Herbert Marshall
and others, devoted itself to social drama.

These developments arose under the influence of a war that had
stirred the English people to the very roots of their national consciousness and were promoted by the moderate Socialistic program of the
British Labour Party immediately after the conflict. England became
the home of continuous and distinguished productions. Perhaps the
most memorable of these were the "Old Vic's" *Henry IV* and its
Oedipus the King, with Laurence Olivier playing Sophocles' king
triumphantly in William Butler Yeats's adaptation. Especially impressive, aside from the diction of British acting, was the sense of
style present in the productions. Actors of the stature of John Gielgud,
Laurence Olivier, Vivian Leigh, Joyce Redman, and Peggy Ashcroft
found their peers in stage directors such as Peter Brook and Martin
Browne, and the actors themselves, notably John Gielgud, excelled
as directors.

A number of already established playwrights contributed to the
dramatic output of the early post-war period. Among these Terence
Rattigan, who provided the Lunts with a smoothly running comic
vehicle, *O Mistress Mine*, in 1945, distinguished himself with the

writing of *The Winslow Boy*. Based on a celebrated law case concerning a young naval cadet who had been innocently charged with theft, *The Winslow Boy* presented the struggles of the boy's father to vindicate him. With the assistance of a famous advocate, the father clears his son's name after years of sacrifice and tribulation. Since the affair of the little boy becomes a national issue and even reaches the House of Commons, the play exemplified the English and American view that even inconsequential matters are of moment to a democratic society whenever an individual's rights are in jeopardy. *The Winslow Boy* was not a masterpiece of original inspiration; but produced in 1946 after the conclusion of a great war in defense of liberty, it was greeted as a stirring affirmation of principle. Liberal idealism also found a strong champion in the novelist, essayist, and playwright J. B. Priestley (1894–). Having developed a strong democratic stand during the war, he continued to write social dramas. *An Inspector Calls*, produced by the "Old Vic" in 1946, was a somewhat fantastic and ironic morality, calling attention to the network of social responsibility in which people are apt to be caught. Here, he continued to play tricks with time as in earlier time-relativity plays, but with more point and substance. "We are members of one body" was the theme of this treatment of an upper-class family's responsibility for the suicide of a lower-class girl.

An inquiring spirit continued to sparkle in the work of the eccentric *causeur* "James Bridie," Dr. Osborne Henry Mavor (1888–1951), the Scottish physician and dramatist. His most attractive new play, *Mr. Gilley*, produced in the London season of 1949–1950, was an affecting fantasy about the heavenly trials of an idealistic schoolmaster who tried to disseminate noble values with less success than persistence. *Mr. Gilley* was of the same order of querulous semi-philosophic drama — caviare to Broadway! — that Bridie wrote earlier in *Mr. Bolfry* (1943), in which the Devil ("Mr. Bolfry") and a minister unite in putting an unbeliever out of countenance. Returning to Biblical matter, previously explored by him delightfully in *Tobias and the Angel* (1930), Bridie also wrote *The Sign of the Prophet Jonah* (1942) and a somewhat raffish treatment of Mary of Egypt, *The Dragon and the Dove* (1942). In *Lancelot,* (1945), Bridie also cast a quizzical eye on famous figures of Arthurian romance and on the wizard Merlin's attempt to practice eugenics and bring forth a perfect human being. Bridie's non-philosophical piece, the rather scrambled *Daphne Laureola*, in its best portions a bizarre character study, won considerable success in London in 1949. Never a sufficiently conscientious craftsman and always too fond of discourse, Bridie was, nevertheless, one of England's most original writers for the stage.

For the record, too, it may be worth noting that R. C. Sherriff (1896– .), who had not won any particular favor since his famous war-drama *Journey's End* in 1929, interested London with a new play, *Miss Mabel*, in 1948 and with *Home at Seven*, a unique melodrama of amnesia in white-collar circles. It provided Sir Ralph Richardson with a successful vehicle.

It is a lamentable fact, however, that the post-war period in England dispensed much trashy drama, and had to get along without a single major dramatist. Shaw's extreme old age removed him from the field. (He could only repeat scraps of his former wit and observation in his last play *Buoyant Billions*.) Shaw's death, coming at the midcentury point (November 2, 1950), could be taken as the official closing of a great era of drama — the drama of ideas and sceptical inquiry inaugurated by Henrik Ibsen a good seventy-five years earlier.

Only one giant was left to the English-speaking theatre across the sea. He was the Dublin-born Sean O'Casey, almost equally neglected, so far as major professional productions are concerned, on both sides of the Atlantic. He was better served in his native Ireland only when the Abbey Theatre, somewhat shorn of its original splendor, produced his lyrical, perhaps too lyrical, Dublin transport strike drama *Red Roses for Me* (1943). In *Red Roses for Me*, O'Casey proved that his power of passionate utterance was undiminished by neglect, and in *Cock-a-doodle Dandy* (1949) he created, if not the sturdiest, surely the most entrancing and incisive of his non-realistic plays. This folk comedy, enlivened with breezy fantasy, pokes glorious fun at provincial philistinism and constitutes a high-hearted, if also rueful, affirmation of love of life and freedom of spirit. The wholesome young exponents of a full life wage war in *Cock-a-Doodle Dandy* against calculating and superstition-ridden middle-aged proponents of village puritanism. The latter, forming a vigilante group under "Father Domineer" to oppose "the onward rush of paganism," finally score a victory by driving out a spirited girl Loreleen. She is joined by Lorna, the young, life-loving wife of one of the girl's persecutors, and together they go away "to a place where life resembles life more than it does here." One by one, the representatives of life depart the village, leaving it to desiccated provincials, among whom are a pair of dimwitted and blustering codgers worthy of O'Casey's earlier imperishable booze-companions "Captain" Boyle and Joxer.

Manifestly a satire on Eire's growing puritanism and censorship of the arts, this comedy leaves the ground of its immediate provocation. It provides rich fancy and symbolism, mainly with a half-real, half-fantastic rooster called the "Demon Cock," who is chased frantically by the timid old men, and with an accordion-playing "Messenger", who might be the great god Pan himself. Weird blasts of wind whip the trousers off the village Sergeant and whirl about the other philistines, while the "Messenger" coaxes a soft tune out of his accordion and the women, unaffected by the blasts, look on with amusement as the fools try to hold on to their clothing. With this play, O'Casey wrote the outstanding poetic extravaganza of the decade, and one of the few masterpieces of Irish drama written since *The Playboy of the Western World.* Along with *Purple Dust,* an uproarious yet poetic farce-comedy about the fiasco of two patronizing Englishman in Ireland, published in 1940, *Cock-a-Doodle Dandy* represented the peak of O'Casey's achievement after he abandoned realistic technique with *The Silver Tassie,* back in 1928.

Untamed poetry, however, could be provided only by the fierce and original talent of Ireland's most distinguished living exile.[3] When another voluntary exile from the Emerald Isle, Paul Vincent Carroll (1900–   ), the author of *Shadow and Substance* (1938) and *The White Steed* (1939), wrote another protest against puritanism in *The Wise Have Not Spoken,* produced in London in 1946, he created a social drama in the realistic vein rather than poetic drama. A third Irish emigré Dennis Johnston (1901–   ), author of the Chekhovian Irish drama *The Moon in the Yellow River* and of the rare expressionistic piece *The Old Lady Says 'No',* had a passionate but unremarkable play about Dean Swift, *Weep for the Cyclops,* produced by the Bristol "Old Vic" company in 1946.

10   ENGLISH POETIC DRAMA: ELIOT AND FRY

A renaissance of poetic drama became the most lauded feature of the English theatre of the 1940's. It was associated chiefly with the work of the American-born T. S. Eliot (1888–   ) and Christopher Fry (1907–   ). Eliot and Fry, along with other less well-known writers of verse drama,[4] specialized in various degrees of literary and dramatic formalism.

It may be also observed that Eliot and Fry made a virtue of traditionalism and were orthodox in thought and religion, striking roots in the High Church of England. They belonged to the "genteel tradition" antipodal to O'Casey's impassioned proletarianism and turbulent heterodoxy.

Eliot, as noted in an earlier chapter, started contributing his talent to the theatre back in 1935 with *Murder in the Cathedral,* his first play, except for the early, pungently written dramatic fragment *Sweeney Agonistes.* Specially conceived as a festival piece of Canterbury Cathedral, *Murder in the Cathedral* was later professionally performed in London and New York. The play was executed formally as ritualistic or liturgical drama. Although universal in theme, *Murder in the Cathedral,* in dealing with the martyrdom of St. Thomas à Becket, was medieval in setting and subject matter. Nor was there anything unique in a playwright's use of verse for historical subjects. Any uniqueness attributable to *Murder in the Cathedral* lay in the rare quality of Eliot's intellect and poetic endowment; in his choruses, so formal and yet so fluid, and so modern by virtue of their freedom from Victorian embellishment; and in the dramatically effective explanations offered by the murderers in the form of speeches from a podium — in Shavian prose!

Murder in the Cathedral was written in the period when the younger English poets — W. H. Auden (1907–   ), Stephen Spender, and Louis MacNeice — were writing contemporary social drama in verse. Eliot also turned to a contemporary subject in his second piece *The Family Reunion* (1939). Without subordinating his poetry to the flabby prose of modern times, Eliot moved into an English countryhouse and peopled it with characters who would have been at home in contemporary English comedy of manners. This marked Eliot's progress toward modern verse drama. The fact that Eliot introduced into the play the classic Furies as the tormentors of his guilt-burdened hero Lord Harry was not fatally anomalous, since these symbols of conscience were used discretely and suited the theme. Nonetheless *The Family Reunion* was a failure. Its author suffered shipwreck on the shoals of a discursive moralism which not only caused confusion to the playgoer, but depleted the work of necessary dramatic concreteness and action.

Evidently resolved to improve his dramatic technique, though without foregoing his philosophy of sin and salvation, Eliot wrote *The Cocktail Party* in 1949, employing richer and more varied characterization than previously, and neatly furnishing the play with acidulous comedy of manners. He accomplished this feat in a story of an upper-class marriage seemingly irreparably damaged and then repaired through the mystical agency of guardian angels in mufti — that is, glib society friends in ordinary life who prove to be supernatural guardians. They bring the married couple and the husband's mistress to a spiritual guide presented by Eliot as a psychiatrist of indeterminate classification. The latter reconciles the superficial couple and sends the husband's lady-love, Celia Copplestone, to self-sacrificing work among the natives of Africa and to a martyr's glorious death, for which he knew her to be qualified by the hunger of her spirit.

It could be argued against the play that Eliot's desire to write poetic dialogue that would not sound like poetry resulted in his not writing poetry at all in most of the scenes. This hardly matters, since Eliot's non-poetic verse constitutes excellent high comedy dialogue. Moreover, this dialogue does rise to a noble elevation whenever the content calls for it. Confusion and difficulty of comprehension were also charged against the work. Yet, this did not prevent the London and New York productions from having long and profitable runs. Considerable protest could be lodged against Eliot on the score of a fundamentally "superior" outlook that makes a sharp theological distinction between a society of the elect, one member of which is assigned to a glorious, if horrible martyrdom, and the garden-variety of men and women, who are restored to commonplace domesticity by the "psychiatrist." Here, too, however, some defense is possible, since, after all, there are differences in spiritual endowment among the characters.

The Cocktail Party suffers as a play mainly from the absence of its most interesting character in the third act, and from the transference of her story to reportage once she departs for Africa. For two acts the work has continuing tension, but loses it thereafter, and precisely at the point when it should mount. As the Times Literary Supplement [5] pointed out, "at the end of the second act the main crises have been virtually resolved." The third act is largely an epilogue.

In the third act, too, the reunited Chamberlaynes display good breeding and sentiment, but what they make of their reunion is hardly of great consequence as drama. Nor does their later life redound to the credit of Sir Henry Harcourt-Reilly, psychiatrist-extraordinary and Harley Street father-confessor. His mystical status cannot be seen in a very impressive light if little more than a cocktail party *status quo* is the end of his endeavors on stage while the spiritual redemption of Celia Copplestone remains off stage. Fortunately, the "high comedy" atmosphere of the third act returns us to the milieu of the first act (though with some deepening of mood), so that the play does not actually disintegrate. It does, however, thin out as a whole, and the weak third act comes as a disappointment after a second-act scene in Harcourt-Reilly's office which is remarkably effective both as drama and as poetry. The Times Literary Supplement called it "the finest scene in modern poetic drama." [5]

With *The Cocktail Party*, T. S. Eliot came closest to writing viable poetic drama for the theatre. More such drama came with greater facility, less depth of thought, and less poetic discipline from his junior Christopher Fry (1907–   ), particularly in *The Lady's Not for Burning*. Fry had previously written a charming pastoral saint play, *The Boy with a Cart* (1937), a pert one-act version of the matron of Ephesus theme from Petronius *A Phoenix Too Frequent* (1946), a weighty Moses-in-Egypt religious piece *The First-born* (1947), and a Canterbury Festival play *Thor, with Angels* (1948). A marked talent for dramatic verse had appeared in these plays, even in the slight and rather familiar wit of *Phoenix Too Frequent*.

The Lady's Not for Burning (1949), staged successfully both in London and New York by John Gielgud, revealed its author at the peak of his abilities as versifier, poet, dramatist, and theatrician. Concerned with an extraordinarily bright and voluble young man's attempt to save an innocent girl from a medieval witch-hunt by pretending that he is the criminal, the play ran the gamut of emotions and theatrical tricks with virtuosity and grace. Mingling horseplay with the imminence of witch-burning, and combining conversational dexterity with dramatic suspense, the play attracted all but those who found Fry too much in love with his own cleverness. Here and there, too, Fry sent his plummet down a fathom deeper than is customary in bright comedy. The anguish of the sceptical savior of the "witch" actually resembles the existentialist sense of isolation and disillusion present in the plays of Sartre and Camus. His despair is, however, a watered down existentialism at best, and it is romantically dissolved when the "witch" overcomes his dread of attachment and prevails upon him to go away with her.

The Lady's Not for Burning was romantic not only in its verbal pyrotechnics but in its breezy defiance of philistinism. It read like a young man's effort, although there was surely no reason to regret this in so scintillating an exercise. Eliot was reported to have said that Fry would be a good poet when he learned not to be so poetical; and this was a valid criticism, as was also any complaint one could lodge against the author's excessive skittishness.

If the author had not been forty-two when he wrote *The Lady's Not for Burning*, one might have located the play in his ultimate development as his *Love's Labour's Lost*; this, on the basis of the writing's embellished prolixity. Like *Love's Labour's Lost*, it was a youthful play, but without having a young author. His next play *Venus Observed* (1950), written for Laurence Olivier, while more chastened in style, actually revealed some retrogression in substance and craftsmanship. Frequently amusing, this comedy of a middle-aged gentleman's encounters with a bevy of eligible women contracted a broken spine after the first act. It failed to reveal a logic of natural development. Next in 1950, Fry made the deft translation and adaptation of Anouilh's *L'Invitation au Château* — the previously described *Ring Round the Moon* — which could do no more, however, than confirm previously formed impressions that Fry was completely at ease in the theatre. (A former schoolmaster, Fry had started his career on the stage as an actor at Bath as long ago as 1927. He had directed plays for a repertory company from 1934 to 1936, and had tried his hand, in 1939 and 1940, at the pageant-plays *Thursday Child* and *The Tower*.) Whether he would ultimately attain the stature that was already being claimed him, could not be determined at the midpoint of the century. Fry's work, nevertheless, signified some freshening of English playwriting.

English drama possesses an unfaded tradition of poetry. It was gratifying to find it reviving in the poetry and skillful verse of Eliot, Fry, and others.[6] There was refreshment for the long neglected ear in having a country saint in *The Boy with the Cart* speak Wordsworthian poetry in referring to "A brushwork sun skidding ahead of me," and in hearing the hero of *The Lady's Not for Burning*, Thomas Mendip, declare

> Flesh
> Weighs like a thousand years, and every morning
> Wakes heavier for an intake of uproariously
> Comic dreams which smell of bane

or, suiting action to statement,

> . . . if existence will
> Molest a man with beauty, how can he help
> Trying to impose on her the boundary
> Of his two bare arms?

(Oxford University Press, 1949–1950)

Fry, however, still had to take his own prescription, as delivered at a London Group Theatre symposium, to the effect that the poet-dramatist "should not be conscious of himself creating a special form" and that "his poetry should come to him from his characters." (Theatre Newsletter, vol. 5, no. 115, February 3, 1951.) In the spring of 1951 he returned to religious drama with *A Sleep of Prisoners,* presenting several Biblical episodes in the form of dreams by prisoners of war in a ruined church. The medieval dream allegory tradition was present here with considerably less stiffness than has been customary, and the relation of the caged soldiers' nightmares to the relevant theme of sin and salvation was sufficiently apparent; the captives' tensions justified their fantasies.

The play, which was first produced at St. Thomas's Church in London, made a strong impression in England. It was interestingly constructed and contained some of Fry's best dramatic poetry. It did not, however, represent any advance toward significant modern drama. Nor did Fry successfully unify his episodes, with the result that the play seemed more like a perfunctory exercise than it actually was.

Americans enjoyed no such minor renaissance of poetic theatre, either Shakespearian or modern, as did the English. Nevertheless, a small sluice of poetic drama was opened by Tennessee Williams, and a "poetry of theatre" (rather than of language) distinguished *Death of a Salesman*, an imaginatively constructed drama by the new playwright Arthur Miller.

The most widespread advances in the American theatre appeared in the field of musical entertainment. Most original were a series of *Ballet Ballads* (1948), one-act syntheses of music, chorus, and ballet written by the lyricist John Latouche to a score by Jerome Moross. This experiment, however, was a lone venture, and the most influential advances were made on the musical comedy stage, to which the major contributions continued to be made by the partnership of Richard Rodgers and Oscar Hammerstein II that had begun with *Oklahoma*!

Rodgers and Hammerstein, who did not quite succeed with their experimental but rather blatant morality-play *Allegro*, made distinct progress in *South Pacific* by allowing the action of their vivid and affecting South Sea island romance to assimilate the conventional musical comedy chorus. Thematically superior to most musicals with its story of racial prejudice defeating one pair of lovers and being overcome by another, *South Pacific* proved as musically and dramatically effective, if not quite as enchanting, as their first triumph *Oklahoma*! In the season of 1949–50, these experts managed to make another meritorious, if rather derivative, musical entertainment, *The King and I*, a comedy of the Westernization of Siam and a paean to tolerance and democratic progress. Other musicals of merit, such as *Finian's Rainbow*, compounded of Celtic fantasy, satire and American idealism by E. Y. Harburg and Fred Saidy, and *Brigadoon*, a tenderly wrought Scottish romantic fantasy by Alan Jay Lerner and Frederick Loewy, enlivened the period. The musical stage also found some austere elevation in the ingenious operatic efforts or "music-dramas" of Gian-Carlo Menotti. *The Medium* (1947) was an original and spine-chilling *grand-guignol* about spiritualism, and *The Consul*, in the season of 1949–50, gave stirring expression to the anxieties and disappointments of would-be emigrés from a totalitarian country. Menotti won an enviable reputation in America, as a playwright and composer, although both his musical score and plot were quite derivative.

Less gratification was provided, in general, by the musically-unaided playwriting on which the estate of drama still must rest, no matter how enriched the theatre can be by musical composition and ballet. Philip Barry (1896–1949), Elmer Rice, and Maxwell Anderson contributed respectable familiar work. Barry's *Second Threshold* (1951), completed after his death by Robert Sherwood, was perhaps his most thoughtful high-comedy, being suffused with the subdued wisdom of disenchantment. Rice exhibited theatrical skill in *Dream Girl*, which made no pretence to world-shaking significance but provided a shrewd, entertaining romance in contemporary terms. Maxwell Anderson, in addition to writing a Joan of Arc play in the form of a stage rehearsal, *Joan of Lorraine*, and making a musical version of the South African social novel *Cry, the Beloved Country* with the composer Kurt Weill (*Lost in the Stars*), supplied his best-written Elizabethan verse drama. It was *Anne of the Thousand Days*, a free treatment of the fateful marriage of Anne Boleyn and Henry VIII.

Among plays by the generation of the nineteen-twenties, O'Neill's *The Iceman Cometh*, produced in 1946, stood out as an imposing edifice erected by Giant Despair. Written in 1939, it expressed this uncompromising author's despair of mankind. The play was a naturalistic picture of failure in the case of denizens of a beach-front saloon who sustain themselves with desperate illusions. This overlong work, which possessed much force and sardonic humor, could have been improved by judicious cutting and by a less lumbering style of production. For all that, however, O'Neill's study of human frailty and self-deception was impressive. One might describe it as a *Lower Depths* written with psychological complexity as well as with flashes of anger and scorn. And it may be added that although the "Waste Land" pessimism of the work displeased the hopeful after the Second World War, world events not long after the close of the production made O'Neill's saturnine attitude quite comprehensible. Here, as in his earlier work, O'Neill was independent of temporal considerations. He remained planted squarely in a sense of original sin and a need for redemption far less theological but far more anguished and turbulent than Eliot's. His negations had heat and fire rather than surface glitter, for O'Neill, as usual, had not set out to please anyone. If the play also had raffish humor, it was there naturally, rather than by clever calculation. The entire work seemed more hewn out of dogged conviction and personal torment than calculatingly composed; and this impression accounted for much of the strength of the play, as well as for the shortcomings that caused dissatisfaction with it.

Later, in the same season of 1946–47, the Theatre Guild also attempted to produce another play by O'Neill, *The Moon for the Mis-*

begotten, the drama of an oversized, unbeautiful farm girl and a dissipated, disillusioned man, written in 1943. The Guild withdrew it after a mid-Western tryout, mainly owing to difficulties in properly casting the "six-foot" Irish heroine of that piece. A third play of his, *A Touch of the Poet,* was not made available to the public, and a fourth, *Long Day's Journey into the Night,* would not be produced until twenty-five years after its author's death because it was, according to O'Neill, "a real story" and one person in it was still alive.

Even without these pieces, however, O'Neill's work since 1914 comprised the most substantial body of dramatic literature produced by an American playwright, and it was no small reflection upon the professional theatre that his plays were not regularly revived. America still lacked a professional repertory company, although an abortive attempt had been made by Margaret Webster, Eva Le Galliene, and Cheryl Crawford to establish one. America also lacked a true National Theatre, for whose repertoire O'Neill's contributions would have qualified better than any other native playwright's work. Although a chartered but precariously financed American National Theatre and Academy ("ANTA") made a valiant beginning with experimental productions that culminated, under the management of Robert Breen, in an ambitious season of ten plays during 1950–51, this organization's professional status awaited strengthening and stabilization. When Robert Whitehead undertook this task, his first act was to provide a powerful revival of O'Neill's farm-tragedy, *Desire Under the Elms.* A situation of crisis had been forming in the commercial theatre after the war, chiefly, if not exclusively, as a result of high costs of production, and this made it still more difficult to keep the works of O'Neill regularly on view.

The contributions of younger playwrights than Anderson and O'Neill, of writers discovered during the nineteen-thirties, also sustained mid-century stage production. Their influence on the theatre, however, was no longer as strong as it had been before 1940, and "social drama" was no longer in great favor with the public and the critics, and, it seemed, with the playwrights themselves.

After many disappointments since *Golden Boy* (1937) Clifford Odets (1906–   ) prevailed in the 1950–51 season with his intense domestic drama *The Country Girl;* and, reflecting the decline of social militancy in the American Theatre during the growing tension with Soviet Russia, this was Odets' first play to lack challenging implications. On one hand, their absence represented a reduction of dimension in his work, which had previously owed much of its significance and force to his social passion. On the other hand, the play gave assurance that Odets, the most gifted discovery of the mid-thirties, was still a powerful dramatist on any terms, and that he could prove himself one whenever he did not strain for analogies between his characters and the social scene.

Continuing to write plays with considerable regularity, Lillian Hellman (1905–) supplied a sequel to her 1939 drama *The Little Foxes* in *Another Part of the Forest* (1946). It presented the members of her Hubbard family in earlier stages of their predatory career. Less effective than *The Little Foxes*, the play, nonetheless, had a fine cutting edge. Moral analysis being this author's major preoccupation, Miss Hellman presented an adaptation of the existentialist play *Montserrat* (by Robles) in 1949, and concluded her stint for the decade of the nineteen-forties with *The Autumn Garden*, produced in the spring of the 1950–51 season. The play considered the misspent and futile lives of a number of characters whose years of indecision had twisted or stalemated them beyond redemption. Neither a water-tight case, nor a surging drama, this seemingly random piece was nonetheless carefully ordered and often absorbing. It contained some half dozen excellently drawn characters (this itself was an unusual achievement in the decade's theatre), as well as some of the most incisive and revealing dialogue of which this vigorous playwright was capable. The play also included a measure of human sympathy, rare in a Hellman trial (for once, there were no downright villains on her calendar), as well as a degree of affecting indirection and stasis unusual for a writer who had usually favored overt conflicts on the stage.

Sidney Kingsley (1906–) also had a trial calendar and used it twice, in *Detective Story* (1949) and in a dramatization of Arthur Koestler's powerful political novel *Darkness at Noon*, produced in the season of 1950–51. The indictment in the first case was directed at too much righteousness, and in the second case, against totalitarianism in Soviet Russia. *Detective Story*, the drama of a guardian of the law whose obsessive tracking down of criminals destroyed his happiness and peace of mind, had a vivid night-court setting and brought a varied yet tense action to a strong climax. In this drama, Kingsley revealed not merely his usual craftsman's skill, but also his particular talent for naturalistic presentation of backgrounds. This talent found scant employment in *Darkness at Noon*, which levied extreme demands, however, on Kingsley's craftsmanship and revealed his skill. He also managed to supply considerable pathos and intense self-examination in the story of the "Old Bolshevik" Rubashov, whose torment resides less in his personal fate as a condemned "traitor" than in his ironic realization that he had helped to establish the communist rule that was betraying his ideals. Endorsement of the play as a work of art rather than as topical drama would, nonetheless, require considerable quali-

fication.   Except for Rubashov, the characterizations were sketchy;
except for his speeches, the dialogue was less than inspired.

Darkness at Noon was indicative of a change of temper in the
post-war American theatre. It had started in 1945 with a rush of
liberal enthusiasm for self-criticism by Americans, and it ended with
pointing a finger at conditions in a country to which many liberals
had once extended much sympathetic patience. As the author of *Ten
Million Ghosts* and *Dead End* (1936), Kingsley himself had been an
outstanding liberal of the same brand.

Immediately after the Second World War, the American theatre
had evinced considerable resolve to safeguard and put into local effect·
the ideals of racial tolerance that had received emphasis during the
conflict with the Germany of genocidal storm-troopers. Even the
American motion picture industry manifested an interest in this cause
with such films as *Gentlemen's Agreement, Home of the Brave*, and
Lost Boundaries. American liberalism was represented on the stage
in general terms by Emmet Lavery's biography of Justice Oliver
Wendell Holmes, *The Magnificent Yankee* (1946). The authors of
the anti-Nazi play *Tomorrow the World* (1943), James Gow and
Arnaud d'Usseau, exposed discriminatory attitudes toward the Negro
in *Deep Are the Roots*. It was a somewhat sensational work for
America, since it touched upon the question of intermarriage. Its best
portions were the least melodramatic ones: a liberal-minded young
woman's realization that prejudice had struck deep roots in her consciousness, and a pair of young lover's renunciation of each other after
acknowledging the incompatibility of their love with the realities of
their environment. This work was followed by a number of undistinguished presentations of the Negro problem in both the North and
the South. One treatment of antisemitism late in 1945, *Home of the
Brave* by Arthur Laurents, however, was written with considerable
ingenuity and force. The subject was presented as a clinical case in
a somewhat expressionistic form and dealt with an inner trauma
rather than with overt examples of prejudice.

The most successful liberal plays were comedies in which messages
were subordinated to humor or were enlivened by it. The best of these
were contributed by facile practitioners; by the successful film director
Garson Kanin and by the playwriting team of Lindsay and Crouse.
Kanin's *Born Yesterday* (1946) was reminiscent of the debunking
farce-comedies that had flourished in the nineteen-twenties and thirties,
during the reign of Kaufman comedy. To the familiar antics and
"wise-cracks" of the Kaufman school, Kanin added an undertone of
serious concern with the efforts of a ruthless promoter to circumvent
the law and subvert legislators, as well as to ride roughshod over

ordinary people's feelings. In *State of the Union* (1945), Lindsay and Crouse confected political comedy from a nomination campaign and a domestic fracas. The two themes merged in the comic intervention of a clever wife, who deflated her husband's ego and political ambitions by routing both her rival, an unscrupulous woman publisher, and the politically unhealthy elements that were clinging to her essentially well-intentioned spouse. Later, a third, less scintillating piece dealing with anti-liberal policies at a girl's college, *Goodbye, My Fancy* by Fay Kanin, completed the round of a *genre* of comedies dedicated to the advocacy of democratic principle.

To what extent the deepening international crisis and the ensuing rise of intolerance for dissident opinion would affect social drama in a serious or even in a comic vein, remained to be seen. At the conclusion of the 1950–51 season, anti-liberal manifestations were inconsequential in the theatre, and it could be argued, indeed, that the very denunciations of the Soviet regime in *Darkness At Noon* were made on behalf of liberalism. Liberalism, after all, consists in looking into one's neighbor's backyard as well as into one's own. The question that arose in 1951 was only whether looking into their own yard might cease to be one way in which playwrights would feel free to exercise their powers of observation and self-expression.

Most people engaged in the American theatre were actually more exercised over the possibility that the professional stage, which had been a shrinking enterprise for some time, would shrink even further. It was quite unusual now for even enthusiastically endorsed Broadway productions to earn back their investment. Consequently there were fewer and fewer plays on the boards. University and community theatres throughout the land strove to take up the slack in stage production, and efforts were made to encourage decentralization of the American stage. The cause of dramatic art coincided with patriotism and American self-esteem. Surely, the greatest republic the world has ever seen deserved a theatre proportionate to its national resources!

For artistic creation, however, honorable ambitions are insufficient, as are also conditions of economic prosperity. Talent is required, and dramatic talent is usually scarce. Interest in contemporary drama must focus, therefore, on the emergence of new writers and the progress of recently established playwrights.

The effectiveness of the able novelist Carson McCullers was not conclusive, since the entrancing comedy of lonely adolescence, *Member of the Wedding*, was her dramatization of her own novel. Robinson Jeffers' exciting free version of Euripides' *Medea* (1947), in which the remarkable tragedienne Judith Anderson gave a celebrated performance, was no indication of halcyon days for the theatre. Jeffers

was a poet rather than a dramatist by profession and he had been
writing for some thirty years. Incisive dramas, such as *The Heiress*
and *Billy Budd*, as well as the two meritorious war-plays *Command
Decision* (1947) and *Mister Roberts* (1948), were all dramatizations
of books.[7]

More confidence was engendered by the newcomer William Inge,
whose first professionally produced play *Come Back, Little Sheba*
revealed insight into commonplace life and a capacity for transfiguring it into consuming pathos. The play dealt with a well-bred man's
sense of failure in marriage and his explosive alcoholism before he
relapses into remorseful quiescence. The tension in this play simmered
for a long time, burst into almost unbearable frenzy in the second
act, and then simmered down again. A fateful rhythm in an alcoholic's
life was established by the playwright. Deliberately making the drama
static at the beginning, the author prepared a tremendous explosion of
nerves and anguish. The alcoholic goes berserk after his wife's irritating behavior, which reminds him of the manner in which he was
trapped into marriage. The author was equally adept in his portrayal
of the wife, a slatternly and crude woman who is, nonetheless, pathetic
in her fluttering anxiety and compensatory *voyeurism*.

One limitation of this kind of naturalism is that it drops us into a
morasses of numbing futility. Horizons are narrowed by such concentration on broken spirits by a playwright who fails to supply compensations of heroic anger or even negation, such as O'Neill provided
in *The Iceman Cometh*. It was, therefore, in the achievements of two
other still young dramatists, Tennessee Williams and Arthur Miller,
that the post-war period in America found the most gratification. A
poetic imagination combined with naturalistic candor was manifest
in Williams, and a force relentlessly judicial, yet compassionate, in
Miller.

12 TENNESSEE WILLIAMS AND ARTHUR MILLER

The Mississippi-born Tennessee (John Lanier) Williams
(1914–) had his first successful production, *The Glass Menagerie*,
in 1945. Hitherto only slightly known for his overwrought study of
small-town frustrations *Battle of Angels* and for his one-act plays
collected under the title 27 *Wagons Full of Cotton and Other One-
Act Plays* (New Directions, 1945), Williams came to be regarded as
the most promising playwright of the decade. There was, in fact,
more than promise in *The Glass Menagerie* and *A Streetcar Named
Desire* (1947), while two other plays, produced between 1948 and
1950, the affecting failure *Summer and Smoke* and the popular
comedy *The Rose Tattoo*, also disclosed a unique talent.

(In all his work, Williams revealed himself a poet of the theatre absorbed in the problem of living an abundant emotional life. His most delicate work, *The Glass Menagerie*, was marred only by some preciosity, mainly in the form of stage directions, most of which were eliminated in Eddie Dowling's memorable Broadway production. Williams presented the depressed family life of a superannuated Southern belle. (The play framed a series of rueful reminiscences by her son, who had made his escape from the stalemate in his home and could now view it with objectivity and rueful compassion.) The play endeared itself to many playgoers as a fusion of realism and poetic theatre. Most notably, however, Williams created here two unforgettable characters, the retiring sister Laura, too shy to face reality, and the mother Amanda, too incompetent to cope with it effectively: the one, unsullied and noble and delicate as thistledown; the other, battered, ineptly designing, querulous — and pathetically ridiculous. These portraits, suggestive of a trapped and frustrated womanhood that Williams had observed in the South, were to recur in *A Streetcar Named Desire* and *Summer and Smoke*.

In the last-mentioned work, which had a rich texture of dramatic experience but depended on a too novelistic or sprawling structure, the Laura type was to dominate the action. Here, moreover, the inhibited "Laura" character, who loses her chance of love as a result of too much fastidiousness, was not allowed to retain her pristine purity. Driven to desperation by ironically losing the man she had kept at a distance too long, Williams' heroine makes an assignation with the first footloose person she meets. Frustration, painstakingly motivated by her sensitivity and her unhappy family life, starts the idealistic girl on a road that may have many widenings but will ultimately bring her to complete moral, as well as psychological, bankruptcy.

Few qualifications greeted the earlier produced, extremely popular *Streetcar Named Desire*, brilliantly staged by Elia Kazan. This play revolved around a woman who bore considerable resemblance to the heroine of *Summer and Smoke* in the last scene. (*Summer and Smoke* was actually written before *A Streetcar Named Desire*.) Blanche Du Bois, the daughter of a plantation family, seeks a last refuge in the home of a sister. Dislodged from her moorings by the decay of her family and by an unfortunate marriage to an abnormal young man, she has become a nymphomaniac and prostitute who sustains her last shreds of dignity on alcohol and delusions. It is Blanche's final misfortune that her state of mind requires her to assume an air of fastidiousness and superiority toward the vivacious Polish workingman her more earthy sister had married. Stanley Kowalsky, defending his honor and marriage against Blanche, succeeds in stripping her of every shred of pitiful pretence and destroys the only opportunity she has of contracting a marriage that might have saved her from total shipwreck. Since this struggle between Blanche and her brother-in-law has not lacked elements of sexual provocation, it ends in his violating her while her sister is in the hospital giving birth to a child. Thoroughly deranged after this traumatic event, she is taken to an asylum with the consent of the sister, who has the hard choice of either sending her away as a mental case or believing Blanche's frantic accusations against Stanley.

A Streetcar Named Desire is subject to criticism on the grounds that it is overmotivated (Pelion is piled on Ossa in order to establish Blanche's psychosis), and that Williams was excessively exercised over a problem more clinical than tragic. The clinical picture is, at the same time, less convincingly clear than it might be, and the rape scene, although powerful theatre in itself, may be designated as naturalism transformed into sensationalism. A shift in the characterization and dramatic function of Kowalsky is also effected by this scene, since the point at issue before Stanley violated Blanche had been his resolve to repel an intruder who was threatening his marriage.

Still, *Streetcar* made pulsating theatre, falling short of tragic austerity and artistic discipline, but also rising above the level of mere pathos. Blanche was too intense in her clinging to the ideal of herself, an ideal of refinement and distinction, to be a mere object of pity. For the most part, the question of pity for the world's bruised lambs, central to the play, was raised by Williams with sensitivity unweakened by sentimentality. The lamb in this instance was on occasion a lioness, fiercely defending her litter of dreams. It was also evident, before the rape scene, that the mercy Blanche failed to meet could not be extended to her, given the circumstances and given her own compulsively irritating behavior. That the wind is not usually tempered to shorn lambs was an essential element of whatever meaning the play suggested and exemplified. Supplied with a vivid background and vital characterization, suffused at the same time with expressive atmosphere, and enriched with a dialogue often salty and often evocative, *A Streetcar Named Desire* made vibrant theatre. A maturer playwright, a more intellectually and artistically disciplined one, might have wrought an imperishable masterpiece out of the story and character.

At the midpoint of the century, Williams did not attempt to exceed his reach. *The Rose Tattoo*, which opened in New York in February 1951, was a rather jerry-built, if vivid, play of no particular consequence. Its attractiveness lay in folk and character comedy, somewhat darkened by a Latin woman's obsession with her late husband's prowess and fidelity as a lover. To some degree too, *The Rose Tattoo* marked a departure from its author's too familiar *motif* of sexual repression. Along with bursts of naturalistic sensationalism, this theme had been too conspicuous in what might be called the "Southern Gothic" phase of Williams' playwriting and was beginning to weary some of his critics. Whether the overcoming of frustration at the conclusion of *The Rose Tattoo* was of great moment is questionable. It was the vitality of the Sicilian-American characters in the play that mattered; this, along with the author's eye for colorful detail and his ear for expressive dialogue. These evidences of Williams' talent, however, were by no means new; they had been apparent for a decade — ever since Theresa Helburn and John Gassner had selected him for a New School playwriting seminar in 1940 and bought his *Battle of Angels* for the Theatre Guild at the end of the semester. Whether he would equal or surpass the steps he had already taken toward major playwriting still remained to be seen. Since, at the writing of *The Rose Tattoo*, Williams was only in his thirty-seventh year, the prospect seemed favorable.

Williams' compeer during the early post-war period was Arthur Miller (1916–   ), the author of *All My Sons* and *Death of a Salesman*. His promise had been recognized in the last years of the 'thirties by Theresa Helburn's Bureau of New Plays, headed by Miss Helburn and John Gassner, and he was financially assisted by the Bureau while studying drama at the University of Michigan under Professor Kenneth E. Rowe. Before winning the New York Drama Critics Circle award with *All My Sons* in 1947, he had been writing plays for some time. He had aroused interest with an uneven novelistic play, *The Man Who Had All the Luck*, on Broadway in 1944, and had won considerable success with a novel about anti-semitism, *Focus* (1945), that had been originally conceived as a play. In 1942, he had also done research for the scenario of the Ernie Pyle war film *The Story of G.I. Joe*, and in 1944 had published a diary of experiences connected with this work in army camps under the title *Situation Normal*.

All My Sons, although somewhat contrived and familiarly plotted, was a strongly characterized and tautly drawn indictment of a war profiteer in particular and of the social philosophy of self-interest in general. More specifically, it was the drama of a factory owner, Joe Keller, who in his anxiety over the possibility of losing war contracts, had sold defective engines to the government, thereby causing the death of a number of American flyers during the Second World War. After having shifted the blame on to an innocent partner, Keller tries to enjoy the harvest of his dishonesty. His guilt, however, is discovered, whereupon he elects to kill himself rather than have his own son deliver him up to the police. Joe Keller's motive had been his desire to preserve his business in order to pass it on to his sons. Instead, one of the sons, an aviator, committed suicide on hearing of his father's guilt, and his other son turns against him. Keller learns at long last that family loyalty is not enough for a member of the human race. The taut, if somewhat overcontrived, play recalled Ibsen's social realism and demonstration of a moral issue.

The competence, rather than creative originality, of *All My Sons* did not prepare one for Miller's next play, *Death of a Salesman* (1949), which presented the calvary of an ordinary man with the help of a discreetly employed expressionistic technique of "flashback" reminiscence and delirium. Considerable technical skill, imagination, and close observation of character and suburban manners went into the work, along with a deep pity that fastidious critics considered somewhat too prodigally expended upon the commonplace salesman Willy Loman. The play had especially vibrant scenes of conflict between Willy and his sons, whose failure to come up to his expectations is the special cross he has to bear in a generally disappointing career as a run-of-the-mill salesman. If the trials of an elderly employee put out to pasture were necessarily pitched only on the ordinary level of pathos, Willy's parental passion assumed huge dimensions.

Miller's hero — like the heroes of all exciting, more or less tragic drama — is an extremist who lives intensely rather than wisely and well. There is no mean in Willy's naive glorification of materialistic success, salesmanship and personal popularity. He is also immoderate in his expectations of filial devotion and in the hopes he entertains for one of his sons, the former high school football hero Biff. Extremists make heroic characters whatever their station in life; and unless all their values are ignoble, extremists are apt to approach the estate of tragedy. Ultimately, Willy, who had first sought death as an escape from failure, kills himself in order to preserve his image of himself as the man who has produced a great son. His suicide is sparked by the resolve to secure the future of the son in whom he continues to repose high hopes. These are not warranted by reality, as the son himself realizes; but since when have tragic and near-tragic characters been sensible? Willy's suburban little man's ambitions and his problems as a superannuated employee do not qualify him for a role in classic tragedy. Yet Willy is a thoroughly human character whose limitations and errors are combined with a noble parental passion and a heroic effort to maintain his self-esteem and dreams. He has misjudged reality, and this error destroys him; but, as Edith Hamilton might have said, this common man belongs to the "aristocracy of passionate souls" — an aristocracy of the tragic temperament.

To place the play on the austere peaks of high tragedy would be to overestimate Willy's sense of values and to overlook his failure to achieve any understanding of himself and of reality; self-understanding is attained only by his son Biff and understanding of Willy's character and circumstances is won only by his wife and his neighbor Uncle Charlie. Miller retained a realistic attitude toward his floundering main character. Willy's lack of insight is, indeed, so great that Arthur Miller had to resort to the old-fashioned method of employing *raisonneurs* in order to give the play its total meaning. Nor was Miller's language capable of soaring sufficiently for supreme tragic effect. Between the extremes of dismissing the play as mere pathos and acclaiming it as "high tragedy," however, there lies a respectable area of "middle tragedy" in modern theatre, and here *Death of a Salesman* is entirely at home.

If any conclusions can be drawn from the work of Williams and Miller, it is that by drawing sustenance from the common man and from raw experience, American playwriting displayed considerable vigor and amplitude. The American "cult of experience" paid dividends in the theatre. Moreover, blunt strength could be combined with sensitiveness; naturalism with poetic or, at least, theatrical imagination; and realistic technique with other (expressionist and symbolist) techniques. All this, it is true, had already been manifest in the work of O'Neill more than a quarter of a century earlier. In order to be effective, however, each generation must rediscover for itself what has already been discovered. Since realism had remained the dominant style of the American theatre and had, in fact, acquired augmented prestige from the pressures of a decade of economic depression and half a decade of total war, the advantage of fusing realism with imagination was a necessary rediscovery. Its possibilities were sufficiently explored by Williams and Miller, as well as sufficiently appreciated by the American public, to provide some hope for a theatre that had become, economically, almost untenable. It is true that a decline of creative energy in the American theatre could be noted at the mid-century point. It did not, however, follow that this decline had to be of long duration.

XXXII

MIDCENTURY SUMMARY

I MODERN THEATRE

A THREE-QUARTER of a century period of more or less distinctive theatre and dràma closed with the season of 1950–51, if we take the year 1875 to be the beginning.[1] In theatrical art, the Western world had run the gamut of a variety of styles of production, theatrical organization, and acting. During that period, style had followed style, and style had *fused* with style, while playgoers became accustomed to accepting every convention of theatre. Especially after World War I, it was not uncustomary in any single season to see, jostling each other on Broadway or London's Shaftsbury Avenue, or in most European theatrical capitals, plays and productions more or less realistic, symbolistic, expressionistic, and even surrealistic. If any conclusion could be drawn from this situation, it was that the modern world was eclectic, curious and restive, as in other historical ages of social and cultural instability. In any case, the period was characterized by a pervasive experimentalism which indicated creative vigor to some observers and decadence or a "decline of the west" to others.

Philosophically-minded critics and historians came to lament that the theatre had ceased to be a communion and had become a gaudy marketplace filled with the miscellaneous gewgaws of a Vanity Fair. That was, to a degree, the case, since eclecticism and variety were the order of the day. There were also in the Western theatre little sideshows by coteries acclaimed as the avant-garde or denounced as mountebanks and decadents. These artists sometimes wore the rue of disenchantment and displayed it with gaiety or with bravura. At the theatres frequented and created by the sophisticates of different decades there could often be seen dramatic oddities: Productions of an *Ubu Roi* (a prank with a sting in its tail by the adolescent Alfred Jarry) in the 1890's;[2] a Cummings *him* in the 1920's; a Gertrude Stein *Four Saints in Three Acts*, in which the words were not intended to make sense; or a Cocteau *jeu d'esprit*, such as *Orpheus* or *The Infernal Machine*, in the 1920's and the 1930's. All this and much more could be noted, including the many extravagant stage performances of German expressionism, Italian futurism, and Russian constructivism.

747

On reflection, however, it will be seen that, in the field of stage production, a general pattern emerges. Viewed in perspective, the bewildering confusion of styles can be subsumed under two developments : Realism and experiments in non-realistic stylization of theatre.

Stage realism was the first major achievement. It represented an advance over the haphazard theatricality and vulgar romanticism that had preempted stage production during the first three quarters of the nineteenth century. The stage was not reformed until after pioneering by the so-called independent theatres, amateur at first and later professional, such as Antoine's *Théâtre Libre* in Paris, and Stanislavsky's *Moscow Art Theatre*. Stage realism, dedicated in its first phase to photographic literalness and anti-theatrical naturalness, came honestly by its label of Naturalism. Maturing and mellowing, however, it recognized the contradiction between literalness and art ; and, indeed, between "naturalness" and "art," since art invariably entails expressive organization and significant form, some stylization and even some artificiality. Naturalism, then, made way for a style or convention of staging that may be properly designated as "Selective Realism".

At the peak of the naturalistic movement, moreover, and in reaction to it, there arose in the eighteen-nineties, largely as a reflection of symbolism in poetry and of the *fin de siècle* "art for art's sake" vogue, a movement devoted to emphatic and sensitively designed stylization. It differed in theory and practice from the pre-naturalistic — haphazardly romantic and realistic — stage in insisting upon unity and expressiveness of style. It differed from the naturalistic theatre in stressing suggestiveness, poetry of mood, and various degrees of symbolization. Propounded under the general term "symbolism" (which should not be equated in most cases with allegory), the directors and scene designers took their cue mainly from Wagner's ideas on theatre as a perfect synthesis of the arts.

This movement's strongholds were the so-called Art Theatres. The first of these, the *Théâtre d'Art*, was founded by the French poet Paul Fort in 1890. The next important one, a few years later, was the *Théâtre de L'Oeuvre*, founded by Lugné-Poë (1869–1940), once an actor in Antoine's naturalistic productions, who staged Maeterlinck's early symbolist plays. Max Reinhardt (1873–1943), who had played old men's parts at the Berlin *Deutsches Theater* under the naturalist producer Otto Brahm, was another stage director who turned to stylization. He adopted, indeed, a variety of styles during his long and flourishing career in Central Europe.

Still, it was not long before the "symbolists" met the realists halfway, just as the realists assimilated the artistry of the symbolists. The Moscow Art Theatre produced plays by Maeterlinck and Andreyev and asked Gordon Craig to stage *Hamlet* for it in 1911. The classic instance of amalgamation of advances in realism and stylization is provided by the distinguished career of Jacques Copeau (1878–1949). He started with antagonism to the realistic stage, establishing his *Théâtre du Vieux Colombier* in Paris to promote symbolist art. Soon, however, he made his enterprise next in. importance to the Moscow Art Theatre by fusing simplified, formalist production style with the "inner realism" of acting developed by Constantin Stanislavsky (1865–1938). His associates and followers were the influential actor-managers Louis Jouvet and Charles Dullin. In later years, after the closing of his theatre, Copeau maintained a school that attracted students from all parts of the world. Among these was Harold Clurman, the eminent New York Group Theatre director, who staged the best of Odets' plays of social realism in the nineteen-thirties.

Together with Selective Realism, a modified symbolism — although often one would be hard put to it to distinguish one style from the other — has been the dominant production style of the century. The more or less aberrant twentieth century styles of expressionism, constructivism, futurism, surrealism, and "epic-theatre" (of the Brecht-Piscator and the "Living Newspaper" variety) all represented facets of the general departure from naturalism initiated by the *fin de siècle* symbolist movement toward the close of the nineteenth century. These styles were not invariably the flotsam of a shipwrecked society, even if some extreme productions seemed to be nothing more than that. In the case of "epic theatre," the productions not only expressed an orderly view of society and moral consistency, but actually made selective use of both realism and symbolism. (The American playgoer in the late nineteen-thirties could most easily note this development in the Federal Theatre "living newspaper" production *One-third of a Nation*, a dramatization of the problems of slum clearance.) In other instances, extreme stylization was justified by a poetic intention (Strindberg's *The Dream Play*), by satiric protest against dehumanization in industrial, mass-production society (*R.U.R.*, *The Adding Machine*, *Beggar on Horseback*), and by psychological interest, as in O'Neill's *Emperor Jones* and *The Great God Brown*. Stylization was employed, indeed, even for an affirmation of the norms in life. This latter procedure was conspicuously apparent in the orientally stylized *Our Town* Broadway production by Jed Harris, and sanity and stability never received a calmer exposition in the American theatre. *Our Town* was an instance (Brecht's *The Good Woman of Setzuan* is another) of the fact that the modern Western theatre, which has raided many nests, could make itself an orderly home. An *Our Town* or *Good Woman of Setzuan* was surely a sign of wholesomeness rather than of deterioration in the Western mind and creative spirit. Nor was even surrealistic effort invariably esoteric, as American playgoers could discover in the vital productions of Saroyan's plays *My Heart's in the Highlands,* as staged by Robert Lewis, and *The Beautiful People,* as staged by the author himself.

Finally, it is to be noted, that a swing against any stylization that overshot the mark was apt to be prompt during the century. For example, too much Gordon Craig symbolism or too much Meyerhold constructivism or theatricalism was likely to result in a marked reaction. The neglect with which Craig was treated in England is regrettable. Yet England's resistance to much exalted Gordon Craig mistiness, to a *mystique* of art, was surely no sign of a civilization intent upon dissolving itself. The treatment meted out by Soviet Russia to Meyerhold is inexcusable — a barbarous reversal of humanism and freedom, both political and artistic. Still, his loss of popularity with playgoers, even before he lost his post and "disappeared," and even before the hounds of officially inspired dramatic criticism began to yelp at his heels, indicated a preference on the part of playgoers for less bizarre theatre. He, himself, had come to realize, in fact, that he had exhausted the possibilities of extreme constructivism and bio-mechanical performance, and had reduced the degree of stylization in his productions before his brilliant career came to an end.

The above paragraphs are intended to qualify cavalier generalizations to the effect that the century's theatre was in utter chaos and reflected the breakdown of Western civilization. When the facts are assembled and the separate integers are allowed to fall into their proper place in the total arithmetic of modern theatre, there is no reason to accept the Soviet critics' freely flung charges of "bourgeois decadence" at face value. Nor are there compelling reasons to assent to the fastidiously made notations of the disciples of T. S. Eliot and the New Criticism concerning footless and anarchic creation for want of hierarchy and an aristocratic or a theological discipline in our civilization. Bumbling and cheapness — and "decadence" — have always been present in the theatre. It may be noted, in passing, that Eliot himself was not quite so fastidious when he courted popular success with *The Cocktail Party.* (Or did he reassure himself that by descending into the market place, he would lead it into godly ways?) As for those who lamented that the theatre has ceased to serve as a rite or constitute a true communion, they would have to acknowledge that this had been the case long before the advent of our modern theatre. It was not "modernism" that had destroyed "ritual" or communion.[3]

2 MODERN DRAMA

In a summary of this nature, a separation of theatre and drama is, of course, quite impossible, for the theatre does as the drama says; or, so it is at least when the drama has anything worth saying. Conversely, dramatic writing is affected by conditions in the theatre, since the success of writing depends upon efficient projection and enrichment by stage art. To a degree, therefore, what has already been set down by way of modern theatrical history, also applies to the modern drama.

One might add, however, that the question of theatre as ritual and communion does have an important bearing on the subject of modern drama, for ritual entails a shared experience and the modern drama was not generally written by playwrights who assumed long-established and inviolable values. This disturbs those who believe that art, especially dramatic art, is most perfect when dramatists can assume moral and social values instead of having to invent, explain, and argue them in a play, as has been the case ever since Ibsen came to the fore.

Although it is self-evident that communication of feeling and thought is essential, it is, nevertheless, by no means so certain that the drama is always at its best when audience and author absolutely share the same values as members of a stable communion. If this were so, the medieval drama would have been *ipso facto* superior to even Athenian tragedy, which was written after 450 B.C. in an atmosphere of considerable scepticism, strain, and dissension. Certainly, the Athenians themselves did not consider their society or its values as unquestionable and unshaken, or there would have been no Sophists and no outcries against the undermining influence of Euripides and Socrates. By the same test, too, medieval dramatists would have to be rated higher than Shakespeare and the sceptical Molière. We might also reflect that there has been no dearth of "shared values" in the Russia of Stalin, and yet dedication to five-year plans or to Stalinism has hardly qualified conforming Soviet playwrights for any Hall of Fame. In contrast, actually, Russia produced its best writers from Pushkin to Gorky (Gogol, Turgenev, Tolstoy, Dostoevsky, and Chekhov) in a time of crumbling values under an absolutist church and state.

It would seem to the present author that the only conformity necessary to good literary art is conformity to humane principles, and that the only "shared values" are the values man has generally revered, if also often violated. Regardless of how formulated, these have added up to a decent respect for justice, honesty, honor, and loving-kindness — that is, for the humane commonplaces. These values have been as apparent, on the whole, in the best examples of modern drama as in the best dramatic works of any other era.

In the modern drama, it was generally assumed that the interplay of man and his environment is important, if not, indeed, in all respects decisive: that both the individual and society were proper fields for rational inquiry; and that both individuals and communities would reveal upon proper investigation error and evil, as well as possibilities of improvement, explainable on grounds other than those of original human perversity and the need for supernatural intervention. Broadly speaking, the drama was ruled by ideas of progress and evolution that had arisen during the eighteenth century Enlightenment and the American and French Revolutions. Under this dispensation arose the concern with relativistic morality, social reform, equality of the sexes, and psychological problems so frequent in modern playwriting. The antithetical acceptance of original sin, of "degree" or hierarchy, and of absolute morality and a supernatural order was a minority manifestation. On one side, although with individual differences, stood many of the most redoubtable dramatists of the age — Ibsen, Strindberg, Chekhov, Gorky, Benavente, Shaw, Galsworthy, O'Casey. On the other side, although also with individual differences, stood Claudel, the latter-day Strindberg, and T. S. Eliot. Between the rationalists and the believers, stood cynics, sceptics, and heterodox anti-rationalists such as Becque, Synge, Sternheim, Pirandello, Wedekind, and O'Neill. These, too, may be assigned to the liberal wing of modern playwriting, since they too had no effective inclination to cast anchor into the sea of religious faith. The choice for most of the modern playwrights lay between some form of postitivist, liberal set of values or scepticism. And in either case they sought new horizons in art and thought.

Still, it is not to be assumed that a widening of horizons is equivalent to a deepening of insight. Even the assembled assault of a brilliance and knowledge perhaps never before noted in theatrical history did not eventuate in such profundity as may be found in Shakespeare or the classic tragedians. Certainly all the formidable intellectual equipment carried by the moderns was no warrant of artistic superiority, no asurance of artistic triumph. Such peaks of tragic art as those represented by *Hamlet* and *Oedipus the King* were not scaled by the moderns. Although there is no fatalistic certainty that these peaks could not be attained in modern times, the likelihood that they would be scaled in the foreseeable future was not great.

It is to be noted, of course, that much that is commonplace in the text of a play was frequently enriched or at least enlivened by the stage director and the actors. As this edition was going to press (in the spring of 1953), William Inge, previously mentioned only as the author of *Come Back, Little Sheba*, had a new play about humdrum life produced on Broadway, *Picnic*. This drama of frustration in a small-town was made remarkably active in the theatre by Joshua Logan's stage direction.

It should also be noted that playwrights known for their concern with commonplace struggles were not invariably content with their achievement. Arthur Miller, who had won an enormous reputation in America with *Death of a Salesman,* had written an unproduced verse-drama *Montezuma* earlier in his career. In the season of 1952–53, he turned to a historical subject, the Salem witchcraft trials, in *The Crucible.* This stark but exalted drama of bigotry and mass-hysteria tested men's conscience and courage on a tragic plane. Regardless of any critical reservations to which the play could be subjected, the effect on New York audiences was extremely stirring. And the audiences of the modern drama had been stirred quite frequently ever since the advent of Ibsen's *A Doll's House* and Hauptmann's *The Weavers,* although the excitement of a contemporary audience could not, of course, guarantee recurrent exhilaration in later decades.

Finally, it must be observed that the mere composition of poetic drama was no assurance that the modern drama would soar to heights unreached by prose plays. Some of the dullest plays of the modern period were written by versifiers and even by poets. Nor could one consider the mere recourse to expressionist devices and symbolism an effective way of overcoming banality. Often the playwright was simply exchanging the banality of the commonplace for the banalities of estheticism. Thus, a return to German expressionism in Wolfgang Borchert's *The Man Outside (Draussen aus der Tür)*, a play about the return of a soldier from the front, did not herald a revived German drama immediately after Hitler's fall. And *Camino Real* (1953), in which Tennessee Williams symbolized his dim view of modern life with extensive literary allusions, proved to be his weakest full-length play.

Modern playwrights, after 1950, would have to steer a clear course between commonplace realism and literary pretensions if they were to come within hailing distance of the gnarled and deceptively simple prose dramas with which Ibsen inaugurated the age of modern playwriting. That the dangers of estheticism were no fewer than those of dramatic journalism had been demonstrated frequently ever since the advent of Maeterlinck. Nor would salvation come from attempts to dissolve reality into suggestive atmosphere in the case of stage production. Evasions are never solutions.

The limitations of modern drama must be noted along with its attainments. In fact, the former were virtually inherent in the latter. For one thing, the noble age of dramatic poetry was long past, whereas the greatest drama of other periods had also been great poetry. In the Athenian, Elizabethan, and Louis the Fourteenth ages, a sharp distinction between drama and poetry was not even made. The most eminent playwrights of Athens were also its ablest poets; the supreme

Elizabethan dramatist was also the greatest Elizabethan poet; the master-tragedian of Louis XIV's France was also its most distinguished poet. Modern drama was largely prose drama. Its resonances were limited, and its capacity for final and therefore imperishable utterance was not much in evidence unless Shaw thundered or Synge and O'Casey lilted. The poets in the theatre were few in number. Nor can it be maintained that they attained their full poetic magnitude in the verse they wrote for the stage. This is true of Yeats, Eliot, Lorca, Alexander Blok, and Robinson Jeffers.

Also, the modern playwrights were impelled, if not indeed compelled, to argue ideas and substantiate premises in the course of creating a meaningful play. They had to waste time and energy upon something that was less properly fulfilled art than preparatory exposition or discussion. This was a necessity in the case of writers who wrote about social problems and tensions for an age in which political discourse was generally free, and often both voluminous and strident. And those playwrights who concentrated on individuality rather than social problems were rarely less analytical. Modern man was making the study of man analytical and scientifically schematic, which is hardly what Alexander Pope had meant when he wrote that the proper study of man is man. "Psychology" is one thing, a breathing man is another. Modern playwrights, responding to the spirit of the age generally "psychologized." More often than not they tried to penetrate into the human heart by dissecting it (and formulating the results) instead of allowing it to remain alive and whole. For one Chekhov or O'Casey there were a dozen mediocrities who blossomed out as amateur psychologists or psychoanalysts. Characterization in art is not "psychology." Sophocles was not a psychologist, and neither was Shakespeare. But O'Neill, for example, was; and the difference is sometimes painfully apparent when we read many of his plays — although O'Neill was, of course, more than a mere psyche-splitter.

In a fragmented world there was a tendency toward a fragmentation of life in dramatic writing. This, to conclude, was especially apparent in the numerous plays in which spiritually impoverished persons aired their petty aims and tepid tribulations endlessly. This had been "new" material when so-called middle-class drama first invaded the theatre. But it became subject to the law of diminishing returns — or diminishing revelations — as time moved on, and too many playwrights were disinclined to face this fact or were unaware of it. Critics, too, were apt to overlook it, no doubt because they, too, were products of a world that tended to contract space, diminish the areas of wonder, and subject man to microscopic (and therefore incomplete) scrutiny when he was not otherwise reduced to the status of "mass-man," whether suburban or proletarian. An epic quality had characterized Greek and Elizabethan drama, and the epic spirit was not entirely lost in seventeenth century and romantic theatre. But, as a rule, both epic stature and extension were deemed to be *de trop* in the modern theatre, except as spectacle. People seemed to be embarrassed by evidences of epic struggle in the drama, and those who tried to create it were usually regarded as mavericks.[4]

"We are living in a levelling period," wrote Ortega y Gasset. In the main, it must be conceded that the modern playwrights ranged on the foothills of great art, rather than on its topmost elevations. Because the playwrights devoted themselves, in the main, to common reality and to the prose of life, they rarely rose to the altitudes of high tragedy. They favored at most a genre of "low" or "middle" tragedy or, more frequently, an indeterminate type of serious drama. That is, they felt serious rather than exalted. Suffering, conducive to social or psychological analysis, was often present in the modern plays. Transfigured suffering evocative of magnificence of mind and spirit was decidedly rarer. Modern playwriting was also apt to be more sceptical than affirmative; and more anti-heroic than heroic, the older view of man's singularity and eminence having undergone reduction by modern sociological and psychological outlooks.

It must be conceded, however, that as an alternative to heroic mouthings and posturings (present, for example, in overwrought Jacobean tragedies, seventeenth century English "heroic plays," and grandiloquent Romantic dramas), the modern anti-heroic piece was more acceptable. Better one *Uncle Vanya, Arms and the Man,* or *Playboy of the Western World* than a dozen *Hernanis*. Affirmations, moreover, were still possible to the moderns in spite of their realistic attitudes and intellectual discourse. This may be seen in such diverse plays as Tolstoy's *Power of Darkness,* Gorki's *The Lower Depths,* Shaws' *Androcles and the Lion* and *Saint Joan,* Sartre's *The Flies,* and Sherwood's *Abe Lincoln in Illinois.* Nor was poetic power completely beyond the compass of playwrights who could give the theatre such plays in prose or verse as *Peer Gynt, The Dream Play, The Sea Gull, The Cherry Orchard, The Playboy of the Western World, Deirdre of the Sorrows, Heartbreak House, Juno and the Paycock,* and *Blood Wedding.*

Combining with these and other forays into inspired drama numerous explorations of reality, modern dramatists made the theatre a total adventure. The accumulation of respectable literature during the first seventy-five years of the modern stage, to which each year was likely to add something somewhere in the western world, made the modern age one of the major epochs of stage history. Its future at the midpoint of the century was not more obscure and uncertain than the future of Western civilization itself. Theatre and society carried the same burdens. But both the theatre and the Western world already had a past to which clung much achievement as well as failure, much light as well as darkness. As in previous ages of transition, both the stage and society were in dire need of the rationality of man and the grace of God. Perhaps the rationality would assert itself and the grace would descend.

APPENDIX

I

JEWISH DRAMA

It is impossible to do justice to the Jewish drama in this general survey. It must be noted, however, that the Jewish theatre has been an active force in Russia, Poland, Rumania, and America ever since 1876 when Abraham Goldfaden founded the Jewish stage in Jassy, Rumania, in response to the Zionist movement. After a long struggle with religious prohibitions, European Jewry developed theatre and drama out of such carnivals as "Purim" (the story of Esther and Haman) as early as the fourteenth century. Rudimentary works like *The Sale of Joseph, David and Goliath,* and *The Sacrifice of Isaac* appeared at the beginning of the eighteenth century, recalling the miracle and mystery plays of the Middle Ages. Still, economic and political difficulties, as well as orthodox inhibitions, made the theatre sporadic and kept it mostly on the level of light entertainment.

Out of this tradition in time arose the operettas of the nineteenth century song-writer Goldfaden, and folk pieces by Sholom Aleykim (Aleichem) followed. Poland and Russia became centers of Jewish theatre toward the end of the nineteenth century. Finally America, Soviet Russia, and Palestine saw interesting developments. In New York the imposing actor Jacob Adler encouraged the growth of serious drama; Maurice Schwartz's Yiddish Art Theatre produced colorful Jewish plays, as well as translations from several languages, with much spectacular effect; and the Artef favored social drama and excellent stylization under its distinguished director Benno Schneider. Under the Soviets there have been the famous Habima, a Hebrew-speaking unit, and Jewish national theatres which have been very highly regarded. The Jewish theatre has erred on the side of the spectacular, but this trend has also provided vivid backgrounds and vigorous rhythms. It has also redeemed itself with some striking theatricality by the Artef and the Habima.

The drama began to outgrow its operatic and sentimental approach. Notable was the crude work of Jacob Gordin who wrote problem plays in the spirit of Brieux, Hauptmann, and Sudermann. Although given to wholesale borrowings and mediocre craftsmanship, Gordin introduced the modern drama of ideas into the Jewish theatre. He was followed by the playwrights Libin and Kobrin who moderated and modified the problem play, and by Sholom Asch who introduced symbolism, poetic moods (*The Sinner* and *Night*), and erotic psychology. The latter's chief work

757

was the strained, popular *God of Vengeance,* a kind of *Anna Christie* revolving around a brothel owner's failure to prevent his daughter from becoming a harlot.

The high-water mark of Jewish drama was reached by David Pinsky, Peretz Hirschbein, and S. Ansky (Rappoport). Pinsky was a master of style, characterization, and imaginativeness. Born in 1872, he first made his mark in naturalism with *Isaac Sheftel,* a labor drama of the *Strife* variety written before Galsworthy's play in 1899. Folk-flavored poetic and imaginative plays like *The Eternal Jew* and *The Dumb Messiah* followed in the next dozen years, and an original series of one-acters *King David and His Wives* in 1915 proved his mettle as a psychological dramatist. His masterpiece *The Treasure,* produced in German by Reinhardt in 1910 and later in English by the Theatre Guild, is a vivid and flavorsome extravaganza on the power of greed, notable for its character drawing.

Hirschbein's addiction to the European symbolists led him into undramatic tenuousness, but his *Idle Inn* is an affecting love drama. In fact, it is through fantasy that the Jewish drama has made its greatest impression upon the outside world. That poem of ecstasy Ansky's *The Dybbuk* is the Jewish theatre's most popular contribution thus far. It is a fantastic tragedy of possession in which the ghost of a frustrated lover enters his beloved's body and is exorcised with the greatest difficulty.

Only experts familiar with the nuances of the language like Isaac Goldberg and N. Buchwald are qualified to render judgment on the literature of the Jewish stage. But it is apparent that although there has been no evidence of a major playwright writing in Yiddish speech (a necessarily small field), the Jewish theatre has enriched the drama with imagination and folk flavor. It would be surprising if this were not so in view of the fact that the modern theatre is obliged to the race for such dramatists as Schnitzler, Heijermans, Toller, Werfel, Molnar, Rice, Behrman, Kaufman and Odets, as well as the work of such performers and directors as Rachel Felix, Sarah Bernhardt, Elisabeth Bergner, Paul Muni, Otto Brahm, Emmanuel Reicher, Max Reinhardt, and Philip Moeller.

The Jewish stage has been distinct from the new Hebrew-speaking theatre, which had its origins in Warsaw in 1907 and found a leader in Nahum Zemach between 1911 and 1914 in Bielystok and achieved importance with the organization of the Habima ("Stage") in Moscow. Stanislavsky's ablest associate, Vakhtangov took charge of the training of the company's actors and staged *The Dybbuk* in Hebrew with memorable stylization. Another famous production was that of *The Golem,* Halper Leivick's folk-fantasy of a magically created robot.

Both plays remained in repertory when this theatrical troupe toured the world in the nineteen-twenties and in 1948. After the Soviet government began suppressing Zionist nationalism within its borders and discouraged the use of the Hebrew language, the Habima settled in Palestine, in 1928. Its rivals in Israel were the Ohel ("Tent"), founded in 1926, and the modernist Chamber Theatre. Free from provincialism in the main, the Israeli stage called in foreign stage directors from time to time, such as the former English "Old Vic" director Tyrone Guthrie and the American, former Group Theatre, director Harold Clurman.

II

POLISH DRAMA

A WORD may also be said for the Polish theatre which revealed some originality during the post-Versailles years of independence tragically cut short in the fall of 1939. Its older masterpiece, Count Zygmunt Krasinski's *The Profane Comedy,* was written in 1835 and is considered the greatest poetic work in the language. Byronism and the influence of *Faust* are discernible in this tragedy of the search for the absolute on the part of Count Henryk, a loveless and demoniac person consumed with frustrated longing for love. An aristocratic bias, excessively strong in the proud Polish upper classes, led Krasinski to conclude with a struggle between his hero and a symbolic figure Pancracy, representing the spirit of demagoguery and mass revolt. Pancracy wins the battle after Count Henryk, like a true aristocrat, has rejected the former's offers of peace. Krasinski's vision, however, ends with Pancracy also overthrown, while the people are celebrating their victory; for Pancracy had a mystic kinship with the Count, as if they were both children of the same demoniacal lovelessness.

In the heyday of the modern Polish theatre (which had parallel developments in some interesting stagecraft by the theatres of Yugoslavia, Rumania and Bulgaria) the cosmic romanticism of Krasinski was not entirely *passé.* Since the Poles seem to be an incurably romantic people, their most distinguished plays continued to be historical poetic pieces like Rostworowski's *Judas* and *Caligula.* Nevertheless, the same author also started the Polish realistic drama in a moralistic trilogy of peasant life *The Surprise, Moving Day,* and *At the Goal.* Psychological drama was developed by Zofya Nalkowska in such plays as *Dom Kobiet* (*House of Women*) and *The Day of his Return,* the tragedy of a bedeviled soldier and prisoner. Handicapped by economic straits and the dictatorship of the aristocracy, which remained in the saddle until the collapse of the temporarily revived nation, the theatre brought forth only timid social drama which generally treated topical questions by analogy with older historical events. (See *The Polish Theatre after the War* by W. Zawistowski, in *The Theater in a Changing Europe,* ed. by Thomas H. Dickinson.) On the whole, however, the colorful Slavic theatre, exclusive of the Russian and the Czech contributions, has thus far revealed no plays of international significance.

no plays of international significance, except perhaps the psychological social drama *Poor Man's Miracle* (1939) by Marian Hemar, adapted by Lennox Robinson in Ireland.

THE DEVELOPMENT OF THE THEATRE IN THE WESTERN WORLD (MAIN LINES)
PRIMITIVE RITES (VEGETATION RITES, TOMB RITES, SEXUAL MAGIC, DITHYRAMBIC DANCES, ETC.)

Passion Plays of Egypt and Asia Minor

Greek Comedy
"Old Comedy" (5th Century B.C.) Aristophanes (c. 450–385 B.C.)
"Middle Comedy" (c. 400–325 B.C.)
"New Comedy" Menander (343–291 B.C.)

Roman Comedy Plautus (c. 254–184 B.C.)
Roman Comedy Terence (c. 190–159 B.C.)

Humanist Comedy (15th and 16th Centuries)

Neo-Classic Comedy Molière (1622–1673)

Holberg (1684–1754)
Goldoni (1707–1793)

Atellan and other folk farces of Italy
Roman Mimes
Commedia dell' arte (16th to 18th centuries)

Greek Tragedy
Aeschylus (525–456 B.C.)
Sophocles (496–406 B.C.)
Euripides (480–406 B.C.)

Greek Satyr Plays (5th Century B.C.)

Roman Tragedy Seneca (3 B.C.–65 A.D.)

Humanist Tragedy (15th and 16th Centuries)

Neo-Classic Tragedy (17th and 18th centuries) Corneille (1606–1684) Racine (1639–1699)

Restoration Comedy (1670–1729) Congreve
Sheridan (1751–1816)

Later Comedy of Manners
Wilde (1856–1900)
Maugham (1874–)
Coward (1899–)
Kaufman (1889–)
Behrman (1893–)

Shaw (1856–(1950)

Elizabethan Drama
Marlowe (1564–1593)
Shakespeare (1564–1616)
Beaumont and Fletcher, etc.

Spanish "Golden Age" Lope de Vega (1562–1635) Calderón (1600–1681)

Christian Ritual

Medieval Drama (9th to 15th Century A.D.)

Romantic Drama and Theatre
Goethe (1749–1832)
Schiller (1759–1805)
Hugo (1802–1885)

Realistic Drama and Theatre
Ibsen (1828–1906)
Strindberg (1849–1912)
Chekhov (1860–1904)

Naturalistic Drama and Theatre
Hauptmann (1862–(1946)
Gorky (1868–1936)
O'Neill (1888–(1953)

Expressionism
Wedekind (1864–1918)
Pirandello (1867–1936)
Toller (1893–1939)
O'Neill
Epic Drama (Piscator, Brecht)
The Living Newspapers

Neo-Romanticism
Maeterlinck (1862–(1919)
d'Annunzio (1863–1938)
Yeats (1865–1939)

THEATRE AND MAN IN THE WESTERN WORLD

Primitive Dramatic Rites	Sympathetic Magic, Totemism	Primitive Society
(CHAPTERS I-VI) Primitive Dramatic Rites Passion Plays in Egypt (2000 B.C.) and Asia Minor	Hieroglyphics, Cuneiform writing, Egyptian poems —*The Book of the Dead*; Code of Hammurabi; Egyptian architecture and sculpture; Mesopotamian architecture and sculpture Homer, c. 900-800 B.C.	Egyptian, Babylonian, Assyrian hegemonies Greece occupied by Greek-speaking peoples, 3000-2000 B.C. Trojan War, c. 1200-1180 B.C.
		Rise of aristocratic rule in Greece, 800-700 B.C. Rome built, 753 B.C.
	Terpander, music, c. 670 B.C.	Law-givers in Greece, 650-600 B.C.
	Arion, development of dithyramb, 625-585 B.C. Sappho and other poets, c. 600 B.C. Thales' natural philosophy, 585 B.C.	
	Pythagoras, philosophy, mathematics (540-500 B.C.)	Pisistratus begins his democratic rule in Athens, 561 B.C.
		Cyrus captures Babylon, founds Persian empire 539 B.C.
Thespis, first Athenian play contest, 535 B.C. Aeschylus, 525-456 B.C.	Pindar, poetry, 522-435 B.C.	Darius' first expedition into Europe, 512 B.C.
	Phidias, sculpture, 500?-432 B.C. Anaxagoras, philosophy, 500-435 B.C.	Revolt of Asiatic Greek colonies, 499 B.C., against Persia

Sophocles, 497-406 B.C.		Battle of Marathon, 490 B.C.
Euripides, 480-406 B.C.		
Prometheus Bound, 479? B.C.		Xerxes invades Greece, Battles of Thermopylae and Salamis, 480 B.C.
The Persians, 472 B.C.		Athenian supremacy, beginning of Athenian imperialism, 478 B.C.
	Herodotus, history, 484-425? B.C.	
		Ephialtes' democratic reforms, 463-461 B.C.
Oresteian Trilogy, 458 B.C.		
	Thucydides, history, 471-400? B.C.	Triumph of Athenian imperialism, treasury of Delian confederacy in Athens, 454-453 B.C. Pericles begins his leadership, 453 B.C.
	Socrates, 469-399 B.C.	
	Democritus, atomic theory, b. 460 B.C.	
Aristophanes, 446?-385 B.C.		
	Parthenon rebuilt 448-438 B.C.	
Antigone, 441 B.C.		
Oedipus the King, after 441 B.C.		Peloponnesian War begins, 431 B.C.
Medea, 431 B.C.		Plague in Athens, 430 B.C.
	Plato, 429-348 B.C.	Death of Pericles in third year of the war, 429; rise of demagogues
		Third invasion of Athens, 428 B.C.

The Clouds, 423 B.C.		Peace of Nicias, 421 B.C.; resumption of the war
The Trojan Women, 415 B.C.		Disaster of Athenian fleet at Syracuse, 413 B.C. Revolt of Athenian allies, 412-411 B.C.
Lysistrata, 411 B.C. The Bacchae, 406 B.C.		Athens blockaded, 405-404 B.C. Surrender of Athens to Sparta, 404 B.C. Spartan garrison in Athens, 403 B.C.
Decline of Greek tragedy; Alexandrian tragedy; heyday of Greek acting; improvement of stage technique, 4th and 3rd centuries B.C.	Praxiteles, 4th century B.C Socrates executed, 399 B.C.	Confederation of Athens, Thebes, etc. vs. Sparta, 395-94 B.C. Long walls of Athens rebuilt, 393 B.C.
	Aristotle, 384-322 B.C. Demosthenes, 384-322 B.C.	Rise of Macedonian power under Philip, 358 B.C.
	Zeno, Greek stoicism, 350-258 B.C.	
Menander, 343-291 B.C.; "New Comedy"	Epicurus, 341-270 B.C.	Philip descends into Greece, 336. Alexander becomes king Alexander the Great in Greece, 335; in Persia, 334; founds Alexandria, 331; Indian campaign, 326; death, 323.
	Theocritus, c. 315-?	Revolt of Greece vs. Macedonia, 323 B.C.

765

Dramatists	Literature	History
		Rome, mistress of Central Italy, 290 B.C.
		Rivalry between Rome and Carthage—the First Punic War, 264 B.C.
	First Roman poets, Livius Andronicus *fl.* 240 B.C.	
Plautus, 254?-184? B.C.	Naevius *fl.* 235, Ennius, 239-169 B.C.	
		Cato the Censor, 224-144 B.C.
		Second Punic War, 218-201 **B.C.**
		Hannibal in Italy, 218 B.C.
		Hannibal crushed, 202 B.C.
Terence, *c.* 190-159 B.C.		
Phormio, 162 B.C.	Greek cultural influences	
		Third Punic War, 149-146 B.C.; Carthage razed to the ground
		Social conflicts, plebs *vs.* aristocracy: Tiberius Gracchus killed, 133 B.C.
		Caius Gracchus killed, 121 B.C.
	Cicero, 106-43 B.C.	Julius Caesar, 100-44 B.C.
	Lucretius, 95-51 B.C.	Social war, 91 B.C.
		Revolt of Spartacus, 71 B.C.
	Catullus, 86-46 B.C.	Conquest of Western Europe by Rome
	Virgil, 70-19 B.C.	
	Horace, 65-8 B.C.	
	Ovid, 43 B.C.-6 A.D.	Augustus Caesar, Roman emperor 27 B.C.-14 A.D

766

Seneca, 3 B.C.-65 A.D.		Birth of Christ, 4 B.C.
		Tiberius becomes Emperor, 14 A.D.
	Pliny the Elder, natural history, 23-79 A.D.	
Decline of Roman drama		Christ crucified, 30 A.D.
Improvement of theatre architecture and production		Spread of Christianity thereafter
Spectacles		
Mimes		Nero, 54-68 A.D.
	Martial, 43-104 A.D.	
	Tacitus, 60-135 A.D.	Roman Empire reaches its greatest extent, 117 A.D.
		Marcus Aurelius, emperor in 161 A.D.
		Teutonic incursions into the Roman empire
		Constantine the Great, emperor in 312 A.D.
		Triumph of Christianity
	Collapse of Roman culture	
	Rise of Christian culture and thought	
	St. Augustine, 354-430 A.D.	
	The Vulgate (Latin) translation of the Bible; St. Jerome, 347-410? A.D.	
		Visigoths under Alaric capture Rome, 410 A.D.
		Britain invaded by Angles and Saxons, c. 425
		Gothic kings in Italy, 453
		End of Western Roman Empire, 476

		Pope Gregory the Great 590 A.D.
		Mohammed's hegira, 622
	The Koran, 634	
	Beowulf, first redaction, 7th century	
		Charles Martel defeats the Saracens, 732
		Charlemagne crowned Emperor of the West, 800
Tropes, 9th century		
	Translations under King Alfred, 871-910	Alfred the Great in England, 871-901
Hrosvitha; drama in the monasteries, 10th century		Otto I crowned Holy Roman Emperor, 962
Liturgical plays in Latin, 10th century and later	*The Poetic Edda*, end of 10th century	
	Song of Roland, end of 10th century	
Introduction of the vernacular into the liturgical drama		William the Conqueror, Norman Conquest of England, 1066
		The First Crusade, 1095
		Godfrey of Bouillon captures Jerusalem, 1099
Saint plays, 11th century and later	Troubadours and minnesingers, 12th-13th centuries	
	Oxford University founded, 1133	
	Nibelungenlied, c. 1140	Second Crusade, 1147
Adam, c. 1150		Henry II, in England, 1154
		St. Francis of Assisi, 1182-1226

Easter and Nativity play cycles	Romances of chivalry; Chrétien de Troyes, c. 1200; metrical romances in England, 1150-1300	Saladin captures Jerusalem, 1187 Third Crusade, 1189
	Cambridge University founded, 1209? Cimabue, c. 1240-c. 1302	Magna Charta, 1215
Feast of Corpus Christi established, 1264; Easter and Nativity play cycles begin to be fused	Dante, 1265-1321 Giotto, c. 1266-1337 Roger Bacon, scientific thought, Opus Majum, 1267 Marco Polo starts his travels, 1271	
	Thomas Aquinas dies, 1274	Edward I, 1272
Mystery Play Cycles, 1300-1450	Petrarch, 1304-1374	
	Boccaccio, 1313-1375 Greek scholars in Italy, 14th century	The Schism, the Popes at Avignon, 1305-1456 and the Great Schism, 1378-1417
	Chaucer, c. 1340-1400	The Hundred Years' War between England and France, 1337-1453
	Piers Plowman, proletarian and Tolstoyan poetry, 1362-1398	The Black Death, 1348 The Jacquerie, peasant revolt in France, 1358

"Paternoster Plays," first mentioned in 1378	Wycliffe translates the Bible into English, 1381; John Huss preaches in Bohemia, 1398; early Protestantism	Richard II, 1377 The Peasant Revolt in England, 1381
Morality Plays, 15th century	Invention of gunpowder in Europe; decline of feudalism, 15th century	Henry IV, 1399
The Castle of Perseverance, 1425	Jan van Eyck, ?-1440 François Villon, 1431–after 1463	Henry V, 1413 Joan of Arc burned at the stake, 1431
Everyman, end of 15th century Medieval farces, Master Pathélin, c. 1469 (CHAPTERS X-XIII)	Memlinc, 1425?-1495 Great age of Italian art—Leonardo da Vinci, Michelangelo, etc.—1450-1576 Botticelli, 1446-1510	Constantinople captured by the Turks, 1453 Wars of the Roses, 1455–1485; Henry VII, Tudor dynasty begins
	Greek scholars flee to Italy, bringing classic culture with them, second half of the 15th century Leonardo da Vinci, 1452-1519. Forerunner of modern science Gutenberg's Bible, 1455 Humanism, late 15th and 16th century Erasmus, 1466-1536 Machiavelli, 1469-1527	Lorenzo de Medici in power in Florence, 1469-1492

Ariosto, 1474-1533	Dürer, 1471-1528	Ferdinand and Isabella conquer Granada, 1492; Spain unified
	Copernicus, 1473-1543	Columbus discovers America, 1492
	Michelangelo, 1475-1564	
	Sir Thomas More, 1478-1535	
	Colet lectures on classics at Oxford, 1491. Humanism in England	
Aretino, 1492-1556		
Transitional farces		
Hans Sachs, 1494-1576	Rabelais, 1495-1553	Vasco da Gama rounds Cape of Good Hope, 1498
John Heywood, c. 1497-1580		
Celestina, 1499-1502		
Decline of mystery plays, 16th century; preserved in Catholic Central Europe		
Morality plays begin to reflect reformation and renaissance, 16th century, and decline		Henry VIII, 1509-1547
Commedia dell' Arte 16th-18th centuries	Wyatt, 1503-42	
Humanist Drama, 1st half of 16th century		
Ariosto's *Suppositi*, 1509		
Lope de Rueda, 1510?-1565	Ariosto's *Orlando Furioso* 1515-1532	
Mandragola, c. 1514	Machiavelli's *The Prince*, 1517; Surrey, 1517?-1547	
Trissino's *Sofonisba*, 1515		

771

		Charles V of Spain inherits Hapsburg dominions; speak of Spanish hegemony
		Cortez conquers Mexico for Spain, 1519
		Magellan sails around the world, 1519-1522
		Luther at the Diet of Worms, 1521; Protestantism
	Palestrina, 1524?-1594	
	Hans Holbein the Younger in England, 1526-1543?	
	Tyndale's translation of the *New Testament* into English, 1526	
		Pizarro seizes Peru for Spain, 1530
English School Plays:		
Ralph Roister Doister, 1533	Montaigne, 1533-1592	
Gammer Gurton's Needle 1552-1553		Henry VIII makes England a Protestant nation, 1534
		Destruction of the Monasteries in England, 1536-1539
Guarini, 1537-1612		Loyola founds the Jesuit sect, 1539; Council of Trent 1545; the reformation within the Catholic Church
Serlio's *Architettura*, 1545	Tasso, 1544-1595	
Cervantes, 1547-1616	Giordano Bruno, philosopher of pantheism and Copernican system, 1548-1600	
	The *Pléiade* in France, 1549-1572	
Jodelle's *Cléopatre Captive*, 1552	Spenser, 1552?-1599	
		Queen Elizabeth, 1558-1603
Gorboduc, 1561	Francis Bacon, apostle of modern science, 1561-1626	
Lope de Vega, 1562-1635		

Marlowe, 1564-1593	Galileo, 1564-1642	Revolt of the Netherlands, 1566
Shakespeare, 1564-1616		
Middleton, 1570-1627	Kepler, 1571-1630	St. Bartholomew's Day, Massacre of Protestants in France, 1572
Ben Jonson, 1573-1637	Harvey, the circulation of the blood, 1578-1657	
Tasso's *Aminta*, pastoral drama, 1573		
John Fletcher, 1579-1625	Montaigne's *Essays*, 1580	
Webster, c. 1580-1625		
Il Pastor Fido, 1585		
Court Drama; *Campaspe*, 1583		
Ford, 1586-1639		
Arden of Feversham, 1586		
The Spanish Tragedy, 1586-7		
Tamburlaine, 1587		Defeat of the Spanish Armada, 1588
Dr. Faustus, 1589		
Edward II, c. 1590		Henry IV becomes King of France in 1589 and unifies the nation, 1594
Shakespeare's romantic comedies and histories, 1590-1600	Spenser's *The Faerie Queene* I-III, 1593	
Every Man in his Humour, 1598	Opera: *Dafne*, 1597	
The Shoemakers' Holiday, c. 1600		

Calderón, 1600-1681	Clement Marot, 1495-1544	
Shakespeare's tragic period, 1600-1608	Ronsard, 1524-1585	James I of England, 1603-1625
A Woman Killed with Kindness, 1603		
Volpone, 1605	Cervantes' *Don Quixote*, 1605-1616	Settlement of Jamestown in Virginia, 1607
Shakespearean romance or tragi-comedy, 1608-1613	Milton, 1608-1674	Expulsion of the Moors from Spain, 1609; Henrik Hudson in America, 1609
Philaster, 1609; *The Maid's Tragedy*, c. 1609		
The Alchemist, 1610; *Fuente Ovejuna*, c. 1610		
The Atheist's Tragedy, 1611; *The White Devil*, 1611-1612	King James *Authorized Version* of the Bible, 1611	
The Duchess of Malfi, 1613-1614		
The Changeling, 1623		Thirty Years' War in Germany, 1618-1648
		Charles I, 1625-49
		Parliament dissolved by Charles I, 1629
	Metaphysical and Cavalier poetry in England, 1st half of 17th century	
'Tis Pity She's a Whore, 1633		
Milton's *Comus*, 1634		
Life Is a Dream, c. 1636	Milton's *Lycidas*, 1638	
The Cardinal, 1641		
English public theatre closed by the Puritans, 1642		The Puritan Rebellion in England, 1642-1646
(CHAPTERS XV-XVI)		The Commonwealth government in England, 1649-1660

	Malherbe, founder of neo-classical school in France, 1555-1628	Henry IV rules France, 1589-1610; Sully's reforms
	Rubens, 1577-1640	
Corneille, 1606-1684	Descartes, 1596-1650	
Molière, 1622-1673	Jean de Balzac, 1597-1654; neo-classic rules for prose	
	Velasquez, 1599-1660	
	Rembrandt, 1606-1669	
	Pascal, 1623-1662	Cardinal Richelieu's rule in France, 1624-1642
Dryden, 1631-1700	Mme. de Sévigné, 1626-1696	
The Cid, 1637	Locke, 1632-1704	
	Boileau, literary dictator of France, 1636-1711	
Racine, 1639-1699		Mazarin's rule in France, 1642-1661
Wycherley, 1640-1715		Charles I beheaded, 1649
	Hobbes' *Leviathan*, 1651	Cromwell's Protectorate in England, 1653-1658
Otway, 1651-1685		
Etherege, 1635-1691		Restoration of Charles II in England, 1660
Les Précieuses Ridicules, 1659	Pepys' *Diary*, 1660-1669	Louis XIV, absolutist regime, 1661-1715
		Colbert, minister of Louis XIV, 1661-1683; financial reform; mercantilism
The Misanthrope, 1666		

Vanbrugh, 1666-1726	Milton's *Paradise Lost*, 1667	
	Swift, 1667-1745	
	La Fontaine's *Fables*, 1668	
Congreve, 1670-1729	Pascal's *Pensées*, 1670	
Milton's *Samson Agonistes*, 1671		
Steele, 1671-1729		
Conquest of Granada, 1672	Addison, 1672-1719	
The Country Wife, 1673	Boileau's *L'Art Poétique*, 1673	
Phèdre, 1677		
The Plain Dealer, 1677		
Farquhar, 1678-1707	*Pilgrim's Progress*, 1678	
All for Love, 1678		
Holberg, 1684-1754	Watteau, 1684-1721	Revocation of Edict of Nantes, religious intolerance in the interests of absolutism, 1685
	J. S. Bach 1685-1750	James II, 1685-1688; the "Bloodless Revolution," beginning of Constitutional monarchy in England
	Newton's *Principia*, 1687	
	Pope, 1688-1744	
Athalie, 1691	Montesquieu, 1689-1755	The English Bill of Rights, 1689
Voltaire, 1694-1778		
		Accession of Peter I, modernization of Russia begun, 1696
	Hogarth, 1697-1764	
Collier's attack on Restoration comedy, 1698		
The Way of the World, 1700		

Steele's *The Tender Husband*, 1703; "sentimental comedy"	First daily newspaper in England, 1702	Queen Anne of England, 1702-1714
The Beaux' Stratagem, 1707	Fielding, 1707-1754	Battle of Blenheim, 1704
Goldoni, 1707-1793		
	The Spectator, 1711-1714	
	Rousseau, 1712-1778	
Cato, 1713		George I of England, 1714-1727
Diderot, 1713-1784		
	Le Sage's *Gil Blas*, 1715	
	Montesquieu's *Persian Letters*, 1721; *The Spirit of the Laws*, 1748. Rationalism	Walpole, prime minister of England, 1721-1742
	Reynolds, 1723-1792	Death of Peter the Great, 1725
	Gulliver's Travels, 1726	
	Gainsborough, 1727-1788	
Goldsmith, 1728-1774		
The Beggar's Opera, 1728		
The London Merchant, 1731. Bourgeois drama	Franklin's *Poor Richard's Almanac*, 1732	
Beaumarchais, 1732-1799	Richardson's *Clarissa Harlowe*, 1748; David, 1748-1825	
	Fielding's *Tom Jones*, 1749	
Sheridan, 1751-1816	The French Encyclopedia, 1751-1786. Rationalism	Clive in India, 1751. British imperialism
		Seven Years' War, 1756-1773
Diderot's *Le Père de Famille*, 1757. Bourgeois drama	Rousseau's *Social Contract*, 1762	

Johnson's edition of Shakespeare, 1765	Sterne's *Sentimental Journey*, 1768	
	Watt's steam engine, 1768. The Industrial Revolution begins in England	American Revolution, 1775-1783
		The American Declaration of Independence, 1776
She Stoops to Conquer, 1773		
The Rivals, 1775		
The Barber of Seville, 1775		
The School for Scandal, 1777		
(CHAPTERS XVI-XVII)		
J. C. Gottsched, 1700-1766	Buffon, 1707-1788; Linnaeus, 1707-1778	
	Thomas Gray, 1716-1771. Romanticism in poetry	
Garrick, 1717-1779		Turgot, 1727-1781. Laissez faire
Lessing, 1729-1781		
	Joseph Priestley, 1733-1804. Modern chemistry	
	Thomas Paine, 1737-1809; Galvani, 1737-1798 (electricity)	
	Beccaria, 1738-1794. Modern penology	Frederick the Great, 1740-1786. Prussian triumphs
	J. G. Herder, 1744-1803	
Goethe, 1749-1832		
	William Godwin, 1756-1836; Mozart, 1756-1791	Seven Years' War, 1756-1763
	Voltaire's *Candide*, 1757	
Schiller, 1759-1805	Robert Burns, 1759-1796	Fall of Quebec, 1759
		Accession of George III, 1760

778

Minna von Barnhelm, 1767	Fichte, 1762-1814. German Romantic philosophy	Catherine the Great, queen of Russia, 1762-1796
Hamburg Dramaturgy, 1767-1768	Rousseau's *Émile*, 1764	
	Lessing's *Laocoon*, 1766	
	Mme. de Staël, 1766-1817	
	August Wilhelm Schlegel, 1767-1845	
	Chateaubriand, 1768-1848	Napoleon Bonaparte, 1769-1821
Emilia Galotti, 1771	Beethoven, 1770-1827; G. W. F. Hegel, 1770-1831	
	Sir Walter Scott, 1771-1832	
Tieck, 1773-1853	Coleridge, 1772-1834	
Götz von Berlichingen, 1773		Warren Hastings, governor of India, 1774-1785. British imperialism
First draft of Faust, 1774		American Revolution, 1775-1783
Klinger's Storm and Stress, 1776	Turner, 1775-1851	Adam Smith's *The Wealth of Nations*, 1776; American Declaration of Independence, 1776
Kleist, 1777-1811	Hazlitt, 1778-1830	
Nathan the Wise, 1779	Beranger, 1780-1857	
The Robbers, 1781	Kant's *Critique of Pure Reason*, 1781	Constitution of the United States, drafted in 1787; effective in 1789
Egmont, 1787	Byron, 1788-1824	French Revolution, 1789
Scribe, 1791-1861; Grillparzer, 1791-1872		

Wallenstein, 1799	Shelley, 1792-1822; Lamartine, 1792-1869	Reign of Terror in France, 1792-1793; Louis XVI guillotined
Pushkin, 1799-1837	The Cotton Gin, 1793	
	Carlyle, 1795-1881	
	Keats, 1795-1821	Napoleon invades Italy, 1796
Hugo, 1802-1885	Heine, 1797-1856; de Vigny, 1797-1863	Napoleon becomes First Consul, 1799
Dumas *Père*, 1802-1870	*Lyrical Ballads*, 1798	
Wilhelm Tell, 1804	Delacroix, 1799-1863	Napoleonic Wars, 1800-1812
Faust, I, 1808		
Musset, 1810-1859		Napoleon becomes Emperor, 1804
	Childe Harold, I, II, 1812; Grimm Brothers' Fairy Tales	
Büchner, 1813-1837		Battle of Waterloo, 1815
		Metternich dominates European reactionary politics, 1815-1848
	Schopenhauer's *The World as Will and Idea*, 1819	
The Cenci, 1820		
Augier, 1820-1889		
Rachel, 1821-1858		
Dumas *fils*, 1824-1895		
Boris Godunov, 1825	The Steam Locomotive, 1825	Greek War of Independence, 1825
Hernani, 1830		
Faust, II, 1831	Stendhal's *The Red and the Black*, 1831	

Sardou, 1831-1908		
		Revolution overthrows Bourbons in France, 1832; middle-class monarchy of Louis-Philippe
Chatterton, 1835	Tennyson, poems, 1833, 1842	
Ruy Blas, 1838	Dickens' *Oliver Twist*, 1837	Accession of Queen Victoria, 1837
The Lady of the Camellias, 1852	Tennyson's *In Memoriam*, 1850	
(CHAPTERS XIX-XXIX)		
Gogol, 1809-1852	Comte, 1798-1857	
	Balzac, 1799-1850	
	Thackeray, 1811-1863	
Hebbel, 1813-1863	Dickens, 1812-1870	
	Thoreau, 1817-1862	
Turgenev, 1818-1883	Walt Whitman, 1819-1892	
	Baudelaire, 1821-1867	
	Dostoyevsky, 1822-1881; Arnold, 1822-1888	
Tolstoy, 1828-1910		Revolutionary ferment in Europe, 1830. The middle-class rises to greater power; greater industrialization of Europe. First Reform Bill in England, 1832
	Manet, 1833-1883; Brahms, 1833-1897	
Björnson, 1832-1910; Echegeray, 1832-1916	Balzac's *Father Goriot*	
	Mark Twain, 1835-1910	
W. S. Gilbert, 1836-1911		
The Inspector General, 1836		

	Swinburne, 1837-1909	Reign of Queen Victoria, 1837-1901
Becque, 1837-1899	Dickens' *Oliver Twist*, 1837	
	Bizet, 1838-1875; Henry Adams, 1838-1918	
Herne, 1839-1901	Cézanne, 1839-1906	
Zola, 1840-1903	Hardy, 1840-1928	Chartist riots in England, 1842
Maria Magdalena, 1844	Nietzsche, 1844-1900; France,1844-1924	
	Verlaine, 1844-1896	
Bernhardt, 1845-1923	Kierkegaard's *Either/Or*, 1843	Revolutions throughout Europe, 1848-1849; second French republic until 1852—Louis Blanc's social reforms in France
Strindberg, 1849-1912; Brunetière, 1849-1906	Maupassant, 1850-1903	Napoleon III, 1852
Henry Arthur Jones, 1851-1929		Perry's visit to Japan, 1853. Westernization of Japan begins
Curel, 1854-1928	*Leaves of Grass* (1st and 2nd editions), 1855, 1856	
Pinero, 1855-1934	Freud, 1856-1939	
Shaw, 1856-1950; Wilde, 1856-1900	Flaubert's *Madame Bovary*, 1857	
Sudermann, 1857-1932		
Brieux, 1858-1932; Antoine, 1858-1943	Darwin's *Origin of Species*, 1859	Unification of Italy; emancipation of serfs in Russia, 1861
Duse, 1859-1924; Lady Gregory, 1859-1932	Tolstoy's *War and Peace*, 1860	American Civil War, 1861-1865
Chekhov, 1860-1904; Barrie, 1860-1937		Bismarck becomes Prime Minister of Prussia, 1862
Hauptmann, 1862-1946;Appia, 1862-1928		

Maeterlinck, 1862–1949		
Stanislavsky, 1863–1938; d'Annunzio, 1863–1938	Dehmel, 1863–1922	
Heijermans, 1864–1924		
Yeats, 1865–1939	*Crime and Punishment*, 1865	
Benavente, 1866		Ascendancy of Prussia; War with Austria, 1866
Brand, 1866		
Galsworthy, 1867–1933; Pirandello, 1867–1937	Marx's *Capital*, 1867	Second Reform Bill in England, 1867
Peer Gynt, 1867	*Anna Karenina*, 1867	
Gorky, 1868–1936; Rostand, 1868–1918		
	Edwin Arlington Robinson, 1869–1935	Franco-Prussian War, 1870–1871; Lenin, 1870–1924
Andreyev, 1870–1919		
Synge, 1871–1909	Proust, 1871–1922; Dreiser, 1871–1945	Paris Commune; the Third Republic of France; the establishment of the German Empire, 1871
Gordon Craig, 1872–	*Erewhon*, 1872	
Reinhardt, 1873–1949		The Spanish Republic, 1873–1875
The Meiningen Company, 1874–1890		Disraeli becomes Prime Minister, 1874
	Robert Frost, 1875; Thomas Mann, 1875–	
	Bell's telephone, 1876	
	Hardy's *Return of the Native*, 1877	
Molnar, 1878–1952; Copeau, 1878–1949	Edison's first practical electric light, 1879; Einstein, 1879–	Bismarck's war on socialism, 1878–1890; Stalin, 1879–1953
Alexander Blok, 1880–1921	*The Brothers Karamazov*, 1880	
Ghosts; *The Vultures*, 1881		
Lenormand, 1882–1938	James Joyce, 1882–1941	
An Enemy of the People; *Iolanthe*, 1882		

Vahktangov, 1883-1922	*Thus Spake Zarathustra*, 1883	The Triple Alliance, Germany, Austria and Italy, 1883
Beyond Our Power, 1883		Mussolini, 1883-1945
The Wild Duck, 1884	*Diana of the Crossways; The Mayor of Casterbridge*, 1885	
The Power of Darkness, 1886	Robinson Jeffers, 1887-	
The Father, 1887		
The *Théâtre Libre* founded, 1887	T. S. Eliot, 1888-	Wilhelm II becomes Emperor of Germany, 1888
O'Neill, 1888-		Hitler, 1889-1945?
The *Freie Bühne* founded, 1889		
Kaufman, 1889-		
Kelly, 1890-; Karel Capek, 1890-1939	*Tess of the D'Urbervilles*, 1891	Franco-Russian Alliance, 1891
Grein's Independent Theatre in London, 1891	*Leaves of Grass* (9th ed.), 1891-1892	
Sidney Howard, 1891-1939		
Hedda Gabler, 1891		
The Weavers; The Master Builder; Widower's Houses; The Fossils, 1892		
Behrman, 1893-; Toller, 1893-1939		
The Second Mrs. Tanqueray; Pelléas and Melisande, 1893		
O'Casey, 1894-	*The Yellow Book*, 1894-1897	
The Importance of Being Earnest, 1895		
Sherwood, 1896-	Verlaine, d. 1896	
The Sea Gull; The Sunken Bell, 1896		
The Moscow Art Theatre founded, 1897		The Victorian Jubilee, 1897
Cyrano de Bergerac, 1897		
Mrs. Warren's Profession; Gioconda, **1898**; Bertolt Brecht, 1898-	Mallarmé, d. 1898; **Radium isolated by Pierre** and Marie Curie, 1898	Spanish-American War, 1898
Lorca, 1899-1936		

Coward, 1899–	Sister Carrie, 1900	The Boer War, 1899-1902
The Good Hope; The Three Sisters, 1900		
The Lower Depths; Man and Superman; Rose Bernd; Riders to the Sea, 1903	*The Way of All Flesh*, 1903; *The Wright Brothers' Flight*, 1903	
Lillian Hellman, 1904–		
The Cherry Orchard; The Lonely Way; Peter Pan, 1904		The Russo-Japanese War; the First Russian Revolution, 1904-1905
Sartre, 1905–	Einstein's first paper on relativity, 1905	Separation of Church and State in France, 1905
Odets, 1906–	*The Man of Property*, beginning of *The Forsyte Saga*, 1906	The first Duma or parliament in Russia, 1906
The Playboy of the Western World; Major Barbara, 1907		
What Every Woman Knows, 1908	Anatole France's *Penguin Island*, 1908	
Saroyan, 1908–		
Strife, 1909	Bleriot flies an airplane from France to England; Peary at the North Pole, 1909	
Justice; The Tragedy of Nan; The Madras House, 1910		
		Establishment of the Chinese Republic, 1912; the Balkan Wars, 1912-1913
Tennessee Williams, 1914–	Lawrence's *Sons and Lovers*, 1914 Frost's *North of Boston*, 1914	The World War, 1914-1918
Heartbreak House, 1914-1917	Einstein's Second Relativity Theory, 1915	
The Provincetown Players, 1915-1929	*Spoon River Anthology*, 1915	
He Who Gets Slapped, 1915; *From Morn to Midnight*, 1916	Robinson's *The Man Against the Sky*; Sandburg's *Chicago Poems*, 1916	Easter Rebellion in Dublin, 1916
		Bolshevik revolution in Russia; Lenin in power, 1917
	Spengler's *Decline of the West*, 1918	
The Theatre Guild founded, 1919		

The Goat Song; Masses and Man; R.U.R.; Beyond the Horizon; Six Characters in Search of an Author, 1921		First meeting of the League of Nations, 1920 American Prosperity, 1920-1929 The Irish Free State established, 1921
Saint Joan, 1923	T. S. Eliot's *The Waste Land; Ulysses*, 1922	Mussolini seizes power, 1922 Hitler's first *Putsch*, 1923; Ramsay MacDonald becomes Labor Prime Minister of England, 1923
What Price Glory; Desire Under the Elms, 1924 *Juno and the Paycock; Processional*, 1925 *The Plough and the Stars*, 1926	Thomas Mann's *The Magic Mountain*, 1924 Gide's *The Counterfeiters*, 1925	
Street Scene, 1929	*A Farewell to Arms*, 1929	The N. Y. Stock Market crash, and world-wide economic depression, 1929
The Green Pastures, 1930 The Group Theatre, 1931-1940 *Mourning Becomes Electra*, 1931		Brüning regime in Germany, 1930-1932 National Government in England, 1931
Blood Wedding; The Three-Penny Opera, 1933	Malraux's *Man's Fate*, 1933	Presidency of Franklin D. Roosevelt, 1933-1945 Hitler seizes power in Germany, 1933
Federal Theatre, 1935-1939 *Awake and Sing*, 1935		Ethiopian War, 1935-1936
Winterset, 1936	Mann's *Joseph and His Brethren*, 1936	Spanish Civil War, 1936-1939; Saar plebiscite, 1936; treason trials in Russia, 1936
High Tor; The Fall of the City; Shadow and Substance, 1937 *Abe Lincoln in Illinois; Our Town*, 1938 *The Little Foxes; The Time of Your Life*, 1939	Steinbeck's *Grapes of Wrath*, 1939	Austria seized by Germany; the Munich agreement and end of Czechoslovakia, 1938
The Skin of Our Teeth, 1942 *The Glass Menagerie; The Winslow Boy; The Madwoman of Chaillot*, 1945		The Second World War, 1939-1945 The United Nations established, 1945 The Atom Bomb, 1945

Philip Barry: *The Philadelphia Story*, 1939	William Faulkner: *The Wild Palms*, 1939	Germany invades Poland, Sept. 1, 1939 France and England declare war, Sept. 3, 1939
Robert Sherwood: *There Shall Be No Night*, 1940		Soviet Russia attacks Finland, 1939–40 Germany conquers Norway, June 10, 1940 Evacuation of Dunkirk, May 26–June 4, 1940 France surrenders, June 22, 1940
Lillian Hellman: *Watch on the Rhine*, 1941 Noel Coward: *Blithe Spirit*, 1941		Germany invades Russia, June 22, 1941 Japan bombs Pearl Harbor, December 7, 1941
	T. S. Eliot: *Little Gidding*, 1942 Shostakovich: Seventh ("Leningrad") Symphony, 1942 Albert Camus: *The Stranger*, 1942	Germans surrender at Stalingrad, February 2, 1943
Sartre: *The Flies*, 1943	Sartre formulates "Existentialism," 1943–46 Mann completes his novel cycle *Joseph and His Brothers*, 1943	
Rodgers and Hammerstein: *Oklahoma!*, 1944		Allies land in Normandy, June 6, 1944
Garson Kanin: *Born Yesterday*, 1946 Eugene O'Neill: *The Iceman Cometh*, 1946 Arthur Miller: *All My Sons*, 1947 Williams: *A Streetcar Named Desire*, 1947 Carl Zuckmayer: *The Devil's General*, 1948 Bertolt Brecht: *The Good Woman of Setzuan*, pub. 1948	Auden's *Collected Poetry*, 1945 John Hersey: *Hiroshima*, 1946 Auden: *The Age of Anxiety*, 1947 Gide receives Nobel Prize, 1947 Camus: *The Plague*, 1947	Franklin D. Roosevelt dies, April 12, 1945 Germany surrenders, May 7, 1945 United Nations first conference begins, June 26, 1945 Labour Party victory in England, July 1945 The atom bomb dropped on Hiroshima, August 6, 1945 Japan surrenders, August 14, 1945 Tension between Western nations and Soviet Russia grows, 1947
Christopher Fry: *The Lady's Not For Burning*, 1948 Miller: *Death of a Salesman*, 1949 T. S. Eliot: *The Cocktail Party*, 1949	T. S. Eliot receives Nobel Prize, 1948 Faulkner: *Intruder in the Dust*, 1948	The Korean War, June 25, 1950

A NOTE ON PARALLELS

THIS comparative table, which may provide some background for this book, proves as little or as much as one may desire. It is not set down here to demonstrate anything beyond the obvious point that the theatre, in its most impressive manifestations, has been part of a larger stream of culture and events. That it should bear their stamp directly or indirectly was natural. That the impress was remarkably vivid was ensured by the sensitive and spectacular nature of an art that revels in crises and in the externalization of conflicts.

As every art has its own momentum and carries over the traditions or trends peculiar to it, the response of the theatre to other artistic, intellectual and historical activities was by no means mathematically precise. No hard and fast parallel can be drawn. There have been periods of uneven development when the drama was far less fruitful than the other arts. This was the case, for example, in Renaissance Italy, the mid-Victorian period and nineteenth century America. The reasons for this may be located in the existence of special requirements for an intellectually vigorous theatre.

It is also noteworthy that the stage prospered or progressed under conditions of both comparative stability and instability. Stability, which should ensure the theatre a sound economic basis, did not invariably promote the physical theatre and the drama, as may be seen in the mid-Victorian period. Social instability, which theoretically should fire those masters of climax the dramatists, did not necessarily prove an incentive, as may be observed during the late Roman Empire or during the French Revolution and the Napoleonic period in France. Supplementary circumstances caused major deviations from any expected results. Conversely, periods of historic crises did not act as a summary deterrent, as may be noted in the great Athenian era during which a momentous war was raging between Athens and Sparta, the harassed post-war German and the American depression period. "As a matter of fact," Brooks Atkinson writes correctly, "men of letters have rarely had the pleasure of practicing their trade in a time of peace, public rest, and well-being."

As a matter of fact, there has never been such a period in the absolute sense, and man's history has run a restless course since time immemorial. Mankind and its artists have, indeed, had to endure greatly. It is in truth from this dynamic nature of man's collective, as well as private, life that a great art like the drama has gathered its impetus and derived its content, meaning, and value to humanity. Only general and overwhelming catastrophes like the collapse of the Roman Empire and the Thirty Years' War in Germany could devastate the theatre.

Notice may also be taken of the fact that the drama has inevitably reflected or represented conflicts of principles, philosophies and interests, whether of states, classes or religious groups. Marxists tend to place special emphasis on this fact, and indeed there is no want of evidence for their opinion. Such conflicts may be found even in the so-called universal art of the Greek tragedians, not excluding that of the serene Sophocles; even in medieval drama—in the fact that the burghers took over the religious drama, filled it with references to their own life, and ignored the feudal aristocracy or referred to it derogatorily, not to mention the direct propaganda in the morality plays; even in the aristocratic art of Racine which reflects the struggle between puritanical, essentially bourgeois Jansenism and the hedonistic court. It is difficult to comprehend how fundamental social, political and cultural oppositions could have escaped the dramatists or the theatre for which they wrote.

Nevertheless, the drama has been equally partial to the reconciliations of warring principles, the resolution of antagonisms. Even this art of conflicts and crises is, after all, an active attempt to make man at home in an alien universe, to salve his wounds, and to pacify him. To a world that is sadly in need of pacification and balm, art is the perfect Paraclete or Comforter, bringing reconciliation and even escape from the intolerable importunities of present fact. Much of the humanism of the drama and the

788

stage comes from this effort; also much of its esthetic nature, which is a matter of balance, order and repose. If man is constantly warring against himself and his kind, he is also ceaselessly striving for appeasement. Those historians who in the name of "dialectics" (when they define it too strictly or too literally) try to find only stridency in dramatic art overlook the nature of both art and man. Reconciliation, synthesis, and unity provide a major esthetic and intellectual gratification in great Attic, medieval, Elizabethan, and neo-classic drama. Even the greatest post-Ibsen dramatic literature evinces this tendency, along with its unmistakable presentation of as yet unresolved antagonisms. Among other plays one may cite the testimony of such radically different examples as Chekhov's, Schnitzler's, Synge's, Carroll's, Galsworthy's work, *The Plough and the Stars, Strange Interlude, Winterset, Our Town,* Gorky's *Yegor Bulychov* and even many Soviet plays like *The Last of the Turbins, Fear, Squaring the Circle* and *Aristocrats.*

The drama, in short, has come to us bearing not only a sword but an olive branch. A broad interpretation of human effort could hardly do otherwise. The stage may not be a home for convalescents, but this does not necessarily make it a cockpit or an arena for gladiators.

NOTES

CHAPTER I
[1] Stubbes: *Anatomie of Abuses.*
[2] Harrison, Jane Ellen: *Ancient Art & Ritual*, p. 62.
[3] *Ibid.*, p. 64.
[4] *Ibid.*, pp. 30-31.
[5] Frazer, James George: *The Golden Bough.* p. 265. One-volume abridged edition, 1922. Macmillan.
[6] *Ibid.*, pp. 362-68.
[7] *Ibid.*, pp. 324-47.
[8] Harrison, Jane Ellen: *Ancient Art & Ritual*, pp. 79-82.
[9] *Ibid.*, p. 90ff.
[10] Frazer, *ibid.*, p. 389.

CHAPTER II
[1] Translation by John Stuart Blackie.
[2] The Greek word for actor was "hypokrites," an answerer, one who replies to the chorus.
[3] Hamilton, Edith: *Three Greek Plays.* Introduction to *Agamemnon.*
[4] Simonson, Lee: *The Stage is Set*, p. 138. See also Allardyce Nicoll's *The Development of the Theatre*, Chapter I.
[5] Norwood, Gilbert: *Greek Tragedy*, pp. 122-23.
[6] *Ibid.*, p. 124.
[7] Symonds, John Addington: *Studies of the Greek Poets.*
[8] Translation by John Stuart Blackie.
[9] Translation by Edith Hamilton.
[10] Translation by Edith Hamilton.

CHAPTER III
[1] Translation by Jebb: lines 1225-28.
[2] *The Dynasts.*
[3] Translation by Sir George Young. (Everyman Edition, E. P. Dutton.).
[4] The italics are of course mine.
[5] Translation in Gilbert Norwood's *Greek Tragedy.*

CHAPTER IV
[1] *The Birth of Tragedy.* Modern Library Edition, p. 250.
[2] Translation by Gilbert Murray.
[3] *Ibid.*
[4] Translation by Woodhill: Everyman edition, vol. 1.
[5] Translation by Gilbert Murray.

⁶ See Gassner, John: "Catharsis and the Theory of Enlightenment," *One Act Play Magazine*, August 1937.

⁷ *Le Théâtre de Sénèque*. Paris, 1924. p. 195.

CHAPTER V

¹ *The Poetics*.

² Introduction, 1820. *The Frogs and Three Other Plays of Aristophanes*. Everyman Edition.

³ See *The Thesmophoriazusae*.

⁴ Translation by B. B. Rogers. *The Comedies of Aristophanes*. Loeb Classical Library.

CHAPTER VII

¹ Sheldon Cheney's *The Theatre*, chapter V, contains an interesting view on the sensuous theatre of the East.

² See the introduction to *Biblical Idyls*.

³ The translation by Professor Ryder is recommended for its grace.

CHAPTER VIII

¹ Cornaby, W. Arthur, *New China Review*, March 1919.

² *The Theatre*, p. 118.

³ Introduction to *Three Tibetan Mysteries* by H. I. Woolf, p. 9.

⁴ *Three Tibetan Mysteries*. Translated by H. I. Woolf. Broadway Translations. E. P. Dutton & Co., N. Y.

⁵ Unless otherwise stated, all quotations are from the translations of Arthur Waley in *The Noh Plays of Japan*. Alfred A. Knopf, 1922.

⁶ *Ibid.*, p. 23.

⁷ London *Observer*, December 11, 1938.

CHAPTER IX

¹ See Adams, Joseph Quincy: *Chief Pre-Shakespearean Dramas*.

² For more detailed accounts the reader is referred to Lee Simonson's *The Stage is Set*, E. K. Chambers' *The Medieval Stage*, and the authoritative books of Professor Gustave Cohen in French.

³ Translation by Babette and Glenn Hughes in Barrett H. Clark's *World Drama*.

⁴ See *Harvard Miracle Plays*. Edited by Donald Fay Robinson. Samuel French, N. Y.

⁵ Translation by C. G. Child, *Everyman and Other Plays*, Riverside Press, Boston.

⁶ See translation by M. Jagendorf reprinted in Barrett H. Clark's *World Drama*, volume 1. D. Appleton & Co.

⁷ Although there is no external evidence, scholars are agreed in attributing this play to Heywood.

CHAPTER X

¹ See *periaktoi*, Chapter III of this book.

² Elson, Arthur: *The Book of Musical Knowledge*, p. 62.

³ Symonds, John Addington: *Renaissance in Italy.* Modern Library edition, v. 2, p. 239.

⁴ And its sequel, *The Red Cock,* translated as *The Conflagration* in the American edition of Hauptmann's Works published by Viking Press.

⁵ Symonds, v. 1, p. 158.

CHAPTER XI

¹ See Ticknor's *History of Spanish Literature,* v. 2, p. 183.

² See Introduction p. xxiii of *Four Plays by Lope de Vega,* translated by Underhill.

³ Laborde's *History of Spanish Literature.*

CHAPTER XII

¹ Michael Drayton's tribute to Marlowe.

² Bakeless, John: *Christopher Marlowe. The Man In His Time,* p. 65.

³ *Ibid.,* p. 80.

⁴ See Appendix to the Mermaid Series edition of the works of Christopher Marlowe, pp. 428-430.

⁵ See Chapter VI, Part 2.

⁶ Other scholars ascribe the authorship to a certain William Stevenson, a fellow of Christ's College.

⁷ Saintsbury, George: *English Literature,* v. 2, p. 57.

⁸ Schilling, Felix: *Elizabethan Playwrights,* p. 200.

⁹ Legouis, Emile: *A History of English Literature* (with Louis Cazamian), Macmillan, p. 418.

¹⁰ Brown, John Mason: *Letters from Greenroom Ghosts,* p. 86.

CHAPTER XIII

¹ In Chettle's *Kind-Hearts' Dream.*

² In matters of chronology I am following E. K. Chambers. See his *William Shakespeare: A Study of Facts & Problems,* Oxford University; and its abridgement by Charles Williams, *A Short Life of Shakespeare with the Sources,* 1933.

³ Brandes, Georg: *William Shakespeare,* p. 131.

⁴ *Ibid.,* p. 139.

⁵ See E. M. Albright's *Shakespeare's Richard II and the Essex Conspiracy.* P.M.L.A. xiii, 3.

⁶ Brandes, p. 80.

⁷ See Smirnov's *Shakespeare.*

⁸ See Hazlitt's splendid analysis in *Characters of Shakespeare's Plays.*

⁹ See *A Short Life of Shakespeare* by Charles Williams (abridgment of Chambers' authoritative work), p. 64.

CHAPTER XIV

¹ Hazlitt, William: *Lectures on the Dramatic Literature of the Age of Elizabeth,* 1820.

² Introduction to *Selected Works of Ben Jonson* by Harry Levin, Random House, p. 3.

CHAPTER XV

[1] *Six Plays by Corneille & Racine*, edited with an introduction by Paul Landis, p. ix. Modern Library.

[2] See introduction to *Six Plays by Corneille and Racine*, p. ix.

[3] See Plekhanov's *Art & Society*, p. 20.

[4] Written with several collaborators.

[5] See his introduction to the Mermaid Series edition of Dryden's works.

[6] See Barrett H. Clark's *European Theories of the Drama*.

CHAPTER XVI

[1] Meredith, George: *On the Idea of Comedy and of the Uses of the Comic Spirit* (1877).

[2] *Ibid.*

[3] See John Palmer's *Comedy*, p. 14.

[4] See my chapter on Racine.

[5] Paul Frischauer's *Beaumarchais*, p. 163.

[6] *The World in Falseface.*

[7] *Comedy and Conscience After the Restoration* by Joseph Wood Krutch, p. 22.

[8] See Thackeray's *The English Humorists*.

CHAPTER XVII

[1] *Three Philosophical Poets.*

CHAPTER XVIII

[1] Lawson's *Theory and Technique of Playwriting*, p. 41.

[2] See Preface in *Four Plays* by Émile Augier, translated by Barrett H. Clark, 1915.

CHAPTER XIX

[1] See the finely reasoned pamphlet *Henrik Ibsen* edited by Angel Flores.

[2] Koht, v. 1, p. 43.

[3] See Koht's standard biography, *The Life of Ibsen*, v. 1, p. 59.

[4] *Quintessence of Ibsenism*, p. 51.

[5] See *Henrik Ibsen, a Marxist Analysis*, Critics Group.

[6] See Koht's *Life of Ibsen*, v. 2, 184-185.

[7] See *The Wallet of Time*, 1913; or p. 100 of *The American Theatre as Seen by Its Critics*, ed. by Montrose J. Moses and John Mason Brown.

[8] Koht, v. 2, p. 205.

[9] *Quintessence of Ibsenism*, p. 112.

[10] *Introduction to Three Plays* by Brieux, p. xiv.

[11] See Koht v. 2, p. 326.

[12] See *Introduction to Three Plays* by Brieux, p. xiv.

[13] *Quintessence of Ibsenism.*

[14] See *Henrik Ibsen, a Marxist Analysis.*

[15] An article on *The Wild Duck* in the Sunday theatre section of the New York *Times*.

CHAPTER XX

[1] "The Spirit of Scandinavian Realism." *New Republic*, March 21, 1923.

CHAPTER XXI

[1] See *Theatre Arts Monthly*, November 1937, p. 902.

[2] See John Mason Brown's *The Modern Theatre in Revolt*, p. 6, as well as the entire first chapter, for an illuminating discussion of the romantic and the naturalistic programs.

[3] Lewisohn's *The Modern Drama*, pp. 36-37.

[4] Matthew Josephson's *Zola and His Time*, p. 78, and the introduction to the novel.

[5] *Ibid.*, p. 123.

[6] See Hugh Allison Smith's *Main Currents of French Drama*, p. 203.

[7] *La vie littéraire.*

[8] *A Study of the Modern Drama*, p. 163.

[9] Introduction to *The Infernal Machine*, vii.

[10] Nicoll's *The Development of the Theatre*, p. 191.

[11] Simonson's *The Stage Is Set*, p. 353ff.

[12] *Ibid.*, p. 360.

[13] Brown's *The Modern Theatre in Revolt*, p. 49.

[14] See Simonson's *The Stage Is Set*, 309-50 for a brilliant polemic against Craig.

CHAPTER XXII

[1] Halfdan Gregersen's *Ibsen and Spain*, pp. 34-35.

[2] See Introduction by H. Granville Barker to *The Plays of Martinez Sierra*. E. P. Dutton & Co.

[3] See review of the Quinteros' "A Hundred Years Old" in *The Nation*.

[4] Lorca's *The Blood Wedding* was given an impressive production in Soviet Russia in the spring of 1939. For his services to the Republican theatre see "The Theatre in the Spanish Republic" by Mildred Adams in *Theatre Arts Monthly*, March 1932.

[5] *Iconoclasts*, p. 324.

[6] Starkie's *Luigi Pirandello*, p. 16.

[7] Vittorini's *The Drama of Pirandello*, p. 10.

[8] James C. Grey's "Luigi Pirandello," *Theatre Arts*, October 1922.

[9] See Fredericka V. Blankner's "Pirandello Paradox," *Theatre Arts Monthly*, December 1928.

[10] Domenico Vittorini's *The Drama of Luigi Pirandello*.

[11] James C. Grey's "Luigi Pirandello," *Theatre Arts*, October 1922.

CHAPTER XXIII

[1] Freytag's *Die Journalisten* (*The Journalists*) and Paul Lindau's *Gräfin Leah* (*Countess Leah*), a picture of decadence in aristocratic circles, reflect the work of Dumas *fils* and Augier.

[2] Anzengruber also possessed a wealth of folk humor; see his other plays.

[3] Eloeser's *Modern German Literature*, p. 36.

[4] See "Otto Brahm and Naturalist Directing," *Theatre Workshop*, April-July 1937.

[5] *Ibid.*

[6] *Iconoclasts*, p. 188.

[7] See Ludwig Lore's reminiscence, "Hauptmann in His Youth," in New York *Herald Tribune Books*, 1932.

[8] See "Hauptmann Returns to America" by Charles H. Meltzer (translator of *The Sunken Bell*) in the magazine section of the New York *Herald Tribune*, March 6, 1932.

[9] *Ibid.*

CHAPTER XXIV

[1] See Ashley Dukes' introduction to *Anatol*, etc., Modern Library, 1917.

[2] See *Contemporary Hungarian Theatre* by Koloman Brogyányi in *The Theatre of Changing Europe*, edited by Thomas H. Dickinson.

[3] Chandler's *Modern Continental Playwrights*, p. 347.

[4] Bruno Frank's *Twelve Thousand*, a romance about the Hessians who were herded to America to fight George III's battle with the colonists, and his *Storm in a Teacup* (adapted by James Bridie) also diverged from the expressionist furor. Vicki Baum's well-known *Grand Hotel* was a kaleidoscopic melodrama of the most marketable kind. Theodor Tagger (Ferdinand Bruckner) moved from psychoanalytical drama like *The Sickness of Youth* to more political work—liberal rather than radical—in *The Criminals*, a provocative picture of the chaos on the eve of the National Socialist reaction; and in *Races*, a lagging exposition of anti-semitism and the problems of bedeviled young storm troopers.

[5] For articles on the contemporary German theatre see among many: A. E. Zucker's "Germany's New Army of Organized Playgoers," *Theatre Guild Magazine*, May, 1931, pp. 24-27. An account of Die Volksbühne.

Sinclair Dombrov's "Post-Expressionism," *Theatre Arts*, January, 1924, pps. 26-37. An illustrated brief account of the work of the progressive German director Leopold Jessner, who in the famous "Jessner-steps" conceived "the word and the scene equally in terms of massed levels rising harmoniously to a dramatic resolution."

Anna Latsis' "Piscator's Theatre," *The International Theatre*, Bulletin No. 5, 1933, pp. 10-14. A study of Piscator's thirteen-year effort to create and develop a stage technique which would express social realities; of his use of conveyors and films to supplement dramatic action; and of his creation of an "epic theatre." An example of his various attempts to relate the drama of the individual to the social environment is his staging of Toller's *Hoppla*, made "complete by a film showing the contradictions of the existence of the proletariat, and of the parasitic bourgeoisie."

Friedrich Wolf's "The Work of the Theatrical Troupe 'Südwest,'" *The International Theatre*, No. 5, 1933, pp. 24-26. An informative note on the agitational theatre in Germany shortly before the Nazi regime.

Mordecai Gorelik's "Epic Realism," *Theatre Workshop*, April-July, 1937, pp. 29-40. A brilliant account of the principles of Brecht's "epic drama" or the "learning play," with excerpts from Brecht's notes on his first successful effort in this direction—*The Three-Penny Opera* (with music by Kurt Weill), a modernistic version of John Gay's *Beggar's Opera*. Regarding the theory of epic realism Gorelik writes: "The epic style does not accept the principle of the emotional 'carrying-away' of the spectator, nor does it accept the principle (as advocated by Wagner, Craig, Appia, etc.) of the fusion of theatrical arts in production. . . . There must be room in the theatre for the mind, as well as the passions." By "mind" is meant, in practice, analytical comment on the action of the play. An answer to these theories will be found in Edmund Fuller's "Epic Realism: An Analysis of Bert Brecht," in *The One Act Play Magazine*, April 1938, pp. 1124-1130.

H. W. L. Dana's "Impressions of Nazi Drama," *New Theatre*, Sept. 1936, pp. 14-15ff.

Ashley Duke's "Nazi Theatre: Second Phase," *Theatre Arts Monthly*, March 1935, pp. 177-184.

Percival Wilde's *Contemporary One-Act Plays from Nine Countries* (Little, Brown & Co., 1936). See chapter: "The Drama and the Nazis," p. 277.

Friedrich Wolf's "Fascist Drama," *International Literature*, 1937, no. 3, p. 79ff.

Winifred Smith's "Four Years of Nazi Drama," *New Masses*, Aug. 11, 1936. The most favorable report despite the radicalism of this magazine.

Cloyd Head's "Prague." *Theatre Arts*, October 1924, pp. 695-712. An early account of the new Czech theatre, its playwrights, and the brilliant modernist directors K. H. Hilar and Jaroslav Kvapil.

Illuminating accounts of the contemporary drama in Central Europe will also be found in various chapters of Thomas H. Dickinson's *The Theater in Changing Europe*, 1937.

CHAPTER XXV

[1] Mirsky's *History of Russian Literature*, p. 73.

[2] See the chapter on *Romanticism Over Europe*.

[3] See William Lyon Phelps' "Turgenev, Ancestor," *Theatre Guild Magaizne*, May 1930.

[4] See Preface to *The Plays of Ivan S. Turgenev* by M. S. Mandell.

[5] William Lyon Phelps, *ibid*.

[6] Mirsky's *History of Russian Literature*, p. 252.

[7] *Ibid.*, p. 310.

[8] *L'Assomoir at the Ba-Ta-Clan, Theatre Arts*, April 1922.

[9] *Reminiscences of Anton Chekhov.*

[10] *My Life in Art*, p. 347.

[11] *Life and Letters of Chekhov.*

[12] Jerome Mellquist's "Chekhov and His One-Act Plays," *One Act Play Magazine*, March 1939, p. 846.

[13] *Ibid.*

[14] *My Life in the Russian Theatre*, p. 14.

[15] *Ibid.* p. 22.

[16] Stark Young's translation, Scribner's.

[17] Nemirovitch-Dantchenko's *My Life in the Russian Theatre*, p. 66.

[18] Dantchenko, p. 154.

[19] Norris Houghton's *Moscow Rehearsals*, pp. 58-62.

CHAPTER XXVI

[1] Nemirovitch-Dantchenko, p. 228.

[2] See Eugenia Knipovich's "The Socialist Humanism of Gorky," *International Literature*, 1936.

[3] See H. W. L. Dana's "Maxim Gorki—Dramatist of the Lower Depths," *New Theatre*, August 1936, pp. 10-12, 28.

[4] H. W. L. Dana, *ibid*.

[5] See excerpts from Court Proceedings in the case of the Anti-Soviet "Bloc of Rights & Trotskyites," March 2-13, 1938, in *International Literature*, 1938, No. 3.

[6] He was, I believe, either exiled to Siberia or imprisoned.

[7] See H. W. L. Dana's *Handbook of Soviet Drama*, p. 40, for the list.

[8] Dickinson's *The Theatre of Changing Europe*, p. 66.

[9] *Ibid.*, p. 82.

CHAPTER XXVII

[1] See Ervine's column in the London *Observer*, April 21, 1939.

[2] Essays, p. 16, 1907.

[3] Essays, p. 206, 1899.

[4] Montrose J. Moses' "With William Butler Yeats," *Theatre Arts Monthly*, June 1924.

[5] *The Countess Cathleen*.

[6] Lady Gregory was born in 1859.

[7] This was less true of Chekhov who sometimes employed banal popular expressions that irk that fine critic Prince Mirsky no end.

[8] See *The Complete Works of Synge* (Random House, N. Y.), pp. 557-616.

[9] See the long sentences of *The Well of the Saints*.

[10] Preface to *The Playboy of the Western World*.

[11] Malone's *The Irish Drama*, p. 151.

[12] English Review, April 1924.

[13] The full text is given in W. G. Fay and Catherine Carswell's *The Fays of the Abbey Theatre*, pp. 218-219. See this book for further details on *The Playboy* riot. Additional material on the reception of the play in Dublin and America will be found in Herbert Farjeon's "The Birth of the Playboy," *Theatre Arts Monthly*, March 1932.

[14] It is still being misunderstood somewhat by authoritative historians like Andrew E. Malone. See pp. 151-52 of *The Irish Drama*.

[15] See pp. 369-79 in *The Collected Works of Synge* (Random House).

[16] *Ibid.*, Preface.

[17] *Treasury of the Theatre* edited by Burns Mantle and John Gassner, p. 442.

[18] Rutherford Mayne an engineer turned actor started writing in 1906 with *The Turn of the Road* and has continued to write for the Ulster Theatre and the Abbey since then. His latest work *Bridge Head* (1934) is a noble but for America a remote picture of the important work of the Irish Land Commission in reapportioning farm land among the needy peasantry.

[19] Review in The London *Observer*, August 15, 1937.

[20] Malone's *Irish Drama*, p. 218.

CHAPTER XXVIII

[1] *History of Modern Europe*, vol. 2, pp. 297 ff., Macmillan, 1921.

[2] *Queen Victoria*, pp. 406 ff.

[3] See *Culture and Anarchy*.

[4] Joseph Wood Krutch, "The Creative Muddle," in *The Nation*.

[5] "Henry Arthur Jones Reconsidered" by Clayton Hamilton, *Theatre Guild Magazine*, December 1930.

[6] *Euripides and Shaw, with other Essays*, p. 65.

[7] Barrett H. Clark's *A Study of the Modern Drama*, p. 252.

[8] "Memories of Oscar Wilde," *The Saturday Review of Literature*, May 27, 1939.

[9] Produced about five weeks before *The Importance of Being Earnest*.

[10] See Charles Shaw's *Bernard's Brethren*.

[11] See Shaw's "In the Days of My Youth," reprinted in *The Living Age*, 1924.

[12] "Bernard Shaw at Eighty" in *The Triple Thinkers*, pp. 245-46.

[13] See his article for the *New Statesman* of London, reprinted in the New York *Journal-American*, October 6, 1939.

[14] *Art of the Night*, 274.

[15] "At Tea with G. B. S." by G. W. Bishop in *Theatre Guild Magazine*, Nov. 1930.

[16] See his Preface to *Three Plays* by Brieux.

[17] Preface to *Nine Plays*, Dodd, Mead & Co. 1935, p. xii.

[18] *Plays Pleasant and Unpleasant*, 1898.

[19] Preface to *Nine Plays*, p. xxv.

[20] "Bernard Shaw's 'Apple Cart.' " Reviewed by Bernard Shaw, *Theatre Guild Magazine*, July 1930.

[21] *The Arts Weekly*, April 16, 1932; also pp. 283-286 *The American Theatre as Seen by its Critics*, edited by Montrose J. Moses and John Mason Brown.

[22] *Some Platitudes Concerning Drama* by Galsworthy.

[23] See Ivor Brown's "London Pioneering" in *Theatre Guild Magazine*, January 1930, for the work of The Stage Society, the Phoenix Society, The Arts Theatre Club, the Gate, and The Pioneer Players. See also the reports on the repertory companies in various issues of the London *Observer*.

CHAPTER XXIX

[1] See Dunlap's *André*, revised and made more patriotic in 1803 under the title of *The Glory of Columbia;* and James Nelson Barker's *Superstition* in 1824. For Indian plays see Barker's *Indian Princess* (1808), Custis' *Pocahontas or The Settlers of Virginia* (1830), and the most popular of them *Metamora* (1829), produced by Edwin Forrest.

[2] *The American Theatre*, p. 49.

[3] In collaboration with Washington Irving.

[4] See Montrose J. Moses' "Harrigan, American" in *Theatre Guild Magazine*, June 1930, for a charming account of Edward Harrigan and Tony Hart's vaudeville comedies.

[5] *The American Dramatist*, p. 317.

[6] For a scrupulously detailed account of the work of Herne, Bronson, Sheldon, Fitch, Thomas and numerous other playwrights see Professor Quinn's book.

[7] See Walt Kuhn's *The Story of the Armory Show*, privately published by Kuhn in 1938.

[8] For some account of this ferment see the early issues of *Theatre Arts*, Macgowan's "Footlights Across America," other books listed in the bibliography, and Cheney's postmortem analysis, "The Art Theatre—Twenty Years After" in *The New Caravan*, W. W. Norton, 1936, pp. 426-445.

[9] See Virgil Geddes' *The Melodramadness of Eugene O'Neill*.

[10] See "Christopher Marlowe to Eugene O'Neill" in *Letters from the Greenroom*.

[11] See Geddes' *The Melodramadness of Eugene O'Neill*, Charmion von Wiegand's "The Quest of O'Neill," *New Theatre*, September 1935, Eleanor Flexner's *American Playwrights 1918-1938*, and John Howard Lawson's *Theory and Technique of Playwriting*, pp. 129-141.

[12] See Eleanor Flexner, John Howard Lawson, and Charmion von Wiegand.

[13] Eleanor Flexner's *American Playwrights 1918-1938*, p. 135.

[14] Pages 262-265, *The American Theatre as Seen by its Critics*, edited by Moses and Brown. See Geddes, and Ervine's "At the Play" in the London *Observer*, June 11, 1937.

[15] See the poems reprinted in *A Bibliography of the Works of Eugene O'Neill* by Ralph Sanborn and Barrett H. Clark.

[16] See Charmion von Wiegand's "The Quest of O'Neill," *New Theatre*, Sept., 1935.

[17] Later expanded into the full-length melodramatic exposé of the acquisitive instinct *Gold*.

[18] See Eleanor Flexner's *American Playwrights 1918-1938*, p. 148.

[19] A first draft, *Chris Christopherson*, was staged on the road in 1919.

[20] See Von Wiegand.

[21] See Eleanor Flexner, p. 153-154, and especially Charmion von Wiegand.

[22] I have found a trend in this direction in science, in the thought of Hogben and Haldane, and the work of the psychoanalysts Otto Fenichel and Wilhelm Reich; it is apparently also present in the studies of Soviet scientists. But O'Neill's intuitive synthesis—which he did not of course systematize or pretend to make a point of—came before and was, apparently, not influenced by any theory.

[23] See Eleanor Flexner and Charmion von Wiegand.

[24] Eleanor Flexner, p. 151.

[25] Introduction to *Nine Plays* by Eugene O'Neill.

[26] See Granville Hicks' *The Great Tradition*, p. 254.

[27] This tendency in O'Neill's work is a main item in Virgil Geddes' indictment in *The Melodramadness of Eugene O'Neill*.

[28] See Lawson, p. 135, for a comparison between Hedda and Nina, to which I take some exception, however, since Nina is much less conventional in conduct.

[29] Joseph Wood Krutch, in his review of *Strange Interlude* in *The Nation*. Also, the chapter on O'Neill, *The American Drama Since 1918*.

[30] John Howard Lawson's point that Nina is driven on by instinct, that she "lives in an emotional trance; she never chooses or refuses" is also well taken. This reduces the possibility of tragic grandeur, though it does not prevent her from impressing us intensely. The praying mantis also fails to choose and yet is morbidly fascinating. Lawson, p. 135.

[31] *The Modern Temper.*

[32] Notes for *Mourning Becomes Electra* deciphered for me by Mr. Edmund Fuller from the facsimile reproduction in the special edition of the play.

[33] The New York *Times*, September 12, 1937, Section II, part 2, x3.·

[34] The young O'Neill, we recall, had been at odds with his father, who wanted him to settle down to a business life.

CHAPTER XXX

[1] The use of masks and expressionism as opposed to literal realism.

[2] The reader is referred to Burns Mantle's *Contemporary American Playwrights*, the 1936 edition of Professor Arthur Quinn's comprehensive *History of the American Drama from the Civil War to the Present Day*, Joseph Wood Krutch's study of *The American Drama since 1918*, and Eleanor Flexner's *American Playwrights 1918-1938* written from the social viewpoint of the younger critics.

[3] *Hans Sonnenstössers Höllenfahrt.*

[4] For an adequate account of their work the reader must be referred to Eleanor Flexner's *American Playwrights 1918-1938*, chapter VII; Joseph Wood Krutch's *The American Drama since 1918*, chapter V; Ben Blake's *The Awakening of the American Theatre;* John Mason Brown's *Two on the Aisle*, chapter V; Anita Block's *The Changing World in Plays and Theatre*, chapter VI; John Gassner's "The One-Act Play in the Revolutionary Theatre," in *The One-Act Play Today*, edited by William Kozlenko, and *Introduction* to *Twenty Best Plays of the Modern American Theatre.*

[5] "Clifford Odets," *Theatre Arts Monthly*, April 1939, pp. 257-264.

[6] This survey has omitted for lack of space a number of writers who have contributed to the vital American theatre. In the Kaufman subheading, note might have been taken of J. P. McEvoy, author of *The Potters*; of Howard Lindsay and Russel Crouse who have turned out highly amusing and pointed musical comedies like *Anything Goes* and *Hooray for What*, as well as a delightful dramatization of Clarence Day's *Life with Father*.

In the field of high comedy, mention might be made of Samson Raphaelson, particularly for his wise comedy of romantic middle age and unromantic youth, *Accent on Youth*; Vincent Lawrence; Zoë Akins, author of the blithe comedy *Papa*; Paul Osborne, for his neat *The Vinegar Tree*, which turns a "Second Mrs. Tanqueray" theme into comedy, as well as for his affecting adaptation *On Borrowed Time*, a fantasy on death; Harry W. Gribble for his *March Hares*, and Lawrence Langner and Armina Marshall for their charming comedy on bundling *The Pursuit of Happiness*.

The poetic drama has been aided by T. S. Eliot in *Murder in the Cathedral* and *Family Reunion*, by Stanley Young, and by Robert Turney with his retelling of the Agamemnon story *The Daughters of Atreus*. Fantasy celebrated a minor triumph in John Balderston's *Berkeley Square*, in which a young man meets up with his ancestors by going backward in time. Romance has found an able practitioner in Edwin Justus Mayer, author of *The Firebrand* and *Children of Darkness*, a distinguished high comedy. John Colton's *Rain*, the successful melodrama of puritanic repressions and their flare-up, belongs in a class by itself. E. P. Conkle, in numerous clever one-acters, and Hatcher Hughes in *Hell Bent for Heaven* added folk drama.

Among the social dramatists at least the following have done some creditable work: Michael Blankfort in *The Brave and the Blind* and *Battle Hymn* (a John Brown drama, written with Michael Gold); Ben Bengal in the charming strike-playlet *Plant in the Sun*; Melvin Levy in *Gold Eagle Guy*; Arthur Arent in his "living newspapers"; John Haynes Holmes and Reginald Lawrence in the pacifist play *If This Be Treason*; Leopold Atlas in the affecting divorce play *Wednesday's Child*; and William Kozlenko in the one-acter *This Earth is Ours*. Unusually penetrative were also the short plays of Philip Stevenson.

CHAPTER XXXI

[1] For those who are puzzled by the term "Existentialism," the following note may be of assistance: The term, used in Sartre's sense, predicates an atheistic existentialism in contrast to "Christian existentialism." Sartre's "Existentialism" predicated, first of all, the primacy (for man) of "existence" rather than of "essence." In philosophy, every object has "essence" and "existence," a constant collection of properties or "essence" and a certain presence effective in the world which is called "existence." For many philosophers, influenced by religion or by Plato, the *essence* comes before the *existence* (the "idea" of the thing comes before its specific individual manifestation) and has greater importance. It is held by many philosophers that everything exists in conformity to its essence, as, for example, when we say that human nature is the essence to which individual men and women conform. For the Existentialist, "existence" — *that which the human being makes himself by his acts and choices or decisions* — is primary. Since Sartre's godless universe has no divine plan — the universe is "irrational" or "absurd" — the individual "makes himself." Men determine what they are by their actions or "existence."

The so-called essence of the species "man" is in the germ from which he is born. But the man is not the germ; nor does it strictly predetermine what he will be. We are what we have developed into; the egg cell contains numerous possibilities, and we give realization to some of these by the life we lead. In this respect, man is "free." He can *choose* among these possibilities, and he can do so all the time. A human being can choose what he will be; that is, he can choose what his individual (although not, of course, his universal, species-determined) essence shall be. The important question is "What kind of a man are you?" and it is up to you to decide this by the life you lead. In this respect, you possess freedom; you are not the slave of circumstance; you are not the product of the irrationalism of the universe. If your situation threatens your integrity, you can choose to surrender it; but you can also elect the alternatives of fighting, suffering or dying.

A man cannot, of course, choose to be what it is impossible for him to be. He may be conditioned in his feelings and thoughts by many factors, such as class and occupation. Still, if we cannot select the class into which we are born, our physique, and our innate capacity for intelligence, we can at least choose our *attitude* toward our condition; we can choose to resign ourselves or to revolt, to be cowardly or courageous, and so on. Existentialist drama, therefore, conforms to the critic Brunetière's "law of the drama" — namely, that dramatic action should be a result of the operations of "free will," rather than of mechanical fatalism or absolute determinism. (Ferdinand Brunetière, *The Law of the Drama*, 1894; translated by Philip M. Hayden, Columbia University Dramatic Museum, 1914.) The characters' moral failure or triumph in Sartre's plays is determined by the nature and the degree of their volition. Moral issues are paramount in existentialist drama, and Sartre presents the moral bankruptcy of individuals in *No Exit* and *The Respectful Prostitute*, heroism in the French resistance drama *The Victors*, and purgation and liberation in the Oresteian drama *The Flies*.

² A more standardized entertainer was André Roussin, author of three brittle pieces — *Bobosse*, *Nina*, and *The Little Hut*, all trifles of boulevard extraction for which there was a curious enthusiasm in English quarters.

³ In 1946, O'Casey also wrote an affecting war play *Oak Leaves and Lavender*. It celebrated England's united stand against Hitler, and expressed faith in a victorious new way of life. It was also a lament for the death of two heroes, one from the upper and another from the lower classes.

⁴ Ronald Duncan (1914–   ), author of *This Way to the Tomb*, a religious drama written in Masque and anti-Masque form, with music supplied by England's ablest new composer, Benjamin Britten: Norman Nicholson, author of *The Old Man of the Mountains*, a retelling of the Elijah story, in which Elijah is a farmer engaged in conflict with an Ahab who is a north-England squire; Mrs. Anne Ridler, author of a devotional play *The Shadow Factory*, which concerns a factory director's salvation.

⁵ London, March 31, 1950.

⁶ The stream of poetic drama appeared to be unabated in 1950, Ronald Duncan publishing a new play, *Stratton*, and Anne Riddler, three one-act pieces in a volume entitled *Henry Bly and Other Plays*.

[7] *The Heiress* (1947) was a dramatization of Henry James's *Washington Square* by Ruth and Augustus Goetz. (Another effective dramatization of a short novel by Henry James, *The Turn of the Screw*, was made by William Archibald under the title of *The Innocents*.) *Billy Budd* (1951) was a dramatization by Louis O. Coxe and Robert Chapman of Herman Melville's allegorical short novel of the sea. The play was a provocative, if not altogether successful, treatment of the conflict between absolute good and absolute evil on one level of significance, and of the inhuman operation of war-time discipline and legal codes on another level. *Command Decision* (1947) was William Wister Haines' dramatization of his Second World War novel revolving around an Air Force general's difficult decisions in dispatching his men on fatal missions over Germany. *Mister Roberts* (1948) was a vivid and brisk dramatization of Thomas Heggen's naval war novel by the author working with the director Joshua Logan.

CHAPTER XXXII

[1] In 1875, Ibsen was moving toward realism. Becque was writing *The Vultures*. Zola, having already had his naturalistic play *Thérèse Raquin* produced and having already published it with its famous *Preface* in 1873, was extending his influence in the theatre. Ibsen was moving toward his middle-period of realistic social drama; his *Pillars of Society* appeared in 1877.

[2] Alfred Jarry was born in 1873 and died in 1907. His *King Ubu*, staged by a small group in 1888, had its official premiere in December 1896 at Lugné-Poë's experimental *Théâtre de l'Oeuvre*.

[3] There is, of course, considerably more to this subject than I can indicate here, and for an admirably thoughtful discussion, even if I cannot agree with it in every respect, I can do no better than refer the reader to Francis Fergusson's *The Idea of a Theatre*, Princeton University Press, 1949.

[4] A few writers generally treated as outsiders by the modern theatre, as were Claudel and Thomas Hardy (when he composed *The Dynasts*), and these made too little effort to overcome the barrier between printed literature and the stage. Others prevailed, more or less, by dint of forceful personality, reputation, or strong theatre sense; Hauptmann did with *The Weavers* and *Florian Geyer*, Shaw with *Back to Methuselah* and *Saint Joan*, O'Casey with *The Plough and the Stars*, Wilder with *The Skin of Our Teeth*. Brecht astutely felt the need for "epic theatre" and produced his unique variant of it in such plays as *Mother Courage*

and *The Caucasian Circle of Chalk*; and a few others, far less talented writers, tried to follow him and the director Erwin Piscator. co-author of *The Good Soldier Schweik.* in creating epic realism. A glimmer of epic possibilities also appeared in the religious festival plays of England, of which *Murder in the Cathedral* was the most noteworthy example. Yet, among the examples cited, only *The Caucasian Circle of Chalk, The Skin of Our Teeth*, and *Saint Joan* had the heroic spirit in the foreground of their matter and treatment. If *Murder in the Cathedral* were cited as another heroic drama. it would invite the large reservation that it does not present its subject as an epic struggle. When Becket's conflict with Henry II is not treated merely reverentially, it is rendered inwardly or "psychologically" (Becket's dialogue with the Tempters) or analytically (the apology of the Knights who murdered Becket).

BIBLIOGRAPHY

SOME COLLECTIONS OF PLAYS

A. GENERAL

Clark, Barrett H.: *World Drama*. 2 volumes. 1347 pp. New York: D. Appleton, 1933. Very inclusive up to Ibsen.

Leverton, Garrett H.: *Plays for the College Theatre*. New York: Samuel French, 1932. 629 pp. From the Middle Ages to the twentieth century.

Mantle, Burns and Gassner, John: *A Treasury of the Theatre*. New York: Simon & Schuster, 1935. 1643 pp. Thirty-four plays from *Agamemnon* to *Of Thee I Sing*.

Matthews, Brander: *Chief European Plays*. Boston: Houghton Mifflin and Co., 1916. 786 pp. From Aeschylus to Ibsen, with notes.

Millett, Fred B. and Bentley, Gerald Eades: *The Play's the Thing*. New York: D. Appleton & Co. An anthology of ancient and modern plays from Sophocles' *Oedipus the King* to O'Neill's *The Hairy Ape*.

Thomas, Lowell: *Plays and the Theatre*. Boston: Little, Brown & Co., 1937. Thirteen plays and sound introductions.

B. PERIODS AND PLAYWRIGHTS

Hamilton, Edith: *Three Greek Plays*. New York: W. W. Norton & Co., 1937. Notable translations of *Prometheus Bound*, *Agamemnon*, and *The Trojan Women*.

Landis, Paul: *Four Greek Plays*. New York: Modern Library, 1929.

Newton, Thomas: *Seneca his Tenne Tragedies*. New York: Alfred A. Knopf, 1927. The famous Elizabethan translations of Seneca. (Roman tragedy.)

Oates, Whitney J. and O'Neill, Eugene, Jr.: *The Complete Greek Drama*. 2 volumes. New York: Random House, 1938. The only complete collection in English; supplied with scholarly introductions to every play, as well as with a general introduction.

Fenollosa, Ernest F. and Pound, Ezra: *"Noh" or Accomplishment*. London: Macmillan & Co., Ltd., 1916. Contains Japanese Noh plays.

Iwasaki, Yozan T. and Hughes, Glenn: *Three Modern Japanese Plays*. Cincinnati: Stewart & Kidd Co., 1923.

New Plays from Japan. New York: D. Appleton and Co., 1930.

Ryder, Ernest: *Translations of Shakuntala and Other Works*. New York: E. P. Dutton & Co., 1920. Valuable for the study of Hindu drama. Excellent translations.

The Little Clay Cart. Adaptation used by the Neighborhood Playhouse of New York. New York: Theatre Arts, Inc., 1934. (See also complete translation by Arthur Ryder.)

Waley, Arthur: *The Nō Plays of Japan*. New York: Alfred A. Knopf, 1922. Excellent translations.

Lieder, P. R., Lovett, R. M. and Root, R. K.: *British Drama*. Boston: Houghton Mifflin Co., 1929. Ten plays from the Middle Ages to Oscar Wilde, supplied with scholarly introductions.

Adams, Joseph Quincy: *Chief Pre-Shakespearean Dramas*. Boston: Houghton Mifflin Co., 1924. Invaluable for the study of the medieval and early Tudor drama; the medieval plays are in Middle English, but the editor's footnotes smooth the way for the layman.

Boas, Frederick S.: *Five Pre-Shakespearean Comedies*. (Early Period.) London: Oxford University Press, 1934.

Child, D. G.: *The Second Shepherds' Play, Everyman and Other Early Plays*. Boston: Houghton Mifflin & Co., 1910. Modernized texts.

Dunn, Esther C.: *Eighteen Famous Elizabethan Plays*. New York: Modern Library Giant, 1932.

Mermaid Series. *The Best Plays of the Old Dramatists*. 22 volumes, 1887-1895. Excellent compilation of Elizabethan, seventeenth- and eighteenth-century English plays, with introductions and editorial matter.

Parks, Edd Winfield and Beatty, Richmond Croom: *The English Drama*. New York: W. W. Norton & Co., 1935. 1495 pp. From medieval drama to Shirley. Also includes translations of two plays by Plautus and Seneca. Contains excellent introductions.

Robinson, Donald Fay: *The Harvard Dramatic Club Miracle Plays*. New York Samuel French, 1928.

Thorndike, Ashley: *The Minor Elizabethan Drama*. 2 volumes. Vol. I, Pre-Shakespearean Comedies; Vol. II, Pre-Shakespearean Tragedies. New York: E. P. Dutton & Co., 1910.

Fitzgerald, Edward: *Six Dramas of Calderon:* London, Routledge, 1904.

Underhill, John Garrett: *Four Plays by Lope de Vega*. New York: Charles Scribner's Sons, 1936.

Landis, Paul: *Six Plays by Corneille and Racine*. New York: Modern Library, 1931.

MacMillan, Dougald and Jones, Howard Mumford: *Plays of the Restoration and 18th Century*. New York: Henry Holt & Co., 1931.

Moore, Cecil A.: *Twelve Plays of the Restoration and Eighteenth Century*. 952 pp. New York: Modern Library, 1933.

Tupper, Frederick and James W.: *Representative Dramas from Dryden to Sheridan*. Revised edition, 722 pp. New York: Oxford University Press, 1934. Contains valuable introductions and notes.

Chandler, Frank W. and Cordell, Richard A.: *Twentieth Century Plays*. New York: Thomas Nelson & Sons, 1934. Twenty important plays.

Dickinson, Thomas H.: *Chief Contemporary Dramatists*. Series 1, 2, and 3. Boston: Houghton Mifflin & Co., 1915, 1921, 1930. The three volumes, totaling nearly 2100 pages of double-column type, are indispensable to the student of modern drama.

Katzin, Winifred: *Eight European Plays*. New York: Brentano's, 1927. Plays by Kaiser, Sternheim, San Secondo and other moderns.

Tucker, S. Marion: *Twenty-Five Modern Plays*. 1045 pp. New York: Harper & Brothers, 1931.

Allen, L. H.: *Three Plays by Frederick Hebbel*. New York: E. P. Dutton. (See the introduction on Hebbel.)

Ibsen, Henrik: *Early Plays*. Tr. by Anders Orbeck. New York: American-Scandinavian Foundation, 1921. Contains *Catiline, The Warrior's Barrow, Olaf Liljekrans*.

Clark, Barrett H.: *Masterpieces of Modern Spanish Drama*. New York: Duffield & Co., 1917. Plays by Echageray, Galdos, and Guimera.

Clark, Barrett H.: *Four Plays of the Free Theatre*. Cincinnati: Stewart & Kidd Co., 1915. Plays of the *Théâtre Libre* by Curel, Jullien, Porto-Riche, and Ancey.

Goldberg, Isaac: *Plays of the Italian Theatre*. Boston: J. W. Luce & Co., 1921.

Bechhofer, C. E.: *Five Russian Plays*. London: K. Paul, Trench, Trubner & Co., Ltd., 1916.

Four Soviet Plays. New York: International Publishers, 1937. Contains *Yegov Bulychov, An Optimistic Tragedy, Aristocrats;* and *Masters of Time*.

Lyons, Eugene: *Six Soviet Plays*. With a Preface by Elmer Rice. Boston: Houghton Mifflin & Co., 1934. Contains *Days of the Turbins, Squaring the Circle, Tempo, Bread, Ingo*, and *Fear*.

Noyes, George Rapall: *Masterpieces of the Russian Drama*. New York: D. Appleton & Co., 1933.

Sayler, Oliver M.: *The Moscow Art Theatre Series of Plays*. 2 volumes. New York: Brentano's, 1923.

Goldberg, Isaac: *Six Plays of the Yiddish Theatre*. First and second series. Boston: John W. Luce & Co., 1918.

Canfield, Curtis: *Plays of the Irish Renaissance, 1880-1930*. New York: Ives Washburn, 1929. A valuable anthology, excellently edited. Plays by Yeats, Synge, Lady Gregory, Padraic Colum, T. C. Murray, Edward Martyn, O'Casey, Lennox Robinson and others.

Plays of Changing Ireland. New York: Macmillan, 1936. A collection of the most recent Irish plays, excellently edited, with useful introductions. Plays by Yeats, Denis Johnston, Lennox Robinson, George Shiels, Mary Manning, Rutherford Mayne, and others.

Moses, Montrose J.: *Representative British Dramas, Victorian and Modern* Boston: Little Brown & Co., 1931.

Coe, Kathryn and Cordell, William H.: *Pulitzer Prize Plays*, New York: Random House, 1937.

Federal Theatre Plays. 2 volumes. New York: Random House, 1938. A collection of six plays, four of which are "Living Newspapers," the latest development in dramatic form.

Mantle, Burns: *The Best Plays of 1919-20.* New York: Dodd, Mead & Co., 1920. The best plays produced in America each year after 1920 have been published annually. Each volume contains, in addition to abstracts of ten plays, a résumé of the year in the theatre and a record of each play produced.

Mantle, Burns and Sherwood, Garrison P.: *The Best Plays of 1909-1919 and the Year Book of the Drama in America.* New York: Dodd, Mead & Co., 1933.

Moses, Montrose J.: *Representative American Dramas, National and Local.* Boston: Little Brown & Co., 1933.

Quinn, Arthur Hobson: *Representative American Plays.* New York: D. Appleton-Century, 1938. Includes plays by Thomas Godfrey, Royall Tyler, William Dunlap, John Howard Payne, Anna Cora Mowath, George Henry Baker, Steele MacKaye, James A. Herne, Bronson Howard, Clyde Fitch, and others, as well as later selections.

The Theatre Guild Anthology. New York: Random House, 1936, 973 pp. Plays by Shaw, O'Neill, Ervine, Molnar, Andreyev, Rice, Werfel, Howard, Barry, Sherwood, Maxwell Anderson, S. N. Behrman, and others.

Gassner, John: *Twenty Best Plays of the Modern American Theatre.* New York: Crown Publishers, 1939. Covers the 1929-1939 period.

Individual Authors

Among numerous editions of the work of individual playwrights, those that will be found most easily available appear under the imprint of The Mermaid Series (T. Fisher Unwin, London), Modern Library, Everyman's Library (E. P. Dutton, N. Y. and J. M. Dent, London), and World's Classics (Oxford University Press, London), Bohn's Classics, and Random House. Scribner's has published the complete works of Ibsen, Strindberg, Chekhov, and Galsworthy; Viking Press, most of the works of Gerhart Hauptmann; Brentano's (succeeded by Dodd, Mead & Co.), the complete works of Bernard Shaw; Dutton, many of Pirandello's plays; Liveright, the plays of O'Neill (the last two by Random House).

C. ONE-ACT PLAY COLLECTIONS

Clark, Barrett H.: *Representative One-Act Plays by British and Irish Authors.* Boston: Little, Brown & Co., 1922.

Kozlenko, William: *The Best Short Plays of the Social Theatre.* New York: Random House, 1939. The social drama of the thirties is represented by ten short plays.

Mayorga, Margaret: *The Best One-Act Plays of 1937.* (1938). New York: Dodd, Mead & Co., 1938; 1939.

Representative One-Act Plays by American authors. Boston: Little, Brown, 1937.

One-Act Plays for Stage and Study. 9 volumes. New York: Samuel French. American and foreign plays (1924-1938).

Shay, Frank: *Fifty More Contemporary One-Act Plays.* New York: D. Appleton & Co., 1928.

Shay, Frank and Loving, Pierre: *Fifty Contemporary One-Act Plays*. Cincinnati: Stewart & Kidd, 1920.

Wilde, Percival: *Contemporary One-Act Plays from Nine Countries*. Boston: Little, Brown & Co., 1936. See the excellent introductions.

GENERAL HISTORIES

A. WORLD HISTORY OF DRAMA AND THEATRE

Bates, Alfred (editor): *The Drama*. 22 volumes. London: The Athenian Society, 1913. An exhaustive but wayward and not always sufficiently critical history of the drama from its beginning to the first decade of our century.

Boehn, Max von: *Dolls and Puppets*. London: Harrap, 1932.

Busse, Bruno: *Das Drama*. 4 volumes. Leipzig: B. G. Teubner, 1922.

Cheney, Sheldon: *The Theatre: Three Thousand Years of Drama, Acting and Stagecraft*. New York: Longmans, Green & Co., 1929.

Fort, Alice B. and Kates, Herbert S.: *Minute History of the Drama*. N. Y.: Grosset and Dunlap, 1935. Useful in schools; too elementary for the adult student.

Gilder, Rosamond: *A Theatre Library*. New York: Theatre Arts, Inc. 1932. A bibliography.

Gilder, Rosamond and Freedley, George: *Theatre Collections in Libraries and Museums*. New York: *Theatre Arts*, 1936.

Hubbell, Jay B. and Beaty, John O.: *An Introduction to Drama*, New York: Macmillan, 1927.

Mantzius, Karl: *A History of Theatrical Art*. 6 volumes. Tr. L. von Cossel. London: Duckworth, 1903-21.

Matthews, Brander: *The Development of the Drama*. New York: Charles Scribner's Sons, 1908.

Millett, Fred B. and Bentley, Gerald Eades: *The Art of the Drama*. New York: Appleton-Century, 1935.

Nicoll, Allardyce: *The Development of the Theatre*. New York: Harcourt, Brace & Co., 1927.

Reinach, Salomon: *Apollo: An Illustrated Manual of the History of Art Throughout the Ages*. New York: Charles Scribner's Sons, 1913. A useful parallel to the history of the theatre.

Orpheus, A History of Religions. New York: Horace Liveright, 1930. A parallel study.

Simonson, Lee: *The Stage Is Set:* New York: Harcourt, Brace & Co., 1932.

Sobel, Bernard: *The Theatre Handbook and Digest*. New York: Crown Publishers, 1939.

Stauffer, Ruth M.: *The Progress of Drama Through the Centuries*. New York: Macmillan, 1928.

Stevens, Thomas Wood: *The Theatre from Athens to Broadway*. New York: D. Appleton & Co., 1932.

Stuart, Donald Clive: *The Development of Dramatic Art:* New York and London: D. Appleton & Co., 1928.

Theatre Arts. A quarterly, 1916-1923. A monthly, 1924 to the present day. An invaluable record of the theatre.

Turner, William: *History of Philosophy*. Boston: Ginn & Co., 1903. A helpful
    parallel study, especially for the section on classic drama.
Van Loon, Hendrik: *The Arts*. New York: Simon & Schuster, 1937. A useful
    parallel study.
Wells, H. G.: *The Outline of History*. One volume edition, Garden City Publish-
    ing Co., 1925. A parallel to the history of the theatre.

B. NATIONAL DRAMA AND THEATRE

Eaton, Walter Prichard: *The Drama in English*. New York: Charles Scribner's
    Sons, 1930. A useful introductory study.
Fitzmaurice-Kelly, J.: *A New History of Spanish Literature*. New York: Oxford
    University Press, 1926. Sections on the drama.
Fowler, Harold N.: *A History of Roman Literature*. New York: Macmillan, 1932.
    Sections on the drama.
Francke, Kuno: *A History of German Literature as Determined by Social Forces*.
    New York: Henry Holt & Co., 1901. Sections on the drama.
Jorgenson, Theodore: *History of Norwegian Literature*. New York: Macmillan,
    1933. Sections on the drama.
Kennard, Joseph Spencer: *The Italian Theatre*. 2 volumes. Tr. by R. T. Weaver.
    New York: Rudge, 1932.
Lancaster, H. C.: *A History of French Dramatic Literature*. Baltimore: Johns
    Hopkins Press, 1935. Sections on the drama.
Legouis, Emile and Cazamian, Louis: *A History of English Literature*. New
    York: Macmillan, 1930. Sections on the drama.
Mirsky, Prince D. S.: *A History of Russian Literature*. London: Routledge,
    1927. From the beginnings of Russian Literature until 1881. Sections on
    the drama.
    Contemporary Russian Literature (1881-1925). New York: Alfred A. Knopf,
    1926. Sections on the drama.
Nicoll, Allardyce: *British Drama*. New York: Crowell Co., 1925. Later edition,
    1933.
Saintsbury, George: *A Short History of French Literature*. Oxford: Clarendon
    Press, 1884. Contains excellent criticism of French classical drama.
Sinclair, T. A.: *A History of Classical Literature from Homer to Aristotle*. New
    York: Macmillan, 1935. Sections on the drama.
Smith, Mabell S. C.: *The Spirit of French Letters*. New York: Chautauqua Press,
    1912. Chapter VII, although extremely inadequate, contains a good an-
    alysis of *The Cid*.
Taine, Hippolyte: *Introduction to the History of English Literature*, 1863. In sev-
    eral English editions. Sections on the drama.
Thorndike, Ashley H.: *English Comedy*. New York: Macmillan, 1928.
Ward, Adolphus William: *A History of English Dramatic Literature to the Death
    of Queen Anne*. London and New York: Macmillan, 1899.

GENERAL CRITICISM

Agate, James: *The English Dramatic Critics*. London: Baker, 1932. An an-
    thology of English Criticism.

Archer, William: *Playmaking, a Manual of Craftsmanship.* New York: Boston: Small, Maynard Co., 1928.

Babbitt, Irving: *The Masters of Modern French Criticism.* Boston: Houghton Mifflin & Co., 1912. See especially Chapter X on Brunetiere.

Baker, George Pierce: *Dramatic Technique.* Boston: Houghton Mifflin Co., 1919.

Beerbohm, Max: *Around the Theaters.* 2 volumes. New York: A. A. Knopf, 1930. A brilliant commentary on the drama of the present century. Papers written for the *London Saturday Review* from 1898 to 1910.

Bergson, Henri: *Laughter—An Essay on the Meaning of the Comic.* Translated by C. Brereton & F. Rothwell. New York: Macmillan, 1911.

Brown, John Mason: *The Art of Playgoing.* New York: W. W. Norton & Co., 1936. An excellent introduction to the drama for contemporary audiences. *Letters from Greenroom Ghosts.* New York: Viking Press, 1934. Charming and illuminating essays. *Upstage.* New York: W. W. Norton & Co., 1928.

Brunetiere, Ferdinand: *The Law of the Drama.* New York: Columbia University Dramatic Museum, 1914.

Clark, Barrett H.: *European Theories of the Drama.* New York: D. Appleton & Co., 1929.

Cooper, Lane: *Aristotle on the Art of Poetry.* An Amplified Version with Supplementary Illustrations for Students of English. New York: Ginn & Co., 1913.

Dryden, John: *Dramatic Essays.* New York: E. P. Dutton. Everyman edition.

Ervine, St. John: *How to Write a Play.* New York: Macmillan, 1928.

Freud, Sigmund: *Wit and Its Relation to the Unconscious.* See Modern Library Giant edition, *The Basic Writings of Sigmund Freud,* 1938.

Freytag, Gustav: *Technique of the Drama.* Tr. by Elias J. MacEwan. Chicago: S. C. Griggs & Co., 1895.

Granville-Barker, Harley: *The Study of Drama.* New York: Macmillan (Cambridge), 1934.

Guerard, Albert: *Literature and Society.* Boston: Lothrop, Lee and Shepard Company, 1935. A temperate study that illuminates the relation between writers and their environment.

Krutch, Joseph Wood: *The Modern Temper.* New York: Harcourt, Brace & Co., 1929. Interesting on tragedy.

Krows, Arthur Edwin: *Playwriting for Profit.* New York: Longmans, Green & Co., 1928.

Lawson, John Howard: *Theory and Technique of Playwriting.* New York: G. P. Putnam's Sons, 1936.

Lessing, Gotthold Ephraim: *The Hamburg Dramaturgy.* Tr. by E. C. Beasley and Helen Zimmern. London: Bohn, 1879. Edited by Ch. Harris-Holt, 1901.

Lewisohn, Ludwig: *A Modern Book of Criticism.* New York: Modern Library, 1919.

Lifshitz, Mikhail: *Philosophy of Art of Karl Marx,* New York: Critics Group Press, 1938.

Lucas, F. L.: *Tragedy in Relation to Aristotle's Poetics.* London: Hogarth Press, 1927.

Ludovici, Anthony M.: *The Secret of Laughter*. New York: Viking Press, 1933. An interesting consideration of comedy and the theories of laughter; particularly pertinent to Greek and Roman comedy.

Nathan, George Jean: *The World in Falseface*. New York: Alfred A. Knopf, 1923.
Art of the Night, 1928.
Testament of a Critic, 1931.
The Morning After the First Night, 1938. (See other books by the author.)

Nicoll, Allardyce: *The Theory of Drama*. London: G. G. Harrap & Co., 1931. A provocative and scholarly work.

Palmer, John: *Comedy*. London: Martin Secker, 1914.

Perry, Henry Ten Eyck: *Masters of Dramatic Comedy and their Social Themes*. Cambridge: Harvard University Press, 1939.

Rowe, Kenneth E.: *Write That Play*. New York: Funk & Wagnalls, 1939.

Shaw, G. Bernard: *Dramatic Opinions and Essays*. 2 volumes. New York: Brentano's, 1907.

Shaw, George Bernard: *The Sanity of Art*. London: Constable & Co., 1911.

Strong, L. A. G.: *Common Sense about Drama*. New York: Alfred A. Knopf, 1937.

Spingarn, Joel: *Literary Criticism in the Renaissance*. New York: Columbia University Press, 1908.

Walkley, A. B.: *Drama and Life*. London: Methuen, 1907.

Wells, Henry: *The Judgment of Literature*. New York: W. W. Norton & Co., 1928. A useful introduction to the judgment of literature, applicable in part to the drama.

Willocks, M. P.: *Between the Old World and the New*. New York: Frederick A. Stokes Co., 1926.

Wilde, Percival: *The Craftsmanship of the One-Act Play*. Boston: Little, Brown & Co., 1931.

Young, Stark: *The Flower in Drama*. New York: Charles Scribner's Sons, 1923.
The Theatre. New York: E. P. Dutton, 1927.

PRIMITIVE THEATRE

Brown, Ivor: *First Player. The Origin of Drama*. New York: William Morrow & Co., 1928.

Budge, E. A. Wallis: *Osiris and the Egyptian Resurrection*. London and New York: P. L. Warner, 1911. Contains a chapter on ancient Egyptian drama.

Calverton, V. F.: *The Making of Man. An Outline of Anthropology*. New York: The Modern Library, 1931.

Frazer, James George: *The Golden Bough. A Study in Magic and Religion*. (One volume edition). New York: Macmillan, 1922.

Harrison, Jane Ellen: *Mythology*. Boston: Marshall Jones, 1924. A provocative introduction to one source of the drama. See also the same author's *Prolegomena to the Study of Greek Religion*. Cambridge: University Press, 1908.
Ancient Art and Ritual. New York: Henry Holt & Co., 1931.

Havemeyer, Loomis: *The Drama of Savage Peoples*. New Haven: Yale University Press, 1916. A study of the origins of the drama.
Malinowski, Bronislaw: *Myth in Primitive Psychology*. New York: W. W. Norton & Co., 1926.
Ridgeway, William: *The Dramas and Dramatic Dances of Non-European Races*. Cambridge: University Press, 1915. An advanced study of primitive drama.
Ròheim, Gèza: "Primitive High Gods." Special number of *The Psychoanalytic Quarterly*, January, 1934. No. 1, Part 2. The psychoanalytic view of religious origins, applicable to dramatic origins.
Thorpe, Evelyn: *Here We Go Round. The Story of the Dance*. New York: Wm. Morrow & Co. 1926.

CLASSIC THEATRE AND DRAMA

Allen, James Turney: *Stage Antiquities of the Greeks and Romans and Their Influence*. New York: Longmans, Green & Co., 1927.
Aristophanes: *The Eleven Comedies*. London: The Athenian Society, 1912. Translator unmentioned. Excellent introductions.
The Frogs and Three Other Plays. New York: E. P. Dutton, 1911. Attention is called to the introduction by John Hookham Frere, 1820.
Bailey, Cyril (editor): *The Legacy of Rome*. Oxford: Clarendon Press, 1923. Articles on Roman literature, religion, philosophy, industry, art, and life.
Beer, M.: *Social Struggles in Antiquity*. Tr. by H. J. Stenning. New York: International Publishers, 1929.
Bieber, Margarete: *The History of the Greek and Roman Theatre*. Princeton: Princeton University Press, 1939.
Blackie, John Stuart: *The Lyrical Dramas of Aeschylus*. New York: E. P. Dutton, 1920. See the Preface, On the Genius and Character of the Greek Tragedy, The Life of Aeschylus, and Introductory Remarks and Notes on the plays. Somewhat dated, since written in 1846, but illuminating.
Bury, J. B.: *A History of Greece to the Death of Alexander the Great*. New York: Modern Library Giant edition, 1937.
Cornford, Francis M.: *The Origin of Attic Comedy*. New York: Macmillan (Cambridge), 1934.
Decharme, P.: *Euripides and the Spirit of the Dramas*. Tr. James Loeb. New York: Macmillan, 1906.
Flickinger, R. S.: *The Greek Theater and Its Drama*. Chicago: Chicago University Press, 1926.
Fowler, Harold N.: *A History of Roman Literature*. New York: Macmillan, 1932.
Goodell, Thomas Dwight: *Athenian Tragedy, A Study in Popular Art*. New Haven: Yale University Press, 1920.
Haigh, A. E.: *The Attic Theatre*. A Description of the Theatre of the Dramatic Performances at Athens. 3rd Edition, revised and in part rewritten. Oxford: Clarendon Press, 1907.
Hamilton, Edith: *Three Greek Plays*. New York: W. W. Norton & Co. 1937. (*Prometheus Bound, Agamemnon, Trojan Women*). See introductions.
The Greek Way. New York: W. W. Norton & Co., 1930.
Herrman, Leon: *Le théâtre de Sénèque*. Paris, 1924.

Hyde, Walter Woodburn: *Greek Religion and its Survivals*. Boston: Marshall Jones & Co., 1923. Provides an illuminating account of some basic meanings of the content and outlook of Greek drama.

Livingstone, R. W. (editor): *The Legacy of Greece*. Oxford: Clarendon Press, 1923. Articles on Greek literature, religion, philosophy, science, and art.

Lord, Louis P.: *Aristophanes: His Plays and Influence*. Boston: Marshall Jones Company, 1925.

Lucas, F. L.: *Euripides and his Influence*. New York: Longmans, Green & Co., 1928.

Mahr, August C.: *The Origin of the Greek Tragic Form*. New York: Prentice-Hall, 1938.

Menander: *Three Plays*. Translated and Interpreted by L. A. Post. New York: E. P. Dutton & Co. 1929. Attention is called to the Introduction by Professor Post.

Murray, Gilbert: *Euripides and his Age*. New York: Henry Holt & Co., 1913.
    The Plays of Euripides. New York: Longmans, Green & Co., 1906. See the Introductions and Notes to the individual plays translated by Murray.
    Euripides' Hippolytus and Bacchae; Aristophanes' Frogs. See Introductions; Appendix on the Lost Tragedies of Euripides; and The Significance of the Bacchae in Athenian History.

Nestle, Wilhelm: *Euripides, der Dichter der Griechischen Aufklärung*. Stuttgart: W. Kohlhammer, 1901.

Newton, Thomas (editor): *Seneca His Tenne Tragedies*. Attention is called to the excellent Introduction by T. S. Eliot. New York: Alfred A. Knopf, 1927.

Nietzsche, Friedrich: *The Birth of Tragedy*. In: *Ecce Homo & The Birth of Tragedy*. Tr. by Clifton Fadiman. New York: Modern Library. A confused but provocative study of Greek tragedy.

Norwood, Gilbert: *Euripides and Shaw*. Boston: John W. Luce, 1921. Also contains an essay: The Present Renaissance of English Drama.
    The Art of Terence. Oxford: Clarendon Press, 1923. A good introduction to Roman comedy.
    Greek Tragedy. Boston: John W. Luce (date missing). A brilliant, if sometimes controversial, interpretation.

Plautus: *Three Plays of Plautus*. Translated by F. A. Wright & H. Lionel Rogers. New York: E. P. Dutton. Attention is called to the Introductions: "Plautus: His Life and Times"; "Plautus the Poet"; "The Plautine Theatre" by F. A. Wright.

Sheppard, J. T.: *Aeschylus and Sophocles, Their Work and Influence*. New York: Longmans, Green & Co., 1927.

Smyth, Herbert Weir: *Aeschylean Tragedy*. Berkeley, Calif.: University of California Press, 1924.

Symonds, John Addington: *Studies of the Greek Poets*, London: A. & C. Black, 1920. 3rd ed.

Verrall, A. W.: *Euripides, the Rationalist*. Cambridge: University Press, 1905. (See also Dr. Verrall's various editions and studies of Euripides' individual plays). Original but controversial analysis of Euripides as a modern thinker.

Young, Sir George: *The Dramas of Sophocles*. Everyman Library. New York: E. P. Dutton, 1920. See the Introduction and Fragments of the Lost Plays.

THE ORIENT

Aston, W. G.: *The History of Japanese Literature.* New York: D. Appleton and Company, 1899. (See especially pp. 197-217, and pp. 273-288.)

Buss, Kate: *Studies in Chinese Drama.* New York: Jonathan Cape and Smith, 1930.

Durant, Will: *The Story of Civilization. Our Oriental Heritage.* New York: Simon and Schuster, 1935.

Giles, Herbert A.: *A History of Chinese Literature.* New York: D. Appleton & Co., 1931. Revised edition.

Gown, Herbert H.: *A History of Indian Literature.* New York: D. Appleton & Co., 1931.

Horrwitz, E. P.: *The Indian Theatre.* London: Blackie & Son, 1912. Interesting but unauthoritative.

Jastrow, Morris: *The Book of Job.* Philadelphia: Lippincott, 1920.

Kallen, Horace M.: *The Book of Job as a Greek Tragedy.* New York: Moffat, Yard & Co., 1918. An interesting study and dramatic Version of *Job,* although weighty scholarship opposes Professor Kallen's view. See Jastrow's book.

Keith, A. Bernedale: *The Sanskrit Drama in Its Origin, Development, Theory and Practice.* Oxford: Clarendon Press, 1924.

Kincaid, Zoë: *Kabuki, the Popular Stage of Japan.* New York: Macmillan, 1925.

Lombard, Frank Alanson: *An Outline History of the Japanese Drama.* London: G. Allen & Unwin, Ltd., 1928.

Stopes, Marie C. and Joji Sakurai: *Plays of Old Japan.* New York: E. P. Dutton, 1913. See the introduction, pp. 1-34.

Waley, Arthur: *The Noh Plays of Japan.* New York: Alfred A. Knopf. 1922. The best translations and excellent introductory material.

Zucker, A. E.: *The Chinese Theater.* Boston: Little, Brown & Co., 1925.

THE MIDDLE AGES

Adams, Joseph Quincy: *Chief Pre-Shakespearean Dramas.* Boston: Houghton Mifflin Co., 1924. See the notes.

Bates, Katharine Lee: *The English Religious Drama.* New York: Macmillan, 1902. An excellent interpretation, although later scholarship affects some facts in the book.

Beer, M.: *Social Struggles in the Middle Ages.* Tr. by H. J. Stenning. New York: International Publishers, 1929.

Chambers, E. K.: *The Medieval Stage.* Oxford: Clarendon Press. 2 volumes. 1903.

Cohen, Gustave: *Histoire de la mise en scène dans le théâtre religieux français du moyen age.* Paris: Champion, 1926.

Nicoll, Allardyce: *Masks, Mimes and Miracles.* New York: Harcourt, Brace & Co., 1932. Excellent on the period between classic Greek and Renaissance drama, containing good material on the *commedia dell' arte.*

Osborn, E. B.: *The Middle Ages.* New York: Doubleday, Doran & Co., 1928. An excellent summary of the background of the medieval drama.

Young, Carl: *The Drama of the Medieval Church.* Oxford: Clarendon Press, 1933.

THE RENAISSANCE AND THE SIXTEENTH CENTURY

Burckhardt, Jacob: *The Civilization of the Renaissance in Italy.* New York: Albert & Charles Boni edition, 1935. An illuminating introduction to the Italian Renaissance drama.

Lea, K. M.: *Italian Popular Comedy. A Study in the Commedia dell' arte.* 2 volumes. Oxford: Clarendon Press, 1934.

Machiavelli, Niccolo: *Mandragola.* Tr. by Stark Young. Includes Macaulay's Essay on Machiavelli. New York: Macaulay Co. 1927.

Smith, Winifred: *The Commedia dell' Arte.* New York: Columbia University Press, 1912.

Symonds, John Addington: *Renaissance in Italy.* 2 volumes. New York: Modern Library Giant, 1935.

Taylor, Henry Osborn: *Thought and Expression in the Sixteenth Century.* New York: Macmillan, 1920.

Welsford, Enid: *The Court Masque.* New York: Macmillan, 1928. A history of the Masques in Italy, France and England.

Chaytor, H. J. (editor): *Dramatic Theory in Spain. Extracts from Literature before and during the Golden Age.* New York: Macmillan (Cambridge), 1926.

"Lope de Vega: Three Hundred Years After." New York: *Theatre Arts Monthly.* Memorial issue. September 1935. An excellent summary.

Rennert, Hugo Albert: *The Life of Lope de Vega.* Philadelphia: Campion & Co., 1904.

The Spanish Stage in the Time of Lope de Vega. New York: Hispanic Society, 1909.

Ticknor, George: *History of Spanish Literature.* Boston: Houghton Mifflin & Co., 1891. See Volume II.

Underhill, John Garrett: *Four Plays by Lope de Vega.* New York: Charles Scribner's Sons, 1936. With a critical essay, "Some Characteristics of the Spanish Theatre of the Golden Age" by Jacinto Benavente.

Bakeless, John: *Christopher Marlowe. The Man in His Time.* New York: William Morrow & Co., 1937.

Baker, Howard: *Introduction to Tragedy*, University, La.: Louisiana State Press, 1939. Presents the view that Elizabethan drama was descended from medieval literature rather than from classic Senecan tragedy.

Barrett, W. P.: *Chart of Plays: 1584 to 1623.* New York: Macmillan (Cambridge), 1934.

Boas, Frederick S.: *Marlowe and his Circle.* London: Humphrey Milford, 1931.

Brooke, Rupert: *John Webster and the Elizabethan Drama.* New York: John Lane Co., 1916.

Bradbrook, M. C.: *Themes and Conventions of Elizabethan Tragedy.* New York: Macmillan (Cambridge), 1935.

Brooke, C. F. Tucker: *The Tudor Drama.* Boston: Houghton Mifflin & Co., 1911.

Campbell, Lily B.: *Scenes and Machines on the English Stage during the Renaissance*. New York: Macmillan, 1923.

Chambers, E. K.: *The Elizabethan Stage*. 4 volumes. Oxford: Clarendon Press, 1923.

Coleridge, S. T.: *Lectures and Notes on Shakespeare and Other Dramatists*. London: Oxford University Press, 1931. Other editions easily accessible.

Cunliffe, J. W.: *Influence of Seneca on Elizabethan Tragedy*. New York: G. E. Stechert, 1925.

Eliot, T. S.: *Elizabethan Essays*. London: Faber & Faber, 1924.

Ellis, Havelock (editor): *Christopher Marlowe*. The Mermaid Series. London: T. Fisher Unwin. See Introductions by John A. Symonds and by Havelock Ellis, and the Appendices.

Fansler, Harriott Ely: *The Evolution of Technic in Elizabethan Tragedy*. Chicago: Row, Peterson & Co., 1914.

Harrison, G. B.: *The Story of Elizabethan Drama*. New York: Macmillan (Cambridge), 1924.

Hotson, J. Leslie: *The Death of Christopher Marlowe*. Cambridge: Harvard University Press, 1925.

Lamb, Charles: *Specimens of the English Dramatic Poets*, published in 1808.

Lawrence, W. J.: *The Elizabethan Playhouse and Other Studies*. (2nd series) Stratford-upon-Avon: Shakespeare Head Press, 1913; also Lippincott & Co., 1913.

The Physical Conditions of the Elizabethan Public House. Cambridge: Harvard University Press, 1927.

Pre-Restoration Stage Studies. Cambridge: Harvard University Press, 1927.

Levin, Harry (editor): *Ben Jonson: Selected Works*. New York: Random House, 1938. Contains an excellent introduction to Jonson's work.

Life in Shakespeare's England. A Book of Elizabethan Prose. Compiled by J. Dover Wilson. New York: Macmillan (Cambridge), 1926.

Lucas, F. L. (editor): *The Complete Works of John Webster*. 4 volumes. New York: Oxford University Press, 1937. Contains valuable introductions to Webster's work.

Palmer, John: *Ben Jonson*. New York: The Viking Press, 1934.

Saintsbury, George: *A History of Elizabethan Literature*. London: Macmillan & Co., 1887.

Schelling, Felix E.: *Elizabethan Playwrights*. New York: Harper & Brothers, 1925.

Sisson, C. J.: *Lost Plays of Shakespeare's Age*. New York: Macmillan (Cambridge), 1936.

Swinburne, Algernon Charles: *The Age of Shakespeare*. London: Chatto and Windus, 1908. Rhapsodically appreciative but interesting as a poet's comment on the minor Elizabethans.

Alexander, Peter and Pollard, Alfred W.: *Shakespeare's Henry VI and Richard III*. New York: Macmillan (Cambridge), 1929.

Baker, George Pierce: *The Development of Shakespeare as a Dramatist*. New York: Macmillan, 1907

Bradby, Anne (editor): *Shakespeare Criticism 1919-35*. London: Oxford University Press, 1936.

Bradley, A. C.: *Shakespearean Tragedy. Hamlet, Othello, King Lear, Macbeth*. London: Macmillan, 1904.
Shakespearean Tragedy. London: Macmillan, 1932.

Brandes, Georg: *William Shakespeare*. London: Macmillan, 1904.

Cairncross, A. S.: *Problem of Hamlet. A Solution*. London: Cambridge, 1936.

Chambers, Edward: *William Shakespeare: A Study of Facts and Problems*. 2 volumes. London: Oxford University Press, 1930. The most authoritative book on Shakespeare.

Chambrun, Clara Longworth de: *Shakespeare Rediscovered*. New York: Charles Scribner's Sons, 1938.

Charlton, H. B.: *Shakespearean Comedy*. New York: Macmillan, 1938.

Dowden, Edward: *Shakespere*. New York: D. Appleton & Co., 1888. Still a good handbook, especially when read in conjunction with Chambers or Williams.

Gilder, Rosamond: *John Gielgud's Hamlet*. New York: Oxford University Press, 1937.

Granville-Barker, H.: *Prefaces to Shakespeare*. London: Sidgwick and Jackson, 1927. An indispensable book.

Granville-Barker, Harley and Harrison, G. B.: *A Companion to Shakespeare Studies*. New York: Macmillan, 1934.

Hazlitt, William: *Characters of Shakespeare*. New York: E. P. Dutton. Everyman Edition.

Knight, G. Wilson: *The Wheel of Fire*. London, Oxford University Press, 1930.
Principles of Shakespearean Production. New York: Macmillan, 1937.

Lawrence, William Witherle: *Shakespeare's Problem Comedies*. New York: Macmillan, 1931.

Lee, Sir Sidney: *A Life of William Shakespeare*. New York: Macmillan, 1929.

Lewis, Wyndham: *The Lion and the Fox. The Role of the Hero in the Plays of Shakespeare*. New York: Harper & Brothers, *c.* 1925.

MacCallum, M. W.: *Shakespeare's Roman Plays and Their Background*. London: Macmillan, 1925.

MacCracken, H. N., Pierce, F. E., and Durham, W. H.: *An Introduction to Shakespeare*. New York: Macmillan, 1910.

Quiller-Couch, Sir Arthur T.: *Shakespeare's Workmanship*. New York: Macmillan (Cambridge), 1931.

Shakespeare and his Times. New York: Theatre Arts, Inc., 1935. One hundred prints.

Smirnov, A. A.: *Shakespeare*. New York: Critics Group, 1936. A short social study.

Smith, D. Nichol (editor): *Shakespeare Criticism*. London: Oxford University Press, 1936.

Spurgeon, Caroline F. E.: *Leading Motives in the Imagery of Shakespeare's Tragedies*. London: Oxford University Press, 1930.

Stoll, Elmer Edgar: *Shakespeare's Young Lovers*. London: Oxford University Press, 1937.

Thorndike, Ashley H.: *Shakespeare's Theatre*. New York: Macmillan, 1916

Tolman, Albert H.: *Falstaff and Other Shakespearean Topics*. New York: Macmillan, 1925.

Van Doren, Mark: *Shakespeare*. New York: Henry Holt & Co., 1939.

Williams, Charles: *A Short Life of Shakespeare*. London: Oxford University Press, 1933. (An abridgment of Chambers' *William Shakespeare* for the laity.)

Wilson, J. Dover: *What Happens in "Hamlet."* New York: Macmillan (Cambridge), 1935.

The Manuscript of Shakespeare's "Hamlet" and the Problems of Its Transmission: An Essay in Critical Bibliography. New York: Macmillan (Cambridge), 1934.

The Essential Shakespeare. New York: Macmillan (Cambridge), 1932.

Winter, William: *Shakespeare's England*. New York: Macmillan, 1893.

NEO-CLASSIC, SEVENTEENTH AND EIGHTEENTH CENTURIES

Darlington, William C.: *Sheridan*. London: Duckworth, 1933.

Elwin, Malcolm: *The Playgoer's Handbook to Restoration Drama*. London: Macmillan, 1928.

Frischauer, Paul: *Beaumarchais: Adventurerer in the Century of Women*. New York: The Viking Press, 1935.

Guizot, M.: *Corneille and his Times*. New York: Harper and Brothers, 1852. Originally published in French in 1813, revised in 1852; translator unmentioned. A valuable study of French drama in the seventeenth-century drama, supplied with documentary material. Omits Racine and Molière, however.

Harbage, Alfred: *Sir William Davenant, Poet Venturer, 1606-1668*. Philadelphia: University of Pennsylvania Press, 1935.

Hawkins, Frederick: *Annals of the French Stage from its Origin to the Death of Racine*. 2 volumes. London: Chapman & Hall, 1884.

Hotson, Leslie: *The Commonwealth and Restoration Stage*. Cambridge: Harvard University Press, 1928.

Krutch, Joseph Wood: *Comedy and Conscience After the Restoration*. New York: Columbia University Press, 1924.

Landis, Paul (editor): *Six Plays by Corneille and Racine*. New York: Modern Library, 1931. See the enlightening Introduction by Professor Landis.

Marzials, Sir Frank T.: *Molière*. London: George Bell & Sons, 1906.

Matthews, Brander: *Molière: His Life and His Works*. New York: Charles Scribner's Sons, 1910.

Nettleton, George Henry: *English Drama of the Restoration and Eighteenth Century, 1642-1780*. New York: Macmillan, 1914.

Nicoll, Allardyce: *A History of Late 18th Century Drama*. Cambridge: University Press, 1925.

A History of Early Eighteenth Century Drama, 1700-1750. Cambridge: University Press, 1925.

A History of Restoration Drama, 1660-1700. New York: Macmillan (Cambridge), 1923.

Stuart Masques and the Renaissance Stage. New York: Harcourt, Brace & Co., 1938.

Page, Eugene R.: *George Colman, the Elder—Essayist, Dramatist and Theatrical Manager, 1732-1794.* New York: Columbia University Press.

Palmer, John: *Molière.* New York: Brown & Warren, 1930.

Strachey, Lytton: *Landmarks in French Literature.* New York: Henry Holt & Co., 1912.

Summers, Montague: *The Playhouse of Pepys.* New York: Macmillan, 1935. *The Restoration Theatre.* New York: Macmillan, 1934.

Thackeray, William Makepeace: *The English Humourists,* 1851. Available in Everyman Library and other editions.

Thirion, Ernest (editor): *Théâtre Choisi de Molière.* Paris: Libraire Hachette, 1922. See the excellent introductions and notes—in French.

Tilley, Arthur: *Molière.* New York: Macmillan (Cambridge), 1921. *Three French Dramatists: Racine, Marivaux, Musset.* New York: Macmillan (Cambridge), 1933. See the part on Racine.

ROMANTICISM

Babbitt, Irving: *Rousseau and Romanticism.* Boston: Houghton, Mifflin & Co., 1919.

Bekker, Paul: *Richard Wagner, His Life and Work.* New York: W. W. Norton, 1931.

Brandes, Georg: *Wolfgang Goethe.* New York: N. L. Brown, 1924.

Carlyle, Thomas: *The Life of Schiller.* London, 1825.

Dunlop, Geoffry (editor and translator): *The Plays of Georg Büchner.* New York: Viking Press, 1928. See the excellent introduction.

Giese, William F.: *Victor Hugo, the Man and the Poet.* New York: The Dial Press, 1926.

Lewes, George Henry: *The Life and Works of Goethe.* London, 1875.

Locke, Arthur Ware: *Music and the Romantic Movement in France.* New York: E. P. Dutton, 1920.

Ludwig, Emil: *Goethe.* New York: Putnam's, 1928.

Madách, Imre: *The Tragedy of Man.* Tr. by Charles Henry Meltzer and Paul Vajda. Budapest: Vojna & Company, 1933. (See Foreword and Introduction.)

Mann, Thomas: *Three Essays.* New York: Alfred A. Knopf, 1929. Contains an excellent study of Goethe.

Mehring, Franz: *The Lessing Legend.* Originally serialized in *Die Neue Zeit,* 1892. Abridged translation by A. S. Grogan. New York: Critics Group, 1938.

Nevinson, Henry W.: *Life of Schiller.* New York: Thomas Whittaker Co., 1889.

Pfeiffer, Arthur: *Georg Büchner: Vom Wesen der Geschichte.* Frankfort am Main: V. Klostermann, 1934.

Rousseau, Jean Jacques: *Confessions,* 1769. The Bibliophilist Society and other editions.

Robertson, John G.: *Goethe: The Romantic Spirit Exhibited*. London: Routledge, 1927.

Runes, Dagobert D. (editor): *Goethe: A Symposium*. New York: Roerich Museum Press, 1932. Essays by Rolland, Mann, Santayana, Robertson, Slochower, and others.

Sanborn, T. B. (editor): *The Life and Genius of Goethe*. Boston: Ticknor and Co., 1886. Lectures at the Concord School of Philosophy.

Santayana, George: *Three Philosophical Poets*. Cambridge: Harvard University Press, 1927. Contains an excellent study of Goethe and romanticism.

Sime, James: *Life and Writings of Goethe*. London: Walter Scott Publishing Co. (No date given.)

Snow, Royall H.: *Thomas Lovell Beddoes*. New York: Covici, Friede, 1928. The biography of a unique romanticism.

Thomas, Calvin (editor): *Goethe's Faust*. 2 volumes. New York: D. C. Heath, 1912. Text in German; valuable introduction in English to each volume.

Waterhouse, Francis A.: *Random Studies in the Romantic Chaos*. New York: Robert M. McBride, 1923. See especially the brief treatment of Victor Hugo.

THE NINETEENTH AND TWENTIETH CENTURIES IN EUROPE

Balmforth, Ramsden: *The Problem Play*. New York: Henry Holt & Co., 1928. A study of the content and influence of modern problem plays.

Block, Anita: *The Changing World in Plays and Theatre*. Boston: Little, Brown & Co., 1939. A study of the drama in relation to contemporary social problems and interests.

Brandes, Georg: *Main Currents in Nineteenth Century Literature*. 5 vols. London: W. Heinemann, 1906.

Brown, John Mason: *The Modern Theatre in Revolt*. New York: W. W. Norton, 1929.

Carter, Huntly: *The New Spirit in the European Theatre 1914-1924*. New York: George H. Doran, 1925.

Chandler, Frank W.: *Modern Continental Playwrights*. New York: Harper & Brothers, 1931. A detailed account of the work of numerous European playwrights.

Chandler, Frank Wadleigh: *Aspects of Modern Drama*. New York: Macmillan, 1914.

Clark, Barrett H.: *A Study of the Modern Drama*. New York: Appleton-Century, 1938.

Cheney, Sheldon: *The Art Theatre*. New York: Alfred A. Knopf, 1925.

Dickinson, Thomas H. (editor): *The Theatre in a Changing Europe*. New York: Henry Holt & Co., 1937. Articles on the theatre since 1914 by reliable foreign authorities.

Dukes, Ashley: *The Youngest Drama*. London: E. Benn, Ltd., 1923.

Flanagan, Hallie: *Shifting Scenes of the Modern European Theatre*. New York: Coward-McCann, 1928.

Goldberg, I.: *The Drama of Transition*. Cincinnati: Stewart & Kidd Co., 1922. Contains a good section on Jewish drama, in addition to interesting studies of European trends.

Hamilton, Clayton: *Conversations on Contemporary Drama*. New York: Macmillan, 1924.

Henderson, Archibald: *European Dramatists*. New York: Appleton & Co., 1926.

Huneker, James: *Iconoclasts*. New York: Charles Scribner's Sons, (1905), 1919.

Lewisohn, Ludwig: *The Modern Drama*. New York: Huebsch, 1921. A review of modern trends. Very inadequate for Irish drama.

Miller, Anna Irene: *The Independent Theatre in Europe*. New York: Long and Smith, 1927. A history of the art theatres beginning in 1887.

Moderwell, Hiram K.: *The Theatre of Today*. New York: John Lane, 1927.

Nicoll, Allardyce: *A History of Early Nineteenth Century Drama, 1800-1850*. Cambridge: University Press, 1930.

Saintsbury, George: *A History of Nineteenth Century Literature*. New York: Macmillan, 1896.

Archer, William: *Introductions* (to individual volumes of Ibsen's plays). 12 volumes. New York: Charles Scribner's Sons, 1929. See volume 12 "From Ibsen's Workshop Notes, scenarios, etc." for further important material.

Firkins, Ina Ten Eyk: *Henrik Ibsen, a Bibliography*. New York: H. W. Wilson Co., 1921. (See this book for numerous studies of Ibsen.)

Flores, Angel (editor): *Ibsen*. New York: Critics Group, 1937. Brief sociological studies by Engels, Mehring, Plekhanov, and Lunacharsky.

Hedén, Erik: *Strindberg, Leben und Dichtung*. Tr. from Swedish into German by Julia Koppel. Munich: C. H. Beck'sche Verlagsbuchhandlung, 1921.

Kildal, Arne and Hollander, L. M.: *Speeches and New Letters of Henrik Ibsen*. Boston: R. G. Badger, 1910.

Koht, Haldan: *The Life of Ibsen*. 2 volumes. New York: W. W. Norton & Co., 1931. The most authoritative general and biographical study of Ibsen.

Letters of Henrik Ibsen. Tr. by John Nilsen Lauvrik and Mary Morison. New York. Duffield & Co., 1905.

Löwenthal, Leo: *Das Individuum in der individualistischen Gesellschaft. Bemerkungen über Ibsen. Zeitschrift für Sozialforschung*, vol. 5, no. 3, 1936. Librairie Felix Alcan, Paris, pp. 321-363. A brilliant analysis of Ibsen's treatment of individuality in relation to society.

McGill, V. J.: *August Strindberg, the Bedevilled Viking*. New York: Brentano's, 1930.

Plays by August Strindberg. Translated by Edwin Bjorkman. New York: Charles Scribner's Sons, 1916. See the excellent introductions by the translator.

Shaw, Bernard: *The Quintessence of Ibsenism*. (1891.) New York: Brentano's, 1914.

Thompson, Vance. *Strindberg and his Plays*. New York: McDevitt-Wilson, 1921.

Weigand, Hermann J.: *The Modern Ibsen*, New York: Henry Holt & Co., 1925.

Zucker, A. E.: *Ibsen, the Master-Builder*. New York: Henry Holt & Co., 1929. An excellent shorter biography, only slightly critical.

Bell, A. F. G.: *Contemporary Spanish Literature*. New York: Alfred A. Knopf, 1925.

Bithell, Jethro: *Life and Writings of Maurice Maeterlinck*. London: Walter Scott Co., 1913.

Brieux, Eugene: *Three Plays by Brieux*. New York: Brentano's, 1911. See Preface by Bernard Shaw.

Chandler, Frank W.: *The Contemporary Drama of France*. Boston: Little, Brown & Co., 1925.

Copeau, Jacques: *Souvenirs du Vieux-Colombier*. Paris: Nouvelles Éditions Latines, 1931.

Crespi, Angelo: *Contemporary Thought of Italy*. New York: Alfred A. Knopf, 1926. This highly specialized book will illuminate Pirandello's thought.

Gregersen, Halfdan: *Ibsen and Spain. A Study in Comparative Drama*. Cambridge: Harvard University Press, 1936.

Josephson, Matthew: *Zola and His Time*. New York: Book League, 1928.

McClintock, L.: *The Contemporary Drama of Italy*. Boston: Little, Brown & Co., 1920. Naturally inadequate for a study of Pirandello, who attained his zenith after 1920. For an exception taken to McClintock's opinion of d'Annunzio see "D'Annunzio and Dr. McClintock" in *Theatre Arts*, April 1920.

Rolland, Romain: *The People's Theater*. Tr. by Barrett H. Clark. New York: Henry Holt & Co., 1918.

Scheifley, W. H.: *Brieux and Contemporary French Society*. New York: G. P. Putnam's, 1917.

Smith, Hugh Allison: *Main Currents of Modern French Drama*. New York: Henry Holt & Co., 1925.

Starkie, Walter: *Jacinto Benavente*. London: H. Milford, 1924.
Luigi Pirandello 1867-1936. New York: E. P. Dutton & Co., 1937.

Suberville, Jean: *Edmond Rostand: Son Théâtre, Son Oeuvre Posthume*. Paris: Chiron, 1922.

Thalasso, A.: *Le théâtre libre*. Paris: Mercure de France, 1909.

Taylor, Una: *Maurice Maeterlinck: A Critical Study*. London: Secker, 1914.

Underhill, John Garrett: *Benavente as a Modern*. Poet Lore, vol. 29.

Vittorini, Domenico: *The Drama of Luigi Pirandello*. Philadelphia: University of Pennsylvania Press, 1935.

Waxman, Samuel M.: *Antoine and the Théâtre Libre*. Cambridge: Harvard University Press, 1926.

Campbell, Thomas M.: *Life and Works of Friedrich Hebbel*. Boston: R. G. Badger, 1919.

Eloesser, Arthur: *Modern German Literature*. New York: Alfred A. Knopf, 1933. A brilliant account of the German drama and its literary background.

Grube, Max: *Geschichte der Meininger*. Berlin-Schöneberg: M. Hesse, 1926.

Henze, Herbert: *Otto Brahm und das deutsche Theater*. Berlin: Mittler u. Sohn, 1930. An abridgment of this valuable book has appeared in English in *Theatre Workshop*, April-July, 1937.)

Jones, W. Tudor: *Contemporary Thought of Germany*. 2 volumes. New York: Alfred A. Knopf, 1931. This study of philosophy throws much light on the basic outlook of dramatic naturalism. See study of Hegelianism, Chapter 3;

"Philosophy and the Sciences," Chapter 4, v. 1, p. 127-193; and trans-
cendentalism, v. 2, chapter 2, which may illuminate neo-romanticism.

Kerr, Alfred: *Das neue Drama*, 1909. Vol. 1 in *Gesammelte Schriften*. Berlin:
S. Fischer, 1917-20.

Klenze, Camille von: *From Goethe to Hauptmann*. New York: Viking Press,
1926.

Reik, Theodor: *Arthur Schnitzler als Psycholog*. Minden: J. C. C. Bruns, 1913.

Sayler, Oliver M.: *Max Reinhardt and His Theatre*. New York: Brentano's,
1924.

Scheffauer, Herman George: *The New Vision in the German Arts*. New York:
Huebsch, 1924. A review of expressionism in the arts.

Schlenther, Paul (enlarged by A. Eloesser): *Gerhart Hauptmann: Leben und
Werke*. Berlin: S. Fischer, 1922.

Schnitzler, Arthur: *The Lonely Way, Intermezzo, Countess Mizzie*. Boston:
Little, Brown & Co., 1927. See Introduction to Schnitzler's work by Edwin
Bjorkman.

Witkowski, Georg: *German Drama of the 19th Century*. Tr. by L. E. Horning.
New York: Henry Holt & Co., 1909.

Brasol, Boris: *The Mighty Three—Pushkin, Gogol, Dostoievsky*. New York:
William Farquhar Payson, 1934.

Carter, Huntly: *The New Spirit in the Russian Theatre. 1917-1928*. London:
Brentano's Ltd., 1929.

Chekhov, Anton: Reminiscences of by Maxim Gorky, Alexander Kuprin, and
I. A. Bunin. New York: Huebsch, 1922.

Letters of A. Tchekov to his Family and Friends. Tr. by Constance Garnett.
New York: Macmillan, 1920.

The Life and Letters of A. Tchekhov. Tr. by S. S. Koteliansky and Philip Tom-
linson. London: Cassell, 1925.

Note-Book of Anton Chekhov. Tr. by S. S. Koteliansky and Leonard Woolf.
New York: Huebsch, 1921.

Dana, H. W. L.: *Handbook on Soviet Drama*. New York: American Russian Institute, 1928. Valuable lists and notes on theatrical activity in Russia.

Freeman, Joseph, etc.: *Voices of October: Art and Literature in Soviet Russia*.
New York: Vanguard, 1930. For a contradictory view on Soviet achieve-
ments see Max Eastman's *Artists in Uniform: A Study in Literature and
Bureaucratism*. New York: Knopf, 1934.

Fülöp-Miller, René and Gregor, Joseph: *The Russian Theatre*. Philadelphia:
Lippincott, 1930. Excellently illustrated.

Gerhardi, William: *Anton Chekhov: A Critical Study*. London: Duckworth, 1923.

Gorky, Maxim: *Reminiscences of Tolstoy*. New York: Huebsch, 1921.

Houghton, Norris: *Moscow Rehearsals*. Introduction by Lee Simonson. New
York: Harcourt, Brace & Co., 1936. A penetrative description of Soviet
stagecraft.

Kaun, Alexander: *Leonid Andreyev. A Critical Study*. New York: Huebsch, 1924.
Maxim Gorky and his Russia. New York: Cape and Smith, 1931. (Also see
H. W. L. Dana's "Maxim Gorki—Dramatist of the Lower Depths," in
New Theatre, August 1936.)

Maude, Aylmer: *The Life of Tolstoy.* 2 volumes. New York: Dodd, Mead & Co., 1910.

Nemirovitch-Dantchenko, Vladimir: *My Life in the Russian Theatre.* Tr. by John Cournos. Boston: Little, Brown & Co., 1936.

Sayler, Oliver M.: *Inside the Moscow Art Theatre.* New York: Brentano's, 1925. *The Russian Theatre.* New York: Brentano's, 1922.

Stanislavsky, Constantin: *My Life in Art.* Tr. by J. J. Robbins. Boston: Little, Brown & Co., 1938.

Turgenev, Ivan S.: *The Plays of Turgenev.* 2 volumes. Translated by M. S. Mandell, with an introduction by William Lyon Phelps. New York: Macmillan, 1924.

Wiener, Leo: *The Contemporary Drama of Russia.* Boston: Little, Brown and Co., 1924. From Ostrovsky to Evreinov.

Boyd, Ernest A.: *Ireland's Literary Renaissance.* New York: J. Lane Co., 1916. *The Contemporary Drama of Ireland.* Boston: Little, Brown & Co., 1928.

Byrne, Dawson: *The Story of Ireland's National Theatre.* Dublin: The Talbot Press, 1929.

Corkery, Daniel: *Synge and Anglo-Irish Literature.* New York: Longmans, Green & Co., 1931.

Fay, W. G. and Carswell, Catherine: *The Fays of the Abbey Theatre: An Autobiographical Record.* New York: Harcourt, Brace & Co., 1935.

Gregory, Lady Isabella A.: *Our Irish Theatre.* New York: G. P. Putnam's Sons, 1913.

Malone, Andrew E.: *The Irish Drama.* New York: Charles Scribner's Sons, 1929.

O'Casey, Sean: *The Flying Wasp.* London: Macmillan, 1937.
I Knock at the Door. New York: Macmillan, 1939. An autobiographical novel of childhood which will probably be followed by other volumes.

Synge, John Millington: *The Aran Islands. In Wicklow, In West Kerry, In the Congested Districts.* See *The Complete Works of John M. Synge,* New York: Random House, 1935.

Weygandt, Cornelius: *Irish Plays and Playwrights.* Boston: Houghton Mifflin & Co., 1913.

Yeats, William Butler: *Autobiography of William Butler Yeats:* New York: Macmillan, 1938.

Bishop, G. W.: *Barry Jackson and the London Theatre.* London: A. Barker, Ltd., 1933. An account of the progressive theatre in England.

Broad, C. Lewis and Violet M.: *Dictionary to the Plays and Novels of George Bernard Shaw.* London: Macmillan, 1929.

Coats, R. H.: *John Galsworthy as a Dramatic Artist.* New York: Charles Scribner's Sons, 1926.

Cordell, Richard A.: *Henry Arthur Jones and the Modern Drama.* New York; 1932.

Cunliffe, J. W.: *English Literature in the Twentieth Century.* New York: Macmillan, 1933.

Modern English Playwrights. From 1825 to 1927. New York: Harper & Brothers, 1927.

Dark, Sidney and Grey, Rowland: *W. S. Gilbert, His Life and Letters.* New York: Doran, 1924.

Darlington, W. A.: *J. W. Barrie.* London: Blackie, 1938.

Dickinson, Thomas H.: *The Contemporary Drama of England.* Boston: Little, Brown & Co., 1931.

Fyfe, H. H.: *Sir Arthur Wing Pinero's Plays and Players.* London: E. Benn, 1930.

Goldberg, Isaac: *The Story of Gilbert & Sullivan.* New York: Simon & Schuster, 1928.

Harris, Frank: *Oscar Wilde: His Life and Confessions.* London: Constable & Co., 1938.

Henderson, Archibald: *G. Bernard Shaw: His Life and Works.* New York: D. Appleton & Co., 1932.

Jones, Doris Arthur: *The Life and Letters of Henry Arthur Jones.* (American title: *Taking the Curtain Call.*) New York: Macmillan, 1930.

Morgan, A. E.: *Tendencies of Modern English Drama.* New York: Charles Scribner's Sons, 1924.

Norwood, Gilbert: *Euripides and Shaw, with Other Essays.* Boston: John W. Luce & Co., 1921.

Roy, James A.: *James Matthew Barrie.* New York: Charles Scribner's Sons, 1938.

Shaw, Charles: *Bernard's Brethren. With Comments by Bernard Shaw.* London: Constable, 1939.

Walker, Hugh and Mrs. Hugh: *Outline of Victorian Literature.* New York: Macmillan (Cambridge), 1925.

Strachey, Lytton: *Queen Victoria.* New York: Harcourt, Brace & Co., 1921. An excellent reference for Victorian life.

Wilson, Edmund: *The Triple Thinkers.* New York: Harcourt, Brace & Co., 1938. See the chapter "Bernard Shaw at Eighty," a brilliant study.

AMERICAN THEATRE AND DRAMA

Anderson, John: *The American Theatre.* New York: The Dial Press, 1938. A brief but illuminating review.

Anderson, Maxwell: *The Essence of Tragedy and Other Footnotes and Papers.* New York: Anderson House, 1939. Statements by an important playwright.

Beard, Charles and Mary: *The Rise of American Civilization.* One-volume edition. New York: Macmillan, 1930.

Beer, Thomas: *The Mauve Decade.* New York: Alfred A. Knopf, 1926. A history of the 1890-1900 period in American life.

Blake, Ben: *The Awakening of the American Theatre.* New York: Tomorrow Publishers, 1935. An account of the proletarian theatre.

Bourne, Randolph: *History of a Literary Radical and Other Essays.* Edited with an Introduction by Van Wyck Brooks. New York: Huebsch, 1920. A cross-section of the intellectual interests of the 1910's, the formative period of Eugene O'Neill and other contemporary playwrights.

Brooks, Van Wyck: *The Flowering of New England.* New York: E. P. Dutton, 1936.

Calverton, V. F.: *The Liberation of American Literature.* New York: Charles Scribner's Sons, 1931.

Clark, Barrett H.: *Eugene O'Neill: The Man and His Plays.* London: J. Cape, 1933.
 Maxwell Anderson: The Man and his Work. New York: Samuel French, 1933.

Coad, Oral S.: *William Dunlap, a Study of his Life and Works.* New York: Dunlap Society, 1917.

Deutsch, Helen and Hanau, Stella: *The Provincetown.* New York: Farrar & Rinehart, 1931. A history of the Provincetown Theatre.

De Voto, Bernard: *Mark Twain's America.* Boston: Little, Brown & Co., 1932.

Dunlap, William: *History of the American Theatre.* New York, 1932; London, 1933. Originally published in 1833.

Eaton, Walter Prichard: *The Theatre Guild. The First Ten Years.* (With articles by the Directors). New York: Brentano's, 1919.

Gassner, John (editor): *Twenty Best Plays of the Modern American Theatre.* New York: Crown, 1939. See Introduction, "An American Decade," for a brief survey of the 1929-1939 drama.

Geddes, Virgil: *The Melodramadness of Eugene O'Neill.* Brookfield, Conn.: Brookfield Players, Inc., 1934. A provocative pamphlet.

Hicks, Granville: *The Great Tradition: An Interpretation of American Literature Since the Civil War.* New York: Macmillan, 1933. A provocative and controversial social study.

Hopkins, Arthur: *To a Lonely Boy.* New York: Doubleday, Doran & Co., 1937. An informal discussion of the contemporary American theatre by the noted producer.

Kozlenko, William (editor): *The One-Act Play Today.* New York: Harcourt, Brace & Co., 1938. A symposium by Walter Prichard Eaton, Glenn Hughes, Alfred Kreymborg, Michael Blankfort, Barrett Clark, Percival Wilde, John Gassner, and others.

Krutch, Joseph Wood: *The American Drama since 1918.* New York: Random House, 1939.

Lewisohn, Ludwig: *Expression in America.* New York: Harper & Brothers, 1932.

MacKaye, Percy: *Epoch, the Life of Steele MacKaye.* 2 volumes. New York: Boni & Liveright, 1927.

Mantle, Burns: *American Playwrights of Today.* New York: Dodd, Mead & Co., 1938. A biographical survey or cyclopedia.

Mayorga, Margaret G.: *A Short History of the American Drama.* New York: Dodd, Mead & Co., 1932.

Moses, Montrose J.: *The American Dramatist.* Boston: Little, Brown & Co., 1925.
 Clyde Fitch and his Letters. Boston: Little, Brown & Company, 1924.

Moses, Montrose J. and Brown, John Mason: *The American Theatre as Seen by*

Its Critics. New York: W. W. Norton & Co., 1934. A valuable compilation of American criticism from 1752 to 1934.

Mumford, Lewis: *The Golden Day: A Study in American Experience and Culture.* New York: Boni & Liveright, 1926.

O'Dell, George C. D.: *Annals of the New York Stage*. 11 volumes. New York: Columbia University Press, 1927-39. Invaluable as a chronicle of the theatre in New York.

Parrington, Vernon Louis: *Main Currents in American Thought: An Interpretation of American Literature from the Beginnings to 1920*. 3 volumes. New York: Harcourt, Brace & Company, 1927-1930.

Parry, Albert: *Garrets and Pretenders: A History of Bohemianism in America.* New York: Covici, Friede, 1933.

Quinn, Arthur Hobson: *A History of the American Drama. From the Civil War to the Present Day*. New York: F. S. Crofts & Co., 1936.

Sanborn, Ralph and Clark, Barrett H.: *A Bibliography of the Works of Eugene O'Neill*. New York: Random House, 1931. Includes O'Neill's early poetry in the New York *Call*, New York *Tribune*, *The Masses*, and *New London Telegraph*.

Santayana, George: *The Genteel Tradition at Bay*. New York: Charles Scribner's Sons, 1931.

Skinner, Richard Dana: *Eugene O'Neill: A Poet's Quest*. New York: Longmans, Green & Co., 1935.

Whitman, Willson: *Bread and Circuses. A Study of Federal Theatre*. New York: Oxford University Press, 1937.

Winther, Sophus Keith: *Eugene O'Neill: A Critical Study*. New York: Random House, 1934.

STAGE TECHNIQUE

Appia, Adolphe: *Die Musik und die Inscenierung*. Munich: F. Bruckmann, 1899. "The Staging of Tristan and Isolde." Tr. by Lee Simonson. In *Theatre Workshop*, April-July 1937, pp. 61-72.

Architecture for the New Theatre. Essays by Norman Bel Geddes, Lee Simonson, and others. New York: Theatre Arts, Inc., 1935.

Barber, Philip W.: *The Scene Technician's Handbook*. New Haven: Whitlock's Book Store, 1928.

Boleslavsky, Constantin: *Acting: The First Six Lessons*. New York: Theatre Arts, Inc., 1933.

Brickell, Herschel L. (editor): *Our Theatre Today*. New York: Samuel French, 1936. A handbook on scenic art, lighting, costuming, "make-up," directing, etc.

Brown, Gilmor and Garwood, Alice: *General Principles of Play Direction*. New York: Samuel French, 1936.

Burris-Meyer, Harold and Cole, Edward C.: *Scenery for the Theatre*. Boston: Little, Brown & Co., 1938.

Cheney, Sheldon: *Stage Decoration*. New York: The John Day Co., 1928.

Craig, Edward Gordon: *On the Art of the Theatre*. Chicago: Browne's Bookstore, 1911. Dodd, Mead & Co., N. Y., 1925.

The Theatre Advancing: Boston: Little, Brown & Co., 1919.

Scene. New York: Oxford University, 1923. Acclaimed by many students of the drama to be epoch-making contributions to the art of the theater. In connection with these volumes the reader is advised to read Lee Simonson's chapters on Gordon Craig in *The Stage Is Set* which dispute Craig's significance.

Eustis, Morton: *Players at Work.* New York: Theatre Arts, Inc., 1937.

Fuchs, Theodore: *Stage Lighting.* Boston: Little, Brown & Co., 1929.

Fuerst, Walter Rene and Hume, S. J.: *Twentieth Century Decoration.* 2 volumes. Introduction by Adolph Appia. London: Alfred A. Knopf, 1928.

Komisarjevsky, Theodore: *The Costume of the Theatre.* London: Geoffrey Bles, 1931.

Mather, Charles Chambers; Spaulding, Alice Howard; Skillen, Melita: *Behind the Footlights.* New York: Silver, Burdett & Co., 1935. A useful practical book for schools; parts 2 and 3 deal with acting and production.

MacGowan, Kenneth and Jones, Robert Edmond: *Continental Stagecraft.* New York: Harcourt, Brace & Co., 1922.

McCandless, Stanley: *A Method of Lighting the Stage.* Revised edition. New York: Theatre Arts, Inc., 1939.

Modern Stage Design. New York: Theatre Arts, Inc., 1935. One hundred and fifty prints.

Oenslager, Donald: *Scenery Then and Now.* New York: W. W. Norton & Co., 1936.

Pichel, Irving: *Modern Theatres.* New York: Harcourt, Brace & Co., 1925.

Selden, S. and Sellman, H. D.: *Stage Scenery and Lighting.* New York: F. S. Crofts, 1930.

Stanislavsky, Constantin: *An Actor Prepares.* New York: Theatre Arts, Inc., 1936.

Urban, Joseph: "Theatres." New York: *Theatre Arts,* 1930.

ADDITIONAL BIBLIOGRAPHY
I. GENERAL HISTORIES AND STUDIES

Bentley, Eric: *The Playwright as Thinker.* New York: Reynal-Hitchcock, 1946. A noteworthy critical evaluation of modern dramatic writings and theatre.

Blanchart. Paul: *Histoire de la Mise en scène.* Paris: Presses Universitaires de France. 1948. A brief but instructive history of the art of staging a play — i.e., the art of the stage director, scene designer, etc.

Brooks. Cleanth and Heilman. Robert B.: *Understanding Drama.* New York: 1948. A probing introduction to the drama, along with the text of representative plays.

Clark. Barrett H. and Freedley. George: *A History of Modern Drama.* New York: D. Appleton-Century Company, Inc., 1947. A thorough account. with contributions by Mildred Adams. H. W. L.

Dana Henry Schnitzler. Domenico Vittorini. and others. The book contains chapters on little known subjects such as Balkan, Baltic and Latin American drama.

Cole, Toby and Chinoy, Helen Krich: *Actors on Acting*, New York: Crown Publishers, 1949. An anthology of views on acting from classic times to the twentieth century.

Directing the Play. New York: Bobbs. Merrill Co.. 1953. A collection of important essays by eminent modern directors.

Dubech. Lucien: *Histoire générale du Théâtre*. Five volumes. Paris: Librairie de France, 1931–34. The most ample treatment of the theatre.

Fergusson. Francis: *The Idea of a Theatre*. Princeton. N. J.: Princeton University Press. 1949. A critical study of drama and theatre in relation to ritual and the communal spirit from the Greeks to the twentieth century. A provocative work.

Friedell. Egon: *Kulturgeschichte der Neuzeit. Die Krisis der Europäischen Seele von der Schwarzen Pest bis zum Weltkrieg*. Unabridged edition. 3 volumes in one. London and Oxford: Phaedon Press Ltd.. 1947. This "cultural History" of Europe from the Black Plague to World War I is invaluable as a companion book to any history of European drama and theatre. The discussions of these subjects are themselves extremely stimulating.

Gassner. John (ed.): *A Treasury of the Theatre: From Agamemnon to a Month in the Country*, New York: The Dryden Press. 1951. College edition of Simon and Schuster publication. The two volumes contain 65 complete plays with numerous introductions and lists of plays. The Simon and Schuster trade edition is in 3 volumes.

A Treasury of the Theatre: From Ghosts to Death of a Salesman. New York: The Dryden Press, 1950. College edition of Simon and Schuster publication.

Gorelik. Mordecai: *New Theatres for Old*. New York: Samuel French, 1940.

Gregor, Josef: *Weltgeschichte des Theatres*. Zürich: Phaidon Varlag, 1933. The best one-volume history of the theatre in a foreign language.

Masks of the World: London: B. T. Batsford. 1936–37.

Hartnoll, Phyllis (ed.): *The Oxford Companion to the Theatre*. London: Oxford University Press. 1951. The best, if not invariably accurate, cyclopedia of the drama and theatre.

Highet. Gilbert: *The Classical Tradition: Greek and Roman Influences on Western Literature*. London and New York: Oxford University Press. 1949. See especially chapter 7, "The Renaissance Drama", and chapter 16. "Baroque Tragedy."

Kronenberger Louis: *The Thread of Laughter*. New York: Alfred Knopf, 1952. A penetrating study of English comedy.

Laver, James: *Drama: Its Costume and Décor*. London: The Studio Publications, 1951.

Lewes, George Henry: *Actors and the Art of Acting*. London: Smith Elder & Co., 1875. Especially interesting is the chapter "Shakespeare as actor and critic."

Nagler, A. M.: *Sources of Theatrical History*. New York: Theatre Annual, Inc., 1952. A brilliantly selected and edited source book.

Nicoll, Allardyce: *World Drama: From Aeschylus to Anouilh*. New York: Harcourt, Brace and Company, 1950. A comprehensive history, carefully organized, accurate and detailed.

Oenslager, Donald: *Scenery, Then and Now*. New York: W. W. Norton & Co., 1936.

Perry, Henry Ten Eyck: *Masters of Dramatic Comedy and Their Social Themes*. Cambridge, Mass.: Harvard University Press, 1939.

Seyler, Athene and Haggard, Stephen: *The Craft of Comedy*. New York: Theatre Arts, 1946.

Schmida, S.: *Theater vom Morgen*. Vienna: Verlag A. Sexel, 1950. A probing study of form in drama and theatre, with a historical consideration of "arena theatre" and future possibilities.

Thompson, Alan Reynold: *The Anatomy of the Drama*. Berkeley, Calif.; University of California Press, 1946. A useful and unpretentious introduction to drama.

Valny-Baysse, Jean: *Naissance et Vie de la Comédie-Française*. Paris: Librairie Floury, 1945. A history of the Comédie Française from 1402 to 1945, a rather anecdotal chronicle.

Wilson, N. Scarlyn: *European Drama*. London: Ivor Nicholson & Watson, Ltd., 1937.

NEW EDITIONS

Butcher, S. H.: *Aristotle's Theory of Poetry and Fine Art*. With a prefatory essay by John Gassner. New York: Dover Publications, 1951.

Clark, Barrett H.: *European Theories of the Drama*. With a new American supplement consisting of essays by Maxwell Anderson, John Mason Brown, John Gassner, Joseph Wood Krutch, Ludwig Lewissohn, Eugene O'Neill, and others. New York: Crown Publishers, 1947.

Lawson, John Howard: *Theory and Technique of Playwriting and Screenwriting*. New York: Putnam, 1949. The practical chapters are informative as well as provocative.

II. CLASSIC THEATRE AND DRAMA

Beare, W.: *The Roman Stage:* Cambridge. Mass.: Harvard University Press, 1951. A short history of the Latin drama in the time of the Roman republic, and an authoritative book on the subject.

Bowra. C. M.: *Sophoclean Tragedy.* Oxford University Press, 1944. (See Waldock on Bowra's book.)

Goheen, Robert F.: *The Imagery of Sophocles' "Antigone."* Princeton: Princeton University Press, 1951. A study of the poetry and dramatic structure.

Little, Alan M. G.: *Myth and Society in Attic Drama.* New York: Columbia University Press, 1942.

Manning, Clarence Augustus: *A Study of Archaisms in Euripides.* New York: Columbia University Press, 1916. An interesting attempt to show how the intellectually adventurous Euripides was the "conserver and the restorer" of the old tragic form and style. "In many ways Euripides undertook successfully to revive and adapt the methods of Aeschylus."

Post, L. A.: *From Homer to Menander: Forces in Greek Poetic Fiction.* Berkeley: University of California Press. 1951. Greek tragedy and comedy is here studied in relation to Greek epic.

Waldock, A. J.: *Sophocles the Dramatist.* London: Cambridge University Press. 1951. A critical study of Sophocles' merits and deficiencies as playwright.

Whitman, Cedric H.: *Sophocles: A Study of Heroic Humanism.* Cambridge, Mass.: Harvard University Press, 1921. An original and brilliant study of Sophoclean tragedy.

III. THE ORIENT

Habimah, *Hebrew Theatre of Palestine.* Tel Aviv, Bamah, *Theatre Art Journal,* 1937.

Martinovich, Nicholas N.: *The Turkish Theatre.* New York: Theatre Arts, Inc.. 1933.

Sakanishi, Shio: *Comic Interludes of Japan.* Boston: Marshall Jones Co., 1938.

Yajnik, R. K.: *The Indian Theatre.* London: George Allen & Unwin, Ltd., 1933.

Zung, Cecilia S. L.: *The Secrets of the Chinese Drama.* Shanghai: Kelly and Walsh, Ltd.. 1937.

IV. THE MIDDLE AGES

Cohen, Gustave: *Le Théâtre en France au Moyen Age*. Paris: Presses Universitaires de France, 1948. (Original edition. 1928.)

Evans, M. Blakemore: *The Passion Play of Lucerne*. New York: Modern Language Association, 1943. A valuable reconstruction of The Passion Play of 1583.

Young, Karl: *The Drama of the Mediæval Church*. 2 vols. Oxford: The Clarendon Press, 1933.

V. THE RENAISSANCE AND EARLY SIXTEENTH CENTURY

Adams, John Cranford: *The Globe Playhouse*. Cambridge, Mass.: Harvard University Press, 1942. An important study.

Barrault, Jean-Louis: *A propos de Shakespeare et du Théâtre*. Paris: "Éditions de la Parade," 1949. A brilliant short study of poetic realism as applied to stage art and an exposition of Barrault's views on acting. Three essays: Shakespeare and the French; Shakespeare's Message; and Concerning the Theatre.

Bere, R. de la: *John Heywood: Entertainer*. London: George Allen & Unwin Ltd., 1937.

Boas, F. S.: *An Introduction to Tudor Drama*. London: Oxford University Press, 1933.

An Introduction to Stuart Drama. London: Oxford University Press, 1936.

Campbell, Oscar James: *Shakespeare's Satire*. London: Oxford University Press, 1943. A penetrating and informative study.

Chute, Marchette: *Shakespeare of London*. New York: E. P. Dutton, 1949. A vivid biography.

Clemen, W. H.: *The Development of Shakespeare's Imagery*. London: Methuen & Co., Ltd., 1951. An outstanding study in the field.

Craig, Hardin: *An Interpretation of Shakespeare:* New York: The Dryden Press, 1948. A noteworthy orthodox scholarly study.

The Enchanted Glass: The Elizabethan Mind in Literature. New York: Oxford University Press, 1950.

Dunn, Esther Cloudman: *Shakespeare in America*. New York: Macmillan Co., 1939.

Granville-Barker, Harley: *Prefaces to Shakespeare*. Two volumes. Princeton, N. J.: Princeton University. Volume 1, 1946. Volume 2, 1947. The most distinguished work of Shakespearean criticism written from the point of view of a modern producer.

Harbage, Alfred A.: *As They Liked It.* New York: A brief, synoptic study of Shakespeare's attitude and his audience's.

Kernodle, George R.: *From Art to Theatre.* Chicago: University of Chicago Press, 1944. A distinguished and remarkably enlightening study of the development of the Renaissance theatre.

Knight, G. Wilson: *The Wheel of Fire: Interpretation of Shakespearean Tragedy with Three New Essays.* New York: Oxford University Press, 1949.

Knights, L. C.: *Drama and Society in the Age of Jonson.* London: Chatto and Windus, 1937.

Kocher, Paul H.: *Christopher Marlowe.* Chapel Hill, N. C.: University of North Carolina Press, 1946.

Levin, Harry: *The Overreacher: A Study of Christopher Marlowe.* Cambridge: Harvard University Press, 1952. A brilliantly written study supported by recent research on the Renaissance.

Parrott, Thomas Marc, and Ball, Robert Hamilton: *A Short View of Elizabethan Drama.* New York: Charles Scribner's Sons, 1943.

Reynolds, George Fullmer: *The Staging of Elizabethan Plays.* London: Oxford University Press, 1940.

Schücking, Levin L.: *Shakespeare und der Tragödientstil seiner Zeit (Shakespeare and the Tragic Style of His Times).* Bern: A. Francke A. G. Verlag, 1947. A provocative study relating Shakespearean tragedy to Elizabethan and Jacobean tragic themes and style.

Sprague, Arthur Colby: *Shakespeare and the Actors.* Cambridge: The Harvard Press, 1944.

Shakespearian Players and Performances. Cambridge: Harvard University Press, 1953. An informative and vivid account of celebrated performances by Betterton, Garrick, Kean, Irving, Booth, and others. Included is a study of William Poel's Shakespearian productions.

Tillyard, E. M. W.: *Shakespeare's History Plays.* New York: The Macmillan Co., 1946.

Shakespeare's Problem Plays. London: Chatto & Windus, 1950.

Van Doren, Mark: *Shakespeare.* New York: Henry Holt & Co., 1939. A simple but brilliant study of Shakespeare's plays.

Venezky, Alice: *Pageantry on the Shakespearean Stage.* New York: Twayne, 1951.

Webster, Margaret: *Shakespeare Without Tears.* New York: Whittlesey House, 1942. A unique, practical study of Shakespeare's work.

Williamson, Claude C. H. (ed.): *Readings on the Character of Hamlet, 1661–1947.* London: George Allen & Unwin, Ltd., 1950.

Winter, William: *Shakespeare on the Stage.* 3 vols. New York: Moffat Yard & Co., 1911, 1915, 1916.

VI. NEO-CLASSIC, SEVENTEENTH AND EIGHTEENTH CENTURIES

Avery, Emmet I.: *Congreve's Plays on the Eighteenth Century Stage.* New York: Modern Language Association, 1951.

Clark, A. F. B.: *Jean Racine.* Cambridge, Mass.: Harvard University Press, 1939.

Dobrée, Bonamy: *Restoration Tragedy, 1660–1720.* London, Oxford, Clarendon Press, 1929.

Mignon, Elizabeth: *Crabbed Age and Youth.* Durham, N. C.: Duke University Press, 1947. An illuminating study of the satirical treatment of elderly people in Restoration comedy.

Rosenfeld, Sybil: *Strolling Players and Drama in the Provinces, 1660–1765.* Cambridge, England, Cambridge University Press, 1939.

Southern, Richard: *The Georgian Playhouse.* London: Pleiades Books, 1948.

Stein, Elizabeth P.: *David Garrick, Dramatist.* New York: Modern Language Association of America, 1938.

Summers, Montague: *The Restoration Theatre.* New York: Macmillan, 1934.

Taylor, Aline Mackenzie: *Next to Shakespeare.* Durham, N. C.: Duke University Press, 1950. A history of Thomas Otway's *Venice Preserved* and *The Orphan* and their productions on the London Stage.

Taylor, D. Crane: *William Congreve.* London: Humphrey Milford, 1931.

VII. ROMANTICISM

Bertault, Jules: *L'époque romantique.* Paris: Éditions Jules Tallandier, 1949. A lucid study of romanticism useful for a study of the "battle of Hernani," Musset, etc.

Blankenagel, John C.: *The Dramas of Heinrich von Kleist.* Chapel Hill, N. C.: University of North Carolina Press, 1931.

Coquelin, Constant: *The Art of the Actor.* London: Allen and Unwin, 1932. (Originally written in 1886).

Art and the Actor. With an introduction by Henry James. New York: Dramatic Museum of Columbia University, 1915.

Kuhn-Foelix, August: *Heinrich von Kleist.* Murnau: Ulrich Riemerschmidt Verlag, 1948. A brief study.

Wehner, Josef Magnus: *Hebbel.* Stuttgart: Cotta Verlag, 1938. A brief study.

VIII.   LATER NINETEENTH AND TWENTIETH CENTURIES IN EUROPE

1.   GENERAL CRITICISM AND THEORY

Bentley, Eric: *In Search of Theatre.* New York: Alfred A. Knopf, 1953. An excellent descriptive and critical study of aspects of modern and contemporary theatre.

Gassner, John: *Theatrer in Our Time.* New York: Crown, 1953.

James, Henry: *The Scenic Art. Notes on Acting and the Drama,* 1872–1901. Edited by Allan Wade. New Brunswick: Rutgers University Press, 1948. A stimulating collection of essays on the late nineteenth century theatre, as well as on playwrights — Augier, Dumas *fils,* Ibsen, and Rostand.

Jones, Robert Edmond: *The Dramatic Imagination.* New York: Duell, Sloan, and Pearce, 1941.

Peacock, Ronald: *The Poet in the Theatre.* New York: Harcourt, Brace and Co., 1946. A study of modern poetic drama.

Young, Stark: *Immortal Shadows.* New York: Scribner, 1948. Distinguished criticism of modern productions.

2.   SCANDINAVIAN THEATRE

Anwand, Oskar: *Strindberg.* Berling: Ullstein, 1924.

Bradbrook, Muriel: *Ibsen, the Norwegian.* London: Chatto and Windus, 1946.

Dahlstrom, C. E. Wm. Leonard: *Strindberg's Dramatic Expressionism:* Ann Arbor: University of Michigan, 1930. A useful study of Strindberg's later plays.

Downs, W.: *Ibsen, The Intellectual Background.* Cambridge: Cambridge University Press, 1946.

Lavrin, Janko: *Ibsen: An Approach.* London: Methuen & Co., Ltd., 1950. A useful new critical analysis.

Sprigge, Elizabeth: *The Strange Life of August Strindberg.* New York: Macmillan, 1949. An informative biography, of marked critical value.

Tennant, P. F. D.: *Ibsen's Dramatic Technique.* Cambridge: Bowes, 1948.

3.   FRENCH, SPANISH AND ITALIAN THEATRE

Arvin, N. C.: *Eugene Scribe and the French Theater,* 1815–1860. Cambridge, Mass.: Harvard University Press, 1924.

Barea, Arturo: *Lorca: The Poet and His People.* New York: Harcourt, Brace & Co., 1949.

Clouard, Henri: *Histoire de la Littérature Française. Du Symbolisme à nos jours.* 2 volumes. Paris: Albin Michel. Volume 1, 1947; volume 2, 1949. An invaluable history of French literature. Volume 1 treats the period between 1885 and 1914; volume 2, the period from 1915 to 1940.

Honig, Edwin: *García Lorca.* Norfolk, Conn.: New Directions, 1944.

Laprade, Jacques de: *Le Théâtre de Montherlant.* Paris: La Jeune Parque, 1950. A stimulating study of the dramatic compositions of Montherlant.

Lorca, Federico García: *Three Tragedies.* Norfolk, Conn., New Directions, 1947. See pp. 1–37.

Peter, René: *Le Théâtre et la vie sous la troisième république. (Première époque.)* Paris: Éditions Littéraires de France, 1945. A chatty account of the theatre of the Third-Republic before the triumph of naturalism.

Yale French Studies. Fifth Biennial Issue, III, 1, 1951: The Modern, Theatre and its Background, with essays by François Mauriac, Jean-Louis Barrault, and others.

4. GERMAN THEATRE

Arnold, R. F. (ed.): *Das deutsche Drama.* München: Beck, 1925.

Bab, Julius: *Die Chronik des deutschen Dramas: 1900–18.* Four volumes. Berlin: Oesterheld u. Co., 1922.

Expressionismus. In *Das deutsche Drama,* ed., by R. F. Arnold. München: Beck, 1925.

Berlau, Brecht, Hubalek, etc.: *Theaterarbeit.* Dresden: Dresdne Verlag, 1952. A discussion of six "Berlin Ensemble" productions from every aspect of production, but with a Marxist bias.

Brecht, Bertolt: *Sinn und Form.* Berlin: Rütten & Loening, n.d. (1950 ?). See especially *Kleines Organon für das Theater,* pp. 11–42 for Brecht's theory of "epic realism."

Diebold, Bernhard: *Anarchie im Drama. (Dritte erweiterte Auflage.)* Frankfurt am Main: Frankfurter Verlags-Anstalt, 1925. A study of German expressionist drama.

Dosenheimer, Elise: *Das deutsche soziale Drama von Lessing bis Sternheim.* Konstanz: Südverlag, 1949. An informative study of German social drama.

Droop, Fritz: *Toller und seine Bühnenwerke.* Berlin: Franz Schneider Verlag, 1922. A brief review of Toller's early plays.

Herald, Heinz: *Max Reinhardt.* Berlin: Felix Lehmann Verlag, 1915.

Nestriepke, S.: *Geschichte der Volksbühne Berlin.* Berlin: Volksbühnen-Verlags und Vertriebs, 1930. A history of the progressive Volksbühne from 1890 to 1914.

Newmark, Maxim: *Otto Brahm. The Man and the Critic.* New York: G. E. Stechert & Co., 1938.

Omankowski, Willibald: *Georg Kaiser und seine besten Bühnenwerke.* Berlin: Franz Schneider Verlag, 1922. A brief review of Kaiser's early plays.

Samuel, Richard and R. Hinton Thomas: *Expressionism in German Life, Literature, and the Theater.* Cambridge: Cambridge University Press, 1939. This covers the period from 1910 to 1924.

Viëtor, Karl: *George Büchner.* Bern: A. Francke, 1949.

5.   RUSSIAN THEATRE

Balukhaty, S. D. (ed.): *The Seagull Produced by Stanislavsky.* New York: Theatre Arts, 1952.

MacLeod, Joseph: *The New Soviet Theatre:* London: George Allen and Unwin, Ltd., 1943.

Magarshack, David: *Stanislavsky.* New York: Chanticleer Press, 1951.

Simmons, Ernest J.: *Leo Tolstoy.* Boston: Little, Brown & Co., 1946.

Toumanova, Nina A.: *Anton Chekhov, The Voice of Twilight Russia.* New York: Columbia University, 1937.

6.   ENGLISH AND IRISH THEATRE

Bentley, Eric: *Bernard Shaw:* Norfolk, Conn.: New Directions, 1947. A brilliant short analysis and evaluation.

Dunkel, Wilbur Wright: *Sir Arthur Wing Pinero: A Critical Biography with Letters.* Chicago: University of Chicago Press, 1941.

Eliot, T. S.: *Poetry and Drama.* Cambridge: Harvard University Press, 1951. Here Eliot discusses his own plays and also discourses on the problems of verse and prose drama.

Fuller, Edmund: *George Bernard Shaw.* New York: Charles Scribner's Sons, 1950.

MacCarthy, Desmond: *Shaw's Plays in Review.* New York: Thames and Hudson, 1951. A collection of brilliant reviews of Shaw's plays from 1907 to 1945.

Marshall, Norman: *The Other Theatre:* London: John Lehmann, 1947. An important history of the non-commercial theatre in England since the nineteen-twenties.

Nicoll, Allardyce: *A History of Late Nineteenth Century Drama, 1850–1900.* Two volumes. London: Cambridge University Press, 1946.

Pearson, Hesketh: *G. B. S. A Full-length Portrait.* New York: Harper & Brothers, 1942.

    The Last Actor-Managers. New York: Harper & Brothers, 1950.

Reynolds, Ernest: *Modern English Drama. A Survey of the Theatre from* 1900. London: George G. Harrap & Co., Ltd., 1949.

Robinson, Lennox (ed.): *The Irish Theatre.* London: Macmillan and Co., Ltd., 1939.

Roditi, Edouard: *Oscar Wilde.* Norfolk, Conn.: New Directions, 1947.

Shaw, Bernard: *The Art of Rehearsal.* Pamphlet. New York: Samuel French, 1922.

Speaight, Robert: *Drama Since* 1939. London: Longman's, 1947. A useful pamphlet on developments in the English theatre.

7. AMERICAN THEATRE

Atkinson, Brooks: *Broadway Scrapbook.* New York: Theatre Arts, 1947. A collection of notable Sunday pieces from the New York *Times* on recent theatre.

Brown, John Mason: *Broadway in Review.* New York: W. W. Norton, 1940.

Seeing Things, New York: Whittlesey House, 1946.

Seeing More Things, New York: Whittlesey House, 1948.

Chapman, John: Continuation of Burns Mantle's series of annual volumes, containing abbreviated versions of ten plays produced each season on Broadway and a comprehensive listing of all other plays of the season, with casts and summaries: *The Burns Mantle Best Plays of* 1947–48, and every year thereafter, prepared by John Chapman, succeeded in 1952 by Louis Kronenberger.

Clurman, Harold: *The Fervent Years.* New York: Alfred A. Knopf, 1945. The story of New York's Group Theatre by its co-founder and co-director.

Flanagan, Hallie: *Arena.* New York: Duell, Sloane & Pearce, 1940. A history of the Federal Theatre in America.

Dynamo, New York: Duell, Sloan & Pearce, 1943. A history of the Vassar Experimental Theatre.

Flexner, Eleanor: *American Playwrights* 1918–1938 (With a *Preface* by John Gassner). New York: Simon & Schuster, 1938.

Gassner, John: *Producing the Play.* New York: The Dryden Press, 1952. (Rev. ed.). See especially the chapter on arena theatre.

Gagey, Edmond M.: *Revolution in the American Drama.* New York: Columbia University Press, 1947.

Hartman, John Geoffrey: *The Development of American Social Comedy from* 1787 *to* 1936. Philadelphia, pub. by author, 1939.

Houghton, Norris: *Advance From Broadway.* New York: Harcourt, Brace & Co., 1941.

Hughes, Glenn: *A History of the American Theatre, 1700–1950.* New York: Samuel French, 1951.

Jones. Margo: *Theatre in the Round.* New York: Rinehart & Co., 1951. A history of the Dallas arena theatre.

Langner, Lawrence: *The Magic Curtain.* New York: E. P. Dutton & Co., 1951. A history of The Theatre Guild and its antecedents.

Morehouse, Ward: *Matinee Tomorrow: Fifty Years of Our Theatre.* New York: Whittlesey House, 1949. A rapid review of the American stage.

Nathan, George Jean: *The Theatre Book of the Year.* New York: Alfred A. Knopf. Annual volumes of play reviews since the New York theatrical season of 1942–43.

O'Hara, Frank Hurlburt: *Today in American Drama.* Chicago: University of Chicago Press, 1939.

Simonson, Lee: *Part of a Lifetime.* New York: Duell, Sloan & Pearce, 1943.

INDEX OF PLAYWRIGHTS

(Italic numerals indicate principal references to the dramatists and their works. For additional listings see Addendum at the end of this index.)

A

B

ADDENDUM (INDEX TO MATERIAL ADDED IN THIRD EDITION)

INDEX OF SUBJECTS

A

ADDENDUM (INDEX TO MATERIAL ADDED IN THIRD EDITION)